EQUITY & TRUSTS

Text, Cases, and Materials

SECOND EDITION

Paul S Davies, MA

Barrister of Lincoln's Inn
Associate Professor in Law
Fellow and Tutor in Law, St Catherine's College, Oxford

Graham Virgo BCL, MA

Bencher of Lincoln's Inn
Professor of English Private Law, University of Cambridge
Pro-Vice-Chancellor for Education, University of Cambridge
Fellow, Downing College, Cambridge

CONSULTANT EDITOR

E H Burn BCL, MA

Barrister and Honorary Bencher of Lincoln's Inn
Emeritus Student of Christ Church, Oxford
Formerly Professor of Law in the City University

OXFORD
UNIVERSITY PRESS

UNIVERSITY PRESS

Great Clarendon Street, Oxford, OX2 6DP,
United Kingdom

Oxford University Press is a department of the University of Oxford.
It furthers the University's objective of excellence in research, scholarship,
and education by publishing worldwide. Oxford is a registered trade mark of
Oxford University Press in the UK and in certain other countries

© Oxford University Press 2016

First edition 2013

Impression: 1

Public sector information reproduced under Open Government Licence v3.0
(http://www.nationalarchives.gov.uk/doc/open-government-licence/open-government-licence.htm)

Published in the United States of America by Oxford University Press
198 Madison Avenue, New York, NY 10016, United States of America

British Library Cataloguing in Publication Data
Data available

Library of Congress Control Number: 2016936814

ISBN 978–0–19–872765–1

Printed in Great Britain by
Bell & Bain Ltd., Glasgow

PREFACE

The first edition of this book emerged, like a butterfly from a chrysalis, from *Maudsley and Burn's Trusts and Trustees: Cases and Materials*, the seventh edition of which was published in 2008. The aim of this book continues the tradition set by Maudsley and Burn: extracts from key cases, articles, and other materials are pieced together to provide the reader with a clear understanding of a complex body of law. But whereas the previous work contained only cases and materials with some commentary, this book includes a significant amount of our own text. We have sought to explain, analyse, and criticize the law by weaving extracts from relevant cases and materials into the text, presenting an accessible and coherent account of Equity and trusts.

The trust is at the heart of the book, and is the most significant contribution of Equity to the law. But other aspects of Equity's contribution, including breach of fiduciary duty and equitable orders, are also covered. Equity and trusts is a body of law that is traditionally considered to be difficult to understand. This is partly because it is sometimes, unfairly, considered to be a subject that is old-fashioned and not relevant today. It is true that much of the law derives from old cases, but its modern significance cannot be doubted. The contemporary and commercial importance of the subject is reflected in the wide variety of new cases, statutes, and law reform proposals that we have been able to include in this new edition. Since the publication of the last edition barely three years ago there have been some very significant judicial developments, particularly in the Supreme Court. In *Pitt v Holt*[1] the equitable jurisdiction to rescind a disposition for mistake or breach of duty by a trustee was examined, and the so-called 'rule in *Re Hastings-Bass*' was restricted. In *FHR v Mankarious*,[2] the Supreme Court resolved a controversial area of the law by holding that a fiduciary who makes profits in breach of fiduciary duty holds those profits on constructive trust for his principal. Moreover, in *Williams v Central Bank of Nigeria*[3] the Supreme Court decided that claims against dishonest assisters and knowing recipients must be brought within a limitation period of six years, and in *AIB Group (UK) Plc v Mark Redler & Co*[4] the Justices offered strong support of the earlier decision of the House of Lords in *Target Holdings Ltd v Redferns*[5] in deciding that a trustee must pay equitable compensation following a breach of trust. Most recently, in *Menelaou v Bank of Cyprus*,[6] the Supreme Court discussed the nature of proprietary remedies and subrogation. Similarly, the Privy Council has also heard important appeals in the area of Equity and trusts; *Crédit Agricole Corp and Investment Bank v Papadimitriou*[7] considered the defence of bona fide purchaser for value without notice, and in *Brazil v Durant International Corp*[8] the Privy Council explicitly recognised the possibility of 'backwards tracing' in some situations. The lower courts have also been active,[9] highlighting further the need for a clear understanding of the key principles underpinning Equity and trusts.

---

1 [2013] UKSC 26; [2013] 2 AC 108.
2 [2014] UKSC 45; [2015] 1 AC 250.
3 [2014] UKSC 10; [2014] AC 1189.
4 [2014] UKSC 58; [2015] AC 1503.
5 [1996] AC 421.
6 [2015] UKSC 66; [2016] AC 176.
7 [2015] UKPC 13; [2015] 1 WLR 4265.
8 [2015] UKPC 35; [2015] 3 WLR 599.
9 E.g. *Santander UK Plc v RA Legal Solicitors* [2014] EWCA Civ 183; [2014] PNLR 20; *Relfo Limited (In Liquidation) v Varsani* [2014] EWCA Civ 360; [2015] 1 BCLC 14.

At the end of each chapter we have included a hypothetical question to encourage the reader to think about the application of the law that has been considered earlier in the chapter and in the book. Guidance is given in the Online Resource Centre as to the issues raised in these questions and the cases and materials that might be used in an answer. Consistent with the goals of the *Text, Cases, and Materials* series, this book can be used as a free-standing book in its own right. But it also complements a 'traditional' textbook that Graham Virgo has written: *The Principles of Equity and Trusts*, also published by OUP and now in its second edition. Both books adopt broadly the same structure, although sometimes different perspectives are adopted and different material is considered.

Although we have each taken primary responsibility for the preparation of particular chapters, we share joint responsibility for the book as a whole. We are both grateful for the support of Edward Burn in his capacity as consultant editor, and would also like to thank Marilyn Kennedy-McGregor, his wife, for her encouragement. We have appreciated the assistance of the publishers, who have compiled the Table of Cases, Statutes and Statutory Instruments, and the Index, and obtained the necessary permissions. We have greatly benefited from the advice and feedback of our students which has assisted our preparation of this new edition. Graham would like to thank Cally, Elizabeth, and Jonathan for their support and encouragement, and Paul is similarly grateful to Marine and Emma.

This edition purports to state the law as it was on 29 February 2016, but it has been possible to incorporate some more recent developments where space has permitted.

Paul S Davies
St Catherine's College
Oxford

Graham Virgo
The Old Schools
Cambridge

25 April 2016

CONTENTS

PART IX ORDERS

ACKNOWLEDGEMENTS

Grateful acknowledgement is made to all the authors and publishers of copyright material which appears in this book, and in particular to the following for permission to reprint material from the sources indicated:

Extracts from Law Commission and Charity Commission Reports, Consultation Papers, and Discussion Papers are Crown copyright material and are reproduced under Class Licence Number C2006010631 with the permission of the Controller of OPSI and the Queen's Printer for Scotland

Bloomsbury Professional: extract from *Trust Law International* (TLI): Edelman and Elliott, *Money Remedies against Trustees* (2004) 18 TLI 116; Lord Browne-Wilkinson, *Equity and its Relevance to Superannuation Schemes Today* (1992) 62 TLI 119; Vinelott J, *Re Beatty's WT (No. 2)* (1997) 11 TLI 77; Judge Paul Baker QC, *Anker Petersen v Anker-Petersen* (1998) 12 TLI 166.

Cambridge University Press via the authors: extracts from *The Cambridge Law Journal*: Lord Neuberger, *The Stuffing of Minerva's Owl? Taxonomy and Taxidermy in Equity* (2009) 68 CLJ 537–49; Etherton, *Constructive Trusts: A New Model for Equity and Unjust Enrichment* (2009) 67 CLJ 265–87; Nolan, *Vandervell v IRC: A Case of Overreaching* (2002) 61 CLJ 169–88; Parkinson, *Reconceptualising the Express Trust* (2002) 61 CLJ 657–75; Thornton, *Ethical Investments: A Case of Disjointed Thinking* (2009) 67 CLJ 396–422.

Columbia Law Review Association Inc.: extract from Fuller, *Consideration and Form*, 41 Columbia Law Review 799 (1941) reproduced with permission of Columbia Law Review Association, Inc.; permission conveyed through Copyright Clearance Center, Inc.

Hart Publishing: extracts from Birks and Pretto, *Breach of Trust*; Conaglen, *Fiduciary Loyalty*; Cornish, Nolan, O'Sullivan, and Virgo, *Restitution: Past Present and Future*; Gardner, *Reliance-based Constructive Trusts* in Mitchell (ed.) *Constructive and Resulting Trusts*; Garton, *National Anti-Vivisection Society v IRC* in Mitchell and Mitchell (eds.) *Landmark Cases in Equity*; Mitchell, *Constructive and Resulting Trusts*; Swadling, *The Quistclose Trust*.

The Incorporated Council of Law Reporting: extracts from *Appeal Cases* (AC); *Chancery Law Reports* (Ch); *Court of Appeal of England and Wales Decisions (Civil Division)* (EWCA Civ); *Law Reports Chancery Appeals* (Ch App); *United Kingdom Upper Tribunal* (UKUT); *Weekly Law Reports* (WLR).

Informa UK Ltd: extracts from *Lloyd's Maritime and Commercial Law Quarterly*: Goode, *Are Intangible Assets Fungible?* [2003] LMCLQ 379; and from Lloyd's Law Reports: *Mareva Compania Naviera SA v International Bulkcarriers SA* [1975] 2 Lloyd's Rep 509. Also extracts from Birks and Rose (eds) *Restitution and Equity Volume 1: Resulting Trusts and Equitable Compensation*.

Legalease Ltd: extracts from *Wills and Trusts Law Reports* (WTLR): *Challinor v Bellis* [2016] WTLR 43]; *Helena Housing Ltd v The Commissioners for Her Majesty's Revenue and Customs* [2012] WTLR 1519; *Re Horley Town Football Club* [2006] WTLR 1817; *Kasperbauer v Griffith* [2000] 1 WTLR 333; *Lohia v Lohia* [2001] WTLR 101; *Murad v Al-Saraj* [2005] WTLR 1573; *Nestlé v National Westminster Bank plc.* [2000] WTLR 795; *Richard v The Hon A. B. Mackay* [2008] WTLR 1667.

Oxford University Press: extract from Matthews, *The New Trust: Obligation Without Rights?* in Oakley (ed.) *Trends in Contemporary Trust Law*; by permission of Oxford University Press.

Rating Publishers Ltd: extracts from *Rating and Valuation Reporter* (RVR): *R v District Auditor, ex parte West Yorkshire Metropolitan County Council* [1986] RVR 24.

LexisNexis: extracts from law reports including *All England Law Reports* (All ER), *Butterworths Company Law Cases* (BCLC), *Encyclopaedia of Forms and Precedents* (EF&P), *New Law Journal* (NLJ), and *Simon's Tax Cases* (STC); reproduced by permission of RELX (UK) Limited, trading as LexisNexis.

Thomson Reuters: extracts from *Australian Law Journal Reports* (ALJR); *British Company Cases* (BCC); *Commercial Law Cases* (CLC); *Conveyancer; Conveyancer and Property Lawyer* (Conv); *Fleet Street Reports* (FSR); *Law Quarterly Review* (LQR); *Property and Compensation Reports* (P & CR); *Property and Compensation Reports Digest* (P & CR D); *Property, Planning and Compensation Reports* (PPC); and *Scots Law Times* (SLT). Also extracts from Goff and Jones, *The Law of Restitution*; Hodge, *Rectification: The Modern Law and Practice Governing Claims for Rectification for Mistake*; Lord Millett, *Proprietary Restitution* in Degeling and Edelman (eds) *Equity in Commercial Law*; Megarry and Wade, *The Law of Real Property*; and McGhee (ed.), *Snell's Equity*; reproduced with permission of THOMSON REUTERS (PROFESSIONAL) UK LIMITED via PLSclear.

Trust Law Committee: extracts from papers *Consultation Paper on Trustee Exemption Clauses* and *Rights of Creditors against Trustees and Trust Funds*.

Every effort has been made to trace and contact copyright holders prior to going to press but this has not been possible in every case. If notified, the publisher will undertake to rectify any errors or omissions at the earliest opportunity.

TABLE OF CASES

Page references in **bold** type indicate where a case is set out in part or full.

TABLE OF STATUTES

This table is sorted as follows: UK legislation, foreign legislation, European legislation, and international instruments. Page references in **bold** type indicate where a statute is set out in part or in full.

TABLE OF STATUTORY INSTRUMENTS

TABLE OF INTERNATIONAL LEGISLATION

PART I

INTRODUCTION TO EQUITY AND TRUSTS

1

INTRODUCTION TO EQUITY

CENTRAL ISSUES

1. Equity is that body of law which has been made and developed by judges in the Chancery courts to modify the rigid application of the Common Law.

2. Equity is grounded on rules, principles, and doctrines that are strictly interpreted, but their application and the remedies awarded can be tempered by the exercise of judicial discretion to ensure a just and fair result.

3. Although the administration of Common Law and Equity has been fused into a single procedural system, this has not resulted in the substantive fusion of Common Law and Equity into a single body of rules.

4. Equity continues to have a significant role in many contemporary aspects of the law, including commercial and corporate law.

5. The core principle which underpins the equitable jurisdiction is that it responds to conscience.

6. At the heart of Equity is a fundamental division between the recognition and protection of property rights and personal rights.

7. There are a variety of equitable maxims that are useful generalizations of complex law.

1. WHAT IS EQUITY?

(a) HISTORICAL FOUNDATIONS OF EQUITY

There is a fundamental division in the legal system between law that is created by the legislature and law that is created by the judges. This judge-made law is called the 'common law'. But 'Common Law' is used in another, more specific sense, to indicate that body of law which was made and developed by the judges in the Common Law courts, as opposed to that body of law which was made and developed by the judges in the Chancery courts. It is this latter body of law that is called 'Equity'.

'Equity' has certain characteristics that distinguish it from the Common Law and that derive from the historical origins of the equitable jurisdiction.[1] From the Middle Ages, the Common Law was a formalistic body of rules which were interpreted strictly. Where the Common Law did not provide a

---

[1] See Baker, *Introduction to Legal History* (4th edn) (Oxford: Oxford University Press, 2002), pp. 97–116.

remedy or where the result reached was harsh, it was possible to petition the King, and later the Lord Chancellor, to provide a remedy through the exercise of his discretion. Eventually, so many petitions came to the Chancellor that it was necessary to establish a separate court, known as the Court of Chancery, to deal with them and it was the law that was developed and applied in this Court that became known as Equity.

There developed a struggle between the Common Law and Chancery courts, with each considering that its approach should prevail over the other. This struggle came to a head in the *Earl of Oxford's case*,[2] in which Equity prevailed. Lord Chancellor Ellesmere in that case recognized that Equity's function was 'to soften and mollify the extremity of the law'. Later, Lord Chancellor Cowper summarized the relationship between Common Law and Equity well when he said:[3]

> Equity is no part of the law, but a moral virtue which qualifies, moderates and reforms the rigour, hardness and edge of the law.

Such modification was based upon ideas of morality and justice. But, ultimately, the intervention of the Lord Chancellor depended upon the exercise of his own conscience. This inherently arbitrary approach meant that it was difficult to predict the outcome of any petition to the Lord Chancellor. In the seventeenth century, John Seldon wrote that:[4]

> Equity is a roguish thing. For Law we have a measure, know what to trust to; Equity is according to the conscience of him that is Chancellor, and as that is larger or narrower, so is Equity. 'Tis all one as if they should make the standard for the measure we call a 'foot' a Chancellor's foot; what an uncertain measure would this be! One Chancellor has a long foot, another a short foot, a third an indifferent foot. 'Tis the same thing in the Chancellor's conscience.

Thus, for some time it was thought that 'Equity varies with the length of the Chancellor's foot', meaning that it was arbitrary and unprincipled. But, over the years, Equity became more rule-based and principled, with identifiable doctrines being recognized. This was largely because the Equity jurisdiction was transferred from the Chancellor to judges, whose decisions had value as precedent for future decisions, so that like cases could be treated alike.

Even though Equity's function in moderating the rigours of the Common Law was clear, the legal system that emerged was far from ideal. The dual court structure resulting from having distinct Common Law and Chancery courts, in which different bodies of law were applied, caused great inconvenience and injustice: it meant that the claimant had to choose the right court in which to pursue the claim. If the wrong court were chosen, the claimant would have to start again in the other court, leading to lengthy delays and high costs.

The perception that proceedings in Chancery were beset by inordinate delays and expense was reflected by Charles Dickens in *Bleak House*, first published in 1853, which starts with the following description of Equity, as practised in the courts of the time:

> On such an afternoon, some score of members of the High Court of Chancery bar ought to be—as here they are—mistily engaged in one of the ten thousand stages of an endless cause, tripping one another up on slippery precedents, groping knee-deep in technicalities, running their goat-hair and

---

[2] (1615) 1 Ch Rep 1. See Ibbetson, 'The *Earl of Oxford's case*', in *Landmark Cases in Equity* (eds Mitchell and Mitchell) (Oxford: Hart, 2012), ch. 1.

[3] *Lord Dudley v Lady Dudley* (1705) Prec Ch 241, 244.

[4] Pollock (ed.), *Table Talk of John Selden* (Selden Society, 1927) p. 43.

> horse-hair warded heads against walls of words, and making a pretence of equity with serious faces, as players might.
>
> ...
>
> [Everyone is] yawning for no crumb of amusement ever falls from Jarndyce and Jarndyce (the cause in hand), which was squeezed dry years upon years ago.
>
> ...
>
> Jarndyce and Jarndyce drones on. This scarecrow of a suit has, in course of time, become so complicated that no man alive knows what it means.

That case involved a disputed inheritance. By the end of the novel, judgment is given, but the legal costs that have been incurred are so great that they devour most of the estate that was disputed in the first place.

The complexity of litigation in the nineteenth century was to some extent resolved by the enactment of the Judicature Acts of 1873 and 1875, which abolished the Common Law and Chancery courts and replaced them with a single High Court. The effect of this legislation was to fuse the administration of Common Law and Equity. The Judicature Acts emphasized that Equity, as a body of law, could be applied in any court within the High Court. This is now recognized by the Senior Courts Act 1981.

SENIOR COURTS ACT 1981

49. Concurrent administration of law and equity.

(2) Every court [exercising jurisdiction in England or Wales] shall give the same effect as hitherto—

    (a) to all equitable estates, titles, rights, reliefs, defences and counterclaims, and to all equitable duties and liabilities; and

    (b) subject thereto, to all legal claims and demands and all estates, titles, rights, duties, obligations and liabilities existing by the common law or by any custom or created by any statute,

and, subject to the provisions of this or any other Act, shall so exercise its jurisdiction in every cause or matter before it as to secure that, as far as possible, all matters in dispute between the parties are completely and finally determined, and all multiplicity of legal proceedings with respect to any of those matters is avoided.

It follows, for example, that remedies derived from the Common Law or Equity jurisdiction can be awarded, regardless of the court in which the claim was heard. However, it is important to appreciate that the Judicature Acts only fused the administration of the Common Law and Equity; they did not fuse the two bodies of law. As Sir Raymond Evershed said, extra-judicially:[5]

> the so-called 'fusion' of law and equity was a procedural matter and (save incidentally and because procedural matters cannot under our system sensibly be divorced from substantive law) the function of equity in relation to the common law was not thereby changed.

The principle that Equity prevails over the Common Law was maintained by the Judicature Acts, and is also now recognized in the Senior Courts Act 1981.

---

[5] Evershed, 'Reflections on the Fusion of Law and Equity after Seventy-Five Years' (1954) LQR 326, 327.

SENIOR COURTS ACT 1981

49. Concurrent administration of law and equity

(1) Subject to the provisions of this or any other Act, every court exercising jurisdiction in England or Wales in any civil cause or matter shall continue to administer law and equity on the basis that, wherever there is any conflict or variance between the rules of equity and the rules of the common law with reference to the same matter, the rules of equity shall prevail.

Although the equitable jurisdiction prevails where there is difference between Common Law and Equity, over the years the operation of Common Law and Equity has become closer.[6]

(b) CHARACTERISTICS OF EQUITY

Equity was originally founded on the Lord Chancellor's discretion, which was exercised with reference to his conscience. As a result, Equity is traditionally characterized as a discretionary jurisdiction, which is grounded on unconscionability, although it is unclear whether the contemporary interpretation of conscience refers to the conscience of the judge or of the parties.

(i) *Discretionary jurisdiction*

There is a tendency to treat Equity as being a discretionary regime that seeks to secure a just and fair result, without necessarily having regard to identifiable rules that produce certainty and predictability. Equity in the seventeenth century was certainly characterized in that way.[7]

But subsequent developments mean that modern Equity is preferably characterized as doctrinal, in the sense that it is made up of identifiable rules that are to be applied strictly without any significant role for judicial discretion. In *Re Diplock*,[8] the Court of Appeal recognized that:

if a claim in equity exists, it must be shown to have an ancestry founded in history and in the practice and precedents of courts administering equity jurisdiction. It is not sufficient that because we may think that the 'justice' of the present case requires it, we should invent such a jurisdiction for the first time.

Lord Denning, writing extra-judicially, noted that:[9]

the Courts of Chancery are no longer courts of equity ... They are as fixed and immutable as the Courts of law ever were.

But it does not follow that Equity itself is immutable. Sir George Jessel MR recognized in *Re Hallett's Estate*[10] that:[11]

the rules of Courts of Equity are not, like the rules of the Common Law, supposed to have been established from time immemorial. It is perfectly well known that they have been established from

---

[6] See further Chapter 1.2, pp. 8–10.

[7] See the comments of Seldon, Chapter 1.1(a), p. 4, in Pollock (ed.), *Table Talk of John Selden* (London: Selden Society, 1927), p. 43.

[8] [1948] Ch 465, 481.

[9] Denning, 'The Need for a New Equity' (1952) 5 CLP 8.

[10] (1880) 13 Ch D 696, 710.

[11] For further consideration of this case, see Chapter 18.3(c)(ii)(c), p. 871.

> time to time—altered, improved, and refined from time to time....in cases of this kind, the older precedents in Equity are of very little value. The doctrines are progressive, refined, and if we want to know what the rules of Equity are, we must look, of course, rather to the more modern than the more ancient cases.

There continues to be a significant role for the exercise of judicial discretion within Equity. The award of equitable remedies lies in the discretion of the court, and it is entirely appropriate that questions of justice and fairness are taken into account when determining the nature and extent of any remedy that is awarded. For example, if the requirements for proprietary estoppel can be established,[12] which will be a matter of application of equitable doctrine, the judge then has a discretion to determine what the most appropriate method for satisfying the Equity might be.

The true characterization of Equity is that it is grounded on rules, principles, and doctrine that are strictly interpreted, but their application and the award of remedies can be tempered by the exercise of judicial discretion to secure a just and fair result.

(ii) *Unconscionability*

Unconscionability is the most important principle which underpins the equitable jurisdiction. In *Westdeutsche Landesbank Girozentrale v Islington LBC*,[13] Lord Browne-Wilkinson recognized that the key justification for the recognition of a trust, Equity's most significant creation,[14] was that 'Equity operates on the conscience of the owner of the legal interest'.[15] The essential function of Equity is that it restrains injustice by stopping the unconscionable conduct of a particular person.[16]

Whilst the notions of conscience and unconscionability are undoubtedly significant to the operation of Equity, it remains unclear how unconscionability is to be determined. Originally, reference was made to the conscience of the Lord Chancellor. It later appears that 'conscience' at one point referred to:[17]

> the judge's and the defendant's private knowledge of facts which could not be proved at common law because of medieval common law conceptions of documentary evidence and of trial by jury.

This procedural interpretation of 'conscience' is no longer relevant, but the language of conscience and unconscionability remains significant. If such language cannot be clearly defined, the doctrinal coherence of Equity might be undermined.

It is, therefore, crucial to decide whether unconscionability is a rule of substance or simply a guiding principle. The former would require a very clear definition of unconscionability, which would be applied in order to determine whether a defendant has acted unconscionably; the latter might be manipulated by the courts in order to fashion rights and remedies to reach the just and fair result. Unconscionability has sometimes been interpreted as a guiding principle. For example, in *Winkworth v Edward Baron Development Co. Ltd*,[18] Lord Templeman memorably said:

> Equity is not a computer. Equity operates on conscience.

---

[12] See Chapter 9.4, p. 469.
[13] [1996] AC 669.
[14] See Chapter 2.2, p. 25.
[15] [1996] AC 669, 705.
[16] Evershed, 'Registrations on the Fusions of Law and Equity after Seventy-five Years' (1954) LQR 326, 329.
[17] Macnair, 'Equity and Conscience' (2007) OJLS 659.
[18] [1986] 1 WLR 1512, 1516.

In Australia,[19] unconscionability is regarded simply as a guiding principle, which gives the court discretion to reach a just result. But, in England and Wales, unconscionability tends to be treated as a substantive doctrine. For example, it has been used to prevent a defendant from relying on his or her strict statutory rights where the defendant had induced the claimant to act to his or her detriment.[20] Further, and very importantly, unconscionability has been used as a basis for creating equitable proprietary rights where the defendant has received property from the claimant that the defendant should have returned, but failed to do so.[21]

Despite the significant role of unconscionability in modern Equity, it needs to be established whose conscience is relevant when applying this concept. Unconscionability might refer to the conscience of the judge, in the sense that the judge considers that it would be unconscionable to deny a remedy; or to the conscience of a reasonable person; or to the defendant's own conscience. Choosing between these options might greatly influence the outcome of a case;[22] its importance will be carefully analysed in subsequent chapters.

2. ASSIMILATION OF COMMON LAW AND EQUITY

As we have seen, the Judicature Act 1873 did not abolish Equity, but simply fused the administration of Common Law and Equity. One of the great controversies concerning the function of Equity today is whether the separate existence of the Common Law and Equity can still be justified, or whether the substantive law of the two jurisdictions should be fused. The approach of those in favour of fusion has been summarized by Burrows:[23]

> the fusion school of thought argues that the fusion of the administration of the courts brought about by the 1873–5 Acts, while not dictating the fusion of the substantive law, rendered this, for the first time, a realistic possibility. While there are areas where common law and equity can happily sit alongside one another, there are many examples of inconsistencies between them. It is important to remove the inconsistencies thereby producing a coherent or harmonized law. In developing the law it is legitimate for the courts to reason from common law to equity and vice versa. A harmonized rule or principle that has features of both common law and equity is at the very least acceptable and, depending on the rule or principle in question, may represent the best way for the law to develop.

For others, the continued existence of Common Law and Equity is not a matter of concern. For example, Lord Millett has said:[24]

> Those who favour the fusion of law and equity might perhaps reflect that the three greatest systems of jurisprudence in the Western world have all been dual systems. Jewish law had its written and oral law; Roman law its civil and praetorian or bonitary law; English law common law and equity. In each case

---

[19] *Muschinski v Dodds* (1985) 160 CLR 583; *Roxborough v Rothmans of Pall Mall Australia Ltd* (2002) 185 ALR 335, 355 (Gummow J).

[20] *Rochefoucauld v Bousted* [1897] 1 Ch 196. See Chapter 4.2(b), p. 122.

[21] *Westdeutsche Landesbank Girozentrale v Islington LBC* [1996] AC 669.

[22] See, in particular, Chapter 7, 'Constructive Trusts'.

[23] See, especially, Burrows, 'We Do This at Common Law But That in Equity' (2002) 22 OJLS 1, 4. See also Worthington, *Equity*, ch. 10.

[24] 'Proprietary restitution', in *Equity in Commercial Law* (eds Degeling and Edelman) (Sydney: Law Book Co., 2005), ch. 12, p. 309.

the duality served a similar function. One system provided certainty; the other the necessary flexibility and adaptability to enable justice to be done. But the common law and equity are not two separate and parallel systems of law. The common law is a complete system of law which could stand alone, but which if not tempered by equity would often be productive of injustice; while equity is not a complete and independent system of law and could not stand alone.

In fact, there is not a great difference between these two approaches. Common Law and Equity are closely intertwined and are not independent legal systems. This has been recognized by Kitto J, extra-judicially:[25]

[I]t will be salutary for the lawyer to remind himself that equity is the appendix that the Chancery was composing for the saving of the common law, and is not an independent system of law.

But the continued existence of a separate body of law known as Equity is essential. For example, complete assimilation of Common Law and Equity would not result in the abolition of the trust, but would render its analysis much more complex; the subtleties and nuances of the law would be lost.[26] Where, however, the rules of Common Law and Equity conflict, there is then scope for assimilation. There is growing evidence of such assimilation occurring. For example, the equitable jurisdiction to pay compound interest has been extended to Common Law claims for breach of contract and tort;[27] the equitable remedy of an account of profits may exceptionally be available where the defendant has breached a contract;[28] and there is growing assimilation of the principles relating to the award of compensatory remedies for equitable wrongs with those concerning Common Law wrongs, at least where the equitable wrong has occurred in a commercial context.[29] Another example of fusion is *Halpern v Halpern (No. 2)*,[30] Carnwath LJ relied on the Senior Courts Act 1981 to conclude that rescission of a contract for duress at Common Law would be subject to the more flexible, equitable interpretation of the bar that the claimant could not restore the defendant to his or her pre-contractual position. Carnwath LJ said:[31]

130 years after the 'fusion' of law and equity by the Judicature Act 1873...an argument based on a material difference in the two systems would have faced an uphill task....

rescission for duress should be no different in principle from rescission for other 'vitiating factors'.

These other 'vitiating factors' include those that are recognized in Equity, such as undue influence and unconscionable conduct. It therefore appears that in this area of rescission, the Common Law is being assimilated with Equity. This illustrates the appropriate response to fusion: complete substantive fusion is not appropriate; rather, where there is conflict or variance between Equity and the Common Law, the equitable rules should prevail, although there are areas of the

---

[25] 'Foreword', in *Equity: Doctrine and Remedies* (eds Meagher, Gummow, and Lehane) (London: Butterworths, 1975).
[26] See Virgo, 'Restitution Through the Looking Glass: Restitution Within Equity and Equity Within Restitution', in *Rationalizing Property, Equity and Trusts: Essays in Honour of Edward Burn* (ed. Getzler) (Oxford: Oxford University Press, 2003), ch. 5, p. 106. See also Martin, 'Fusion, Fallacy and Confusion: A Comparative Study' [1994] Conv 13.
[27] *Sempra Metals Ltd v IRC* [2007] UKHL 34; [2008] 1 AC 561. See further Chapter 17.5, p. 839.
[28] *Attorney-General v Blake* [2001] 1 AC 268.
[29] *AIB Group (UK) plc v Redler* [2014] UKSC 58; [2015] AC 1503. See further Chapter 17.3(a)(ii), p. 821.
[30] [2007] EWCA Civ 291; [2008] QB 195, [70].
[31] Ibid.

law where it has been argued that Equity should be influenced by the approach adopted by the Common Law.[32]

3. THE CONTEMPORARY CONTRIBUTION OF EQUITY

Equity in the nineteenth century was concerned with death and succession, taxes, and debts. This is dry and technical law. But Equity today is very different. Although the modern subject is built on the old cases, the principles that underpin those cases have been refined over the years and are still of real significance, often in very different contexts. Equity remains relevant, both in terms of explaining long-established doctrines of private law and also as a mechanism for providing new solutions to contemporary problems. As Lord Denning MR noted in *Eves v Eves*, 'Equity is not past the age of child bearing.'[33]

Equity has made a profound contribution to many areas of the law, especially as regards the identification of rights and the development of important remedies. Examples include the order of specific performance to make the defendant perform his or her obligations under a contract, and injunctions to prevent the defendant from committing a wrong.[34] But Equity has also been influential in many other ways. For instance, it can be used to regulate exploitative transactions, such as where one party unduly influences another to enter into a disadvantageous contract or to make a gift.[35] Equity recognizes an action for breach of confidence in cases in which the defendant is in a relationship with the claimant by virtue of which there is a duty to maintain confidences, and the defendant breaches that duty by disclosing the confidential information to another.[36] This is being expanded to encompass liability for invasion of privacy.[37] Equity is also responsible for the recognition and regulation of certain types of relationship known as fiduciary relationships.[38] A fiduciary is somebody who is in a relationship of trust and confidence with somebody else, known as the principal. The fiduciary is expected to be loyal to the principal and to maintain the highest standards of behaviour in looking after the principal's interests. Typical fiduciary relationships are those of company directors with their company and solicitors with their clients.

The most important contribution of Equity to English law is undoubtedly the trust. The essence of the trust is that property is held by one person for the benefit of another. This is recognized through the division of property rights. One person, known as the 'trustee', holds the legal title to the property. That person is, therefore, the legal owner at Common Law. That legal owner does not, however, have absolute, beneficial ownership. Whereas the Common Law cannot see past legal ownership, Equity is able to recognize that the legal owner holds the property not for themselves but for the benefit of somebody else, known as the beneficiary. In Equity, the beneficiaries under a trust are the owners of the beneficial interests given to them. The trustee's ownership is wholly burdensome. Trusteeship imposes onerous duties and liabilities upon trustees, who have to manage the trust property in the exclusive interest of the beneficiaries.

---

[32] See liability for unconscionable receipt, Chapter 19.3, pp. 951–70 and rectification, Ch. 20, 4, pp. 1010–13.
[33] [1975] 1 WLR 1338, 1341.
[34] See Chapter 20.2–3, pp. 977–1010.
[35] *Royal Bank of Scotland plc v Etridge (No. 2)* [2002] 2 AC 773.
[36] *Coco v AN Clark (Engineers) Ltd* [1969] RPC 41.
[37] *OBG Ltd v Allan* [2007] UKHL 21; [2008] AC 1, [255] (Lord Nicholls), and [272] (Lord Walker); *Primary Group (UK) Ltd v Royal Bank of Scotland plc* [2014] EWHC 1082 (Ch).
[38] See further Chapter 14, 'Fiduciary Obligations'.

4. EQUITABLE RIGHTS

At the heart of Equity is a fundamental division between the recognition and protection of property rights and personal rights. In a variety of situations, Equity will recognize that the claimant has an interest in property, or that the defendant is personally liable to pay the claimant a sum of money to compensate for loss suffered or to give up a gain made. Sometimes, the claimant may have both property and personal rights at the same time. It is then important to determine which right it is better for the claimant to assert.

(a) PROPRIETARY RIGHTS

(i) *Advantages of proprietary rights*

Often, but not always, it will be preferable for the claimant to rely on a right to property that is in the defendant's hands. Generally, these property rights take one of two forms. First, the claimant may be able to assert a right to recover particular property from the defendant. Secondly, the claimant may have a right to a security interest in the property.

Claiming property rights has two advantages for the claimant, depending on the nature of the property right that is claimed. First, the claimant's property right will give him or her priority over other creditors of the defendant. This will be significant where the defendant is insolvent. For example, in *Re Lehman Brothers International (Europe) (in administration)*, Patten LJ said:[39]

> a beneficiary under a trust is not ipso facto a creditor of the trustee. Although the trust relationship may give rise to unsecured claims against the trustee for breach of trust or even negligence and may sometimes exist in a wider contractual framework, it remains at its core a different legal relationship. Subject to the terms of the trust instrument, the trustee holds the trust property for the benefit of those beneficially entitled to it and has a primary obligation to maintain those particular assets (or any which replace them) to the exclusion of all other claims. The trust property does not form part of the trustee's estate in the event of insolvency so as to be available to meet the claims of general creditors and the beneficiary is entitled to the property in specie free of any such claims.

Where a trustee becomes insolvent, all the assets belonging to the trustee are divided up amongst his or her creditors. But, if a beneficiary has an equitable property right to assets held by the trustee, it cannot be said that those assets belong to the trustee beneficially. Those assets are, therefore, removed from the pool of the trustee's assets, as they belong in Equity to the beneficiary. Only the remaining assets that belong to the trustee beneficially are then distributed amongst the remaining creditors (generally *pari passu*, or proportionally). Clearly, this puts a beneficiary in a much stronger position than other creditors. Similarly, if a claimant has a security interest in the property held by a defendant who becomes insolvent, that property interest will be satisfied before the claims of any other unsecured creditors are satisfied.

Secondly, where the claimant has a property interest that is not a security interest, if the property has increased in value the claimant will get the benefit of that increase. This is because the property itself[40] belongs, in Equity, to the claimant. But this also means that, if the property has fallen in value, the claimant would suffer from the loss of value. In such circumstances, the claimant would generally

---

[39] [2009] EWCA Civ 1161, [33].
[40] Or at least a share in the property: see Chapter 18.5(b)(ii), pp. 894–9.

prefer to assert a personal right against the defendant for the value of the losses suffered by the claimant or the gains made by the defendant.

(ii) *Creation of property rights*

Equitable proprietary rights need to be created specifically. If somebody is the legal owner of property, it does not follow that that person also has an equitable interest in that property. Indeed, that person will commonly be the absolute legal owner of property in which there is no equitable interest. As Lord Browne-Wilkinson observed in *Westdeutsche Landesbank Girozentrale v Islington LBC*:[41]

> A person solely entitled to the full beneficial ownership of money or property, both at law and in equity, does not enjoy an equitable interest in that property. The legal title carries with it all rights. Unless and until there is a separation of the legal and equitable estates, there is no separate equitable title.

There are a variety of events that will operate to separate the legal and equitable estates and thereby create an equitable interest in property. By far the most significant is the intentional creation of that interest, as occurs where an express trust is created. Secondly, an equitable interest may arise by virtue of a presumed intent that property should be held by the legal owner on behalf of the claimant.[42] Thirdly, an equitable proprietary interest may arise by operation of law, often because the defendant can be considered to have acted unconscionably.[43]

(iii) *Beneficial interest*

The distinction between legal and equitable proprietary rights is significant for a number of reasons. Each type of property right functions in a different way. Where an equitable property interest has not been created, the legal owner of property will also be its beneficial owner in the sense that he or she can obtain the benefits of the property, including its use and income arising from the property such as the dividends paid in respect of shares. Once an equitable interest has been created, however, the legal owner will no longer have the beneficial ownership of the property; it is the equitable owner who is the beneficial owner and who has the right to receive the benefits of the property. In this situation, the legal owner will be obliged to administer and manage the property on behalf of the equitable owner. The legal owner of the property will determine how that property is to be used and is obliged to bring legal proceedings if that property is destroyed or damaged.[44]

(iv) *Successive proprietary rights*

A further characteristic of equitable proprietary rights is that it is possible to plan for successive rights to property, so that provision can be made for the present and future beneficial use of the property. For example, a testator can leave his estate to his wife for life, with remainder to a child. It will follow that, on the testator's death, the wife will get the benefit of the property whilst she is alive, but on her death it will pass to the child. The ability to provide for consecutive interests in property is an important

---

[41] [1996] AC 669, 706.
[42] See Chapter 8.2, pp. 364–84.
[43] See Chapter 7.2(a), pp. 332–6.
[44] *Leigh and Sillivan Ltd v The Aliakmon Shipping Co. Ltd* [1986] AC 785; *MCC Proceeds Inc. v Lehman Brothers International (Europe)* [1998] 4 All ER 675.

feature of Equity. It is possible to provide for such consecutive interests at Common Law too, but only as regards land; in Equity, this can occur as regards both land and personal property.

A present equitable proprietary interest is described as an 'interest in possession'. A beneficiary with an interest in possession has a right to the present enjoyment of trust property. Future proprietary interests are divided between vested and contingent interests. A vested interest is an interest where the person entitled to it is ascertained and 'the interest is ready to take effect in possession immediately, subject only to any prior interest'.[45] So, for example, in a trust of land held for A for life with remainder to B, B will have a vested interest, which will become an interest in possession on A's death. As Megarry and Wade recognize:[46]

> [a vested interest] is a 'future interest', since the right of enjoyment is postponed. However, it is also an already subsisting right in property vested in its owner: it is a present right to future enjoyment.

A contingent interest 'is one which will give no right at all unless or until some future event happens'.[47] For example, where property is left to A for life and remainder to B if she attains the age of 21, then, until B attains that age, the interest will be contingent. On attaining that age it will be vested. On the death of A it will be vested in possession.

A beneficiary's entitlement to a vested interest may depend on the satisfaction of a condition, known as a 'condition precedent'. An existing interest may be determined if a condition, known as a 'condition subsequent', is satisfied.

Whether an interest is in possession, vested, or contingent, and whether the interest is subject to a condition precedent or subsequent, is significant as regards the operation of a number of rules within the law of trusts.[48]

(v) *Shared property ownership*

There are two types of shared ownership of property. One is joint tenancy, whereby the owners own the whole of the property together and do not have a particular share in it. It follows that, if one of two joint tenants dies, the other automatically becomes the sole owner of the property. The alternative method of shared ownership is tenancy in common, whereby the owners own a definite share of the property, which can be devised in a will. Typically joint tenancy and tenancy in common can be distinguished by reference to whether there is evidence of a separation of interest. If there is no indication that the parties are to have distinct and separate shares in the property, there will be a joint tenancy. Where, however, there is an indication that the parties are to take separate and distinct interests, such as where property is transferred to A and B equally, there will be a tenancy in common.

(b) PERSONAL RIGHTS

Equitable personal rights have also proved to be significant. Such rights might arise from a fiduciary relationship of trust and confidence: for example, a solicitor, as a fiduciary, will owe particular

---

[45] Burn and Cartwright (eds), *Cheshire and Burn's Modern Law of Real Property* (18th edn) (Oxford: Oxford University Press, 2011), p. 532.

[46] Harpum, Dixon, and Bridge (eds), *Megarry and Wade: The Law of Real Property* (8th edn) (London: Sweet & Maxwell, 2012), p. 310.

[47] Ibid.

[48] See Chapter 13.5, pp. 651–9.

personal obligations to his or her client, as a principal. Such fiduciary obligations are distinct from, and in addition to, the ordinary duties imposed by the Common Law in contract and tort.[49]

A claimant may have both proprietary and personal rights in Equity. For example, trustees will often owe fiduciary duties to their beneficiaries. So, if a trustee misappropriates trust property, the beneficiaries may be able to rely not only on their equitable proprietary rights to make a claim to recover the property,[50] but alternatively on their personal rights against the trustee: the trustee may consequently be liable either to compensate the beneficiaries for the loss that they have suffered or to account for the profit the trustee made as a result of the breach of his or her personal obligations.[51]

Personal equitable rights may arise as a result of wrongdoing, such as breach of trust. But they can also arise from unjust enrichment. The law of unjust enrichment was recognized by the House of Lords in 1991,[52] but this was simply the formal recognition of a principle that had been developing for many hundreds of years. Much of this development had occurred at Common Law, but Equity has had a significant influence on that development too. The essence of the law of unjust enrichment was recognized by Lord Steyn in *Banque Financière de la Cité v Parc (Battersea) Ltd*:[53]

> unjust enrichment ranks next to contract and tort as part of the law of obligations. It is an independent source of rights and obligations.
>
> Four questions arise. (1) Has [the defendant] benefited or been enriched? (2) Was the enrichment at the expense of [the claimant]? (3) Was the enrichment unjust? (4) Are there any defences?

If a defendant's enrichment is unjust, he or she will be required to give back the value of the gain made to the claimant. This is a restitutionary remedy: restitution is concerned with depriving the defendant of gains rather than compensating the claimant for loss suffered.

All four questions identified by Lord Steyn are crucial.[54] The third question will be satisfied where a ground of restitution can be identified. The recognized grounds of restitution include mistake,[55] total failure of basis,[56] and undue influence.[57] The most significant defence to a claim in unjust enrichment is that of change of position, which was recognized by Lord Goff in *Lipkin Gorman (a firm) v Karpnale Ltd*:[58]

> I am most anxious that, in recognising this defence [of change of position] to actions of restitution, nothing should be said at this stage to inhibit the development of the defence on a case by case basis, in the usual way. It is, of course, plain that the defence is not open to one who has changed his position in bad faith, as where the defendant has paid away the money with knowledge of the facts entitling the plaintiff to restitution; and it is commonly accepted that the defence should not be open to a wrongdoer.... At present I do not wish to state the principle any less broadly than this: that the defence is available to a person whose position has so changed that it would be inequitable in all the circumstances to require him to make restitution, or alternatively to make restitution in full. I wish to

---

[49] See Chapter 14.
[50] See further Chapter 18, 'Proprietary Claims and Remedies'.
[51] See further Chapter 17, 'Personal Claims and Remedies'.
[52] *Lipkin Gorman (a firm) v Karpnale Ltd* [1991] 2 AC 548.
[53] [1999] 1 AC 221, 227 (Lord Steyn).
[54] Although in *Bank of Cyprus UK Ltd v Menelaou* [2015] UKSC 66, [2016] AC 176, [19] Lord Clarke described them as 'broad headings for ease of exposition'.
[55] *Pitt v Holt* [2013] UKSC 26; [2013] 2 AC 108. See Chapter 7.2(c), pp. 337–41.
[56] *Fibrosa Spolka Akcyjna v Fairbairn Lawson Combe Barbour Ltd* [1943] AC 32.
[57] *Allcard v Skinner* (1887) 36 Ch D 145.
[58] [1991] 2 AC 548, 580.

stress however that the mere fact that the defendant has spent the money, in whole or in part, does not of itself render it inequitable that he should be called upon to repay, because the expenditure might in any event have been incurred by him in the ordinary course of things. I fear that the mistaken assumption that mere expenditure of money may be regarded as amounting to a change of position for present purposes has led in the past to opposition by some to recognition of a defence which in fact is likely to be available only on comparatively rare occasions.

Consequently, the defence will apply where the defendant has received an enrichment and, in reliance on that receipt, has changed his or her position, such as by buying something which he or she would not otherwise have bought. The defence will not be available where the defendant has acted in bad faith or can be considered to be a wrongdoer.

It is important to appreciate that unjust enrichment leads to a personal remedy to give back the value of the gain received by the defendant. It does not create proprietary rights,[59] but the Supreme Court has recognized that unjust enrichment can create a security interest in property by means of subrogation.[60] Liability in unjust enrichment is strict: a defendant may have to effect restitution even if he or she is not at fault.

5. EQUITABLE MAXIMS

There are various established equitable maxims that are often cited by judges when reaching a decision. Sometimes these maxims are referred to simply as a 'mantra',[61] without any obvious understanding as to why they are being used. Certainly, these maxims must be approached with care, and it is important not to apply them literally but to be sensitive to the particular facts at issue. However, an understanding of the more important maxims, considered in this section, remains helpful: they are used by the Courts and continue to be significant. As Lord Upjohn recognized in *Boardman v Phipps:*[62]

Rules of equity have to be applied to such a great diversity of circumstances that they can be stated only in the most general terms and applied with particular attention to the exact circumstances of each case.

The maxims may, therefore, serve as useful generalizations of complex law, even if the application of a maxim will rarely be decisive in isolation.

(a) THOSE WHO SEEK EQUITY MUST DO EQUITY

When a judge decides whether it is appropriate to award an equitable remedy, one relevant consideration is whether the claimant is willing to act fairly to the defendant in the future. In *Chappell v Times Newspapers Ltd,*[63] an injunction was denied to employees who wished to restrain their employer from

---

[59] *Bank of Cyprus UK Ltd v Menelaou* [2015] UKSC 66 [2016] AC 176.
[60] Ibid. See further Chapter 18.5(b)(ii)(c), pp. 900–11.
[61] *Jones v Kernott* [2011] UKSC 53; [2012] 1 AC 776, [19] (Lord Walker and Lady Hale).
[62] [1967] 2 AC 46, 123.
[63] [1975] 1 WLR 482.

dismissing them because they had refused to undertake that they would not strike in the future. Megarry J said:[64]

> Instead of looking to the past, I would look to the future. There is a general principle which lies enshrined in the maxim 'He who seeks equity must do equity.' That maxim, like the other maxims of equity, is not to be construed or enforced as if it were a section in an Act of Parliament; but it expresses in concise form one approach made by the court when the discretionary remedy of an injunction is sought. If the plaintiff asks for an injunction to restrain a breach of contract to which he is a party, and he is seeking to uphold that contract in all its parts, he is, in relation to that contract, ready to do equity. If on the other hand he seeks the injunction but in the same breath is constrained to say that he is ready and willing himself to commit grave breaches of the contract at the behest of a body or person (whether his union or not) engaged in an active campaign of organising the repeated commission of such breaches, then it seems to me that the plaintiff cannot very well contend that in relation to that contract he is ready to do equity. One may leave on one side any technicalities of law or equity and simply say, in the language of childhood, that he is trying to have it both ways: he is saying 'You must not break our contract but I remain free to do so.'

(b) THOSE WHO COME TO EQUITY MUST COME WITH CLEAN HANDS

Whereas the previous maxim was concerned with the claimant's conduct in the future, the maxim that those who come to Equity must have clean hands[65] relates to the claimant's past conduct. The maxim has been described as:[66]

> a principle of justice designed to prevent those guilty of serious misconduct from securing a discretionary remedy, such as an injunction.

In *Dering v Earl of Winchelsea*,[67] Eyre CB said that the principle of coming to Equity with clean hands:

> does not mean a general depravity; it must have an immediate and necessary relation to the equity sued for; it must be a depravity in a legal as well as in a moral sense.

It follows that the improper conduct must relate to the relief that is sought in some way. Just because the claimant's general conduct is unacceptable does not mean that Equity will deny relief to the claimant. So, for example, in *Argyll (Duchess) v Argyll (Duke)*,[68] the Duchess was able to obtain an injunction to restrain her former husband from publishing confidential information, even though it was her adultery that had led to the breakdown of the marriage in the first place. That adultery was unrelated to the claimant's attempt to prevent the publishing of confidential information. Ungoed-Thomas J said:[69]

> Should, then, the plaintiff be denied the injunction which she would otherwise get because she has herself to an extent broken confidence and because she, after the confidences of whose breach she

---

[64] Ibid, 495.
[65] *Fitzroy v Twilim* (1786) 1 TR 153. See Chafee, 'Coming into Equity with Clean Hands' (1949) 47 Mich L Rev 877 and 1065.
[66] *Dunbar v Plant* [1998] Ch 412, 422 (Mummery LJ).
[67] (1787) 1 Cox Eq Cas 318, 319.
[68] [1967] Ch 302.
[69] Ibid, 322.

> complains, adopted an immoral attitude towards her marriage? A person coming to Equity for relief—and this is equitable relief which the plaintiff seeks—must come with clean hands; but the cleanliness required is to be judged in relation to the relief that is sought.

The clean hands maxim will not, however, deny relief where it is not necessary for the claimant to rely on improper conduct to establish an equitable claim. In *Tinsley v Milligan*,[70] one party was able to assert an equitable right to property that was registered in the name of her partner, even though the purpose of the arrangement had been to enable her to perpetrate a fraud. It was held that she could assert an equitable property right, because she did not need to rely on her illegality to do so. Lord Browne-Wilkinson said:[71]

> In my judgment the court is only entitled and bound to dismiss a claim on the basis that it is founded on an illegality in those cases where the illegality is of a kind which would have provided a good defence if raised by the defendant. In a case where the plaintiff is not seeking to enforce an unlawful contract but founds his case on collateral rights acquired under the contract (such as a right of property) the court is neither bound nor entitled to reject the claim unless the illegality of necessity forms part of the plaintiff's case.

The claimant's fraudulent conduct was clearly reprehensible, but did not need to be invoked for her to establish her equitable property right. As a result, the maxim did not apply. Lord Goff dissented in *Tinsley* because he considered that the maxim was applicable:[72]

> once it comes to the attention of a court of equity that the claimant has not come to the court with clean hands, the court will refuse to assist the claimant, even though the claimant can prima facie establish his claim without recourse to the underlying fraudulent or illegal purpose.

On the facts of *Tinsley*, it may be that the claimant had 'cleaned' her hands: she had repaid the benefits obtained from the fraudulent scheme and so may no longer have had 'unclean' hands at all. But, in any event, any uncleanliness was surely too remote from the claimant's claim to prevent her from asserting an equitable interest in the property.

The operation of the 'clean hands' maxim was justified by Murphy J in the High Court of Australia in *Time-Life International (Nederlands) BV v Interstate Parcel Express Co Pty Ltd*[73] as follows:

> [it] is far more than a mere banality. It is a self-imposed ordinance that closes the doors of a court of equity to one tainted with inequitableness or bad faith relative to the matter in which he seeks relief, however improper may have been the behaviour of the defendant. That doctrine is rooted in the historical concept of a court as a vehicle for affirmatively enforcing the requirements of conscience and good faith.

---

[70] [1994] 1 AC 340. See further Chapter 8.2(d)(i), pp. 377–9.
[71] Ibid, 377.
[72] Ibid, 358.
[73] (1978) FSR 215.

This maxim is clearly based upon the historical origins of Equity as being founded on conscience. This was considered by Pettit:[74]

> Unconscionability is perhaps the common factor. The clean hands doctrine is perhaps no more than a background principle from which have developed particular equitable defences—innocent misrepresentation, equitable fraud, laches and acquiescence and unfairness and hardship...Most cases where the clean hands maxim is found in fact involve one or other of these defences and the reference to clean hands is otiose. There remain exceptional cases which do not readily fall into any of these categories yet where the courts have taken the view that it would be unconscionable for the plaintiff to succeed, and these cases can be regarded as applications of a clean hands doctrine. They include cases where the plaintiff has been seeking to further a deception of the public;[75] where the plaintiff is shown to have materially misled the court or to have abused its process[76]...where a tenant notoriously using the premises as a disorderly house sought relief against forfeiture.[77]

(c) EQUITY TREATS AS DONE THAT WHICH OUGHT TO BE DONE

This maxim has been particularly significant in the development of Equity,[78] but there is a tendency to rely on it too readily without regard to its rationale. The maxim has proved to be particularly significant where the parties have entered into a contract that is specifically enforceable; for then Equity will treat the contract as having been performed. This was recognized by Lindley LJ in *Re Anstis*:[79]

> Equity, no doubt, looks on that as done which ought to be done; but this rule, although usually expressed in general terms, is by no means universally true. Where the obligation to do what ought to be done is not an absolute duty, but only an obligation arising from contract, that which ought to be done is only treated as done in favour of some person entitled to enforce the contract as against the person liable to perform it.

So, for example, where the defendant has agreed to sell land to the claimant but has not done so, the defendant will still own the land at Law, but Equity will treat the land as having been transferred to the claimant so the vendor will hold the land on constructive trust for the purchaser.[80] The maxim was applied in *Walsh v Lonsdale*,[81] in which Equity treated a person who had entered into a specifically enforceable agreement to take a lease as though that person was a lessee of the property. Sir George Jessel MR said:[82]

> There is an agreement for a lease under which possession has been given. Now since the Judicature Act the possession is held under the agreement. There are not two estates as there were formerly, one estate at common law by reason of the payment of the rent from year to year, and an estate in equity under the agreement. There is only one Court, and the equity rules prevail in it. The tenant holds under an agreement for a lease. He holds, therefore, under the same terms in equity as if a lease had been

---

[74] 'He Who Comes into Equity Must Come with Clean Hands' [1990] Conv 416, 425.
[75] *Leather Cloth Co Ltd v American Leather Cloth Co Ltd* (1863) 4 De GJ & S 137.
[76] *Armstrong v Sheppard & Short Ltd* (1959) 2 QB 384.
[77] *Gill v Lewis* [1956] 2 QB 1.
[78] *Banks v Sutton* (1732) 2 P Wms 700, 715.
[79] (1886) 31 Ch D 596, 695.
[80] *Rayner v Preston* (1881) 18 Ch D 1. See Chapter 7.2(f), p. 351.
[81] (1882) 21 Ch D 9.
[82] Ibid, 14.

> granted, it being a case in which both parties admit that relief is capable of being given by specific performance. That being so, he cannot complain of the exercise by the landlord of the same rights as the landlord would have had if a lease had been granted.

There have, however, been cases in which the maxim has been applied outside the context of specifically enforceable contracts. It has been applied, for example, where a donor has failed to make an effective gift at Law.[83] In such circumstances, the use of the maxim is much more difficult to justify.

(d) EQUITY FOLLOWS THE LAW

Although the maxim that Equity follows the law has long been recognized, its meaning is ambiguous. It is certainly the case that Equity recognizes legal rules, but if Equity were to have followed the law absolutely, there would have been no scope for the development of separate equitable doctrines. It is for this reason that the American judge Cardozo J recognized that 'Equity follows the law, but not slavishly nor always.'[84]

One example of Equity following the law arises where two parties own a house that is registered in their joint names. It was recognized in *Jones v Kernott*[85] that:

> The starting point is that equity follows the law and they are joint tenants both in law and in equity.

Equity will consequently presume that the beneficial interest in the property corresponds to their legal interest, so that they will share the beneficial interest equally, although this presumption can be rebutted by a contrary intention.

(e) EQUITY WILL NOT ASSIST A VOLUNTEER

A 'volunteer' is somebody who has not provided consideration for a particular transaction, such as the recipient of a gift. Where a donor purports to make a gift but it is not effective at law, Equity will not perfect the imperfect gift,[86] this being founded on the principle that Equity will not assist a volunteer. So, if a settlor fails to transfer property to a trustee, Equity will not intervene to perfect the transfer. This maxim is, however, subject to a number of exceptions, where Equity will assist a volunteer and will perfect an imperfect gift, such as where the transferor has done everything necessary to transfer title.[87] Importantly, once a trust has been fully constituted, the beneficiary will be able to enforce the trust, even if the beneficiary has provided no consideration. As Lord Browne-Wilkinson said in *T Choithram International SA v Pagarani*:[88]

> Until comparatively recently the great majority of trusts were voluntary settlements under which beneficiaries were volunteers having given no value. Yet beneficiaries under a trust, although volunteers,

---

[83] See Chapter 4.3(c)(i), pp. 153–6.
[84] *Graf v Hope Building Corpn;* (1920) 254 NY 1, 9.
[85] *Jones v Kernott* [2011] UKSC 53; [2012] 1 AC 776, [51](1) (Lady Hale and Lord Walker). See Chapter 9.2(b), pp. 434–47.
[86] *Milroy v Lord* (1862) 4 De GF & J 264, 275 (Turner LJ). See Chapter 4.3(c), p. 152.
[87] See Chapter 4.3(c)(i), pp. 153–6.
[88] [2001] 1 WLR 1, 12.

can enforce the trust against the trustees. Once a trust relationship is established between trustee and beneficiary, the fact that a beneficiary has given no value is irrelevant.

(f) EQUITY IS EQUALITY

The maxim that Equity is equality means that, where there are equitable interests in property, Equity presumes that they are equal interests. For example, where the trustees have a power to appoint to a charitable purpose and a non-charitable purpose, if the power is not exercised the court will allocate half of the fund for charitable purposes and half for non-charitable purposes.[89] The maxim will not be applied, however, where it is not considered to reflect the intention of the parties. In *McPhail v Doulton*,[90] the trustees had a discretion to appoint property amongst a large class of beneficiaries, but the Court thought it would be inappropriate to apply the maxim that 'Equity is equality' in that context. Lord Wilberforce said:[91]

As a matter of reason, to hold that a principle of equal division applies to trusts such as the present is certainly paradoxical. Equal division is surely the last thing the settlor ever intended: equal division among all may, probably would, produce a result beneficial to none. Why suppose that the court would lend itself to a whimsical execution? and as regards authority, I do not find that the nature of the trust, and of the court's powers over trusts, calls for any such rigid rule. Equal division may be sensible and has been decreed, in cases of family trusts, for a limited class, here there is life in the maxim 'equality is equity', but the cases provide numerous examples where this has not been so, and a different type of execution has been ordered, appropriate to the circumstances.

On the facts of *McPhail v Doulton*, if the trust property had been distributed according to the maxim that 'Equity is equality', each beneficiary would have received very little indeed, given the large number of beneficiaries in the class. This would not have been a sensible result, so the maxim was not applied.

The maxim that Equity is equality was, however, applied literally in *Re Bower's Settlement Trusts*.[92] A settlement provided that if one of the beneficiaries were to die, his share should accrue to the other beneficiaries. One of the beneficiaries had died and Morton J applied the equitable maxim so that the deceased beneficiary's share was distributed equally between the other beneficiaries, rather than proportionately in accordance with their existing share of the residue. Whether this literal application of the maxim was appropriate was considered in *Re Steel*.[93] In that case, legacies of different amounts were left in a will, which also contained a clause stating: 'Any residue remaining to be divided between those beneficiaries who have only received small amounts.' In interpreting this clause, Megarry V-C applied the maxim and divided the residue equally among the beneficiaries. But he considered the interpretation of the maxim more generally:[94]

there is then the question of what is to be the basis of division. There were two rival contentions on this. One was that the residue should be divided equally between all the legatees whose legacies had not lapsed, irrespective of the size of those legacies. The other was that the residue should be divided

---

[89] *Hoare v Osborne* [1866] LR 1 Eq 585.
[90] *McPhail v Doulton* [1971] AC 424.
[91] Ibid, 451.
[92] [1942] Ch 197.
[93] [1979] Ch 218.
[94] Ibid, 225.

proportionately among those legatees, in proportion to the size of each legacy, so that, for instance, a £200 legatee would get twice the share of residue of a £100 legatee. In support of equal division, it could be said by the £100 legatee to the £200 legatee: 'You were intended to get £100 more than me, and if we each get an equal share of residue, you will still get £100 more than me.' The riposte of the £200 legatee is: 'I was intended to get twice as much as you: equal division of the residue will alter that proportion, and so to carry out the proportions originally intended, the residue should be divided proportionately to our respective legacies. In favour of equal division there is the maxim 'equality is equity', and In Re Bower's Settlement Trusts [1942] Ch 197 . . .

. . . in [that case] the property was settled in terms of shares, rather than fixed amounts. It can therefore be said that the natural form of comparison in that case was on a proportionate basis, and that there was not the same freedom to choose between a comparison of proportions and a comparison of amounts, such as that one legatee is getting £100 more than another, as there is in this case.

Thus far, the concept of equality may be said to be in the ascendant. But does equality in this context necessarily mean a simple mathematical equality? . . .

When the maxim 'equality is equity' comes to be applied, it often, and I think usually, will mean mathematical equality, in that no other basis of equality can be discerned: but given suitable circumstances a true equality of treatment may require the application of a mathematical inequality, and instead a proportionate equality. So far as can be judged from the short report, this consideration was not put before Morton J in In Re Bower's Settlement Trusts.

The subject is one on which I feel considerable doubt. With all the respect due to a great equity lawyer, I might well, I think, have reached the opposite conclusion had the facts of In Re Bower's Settlement Trusts come before me without the benefit of the decision of Morton J. But there stands the decision. Further, I think that it would be easier to support the cause of proportionate division on the facts of that case than it is on the facts of the case now before me. There seems to me to be a real difference between shares of a fund on the one hand and legacies of fixed amounts on the other hand: one moves in a world of proportions, and the other in a world of determinate sums . . . I find it difficult, too, to see why in dividing the residue the intention should be treated as being to preserve the proportions rather than the gaps in amount, instead of being the opposite. In the end, I think that on the whole, in a case of real doubt . . . and as a matter of last resort, the simplicity of mathematical equality is to be preferred to any process of proportionate division.

(g) EQUITY LOOKS TO SUBSTANCE RATHER THAN FORM

In *Parkin v Thorold*,[95] Lord Romilly MR recognized that:

Courts of Equity make a distinction in all cases between that which is matter of substance and that which is matter of form; and, if they do find that by insisting on the form, the substance will be defeated, they hold it to be inequitable to allow a person to insist on such form, and thereby defeat the substance.

This provides the basis for the equitable remedy of rectification.[96] Where the words of a contract do not reflect the common intentions of the parties, Equity is willing to rewrite the document to reflect those intentions.[97] Similarly, where it is possible to identify an obligation that the recipient of

[95] (1852) 16 Beav 59, 66.
[96] See Chapter 20.4, pp. 1010–14.
[97] *The Olympic Pride* [1980] 2 Lloyds Rep 67.

property holds that property for somebody else, Equity will recognize that a trust has been created, even though the settlor has not explicitly stated that he or she intended to create a trust.[98] At the other extreme are circumstances in which the settlor has purported to create a trust, but Equity, having regard to the substance of the transaction, concludes that the trust is a sham.[99]

(h) WHERE THE EQUITIES ARE EQUAL, THE FIRST IN TIME SHALL PREVAIL

Equitable interests usually rank in the order in which they were created. So where there are two competing equitable interests in property, the usual rule is that the interest that was created first will have priority over the interest that was created later. As Millett J said in *Macmillan Inc. v Bishopsgate Trust (No. 3)*:[100]

> In English law the order of priority between two competing interests in the same property depends primarily on whether they are legal or merely equitable interests. Where both interests are equitable— or both legal, for that matter—the basic rule is that the two interests rank in the order of their creation. In the case of equitable interests the order of priority may be reversed in special circumstances, but 'where the equities are equal, the first in time prevails'.

An example of the 'special circumstances' to which Millett J referred arises where an interest has been appropriately registered: registration ensures that an interest has priority over an unregistered interest.[101] It is important to appreciate that this rule of 'first in time' only applies as regards two equitable interests. A subsequently acquired legal interest may have priority over a previously created equitable interest if the legal interest was acquired by a bona fide purchaser for value without notice. In such a situation, the legal interest has priority over the equitable interest in both Equity and at Law.[102]

QUESTION

Alan has a mistress, Brenda, with whom he has a child, Christopher. Alan is preparing his will and wants to leave property to Brenda and Christopher, but without revealing this to his wife. Alan asks his best friend, David, whether, if Alan left property to David in his will, David would transfer it to Brenda. David agrees to do so and Alan leaves £10,000 to David in his will. After Alan's death, David receives £10,000, but refuses to transfer it to Brenda because 'the will could not be clearer: this is my money'.

Should Brenda and Christopher have a remedy? If so, how might Equity help?

FURTHER READING

Baker, *Introduction to Legal History* (4th edn) (Oxford: Oxford University Press, 2002), pp. 97–116.

Burrows, 'We Do This at Common Law But That in Equity' (2002) 22 OJLS 1.

---

[98] See Chapter 3.2(a), pp. 67–9.
[99] See Chapter 3.2(b), pp. 69–73.
[100] [1995] 1 WLR 978, 999–1000.
[101] See e.g. Land Registration Act 2002, section 29.
[102] *Pilcher v Rawlins* (1872) LR 7 Ch. App. 259; *Macmillan Inc. v Bishopsgate Trust (No. 3)* [1995] 1 WLR 978, 1000 (Millett J). See further Chapter 18.6(a), pp. 911–6.

Martin, 'Fusion, Fallacy and Confusion; A Comparative Study' [1994] Conv 13.

Pettit, 'He Who Comes into Equity Must Come with Clean Hands' [1990] Conv 416.

Virgo, 'Restitution Through the Looking-glass: Restitution Within Equity and Equity Within Restitution', in *Rationalizing Property, Equity and Trusts: Essays in Honour of Edward Burn* (ed. Getzler) (London: Butterworths Lexis-Nexis, 2003), p. 106.

Worthington, *Equity* (2nd edn) (Oxford: Oxford University Press, 2006), chs 1 and 10.

2

INTRODUCTION TO TRUSTS

CENTRAL ISSUES

1. The trust involves a trustee or trustees holding property rights on behalf of another or for an identified purpose. A trustee is obliged in Equity to exercise those rights for that person or purpose.

2. It is unconscionable for a trustee appointed by a settlor to deny the trust and keep the property for him or herself.

3. There are a number of different categories of trust, the operation of which is influenced by the context in which the trust arises.

4. There are a variety of reasons why someone would wish to create a trust, with the consequent separation of legal and equitable title, whether in the context of the family, or business and finance.

5. It is important to distinguish the trust from other legal mechanisms, such as agency and bailment, which have different legal implications to the trust.

6. The law of trusts is primarily concerned with the different rights that various people might have following the creation of a trust. There is particular controversy about the nature of the beneficiary's rights to trust property.

1. HISTORY OF THE TRUST

Although the trust has been recognized for hundreds of years, its nature and function has not been constant. Grbich recognized that:[1]

> the term 'trust' is not clear and unchanging like a crystal, it is the skin round a living and growing concept.

The origins of the trust can be traced back to the thirteenth century, when it was essentially a conveyancing device for the holding of land to avoid financial liabilities and restrictions on the inheritance of property.[2] This forerunner of the modern trust was called the use. At its most basic, this device was used to transfer land to people who would hold it for the use of the transferor for life and then for selected family members. In that way, the transferor could ensure that the land was inherited by a

---

[1] *'Baden*: Awakening the Conceptually Moribund Trust' (1974) MLR 643, 648.
[2] See Milsom, *Historical Foundations of the Common Law* (2nd edn) (London: Butterworths, 1981), ch. 9; Baker, *An Introduction to English Legal History* (4th edn) (Oxford: Oxford University Press, 2002), ch. 14.

member of his family rather than forfeited to a lord. The use was also deployed where a tenant of land was fighting abroad, for example in the Crusades, so that trustees could be appointed to manage the land on his behalf. The person who transferred the land would today be called the settlor, but he might alternatively be described as the trustor, since he trusted the transferee to hold the land for the benefit of himself or somebody else. The transferee of the land was called a trustee, because he was trusted by the transferor. The person for whom the land was held was called the beneficiary, because he or she benefited from the use of the land.

Although this tripartite structure of the trust can be identified in the modern trust device, the context in which the trust arises today is very different. The trust has developed from a trust of land, to a trust of all kinds of property within the family, including money and shares, and has further expanded to its significant use today as a commercial device for the management of a portfolio of financial assets.[3] Although many of the essential components of the modern commercial trust can be traced back to the medieval use, the context in which the trust arises is completely different, and this has had a significant impact on the development of the law of trusts.

2. DEFINITION OF THE TRUST

The trust has been defined in many different ways,[4] but one of the most helpful definitions was suggested by Maitland:[5]

> I should define a trust in some such way as the following—when a person has rights which he is bound to exercise upon behalf of another or for the accomplishment of some particular purpose he is said to have those rights in trust for that other or for that purpose and he is called a trustee. It is a wide, vague definition, but the best that I can make.

This definition identifies certain key features of the trust. It is concerned with one person, the trustee, acting on behalf of another or for an identified purpose. It is concerned with the exercise of rights. It is concerned with the imposition of obligations on the trustee.

A useful definition of the trust can be found in the Recognition of Trusts Act 1987, which ratified the 1984 Hague Convention on the Law Applicable to Trusts and their Recognition, which establishes uniform conflict of law rules for the international recognition of the trust. Whilst the definition of the trust in the 1987 Act does not purport to define the trust domestically, its definition does accord with the understanding of the trust in English law.

RECOGNITION OF TRUSTS ACT 1987

SCHEDULE Convention on the Law Applicable to Trusts and their Recognition

Article 2

For the purposes of this Convention, the term 'trust' refers to the legal relationship created—*inter vivos* or on death—by a person, the settlor, when assets have been placed under the control of a trustee for the benefit of a beneficiary or for a specified purpose.

---

[3] See Langbein, 'The Secret Life of the Trust: The Trust as an Instrument of Commerce' (1997) 107 Yale LJ 165.
[4] See Hart, 'What is a Trust?' (1899) LQR 294.
[5] *Equity: A Course of Lectures* (2nd edn) (ed. Brunyate) (Cambridge: Cambridge University Press, 1936), p. 44.

A trust has the following characteristics—

(a) the assets constitute a separate fund and are not a part of the trustee's own estate;

(b) title to the trust assets stands in the name of the trustee or in the name of another person on behalf of the trustee;

(c) the trustee has the power and the duty, in respect of which he is accountable, to manage, employ or dispose of the assets in accordance with the terms of the trust and the special duties imposed upon him by law.

The reservation by the settlor of certain rights and powers, and the fact that the trustee may himself have rights as beneficiary, are not necessarily inconsistent with the existence of a trust.

Article 11

[Recognition of a trust] shall imply, as a minimum, that the trust property constitutes a separate fund, that the trustee may sue and be sued in his capacity as trustee, and that he may appear or act in this capacity before a notary or any person acting in an official capacity.

In so far as the law applicable to the trust requires or provides, such recognition shall imply in particular—

(a) that personal creditors of the trustee shall have no recourse against the trust assets;

(b) that the trust assets shall not form part of the trustee's estate upon his insolvency or bankruptcy;

(c) that the trust assets shall not form part of the matrimonial property of the trustee or his spouse nor part of the trustee's estate upon his death;

(d) that the trust assets may be recovered when the trustee, in breach of trust, has mingled trust assets with his own property or has alienated trust assets.

There are consequently two fundamental features of the trust: [6]

(1) a trustee holds property rights for a person or purpose—the property component; and

(2) the trustee is obliged in Equity to exercise those rights for that person or purpose—the obligation component.

The trust is distinguished from other legal concepts by these two components.[7] Their significance has been identified particularly well in Parkinson's definition of the trust that is intentionally created, known as an express trust:[8]

An express trust is an equitable obligation...binding a person ('the trustee') to deal with identifiable property to which he or she has legal title...for the benefit of others to whom he or she is in some way accountable. Such obligations may either be for the benefit of persons who have proprietary rights in equity, of whom he or she may be one, or for the furtherance of a sufficiently certain purpose...which can be enforced by someone intended to have a right of enforcement under the terms of the trust... or by operation of law.

Of these core components of the trust, it is the property component involving the split of legal and equitable title to property that is usually considered to be the essence of the trust. Whilst this component is undoubtedly significant, more recent analysis of the trust has emphasized the obligation

---

[6] Jaffey, 'Explaining the Trust' (2015) 131 LQR 377, 393.
[7] See Chapter 2.6, pp. 39–55.
[8] 'Reconceptualising the Express Trust' (2002) 61 CLJ 657, 683.

component.[9] Most significantly, Langbein has developed the 'contractarian account of the trust',[10] by virtue of which he concludes that the trust should be considered to be a bargain concerning how the trust assets should be managed and distributed. In particular, the 'trust deal', as he puts it, defines the powers and responsibilities of the trustee in managing the trust property. Langbein does not purport to argue that the trust should be defined only by reference to the obligation component, with that obligation deriving from a contract. He considers that the trust is a 'hybrid of contract and property', and that it 'straddles our categories of property and contract, because it embodies a contract about how property is to be deployed'.[11]

Langbein, 'The Contractarian Basis of the Law of Trusts' (1995) 105 Yale LJ 625[12]

We are accustomed to think of the trust as a branch of property law. The *Restatement (Second) of Trusts* defines the trust as 'a fiduciary relationship with respect to property', and the codes and treatises say similar things. This way of speaking about the trust omits an important dimension.

The contractarian claim. In truth, the trust is a deal, a bargain about how the trust assets are to be managed and distributed. To be sure, the trust originates exactly where convention says it does, with property. The *Restatement* says, 'A trust cannot be created unless there is trust property.' The owner, called the settlor, transfers the trust property to an intermediary, the trustee, to hold it for the beneficiaries. We treat the trustee as the new owner for the purpose of managing the property, while the trust deal strips the trustee of the benefits of ownership.

The distinguishing feature of the trust is not the background event, not the transfer of property to the trustee, but the trust deal that defines the powers and responsibilities of the trustee in managing the property. Sometimes the trust deal also confers significant discretion upon the trustee over dispositive provisions, that is, in allocating the beneficial interests among the beneficiaries. The settlor and the trustee may express their deal in detailed terms drafted for the particular trust, or they may be content to adopt the default rules of trust law. Either way, the deal between settlor and trustee is functionally indistinguishable from the modern third-party-beneficiary contract. Trusts are contracts.

This contractarian account of the trust is undoubtedly useful, especially because it does not undermine the significance of the property component to the trust. It is clearly the case that the nature of a trustees' duties and powers and the operation of the trust depend on the terms of the document that governs the trust. In many cases, the 'law of trusts' is simply a body of default rules that can be rejected by the settlor in creating the trust and which apply where no alternative provision has been made in the trust instrument.

But the key problem with Langbein's thesis is his emphasis on a contract or bargain between the settlor and the trustee, which is unrealistic. This is because, once the trust has been created, the settlor has no rights to enforce the bargain and usually has no rights relating to the trust, except where he or she has reserved powers to revoke the trust,[13] to appoint trustees, to direct investment by the trustees,[14] or to amend the trust. Enforcement of the trust is left to the beneficiaries who were not parties to the bargain. Further, the trustee of a testamentary trust cannot usually be considered

---

[9] Ibid.

[10] 'The Contractarian Basis of the Law of Trusts' (1995) 105 Yale LJ 625. See also Maitland, *Equity: A Course of Lectures* (2nd edn), p. 28.

[11] 'The Contractarian Basis of the Law of Trusts' (1995) 105 Yale LJ 625, 669 and 671.

[12] Footnotes omitted.

[13] *Choithram International SA v Pagarani* [2002] 1 WLR 1, 11 (PC).

[14] *Vestey's Executors v IRC* [1949] 1 All ER 1108.

to have entered into any bargain with the testator. Finally, it is possible for a settlor to declare him or herself a trustee and there clearly cannot be a contract between the settlor and trustee in such circumstances.

The 'contractarian' analysis of the trust cannot be regarded as a universal explanation of the express trust, but it does not follow that the thesis should be rejected completely. Langbein identifies an important truth relating to the law of trusts, namely that the obligations of the trustee can be modified by the terms of the trust instrument. It is not helpful to consider that instrument as inevitably being a bargain or a contract, but it clearly has a vital role in determining the nature of the trustee's obligations.

It follows that, however the trust might be defined, the definition must consist of two components. The property component emphasizes that it is only possible to have a trust of property, and that the rights relating to that property are split between the legal proprietary rights of the trustee[15] and the equitable proprietary rights of the beneficiary. This is significant because, if the trustee becomes insolvent, the trust property cannot be transferred to the trustee's creditors, since that property belongs to the beneficiaries in Equity.[16] Also, if that property has been misappropriated and transferred to a third party, the beneficiaries have a claim based on their equitable property rights to recover that property or its identifiable substitute.[17] The obligation component emphasizes that the trustee owes an obligation to the beneficiaries as regards the management and use of that property. This is significant because it means that the trustee is unable to benefit from that property for him or herself, save to the extent that he or she might also be a beneficiary of the trust.

3. THE ESSENCE OF THE TRUST

In *Westdeutsche Landesbank Girozentrale v Islington LBC*,[18] Lord Browne-Wilkinson identified four fundamental principles relating to all trusts, which he considered to be uncontroversial:[19]

> The relevant principles of trust law
>
> (i) Equity operates on the conscience of the owner of the legal interest. In the case of a trust, the conscience of the legal owner requires him to carry out the purposes for which the property was vested in him (express or implied trust) or which the law imposes on him by reason of his unconscionable conduct (constructive trust).
>
> (ii) Since the equitable jurisdiction to enforce trusts depends upon the conscience of the holder of the legal interest being affected, he cannot be a trustee of the property if and so long as he is ignorant of the facts alleged to affect his conscience, i.e. until he is aware...in the case of a constructive trust, of the factors which are alleged to affect his conscience.
>
> (iii) In order to establish a trust there must be identifiable trust property. The only apparent exception to this rule is a constructive trust imposed on a person who dishonestly assists in a breach of trust who may come under fiduciary duties even if he does not receive identifiable trust property.[20]

---

[15] Although it is sometimes possible for a trustee to hold equitable property rights on trust for the beneficiary. See Chapter 2.7(b), p. 55.

[16] See Chapter 1.4(a), p. 11.

[17] See Chapter 18, 'Proprietary Claims and Remedies'.

[18] [1996] AC 669.

[19] Ibid, 705.

[20] The better view is that there is no constructive trust in such a situation, but only a personal liability to the claimant. See Chapter 7.1(b)(iv), p. 331.

(iv) Once a trust is established, as from the date of its establishment the beneficiary has, in equity, a proprietary interest in the trust property, which proprietary interest will be enforceable in equity against any subsequent holder of the property (whether the original property or substituted property into which it can be traced) other than a purchaser for value of the legal interest without notice.

These principles are significant to the interpretation and operation of trusts, although they are more controversial than Lord Browne-Wilkinson appeared to think. For example, although his Lordship is generally correct to state that it is unconscionable for a trustee appointed by a settlor to deny the trust and keep the property for him or herself, this will only be the case where the trustee is aware that he or she has been appointed as trustee. But a person may become a trustee despite not knowing this;[21] in such circumstances, the trustee will not be aware of significant facts that affect his or her conscience. It is correct, however, that for there to be a valid trust there must be identifiable trust property in which the beneficiary has an equitable proprietary interest. As a general rule, the trustee should keep trust property segregated from his or her own property.[22] If a defendant is allowed to mix the property that has been received with his or her own property, this may be a significant factor which suggests that the property is not held on trust, but by the defendant beneficially.[23]

4. CLASSIFICATION OF TRUSTS

There are a variety of ways in which trusts can be classified, but the most significant methods are by reference to the event that creates the trust and by the context in which the trust arises.

(a) BY EVENT

Trusts can be classified by reference to particular events to determine when the trust arises. This event-based scheme was propounded by Birks,[24] and has been summarized by Chambers:[25]

Much more useful than the conventional classification of trusts, as express, implied, resulting or constructive, would be a classification distinguishing trusts as generated by consent, wrongs, unjust enrichment or other events. The advantage of this approach would be the greater ease of aligning the law of trusts with other areas of law responding to the same ideas.

Although this event-based classification has proved useful to some commentators, it has not been endorsed by the courts and, as regards the classification of trusts, it does not reflect the state of the law and is too uncertain to be of any predictive value. For example, the final category of 'other events' is potentially very wide, since there are a variety of other events that trigger the recognition of trusts but which cannot be considered to fall within the first three categories; examples include trusts arising from unconscionable conduct not amounting to a recognized wrong[26] or estoppel.[27]

---

[21] See Chapter 2.4(b)(x)(xi), p. 36.
[22] *Re Lehman Brothers International (Europe) (in administration)* [2012] UKSC 6; [2] (Lord Hope).
[23] *Pearson v Lehman Brothers Finance SA* [2010] EWHC 2914 (Ch), [225] (Briggs J).
[24] Birks, 'Equity in the Modern Law: An Exercise in Taxonomy' (1996) Univ WALR 1, 9.
[25] *Resulting Trusts* (Oxford: Clarendon Press, 1997), p. 5.
[26] See Chapter 7.2(a), p. 332.
[27] See Chapter 9.4, pp. 469–80.

Further, no case has explicitly recognized that a trust arises where the defendant is unjustly enriched at the expense of the claimant. Similarly, the commission of most wrongs, such as breach of contract and tort, will not trigger the recognition of a trust; even where the defendant has committed an equitable wrong of breach of fiduciary duty, a trust will only be triggered exceptionally.[28] Finally, whilst express trusts, which are intended to be created by a trustee or settlor, might fall within the category of 'consensual trusts', the language of consent is inappropriate since it might suggest that the creation of an express trust is contractual. There is, however, usually no contract between any of the settlor, trustee, or beneficiary, primarily because of the absence of consideration between the parties.

It follows that classification of trusts by event is, at best, unhelpful and, at worst, distorts our understanding of when trusts can and should arise.

(b) BY CONTEXT

It is preferable to characterize trusts by reference to the context in which the trust arises. As McBride has recognized:[29]

> If you want to know what a trust is then you will want to consult or construct an 'identity-based' classification of trusts which classifies trusts as instances of irreducibly dissimilar legal concepts. If the word 'trust' describes one discrete legal concept then under an identity-based classification of trusts all trusts will be classified as instances of the same type of legal concept, the features of which can then be delineated and used to define what a trust is.

Various categories of trust can be identified. In fact, the categories are not mutually exclusive, since a particular trust might fall within more than one category.

(i) *Express trusts*

An express trust is created intentionally by the settlor (if the trust is created by somebody whilst he or she is alive, who 'settles' property on trust) or the testator (if the trust is created by somebody in a will). The settlor of a trust may either declare that he or she holds property on trust for somebody else or transfer property to somebody else to hold on trust for the settlor or for another person.

(ii) *Fixed trusts*

In a fixed trust, the beneficiaries' interests are specified in the trust instrument. For example, £9,000 may be held by Alan on trust for Brenda, Carol, and Debbie in equal shares, so that each of the beneficiaries has a one-third interest in the trust fund.

(iii) *Discretionary trusts*

Another form of express trust is the discretionary trust under which the trustees have discretion to 'appoint' (meaning 'to distribute') the property as they wish to people from a particular class of potential beneficiaries, known as the objects. For example, £1 million may be settled on trust for the

---

[28] See Chapter 7.2(g), pp. 000–00.
[29] 'On the classification of trusts', in *Restitution and Equity, Volume 1: Resulting Trusts and Equitable Compensation* (eds Birks and Rose) (Oxford: Mansfield Press, 2000), p. 23.

trustees in their absolute discretion to use it to pay for the education of the children of employees of a particular company. The trustees could then allocate the fund to such children of employees and in such amounts as they considered appropriate. The objects of a discretionary trust do not have an equitable proprietary interest in the trust property, since the trustee's discretion may not be exercised in their favour. Instead, they have only an expectation that the trustees might exercise the discretion in their favour.

(iv) Inter vivos *trusts*

Trusts may be created *inter vivos*, which simply means that they are created whilst the settlor remains alive.

(v) *Testamentary trusts*

A testator may leave property in his or her will to a beneficiary, known as a 'devisee' or 'legatee', absolutely, so that, following the death of the testator and once his or her estate has been administered, the property will be transferred to the legatee. But the testator may instead wish to leave some property on trust. Once the estate has been administered, the trust property will then be transferred to a trustee to hold on the trusts identified in the will. This could be a discretionary trust or it could be a fixed trust in which the testator has created successive interests.

(vi) *Bare trusts*

A bare trust arises where property is vested in the trustee for the sole benefit of the beneficiary, who is of full age. The trustee of a bare trust has no active duties relating to the management and disposal of the trust property,[30] but is bound to follow the instructions of the beneficiary. This can be compared with a so-called 'special trust', where special duties are imposed on the trustee to manage the property and to distribute it to the beneficiaries.

(vii) *Public and private trusts*

Trusts may be created for public purposes as well as for individuals or a class of people. Trusts for individuals or classes of people are private trusts, since they are not created for the benefit of the public. Public trusts, known as charitable trusts, must operate for the benefit of the public.[31]

(viii) *Protective trusts*

A protective trust protects a beneficiary's assets against the effects of bankruptcy or other misfortune.[32] The typical protective trust involves the beneficiary being given a life interest that is determinable on the occurrence of a designated event, such as the beneficiary's bankruptcy or the assignment of the interest. If the designated event occurs, the life interest is forfeited, but the property will then be held on a discretionary trust, with the original beneficiary being a member of the class who might still be able to benefit from the exercise of the trustees' discretion.

---

[30] *Re Cunningham and Frayling* [1891] 2 Ch 567.
[31] See Chapter 5.3(c)(ii), pp. 191–205.
[32] See Sheridan, 'Protective Trusts' [1957] 21 Conv 110.

The trust is called 'protective' because it provides a mechanism for protecting the beneficiary from adverse events. Donovan LJ recognized that this trust 'is intended as protection to spendthrift or improvident or weak life tenants'.[33] The use of the trust has proved to be especially important where a parent is concerned about a profligate child losing property on being declared bankrupt. So, if the beneficiary becomes bankrupt, the termination of his or her life interest would mean that there is no property available to the beneficiary's creditors, because he or she no longer has an equitable proprietary interest in that property.

The protective trust is a particularly significant mechanism for defeating the claims of creditors and so is subject to a number of restrictions. For example, it cannot be created by a settlor to protect his or her own property from creditors on being declared bankrupt.[34] The nature of the protective trust and the consequences of forfeiture can be determined expressly by the trust instrument, but if that instrument simply says that the beneficiary has a life interest and the property is held on protective trust,[35] the statutory regime under section 33 of the Trustee Act 1925 applies.

TRUSTEE ACT 1925

33. Protective Trusts

(1) Where any income . . . is directed to be held on protective trusts for the benefit of any person (in this section called 'the principal beneficiary') for the period of his life or for any less period, then, during that period (in this section called the 'trust period') the said income shall, without prejudice to any prior interest, be held on the following trusts, namely:

(a) Upon trust for the principal beneficiary during the trust period or until he, whether before or after the termination of any prior interest, does or attempts to do or suffers any act or thing, or until any event happens, other than an advance under any statutory or express power, whereby, if the said income were payable during the trust period to the principal beneficiary absolutely during that period, he would be deprived of the right to receive the same or any part thereof, in any of which cases, as well as on the termination of the trust period, whichever first happens, this trust of the said income shall fail or determine.

(b) If the trust aforesaid fails or determines during the subsistence of the trust period, then, during the residue of that period, the said income shall be held upon trust for the application thereof for the maintenance or support, or otherwise for the benefit, of all or any one or more exclusively of the other or others of the following persons (that is to say)—

(i) the principal beneficiary and his or her spouse or civil partner, if any, and his or her children or more remote issue, if any; or

(ii) if there is no spouse or civil partner or issue of the principal beneficiary in existence, the principal beneficiary and the persons who would, if he were actually dead, be entitled to the trust property or the income thereof or to the annuity fund, if any, or arrears of the annuity, as the case may be;

as the trustees in their absolute discretion, without being liable to account for the exercise of such discretion, think fit.

---

[33] *General Accident Fire and Life Assurance Corporation Ltd v IRC* [1963] 1 WLR 1207, 1218.
[34] *Re Burroughs-Fowler* [1916] 2 Ch 251.
[35] *Re Wittke* [1944] Ch 166.

The consequences of forfeiture may be beneficial to the beneficiary, especially where the effect is to protect trust property from creditors. But it may sometimes have adverse consequences for the beneficiary. For example, in *Re Baring's Settlement Trusts*,[36] a wife had a protected life interest with income payable to her until some event happened by virtue of which the income would become payable to somebody else. She failed to obey a court order to return her infant children to the jurisdiction of the court and consequently her husband obtained a sequestration order against her property. This was sufficient to forfeit her life interest, because she no longer had a right to receive the income from the trust property; a discretionary trust, therefore, arose, even though the sequestration order was only temporary. Morton J said:[37]

> [the settlor] intended that there should be a continuous benefit to the beneficiaries so that either the tenant for life should be in a position to have the income or the discretionary trust should arise.

This can be compared with *Re Oppenheim's Will Trusts*,[38] where a tenant for life under a protective trust had been certified as a person of unsound mind. A receiver was consequently appointed to conduct his affairs. Harman J held that this did not effect a forfeiture and said:[39]

> I think that a man who has a statutory agent, as this man has, can give by his agent a personal discharge no less than...if he were on the top of Mount Everest, his banker could give a personal discharge on his behalf. It seems to me also that the forfeiture was not intended to operate in a case of this kind where no one else will be entitled to the benefit of the income in the event which has happened. It was intended to prevent the income from getting into other hands. That does not occur in the present case.

Once the life interest has been forfeited the discretionary trust comes into effect and the trustees are obliged to exercise their discretion to dispose of the property to one of the members of the class.[40] This could be the beneficiary who formerly had the life interest, but only if the trustees consider it to be appropriate to exercise their discretion in this way.

If the principal beneficiary acts in such a way as to inadvertently forfeit his or her protected life interest, it might be possible for the act to be set aside through the exercise of the equitable jurisdiction relating to mistake.[41] For example, in *Gibbon v Mitchell*,[42] the claimant voluntarily surrendered his protected life interest in favour of his children by a deed, in order to minimize his inheritance tax liability. However, he did not realize that this would result in the forfeiture of the life interest and bring a discretionary trust into effect. Consequently, the deed of surrender was set aside on the ground that he had made a serious mistake.

(ix) *Pension fund trusts*

A typical contributory pension scheme involves members of the scheme, who are employees of a company or a group of companies, contributing a percentage of their salary to the scheme. Their employer also makes contributions. On retirement, the members of the scheme receive defined

---

[36] [1940] Ch 737.
[37] Ibid, 753.
[38] [1950] Ch 633.
[39] Ibid, 636.
[40] *Re Gourju's Will Trusts* [1943] Ch 24.
[41] On the role of mistake generally to set aside trusts and dispositions to trusts, see Chapter 7.2(c), pp. 337–41.
[42] [1990] 1 WLR 1304.

benefits, either as a proportion of their final salary or of their average salary. Although contributory pension schemes can be established contractually without using a trust, the trust mechanism is used for large pension schemes as a way of managing substantial sums of money for the benefit of the employees who participate in the scheme. This was considered by Lord Millett in *Air Jamaica Ltd v Charlton*:[43]

A pension scheme can, in theory at least, be established by contract between the employer and each employee and without using the machinery of a trust. Such a scheme would have to be very simple. It would look very like a self-employed pension policy. There would be no trust fund and no trustees. The employer would simply contract with each of his employees that, if the employee made weekly payments to the employer, the employer would pay the employee a pension on retirement or a lump sum on death. The employer would not make any contributions itself, since there would be no one to receive them. But the benefits would be calculated at a higher level than would be justified by the employee's contributions alone.

The company's pension scheme was, however, of a very different kind. A trust fund was established with its own trustees. Contributions, whether by members or by the company, were paid into the trust fund, and the trustees were given powers of investment over the fund. The benefits were funded in part by contributions and in part by the income of the investments held in the fund. The interposition of a trust fund between the company and the members meant that payment of benefits to members was the responsibility of the trustees, not the company. The machinery employed was that of a trust, not a contract.

This is not to say that the trust is like a traditional family trust under which a settlor voluntarily settles property for the benefit of the object of his bounty. The employee members of an occupational pension scheme are not voluntary settlors. As has been repeatedly observed, their rights are derived from their contracts of employment as well as from the trust instrument. Their pensions are earned by their services under their contracts of employment as well as by their contributions. They are often not inappropriately described as deferred pay. This does not mean, however, that they have contractual rights to their pensions. It means only that, in construing the trust instrument, regard must be had to the nature of an occupational pension and the employment relationship that forms its genesis.

In the present case prospective employees were informed that the company maintained a pension scheme for its staff and that membership was compulsory for those under 55 years of age. They were told the amount of the employee's contribution, and that the company paid 'an amount not less than the employee's contribution, plus any amount necessary to support the financial viability of the scheme'. Even if these can be regarded as imposing contractual obligations on the company, the only obligation which was undertaken by the company, and one which it has fully performed, was to make contributions to the fund. The obligation to make pension payments was not a contractual obligation undertaken by the company, but a trust obligation imposed on the trustees. . . . each employee becomes a member of the pension scheme by virtue of his employment, but . . . his entitlement to a pension arises under the trusts of the scheme.

Their Lordships should add for completeness that, while the members' entitlements arise under the trusts of the pension plan, the company's obligation to deduct contributions from members and to pay them to the trustees together with its own matching contributions, is contractual. The company undertook this obligation by its covenant with the trustees in the trust deed. The obligation was, however, subject to the power of the company unilaterally to discontinue the plan under section 13.2 of the plan.

---

[43] [1999] 1 WLR 1399, 1407.

> It is well established that, absent statutory intervention, such pensions schemes are subject to the rule against perpetuities...the Social Security Act 1973[44]...makes special provision for all qualifying occupational pension schemes to be exempt from the rule.

Hayton has noted that:[45]

> the species of pension trust should be regarded as having evolved from the trust genus as a drastically different species from the species of traditional family trust.

This may well be true, but the pension trust is a genuine trust and is influenced by fundamental principles of trust law.[46] In fact, some of the leading cases on the modern law of trusts are pension trust cases.[47] But, as Lord Millett recognized in *Air Jamaica*, the existence of the employees' contract of employment means that some of the principles are applied differently.[48] So, for example, the typical tripartite structure of the traditional trust, in which the settlor, trustee, and beneficiary are all independent and distinct, does not operate in the same way for pension trusts. This was recognized by Browne-Wilkinson V-C in *Imperial Group Pension Trust v Imperial Tobacco Ltd*:[49]

> Pension scheme trusts are of quite a different nature to traditional trusts. The traditional trust is one under which the settlor, by way of bounty, transfers property to trustees to be administered for the beneficiaries as objects of his bounty. Normally, there is no legal relationship between the parties apart from the trust. The beneficiaries have given no consideration for what they receive. The settlor, as donor, can impose such limits on his bounty as he chooses, including imposing a requirement that the consent of himself or some other person shall be required to the exercise of the powers.
>
> ...a pension scheme is quite different. Pension benefits are part of the consideration which an employee receives in return for the rendering of his services. In many cases, including the present, membership of the pension scheme is a requirement of employment. In contributory schemes, such as this, the employee is himself bound to pay his or her contributions. Beneficiaries of the scheme, the members, far from being volunteers have given valuable consideration. The company employer is not conferring a bounty.

In a pension trust, each member is a settlor of a separate settlement within the head trust, but that member is also the beneficiary. The employees' contract of employment treats the provision of their pension rights as part of their pay; the receipt of benefits by the employee subsequently can be considered to be deferred remuneration for their services to their employer.

---

[44] See now the Pension Schemes Act 1993, s. 163. See generally Chapter 3.7, pp. 112–6.

[45] 'Pension Trusts and Traditional Trusts: Drastically Different Species of Trusts' [2005] Conv 229, 245.

[46] See, for example, the law on distribution of surplus funds following the termination of a pension trust, at Chapter 8.3(c)(ii), pp. 393–7.

[47] *Air Jamaica Ltd v Charlton* [1999] 1 WLR 1399 (resulting trust), Chapter 8.3(b), pp. 385–92; *Cowan v Scargill* [1985] Ch 270 (ethical considerations in making investment decisions), Chapter 12.4(c)(ii), pp. 601–8; *Mettoy Pension Trustees Ltd v Evans* [1990] 1 WLR 1587 (release of fiduciary power), Chapter 11.7(e), p. 570; *Edge v Pensions Ombudsman* [2000] Ch 602 (duty to exercise discretion for proper purpose).

[48] Milner, 'Pension Trust: A New Trust Form' [1997] Conv 89.

[49] [1991] 1 WLR 589, 597.

Whereas trustees of traditional trusts are required to promote the best interests of the beneficiaries exclusively, this is not true of pension trustees. As Fox has observed:[50]

> pension trusts do not operate in a narrow setting where the trustees' exclusive concern is to promote the members' best interests. The view of Sir Robert Megarry V-C in *Cowan v Scargill* [1985] Ch. 270, 288–89 that pension trustees, like traditional donative trustees, must aim to promote their beneficiaries' best financial interests might have been true for their investment powers but it is not necessarily true for all powers of pension trustees. The members are one section of a larger network of relevant participants in the pension scheme. So the trustees must also have regard to the employer's interest in operating the scheme... This is entirely appropriate. The scheme is an adjunct to the employer's business. The employer carries the immediate risk of moral hazard arising from the trustees' decisions since it is liable to pay the balance of cost of funding the scheme if it falls into deficit.

Another participant in this network is the Pensions Protection Fund, an insurance scheme that underwrites pension schemes that are in deficit when they are wound up. Trustees of the pension fund cannot, however, exercise their discretion in such a way as to increase the trust fund's surplus whilst relying on the Pensions Protection Fund to underwrite the effect of their actions, since that Fund was only intended to provide compensation in the last resort.[51]

The financial significance of pension trusts to many employees, and the dangers of abuse of powers and misappropriation of trust assets by employers, has meant that these trusts are regulated by statute, notably the Pensions Act 1995. This provides safeguards for the protection of beneficiaries, including a requirement to appoint professional advisers and a minimum funding requirement to prevent a shortfall of funds.[52] The Pensions Act 2004 resulted in the creation of a Pensions Regulator to reduce the possibility of pension funds being misappropriated.

(x) *Resulting trusts*

In certain recognized situations, a trustee will hold property on trust for the person who transferred property to the trustee. This fact-pattern is not exclusive to resulting trusts: a trustee may hold property for the settlor under an express trust, for example. But, whereas an express trust arises because it was expressly intended, the resulting trust arises where the intentions of the transferor have not been made express but the transferor is presumed to have intended that the property transferred be held on trust for him or her. The property is said to 'result' back to the settlor or the estate of the testator, and so the trust is called a resulting trust.[53] A trustee will hold property on resulting trust for the settlor who sought to create an express trust that has failed. Similarly, where a transferor has transferred property to the transferee for no consideration in return, it will generally be presumed that the transferor intended the transferee to hold the property on trust for him or herself.

(xi) *Constructive trusts*

The constructive trust[54] arises through the application of legal rules, rather than the express or presumed intent of a settlor. These trusts are recognized in a number of different circumstances, but

---

[50] 'Discretion and Moral Hazard in Pension Trusts' (2010) 69 CLJ 240, 242.
[51] *Independent Trustee Services Ltd v Hope* [2009] EWHC 2810 (Ch), [119] (Henderson J).
[52] Nobles, 'Pensions Act 1995' (1996) 59 MLR 241.
[53] See Chapter 8, 'Resulting Trusts'.
[54] See Chapter 7, 'Constructive Trusts' and Chapter 9, 'Informal Arrangements Relating to Land'.

primarily where the recipient of property can be considered to have acted unconscionably, such as where the property was obtained fraudulently.

5. REASONS FOR CREATING AN EXPRESS TRUST

There are a variety of reasons why someone would wish to create a trust, with the consequent separation of legal and equitable title, whether in the context of the family, or business and finance.

(a) SEGREGATION OF ASSETS

The trust enables trust assets to be segregated from other assets of the settlor. Provided that the settlor is not also the beneficiary under the trust, this arrangement will protect the trust assets from the consequences of the settlor's insolvency. If the settlor becomes insolvent, he or she will no longer have any proprietary interest in the assets, so they will not be available to his or her creditors. Segregation of assets is also relevant as regards the trustee, since, if the trustee becomes insolvent, the trust assets will not be available for the trustee's creditors, because the assets belong to the beneficiaries in Equity.

(b) ASSET PARTITIONING

Asset partitioning refers to the ability to take an asset and to create different rights in it. In the family context, asset partitioning can be especially significant because it enables the settlor or testator to provide for the successive enjoyment of property, such as when property is left to a wife for life with remainder to the testator's children. This means that the wife will have the benefit of the property for her life, but, on her death, the property will pass to the children.

(c) MANAGEMENT OF PROPERTY

There may be a particular advantage in having trustees manage and administer the property on behalf of the beneficiaries. For example, the trustees might have particular financial and investment experience. Alternatively, the beneficiaries may be too young to manage the property themselves, or it might be that they cannot be trusted with the property; in either event, it is preferable for somebody else to manage the property on their behalf. This is one of the main reasons why the trust is used in the commercial world, such as for pension funds. It is commercially useful for a group of people to be able to invest their funds by means of a unit or investment trust, under which trustees hold investments in a range of securities in trust for investors who have purchased units or shares in the trust fund.

(d) TAX AVOIDANCE

Taxation is often a prominent consideration in the decision to create a trust. The use of the trust can provide a mechanism for avoiding or minimizing a tax liability. The trust is significant in this respect because it enables more than one person to have an interest in property; it is, therefore, possible to structure the ownership of property in such a way as to ensure that one person benefits from the property but that another owns it at law. For example, a settlor may name his or her infant children as beneficiaries of some of his or her assets; if the settlor is a higher rate taxpayer, this might be advantageous as the trust may be charged a lower rate of tax. Another option is for the settlor to transfer title to property to a trustee who is resident in another country that is a tax haven, where little or no tax is paid, so that the trust would be taxed in that country.

The trust cannot be used as a mechanism to evade the payment of tax that is already due, since that is a criminal offence. The trust can, however, be used to avoid or mitigate a tax liability. The distinction between tax avoidance and mitigation was recognized by Lord Nolan in *Inland Revenue Commissioners v Willoughby*:[55]

> The hallmark of tax avoidance is that the taxpayer reduces his liability to tax without incurring the economic consequences that Parliament intended to be suffered by any taxpayer qualifying for such reduction in his tax liability. The hallmark of tax mitigation, on the other hand, is that the taxpayer takes advantage of a fiscally attractive option afforded to him by the tax legislation, and genuinely suffers the economic consequences that Parliament intended to be suffered by those taking advantage of the option.

Tax mitigation is always legitimate. Tax avoidance is generally legitimate, although the more artificial the scheme the more likely that it will be found to be ineffective.

A wide variety of tax-avoidance schemes have been developed, which use the trust as their means of implementation. The fundamental principle relating to the validity of such schemes was recognized by Lord Tomlin in *IRC v Duke of Westminster*:[56]

> Every man is entitled if he can to arrange his affairs so that the tax attaching under the appropriate Acts is less than it otherwise would be. If he succeeds in ordering them so as to secure that result, then, however unappreciative the Commissioners of Inland Revenue or his fellow taxpayers may be of his ingenuity, he cannot be compelled to pay an increased tax.

If, however, the main purpose or one of the main purposes of creating the trust is to avoid or reduce tax and this is considered to be abusive, in the sense that the creation of the trust is not a reasonable course of action, the 'general anti-abuse rule' will apply so that the tax advantage obtained will be counteracted by making an adjustment to the tax liability.[57]

Where income arises from a trust, its taxation takes place at two different stages. The trustees are chargeable because they receive the income,[58] and the beneficiaries are also assessable on any income they received under the trust, but such assessment will take account of any Income Tax already paid by the trustees. Where, however, the trust is a bare trust,[59] the beneficiary is taxed as though he or she were the absolute owner of the property.[60]

The trustees will be chargeable to Capital Gains Tax on any increase in the capital value of trust assets made in disposing of trust assets in the course of administering the trust. A settlor who settles property on trust will not, however, be liable to pay tax on any gain in the capital value of the property unless he or she retains an interest in that property. Inheritance Tax is the tax that most concerns the trust lawyer. This is the tax that is paid on the value of a deceased's estate. The use of the trust can

---

[55] [1997] 1 WLR 1071, 1079.
[56] [1936] AC 1, 19.
[57] Finance Act 2013, Part 5 and Sch 43. See further on the doctrine of sham trusts at Chapter 3.2(b), pp. 69–73.
[58] *Williams v Singer* [1921] 1 AC 65.
[59] See Chapter 2.4(b)(vi), p. 31.
[60] *Baker v Archer-Shee* [1927] AC 844.

be especially significant in reducing Inheritance Tax liability, especially where property is settled on trust and the settlor does not die within the next seven years.[61]

6. DISTINGUISHING TRUSTS FROM OTHER LEGAL MECHANISMS

To understand the trust it is important to determine how it differs from other legal mechanisms. Sometimes the boundaries are clear, but they are becoming increasingly difficult to define.

(a) CONTRACT

Trust and contract are very different concepts. Contract is based upon agreement, requiring either a deed or consideration, and creates a personal right against the other party. The trust is an equitable concept, arising typically by virtue of the intention of the settlor or testator, and creates proprietary and personal rights in the beneficiary, which he or she is able to enforce despite being a volunteer and not a party to any bargain. Whereas one contracting party can sue the other for breach of contract, once the trust has been created, the settlor cannot sue the trustee for breach of trust and cannot seek the termination of the trust; it is the beneficiary who is able to sue for breach of trust.

It is important also to distinguish between the creation of a trust and a contract or covenant to create one. Once a trust is created, the beneficiaries become owners in Equity of their share of the settled property. But, if the settlor has only promised to create a trust or to add property to an existing settlement, by means of a covenant, the rights of the intended beneficiaries depend on whether they can compel the settlor to perform the covenant. Traditionally, they cannot do so if they are volunteers, for Equity does not assist a volunteer.[62] The effect of this rule has now been modified by the Contracts (Rights of Third Parties) Act 1999.[63]

Despite these differences between trust and contract, there are a growing number of situations in which the dividing line between them is blurred. For example, the trust might derive from a contract, such as the pension fund trust that derives from the employment contract.[64] It has been recognized that a single transaction can give rise to both a trust and a contract.[65] Contracts can also modify the application of the rules in the law of trusts and even exclude them.[66] This is particularly important since many trustees are professionals whose duties and responsibilities are determined by their contract of appointment, which will often exclude their liability for breach of trust.[67]

(b) DEBT

The relationship of creditor and debtor is one of personal obligation, since the debtor is personally liable to the creditor for the value of the debt. If the debtor becomes insolvent, his or her assets will

---

[61] See *Pitt v Holt* [2013] UKSC 26; [2013] 2 AC 108, Chapter 11.7(g), pp. 577–83.

[62] See Chapter 4.3(c), p. 152.

[63] See Chapter 4(3)(d)(i), pp. 162–3.

[64] See Chapter 2.4(b)(ix), pp. 33–6. See also the role of contract in explaining how property can be held for the purposes of an unincorporated association: see Chapter 6.4(b)(v), pp. 305–11.

[65] *Charity Commission for England and Wales v Framjee* [2014] EWHC 2507 (Ch); [2015] 1 WLR 16, [42] (Henderson J).

[66] See Chapter 16.2, pp. 744–60.

[67] See Chapter 16.2(b)(iii)(a), pp. 750–2.

be available to all his or her creditors, who will not have priority over each other unless one of them has a security interest over the debtor's property. The relationship of beneficiary and trustee is different, because the beneficiary has an equitable proprietary interest in the trust assets, so that he or she will be able to claim those assets in priority to the trustee's creditors if the trustee becomes insolvent.

The distinction between trust and debt is illustrated by *Duggan v Governor of Full Sutton Prison*.[68] A rule in the Prison Rules provided that any prisoner who had cash in prison was required to pay it into an account under the Governor's control. The Court of Appeal held that this created a relationship of debtor and creditor, but did not impose a trust, because there was nothing in the Prison Rules to indicate that a trust was intended. It followed that, since the Governor had not received the money as trustee, he was not obliged to invest the money in an interest-bearing account for the benefit of the prisoners.

The creditor–debtor relationship is not, however, entirely alien to the trust. The trustee may be personally liable to the beneficiary for breach of trust, and this liability will create a debt owed to the beneficiary, so that, to this extent, the beneficiary is the creditor of the trustee.[69]

Whether the beneficiary can be considered to be creditor of the trustee was significant in *Re Lehman Brothers International (Europe) (No. 2)*.[70] A bank, Lehman Brothers, had collapsed, leaving a lot of money owing to creditors. To ensure that the creditors were paid some of what they were owed, the bank's administrators applied for a so-called 'scheme of arrangement'[71] to reduce some of the bank's liabilities, which required the consent of creditors to be effective. One issue for the court concerned the determination of who was a creditor. Patten LJ said:[72]

a 'creditor' will consist of anyone who has a monetary claim against the company which, when payable, will constitute a debt. Contingent claims are included for this purpose. A claim (e.g.) for damages in tort is still a legal liability of the company which will ultimately result in either an agreed payment or a judgment debt. The Scheme has been drafted so as to exclude anyone whose only claim against the company will be one *in rem*. To be a Scheme Creditor one has to have a current or contingent claim for damages or equitable compensation against the company, either of which is sufficient to render the claimant a creditor at least in that respect...

It is obvious that someone with a purely proprietary claim against the company is not its creditor in any conventional sense of that word. As a matter of ordinary language, a creditor is someone to whom money is owed...

No one can dispute that a creditor with security for what is owed remains a creditor of the company. Their security exists and is only enforceable to the extent and for so long as the underlying indebtedness continues....The interests granted to secured creditors (which, in the case of real property, amount to a legal estate) are only ever held as security interests subject to the debtor's equity of redemption. An arrangement under which that indebtedness is re-organised will therefore necessarily impact on any security held in respect of it and may involve the repatriation of the debtor's property free from the charge. When this occurs the secured creditor is simply returning to the debtor property which the creditor never owned beneficially and was only ever held as security for the debt. Blackburne J was quite right to regard this as wholly different from the converse case of property which has never formed part of the company's assets but is held by it only as trustee.

---

[68] [2004] 1 WLR 1010.
[69] *Sharp v Jackson* [1899] AC 441, 426 (Earl of Halsbury LC).
[70] [2009] EWCA Civ 1161; [2010] BCC 272.
[71] Under Companies Act 2006, Pt 26.
[72] [2009] EWCA Civ 1161; [2010] BCC 272, [58] (Patten LJ).

It followed that former clients of the bank who had equitable rights in property that was held by the company on trust for them were not creditors, because a proprietary claim to trust property did not constitute a claim in respect of a debt owed by the company: the beneficiaries of the trust would have a claim to the property that was held on trust rather than to the value of that property. By contrast, those who had security rights in the company's property would be classed as creditors of the company, since they would not have a claim to recover particular property, but a claim only to the value of what was due to them. Admittedly, by virtue of such creditors' security over property, their claims would rank above those of other unsecured creditors of the bank, but the creditor with a security interest is still properly characterized simply as a creditor.

The boundary between trust and debt is sometimes blurred. It is, for example, possible for a debt itself to be the subject matter of a trust.[73] It is also possible to ensure that what might otherwise be a simple debt is considered to be a trust where money is lent for a particular purpose and, if that purpose fails, the borrower will hold the money on trust for the creditor.[74]

(c) BAILMENT

The trust and bailment appear to have much in common, since both involve obligations to look after property for the benefit of another, with the trustee holding the property for the beneficiary and the bailee for the bailor. This was considered by Maitland:[75]

We must distinguish the trust from the bailment. This is not very easy to do, for in some of our classical text-books perplexing language is used about this matter. For example, Blackstone defines a bailment thus: 'Bailment, from the French *bailler*, is a delivery of goods in trust, upon a contract expressed or implied, that the trust shall be faithfully executed on the part of the bailee' (Comm. II, 451).

Here a bailment seems to be made a kind of trust. Now of course in one way it is easy enough to distinguish a bailment from those trusts enforced by equity, and only by equity, of which we are speaking. We say that the rights of a bailor against his bailee are legal, are common law rights, while those of a *cestui que trust* against his trustee are never common law rights. But then this seems to be a putting of the cart before the horse; we do not explain why certain rights are enforced at law while other rights are left to equity.

Let us look at the matter a little more closely. On the one hand we will have a bailment—A lends B a quantity of books—A lets to B a quantity of books in return for a periodical payment—A deposits a lot of books with B for safe custody. In each of these cases B receives rights from A, and in each of these cases B is under an obligation to A; he is bound with more or less rigour to keep the books safely and to return them to A. Still we do not I think conceive that B is bound to use on A's behalf the rights that he, B, has in the books. Such rights as B has in them he has on his own behalf, and those rights he may enjoy as seems best to him. On the other hand, S is making a marriage settlement and the property that he is settling includes a library of books; he vests the whole ownership of these books in T and T' who are to permit S to enjoy them during his life and then to permit his firstborn son to enjoy them and so forth. Not unfrequently valuable chattels are thus settled so that whoever dwells in a certain mansion during the continuance of the settlement shall have the use of the pictures, books, plate, and so forth. Now here T and T' are full owners of the chattels. S and the other *cestui que trusts* have no rights in the chattels, but T and T' are bound to use their rights according to the words of the settlement, words which compel them to allow S and the other *cestui que trusts* to enjoy those things.

---

[73] *Don King Productions v Warren* [2000] Ch 291.
[74] As recognized in *Barclays Bank plc v Quistclose Investments Ltd* [1970] AC 567. See Chapter 8.5(a), pp. 410–17.
[75] *Lectures on Equity* (2nd edn), p. 45.

> You may say the distinction is a fine one, almost a metaphysical one—and very likely I am not stating it well—but there are two tests which will bring out the distinction. The one is afforded by the law of sale...
>
> A is the bailor, B is the bailee of goods; B sells the goods to X, the sale not being authorised by the terms of the bailment...X, though he purchases in good faith, and though he has no notice of A's rights, does not get a good title to the goods. A can recover them from him; if he converts them to his use he wrongs A. Why? Because he bought them from one who was not owner of them. Turn to the other case. T is holding goods as trustee of S's marriage settlement. In breach of trust he sells them to X; X buys in good faith and has no notice of the trust. X gets a good title to the goods. T was the owner of the goods; he passed his rights to X; X became the owner of the goods and S has no right against X—for it is an elementary rule...that trust rights can not be enforced against one who has acquired legal (i.e. common law) ownership bona fide, for value, and without notice of the existence of those trust rights. Here you see one difference between the bailee and the trustee...
>
> Cases can be conceived where it would be difficult to say whether there was a bailment by deposit or a trust. For instance, I go abroad in a hurry and do not know whether I shall return. I send a piano to a friend, and I say to him, 'Take care of my piano and if I don't return give it to my daughter'. This may be construed both ways, as a bailment or as a trust. Perhaps the age of my daughter—a thing strictly irrelevant—would decide which way it would go.

The crucial difference between bailment and trust turns on the location of the legal ownership: the trustee typically obtains legal ownership to property and manages the property for the benefit of those who have an equitable proprietary interest, whereas the bailee does not obtain legal ownership, and manages the property for the legal owner, the bailor.[76] The nature of the duties of management and the consequences of misapplication of the property will depend on whether a trust or a bailment can be identified, and this will turn on what the transferor of the property intended. As Maitland observed, where the property is sold to a third party in good faith the differences between trust and bailment are stark: the bailor may rely upon his or her legal title to sue the third party for the tort of conversion, even if the third party purchaser bought the property for value and in good faith, but the equitable owner of the property will not be able to bring any claim against such a third party, since any equitable interest in the property will be defeated by the third party's being a bona fide purchaser for value without notice.[77]

There will sometimes be circumstances under which a bailment will be converted into a trust, such as where the bailee has sold the property that he or she was looking after and the proceeds of sale are mixed with his or her own money. Legal title will then be transferred to the bailee, but he or she will hold the value of the property that was sold on trust for the bailor.[78]

(d) AGENCY

Although both trustees and agents are subject to fiduciary duties—such as the duty not to make an unauthorized profit[79]—the essential difference between a trust and agency relationship again relates to proprietary rights. The agency relationship is a personal relationship. This means that any property transferred by the principal to the agent either still belongs to the principal at law or, if legal title has

---

[76] *MCC Proceeds Inc. v Lehman Bros International (Europe)* [1998] 4 All ER 675, 688 (Mummery LJ).
[77] See Chapter 18.6(a), pp. 911–16.
[78] *Re Hallett's Estate* (1879) 13 Ch D 696.
[79] See Chapter 14.4, pp. 682–704.

passed to the agent, the principal will not have any equitable proprietary interest in the property; rather, the agent is simply liable to account to the principal for the value of the property received, so the relationship is one of creditor and debtor.

There will be circumstances, however, where the line between agency and trust is difficult to discern and the agency relationship can be converted into a trust relationship. This will occur where the agent has received property from the principal or from a third party on behalf of the principal, so that the agent holds the property on trust for the principal. Whether a trust can be identified from an agency relationship will depend on the principal's intention. But a very significant factor in determining what the principal intended concerns whether the agent was under a duty to keep goods or money received separate from his or her own goods or money, since this suggests that the agent has not received the property beneficially for his or her own purposes. This was recognized by Millett LJ:[80]

Whether [the defendant agent] was in fact a trustee of the money may be open to doubt. Unless I have misunderstood the facts [of *Nelson v Rye* [1996] 1 WLR 1378, (explained in the following extract)] or they were very unusual it would appear that the defendant was entitled to pay receipts into his own account, mix them with his own money, use them for his own cash flow, deduct his own commission, and account for the balance to the plaintiff only at the end of the year. It is fundamental to the existence of a trust that the trustee is bound to keep the trust property separate from his own and apply it exclusively for the benefit of his beneficiary. Any right on the part of the defendant to mix the money which he received with his own and use it for his own cash flow would be inconsistent with the existence of a trust. So would a liability to account annually, for a trustee is obliged to account to his beneficiary and pay over the trust property on demand...His liability arose from his failure to account, not from his retention and use of the money for his own benefit, for this was something which he was entitled to do.

For example, where a client transfers money to his or her solicitor, the solicitor must keep that money in a separate account.[81] A solicitor might act as an agent for his or her client in negotiating the purchase of property, and, when the client later transfers money to the solicitor to complete the purchase, that money is held by the solicitor on trust for the client in a separate client account.

The decision whether a particular relationship should be characterized as an agency or a trust relationship will ultimately depend on the intention of the party creating the relationship. To assist with the identification of this intention, various principles were identified by Briggs J in *Pearson v Lehman Brothers Finance SA*:[82]

v) ...the question whether B has a proprietary interest in the property acquired by A for B's account depends upon their mutual intention, to be ascertained by an objective assessment of the terms of the agreement or relationship between A and B with reference to that property.

vi) The words used by the parties such as 'trust', 'custody', 'belonging', 'ownership', title', may be persuasive, but they are not conclusive in favour of the recognition of B's proprietary interest in the property, if the terms of the agreement or relationship, viewed objectively, compel a different conclusion.

vii) The identification of a relationship in which A is B's agent or broker is not conclusive of a conclusion that A is, in relation to the property, B's trustee, although it may be a pointer towards that conclusion.

---

[80] *Paragon Finance v DB Thakerar and Co.* [1999] 1 All ER 400, 416.
[81] Solicitors' Regulation Authority Accounts Rules 2011, rules 13 and 14.
[82] [2010] EWHC 2914 (Ch), [225]. Appeal dismissed [2011] EWCA Civ 1544; [2012] 2 BCLC 151, without considering this issue.

viii) A relationship which absolves A from one or more of the basic duties of trusteeship towards B is not thereby rendered incapable of being a trustee beneficiary relationship, but may be a pointer towards a conclusion that it is not.

ix) Special care is needed in a business or commercial context. Thus:

   (a) The law should not confine the recognition and operation of a trust to circumstances which resemble a traditional family trust, where the fulfilment of the parties' commercial objective calls for the recognition of a proprietary interest in B.

   (b) The law should not unthinkingly impose a trust where purely personal rights between A and B sufficiently achieve their commercial objective.

x) There is, at least at the margin, an element of policy. For example, what appears to be A's property should not lightly be made unavailable for distribution to its unsecured creditors in its insolvency, by the recognition of a proprietary interest in favour of B. Conversely, the clients of intermediaries which acquire property for them should be appropriately protected from the intermediary's insolvency . . .

A conclusion that, as between them, A acts as B's agent in the acquisition of property from C by no means leads to the inevitable result that B thereby obtains a proprietary interest in the property, such that it is held by A as his trustee. *Nelson v Rye* [1996] 1 WLR 1378 is a classic example of a case in which that assumption was wrongly made, as is illustrated by the devastating critique of that judgment by Millett LJ in *Paragon Finance v DB Thakerar & Co* [1999] 1 All ER 400, at 415–6. Nelson was a solo musician, managed by Rye, who collected Nelson's fees and royalties as his agent, with an undoubted duty to account. Nonetheless the terms of the agency relationship permitted Rye to mix Nelson's fees and royalties with his own money, to use them for his own cash-flow, to deduct his own commission and to account for the balance to Nelson only at the year end. Those features of the relationship were inconsistent with the existence of any trust of the receipts, and therefore with any proprietary interest of Nelson in them, for as long as they remained with Rye.

The true principles are in my judgment admirably summarised in *Bowstead & Reynolds on Agency* (19th ed) in paragraph 6-041, from which I have drawn the following extracts (although the whole passage deserves reading in full):

'The analogy with trust might be taken to suggest first, that when an agent holds title to money or other property for his principal, he always does so (in situations where the principal does not himself own it) as trustee. This would often be impractical and has never been the rule. It is perfectly possible for property so held, especially money, to be the agent's own, and mixed with his own assets subject only to a duty to transfer or account for it to his principal. Equally however he may certainly hold as trustee.

Sometimes the answer turns on the contract between principal and agent. It is clear in this context and in general that the existence of a contractual relationship of debtor and creditor between the parties does not prevent the existence of a simultaneous trust relationship, or a fiduciary relationship of a less onerous nature, involving nevertheless that certain money or property is held on trust.

Thus it may be provided expressly between principal and agent that money received is so held. At other times the intention to create a trust may be inferred; the matter turns on the objective interpretation, according to general principles, of the intentions of the parties.

. . . the present trend seems to be to approach the matter more functionally and to ask whether the trust relationship is appropriate to the commercial relationship in which the parties find themselves; whether it was appropriate that money or property should be, and whether it was, held separately, or whether it was contemplated that the agent should use the money, property or proceeds of the property as part of his normal cash flow in such a way that the relationship of debtor and creditor is more appropriate.

A relevant consideration also is whether money or property was received in pursuance of a single transaction for which the agent was appointed, or as part of a group of transactions in respect of which a general account was to be rendered later or periodically.

Although the issue does not arise in many of the cases, a central question, really one of policy, and perhaps too often overlooked (because not in issue) is whether the rights of the principal are sufficiently strong, and differentiatable from other claims, for him to be given priority in respect of them in the agent's bankruptcy. . . .

Sometimes the position is secured by statute or regulation providing that particular types of functionary (e.g. estate agents and solicitors) hold clients' money on trust, pay into client accounts and keep trust accounts.' . . .

In my judgment there is no immutable principle that an arrangement between A and B (where A acquires property for B's account) which includes a consensual disapplication of some fiduciary obligation generally regarded as a basic feature of a trust, thereby prevents the existence of a trustee beneficiary relationship arising between the parties, or the recognition of A's proprietary interest in the property.

An example of the disapplication of a basic fiduciary obligation would be where the agent is permitted to use the principal's money for the agent's own purposes. Briggs J continued:[83]

In my judgment the true principle which emerges from these cases is that, while there are no hard and fast rules whereby the consensual disapplication of some basic trustee duty precludes the recognition of a trustee beneficiary relationship between the parties, nonetheless the greater the extent to which those duties are disapplied, the harder it will be for the court to conclude, taking all relevant matters into account, that the parties objectively intended to create such a relationship between them.

The recognition of these principles by Briggs J is important, although the emphasis on questions of policy when determining whether a trust was intended gives the judge significant discretion in recognizing a trust. This is at odds with some other recent decisions and judicial pronouncements that are critical of the role of judicial discretion in identifying proprietary interests.[84]

(e) ASSIGNMENT

An assignment involves transferring rights from one person, the assignor, to another, the assignee. For example, if B owes money to A, A can assign the debt to C so that B will then owe the money to C. This does not involve the creation of any trust, since the essence of assignment is the transfer of existing rights rather than the creation of new rights.

The boundary between assignment and trust may be significant, particularly because the creation of a trust can be used to avoid limitations on the assignment of rights. For example, in *Don King Productions Ltd v Warren*,[85] two boxing promoters entered into a partnership. They agreed that the benefit of all their existing contracts with particular boxers should be brought into the partnership. The promoters later fell out and the partnership needed to be dissolved. One of the questions for the court concerned whether all the boxing contracts had been transferred to the partnership. On the facts, an assignment of rights to the partnership appeared to have occurred, but this would not have been valid because many of the contracts contained anti-assignment clauses. But the court got around this

---

[83] Ibid, 260.
[84] See in particular the rejection of the remedial constructive trust, at Chapter 7.3, pp. 355–8.
[85] [2000] Ch 291. See also *Barbados Trust Co. v Bank of Zambia* [2007] EWCA Civ 148; [2007] 1 Lloyd's Rep 495.

restriction by holding that the anti-assignment clauses did not prevent the person who was to receive the benefit of the contracts from holding those benefits on trust for somebody else. Lightman J said:[86]

> Accordingly in principle I can see no objection to a party to contracts involving skill and confidence or containing non-assignment provisions from becoming trustee of the benefit of being the contracting party as well as the benefit of the rights conferred. I can see no reason why the law should limit the parties' freedom of contract to creating trusts of the fruits of such contracts received by the assignor or to creating an accounting relationship between the parties in respect of the fruits . . . most importantly this view accords with common sense and justice and achieves the commercial objective of the parties.

Since the contracts referred only to a prohibition on assignment and did not refer to a prohibition on creating a trust, they were not construed as prohibiting the transfer of rights by trust, because assignment and trust are functionally different. An assignment involves the transfer of an existing right and a trust involves the creation of a new right. In other words, where a right to the benefit of a contract is transferred directly from A to B, this involves an assignment. If, however, A declares that he holds those rights for the benefit of B, this involves the creation of a new equitable proprietary right.

(f) GIFT

Gifts and trusts are distinct. A typical gift involves transferring all rights to property to the donee absolutely and without obligation, whereas the typical trust involves the transfer of property to the trustee, subject to an obligation to hold that property on trust for the beneficiary. Since the trustee does not receive the property beneficially, it cannot be considered to have been given to him or her as a gift.

In between the categories of gift and trust is a third category where property is transferred subject to a condition. Whether a conditional transfer is a gift or a trust will depend on the intention of the transferor, objectively determined by the courts.[87] This is illustrated by *Attorney-General v The Cordwainers' Co.*,[88] in which the testator had left an inn to the Cordwainers' Company on condition that it paid annuities to certain relatives of the testator and made some payments for charitable purposes. Over the years, the rents obtained from the inn increased, so that there was a substantial surplus; the question for the court concerned the identification of who was entitled to it. It was held that the original bequest of the inn constituted a gift subject to a condition, rather than a trust, and, subject to satisfactory performance of the condition, the company was entitled to keep the surplus rents from the property beneficially. In other words, the testator intended that the company should receive the inn absolutely as a gift subject to the continued performance of the condition. Sir John Leach MR said:[89]

> The first question is whether this testator intended the corporation to take as mere trustees, or whether he intended to give them any beneficial interest . . .
>
> It does not appear to me that the words of this devise do constitute this corporation mere trustees. The estate is absolutely given to them; not upon trust, but for the use, interest, and performance of the testator's will. It is rather a gift upon condition, than a gift upon trust. They are to take the estate so devised to them, upon condition that they perform the duties which by the terms of the will are imposed upon

---

[86] [2000] Ch 291, 321. This was approved by the Court of Appeal in *Barbados Trust Co. v Bank of Zambia*, ibid.
[87] See Thomas, 'Conditions in Favour of Third Parties' (1952) 11 CLJ 240.
[88] (1833) 3 My & K 534.
[89] Ibid, 542.

them. Those duties are not for mere charitable purposes. Half the property that this testator disposes of is disposed of to his brother; an annuity of £6 is given to his brother for his life; and after his brother's death there is no disposition of this annuity, except that £2 a year are given to his widow if she survived him. These are not charitable purposes. It is plain that a beneficial estate was intended to be given to the Cordwainers' Company, because the testator expressly declares that, if the condition upon which this estate is devised to the corporation be not performed, the brother shall enter and defeat the estate given to the Cordwainers' Company. Defeat what estate? An estate given to them in mere trust, from which they were to derive no benefit? Is it to be supposed that this was considered by the testator in the nature of a penalty? The imposition of a penalty for non-performance of the condition implies a benefit, if the condition be performed, and is inconsistent with any other intention, than that the testator meant to give a beneficial interest to the company upon the terms of complying with the directions contained in his will.

This can be compared with *Re Frame*,[90] in which property was bequeathed to a housekeeper, Mrs Taylor, on condition that she adopted one of the testator's daughters and made payments to the testator's other children. The housekeeper's application to adopt the daughter was unsuccessful, so the condition was not satisfied. The housekeeper consequently argued that the testator had made a gift subject to a condition and that, since the condition had become impossible to perform, she was entitled to receive the property absolutely. It was held that the testator had actually intended to create a trust for his children, as was made clear from the imposition of the obligation to pay money to his other children. The housekeeper was therefore obliged to provide maintenance for the daughter. Simonds J said:[91]

The question is what those words mean. I have listened to an able and interesting argument on these questions: whether the condition is a condition subsequent or a condition precedent;[92] whether, if it be a condition precedent, the condition has become impossible of performance, and whether, if so, the gift fails; whether, if it be a condition subsequent, the donee has failed, through no fault of her own, to comply with the condition, and whether, in that event, the gift has failed. As I listened to that argument it impressed itself more and more on me that, after all, this was not a condition at all, for, in my view, on the true construction of this clause, the word 'condition' is not used in its strict legal sense. It is a gift to Mrs. Taylor on condition, in the sense of on the terms or on the trust that she does certain things, and that, I think, becomes clearer when it is realized that the condition relates not only to the adoption of one daughter, but to the payment of certain sums to other daughters. A devise, or bequest, on condition that the devisee or legatee makes certain payments does not import a condition in the strict sense of the word, but a trust, so that, though the devisee or legatee dies before the testator and the gift does not take effect, yet the payments must be made; for it is a trust, and no trust fails for want of trustees. When I come to look at the condition, it seems clear that what the testator intended was that Mrs. Taylor should receive certain moneys on the term that she performed certain acts. Much argument has been directed to what is involved in the condition that 'she adopts my daughter'. It seems clear that whether or not an adoption under the authority of an order made under [statute] is necessary, what is intended is not any single formal act, but a series of acts to establish as between Mrs. Taylor and the testator's daughter the relationship of parent and child—in a word, Mrs. Taylor was to treat the child as if she were her daughter, because that is what adoption means. Is that a trust which the Court can enforce? It includes not only the parental duties of care, advice, and affection, but also the duty of maintenance. This Court cannot compel, so far as adoption involves the giving of care, advice and

---

[90] [1939] Ch 700.
[91] Ibid, 703.
[92] See Chapter 1.4(a)(iv), pp. 12–13.

> affection that such things be given. But, seeing that it involves the duty of maintenance, that is a trust which the Court can enforce, directing, if necessary, an inquiry in that regard. It will not allow the whole trust to fail because in part it cannot be enforced.

As always, whether a trust was intended requires careful analysis by the court of the context of the transfer.

(g) INTERESTS UNDER A WILL OR INTESTACY

Where a testator dies, his or her property will pass to executors, who will receive the property absolutely, but subject to a fiduciary duty to ensure that it is transferred to those entitled under the will. Where the deceased has not left a will, he or she will have died intestate. There will be no executors of the estate, but the courts will appoint administrators to ensure that the deceased's property is transferred to those who are entitled to it under the law of intestacy. Executors and administrators are collectively described as the 'personal representatives' of the deceased.

The personal representatives have legal title to the estate. Title to property will pass to those entitled under the will once the executors have assented. This assent can be implied where the property is personalty,[93] but written assent is required if the property is land.[94] It follows that, if the will creates a testamentary trust, once the necessary assent has been obtained, title will then pass to the trustees, who may be the same people as the executors, but who will receive the property in a different capacity. The significance of this distinction between personal representative and trustee is illustrated by *Attenborough v Solomon*.[95] The testator bequeathed his residuary estate to his two sons. Before the estate was distributed, one of the sons delivered some silver plate from the residuary estate to a pawnbroker, in order to secure a personal loan. If the son had acted as an executor, the pawnbroker would have obtained rights over the plate, because the power of disposal of personalty by executors is several, which means that any executor could pawn the plate. But, if the son had acted as a trustee, he could not have pawned the plate, because the trustees' power of disposal is joint, which requires them all to agree. It was held that the son had acted as a trustee, so the pawnbroker had no rights to the plate. Viscount Haldane LC said:

> The position of an executor is a peculiar one. He is appointed by the will, but then, by virtue of his office, by the operation of law and not under the bequest in the will, he takes a title to the personal property of the testator, which vests him with the *plenum dominium* [full ownership] over the testator's chattels. He takes that, I say, by virtue of his office. The will becomes operative so far as its dispositions of personalty are concerned only if and when the executor assents to those dispositions. It is true that by virtue of his office he has a general power to sell or pledge for the purpose of paying debts and getting in the money value of the estate. He is executor and he remains executor for an indefinite time.... the office of executor remains, with its powers attached, but the property which he had originally in the chattels that devolved upon him, and over which these powers extended, does not necessarily remain. So soon as he has assented, and this he may do informally and the assent may be inferred from his conduct, the dispositions of the will become operative, and then the beneficiaries have vested in them the property in those chattels. The transfer is made not by the mere force of the assent of the executor, but by virtue of the dispositions of the will which have become operative because of this assent.

---

[93] *Re King's Will Trusts* [1964] Ch 542.
[94] Administration of Estates Act 1925, s. 36(4).
[95] [1913] AC 76.

> Now, my Lords...and in view of the fourteen years which had passed since the testator died before the time when [the son] made the pledge to the appellants in 1892, I am of opinion that the true inference to be drawn from the facts is that the executors considered that they had done all that was due from them as executors by 1879, and were content when the residuary account was passed that the dispositions of the will should take effect. That is the inference I draw from the form of the residuary account; and the inference is strengthened when I consider the lapse of time since then, and that in the interval nothing was done by them purporting to be an exercise of power as executors. My Lords, if this be so, this appeal must be disposed of on the footing that in point of fact the executors assented at a very early date to the dispositions of the will taking effect. It follows that under these dispositions the residuary estate, including the chattels in question, become vested in the trustees as trustees. That they were the same persons as the executors does not affect the point, or in my opinion present the least obstacle to the inference. But if that was so, then the title to the silver plate of [the son] as executor had ceased to exist before he made the pledge of 1892. What then was the position of the appellants?...When [the son] handed over these articles of silver to [the pawnbroker] he had no property to pass as executor; and they got no contractual rights which could prevail against the trustees. The latter were the true owners and they are now in a position to maintain an action...to recover possession of the chattels.

The nature of the proprietary interest of the executor or administrator is significant. Legal title to the property in the deceased's estate will be automatically vested in the personal representatives on the deceased's death. There will be no equitable proprietary interest in that property, since there will have been no event to create such an interest and nobody other than the personal representative who could have it; as we have already seen,[96] one person alone cannot have both the legal and equitable proprietary interest. But the personal representative cannot be considered to have the beneficial interest in the property,[97] since, as fiduciaries, they are not in a position to benefit from the property. So where is the beneficial interest? It might be considered to be located in those people who are entitled to the estate. But such persons have only an expectation of benefit, which is characterized as a mere equity, and they cannot enforce this interest by, for example, requiring the personal representative to transfer possession of the property to them. The better view, therefore, is that the beneficial interest in the property should simply be considered to be in suspense pending the administration of the estate.[98]

A legatee under a will has neither a legal nor an equitable interest in any of the deceased's property until the executors have discharged all the deceased's debts or have taken the risk of conveying the property prematurely to the relevant beneficiary.[99] The same is true of those who are entitled on intestacy.[100] This is because, until the estate has been completely administered with all debts paid, it is impossible to say of what the estate consists.[101] This illustrates the key difference between a beneficiary's interests under a will or intestacy and interests under a fixed trust. The former interests are not proprietary; they consist only of a personal right to ensure that the estate is administered, rather than a right that attaches to a specific piece of property. Interests under a fixed trust are properly characterized as proprietary, since they relate to identifiable trust assets.[102] Despite this, if property from an unadministered estate has been misappropriated, the person entitled to the estate can bring a proprietary claim to recover the property from a third party.[103] This might suggest that the beneficiary

[96] See Chapter 1.4(a)(ii), p. 12.
[97] *Commissioner of Stamp Duties (Queensland) v Livingston* [1965] AC 694, 707 (Viscount Radcliffe).
[98] By analogy with the trust created by a testator, but which arises on the death of a legatee: see *Ottaway v Norman* [1972] Ch 698, discussed at Chapter 4.2(c)(1), pp. 138–40.
[99] *Commissioner of Stamp Duties (Queensland) v Livingston* [1965] AC 694.
[100] *Eastbourne Mutual Building Society v Hastings Corporation* [1965] 1 WLR 861.
[101] *Commissioner of Stamp Duties (Queensland) v Livingston* [1965] AC 694, 708 (Viscount Radcliffe).
[102] See Chapter 2.7(e)(i), pp. 57–8.
[103] *Re Diplock's Estate* [1948] Ch 465.

does have a proprietary interest in the estate before it is administered. In fact, the beneficiary is acting only on behalf of the estate and in lieu of the personal representatives, who might themselves be implicated in the misappropriation of the property.[104] Consequently, if that property is recovered, it will be restored to the estate rather than to the beneficiary; this is simply a consequence of the beneficiary's right to ensure that the estate is properly administered.[105]

The significance of this analysis of interests under a will is illustrated by *Commissioner of Stamp Duties (Queensland) v Livingston*.[106] A testator had left his estate to his wife, Mrs Coulson. Following his death, and whilst the estate was still being administered, the widow died intestate. Her estate was liable to pay tax if she held a beneficial interest in the property left to her by her husband. It was held that she did not have such an interest because administration of the estate was not complete. On her husband's death, full ownership of the estate had passed to the executors and the wife had not acquired any proprietary interest in it. Viscount Radcliffe said:[107]

> whatever property came to the executor *virtue officii* [by virtue of office] came to him in full ownership, without distinction between legal and equitable interests. The whole property was his. He held it for the purpose of carrying out the functions and duties of administration, not for his own benefit; and these duties would be enforced upon him by the Court of Chancery, if application had to be made for that purpose by a creditor or beneficiary interested in the estate. Certainly, therefore, he was in a fiduciary position with regard to the assets that came to him in the right of his office, and for certain purposes and in some aspects he was treated by the court as a trustee. 'An executor,' said Kay J in *Re Marsden* (1884) 26 Ch D 783 at 789, 'is personally liable in equity for all breaches of the ordinary trusts which in Courts of Equity are considered to arise from his office.' He is a trustee 'in this sense'.
>
> It may not be possible to state exhaustively what those trusts are at any one moment. Essentially, they are trusts to preserve the assets, to deal properly with them, and to apply them in a due course of administration for the benefit of those interested according to that course, creditors, the death duty authorities, legatees of various sorts, and the residuary beneficiaries. They might just as well have been termed 'duties in respect of the assets' as trusts. What equity did not do was to recognise or create for residuary legatees a beneficial interest in the assets in the executor's hands during the course of administration. Conceivably, this could have been done, in the sense that the assets, whatever they might be from time to time, could have been treated as a present, though fluctuating, trust fund held for the benefit of all those interested in the estate according to the measure of their respective interests. But it never was done. It would have been a clumsy and unsatisfactory device from a practical point of view; and, indeed, it would have been in plain conflict with the basic conception of equity that to impose the fetters of a trust upon property, with the resulting creation of equitable interests in that property, there had to be specific subjects identifiable as the trust fund. An unadministered estate was incapable of satisfying this requirement. The assets as a whole were in the hands of the executor, his property; and until administration was complete no one was in a position to say what items of property would need to be realised for the purposes of that administration or of what the residue, when ascertained, would consist or what its value would be...
>
> At the date of Mrs. Coulson's death, therefore, there was no trust fund consisting of Mr. Livingston's residuary estate in which she could be said to have any beneficial interest, because no trust had as yet come into existence to affect the assets of his estate...

---

[104] *Commissioner of Stamp Duties (Queensland) v Livingston* [1965] AC 694, 714 (Viscount Radcliffe).
[105] Bailey, 'Equitable Interests: Position of Beneficiaries Under Will or Intestacy—Whether Administration Complete: Tracing' (1965) 23 CLJ 44, 46.
[106] [1965] AC 694.
[107] Ibid, 707.

What she was entitled to in respect of her rights under her deceased husband's will was a chose in action, capable of being invoked for any purpose connected with the proper administration of his estate.

The fact that the right to have the estate properly administered is a mere equity that is transmissible means that a legatee (otherwise known as a devisee) who is entitled to land under the testator's estate can enter into a valid contract to sell the land even before the estate has been administered. This was recognized by Lord Browne-Wilkinson in *Wu Koon Tai v Wu Yau Loi*:[108]

In principle, there is no reason why a devisee of land comprised in an unadministered estate cannot enter into a binding contract to sell that land. True, until completion of the administration and the vesting of the property in the devisee, the devisee cannot convey the land in specie.

But their Lordships were referred to no authority to suggest that such devisee cannot validly contract to sell the land at a time when his interest is a mere chose in action or expectancy. Their Lordships can see no distinction in principle between such a contract and a contract for value to assign a future chose in action. As and from the date when the chose in action comes into existence, the contract becomes specifically enforceable.

(h) POWERS

Trusts and powers are fundamentally different. Trusts impose obligations that *must* be exercised. Powers are discretionary, so they *may* be exercised. It is important to distinguish between trusts and powers, not only because it is necessary to determine whether the trustee must or may act, but also because trusts can be executed by the court, whereas powers cannot.[109] So, for example, where a trustee dies without making an appointment of trust property to the beneficiaries, if there is a trust obligation to make such an appointment, the court will do so, but if there is only a power, it will lapse on the trustee's death.[110] The distinction between trusts and powers was once more significant, because there were different tests to determine whether a disposition to trustees was void for uncertainty depending on whether the disposition was coupled with a trust or a power. But the tests of certainty have now been assimilated.[111] It is important to note that trusts and powers do not invariably operate in isolation: a single trust instrument might both impose trust obligations on the trustees and create discretionary powers that may be exercised by the trustees.

(i) *Trusts and powers*

The distinction between trusts and powers is significant when determining the obligations of a trustee when distributing trust property to objects of the trust. This was considered by Park J in *Breadner v Granville-Grossman*:[112]

It is trite law that there is a distinction between two kinds of dispositive discretions which may be vested in trustees. There are discretions which the trustees have a duty to exercise (sometimes

---

[108] [1997] AC 179, 188.
[109] See Chapter 13.2(b), pp. 632–8.
[110] *Brown v Higgs* (1803) 8 Ves 561.
[111] See Chapter 3.4(b), (c), pp. 91–109.
[112] [2001] Ch 523, 540.

called 'trust powers'), and discretions which the trustee may exercise but have no duty to exercise (sometimes called 'mere powers'). The distinction is most familiar in the context of discretions to distribute income. In cases of trust powers the trustees are bound to distribute the income, but have a discretion as to how it should be divided between the beneficiaries. In cases of mere powers the trustees have two discretions—first a discretion whether to distribute the income or not, and second, if they decide that they will exercise the first discretion, a further discretion as to how to divide the income between the beneficiaries. In the latter kind of case there will usually be a default trust which deals with the income if the trustees do not exercise their discretion to distribute it. Typically the default trust will provide for the undistributed income to be accumulated or to be paid as of right to a beneficiary whose interest in it is vested but defeasible by the trustees exercising their discretion to distribute...

Sometimes the distinction does not matter, but there is an important difference between the two kinds of case if the trustees do not exercise the discretion to distribute income within the normal time for exercising it. That time is usually 'a reasonable time'. If there is a trust power and, although the trustees are required to exercise it within a reasonable time, they do not do so, the discretion still exists. If the trustees are willing to exercise it, albeit later than they should have done, the court will probably permit them to do so...Alternatively the court will exercise the discretion itself. But if the discretion to distribute income is a mere power, and the trustees do not exercise it within a reasonable time of the receipt of an item of income, the discretion no longer exists as respects that income. The default trusts take effect indefeasibly.

This passage was described by the Privy Council in *Schmidt v Rosewood Trust Ltd*[113] as 'a very clear and eminently realistic account of both the points of difference and the similarities between a discretionary trust and a fiduciary dispositive power'.

However, this comment in itself highlights the scope for confusion in this area: the same things are sometimes given different names. What the Privy Council in *Schmidt* called a 'fiduciary dispositive power', is exactly the same as what Park J in *Breadner* called 'a mere power'. This type of power is given to a fiduciary, such as a trustee, in his or her capacity as a fiduciary. It is a true power because the trustee is not obliged to exercise it at all. But its fiduciary nature means that the trustee must consider whether or not the power should be exercised.[114] Such fiduciary powers can be contrasted with 'non-fiduciary' powers. Confusingly, such powers are also often called 'mere powers'; if the term 'mere powers' is to be used, it is better if it is used in this non-fiduciary sense. In contrast to the holder of a fiduciary power, the donee of a mere power is not even required to consider exercising the power.[115] The holder of a mere power is generally not a fiduciary. It is, however, possible for a mere power to be given to a trustee, but it must be made clear that the recipient of the power is to hold the power in a personal capacity rather than as a trustee.

Although powers and trusts are conceptually distinct, the terminology again becomes confusing, because discretionary trusts are sometimes also known as 'trust powers'. This is because of the dual components of a discretionary trust: it is clearly a trust, since the trustee must make an appointment, but that trust is coupled with a power, since the trustees can choose which of the objects are to benefit from the exercise of the power.[116]

---

[113] [2003] UKPC 26; [2003] 2 AC 709, [40].
[114] *Re Gulbenkian* [1970] AC 508, 525 (Lord Upjohn).
[115] Ibid, 518 (Lord Reid).
[116] *Brown v Higgs* (1803) 8 Ves 561, 570 (Lord Eldon).

(ii) *Determining whether a trust or power has been created*

Whether the settlor or testator has created a trust obligation or a discretionary power depends on his or her intent, as deduced from careful construction of the trust instrument. If mandatory language is used, this suggests that there is a trust obligation that must be exercised, such as by use of the phrase 'to be distributed'. Discretionary language suggests a fiduciary power, such as the trustee 'may appoint'. If there is express provision for what should happen to the property if the power is not exercised—known as a 'gift-over' provision—this is a clear sign that a power and not a trust has been created: since the exercise of the trustees' discretion under a trust is mandatory, it is incompatible with the notion of there being any 'gift-over'.[117] So, if a settlor gives to his trustees a sum of money 'with power to appoint in favour of such of my children and in such proportions as my trustees shall think fit, and, in default of appointment, the money is to be given to my brother', this will create a power. The trustees do not *have* to exercise the power, although they *may* choose to do so, and the clear gift-over provision in favour of the settlor's brother means that it cannot be a trust, since provision has been made for what should happen to the property if the power is not exercised.

The process of construction of the trust instrument is illustrated by the decision of the House of Lords in *McPhail v Doulton*.[118] A clause in a deed stated that the trustees 'shall apply the net income of the fund...in such amounts, at such times, and subject to such conditions (if any) as they think fit'. It was held that this had created a discretionary trust rather than a fiduciary power, because of the mandatory words used in the deed. Lord Wilberforce said:[119]

> It is striking how narrow and in a sense artificial is the distinction, in cases such as the present, between trusts or as the particular type of trust is called, trust powers, and powers. It is only necessary to read the learned judgments in the Court of Appeal to see that what to one mind may appear as a power of distribution coupled with a trust to dispose of the undistributed surplus, by accumulation or otherwise, may to another appear as a trust for distribution coupled with a power to withhold a portion and accumulate or otherwise dispose of it. A layman and, I suspect, also a logician would find it hard to understand what difference there is...
>
> Naturally read, the intention of the deed seems to me clear: clause 9(a), whose language is mandatory ('shall'), creates, together with a power of selection, a trust for distribution of the income, the strictness of which is qualified by clause 9(b), which allows the income of any one year to be held up and (under clause 6(a)) either placed, for the time, with a bank, or, if thought fit, invested...I therefore...declare that the provisions of clause 9(a) constitute a trust.

(iii) *Power coupled with a trust*

The trustee may be given a power to determine whether or not to make an appointment, but, if the power is not exercised before the trustee dies, it will lapse and be replaced with a trust obligation in favour of the objects of the power. For example, in *Burrough v Philcox*,[120] the testator gave life interests in his property to his two children with remainder to their issue. His will provided that, if his children should die without issue, the survivor had a power to dispose of the property in his will amongst the testator's nephews and nieces in such proportions as the surviving child thought proper. It was held

---

[117] Hopkins, 'Certain Uncertainties of Trusts and Powers' (1971) 29 CLJ 68, 72.
[118] [1971] AC 424. See further Chapter 3.4(b), pp. 91–105.
[119] Ibid, 448.
[120] (1840) 5 My & Cr 72.

that the testator had created a trust in favour of his nephews and nieces, but this was subject to a power of selection in the surviving child, which lapsed on that child's death. Lord Cottenham said:[121]

> The question is, whether these nephews and nieces and their children, take any interest in the property, independently of the power; that is, whether the power given to the survivor of the son and daughter is a mere power, and the interests of the nephews and nieces and their children were, therefore, to depend upon the exercise of it, or whether there was a gift to them, subject only to the power of selection given to the survivor of the son and daughter . . .
>
> These and other cases shew that when there appears a general intention in favour of a class, and a particular intention in favour of individuals of a class to be selected by another person, and the particular intention fails, from that selection not being made, the Court will carry into effect the general intention in favour of the class. When such an intention appears, the case arises, as stated by Lord Eldon in *Brown v Higgs* (1803) 8 Ves 561 at 574, of the power being so given as to make it the duty of the donee to execute it; and, in such case, the Court will not permit the objects of the power to suffer by the negligence or conduct of the donee, but fastens upon the property a trust for their benefit.

If the surviving child had made a selection in his own will, this would have been effective, but no such selection had been made, so the property was held on trust for the nephews and nieces who took in equal shares. This construction was justifiable because the testator was considered to have a general intention to benefit the class of nephews and nieces as a whole, although this was subject to a particular intention for his surviving child to have a discretion to select from that class. This can be compared with *Re Weekes' Settlement*.[122] The testatrix gave a life interest in the property to her husband and also gave to him a power to dispose of the property by will amongst their children. The husband did not leave the property to their children in his will. In holding that the children were not entitled to the property, Romer J said:[123]

> I should gather from the terms of the will that it was a mere power that was conferred on the husband, and not one coupled with a trust that he was bound to exercise. I see no words in the will to justify me in holding that the testatrix intended that the children should take if her husband did not execute the power.
>
> This is not a case of a gift to the children with power to the husband to select, or to such of the children as the husband should select by exercising the power.
>
> If in this case the testatrix really intended to give a life interest to her husband and a mere power to appoint if he chose, and intended if he did not think fit to appoint that the property should go as in default of appointment according to the settlement, why should she be bound to say more than she has said in this will?
>
> I come to the conclusion on the words of this will that the testatrix only intended to give a life interest and a power to her husband—certainly she has not said more than that.
>
> Am I then bound by the authorities to hold otherwise? I think I am not. The authorities do not shew, in my opinion, that there is a hard and fast rule that a gift to A for life with power to A to appoint among a class and nothing more must, if there is no gift over in the will, be held a gift by implication to the class in default of the power being exercised. In my opinion the cases shew . . . that you must find in the will an indication that the testatrix did intend the class or some of the class to take—intended in fact that the power should be regarded in the nature of a trust—only a power of selection being given, as, for example, a gift to A for life with a gift over to such of a class as A shall appoint.

---

[121] Ibid, 89.
[122] [1897] 1 Ch 289.
[123] Ibid, 292.

As always, when construing trusts and powers the intention of the settlor or testator must be interpreted carefully.

7. RIGHTS AND INTERESTS UNDER A TRUST

The law of trusts is primarily concerned with the different rights that various people might have following the creation of a trust.

(a) EVENT CREATING EQUITABLE INTERESTS

It is a fundamental principle of the law of trusts that, where one person has both legal title to property and the sole right to the benefit of that property, there is no equitable interest in it. A particular event needs to be identified to create the equitable interest which will be separate from the legal interest. This was recognized by Lord Browne-Wilkinson in *Westdeutsche Landesbank Girozentrale v Islington LBC*:[124]

> A person solely entitled to the full beneficial ownership of money or property, both at law and in equity, does not enjoy an equitable interest in that property. The legal title carries with it all rights. Unless and until there is a separation of the legal and equitable estates, there is no separate equitable title.

(b) INTERESTS OF TRUSTEE

Although many trusts involve the trustee having legal title to property, it is possible to declare a trust of an equitable proprietary interest in property. This would create a sub-trust, as it operates 'under' the main trust.[125] This possibility was recognized by Briggs J in *Pearson v Lehman Brothers Finance SA*:[126]

> It is common ground that a trust may exist not merely between legal owner and ultimate beneficial owner, but at each stage of a chain between them, so that, for example, A may hold on trust for X, X on trust for Y and Y on trust for B. The only true trust of the property itself (ie of the legal rights) is that of A for X. At each lower stage in the chain, the intermediate trustee holds on trust only his interest in the property held on trust for him. That is how the holding of intermediated securities works under English law, wherever a proprietary interest is to be conferred on the ultimate investor.

(c) MERGER OF LEGAL AND EQUITABLE INTERESTS

Once an equitable interest has been created, it will be lost if the property is transferred to a person who has sole legal and beneficial title to it. This was recognized by Farwell J in *Re Selous*:[127]

> where equitable and legal estates, equal and coextensive, unite in the same person, the former merges, or, in other words, that a person cannot be trustee for himself.

---

[124] [1996] AC 669, 706.
[125] See further Chapter 10.2(e), pp. 510–12.
[126] [2010] EWHC 2914 (Ch), [226]. Upheld on appeal: [2011] EWCA Civ 1544, [2012] 2 BCLC 151.
[127] [1901] 1 Ch 921, 922 (Farwell J).

This is illustrated by *Re Cook*,[128] in which land was held on trust by a husband and wife for themselves. Since there were two of them, each could hold the legal title to the land on trust for him or herself and the other. But, when the husband died, the entire interest in the property, both legal and equitable, vested in the wife. It was held that the legal interest had swallowed up the equitable, so that there was a merger of the two interests. It followed that the trust was terminated. As Harman J recognized:[129]

> you cannot have a trust existing when nobody is interested under it except the trustee, because nobody can enforce it and there is, in fact, no trust in existence.

This is entirely consistent with Lord Browne-Wilkinson's remarks in *Westdeutsche*:[130] a trust cannot exist where a person has both legal and beneficial title to property. Legal and equitable title needs to be split in order to create a trust, but, if they later merge together, the trust will no longer exist.

(d) OVERREACHING OF EQUITABLE INTERESTS

Where trust property is transferred by the trustee to a third party, it is a matter of some significance whether the transferee holds the property on the original trust or obtains the property free from the trust by virtue of the doctrine of overreaching. This has been explained by Fox as follows:[131]

> In the context of trusts, overreaching is primarily a mechanism by which T [the trustee] is enabled to transfer individual assets out of the trust fund so as to confer on the transferee a title clear of any beneficial interests or powers which affected the assets when T held them. The secondary aspect of overreaching is that any substituted asset which T acquires in exchange for the original trust asset becomes subject to the same equitable interests or powers as affected the original asset...By operation of the law, B's [the beneficiary's] interest in the original asset is transposed to the substitute without the need for any express re-settlement or attornment by T.

Overreaching will operate in this manner where the transfer is authorized: the effect of such a transaction is to overreach the beneficiary's equitable proprietary interest. So, if the trustee sells some shares for cash, and this is authorized, the beneficiary's interest in the shares is overreached and transposed into the cash.

Where, however, a trustee transfers trust property to a third party by a transaction that is unauthorized, the overreaching doctrine will not apply. Fox has written that:[132]

> Suppose now a second transaction in which T [the trustee] has limited powers of sale and investment over the trust fund. T sells an original holding of shares held for B as life tenant without obtaining the consent of some third person, as the terms of the trust require him to...This is an unauthorized sale, beyond T's power of disposition. It is also a breach of trust. T's ability to overreach B's interest is an incident of a properly exercised power of disposition. If therefore T acts without the authority conferred by that power, overreaching can have no place in the transaction. *Prima facie* B's equitable interest in the shares can subsist so as to bind P [the purchaser], though it would be extinguished if P acquired the legal title to them as a bona fide purchaser.

---

[128] [1948] Ch 212.
[129] Ibid, [215].
[130] See Chapter 2.7(a), p. 55.
[131] 'Overreaching', in *Breach of Trust* (eds Birks and Pretto) (Oxford: Hart, 2002), p. 95.
[132] Ibid, 96.

Consequently, where the transfer is unauthorized, the beneficiary's equitable proprietary interest will not be overreached, so the third party recipient will hold the property on trust for the beneficiary, even if the third party was unaware of the beneficiary's equitable proprietary interest. This equitable proprietary interest will be destroyed, however, if the third party was a bona fide purchaser for value of the trust property.[133] So, if the trust property is sold by the trustee without authority under the trust instrument, and the purchaser has provided some value for the transfer in good faith and without notice of the existence of the beneficiary's equitable proprietary interest, the purchaser will take free of that proprietary interest.[134] In such circumstances, the beneficiary's only claim is against the trustee for breach of trust.

(e) THE NATURE OF A BENEFICIARY'S RIGHT

Although it is clear that where a trustee holds property on trust the beneficiaries have an equitable right to the trust property, the nature of this right is a matter of some controversy. The right can be characterized in three different ways.

(i) *Proprietary right*

The beneficiary's right can be characterized as a proprietary right against a particular asset, known as a right *in rem*. This is the most common way of analyzing the right.[135] This has been described by Nolan as follows:[136]

> In short, a beneficiary's core proprietary rights under a trust consist in the beneficiary's primary, negative, right to exclude non-beneficiaries from the enjoyment of trust assets. Infringement of this primary right will generate secondary rights by which a beneficiary may also prevent (or at least restrict) access to assets by non-beneficiaries.

This proprietary right is not, however, as strong as a legal proprietary right. It will be defeated if a third party obtains the property in good faith and for value. If a third party steals the trust property, the beneficiary has no claim in the tort of conversion,[137] because that tort depends on the claimant having a possessory right,[138] which the beneficiary lacks. Similarly, where the property is negligently damaged, the beneficiary has no direct claim against the tortfeasor for property damage or economic loss, because such a claim can be brought only by a person who has a legal proprietary interest or possessory interest in the property.[139] A claim can only be brought if the trustee is made a party to the proceedings. This was acknowledged by the Court of Appeal in *Shell UK Ltd v Total UK Ltd*.[140] In that case, the claimant, Shell, stored oil at a terminal. The tanks and pipelines were held on trust for the claimant by two companies. The defendant, Total, negligently overfilled a fuel storage tank, which consequently exploded and damaged the tanks and pipelines in which the claimant had a beneficial interest. The court had to decide whether the claimant could sue for damage to property in which it had a beneficial interest and whether

---

[133] *Thomson v Clydesdale Bank Ltd* [1893] AC 282.
[134] See Chapter 18.6(a), pp. 911–16.
[135] See Scott, 'The Nature of the Rights of the *Cestuis Que* Trust' (1917) 17 Columbia L Rev 269.
[136] 'Equitable Property' (2006) 122 LQR 232, 234.
[137] *MCC Proceeds Inc. v Lehman Bros International (Europe)* [1994] 4 All ER 675.
[138] *Healey v Healey* [1915] 1 KB 938.
[139] *Leigh and Sillivan Ltd v Aliakmon Shipping Co. Ltd* [1986] AC 785, 809 (Lord Brandon).
[140] [2010] EWCA Civ 180; [2011] QB 86.

it could also sue for consequential economic loss. The issue for the court was summarized as follows:[141]

> The explosion caused damage to property in which and through which Shell stored or distributed its oil. Legal title to the tanks and pipelines were in a vehicle company which held the same on trust for Shell and others. Total has accepted liability for the destruction of anything which was the property of Shell, but disputed liability for the loss of profits that Shell claims flowed from the destruction of or damage to the tanks or pipelines. Total relies on what it asserts is 'the rule recognised by many authorities' to the effect that only a legal owner or someone with an immediate right to possession has the right to claim damages for economic loss [sic] the consequence of damage to property.

Waller LJ held:[142]

> [We] would be prepared to hold that a duty of care is owed to a beneficial owner of property (just as much as to a legal owner of property) by a defendant, such as Total, who can reasonably foresee that his negligent actions will damage that property. If, therefore, such property is, in breach of duty, damaged by the defendant, that defendant will be liable not merely for the physical loss of that property but also for the foreseeable consequences of that loss, such as the extra expenditure to which the beneficial owner is put or the loss of profit which he incurs. Provided that the beneficial owner can join the legal owner in the proceedings, it does not matter that the beneficial owner is not himself in possession of the property...
>
> It should not be legally relevant that the co-owners of the relevant pipelines, for reasons that seemed good to them, decided to vest the legal title to the pipelines in their service companies and enjoy the beneficial ownership rather than the formal legal title. Differing views about the wisdom of the exclusionary rule are widely held but however much one may think that, in general, there should be no duty to mere contracting parties who suffer economic loss as a result of damage to a third party's property, it would be a triumph of form over substance to deny a remedy to the beneficial owner of that property when the legal owner is a bare trustee for that beneficial owner.
>
> ...[we] hold that Shell can recover for its provable loss or, if formality is necessary, that [the trustees] can recover the amount which Shell has lost but will hold the sums so recovered as trustees for Shell.

Whilst the Court of Appeal expanded the possibility of a tort claim being brought by a beneficiary, by finding that a tortfeasor can owe a duty of care to the beneficiary, the Court of Appeal acknowledged the lesser nature of the beneficiary's proprietary interest by recognizing that, for reasons of formality, the claimant beneficiary did not have a direct claim against the defendant tortfeasor for consequential economic loss, because the claimant was neither the legal owner of the property nor in possession of it. But it was held that such a claim could be brought if the trustees were joined as parties to the proceedings, since their legal title to the property could be used to establish the claim, even though the loss was suffered by the beneficiary. If the trustees were to refuse to sue, the beneficiary could then either sue the trustees for breach of trust or use the exceptional procedure known as the *Vandepitte* procedure,[143] whereby the beneficiary can name the trustees as defendant and also bring proceedings against the third party. This is what happened in *Shell UK*.

---

[141] Ibid, [5].

[142] Ibid, [142].

[143] After *Vandepitte v Preferred Accident Insurance Corporation of New York* [1933] AC 70, 79 (PC) (Lord Wright). See further Chapter 10.1(a)(ii)(e), pp. 489–90.

(ii) *Personal rights*

Maitland characterized the beneficiary's equitable rights as being personal rights against the trustee, known as rights *in personam*, rather than property rights against a thing. He said:[144]

> Equitable estates and interests are rights *in personam* but they have a misleading resemblance to rights *in rem*.

That is because, he said, a bona fide purchaser for value can acquire legal title to property and defeat the beneficiary's interest.

But this does not explain how the beneficiary acquires rights that can bind third parties even if the third party is unaware of the rights.[145] Similarly, if the trustee is declared bankrupt, the trustee in bankruptcy cannot claim the trust property in priority to the beneficiary's rights, which would be the case if the beneficiary's rights against the trustee were only personal. Further, where the subject matter of the trust is a personal right, such as where a trustee holds the value credited to a bank account on trust, if the trustee becomes insolvent, the beneficiary will still have a claim to the money credited to the account, even though the bank was contractually liable to pay only the value that is credited to the account. In other words, the bank has a personal right to the money credited to the bank at Common Law, but the beneficiary has an equitable proprietary right to it.

(iii) *Rights against rights*

McFarlane and Stevens[146] treat the beneficiary's equitable right as being a right against rights, namely the beneficiary's right against the trustee's rights of ownership:

> An equitable property right is neither a right against a person not a right against a thing. Rather, it is a right against a right. As a result, it cannot be fitted into the Roman dichotomy of rights *in personam* and *rights in rem*...
>
> whenever a party (B) has a right against a right of another (A), B's right is prima facie binding on anyone who acquires a right that derives from A's right.... there remains a difference between a right against a thing and a right against a right. The key attribute of a right against a thing is its universal exigibility: if B has a right against a thing, B's right is prima facie binding on the rest of the world. The key attribute of a right against a thing can be labelled persistence: if B has a right against A's right, B's right is prima facie binding on anyone who acquires a right that derives from A's right.
>
> B will acquire such a persistent right *whenever* A is under a duty to hold a specific claim-right or power, in a particular way, for B.

In other words, rather than saying that the trustee holds property on trust for the beneficiary, McFarlane and Stevens consider that the trustee holds his or her right of ownership of the property on trust for the beneficiary, who has an equitable right exigible against that right of ownership.

---

[144] Maitland, *Lectures on Equity* (2nd edn), p. 117.

[145] Jaffey, 'Explaining the Trust' (2015) 131 LQR 377, 379.

[146] 'The nature of equitable property' (2010) 4 JoE 1. See also Edelman, 'Two Fundamental Questions for the Law of Trusts' (2013) 129 LQR 66, 85.

This analysis is used to explain the characteristics of equitable rights, especially that they persist against third parties who acquire rights that derive from the trustee's rights, such as where the trustee transfers ownership to a third party. The third party is then bound by the beneficiary's right as against the third party's right to ownership, save where the third party is a bona fide purchaser for value. The thesis is also used to explain how the beneficiary obtains equitable rights where the trustee has only a personal right. So, for example, where the beneficiary asserts an equitable right in respect of a bank account, he or she is not asserting a right to the bank account, but instead to the trustee's personal right to be paid by the bank; this is the beneficiary's right against a right. If this personal right is acquired by a third party, such as the trustee in bankruptcy of the trustee, it will be a right that can continue to be enforced by the beneficiary even though the trustee in bankruptcy was unaware of the beneficiary's existence, in the same way as a third party who acquires ownership of property from the trustee will automatically be bound by the beneficiary's right against the third party's right of ownership.

McFarlane and Stevens' thesis is useful in explaining the characteristics of equitable rights by avoiding the need to characterize them as proprietary or personal. It also avoids the need to distinguish between legal and equitable ownership of property, since it rejects any notion of equitable ownership and replaces it with a notion of equitable rights. It also explains how there can be trusts of equitable rights. So, for example, B's equitable right as a beneficiary can be held on trust for C, so that C has a right against B's equitable right against the trustee's right of ownership to the property. The thesis also enables notions of equitable rights to be exported to jurisdictions with no tradition of Equity, because any legal system can recognize the concept of a right against a right.

Although McFarlane and Stevens' thesis does purport to explain the nature of a beneficiary's equitable right, it should be rejected primarily because it involves an artificial and unnecessarily complex analysis for the following specific reasons.

(1) The language of a right against a right is alien to Equity jurisprudence. This language is not used by the courts, in which the focus is instead on property rights, and the courts recognize that a beneficiary does have a proprietary interest in the trust property.[147] Similarly, there are statutes that refer to interests under a trust as being 'interests in property'.[148]

(2) The thesis fails to explain adequately the essentially proprietary nature of the beneficiary's interest under a trust. That interest is assignable, can be traded, can be held on trust for another, can sometimes enable the beneficiary to direct the transfer of trust property to him- or herself,[149] and may result in a tax liability because the beneficiary has an immediate claim to the trust property.

(3) It is a fundamental principle of Equity that a trust will not fail for want of a trustee.[150] If a trust is created by the settlor, but the trustee declines to act as trustee, the beneficiary can apply to the court to have a trustee appointed. The right of the beneficiary to have a trustee appointed cannot be considered to be a right against the trustee's right of ownership, because there will be no trustee at that particular moment. It is much more satisfactory to analyse this

---

[147] See, e.g. *Westdeutsche Landesbank Girozentrale v Islington LBC* [1996] AC 699, 705 (Lord Browne-Wilkinson); *Re Lehman Brothers International (Europe) (No. 2)* [2009] EWCA Civ 1161; *Pearson v Lehman Brothers Finance SA* [2010] EWHC 2914 (Ch), [225] (Briggs J). Upheld by Court of Appeal: [2011] EWCA Civ 1544; [2012] 2 BCLC 151.

[148] See, e.g. Trusts of Land and Appointment of Trustees Act 1996, s. 22(1).

[149] See Chapter 10.3, pp. 519–23.

[150] See Chapter 11.3(f), p. 544.

right as arising because Equity will ensure that the beneficiary's proprietary right to the trust property is respected.

Despite its flaws, the rights-against-rights thesis does at least purport to explain the key characteristics of equitable rights, which the *in rem* and *in personam* theories cannot satisfactorily do. The preferable view is that equitable rights should be regarded as proprietary, which is why they can persist against third parties. But equitable proprietary rights are modified rights, in that they do not have the same characteristics as legal proprietary rights. This is because equitable proprietary rights are properly treated as subsidiary property rights; they are subsidiary to legal proprietary rights. That is why legal proprietary rights are not defeated by the property being received by a bona fide purchaser for value and why the legal owner of property can bring the full range of claims for tortious interference with the property.

The modified nature of equitable proprietary rights also explains how, although the trustee's claim against a bank for money credited to a bank account is a personal claim, it is transformed into a proprietary right of the beneficiary if the trustee became insolvent or if the money credited to the account was misappropriated by a third party. This arises because of the ability of Equity to identify property in a fund.[151] Equity sees that, where trust money is credited to a bank account, the beneficiary of the trust has a right to the value in the fund. It is not the fund itself that is held on trust, but rather the value in the fund, the credit, even where the fund is made up of value from different sources, such as where money from the trustee is credited to the account as well. Once it is recognized that Equity can identify property in a fund, it is easy to treat the beneficiary's rights to the value in the fund as a proprietary right that persists against third parties apart from a bona fide purchaser for value, even though the trustee has only a personal right against the bank. This was recognized by Briggs J in *Pearson v Lehman Brothers Finance SA*:[152]

> [N]o-one doubts the beneficial interest of clients in a solicitor's client account. Yet the subject matter of that fund consists entirely of the solicitor's purely personal rights as a customer of the client account bank or banks.

This modified nature of the beneficiary's equitable proprietary rights against trust property is especially important when analysing the claims of beneficiaries to recover trust property that has been received by third parties, even where the original property has been substituted for new property.[153] So, for example, where shares are held on trust and have been misappropriated by the trustee and given to a third party, who then sells the shares and uses the proceeds to buy a car, the beneficiary of the trust can assert an equitable proprietary right against the car. This could be explained, using the language of McFarlane and Stevens, on the basis that the beneficiary has a right against the trustee's right to the ownership of the shares that persists against the third party, and which continues when the shares are sold and the car is purchased in its place. But it is so much easier, conceptually and analytically, to recognize that the beneficiary has an equitable proprietary right to the shares that can then be asserted against the car when it is substituted for the shares. But, being recognized in Equity, this proprietary right is modified and would be defeated if the shares had been purchased by the third party in good faith.

---

[151] Nolan, 'Property in a Fund' (2004) 120 LQR 108.
[152] [2010] EWHC 2914 (Ch), [227]. Upheld by Court of Appeal: [2011] EWCA Civ 1544; [2012] 2 BCLC 151.
[153] See Chapter 18.3(b), pp. 854–9.

QUESTION

Alan is a soldier who is about to be deployed to a foreign country for over a year. He asks his friend Brian to look after Alan's dog, Clive, and also to receive £10,000 from Alan, which Alan wants Brian to use to buy shares in a company for him. Brian agrees to do so. Brian pays the money into his own bank account, which is already credited with £10,000. After Alan has left the country, Brian sells Clive to Debbie for £1,000, and credits this money to his bank account. Brian withdraws £20,000 from his bank account, which he uses to buy 20,000 shares in Europa Ltd for £1 each. A year later Alan returns to the country. Debbie still has Clive and the shares in Europa Ltd are now worth £2 each.

Alan seeks your advice as to the nature of any claims he might have against Brian and Debbie.

FURTHER READING

Edelman, 'Two Fundamental Questions for the Law of Trusts' (2013) 129 LQR 66.

Fox, 'Overreaching', in *Breach of Trust* (eds Birks and Pretto) (Oxford: Hart, 2002), ch. 4.

Hayton, 'Pension Trusts and Traditional Trusts: Drastically Different Species of Trusts' [2005] Conv 229.

Jaffey, 'Explaining the Trust' (2015) 131 LQR 377.

Langbein, 'The Contractarian Basis of the Law of Trusts' (1995) 105 Yale LJ 625.

McBride, 'On the Classification of Trusts', in *Restitution and Equity, Volume 1: Resulting Trusts and Equitable Compensation* (eds Birks and Rose) (Oxford: Mansfield Press, 2000), ch. 2.

McFarlane and Stevens, 'The Nature of Equitable Property' (2010) 4 JoE 1.

Nolan, 'Equitable Property' (2006) 122 LQR 232.

Parkinson, 'Reconceptualising the Express Trust' (2002) 61 CLJ 657.

Sheridan, 'Protective Trusts' (1957) 21 Conv 110.

PART II

EXPRESS PRIVATE TRUSTS

3

THE REQUIREMENTS OF
AN EXPRESS TRUST

CENTRAL ISSUES

1. A valid express trust requires certainty of intention, certainty of subject matter, and certainty of objects ('the three certainties').

2. Express trusts respond to the intention of the creator of the trust, whether settlor or testator. This intention is assessed objectively. However, if the settlor or testator actually intended a relationship other than a trust, then the trust may be a sham.

3. There must be property upon which the trust can bite. Certainty of subject matter is assessed objectively. Problems arise if the property is not clearly ascertained. It appears that a trust over tangible property that has not been clearly segregated from similar property will be uncertain, but a trust over intangible property in such circumstances will be certain.

4. It must be clear to which objects, whether people or purposes, the trustees can and cannot appoint the property. Different tests are used to establish the certainty of objects: for a fixed trust, a complete list of beneficiaries is needed unless the trust is subject to a condition precedent, in which case the trust will be valid if one person fulfils the condition. For discretionary trusts and fiduciary powers, it needs to be certain whether any given person is or is not within the scope of the class of objects.

5. There needs to be someone in whose favour the trustees, and in default the court, can enforce the trust. This is known as the 'beneficiary principle'.

6. Settlors may not tie up their wealth forever. The perpetuity rules are therefore important. The property under the trust must vest within the perpetuity period.

1. INTRODUCTION

This chapter considers the requirements which need to be fulfilled for an express trust to be valid. The trust must be sufficiently certain; there must be beneficiaries who are able to enforce the trust; and the trust must comply with the perpetuity rules. Formalities for the creation of a trust are considered in Chapter 4. This chapter is only concerned with trusts for people and not trusts for purposes. Charitable and non-charitable purpose trusts, will be examined in Chapters 5 and 6.

Crucially, an express trust must fulfil the 'three certainties', which were influentially formulated by Lord Langdale MR in *Knight v Knight* as follows:[1]

> First, if the words are so used, that upon the whole, they ought to be construed as imperative;
>
> Secondly, if the subject of the recommendation or wish be certain; and,
>
> Thirdly, if the objects or persons intended to have the benefit of the recommendation or wish be also certain.

Thus, a trust cannot be created unless there is certainty in respect of (i) the intention to create a trust; (ii) the property that is the subject matter of the trust; and (iii) the objects of the trust. Although the three aspects of 'certainty' are here treated separately, in many cases they overlap. So, for example, it has been recognized that 'uncertainty in the subject of the gift has a reflex action upon the previous words, and throws doubt upon the intention of the testator'.[2] Similarly, a division of property among various beneficiaries may create uncertainty as to both the property and the beneficiaries.[3]

Nevertheless, it remains important that all aspects of the certainty requirement be fulfilled. Express trusts respond to the express intentions of the settlor or testator; without a certain intention to create a trust no trust can arise. Certainty of subject matter and objects are also necessary, primarily because if they are uncertain then it will not be possible for the court to administer the trust if the trustee fails to do so. In *McPhail v Doulton*, considered later,[4] Lord Wilberforce was prepared to accept that 'the test of validity is whether the trust can be executed by the court'.[5]

Deciding whether or not a trust satisfies the requirement of certainty calls for careful consideration of the language used to establish the trust. Often, this means interpreting the trust deed or will carefully. Although a thorough examination of the doctrine of interpretation lies beyond the scope of this book,[6] it is important to appreciate that the principles that apply to the interpretation of contracts apply equally to trust deeds.[7] The meaning of the words used to create the trust needs to be ascertained objectively, taking into account the context in which the language was used.[8] Careful drafting of the trust instrument should help to reduce problems of uncertainty.[9] However, the courts will 'not lightly allow contracting parties' purposes and intentions to be defeated by supposed uncertainty',[10]

---

[1] *Knight v Knight* (1840) 3 Beav 148, 173 (Lord Langdale MR). However, a mere 'recommendation' or 'wish' may no longer be sufficient to create a trust: see the discussion of precatory words in Chapter 3.1(a), pp. 67–8.

[2] *Mussoorie Bank v Raynor* (1882) 7 App Cas 321, 331 (Sir Arthur Hobhouse).

[3] *Boyce v Boyce* (1849) 16 Sim 476.

[4] See Chapter 3.4(b), pp. 91–4.

[5] [1971] AC 424, 451.

[6] See e.g. Lewison, *The Interpretation of Contracts* (6th edn) (London: Sweet & Maxwell, 2015); McMeel, *The Construction of Contracts: Interpretation, Implication and Rectification* (2nd edn) (Oxford: Oxford University Press, 2011).

[7] *Re Sigma Finance Corporation (in administrative receivership)* [2009] UKSC 2.

[8] See notably *Investors Compensation Scheme Ltd v West Bromwich Building Society* [1998] 1 WLR 896, 912–13 (Lord Hoffmann). The literal meaning of words may not represent the true interpretation of the language. See recently *Arnold v Britton* [2015] UKSC 36; [2015] AC 1619.

[9] As might giving another party the power to resolve any uncertainty: see Chapter 3.4(b)(i), pp. 99–102.

[10] *Pearson v Lehman Brothers Finance SA* [2010] EWHC 2914 (Ch), at [245] (Briggs J) (upheld on appeal: [2011] EWCA Civ 1544; [2012] 2 BCLC 151).

and generally seek to resolve any ambiguity in favour of upholding the trust if possible. As Sir Robert Megarry V-C held in *Re Hay's S.T.*:[11]

> Dispositions ought if possible to be upheld, and the court ought not to be astute to find grounds upon which a power can be invalidated.

In *Re Gulbenkian's Settlements* Lord Upjohn insisted that mistakes in drafting would not necessarily mean that there was insufficient certainty for a valid trust. Common sense is required to ascertain the meaning of the language used:[12]

> very frequently, whether it be in wills, settlements or commercial agreements, the application of such fundamental canons [of construction] leads nowhere, the draftsman has used words wrongly, his sentences border on the illiterate and his grammar may be appalling. It is then the duty of the court by the exercise of its judicial knowledge and experience in the relevant matter, innate common sense and desire to make sense of the settlor's or party's expressed intentions, however obscure and ambiguous the language that may have been used, to give a reasonable meaning to that language if it can do so without doing violence to it. The fact that the court has to see whether the clause is 'certain' for a particular purpose does not disentitle the court from doing otherwise than, in the first place, trying to make sense of it.

2. CERTAINTY OF INTENTION

(a) GENERAL PRINCIPLES

The key requirement of an express trust is that the settlor or testator intended to create a trust. If a trust was not intended, an express trust cannot be found.

The settlor or testator must have capacity to create a trust. Consequently, a settlement made by a child is voidable by the child before or reasonably soon after he or she attained the age of 18,[13] and a settlement made by a mentally incapacitated person is void.[14]

The intention to create a trust is particularly important because, once established, the trust is generally considered to be irrevocable. A contract might be varied by the contracting parties themselves,[15] but the settlor cannot usually vary a trust once it has been created.[16] Strong evidence is, therefore, needed to show that a trust rather than a mere agreement was intended.[17]

However, it is not necessary for the word 'trust' to be used. As Megarry J said in *Re Kayford Ltd*:[18]

> It is well settled that a trust can be created without using the word 'trust' or 'confidence' or the like: the question is whether in substance a sufficient intention to create a trust has been manifested.

---

[11] *Re Hay's Settlement Trusts* [1982] 1 WLR 202, 212.
[12] [1970] AC 508, 522 (Lord Upjohn). The case itself concerned a power: see Chapter 3.4(c), pp. 105–8.
[13] *Edwards v Carter* [1893] AC 360.
[14] *Re Beaney* [1978] 1 WLR 770. But note the Mental Capacity Act 2005 by virtue of which the court may make a settlement of property or execute a will on behalf of a person who lacks mental capacity: s. 18(1)(h), (i).
[15] Subject to any third party rights: see the Contracts (Rights of Third Parties) Act 1999, s. 2.
[16] *Re Schebsman* [1944] Ch 83. For variation, see Chapter 15.
[17] *Vandepitte v Preferred Accident Insurance Corp of New York* [1933] AC 70.
[18] [1975] 1 WLR 279, 28.

Similarly, Henderson J has recently said that:[19]

> In order for a trust to be established, it is not necessary for a settlor to use the word 'trust' or any other formal language, or to have any knowledge of trust law, so long as the traditional 'three certainties' (of words, subject-matter and objects) are satisfied.

It is necessary for the settlor to use 'imperative' words: if the trustees do not have to distribute the property, then a power, not a trust, will have been created.[20] Although it was once the case that mere 'precatory words', expressing a desire[21] or wish[22] or confidence[23] that a person act in a certain way, were sufficient for an express trust to be intended, that is no longer necessarily true.[24] Instead, whether or not a trust is intended will always be a question of interpretation. This is apparent from the following case.[25]

Re Adams and the Kensington Vestry [1884] 27 Ch D 394

George Smith, the testator, provided in his will as follows: 'I give, devise, and bequeath all my real and personal estate and effects whatsoever and wheresoever unto and to the absolute use of my wife, Harriet Smith, her executors, administrators and assigns, in full confidence that she will do what is right as to the disposal thereof between my children, either in her lifetime or by will after her decease.'

The question was whether this was an absolute gift, or whether the property was subject to a trust in favour of the children. The court held that the widow took absolutely; no trust was intended.

Cotton LJ:

Undoubtedly confidence, if the rest of the context shews that a trust is intended, may make a trust, but what we have to look at is the whole of the will which we have to construe, and if the confidence is that she will do what is right as regards the disposal of the property, I cannot say that that is, on the true construction of the will, a trust imposed upon her. Having regard to the later decisions, we must not extend the old cases in any way, or rely upon the mere use of any particular words, but, considering all the words which are used, we have to see what is their true effect, and what was the intention of the testator as expressed in his will. In my opinion, here he has expressed his will in such a way as not to shew an intention of imposing a trust on the wife, but on the contrary, in my opinion, he has shewn an intention to leave the property, as he says he does, to her absolutely.

Although examples can be given where the threshold of certainty regarding an intention to create a trust was set very high,[26] there are also instances where the court has been more generous in finding a trust. *Paul v Constance*[27] illustrates this point. Dennis Constance was married to Bridget Constance, but, when the marriage broke down, he left his wife and later began a relationship with Doreen Paul. Whilst together with Doreen, Dennis deposited money in an account in his name, from which Doreen could also withdraw money. Dennis also put some of his and Doreen's bingo winnings into

---

[19] *Charity Commission for England and Wales v Framjee* [2014] EWHC 2507; [2015] 1 WLR 16.
[20] See *Knight v Knight*, Chapter 3.1, p. 66.
[21] *Re Diggles* (1888) 39 Ch D 253.
[22] *Re Hamilton* [1895] 2 Ch 370.
[23] *Mussorie Bank Ltd v Raynor* (1882).
[24] *Lambe v Eames* (1871) 6 Ch App 597.
[25] See also *Re Steele's Will Trusts* [1948] Ch 603.
[26] *Jones v Lock* (1865) 1 Ch App 25, Chapter 4.3(a), pp. 146–7; *Swiss Bank Corpn v Lloyds Bank Ltd* [1982] AC 584; *Re Multi Guarantee Co. Ltd* [1987] BCLC 257.
[27] [1977] 1 WLR 527.

the account, telling her that 'the money is as much yours as mine'. Dennis then died intestate, and Bridget claimed all the money in the account as Dennis' wife. Doreen argued that Dennis was holding the money on trust for the benefit of Doreen and himself in equal shares. Both the judge and the Court of Appeal agreed that Doreen was entitled to half of the money in the account as a beneficiary under a trust. In their particular context, the words 'the money is as much yours as mine' was sufficient to evince an intention to create an express trust. Scarman LJ recognized that 'it might, however, be thought that this was a borderline case',[28] and it is suggested that the decision in *Paul v Constance* is probably at the limit of how far the courts will go to find a sufficiently certain intention to create a trust. It is obvious that clearer words are desirable.

(b) SHAM TRUSTS

Although it may seem, on an objective interpretation of the facts, that it can be established with sufficient certainty that the settlor did intend to create a trust, in some instances this conclusion will be undermined because the trust is a pretence, or a sham. Where the real, subjective intentions of the settlor and trustee are to mislead or deceive in some way, the appearance of an express trust conceals the true intentions which do not involve a trust relationship at all. In such cases, the subjective intentions of the parties trump the objective appearance of a trust, and the court will find the trust to be a sham. In *Hitch v Stone*, Arden LJ said:[29]

> It is of the essence of this type of sham transaction that the parties to a transaction intend to create one set of rights and obligations but do acts or enter into documents which they intend should give third parties, in this case the Revenue, or the court, the appearance of creating different rights and obligations.

A good indicator that a trust is a sham is if the trustee does not truly have the power to administer the trust property as his or her own, and the settlor continues to exercise real control over the 'trust' property. Ultimately, it is a question of degree whether or not the settlor retains such power over the property that the trust is a sham. This point has been well made by Conaglen.

Conaglen, 'Sham Trusts' (2008) 67 CLJ 176, 196–7

> The question is one of degree: does the settlor have such a degree of control over the trustee's conduct that it is proper to infer that the settlor and the trustee entered into the supposed trust arrangement in order to mislead others into believing that the apparent trust was valid? It is important in this regard to emphasise that the mere fact that the trustee has abdicated some of its decision-making powers to the settlor after the trust was created does not necessarily indicate that the trust was a sham when it was originally created: such subsequent conduct may instead amount to no more than a breach of trust on the trustee's part (or potentially a valid delegation of powers by the trustee). But where the pattern of conduct indicates that the trustee has never exercised its discretionary powers and has always been prepared to act simply as the settlor directs, the court may legitimately conclude that both the settlor and the trustee never intended to give effect to the trust instrument and instead entered into it only in order to disguise the true arrangement. It is important to emphasise this high threshold: the mere

---

[28] Ibid, 532.
[29] [2001] EWCA Civ 63; [2001] STC 214 at [63]. See also *Snook v London and West Riding Investments Ltd* [1967] 2 QB 786, 802.

inclusion in a trust instrument of a power for the settlor to revoke the trust, or to control the trust's investments, does not necessarily mean that the trust is a sham.

It might be helpful to think of the courts applying some sort of 'trustometer' device:[30] the more powers the settlor retains for him or herself, the more likely it is that the trust is a sham.

Although a sham need only be proved on the general civil standard of a balance of probabilities, convincing evidence will be required; given that a sham generally involves a finding of dishonesty,[31] courts will not readily conclude that an apparently legitimate trust is in fact a sham.

National Westminster Bank plc v Jones [2001] 1 BCLC 98, [59]

Neuberger J:

Because a finding of sham carries with it a finding of dishonesty, because innocent third parties may often rely upon the genuineness of a provision or an agreement, and because the court places great weight on the existence and provisions of a formally signed document, there is a strong and natural presumption against holding a provision or a document a sham.

There has been some discussion about whether the intentions of the settlor *and* the trustee need to be found. Is it sufficient if the settlor *alone* did not truly intend to set up a real trust? Or does the trustee *also* need to intend that the trust not operate as a true trust?

In *Shalson v Russo*,[32] Rimer J thought that both the settlor and the trustee must intend the trust to be a sham. So, if the settlor lacks the intention to create a trust, but the trustee does not share this intention, the trust could still be valid.[33] This seems satisfactory: if the settlor intends a sham, but the trustee is unaware of this and operates the trust as a proper trust, the court should not interfere by declaring the trust a sham. The settlor's intentions have been defeated, but since they were improper from the outset, this is not objectionable. Any other conclusion may disadvantage innocent third parties who have relied upon the outward appearance of a valid trust. As Patten LJ remarked in *Pankhania v Chandegra*:[34]

The question of what constitutes a sham trust has been the subject of considerable discussion in recent years, particularly in the context of attempts to shield assets from the claims of divorced spouses or creditors. But what is, I think, clear is that it must be shown both that the parties to the trust deed (in this case, the claimant and the defendant) never intended to create a trust and that they did intend to give that false impression to third parties or to the court. So in *Snook v London and West Riding Investments Ltd* [1967] 2 QB 786, at page 802, Lord Diplock said that:

'As regards the contention of the plaintiff that the transactions between himself, Auto Finance and the defendants were a "sham," it is, I think, necessary to consider what, if any, legal concept is involved in the use of this popular and pejorative word. I apprehend that, if

---

[30] Harris, 'No Such Thing as a Sham Trust?' [2004] Private Client Business 95.

[31] Although in *Midland Bank plc v Wyatt* [1997] 1 BCLC 242, 252 it was held that a trust may be a sham even if it was the result of mistaken legal advice, rather than the result of dishonesty. Such circumstances will, however, be very rare.

[32] [2003] EWHC 1637 (Ch); [2005] Ch 281.

[33] See also *Chase Manhattan Equities Ltd v Goodman* [1991] BCLC 897; *Grupo Torras SA v Al Sabah* [2004] WTLR 1 (Deputy Bailiff of the Royal Court of Jersey).

[34] [2012] EWCA Civ 1438; [2013] 3 FCR 16, [20]–[21].

it has any meaning in law, it means acts done or documents executed by the parties to the "sham" which are intended by them to give to third parties or to the court the appearance of creating between the parties legal rights and obligations different from the actual legal rights and obligations (if any) which the parties intend to create.'

This is now recognised as an authoritative statement of what has to be proved in order to set aside a transaction as a sham and applies as much to a trust as to any other kind of instrument: see *Hitch v Stone (Inspector of Taxes)* [2001] EWCA Civ 63; *Shalson v Russo* [2003] EWHC 1637 (Ch).

This argument had been accepted by Munby J, the judge in *A v A*, and in the following extract Munby J provides thoughtful discussion of sham trusts. At the end of the passage, the judge also offers a good explanation of *dicta* in *Midland Bank plc v Wyatt*,[35] which have sometimes been thought to be inconsistent with the proposition that all the parties to the sham trust need to share the dishonest intention. In *Wyatt*, the trust was created by a declaration made by the settlor that he hold property on trust for another; in such circumstances of self-declaration, it seems reasonable only to examine the settlor's intention, given that the settlor is also meant to be the trustee.[36]

A v A [2007] EWHC 99 (Fam), [41]–[50]

Munby J:

In the present case there have been, from time to time, a number of different trustees of the trusts. The question therefore arises as to which of the trustees' intentions are relevant for this purpose. Put somewhat differently, the question arises as to whether a trust which is not a sham can subsequently become a sham and, conversely, whether a trust which is a sham can subsequently lose that character...

It seems to me that as a matter of principle a trust which is not initially a sham cannot subsequently become a sham...Once a trust has been properly constituted, typically by the vesting of the trust property in the trustee(s) and by the execution of the deed setting out the trusts upon which the trust property is to be held by the trustee(s), the property cannot lose its character as trust property save in accordance with the terms of the trust itself, for example, by being paid to or applied for the benefit of a beneficiary in accordance with the terms of the trust deed. Any other application of the trust property is simply and necessarily a breach of trust; nothing less and nothing more.

A trustee who has bona fide accepted office as such cannot divest himself of his fiduciary obligations by his own improper acts. If therefore, a trustee who has entered into his responsibilities, and without having any intention of being party to a sham, subsequently purports, perhaps in agreement with the settlor, to treat the trust as a sham, the effect is not to create a sham where previously there was a valid trust. The only effect, even if the agreement is actually carried into execution, is to expose the trustee to a claim for breach of trust and, it may well be, to expose the settlor to a claim for knowing assistance[37] in that breach of trust. Nor can it make any difference, where the trust has already been properly constituted, that a trustee may have entered into office—may indeed have been appointed a trustee in place of an honest trustee—for the very purpose and with the intention of treating the trust for the future as a sham. If, having been appointed trustee, he has the trust property under his control, he cannot be heard to dispute either the fact that it is trust property or the existence of his own fiduciary duty...

---

[35] [1997] 1 BCLC 242.
[36] See also *Painter v Hutchison* [2007] EWHC 758 (Ch); [2008] BPIR 170, [109]–[115] (Lewison J).
[37] See Chapter 19, 'Third Party Liability'.

I turn to consider the converse case. Can a trust which is initially a sham subsequently lose that character? I see no reason in principle why that should not be possible. The situation is best explained by an example. S has purportedly vested property in T1 as trustee of a trust which is in fact, consistently with their common intention, a sham from the outset. T1 now wishes to retire as 'trustee.' S, executing all the appropriate documents, purports to appoint T2 as T1's successor and to transfer the 'trust property' into T2's name. Now if T2 knows that the 'trust' is a sham and accepts appointment as 'trustee' intending to perpetuate the sham, then nothing has changed. The 'trust' was a sham whilst T1 was the 'trustee' and remains a sham even though T1 has been replaced by T2. But what if T2 does not know that the 'trust' was a sham, and accepts appointment believing the 'trust' to be entirely genuine and intending to perform his fiduciary duties conscientiously and strictly in accordance with what he believes to be a genuine trust deed? I cannot see any reason why, in that situation, what was previously a sham should not become, even if only for the future, a genuine trust.

On the contrary, principle argues compellingly that in such circumstances there is indeed, for the future, a valid and enforceable trust. After all, in the circumstances I have postulated, the trust property has been vested in someone who accepts that he holds the property as trustee on the trusts of a document which he believes to be a genuine instrument. He has no intention that the arrangement should be a sham...

The corollary of all this can be stated very simply. Whatever the settlor or anyone else may have intended, and whatever may have happened since it was first created, a trust will not be a sham—in my judgment cannot as a matter of law be a sham—if *either* • i) the original trustee(s), *or* • ii) the current trustee(s), were not, because they lacked the relevant knowledge and intention, party to the sham at the time of their appointment. In the first case, the trust will never have been a sham. In the second case, the trust, even if it was previously a sham, will have become a genuine—a valid and enforceable—trust as from the date of appointment of the current trustee(s).

There has been some debate in the authorities as to what is required to establish the requisite common *intention*. In *Midland Bank plc v Wyatt* [1995] 1 FLR 696, the Deputy Judge, Mr David Young QC, said at page 699 that:

> 'a sham transaction will still remain a sham transaction even if one of the parties to it merely went along with the 'shammer' not either knowing or caring about what he or she was signing. Such a person would still be a party to the sham and could not rely on any principle of estoppel such as was the case in *Snook*[38]...'

What is required is a common *intention*, but reckless indifference will be taken to constitute the necessary intention.

This recognition that reckless indifference can be equated with intention seems satisfactory and is consistent with how intention is defined in other areas of the law.[39]

Generally, a sham trust is considered to be void. But it should be remembered that sham trusts are often established in order to hide or conceal something. For example, a settlor may give the impression of setting up a trust in order to deceive his creditors. In such instances, the trust can also be said to be tainted by illegality, since the trust mechanism is being exploited in order to defraud his or her creditors. The principles of illegality must, therefore, be borne in mind when considering the impact of sham trusts in this area. These will be considered in more detail in Chapter 8.[40] However, it is important to appreciate that any illegality should not affect the right of a third party, such as the Revenue, to establish that a trust is a sham. But the fact that the parties are tainted by illegality means

---

[38] *Snook v London and West Riding Investments Ltd* [1967] 2 QB 786.
[39] See e.g. in the context of the tort of inducing a breach of contract, *OBG Ltd v Allan* [2007] UKHL 21; [2008] 1 AC 1 at [40]–[41] (Lord Hoffmann); [192] (Lord Nicholls).
[40] See Chapter 8.2(d)(i), pp. 377–83.

that they may not be able *themselves* to claim that a trust is a sham. This is because a party may not lead any evidence of illegality in order to establish his or her claim.[41] But if one of the parties withdraws from the illegal transaction before any part of the illegal purpose is implemented, then that party may be able to rely upon the illegal intentions in order to establish that a trust is a sham.[42]

If the trust is a sham, then that generally leads to the conclusion that the trust is void.[43] However, holding the trust to be void may, in some circumstances, adversely affect innocent third parties who have relied upon the apparently valid express trust. In such cases, third parties should be protected and the doctrine of estoppel might be employed to prevent parties to the sham from denying the existence of a trust to the detriment of those who have innocently relied upon the trust.[44] In *Carman v Yates*, Charles J insisted that:[45]

> as against an innocent third party it cannot lie in the mouths of the pretenders to assert to the disadvantage of that innocent third party that the transaction is a sham, or pretence, and thus of no effect.

This seems entirely appropriate, but it is not clear how the court would deal with the situation where the interests of various innocent third parties conflict, such that some would insist on the trust being a sham, and others precisely the contrary.[46] Charles J in *Carman v Yates* suggested that the courts would benefit from a degree of flexibility in such a situation.[47] Conaglen has cautioned against unconstrained judicial discretion in this area, preferring instead to focus upon established principles concerning estoppel and the priority of competing equities.[48] This may be the most appropriate approach. However, there is some merit in allowing the courts the flexibility to achieve the most satisfactory outcome from a highly unsatisfactory situation. Indeed, the Law Commission has recently recommended a slightly more flexible approach when establishing what the consequences of a trust tainted by illegality should be.[49]

(c) INSOLVENCY ACT 1986

Similar to the discussion on shams in Section (b), a declaration of trust may also be set aside where it is made to the unfair prejudice of creditors. Section 423 of the Insolvency Act 1986[50] provides that a transaction, including a gift, which was at an undervalue[51] and which was intended to put assets beyond the reach of creditors[52] or to prejudice their interests in a claim against the transferor,[53] may

---

[41] *Tinsley v Milligan* [1994] 1 AC 340.

[42] *Tribe v Tribe* [1996] Ch 107; *Painter v Hutchison* [2007] EWHC 758 (Ch).

[43] *Midland Bank plc v Wyatt* [1995] 1 FLR 696, 707; *Rahman v Chase Bank (C.I.) Trust Co Ltd* [1991] JLR 103, 168; *Hitch v Stone* [2001] EWCA Civ 63; [2001] STC 214, at [87].

[44] *Hitch v Stone* [87]; *National Westminster Bank v Jones* [2001] 1 BCLC 98, [60].

[45] [2004] EWHC 3448 (Ch); [2005] BPIR 476, [219].

[46] Neuberger J has said that the court would have to consider such a scenario if and when it arises: *Natwest v Jones* [2001] 1 BCLC 98, [60].

[47] [2004] EWHC 3448 (Ch); [2005] BPIR 476, [220].

[48] Conaglen, 'Sham Trusts' (2008) 67 CLJ 176, 205–6.

[49] Draft Trusts (Concealment of Interests) Bill, to be found in Law Commission, *The Illegality Defence* Law Com. No. 320 (2010). See Chapter 8.2(d)(i), p. 382.

[50] See also Insolvency Act, s. 339: transactions at an undervalue where the transferor is declared bankrupt within five years of the transaction, but there is no need to prove an intent to defraud creditors. See e.g. *Hill v Haines* [2007] EWCA Civ 1284; [2007] 50 EG 109 (CS).

[51] See *Re MC Bacon Ltd* [1990] BCLC 324; *Agricultural Mortgage Corpn plc v Woodward* [1995] 1 EGLR 1 (creation of tenancy for wife set aside, even though it was at full value, since wife achieved benefits greater than those conferred by the tenancy itself).

[52] *IRC v Hashmi* [2002] EWCA Civ 981; [2002] WTLR 1027.

[53] *Hill v Spread Trustee Co. Ltd* [2006] EWCA Civ 542; [2007] 1 WLR 2404 (purpose in making a settlement to induce the revenue to make an incorrect assessment of capital gains tax: within s. 423).

be set aside and the court may order that any property transferred under the transaction is to be returned. So, for example, if a settlor creates a settlement not for value in order to defraud creditors, this trust can be set aside and the settled property be restored to the settlor.

This is illustrated by *IRC v Hashmi*,[54] where a tenant had acquired the freehold of the property and purported to declare a trust of this for his son. The tenant had been under-declaring his profits. In concluding that he had intended to defraud his creditors, Arden LJ said:[55]

> [Section 423 of the Insolvency Act 1986] does not require the inquiry to be made whether the purpose was a dominant purpose. It is sufficient if the statutory purpose can properly be described as a purpose and not merely as a consequence…it will often be the case that the motive to defeat creditors and the motive to secure family protection will co-exist in such a way that even the transferor himself may be unable to say what was uppermost in his mind…for something to be a purpose it must be a real substantial purpose.

Moreover, it is unlawful for a person to declare himself to be holding property on trust for one creditor, or group of creditors, to the detriment of other creditors: this is known as a 'voidable preference'. In such circumstances, a sufficiently certain intention to create a trust may be established, but that intention is not given effect due to the policy underpinning the Insolvency Act 1986, sections 238 and 239, which insists that unsecured creditors should be treated equally amongst themselves. Thus, if a company declares itself to be holding the property of a customer on trust, it is difficult to ascertain whether the customer should truly be able to rely upon a proprietary interest, rather than simply a contractual claim in debt. This is particularly significant when considering the *Quistclose* mechanism, considered in Chapter 8.[56] But, for present purposes, it is important to note that the intention of the company declaring a trust may not be given effect by the court. Whether or not an unfair preference is at issue depends on the particular circumstances of a case. In *Re Kayford Ltd*,[57] Megarry J held that the trust was valid where a mail order company, experiencing financial difficulties, set up a separate account called the 'Customer's Trust Deposit Account', in order to try to ring-fence deposits received from its customers. The company only intended to take the money out of the account once the goods were delivered to the customers. The judge held that this was not an unlawful preference in favour of the new depositors:[58]

> I may say at the outset that on the facts of the case [counsel] was unable to contend that any question of a fraudulent preference arose. If one leaves on one side any case in which an insolvent company seeks to declare a trust in favour of creditors, one is concerned here with the question not of preferring creditors but of preventing those who pay money from becoming creditors, by making them beneficiaries under a trust.

This decision can be justified, since, without the protection offered by a trust, the company may have been less likely to receive orders from customers. Without such orders, the company may simply have entered liquidation even earlier, so its other creditors would not have been in any better position by opposing the creation of a trust. Nevertheless, it was something of a boon to the customers to find themselves beneficiaries under a trust, and companies must remain cautious about preferring one group of creditors over another through the trust mechanism.

---

[54] [2002] EWCA Civ 981; [2002] WTLR 1027.
[55] Ibid, [23]–[25].
[56] *Barclays Bank Ltd v Quistclose Investments Ltd* [1970] AC 567, see Chapter 8.5, pp. 410–26.
[57] [1974] 1 WLR 279.
[58] Ibid, 281.

3. CERTAINTY OF SUBJECT MATTER

The subject matter of a trust must be sufficiently certain. Without property upon which the trust can bite, there can be no valid trust. Exactly what property is held on trust must be defined with certainty. Otherwise, it is difficult to administer the trust properly: trustees, and in default the court, need to know exactly what property must be distributed. Defining the subject matter of the trust also makes it clear which property is unavailable to be distributed to creditors in the event of the trustee's insolvency.

(a) NATURE OF SUBJECT MATTER

Property is defined broadly and is not limited to tangible goods.[59] For example, in *Swift v Dairywise Farms Ltd*[60] it was held that milk quotas (which gave the holder an exemption from a levy that would otherwise be payable) could form the subject matter of a trust. In justifying this decision, Jacob J referred to the wide definition of property in section 436 of the Insolvency Act 1986:

> 'property' includes money, goods, things in action, land and every description of property wherever situated and also obligations and every description of interest, whether present or future or vested or contingent, arising out of, or incidental to property.

(b) OBJECTIVE INTERPRETATION

Identifying the subject matter of the trust and whether it meets the certainty requirement requires careful construction of the language used. The following two cases are instructive in this regard.

Palmer v Simmonds [1854] 2 Drew 221

The testatrix, by her will, gave her residuary estate to Thomas Harrison 'for his own use and benefit, as I have full confidence in him, that if he should die without lawful issue he will...leave the bulk of my said residuary estate unto' certain named persons.

The expression of confidence was sufficient, according to the practice at that time, to manifest an intention to create a trust.[61] The question was whether the subject matter of the trust was sufficiently certain. It was held that it was not.

Kindersley V-C:

What is the meaning then of bulk? The appropriate meaning, according to its derivation, is something which bulges out, &c. [His Honour referred to *Todd's Johnson and Richardson's Dictionary* for the different meanings and etymology of the word.] Its popular meaning we all know. When a person is said

---

[59] In *Don King Productions v Warren* [2000] Ch 291 the Court of Appeal accepted that personal and unassignable rights could be held on trust. This has been criticized: Tettenborn, 'Trusts and Unassignable Agreements—Again' [1999] LMCLQ 353 (A. Tettenborn).

[60] [2000] 1 WLR 1177. See [2000] All ER Rev 247 (Clarke).

[61] For discussion of precatory words, see Chapter 3.2(a), p. 68.

to have given the bulk of his property, what is meant is not the whole but the greater part, and that is in fact consistent with its classical meaning. When, therefore, the testatrix uses that term, can I say she has used a term expressing a definite, clear, certain part of her estate, or the whole of her estate? I am bound to say she has not designated the subject as to which she expresses her confidence; and I am therefore of opinion that there is no trust created; that *Harrison* took absolutely, and those claiming under him now take.

Re Golay's Will Trusts [1965] 1 WLR 969 (ChD)

By his will, the testator directed his executors 'to let Tossy—Mrs F. Bridgewater—to enjoy one of my flats during her lifetime and to receive a reasonable income from my other properties....' The question was whether the gift of the income was void for uncertainty. It was held that the gift was valid.

Ungoed-Thomas J:

The question therefore comes to this: Whether the testator by the words 'reasonable income' has given a sufficient indication of his intention to provide an effective determinant of what he intends so that the court in applying that determinant can give effect to the testator's intention.

Whether the yardstick of 'reasonable income' were applied by trustees under a discretion given to them by a testator or applied by a court in course of interpreting and applying the words 'reasonable income' in a will, the yardstick sought to be applied by the trustees in the one case and the court in the other case would be identical. The trustees might be other than the original trustees named by the testator and the trustees could even surrender their discretion to the court. It would seem to me to be drawing too fine a distinction to conclude that an objective yardstick which different persons sought to apply would be too uncertain, not because of uncertainty in the yardstick but as between those who seek to apply it.

In this case, however, the yardstick indicated by the testator is not what he or some other specified person subjectively considers to be reasonable but what he identifies objectively as 'reasonable income'. The court is constantly involved in making such objective assessments of what is reasonable and it is not to be deterred from doing so because subjective influences can never be wholly excluded. In my view the testator intended by 'reasonable income' the yardstick which the court could and would apply in quantifying the amount so that the direction in the will is not in my view defeated by uncertainty.

These two cases show that the subject matter of the trust must be *objectively* clear. Different parties could have had different views about what constituted the 'bulk' of an estate, and, therefore, the scope of the trust could have varied considerably between, for example, the original trustees, subsequent trustees, and the court. By contrast, 'reasonableness' is a concept with which lawyers and courts regularly grapple across a wide variety of concepts; as a result, a 'reasonable amount' can be ascertained with a higher degree of certainty than 'bulk'. Nevertheless, it must also be accepted that 'reasonable income' cannot be precisely defined, and that trustees and the court may differ about what exactly constitutes a 'reasonable' amount. It is suggested that the room for disagreement within the confines of 'reasonableness' is perhaps sufficiently narrow for the courts to feel able to uphold the trust. After all, courts do not strive to defeat gifts. But there are limits to how far the court will go to uphold a trust—and the 'bulk' of an estate in *Palmer v Simmonds* clearly crossed the boundary of certainty.

(c) PROPERTY IN A LARGER BULK NOT CLEARLY SEGREGATED

The property that is subject to the trust must be identifiable.[62] If the subject matter of the trust is segregated and clearly separated from other property of the trustee, that clearly helps to ensure that the certainty requirement is met. So, if a trust is declared over a part of a larger quantity of property, it is advisable to segregate the property that forms the subject matter of the trust. Problems arise where this is not done. For example, in *Re London Wine Co (Shippers) Ltd*[63] the London Wine Company (LWC) allowed people to purchase wine, generally as an investment. Upon purchase, LWC provided the customer with a document of title confirming that the wine belonged to the purchaser. The wine bought by the customers would remain in warehouses. However, the customers' bottles of wine were not segregated from the rest of LWC's stock. When LWC later entered liquidation, it became necessary to establish whether all the relevant bottles of wine belonged to LWC, or whether some were held on trust for the customers. Oliver J held that there could be no trust, since the subject matter of the trust was uncertain: it was not clear *which* bottles of wine were held on trust for the customers.

This decision is entirely orthodox: it must be clear upon which property the trust bites. However, the decision might seem harsh upon the purchasers; after all, the purchasers might have believed that the wine belonged to them, and that LWC would ensure that this was the case. Indeed, given that the case involved the sale of goods, the *result* of the case would now be affected by the Sale of Goods (Amendment) Act 1995, which introduced section 20A into the Sale of Goods Act 1979:

Sale of Goods Act 1979, s. 20A—Undivided shares in goods forming part of a bulk.

(1) This section applies to a contract for the sale of a specified quantity of unascertained goods if the following conditions are met—

    (a) the goods or some of them form part of a bulk which is identified either in the contract or by subsequent agreement between the parties; and

    (b) the buyer has paid the price for some or all of the goods which are the subject of the contract and which form part of the bulk.

(2) Where this section applies, then (unless the parties agree otherwise), as soon as the conditions specified in paragraphs (a) and (b) of subsection (1) above are met or at such later time as the parties may agree—

    (a) property in an undivided share in the bulk is transferred to the buyer, and

    (b) the buyer becomes an owner in common of the bulk.

But statutory reform in a specific context of sale—as opposed to gift or declaration of trust—should not cloud the general principle of trust law: for a trust to be valid, the property in question should be certain. In *Re Stapylton Fletcher Ltd*[64] there was a valid trust where, on similar facts to *Re London Wine Company*, the wine company in question *did* separate the stock designated for the customers from its general stock. This made it easy to ascertain which bottles or cases were being held for the

---

[62] *Westdeutsche Landesbank Girozentrale v Islington London Borough Council* [1996] AC 669, 705 (Lord Browne-Wilkinson).

[63] [1986] PCC 121.

[64] [1994] 1 WLR 1181.

purchasers. By contrast, in *Re Goldcorp Exchange Ltd*[65] the purchasers of gold bullion were not able to prove the existence of a valid trust where the bullion was never segregated[66] and it was impossible to distinguish which property might be the subject matter of a trust.

From these cases, the need clearly to demarcate the property that is subject to the trust might be considered to be apparent. However, the following decision held that a trust of 50 out of 950 shares was valid, despite those shares not being clearly segregated.

Hunter v Moss [1994] 1 WLR 452

The defendant was the registered owner of 950 shares in a company (MEL) with an issued share capital of 1,000 shares. He made an oral declaration of trust in favour of the plaintiff in respect of 5 per cent of the company's issued share capital (i.e. 50 shares). The Court of Appeal held that the trust was not void for uncertainty.

Dillon LJ:

It is well established that for the creation of a trust there must be the three certainties referred to by Lord Langdale in *Knight v Knight* (1840) 3 Beav 148. One of those is, of course, that there must be certainty of subject matter. All these shares were identical in one class: 5 per cent was 50 shares and the defendant held personally more than 50 shares. . . . Again, it would not be good enough for a settlor to say 'I declare that I hold 50 of my shares on trust for B,' without indicating the company he had in mind of the various companies in which he held shares. There would be no sufficient certainty as to the subject matter of the trust. But here the discussion is solely about the shares of one class in the one company.

It is plain that a bequest by the defendant to the plaintiff of 50 of his ordinary shares in MEL would be a valid bequest on the defendant's death which his executors or administrators would be bound to carry into effect. [Counsel] sought to dispute that and to say that if, for instance, a shareholder had 200 ordinary shares in ICI and wanted to give them to A, B, C and D equally he could do it by giving 200 shares to A, B, C and D as tenants in common, but he could not validly do it by giving 50 shares to A, 50 shares to B, 50 shares to C and 50 shares to D, because he has not indicated which of the identical shares A is to have and which B is to have. I do not accept that. That such a testamentary bequest is valid, appears sufficiently from *Re Clifford* [1912] 1 Ch 29 and *Re Cheadle* [1900] 2 Ch 620. . . .

[Counsel], however, relied on two authorities in particular. One is a decision of Oliver J in *Re London Wine Co (Shippers) Ltd* [1986] PCC 121 which was decided in 1975. That was a case in which the business of the company was that of dealers in wine and over a period it had acquired stocks of wine which were deposited in various warehouses in England. Quantities were then sold to customers by the company, but in many instances the wine remained at the warehouse. There was no appropriation—on the ground, as it were—from bulk, of any wine, to answer particular contracts. But the customer received from the company a certificate of title for wine for which he had paid which described him as the sole and beneficial owner of such-and-such wine of such-and-such a vintage. The customer was charged for storage and insurance, but specific cases were not segregated or identified.

Subsequently, at a stage when large stocks of wine were held in various warehouses to the order of the company and its customers, a receiver was appointed by a debenture holder. The question that arose was whether the customers who had received these certificates of title had a good title to the

---

[65] [1995] 1 AC 74 (PC). This case, as well as *Re London Wine*, pre-dated section 20A of the Sale of Goods Act 1979.
[66] Apart from for a small number of purchasers.

quantity of wine referred to in the certificate as against the receiver appointed under a floating charge. The judge held that it could not be said that the legal title to the wine had passed to individual customers and the description of the wine did not adequately link it with any given consignment or warehouse. And, furthermore, it appeared that there was a lack of comparison at the time the certificates were issued in that, in some cases, the certificates were issued before the wine which had been ordered by the company had actually been received by the company. It seems to me that that case is a long way from the present. It is concerned with the appropriation of chattels and when the property in chattels passes. We are concerned with a declaration of trust, accepting that the legal title remained in the defendant and was not intended, at the time the trust was declared, to pass immediately to the plaintiff. The defendant was to retain the shares as trustee for the plaintiff.

[Counsel] also referred to *MacJordan Construction Ltd v Brookmount Erostin Ltd* (1991) 56 BLR 1, a decision of this court. The position there was that MacJordan were sub-contractors for Brookmount as main contractors. There was retention money kept back by Brookmount which, on the documents, was to be held on a trust for the sub-contractors, but it had not been set aside as a separate fund when a receiver was appointed by the main contractor, Brookmount's bank. It was, consequently, held that MacJordan were not entitled to payment in full of the retention moneys in priority to the receiver and the secured creditor. It was common ground in that case that, prior to the appointment of the receivers, there were no identifiable assets of Brookmount impressed with the trust applicable to the retention fund. At best, there was merely a general bank account.

In reliance on that case [Counsel] submitted that no fiduciary relationship can attach to an unappropriated portion of a mixed fund. The only remedy is that of a floating charge. He referred to a passage in the judgment of Lord Greene MR in *Re Diplock* [1948] Ch 465 at 519–520 where he said:

> 'The narrowness of the limits within which the common law operated may be linked with the limited nature of the remedies available to it…In particular, the device of a declaration of charge was unknown to the common law and it was the availability of that device which enabled equity to give effect to its wider conception of equitable rights.'

So [Counsel] submitted that the most that the plaintiff could claim is to have an equitable charge on a blended fund….

As I see it, however, we are not concerned in this case with a mere equitable charge over a mixed fund. Just as a person can give, by will, a specified number of his shares of a certain class in a certain company, so equally, in my judgment, he can declare himself trustee of 50 of his ordinary shares in MEL or whatever the company may be and that is effective to give a beneficial proprietary interest to the beneficiary under the trust. No question of a blended fund thereafter arises and we are not in the field of equitable charge.

The reasoning used by the Court of Appeal in *Hunter v Moss* has been criticized. In particular, the analogy with testamentary trusts is dubious.

Hayton, 'Uncertainty of Subject Matter of Trusts' 110 (1994) LQR 335, 338–9

[Dillon LJ] ignored the fact that there is a crucial difference between such a testamentary bequest, where undoubtedly the testator has effectively divested himself of his legal and beneficial ownership, and an *inter vivos* declaration of oneself as trustee for another, where the disputed question is whether or not the settlor has effectively divested himself of this beneficial ownership in specific property.

It is elementary that a bequest is a perfect gift that is completed by the testator's death. Thereupon, certain property, namely the testator's whole estate, passes to the executor, who has full ownership without distinction between legal and equitable interests therein, subject to fiduciary obligations to administer it by paying debts, expenses, taxes, etc., and then implementing the executory trusts of the testator to the extent that there is sufficient property left to satisfy such trusts. The intended beneficiaries only have an equitable chose in action until the executor has completed the administration of the estate: *Comr of Stamp Duties v Livingston* [1965] AC 694.[67]

It follows that the only *inter vivos* situation analogous to the testamentary situation instanced by Dillon LJ is that where the settlor makes a perfect gift of specific property to a trustee so as to divest himself of legal and beneficial ownership thereof, e.g. by transferring 950 shares to a trustee and imposing equitable obligations upon the trustee to distribute 50 to X and 900 to Y.

The position is very different where the settlor, S, retains the legal title and intends to declare a trust so as to make a perfect gift to X of the equitable interest in specific property. S can intend either that X is to be equitably entitled to one-nineteenth of each of S's 950 shares, so that S and X are equitable tenants in common, or, as in *Hunter v Moss*, that X is to be exclusively entitled in equity to 50 of S's 950 shares. In the former case, X has a certain equitable interest in one-nineteenth of every share; but in the latter case S has not yet divested himself of any beneficial interest in any specific shares because he has not set aside a specific 50 shares for X, so surely the equitable gift is imperfect and X has no equitable rights in any shares. If S then changes his mind, it follows that equity will not compel him to perfect his imperfect gift by treating the latter type of intention as the former: cp. *Milroy v Lord* (1852) 4 De G F & J 264.[68] In contrast, if S had declared himself trustee of 50 for X and 900 for Y, then he would have divested himself of all beneficial interest in his 950 shares. Thus, under the rule in *Saunders v Vautier* (1841) 4 Beav 115,[69] if X and Y agreed, being between them absolutely entitled to the whole equitable interest in the 950, they could jointly call for the shares.

As Hayton observes, if the trust had been for one-nineteenth of the 950 shares, as opposed to 50 out of 950 shares, the subject matter of the trust would have been sufficiently certain.[70] This is because the court does not have to decide *which* 50 shares are held on trust, but rather can say that all the shares are held on trust in the proportions of 1:18. Indeed, this approach was adopted in Australia in *White v Shortall*. Campbell J[71] found the reasoning in *Hunter v Moss* to be unpersuasive, but did conclude that the declaration of a trust of 222,000 shares out of 1.5 million was valid.

White v Shortall [2006] NSWC 1379, [210] (Campbell J)[72]

The declaration of trust left him free to deal with the parcel of 1.5 million shares as he pleased, provided that it was not reduced below 222,000, provided that any encumbrances on the shareholding were such that at least 220,000 were left unencumbered, and provided that the plaintiff was entitled to call for the transfer of 222,000 shares at any time...If there were to be any declaration of dividend or return of capital prior to the time that the plaintiff had the 222,000 shares transferred to her, the

---

[67] See Chapter 2.6(g), pp. 50–1.

[68] See Chapter 4.3, p. 146.

[69] See Chapter 10.3, pp. 519–23.

[70] The Court of Appeal certainly considered the case to turn upon whether a trust over 50 shares was valid. Yet the actual declaration of trust was for 5 per cent of the shareholding, and it is suggested that this could have been interpreted as a trust for one-nineteenth of the whole.

[71] [2006] NSWSC 1379. Not disturbed on appeal: [2007] NSWCA 372.

[72] See Chapter 18, 'Proprietary Claims and Remedies', for an analogous analysis of equitable proprietary interests in a mixed fund.

plaintiff would be entitled to receive an appropriate proportionate part of the dividend or return of capital…A trust of this kind is not analogous to a simple trust, where a single and discrete item is held on a bare trust for a single beneficiary. Rather, it is a trust of the fund (the entire shareholding of 1.5 million shares) for two different beneficiaries…It is because the trust is construed as being of the entire shareholding that it is not necessary for the plaintiff to be able to point to some particular share and be able to say 'That share is mine.'…In the present case, one can identify the property that is subject to the trust (the entire shareholding) one can identify the trustee (the defendant), and one can identify the beneficiaries (the plaintiff as to 220,000 shares, the defendant as to the rest). That is all that is needed for a valid trust.

If the trust can be construed in this manner, such that the entire fund is being held on trust, then this is the preferable approach, which can resolve many of the difficulties surrounding *Hunter v Moss*. This was confirmed by Briggs J in *Pearson v Lehman Brothers Finance SA*,[73] who said that:

The analysis which I have found the most persuasive is that such a trust works by creating a beneficial co-ownership share in the identified fund, rather than in the conceptually much more difficult notion of seeking to identify a particular part of that fund which the beneficiary owns outright. A principal academic advocate for the co-ownership approach is Professor Roy Goode: see for example 'Are Intangible Assets Fungible?' [2003] LMCLQ 379.[74] Among the judicial commentators I have found the analysis of Campbell J in *White v Shortall* at paragraph 212 to be the most persuasive.

Be that as it may, the *approach* adopted by the Court of Appeal in *Hunter v Moss* was different, even if the *result* is consistent with such an analysis. Moreover, although Dillon LJ in *Hunter* thought *London Wine* was 'a long way' from the facts of *Hunter*, it is not immediately obvious why this should be true. His Lordship hinted that the difference may lie in the fact that *London Wine* concerned tangible property, whereas *Hunter* concerned intangible property. This distinction was approved by Neuberger J in *Re Harvard Securities Ltd*.[75]

Re Harvard Securities Ltd [1998] BCC 567

A company purchased shares on behalf of clients and retained legal title in the shares as nominee for each client. The company later went into liquidation. The question for the court was whether the clients of the company had a beneficial interest in the shares even though the shares had not been allocated to them.

Neuberger J:

I refer again to the way in which Dillon LJ distinguished *London Wine*: he said it was 'concerned with the appropriation of chattels and when the property in chattels passes', whereas in *Hunter* the Court of Appeal was concerned with shares and a declaration of trust. In my judgment, therefore, the ground upon which the Court of Appeal in *Hunter* distinguished *London Wine* is substantially the same ground upon which *Goldcorp* can be distinguished from *Hunter*.

---

[73] [2010] EWHC 2914 (Ch), [244]; upheld on appeal: [2011] EWCA Civ 1544; [2012] 2 BCLC 151, [69]–[77].
[74] See Chapter 3.3, p. 83.
[75] See also *Re CA Pacific Finance Ltd* [2000] 1 BCLC 494 (Court of First Instance, Hong Kong Special Administrative Region).

[Counsel's] alternative argument was that *Hunter* could be properly distinguished from *Wait*,[76] *London Wine* and *Goldcorp* on a ground on which the present case could be properly distinguished from *Hunter*, namely that *Hunter* was concerned with an express declaration of trust, whereas the other cases (including the present one) are not. While it is true that this is a point mentioned by Dillon LJ when distinguishing *London Wine* (see at p. 458H) I have come to the conclusion that it is not a proper ground for distinguishing Hunter from *Wait, London Wine* and, indeed, *Goldcorp* and the present case. First, it is clear from the reasoning in *Wait* and *London Wine* that this is not a valid ground for distinction. The point is well illustrated by Oliver J's inability to see how:

> 'a farmer who declares himself to be trustee of two sheep (without identifying them) can be said to have created a perfect and complete trust of whatever rights he may confer by such declaration as a matter of contract'

...

While I am not particularly convinced by the distinction, it appears to me that a more satisfactory way of distinguishing *Hunter* from the other cases is that it was concerned with shares, and not with chattels. First, that is a ground which is consistent with Dillon LJ's reliance on *Re Rose*[77] (a case concerned with shares) and his ground for distinguishing *London Wine* (and, by implication, *Wait*) which, it will be remembered, he described as being 'concerned with the appropriation of *chattels* and when *property in chattels* passes'. Secondly, it is on this basis that the editors of Underhill and Hayton believe that *Hunter* is explained (although they regard it on an unsatisfactory basis). Thirdly, the observations of Atkin LJ in *Wait* at p. 630 referring to the 'ordinary operations of buying and selling goods' could be said to provide a policy ground for there being one rule for chattels and another for shares.

Fourthly, as the editors of Meagher Gummow & Lehane on *Equity Doctrines & Remedies* (3rd edn, 1993, Butterworth Law NZ)) point out, the need for appropriation before any equitable interest can exist in relation to chattels can be contrasted with the absence of any such need before there can be an effective equitable assignment of an unascertained part of a whole debt or fund (see at para. 679–682). This distinction is described by the editors as 'very difficult to see'; nonetheless, they accept that, despite the criticism to which cases such as *Wait* have been subjected, it is unlikely that they will be overruled.

...

The description of the sub-contracted grain in *Wait*, the client's wine in *London Wine*, and the customer's bullion in *Goldcorp* as 'an unascertained part of a mass of goods' is quite apt. It would not, however, be a sensible description of the 50 shares in *Hunter* or, indeed, the shares in the present case. Mr Halpern pointed out that it is not really possible to identify, whether physically or by words, a proportion of a debt, whereas it is possible to identify chattels (by labelling or segregation) or shares (by reference to their number); he also pointed out that part of a debt or fund is fungible with the balance. For those two reasons, he submitted that the inconsistency suggested in Meagher Gummow & Lehane is not valid. There is obvious force in that point, but, in the end, it seems to me that, given that the distinction exists between an assignment of part of a holding of chattels and an assignment of part of a debt or fund, the effect of the decision in *Hunter* is that, in this context, shares fall to be treated in this context in the same way as a debt or fund rather than chattels.

In all the circumstances, therefore, it seems to me that the correct way for me, at first instance, to explain the difference between the result in *Hunter*, and that in *Wait, London Wine* and *Goldcorp*, is on the ground that *Hunter* was concerned with shares, as opposed to chattels.

---

[76] *Re Wait* [1927] 1 Ch 606.
[77] [1952] Ch 499; see Chapter 4.3(c)(i), pp. 153–6.

Even Neuberger J himself was not convinced that this distinction between intangibles and tangibles is satisfactory, but he thought that was how he must decide the case, given that he was sitting only at first instance. Hayton has described this distinction as 'a possible, old-fashioned, but surely specious, distinction'.[78] But Martin has defended the contrary point of view.

Martin, 'Certainty of Subject-matter: A Defence of *Hunter v Moss*' [1996] Conv 223, 224

Although no doubt some chattels can be regarded as identical to other chattels of the same description, the rationale of the rule that there cannot be a trust of chattels which have not been segregated from a mass of similar chattels is that they are not necessarily identical. Even bottles of wine of the same label may not be identical; some may be 'corked' and undrinkable.... The chattels rule does not apply to money, shares and other choses in action because, in the nature of things, there is no difference between one pound and another pound, or one share and another share of the same class in the same company.

The tangible/intangible distinction is a clear statement of the current orthodoxy. But it has been suggested that a better distinction would be between fungibles and non-fungibles. There is a difference: fungibles are not necessarily tangibles.

Goode, 'Are Intangible Assets Fungible?' [2003] LMCLQ 379, 383[79]

Fungibility presupposes that performance is to be rendered or procured by selection and segregation from an indeterminate source or from a larger, identified collection or bulk, each unit within the collection and each part of the bulk being legally the equivalent of any other unit or part. In short, the obligation is to deliver or transfer not an identified asset but anything which corresponds to the contract description....

But fungibility in its proper legal sense is not confined to tangibles; it is equally applicable to intangible property, such as debts and shares. The fundamental requirement of interchangeability means that the property subject of the enquiry must be susceptible of being divisible into separate units capable in law of being separately owned.

Goode suggests that wine, grain, flour, and money, although tangible, are fungibles, because they are interchangeable. Yet a trust declared over 10 kilos out of 50 kilos of flour, if unsegregated and unascertainable, seems likely to fail because the property is not intangible. In *Re London Wine*, Oliver J explicitly said:[80]

I appreciate the point taken that the subject-matter is part of a homogeneous mass so that specific identity is of little importance as it is, for instance, in the case of money. Nevertheless, as it seems to me, to create a trust it must be possible to ascertain with certainty not only what the interest of the beneficiary is to be but to what property it is to attach.

This may help to explain why Neuberger J in *Re Harvard* confined the distinction to tangible/intangible. But it is not clear why the logic of the later decision in *Hunter v Moss*, which led to the trust over

---

[78] (1994) 110 LQR 335, 337.
[79] See also Worthington, 'Sorting Out Ownership Interests in Bulk: Gifts, Sales and Trusts' [1999] JBL 1.
[80] [1986] PCC 121, 137.

shares being valid, should not extend to tangible fungibles. Indeed, although not crucial to deciding the case, Briggs J recently said in *Pearson v Lehman Brothers Finance SA*:[81]

> A trust of part of a fungible mass without the appropriation of any specific part of it for the beneficiary does not fail for uncertainty of subject matter, provided that the mass itself is sufficiently identified and provided also that the beneficiary's proportionate share of it is not itself uncertain.

It may therefore be that there is scope for the tangible/intangible reconciliation of *Re London Wine* and *Hunter v Moss* to be tweaked so that the dividing line is drawn between fungibles and non-fungibles. This would be a welcome development.

However, distinguishing between tangible and intangible property may not be the only way to reconcile the case law in this area. It has also been suggested that *Hunter v Moss* and *Re London Wine Company* are consistent since only in the former case was the larger bulk identified—the 950 shares which the defendant owned—whereas in the latter case the stock of wine owned by LWC fluctuated.

Parkinson, 'Reconceptualising the Express Trust' (2002) CLJ 657, 671–2, and 675–6

> However, a further ground for distinction is that in these cases also, there was a fluctuating mass, and so one could not identify the assets owned in equity by each customer by reference to proportions. In *London Wine*, for example, the mass of which the purchased bottles usually represented a portion was subject to fluctuation and change. It so happened that in some cases a customer or customers between them had purchased the entire company stock; but there was no reason why the company should not at some later stage purchase more wine of that vintage and also no reason why it should not satisfy the customers' contracts out of newly purchased stock. It was thus not possible to say either that certain bottles or cases were held on trust or that a particular customer owned a definite percentage of the company's entire stock. This might not matter perhaps if the bottles stored increased in number but it could matter very much if the numbers decreased. This is illustrated by *Re Goldcorp*. In this case, the levels of bullion held by the company varied from time to time. Thus not only was it impossible to say what bullion each customer owned but it was also impossible to know what fraction of the total bullion each customer owned especially since the amount purchased exceeded the gold bullion which was stored.
>
> …
>
> It follows from analysis of the requirements of certainty in relation to trust property that at the heart of the doctrine, it is the *obligation* which must be described with sufficient certainty, not the trust property. It is enough that the subject-matter of the trust can be ascertained, that is the pool of property from which the trust fund must come, and that the trust obligation with respect to that property is defined with sufficient clarity. This is the thread which runs through all the cases concerning uncertainty of subject-matter which have been discussed. If, as in *Hunter v. Moss*, a trustee declares that 50 shares out of a parcel of 950 shares are held on trust, that is a sufficient definition of his obligation with respect to the parcel of 950 shares. If the trustee indicates that all the money in a particular bank account, less £50, is held on trust, that is a sufficient definition of the obligation. And if there is an obligation to collect sales taxes as a trustee or to account as a trustee for the proceeds of sale of airline tickets, then it is sufficiently certain if the obligation is defined clearly enough to provide a proper basis for computation of how much money which has been collected from customers is impressed with a trust.

---

[81] [2010] EWHC 2914 (Ch) [225]. This was cited with apparent approval on appeal: [2011] EWCA Civ 1544; [2012] 2 BCLC 151, [70].

Focussing on the obligations owed may be helpful in these circumstances. In particular, if it is clear that the defendant should have been holding 50 shares on trust, and then he sells some of his shares, the ordinary presumptions of tracing might apply such that the innocent claimant beneficiary of the shares can choose to say whether the trustee sold his own shares or those of the claimant.[82]

(d) 'WHATEVER IS LEFT' TRUSTS

In *Pearson v Lehman Brothers Finance SA*, Briggs J stated:[83]

> A trust does not fail for want of certainty merely because its subject matter is at present uncertain, if the terms of the trust are sufficient to identify its subject matter in the future.

So, if a testator provides that the 'residue' of his property should be held on trust, then that 'residue' will not fail for want of certainty of subject matter: the residue of the testator's estate becomes clear upon his death.

Re Last [1958] P 137

A woman left property to her brother in her will, further providing that: 'At his death anything that is left, that came from me to go to my late husband's grandchildren.' The brother then died intestate, and the question arose as to whether he was holding the remaining property on trust for the grandchildren. It was held that there was sufficient certainty of subject-matter for a trust.

Karminski J:

In a matter of construction of this kind it is clearly essential to pay particular attention to the terms of the instrument which is being construed and to avoid too close comparisons with words used in wills in other cases. In this case, looking at the will as a whole, I have come to the conclusion that the words used are sufficiently clear to cut down [the brother's] interest from an absolute to a life interest. Clearly there is an ambiguity, but I have attempted to read the will as a whole, and then to reach that construction which most effectively, in my view, expresses the intentions of the testatrix. I remind myself of the words of Joyce J. in *In Re Sanford*:[84] 'Weight may be given to the consideration that it is better to effectuate than to frustrate the testator's intentions.'

In *Re Last*, the court felt able to construe the trust instrument as giving the brother a life interest in the property along with a power to dispose of the property during his lifetime. But, on similar facts, the court had previously held that the initial recipient took the property absolutely, because the subject matter of what was held on trust for the subsequent recipients was uncertain.[85] It is suggested that the construction favoured in *Re Last* is preferable.

An alternative possibility is to recognize a 'floating trust': if property is given to A on the understanding that A will leave to B whatever of the property is left at his or her death, a valid trust might be created in favour of B that is 'floating' or 'in suspense' during the lifetime of A, but attaches to the

---

[82] See Chapter 18.3(c)(ii)(c), pp. 870–3. See also Martin [1996] Conv 223.
[83] [2010] EWHC 2914 (Ch) [225]; upheld on appeal: [2011] EWCA Civ 1544; [2012] 2 BCLC 151.
[84] [1901] 1 Ch 939.
[85] *Sprange v Barnard* [1789] 2 Bro CC 585.

estate of A upon A's death. In *Ottaway v Norman*,[86] Brightman J was happy to assume that such a trust was valid, without recourse to the *Re Last* construction of the initial recipient enjoying a life interest coupled with a power to benefit from the property himself. Admittedly, *Ottaway* concerned a secret trust,[87] but it is conceivable that a similar approach may be adopted beyond the context of secret trusts.

Ottaway v Norman [1972] Ch 698

A testator left his bungalow to his housekeeper, as well as £1,500 and half the residue of his estate, on the understanding that the housekeeper would leave the bungalow and whatever money was left to the testator's son in her own will. The housekeeper failed to do this, but the court held that there was a secret trust in favour of the son.

Brightman J:

If property is given to the primary donee on the understanding that the primary donee will dispose by his will of such assets, if any, as he may have at his command at his death in favour of the secondary donee, a valid trust is created in favour of the secondary donee which is in suspense during the lifetime of the primary donee, but attaches to the estate of the primary donee at the moment of the latter's death. There would seem to be at least some support for this proposition in an Australian case to which I was referred: *Birmingham v. Renfrew* (1937) 57 C.L.R. 666.

4. CERTAINTY OF OBJECTS

It is crucial that the objects of a trust be defined with sufficient certainty so that trustees, or in default the court, know to whom the trust property can and cannot be appointed. In *Re Gulbenkian's Settlements*, Lord Upjohn said:[88]

The principle is, in my opinion, that the donor must make his intentions sufficiently plain as to the objects of his trust and the court cannot give effect to it by misinterpreting his intentions by dividing the fund merely among those present. Secondly, and perhaps it is the more hallowed principle, the Court of Chancery, which acts in default of trustees, must know with sufficient certainty the objects of the beneficence of the donor so as to execute the trust.

This certainty requirement has been broken down into further elements by Carl Emery.

Emery, 'The Most Hallowed Principle—Certainty of Beneficiaries of Trusts and Powers of Appointment' (1982) 98 LQR 551, 552

(a) 'Conceptual certainty': this refers to the precision of language used by the settlor to define the classes of person whom he intends to benefit.

---

[86] [1972] Ch 698.
[87] For discussion of secret trusts, see Chapter 4.3(c)(iii), pp. 127–45.
[88] [1970] AC 508, 524.

(b) 'Evidential certainty': this refers to the extent to which the evidence available in a particular case enables specific persons to be identified as members of those classes—and so as beneficiaries or potential beneficiaries.

(c) 'Ascertainability': this refers to the extent to which 'the whereabouts or continued existence'[89] of persons identified as beneficiaries or potential beneficiaries can be ascertained.

(d) 'Administrative workability': this refers to the extent to which it is practicable for trustees to discharge the duties laid upon them by the settlor towards beneficiaries or potential beneficiaries.

It is useful to analyse certainty of objects not as a monolithic whole, but rather as discrete elements. Conceptual certainty is generally a question of law, and, as such, needs to be able to be resolved by the courts.[90] Evidential certainty, on the other hand, is a question of evidence which, in accordance with general principles of civil law, needs to be proved on a balance of probabilities. These first two types of certainty merit the most attention; the other two forms of certainty identified by Emery are of lesser importance. As will be seen, problems surrounding ascertainability do not seem to render any trust void, and, although administrative unworkability has rendered a purported discretionary trust void, this result has been much criticized.[91]

Before examining the different types of trusts and powers, it should be noted that the terminology in this area often leads to confusion. The dividing line between trusts and powers is not always made clear; the very use of phrases such as 'trust powers' and 'powers in the nature of a trust'[92] shows this. Such phrases refer to trusts in which the trustees have a power of selection; they essentially mean the same thing as 'discretionary trust'.[93] Trustees are required to exercise a trust power. This should be contrasted with a mere power, which need not be exercised.[94]

(a)   FIXED TRUSTS

Under a fixed trust, the trustees have no discretion regarding how the trust property should be distributed: exactly how much each beneficiary should receive has already been determined by the settlor. This means that the trustees, and in default the court, must know to whom the property should be appointed. Both conceptual certainty and evidential certainty need to be established.

Re Gulbenkian's Settlements [1970] AC 508, 524[95]

Lord Upjohn:

Suppose the donor directs that a fund be divided equally between 'my old friends,' then unless there is some admissible evidence that the donor has given some special 'dictionary' meaning to that phrase which enables the trustees to identify the class with sufficient certainty, it is plainly bad as being too uncertain. Suppose that there appeared before the trustees (or the court) two or three individuals who

---

[89] These words are those of Lord Upjohn in *Re Gulbenkian* [1970] AC 508, 524.
[90] *Re Wynn* [1952] Ch 271. See Chapter 3.4(b)(i), pp. 99–102.
[91] *R v District Auditor, ex p West Yorkshire Metropolitan County Council* [1986] RVR 24; see Chapter 3.4(b)(ii), pp. 102–5.
[92] See *Breadner v Granville-Grossman* [2001] Ch 523 at 540 (Park J).
[93] See [1984] Conv 227 (Bartlett and Stebbings).
[94] See Chapter 2.6(h), pp. 51–5.
[95] Admittedly this case concerned a power rather than a trust. See Chapter 2.6(h), pp. 51–5.

> plainly satisfied the test of being among 'my old friends,' the trustees could not consistently with the donor's intentions accept them as claiming the whole or any defined part of the fund. They cannot claim the whole fund for they can show no title to it unless they prove they are the only members of the class, which of course they cannot do, and so, too, by parity of reasoning they cannot claim any defined part of the fund and there is no authority in the trustees or the court to make any distribution among a smaller class than that pointed out by the donor.

Although it might be argued that there is a 'core of certain meaning'[96] to 'old friends', the court cannot allow such a trust to stand, as both 'old' and 'friends' are insufficiently certain and may have a range of meanings.

In essence, trustees have to be able to draw up a 'complete list' of the beneficiaries when dealing with a fixed trust.[97] Otherwise, the trustees would not be able to give effect to the settlor's intentions; 'equal shares', for example, can only be calculated once all the beneficiaries are known. As a result, both 'conceptual certainty' and 'evidential certainty' are required. However, 'ascertainability' does not appear to be necessary: there is no reason why all the beneficiaries need to be ascertained; if one of the beneficiaries cannot be found, then his share could simply be paid into the court. As Lord Upjohn remarked in *Re Gulbenkian*:[98]

> if the class is sufficiently defined by the donor the fact that it may be difficult to ascertain the whereabouts or continued existence of some of its members at the relevant time matters not. The trustees can apply to the court for directions or pay a share into court.

Nor should a fixed trust be afflicted by administrative unworkability: if a complete list can be drawn up, then it should always be practicable for the trustees to give effect to the settlor's intention.

(i) *An exception—fixed trusts subject to a condition precedent*

It is possible for a settlor to give a gift provided that the recipient first fulfils a given condition. This may be construed as a fixed trust of a series of individual gifts subject to a condition precedent: the trustee is obliged to distribute the property to any individual who satisfies the condition. The onus lies on each potential object of the trust to show that he satisfies the relevant condition. As a result, the trust will not fail for evidential certainty: the presumption is that the object does not satisfy the condition unless he produces evidence that proves the contrary. Nor will such a trust fail for unascertainability: it is not for the trustees to seek out objects, but for the potential objects to establish that they satisfy the condition. For similar reasons, it is difficult to imagine such a trust being administratively unworkable.

More difficult is the relevant test of conceptual certainty. It appears to be more lax[99] than the 'complete list' test generally required for fixed trusts. A more relaxed approach is justifiable since it is sufficient if only one person satisfies the condition, so there is no need to know *all* the possible beneficiaries. Nor is there any need for the trustees to undertake a wide survey of potential objects:[100] each

---

[96] Emery, 'The Most Hallowed Principle—Certainty of Beneficiaries of Trusts and Powers of Appointment' (1982) 98 LQR 551, 564.

[97] See *IRC v Broadway Cottages Trust* [1955] Ch 20, albeit concerning a discretionary trust. There is an exception if the fixed trust can be interpreted as a series of individual gifts subject to a condition precedent: see Chapter 3.4(c)(i), pp. 108–9.

[98] [1970] AC 508, 524.

[99] Although a stricter test seems to apply for conditions subsequent: *Re Tuck's Settlement Trust* [1978] Ch 49, 60; *Re Tepper's Will Trusts* [1987] Ch 49.

[100] As is the case for both discretionary trusts (Chapter 3.4(b), pp. 91–4) and fiduciary powers Chapter 3.4(c), pp. 105–7.

potential beneficiary needs to take the initiative and show that he or she satisfies the relevant condition. Thus, even though a concept such as 'old friends' may be insufficiently certain for fixed trusts *not* subject to a condition precedent, it is unproblematic here: there may be individuals who on any conceivable test definitely satisfy the condition.

This approach has been clearly expounded by Browne-Wilkinson J in *Re Barlow's Will Trusts*.

Re Barlow's Will Trusts [1979] 1 WLR 278

A testatrix died in 1975, owning a large collection of valuable pictures. By her will she gave some of them to her executor upon trust for sale, and added a direction to him 'to allow any member of my family and any friends of mine who may wish to do so to purchase any of such pictures' at a valuation made in 1970, or at probate value, whichever should be the lower. The court held that this was valid.

Browne-Wilkinson J:

The main questions which arise for my decision are (a) whether the direction to allow members of the family and friends to purchase the pictures is void for uncertainty since the meaning of the word 'friends' is too vague to be given legal effect; and (b) what persons are to be treated as being members of the testatrix's family. I will deal first with the question of uncertainty.

Those arguing against the validity of the gift in favour of the friends contend that, in the absence of any guidance from the testatrix, the question 'Who were her friends?' is incapable of being answered. The word is said to be 'conceptually uncertain' since there are so many different degrees of friendship and it is impossible to say which degree the testatrix had in mind. In support of this argument they rely on Lord Upjohn's remarks in *Re Gulbenkian's Settlements* [1970] AC 508,[101] and the decision of the House of Lords in *Re Baden's Deed Trusts* [1971] AC 424,[102] to the effect that it must be possible to say who is within and who without the class of friends. They say that since the testatrix intended all her friends to have the opportunity to acquire a picture, it is necessary to be able to ascertain with certainty all the members of that class.

Mr. Shillingford, who argued in favour of the validity of the gift, contended that the test laid down in the *Gulbenkian* and *Baden* cases was not applicable to this case; the test, he says, is that laid down by the Court of Appeal in *Re Allen* [1953] Ch 810, as appropriate in cases where the validity of a condition precedent or description is in issue, namely, that the gift is valid if it is possible to say of one or more persons that he or they undoubtedly qualify even though it may be difficult to say of others whether or not they qualify.

The distinction between the *Gulbenkian* test and the *Re Allen* test is, in my judgment, well exemplified by the word 'friends'. The word has a great range of meanings; indeed, its exact meaning probably varies slightly from person to person. Some would include only those with whom they had been on intimate terms over a long period; others would include acquaintances whom they liked. Some would include people with whom their relationship was primarily one of business; others would not. Indeed, many people, if asked to draw up a complete list of their friends, would probably have some difficulty in deciding whether certain of the people they knew were really 'friends' as opposed to 'acquaintances'. Therefore, if the nature of the gift was such that it was legally necessary to draw up a complete list of 'friends' of the testatrix, or to be able to say of any person that 'he is not a friend', the whole gift would probably fail even as to those who, by any conceivable test, were friends.

---

[101] Chapter 3.4(c), pp. 105–6.
[102] Chapter 3.4(b), pp. 91–4.

But in the case of a gift of a kind which does not require one to establish all the members of the class (e.g. 'a gift of £10 to each of my friends'), it may be possible to say of some people that on any test, they qualify. Thus in *Re Allen* at 817, Sir Raymond Evershed MR took the example of a gift to X 'if he is a tall man'; a man 6 ft. 6 ins. tall could be said on any reasonable basis to satisfy the test, although it might be impossible to say whether a man, say, 5ft. 10ins. high satisfied the requirement.

So in this case, in my judgment, there are acquaintances of a kind so close that, on any reasonable basis, anyone would treat them as being 'friends'. Therefore, by allowing the disposition to take effect in their favour, one would certainly be giving effect to part of the testatrix's intention even though as to others it is impossible to say whether or not they satisfy the test.

In my judgment, it is clear that Lord Upjohn in *Re Gulbenkian's Settlements* [1970] AC 508 was considering only cases where it was necessary to establish all the members of the class. He makes it clear, at 524, that the reason for the rule is that in a gift which requires one to establish all the members of the class (e.g. 'a gift to my friends in equal shares') you cannot hold the gift good in part, since the quantum of each friend's share depends on how many friends there are. So all persons intended to benefit by the donor must be ascertained if any effect is to be given to the gift. In my judgment, the adoption of Lord Upjohn's test by the House of Lords in the *Baden* case is based on the same reasoning, even though in that case the House of Lords held that it was only necessary to be able to survey the class of objects of a power of appointment and not to establish who all the members are.

But such reasoning has no application to a case where there is a condition or description attached to one or more individual gifts; in such cases, uncertainty as to some other persons who may have been intended to take does not in any way affect the quantum of the gift to persons who undoubtedly possess the qualification. Hence, in my judgment, the different test laid down in *Re Allen* [1953] Ch 810.

The recent decision of the Court of Appeal in *Re Tuck's Settlement Trusts* [1978] Ch 49,[103] establishes that the test in *Re Allen* is still the appropriate test in considering such gifts, notwithstanding the *Gulbenkian* and *Baden* decisions: see per Lord Russell of Killowen at 65.

Accordingly, in my judgment, the proper result in this case depends on whether the disposition in clause 5 (a) is properly to be regarded as a series of individual gifts to persons answering the description 'friend' (in which case it will be valid), or a gift which requires the whole class of friends to be established (in which case it will probably fail).

The effect of clause 5 (a) is to confer on friends of the testatrix a series of options to purchase. Although it is obviously desirable as a practical matter that steps should be taken to inform those entitled to the options of their rights, it is common ground that there is no legal necessity to do so. Therefore, each person coming forward to exercise the option has to prove that he is a friend; it is not legally necessary, in my judgment, to discover who all the friends are. In order to decide whether an individual is entitled to purchase, all that is required is that the executors should be able to say of that individual whether he has proved that he is a friend. The word 'friend', therefore, is a description or qualification of the option holder.

It was suggested that by allowing undoubted friends to take I would be altering the testatrix's intentions. It is said that she intended all her friends to have a chance to buy any given picture, and since some people she might have regarded as friends will not be able to apply, the number of competitors for that picture will be reduced. This may be so; but I cannot regard this factor as making it legally necessary to establish the whole class of friends. The testatrix's intention was that a friend should acquire a picture. My decision gives effect to that intention.

I therefore hold that the disposition does not fail for uncertainty, but that anyone who can prove that by any reasonable test he or she must have been a friend of the testatrix is entitled to exercise the option.

---

[103] Chapter 3.4(b)(i), pp. 101–2.

Without seeking to lay down any exhaustive definition of such test, it may be helpful if I indicate certain minimum requirements: (a) the relationship must have been a longstanding one. (b) The relationship must have been a social relationship as opposed to a business or professional relationship. (c) Although there may have been long periods when circumstances prevented the testatrix and the applicant from meeting, when circumstances did permit they must have met frequently. If in any case the executors entertain any real doubt whether an applicant qualifies, they can apply to the court to decide the issue.

(b) DISCRETIONARY TRUSTS

Under a discretionary trust, also known as a trust power, the trustees enjoy a discretion as to which objects should receive the trust property, and how much each object should receive. The potential objects need to be defined with sufficient certainty to enable the trustees, or in default the court, to exercise their discretion appropriately. Since a trust obligation is concerned, the appointment of the trust property is mandatory: a trust power must be exercised.[104]

In *IRC v Broadway Cottages Trust*[105] it was held that a trust was void for uncertainty unless it was possible to make, at the time when the trust came into operation, a list of all the beneficiaries; this is known as the 'complete list test'. This rule was thought to be necessary in order to make a distribution possible if the trustees, in breach of their duty, failed to make a selection. The method of distribution, it was said, would be by equal division amongst the members of the class of beneficiaries on the principle that 'equality is equity'; and equal division was only possible if it was known how many shares there would be.[106] However, the problem was artificial, in that it had never arisen in the form of trustees refusing to select beneficiaries. Rather, the issue had only arisen when the trustees had asked the court whether a selection would be valid. Reluctant trustees could in any case be replaced. Further, in modern trusts with the employees of a business as objects, and not merely members of the family as was usually the case with older trusts, equal division would be absurd. The problem of determining the division if the trustees failed to select was not insuperable: the court could find a way.

These criticisms were recognized by the House of Lords in *McPhail v Doulton* (also known as *Re Baden's Deed Trusts (No. 1)*), which departed from the test in *Broadway Cottages* and instead adopted, as the test for certainty of beneficiaries under a *discretionary* trust, the test which had been applied to mere powers in *Re Gulbenkian's Settlements*.[107] This has become known as the 'given postulant' test,[108] or the 'is or is not' test: it needs to be possible to determine with certainty whether any given postulant is or is not a member of the class.

McPhail v Doulton [1971] AC 424

A deed, executed on July 17, 1941, by the settlor, Mr Bertram Baden, provided that a fund was to be held upon certain trusts in favour of the staff of Matthew Hall and Co Ltd and their relatives and dependants.

---

[104] Chapter 2.6(h)(i), pp. 51–4.
[105] [1955] Ch 20.
[106] *Burrough v Philcox* (1840) 5 My & Cr 72.
[107] Chapter 3.4(c), pp. 105–6.
[108] Following the formulation of the rule by Harman J in *Re Gestetner Settlement* [1953] Ch 672, 688: 'whether any given postulant is a member of the specified class'.

The deed provided (clause 9 (a)) that the trustees should apply the net income in making grants at their absolute discretion 'to or for the benefit of any of the officers and employees or ex-officers or ex-employees of the company or to any relatives or dependants of any such persons in such amounts at such times and on such conditions (if any) as they think fit...'

Two main questions arose: whether the deed created a power or a trust; and whether it was void for uncertainty. At first instance,[109] Goff J held that it was a power and not a trust and that it was valid, applying as the test of certainty that was used by the Court of Appeal in *Re Gulbenkian's Settlements*:[110] a power was valid if it was sufficiently certain to enable any one claimant to show that he or she comes within the description.

The Court of Appeal[111] agreed that it was a power and not a trust; but remitted the case to the Chancery Division to determine the validity upon the application of the test for certainty of powers which had been laid down by the House of Lords in *Re Gulbenkian's Settlements*.[112] The decision of the Court of Appeal was appealed to the House of Lords.

The House of Lords held that: (i) the deed created a trust and not a power; (ii) the test for certainty for discretionary trusts was the same as that for powers i.e. whether it could be said with certainty that any given individual was or was not a member of the class.[113]

The case was remitted to the Chancery Division for the determination of validity upon this basis. Brightman J upheld its validity and this was affirmed by the Court of Appeal in *Re Baden's Deed Trusts (No. 2)*.[114]

Lord Wilberforce:

In this House, the appellants contend, and this is the first question for consideration, that the provisions of clause 9 (a) constitute a trust and not a power. If that is held to be the correct result, both sides agree that the case must return to the Chancery Division for consideration, on this footing, whether this trust is valid. But here comes a complication. In the present state of authority, the decision as to validity would turn on the question whether a complete list (or on another view a list complete for practical purposes) can be drawn up of all possible beneficiaries. This follows from the Court of Appeal's decision in *IRC v Broadway Cottages* [1955] Ch 20, as applied in later cases by which, unless this House decides otherwise, the Court of Chancery would be bound. The respondents invite your Lordships to review this decision and challenge its correctness. So the second issue which arises, if clause 9(a) amounts to a trust, is whether the existing test for its validity is right in law and, if not, what the test ought to be.

[Having concluded that clause 9(a) constituted a trust his Lordship continued:]

This makes it necessary to consider whether, [in remitting the case to the Chancery Division to determine whether clause 9(1) was void for uncertainty], the court should proceed on the basis that the relevant test is that laid down in *IRC v Broadway Cottages Trust* [1955] Ch 20 or some other test.

That decision gave the authority of the Court of Appeal to the distinction between cases where trustees are given a *power* of selection and those where they are bound by a *trust* for selection. In the former case the position, as decided by this House, is that the power is valid if it can be said with certainty

[109] [1967] 1 WLR 1457.
[110] [1968] Ch 126, following *Re Allen* [1953] Ch 810; *Re Leek* [1967] Ch 1061; affd [1969] 1 Ch 563; *Re Gibbard's Will Trusts* [1967] 1 WLR 42.
[111] [1969] 2 Ch 388 (Harman and Karminski LJJ, Russell LJ dissenting).
[112] [1970] AC 508.
[113] On this issue, Lord Reid, Viscount Dilhorne, and Lord Wilberforce formed the majority; Lord Hodson and Lord Guest dissented.
[114] [1973] Ch 9, Chapter 3.4(b), pp. 94–9.

whether any given individual is or is not a member of the class and does not fail simply because it is impossible to ascertain every member of the class: *Re Gulbenkian's Settlements* [1970] AC 508. But in the latter case it is said to be necessary, for the trust to be valid, that the whole range of objects (I use the language of the Court of Appeal) should be ascertained or capable of ascertainment.

The respondents invited your Lordships to assimilate the validity test for trusts to that which applies to powers. Alternatively they contended that in any event the test laid down in the *Broadway Cottages* case was too rigid, and that a trust should be upheld if there is sufficient practical certainty in its definition for it to be carried out, if necessary with the administrative assistance of the court, according to the expressed intention of the settlor. I would agree with this, but this does not dispense from examination of the wider argument. The basis for the *Broadway Cottages* principle is stated to be that a trust cannot be valid unless, if need be, it can be executed by the court, and (though it is not quite clear from the judgment where argument ends and decision begins) that the court can only execute it by ordering an equal distribution in which every beneficiary shares. So it is necessary to examine the authority and reason for this supposed rule as to the execution of trusts by the court.

Assuming, as I am prepared to do for present purposes, that the test of validity is whether the trust can be executed by the court, it does not follow that execution is impossible unless there can be equal division.

As a matter of reason, to hold that a principle of equal division applies to trusts such as the present is certainly paradoxical. Equal division is surely the last thing the settlor ever intended: equal division among all may, probably would, produce a result beneficial to none. Why suppose that the court would lend itself to a whimsical execution? And as regards authority, I do not find that the nature of the trust, and of the court's powers over trusts, calls for any such rigid rule. Equal division may be sensible and has been decreed, in cases of family trusts, for a limited class; here there is life in the maxim 'equality is equity', but the cases provide numerous examples where this has not been so, and a different type of execution has been ordered, appropriate to the circumstances.

...

So I come to *IRC v Broadway Cottages Trust* [1955] Ch 20. This was certainly a case of trust, and it proceeded on the basis of an admission, in the words of the judgment, 'that the class of 'beneficiaries' is incapable of ascertainment'. In addition to the discretionary trust of income, there was a trust of capital for all the beneficiaries living or existing at the terminal date. This necessarily involved equal division and it seems to have been accepted that it was void for uncertainty since there cannot be equal division among a class unless all the members of the class are known. The Court of Appeal applied this proposition to the discretionary trust of income, on the basis that execution by the court was only possible on the same basis of equal division. They rejected the argument that the trust could be executed by changing the trusteeship, and found the relations cases of no assistance as being in a class by themselves. The court could not create an arbitrarily restricted trust to take effect in default of distribution by the trustees. Finally they rejected the submission that the trust could take effect as a power: a valid power could not be spelt out of an invalid trust.

My Lords, it will have become apparent that there is much in this which I find out of line with principle and authority but before I come to a conclusion on it, I must examine the decision of this House in *Re Gulbenkian's Settlements* on which the appellants placed much reliance as amounting to an endorsement of the *Broadway Cottages* case. But is this really so?

[His Lordship examined the case and continued:] What this does say, and I respectfully agree, is that, in the case of a trust, the trustees must select from the class. What it does not say, as I read it, or imply, is that in order to carry out their duty of selection they must have before them, or be able to get, a complete list of all possible objects.

So I think that we are free to review the *Broadway Cottages* case. The conclusion which I would reach, implicit in the previous discussion, is that the wide distinction between the validity test for powers and that for trust powers is unfortunate and wrong, that the rule recently fastened upon the courts by *IRC v Broadway Cottages Trust* ought to be discarded, and that the test for the validity of trust powers ought to be similar to that accepted by this House in *Re Gulbenkian's Settlements* for powers, namely, that the trust is valid if it can be said with certainty that any given individual is or is not a member of the class.

...

Assimilation of the validity test does not involve the complete assimilation of trust powers with powers. As to powers, I agree with my noble and learned friend Lord Upjohn in *Re Gulbenkian's Settlements* that although the trustees may, and normally will, be under a fiduciary duty to consider whether or in what way they should exercise their power, the court will not normally compel its exercise. It will intervene if the trustees exceed their powers, and possibly if they are proved to have exercised it capriciously. But in the case of a trust power, if the trustees do not exercise it, the court will: I respectfully adopt as to this the statement in Lord Upjohn's opinion at 525. I would venture to amplify this by saying that the court, if called upon to execute the trust power, will do so in the manner best calculated to give effect to the settlor's or testator's intentions. It may do so by appointing new trustees, or by authorising or directing representative persons of the classes of beneficiaries to prepare a scheme of distribution, or even, should the proper basis for distribution appear by itself directing the trustees so to distribute. The books give many instances where this has been done, and I see no reason in principle why they should not do so in the modern field of discretionary trusts (see *Brunsden v Woolredge* (1765) Amb 507; *Supple v Lowson* (1773) Amb 729; *Liley v Hey* (1842) 1 Hare 580 and *Lewin on Trusts* (16th edn, 1964) p. 630). Then, as to the trustees' duty of inquiry or ascertainment, in each case the trustees ought to make such a survey of the range of objects or possible beneficiaries as will enable them to carry out their fiduciary duty (cf. *Liley v Hey*). A wider and more comprehensive range of inquiry is called for in the case of trust powers than in the case of powers.

Two final points: first, as to the question of certainty. I desire to emphasize the distinction clearly made and explained by Lord Upjohn at 524, between linguistic or semantic uncertainty which, if unresolved by the court, renders the gift void, and the difficulty of ascertaining the existence or whereabouts of members of the class, a matter with which the court can appropriately deal on an application for directions. There may be a third case where the meaning of the words used is clear but the definition of beneficiaries is so hopelessly wide as not to form 'anything like a class' so that the trust is administratively unworkable or in Lord Eldon's words one that cannot be executed: *Morice v Bishop of Durham* (1805) 10 Ves 522 at 527. I hesitate to give examples for they may prejudice future cases, but perhaps 'all the residents of Greater London' will serve. I do not think that a discretionary trust for 'relatives' even of a living person falls within this category.

This last paragraph suggests that the given postulant test requires conceptual certainty, evidential certainty, and administrative workability. Once again, ascertainability need not be an issue: if a potential object cannot be found, that simply means that the trustees will not appoint the trust property in his favour.

Although *McPhail v Doulton* set out the appropriate test of certainty, it did not decide whether or not the discretionary trust at issue satisfied the given postulant test. This was the task of the Court of Appeal in *Re Baden's Deed Trusts (No. 2)*.

Re Baden's Deed Trusts (No. 2) [1973] Ch 9

On remittance to the Chancery Division, Brightman J and the Court of Appeal found that the test of certainty was satisfied. The wide differences in their application of the test demonstrates how difficult it may prove to be in practice.

Sachs LJ:

The next point as regards [the] approach that requires consideration is the contention, strongly pressed by Mr. Vinelott, that the court must always be able to say whether any given postulant is *not* within the relevant class as well as being able to say whether he is within it. In construing the words already cited from the speech of Lord Wilberforce in the *Baden* case (as well as those of Lord Reid and Lord Upjohn in the *Gulbenkian* case), it is essential to bear in mind the difference between conceptual uncertainty and evidential difficulties…

As Mr. Vinelott himself rightly observed, 'the court is never defeated by evidential uncertainty', and it is in my judgment clear that it is conceptual certainty to which reference was made when the 'is or is not a member of the class' test was enunciated. (Conceptual uncertainty was in the course of argument conveniently exemplified, rightly or wrongly matters not, by the phrase 'someone under a moral obligation' and contrasted with the certainty of the words 'first cousins'.) Once the class of person to be benefited is conceptually certain it then becomes a question of fact to be determined on evidence whether any postulant has on inquiry been proved to be within it: if he is not so proved, then he is not in it. That position remains the same whether the class to be benefited happens to be small (such as 'first cousins') or large (such as 'members of the X Trade Union' or 'those who have served in the Royal Navy'). The suggestion that such trusts could be invalid because it might be impossible to prove of a given individual that he was *not* in the relevant class is wholly falla-cious—and only Mr. Vinelott's persuasiveness has prevented me from saying that the contention is almost unarguable…

In agreement with the practical approach of Brightman J [1972] Ch 607 at 625, I consider that the trustees, or if necessary the court, are quite capable of coming to a conclusion in any given case as to whether or not a particular candidate could properly be described as a dependant—a word that, as the judge said, 'conjures up a sufficiently distinct picture'. I agree, too, that any one wholly or partly depend-ent on the means of another is a 'dependant'. There is thus no conceptual uncertainty inherent in that word and the executors' contentions as to the effect of its use fail.

As regards 'relatives' Brightman J, after stating, at 625, 'It is not in dispute that a person is a relative of an…employee…, if both trace legal descent from a common ancestor': a little later said: 'In practice, the use of the expression "relatives" cannot cause the slightest difficulty.' With that view I agree for the reasons he gave when he correctly set out the evidential position.

Megaw LJ:

The executors' argument concentrates on the words 'or is not' in the [given postulant test]: 'if it can be said with certainty whether any given individual is *or is not* a member of the class'. It is said that those words have been used deliberately, and have only one possible meaning; and that, however startling or drastic or unsatisfactory the result may be—and Mr. Vinelott does not shrink from saying that the con-sequence is drastic—this court is bound to give effect to the words used in the House of Lords' defini-tion of the test. It would be quite impracticable for the trustees to ascertain in many cases whether a particular person was *not* a relative of an employee. The most that could be said is: 'There is no proof that he is a relative.' But there would still be no 'certainty' that such a person was not a relative. Hence, so it is said, the test laid down by the House of Lords is not satisfied, and the trust is void. For it cannot be said with certainty, in relation to any individual, that he is not a relative.

I do not think it was contemplated that the words 'or is not' would produce that result. It would, as I see it, involve an inconsistency with the latter part of the same sentence: 'does not fail simply because it is impossible to ascertain every member of the class'. The executors' contention, in sub-stance and reality, is that it *does* fail 'simply because it is impossible to ascertain every member of the class'.

The same verbal difficulty, as I see it, emerges also when one considers the words of the suggested test which the House of Lords expressly rejected. That is set out by Lord Wilberforce in a passage immediately following the sentence which I have already quoted. The rejected test was in these terms [1971] AC 424 at 450: '...it is said to be necessary...that the whole range of objects...should be ascertained or capable of ascertainment'. Since that test was rejected, the resulting affirmative proposition, which by implication must have been accepted by their Lordships, is this: a trust for selection will not fail simply because the whole range of objects cannot be ascertained. In the present case, the trustees could ascertain, by investigation and evidence, many of the objects: as to many other theoretically possible claimants, they could not be certain. Is it to be said that the trust fails because it cannot be said with certainty that such persons are not members of the class? If so, is that not the application of the rejected test: the trust failing because 'the whole range of objects cannot be ascertained'?

In my judgment, much too great emphasis is placed in the executor's argument on the words 'or is not'. To my mind, the test is satisfied if, as regards at least a substantial number of objects, it can be said with certainty that they fall within the trust; even though, as regards a substantial number of other persons, if they ever for some fanciful reason fell to be considered, the answer would have to be, not 'they are outside the trust', but 'it is not proven whether they are in or out'. What is a 'substantial number' may well be a question of common sense and of degree in relation to the particular trust: particularly where, as here, it would be fantasy, to use a mild word, to suggest that any practical difficulty would arise in the fair, proper and sensible administration of this trust in respect of relatives and dependants.

I do not think that this involves, as Mr. Vinelott suggested, a return by this court to its former view which was rejected by the House of Lords in the *Gulbenkian* case. If I did so think, I should, however reluctantly, accept Mr. Vinelott's argument and its consequences. But as I read it, the criticism in the House of Lords of the decision of this court in that case related to this court's acceptance of the view that it would be sufficient if it could be shown that *one single person* fell within the scope of the power or trust. The essence of the decision of the House of Lords in the *Gulbenkian* case, as I see it, is *not* that it must be possible to show with certainty that any given person is *or is not* within the trust; but that it is not, or may not be, sufficient to be able to show that one individual person is within it. If it does not mean that, I do not know where the line is supposed to be drawn, having regard to the clarity and emphasis with which the House of Lords has laid down that the trust does not fail because the whole range of objects cannot be ascertained.

Stamp LJ:

Mr. Vinelott, fastening on those words, 'if it can be said with certainty that any given individual is or is not a member of the class', submitted in this court that a trust for distribution among officers and employees or ex-officers or ex-employees or any of their relatives or dependants does not satisfy the test. You may say with certainty that any given individual is or is not an officer, employee, ex-officer or ex-employee. You may say with certainty that a very large number of given individuals are relatives of one of them; but, so the argument runs, you will never be able to say with certainty of many given individuals that they are not. I am bound to say that I had thought at one stage of Mr. Vinelott's able argument that this was no more than an exercise in semantics and that the phrase on which he relies indicated no more than that the trust was valid if there was such certainty in the definition of membership of the class that you could say with certainty that some individuals were members of it: that it was sufficient that you should be satisfied that a given individual presenting himself has or has not passed the test and that it matters not that having failed to establish his membership—here his relationship—you may, perhaps wrongly, reject him. There are, however, in my judgment serious difficulties in the way of a rejection of Mr. Vinelott's submission.

The first difficulty, as I see it, is that the rejection of Mr. Vinelott's submission involves holding that the trust is good if there are individuals—or even one—of whom you can say with certainty that he is a member of the class. That was the test adopted by and the decision of the Court of Appeal in the *Gulbenkian* case where what was under consideration was a power of distribution among a class conferred upon trustees as distinct from a trust for distribution: but when the *Gulbenkian* case came before the House of Lords that test was decisively rejected and the more stringent test upon which Mr. Vinelott insists was adopted. Clearly Lord Wilberforce in expressing the view that the test of validity of a discretionary trust ought to be similar to that accepted by the House of Lords in the *Gulbenkian* case did not take the view that it was sufficient that you could find individuals who were clearly members of the class; for he himself remarked, towards the end of his speech as to the trustees' duty of inquiring or ascertaining, that in each case the trustees ought to make such a survey of the range of objects or possible beneficiaries as will enable them to carry out their fiduciary duty. It is not enough that trustees should do nothing but distribute the fund among those objects of the trust who happen to be at hand or present themselves. Lord Wilberforce, after citing that passage which I have already quoted from the speech of Lord Upjohn in the *Gulbenkian* case, put it more succinctly by remarking that what this did say (and he agreed) was that the trustees must select from the class, but that passage did not mean (as had been contended) that they must be able to get a complete list of all possible objects. I have already called attention to Lord Wilberforce's opinion that the trustees ought to make such a survey of the range of objects or possible beneficiaries as will enable them to carry out their fiduciary duty, and I ought perhaps to add that he indicated that a wider and more comprehensive range of inquiry is called for in the case of what I have called discretionary trusts than in the case of fiduciary powers. But, as I understand it, having made the appropriate survey, it matters not that it is not complete or fails to yield a result enabling you to lay out a list or particulars of every single beneficiary. Having done the best they can, the trustees may proceed upon the basis similar to that adopted by the court where all the beneficiaries cannot be ascertained and distribute upon the footing that they have been: see, for example, *Re Benjamin* [1902] 1 Ch 723. What was referred to as 'the complete ascertainment test' laid down by this court in the *Broadway Cottages* case is rejected. So also is the test laid down by this court in the *Gulbenkian* case. Validity or invalidity is to depend upon whether you can say of any individual—and the accent must be upon that word 'any', for it is not simply the individual whose claim you are considering who is spoken of—'is or is not a member of the class', for only thus can you make a survey of the range of objects or possible beneficiaries.

If the matter rested there, it would in my judgment follow that, treating the word 'relatives' as meaning descendants from a common ancestor, a trust for distribution such as is here in question would not be valid. Any 'survey of the range of the objects or possible beneficiaries' would certainly be incomplete, and I am able to discern no principle upon which such a survey could be conducted or where it should start or finish. The most you could do, so far as regards relatives, would be to find individuals who are clearly members of the class—the test which was accepted in the Court of Appeal, but rejected in the House of Lords, in the *Gulbenkian* case.

The matter does not, however, rest there ... *Harding v Glyn* (1739) 1 Atk 469 ... was an early case where the court executed a discretionary trust for 'relations'—and it is a discretionary trust for relations that I am considering—by distributing to the next of kin in equal shares[115] ...

Harding v Glyn accordingly cannot be regarded simply as a case where in default of appointment a gift to the next of kin is to be implied as a matter of construction, but as authority endorsed by the decision of the House of Lords [1971] AC 424, that a discretionary trust for 'relations' was a valid trust to be executed by the court by distribution to the next of kin. The class of beneficiaries thus

---

[115] Cf *Re Barlow's Will Trusts* [1979] 1 WLR 278, Chapter 3.4(a)(i), pp. 89–91, where 'relations' was held to mean everyone related by blood to the testatrix.

becomes a clearly defined class and there is no difficulty in determining whether a given individual is within it or without it.

Does it then make any difference that here the discretionary trust for relations was a reference not to the relations of a deceased person but of one who was living? I think not. The next of kin of a living person are as readily ascertainable at any given time as the next of kin of one who is dead.

The decision in *Re Baden's Deed Trusts (No. 2)* creates considerable difficulty because all three judges adopted different approaches. When considering the merits of the respective speeches of Sachs LJ, Megaw LJ, and Stamp LJ, it must be remembered that the task of the Court of Appeal was to apply the judgment of the House of Lords in *McPhail v Doulton*. It is against this background that the decision of their Lordships must be judged.

The *result* of the *Baden* litigation tells us that a trust in favour of 'dependants' or 'relatives' is sufficiently certain. But *why* this is so, and how difficult terms such as 'relatives' should be interpreted, remain tricky questions, which could pose problems to trustees in the future.

Regarding conceptual certainty, the judges in the Court of Appeal disagreed on the correct meaning of 'relatives'. Megaw LJ and Sachs LJ thought relatives would still be conceptually certain if defined as 'descendants from a common ancestor', whereas Stamp LJ considered that to be too wide—since it would be impossible to state with certainty whether any and every person is or is not within the class—and interpreted relatives as meaning 'statutory next-of-kin'. The restrictive approach of Stamp LJ is consistent with his approach to evidential certainty, discussed in the immediately following paragraphs. But it greatly restricts the scope of the class. Whether or not this is appropriate presents a question of construction that will turn upon the facts of each particular case.

Significantly, the judges also differed on the meaning of the 'is or is not' test. In particular, they did not agree on the weight that should be attached to the 'is not' part of the test. In a sense this is misleading: if it cannot be proved with certainty that a person is not within the class, that necessarily means that it cannot be established with certainty that that person is within the class. Essentially, the crux of the debate is whether it is permissible to have some given postulants about whom it cannot be said with certainty either that they fall within, or that they fall outside, the scope of the class. Stamp LJ insisted that it was impermissible: it must be possible to say of *any* given postulant whether he or she is or is not a member of the class. If the evidence is inconclusive either way, the trust must fail. On the other hand, Megaw LJ thought that if it could be shown, with certainty, that a substantial number of postulants were within the class, then the trust would not fail for evidential uncertainty, even if the position of some postulants was unclear. Sachs LJ favoured an evidential presumption that any postulant would not be within the scope of the class unless he or she could prove with certainty that he or she was.

Which interpretation should be favoured? The approach of Stamp LJ is most faithful to that put forward by the House of Lords, whereas the approaches of Megaw LJ and Sachs LJ perhaps shift the law back in the direction of the 'one person' test rejected by the House of Lords in *Re Gulbenkian* and *McPhail v Doulton*. Nevertheless, the rigidity in Stamp LJ's insistence upon the need to prove with certainty whether *any*, and therefore every, postulant is or is not within the scope of the class will often prove difficult to meet and lead to many trusts failing for want of certainty. This is unsatisfactory, and will generally be contrary to the intentions of the settlor. It would be preferable to adopt the approach of Sachs LJ, and make postulants themselves prove that they are within the scope of the class. In effect, this would mean that a trust will never fail for lack of evidential certainty. Whilst desirable, it must be admitted that this does appear to be inconsistent with Lord Wilberforce's insistence in *McPhail v Doulton* that *both* conceptual *and* evidential certainty needed to be established.

In any event, it should be noted that such difficulties have not much appeared in subsequent cases, probably because there are so many ways for settlors to avoid difficulties regarding certainty of objects through careful drafting of the trust instrument. Moreover, a settlor could simply create a trust in favour of a small, certain class of persons, but then give the trustees the power to add beneficiaries to the class,[116] providing guidance to the trustees regarding who should be added through a letter of wishes.[117] Another potential means of dealing with uncertainty is to allow third parties to resolve questions of interpretation.

(i) 'Curing' uncertainty through delegation

A settlor or testator may seek to circumvent any uncertainty by providing that somebody else—either a trustee or third party—can resolve any uncertainty relating to the identity of objects. There is, however, a need to balance two conflicting principles where the validity of such a power is considered. First, it is not acceptable to exclude the jurisdiction of the court to determine whether the objects are certain. Conceptual certainty being a question of law, it is traditionally thought to be the case that if the court is unable to define a class of objects with sufficient certainty, then nobody else is able to establish that the class is conceptually certain, regardless of what is provided in the instrument creating the trust. Further, there is the principle against excessive delegation to a trustee by the settlor and especially the testator, who cannot rely on the trustee to effectively make the will for him or her, for example by saying that all the testator's property is to be distributed by the trustee as he or she wishes.[118] Against this is the principle that the settlor's or testator's intention should be respected, so if the creator of the trust wishes the trustees to be the arbiters to resolve uncertainty, then so be it. Upholding such 'curing clauses' would mean that fewer trusts fail for lack of certainty, and the intentions of the settlor or testator would, therefore, be less likely to be frustrated.

The importance of preserving the court's jurisdiction to decide questions of law was highlighted in the following case.

Re Wynn [1952] Ch 271

A clause in a will stated: 'I authorise and empower my trustees to determine what articles pass under any specific bequest contained in this my will...and whether any moneys are to be considered as capital or income and how valuations are to be made and or value determined for any purpose in connexion with the trusts and provisions of this my will...and to apportion blended trust funds and to determine all questions and matters of doubt arising in the execution of the trusts of this my will...and I declare that every such determination whether made upon a question actually raised or only implied in the acts and proceedings of...my trustees shall be conclusive and binding upon all persons interested under this my will.'

The clause was held to be void.

Danckwerts J:

No doubt it may be said that it is convenient to have matters regarding the apportionment of capital moneys and the application of moneys in the payment of expenses referred to some informal decision, and that in that way expense may be saved which would be necessarily incurred if the matters had to

---

[116] *Re Manisty's Settlement* [1974] Ch. 17.
[117] See Chapter 10.1(b)(ii), pp. 494–8. As a letter of wishes is not legally binding, it could not be void for uncertainty.
[118] *In Bonis Smith* (1869) LR 1 P & D 717 (Lord Penzance); Gordon (1953) 69 LQR 334.

be referred to the court; but in my view a clause of this kind has no effect if it is attempted to use it so as to prevent the beneficiaries requiring the matter to be decided by the court. As long as the clause is not contested, it may be that the beneficiaries will be content to have the matters dealt with by the trustees in the course of their operations in the administration of the estate; and it may, of course, be that the trustees have applied their minds and carried out their duties in a perfectly proper manner in the way in which they deal with matters connected with the estate; but it seems to me that the result is that any beneficiary is entitled to go to the court to have his rights considered and, if necessary, upheld; and that a testator may not by the provisions of his will exclude the right of the court to decide the matters, even though the trustees have considered them and reached a certain decision.

By contrast, evidential certainty is a question of fact, not law, and the court is not concerned about having exclusive jurisdiction over questions of fact.

Re Coxen [1948] Ch 747 (Ch D)

The testator left a house to trustees upon trust for his wife to live in; and he declared that, 'if in the opinion of my trustees she shall have ceased permanently to reside therein', the house was to fall into residue. The question was whether this proviso constituted a valid limitation upon the gift.

Jenkins J held that the condition was not void for uncertainty: the decision of the trustees would be sufficient to determine the widow's interest.

Jenkins J:

I have so far treated the condition as if it was simply in the terms 'if she shall have ceased permanently to reside', whereas its actual terms are 'if in the opinion of my trustees she shall have ceased permanently to reside'. That I think makes a very material difference. The opinion of the trustees that the double event has happened, and not simply the happening of the double event, is what brings about the cesser of Lady Coxen's interest. If the testator had insufficiently defined the state of affairs on which the trustees were to form their opinion, he would not I think have saved the condition from invalidity on the ground of uncertainty merely by making their opinion the criterion, although the declaration by the trustees of this or that opinion would be an event about which in itself there could be no uncertainty. But as I have already indicated, I think the relevant double event is sufficiently defined to make it perfectly possible for the trustees (as the judges of fact for this purpose) to decide whether it has happened or not, and in my view the testator by making the trustees' opinion the criterion has removed the difficulties which might otherwise have ensued from a gift over in a double event the happening of which, though in itself sufficiently defined, may necessarily be a matter of inference involving nice questions of fact and degree.

There might be thought to be a divide between a clause that purports to resolve evidential uncertainty and one that seeks to cure conceptual uncertainty. But it has been suggested that the importance of giving effect to the settlor's intention means that even conceptual uncertainty might be curable. For example, in *Dundee General Hospitals Board of Management v Walker*,[119] a Scottish case, the House of Lords held that a clause in a will that provided that trustees in their 'sole and absolute' discretion could determine whether a hospital had been taken over by the State was valid. Lord Denning MR

---

[119] [1952] 1 All ER 896.

has subsequently interpreted this decision to mean that a testator or settlor can delegate to another in order to cure conceptual uncertainty of objects.

Re Tuck's Settlement Trusts [1978] Ch 49

The settlor provided an income for the holder for the time being of the family baronetcy if and when and so long as he should be of the Jewish faith, and married and living with 'an approved wife' or, if separated, being so separated through no fault of his. An 'approved wife' was defined as a wife of Jewish blood by one or both of her parents, who had been brought up in the Jewish faith, had never departed from it, and, who, at the date of the marriage, continued to worship according to the Jewish faith. The Chief Rabbi in London of either the Portuguese or the Anglo-German community was designated to decide any question as to who was an approved wife, and whether any separation was or was not due to the fault of the baronet.

The question was whether the trusts were void for uncertainty; and whether the reference to the Chief Rabbi was effective, or void as an ouster of the jurisdiction of the court. The Court of Appeal held that the condition was sufficiently certain. On the question whether, if it had been void for uncertainty, the trust would have been saved by the provision making the Chief Rabbi's decision conclusive, Lord Denning MR said:

[Counsel] submitted that, in a case where there was conceptual uncertainty (where the words were not clear enough for the court) it followed inexorably that they were not clear enough for a rabbi either.

He based this on the words of Jenkins J. in *In Re Coxen* [1948] Ch. 747, 761 and on *In Re Jones, Decd.* [1953] Ch. 125. Alternatively he said that, by entrusting the decision to a rabbi instead of to the court, the settlor was ousting the jurisdiction of the court. He based this on *In Re Raven* [1915] 1 Ch. 673 and *In Re Wynn, Decd.* [1952] Ch. 271.

I cannot accept either of these submissions. Nor can I accept the decisions on which Mr. Dillon relies. All the cases on this subject need to be reconsidered in the light of *Dundee General Hospitals Board of Management v. Walker* [1952] 1 All E.R. 896. A testator there gave money to a hospital provided that at his death it should not have been taken over by the state. He gave his trustees 'sole and absolute discretion' to decide whether it had been taken over by the state. The House held that this entrusting to his trustees was perfectly valid: and their decision was to be upheld. It was a decision of the House of Lords in a Scottish case. It may not be binding on the English courts in an English case. But it is of the highest persuasive value. *Donoghue v. Stevenson* [1932] A.C. 562 was a Scottish appeal. But it transformed the law of England. I venture to suggest that, on questions of principle, it is most desirable that the laws of England and Scotland should be uniform: and, accordingly, that a decision of the House of Lords—when founded on principle and not on authority—should be regarded as applicable to both countries: unless the House itself says otherwise. Why otherwise should we have Scottish Law Lords sitting on English cases or English Law Lords sitting on Scottish cases? The very constitution of the House shows that each system of law has much to learn from the other: and that a decision on a point of principle should reflect the best of both.

I see no reason why a testator or settlor should not provide that any dispute or doubt should be resolved by his executors or trustees, or even by a third person. To prove this, I will first state the law in regard to contracts. Here the general principle is that whenever persons agree together to refer a matter to a third person for decision, and further agree that his decision is to be final and binding upon them, then, so long as he arrives at his decision honestly and in good faith, the two parties are bound by it. . . .

> If two contracting parties can by agreement leave a doubt or difficulty to be decided by a third person, I see no reason why a testator or settlor should not leave the decision to his trustees or to a third party. He does not thereby oust the jurisdiction of the court. If the appointed person should find difficulty in the actual wording of the will or settlement, the executors or trustees can always apply to the court for directions so as to assist in the interpretation of it. But if the appointed person is ready and willing to resolve the doubt or difficulty, I see no reason why he should not do so. So long as he does not misconduct himself or come to a decision which is wholly unreasonable, I think his decision should stand. After all, that was plainly the intention of the testator or settlor.

Clearly, Lord Denning's approach helps to protect the intention of the testator or settlor. But it did not receive the support of the other judges in the Court of Appeal. For example, Eveleigh LJ thought that the Chief Rabbi was not resolving uncertainty, but that the class should be defined as those whom the Chief Rabbi considers to be of the Jewish faith. Eveleigh LJ said:

> I therefore do not regard the settlor as leaving it to the Chief Rabbi to discover what the settlor meant or to provide a meaning for the expression used by the settlor when the meaning is in doubt. The court itself will not do so and I doubt if *Dundee General Hospitals Board of Management v. Walker* [1952] 1 All E.R. 896 allows me to say that the court will permit the Chief Rabbi to do so. The fact is that the Chief Rabbi knows what he means by 'Jewish faith' and the testator has said that he means the same thing. There is no element of speculation here. Id certum est.

The approach of Eveleigh LJ may well be preferable and a better interpretation of *Dundee General Hospitals*. In defining the class such that the 'arbiter' is part of the definition of the class, there is no danger of the court's jurisdiction over questions of law being usurped. Indeed, no mention was made of Lord Denning's remarks in *Re Wright's Will Trusts*,[120] which insisted that conceptual uncertainty could not be cured by delegation.

However, even if it is accepted that conceptual uncertainty can be cured by delegation, this does not render the courts redundant. The person resolving the uncertainty must act reasonably, and can be required to explain his or her decision to the court. In *Dundee General Hospitals*, Lord Reid said:[121]

> But, by making his trustees the sole judges of a question, a testator does not entirely exclude recourse to the Court by persons aggrieved by the trustees' decision. If it can be shown that the trustees considered the wrong question, or that, although they purported to consider the right question, they did not really apply their minds to it or perversely shut their eyes to the facts, or that they did not act honestly or in good faith, then there was no true decision and the Court will intervene.

(ii) *Administrative unworkability*

In *McPhail v Doulton*, Lord Wilberforce hinted that a class may be so 'hopelessly wide' as to be administratively unworkable.[122] This was the problem at issue in the following case.

---

[120] [1981] LS Gaz 841.

[121] [1952] 1 All ER 896, 905 (Lord Reid). See too *Re Coates* [1955] 1 Ch 495, 500 (Roxburgh J); *Re Tuck's Settlement Trust* [1978] Ch 49, 62 (Lord Denning).

[122] See Chapter 3.4(b), p. 94.

R v District Auditor, ex p West Yorkshire Metropolitan County Council [1986] RVR 24 (QB)

A local authority resolved to create a trust under which the trustees were 'to apply and expend the Trust Fund for the benefit of any or all or some of the inhabitants of the County of West Yorkshire' in four specified ways. It was conceded that this was not a charitable trust, because one of its objects, the dissemination of information about the proposed abolition of the metropolitan county councils, was not charitable.[123] The Court held that the trust could not take effect as an express private trust.

Lloyd LJ:

Counsel for the county council...argued that the beneficiaries of the trust were all or some of the inhabitants of the county of West Yorkshire. The class might be on the large side, containing as it does some 2½ million potential beneficiaries. But the definition, it was said, is straightforward and clear cut. There is no uncertainty as to the concept. If anyone were to come forward and claim to be a beneficiary, it could be said of him at once whether he was within the class or not.

I cannot accept counsel for the county council's argument. I am prepared to assume in favour of the council, without deciding, that the class is defined with sufficient clarity. I do not decide the point because it might, as it seems to me, be open to argument what is meant by 'an inhabitant' of the county of West Yorkshire. But I put that difficulty on one side. For there is to my mind a more fundamental difficulty. A trust with as many as 2½ million potential beneficiaries is, in my judgment, quite simply unworkable. The class is far too large. In *Re Gulbenkian's Settlements* [1970] AC 508 Lord Reid said at 518:

> 'It may be that there is a class of case where, although the description of a class of beneficiaries is clear enough, any attempt to apply it to the facts would lead to such administrative difficulties that it would for that reason be held to be invalid.'

[His Lordship quoted Lord Wilberforce's final paragraph in *McPhail v Doulton* [1971] AC 424 at 457,[124] and continued:]

It seems to me that the present trust comes within the third case to which Lord Wilberforce refers. I hope I am not guilty of being prejudiced by the example which he gave. But it could hardly be more apt, or fit the facts of the present case more precisely.

I mention the subsequent decisions in *Re Baden's Deed Trusts (No 2)* [1972] Ch 607, and on appeal [1973] Ch 900, and *Re Manisty's Settlement* [1974] Ch 17, with misgiving, since they were not cited in argument. The latter was a case of an intermediate power, that is to say, a power exercisable by trustees in favour of all the world, other than members of an excepted class. After referring to *Gulbenkian* and the two *Baden* cases, Templeman J (as he then was) said:

> 'I conclude...that a power cannot be uncertain merely because it is wide in ambit.'

A power to benefit, for example, the residents of Greater London might, he thought, be bad, not on the ground of its width but on the ground of capriciousness, since the settlor could have no sensible intention to benefit 'an accidental conglomeration of persons' who had 'no discernible link with the settlor'. But that objection could not apply here. The council had every reason for wishing to benefit the inhabitants of West Yorkshire.

Lord Wilberforce's dictum has also been the subject of a good deal of academic comment and criticism, noticeably by L. McKay (1974) 38 Conv 269 and C.T. Emery (1982) 98 LQR 551. I should have

---

[123] See Chapter 5.5, pp. 255–8.
[124] Chapter 3.4(b), p. 94.

welcomed further argument on these matters, but through no fault of counsel for the county council this was not possible. So I have to do the best I can.

My conclusion is that the dictum of Lord Wilberforce remains of high persuasive authority, despite *Re Manisty*. *Manisty's* case was concerned with a power, where the function of the court is more restricted. In the case of a trust, the court may have to execute the trust. Not so in the case of a power. That there may still be a distinction between trusts and powers in this connection was recognized by Templeman J himself in the sentence immediately following his quotation of Lord Wilberforce's dictum, when he said:

> 'In these guarded terms Lord Wilberforce appears to refer to trusts which may have to be executed and administered by the court and not to powers where the court has a very much more limited function.'

There can be no doubt that the declaration of trust in the present case created a trust and not a power. Following Lord Wilberforce's dictum, I would hold that the definition of the beneficiaries of the trust is 'so hopelessly wide' as to be incapable of forming 'anything like a class'. I would therefore reject counsel for the county council's argument that the declaration of trust can take effect as an express private trust.[125]

There is, therefore, no doubt that a trust may be void because of administrative unworkability. Indeed, in *Re Harding* it was accepted as 'common ground that a private trust for such a large class as the black community in four London Boroughs would be so large as to make a private trust unworkable, and hence void'.[126]

However, it is not clear *why* the sheer size of a class should render a trust void for administrative unworkability. For example, the class in *Re Baden's Deed Trusts (No. 2)* was large, such that the trustees would be unable to survey every potential beneficiary, but the trust was nevertheless held to be valid. This is entirely appropriate: trustees should always be able to make a *reasonable* survey of the class in general terms. As long as the trust property is then appointed to objects who fall within the scope of the class, the size of the class should not matter. Administrative workability should be an irrelevant consideration.[127] To adopt such an approach would simply require the court not to be too exigent in its expectations of what actions trustees should take. On the basis that the settlor's intention should be respected as much as possible, courts should not interfere and declare a trust administratively unworkable solely because the settlor gave his trustees a wide discretion to appoint property within a huge class of potential objects.

McKay, *'Re Baden* and the Third Class of Uncertainty' [1974] Conv 269, 280–2

On one view it is possible to argue that...if [the court] is to be in a position to make the selection contemplated then it must have a more precise notion of the aims and ambitions of the settlor than a broad intention to 'benefit' the stated class....

The most compelling argument against the 'third class' [of administrative unworkability] requiring the provision of rules of a more specific character than 'benefit' is that to so require would undo most of the

---

[125] Cf *Re Beatty* [1990] 1 WLR 1503 (fiduciary power given to trustees in favour of 'such person or persons as they think fit' held valid without consideration of administrative unworkability); Martin [1991] Conv 138.

[126] [2007] EWHC 3 (Ch); [2008] Ch 235, [15], although it was held that the trust in question was charitable.

[127] See the academic criticism cited by Lloyd LJ: McKay [1974] Conv 269 and Emery (1982) 98 LQR 551.

good work performed in *Re Baden* by Lord Wilberforce himself. The *Baden* deed, and most other establishing quasi-public employee trusts, was both prompted by that broad sentiment and appropriately expressed in those broad terms. The multifarious forms in which benefit may legitimately be conferred by trustees should not cloud the fact that, if it has to, the court through its own determination or with the aid of persons acting on its behalf is just as capable of determining whether a particular proposal is one of those forms. Flexibility in the realm of execution is at the heart of the *Re Baden* decision, and it would be inconsistent with that decision were the courts to falter and refuse to make such a determination. And if they should and would make it in the *Baden* deed context, there is no reason for affording different treatment to the Greater London trust.

However, such arguments are unlikely to succeed given the decision in *West Yorkshire*. As mentioned already, settlors would be better advised to create a trust in favour of a small, certain class of persons, but then give the trustees the power to add beneficiaries to the class, providing guidance to the trustees regarding who should be added through a letter of wishes.[128] But it is interesting to wonder whether the result in *West Yorkshire* would have been the same had the fund been larger. In *West Yorkshire*, £400,000 was to be held on trust for a class containing around 2.5 million people. It may be that administering such a fund for such a huge class was thought to be impractical and that, therefore, the trust was deemed 'administratively unworkable'. Perhaps the outcome might have been different if a much greater sum—say, £50 million—had been given to 'the inhabitants of West Yorkshire'. It is suggested that such a trust *could* be administered properly, given the increased size of the fund at the trustees' disposal. It might be that administrative unworkability involves some sort of assessment of proportionality of the size of the fund with the size of the class. Admittedly, though, there is no suggestion of this either in Lord Wilberforce's *dicta* in *McPhail v Doulton* or in *West Yorkshire*.

(c) FIDUCIARY POWERS

The crucial difference between powers and discretionary trusts is that powers do not *have* to be exercised.[129] However, if the power is a fiduciary power,[130] then the holders of the power (often trustees) must *consider* the exercise of the power, even if they ultimately choose not to distribute the property at their disposal.[131] The fact that the holders of such powers need to consider their exercise means that it must be possible for them to make a reasonable survey of potential objects in order to make a sensible decision whether or not to appoint any of the property to potential objects.[132] As a result, such powers must be certain. In *McPhail v Doulton*, Lord Wilberforce noted that the difference between trusts and fiduciary powers is 'narrow'.[133] Indeed, in *McPhail* Lord Wilberforce essentially adopted the test for certainty of fiduciary powers enunciated in *Re Gulbenkian*.

Re Gulbenkian's Settlements [1970] AC 508

A settlement contained a power to appoint in favour of Nubar Gulbenkian 'any wife and his children or remoter issue...and any person...in whose house or apartments or in whose company or under whose care or control or by or with whom [he] may from time to time be employed

---

[128] See Chapter 3.4(b), p. 99.
[129] See Chapter 2.6(h), p. 51.
[130] See Chapter 2.6(h)(i), pp. 51–2.
[131] Ibid.
[132] Even this is not required under a non-fiduciary mere power: ibid.
[133] Chapter 2.6(h)(ii), p. 53.

or residing'. The question was whether the power was void for uncertainty. It was unanimously upheld by the House of Lords. A power is valid if it could be said with certainty whether any given individual was or was not a member of the class.

Lord Upjohn:

In my opinion, this clause is not void for uncertainty, and the Court of Appeal were quite right to over-rule the decision of Harman J in *Re Gresham's Settlement* [1956] 1 WLR 573, where he held a similar clause was void on that ground.

My Lords, that is sufficient to dispose of the appeal, but, as I have mentioned earlier, the reasons of two members of the Court of Appeal went further and have been supported by counsel for the respondents with much force and so must be examined.

Lord Denning MR [1968] Ch 126 at 134E, propounded a test in the case of powers collateral, namely, that if you can say of one particular person meaning thereby, apparently, any one person only that he is clearly within the category the whole power is good though it may be difficult to say in other cases whether a person is or is not within the category, and he supported that view by reference to author-ity. Winn LJ at 138E said that where there was not a complete failure by reason of ambiguity and uncertainty the court would give effect to the power as valid rather than hold it defeated since it will have wholly failed, which put—though more broadly—the view expressed by the Master of the Rolls. Counsel for the respondents in his second line of argument relied upon these observations as a matter of principle but he candidly admitted that he could not rely upon any authority. Moreover, the Master of the Rolls at 133B, expressed the view that the different doctrine with regard to trust powers should be brought into line with the rule with regard to conditions precedent and powers collateral...

But with respect to mere powers, while the court cannot compel the trustees to exercise their powers, yet those entitled to the fund in default must clearly be entitled to restrain the trustees from exercising it save among those within the power. So the trustees or the court must be able to say with certainty who is within and who is without the power. It is for this reason that I find myself unable to accept the broader proposition advanced by Lord Denning MR and Winn LJ mentioned earlier, and agree with the proposition as enunciated in *Re Gestetner Settlement* [1953] Ch 672 and the later cases.

It would seem that fiduciary powers are also subject to the same requirements of conceptual and evidential certainty that concern discretionary trusts.[134] Ascertainability will not pose a problem for powers because they do not *need* to be exercised anyway.

It might be thought that administrative unworkability also afflicts fiduciary powers. For example, in *Blausten v IRC*, Buckley LJ, albeit *obiter*, suggested that:[135]

If the class of persons to whose possible claims they would have to give consideration were so wide that it really did not amount to a class in any true sense at all no doubt that would be a duty which it would be impossible for them to perform and the power could be said to be invalid on that ground.

Nevertheless, such a result seems unlikely.[136] Indeed, *Blausten* was not thought to decide the issue in either *Re Manisty's Settlement*[137] or *Re Hay's Settlement Trust*.[138] In both these cases, fiduciary

---

[134] Chapter 3.4(b), p. 91.
[135] [1972] Ch 256, 271.
[136] Although see Chapter 3.4(c)(i), pp. 108–9 for discussion of *Mettoy Pension Trustees Ltd v Evans* and the amalga-mation of powers and discretionary trusts.
[137] [1974] Ch 17.
[138] [1982] 1 WLR 202.

powers were recognized as valid where the trustee holders of the power could exercise the power in favour of absolutely anybody with the exception of a limited class. In *Re Hay's Settlement Trust* Sir Robert Megarry V-C explicitly departed from the view of Buckley LJ in *Blausten*, pointing out that Buckley LJ's comments were made before the decision of the Court of Appeal in *Re Baden's Deed Trusts (No. 2)*, and concluded:[139]

> I do not see how mere numbers can inhibit the trustees from considering whether or not to exercise the power, as distinct from deciding in whose favour to exercise it.... Nor can I see that the power is administratively unworkable. The words of Lord Wilberforce in *In re Baden (No. 1)* [1971] A.C. 424, 457 are directed to discretionary trusts, not powers.

It therefore seems as if sheer size does not appear to be an issue. This is entirely appropriate; after all, a potentially huge range of objects does not prevent the holder of a power from *considering* its exercise.

However, distinct from size is the issue of 'capriciousness'. It may be that a fiduciary power could be declared void on this basis. This was suggested by Templeman J in *Re Manisty*:

> The court may also be persuaded to intervene if the trustees act 'capriciously,' that is to say, act for reasons which I apprehend could be said to be irrational, perverse or irrelevant to any sensible expectation of the settlor; for example, if they chose a beneficiary by height or complexion or by the irrelevant fact that he was a resident of Greater London....
>
> A power to benefit 'residents of Greater London' is capricious because the terms of the power negative any sensible intention on the part of the settlor.[140] If the settlor intended and expected the trustees would have regard to persons with some claim on his bounty or some interest in an institution favoured by the settlor, or if the settlor had any other sensible intention or expectation, he would not have required the trustees to consider only an accidental conglomeration of persons who have no discernible link with the settlor or with any institution. A capricious power negatives a sensible consideration by the trustees of the exercise of the power.[141]

This notion of capriciousness was also discussed in *Re Hay*, so it appears to be relevant when considering the validity of powers. However, it is not clear why this should be the case.[142] After all, why should the law prevent a settlor from being capricious? Surely the goal of upholding the settlor's intention should trump any qualms surrounding capriciousness? Moreover, it has been held that a testator *can* be capricious in his will. For example, in *Re Allsopp*, Lord Denning MR said:[143]

> If you find that a literal interpretation gives rise to a capricious result which you are satisfied the testator can never have intended, then you should reject that interpretation and seek for a sensible interpretation which does accord with his intention. It is sometimes said that a testator can be capricious if he likes. Yes, if you are sure that he intended to be; but you should not impute capriciousness to him merely to justify yourself in giving the words a literal interpretation.

---

[139] [1982] 1 WLR 202, 211.
[140] But note that in *West Yorkshire* it was accepted that the trust was not capricious, since there were good reasons why the council wanted to benefit the people of West Yorkshire.
[141] [1974] Ch 17, 26–7.
[142] McKay, '*Re Baden* and the Third Class of Uncertainty' [1974] Conv 269, 282–3.
[143] [1968] Ch 39, 47.

Although capriciousness has been discussed by the courts, it has never rendered a fiduciary power void, and it is suggested that it is unlikely ever to do so. The very test of capriciousness is vague; even if a settlor has created a trust capriciously, it is difficult to envisage that ever preventing a sensible consideration by the trustees of the exercise of the power. The court should not strive to defeat the power the settlor intended.

(i) *Amalgamating the tests for powers and discretionary trusts*

The difference between fiduciary powers and discretionary trusts is very thin. This has led some to argue that there should be greater amalgamation of the two areas. For example, in *Mettoy Pension Trustees Ltd v Evans*,[144] Warner J suggested that the remedies available for the enforcement of discretionary trusts could also be used regarding mere powers. Gardner has contemplated what consequences this approach might have.

Gardner, 'Fiduciary Powers in Toytown' (1991) 107 LQR 214, 218–19

This adoption of discretionary trust remedies for fully fiduciary powers of appointment is of considerable doctrinal importance. *Ubi remedium, ibi jus.* The idea of such powers involving duties to their objects no longer rests even partly on statements about these duties in the abstract: the new position on remedies means that they have now been given the most comprehensive available concrete form.

So Warner J.'s judgment can be seen as topping out the development of fully fiduciary powers of appointment. One should not, however, think of this in terms of a progression from darkness to enlightenment. Of course, an element of such a perception may have helped motivate the development. Judges may have felt that it was simply 'not fair' that the objects of such powers should be so much less favoured than the takers in default, and have set about rectifying the situation by according the former greater rights. But it would be more accurate to think of the two types of power—those with duties to the objects, and those without—in terms of the law offering these two different facilities to those setting up such powers, allowing them to choose whichever is more appropriate for their needs. Perhaps few settlors would want to negate duties towards their objects merely for the sake of it. But one countervailing consideration is that the higher duties and remedies of fully fiduciary powers may carry a price in the form of a more stringent certainty test. By *Morice* v. *Bishop of Durham* (1805) 10 Ves. 522, the terms of a trust—or power—must be sufficiently certain for the performance of the relevant duties and the application of the relevant remedies. This might, therefore, mean that not all powers of appointment which could be valid without the new duties and remedies will necessarily be valid with them.

The standard 'is or is not' certainty test, established by *Re Gulbenkian's Settlement Trusts* [1970] A.C. 508, should remain unaffected, since it is directed at the duty not to pay non-objects, which has always been owed to the takers in default anyway. But it is at least arguable that the assimilation of duties and remedies in fiduciary powers with those encountered in discretionary trusts means that such powers now need additionally to satisfy the requirement, hitherto found only in discretionary trusts, that the objects must represent 'something like a class,' which apparently rules out groups such as 'the residents of Greater London' (*McPhail* v. *Doulton* [1971] A.C. 424 at p. 457). Unfortunately, even in discretionary trusts themselves, although it seems reasonably clear that this test has to do with the duties involved in the discretion, it is not easy to see just what difficulty it is aimed at pre-empting. Commentators have made valiant efforts to explain it, but most ultimately seem unconvinced of its role. The sole decision of which it forms the ratio, *R.* v. *District Auditor, ex p. West Yorkshire Metropolitan County Council*

---

[144] [1990] 1 WLR 1587. See Chapter 13.2(b)(ii), pp. 634–6.

[1986] R.V.R. 24, was heard under the Crown List and provides no illumination. Megarry J. was not demonstrably wrong, therefore, in holding the test inapplicable to fully fiduciary powers of appointment in *Re Hay's Settlement Trusts* [1982] 1 W.L.R. 202. But that decision's less developed treatment of remedies still left its commitment to the idea of such fully fiduciary powers a little less certain than that of the *Mettoy* case. The newly unequivocal commitment in the latter ought to mean that the question of applying the 'something like a class' test to them will need to be at least looked at once more. At all events, however, its application would have presented no problem in the *Mettoy* case, since the class of objects there—the pensioners—was certainly no more diffuse than the class which apparently occasioned no concern in *McPhail* v. *Doulton* itself.

Gardner is ultimately critical of administrative unworkability, and appears reluctant to accept its application in the context of fiduciary powers. This seems correct. Moreover, any amalgamation that *Mettoy* may or may not bring about should not see trusts being struck down for capriciousness. It may, therefore, be that administrative unworkability afflicts trusts but not powers, whereas capriciousness concerns powers but not trusts. The two are certainly different: in the *West Yorkshire* case, for example, there was a sensible reason why the council wanted to benefit the inhabitants of West Yorkshire. Capriciousness was, therefore, not at issue, although administrative unworkability was. In any event, both administrative unworkability and capriciousness have been criticized, since their application runs counter to the important aim of giving effect to the settlor's intentions, and it might be preferable for neither doctrine to apply either to discretionary trusts or to fiduciary powers. However, this clearly conflicts with the judgment of Warner J in *Mettoy*, who suggested that a fiduciary power could be afflicted by administrative unworkability. But it might simply be that *Mettoy* was a difficult case and too much weight should not be placed upon it;[145] the particular nature of pension trusts, at issue in the case, perhaps means that the comments of Warner J should be limited to that context.

5. ABSENCE OF CERTAINTIES

If there is insufficient certainty of intention, subject matter, or objects, then the trust will fail. If the trust was created by a declaration of the settlor, then the trust simply will not take effect. But often the property that was the subject of the purported trust will have been transferred to the purported trustee. In such circumstances, different results may follow.

If it is clear that the settlor intended the recipient of the property to hold that property on trust for others, but there is insufficient certainty of subject matter or objects, then it will often be the case that the putative trustee cannot hold the property for her- or himself. This is because it would be unconscionable for such a person to claim the property absolutely and beneficially when he knew that the settlor intended otherwise. Thus, the recipient of the property will be holding the property on trust, but not in accordance with the express trust that failed for lack of certainty, but rather for the settlor on a resulting trust.[146]

However, in some instances the recipient of the property will be able to hold the received property beneficially. For example, if there is uncertainty as to subject matter, it might not be clear upon which part of the received property the trust should bite. If the facts can be interpreted as the purported settlor giving an absolute gift of property to the putative trustee, which was then to be supplemented

---

[145] And it has been overruled on its interpretation of *Re Hastings-Bass* by *Pitt v Holt* [2011] EWCA Civ 197; [2011] 3 WLR 19: see Chapter 11.7(g), pp. 577–83.

[146] See Chapter 8.3, p. 384.

by an express trust,[147] then that supposed trustee may take the property beneficially under the 'rule in *Hancock v Watson*'.[148] In that case, Lord Davey said:[149]

> in my opinion, it is settled law that if you find an absolute gift to a legatee in the first instance, and trusts are engrafted or imposed on that absolute interest which fail, either from lapse or invalidity or any other reason, then the absolute gift takes effect so far as the trusts have failed to the exclusion of the residuary legatee or next of kin as the case may be.

Difficulties also arise where there is uncertainty because *part* of the trust instrument fails one of the certainties. For example, what would have been the result if, in *Re Baden*,[150] the court had decided that 'dependant' was sufficiently certain, but 'relatives' was not? Would the trust have failed entirely? Or would it be possible for the court to sever 'relatives', in order that the trustees could still appoint the trust property to the dependants?

Although it has sometimes been suggested that the term giving rise to the uncertainty could be severed,[151] in *Re Wright's Will Trusts*,[152] where the relevant class consisted of identifiable named charities and other bodies that could not be identified, the Court of Appeal refused to give effect to the gift in favour of the named charities only. Templeman LJ said:

> where a trust creates beneficiaries some of whom cannot be ascertained by virtue of uncertainty while including certain beneficiaries or charities, the trust must be wholly invalid. Where, of course, a testator gives part of his property to charitable purposes, so that part can be segregated, that principle does not apply; but where, as here, the trustees have power to distribute the trust fund between objects who are uncertain and between charities, then, as a general rule, the whole trust must fail and the charities are deprived.

Yet Templeman LJ recognized that severance is possible in the context of charitable trusts, in order to give effect to the settlor's wishes as much as possible.[153] It is unclear why the same consideration does not have equal importance in the private sphere. Surely it would be better to permit the possibility of severance, such that at least some of those intended to benefit by the settlor can do so. Of course, if severance would run counter to the intentions of the settlor[154] then it should not be employed, but it is suggested the courts should be able to employ this device where it would help to uphold the trust and the settlor's intention to the greatest extent possible.

6. THE BENEFICIARY PRINCIPLE

The orthodox view is that a private trust can only exist if the trustees hold the trust property on trust for ascertainable individuals—or for such as will be ascertained during the period of perpetuity.[155]

---

[147] Although if the property was always to be held beneficially for others then the trustee cannot take beneficially: e.g. *Boyce v Boyce* (1849) 6 Sim 476.

[148] [1902] AC 14.

[149] [1902] AC 14, 22.

[150] Chapter 3.4(b), pp. 94–8.

[151] *Re Leek* [1969] 1 Ch 563, 586 (Sachs LJ); *Re Gulbenkian's Settlements* [1968] Ch 126, 138 (CA, Winn LJ); cf. decisions on trusts which are not exclusively charitable: see Chapter 5.5(b)(iii), p. 260.

[152] (1999) 13 TLI 48 (decided in 1982).

[153] See *Re Clarke* [1923] 2 Ch 407.

[154] For example, if a letter of wishes indicates that the settlor intended that the 'uncertain group' receive the larger share of the trust property to the (almost) exclusion of the 'certain group'.

[155] *Re Flavel's Will Trusts* [1969] 1 WLR 444, especially at 446–7.

The court must be able to enforce a trust, and there must be ascertainable persons in whose favour the court can decree performance. A trust is obligatory; and there cannot be an obligation unless there is a corresponding right, held by the beneficiaries.

The beneficiary principle was crucial to the decision in *Morice v Bishop of Durham*.

Morice v Bishop of Durham [1804] 9 Ves 399 (upheld on appeal (1805) 10 Ves 522)

There was a bequest to the Bishop upon trust for 'such objects of benevolence and liberality as the Bishop of Durham in his own discretion shall most approve of'. This was held not to be a charitable trust. As there were no ascertainable beneficiaries, the trust failed.

Sir William Grant MR:

The only question is whether the Trust, upon which the residue of the personal Estate is bequeathed, be a trust for charitable purposes. That it is upon some trust, and not for the personal benefit of the Bishop is clear from the words of the Will; and is admitted by his Lordship; who expressly disclaims any beneficial interest. That it is a Trust, unless it be of a charitable nature, too indefinite to be executed by this Court, has not been, and cannot be denied. There can be no Trust over the exercise of which this Court will not assume a control; for an uncontrollable power of disposition would be Ownership, and not Trust. If there be a clear Trust, but for uncertain objects, the property, that is the subject of the trust, is undisposed of, and the benefit of such Trust must result to those, to whom the Law gives Ownership in default of disposition by the former owner. But this doctrine does not hold good with regard to Trusts for Charity. Every other Trust must have a definite object. There must be somebody, in whose favour the Court can decree performance.

As the Master of the Rolls made clear, the beneficiary principle does not apply to charitable trusts. Charitable trusts are a special type of purpose trust, one that is of special importance to society, and is therefore given special privileges in terms of perpetuity, taxation, and enforcement.[156] The Attorney-General and the Charity Commission are charged with the duty of enforcement of charitable trusts.

Some cases at first instance have upheld non-charitable purpose trusts.[157] The modern trend however is to declare them void; and the court will not extend the confines of existing decisions. Even those have been described by Harman LJ as 'troublesome, anomalous and aberrant'.[158] We will consider in Chapter 6 the ways in which it is possible to achieve a non-charitable purpose without setting up a trust.[159]

It has been argued that the orthodox view that English law does not recognize purpose trusts is incorrect.[160] Although this may be correct when the old authorities are examined, it is clear from the more recent authorities that the settled view is that non-charitable purpose trusts are not generally considered to be valid in English law. This view is now so entrenched that it is unlikely to be overturned save by legislation. Nevertheless, other jurisdictions have recognized non-charitable purpose trusts, and it has been suggested that English law should develop in a similar manner.[161]

[156] See Chapter 5.1(a), pp. 177–8.
[157] See Chapter 6.2, pp. 289–94. Further, article 2 of the Hague Convention on the Law Applicable to Trusts and on their Recognition (1984), incorporated into English law by the Recognition of Trusts Act 1987, defines a trust to include one 'for a specified purpose'.
[158] *Re Endacott* [1960] Ch 232, 251; *Re Wood* [1949] Ch 498.
[159] See Chapter 6.3, pp. 294–9.
[160] Baxendale-Walker, *Purpose Trusts* (2nd edn) (Tottel 1999).
[161] See also Matthews, 'The New Trust: Obligations Without Rights?' in A.J. Oakley, *Trends in Contemporary Trust Law* (Oxford: Oxford University Press, 1996).

Hayton, 'Developing the Obligation Characteristic of the Trust' (2001) 117 LQR 96, 100–1

Underlying and underpinning the trust obligation is the fundamental principle that just as a car needs an engine, so a trust needs an enforcer (whether the enforcer be a beneficiary or the Attorney-General or the Charity Commissioners or some person expressly appointed by the settlor to be enforcer with *locus standi* positively to enforce the trust). Is it seriously to be suggested that the English court would invoke the orthodox beneficiary principle to refuse to give effect to a foreign non-charitable purpose trust of English assets where under the foreign governing law as a result of legislation (like that of Jersey or Bermuda or the Isle of Man or the Cayman Islands or the British Virgin Islands) such a trust is valid where the trust instrument expressly provides for an enforcer? Would the English court really hold the assets to be subject to a resulting trust for the settlor? It is submitted that, because the beneficiary principle should be regarded as the 'enforcer principle', the English court would regard the foreign trust concept neither as repugnant to the English trust concept nor contrary to English public policy, the trust being one that the English court can 'both enforce and control'.

Thus, where a trust instrument provides for an enforcer to enforce a non-charitable purpose trust, the beneficiary principle should not vitiate such a trust, whether the trust be governed by a *foreign law* with legislation accepting such a trust as valid (and whether the trust is wholly foreign, except for some trust assets located in England, or is wholly internal to England except for the choice of the foreign governing law) or be governed by *English law* under general equitable principles. Of course, it should not matter that the settlor appoints himself the first enforcer under the terms of his trust deed as the person best fitted for the enforcement task, with provision for subsequent enforcers.

7. PERPETUITY RULES

For a trust to be valid it must comply with a variety of rules known as the perpetuity rules. Failure to comply with these rules will render the trust void.[162] The essence of the perpetuity rules is to prevent property being tied up forever by one person, able to control the property for an unduly long period after his death. This fear of the power of the 'dead hand' has led to perpetuity rules, which insist that an interest must vest[163] in a party within a given period. As Simes wrote:[164]

The Rule against Perpetuities furthers alienability; if it were not for this Rule, property would be unproductive, and society would have less income.

Simes was of the view that it was necessarily desirable for property to be controlled by the living rather than the dead, since only the former could respond to changes in circumstances as they arose. Deech was also sympathetic to this rationale:[165]

The most convincing modern explanation of the functions of the Rule [against perpetuities] is the so-called Dead Hand Rationale. According to this doctrine, the Rule is necessary in order to strike a balance

---

[162] But see Jaconelli, 'Independent Schools, Purpose Trusts and Human Rights' [1996] Conv 24, 27–8 arguing that such trusts are voidable, i.e. they stand until they are terminated.

[163] An interest will be vested when it does not depend upon a prior condition being fulfilled: see Chapter 1.4(a)(iv), p. 13.

[164] Simes, *Public Policy and the Dead Hand* (Ann Arbor: University of Michigan Press, 1955) 36.

[165] Deech, 'Lives in Being Revived' (1981) 97 LQR 593, 594.

between on the one hand the freedom of the present generation and, on the other, that of future generations to deal as they wish with the property in which they have interests. If a settlor or testator had total liberty to dispose of his property among future beneficiaries, the recipients, being fettered by his wishes, would never enjoy that same freedom in their turn. The liberty to make fresh rearrangements of assets is necessary not only in order to be rid of irksome conditions attached by earlier donors to the enjoyment of income but also in order to be able to manoeuvre in the light of new tax laws, changes in the nature of the property and in the personal circumstances of the beneficiaries, unforeseeable by the best intentioned and most perspicacious of donors.

It is appropriate that a balance be struck between the interests of testators to dispose of their assets as they wish, and the public interest in not having property tied up and unable to be used in an economically advantageous fashion for excessive periods of time.

(a) THE RULE AGAINST REMOTENESS OF VESTING

The rule against remoteness of vesting is of broad scope:[166]

Perpetuities and Accumulations Act 2009

1 Application of the rule

(1) The rule against perpetuities applies (and applies only) as provided by this section.

(2) If an instrument limits property in trust so as to create successive estates or interests the rule applies to each of the estates or interests.

(3) If an instrument limits property in trust so as to create an estate or interest which is subject to a condition precedent and which is not one of successive estates or interests, the rule applies to the estate or interest.

(4) If an instrument limits property in trust so as to create an estate or interest subject to a condition subsequent the rule applies to—

    (a) any right of re-entry exercisable if the condition is broken, or

    (b) any equivalent right exercisable in the case of property other than land if the condition is broken.

(5) If an instrument which is a will limits personal property so as to create successive interests under the doctrine of executory bequests, the rule applies to each of the interests.

(6) If an instrument creates a power of appointment the rule applies to the power.

(7) For the purposes of subsection (2) an estate or interest includes an estate or interest—

    (a) which arises under a right of reverter on the determination of a determinable fee simple, or

    (b) which arises under a resulting trust on the determination of a determinable interest.

(8) This section has effect subject to the exceptions made by section 2 and to any exceptions made under section 3.

…

---

[166] Although in the United States of America there is a growing tendency to allow settlors to create family trusts which are perpetual: see Waggoner 'US Perpetual Trusts' (2011) 127 LQR 423.

Under section 3, exceptions may be specified by statutory instrument. Of more importance is section 2, which provides that charitable purpose trusts are exempt from the rule against perpetuities:

2 Exceptions to rule's application

(1) This section contains exceptions to the application of the rule against perpetuities.

(2) The rule does not apply to an estate or interest created so as to vest in a charity on the occurrence of an event if immediately before the occurrence an estate or interest in the property concerned is vested in another charity.

(3) The rule does not apply to a right exercisable by a charity on the occurrence of an event if immediately before the occurrence an estate or interest in the property concerned is vested in another charity.

(4) The rule does not apply to an interest or right arising under a relevant pension scheme.

(5) The exception in subsection (4) does not apply if the interest or right arises under—

    (a) an instrument nominating benefits under the scheme, or

    (b) an instrument made in the exercise of a power of advancement arising under the scheme.

However, the 2009 Act only applies to trusts taking effect, or wills executed, before 6 April 2010, so the previous rules remain of some relevance.[167] As a result, the length of the perpetuity period will depend upon when the trust was created. There are three possibilities: (i) the old Common Law regime; (ii) under the Perpetuities and Accumulation Act 1964; and now (iii) under the Perpetuities and Accumulation Act 2009. Both statutes apply prospectively only, so all three regimes remain relevant.

The perpetuity period at Common Law is assessed by reference to a relevant life in being plus 21 years. For example, if Alan's will creates successive interests, with a life interest for his daughter Brenda, then for her son Clive for life and remainder to Clive's first-born child, each interest will only be valid if it is vested in each person within the perpetuity period.[168] So, whilst the life interests of Brenda and Clive would clearly vest within the perpetuity period, if Clive had no children when Brenda died, the interest of any children he might later have would be void under the Common Law perpetuity rules, since that interest might not vest until more than 21 years after Brenda's death.

Legislation has now provided for the possibility of fixed perpetuity periods. Under the Perpetuities and Accumulation Act 1964, section 1, it became possible to specify that the perpetuity period would be no more than 80 years long. Under the Perpetuities and Accumulations Act 2009, section 5, this period has been extended to 125 years and has become mandatory.

Perpetuities and Accumulations Act 2009

5 Perpetuity period

(1) The perpetuity period is 125 years (and no other period).

(2) Subsection (1) applies whether or not the instrument referred to in section 1(2) to (6) specifies a perpetuity period; and a specification of a perpetuity period in that instrument is ineffective.

Whether the perpetuity period was satisfied was originally determined at Common Law at the time when the trust was created. This determination was definitive, and if it was possible that the

---

[167] Perpetuities and Accumulations Act 2009 (Commencement) Order 2010/37.
[168] Perpetuities and Accumulations Act 2009, s. 1(2).

property might vest outside the perpetuity period, the interest in that property would be void. Under the Perpetuities and Accumulations Act 2009 there is a 'wait and see' rule,[169] which applies where an interest would be void on the ground that property might not vest until after the perpetuity period has passed. In such circumstances, the interest in the trust property is not to be treated as void until it is clear that the property must vest, if at all, after the end of the perpetuity period. Everything done before this point remains valid. This principle of 'wait and see' is a sensible way to seek to give effect to the intentions of the settlor or testator, and avoids unduly harsh results where a gift is declared void, even though an interest might have vested well within the perpetuity period.

Perpetuities and Accumulations Act 2009

7 Wait and see rule

(1) Subsection (2) applies if (apart from this section and section 8) an estate or interest would be void on the ground that it might not become vested until too remote a time.

(2) In such a case—

    (a) until such time (if any) as it becomes established that the vesting must occur (if at all) after the end of the perpetuity period the estate or interest must be treated as if it were not subject to the rule against perpetuities, and

    (b) if it becomes so established, that does not affect the validity of anything previously done (whether by way of advancement, application of intermediate income or otherwise) in relation to the estate or interest.

(3) Subsection (4) applies if (apart from this section) any of the following would be void on the ground that it might be exercised at too remote a time—

    (a) a right of re-entry exercisable if a condition subsequent is broken;

    (b) an equivalent right exercisable in the case of property other than land if a condition subsequent is broken;

    (c) a special power of appointment.

(4) In such a case—

    (a) the right or power must be treated as regards any exercise of it within the perpetuity period as if it were not subject to the rule against perpetuities, and

    (b) the right or power must be treated as void for remoteness only if and so far as it is not fully exercised within the perpetuity period.

(5) Subsection (6) applies if (apart from this section) a general power of appointment would be void on the ground that it might not become exercisable until too remote a time.

(6) Until such time (if any) as it becomes established that the power will not be exercisable within the perpetuity period, it must be treated as if it were not subject to the rule against perpetuities.

Similarly, a power of appointment will not be treated as void until it is established that the power will not be exercised within the perpetuity period. If a gift is made in favour of a class of people, it might not be possible to ascertain all members of the class within the perpetuity period because, for example, some of the members of the class are unborn, such as where there is a trust for 'my children, grandchildren, and great-grandchildren'. In such a case, rather than treating the whole trust as void

---

[169] See similarly Perpetuities and Accumulations Act 1964, s. 3.

because part of the property might vest outside the perpetuity period, it is possible artificially to close the class so that those who are ascertainable within the perpetuity period will benefit from the trust. This is done by excluding from the class those whose interests might vest outside the perpetuity period, as long as their exclusion does not mean that there are no members of the class:

8 Exclusion of class members to avoid remoteness

(1) This section applies if—

    (a) it is apparent at the time an instrument takes effect or becomes apparent at a later time that (apart from this section) the inclusion of certain persons as members of a class would cause an estate or interest to be treated as void for remoteness, and

    (b) those persons are potential members of the class or unborn persons who at birth would become members or potential members of the class.

(2) From the time it is or becomes so apparent those persons must be treated for all the purposes of the instrument as excluded from the class unless their exclusion would exhaust the class.

(3) If this section applies in relation to an estate or interest to which section 7 applies, this section does not affect the validity of anything previously done (whether by way of advancement, application of intermediate income or otherwise) in relation to the estate or interest.

(4) For the purposes of this section—

    (a) a person is a member of a class if in that person's case all the conditions identifying a member of the class are satisfied, and

    (b) a person is a potential member of a class if in that person's case some only of those conditions are satisfied but there is a possibility that the remainder will in time be satisfied.

(b) RULE AGAINST INALIENABILITY

The rule against perpetuities may also affect the duration of a trust, since a trust will be void if, by its terms, the capital is required to be tied up for a time in excess of the perpetuity period.[170] This is known as the rule against excessive duration or the 'Rule against Inalienability'.[171] It is not applicable to trusts for charitable purposes; the community interest is that charitable trusts should last forever.[172] However, it does apply to non-charitable purpose trusts, although the statutory perpetuity period does not apply to such trusts and instead the Common Law perpetuity period will apply.[173]

Perpetuities and Accumulations Act 2009[174]

18 Rule as to duration not affected

This Act does not affect the rule of law which limits the duration of non-charitable purpose trusts.

---

[170] See *Re Lipinski's Will Trusts* [1976] Ch 235.
[171] Dawson, 'The Rule Against Inalienability—A Rule Without A Purpose' (2006) 26 LS 414 (I. Dawson).
[172] See Chapter 5, 'Charitable Purpose Trusts'.
[173] See further Chapter 5, 'Charitable Purpose Trusts'.
[174] See similarly Perpetuities and Accumulations Act 1964: s. 15(4).

QUESTION

Phil makes the following provisions in his will:

(i) £10,000 to my wife, Claire, to be distributed amongst my best friends and relatives at her discretion. Claire is able to determine conclusively who my best friends are.

(ii) 10 bottles of 1953 Château Pétrus claret to my son, Luke.

(iii) £5,000 to my wife, Claire, who is able, in her absolute discretion, to divide the fund amongst the people of Mansfield, my home town.

(iv) The bulk of my remaining estate to my brother, Ed.

(v) Whatever is left of my estate should be given to my surviving children equally.

There are 50 bottles of wine in Phil's cellar upon his death. The population of Mansfield is 100,000 inhabitants.

Are all the above gifts valid? Would your answer differ if Phil had made these gifts when he was alive, rather than in a will?

FURTHER READING

Conaglen, 'Sham Trusts' (2008) 67 CLJ 176.

Emery, 'The Most Hallowed Principle—Certainty of Beneficiaries of Trusts and Powers of Appointment' (1982) 98 LQR 551.

Gardner, 'Fiduciary Powers in Toytown' (1991) 107 LQR 214.

Goode, 'Are Intangible Assets Fungible?' (200)] LMCLQ 379.

Hayton, 'Uncertainty of Subject Matter of Trusts' (1994) 110 LQR 335.

Hayton, 'Developing the Obligation Characteristic of the Trust' (2001) 117 LQR 96.

Martin, 'Certainty of Subject-matter: A Defence of *Hunter v Moss*' [1996] Conv 223.

Matthews, 'The New Trust: Obligations Without Rights?' in Oakley, *Trends in Contemporary Trust Law* (Oxford: Oxford University Press, 1996).

McKay, '*Re Baden* and the Third Class of Uncertainty' [1974] Conv 269.

Parkinson, 'Reconceptualising the Express Trust' (2002) 61 CLJ 657.

Worthington, 'Sorting Out Ownership Interests in Bulk: Gifts, Sales and Trusts' (1999) JBL 1.

4

CREATION OF EXPRESS TRUSTS

CENTRAL ISSUES

1. Certain formality requirements must be met for the creation of express trusts. For example, a declaration of an express trust over land requires signed writing.

2. Equity will not allow a statute to be used as an instrument of fraud. As a result, a person may not deny the existence of a trust by relying upon another's lack of compliance with the requisite formalities if that would allow a fraud to be perpetrated on the settlor or beneficiary.

3. Trusts created by a will also need to satisfy formality requirements. These requirements can be modified in certain circumstances, such as by the incorporation of other documents.

4. A testator might wish to create a testamentary trust without disclosing the identity of the beneficiaries. This can be done by declaring a trust and stating in the will that the identity of the beneficiaries has already been disclosed to the trustee. This is called a half-secret trust.

5. Alternatively, the testator may leave property to a legatee apparently absolutely, but the testator will have previously requested the legatee to hold the property on trust. This is called a fully secret trust.

6. Neither half-secret nor fully secret trusts will comply with statutory formality requirements but, subject to the fulfilment of certain conditions, they will be regarded as valid to ensure that the statutory formalities are not used as an instrument of fraud.

7. A trust must be constituted by title to the trust property being vested in the trustee. A trust can be constituted in two ways: by declaration of oneself as a trustee or by transfer of property to trustees. These two methods of constitution are mutually exclusive.

8. For the effective transfer of legal title to property, compliance with any relevant formalities required at law is necessary. But even if all the requirements for the transfer of legal title are not fulfilled, the person to whom the property is intended to be transferred may obtain an equitable proprietary interest if the transferor has done everything in his or her power to effect the transfer. Such an equitable interest may even arise earlier, if at that point it would be unconscionable for the donor to pull out of the transfer.

1. INTRODUCTION

In Chapter 3 we considered the requirements for an express trust to be valid. In this chapter we are concerned with the formalities relating to the creation of trusts. In order to create an express trust two distinct formality issues need to be considered. The first relates to the formalities for the declaration of trusts. The second concerns the formalities for the constitution of trusts, by which property is vested in trustees.

2. FORMALITIES FOR THE DECLARATION OF TRUSTS

(a) FUNCTION OF FORMALITIES

Fuller has identified three crucial purposes served by formality rules.

Fuller, 'Consideration and Form' (1941) 41 Columbia Law Review 799, 800–4

§ 2. *The Evidentiary Function.*-The most obvious function of a legal formality is, to use Austin's words, that of providing 'evidence of the existence and purport of the contract, in case of controversy.' The need for evidentiary security may be satisfied in a variety of ways: by requiring a writing, or attestation, or the certification of a notary....

§ 3. *The Cautionary Function.*-A formality may also perform a cautionary or deterrent function by acting as a check against inconsiderate action. The seal in its original form fulfilled this purpose remarkably well. The affixing and impressing of a wax wafer-symbol in the popular mind of legalism and weightiness was an excellent device for inducing the circumspective frame of mind appropriate in one pledging his future. To a less extent any requirement of a writing, of course, serves the same purpose, as do requirements of attestation, notarization, etc.

§ 4. *The Channeling Function.*-Though most discussions of the purposes served by formalities go no further than the analysis just presented, this analysis stops short of recognizing one of the most important functions of form. That a legal formality may perform a function not yet described can be shown by the seal. The seal not only insures a satisfactory memorial of the promise and induces deliberation in the making of it. It serves also to mark or signalize the enforceable promise; it furnishes a simple and external test of enforceability. This function of form Ihering described as 'the facilitation of judicial diagnosis,'... The thing which characterizes the law of contracts and conveyances is that in this field forms are deliberately used, and are intended to be so used, by the parties whose acts are to be judged by the law. To the business man who wishes to make his own or another's promise binding, the seal was at common law available as a device for the accomplishment of his objective. In this aspect form offers a legal framework into which the party may fit his actions, or, to change the figure, it offers channels for the legally effective expression of intention. It is with this aspect of form in mind that I have described the third function of legal formalities as 'the channeling function.'...

§ 5. *Interrelations of the Three Functions.*-Though I have stated the three functions of legal form separately, it is obvious that there is an intimate connection between them. Generally speaking, whatever tends to accomplish one of these purposes will also tend to accomplish the other two....

Just as channeling may result unintentionally from formalities directed toward other ends, so these other ends tend to be satisfied by any device which accomplishes a channeling of expression. There is an evidentiary value in the clarity and definiteness of contour which such a device accomplishes. Anything which effects a neat division between the legal and the non-legal, or between different kinds

> of legal transactions, will tend also to make apparent to the party the consequences of his action and will suggest deliberation where deliberation is needed.

Fuller is here primarily concerned with consideration in contract law, but his analysis of formalities extends beyond that context and is important for trusts. It explains why we insist upon certain formal requirements before holding a trust to be valid. These formalities make it easier for the court to establish, on the evidence, that a trust was created (the evidentiary function). They also tend to ensure that the settlor has thought carefully about the consequences of his or her actions (the cautionary function). Formalities also help to ensure that the trusts created are easily recognizable as trusts, within acceptable parameters, and may be dealt with routinely (the channelling function).

Thus, there are good reasons for formality rules being in place. It should, however, be recognized that a strict insistence upon formalities will inevitably mean that the intention of the settlor is frustrated in some instances. There is, therefore, a tension between giving effect to the clear and unambiguous intention of the settlor and ensuring compliance with the relevant formalities. This tension has produced some difficult cases, which will be examined in this chapter.

It is helpful to consider the formalities relating to *inter vivos* trusts and testamentary trusts separately. This is because the Wills Act 1837 applies only to the latter and has an important impact upon the formality requirements necessary for a valid trust.

(b) *INTER VIVOS* DECLARATION OF TRUSTS

Writing is not required for trusts of pure personalty.[1] Trusts of land or interests in land must, however, be evidenced by writing. The crucial provision is section 53 of the Law of Property Act 1925.

LAW OF PROPERTY ACT 1925

s. 53 Instruments required to be in writing

(1) Subject to the provision hereinafter contained with respect to the creation of interests in land by parol—

    (a) no interest in land can be created or disposed of except by writing signed by the person creating or conveying the same, or by his agent thereunto lawfully authorised in writing, or by will, or by operation of law;

    (b) a declaration of trust respecting any land or any interest therein must be manifested and proved by some writing signed by some person who is able to declare such trust or by his will;

    (c) a disposition of an equitable interest or trust subsisting at the time of the disposition, must be in writing signed by the person disposing of the same, or by his agent thereunto lawfully authorised in writing or by will.

(2) This section does not affect the creation or operation of resulting, implied or constructive trusts.

This provision is of the utmost importance but not easy to interpret. Some initial points regarding its scope are, therefore, worth emphasizing.

---

[1] E.g. *Paul v Constance* [1977] 1 WLR 527.

First, it must be appreciated that section 53(1)(c) is relevant to the disposition of equitable interests that are *already existing* at the time of the disposition. This is considered in Chapter 10. In this chapter, the focus is upon the *creation* of a trust, and we are only concerned with the formality requirements relating to the creation of an *express* trust. Section 53(2) makes it clear that section 53(1) does not apply to resulting, implied, or constructive trusts.

Within section 53(1), there is, potentially, some overlap between paragraphs (a) and (b). Paragraph (a) concerns the creation of an interest in land, whereas paragraph (b) concerns the declaration of a trust respecting land. The two are not mutually exclusive: the absolute legal owner of land might declare himself to be holding the property on trust for his children. In such an event, should paragraph (a) or (b) apply? The answer is not obvious, but it is suggested that, if paragraph (b) is to have any scope of its own, then it should apply to such situations.

Choosing between paragraphs (a) and (b) has potentially significant consequences. Before considering the *effect* of non-compliance, it is helpful to think about what the writing requirement for a trust over land actually entails. Paragraphs (a) and (c) explicitly contemplate the formality being satisfied by an agent, but not (b). This might suggest that an agent cannot satisfy the requirement of writing in paragraph (b)—otherwise, as in (a) and (c), 'agent' would have been specifically mentioned. However, paragraph (b) does provide that the signed writing may come from 'some person who is able to declare such trust', and this may include an agent. This would be a sensible, practical interpretation; indeed, it has been held that this requirement of writing in paragraph (b) might be fulfilled by the trustee who is to hold the property on trust.[2] The written document used to 'manifest and prove' the existence of a trust in accordance with paragraph (b) can be provided after the time at which the trust was declared.[3]

Failure to comply with paragraph (a) means that no interest in land could have been created or disposed. However, failure to comply with paragraph (b) does not mean that there was no trust, only that it is unenforceable.[4] Thus, if A declares himself to be holding land on trust for B, but there is no signed writing to prove this, then B cannot enforce the trust. In such a scenario, the result is relatively straightforward: A remains absolutely entitled to the property.

It is much more difficult where the settlor no longer has legal title to the property because the property has been transferred to B, on the understanding that B was to hold the property on trust. If it has been intended by the settlor that B hold on trust, and B knows that this was the intention, then it would be unconscionable for B to rely upon his having legal title to claim beneficial ownership of the property just because the trust cannot be proved by signed writing. This is because a statute[5] cannot be used as an instrument of fraud. By relying upon the absence of writing to assert absolute ownership, B would be committing a fraud, and the law simply will not allow this. B must be holding the property on trust. In *Bannister v Bannister*, the Court of Appeal considered that B would be holding the property on a constructive trust, since it would be unconscionable for B to deny that he was holding the property on trust.[6]

Bannister v Bannister [1948] 2 All ER 133, CA

A widow agreed to sell a cottage to her brother-in-law, on the understanding that she could live in the property as long as she liked without paying rent. The brother-in-law reneged on the agreement and later sought to evict the widow. The court held that he could not rely upon the lack

---

[2] *Gardner v Rowe* [1828] 5 Russ. 258, 38 ER 1024.
[3] *Gardner v Rowe* [1828] 5 Russ. 258, 38 ER 1024; *Rochefoucauld v Boustead* [1897] 1 Ch 196.
[4] *Gardner v Rowe* [1828] 5 Russ. 258, 38 ER 1024.
[5] Of particular relevance here is the Law of Property Act 1925, previously the Statute of Frauds 1677.
[6] See Chapter 7, 'Constructive Trusts'.

of signed writing fraudulently to deny that he was holding the property on trust for the widow for life.

Scott LJ:

It is, we think, clearly a mistake to suppose that the equitable principle on which a constructive trust is raised against a person who insists on the absolute character of a conveyance to himself for the purpose of defeating a beneficial interest, which, according to the true bargain, was to belong to another, is confined to cases in which the conveyance itself was fraudulently obtained. The fraud which brings the principle into play arises as soon as the absolute character of the conveyance is set up for the purpose of defeating the beneficial interest, and that is the fraud to cover which the Statute of Frauds or the corresponding provisions of the Law of Property Act, 1925, cannot be called in aid in cases in which no written evidence of the real bargain is available. Nor is it, in our opinion, necessary that the bargain on which the absolute conveyance is made should include any express stipulation that the grantee is in so many words to hold as trustee. It is enough that the bargain should have included a stipulation under which some sufficiently defined beneficial interest in the property was to be taken by another. The above propositions are, we think, clearly borne out by the cases to which we were referred of [various cases including] *Rochefoucauld v Boustead*.[7] We see no distinction in principle between a case in which property is conveyed to a purchaser on terms that the entire beneficial interest in some part of it is to be retained by the vendor (as in *Booth v Turle*[8]) and a case, like the present, in which property is conveyed to a purchaser on terms that a limited beneficial interest in some part of it is to be retained by the vendor.

In *Bannister*, Scott LJ held that the relevant trust was constructive: it would be unconscionable for the brother-in-law to deny that he was holding the property on trust for the widow for the duration of her life, so the law should impose a constructive trust. However, this analysis is not universally accepted. Indeed, the Court of Appeal referred to *Rochefoucauld v Boustead*, but in that case the court insisted that, despite the lack of formalities, the settlor could still rely upon an *express* trust.

Rochefoucauld v Boustead [1897] 1 Ch 196

The claimant owned coffee plantations in Ceylon which were the subject of a mortgage. The mortgagee sold the property to the defendant, who had previously agreed to hold the property on trust for the claimant. There was no signed writing to prove the existence of a trust, which was required under the Statute of Frauds 1677 (now replaced by section 53 of the Law of Property Act 1925). Lindley LJ said:[9]

[It is] necessary to consider whether the Statute of Frauds affords a defence to the plaintiff's claim.... [I]t is necessary to prove by some writing or writings signed by the defendant, not only that the conveyance to him was subject to some trust, but also what that trust was. But it is not necessary that the trust should have been declared by such a writing in the first instance; it is sufficient if the trust can be proved by some writing signed by the defendant, and the date of the writing is immaterial. It is further established by a series of cases, the propriety of which cannot now be questioned, that the Statute of Frauds does not prevent the proof of a fraud; and that it is a fraud on the part of a person to whom

---

[7] See discussion immediately below.

[8] (1873), LR 16 Eq 182, 37 JP 710.

[9] [1897] 1 Ch 196, 205–8.

land is conveyed as a trustee, and who knows it was so conveyed, to deny the trust and claim the land himself. Consequently, notwithstanding the statute, it is competent for a person claiming land conveyed to another to prove by parol evidence that it was so conveyed upon trust for the claimant, and that the grantee, knowing the facts, is denying the trust and relying upon the form of conveyance and the statute, in order to keep the land himself.

...

The trust which the plaintiff has established is clearly an express trust within the meaning of that expression as explained in *Soar v. Ashwell* [1893] 2 QB 390. The trust is one which both plaintiff and defendant intended to create. This case is not one in which an equitable obligation arises although there may have been no intention to create a trust. The intention to create a trust existed from the first.

The Court in *Rochefoucauld* thought that the trust which arose was express. The nature of the trust was important because the defendant sought to rely upon a limitation period, which would only have assisted his defence if the trust were constructive rather than express. Swadling has strongly defended this result.

Swadling, 'The nature of the trust in *Rochefoucauld v Boustead*' in *Constructive and Resulting Trusts* (ed. Mitchell) (Oxford: Hart, 2010) p. 113

[S]ection 7 of the Statute of Frauds 1677[10] is potentially in play, but ... this was a rule of evidence which the court disapplied on perfectly orthodox and long-settled grounds. That in turn meant there was no barrier to the admission of the claimant's oral testimony to prove a declaration of trust by the defendant in her favour, and an ordering of accounts on the basis of the declared trust. That the trust was express can be tested in another way. Assume the legislature repealed section 7/section 53(1)(b). Were the facts of *Rochefoucauld* to recur, there could be no argument but that the trust was express. What in fact happened is that the Court of Appeal in *Rochefoucauld* did effectively repeal the statute, at least so far as the claimant was concerned, with the result that the trust there could likewise only be express.

The arguments that the trust was constructive either ignore the reasoning of the court altogether or mistake the nature of section 7 or both. ... When properly analysed, the only possible categorization of the *Rochefoucauld* trust which accords with both the *ratio* of the case and the wording of section 7 of the Statute of Frauds 1677 is that the trust enforced in the case was an express trust.

Swadling's analysis is forceful and persuasive; he dismisses the suggestion, often made,[11] that the importance of the limitation period distorted *Rochefoucauld*. Nevertheless, *Rochefoucauld* has regularly been explained as concerning a constructive trust, and the approach in *Bannister* has been followed.[12]

In a simple two-party case such as *Bannister*, where there are no problems concerning limitation, it does not make much difference whether the trust is described as constructive or express. Indeed, a resulting trust[13]—which arises to fill the gap caused by the failure of an express trust—would have led to the same result on the facts. But choosing which type of trust arises where the formality requirement is not satisfied is of particular importance where A transfers property to B to hold on trust for C.

---

[10] The forerunner of section 53 of the Law of Property Act 1925.

[11] E.g. TG Youdan, 'Formalities for Trusts of Land, and the Doctrine in *Rochefoucauld v Boustead*' (1984) 43 CLJ 306, 331.

[12] E.g. *Binions v Evans* [1972] Ch 359.

[13] See Chapter 8.3, p. 384.

In such three-party scenarios, a resulting trust would mean that B would be holding the property on trust for A, whereas identification of an express trust or, possibly, a constructive trust would mean that B would be holding the property on trust for C. These issues have been well canvassed by Youdan, who ultimately favoured an analysis based upon constructive trust.

Youdan, 'Formalities for Trusts of Land, and the Doctrine in *Rochefoucauld v Boustead*' (1984) 43 CLJ 306, 334

A view about the nature of the trust enforced may suggest important consequences. The most obvious whose outcome may be so affected is where A conveys property to B on the terms of an oral trust for C. If the view is taken that the trust enforced is the express trust created by the parties then it seems to follow that C can take the benefit of the *Rochefoucauld* doctrine and enforce the trust. If the trust enforced is a constructive trust the conclusion is less obvious. It might be argued that the constructive trust should be used only to effect restitution of the property back to where it came from. The remedy of constructive trust is, however, sufficiently malleable that its adoption in the present context should not foreclose debate about whether the benefit of it is taken by A or C.

Youdan ultimately reached the conclusion that if a constructive trust arises, it operates in favour of C. B may not in good conscience deny that he or she should be holding the property on trust for C. This sort of trust is not incompatible with section 53, since section 53(2) states that the formality requirements do not affect the creation or operation of constructive trusts.

Youdan, 'Formalities for Trusts of Land, and the Doctrine in *Rochefoucauld v Boustead*' (1984) 43 CLJ 306, 335–6

I suggest, however, that the third party beneficiary should be entitled to enforce the trust—whether or not the settlor is dead—under the *Rochefoucauld* doctrine as well as in secret trusts. As I already mentioned, it seems to be established that an oral trust of land is valid despite non-compliance with section 7; it is merely unenforceable. Consequently, where A conveys land to B on an oral trust for C, A has ordinarily no right to restitution since B is holding the property on a valid trust for C, and he may carry out that trust if he chooses to do so. The problem arises where B refuses to carry out the trust; the question then is whether A or C can claim the benefit of the *Rochefoucauld* doctrine. The claim of C is, I suggest, stronger for three main, related, reasons. First, it seems inappropriate that B, the trustee, should have the power to determine whether C or A should get the benefit of the property. Secondly, A has effectively divested himself of the property. It is he who is seeking equity to obtain the return of property he has given away on a valid trust. Thirdly, the allowance of C's claim is not contrary to the purpose of the formality requirement. If A had simply conveyed the land to B as a gift for B he obviously could not recover it since he effectively divested himself, the presumption of resulting trust (even assuming there was one) could be rebutted by evidence of the gift, and section 7 of the Statute of Frauds would have no application to such a case. There is no reason why A should be in a stronger position merely because the beneficial gift was to C with the interposition of B's trusteeship.

However, the objection has been raised that such a constructive trust has exactly the same effect as the express trust that fell foul of section 53(1)(b). Scott has preferred to argue that B should be holding the property on trust for A. After all, if neither the settlor nor the trustee is willing to provide signed writing, perhaps the beneficial interest should not be held by C.

Scott, 'Conveyances upon Trusts Not Properly Declared' (1924) 37 Harvard L Rev 653, 666–7

To the writer it would seem that [a trust in favour of C] can be reached only by a violation of the Statute of Frauds. When the land was conveyed by A to B, C acquired no enforceable right under the oral trust or contract; and it seems unsound to say that the refusal to perform an obligation, which because of the Statute of Frauds cannot be enforced, creates any enforceable right in C. It seems strange to hold that although the making of a promise gives no enforceable right to C, the breaking of the promise should give such a right. So to hold would seem to violate the purpose of the Statute.

...

Since B would be unjustly enriched if he were allowed to keep the property, but since that enrichment is not at the expense of C but of A, B should be compelled to return the property to A, and in the meantime should be held as constructive trustee for A. The policy of the Statute of Frauds, which does indeed forbid going forward, with the transaction, does not forbid going backward and putting the parties *in statu quo*. In this class of cases, unlike the cases of a transfer upon an oral trust or contract for the transferor, the result of imposing a constructive trust for the transferor is entirely different from enforcing the oral trust or contract.

Scott's use of unjust enrichment here might be criticized,[14] but his use of a constructive trust in favour of A provides the same result as finding a resulting trust arising upon the failure of an express trust in favour of A.

If an analogy is made with secret trusts,[15] then Youdan's analysis should be preferred. It would be unconscionable for B to deny that he is holding the property on trust for C. Such a constructive trust provides the same outcome as would be reached if the B–C trust is considered to be an express trust, as in *Rochefoucauld*. Even though later decisions seem to have largely considered the trust to be constructive, an analysis based upon the B–C trust being an express trust seems most consistent with *Rochefoucauld* itself. This may be particularly appropriate since it appears that B is able to provide the signed writing necessary to fulfil the requirement of section 53(1)(b), even after he acquires legal title.[16]

(c) BY WILL

(i) *Formalities for testamentary dispositions*

Where a testator intends to create a trust in a will, the formality requirements under the Wills Act 1837 need to be satisfied.

WILLS ACT 1837

9. Signing and attestation of wills

No will shall be valid unless—

(a) it is in writing, and signed by the testator, or by some other person in his presence and by his direction; and

(b) it appears that the testator intended by his signature to give effect to the will; and

---

[14] See Chapter 1.4(b), pp. 13–15.
[15] Considered in Chapter 4.2(c)(iii), pp. 127–45.
[16] *Gardner v Rose* [1828] 5 Russ 258, 38 ER 1024; *Rochefoucauld v Bonstead* [1897] 1 Ch 196.

(c) the signature is made or acknowledged by the testator in the presence of two or more witnesses present at the same time; and

(d) each witness either—

   (i) attests and signs the will; or

   (ii) acknowledges his signature, in the presence of the testator (but not necessarily in the presence of any other witness),

but no form of attestation shall be necessary.

If any of these requirements is not satisfied the will is invalid and any testamentary trust will be void too. It is important that strict formalities must be satisfied before a will can be considered to be valid. If a problem should arise, the testator is no longer available to explain his or her intention. Also the imposition of certain formalities reduces the chance of mistake, fraud, and undue influence as well as ill-considered and hasty dispositions.

A further function of the formalities under the Wills Act is to ensure that the testator does not reserve for him or herself a power to dispose of property by a future document that fails to comply with the statutory formality safeguards. It was for this reason that a gift in a will in *Re Jones*,[17] that purported to reserve to the testator the power to alter the settlement in the future, was held not to be valid.

(ii) *Modification of formality requirements*

Various mechanisms have been developed by Equity to ensure that the strict formality rules for wills do not unnecessarily frustrate the testator's intent. So, for example, informal documents can be incorporated into a will, provided that they are expressly identified by the will and existed when the will was executed. This is called the 'doctrine of incorporation by reference'. The operation of this doctrine is illustrated by *In the Goods of Smart*.[18] The testatrix's will directed that her trustees should give to her friends certain articles which would be specified in a book which was to be found with her will. Since the book was not prepared until three or four years after the testatrix made her will, the book was a future document and could not be incorporated into the will. Gorell Barnes J said:[19]

> It seems to me that it has been established that if a testator, in a testamentary paper duly executed, refers to an existing unattested testamentary paper, the instrument so referred to becomes part of his will; in other words, it is incorporated into it; but it is clear that, in order that the informal document should be incorporated in the validly executed document, the latter must refer to the former as a written instrument then existing—that is, at the time of execution—in such terms that it may be ascertained.

Informal documents can, nevertheless, be incorporated into the will after it has been executed if the reference to these documents in the will is confirmed by another formal document, known as a 'codicil', which refers to the same documents. This was also recognized by Gorell Barnes J in *In the Goods of Smart*:[20]

> If the document is not existing at the time of the will, but comes into existence afterwards, and then, after that again, there is a codicil confirming the will, the question arises, as it has done in a number of

---

[17] [1942] Ch 328.
[18] [1902] P 238.
[19] Ibid, 240.
[20] Ibid, 241.

these cases, whether that document is incorporated. It appears to me that, following out the principle which I have already referred to, the will may be treated, by the confirmation given by the codicil, as executed again, and as speaking from the date of the codicil, and if the informal document is existing then, and is referred to in the will as existing, so as to identify it, there will be incorporation; but if the will, treated as being re-executed at the date of the codicil, still speaks in terms which shew that it is referring to a future document, then it appears to me there is no incorporation.

Another device with which to fulfil the testator's intent arises where property is left in a will to people who are to be identified subsequently, in which case the validity of the bequest may be upheld if the identification of the legatees is made by reference to so-called facts of 'independent legal significance', which are not dependent on the testator's subsequent decision. It does not then matter that the identification of the legatees is made subsequently to the making of the will and outside of the will. So, for example, if a father states in his will that he will leave his property to whichever of his two sons does not obtain property from a third party, the decision of the third party will determine who will benefit under the father's will. This is valid because it is determined by reference to a decision that is both verifiable and independent of the testator. In *Stubbs v Sargon*,[21] it was held that a bequest to trustees to divide property amongst the testatrix's partners at the time of her death was valid, because it was possible to ascertain who the partners were. Lord Langdale MR said:[22]

[It is objected] that it is imperfect, as not designating the devisees, and leaving them to be constituted afterwards by some act of the testatrix herself, requiring none of the solemnities rendered necessary by the Statute of Frauds. The devisees, according to the words, were to be the partners of the testatrix at the time of her decease, or the persons to whom she might have disposed of her business; and as persons might be such partners or disponees by acts of the testatrix, done without formality, it was argued that the devise was void. I think that this objection cannot be sustained; a man, though not married when he makes his will, may devise to such persons as shall be his children at the time of his death. And if the description be such as to distinguish the devisee from every other person, it seems sufficient without entering into the consideration of the question, whether the description was acquired by the devisee after the date of the will, or by the testator's own act in the ordinary course of his affairs, or in the management of his property, and I think that a devise to such person as may be the testator's partners or the disponees of his business may be good.

(iii) *Secret trusts*

Failure to comply with the testamentary formalities may be intended by the testator, and this raises distinct and complex problems for Equity. There might be particular reasons why a testator does not want it to be generally known who is to benefit under his or her will. The testator might, therefore, decide to leave property to a named person in a will, but only in the expectation that the property will be used for the benefit of these unnamed people. This may occur in two different ways. First, the testator may state in the will that property is to be held on trust by a named legatee for the benefit of people whose names are to be communicated separately. This is known as a 'half-secret trust'. In this case, it is clear from the will that the trustee is receiving property as a trustee and not beneficially, so the opportunity to act contrary to the testator's intent is reduced because the legatee cannot fraudulently take the property for him or herself. But is such a trust valid, when the name of the beneficiary is not

---

[21] (1837) 2 Keen 255.
[22] Ibid, 269.

disclosed on the face of the will? This certainly appears to be contrary to the Wills Act 1837, since this involves a disposition of property to take effect after the testator's death where significant terms of the trust have not been incorporated in the will.

The other scenario is known as a 'fully secret trust'. Here, the will purports to leave property to a named person absolutely, but the testator actually intends the legatee to hold the property on trust for the benefit of another, and this intention will have been communicated to the legatee separately.[23] In this situation, there is much greater scope for the testator's intention to be defeated because, according to the will, the legatee is to have the property absolutely and there is nothing to indicate a trust. But, if the legatee, being aware of the testator's intention, seeks to rely on his or her legal rights to the property under the will, he or she would be seeking to use the formality requirements of the Wills Act as an instrument with which to perpetrate fraud. There would appear, therefore, to be a strong case for equitable intervention in such circumstances.

Since half-secret and fully secret trusts raise distinct issues, it is appropriate to consider them separately. But there are certain general principles relating to all secret trusts that need to be considered first.

(a) General principles relating to secret trusts

The key controversy involving secret trusts relates to whether their recognition is compatible with the Wills Act 1837. In both cases, property is to be disposed after the testator's death according to terms that are not declared in the will, which is contrary to the strict formality requirements of that Act.

The recognition of secret trusts has sometimes been justified on the basis that the legatee, who receives property under the will knowing that the testator intended him or her to hold it on trust for somebody else, cannot then rely on the formality requirements of the Wills Act to invalidate the trust, since this would involve the use of that statute as an instrument of fraud. Such trusts are commonly treated as testamentary trusts, which are recognized despite the failure to comply with the formalities of the Wills Act. The preferable view, however, is that both fully secret and half-secret trusts are valid not as exceptions to the formality requirements under the Wills Act, but because they operate outside the will and are, therefore, not caught by those requirements. This is known as the 'dehors (or outside) the will' theory. Secret trusts are properly analysed as express trusts that are validly declared during the testator's lifetime,[24] following communication by the testator and acceptance by the trustee. These trusts arise independently of the will by reason of the personal obligation that has been accepted by the legatee. Although these trusts are not constituted until the subject matter of the trust is vested in the trustee by the executor following the testator's death, it does not follow that they are testamentary trusts, because they have already been created *inter vivos*; it is only the constitution that occurs after the testator's death and this constitution of the trust happens automatically once property has been transferred by the executors to the trustee. This has been recognized by Rickett:[25]

> the Court looks for the expression of the trusteeship by the testatrix, and the acceptance of the trusteeship by the devisee. The trust obligation is owed to the beneficiaries once the trust is duly constituted by the (testamentary) transfer of property to the trustee (devisee)....The secret trust is express; where necessary it must satisfy the formal requirements (meaning that a fully secret trust of land will be caught by the relevant statutory provision); and the matter of constructiveness of any trust is a red herring. A restitutionary approach is not necessary. This is a case of an express trust in a particular

---

[23] See, for example, *Re Freud (deceased)* [2014] EWHC 2577 (Ch); [2014] WTLR 1453.
[24] Oakley, *Constructive Trusts* (3rd edn) (London: Sweet and Maxwell, 1996), p. 262.
[25] 'Thoughts on Secret Trusts from New Zealand' [1996] Conv 302, 306.

factual context.... Of course, the court is tolerating a devolution of the beneficial (equitable) ownership of property on death outside the form 'required' by the statute, but where the factual context demands it the court must so act. The context making the demand is the declaration of a trust independently of the will, but intimately involved with the will in that the latter is the chosen technique for vesting in the trustee the ownership of the trust property... In fact, the will *is* recognised in so far as the devisee acquires legal title by virtue of its operation.

The 'dehors the will' theory of secret trusts was recognized by Sir Robert Megarry V-C in *Re Snowden*:[26]

the whole basis of secret trusts... is that they operate outside the will, changing nothing that is written in it, and allowing it to operate according to its tenor, but then fastening a trust on to the property in the hands of the recipient.

The 'dehors the will' theory is not, however, a perfect explanation of the secret trust. The fact that the trust is declared whilst the testator is still alive, but is constituted only following the testator's death, means that Equity allows the trust to bind property in the testator's estate that may have been acquired after the trust had been declared. This contravenes the usual rule that it is not possible to declare an immediate trust of future property,[27] although this might instead be treated as a trust of the testator's promise to leave future-acquired property to the trustee rather than a trust of the property itself.[28]

Analysing both fully secret and half-secret trusts as express trusts that are created *inter vivos* and not by the will is important when considering how both types of trust are created and operate. Certain key principles can be identified:

(1) The formality requirements of the Wills Act 1837 are not relevant to the recognition of secret trusts. For example, in *Re Young*,[29] a testator made a bequest to his wife and imposed a condition that she should make certain bequests that he had previously communicated to her, including a gift of £2,000 to his chauffeur, Mr Cobb. The chauffeur had witnessed the will, which meant that he could not receive a legacy under it.[30] It was held, however, that the chauffeur was still entitled to the gift, because it arose from an oral trust declared by the testator and was not a bequest under the will. The testamentary formalities were therefore irrelevant to the trust. Danckwerts J said:[31]

The whole theory of the formation of a secret trust is that the Wills Act has nothing to do with the matter because the forms required by the Wills Act are entirely disregarded, since the persons do not take by virtue of the gift in the will, but by virtue of the secret trusts imposed upon the beneficiary, who does in fact take under the will... [E]very consideration connected with this principle requires me to reach the conclusion that a beneficiary under a secret trust does not take under the will...

(2) Since secret trusts are not constituted until after the testator's death, the terms of the trust can be changed by the testator, for example by the will being revoked or altered, or by the property being disposed of in some other way.

---

[26] [1979] Ch 528, 535.
[27] *Re Ellenborough* [1903] 1 Ch 697.
[28] See further Chapter 4.3(e), pp. 167–8.
[29] [1951] Ch 344.
[30] Wills Act 1837, s. 15. Now see the Wills Act 1968, which allows a witness to a will to take under it if the will would have been valid without the particular witness's attestation.
[31] [1951] Ch 344, 350.

Kincaid, 'The tangled web: the relationship between a secret trust and the will'
[2000] Conv 420, 426

It would therefore appear that the trust is not completely constituted at the time of the acceptance by the secret trustee. It does not become constituted and therefore irrevocable until it crystallises on the death of the secret settlor. Thus a secret settlor may revoke the will at any time until death.

What of the revocation not of the will nor the legacy to the secret trustee but of the secret trust itself? It is generally assumed that a secret trust created by will can be revoked as can any other provision of the will....it would appear that because the trust is not constituted until the death of the settlor, the settlor can revoke a secret trust, either by revoking the will (or the legacy) altogether, or by revoking the secret trust aspect of the legacy...it appears that a secret trust is not sufficiently constituted to stand on its own and thus be irrevocable; it requires the death of the secret settlor to crystallise the trust and enable the transfer of the property to the trustee.

Another possible argument is that, unlike other trusts, revocability can be implied into a secret trust because of the secret trust's intimate connection with the epitome of revocable instruments, the will.

It might, however, be possible to invoke the doctrine of proprietary estoppel to invalidate any attempt to revoke the trust or to change its terms.[32] This will apply where the testator has made a clear representation about the validity of the trust, followed by detrimental reliance on the part of the beneficiary.[33]

(3) If the trustee were to die before the testator, it is matter of some uncertainty as to whether this would invalidate the trust. As regards half-secret trusts, it might be argued that the death of the trustee should not invalidate the trust because of the maxim that a trust will not be allowed to fail for want of a trustee,[34] unless the identity of the trustee is especially significant. This maxim would be relevant to half-secret trusts, because the existence of the trust is clear on the face of the will. As regards fully secret trusts, it has been recognized that the death of the trustee before the testator would invalidate the trust.[35] But there is no reason why the maxim that a trust should not be allowed to fail for want of a trustee should not be extended to fully secret trusts as well, since the testator will have relied on the legatee to hold the property on trust after the testator's death.[36] Of course, where the trustee has died before the testator, the testator will usually have the opportunity to appoint another trustee.

(4) The trustee is free to revoke his or her acceptance of the trust before the testator's death, so that the trustee will no longer be bound by his or her undertaking to hold the property on trust. Again, the testator will have the opportunity to appoint a new trustee, but if there were not sufficient time to do so before the testator's death, it would be appropriate for the court to appoint a new trustee.[37] If a trustee seeks to renounce the trust after the testator's death, this will be too late and the trustee will be bound by the trust until a replacement trustee can be appointed.[38]

(5) What should happen where the beneficiary of the trust dies before the testator? In *Re Gardner (No. 2)*,[39] it was held that the personal representatives of the deceased beneficiary could claim his or

---

[32] Pawlowski and Brown, 'Constituting a Secret Trust by Estoppel' [2004] Conv 388.

[33] See further Chapter 9.4, p. 469.

[34] For the view that a half-secret trust would also fail, see Wilde, 'Secret and Semi-secret Trusts: Justifying Distinctions Between the Two' [1995] Conv 366, 373.

[35] *Re Maddock* [1902] 2 Ch 220, 231 (Cozens-Hardy LJ).

[36] Kincaid [2000] Conv 420, 440.

[37] Ibid, at 441.

[38] See further Chapter 11.4, p. 548.

[39] [1923] 2 Ch 230.

her share of the estate. But, usually, where a legatee dies before the testator and the legatee has not acquired a prior interest in the property, the gift simply lapses, and the property passes to the residuary beneficiary under the will. The putative beneficiary under a secret trust does not have any already-acquired interest, because the trust will not be constituted until after the testator's death, when legal title is vested in the trustee. *Re Gardner (No. 2)* should consequently be regarded as wrongly decided. The lapsed gift should instead have been held by the trustee on resulting trust for those entitled to the residuary estate of the testator.

(6) If secret trusts are properly characterized as express trusts, the declaration of the trust must be evidenced by signed writing where the subject matter of the trust is land.[40] This was recognized in *Re Baillie*,[41] as regards a half-secret trust of land. In *Ottaway v Norman*,[42] however, a fully secret trust of land was held to be valid even though it was not evidenced in writing. This might indicate that fully secret trusts of land operate as constructive trusts, since such trusts of land are valid despite the absence of writing;[43] or the trust is valid because otherwise the trustee would be seeking to use a statute as an instrument of fraud; or perhaps the court simply failed to appreciate the significance of the oral declaration of the trust in that case. The preferable view is that, regardless of whether the trust is a fully secret or half-secret trust of land, the trust can be validly declared even though it is not evidenced by signed writing because the trustee's conduct in consciously allowing the testator to leave him or her the land in the expectation that the trustee will hold it on trust for another means that the trustee should not be allowed to use the formality requirements of the Law of Property Act 1925 as an instrument of fraud. The use of this doctrine does not mean that the trust itself is not an express trust.[44]

(b) Half-secret trusts

A half-secret trust arises where a testator leaves property to a named person in a will to hold on a trust that has been, or will be, declared.[45] Since the intended beneficiary is not identified in the will, the strict formalities of the Wills Act 1837 are not satisfied. Despite this, the courts have been willing to enforce such trusts, albeit subject to stringent conditions.

If evidence of the terms of the half-secret trust were not admitted, the trustee would hold the property on resulting trust for those entitled to the testator's residuary estate,[46] because it is clear that the trustee cannot receive the property beneficially. Two different explanations have been suggested as to why it is possible to allow evidence of the terms to be admitted so that the trustee holds the property on the secret trust for the beneficiaries chosen by the testator.

The first is the doctrine of incorporation by reference.[47] The requirements for this doctrine[48] do appear to be consistent with the requirements for the half-secret trust, since the testator must have communicated the terms of the trust, including the identity of the beneficiaries, to the intended trustee before, or at the time that, the will was made and reference to the trust must be made in the will.[49] Once these conditions are satisfied, it would then be possible to incorporate the terms of the secret trust into the will, so that the formality requirements of the Wills Act 1837 could then be considered

---

[40] Law of Property Act 1925, s. 53(1)(b). See Chapter 4.2(b), p. 120.

[41] (1886) 2 TLT 660, 661 (North J).

[42] [1972] Ch 698. See Chapter 4.2(c)(iii)(c), pp. 138–40.

[43] Law of Property Act 1925, s. 53(2).

[44] As in *Rochefoucauld v Bousted* [1897] 1 Ch 196. See Chapter 4.2(b), pp. 122–3.

[45] If the trusts are declared in writing subsequently, it may be possible to incorporate them into the will if the conditions for incorporation are satisfied. See Chapter 4.2(c)(ii), pp. 126–7.

[46] *Re Pugh's Will Trusts* [1967] 1 WLR 1262.

[47] Matthews, 'The True Basis of the Half-secret Trust?' [1979] Conv 360.

[48] See Chapter 4.2(c)(ii), pp. 126–7.

[49] See Chapter 4.2(c)(iii)(b), pp. 134–5.

to be satisfied. This theory also explains why communication of the terms of the trust after the will has been executed will not be effective, unless the will is confirmed by a codicil that refers to the communication.[50]

Although the use of the doctrine of incorporation by reference to explain the law on half-secret trusts appears to explain the requirements of that trust, this is not a sufficient explanation for a number of reasons. First, that doctrine relates only to the incorporation of documents into the will and does not extend to the incorporation of oral communications, which clearly do not comply with the formality requirements of the Wills Act 1837 that all parts of the will need to be in writing. But it has been recognized that oral communication of the terms of the trust are sufficient for a half-secret trust to be valid.[51] Secondly, a document can be incorporated into a will even though it has not been communicated to the trustee, whereas communication of the terms of the trust to the trustee is a vital requirement for a half-secret trust to be valid. Thirdly, the main advantage of the doctrine of incorporation by reference to explain the half-secret trust is to justify the requirement of communication of terms before execution of the will. But that requirement has already been criticized as being inconsistent with the requirements for fully secret trusts and also the 'dehors the will' theory. As Critchley has recognized:[52]

> All in all, the argument by analogy with incorporation by reference is not compelling. It would be considerably stronger were half secret trusts to be limited to written communications, but this would then create yet another odd discrepancy between fully and half secret trusts. It is therefore perhaps better to conclude that, whilst there may have been cross-fertilisation between incorporation by reference and half secret trusts, they are properly viewed as separate doctrines. This means that it is necessary to find some other justification for the informality permitted to half secret... trusts.

An alternative explanation of the half-secret trust is that such trusts should be recognized to prevent a fraud from being perpetrated on the intended beneficiaries if a legatee, having agreed to hold property on trust, fails to do so.[53] Although fraud has proved significant to the recognition of the fully secret trust,[54] it appears not to be relevant to the half-secret trust, since, as the trust is apparent on the face of the will, there is little scope for the trustee to defraud the beneficiaries, save where the trustee might assert that the communication of the terms of the trust occurred after the will had been executed. Even then, there is no scope for the trustee benefiting from the half-secret trust failing, unless he or she was otherwise entitled to the testator's residuary estate.

Fraud cannot, therefore, explain why half-secret trusts are recognized if fraud is interpreted restrictively so that it only applies where the trustee wishes to benefit from the invalidity of the trust. But if fraud were instead interpreted as encompassing unconscionable conduct, it could be used to justify the recognition of these trusts. Trustees can be considered to act unconscionably where they seek not to be bound by their undertaking to the testator to hold property on trust for another. The trust could then be recognized to prevent such unconscionable behaviour from occurring. Such a principle was effectively recognized by the House of Lords in *Blackwell v Blackwell*,[55] in which the testator had left money in his will to five legatees to be applied for the benefit of people whose names he had previously communicated to them. Before the will was executed, the testator had informed the trustees orally

---

[50] See Chapter 4.2(c)(ii), pp. 126–7.
[51] *Blackwell v Blackwell* [1929] AC 318.
[52] 'Instruments of Fraud, Testamentary Dispositions and the Doctrine of Secret Trusts' (1999) 115 LQR 631, 646.
[53] *Blackwell v Blackwell* [1929] AC 318.
[54] See Chapter 4.2(c)(iii)(c), p. 136.
[55] [1929] AC 318.

that the money was to be used for the benefit of his mistress and his illegitimate son. It was held that this was a valid trust. Viscount Sumner said:[56]

In itself the doctrine of equity, by which parol evidence is admissible to prove what is called 'fraud' in connection with secret trusts, and effect is given to such trusts when established, would not seem to conflict with any of the Acts under which from time to time the Legislature has regulated the right of testamentary disposition. A Court of conscience finds a man in the position of an absolute legal owner of a sum of money, which has been bequeathed to him under a valid will, and it declares that, on proof of certain facts relating to the motives and actions of the testator, it will not allow the legal owner to exercise his legal right to do what he will with his own. This seems to be a perfectly normal exercise of general equitable jurisdiction. The facts commonly but not necessarily involve some immoral and selfish conduct on the part of the legal owner. The necessary elements, on which the question turns, are intention, communication, and acquiescence. The testator intends his absolute gift to be employed as he and not as the donee desires; he tells the proposed donee of this intention and, either by express promise or by the tacit promise, which is signified by acquiescence, the proposed donee encourages him to bequeath the money in the faith that his intentions will be carried out. The special circumstance, that the gift is by bequest only makes this rule a special case of the exercise of a general jurisdiction, but in its application to a bequest the doctrine must in principle rest on the assumption that the will has first operated according to its terms. It is because there is no one to whom the law can give relief in the premises, that relief, if any, must be sought in equity. So far, and in the bare case of a legacy absolute on the face of it, I do not see how the statute-law relating to the form of a valid will is concerned at all, and the expressions, in which the doctrine has been habitually described, seem to bear this out. For the prevention of fraud equity fastens on the conscience of the legatee a trust, a trust, that is, which otherwise would be inoperative; in other words it makes him do what the will in itself has nothing to do with; it lets him take what the will gives him and then makes him apply it, as the Court of conscience directs, and it does so in order to give effect to wishes of the testator, which would not otherwise be effectual.

To this two circumstances must be added to bring the present case to the test of the general doctrine, first, that the will states on its face that the legacy is given on trust but does not state what the trusts are, and further contains a residuary bequest, and, second, that the legatees are acting with perfect honesty, seek no advantage to themselves, and only desire, if the Court will permit them, to do what in other circumstances the Court would have fastened it on their conscience to perform.

Since the current of decisions down to *Re Fleetwood* (1880) 15 Ch D 594 and *Re Huxtable* [1902] 2 Ch 793 has established that the principles of equity apply equally when these circumstances are present as in cases where they are not, the material question is whether and how the Wills Act affects this case. It seems to me that, apart from legislation, the application of the principle of equity, which was made in *Fleetwood*'s and *Huxtable*'s cases, was logical, and was justified by the same considerations as in the cases of fraud and absolute gifts. Why should equity forbid an honest trustee to give effect to his promise, made to a deceased testator, and compel him to pay another legatee, about whom it is quite certain that the testator did not mean to make him the object of this bounty? In both cases the testator's wishes are incompletely expressed in his will. Why should equity, over a mere matter of words, give effect to them in one case and frustrate them in the other? No doubt the words 'in trust' prevent the legatee from taking beneficially, whether they have simply been declared in conversation or written in the will, but the fraud, when the trustee, so called in the will, is also the residuary legatee, is the same as when he is only declared a trustee by word of mouth accepted by him. I recoil from interfering with decisions of long standing, which reject this anomaly, unless constrained by statute.

---

[56] Ibid, 334.

The answer is put in the phrase, 'this is making the testator's will for him', instead, that is, of limiting him to the will made in statutory form. What then of the legislation? Great authorities seem to have expressed an opinion, that this equitable principle, as a whole, conflicts with section 9 of the Wills Act. Lord Cairns in 1868 says that when a devisee seeks to apply what has been devised to him otherwise than in accordance with the testator's intentions, communicated by him and accepted, 'it is in effect a case of trust, and in such case the Court will not allow the devisee to set up the Statute of Frauds, or, rather, the Statute of Wills. . . . But in this the Court does not violate the spirit of the statutes; but for the . . . prevention of fraud, it engrafts the trusts on the devise by admitting evidence which the statute would in terms exclude, in order to prevent a devisee from applying property to a purpose foreign to that for which he undertook to hold it': *Jones v Badley* (1868) 3 Ch App 362 at 364 . . .

I think the conclusion is confirmed, which the frame of section 9 of the Wills Act seems to me to carry on its face, that the legislation did not purport to interfere with the exercise of a general equitable jurisdiction, even in connection with secret dispositions of a testator, except in so far as reinforcement of the formalities required for a valid will might indirectly limit it. The effect, therefore, of a bequest being made in terms on trust, without any statement in the will to show what the trust is, remains to be decided by the law as laid down by the Courts before and since the Act and does not depend on the Act itself.

It follows that the essential condition for recognizing a half-secret trust is that the testator has communicated the purpose of the trust to the legatee, who then either acquiesces or promises to comply with this purpose, and the testator consequently relies on this by executing the will so as to leave property to the trustee.[57] In other words, this acquiescence or promise operates as a form of estoppel, because of the key requirements of communication, acceptance, and reliance. It will then be unconscionable for the legatee not to fulfil the undertaking that he or she has given to carry out the purposes for which the bequest was made.[58] This satisfactorily explains why half-secret trusts are recognized and why there are particular requirements for the recognition of such a trust.

The terms of the trust must be communicated to the trustee before, or contemporaneously with, the execution of the will.[59] Communication of the terms after the will has been executed will mean that the half-secret trust fails and the property will be held by the trustee on resulting trust for residuary beneficiaries of the testator's estate; similarly where the terms are not communicated to the trustee at all.[60] It was recognized in *Re Keen*[61] that the reason why communication of the terms of the trust after the will has been executed cannot be effective to declare a half-secret trust is because this involves the testator reserving a power to change a will informally, contrary to the Wills Act 1837. But communication before execution of the will is not a requirement for fully secret trusts[62] and is inconsistent with the 'dehors the will' theory of secret trusts. It follows that it should be sufficient that the terms of the half-secret trust are communicated before the testator's death,[63] because then the testator can be considered to have relied on the trustee's acquiescence by not changing the terms of the will.

In *Re Keen*,[64] it was recognized by the Court of Appeal that giving a sealed envelope to one trustee was sufficient communication of the identity of the beneficiary, even though it was not read until after the testator's death, because the trustee was aware that it contained the name of the beneficiary.

---

[57] *Re Cooper* [1939] Ch 811, 816 (Sir Wilfrid Greene MR).
[58] *Re Keen* [1937] Ch 236, 245 (Lord Wright MR).
[59] *Johnson v Ball* (1851) 5 De G & Sm 85.
[60] *Re Pugh* [1967] 1 WLR 1262.
[61] [1937] Ch 236.
[62] See Chapter 4.2(c)(iii)(c), p. 140.
[63] Communication of the terms after the testator's death will not suffice for a fully secret trust (*Re Boyes* (1884) 26 Ch D 531) and should not do so either for a half-secret trust.
[64] [1937] Ch 236.

Further, it did not matter that the envelope was given to only one of the two trustees named in the will. Lord Wright MR said:[65]

> To take a parallel, a ship which sails under sealed orders, is sailing under orders though the exact terms are not ascertained by the captain till later. I note that the case of a trust put into writing which is placed in the trustees' hands in a sealed envelope, was hypothetically treated by Kay J as possibly constituting a communication in a case of this nature: *Re Boyes* (1884) 26 Ch D 531 at 536. This, so far as it goes, seems to support my conclusion. The trustees had the means of knowledge available whenever it became necessary and proper to open the envelope.

Nevertheless, the trust was declared void because the communication of the terms of the will before the trust was executed was inconsistent with the terms of the will, which stated 'as [the testator] would notify' rather than 'as he had notified'. In *Re Bateman's Will Trusts*,[66] the testator had directed his trustees to pay income 'to such persons and in such proportions as shall be stated by me in a sealed letter in my own handwriting addressed to my trustees'. Since there was no evidence as to whether a sealed letter had been written and addressed to the trustees by the testator at the date of the will, the trust was declared void. Pennycuick V-C said:[67]

> These words clearly, I think, import that the testator may, in the future, after the date of the will, give a sealed letter to his trustees. It is impossible to confine the words to a sealed letter already so given. If that is the true construction of the wording, it is not in dispute that the direction is invalid...it is really clear and not in dispute that once one must construe the direction as admitting of a future letter then the direction is invalid, as an attempt to dispose of the estate by a non-testamentary instrument.

In *Re Rees*,[68] the testator declared a half-secret trust. When the will was executed, he told the trustees that any surplus after making certain payments could be retained by them for their own use. It was held that the surplus could not belong to the trustees, but rather was held on resulting trust for those entitled to the testator's residuary estate. This was because the testator's oral communication to the trustees about the surplus conflicted with the terms of the will, which stated that the trustees were to receive the property as trustees rather than beneficially. Evershed MR said:[69]

> [the testator] intended [the trustees] to take beneficial interests and that his wishes included that intention, would be to conflict with the terms of the will...for the inevitable result of admitting that evidence and giving effect to it would be that the will would be regarded not as conferring a trust estate only upon the two trustees, but as giving them a conditional gift which on construction is the thing which, if I am right, it does not do.

In *Re Tyler*,[70] Pennycuick J said that he did not find the reasoning in *Re Rees* to be easy. On the face of it, the reasoning of Evershed MR in *Re Rees* is unconvincing: if the will says that the property is held on trust for certain people, why cannot some of those people be the trustees who could benefit from the surplus? But, although this was not acknowledged in *Re Rees*, it is surely because the trustees were asserting that they were entitled to the surplus that there was a real danger of fraud on their part, since

---

[65] Ibid, at 242.
[66] [1970] 1 WLR 1463.
[67] Ibid, 1468.
[68] [1950] Ch 204.
[69] Ibid, 207.
[70] [1967] 1 WLR 1269, 1278.

they were seeking to obtain a personal benefit that was not identified on the face of the will. Where the trustees are intended to benefit from the testator's estate, but this is not expressed in the will, the high standards of behaviour expected from the trustees should be such that they should not receive the property beneficially. If this is the correct analysis, it means that even if the trustees in *Re Rees* were intended to benefit under the half-secret trust itself rather than to obtain any surplus, they would not have been able to do so.

Changes to the terms of a half-secret trust after the will has been executed will not be effective if the changes have not been communicated to the trustees. In *Re Cooper*,[71] the testator declared a half-secret trust of £5,000 in his will, having communicated the terms of the trust to his trustees before the will was executed. A month later, the testator made a new will which purported to cancel the previous one. This new will stated that the £5,000 bequeathed to his trustees was to be increased to £10,000 and that the trustees knew the testator's wishes as regards the use of this sum. The fact that the amount had been increased was not, however, communicated to the trustees. It was held that the first £5,000 was held on the terms of the secret trust, as had previously been communicated, but the additional £5,000 was held on resulting trust for those entitled to the testator's residuary estate, because this additional amount had not been communicated to the trustees. Sir Wilfrid Greene MR said:[72]

> It seems to me that upon the facts of this case it is impossible to say that the acceptance by the trustees of the onus of trusteeship in relation to the first and earlier legacy is something which must be treated as having been repeated in reference to the second legacy or the increased legacy, whichever way one chooses to describe it. In order that a secret trust might be made effective with regard to that added sum in my opinion precisely the same factors were necessary as were required to validate the original trusts, namely, communication, acceptance or acquiescence, and the making of the will on the faith of such acceptance or acquiescence. None of these elements, as I have said, were present. It is not possible, in my opinion, to treat the figure of [£] 5000. in relation to which the consent of the trustees was originally obtained as something of no essential importance. I cannot myself see that the arrangement between the testator and the trustees can be construed as though it had meant [£] 5000. or whatever sum I may hereafter choose to bequeath'. That is not what was said and it was not with regard to any sum other than the [£] 5000. that the consciences of the trustees (to use a technical phrase) were burdened. It must not be thought from what I have been saying that some trifling excess of the sum actually bequeathed over the figure mentioned in the first bequest to the trustees would necessarily not be caught. Such an addition might come within the rule of de minimis if the facts justified it. Similarly it must not be thought that, if a testator, having declared to his trustees trusts in relation to a specified sum, afterwards in his will inserts a lesser sum, that lesser sum would not be caught by the trusts. In such a case the greater would I apprehend be held to include the less.

(c) Fully secret trusts

In a fully secret trust the will indicates that a gift is made to a particular person absolutely, but the testator intends the legatee to hold the gift on trust for somebody else. This may be because the testator wants to benefit somebody without anybody knowing or suspecting that there is a different beneficiary, such as a mistress or illegitimate child. Alternatively, the testator might be uncertain as to who should be benefited at the time that the will is executed, and so leaves property to some trusted person, such as a solicitor, to dispose of according to instructions that are to be communicated subsequently.[73]

---

[71] [1939] Ch 811.
[72] Ibid, 817.
[73] See, e.g. *Re Snowden* [1979] Ch 528.

Whatever the reason for their creation, such fully secret trusts do not comply with the necessary formalities of the Wills Act 1837. If they are not to be enforced in favour of the intended beneficiaries, what should happen? It is inequitable for the legatee to keep it for him or herself and Equity will not allow a statute to be used as an instrument of fraud. Fraud would be prevented if the legatee were required to hold upon a resulting trust for the testator's estate, but this would be a denial of the testator's intention. Provided that the intended trusts are communicated to the legatee before the testator's death, such trusts are enforced in favour of the intended beneficiary because otherwise the legatee's reliance on the strict terms of the will to ignore the testator's intention to hold property on trust for another would be unconscionable.

Re Freud (deceased)[74] concerned the interpretation of the will of the artist Lucien Freud, who allegedly had at least 14 illegitimate children. Richard Spearman QC, sitting as a Deputy Judge, recognized that:[75]

> it is common place for solicitors to be appointed as trustees, and one reasonable explanation for a clause which confers a beneficial gift on a solicitor is that the testator intended to impose a fully secret trust.

On the face of the will, Freud's residuary estate was left to the claimants, who were his solicitor and one of his children, absolutely. The defendant, one of Freud's other children, argued that the estate was not given to the claimants for their absolute benefit, but was held on trust, the terms of which were not set out in the will, so that it was a half secret trust. It was held that Freud had not intended to declare a trust, so the residuary estate was indeed given to the claimants absolutely. The claimants had, however, acknowledged that they had received communications from Freud before his death as to how the residuary estate should be used. It therefore appears that this was in fact a fully secret trust.

That the recognition of a fully secret trust is prompted by a desire to prevent fraud is illustrated most clearly by *Thynn v Thynn*.[76] A father, in his will, had made his wife his executrix. Their son persuaded his mother that it would be better for him to be the executor and that he would hold the estate on trust for her. The son arranged for the father's will to be cancelled and a new will was prepared that made the son the executor. When it came to the father signing the new will, which was read out to him by the will-writer, the father said that he could not hear what was being said. He did sign the will, but clearly in very suspicious circumstances. On the father's death, the son obtained the estate and denied that he held this on trust for his mother. It was held that the trust was valid, even though it had not been declared in writing as required by statute, because of the son's fraud. The Lord Keeper held that 'it appeared to be, as well as Fraud, as also a Trust'.

In *Kasperbauer v Griffith*,[77] Peter Gibson LJ recognized that a fully secret trust will only be valid if the following conditions are satisfied:

> the authorities make plain that what is needed is (i) an intention by the testator to create a trust, satisfying the traditional requirement of three certainties (that is to say certain language in imperative form, certain subject matter and certain objects or beneficiaries); (ii) the communication of the trust to the legatees, and (iii) acceptance of the trust by the legatee, which acceptance can take the form of silent acquiescence. The crucial question in the present case is whether there was that intention and...it is an essential element that the testator must intend to subject the legatee to an obligation in favour of the intended beneficiary. That will be evidenced by appropriately imperative, as distinct from precatory language.

---

[74] [2014] EWHC 2577 (Ch); [2014] WTLR 1453.
[75] Ibid, [56].
[76] (1684) 1 Vern 296.
[77] (2000) 1 WTLR 333.

Each of these requirements needs to be examined in turn.

(1) *Testator's intention*: the testator must intend the legatee to be subject to an obligation to hold identified property on trust for identified beneficiaries. But the fully secret trust may not be intended to arise immediately on the testator's death. So, for example, the testator might intend to create an obligation on the legatee to dispose of the property in a particular way by his or her own will. This type of trust is illustrated by *Ottoway v Norman*.

Ottoway v Norman [1972] Ch 698

The testator, Harry Ottoway, left his bungalow, its contents, and some money to his house-keeper, Miss Hodges, in his will. The testator made an agreement with the housekeeper that she would leave the bungalow in her will to the testator's son. She made a will in accordance with this arrangement. But, four years later, she made a new will that left the bungalow to the defendant, Mr Norman. The testator and the housekeeper died, and the testator's son then sought a declaration that the defendant held the bungalow on a fully secret trust for him. The son's claim was upheld.

Brightman J

It will be convenient to call the person upon whom such a trust is imposed the 'primary donee' and the beneficiary under that trust the 'secondary donee'. The essential elements which must be proved to exist are: (i) the intention of the testator to subject the primary donee to an obligation in favour of the secondary donee; (ii) communication of that intention to the primary donee; and (iii) the acceptance of that obligation by the primary donee either expressly or by acquiescence.

It is immaterial whether these elements precede or succeed the will of the donor. I am informed that there is no recent reported case where the obligation imposed on the primary donee is an obligation to make a will in favour of the secondary donee as distinct from some form of *inter vivos* transfer. But it does not seem to me that there can really be any distinction which can validly be taken on behalf of the defendant in the present case. The basis of the doctrine of a secret trust is the obligation imposed on the conscience of the primary donee and it does not seem to me that there is any materiality in the machinery by which the donor intends that that obligation shall be carried out.

[Counsel] for Mr. Norman, relied strongly on *McCormick v Grogan* (1869) LR 4 HL 82. In that case a testator in 1851 had left all his property by a three-line will to his friend Mr. Grogan. In 1854 the testator was struck down by cholera. With only a few hours to live he sent for Mr. Grogan. He told Mr. Grogan in effect that his will and a letter would be found in his desk. The letter named various intended beneficiaries and the intended gifts to them. The letter concluded with the words:

'I do not wish you to act strictly on the foregoing instructions, but leave it entirely to your own good judgment to do as you think I would, if living, and as the parties are deserving.'

An intended beneficiary whom Mr. Grogan thought it right to exclude sued. I will read an extract from the speech of Lord Westbury, at 97, because [counsel] relied much upon it.

'. . .the jurisdiction which is invoked here by the appellant is founded altogether on personal fraud. It is a jurisdiction by which a Court of Equity, proceeding on the ground of fraud, converts the party who has committed it into a trustee for the party who is injured by that fraud. Now, being a jurisdiction founded on personal fraud, it is incumbent on the court to see that a fraud, a *malus animus*, is proved by the clearest and most indisputable evidence.'

Lord Westbury continued, at 97:

'You are obliged, therefore, to shew most clearly and distinctly that the person you wish to convert into a trustee acted *malo animo*. You must shew distinctly that he knew that the testator or the intestate was beguiled and deceived by his conduct. If you are not in a condition to affirm that without any misgiving, or possibility of mistake, you are not warranted in affixing on the individual the delictum of fraud, which you must do before you convert him into a trustee. Now are there any indicia of fraud in this case?'...

Founding himself on Lord Westbury [counsel] sought at one stage to deploy an argument that a person could never succeed in establishing a secret trust unless he could show that the primary donee was guilty of deliberate and conscious wrongdoing of which he said there was no evidence in the case before me. That proposition, if correct, would lead to the surprising result that if the primary donee faithfully observed the obligation imposed on him there would not ever have been a trust at any time in existence. The argument was discarded, and I think rightly. [Counsel] then fastened on the words 'clearest and most indisputable evidence' and he submitted that an exceptionally high standard of proof was needed to establish a secret trust. I do not think that Lord Westbury's words mean more than this: that if a will contains a gift which is in terms absolute, clear evidence is needed before the court will assume that the testator did not mean what he said. It is perhaps analogous to the standard of proof which this court requires before it will rectify a written instrument, for there again a party is saying that neither meant what they have written...

I find as a fact that Mr. Harry Ottaway intended that Miss Hodges should be obliged to dispose of the bungalow in favour of the plaintiffs at her death; that Mr. Harry Ottaway communicated that intention to Miss Hodges; and that Miss Hodges accepted the obligation. I find the same facts in relation to the furniture, fixtures and fittings which passed to Miss Hodges under clause 4 of Mr. Harry Ottaway's will. I am not satisfied that any similar obligation was imposed and accepted as regards any contents of the bungalow which had not devolved on Miss Hodges under clause 4 of Mr. Harry Ottaway's will.

I turn to the question of money. In cross-examination William said the trust extended to the house, furniture and money:

'Everything my father left to Miss Hodges was to be in the trust. The trust comprised the lot. She could use the money as she liked. She had to leave my wife and me whatever money was left.'

In cross-examination Mrs. Dorothy Ottaway [the testator's daughter-in-law] said that her understanding was that Miss Hodges was bound to make a will giving her and her husband the bungalow, contents and any money she had left. 'She could please herself about the money. She did not have to save it for us. She was free to spend it.' It seems to me that two questions arise. First, as a matter of fact, what did the parties intend should be comprised in Miss Hodges's obligation? All money which Miss Hodges had at her death including both money which she had acquired before Mr. Harry Ottaway's death and money she acquired after his death from all sources? Or only money acquired under Mr. Harry Ottaway's will? Secondly, as a matter of law, if such an obligation existed would it create a valid trust? On the second question I am content to assume for present purposes but without so deciding that if property is given to the primary donee on the understanding that the primary donee will dispose by his will of such assets, if any, as he may have at his command at his death in favour of the secondary donee, a valid trust is created in favour of the secondary donee which is in suspense during the lifetime of the primary donee, but attaches to the estate of the primary donee at the moment of the latter's death. There would seem to be at least some support for this proposition in an Australian case to which I was referred: *Birmingham v Renfrew* (1937) 57 CLR 666. I accept that the parties mentioned money on at least some occasions when they talked about Mr. Harry Ottaway's intentions for the future disposition of Ashcroft. I do not, however, find sufficient evidence that it was the intention of Mr. Harry

Ottaway that Miss Hodges should be compelled to leave all her money, from whatever source derived, to the plaintiffs. This would seem to preclude her giving even a small pecuniary legacy to any friend or relative. I do not think it is clear that Mr. Harry Ottaway intended to extract any such far-reaching undertaking from Miss Hodges or that she intended to accept such a wide obligation herself. Therefore the obligation, if any, is in my view, to be confined to money derived under Mr. Harry Ottaway's will. If the obligation is confined to money derived under Mr. Harry Ottaway's will, the obligation is meaningless and unworkable unless it includes the requirement that she shall keep such money separate and distinct from her own money. I am certain that no such requirement was ever discussed or intended. If she had the right to mingle her own money with that derived from Mr. Harry Ottaway, there would be no ascertainable property upon which the trust could bite at her death...

There is another difficulty. Does money in this context include only cash or cash and investments, or all movable property of any description? The evidence is quite inconclusive. In my judgment the plaintiff's claim succeeds in relation to the bungalow and in relation to the furniture, fixtures and fittings which devolved under paragraph 4 of Mr. Harry Ottaway's will subject, of course, to normal wastage, fair wear and tear, but not to any other assets.

Although the analysis of the suspensory trust obligation in *Ottaway v Norman* was *obiter*, it is nonetheless significant. It follows that, if the testator in that case had intended the housekeeper to leave any residue to the testator's son, the son would have had an equitable proprietary interest in that residue. But what sort of trust would this be? The normal secret trust that arises immediately on the testator's death has been analysed as an express trust that is made *inter vivos*, but which is constituted on death. But that cannot be true of the suspensory trust, since, on the testator's death, the trust property is still uncertain and might never exist if the legatee dissipates all of it. Any trust of the residue could be constituted only on the death of the legatee. Consequently, this suspensory trust is better analysed as a constructive trust that attaches to any residue of the testator's estate at the time of the legatee's death.[78] It is only at that point that the subject matter of the trust will be certain. During the period from the testator's death until the legatee has died, the legatee is best regarded as the absolute owner of the property subject to fiduciary responsibilities arising out of the arrangements with the testator to prevent him or her making gifts and settlements *inter vivos* with the purpose of defeating the undertaking. The potential interest of the person whom the testator intended to receive the residue enables him or her to obtain an injunction to prevent such a disposition and to recover any property that has been so disposed. On the death of the legatee, if no provision has been made in his or her will for the residue to be given to the other person, the executor of the legatee's estate will hold the residue on constructive trust for that person. But, crucially, if the legatee legitimately dissipates the legacy received from the testator, there will be no property to be held on trust for the other person.

(2) *Communication to legatee*: the testator must have communicated the trust, its terms, the identity of the trust property, and the beneficiaries to the legatee before the testator's death.[79] So, for example, in *Re Boyes*,[80] the testator left a legacy to his solicitor, who was told that it was to be held on trust, but who was not told for whom. After the testator's death, a letter was found amongst the testator's papers stating that the residuary estate was to be held for the testator's mistress. It was held that this was not sufficient to create a valid secret trust and so the estate was held on resulting trust for the testator's next of kin. The delivery of a sealed letter during the testator's lifetime is a sufficient communication provided that it is known to contain the terms of a trust and is accepted as such.[81]

---

[78] Hayton, '*Ottaway v Norman*' [1972] Conv 129, 132.
[79] *Wallgrave v Tebbs* (1855) 2 K & J 313.
[80] (1884) 26 Ch D 531.
[81] *Re Keen* [1937] Ch 236, 242 (Lord Wright MR). See Chapter 4.2(c)(iii)(b), pp. 134–5.

Presumably this requirement is needed because, if communication after the testator's death was sufficient to validate the trust, this is a step too far in allowing a trust to be valid outside the terms of the will.

(3) *Acceptance by legatee*: the trust must be accepted by the legatee expressly or by acquiescence before the testator's death.[82] Once the legatee has accepted the trust it cannot be disclaimed.[83] Where testamentary gifts are made to two or more people a significant distinction is drawn, depending on whether they were tenants in common or joint tenants.[84] This was recognized in *Re Stead*,[85] where Farwell J said:[86]

> If A induces B either to make, or to leave unrevoked, a will leaving property to A and C as tenants in common, by expressly promising, or tacitly consenting, that he and C will carry out the testator's wishes, and C knows nothing of the matter until after A's death, A is bound, but C is not bound: *Tee v Ferris* (1856) 2 K & J 357; the reason stated at 368 being, that to hold otherwise would enable one beneficiary to deprive the rest of their benefits by setting up a secret trust. If, however, the gift were to A and C as joint tenants, the authorities have established a distinction between those cases in which the will is made on the faith of the antecedent promise by A and those in which the will is left unrevoked on the faith of a subsequent promise. In the former case, the trust binds both A and C: *Russell v Jackson* (1852) 10 Hare 204; *Jones v Badley* (1868) 3 Ch App 362, the reason stated being that no person can claim an interest under a fraud committed by another; in the latter case A and not C is bound: *Burney v Macdonald* (1845) 15 Sim 6 and *Moss v Cooper* (1861) 1 John & H 352, the reason stated at 367 being that the gift is not tainted with any fraud in procuring the execution of the will. Personally I am unable to see any difference between a gift made on the faith of an antecedent promise and a gift left unrevoked on the faith of a subsequent promise to carry out the testator's wishes; but apparently a distinction has been made by the various judges who have had to consider the question. I am bound, therefore, to decide in accordance with these authorities.

The reason for this distinction has been explained by Perrins:[87]

> The 'reasons stated' by Farwell J in *Re Stead* are at first sight contradictory. One consideration is that a person must not be allowed, by falsely setting up a secret trust, to deprive another of his benefits under the will. Apparently this is decisive if the parties are tenants in common but not if they are joint tenants. On the other hand one person must not profit by the fraud of another. Apparently this is decisive only if the parties are joint tenants and not if they are tenants in common. Yet again it is apparently only fraud in procuring the execution of a will that is relevant, and not fraud in inducing a testator not to revoke a will already made. All very confusing, but add *Huguenin v Baseley* (1807) 14 Ves 273 and the whole picture springs into focus and the confusion disappears. Returning to A and C, whether they are tenants in common or joint tenants, C is not bound if his gift was not induced by the promise of A because to hold otherwise would be to enable A to deprive C of his benefit by setting up a secret trust; but C is bound if his gift was induced by the promise of A because he cannot profit by the fraud of another; and if the trust was communicated to A after the will was made, then C takes free if his gift was not induced by the promise of A because if there is no inducement there is no fraud affecting C.
>
> This, it is submitted, is what was decided by the cases cited in Farwell J's judgment.

---

[82] *Moss v Cooper* (1861) 1 J & H 352, 367 (Wood VC).
[83] See Glister, 'Disclaimer and Secret Trusts' [2014] Conv 11.
[84] See Chapter 1.4(a)(v), p. 13.
[85] [1900] 1 Ch 237.
[86] Ibid, 241.
[87] 'Can You Keep Half a Secret?' (1972) 88 LQR 225, 228.

Consequently, the preferable view is that if the testator has been induced by the promise of one of the parties to leave property on secret trust, such that the gift would not have been made without the promise, the trust should bind all parties regardless of whether they are joint tenants or tenants in common.

(d) Standard of proof

The person seeking to establish the secret trust bears the burden of proving that the trust has been created.[88] As regards the standard of proof, it was recognized in *Ottaway v Norman*[89] that clear evidence was required before the court would be willing to conclude that the testator had intended something different from what appeared on the face of the will. In *Re Snowden*,[90] however, Megarry V-C accepted that the ordinary civil standard of proof on a balance of probabilities applied to establish a fully secret trust, save where fraud was asserted against the alleged trustee. In that case, the testatrix made her will six days before she died. She left her residuary estate to her brother absolutely. Six days after her death, the brother died. He left his property to his son. The testatrix's solicitors, who had prepared and witnessed the will, gave evidence that she wanted her brother to divide her estate for her so that she could be 'fair to everyone'. In holding that there was no secret trust, Megarry V-C considered the standard of proof:[91]

> One question that arises is whether the standard of proof required to establish a secret trust is merely the ordinary civil standard of proof, or whether it is a higher and more cogent standard. If it is the latter, I feel no doubt that the claim that there is a secret trust must fail. On this question, *Ottaway v Norman* [1972] Ch 698 was cited; it was, indeed, the only authority that was put before me. According to the headnote, the standard of proof 'was not an exceptionally high one but was analogous to that required before the court would rectify a written instrument'. When one turns to the judgment, one finds that what Brightman J said at 712, was that Lord Westbury's words in *McCormick v Grogan* (1869) LR 4 HL 82 at 97, a case on secret trusts, did not mean that an exceptionally high standard of proof was needed, but meant no more than that:
>
> > 'if a will contains a gift which is in terms absolute, clear evidence is needed before the court will assume that the testator did not mean what he said. It is perhaps analogous to the standard of proof which this court requires before it will rectify a written instrument, for there again a party is saying that neither meant what they have written.' ...
>
> I feel some doubt about how far rectification is a fair analogy to secret trusts in this respect. Many cases of rectification do of course involve a party in saying that neither meant what they have written, and requiring that what they have written should be altered. On the other hand, the whole basis of secret trusts, as I understand it, is that they operate outside the will, changing nothing that is written in it, and allowing it to operate according to its tenor, but then fastening a trust on to the property in the hands of the recipient. It is at least possible that very different standards of proof may be appropriate for cases where the words of a formal document have to be altered and for cases where there is no such alteration but merely a question whether, when the document has been given effect to, there will be some trust of the property with which it dealt. ... I am not sure that it is right to assume that there is a single, uniform standard of proof for all secret trusts. The proposition of Lord Westbury in

---

[88] *Jones v Badley* (1868) LR 3 Ch App 362.
[89] [1972] Ch 698. See Chapter 4.2(c)(iii)(c)(1), pp. 138–40.
[90] [1979] Ch 528.
[91] Ibid, 534.

McCormick v Grogan with which Brightman J was pressed in *Ottaway v Norman* was that the jurisdiction in cases of secret trust was

> 'founded altogether on personal fraud. It is a jurisdiction by which a Court of Equity, proceeding on the ground of fraud, converts the party who has committed it into a trustee for the party who is injured by that fraud. Now, being a jurisdiction founded on personal fraud, it is incumbent on the court to see that a fraud, a *malus animus*, is proved by the clearest and most indisputable evidence.'

Of that, it is right to say that the law on the subject has not stood still since 1869, and that it is now clear that secret trusts may be established in cases where there is no possibility of fraud. *McCormick v Grogan* has to be read in the light both of earlier cases that were not cited, and also of subsequent cases, in particular *Blackwell v Blackwell* [1929] AC 318. It seems to me that fraud comes into the matter in two ways. First, it provides an historical explanation of the doctrine of secret trusts; the doctrine was evolved as a means of preventing fraud. That, however, does not mean that fraud is an essential ingredient for the application of the doctrine; the reason for the rule is not part of the rule itself. Second, there are some cases within the doctrine where fraud is indeed involved. There are cases where for the legatee to assert that he is a beneficial owner, free from any trust, would be a fraud on his part.

It is to this latter aspect of fraud that it seems to me that Lord Westbury's words are applicable. If a secret trust can be held to exist in a particular case only by holding the legatee guilty of fraud, then no secret trust should be found unless the standard of proof suffices for fraud. On the other hand, if there is no question of fraud, why should so high a standard apply? In such a case, I find it difficult to see why the mere fact that the historical origin of the doctrine lay in the prevention of fraud should impose the high standard of proof for fraud in a case in which no issue of fraud arises. In accordance with the general rule of evidence, the standard of proof should vary with the nature of the issue and its gravity: see *Hornal v Neuberger Products Ltd* [1957] 1 QB 247.

Now in the present case there is no question of fraud. The will directed the residue to be held in trust for the brother absolutely, and the only question is whether or not the beneficial interest thus given to him has been subjected to a trust, and if so, what that trust is. The trust, if it is one, is plainly one which required the brother to carry it out: it was he who was to distribute the money and see that everything was dealt with properly, and not the trustees of the will. There was thus no attempt to cancel the testamentary trust of residue for the brother and require the trustees of the will to hold the residue on the secret trust instead. Accordingly I cannot see that rectification provides any real analogy. The question is simply that of the ordinary standard of evidence required to establish a trust.

I therefore hold that in order to establish a secret trust where no question of fraud arises, the standard of proof is the ordinary civil standard of proof that is required to establish an ordinary trust. I am conscious that this does not accord with what was said in *Ottaway v Norman* [1972] Ch 698; but I think the point was taken somewhat shortly there, and the judge does not seem to have had the advantage of having cited to him the authorities that I have considered. For those reasons I have overcome my hesitation in differing from him. I cannot therefore dispose of the case summarily on the footing that a high standard of proof has plainly not been achieved, but I must consider the evidence in some detail to see whether the ordinary standard of proof has been satisfied. The initial question, of course, is whether the brother was bound by a secret trust, or whether he was subject to no more than a moral obligation...

The general picture which seems to me to emerge from the evidence is of a testatrix who for long had been worrying about how to divide her residue and who was still undecided. She had a brother whom she trusted implicitly and who knew her general views about her relations and her property. She therefore left her residue to him in the faith that he would, in due time and in accordance with her general wishes, make in her stead the detailed decisions about the distribution of her residue which had for so long troubled her and on which she was still undecided. He was her trusted brother, more wealthy than

> she, and a little older. There was thus no need to bind him by any legally enforceable trust; and I cannot see any real indication that she had any thought of doing this. Instead, she simply left him, as a matter of family confidence and probity, to do what he thought she would have done if she had ever finally made up her mind. In short, to revert to the language of Christian LJ in *McCormick v Grogan* (1867) IR 1 Eq 313 at 328, I cannot see any real evidence that she intended the sanction to be the authority of a court of justice and not merely the conscience of her brother. I therefore hold that her brother took the residue free from any trust.

Since it had not been established that there was a clear intention that the property should be held on trust, the first requirement of a fully secret trust had not been satisfied.

The difficulty with *Re Snowden* relates to what is meant by 'fraud' for these purposes. It appears that fraud is to be interpreted narrowly to mean deliberate and conscious wrongdoing amounting to deceit. Consequently, where the alleged secret trustee denies the existence of the trust and claims to take the property beneficially, a higher standard of proof than the normal balance of probabilities standard must be satisfied, as in *Ottaway v Norman*. Where, however, the issue is simply whether the conditions for establishing a fully secret trust have been satisfied, such as whether the testator intended such a trust to be declared, as in *Re Snowden*, there is no allegation of fraud in this narrow sense and the normal balance of probabilities standard applies. Similarly, for half-secret trusts, there will usually be no fraud in this narrow sense because the trust is clear on the face of the will. But, even with half-secret trusts, fraud in the narrow sense might be relevant if, for example, the trustee denies that the communication of the terms of the trust occurred before the will was executed and the trustee is entitled to the residuary estate, and so would take the property beneficially if the trust fails.

But this analysis of *Re Snowden* creates a paradox: it means that the worse the trustee's conduct is alleged to be, the higher the standard of proof that needs to be satisfied before the trust is recognized. It follows that, since fraud in this narrow sense of deceit need not be proved to establish a fully secret trust, it would be preferable not to plead it and for the beneficiary of the trust simply to satisfy the standard of proof on the balance of probabilities.

(e) Failure to establish all requirements of a fully secret trust

If it is possible to prove that the testator intended a trust, and that this was communicated to and accepted by the legatee, but it is not possible to prove, for example, who the intended beneficiaries were, or if the terms of the trust are unlawful or uncertain,[92] the property will be held on resulting trust for those entitled to the testator's residuary estate,[93] because of failure of the express trust. Where it is not possible to prove even that the testator intended the legatee to take the property as a trustee, he or she will take the property beneficially.

(f) Non-testamentary applications

Although a fully secret trust can arise only in the testamentary context, the principles recognized in the secret trust cases have been applied to transactions outside of wills. So, for example, in *Gold v Hill*,[94] the testator nominated his solicitor as the beneficiary of a life insurance policy. He then told the solicitor that he wanted him to use the proceeds of the policy to look after his partner and children. Following the testator's death, the solicitor received the proceeds of the policy. It was held that

---

[92] *Re Pugh's Will Trust* [1967] 1 WLR 1262.
[93] *Re Boyes* (1884) 26 Ch D 531.
[94] [1999] 1 FLR 54.

the solicitor held this money on trust for the partner and children, by analogy with a secret trust. Carnwath J said:[95]

> The nomination, like a testamentary disposition, does not transfer or create any interest until death. It is consistent with the principle of *Blackwell v Blackwell* that the nominee should take under the rules of the policy, but then be required to 'apply it as the court of conscience directs' and so 'to give effect to the wishes of the testator'. Such doubts as there may be, in the case of testamentary dispositions, as to the effectiveness of an intention communicated after the execution of the will, appear to be derived from the particular rules applying to wills. There is no reason why they should create similar difficulties in the case of nominations. Since the nomination has no effect until the time of death, it should be sufficient that the nature of the trust is sufficiently communicated prior to that time.

This was not precisely the same mechanism as a secret trust because the solicitor was nominated as beneficiary of the policy rather than in a will, but the effect was the same since the solicitor was intended to hold the money on trust for others and this became effective only on the death of the testator. At that point, the solicitor received the proceeds of the policy, but he was then obliged to apply the money for the benefit of the testator's partner and children.

(g) A unified theory of secret trusts?

Although half-secret and fully secret trusts appear to be juridically different, since one appears on the face of the will and the other does not, the preferable view is that they are not. They are both express trusts that arise 'dehors the will', even though they are constituted only once the testator has died. Both types of trust should be recognized. The trustee can be considered to have acted unconscionably in receiving property in the will and denying the existence of any trust when the testator expected the trustee to hold the property on trust for another. In other words, secret trusts are recognized to prevent fraud in the wider sense of unconscionable conduct in betraying the undertaking made to the testator.[96] It follows that the requirements for both types of trust should be the same, namely an intention to create a trust, communication of the terms to the trustee before the testator's death, and acknowledgement or acquiescence of the trust by the trustee. Analysed like this, half-secret and fully secret trusts are defensible and workable.

3. CONSTITUTION OF TRUSTS

An express trust only exists if the trust is constituted by title to the trust property being vested in the trustee. This is because there must be property upon which the trust obligations can bite; if the trustee has no property, there can be no trust. A trust can be constituted in two ways: by declaration of oneself as a trustee or by transfer of property to trustees.

(a) DECLARATION OF SELF AS TRUSTEE

If the settlor declares him or herself to be a trustee, there is no problem of constitution of the trust since the property is already vested in the settlor. The problem in this context relates to whether there

---

[95] Ibid, at 63.
[96] Hodge, 'Secret Trusts: The Fraud Theory Revisited' [1980] Conv 341.

has been a declaration of trust. It is necessary to show that the settlor manifested an intention to declare him or herself to be a trustee. Nothing else will do.[97] As Maitland observed:[98]

> [m]en often mean to give things to their kinsfolk, they do not often mean to constitute themselves trustees.

It is important to note that the two methods of constituting a trust—declaration and transfer—cannot be meshed together, so that if neither is quite effective but both are almost satisfied the court will still not find that a trust has been constituted. An intention to give will not be construed as an intention to declare oneself to be a trustee: 'An imperfect gift is no declaration of trust.'[99] As Turner LJ said in *Milroy v Lord*:[100]

> if the settlement is intended to be effectuated by one of the modes to which I have referred [either self-declaration as trustee or transfer to another to hold on trust], the Court will not give effect to it by applying another of those modes. If it is intended to take effect by transfer, the Court will not hold the intended transfer to operate as a declaration of trust, for then every imperfect instrument would be made effectual by being converted into a perfect trust.

A good illustration of this approach can be found in the following case.

Jones v Lock [1865] 1 Ch App 25

On returning from a business visit to Birmingham, Mr Jones was reproved by his family for not bringing a present for his baby son. He produced a cheque for £900 payable to himself, and said: 'Look you here, I give this to baby; it is for himself, and I am going to put it away for him, and will give him a great deal more along with it.' He placed the cheque in the baby's hand. His wife feared that the baby might tear it, and Jones added: 'Never mind if he does; it is his own, and he may do what he likes with it.' He then took the cheque back and locked it in a safe. Six days later he died. The question was whether the baby was entitled to the cheque.

It was held that there had been no gift to the baby;[101] and no declaration of trust in his favour.

Lord Cranworth LC:

This is a special case, in which I regret to say that I cannot bring myself to think that, either on principle or on authority, there has been any gift or any valid declaration of trust. No doubt a gift may be made by any person *sui juris* and *compos mentis*, by conveyance of a real estate or by delivery of a chattel; and there is no doubt also that, by some decisions, unfortunate I must think them, a parol[102] declaration of trust of personalty may be perfectly valid even when voluntary. If I give any chattel that, of course, passes by delivery, and if I say, expressly or impliedly, that I constitute myself a trustee of personalty,

---

[97] See Chapter 3.2, p. 67.
[98] Maitland, *Equity* (2nd edn) (Cambridge: Cambridge University Press, 1929) p. 72.
[99] Maitland, *Equity* (2nd edn) p. 72.
[100] *Milroy v Lord* (1862) 4 De GF & J 264 at 274. See Chapter 4.3(b)(i), pp. 150–1. For other examples of the court not saving a trust, see e.g. *Richards v Delbridge* (1874) LR 18 Eq 11.
[101] Because the gift of a non-bearer cheque requires endorsement.
[102] Meaning 'without writing'.

that is a trust executed, and capable of being enforced without consideration. I do not think it necessary to go into any of the authorities cited before me; they all turn upon the question, whether what has been said was a declaration of trust or an imperfect gift. In the latter case the parties would receive no aid from a Court of equity if they claimed as volunteers.[103] But when there has been a declaration of trust, then it will be enforced, whether there has been consideration or not. Therefore the question in each case is one of fact; has there been a gift or not, or has there been a declaration of trust or not? I should have every inclination to sustain this gift, but unfortunately I am unable to do so; the case turns on the very short question whether Jones intended to make a declaration that he held the property in trust for the child; and I cannot come to any other conclusion than that he did not. I think it would be of very dangerous example if loose conversations of this sort, in important transactions of this kind, should have the effect of declarations of trust.

Lord Cranworth obviously regretted the result, but it was difficult to establish *how* the child could receive the money. The transfer by gift was ineffective, and the situation could not be rescued by saying the father had declared himself a trustee: he did not intend a trust, but a gift.

Nevertheless it should be remembered that the word 'trust' does not need to be used explicitly in order to find that a person declared him or herself to be holding property as a trustee. For example, in *Paul v Constance*,[104] the court held that the words 'the money is as much yours as mine' in their particular context were sufficient to find that the speaker was declaring himself to hold the property as trustee for himself and the addressee of the words beneficially. Scarman LJ said:[105]

When one bears in mind the unsophisticated character of the deceased and his relationship with the plaintiff during the last few years of his life, Mr. Wilson submits that the words that he did use on more than one occasion, 'this money is as much yours as mine', convey clearly a present declaration that the existing fund was as much the plaintiff's as his own. The judge accepted that conclusion. I think that he was well justified in doing so and, indeed, I think that he was right to do so.

One case which has caused difficulty in this area, and has often been misinterpreted,[106] is that of *T Choithram International SA v Pagarani*, where the method of constitution of the trust was essentially by self-declaration.

T Choithram International SA v Pagarani [2001] 1 WLR 1 (PC)

The donor (TCP), who was seriously ill, executed a trust deed to establish a philanthropic foundation. Having appointed himself one of the trustees, he stated orally that he gave all his estate to the foundation. TCP died before deposit balances and shares had been transferred to the foundation. The claimants claimed that they were entitled to TCP's estate on an intestacy because he had not made a valid gift to the foundation.

It was held that TCP had intended to make an immediate irrevocable gift to the foundation. Since TCP was one of the trustees of the foundation he was bound by the trust and so the gift to the foundation was properly vested in all the trustees.

---

[103] See Chapter 1.5(e), pp. 19–20.
[104] [1977] 1 WLR 527. See Chapter 3.2(a), pp. 68–9.
[105] Ibid, 531.
[106] See Chapter 4.3(c)(ii), pp. 159–60.

Lord Browne-Wilkinson:

Their Lordships then turn to the central and most important question: on the basis that TCP intended to make an immediate absolute gift 'to the foundation' but had not vested the gifted property in all the trustees of the foundation, are the trusts of the foundation trust deed enforceable against the deposits and the shares or is this (as the judge and the Court of Appeal held) a case where there has been an imperfect gift which cannot be enforced against TCP's estate whatever TCP's intentions[?] . . .

So, it is said, in this case TCP used words of gift to the foundation (not words declaring himself a trustee): unless he transferred the shares and deposits so as to vest title in all the trustees, he had not done all that he could in order to effect the gift. It therefore fails. Further it is said that it is not possible to treat TCP's words of gift as a declaration of trust because they make no reference to trusts. Therefore the case does not fall within either of the possible methods by which a complete gift can be made and the gift fails. Though it is understandable that the courts below should have reached this conclusion since the case does not fall squarely within either of the methods normally stated as being the only possible ways of making a gift, their Lordships do not agree with that conclusion. The facts of this case are novel and raise a new point. It is necessary to make an analysis of the rules of equity as to complete gifts. Although equity will not aid a volunteer, it will not strive officiously to defeat a gift. This case falls between the two common-form situations mentioned above. Although the words used by TCP are those normally appropriate to an outright gift—'I give to X'—in the present context there is no breach of the principle in *Milroy v Lord* if the words of TCP's gift (i.e. to the foundation) are given their only possible meaning in this context. The foundation has no legal existence apart from the trust declared by the foundation trust deed. Therefore the words 'I give to the foundation' can only mean 'I give to the trustees of the foundation trust deed to be held by them on the trusts of foundation trust deed'. Although the words are apparently words of outright gift they are essentially words of gift on trust.

But, it is said, TCP vested the properties not in all the trustees of the foundation but only in one, i.e. TCP. Since equity will not aid a volunteer, how can a court order be obtained vesting the gifted property in the whole body of trustees on the trusts of the foundation[?] Again, this represents an over-simplified view of the rules of equity. Until comparatively recently the great majority of trusts were voluntary settlements under which beneficiaries were volunteers having given no value. Yet beneficiaries under a trust, although volunteers, can enforce the trust against the trustees. Once a trust relationship is established between trustee and beneficiary, the fact that a beneficiary has given no value is irrelevant. It is for this reason that the type of perfected gift referred to in class (b) above is effective since the donor has constituted himself a trustee for the donee who can as a matter of trust law enforce that trust.

What then is the position here where the trust property is vested in one of the body of trustees, viz. TCP? In their Lordships' view there should be no question. TCP has, in the most solemn circumstances, declared that he is giving (and later that he has given) property to a trust which he himself has established and of which he has appointed himself to be a trustee. All this occurs at one composite transaction taking place on 17 February. There can in principle be no distinction between the case where the donor declares himself to be sole trustee for a donee or a purpose and the case where he declares himself to be one of the trustees for that donee or purpose. In both cases his conscience is affected and it would be unconscionable and contrary to the principles of equity to allow such a donor to resile from his gift. Say, in the present case, that TCP had survived and tried to change his mind by denying the gift. In their Lordships' view it is impossible to believe that he could validly deny that he was a trustee for the purposes of the foundation in the light of all the steps that he had taken to assert that position and to assert his trusteeship. In their Lordships' judgment in the absence of special factors where one out of a larger body of trustees has the trust property vested in him he is bound by the trust and must give effect to it by transferring the trust property into the name of all the trustees.

> The plaintiffs relied on the decision of Sir John Romilly MR in *Bridge v Bridge* (1852) 16 Beav 315 as showing that the vesting of the trust property in one trustee, the donor, out of many is not sufficient to constitute the trust: see at 324. Their Lordships have some doubt whether that case was correctly decided on this point, the judge giving no reasons for his view. But in any event it is plainly distinguishable from the present case since the judge considered that the trust could not be fully constituted unless the legal estate in the gifted property was vested in the trustees and in that case the legal estate was vested neither in the donor nor in any of the other trustees.

It must be wondered, contrary to the opinion of the Privy Council, whether *Pagarani* was in fact all that novel at all. Noting the case, Rickett wrote:[107]

> at the end of the day the case does not fall 'between the two common form situations' and is really not novel. In effect, a different conclusion is reached on the effective constitution of the trust because their Lordships construe the case as one of a successful declaration by TCP of himself as trustee, rather than as one of transfer to trustees.

Despite Rickett's doubts as to whether this is satisfactory, the outcome seems appropriate. TCP was one of the trustees, had the relevant property, and declared himself to be holding it on trust. Admittedly, he used the language of 'handing over' the property to trustees, but to whom was he supposed to hand over the property? TCP was one of the trustees himself, and referring to him as handing money to himself might legitimately be interpreted as him holding the property he already owned on the trusts already established. This interpretation is strengthened by the Privy Council's recognition that, if the property is vested in one of a number of trustees, then the trust will be fully constituted. This is sensible: if a trustee has title to property on the understanding that it is held on trust, then it would be unconscionable for that trustee to deny that legal title should be vested in all trustees. As Lord Browne-Wilkinson memorably put it, Equity 'will not strive officiously to defeat a gift'.

(b) TRANSFER OF TRUST PROPERTY TO THE TRUSTEE

The other method of constituting a trust is for the settlor to transfer the property to the trustees. The vesting of the trust property in the trustee constitutes the trust. In a completely constituted trust, there is no need for consideration and the question of whether a beneficiary is a volunteer is immaterial.[108]

The transfer of property from the settlor to the trustee in itself has little to do with the law of trusts, and much to do with the law of gifts. The requirements for A to give property to B are found in the law concerning the transfer of property. If B happens to be a trustee, then a valid transfer will *also* mean that the trust is fully constituted. In most circumstances, the transferor will seek to transfer legal title to the trustee, but in some situations the trustee might only receive equitable title.

(i) *Legal interests*

The method of transfer of legal title varies with the property in question. A legal estate in unregistered land must be transferred by deed,[109] and in registered land by registration;[110] stocks and shares by an

---

[107] 'Completely constituting an inter vivos trust: property rules?' [2001] Conv 515, 519.
[108] See *Paul v Paul* (1882) 20 Ch D 742.
[109] Law of Property Act 1925, s. 52(1).
[110] Land Registration Act 2002.

appropriate form of transfer followed by registration of title in the share register;[111] chattels by deed of gift[112] or by an intention to give coupled with a delivery of possession.[113]

As long as the trustee receives legal title of the property, the trust will be constituted, regardless of the reason why title is vested in the trustee. This principle was made clear in *Re Ralli's Will Trusts*.[114] A testator left his residuary estate on trust for his wife for life, and then for his two daughters, Helen and Irene absolutely. Helen, by her marriage settlement, covenanted to settle property acquired subsequently in favour of the children of Irene. Helen and the testator's widow later died, leaving the claimant, who was Irene's husband, as the sole surviving trustee both of the testator's will and of the marriage settlement. Helen's share of the testator's residuary estate was thus vested in the claimant, and the question was whether the claimant held it on trust for those interested under Helen's will, or on the trusts of Helen's marriage settlement, the beneficiaries of which were the claimant's three children. Buckley J held that the property was held upon the trusts of the marriage settlement: the property was vested in the trustee of the marriage settlement, and it made no difference that it came to him in his capacity as trustee of the will trusts:[115]

> The fund, having come without impropriety into [the claimant's] hands, is now, he says, impressed in his hands with the trusts upon which he ought to hold it under the settlement; and because of the covenant it does not lie in the mouth of the defendants to say that he should hold the fund in trust for Helen's estate. . . .
>
> In my judgment the circumstance that the plaintiff holds the fund because he was appointed a trustee of the will is irrelevant. He is at law the owner of the fund, and the means by which he became so have no effect upon the quality of his legal ownership. The question is: for whom, if anyone, does he hold the fund in equity? In other words, who can successfully assert an equity against him disentitling him to stand upon his legal right? It seems to me to be indisputable that Helen, if she were alive, could not do so, for she has solemnly covenanted under seal to assign the fund to the plaintiff, and the defendants [as representatives of Helen] can stand in no better position.

Helen's representatives were unable to assert any right against the claimant, and the claimant was considered to be holding the property on the trusts of the marriage settlement. The fact that he received the property in an unanticipated manner did not affect the nature of his holding the property as such a trustee.

It is worth emphasizing again that a failed attempt to transfer title will not be reinterpreted as a declaration of trust simply in order to ensure that the gift is fully constituted. A good example of this in the context of property transfers is *Milroy v Lord*.

Milroy v Lord [1862] 4 De GF & J 264

The settlor executed a voluntary deed, purporting to transfer fifty shares in the Bank of Louisiana to Mr Lord to be held on trust for the claimants, and later handed to him the share certificates. At the time, Lord held a general power of attorney, which would have entitled him to transfer the settlor's shares. However, the shares could only be transferred by registration of the transferee in

---

[111] See Companies Act 2006 ss. 544, 770–4; Stock Transfer Act 1963, s. 1.
[112] *Jaffa v Taylor Gallery Ltd* (1990) *The Times*, 21 March.
[113] *Re Cole* [1964] Ch 175; *Thomas v Times Book Co Ltd* [1966] 1 WLR 911.
[114] [1964] Ch 288 (ChD, Buckley J).
[115] Ibid, 300–1.

the books of the bank, and this was never done. The court held that no trust of the shares had been created in favour of the claimants.

Turner LJ:

Under the circumstances of this case, it would be difficult not to feel a strong disposition to give effect to this settlement to the fullest extent, and certainly I spared no pains to find the means of doing so, consistently with what I apprehend to be the law of the Court; but, after full and anxious consideration, I find myself unable to do so. I take the law of this Court to be well settled, that, in order to render a voluntary settlement valid and effectual, the settlor must have done everything which, according to the nature of the property comprised in the settlement, was necessary to be done in order to transfer the property and render the settlement binding upon him. He may of course do this by actually transferring the property to the persons for whom he intends to provide, and the provision will then be effectual, and it will be equally effectual if he transfers the property to a trustee for the purposes of the settlement, or declares that he himself holds it in trust for those purposes; and if the property be personal, the trust may, as I apprehend, be declared either in writing or by parol; but, in order to render the settlement binding, one or other of these modes must, as I understand the law of this Court, be resorted to, for there is no equity in this Court to perfect an imperfect gift. The cases I think go further to this extent, that if the settlement is intended to be effectuated by one of the modes to which I have referred, the Court will not give effect to it by applying another of those modes. If it is intended to take effect by transfer, the Court will not hold the intended transfer to operate as a declaration of trust, for then every imperfect instrument would be made effectual by being converted into a perfect trust. These are the principles by which, as I conceive, this case must be tried.

Applying, then, these principles to the case, there is not here any transfer either of the one class of shares or of the other to the objects of the settlement, and the question therefore must be, whether a valid and effectual trust in favour of those objects was created in the defendant Samuel Lord or in the settlor himself as to all or any of these shares. Now it is plain that it was not the purpose of this settlement, or the intention of the settlor, to constitute himself a trustee of the bank shares. The intention was that the trust should be vested in the defendant Samuel Lord, and I think therefore that we should not be justified in holding that by the settlement, or by any parol declaration made by the settlor, he himself became a trustee of these shares for the purposes of the settlement. By doing so we should be converting the settlement or the parol declaration to a purpose wholly different from that which was intended to be effected by it, and, as I have said, creating a perfect trust out of an imperfect transaction. . . .

(ii) *Equitable interests*

The settlor may transfer equitable title to the trustee. This could create a sub-trust.[116] In order to transfer a subsisting equitable interest, compliance with section 53(1)(c) of the Law of Property Act 1925 is required,[117] such that signed writing is needed. In *Kekewich v Manning*,[118] for example, trustees held shares on trust for A for life, remainder to B absolutely. B assigned his equitable interest to C to hold on trust for D. This was held to create a completely constituted trust of B's equitable interest in remainder.

[116] Chapter 10.2(e), p. 510.
[117] See Chapter 10.2, p. 501.
[118] (1851) 1 De GM and G 176.

(c) FAILED GIFTS: INCOMPLETELY CONSTITUTED TRUSTS

In *Milroy v Lord*, in concluding that the transfer failed, Turner LJ relied upon the fundamental principles that 'equity will not assist a volunteer' and 'there is no equity to perfect an imperfect gift'. Thus in *Re Fry*[119] a purported gift of shares failed since the consent of the Treasury to the transfer was required, and the donor died before the consent was given. Even though the donor had applied for consent and clearly intended the transfer to occur at the time of his death, Romer J was clear that further steps were necessary for the gift to be perfected:[120]

> Now I should have thought it was difficult to say that the testator had done everything that was required to be done by him at the time of his death, for it was necessary for him to obtain permission from the Treasury for the assignment and he had not obtained it. Moreover, the Treasury might in any case have required further information of the kind referred to in the questionnaire which was submitted to him, or answers supplemental to those which he had given in reply to it; and, if so approached, he might have refused to concern himself with the matter further, in which case I do not know how anyone could have compelled him to do so.

Cases such as *Milroy* and *Fry* have sometimes been thought to be too harsh: for the gift to fail in its entirety might appear to frustrate the intentions of the donor. In order to alleviate the strict and unforgiving nature of *Milroy*, emphasis is sometimes placed upon the different maxim that 'Equity will not strive officiously to defeat a gift.'[121] This was certainly the case in *Pennington v Waine*, discussed further below, in which Arden LJ commented that:[122]

> the principle that equity will not assist a volunteer at first sight looks like a hard-edged rule of law not permitting much argument or exception. Historically the emergence of the principle may have been due to the need for equity to follow the law rather than an intuitive development of equity. The principle against imperfectly constituted gifts led to harsh and seemingly paradoxical results. Before long, equity had tempered the wind to the shorn lamb (i.e. the donee). It did so on more than one occasion and in more than one way.

There are two major ways in which it will be seen that Equity has enabled a transfer to be effective in Equity, even though it is not effective at Law: (i) where the donor has done everything in his or her power to transfer title under the 'rule in *Re Rose*'; (ii) where it would be unconscionable for the donor to deny the gift under the 'rule in *Pennington v Waine*'. Although the latter is by far the more controversial, it is important to bear in mind that *both* exceptions are open to criticism.[123] There is a respectable argument that Equity should *not* decline to follow the Law here. As Jenkins LJ observed in *Re McArdle*, if the required formalities are not fulfilled, then:[124]

> the voluntary assignment suffers the fate of other incomplete gifts: the donor has a *locus poenitentiæ* and can change his mind at any time. No question of conscience enters into the matter, for there is no consideration, and there is nothing dishonest on the part of an intending donor if he chooses to change his mind at any time before the gift is complete.

---

[119] [1946] Ch 312.
[120] [1946] Ch 312, 318-8.
[121] E.g. *T Choithram International SA v Pajarani* [2001] 1 WLR 1, 11; see Chapter 4.3(b), p. 148.
[122] [2002] EWCA Civ 227; [2002] 1 WLR 2075, [54]; see Chapter 4.3(c)(ii), pp. 159–60.
[123] See too Edelman, 'Two Fundamental Questions for the Law of Trusts' (2013) 129 LQR 66, 77–81.
[124] [1951] 1 Ch 677.

This seems sensible: if the gift is not yet completed, and the donee has not provided any consideration, then the donor might legitimately expect to be able to change his or her mind. The problem that tends to arise is that the donor dies just before the gift is perfected, and all the evidence suggests that the donor would *not* have changed his or her mind. There is clearly a desire of the courts to try to give effect to the wishes of a testator. Yet even this might be questioned. After all, it is always possible, although admittedly unusual, for a donor to declare him or herself to be holding the property on trust for the donee, pending completion of the transfer.[125]

(i) Donor or settlor has done all necessary to transfer title

The strict approach of *Milroy* and *Fry* has clearly been softened by the intervention of Equity. Of particular significance is the 'rule in *Re Rose*', which provides that if the donor has done everything in his power to complete the transfer, then the gift will be effective.

Re Rose [1952] Ch 499

On 30 March, 1943 the settlor made two transfers of shares in an unlimited company in the form required by its Articles of Association. Under the Articles, the directors of the company could refuse, at their discretion, to register a transfer. The transfers were registered on 30 June, 1943. The settlor died at a time when estate duty would have been payable on the shares if the effective date of the transfer was 30 June, but not if it was 30 March. The Court held that no duty was payable.

Evershed MR:

the Crown's argument . . . is founded [on] the broad, general proposition that if a document is expressed as, and on the face of it intended to operate as, a transfer, it cannot in any respect take effect by way of trust—so far I understand the argument to go. In my judgment, that statement is too broad and involves too great a simplification of the problem; and is not warranted by authority. I agree that if a man purporting to transfer property executes documents which are not apt to effect that purpose, the court cannot then extract from those documents some quite different transaction and say that they were intended merely to operate as a declaration of trust, which *ex facie* they were not: but if a document is apt and proper to transfer the property—is in truth the appropriate way in which the property must be transferred—then it does not seem to me to follow from the statement of Turner LJ that, as a result, either during some limited period or otherwise, a trust may not arise, for the purpose of giving effect to the transfer. The simplest case will, perhaps, provide an illustration. If a man executes a document transferring all his equitable interest, say, in shares, that document, operating, and intended to operate, as a transfer, will give rise to and take effect as a trust; for the assignor will then be a trustee of the legal estate in the shares for the person in whose favour he has made an assignment of his beneficial interest. And, for my part, I do not think that the case of *Milroy v Lord* (1862) 4 De GF & J 264 is an authority which compels this court to hold that in this case—where, in the terms of Turner LJ's judgment, the settlor did everything which, according to the nature of the property comprised in the settlement, was necessary to be done by him in order to transfer the property—the result necessarily negatives the conclusion that, pending registration, the settlor was a trustee of the legal interest for the transferee.

The view of the limitations of *Milroy v Lord*, which I have tried to express, was much better expressed by Jenkins J in the recent case which also bears the same name of *Re Rose* [1949] Ch 78 (though that is a coincidence). It is true that the main point, the essential question to be determined, was whether

---

[125] *Re Ralli's Will's Trusts*, 298.

there had been a transfer *eo nomine*[126] of certain shares within the meaning of a will. The testator in that case, Rose, by his will had given a number of shares to one Hook but the gift was subject to this qualification, 'if such shares have not been transferred to him previously to my death'. The question was, had the shares been transferred to him in these circumstances? He had executed (as had this Mr. Rose) a transfer in appropriate form and handed the transfer and the certificate to Hook; but, at the time of his death, the transfer had not been registered. It was said, therefore, that there had been no transfer; and...there had been no passing to Hook of any interest, legal or beneficial, whatever, by the time the testator died. If that view were right then, of course, Hook would be entitled to the shares under the will. But my brother went a little more closely into the matter, because it was obvious that on one view of it, if it were held that there was a 'transfer' within the terms of the will, though the transfer was inoperative in the eye of the law and not capable of being completed after the death, then Mr. Hook suffered the misfortune of getting the shares neither by gift *inter vivos* nor by testamentary benefaction. Therefore, my brother considered the case of *Milroy v Lord*, and in regard to it he used this language [1949] Ch 78 at 89:

> 'I was referred on that to the well known case of *Milroy v Lord*, and also to the recent case of *Re Fry* [1946] Ch 312. Those cases, as I understand them, turn on the fact that the deceased donor had not done all in his power, according to the nature of the property given, to vest the legal interest in the property in the donee. In such circumstances it is, of course, well settled that there is no equity to complete the imperfect gift. If any act remained to be done by the donor to complete the gift at the date of the donor's death the court will not compel his personal representatives to do that act and the gift remains incomplete and fails. In *Milroy v Lord* the imperfection was due to the fact that the wrong form of transfer was used for the purpose of transferring certain bank shares. The document was not the appropriate document to pass any interest in the property at all.'

Then he refers to *Re Fry*, which is another illustration.

> 'In this case, as I understand it, the testator had done everything in his power to divest himself of the shares in question to Mr. Hook. He had executed a transfer. It is not suggested that the transfer was not in accordance with the company's regulations. He had handed that transfer together with the certificate to Mr. Hook. There was nothing else the testator could do.'

I venture respectfully to adopt the whole of the passage I have read which, in my judgment, is a correct statement of the law. If that be so, then it seems to me that it cannot be asserted on the authority of *Milroy v Lord*, and I venture to think it also cannot be asserted as a matter of logic and good sense or principle, that because, by the regulations of the company, there had to be a gap before Mrs. Rose could, as between herself and the company, claim the rights which the shares gave her vis-à-vis the company, the deceased was not in the meantime a trustee for her of all his rights and benefits under the shares. That he intended to pass all those rights, as I have said, seems to be too plain for argument. I think the matter might be put perhaps in a somewhat different fashion, though it reaches the same end. Whatever might be the position during the period between the execution of this document and the registration of the shares, the transfers were on 30 June, 1943, registered. After registration, the title of Mrs. Rose was beyond doubt complete in every respect; and if the deceased had received a dividend between execution and registration and Mrs. Rose had claimed to have that dividend handed to her, what would have been the deceased's answer? It could no longer be that the purported gift was imperfect; it had been made perfect. I am not suggesting that the perfection was retroactive. But what else could he say? How could he, in the face of his own statement under seal, deny the proposition that he had, on 30 March, 1943, transferred the shares to his wife?—and by the phrase 'transfer the shares' surely must be meant transfer to her 'the shares and all my right title and interest thereunder'. Nothing else could sensibly have been meant.

---

[126] Meaning 'by that name'.

The Court of Appeal in *Re Rose* recognized the creation of an equitable proprietary interest, even though title had not yet passed at Law. This might appear to depart from *Re Fry*. After all, in *Re Fry*[127] the donor had done everything that was in his power to do to transfer the shares: consent was conditional upon the Treasury, a third party. Similarly, in *Re Rose*, the transfer was still conditional upon the discretion of the directors of the company to register the share transfer. After examining these cases, McKay struggled to reconcile them and ultimately favoured *Re Fry* on the basis that:[128]

> if the consent of a third person to a transfer of legal title is required, that consent must be forthcoming before the gift may be complete and perfect. With even more confidence it is submitted that even if this conclusion is incorrect, the *Re Rose* decisions are incorrect for the quite separate reason that neither donor could be said to have done all that he only could do to transfer the legal title.

However, there is little doubt that the rule in *Re Rose* is good law, at least at the level of the Court of Appeal. It has even been applied in the context of a transfer of registered land. In *Mascall v Mascall*,[129] the claimant executed a transfer of a house with registered title in favour of his son, and also handed the land certificate to him. Before the documents were sent to the Land Registry for the registration of the son as proprietor, the claimant and his son had a serious row. The claimant then sought a declaration that the transfer was void. In holding that there had been an effective gift to the son, Lawton LJ referred to *Milroy v Lord* and *Re Rose* and said:[130]

> The plaintiff had done everything in his power to transfer the house to the defendant. He had intended to do it. He had handed over the land certificate. He had executed the transfer and all that remained was for the defendant, in the ordinary way of conveyancing, to submit the transfer for stamping and then to ask the Land Registry to register his title. Mr. Pearson sought to say that, in relation to registered land, if not to unregistered land, the plaintiff could have done more because he himself, pursuant to section 18 of the Land Registration Act 1925, could have asked the Land Registry to register the transfer and he had not done so; therefore he had not done everything within his power. In my judgment, that is a fallacious argument. He had done everything in his power in the ordinary way of the transfer of registered property and, in the ordinary way, it was for the defendant to get the Land Registry to register him as the proprietor of the property.

Mascall might be thought to be something of an extension of *Re Rose* not only because of the nature of the subject matter involved, but also because the application of the rule frustrated the changed intention of the donor. But it clearly shows that title is created in Equity at the moment that the donor has nothing further to do to enable title to pass at Law.

Given that title is created in Equity, but does not pass at law, one would expect a trust relationship to arise. But what sort of a trust is created by *Re Rose*? It surely cannot be an express trust: the donor intended a gift, not a trust, so certainty of intention is lacking. It is suggested that the trust must be

---

[127] [1946] Ch 312; see Chapter 4.3(c), p. 152.
[128] McKay, 'Share Transfers and the Complete and Perfect Rule' [1976] Conv 139, 155.
[129] (1984) 50 P & CR 119.
[130] Ibid, 125. In *Brown & Root Technology Ltd v Sun Alliance and London Assurance Co Ltd* [2001] Ch 733 it was held, in the context of a dispute about the assignment of a lease that had not been registered, that the *Re Rose* principle did not apply as regards legal, rather than equitable, rights. See Dowling, 'Can Roses Survive on Registered Land?' (1999) 50 Northern Ireland Law Quarterly 90.

constructive: once the donor has done all that he can to complete the gift, it would be unconscionable for him to deny the gift, so a constructive trust arises by operation of law. This approach has been favoured by Garton,[131] who has argued that:

> it is in fact entirely possible to view all the situations where equity has intervened to perfect the transfer…as being based on unconscionability. In *Re Rose, Midland Bank v Rose* and *Mascall v Mascall* each transferor, by completing those formalities necessary of him personally, created a state of affairs whereby a third party could complete the transfer at law. In doing this, he relinquished the right to stop the legal transfer, and any attempt to prevent its completion would therefore have been unconscionable.

Considering *Re Rose* to involve the creation of a constructive trust is consistent with the approach taken by the High Court of Australia.[132] But, especially in the light of comments made in *Re McArdle*, it remains unclear *why* it would be unconscionable for the donor to resile from the gift when the donee has not given any consideration for the transfer. In any event, if the donor is to become a trustee, it would be unfortunate for him to be burdened and surprised by all the fiduciary duties which trusteeship of an express trust normally entails. The donor should become a bare constructive trustee and escape onerous fiduciary duties.[133] This analysis is consistent with the cases and explains how the donee has enforceable rights against the relevant property.

(ii) *Beyond* Re Rose: *exploiting unconscionability*

Given the controversial nature of *Re Rose*, it might be expected that the courts would be unlikely to *extend* the intervention of Equity in perfecting a gift that was imperfect at law. Yet in *Pennington v Waine*,[134] this is exactly what the Court of Appeal did. Mrs Ada Crampton told her nephew, Harold Crampton, that she wanted to give him 400 shares in a company and for him to become a director of the company, for which he needed to own at least one share. They both signed the share transfer form, which was delivered to the company's auditor, Mr Pennington, but was not delivered to the company before Ada died. Clearly, title to the shares did not pass at Law, but the Court of Appeal insisted that, because the nephew had been informed of the gift and had been made a director, it would have been unconscionable for the aunt to revoke the gift. It was held that the aunt must have been holding the shares on trust for her nephew.

When reading the case, it is important to appreciate why a 'simple' application of *Re Rose* was insufficient for title to the shares to be created in Equity. Crucially, Ada had given the transfer form to Mr Pennington, who was considered to be Ada's agent and, therefore, on her 'side'. By giving the form to her own agent, she had not done everything that was in her power to effect the transfer. After all, her own agent can be considered to be an extension of herself, and since her own agent had more to do to effect the transfer, the rule in *Re Rose* could not apply. By contrast, if Mr Pennington had been the agent of Harold, then there would be nothing more that Ada could have done, and Harold—through his own agent—would have been in the position of completing the transfer at law: *Re Rose* would therefore have applied.

---

[131] 'The Role of the Trust Mechanism in *Re Rose*' [2003] Conv 364, 374–5.

[132] *Corin v Patton* [1990] HCA 12, [38].

[133] See Chapter 14.1(c), p. 663. Indeed, Todd and Lowrie have argued that if *Re Rose* is to be accepted, the donor should not be a trustee at all, although it is unclear how this would work: Todd and Lowrie, '*Re Rose* Revisited' (1998) CLJ 46.

[134] [2002] EWCA Civ 227; [2002] 1 WLR 2075.

As a result, *Pennington* is distinguishable from *Re Rose*. But precisely why such an extension to the equitable jurisdiction was made is difficult to discern from the reasoning of the Court of Appeal. Clarke LJ said:

> I would accept [the] submission that equity will intervene only where the donor has done everything in his power to perfect the gift cannot be absolutely true since there is always something more that the donor could have done. Thus, even if Ada had delivered the transfer form to Harold, she could have done more by making a specific request to the company to register the shares in Harold's name. In my opinion Ada executed a valid equitable assignment in favour of Harold by signing the form in circumstances in which she had no intention of revoking it in the future. This is not, therefore a case of an imperfect gift (or assignment) of her equitable interest. As I see it, she thereafter held the legal interest in the shares in trust for Harold, who, as between him and her, would thereafter have been beneficially entitled to any dividend declared on the shares.

This reasoning must be doubted: it seems premature for title to be transferred at the moment of signature. If Ada signs the form, does nothing further with it, and then changes her mind the following day and destroys the form, it would seem unfair to hold that title to the shares has already passed to Harold in Equity and it is 'too late' for Ada to change her mind. After all, Harold has no right to expect the gift: he has not provided any consideration. Moreover, the suggestion that Ada becomes a trustee at the point of signature appears to confuse the two methods of constituting a trust: Ada intended to transfer the shares, not declare herself to be a trustee.

The better reasoning in the case was provided by Arden LJ, with whom Schiemann LJ agreed:[135]

> This appeal raises the question of what is necessary for the purposes of a valid equitable assignment of shares by way of gift. If the transaction had been for value, a contract to assign the share would have been sufficient: neither the execution nor the delivery of an instrument of transfer would have been required. However, where the transaction was purely voluntary, the principle that equity will not assist a volunteer must be applied and respected. . . . Accordingly the gift must be perfected, or 'completely constituted' . . .
>
> . . . for [the *Re Rose*] exception to apply it was not necessary that the donor should have done all that it was necessary to be done to complete the gift, short of registration of the transfer. On the contrary it was sufficient if the donor had done all that it was necessary for him or her to do.
>
> There is a logical difficulty with this particular exception because it assumes that there is a clear answer to the question, when does an equitable assignment of a share take place? In fact the question is circular. For if by handing the form of transfer to Mr. Pennington in this case, Ada completed the transaction of gift and the equitable assignment of the 400 shares, Harold can bring an action against Mr. Pennington to recover the shares as his property, and the principle that equity will not assist a volunteer is not infringed. If on the other hand, by handing the share transfer to Mr. Pennington, Ada did not complete the transaction of gift or the equitable assignment of the shares, Harold cannot recover the shares because to do so would mean compelling the donor or the donor's agent to take some further step. The equitable assignment clearly occurs at some stage before the shares are registered. But does it occur when the share transfer is executed, or when the share transfer is delivered to the transferee, or when the transfer is lodged for registration . . .? I return to this point below.
>
> Secondly equity has tempered the wind (of the principle that equity will not assist a volunteer) to the shorn lamb (the donee) by utilising the constructive trust. This does not constitute a declaration of trust

---

[135] Ibid; at [52]–[66].

and thus does not fall foul of the principle (see *Milroy v Lord* (1862) 4 De GF & J 264 and *Jones v Lock* (1865) LR 1 Ch App 25) that an imperfectly constituted gift is not saved by being treated as a declaration of trust. Thus, for example, in *T Choithram International SA v Pagarani* [2001] 1 WLR 1, the Privy Council held that the assets which the donor gave to the foundation of which he was one of the trustees were held upon trust to vest the same in all the trustees of the foundation on the terms of the trusts of the foundation. This particular trust obligation was not a term of the express trust constituting the foundation but a constructive trust adjunct to it. So, too, in *Rose v Inland Revenue Comrs* [1952] Ch 499, the Court of Appeal held that the beneficial interest in the shares passed when the share transfers were delivered to the transferee, and that consequently the transferor was a trustee of the legal estate in the shares from that date. At one stage in his judgment Sir Raymond Evershed MR went further and held that an equitable interest passed when the document declaring a gift was executed....

Thirdly equity has tempered the wind to the shorn lamb by applying a benevolent construction to words of gift. As explained above an imperfect gift is not saved by being treated as a declaration of trust. But where a court of equity is satisfied that the donor had an intention to make an immediate gift, the court will construe the words which the donor used as words effecting a gift or declaring a trust if they can fairly bear that meaning and otherwise the gift will fail. This point can also be illustrated by reference to *T Choithram International SA v Pagarani* [2001] 1 WLR 1....

Accordingly the principle that, where a gift is imperfectly constituted, the court will not hold it to operate as a declaration of trust, does not prevent the court from construing it to be a trust if that interpretation is permissible as a matter of construction, which may be a benevolent construction. The same must apply to words of gift. An equity to perfect a gift would not be invoked by giving a benevolent construction to words of gift or, it follows, words which the donor used to communicate or give effect to his gift.

The cases to which counsel have referred us do not reveal any, or any consistent single policy consideration behind the rule that the court will not perfect an imperfect gift. The objectives of the rule obviously include ensuring that donors do not by acting voluntarily act unwisely in a way that they may subsequently regret. This objective is furthered by permitting donors to change their minds at any time before it becomes completely constituted. This is a paternalistic objective, which can outweigh the respect to be given to the donor's original intention as gifts are often held by the courts to be incompletely constituted despite the clearest intention of the donor to make the gift. Another valid objective would be to safeguard the position of the donor: suppose, for instance, that (contrary to the fact) it had been discovered after Ada's death that her estate was insolvent, the court would be concerned to ensure that the gift did not defeat the rights of creditors. But, while this may well be a relevant consideration, for my own part I do not consider that this need concern the court to the exclusion of other considerations as in the event of insolvency there are other potent remedies available to creditors where insolvents have made gifts to defeat their claims: see for example sections 339 and 423 of the Insolvency Act 1986. There must also be, in the interests of legal certainty, a clearly ascertainable point in time at which it can be said that the gift was completed, and this point in time must be arrived at on a principled basis.

There are countervailing policy considerations which would militate in favour of holding a gift to be completely constituted. These would include effectuating, rather than frustrating, the clear and continuing intention of the donor, and preventing the donor from acting in a manner which is unconscionable. As [counsel] pointed out, both these policy considerations are evident in *T Choithram International SA v Pagarani* [2001] 1 WLR 1. It does not seem to me that this consideration is inconsistent with what Jenkins LJ said in *Re McArdle* [1951] Ch 669. His point was that there is nothing unconscionable in simply (without more) changing your mind....

If one proceeds on the basis that a principle which animates the answer to the question whether an apparently incomplete gift is to be treated as completely constituted is that a donor will not be permitted to change his or her mind if it would be unconscionable, in the eyes of equity, vis-à-vis the donee to do so, what is the position here? There can be no comprehensive list of factors which makes it unconscionable for the donor to change his or her mind: it must depend on the court's evaluation of all the relevant considerations. What then are the relevant facts here? Ada made the gift of her own free will: there is no finding that she was not competent to do this. She not only told Harold about the gift and signed a form of transfer which she delivered to Mr. Pennington for him to secure registration: her agent also told Harold that he need take no action. In addition Harold agreed to become a director of the company without limit of time, which he could not do without shares being transferred to him. If Ada had changed her mind on (say) 10 November 1998, in my judgment the court could properly have concluded that it was too late for her to do this as by that date Harold signed the form 288A, the last of the events identified above, to occur.

There is next the pure question of law: was it necessary for Ada [to] deliver the form of transfer to Harold? . . .

Even if I am correct in my view that the Court of Appeal took the view in *Rose v Inland Revenue Comrs* that delivery of the share transfers was there required, it does not follow that delivery cannot in some circumstances be dispensed with. Here, there was a clear finding that Ada intended to make an immediate gift. Harold was informed of it. Moreover, I have already expressed the view that a stage was reached when it would have been unconscionable for Ada to recall the gift. It follows that it would also have been unconscionable for her personal representatives to refuse to hand over the share transfer to Harold after her death. In those circumstances, in my judgment, delivery of the share transfer before her death was unnecessary so far as perfection of the gift was concerned.

Clearly, Arden LJ considered that the trust arose *before* delivery from 'Ada's side' to 'Harold's side'. So even though there was more that Ada *could* have done to complete the transfer, Equity would still consider title to have passed. Arden LJ and Clarke LJ, were evidently concerned that a dead woman's clear intention be respected rather than frustrated, and it would appear that this greatly influenced the result. Yet in other cases, the donor may not die and simply change his or her mind prior to delivery to the donee; in such circumstances, given *Pennington*, it may now be arguable that a trust has arisen and it is too late for the donor to change his or her mind. This is surely undesirable. Indeed, Arden LJ cited the following passage in her judgment:[136]

According to counsel's researches, the situation in the present case has not arisen in any reported cases before. I note that in her recent work, *Personal Property Law, Text, Cases and Materials* (2000), p 241 Professor Sarah Worthington takes it as axiomatic that 'notwithstanding any demonstrable intention to make a gift, there will be no effective gift in equity if the donor simply places matters (such as completed transfer forms accompanied by the relevant share certificates) in the hands of the donor's agents. In those circumstances the donor remains at liberty to recall the gift simply by revoking the instructions previously given to the agent. The donor has not done all that is necessary, and the donee is not in a position to control completion of the transfer. It follows that the intended gift will not be regarded as complete either at law or in equity.'

Worthington thought the contrary result to *Pennington* to be 'axiomatic'.

Pennington gives rise to numerous difficulties, and it may be that the reasoning was flawed: reliance was placed upon *Pagarani*, but, as has already been seen, that case was an example of *declaration* of trust, not transfer of property. As such, different considerations apply, but this was not recognized by the Court of Appeal. Instead, reliance was placed upon 'unconscionability', but it was used for very different purposes in the two cases. In *Pagarani*, it was considered to be unconscionable to refuse to

[136] Ibid, [58].

transfer title to the other trustees jointly, given that the person was *already* a trustee given his declaration. But in *Pennington*, unconscionability was used to *impose* trusteeship.

Such reliance upon *Pagarani* might mean that the reasoning is irretrievably contaminated and should not be followed. *Pennington* may just be a 'hard case' where the Court strove to give effect to a donor's clear wish that title pass to her nephew. On the other hand, using unconscionability as the touchstone for the constructive trust seems consistent with general principles of Equity and might be supported. For example, Garton has argued that:[137]

> the effect of *Pennington v Waine* should not be seen as introducing a new exception to the rule against perfecting imperfect gifts; rather it is an opportunity to recast *Re Rose* in a theoretically sound fashion by shifting the focus away from the extent of the formalities completed and onto the conscience of the transferor. In addition, a broad attitude to unconscionability, enabling the courts to take the surrounding circumstances of the transfer into account, would resolve many of the practical problems inherent in the rule as it stands.

But if unconscionability is to be used here, it must be established what factors are relevant. This is especially important given that it has long been thought not to be unconscionable to change one's mind about a gift, at least at any point before the donor has done everything in his power to effect the gift. In *Pennington*, Arden LJ stated that there can be no complete list of relevant considerations. But some guidance might be gleaned from the facts of the case itself. Thus, Doggett has written:[138]

> The donee in *Pennington* had agreed to become a director in the company, which required a share qualification, and the donor had expressly told the donee that he need not do anything further to secure the transfer of shares. These were the factors that justified a finding of unconscionability. Yet these do not constitute detriment to the donee. In *Banner Homes Group plc v. Luff Developments Ltd. (No. 2)* [2000] Ch. 372[139] two parties agreed that one would buy land and then both would own the land together, as part of a joint venture. The party making the acquisition gained from this agreement by not having the other party as a rival in the buying process. Thus it was unconscionable for this party to renege on the previous agreement, and a constructive trust arose to prevent this. Yet the donor in *Pennington* had not gained anything. So why was equity's preemptive strike, precluding a retraction which had not actually been attempted, justified in the name of unconscionability when the donee had not incurred any detriment in reliance upon the gift and the donor had not gained any benefit? On other facts disclosing genuine unconscionability the imposition of a constructive trust may be justified, but on the facts of *Pennington* and *Re Rose* the search for an explanation continues.

In *Zeital v Kaye*, Rimer LJ said that *Pennington* concerned 'special facts'.[140] But in *Curtis v Pulbrook*,[141] Briggs J took an approach contrary to that of Doggett in the extract above and said that *Pennington did* involve detrimental reliance:

> On its facts, *Pennington v Waine* appears to have been an example of a sufficient detrimental reliance by the donee, who had agreed to become a director of the subject company upon an assumption that he had received an effective gift of qualifying shares in it . . .

---

[137] 'The Role of the Trust Mechanism in *Re Rose*' [2003] Conv 364, 376.
[138] 'Explaining *Re Rose*: The Search Goes On?' (2003) 62 CLJ 263, 266.
[139] See Chapter 9.3(c), pp. 467–9.
[140] [2010] EWCA Civ 159; [2010] 2 BCLC 1, [40].
[141] [2011] EWHC 167 (Ch); [2011] 1 BCLC 638, [43].

Such detriment is to be found in assuming the onerous duties placed upon a director.[142] However, it is not clear that the donee actually suffered any detriment at all, or that losing his directorship would leave Harold in a worse position, so this explanation remains controversial. Indeed, Briggs J then continued:[143]

> I reach [my] conclusion without any great comfort that the existing rules about the circumstances when equity will and will not perfect an apparently imperfect gift of shares serve any clearly identifiable or rational policy objective.... I have thus far arrived at [my] conclusion on highly technical grounds in relation to an area of law that may warrant further examination.

Briggs J's task of reconciling conflicting cases was not easy and it may be that his conclusions are best-suited to achieving some degree of consistency with general equitable principles. However, Luxton has continued to urge caution:[144]

> The decision in *Curtis* is consistent with established principles, and Briggs J. dealt effectively with the unsatisfactory reasoning in *Pennington*. However, his Lordship's admission in *Curtis* that, but for the application of insolvency law, he 'might have been straining to find a way in which to give effect to the attempted gifts', could indicate a more general judicial readiness to depart from those principles when the opportunity arises. In *Pennington*, Arden LJ's attempt to find a rationale for equity's involvement in this area concentrated on a donor's intention at the expense of a donor's acts; and, in *Curtis*, Briggs J. was similarly attracted to treating perfection as dependent on intention. This approach risks uncertainty. An intention (even a fervent desire) to give, no matter how clearly expressed and repeated, is not enough; the donor must also do everything 'necessary to be done' as stated in *Milroy* and applied by the Court of Appeal in *Re Rose*. Recognising the judgments in *Pennington* to be less than persuasive is no reason to reject the unspoken rationale that underlies the leading cases on perfect gifts and voluntary transfers to trustees.

The judgments in *Pennington* remain difficult to explain. One commentator has suggested that we can explain the result in *Pennington* using orthodox contractual principles,[145] but it is unclear whether such an analysis would be consistent with the decided cases in the event of the donor's insolvency, for example. In *Pennington*, the nephew obtained an equitable proprietary interest under a trust. It therefore seems most likely that future cases will follow the lead of decisions such as *Zeital* and *Curtis* and will continue to try to squeeze *Pennington* within general equitable principles. Given the difficulties inherent in the latter decision, this may well lead to unfortunate contortions.

(d) COVENANTS TO SETTLE

It is important to distinguish between the creation of a trust or settlement and a covenant or contract to create one. Once a settlement is created, the beneficiaries have an equitable proprietary interest in their share of the settled property. But if the settlor has covenanted to create a settlement or to add property to an existing settlement, the rights of the intended beneficiaries depend on whether or not they can compel the settlor to complete the settlement. Traditionally, they could not do so if they were volunteers, since Equity does not assist a volunteer. If, however, a person had provided consideration,

---

[142] See Chapter 14(1)(f), pp. 669–72.
[143] [2011] EWHC 167 (Ch); [2011] 1 BCLC 638, [47]–[48].
[144] 'In Search of Perfection: The *Re Rose* Rule Rationale' [2012] Conv 70, 74–5.
[145] Tham, 'Careless Share Giving' [2006] Conv 411.

including marriage consideration,[146] he or she could enforce the covenant. This Common Law rule has now been supplemented by the Contracts (Rights of Third Parties) Act 1999, which makes it easier for a third party who has not provided consideration to be able to enforce the covenant in his or her own right.

(i) Contracts (Rights of Third Parties) Act 1999

This statute greatly improves the position of a third party to a contract who has not provided consideration.

CONTRACTS (RIGHTS OF THIRD PARTIES) ACT 1999

1. Rights of third party to enforce contractual term

Subject to the provisions of this Act, a person who is not a party to a contract (a 'third party') may in his own right enforce a term of the contract if—

 (a) the contract expressly provides that he may, or

 (b) subject to subsection (2), the term purports to confer a benefit on him.

(2) Subsection (1)(b) does not apply if on a proper construction of the contract it appears that the parties did not intend the term to be enforceable by the third party.

(3) The third party must be expressly identified in the contract by name, as a member of a class or as answering a particular description but need not be in existence when the contract is entered into.

(4) This section does not confer a right on a third party to enforce a term of a contract otherwise than subject to and in accordance with any other relevant terms of the contract.

(5) For the purpose of exercising his right to enforce a term of the contract, there shall be available to the third party any remedy that would have been available to him in an action for breach of contract if he had been a party to the contract (and the rules relating to damages, injunctions, specific performance and other relief shall apply accordingly).

(6) Where a term of a contract excludes or limits liability in relation to any matter references in this Act to the third party enforcing the term shall be construed as references to his availing himself of the exclusion or limitation.

(7) In this Act, in relation to a term of a contract which is enforceable by a third party—

'the promisor' means the party to the contract against whom the term is enforceable by the third party, and 'the promisee' means the party to the contract by whom the term is enforceable against the promisor.

As a result of this Act, the complicated Common Law rules may be circumvented by a claimant. If A enters into a contract with B to provide a benefit to C, then C may be able to invoke the Act in order sue A in his own name. However, the Act only applies to covenants entered into after 11 May, 2000,[147] and the claimant must be expressly identified in the covenant; even then, it may be that, on the true construction of the covenant, the covenantor did not intend the beneficiary to be able to enforce the relevant terms. In any event, it might be preferable for a claimant not to rely upon the Act and find a

---

[146] For example, if A offers B property on the condition that B marry A's daughter, then B offers 'marriage consideration' to A.

[147] Contracts (Rights of Third Parties) Act 1999, s. 10(2). Alternatively, the Act will apply to covenants entered into after 11 November, 1999 if the contract expressly provides that the Act shall apply: s.10(3).

trust:[148] a trust, once constituted, is irrevocable, but a claimant's rights under the Act might be extinguished by the parties to the covenant as provided for by section 2.

2. Variation and rescission of contract

(1) Subject to the provisions of this section, where a third party has a right under section 1 to enforce a term of the contract, the parties to the contract may not, by agreement, rescind the contract, or vary it in such a way as to extinguish or alter his entitlement under that right, without his consent if—

    (a) the third party has communicated his assent to the term to the promisor,

    (b) the promisor is aware that the third party has relied on the term, or

    (c) the promisor can reasonably be expected to have foreseen that the third party would rely on the term and the third party has in fact relied on it.

(2) The assent referred to in subsection (1)(a)—

    (a) may be by words or conduct, and

    (b) if sent to the promisor by post or other means, shall not be regarded as communicated to the promisor until received by him.

(3) Subsection (1) is subject to any express term of the contract under which—

    (a) the parties to the contract may by agreement rescind or vary the contract without the consent of the third party, or

    (b) the consent of the third party is required in circumstances specified in the contract instead of those set out in subsection (1)(a) to (c).

(ii) *Covenants to settle: the Common Law*

The general rule that Equity will not assist a volunteer means that it is difficult for beneficiaries to enforce the covenant. However, the beneficiary will not necessarily be without a remedy; for example, a covenant may have been made with the beneficiary by deed, upon which the beneficiary would be able to sue.[149] Similarly, if the property is actually received by the trustees, then the trust will be fully constituted and the beneficiaries will be able to enforce the trust.[150] A party is not a volunteer if he or she has provided consideration, and in Equity consideration is defined more broadly than at Common Law. Unlike at Common Law, consideration in Equity includes 'marriage consideration': where a covenant to transfer property to be held on trust is made in consideration of a marriage, the husband, wife, and any issue of the marriage[151] are able to enforce the covenant. Thus, in *Pullan v Koe*,[152] Swinfen Eady J stated:[153]

the trustees are entitled to come into a Court of Equity to enforce a contract to create a trust, contained in a marriage settlement, for the benefit of the wife and the issue of the marriage, all of whom are within the marriage consideration. The husband covenanted that he and his heirs, executors, and

---

[148] Section 7(1) provides that the Act is in addition to, and does not replace, the Common Law. See too *Nisshin Shipping Co. Ltd v Cleaves & Co. Ltd* [2003] EWHC 2602 (Comm); [2004] 1 All ER (Comm) 481.

[149] *Cannon v Hartley* [1949] Ch 213.

[150] *Paul v Paul* (1882) 20 Ch D 742.

[151] This includes grandchildren and great-grandchildren: *MacDonald v Scott* [1893] AC 642, 650.

[152] [1913] 1 Ch 9.

[153] Ibid, at 14.

administrators should, as soon as circumstances would admit, convey, assign, and surrender to the trustees the real or personal property to which his wife should become beneficially entitled. The trustees are entitled to have that covenant specifically enforced by a Court of Equity. In *Re D'Angibau* (1879) 15 Ch D 228 at 242 and in *Re Plumptre's Marriage Settlement* [1910] 1 Ch 609 at 616 it was held that the Court would not interfere in favour of volunteers, not within the marriage consideration, but here the plaintiffs are the contracting parties and the object of the proceeding is to benefit the wife and issue of the marriage.

The two cases cited by the judge in this passage highlight the limits of marriage consideration: only the legitimate children of the marriage will be within the marriage consideration, not other relatives, including illegitimate children and children from other marriages. It is common in marriage settlements to include an ultimate remainder in favour of the next-of-kin of one of the spouses, given that it is not normally known when a marriage settlement is made whether or not the marriage will produce any children. However, the next of kin is not within the marriage consideration and, therefore, cannot enforce any of the obligations it contains.[154]

Although consideration is defined more broadly in Equity than at Common Law, some difficulties remain. As at Common Law, it is important that the consideration moves from the claimant, rather than from a third party. If valuable consideration for the covenant is provided by a third party, it will not have come from the beneficiary, so the beneficiary will not be able to enforce the covenant.

Re Cook's Settlement Trusts [1965] Ch 902

In 1934, by an agreement and subsequent settlement of family property, made between Sir Herbert Cook, Sir Francis Cook (his son), and the trustees of the settlement, certain pictures became the absolute property of Sir Francis Cook. In the settlement, Sir Francis covenanted (clause 6) for valuable consideration that if any of those pictures should be sold during his lifetime, the net proceeds of sale should be paid to the trustees of the settlement to be held upon the trusts of the settlement.

In 1962, Sir Francis gave a picture by Rembrandt to his wife, who wanted to sell it. The question was whether, on the sale of the Rembrandt, the trustees were obliged to take steps to enforce the performance of the covenant. Buckley J held that as the beneficiaries had given no consideration for the covenant, they could not require the trustees to take steps to enforce it.

Buckley J:

Mr. Goff, appearing for Sir Francis, has submitted first that, as a matter of law, the covenant contained in clause 6 of the settlement is not enforceable against him by the trustees of the settlement...[He] submits that the covenant was a voluntary and executory contract to make a settlement in a future event and was not a settlement of a covenant to pay a sum of money to the trustees. He further submits that as regards the covenant all the beneficiaries under the settlement are volunteers, with the consequence that not only should the court not direct the trustees to take proceedings on the covenant but it should positively direct them not to take proceedings. He relies upon *Re Pryce* [1917] 1 Ch 234 and *Re Kay's Settlement* [1939] Ch 329.

---

[154] *Re Plumptre's Settlement* [1910] 1 Ch 609.

Counsel for the second and third defendants have contended that on the true view of the facts there was an immediate settlement of the obligation created by the covenant, and not merely a covenant to settle something in the future. It was said, as Mr. Monckton put it, that by the agreement Sir Herbert bought the rights arising under the covenant for the benefit of the *cestuis que trustent* under the settlement and that, the covenant being made in favour of the trustees, these rights became assets of the trust. He relied on *Fletcher v Fletcher* (1844) 4 Hare 67; *Williamson v Codrington* (1750) 1 Ves Sen 511 and *Re Cavendish Browne's Settlement Trusts* [1916] WN 341. I am not able to accept this argument. The covenant with which I am concerned did not, in my opinion, create a debt enforceable at law, that is to say, a property right, which, although to bear fruit only in the future and upon a contingency, was capable of being made the subject of an immediate trust, as was held to be the case in *Fletcher v Fletcher*. Nor is this covenant associated with property which was the subject of an immediate trust as in *Williamson v Codrington*. Nor did the covenant relate to property which then belonged to the covenantor, as in *Re Cavendish Browne's Settlement Trusts*. In contrast to all these cases, this covenant upon its true construction is, in my opinion, an executory contract to settle a particular fund or particular funds of money which at the date of the covenant did not exist and which might never come into existence. It is analogous to a covenant to settle an expectation or to settle after-acquired property. The case, in my judgment, involves the law of contract, not the law of trusts.

As an alternative argument, Mr. Brightman formulated this proposition, which he admitted not to be directly supported by any authority, but he claimed to conflict with none: that where a covenantor has for consideration moving from a third party covenanted with trustees to make a settlement of property, the court will assist an intended beneficiary who is a volunteer to enforce the covenant if he is specially an object of the intended trust or (which Mr. Brightman says is the same thing) is within the consideration of the deed. In formulating this proposition Mr. Brightman bases himself on language used by Cotton LJ in *Re D'Angibau* (1879) 15 Ch D 228 at 242 and by Romer J in *Cannon v Hartley* [1949] Ch 213 at 223. As an example of a case to which the proposition would apply, Mr. Brightman supposes a father having two sons who enters into an agreement with his elder son and with trustees whereby the father agrees to convey an estate to his elder son absolutely in consideration of the son covenanting with his father and the trustees, or with the trustees alone, to settle an expectation on trusts for the benefit of the younger son. The younger son is a stranger to the transaction, but he is also the primary (and special) beneficiary of the intended settlement. A court of equity should, and would, Mr. Brightman contends, assist the younger son to enforce his brother's covenant and should not permit the elder son to frustrate the purposes of the agreement by refusing to implement his covenant although he has secured the valuable consideration given for it. The submission is not without attraction, for it is not to be denied that, generally speaking, the conduct of a man who, having pledged his word for valuable consideration, takes the benefits he has so obtained and then fails to do his part, commands no admiration. I have, therefore, given careful consideration to this part of the argument to see whether the state of the law is such as might justify me (subject to the construction point) in dealing with the case on some such grounds.

There was no consideration for Sir Francis's covenant moving from the trustees; nor, of course, was there any consideration moving from Sir Francis's children.

... there is an equitable exception to the general rule of law which I have mentioned where the contract is made in consideration of marriage and the intended beneficiary who seeks to have the contract enforced is within the marriage consideration. They do not support the existence of any wider exception save perhaps in the case of a beneficiary who is not within the marriage consideration but whose interests under the intended trusts are closely interwoven with interests of others who are within that consideration. They do not support the view that any such exception exists in favour of a person who was not a party to the contract and is not to be treated as though he had been and who has given no consideration and is not to be treated as if he had given consideration. Where the obligation to settle property has been assumed voluntarily it is clear that no object of the intended trusts can enforce the obligation. Thus in *Re Kay's*

Settlement [1939] Ch 329, a spinster made a voluntary settlement in favour of herself and her issue which contained a covenant to settle after-acquired property. She later married and had children who, as volunteers, were held to have no right to enforce the covenant. Mr. Brightman distinguishes that case from the present on the ground that in *Re Kay's Settlement* the settlement and covenant were entirely voluntary, whereas Sir Francis received consideration from Sir Herbert; but Sir Francis received no consideration from his own children. Why, it may be asked, should they be accorded an indulgence in a court of equity which they would not have been accorded had Sir Herbert given no consideration? As regards them the covenant must, in my judgment, be regarded as having been given voluntarily. A plaintiff is not entitled to claim equitable relief against another merely because the latter's conduct is unmeritorious. Conduct by A which is unconscientious in relation to B so as to entitle B to equitable relief may not be unconscientious in relation to C so that C will have no standing to claim relief notwithstanding that the conduct in question may affect C. The father in Mr. Brightman's fictitious illustration could after performing his part of the contract release his elder son from the latter's covenant with him to make a settlement on the younger son, and the younger son could, I think, not complain. Only the covenant with the trustees would then remain, but this covenant would be a voluntary one, the trustees having given no consideration. I can see no reason why in these circumstances the court should assist the younger son to enforce the covenant with the trustees. But the right of the younger son to require the trustees to enforce their covenant, could not, I think, depend on whether the father had or had not released his covenant. Therefore, as it seems to me, on principle the younger son would not in any event have an equitable right to require the trustees to enforce their covenant. In other words, the arrangement between the father and his elder son would not have conferred any equitable right or interest upon his younger son.

I reach the conclusion that Mr. Brightman's proposition is not well-founded.... Accordingly, the second and third defendants are not, in my judgment, entitled to require the trustees to take proceedings to enforce the covenant even if it is capable of being construed in a manner favourable to them.

This passage from *Cook* highlights various issues. One is the suggestion that the trustees should be directed by the court not to sue on the covenant. This is surprising: after all, even though the beneficiary has not given consideration and is a volunteer, the trustee *is* a party to the contract, so would be expected to be able to bring a claim at Common Law. Yet the contrary was suggested in *Cook*, relying on the previous cases of *Re Pryce* and *Re Kay*. The fear seems to be that any other approach would allow the beneficiaries to achieve indirectly what they could not achieve directly. This has been powerfully criticized.

Elliott, 'Enforcing Covenants in Favour of Volunteers' (1960) 76 LQR 100, 114

Suppose the covenant is made directly with the volunteer and not with a person expressed to be a trustee for him. In this situation the volunteer may sue at law on the covenant. Equity will not stand in his light, he is given full damages, and the fact that he gave no consideration is immaterial, since he is suing on a promise under seal. In what way is the volunteer-covenantee more deserving of equity's indulgence than [a purported beneficiary]? That feature which equity regards with something less than enthusiasm in a litigant (*i.e.*, the fact that he gave no consideration) is common to them both. It may be answered that the volunteer-covenantee does not need equity's indulgence, but neither does [the purported beneficiary]—he merely asks to be free of gratuitous interference....

In truth, the interposition of a trustee-covenantee cannot make any material difference to the volunteer, provided that the trustee is willing to sue at law; yet if *Re Pryce* and *Re Kay's Settlement* are right, even a willing trustee will be directed not to sue. Since there is no discernible difference between the volunteer-covenantee and the volunteer with a trustee-covenantee who is willing to help him the conclusion must be that these cases are wrong on this point.

The logic underpinning this argument is compelling. A trustee-covenantee should be able to assert his or her legal rights. There is no good reason for suppressing his or her claim. Nor is it correct that he or she would only be able to recover nominal damages for breach of the covenant, since it is the beneficiary and not the trustee who bears a substantial loss: in *Re Cavendish Browne's Settlement Trusts*,[155] Younger J decided that:

> the trustees were entitled to recover...substantial damages for breach of the covenant to assure, and that the measure of damages was the value of the property which would have come to the hands of the trustees if the covenant had been duly performed.

(e) TRUSTS OF A PROMISE

The passage from *Cook* also raises issues concerning covenants relating to property to be acquired in the future. One difficulty here is that it is impossible to have a trust over future property. However, the covenant can operate as a promise to transfer the property once acquired, so that when the covenantor does get the property, Equity will assume that it has already been transferred to the trust so that the covenantee obtains an equitable interest in it.[156] As a result, the covenantor holds the property on constructive trust for the covenantee. This helps to explain the result in *Pullan v Koe*.[157] The effect of a marriage settlement was that property was settled on the husband, wife, and any children of the marriage. The wife covenanted to settle on the same trusts any property worth £100 or more that she acquired after the marriage. She received a present of £285 from her mother, which was credited to her husband's bank account. Some of this money was used to buy bonds and the interest on these bonds was also credited to the account. Her husband died and the trustees of the marriage settlement claimed the bonds from her husband's executors. It was held that the gift from her mother was held on trust and, since the bonds had been bought with this money, they became trust property as well. When the wife received the gift from her mother, Equity assumed that it had already been transferred to the trust by virtue of the wife's covenant.[158]

A possible alternative approach, which might apply on certain facts, is that the settlor's promise to transfer property to the trust is a chose in action and, therefore, property in its own right; this chose in action is capable of being held on trust by the trustees for the benefit of the beneficiary. Such 'trusts of the promise' are constituted immediately the promise is made, so the fact the beneficiary is a volunteer is irrelevant; the trustee can enforce the promise for the benefit of the beneficiary,[159] or the beneficiary can enforce the promise him or herself, joining the trustee as co-claimant or as defendant.[160]

In *Re Cook's Settlement Trusts*, Buckley J doubted whether a covenant to settle future property can be the subject matter of a trust, but the better view is that it is entirely possible, since the subject matter of the trust is not the property that will be acquired in the future but rather the existing promise. *Fletcher v Fletcher*, one of the cases cited by Buckley J in *Re Cook*, illustrates this point.

---

[155] [1916] WN 341.
[156] *Norman v Federal Commissioner of Taxation* (1963) 109 CLR 9, 24 (Windeyer J) (High Court of Australia).
[157] [1913] 1 Ch 9; see Chapter 4.3(d)(ii), pp. 163–4.
[158] See *Smith v Lucas* (1881) 18 Ch D 531, 543 (Jessel MR).
[159] *Lloyd's v Harper* (1880) 16 Ch D 290. See also *Barclays Bank plc v Willowbrook International Ltd* [1987] 1 FTLR 386; *Harrison v Tew* [1989] QB 307.
[160] *Affréteurs Réunis SA v Leopold Walford (London) Ltd* [1919] AC 801.

Fletcher v Fletcher [1844] 4 Hare 67

By a voluntary deed, Mr Fletcher covenanted with trustees to pay to them £60,000, which the trustees were to hold upon trust for, in the events which happened, his illegitimate son. The trustees were unaware of the deed, which was found among Fletcher's papers after his death. The trustees did not wish to establish the trust except under an order of the court. The court held that the son was entitled to enforce the covenant against the father's executor.

Wigram V-C:

It is not denied that, if the plaintiff in this case had brought an action in the name of the trustees, he might have recovered the money; and it is not suggested, that if the trustees had simply allowed their name to be used in the action, their conduct could have been impeached. There are two classes of cases, one of which is in favour of, and the other, if applicable, against, the plaintiff's claim. The question is, to which of the two classes it belongs.

In trying the equitable question I shall assume the validity of the instrument at law. If there was any doubt of that it would be reasonable to allow the Plaintiff to try the right by suing in the name of the surviving trustee. The first proposition relied upon against the claim in equity was, that equity will not interfere in favour of a volunteer. That proposition, though true in many cases, has been too largely stated. A court of equity, for example, will not, in favour of a volunteer, enforce the performance of a contract in specie. That it will, however, sometimes act in favour of a volunteer is proved by the common case of a volunteer on a bond who may prove his bond against the assets. Again, where the relation of trustee and cestui que trust is constituted, as where property is transferred from the author of the trust into the name of a trustee, so that he has lost all power of disposition over it, and the transaction is complete as regards him, the trustee, having accepted the trust, cannot say he holds it, except for the purposes of the trust; and the Court will enforce the trust at the suit of a volunteer. According to the authorities, I cannot, I admit, do anything to perfect the liability of the author of the trust, if it is not already perfect. This covenant, however, is already perfect. The covenantor is liable at law, and the Court is not called upon to do any act to perfect it. One question made in argument has been, whether there can be a trust of a covenant the benefit of which shall belong to a third party; but I cannot think there is any difficulty in that. Suppose, in the case of a personal covenant to pay a certain annual sum for the benefit of a third person, the trustee were to bring an action against the covenantor; would he be afterwards allowed to say he was not a trustee? If he cannot do so after once acknowledging the trust, then there is a case in which there is a trust of a covenant for another. In the case of *Clough v Lambert* (1839) 10 Sim 174 the question arose; the point does not appear to have been taken during the argument, but the Vice-Chancellor of England was of opinion that the covenant bound the party; that the *cestui que trust* was entitled to the benefit of it; and that the mere intervention of a trustee made no difference. The proposition, therefore, that in no case can there be a trust of a covenant is clearly too large, and the real question is whether the relation of trustee and *cestui que trust* is established in the present case.

However, although the courts may have been more generous in the past,[161] it is now clear that the courts will not readily infer that a promise is to be held on trust. In *Vandepitte v Preferred Accident Insurance Corpn of New York*,[162] Lord Wright held that:

the intention to constitute the trust must be affirmatively proved: the intention cannot necessarily be inferred from the mere general words of the [contract].

A clear intention of the settlor that the promise be held on trust must be established.

---

[161] Cf *Affréteurs Réunis SA v Leopold Walford (London) Ltd* [1919] AC 801.
[162] [1933] AC 70, 79–80. See too *Re Schebsman* [1944] Ch 83.

(f) *DONATIO MORTIS CAUSA*

'*Donatio mortis causa*' means 'deathbed gift'. This equitable doctrine operates to render a gift effective in Equity, even where the requisite formalities have not been complied with, if: (i) it was made by the donor in contemplation of death; (ii) the gift was conditional upon his death; and (iii) the property or essential indicia of title to the property were given to the donee. This last requirement might be fulfilled by giving the keys to a car to the donee, for example, without actually handing over the car itself.[163] It is important to appreciate that the gift only becomes irrevocable upon the donor's death, and before that point he is free to change his mind.[164] However, if the three criteria given here are fulfilled, it is just for Equity to perfect the imperfect gift by compelling the personal representatives of the deceased to perfect the donee's title, even though the donee is a volunteer.

Sen v Headley[165] held that land could be the subject of a *donatio mortis causa*. In that case, the donor, on his deathbed, gave the donee the keys to a box containing the title deeds to a house he owned, and he told the donee that he was giving the house to her. Clearly, the necessary formalities for the transfer of land were not fulfilled, but the Court of Appeal insisted that the gift took effect in equity. Nourse LJ said:[166]

> the three general requirements for such a gift may be stated very much as they are stated in *Snell's Equity*...First, the gift must be made in contemplation, although not necessarily in expectation, of impending death. Secondly, the gift must be made upon the condition that it is to be absolute and perfected only on the donor's death, being revocable until that event occurs and ineffective if it does not. Thirdly, there must be a delivery of the subject matter of the gift, or the essential indicia of title thereto, which amounts to a parting with dominion and not mere physical possession over the subject matter of the gift....
>
> It cannot be doubted that title deeds are the essential indicia of title to unregistered land. Moreover, on the facts found by the judge, there was here a constructive delivery of the title deeds of 56, Gordon Road equivalent to an actual handing of them by Mr. Hewett to Mrs. Sen. and it could not be suggested that Mr. Hewett did not part with dominion over *the deeds*. The two questions which remain to be decided are, first, whether Mr. Hewett parted with dominion over *the house*; secondly, if he did, whether land is capable of passing by way of a *donatio mortis causa*....
>
> It is true that in the eyes of the law Mr. Hewett, by keeping his own set of keys to the house, retained possession of it. But the benefits which thereby accrued to him were wholly theoretical. He uttered the words of gift, without reservation, two days after his readmission to hospital, when he knew that he did not have long to live and when there could have been no practical possibility of his ever returning home. He had parted with dominion over the title deeds. Mrs. Sen had her own set of keys to the house and was in effective control of it. In all the circumstances of the case, we do not believe that the law requires us to hold that Mr. Hewett did not part with dominion over the house. We hold that he did....
>
> Let it be agreed that the doctrine is anomalous. Anomalies do not justify anomalous exceptions. If due account is taken of the present state of the law in regard to mortgages and choses in action, it is apparent that to make a distinction in the case of land would be to make just such an exception. A *donatio mortis causa* of land is neither more nor less anomalous than any other. Every such gift is a circumvention of the Wills Act 1837. Why should the additional statutory formalities for the creation and

---

[163] *Woodard v Woodard* [1995] 3 All ER 980.
[164] *Jones v Selby* (1710) Prec. Ch 300.
[165] [1991] Ch 425.
[166] [1991] Ch 425, 431.

> transmission of interests in land be regarded as some larger obstacle? The only step which has to be taken is to extend the application of the implied or constructive trust arising on the donor's death from the conditional to the absolute estate.

If the requirements of *donatio mortis causa* are satisfied, a constructive trust arises so that the personal representative of the donor holds the property on trust for the donee. If the donee is him- or herself a trustee, this will fully constitute a trust.

However, it is clear that *donatio mortis causa* is an anomalous doctrine that has been greatly restricted. This was again pointed out by the Court of Appeal in *King v Dubrey*,[167] a case where *donatio mortis causa* (referred to as 'DMC') failed because the donor ('D') was not on her deathbed or suffering from a fatal illness that meant that she was acting in contemplation of her imminent death. Jackson LJ said:[168]

> ...I must confess to some mystification as to why the common law has adopted the doctrine of DMC at all. The doctrine obviously served a useful purpose in the social conditions prevailing under the later Roman Empire. But it serves little useful purpose today, save possibly as a means of validating death bed gifts. Even then considerable caution is required. What D says to those who are ministering to him in the last hours of his/her life may be a less reliable expression of his/her wishes than a carefully drawn will. The will may have been prepared with the assistance of a solicitor and in the absence of the beneficiaries. There are no such safeguards during a deathbed conversation. The words contained in a will are there for all to see. There may be much scope for disagreement about what D said to those visiting or caring for him in the last hours of his life.
>
> In my view therefore it is important to keep DMC within its proper bounds. The court should resist the temptation to extend the doctrine to an ever wider range of situations.

(g) THE RULE IN *STRONG V BIRD*

Another method for perfecting an imperfect gift is known as the 'rule in *Strong v Bird*'. Essentially, this rule provides that if the donee of a promised gift obtains title to the gift in another capacity, this will be sufficient to perfect the gift in Equity. Usually, the other capacity in which the donee receives the gift is that of executor.

In *Strong v Bird*,[169] the donor was Mr Bird's step-mother, who lived with him. She paid a sum of money to Bird each month. He then borrowed money from her and it was agreed that Bird would repay the debt over time by deducting a sum each month from what she paid to him. The step-mother did this for two months and then continued to pay the full amount to Bird. On her death, Bird was appointed her executor. The question for the court was whether the debt which Bird continued to owe his step-mother could be considered to have been released through his appointment as executor. It was held that the debt was released when he obtained probate of the will. Sir George Jessel MR said:[170]

> First of all, it is said, and said quite accurately, that the mere saying by a creditor to a debtor, 'I forgive you the debt,' will not operate as a release at law. It is what the law calls *nudum pactum*,

---

[167] [2015] EWCA Civ 581; [2016] 2 WLR 1.
[168] Ibid, [53]–[54].
[169] (1874) LR 18 Eq 315.
[170] Ibid, at 317.

a promise made without an actual consideration passing, and which consequently cannot be supported as a contract. It is not a release, because it is not under seal. Therefore the mere circumstance of saying, 'I will forgive you,' will not do. There are, however, two modes in which, as it
appears to me, the validity of this transaction can be supported. First of all, we must consider what
the law requires. The law requires nothing more than this, that in a case where the thing which is
the subject of donation is transferable or releasable at law, the legal transfer or release shall take
place. The gift is not perfect until what has been generally called a change of the property at law
has taken place. Allowing that rule to operate to its full extent, what occurred was this. The donor,
or the alleged donor, had made her will, and by that will had appointed Mr. *Bird*, the alleged donee,
executor. After her death he proved the will, and the legal effect of that was to release the debt in
law, and therefore the condition which is required, namely, that the release shall be perfect at law,
was complied with by the testatrix making him executor. It is not necessary that the legal change
shall knowingly be made by the donor with a view to carry out the gift. It may be made for another
purpose; but if the gift is clear, and there is to be no recall of the gift, and no intention to recall it,
so that the person who executes the legal instrument does not intend to invest the person taking
upon himself the legal ownership with any other character, there is no reason why the legal instrument should not have its legal effect. For instance, suppose this occurred, that a person made a
memorandum on the title-deeds of an estate to this effect: 'I give *Blackacre* to A. B.,' and afterwards conveyed that estate to A. B. by a general description, not intending in any way to change
the previous gift, would there be any equity to make the person who had so obtained the legal
estate a trustee for the donor? The answer would be that there is no resulting trust; that is rebutted
by shewing that the person who conveyed did not intend the person taking the conveyance to be
a trustee, and although the person conveying actually thought that that was not one of the estates
conveyed, because that person thought that he had well given the estate before, still the estate
would pass at law, notwithstanding that idea, and there being no intention to revoke the gift, surely
it would get rid of any resulting trust. On the same principle, when a testator makes his debtor
executor, and thereby releases the debt at law, he is no longer liable at law. It is said that he would
be liable in this Court: and so he would, unless he could shew some reason for not being made
liable. Then what does he shew here? Why he proves to the satisfaction of the Court a continuing
intention to give; and it appears to me that there being the continuing intention to give, and there
being a legal act which transferred the ownership or released the obligation—for it is the same
thing—the transaction is perfected, and he does not want the aid of a Court of Equity to carry it
out, or to make it complete, because it is complete already, and there is no equity against him to
take the property away from him.

This reasoning has been applied to perfect imperfect gifts.[171] So, even if the donor does not fall
within the rule in *Re Rose*, as long as he or she had the intention to make an immediate gift of
the property, and still had that intention at the time of his or her death, then the gift will be
perfected if the donee obtains title to the property by becoming the executor. The rule applies in
the same way if the donee receives the property through being the administrator of the donor's
estate.[172] If the donee is to be a trustee, the rule in *Strong v Bird* can operate to constitute the
trust.[173]

[171] *Re Stewart* [1908] 2 Ch 251.
[172] *Re James*[1935] Ch 449; cf *Re Gonin* [1979] Ch 16, 34.
[173] Cf. *Re Ralli's Will Trust* [1964] Ch 288; see Chapter 4.3(b)(i), p. 150.

QUESTION

James transferred title to a property he owned to Richard. He orally told Richard to hold the land on trust for Barry. James also told his agent, Steve, to transfer shares in Lucrative Ltd to Sarah and Jenna to hold on trust for Amy.

James fell ill one week later. Aware he was about to die, he asked his brother, Colin, to come to see him in hospital. James gave Colin the keys to the lock on his bicycle, and told Colin that the bicycle was his. James died the following day.

Steve gave the share transfer form to Sarah that same day. In his will, James had provided that those shares should be held by Barry. James had told Barry some years earlier that he was to hold those shares on trust for James' lover, Kate.

Advise Barry, Sarah, and Colin.

FURTHER READING

Critchley, 'Instruments of Fraud, Testamentary Dispositions and the Doctrine of Secret Trusts' (1999) 115 LQR 631.

Fuller, 'Consideration and Form' (1941) 41 Columbia Law Review 799.

Garton, 'The Role of the Trust Mechanism in *Re Rose*' [2003] Conv 364.

Glister, 'Disclaimer and Secret Trusts' [2014] Conv 11.

Hayton, '*Ottaway v Norman*' [1972] Conv 129.

Hodge, 'Secret Trusts: The Fraud Theory Revisited' [1980] Conv 341.

Kincaid, 'Secret and Semi-secret Trusts: Justifying Distinctions between the Two' [1995] Conv 366.

Kincaid, 'The Tangled Web: The Relationship Between a Secret Trust and the Will' [2000] Conv 420.

Luxton, 'In Search of Perfection: The *Re Rose* Rule Rationale' [2012] Conv 70.

Matthews, 'The True Basis of the Half-secret Trust?' [1979] Conv 360.

McKay, 'Share Transfers and the Complete and Perfect Rule' [1976] Conv 139.

Pawlowski and Brown, 'Constituting a Secret Trust by Estoppel' [2004] Conv 388.

Rickett, 'Thoughts on Secret Trusts from New Zealand' [1996] Conv 302.

Rickett, 'Completely Constituting an *Inter Vivos* trust: Property Rules?' [2001] Conv 515.

Scott, 'Conveyances upon Trusts Not Properly Declared' (1924) 37 Harvard L Rev 653.

Swadling, 'The Nature of the Trust in *Rochefoucauld v Boustead*', in *Constructive and Resulting Trusts* (ed. Mitchell) (Oxford: Hart, 2010).

Wilde, 'Secret and Semi-secret Trusts: Justifying Distinctions between the Two' [1995] Conv 366.

Youdan, 'Formalities for Trusts of Land, and the Doctrine in *Rochefoucauld v Boustead*' (1984) 43 CLJ 306.

PART III

PURPOSE TRUSTS

5

CHARITABLE PURPOSE TRUSTS

CENTRAL ISSUES

1. A charitable trust is a public trust for purposes that provide a benefit to the public or a section of the public.

2. Charitable trusts are heavily regulated and subject to supervision by the Charity Commission.

3. A trust will only be charitable if established for a purpose that the law regards as charitable. There are a large number of charitable purposes recognized by statute, including the relief and prevention of poverty and the advancement of education and religion.

4. When determining whether a sufficient section of the public is benefited, generally there must not be a personal nexus between

the settlor of the trust and those who will benefit from it.

5. The purposes of the trust must be wholly and exclusively charitable otherwise the trust will be void.

6. The consequences of the charitable trust failing depend on whether the failure occurs initially or subsequently. If the purpose fails initially and the settlor had a general charitable intention, the trust property can be applied for a similar charitable purpose through the application of a body of rules known as the cy-près doctrine. If the purpose fails subsequently the cy-près doctrine will apply automatically.

1. THE ESSENTIAL CHARACTERISTICS OF A CHARITY

In Part II, we examined private trusts for individual beneficiaries. In Part III, we are concerned with trusts for purposes. The beneficiary principle requires there to be identifiable people who are able to enforce the trust.[1] It follows that a trust for purposes will generally not be valid. One significant exception to this principle is that charitable trusts have long been recognized as valid even though they are trusts for purposes rather than for particular people. These express trusts are treated with special favour by the law because they provide a benefit to the public or a section of the public. Charitable trusts can usefully be characterized as public trusts since they promote purposes beneficial to the community,[2] as distinct from trusts for people, which are private trusts because they provide benefits to private individuals. Charitable trusts operate in a very different legal, fiscal, and social context

---

[1] See Chapter 3.6, pp. 110–12.
[2] *Gaudiya Mission v Brahmachary* [1998] Ch 341, 350 (Mummery LJ).

to private trusts. There are over 165,000 charities registered with the Charity Commission, with an annual income of over £70 billion.[3] Equity has had a very important role in developing the law relating to the creation, definition, and operation of charities.

A charitable institution is defined by statute.

CHARITIES ACT 2011

1 Meaning of 'charity'

(1) For the purposes of the law of England and Wales, 'charity' means an institution which—

    (a) is established for charitable purposes only, and

    (b) falls to be subject to the control of the High Court in the exercise of its jurisdiction with respect to charities.

9 Interpretation

(3) In this Act 'institution' means an institution whether incorporated or not, and includes a trust or undertaking.

Since a charity must be subject to the jurisdiction of the High Court it follows that the charity must be established under English law, even if the charitable purpose is to be fulfilled abroad.

The essential characteristics of a charity were recognized by Mummery LJ in *Gaudiya Mission v Brahmachary*:[4]

> A charity does not have to take any particular legal form; it may be a trust or an undertaking; it may be incorporated or unincorporated. But it must satisfy both requirements for the definition in section 96(1).[5] It must be 'established for charitable purposes'. It will be noted that 'charitable purposes' is a defined term, meaning those 'purposes which are exclusively charitable according to the law of England and Wales';[6] and it must be 'subject to the control of the High Court in the exercise of the court's jurisdiction with respect to charities'...
>
> Under English law charity has always received special treatment. It often takes the form of a trust; but it is a public trust for the promotion of purposes beneficial to the community, not a trust for private individuals. It is therefore subject to special rules governing registration, administration, taxation and duration. Although not a state institution, a charity is subject to the constitutional protection of the Crown as *parens patriae*, acting through the Attorney-General, to the state supervision of the Charity Commissioners and to the judicial supervision of the High Court. This regime applies whether the charity takes the form of a trust or of an incorporated body.

So charitable purposes can be satisfied without resorting to a trust device. For example, it is possible to incorporate a charitable company[7] or to use an unincorporated association to effect a charitable purpose. Regardless of the type of legal mechanism that is used to implement a charitable purpose,

---

[3] www.gov.uk/government/publications/charity-register-statistics/recent-charity-register-statistics-charity-commission.

[4] [1998] Ch 341, 349.

[5] Charities Act 1993. See now Charities Act 2011, s. 1.

[6] See now Charities Act 2011, s. 11.

[7] The Charities Act 2011, Part 11, creates a new form of incorporation specifically for charities, called a 'charitable incorporated organization'. This is not a company, but has some of the hallmarks of a company, such as limited liability.

the people who have the general control and management of the administration of a charity are called the 'charity trustees'.[8] The 'charity trustee' is strictly distinct from 'trustees of a charity', which refers only to the trustees of a charitable trust. If the mechanism for implementing a charitable purpose is not a trust, those people who control and manage the charity will still be called charity trustees, but they are not trustees of a charity. So, for example, the directors of an incorporated charity are charity trustees for the purposes of the Charities Act 2011, but are not trustees of the charity. This is generally a distinction of only technical, rather than practical, significance, since charity trustees are still subject to fiduciary duties and have administrative responsibilities in just the same way as they would if they were trustees of a charitable trust.

Whatever mechanism is used to effect a charitable purpose, an institution can be considered to be charitable only if three conditions are satisfied:

(1) it must be established for a purpose that the law regards as charitable;[9]

(2) its purposes must benefit the public or a sufficient section of the public;[10]

(3) it must be wholly and exclusively charitable in both its purpose and operation.[11]

(a) ADVANTAGES OF BEING A CHARITABLE TRUST

A charitable trust has a number of advntages over private express trusts, as was recognized in *The Independent Schools Council v The Charity Commission for England and Wales*:[12]

> Where a trust or corporation is a 'charity'...certain legal consequences follow. For instance, a charitable trust, unlike a private trust, can have perpetual duration; it is not, in legal jargon, subject to the rule against perpetuities; it is entitled to a number of favourable tax reliefs; and, of course, it is subject to regulation by the Charity Commission or other regulators and, possibly, intervention by the Attorney General. Charitable status also confers reputational benefits, with a consequential greater ability to raise funds.

More specifically, the advantages of a trust being charitable are:

(i) Whereas private trusts are subject to the perpetuity rule,[13] so that they can last for only a limited time, charitable trusts can exist perpetually. However, the rules on vesting of property within the perpetuity period do operate in the same way for charitable trusts as for private trusts,[14] so the property must vest in the charity within 125 years.[15]

(ii) Whereas, for private trusts, there are strict rules as to certainty of intent to create a trust, and certainty in defining the objects,[16] the equivalent rules are much more flexible regarding charitable trusts. It is no objection that the trust fails to provide with reasonable certainty what are the charitable purposes for which the property must be applied;[17] certainty of intention to apply the property for

---

[8] Charities Act 2011, s. 177.
[9] See Chapter 5.3(c)(i), pp. 190–1.
[10] See Chapter 5.3(c)(ii), pp. 191–205.
[11] See Chapter 5.5, pp. 255–60.
[12] [2011] UKUT 421 (TCC); [2012] Ch 214, [14].
[13] See Chapter 3.7, pp. 112–16.
[14] *Re Lord Stratheden and Campbell* [1894] 3 Ch 265. Also, a charity's power to accumulate income is restricted to 21 years: Perpetuities and Accumulations Act 2009, s. 14(4).
[15] Ibid, s. 5. See Chapter 3.7(a), p. 114.
[16] See Chapter 3.2, pp. 67–74; Chapter 3.4, pp. 86–109.
[17] *Moggridge v Thackwell* (1802) 7 Ves Jun 36.

charitable purposes is sufficient, although the purposes must be wholly and exclusively charitable.[18] In *Charity Commission for England and Wales v Framjee*[19] Henderson J said:

> The court is more likely to find that a trust was intended in a charitable context than in a commercial context. So, for example, in *R Jones v Attorney General* (9 November 1976, unreported) Brightman J said, at p 3H of the transcript of his judgment:
>
> > 'a person who solicits money for a charity is a trustee of the money for the purpose of handing it to the charity. A member of the public who puts money in the box is a donor of his contribution, not distinguishable in principle from any other donor or settlor of trust funds.'

If there is doubt as to the particular charitable purposes, the Charity Commission or the courts may prepare a scheme for the use of the property for particular charitable purposes. The courts will, however, generally seek to construe the trust document in a manner that avoids problems regarding the validity of the trust.[20] In *IRC v McMullen*[21] Lord Hailsham said:

> in construing trust deeds the intention of which is to set up a charitable trust...where it can be claimed that there is an ambiguity, a benignant construction should be given if possible.

For example, if a potential charitable trust can be construed in two ways, with one way making it charitable and effectual, and the other non-charitable and void, the courts will adopt the former construction, if at all possible, so as to ensure that property is used for the benefit of charitable purposes.

(iii) There are numerous tax advantages for charities and donors to charities. A number of the key charity cases that have reached the courts have involved disputes with HM Revenue and Customs as to whether or not a trust is charitable, with a decision that the institution is not charitable, resulting in a significant tax liability. For example, the decision of the Upper Tribunal in *The Independent Schools Council v The Charity Commission for England and Wales*,[22] essentially concerned the tests to determine whether independent schools fulfilled charitable purposes for the benefit of the public. If such schools lost their charitable status, this would have a significant financial impact on such schools through the imposition of tax liability.[23]

(iv) Where a private trust fails and there are still trust funds available, those funds will usually be returned to the settlor by means of a resulting trust.[24] Where a charitable trust fails, however, the surplus funds will be applied for a similar charitable purpose, by virtue of the cy-près doctrine;[25] cy-près means 'as near as may be'. This is advantageous in that the creator of the trust and donors to it will know that, once property has been received by that trust, it will be used for charitable purposes even if the particular trust fails.

(b) DISADVANTAGES OF BEING A CHARITABLE TRUST

There are also some disadvantages that arise from charitable status, such as restrictions on permitted activities and the application of funds. There are significant administrative and bureaucratic obligations

---

[18] See Chapter 5.5, pp. 255–60.
[19] [2014] EWHC 2507 (Ch); [2015] 1 WLR 16, [28].
[20] *IRC v Oldham Training and Enterprise Council* [1996] STC 1218, 1235 (Lightman J).
[21] [1981] AC 1, 14.
[22] [2011] UKUT 421 (TCC); [2012] Ch 214, [14].
[23] See further Chapter 5.4(b)(ii)(b), pp. 220–5.
[24] See Chapter 8.3(c), pp. 392–9.
[25] See Chapter 5.6, pp. 260–83.

imposed upon charities as well. All charities need to be registered by the Charity Commission, which can involve an administrative burden in establishing that the hallmarks of a charity are satisfied. Once registered, Part 8 of the Charities Act 2011 imposes strict duties on charity trustees to prepare annual accounts, to arrange for their audit, and to send annual reports to the Charity Commission on their activities. There are criminal penalties for failure to submit reports and returns.

2. REGULATION AND SUPERVISION OF CHARITIES

There are a variety of mechanisms for regulating and supervising charities: (a) the Attorney-General; (b) the Charity Commission; and (c) the Tribunals and courts.

(a) THE ATTORNEY-GENERAL

The Attorney-General is responsible for enforcing the charitable trust in the name of the Crown.[26] He or she acts as the protector of the charity and has been described as the 'representative of the beneficial interest'.[27] There is a need for the Attorney-General to intervene to protect the property of the charitable trust because no private person has a beneficial interest in the trust's property.

(b) CHARITY COMMISSION

The general administration of charities is carried out by the Charity Commission.

CHARITIES ACT 2011

13 The Charity Commission

(1) There continues to be a body corporate known as the Charity Commission for England and Wales (in this Act referred to as "the Commission").

(3) The functions of the Commission are performed on behalf of the Crown.

(i) *Objectives and functions of the Charity Commission*

The Charity Commission has a number of identified objectives and functions.

CHARITIES ACT 2011

14 The Commission's objectives

The Commission has the following objectives—

1. The public confidence objective

The public confidence objective is to increase public trust and confidence in charities.

---

[26] *Gaudiya Mission v Brahmachary* [1998] Ch 341, 350 (Mummery LJ).
[27] *Weth v A-G* [1999] 1 WLR 686, 691 (Nourse LJ).

2. *The public benefit objective*

The public benefit objective is to promote awareness and understanding of the operation of the public benefit requirement.[28]

3. *The compliance objective*

The compliance objective is to promote compliance by charity trustees with their legal obligations in exercising control and management of the administration of their charities.

4. *The charitable resources objective*

The charitable resources objective is to promote the effective use of charitable resources.

5. *The accountability objective*

The accountability objective is to enhance the accountability of charities to donors, beneficiaries and the general public.

15 The Commission's general functions

(1) The Commission has the following general functions—

1. Determining whether institutions are or are not charities.

2. Encouraging and facilitating the better administration of charities.

3. Identifying and investigating apparent misconduct or mismanagement in the administration of charities and taking remedial or protective action in connection with misconduct or mismanagement in the administration of charities.

4. Determining whether public collections certificates should be issued, and remain in force, in respect of public charitable collections.

5. Obtaining, evaluating and disseminating information in connection with the performance of any of the Commission's functions or meeting any of its objectives.

6. Giving information or advice, or making proposals, to any Minister of the Crown on matters relating to any of the Commission's functions or meeting any of its objectives.

(2) The Commission may, in connection with its second general function, give such advice or guidance with respect to the administration of charities as it considers appropriate.

(3) Any advice or guidance so given may relate to—

(a) charities generally,

(b) any class of charities, or

(c) any particular charity,

and may take such form, and be given in such manner, as the Commission considers appropriate.

(4) The Commission's fifth general function includes (among other things) the maintenance of an accurate and up-to-date register of charities under sections 29 (the register) and 34 (removal of charities from register).

(5) The Commission's sixth general function includes (among other things) complying, so far as is reasonably practicable, with any request made by a Minister of the Crown for information or advice on any matter relating to any of its functions.

---

[28] See Chapter 5.3(c)(ii), pp. 191–205.

(ii) *The register of charities*

The register of charities contains the name of every charity registered by the Charity Commission.

CHARITIES ACT 2011

29 The register

(1) There continues to be a register of charities, to be kept by the Commission in such manner as it thinks fit.

(2) The register must contain—

    (a) the name of every charity registered in accordance with section 30, and

    (b) such other particulars of, and such other information relating to, every such charity as the Commission thinks fit.

An institution that is included on the register is conclusively presumed to be a charity, save where the register is rectified.

CHARITIES ACT 2011

37 Effect of registration

(1) An institution is, for all purposes other than rectification of the register, conclusively presumed to be or to have been a charity at any time when it is or was on the register.

If an institution is not registered it does not follow that it is not a charity, since the requirements for registration may have been satisfied, but the trustees may simply have failed to register the charity.[29]

By section 30 of the Charities Act 2011, all charities are required to be registered other than charities that are exempted by statute, charities with a gross income of less than £5,000, and certain charities with a gross income of less than £100,000 that are excepted from registration either by the Commission or under regulations made by the Secretary of State. Where a charity is required to be registered, it is the duty of the charity trustees to apply for registration.[30] Charity trustees are also under a duty to inform the Commission if the charity ceases to exist or if there is a change in the charity's trusts.[31]

The Charity Commission is required to remove charities from the register in certain circumstances.

CHARITIES ACT 2011

34 Removal of charities from register

(1) The Commission must remove from the register—

    (a) any institution which it no longer considers is a charity, and

    (b) any charity which has ceased to exist or does not operate.

---

[29] *Helena Partnerships Ltd v The Commissioners for Her Majesty's Revenue and Customs* [2012] EWCA Civ 569; [2012] WTLR 1519, [14] (Lloyd LJ).

[30] Charities Act 2011, s. 35(1).

[31] Ibid, s. 35(3).

Anybody who might be affected by the registration of an institution as a charity, such as a testator's next of kin, can object to its inclusion on the register or apply for it to be removed.[32]

(iii) *Regulatory powers*

The Charity Commission has various regulatory powers. For example, it can institute an inquiry with regard to a charity or a class of charities;[33] it can give directions to the charity trustees to take particular actions in the interests of the charity;[34] it can give advice to charity trustees relating to the administration of the charity or the performance of the trustees' duties;[35] and it can also sanction actions that are expedient in the administration of the charity, such as a particular application of charity property, even if the charity trustees do not have the power to take such action.[36]

(iv) *Concurrent jurisdiction with the High Court*

The Charity Commission has jurisdiction, which is concurrent with that of the High Court, as regards various matters,[37] such as establishing a scheme for the administration of the charity; appointing, discharging, or removing a charity trustee; and transferring property. But the Charity Commission does not have jurisdiction to determine title to property, or to determine the existence or extent of any trust,[38] and it should not exercise its concurrent jurisdiction if the matter is more appropriately adjudicated by the court because of its contentious nature, or because it raises special questions of law or fact.[39]

(v) *Critique of the role of the Charity Commission*

It has been suggested that the Charity Commission has not been exercising its powers appropriately in determining whether an institution is or is not a charity. The function of the Charity Commission is to apply the law as it has been developed by the courts and by Parliament, but it appears to be developing its own interpretation of those principles.

Luxton and Evans, 'Cogen and Cohesive? Two Recent Charity Commission Decisions on the Advancement of Religion' [2011] 75 Conv 144, 151

The Commission's new approach is of concern because the Commission's guidance and its own analysis of the law underpinning that document are not sources of law, but merely the Commission's understanding of the law generally. The Commission however, which is a government department, relies on, and quotes extensively from, its own guidance and analysis as if these documents were entitled to the same regard as decisions of the higher courts; whereas the Commission's guidance is produced for the limited purpose of assisting those not conversant with charity law...Worryingly, when this has been pointed out, ...the Commission's response has been simply to state that its decisions are 'based on the application of existing charity case law and the Commission's public guidance, which is itself based on

---

[32] Ibid, s. 36.
[33] Ibid, s. 46.
[34] Ibid, s. 84.
[35] Ibid, s. 110.
[36] Ibid, s. 86.
[37] Ibid, s. 69(1).
[38] Ibid, s. 70(1).
[39] Ibid, s. 70(8).

case law'....This demonstrates the Commission's lack of awareness of the need for legal rigour when making a legal decision, such as a decision whether or not to register a body as a charity.

Instead of trying to pull itself up with its own boot straps, the Commission should be interpreting and applying the law on the particular facts of the application before it.

The courts have started to respond to such concerns, most notably by reviewing and in some cases rejecting the Charity Commission's interpretation of the law, particularly its guidance on the interpretation of the public benefit requirement.[40]

(c) THE TRIBUNALS AND COURTS

The First-tier Tribunal and Upper Tribunal[41] have jurisdiction to hear appeals and applications in respect of decisions, orders, and directions of the Charity Commission, such as a decision to register or not to register a charity, or to remove an institution from the register of charities. It is possible to appeal from the First-tier Tribunal to the Upper Tribunal on a point of law.[42]

The Charity Commission or the Attorney-General may also refer matters to the Tribunals, including matters relating to the powers of the Commission itself and to the operation of the law of charity. The Tribunals have a potentially very important role in developing charity law, as illustrated by the Upper Tribunal's decision relating to the charitable status of independent schools.[43] It is possible to appeal from decisions of the Upper Tribunal to the Court of Appeal or to take certain proceedings directly to the High Court.

(i) Charity proceedings

The tribunals have jurisdiction with respect to disputes relating to the internal or functional administration of a charitable trust, so-called 'charity proceedings'.

CHARITIES ACT 2011

115 Proceedings by other persons

(1) Charity proceedings may be taken with reference to a charity by—

  (a) the charity,

  (b) any of the charity trustees,

  (c) any person interested in the charity, or

  (d) if it is a local charity, any two or more inhabitants of the area of the charity,

  but not by any other person.

---

[40] See *The Independent Schools Council v The Charity Commission for England and Wales* [2011] UKUT 421 (TCC); [2012] Ch 214. See Chapter 5.4(b)(ii)(b), pp. 220–5.
[41] Charities Act 2011, Part 17.
[42] Tribunals, Courts and Enforcement Act 2007, s. 11.
[43] *The Independent Schools Council v The Charity Commission for England and Wales* [2011] UKUT 421 (TCC); [2012] Ch 214. See Chapter 5.4(b)(ii)(b), pp. 220–5.

(2) Subject to the following provisions of this section, no charity proceedings relating to a charity are to be entertained or proceeded with in any court unless the taking of the proceedings is authorised by order of the Commission....

(8) In this section 'charity proceedings' means proceedings in any court in England or Wales brought under—

(a) the court's jurisdiction with respect to charities, or

(b) the court's jurisdiction with respect to trusts in relation to the administration of a trust for charitable purposes.

A person is 'interested in the charity' if he or she has an interest in securing the due administration of the charity which is greater than or different from that possessed by ordinary members of the public.[44] Generally, such proceedings must be authorized by the Charity Commission and they will not be if they can be dealt with under the Commission's own regulatory powers.

In *Muman v Nagasena*,[45] Mummery LJ said:

This...is a trust for charitable purposes, and it is clear that there are now issues in the possession proceedings which relate to the administration of those trusts, namely: (i) who are the trustees of the charity; and (ii) who is the patron of the charity. There is a possible third issue as to who are the members. Those are matters of internal or domestic dispute and are not a dispute with an outsider to the charity. These are charity proceedings...That means that they cannot be continued without the authorisation either of the order of the Charity Commissioners or of a judge of the High Court of Justice, Chancery Division. No such authorisation has been obtained. To allow the proceedings to continue without authorisation would be to offend the whole purpose of requiring authorisation for the charity proceedings. That is to prevent charities from frittering away money subject to charitable trusts in pursuing litigation relating to internal disputes.

(ii) *Judicial review*

Decisions of the Charity Commission,[46] and of certain charities that have the characteristics of a public body, may be examined by the courts through judicial review proceedings.

In *Scott v National Trust*,[47] the National Trust had decided not to renew licences to hunt deer on some of its land. Members of various hunts affected by this decision, along with tenant farmers on the relevant land, sought a judicial review of this decision and also commenced 'charity proceedings'. In holding that the claimants could bring charity proceedings but not an action for judicial review, Robert Walker J said:[48]

It is easy to recognise a public element in charitable institutions, and especially in a charitable institution which is regulated by Act of Parliament and is of such great national importance as the National Trust. Charitable trusts were being commonly referred to as 'public' trusts long before the expression 'public law' was in common use...

---

[44] *Re Hampton Fuel Allotment Charity* [1989] Ch 484, 494 (Nicholls LJ) (interpreting the same provision as now occurs in the Charities Act 2011).

[45] [2000] 1 WLR 299, 305.

[46] See, for example, *The Independent Schools Council v The Charity Commission for England and Wales* [2011] UKUT 421 (TCC); [2012] Ch 214, Chapter 5.3(c)(ii), pp. 191–205.

[47] [1998] 2 All ER 705.

[48] Ibid, 712.

The questions of how the law should monitor charities, and of how the law should monitor those public officers and non-charitable bodies which are obviously amenable to judicial review, raise similar problems, to which the law has, it seems to me, provided similar although by no means identical solutions.

The way in which these entities exercise their powers and discretions may affect directly or indirectly many different sections of the public; and even members of the general public who are not personally affected financially or otherwise in any way, may still have very strong and sincerely held views about the rights or wrongs of decisions, whether by a charity or a local authority on a subject such as hunting. The court has jurisdiction to prevent misuse of public powers either by judicial review or (in the case of a charity) by charity proceedings…

Moreover, in each case there is a 'protective filter'…[which] is intended to protect public officers, public bodies and charities from being harassed by a multiplicity of hopeless challenges…The efficacy of the protective screen is, of course, enhanced by the need for the complainant to have a sufficient interest or an interest in the charity.

In this case the Devon and Somerset staghounds and the Quantock staghounds have been hunting deer on Exmoor and the Quantocks since long before the National Trust owned land there. Whether their activities are regarded as laudable or deplorable, the affidavit evidence makes out a strong case that they are an important part of the rural economy in contributing to deer culling, in providing a service in destroying and removing sick and injured beasts, and generally in deer management…

For those reasons I conclude that the plaintiffs in the originating summons proceedings have a sufficient interest…to bring charity proceedings…

I do not think it is helpful, or even possible, to consider the broad question of whether any charity, or even any charity specially established by statute, is subject to judicial review…But the National Trust is a charity of exceptional importance to the nation, regulated by its own special Acts of Parliament…It seems to me to have all the characteristics of a public body which is, *prima facie*, amenable to judicial review, and to have been exercising its statutory public functions in making the decision which is challenged.

However, it is well established that judicial review will not normally be granted where an alternative remedy is available…But it seems to me that Parliament has laid down a special procedure—charity proceedings in the Chancery Division—for judicial monitoring of charities, and that in all but the most exceptional cases that is the procedure which should be followed. A possible exception (and this is mere speculation) might be where a local authority held land on charitable trusts and questions about its dealings with that land were caught up with other questions about its dealings with land which it owned beneficially (though subject, of course, to statutory constraints). But I can see no good reason for making an exception in this case…it seems to me that the right course is for the plaintiffs to proceed with their charity proceedings—that is the originating summons—and that to have parallel judicial review proceedings would simply be wasteful duplication. I do not however, for myself, regard the protective filter and the need for a sufficient interest as matters of technicality, but (for reasons which I have tried to explain) as a sensible and necessary requirement in the public law field, including the law of public (or charitable) trusts.

A further restriction on the availability of judicial review proceedings was recognized in *RSPCA v Attorney-General*,[49] which concerned the legitimacy of the charity's policy of excluding existing members and preventing new members from joining if their reason for wishing to be members was to challenge the charity's policy against hunting with dogs. It was held that an existing member of the charity who was then excluded would have *locus standi* to bring charity proceedings. An unsuccessful

---

[49] [2002] 1 WLR 448.

applicant for membership was not sufficiently interested in the charity to bring charity proceedings, but could also not bring judicial review proceedings because this would circumvent the statutory requirements of charity proceedings. Lightman J said:[50]

> The question raised is whether [the complainants] are able to bring judicial review proceedings if they do not have the necessary interest to bring charity proceedings. The answer to this question is in the negative. There is a serious question whether the Society is the sort of public body which is amenable to judicial review, most particularly in respect of decisions made in relation to its membership (consider *Scott's case* (at 716)). The fact that a charity is by definition a public, as opposed to a private, trust means that the trustees are subject to public law duties and judicial review is in general available to enforce performance of such duties. There is therefore a theoretical basis for allowing recourse to judicial review. It is also true that the Society is a very important charity and its activities (in particular, the inspectorate and its prosecutions for cruelty to animals) are of great value to society…But in carrying out these activities the Society is in law in no different position from that of any citizen or other organisation. Unlike the National Trust, the subject of consideration by Walker J in *Scott's case*, the Society has no statutory or public law role. All I will say is that, though theoretically and in a proper case an application for judicial review may lie, it would not (at any rate in any ordinary case) lie at the instance of disappointed applicants for membership whose interest was insufficient to meet the statutory standard for the institution of charity proceedings. The statutory standard is laid down as a form of protection of charity trustees and the Administrative Court would rarely (if ever) be justified in allowing that protection to be circumvented by the expedient of commencing (in place of charity proceedings) judicial review proceedings. That does not mean that a disappointed applicant for membership is without recourse, for he can complain to the Charity Commission or the Attorney-General and request them to take action.

It is possible for the court to require internal disputes arising within a charity to be resolved by mediation before legal proceedings are pursued.[51] A combined mediation service for charities has been established by the Centre for Dispute Resolution jointly with the National Council for Voluntary Organisations. Mummery LJ in *Muman v Nagasena*[52] recognized that the purpose of this service is to:

> achieve, by voluntary action confidentially conducted, a healing process under which disputes within a charity can be resolved at a modest fee and without diminishing the funds which have been raised for charitable purposes.

3. THE DEFINITION OF CHARITY

There was no formal definition of 'charity' in English law until the enactment of the Charities Act 2006, now consolidated in the Charities Act 2011. Before then, the definition of charity emerged through limited Parliamentary involvement, decisions of the courts, and, more recently, decisions of the Charity Commission as to whether or not to register a charity. The history of the definition of charity remains significant today because the new statutory definition builds on these earlier

---

[50] Ibid, 458.
[51] *Muman v Nagasena* [2000] 1 WLR 299, 305.
[52] Ibid.

developments. As the Upper Tribunal observed in *The Independent Schools Council v The Charity Commission for England and Wales*:[53]

the words 'charity' and 'charitable' have become terms of art. The legal concept of charity has developed incrementally, and not altogether consistently...The meaning which the law and lawyers give to 'charity' does not correspond entirely with the meaning of the word as ordinarily understood. It is important to remember that, in the proceedings before us, we are concerned with the legal concept of charity and not with the ordinary meaning of the word, although it is no doubt the case that ordinary concepts must inform the legal meaning, a meaning which is not frozen at some time in the past.

(a) THE PREAMBLE TO THE CHARITABLE USES ACT 1601

The Charitable Uses Act 1601 featured a Preamble that identified a number of charitable objects. These proved to be highly significant to the subsequent development of the law of charity.

CHARITABLE USES ACT 1601

43 Eliz. I, c. 4: The Preamble

Whereas Lands, Tenements, Rents, Annuities, Profits, Hereditaments, Goods, Chattels, Money and Stocks of Money, have been heretofore given, limited, appointed and assigned, as well by the Queen's most excellent Majesty, and her most noble Progenitors, as by sundry other well disposed Persons; some for Relief of aged, impotent and poor People, some for Maintenance of sick and maimed Soldiers and Mariners, Schools of Learning, Free Schools, and Scholars in Universities, some for Repair of Bridges, Ports, Havens, Causeways, Churches, Sea-Banks and Highways, some for Education and Preferment of Orphans, some for or towards Relief, Stock or Maintenance for Houses of Correction, some for Marriages of poor Maids, some for Supportation, Aid and Help of young Tradesmen, Handicraftsmen and Persons decayed, and others for Relief or Redemption of Prisoners or Captives, and for Aid or Ease of any poor Inhabitants concerning Payments of Fifteens, setting out of Soldiers and other Taxes; which Lands, Tenements, Rents, Annuities, Profits, Hereditaments, Goods, Chattels, Money and Stocks of Money, nevertheless have not been employed according to the charitable Intent of the givers and Founders thereof, by reason of Frauds, Breaches of Trust, and Negligence in those that should pay, deliver and employ the same: For Redress and Remedy whereof, Be it enacted...

The Preamble was repealed by the Charities Act 1960, but, for a trust to be charitable, its purposes still had to fall within the spirit and 'intendment' of the Preamble. The effect of the Preamble was considered by Lloyd LJ in *Helena Housing Ltd v The Commissioners for Her Majesty's Revenue and Customs*:[54]

The law as to the purposes that are charitable is notoriously difficult and unsatisfactory, partly because of its historical development. It is strange enough to find that reference needs to be made in the 21st century, well into the reign of Queen Elizabeth II, to the text of the preamble to a statute passed in the last years of the reign of Queen Elizabeth I, the Statute of Charitable Uses 1601, in order to find what categories of purpose should be regarded as charitable. It is all the more odd to do so when one realises that the 1601 statute was passed in order to reform the procedure for enforcing certain kinds of

---

[53] [2011] UKUT 421 (TCC); [2012] Ch 214, [14].
[54] [2012] EWCA Civ 569, [2012] WTLR 1519, [22].

charitable uses, to the exclusion of others which, accordingly, although charitable were not mentioned in the statute or in the preamble. The most obvious exclusion is religious purposes, other than the repair of churches. As to the context and scope of the Act, see Gareth Jones, *History of the Law of Charity 1532 to 1827*, CUP 1969, page 22 and following. The list of purposes in the preamble may have a more ancient provenance. As Jones observes at page 25 footnote 2, the language of the preamble is in part remarkably similar to that of a passage in William Langland's fourteenth century work *The Vision of Piers Plowman*, which mentions the repair of hospitals, roads and bridges, helping maidens to marry, helping the poor and prisoners, and providing education or training, and other causes reflected in the preamble.

The preamble was first used as a guide to the identification of what was or was not a charitable purpose in the case of *Morice v Bishop of Durham*, which is of seminal importance in this as well as in other contexts as regards the development of the law of trusts: (1804) 9 Ves 399 (Sir William Grant MR) and (1805) 10 Ves 522 (Lord Eldon)…

The issue in that case which is relevant for our purposes was whether a gift of residue to be applied 'to such objects of benevolence and liberality as the Bishop of Durham in his own discretion shall most approve of' was valid as being confined to purposes that were charitable. The decision, at first instance and on appeal, was that objects of benevolence and liberality were not so limited, and that the gift therefore failed.

Sir William Grant stated the significance of the 1601 statute in the following words, which do not seem to have been based on any submissions made to him in the argument as reported, at 9 Ves 405:

> 'Here [i.e. in Court] its signification [i.e. that of the word charity] is derived chiefly from the Statute of Elizabeth. Those purposes are considered charitable, which that Statute enumerates, or which by analogies are deemed within its spirit and intendment.'

If a particular purpose did not fall within the Preamble expressly or by analogy, it could not be regarded as charitable, even though it was beneficial to the public.

(b) THE FOUR HEADS OF CHARITY

The next significant step in the historical development of charity law was the identification of four distinct heads of charitable purpose. In *Commissioners for Special Purposes of Income Tax v Pemsel*,[55] Lord Macnaghten said:

> 'Charity' in its legal sense comprises four principal divisions: trusts for the relief of poverty; trusts for the advancement of education; trusts for the advancement of religion; and trusts for other purposes beneficial to the community, not falling under any of the preceding heads. The trusts last referred to are not the less charitable in the eye of the law, because incidentally they benefit the rich as well as the poor, as indeed, every charity that deserves the name must do either directly or indirectly. It seems to me that a person of education, at any rate, if he were speaking as the Act is speaking with reference to endowed charities, would include in the category educational and religious charities, as well as charities for the relief of the poor. Roughly speaking, I think he would exclude the fourth division. Even there it is difficult to draw the line. A layman would probably be amused if he were told that a gift to the Chancellor of the Exchequer for the benefit of the nation was a charity. Many people, I think, would consider a gift for the support of a lifeboat a charitable gift, though its object is not the advancement of religion, or the advancement of education, or the relief of the poor. And even a layman might take the same favourable view of a gratuitous supply of pure water for the benefit of a crowded neighbourhood. But after all, this is rather an academical discussion. If a gentleman of education, without legal training, were asked what is the meaning of 'a trust for charitable purposes', I think he would most probably reply, 'That sounds like a legal phrase. You had better ask a lawyer'.

---

[55] [1891] AC 531, 583.

In *Scottish Burial Reform and Cremation Society v Glasgow Corporation*,[56] Lord Wilberforce clarified the definition of charity further:

> On this subject, the law of England, though no doubt not very satisfactory and in need of rationalisation, is tolerably clear. The purposes in question, to be charitable, must be shown to be for the benefit of the public, or the community, in a sense or manner within the intendment of the preamble to the statute 43 Eliz. I, c.4. The latter requirement does not mean quite what it says; for it is now accepted that what must be regarded is not the wording of the preamble itself, but the effect of decisions given by the courts as to its scope, decisions which have endeavoured to keep the law as to charities moving according as new social needs arise or old ones become obsolete or satisfied. Lord Macnaghten's grouping of the heads of recognised charity in *Pemsel's case* is one that has proved to be of value and there are many problems which it solves. But three things may be said about it, which its author would surely not have denied: first that, since it is a classification of convenience, there may well be purposes which do not fit neatly into one or other of the headings; secondly, that the words used must not be given the force of a statute to be construed; and thirdly, that the law of charity is a moving subject which may well have evolved even since 1891.

The effect of these decisions is that a trust would be considered to be charitable if it were to fall within the spirit and intendment of the Preamble, but the four heads of charity identified by Lord Macnaghten provided a useful checklist with which to test whether the purpose was charitable. But it was also necessary to establish that the purpose was for the public benefit. Benefit was presumed[57] for trusts for the relief of poverty and for the advancement of education and religion, although this presumption could be rebutted by showing that the particular charity was not for the public benefit.[58] Benefit needed to be proved for a trust to fall within the fourth head of being another purpose that was beneficial to the community. Under each of the heads it was necessary to determine that the public or a sufficient section of the public was benefited. Different tests were adopted for the identification of the public for each head of charity.

(c) THE CHARITIES ACTS 2006 AND 2011

The Charities Act 2006, which came into force in 2008, provided, for the first time, a statutory definition of 'charity', albeit one that built on the previous law. The Charities Act 2011 came into force in 2012 and consolidated the various statutory provisions relating to charities into one statute, but without significantly adding to or altering existing law.

CHARITIES ACT 2011

2. Meaning of 'charitable purpose'

(1) For the purposes of the law of England and Wales, a charitable purpose is a purpose which—

    (a) falls within section 3(1), and

    (b) is for the public benefit (see section 4).

---

[56] [1968] AC 138, 154.
[57] *National Anti-Vivisection Society v IRC* [1948] AC 31, 56 (Viscount Simonds). This presumption has been abolished by statute. See Chapter 5.3(c)(ii), p. 191.
[58] See e.g. *Gilmour v Coats* [1949] AC 426, discussed in Chapter 5.4(c)(ii), pp. 230–5.

(i) *Heads of charity*

The Charities Act 2011 identifies thirteen descriptions of recognized charitable purposes. The purposes of a charity must satisfy at least one of these descriptions, although they do overlap and so a charity may satisfy more than one of them.

CHARITIES ACT 2011

3 Descriptions of purposes

(1) A purpose falls within this subsection if it falls within any of the following descriptions of purposes—

    (a)   the prevention or relief of poverty;

    (b)   the advancement of education;

    (c)   the advancement of religion;

    (d)   the advancement of health or the saving of lives;

    (e)   the advancement of citizenship or community development;

    (f)   the advancement of the arts, culture, heritage or science;

    (g)   the advancement of amateur sport;

    (h)   the advancement of human rights, conflict resolution or reconciliation or the promotion of religious or racial harmony or equality and diversity;

    (i)   the advancement of environmental protection or improvement;

    (j)   the relief of those in need because of youth, age, ill-health, disability, financial hardship or other disadvantage;

    (k)   the advancement of animal welfare;

    (l)   the promotion of the efficiency of the armed forces of the Crown or of the efficiency of the police, fire and rescue services or ambulance services;

    (m) any other purposes—

        (i)   that are not within paragraphs (a) to (l) but are recognised as charitable purposes by virtue of section 5 (recreational and similar trusts, etc.)[59] or under the old law,

        (ii) that may reasonably be regarded as analogous to, or within the spirit of, any purposes falling within any of paragraphs (a) to (l) or sub-paragraph (i), or

        (iii) that may reasonably be regarded as analogous to, or within the spirit of, any purposes which have been recognised, under the law relating to charities in England and Wales, as falling within sub-paragraph (ii) or this sub-paragraph.

(3) Where any of the terms used in any of paragraphs (a) to (l) of subsection (1), or in subsection (2), has a particular meaning under the law relating to charities in England and Wales, the term is to be taken as having the same meaning where it appears in that provision.

Some of these descriptors replicate previously recognized heads of charity, such as the advancement of education and religion. Others simply codify subsequent developments in the definition of charity, either through decisions of the courts or the Charity Commission, such as the advancement of

---

[59] See Chapter 5.4(g), pp. 242–5.

culture or environmental protection. The Charity Commission has provided guidance on charitable purposes which gives examples of relevant purposes under each head.[60]

(ii) *Public benefit*

CHARITIES ACT 2011

4 The public benefit requirement

(1) In this Act "the public benefit requirement" means the requirement in section 2(1)(b) that a purpose falling within section 3(1) must be for the public benefit if it is to be a charitable purpose.

(2) In determining whether the public benefit requirement is satisfied in relation to any purpose falling within section 3(1) it is not to be presumed that a purpose of a particular description is for the public benefit.

(3) In this Chapter any reference to the public benefit is a reference to the public benefit as that term is understood for the purposes of the law relating to charities in England and Wales…

The effect of this provision is that all charities, new and existing, have to satisfy the test of public benefit. This is a test that has been developed over many years through the courts and is not a new test under the 2011 Act. The old presumptions of benefit have been abolished, which means that in each case an organization will have to demonstrate that its purposes do benefit the public. If this cannot be established then a new charity will not be registered and an existing charity will cease to be registered. Once a charity has been registered, charity trustees are under statutory duties both to ensure that the charity acts for the public benefit and to avoid making decisions that adversely affect the charity's public benefit.

The Charities Act 2011 does not provide any definition of public benefit. That definition is derived from previous cases and decisions of the Charity Commission. The Charity Commission is required to produce guidance as to the interpretation of public benefit.

CHARITIES ACT 2011

17 Guidance as to operation of public benefit requirement

(1) The Commission must issue guidance in pursuance of its public benefit objective…

(2) The Commission may from time to time revise any guidance issued under this section.

(3) The Commission must carry out such public and other consultation as it considers appropriate—

    (a) before issuing any guidance under this section, or

    (b) (unless it considers that it is unnecessary to do so) before revising any guidance under this section.

(4) The Commission must publish any guidance issued or revised under this section in such manner as it considers appropriate.

(5) The charity trustees of a charity must have regard to any such guidance when exercising any powers or duties to which the guidance is relevant.

---

[60] Charity Commission, *Guidance on Charitable Purposes* (2013).

The Charity Commission, having undertaken a public consultation, published its guidance in January 2008.[61] This identified two key principles of public benefit, namely that there is an identifiable benefit, which is to the public or a section of the public, and a number of factors that need to be considered when determining whether this public benefit requirement is met. These principles and factors had purportedly been distilled from the myriad of cases on the interpretation of public benefit.

The validity of this guidance was considered by the Upper Tribunal in *The Independent Schools Council v The Charity Commission for England and Wales*.[62] The guidance had been challenged on the ground that it contained errors of law in respect of the public benefit requirement as it applied to charities that charged fees for their charitable activities, specifically independent schools. Various aspects of the guidance were found wanting by the Upper Tribunal, either as being incorrect as a matter of law or as being ambiguous and obscure. Some aspects of the guidance were consequently withdrawn. The Charity Commission consulted on the publication of new guidance, which was published in 2013.

Charity Commission, *Public Benefit: the Public Benefit Requirement* (2013)[63]

The law relating to public benefit

The commission's public benefit guidance is not the law on public benefit. The law on public benefit is contained in charities' legislation and decisions of the courts.

The commission's public benefit guidance is high level general guidance, written for charity trustees, to explain what the law says on public benefit and how it interprets and applies that law....

Part 2: What 'for the public benefit' means

...There are two aspects of public benefit:

- the 'benefit aspect'
- the 'public aspect'

Legal requirement: In general, for a purpose to be 'for the public benefit' it must satisfy both the 'benefit' and 'public' aspects. However, if the purpose is to relieve or prevent poverty, different rules apply.[64]...

The 'benefit aspect'

The 'benefit aspect' of public benefit is about whether the purpose is beneficial.

Legal requirement: to satisfy the 'benefit aspect' of public benefit

- a purpose must be beneficial (see part 3 of this guide)
- any detriment or harm that results from the purpose must not outweigh the benefit (see part 4 of this guide)

The 'public aspect'

The 'public aspect' of public benefit is about whom the purpose benefits.

Legal requirement: to satisfy the 'public aspect' of public benefit the purpose must

- benefit the public in general, or a sufficient section of the public (see part 5 of this guide)
- not give rise to more than incidental personal benefit (see part 6 of this guide)

---

[61] Charity Commission, *Charities and Public Benefit*.
[62] [2011] UKUT 421 (TCC); [2012] Ch 214.
[63] www.gov.uk/government/publications/public-benefit-the-public-benefit-requirement-pb1.
[64] See Chapter 5.4(a)(ii) p. 211.

The commission's decisions about public benefit

Each of a charity's purposes must be for the public benefit.

Many charities have more than one purpose. Where that is the case, the commission will look at each purpose on its own to decide if it is for the public benefit. The public benefit of one purpose cannot be used to offset any lack of public benefit in another.

As the courts would, it will weigh up all the relevant factors and evidence to decide whether each purpose on its own:

- is beneficial
- benefits the public in general, or a sufficient section of it

In most cases this is likely to be clear.

The two aspects of public benefit can overlap. A factor can frequently be regarded as having an impact on both aspects.

Sometimes the commission might need to consider the relationship between what is beneficial and what is harmful, and public and personal benefit.

Some cases require fine judgment to consider whether all the factors, taken together, result in a purpose that is for the public benefit. The commission considers all cases in their own context....

In rare cases where it is not possible for the trustees or applicant to put things right and the commission decides that the organisation's purpose is not for the public benefit, this would mean that, in its view, the organisation is not a charity.

Where it decides this is the case for an organisation applying for registration, it would decline to register it.

Where it decides this is the case for an existing charity, the charity trustees will need to consider changing the purpose and should seek advice....

In the very rare case where changing the purpose is not possible, the commission would have to remove the organisation from the register of charities....

Part 3: Beneficial purpose

What is beneficial

Legal requirement: for a purpose to be charitable it must be beneficial in a way that is identifiable and

- capable of being proved by evidence where necessary
- not based on personal views

Providing evidence of benefit

In some cases the purpose is so clearly beneficial that there is little need for trustees to provide evidence to prove this.

For example, the trustees of an organisation whose purpose is to provide emergency aid in the context of a natural disaster would not need to provide evidence that the purpose is beneficial.

Where it is not clear that a purpose is beneficial, the commission may need to ask for evidence of this.

For example, the commission may need to ask for evidence of:

- the architectural or historical merit of a building preserved under an advancement of heritage purpose
- the artistic merit of an art collection displayed under an advancement of art purpose
- the healing benefits of a therapy provided under an advancement of health purpose
- the educational merit of a training programme offered under an advancement of education purpose

Measuring what is beneficial

It should always be possible to identify and describe how a charity's purpose is beneficial, whether or not that can be quantified or measured.

For example, developing a person's artistic taste by viewing works of art can be beneficial even though it is difficult to quantify or measure.

Not beneficial

If it cannot be shown that an organisation's purpose is beneficial (based on evidence that a court could accept where necessary) then it will not be a charitable purpose.

Part 4: Detriment or harm

How detriment or harm might affect the public benefit requirement

Legal requirement: a purpose cannot be a charitable purpose where any detriment or harm resulting from it outweighs the benefit.

Evidence of detriment or harm

The commission take detriment or harm into account where it is reasonable to expect that it will result from the individual organisation's purpose. This will be based on evidence, not on personal views.

Where the benefit of a purpose is obvious and commonly recognised, there is an even greater need for evidence of detriment or harm to be clear and substantial, if it is to outweigh that benefit.

Part 5: Benefiting the public or a sufficient section of the public

The public

Legal requirement: for a purpose to be charitable it must benefit either

- the public in general or
- a sufficient section of the public

What 'the public in general' means

This means that all of the public can benefit from the purpose.

The benefit of the purpose is not limited to people with a particular need or who have to satisfy some other criteria.

If a purpose does not specify who can benefit, it will generally be taken to mean that it will benefit the public in general.

An example of a purpose which is for the benefit of the public in general is one which is concerned with conserving an endangered species.

What a 'sufficient section of the public' means

Legal requirement: a charitable purpose can benefit a section of the public, but the section must be appropriate (or 'sufficient') in relation to the specific purpose.

A sufficient section of the public are called a 'public class' of people.

There is not a set minimum number of people who have to benefit in order to be a 'public class'.

Whether a section of the public is or is not a 'public class' is not the same for every purpose. What is sufficient for one purpose may not be sufficient for another.

Defining who can benefit on the basis of where people live

In most cases people living in any geographical area (local, national or international) will be a sufficient section of the public.

An example of circumstances in which it might not be sufficient is where the geographical area is too narrowly defined (such as people living in a few named houses)

The geographical area does not have to be in England and Wales. An organisation that is set up and registered in England and Wales can be a charity, even if its purpose is to benefit people entirely outside that area.

Defining who can benefit as people or communities with a particular charitable need

This is often a sufficient section of the public.

Defining who can benefit by reference to 'protected characteristics'

Legal requirement: the Equality Act permits charities to benefit people defined by reference to a 'protected characteristic', provided the restriction of benefits to people having that characteristic is justified in relation to the purpose.

The following are 'protected characteristics':

- age
- disability
- sex
- sexual orientation
- gender reassignment
- marriage and civil partnership
- pregnancy and maternity
- race or nationality
- religion or belief…

Defining who can benefit by reference to a person's skin colour

Legal requirement: charities must not define their beneficiaries by reference to their skin colour. The law does not allow this.

Where a charity's purpose defines who can benefit by reference to their skin colour, the purpose will be read as if that reference to skin colour did not exist.

Defining who can benefit by reference to a person's occupation or profession

This can be a sufficient section of the public depending on the circumstances.

An example of a charity that could define who it benefits by reference to occupation or profession is a charity whose purpose is to relieve the sickness and disability of serving, former and retired teachers and their dependents.

Defining who can benefit by reference to a person's family relationship, contractual relationship (eg employment by an employer) or membership of an unincorporated association

Legal requirement: in general, a charity must not have a purpose which defines who can benefit by reference to:

- their family relationship

- their employment by an employer
- their membership of an unincorporated association

The law allows this only where the purpose is the relief (and in some cases the prevention) of poverty.[65] ...

Defining who can benefit by reference to other sorts of personal characteristic, such as their employment status

Whether this is a section of the public depends on the purpose that will be advanced and the specific circumstances.

For example, 'people who are unemployed' can be a sufficient section of the public where the purpose is the relief of unemployment or the relief of poverty. But it may not be a sufficient section where the purpose is to advance religion.

Deciding what is a 'sufficient' section of the public

This is decided on a case by case basis.

Decisions about this are informed by what the courts have or have not accepted in other cases.

For example, the courts will generally accept that a purpose benefits a sufficient section of the public if its beneficiaries are defined by:

- where they live
- a charitable need
- a 'protected characteristic'

Legal requirement: charities must not define their beneficiaries in the following ways as these will not benefit a sufficient section of the public:

- a purpose which defines who can benefit on the basis of a 'protected characteristic' but which does not satisfy the requirements of the Equality Act
- a purpose which defines who can benefit by reference to their skin colour
- a purpose which defines who can benefit on the basis of a personal connection (unless the purpose is for the relief, and in some cases the prevention, of poverty)
- a purpose which excludes the poor from benefiting - charity law recognises that 'the poor' is a relative term which depends upon the circumstances. However, 'the poor' does not just mean the very poorest in society and can include people of modest means
- a purpose which is confined to a closed religious organisation
- a purpose where all the potential beneficiaries (now and in the future) are named, such as an individual or individuals or a fixed group of individuals
- a purpose where the number of people who can benefit (now and in the future) is numerically negligible (unless the purpose is for the relief, and in some cases the prevention, of poverty)
- a purpose which defines who can benefit in a manner which, when related to the purpose, is 'capricious' (eg wholly irrelevant, irrational or without good reason)
- a purpose which benefits members of a mutual benefit society
- (unless the purpose is for the relief, and in some cases the prevention, of poverty) a purpose which exists for the benefit of an organisation's members only unless:
  - a sufficient section of the public can access those benefits by becoming members and
  - the membership is a suitable way of carrying out the charity's purpose for the public benefit

---

[65] See Chapter 5.4(a)(ii), p. 211, below.

- A private (or 'self-regarding') members' club generally exists for the benefit of its members only, and so cannot be for the public benefit. Even if it has an open membership, an organisation that is 'inward-looking', supported by its members for the purpose of providing benefits for the members, does not benefit a public class of people and so cannot be a charity....

Part 6: Personal benefit

Legal requirement: a charitable purpose may only confer personal benefits if these are 'incidental' to carrying out the purpose.

What 'personal benefit' means

A 'personal benefit' (sometimes also called a 'private benefit') means a benefit that someone receives from a charity. That 'someone' might be an individual or an organisation.

What 'incidental' means

Personal benefit is 'incidental' where (having regard both to its nature and to its amount) it is a necessary result or by-product of carrying out the purpose.

The possibility that a purpose may provide incidental personal benefit does not prevent the purpose being for the public benefit....

When establishing whether the public benefit requirement is satisfied, there are, therefore, two distinct principles that must be considered, relating to the identification of benefit and a sufficient section of the public. This had been confirmed by the Upper Tribunal in *The Independent Schools Council v The Charity Commission for England and Wales*:[66]

> The courts have adopted an incremental and somewhat *ad hoc* approach in relation to what benefits the community or a section of the community. There has never been an attempt comprehensively to define what is, or is not, of public benefit. It is possible, however, to discern from the cases two related aspects of public benefit. The first aspect is that the nature of the purpose itself must be such as to be a benefit to the community: this is public benefit in the first sense...The second aspect is that those who may benefit from the carrying out of the purpose must be sufficiently numerous, and identified in such manner as, to constitute what is described in the authorities as 'a section of the public': this is public benefit in the second sense...
>
> One result of this *ad hoc* development is that what satisfies the public benefit requirement may differ markedly between different types of allegedly charitable purposes. This is why caution must be exercised in applying authorities decided in one area of charity to another area.

These two key principles will be considered in turn.

(a) Identifiable benefit

The charity must provide a benefit that is capable of being recognized or described, but it need not be measured. The use of the word 'benefit' in the context of the public benefit test has sometimes caused confusion to the courts, since 'benefit' is sometimes used to describe the charitable purpose. An important distinction, therefore, needs to be drawn between two uses of the word 'benefit'. A charitable purpose does need to be beneficial, but this is determined as a matter of law with reference to the heads of recognized charitable purposes and the spirit of the Preamble. On the other hand, 'benefit' for purposes of the public benefit test needs to be identified as a question of fact. The Upper

---

[66] [2011] UKUT 421 (TCC); [2012] Ch 214, [44].

Tribunal recognized this in *The Independent Schools Council v The Charity Commission for England and Wales*:[67]

> A gift which fell within the express words of the Preamble might nevertheless fail to be charitable if the nature of the purpose was not such as to be beneficial to the community and so fell outside the spirit of the Preamble. Even a trust for the advancement of education in the form of a school would not have been charitable regardless of the form of education offered simply because it provided for a sufficient section of the community. In the well known example, a trust to train pickpockets would not be charitable; and that, we think, would be because such a trust would not be for the advancement of education within the scope or spirit of the Preamble...
>
> One reason for holding the gift in [*In re Hummeltenberg* [1923] 1 Ch 237] ('for training and developing suitable persons, male and female, as mediums') not to be charitable was that the judge was not satisfied that the gift would or might be operative for the public benefit. As Russell J said, at p 241: 'There is no evidence worthy of the name—nothing but vague expressions of opinions and belief, directed in the main to alleged powers of diagnosis and healing attributed to some mediums' which was the basis on which the gift was said to have the requisite benefit. This absence of 'public benefit' was not related to the second aspect of the public benefit requirement (whether the benefit was directed to the public or a sufficient section of it); it was related only to the first aspect (whether the nature of the gift was such as to be a benefit to the community).

Similarly, in *Re Shaw*,[68] George Bernard Shaw's request in his will that his estate should be used to create a forty-letter alphabet to replace the existing twenty-six letter one was not considered to be of any general utility to the public. The opinion of the testator or the donor of a gift that the public benefit test is satisfied is not relevant.

Any identifiable benefit will be balanced against any detriment or harm arising from that charitable purpose, so that if the detriment exceeds the benefit the public benefit requirement will not be satisfied. In *The Independent Schools Council v The Charity Commission for England and Wales*,[69] the Upper Tribunal said:

> The court, we conclude, has to balance the benefit and disadvantage in all cases where detriment is alleged and is supported by evidence. But great weight is to be given to a purpose which would, ordinarily, be charitable; before the alleged disadvantages can be given much weight, they need to be clearly demonstrated. There is, we think, a considerable burden on those seeking to change the status quo.

So, for example, in *National Anti-Vivisection Society v IRC*,[70] it was held that the public benefit test was not satisfied where an organization sought to ban experimentation on animals, because the detriment to the public through adverse effects on medical research arising from such a ban outweighed the putative benefit arising from the welfare of the animals. As Lord Wright said:[71]

> What [anti-vivisection] seems to do however is to destroy a source of enormous blessings to mankind. That is a positive and calamitous detriment of appalling magnitude. Nothing is offered by way of

---

[67] Ibid, [48].
[68] [1957] 1 WLR 729.
[69] [2011] UKUT 421 (TCC); [2012] Ch 214, [106].
[70] [1948] AC 31.
[71] Ibid, 49.

counterweight but a vague and problematical moral elevation. The law may well say that quite apart from any question of balancing values, an assumed prospect, or possibility of gain so vague, intangible and remote cannot justly be treated as a benefit to humanity, and that the appellant cannot get into the class of charities at all unless it can establish that benefit.

This case also illustrates how the interpretation of public benefit can change over time. A decision fifty years earlier[72] had held that a society whose purpose was to stop experiments on animals was charitable, as being for a purpose that was beneficial to the community. By the time of *National Anti-Vivisection Society*, an awareness of the benefits to medical research arising from experiments on animals meant that a purpose of banning experiments on animals was no longer considered to be beneficial to the public.

In assessing the balance of benefits, it is also necessary to consider any private benefits that are received by people or organizations that are not beneficiaries of the charity. Such private benefits will not necessarily defeat the public benefit test, but they must be incidental to the fulfilment of the charity's aims, such as where they are a necessary by-product of the fulfilment of those aims.

It has been recognized that indirect benefits to the general public arising from the fulfilment of the charitable purpose may be relevant to the public benefit inquiry. This was considered by the Upper Tribunal in *The Independent Schools Council v The Charity Commission for England and Wales*:[73]

Given the very wide range of potential charitable purposes, it is obvious that some charities have purposes which have the primary effect of conferring direct benefits on certain individuals, while other charities have purposes which confer benefits on the public, whether individually or collectively, much more indirectly. An educational charity such as a school is a clear example of the first class of charity, while a charity for the advancement of animal welfare is a clear example of the second class. A trust for maintaining a bridge is somewhere in between: it is of direct benefit to those who use it but of indirect benefit to the relevant community. [Counsel] has put forward a terminology which we have found helpful in illuminating the subject and we adopt it in this judgment. It distinguishes the following three types of benefit. (1) Direct benefits: benefits to persons whose needs it is a purpose of the charity to relieve which are received by such persons as recipients of the main service which the charity provides. (2) Indirect benefits: benefits to persons whose needs it is a purpose of the charity to relieve which are received by such persons otherwise than as recipients of the main service which the charity provides. (3) Wider benefits: benefits other than direct and indirect benefits which are received by the community at large from the activities of the charity.

We recognise the cases do not use a consistent terminology to distinguish public benefit of different degrees. For instance, the term 'indirect benefit' is sometimes used to include both (2) and (3) in [the] classification.

The Upper Tribunal had to consider the relevance of indirect benefits in respect of the advancement of education. It was emphasized that the relevant benefit must relate to the charitable purpose, namely the advancement of education. Consequently, allowing members of the public to use the school's facilities was held not to be a relevant benefit to the public, since it would not advance education. But other indirect benefits would be relevant to establishing the public benefit requirement, such as where students from the school are involved in community projects as part of the school's citizenship education programme. Crucially, whilst the Upper Tribunal acknowledged the argument that education in

---

[72] *Re Fouveaux* [1895] 2 Ch 501.
[73] [2011] UKUT 421 (TCC); [2012] Ch 214, [37].

independent schools might benefit the public because it takes students out of the State sector, it concluded that this would make little, if any, difference to the determination of an independent school's charitable status. The Upper Tribunal stated:[74]

> It might indeed be said…that the provision of private education is a considerable benefit to the community, in that each school takes students out of the state sector who would otherwise have to be educated at the expense of the state. Across the whole independent sector, that amounts to some hundreds of thousands of students.
>
> There is obviously something in that point, although it must not be taken too far…We are therefore concerned with how, if at all, this factor would impact on the way in which a school must operate in order to be doing so for the public benefit. This comes down to whether this saving to the state justifies a lesser provision of public benefit than might otherwise be expected.
>
> We think this factor would be likely to make very little, if any, difference. First, we anticipate that, even ignoring this factor, many schools would have no difficulty acting in a way consistent with their duties to act for the public benefit. For such a school, this factor does not provide much justification for requiring less of it than would otherwise be the case. Secondly, we have no idea how many schools would find it impossible or very difficult, ignoring the benefit to the state, to operate in a way which was for the public benefit. Nor do we have any idea of the number of schools within that class which would with comparative ease be able to operate in a way which was for the (lesser) public benefit if that factor could be taken into account. Accordingly, the suggested benefit to the state is highly speculative and the implicit suggestion that local authorities simply could not cope is not established.

(b) To the public

The benefit must be available to the public or to a section of the public. This is crucial in order to distinguish between public and private trusts. The policy of the law is clear: it is not appropriate for a settlor to obtain the benefits of charitable status through the mechanism of a trust where the beneficiaries are, in fact, a private group of people, such as the settlor's close family or friends. Consequently, the class of actual and potential beneficiaries must be a 'public class'. Although relatively small numbers are likely to benefit from a charity's purpose, it is crucial that the opportunity to benefit be available to a sufficient section of the public. But the size of the class must not be numerically negligible and its members must not be linked by a contract or by a quality that depends on their relationship to a particular individual.[75]

The opportunity to benefit must not be unreasonably restricted, for example, by reference to geographical location. It does not follow that the benefit cannot be restricted to a particular area, but such a restriction must be reasonable. Restricting the benefit to people living in a particular town is likely to be acceptable, as constituting an appropriate section of the public, whereas limiting it to people living in a particular street will not, although this will depend on the particular aims of the charity. The public benefit test can still be satisfied even though the beneficiaries are abroad,[76] but the charity must be registered in England and Wales.[77]

The opportunity to benefit must also not be unreasonably restricted by the ability of potential beneficiaries to pay fees. It does not follow that charities cannot charge for the services or facilities that they

---

[74] Ibid, [205].
[75] *Oppenheim v Tobacco Securities Trust Co Ltd* [1951] AC 297. See Chapter 5.4(b)(ii)(a), pp. 215–20.
[76] *Re Niyazi's Will Trusts* [1978] 1 WLR 910.
[77] *Gaudiya Mission v Brahmachary* [1998] Ch 341.

provide, such as charging school fees[78] or fees for a private hospital,[79] and they can even make a profit as long as this is reasonable and necessary to carry out the charity's aims, such as by enhancing the facilities that are provided. In other words, the profit must be ploughed back into the charitable work.[80] In *Scottish Burial Reform and Cremation Society Ltd v Glasgow Corporation*,[81] Lord Wilberforce, in holding that provision of a cremation service was charitable, even though a fee was charged, said:

> The company makes charges for its services to enable it, in the words of the joint agreed minute, to fulfil effectively the objects for which it was formed. These charges, though apparently modest, are not shown to be higher or lower than those levied for other burial services. In my opinion, the fact that cremation is provided for a fee rather than gratuitously does not affect the charitable character of the company's activity, for that does not consist in the fact of providing financial relief but in the provision of services.

If, however, the charges restrict the benefits only to those who can afford the fees, it may follow that the benefits are not available to a sufficiently large section of the public. This is all a matter of degree, however, and the Charity Commission will consider all the benefits that are provided by a charity that charges fees, since there may be sufficient benefits available to people who cannot afford fees to satisfy the public benefit requirement. This has proved particularly significant as regards independent schools. The fact that fees are charged does not automatically render the school non-charitable, but it will be necessary for the school to show that sufficient benefit is provided to members of the public who are unable to afford fees, such as through the provision of scholarships and bursaries, for otherwise the poor will be excluded from the charity's work.[82]

(c) Political objectives

An institution will not be charitable if its purposes are political. This is related to the identification of a benefit within the public benefit requirement. In *Bowman v Secular Society Ltd*[83] Lord Parker recognized that:

> a trust for the attainment of political objects has always been held invalid, not because it is illegal…but because the court has no means of judging whether a proposed change in the law will or will not be for the public benefit.

Even if there was evidence of the public being benefited by the change in law or policy, additional reasons have been identified as to why political purposes should not be charitable. Lewison J in *Hanchett-Stamford v Attorney General*[84] considered the dictum of Lord Parker and said:

> However, this may be too dogmatic a view. In *National Anti-Vivisection Society v Inland Revenue Commissioners* [1948] AC 31 the House of Lords did evaluate the competing arguments for and against

---

[78] *Independent Schools Council v The Charity Commission for England and Wales* [2011] UKUT 421; [2012] Ch 214 (TCC).

[79] *Re Resch's Will Trusts* [1969] 1 AC 514.

[80] *IRC v Falkirk Temperance Café Trust* 1927 SC 261.

[81] [1968] AC 138, 156.

[82] *The Independent Schools Council v The Charity Commission for England and Wales* [2011] UKUT 421 (TCC), [178]; [2012] Ch 214. See further Chapter 5.4(b)(ii)(b), pp. 220–5.

[83] [1917] AC 406, 442.

[84] [2008] EWHC 330 (Ch); [2009] Ch 173, [16].

the abolition of vivisection; and came to the clear conclusion that the benefits to the public in terms of scientific and medical research outweighed the harm caused by the suffering of animals that vivisection necessarily entailed. A second reason that has been given is that law cannot stultify itself by holding that it is for the public benefit that the law itself should be changed; and that each court must decide on the principle that the law is right as it stands. This was the reason put forward by both Lord Wright and Lord Simonds in the *National Anti-Vivisection Society* case. A third reason is that if the courts sanction as charitable trusts with the purpose of changing the law, they would be trespassing on the role of the legislature, whose constitutional responsibility it is to evaluate the need for such changes. This was one of the reasons given by Slade J in *McGovern v Attorney General* [1982] Ch 321 and by Chadwick LJ in *Southwood v Attorney General* [2000] WTLR 1199. This last reason seems to me to be the most persuasive. But whatever the rationale, there is no doubt that the principle remains that a trust, one of whose purposes is to change the law, cannot be charitable.

When analysing whether a charity is pursuing a political objective, an important distinction needs to be drawn between those cases in which an organization's main purpose is political and those in which the political objective is merely incidental to the charity's principal non-political purpose. An organization will be considered to be pursuing a political purpose not only where its main purpose is of a party-political nature, but also where it advocates or opposes a change in the law or policy, or decisions of central or local government authorities, either in England or abroad.[85] Courts are unwilling to consider whether the pursuit of party-political purposes is for the benefit of the public because the law wishes to remain politically neutral.

However, a charity is able to use political means to further a non-political purpose in a variety of situations, such as where the charity is campaigning for a change in the law for the benefit of those who are objects of the charity's purpose, or where the charity seeks to raise awareness of a particular issue, and/or influence public attitudes and government policy or legislation. Such political means are allowed because the campaigning and demonstrations are a means of furthering the organization's charitable purposes, but without becoming the dominant means by which it carries out those purposes. The Charity Commission has provided guidance on campaigning and political activities:[86]

Campaigning and political activity can be legitimate and valuable activities for charities to undertake

…

However, political campaigning, or political activity, as defined in this guidance, must be undertaken by a charity only in the context of supporting the delivery of its charitable purposes. Unlike other forms of campaigning, it must not be the continuing and sole activity of the charity…

(1) **Campaigning:** We use this word to refer to awareness-raising and to efforts to educate or involve the public by mobilising their support on a particular issue, or to influence or change public attitudes. We also use it to refer to campaigning activity which aims to ensure that existing laws are observed. We distinguish this from an activity which involves trying to secure support for, or oppose, a change in the law or in the policy or decisions of central government, local authorities or other public bodies, whether in this country or abroad, and which we refer to in this guidance as 'political activity'. Examples of campaigning might include:

- a health charity promoting the benefits of a balanced diet in reducing heart problems;
- a refugee charity, emphasising the positive contribution that refugees have made to society and calling for Government to enforce existing legislation that supports the rights of refugees;

---

[85] *McGovern v Attorney-General* [1982] Ch 321, 339 (Slade J).
[86] *Speaking out: guidance on campaigning and political activity by charities* CC9 (London: HMSO, 2008).

- a children's charity, drawing attention to the dangers of domestic violence and child abuse;

- a human rights charity calling on a government to observe certain fundamental human rights, and for the practice of torture to be abolished;

- a charity concerned with poverty and the environment campaigning against investment by some banks in fossil fuel extraction projects; or

- a disability charity calling for existing legislation to be adhered to in order to ensure that all children with special educational needs receive the support they are entitled to in order to access learning…

(2) **Political activity:** Political activity, as defined in this guidance, must only be undertaken by a charity in the context of supporting the delivery of its charitable purposes. We use this term to refer to activity by a charity which is aimed at securing, or opposing, any change in the law or in the policy or decisions of central government, local authorities or other public bodies, whether in this country or abroad. It includes activity to preserve an existing piece of legislation, where a charity opposes it being repealed or amended. This differs from activity aimed at ensuring that an existing law is observed, which falls under (1), Campaigning.

Political activity might include some or all of:

- raising public support for such a change;

- seeking to influence political parties or independent candidates, decision-makers, politicians or public servants on the charity's position in various ways in support of the desired change; and responding to consultations carried out by political parties.

Although this guidance from the Law Commission summarizes the current state of English law accurately, the rule preventing charities from pursuing political purposes has been criticized as being outdated.[87]

Stevens and Feldman, 'Broadcasting Advertisements by Bodies with Political Objects, Judicial Review, and the Influence of Charities Law' [1997] PL 615, 62

Those cases which established that charitable status could not extend to purposes which are political belong to an earlier social era. The fundamental objection to according such status, namely that the law is incapable of judging whether a change in the law or government policy is good or bad, is plainly spurious. In a relativistic age and a mature democracy the law should be able to uphold as charitable objects which are diametrically opposed to each other, provided that they are for the 'public benefit' in the view of a sizeable body of adherents. Religious purposes which are diametrically opposed are already upheld as equally charitable. A Christian missionary organisation seeking to convert Muslims would be just as charitable as a Muslim organisation seeking to convert Christians. There is no reason why a body seeking to promote research into the benefits of vegetarianism should not be charitable alongside a body to promote research into the health benefits of meat consumption. As Lord Wilberforce observed in *Scottish Burial Reform and Cremation Society Ltd v Glasgow City Corpn*[88] the law of charities is not static. It should be allowed to evolve so as to encompass the promotion of the observance of human rights, whether in this country or overseas, and the honouring of international obligations which have

---

[87] Santow, 'Charity in its Political Voice: A Tinkling Cymbol or a Sounding Brass?' (1999) CLP 255. But note the more liberal approach to the recognition of the advancement of human rights as a specific charitable purpose following the enactment of the Charities Act 2011. See Chapter 5.4(h), pp. 245–8.

[88] [1968] AC 138.

been entered into. The very fact that the UK has acceded to such international conventions is indicative that the pursuit of such objectives should be conclusive evidence of benefit to the community. If…it is regrettable that the laws and policies of many countries do not comply with the Charter of the United Nations of which they are members, and that campaigning to change incompatible laws and policies is commendable[89] the law of charities should be allowed to treat such campaigns as charitable notwithstanding their political character.

Feldman and Stevens are right to emphasize that the reasons given for the illegitimacy of pursuing such objectives are unconvincing. Indeed, in *National Anti-Vivisection Society v IRC*,[90] the House of Lords judged that a proposed change in the law, in the form of the abolition of vivisection, was not in the public interest because benefits to the public in terms of scientific and medical research outweighed the harm to animals arising from vivisection. It does not, therefore, seem to be the case that a judge is invariably incapable of determining whether a change in the law or government policy is good or bad. Also, the crucial distinction between political purposes that are a main objective of an organization or only incidental to a dominant charitable purpose, is a distinction that can be very difficult to draw in practice. Consequently, there should be no objection to a charity pursuing political objectives in the sense that the charity is seeking a change in law or policy, whether at home or abroad. This has been recognized by the High Court of Australia in *Aid/Watch Incorporated v Commissioner of Taxation*,[91] which concerned an organization that campaigned for effective Australian and multinational foreign aid policies, albeit not for a specific change in the law but to encourage public debate. This was considered to be for the public benefit. Similarly, in New Zealand the Supreme Court has recognized that a political objective can legitimately be charitable purposes if it generates a public benefit.[92]

The pursuit of political objectives by a charity should only be qualified in two respects. First, a charity should not be allowed to pursue such a political objective if the detriment to the public outweighs the benefit, as determined either by the courts or the Charity Commission. So, for example, a charity that seeks a change in the law in favour of racial or sexual discrimination should not be regarded as pursuing an objective that is beneficial to the public. Secondly, a charity should not pursue party-political objectives, since the benefits of charity law, particularly the fiscal advantages, should not be available in support of such purposes. Essentially, this analysis suggests there is no need for a special rule relating to political objectives; whether or not trusts for such purposes are charitable should be assessed in the normal way by reference to the public benefit criteria.

But as English law stands, it is clear that where a main purpose of an organization is political, the trust will be invalid as a charitable trust. This is the case even if there are other charitable purposes, because a charity's purposes must be wholly and exclusively charitable.[93] Where, however, the organization's purposes might be carried out either in a way that is non-political, or in a way that is political, the courts will adopt a benign approach to the construction of the purpose, and will assume that the trustees will act in a lawful and proper manner and not in a way that can be considered to be political.[94] Such a trust may therefore be charitable, but it is important that the trust is then run exclusively for charitable purposes.

---

[89] *R v Radio Authority, ex p Bull* [1998] QB 294, 306 (Lord Woolf MR).
[90] [1948] AC 31.
[91] [2010] HCA 42; (2010) 241 CLR 539. See Turner 'Charitable Trusts with Political Objects' (2011) CLJ 504.
[92] *Re Greenpeace of New Zealand Inc* [2014] NZSC 105. See Harding, 'An Antipodean view of political purposes and charity law' (2015) 131 LQR 181.
[93] See Chapter 5.5, pp. 255–60.
[94] *Re Koeppler's Will Trusts* [1986] Ch 423, 437 (Slade LJ).

Garton has criticized the state of English law:[95]

> When the House of Lords confirmed the prohibition of political purposes in the *National Anti-Vivisection Society* case it relied on scant authority, none of which was binding on it, and unconvincing justifications which fail to withstand serious scrutiny. In doing so, the House missed an important opportunity to recognise the numerous benefits of a politically active organised civil society with charities beating at its heart. The case continues to limit the extent to which charities can engage with political issues in England to this day.

The better view is that there is no need for a special rule relating to political objectives; this should be assessed in the normal way by reference to the public benefit criteria.[96]

4. CHARITABLE PURPOSES

(a) PREVENTION OR RELIEF OF POVERTY

(i) *Charitable purpose*

Under the old law of charity, the first of the four heads of charitable purpose recognized in *Pemsel's case*[97] was the relief of aged, impotent, and poor people. This head has now been divided into the relief of the poor in section 3(1)(a) of the Charities Act 2011, with 'relief of those in need' now covered by section 3(1)(j).[98] It is important to note that section 3(1)(a) covers both the relief and the prevention of poverty. These provisions may overlap.

'Poverty' is a relative term.[99] In *The Independent Schools Council v The Charity Commission for England and Wales*,[100] the Upper Tribunal recognized:

> 'poor' does not mean destitute even in the context of a trust for the relief of poverty. Broadly speaking, and in the present context, a poor person is a person who cannot reasonably afford to meet a particular need by purchasing at the full cost price the service which it is the charity's purpose to provide.

Poverty can extend to people of moderate means and may even include people who suffer only temporary financial hardship arising from a sudden change in their circumstances. In *Re Coulthurst*,[101] a fund for the widows and orphans of officers of a bank whose financial circumstances were such that they were considered to deserve assistance was held to be charitable. In *AITC Foundation's Application for Registration as a Charity*,[102] the Charity Commission registered a charity to relieve poverty, need, hardship, and distress suffered by people who had invested in companies that had collapsed. These investors, possibly fewer than 300, might have been eligible for compensation, but

---

[95] Garton, '*National Anti-Vivisection Society v Inland Revenue Commissioners*' *Landmark Cases in Equity*, (ed. Mitchell and Mitchell) (Hart Publishing, 2012) 555.

[96] Walton, '*McGovern v Attorney-General*: Constraints on Judicial Assessment of Charitable Benefit' [2014] Conv 317.

[97] *Income Tax Special Purposes Comrs v Pemsel* [1891] AC 531.

[98] See Chapter 5.4(j), pp. 248–51.

[99] *Re Clarke* [1923] 2 Ch 407.

[100] [2011] UKUT 421 (TCC); [2012] Ch 214, [40].

[101] [1951] Ch 661.

[102] [2005] WTLR 1265.

only after an investigation had been concluded and liability determined and they would have suffered financial hardship in the meantime. In *IRC v Oldham Training and Enterprise Council*, a trust to set up the unemployed in trade or business was held to be charitable as being for the relief of poverty because, as Lightman J recognized,[103] it was a

> trust for the improvement of the conditions in life of those 'going short' in respect of employment and providing a fresh start in life for those in need of it.

In *Re de Carteret*[104] the imposition of a minimum income qualification did not prevent a trust from being for the relief of poverty. The trust provided for the payment of 'annual allowances of forty pounds each to widows or spinsters in England whose income otherwise shall not be less than eighty or more than one hundred and twenty pounds per annum'. In recognizing that the trust was charitable, Maugham J emphasized the fact that preference was to 'be given to widows with young children dependent on them'. He said:

> I should have hesitated to hold that it was a good charitable gift had it merely been for 'widows and spinsters'; but I think that, in confining it, as I do, in effect, to widows with young children dependent on them, I am within the decisions to which I have referred.

Imposing a minimum income requirement is, however, surely incompatible with the notion of relieving 'poverty'.

In *Re Sanders' Will Trusts*, a trust to provide 'dwellings' for the 'working classes' was held not to be charitable because there was no requirement of being poor to benefit from it,[105] whereas in *Re Niyazi's Will Trusts*,[106] a testamentary gift to construct a working men's hostel in Cyprus was held to be charitable. This was considered to be different because, as Megarry V-C said:[107]

> The word 'hostel' has to my mind a strong flavour of a building which provides somewhat modest accommodation for those who have some temporary need for it and are willing to accept accommodation of that standard in order to meet the need. When 'hostel' is prefixed by the expression 'working men's', then the further restriction is introduced of the hostel being intended for those with a relatively low income who work for their living, especially as manual workers. The need, in other words, is to be the need of working men, and not of students or battered wives or anything else. Furthermore, the need will not be the need of the better-paid working men who can afford something superior to mere hostel accommodation, but the need of the lower end of the financial scale of working men, who cannot compete for the better accommodation but have to content themselves with the economies and shortcomings of hostel life. It seems to me that the word 'hostel' in this case is significantly different from the word 'dwellings' in *Re Sanders' Will Trusts* [1954] Ch 265, a word which is appropriate to ordinary houses in which the well-to-do may live, as well as the relatively poor.
>
> Has the expression 'working men's hostel' a sufficient connotation of poverty in it to satisfy the requirements of charity? On any footing the case is desperately near the border-line, and I have hesitated in reaching my conclusion. On the whole, however, for the reasons that I have been discussing, I think

---

[103] [1996] STC 1218, 1233. See further Chapter 5.4(e), pp. 238–9.
[104] [1933] Ch 103.
[105] [1954] Ch 265.
[106] [1978] 1 WLR 910.
[107] Ibid, 915.

that the trust is charitable, though by no great margin. This view is in my judgment supported by two further considerations. First, there is the amount of the trust fund, which in 1969 was a little under £15,000. I think one is entitled to assume that a testator has at least some idea of the probable value of his estate. The money is given for the purpose 'of the construction of or as a contribution towards the cost of the construction of a working men's hostel'. £15,000 will not go very far in such a project...

The other consideration is that of the state of housing in Famagusta. Where the trust is to erect a building in a particular area, I think it is legitimate, in construing the trust, to have some regard to the physical conditions existing in that area. Quite apart from any question of the size of the gift, I think that a trust to erect a hostel in a slum or in an area of acute housing need may have to be construed differently from a trust to erect a hostel in an area of housing affluence or plenty. Where there is a grave housing shortage, it is plain that the poor are likely to suffer more than the prosperous, and that the provision of a 'working men's hostel' is likely to help the poor and not the rich.

Clearly, the determination of whether a gift is for the poor requires some very subtle distinctions to be drawn.

Sometimes, the creators of trusts have tried hard to squeeze their gifts within the charitable definition of poverty. For example, in *Re Gwyon*,[108] the testator left a fund to provide trousers for boys in Farnham, subject to various conditions. The motive for this gift is unclear, but it was held not to be for the relief of poverty because the conditions did not identify clearly that the eligible boys had to be children of poor parents. Eve J said:[109]

The question is whether the testator has effectively created such a charity as he contemplated, a charity in the legal sense of the word. Is the object of his benefaction the relief of poverty, are the gifts for the benefit of the poor and needy? I do not think they are. Apart from residential and age qualifications, the only conditions imposed on a recipient are (1) that he shall not belong to or be supported by any charitable institution, (2) that neither he nor his parents shall be in receipt of parochial relief, (3) that he shall not be black,[110] (4) that on a second or subsequent application he shall not have disposed of any garment received within the then-preceding year from the Foundation and that when he comes for a new pair of knickers or trousers the legend 'Gwyon's Present' shall still be decipherable on the waistband of his old ones.

None of these conditions necessarily imports poverty nor could the recipients be accurately described as a class of aged, impotent or poor persons. The references to the receipt of parochial relief and to the possibility of last year's garment having been disposed of show, no doubt, that the testator contemplated that candidates might be forthcoming from a class of society where incidents of this nature might occur, but although a gift to or for the poor other than those who were in receipt of parochial relief—that is, paupers—would be a good charitable gift, it does not follow that a gift to all and sundry in a particular locality and not expressed to be for the poor ought to be construed as evidencing an intention to relieve poverty merely because the testator is minded to exclude paupers. I think that according to the true construction of these testamentary documents the benevolence of the testator was intended for all eligible boys other than paupers, and I cannot spell out of them any indication which would justify the Foundation Trustees refusing an applicant otherwise eligible on the ground that his material circumstances were of too affluent a character. In these circumstances I cannot hold this trust to be within the description of a legal charitable trust.

[108] [1930] 1 Ch 255.
[109] Ibid, 260.
[110] The Equality Act 2010, s. 193(4) states that a provision contained in any charitable instrument which provides for conferring benefits on people in a class defined by reference to colour shall be interpreted as conferring the benefits on the class without the restriction by reference to colour. See *Gibbs v Harding* [2007] EWHC 3 (Ch); [2008] Ch 235.

(ii) *Public benefit*

The presumption that trusts for the relief of the poor would be beneficial has been removed by the Charities Act 2011. It is now necessary to establish in each case that such trusts do indeed satisfy the public benefit test. The old law remains relevant, however, in determining what the public benefit might be regarding trusts for the prevention of poverty or for the relief of the poor. The real significance of previous case law is the long-standing recognition that the test of public benefit is interpreted more liberally where the purpose is for the relief of the poor than for other charitable purposes, primarily because of the benefit to the State from poverty being relieved—which means that it is easier to justify allowing fiscal privileges to such charities. As a result, the 'public' requirement of public benefit might relate to a much smaller class of potential beneficiaries than is the case with the other heads of charity, such as poor relatives of the testator,[111] or poor people from a small geographical area, such as a parish or town.[112] Consequently, there can be a family connection between the creator of the charitable trust and the pool from which the beneficiaries are drawn where the charitable purpose is for the relief of poverty, when this would not be allowed for other charitable purposes. For example, in *Re Scarisbrick*[113] it was held that a trust for the relations of the testator's son and daughter who were in 'needy circumstances' was a valid charitable trust. Jenkins LJ said:[114]

> this is a trust for the relief of poverty in the charitable sense amongst the class of relations described, and, being a trust for the relief of poverty, is…not disqualified from ranking as a legally charitable trust by the circumstances that its application is confined to a class of relations (albeit a wide class), with the result that its potential beneficiaries do not comprise the public or a section thereof under the decisions to which I have referred.
>
> I think the true question in each case has really been whether the gift was for the relief of poverty amongst a class of persons, or rather…a particular description of poor, or was merely a gift to individuals, albeit with relief of poverty amongst those individuals as the motive of the gift, or with a selective preference for the poor or poorest amongst those individuals.

Similarly, in *Re Seglman*[115] it was held that a trust for the benefit of the poor and needy members of a designated group of the testator's family created a charitable trust. Chadwick J said:[116]

> most members of the class are comfortably off, in the sense that they are able to meet their day-to-day expenses out of income, but not affluent. Like many others in similar circumstances, they need a helping hand from time to time in order to overcome an unforeseen crisis: the failure of a business venture, urgent repairs to a dwelling house or expenses brought on by reason of failing health. Further, the…class includes the issue of named individuals, many of whom are still minors. It is impossible to conclude that the minors have been selected because they are, or are likely to be, poor. No doubt, in common with most of their contemporaries, they will experience relative poverty as students. There will be periods when their income from grants or parental resources fails to cover expenditure on their actual or perceived needs. But they are not as a class 'poor persons' within any ordinarily accepted meaning of that expression. The conclusion that I draw from the evidence is that the testator selected the members of the…class on the basis that they were persons who might need financial help from

---

[111] *Re Segelman* [1996] Ch 171.
[112] *Re Lucas* [1922] 2 Ch 52.
[113] [1951] Ch 622.
[114] Ibid, 650.
[115] [1996] Ch 171.
[116] Ibid, 190.

time to time in the future—as had been the case, at least in relation to some of them, in the past—and that they were persons who, by reasons of ties of blood or affection, he would wish to help after his death, as he had done from time to time during his lifetime.

Wherever the line is to be drawn, it is clear that the present gift is nearer to it than that which the Court of Appeal had to consider in *Re Scarisbrick* [1951] Ch 622. The…class is narrower than a class of relations of every degree on both sides of the family. The question is whether the class is so narrow that the gift must be disqualified as a trust for the relief of poverty in the charitable sense…Is this properly to be regarded as a gift to such of a narrow class of near relatives as at the testator's death shall be in needy circumstances?

The basis for disqualification as a charitable gift must be that the restricted nature of the class leads to the conclusion that the gift is really a gift to the individual members of the class. In my view, the gift…is not of that character. The gift with which I am concerned has, in common with the gift which the Court of Appeal had to consider in *Re Scarisbrick*, the feature that the class of those eligible to benefit was not closed upon the testator's death. It remained open for a further period of 21 years. During that period issue of the named individuals born after the death of the testator will become members of the class. It is, in my view, impossible to attribute to the testator an intention to make a gift to those after-born issue as such. His intention must be taken to have been the relief of poverty amongst the class of which they would become members.

In *Dingle v Turner*,[117] the House of Lords considered whether these 'poor relation' cases could be extended to 'poor employees'.

Dingle v Turner [1972] AC 601

The testator sought to create a trust fund 'to apply the income thereof in paying pensions to poor employees of E. Dingle and Co Ltd' who were aged or incapacitated. At the date of the testator's death in 1950, the company had over 600 employees and there was a substantial number of ex-employees. It was held that the will created a valid charitable trust.

Lord Cross of Chelsea:

Your Lordships…are now called upon to give to the old 'poor relations' cases and the more modern 'poor employees' cases that careful consideration which, in his speech in *Oppenheim v Tobacco Securities Trust Co Ltd* [1951] AC 297 at 313[118] Lord Morton of Henryton said that they might one day require.

The contentions of the appellant and the respondents may be stated broadly as follows. The appellant says that in the *Oppenheim* case this House decided that in principle a trust ought not to be regarded as charitable if the benefits under it are confined either to the descendants of a named individual or individuals or to the employees of a given individual or company and that though the 'poor relations' cases may have to be left standing as an anomalous exception to the general rule because their validity has been recognised for so long the exception ought not to be extended to 'poor employees' trusts which had not been recognised for long before their status as charitable trusts began to be called in question. The respondents, on the other hand, say, first, that the rule laid down in the *Oppenheim* case with regard to educational trusts ought not to be regarded as a rule applicable in principle to all kinds of charitable trust, and, secondly, that in any case it is impossible to draw any logical distinction between 'poor relations' trusts and 'poor employees' trusts, and that, as the former cannot be held invalid today after having been recognised as valid for so long, the latter must be regarded as valid also.…

---

[117] [1972] AC 601.
[118] See Chapter 5.4(b)(ii)(a), pp. 215–20.

Most of the cases on the subject were decided in the eighteenth or early nineteenth centuries and are very inadequately reported, but two things at least were clear. First, that it never occurred to the judges who decided them that in the field of 'poverty' a trust could not be a charitable trust if the class of beneficiaries was defined by reference to descent from a common ancestor. Secondly, that the courts did not treat a gift or trust as necessarily charitable because the objects of it had to be poor in order to qualify, for in some of the cases the trust was treated as a private trust and not a charity. The problem in *Re Scarisbrick's Will Trusts* [1951] Ch 622 was to determine on what basis the distinction was drawn....The Court of Appeal...held that in this field the distinction between a public or charitable trust and a private trust depended on whether as a matter of construction the gift was for the relief of poverty amongst a particular description of poor people or was merely a gift to particular poor persons, the relief of poverty among them being the motive of the gift. The fact that the gift took the form of a perpetual trust would no doubt indicate that the intention of the donor could not have been to confer private benefits on particular people whose possible necessities he had in mind; but the fact that the capital of the gift was to be distributed at once did not necessarily show that the gift was a private trust....

Even on [the assumption that the 'poor relations' cases, the 'poor members' cases, and the 'poor employees' cases are all anomalous] the appeal must fail. The status of some of the 'poor relations' trusts as valid charitable trusts was recognised more than 200 years ago and a few of those then recognised are still being administered as charities today....But the 'poor members' and the 'poor employees' decisions were a natural development of the 'poor relations' decisions and to draw a distinction between different sorts of 'poverty' trusts would be quite illogical and could certainly not be said to be introducing 'greater harmony' into the law of charity. Moreover, though not as old as the 'poor relations' trusts 'poor employees' trusts have been recognised as charities for many years; there are now a large number of such trusts in existence; and assuming, as one must, that they are properly administered in the sense that benefits under them are only given to people who can fairly be said to be, according to current standards, 'poor persons', to treat such trusts as charities is not open to any practical objection.

That the Charities Act 2011, as initially enacted in 2006, did not change the law on the interpretation of public benefit for charities for the relief of poverty was confirmed by the Upper Tribunal in *Attorney-General v Charity Commission for England and Wales*.[119] The Upper Tribunal answered three questions that had been posed to it by the Attorney-General, as follows:

Question 2.1: Whether a trust for the relief of poverty amongst a class of potential objects of the trust's bounty defined by reference to the relationship of the potential objects to one or more individuals is capable of being a charitable trust.

Answer: Yes

Question 2.2: Whether a trust for the relief of poverty amongst a class of potential objects of the trust's bounty defined by reference to their or a member of their family's employment or former employment by one or specified commercial companies is capable of being a charitable trust.

Answer: Yes

Question 2.3: Whether a trust for the relief of poverty amongst the members of an unincorporated association or their families is capable of being a charitable trust.

Answer: Yes

It follows that the public benefit test for trusts for the relief of poverty can encompass a potentially narrow class of beneficiaries and the fact that the class is defined by reference to a personal nexus, such

---

[119] (2012) UKUT 420 (TCC), [2012] WTLR 521.

as having a common relative or employer or being a member of the same club, will not prevent the test from being satisfied. This has been confirmed by the Charity Commission's guidance on public benefit which was published in 2013.

Charity Commission, *Public Benefit: the Public Benefit Requirement*

Annex A: Different rules for poverty charities

What is required for a purpose to prevent or relieve poverty to be 'for the public benefit'

Legal requirement: in general, for a purpose to be charitable it must satisfy both the 'public' and 'benefit' aspects of public benefit.

However, if the purpose is to prevent or relieve poverty, the position is different.

In the case of charities for the relief (and in some cases the prevention) of poverty the courts consider the public benefit requirement can be met by satisfying the 'benefit' aspect only. In these cases there is no separate consideration of the 'public' aspect.

Legal requirement: only charities with a purpose to relieve (and in some cases to prevent) poverty can define who can benefit by reference to:

- their family relationship (that means their descent from one individual)
- their employment by an employer
- their membership of an unincorporated association

Legal requirement: a charity must not have a purpose which is for the benefit of named individuals, whether or not they are poor. This is so even if the motive is to relieve poverty and the named individuals happen to be poor.

Providing a service to people with a 'protected characteristic'

In general, charities for the relief (and in some cases the prevention) of poverty may be able to benefit a more narrowly defined section of the public than may be the case for charities with other purposes.

Legal requirement: however, even in the case of 'poverty charities', where the purpose is to provide a service only to people defined by a 'protected characteristic' in the Equality Act (such as age, gender, disability, race) the requirements of the Equality Act must still be met. That means that limiting the service only to those people must be justified.

(b) ADVANCEMENT OF EDUCATION

(i) *Charitable purpose*

The concept of education has progressed a long way since the Preamble to the Charitable Uses Act 1601 identified 'the maintenance of schools of learning, free schools and scholars in universities' and 'the education and preferment of orphans'. Buckley LJ has said that 'Education' is now:[120]

> regarded as extending to the improvement of a useful branch of human knowledge and its public dissemination.

---

[120] *Incorporated Council of Law Reporting for England and Wales v A-G* [1972] Ch 73, 102 (Buckley LJ).

Prior to the Charities Act 2006, education was widely interpreted to include the promotion of the arts and culture. This has now been separated from the advancement of education to form a new head of charity, along with the promotion of heritage and science.[121] In the light of this, it is no longer necessary for 'education' to be given an artificially wide interpretation.

Various principles can be identified relating to the determination of educational charitable purposes. At its core, 'education' relates to teaching, including paying teachers,[122] whether at home or abroad.[123] But it is not confined to formal instruction in the classroom, and encompasses vocational training[124] and practice containing spiritual, moral, mental, and physical elements.[125]

Education also encompasses research. In assessing whether the research is educational, the court will have regard to its aims and utility. In *Re Hopkins' Will Trust*,[126] the key issue was whether a gift to the Francis Bacon Society to identify evidence in support of his authorship of the plays attributed to Shakespeare was charitable. Wilberforce J said:[127]

> Let me say at once that no determination of the authorship of the 'Shakespeare' plays, or even of any subsidiary question relating to it, falls to be made in the present proceedings. The court is only concerned, at this point, with the practicability and later with the legality of carrying [the testator's] wishes into effect, and it must decide this, one way or the other, upon the evidence of the experts which is before it…
>
> On this evidence, should the conclusion be reached that the search for the Bacon–Shakespeare manuscripts is so manifestly futile that the court should not allow this bequest to be spent upon it as upon an object devoid of the possibility of any result? I think not. The evidence shows that the discovery of any manuscript of the plays is unlikely; but so are many discoveries before they are made (one may think of the Codex Sinaiticus, or the Tomb of Tutankhamen, or the Dead Sea Scrolls); I do not think that that degree of improbability has been reached which justifies the court in placing an initial interdict on the testatrix's benefaction…
>
> a bequest for the purpose of search, or research, for the original manuscripts of England's greatest dramatist (whoever he was) would be well within the law's conception of charitable purposes. The discovery of such manuscripts, or of one such manuscript, would be of the highest value to history and to literature. It is objected, against this, that as we already have the text of the plays, from an almost contemporary date, the discovery of a manuscript would add nothing worth while. This I utterly decline to accept. Without any undue exercise of the imagination, it would surely be a reasonable expectation that the revelation of a manuscript would contribute, probably decisively, to a solution of the authorship problem, and this alone is benefit enough. It might also lead to improvements in the text. It might lead to more accurate dating.
>
> Is there any authority, then, which should lead me to hold that a bequest to achieve this objective is not charitable? By [counsel] for the next-of-kin much reliance was placed on the decision on Bernard Shaw's will, the 'British Alphabet' case (*Re Shaw* [1957] 1 WLR 729). Harman J held that the gift was not educational because it merely tended to the increase of knowledge…But the judge did say this at 737: 'if the object be merely the increase of knowledge, that is not in itself a charitable object unless it be combined with teaching or education'; and he referred to the House of Lords decision, *Whicker v*

---

[121] See Chapter 5.4(f), pp. 239–42.
[122] *Case of Christ's College, Cambridge* (1757) 1 Wm Bl 90.
[123] *Manoogian v Sonsino* [2002] EWHC 1304; [2002] WTLR 989.
[124] *IRC v Oldham Training and Enterprise Council* [1996] STC 1218, 1233 (Lightman J).
[125] *IRC v McMullen* [1981] AC 1, 15 (Lord Hailsham).
[126] [1965] Ch 669.
[127] Ibid, 675.

Hume (1858) 7 HL Cas 124, where, in relation to a gift for advancement of education and learning, two of the Lords read 'learning' as equivalent to 'teaching', thereby in his view implying that learning, in its ordinary meaning, is not a charitable purpose.

This decision certainly seems to place some limits upon the extent to which a gift for research may be regarded as charitable. Those limits are that…it must be 'combined with teaching or education'…The words 'combined with teaching or education', though well explaining what the judge had in mind when he rejected the gift in *Shaw's case* [1957] 1 WLR 729, are not easy to interpret in relation to other facts. I should be unwilling to treat them as meaning that the promotion of academic research is not a charitable purpose unless the researcher were engaged in teaching or education in the conventional meaning; and I am encouraged in this view by some words of Lord Greene MR in *Re Compton* [1945] Ch 123 at 127. The testatrix there had forbidden the income of the bequest to be used for research, and Lord Greene MR treated this as a negative definition of the education to be provided. It would, he said, exclude a grant to enable a beneficiary to conduct research on some point of history or science. This shows that Lord Greene MR considered that historic research might fall within the description of 'education'. I think, therefore, that the word 'education' as used by Harman J in *Re Shaw* must be used in a wide sense, certainly extending beyond teaching, and that the requirement is that, in order to be charitable, research must either be of educational value to the researcher or must be so directed as to lead to something which will pass into the store of educational material, or so as to improve the sum of communicable knowledge in an area which education may cover—education in this last context extending to the formation of literary taste and appreciation (compare *Royal Choral Society v IRC* [1943] 2 All ER 101). Whether or not the test is wider than this, it is, as I have stated it, amply wide enough to include the purposes of the gift in this case.

On the other side there is *Re British School of Egyptian Archaeology* [1954] 1 WLR 546, also a decision of Harman J, a case much closer to the present. The trusts there were to excavate, to discover antiquities, to hold exhibitions, to publish works and to promote the training and assistance of students—all in relation to Egypt. Harman J held that the purposes were charitable, as being educational. The society was one for the diffusion of a certain branch of knowledge, namely, knowledge of the ancient past of Egypt; and it also had a direct educational purpose, namely, to train students. The conclusion reached that there was an educational charity was greatly helped by the reference to students, but it seems that Harman J must have accepted that the other objects—those of archaeological research—were charitable, too. They were quite independent objects on which the whole of the society's funds could have been spent, and the language 'the school has a direct educational purpose, namely, to train students' seems to show that the judge was independently upholding each set of objects.

[Counsel for the next-of-kin] correctly pointed out that in that case there was a direct obligation to diffuse the results of the society's research and said that it was this that justified the finding that the archaeological purposes were charitable. I accept that research of a private character, for the benefit only of the members of a society, would not normally be educational—or otherwise charitable—as did Harman J [1954] 1 WLR 546 at 551, but I do not think that the research in the present case can be said to be of a private character, for it is inherently inevitable, and manifestly intended, that the result of any discovery should be published to the world. I think, therefore, that the *British School of Egyptian Archaeology* case supports the Society's contentions.

Wilberforce J's suggestion that an attribute of research as a charitable object is that it is of educational value to the researcher is doubtful, especially because this would not appear to meet the public benefit requirement. Consequently, the preferable view is that research should be considered to be educational only where it involves some element of dissemination of the results.

In *Incorporated Council of Law Reporting for England and Wales v Attorney-General*,[128] a trust for the publication of law reports was considered to advance education because it assisted research into the law and disseminated knowledge of the law. As Buckley LJ recognized:

in a legal system such as ours, in which judges' decisions are governed by precedents, reported decisions are the means by which legal principles (other than those laid down by statutes) are developed, established and made known, and by which the application of those legal principles to particular kinds of facts are illustrated and explained. Reported decisions may be said to be the tissue of the body of our non-statutory law. Whoever, therefore, would carry out any anatomical researches upon our non-statutory corpus juris must do so by research amongst, and study of, reported cases...

The legal profession has from times long past been termed a learned profession, and rightly so, for no man can properly practise or apply the law who is not learned in that field of law with which he is concerned. He must have more than an aptitude and more than a skill. He must be learned in a sense importing true scholarship. In a system of law such as we have in this country this scholarship can only be acquired and maintained by a continual study of case law.

The service which publication of The Law Reports provides benefits not only those actively engaged in the practice and administration of the law, but also those whose business it is to study and teach law academically, and many others who need to study the law for the purposes of their trades, businesses, professions or affairs. In all these fields, however, the nature of the service is the same: it enables the reader to study, and by study to acquaint himself with and instruct himself in the law of this country. There is nothing here which negatives an exclusively charitable purpose.

Although the objects of the council are commercial in the sense that the council exists to publish and sell its publications, they are unself-regarding. The members are prohibited from deriving any profit from the council's activities, and the council itself, although not debarred from making a profit out of its business, can only apply any such profit in the further pursuit of its objects. The council is consequently not prevented from being a charity by reason of any commercial element in its activities.

In *Re South Place Ethical Society*,[129] the objects of the Society were 'the study and dissemination of ethical principles and the cultivation of a rational religious sentiment'. In holding that this was a trust for the advancement of education, as well as being for other purposes beneficial to the community, Dillon LJ said:[130]

The first part of the objects is the study and dissemination of ethical principles. Dissemination, I think, includes dissemination of the fruits of the study, and I have no doubt that that part of the objects satisfies the criterion of charity as being for the advancement of education. The second part, the cultivation of a rational religious sentiment, is considerably more difficult. As I have already said, I do not think that the cultivation is limited to cultivation of the requisite sentiment in the members of the Society and in no one else. In the context the Society is outward looking, and the cultivation would extend to all members of the public whom the Society's teachings may reach. The sentiment or state of mind is to be rational, that is to say founded in reason. As I see it, a sentiment or attitude of mind founded in reason can only be cultivated or encouraged to grow by educational methods, including music, and the development of the appreciation of music by performances of high quality. The difficulty in this part of the Society's objects lies in expressing a very lofty and possibly unattainable ideal in a very few words, and the difficulty is compounded by the choice of the word 'religious', which while giving the flavour of what is in mind, is not in my view used in its correct sense.

---

[128] [1972] Ch 73.
[129] [1980] 1 WLR 1565.
[130] Ibid, 1576.

In *Living in Radiance's Application for Registration as a Charity*,[131] an institution that provided information, services, and education about the science of meditation and peace education was not registered as a charity because it failed to add to the participants' factual knowledge or skills base. The organization of conferences to discuss issues of public and international interest at which the participants learned from and instructed each other was, however, held to be educational in *Re Koeppler's Will Trusts*.[132] Slade LJ said:[133]

> the following salient points emerged from the evidence: (i) the conferences sought to improve the minds of participants, not necessarily by adding to their factual knowledge but by expanding their wisdom and capacity to understand; (ii) the subjects discussed at conferences were recognised academic subjects in higher education; (iii) the conferences operated by a process of discussion designed to elicit an exchange of views in a manner familiar in places of higher education; (iv) the conferences were designed to capitalise on the expertise of participants who were there both to learn and to instruct.

(ii) *Public benefit*

(a) *Definition of the public*

The requirement of public benefit has proved especially significant when determining whether trusts for the advancement of education are charitable, and will be even more so now that benefit can no longer be presumed.[134] It has been in the context of this charitable purpose that the tax advantages of being a charity have proved to be particularly important, especially as regards whether independent schools should be treated as charitable. Also, employers might seek to provide tax-free benefits to employees by providing for the education of their children, but this will be effective only if a sufficient section of the public can be identified. This was the key issue in the leading decision of the House of Lords in *Oppenheim v Tobacco Securities Trust Co Ltd*.[135]

Oppenheim v Tobacco Securities Trust Co Ltd [1951] AC 297

The income of a trust fund was directed to be applied 'in providing for...the education of children of employees or former employees of the British-American Tobacco Co Ltd...or any of its subsidiary or allied companies in such manner...as the acting trustees shall in their absolute discretion...think fit', with power to apply the capital for the same purposes. The number of employees of the company and their subsidiary and allied companies exceeded 110,000. The question was whether the class to be benefited was a sufficient section of the public. It was held that because the qualification to benefit was based upon a personal nexus between those who might benefit and the settlors, the class of beneficiaries was not a section of the public and the trust was void.

Lord Simonds:

In the case of trusts for educational purposes the condition of public benefit must be satisfied. The difficulty lies in determining what is sufficient to satisfy the test, and there is little to help your Lordships to solve it.

---

[131] [2007] WTLR 683.
[132] [1986] Ch 423.
[133] Ibid, 436.
[134] Charities Act 2011, s. 4(2).
[135] [1951] AC 297.

If I may begin at the bottom of the scale, a trust established by a father for the education of his son is not a charity. The public element, as I will call it, is not supplied by the fact that from that son's education all may benefit. At the other end of the scale the establishment of a college or university is beyond doubt a charity. 'Schools of learning and free schools and scholars of universities' are the very words of the preamble to the Statute of Elizabeth. So also the endowment of a college, university or school by the creation of scholarships or bursaries is a charity and none the less because competition may be limited to a particular class of persons. It is upon this ground, as Lord Greene MR pointed out in *Re Compton* [1945] Ch 123 at 136 that the so-called Founder's Kin cases can be rested. The difficulty arises where the trust is not for the benefit of any institution either then existing or by the terms of the trust to be brought into existence, but for the benefit of a class of persons at large. Then the question is whether that class of persons can be regarded as such a 'section of the community' as to satisfy the test of public benefit. These words 'section of the community' have no special sanctity, but they conveniently indicate first, that the possible (I emphasize the word 'possible') beneficiaries must not be numerically negligible, and secondly, that the quality which distinguishes them from other members of the community, so that they form by themselves a section of it, must be a quality which does not depend on their relationship to a particular individual. It is for this reason that a trust for the education of members of a family or, as in *Re Compton*, of a number of families cannot be regarded as charitable. A group of persons may be numerous but, if the nexus between them is their personal relationship to a single [person] or to several [people], they are neither the community nor a section of the community for charitable purposes.

I come, then, to the present case where the class of beneficiaries is numerous but the difficulty arises in regard to their common and distinguishing quality. That quality is being children of employees of one or other of a group of companies. I can make no distinction between children of employees and the employees themselves. In both cases the common quality is found in employment by particular employers. The latter of the two cases by which the Court of Appeal held itself to be bound, *Re Hobourn Aero Components Ltd's Air Raid Distress Fund* [1946] Ch 194, is a direct authority for saying that such a common quality does not constitute its possessors a section of the public for charitable purposes. In the former case, *Re Compton*, Lord Greene MR had by way of illustration placed members of a family and employees of a particular employer on the same footing, finding neither in common kinship nor in common employment the sort of nexus which is sufficient... It appears to me that it would be an extension, for which there is no justification in principle or authority, to regard common employment as a quality which constitutes those employed a section of the community.

Since there was a personal nexus the trust was a private trust which was void for perpetuity.

The decision of the House of Lords in *Oppenheim* does not sit easily with the later decision of the same court in *Dingle v Turner*,[136] which concerned the provision of benefits by an employer for employees for the relief of poverty. Despite the existence of a personal nexus, the public benefit test was satisfied. The cases are distinguishable because they involved different charitable purposes, but why should this make a difference? In *Oppenheim*, Lord MacDermott dissented:[137]

The numerical strength of the class is considerable on any showing. The employees concerned number over 110,000, and it may reasonably be assumed that the children, who constitute the class in question, are no fewer. The large size of the class is not, of course, decisive but in my view it cannot be left out of account when the problem is approached in this way. Then it must be observed that the [beneficiaries] are not limited to those presently employed. They include former employees (not reckoned in the figure

---

[136] [1972] AC 601. See Chapter 5.4(a)(ii), pp. 208–11.
[137] [1951] AC 297, 314.

I have given) and are, therefore, a more stable category than would otherwise be the case. And, further, the employees concerned are not limited to those in the service of the 'British-American Tobacco Co Ltd or any of its subsidiary or allied companies'—itself a description of great width—but include the employees, in the event of the British-American Tobacco Co Ltd being reconstructed or merged on amalgamation, of the reconstructed or amalgamated company or any of its subsidiary companies. No doubt the settlors here had a special interest in the welfare of the class they described, but, apart from the fact that this may serve to explain the particular form of their bounty, I do not think it material to the question in hand. What is material, as I regard the matter, is that they have chosen to benefit a class which is, in fact, substantial in point of size and importance and have done so in a manner which, to my mind, manifests an intention to advance the interests of the class described as a class rather than as a collection or succession of particular individuals....

But can any really fundamental distinction, as respects the personal or impersonal nature of the common link, be drawn between those employed, for example, by a particular university and those whom the same university has put in a certain category as the result of individual examination and assessment? Again, if the bond between those employed by a particular railway is purely personal, why should the bond between those who are employed as railway men be so essentially different? Is a distinction to be drawn in this respect between those who are employed in a particular industry before it is nationalized and those who are employed therein after that process has been completed and one employer has taken the place of many? Are miners in the service of the National Coal Board now in one category and miners at a particular pit or of a particular district in another? Is the relationship between those in the service of the Crown to be distinguished from that obtaining between those in the service of some other employer? Or, if not, are the children of, say, soldiers or civil servants to be regarded as not constituting a sufficient section of the public to make a trust for their education charitable?

It was conceded in the course of the argument that, had the present trust been framed so as to provide for the education of the children of those engaged in the tobacco industry in a named county or town, it would have been a good charitable disposition, and that even though the class to be benefited would have been appreciably smaller and no more important than is the class here. That concession follows from what the Court of Appeal has said. But if it is sound and a personal or impersonal relationship remains the universal criterion I think it shows, no less than the queries I have just raised in indicating some of the difficulties of the problem, that the *Compton* [personal nexus] test is a very arbitrary and artificial rule. This leads me to the second difficulty that I have regarding it. If I understand it aright it necessarily makes the quantum of public benefit a consideration of little moment; the size of the class becomes immaterial and the need of its members and the public advantage of having that need met appear alike to be irrelevant. To my mind these are considerations of some account in the sphere of educational trusts for, as already indicated, I think the educational value and scope of the work actually to be done must have a bearing on the question of public benefit.

Finally, it seems to me that, far from settling the state of the law on this particular subject, the *Compton* test is more likely to create confusion and doubt in the case of many trusts and institutions of a character whose legal standing as charities has never been in question. I have particularly in mind gifts for the education of certain special classes such, for example, as the daughters of missionaries, the children of those professing a particular faith or accepted as ministers of a particular denomination, or those whose parents have sent them to a particular school for the earlier stages of their training. I cannot but think that in cases of this sort an analysis of the common quality binding the class to be benefited may reveal a relationship no less personal than that existing between an employer and those in his service. Take, for instance, a trust for the provision of university education for boys coming from a particular school. The common quality binding the members of that class seems to reside in the fact that their parents or guardians all contracted for their schooling with the same establishment or body. That the school in such a case may itself be a charitable foundation seems altogether beside the point and quite insufficient to hold the *Compton* test at bay if it is well founded in law.

Lord MacDermott's approach to the identification of a section of the community commended itself to the judges in *Dingle v Turner*.[138] Lord Cross said:[139]

> *Oppenheim* [1951] AC 297 was a case of an educational trust and though the majority evidently agreed with the view expressed by the Court of Appeal in the *Hobourn Aero* case [1946] Ch 194 that the *Compton* rule [1945] Ch 123 was of universal application outside the field of poverty it would no doubt be open to this House without overruling *Oppenheim* to hold that the scope of the rule was more limited. If ever I should be called upon to pronounce on this question—which does not arise in this appeal—I would as at present advised be inclined to draw a distinction between the practical merits of the *Compton* rule and the reasoning by which Lord Greene MR sought to justify it. That reasoning—based on the distinction between personal and impersonal relationships—has never seemed to me very satisfactory and I have always if I may say so—felt the force of the criticism to which my noble and learned friend Lord MacDermott subjected it in his dissenting speech in *Oppenheim*. For my part I would prefer to approach the problem on far broader lines. The phrase a 'section of the public' is in truth a vague phrase which may mean different things to different people. In the law of charity judges have sought to elucidate its meaning by contrasting it with another phrase: 'a fluctuating body of private individuals.' But I get little help from the supposed contrast for as I see it one and the same aggregate of persons may well be describable both as a section of the public and as a fluctuating body of private individuals. The ratepayers of the Royal Borough of Kensington and Chelsea, for example, certainly constitute a section of the public; but would it be a misuse of language to describe them as a 'fluctuating body of private individuals'? After all, every part of the public is composed of individuals and being susceptible of increase or decrease is fluctuating. So at the end of the day one is left where one started with the bare contrast between 'public' and 'private'. No doubt some classes are more naturally describable as sections of the public than as private classes while other classes are more naturally describable as private classes than as sections of the public. The blind, for example, can naturally be described as a section of the public; but what they have in common—their blindness—does not join them together in such a way that they could be called a private class. On the other hand, the descendants of Mr. Gladstone might more reasonably be described as a 'private class' than as a section of the public, and in the field of common employment the same might well be said of the employees in some fairly small firm. But if one turns to large companies employing many thousands of men and women most of whom are quite unknown to one another and to the directors the answer is by no means so clear. One might say that in such a case the distinction between a section of the public and a private class is not applicable at all or even that the employees in such concerns as ICI or GEC are just as much 'sections of the public' as the residents in some geographical area. In truth the question whether or not the potential beneficiaries of a trust can fairly be said to constitute a section of the public is a question of degree and cannot be by itself decisive of the question whether the trust is a charity. Much must depend on the purpose of the trust. It may well be that, on the one hand, a trust to promote some purpose, prima facie charitable, will constitute a charity even though the class of potential beneficiaries might fairly be called a private class and that, on the other hand, a trust to promote another purpose, also prima facie charitable, will not constitute a charity even though the class of potential beneficiaries might seem to some people fairly describable as a section of the public. In answering the question whether any given trust is a charitable trust the courts—as I see it—cannot avoid having regard to the fiscal privileges accorded to charities. As counsel for the Attorney-General remarked in the course of the argument the law of charity is bedevilled by the fact that charitable trusts enjoy two quite different sorts of privilege. On the one hand, they enjoy immunity from the rules against perpetuity and uncertainty and though individual potential beneficiaries cannot sue to enforce them the public interest

---

[138] [1972] AC 601. See Chapter 5.4(a)(ii), pp. 208–11.
[139] Ibid, 623.

arising under them is protected by the Attorney-General. If this was all there would be no reason for the courts not to look favourably on the claim of any 'purpose' trust to be considered as a charity if it seemed calculated to confer some real benefit on those intended to benefit by it whoever they might be and if it would fail if not held to be a charity. But that is not all. Charities automatically enjoy fiscal privileges which with the increased burden of taxation have become more and more important and in deciding that such and such a trust is a charitable trust the court is endowing it with a substantial annual subsidy at the expense of the taxpayer. Indeed, claims of trusts to rank as charities are just as often challenged by the revenue as by those who would take the fund if the trust was invalid. It is, of course, unfortunate that the recognition of any trust as a valid charitable trust should automatically attract fiscal privileges, for the question whether a trust to further some purpose is so little likely to benefit the public that it ought to be declared invalid and the question whether it is likely to confer such great benefits on the public that it should enjoy fiscal immunity are really two quite different questions. The logical solution would be to separate them and to say—as the Radcliffe Commission[140] proposed—that only some charities should enjoy fiscal privileges. But, as things are, validity and fiscal immunity march hand in hand and the decisions in the *Compton* [1945] Ch 123 and *Oppenheim* [1951] AC 297 cases were pretty obviously influenced by the consideration that if such trusts as were there in question were held valid they would enjoy an undeserved fiscal immunity. To establish a trust for the education of the children of employees in a company in which you are interested is no doubt a meritorious act; but however numerous the employees may be the purpose which you are seeking to achieve is not a public purpose. It is a company purpose and there is no reason why your fellow taxpayers should contribute to a scheme which by providing 'fringe benefits' for your employees will benefit the company by making their conditions of employment more attractive. The temptation to enlist the assistance of the law of charity in private endeavours of this sort is considerable—witness the recent case of the Metal Box scholarships—*Inland Revenue Commissioners v Educational Grants Association Ltd* [1967] Ch 993[141] —and the courts must do what they can to discourage such attempts. In the field of poverty the danger is not so great as in the field of education—for while people are keenly alive to the need to give their children a good education and to the expense of doing so they are generally optimistic enough not to entertain serious fears of falling on evil days much before they fall on them. Consequently the existence of company 'benevolent funds' the income of which is free of tax does not constitute a very attractive 'fringe benefit.' This is a practical justification—though not, of course, the historical explanation—for the special treatment accorded to poverty trusts in charity law. For the same sort of reason a trust to promote some religion among the employees of a company might perhaps safely be held to be charitable provided that it was clear that the benefits were to be purely spiritual. . . . As I see it, it is on these broad lines rather than for the reasons actually given by Lord Greene MR that the *Compton* rule [1951] AC 123 can best be justified.

Lord Cross's suggestion that the availability of fiscal privileges should be taken into account when assessing public benefit was not supported by three of the other judges in *Dingle v Turner*, one of whom being Lord MacDermott.[142] So, where is the law left concerning the identification of public benefit for the advancement of education following *Oppenheim* and *Dingle*? Although it has been suggested that the consequence of the comments in *Dingle* is that *Oppenheim* must be treated as wrongly decided,[143] those comments were *obiter* and nothing was said in *Dingle v Turner* to suggest that *Oppenheim* should have been decided differently. *Oppenheim* was subsequently followed in *IRC v Educational*

---

[140] *Report of the Radcliffe Commission*, Cmd 9474 (London: HMSO, 1955), [54]–[60].
[141] See Chapter 5.4(b)(ii)(a), p. 220.
[142] Similar doubts were expressed by the Upper Tribunal in *The Independent Schools Council v The Charity Commission for England and Wales* [2011] UKUT 421 (TCC); [2012] Ch 214, [176].
[143] Hayton, '*Dingle v Turner*' (1972) 36 Conv 209, 212.

Grants Association Ltd,[144] although this was decided before *Dingle v Turner*. The Educational Grants Association Ltd was an association established for the advancement of education. It had a close relation with Metal Box Co. Ltd, and the bulk of its income came from that company. Much of the income of the Association was applied for the education of children of persons connected with Metal Box. It was held that the income was not applied for charitable purposes only. Salmon LJ said:

> If a trust established for the purpose of making grants for the education of children of employees or former employees of Metal Box would not be established for charitable purposes only, it seems to me to follow, as the night follows the day, that annual payments applied for the purpose of educating the children of employees or former employees of the company are not applied for charitable purposes only. I do not mean that any child of a Metal Box employee is necessarily excluded from the ambit of this beneficence. If it had been shown, for example, that by chance a few such children had been amongst the members of the general public to have benefited from the grants, I should not have thought that this was in any way breaching the requirement that the annual payments must be applied for charitable purposes only. The trouble in this case is that when one looks at all the facts which have been recited by my Lords and which I need not repeat, one is driven to the same inescapable conclusion as was the judge, namely, that 75% to 85% of the annual payments were in fact not applied for the benefit of a sector of the public but for the benefit of children of employees or former employees of Metal Box as such.

If the facts of *Oppenheim* and *Educational Grants Association* were to arise today, it is clear that the Charity Commission, the Tribunals, and the courts would apply the personal nexus test to determine whether the beneficiaries constituted a sufficient section of the public. But in assessing this, it would be appropriate to have regard to the factors identified by Lord MacDermott in *Oppenheim* and affirmed by Lord Cross in *Dingle v Turner*. The fact that the creator of the trust is seeking to obtain tax advantages should also be regarded as a relevant factor; this is a legitimate motive for seeking charitable status, but cannot be regarded as a purpose in its own right. It is not appropriate for companies to use the law of charity to provide tax-free benefits to employees. This unacceptably confuses the public law of charity with the private endeavours of companies.

Although much of the discussion about public benefit in respect of the advancement of education has focused on the personal nexus test, it must not be forgotten that a factual benefit must be shown and that this benefit is available to the public or a section of the public, so even though there is no personal nexus it must still be established that the public benefit test has been satisfied.[145] So, for example, if the charitable purpose relates to research, this needs to be disseminated and not restricted to the use of the researcher or to the members of a particular society.[146]

Where eligibility to obtain the benefits of the charity are restricted, this does not mean that the benefit is no longer available to a section of the public, as long as the restriction is reasonable and is not based on a personal nexus. So, for example, a scholarship to study at a particular school or university may legitimately be restricted to people from a particular town or to people who attain a certain level of academic achievement, but it cannot be restricted to relatives of the donor.

(b) Public schools

A matter of long-standing controversy has related to the satisfaction of the public benefit requirement by public schools in the UK. Charitable status is very important to such schools

---

[144] [1967] Ch 993.
[145] *The Independent Schools Council v The Charity Commission for England and Wales* [2011] UKUT 421 (TCC); [2012] Ch 214, [52] and [141].
[146] *Re Hopkins' Will Trust* [1965] Ch 669, 681 (Wilberforce J). See Chapter 5.4(b)(i), p. 212.

because it provides significant fiscal advantages. About 5 per cent of the school population in England and Wales attend a private school, and their families pay an average fee of £12,000 per year. Whether such schools satisfy both elements of the public benefit requirement was considered by the Upper Tribunal in *The Independent Schools Council v The Charity Commission for England and Wales*.

The Independent Schools Council v The Charity Commission for England and Wales
[2011] UKUT 421 (TCC); [2012] Ch 214, [111]

Educational trusts of an ordinary sort are seen as being for the public benefit in the first sense [of being beneficial] because of the value to society of having an educated population. It is no more and no less of benefit to the community in the case of a rich person than a poor person. Thus the trust in *Oppenheim v Tobacco Securities Trust Co Ltd* [1951] AC 297 is properly to be seen as for the benefit of the community in the first sense; but it failed to be a charitable trust because it was a private trust lacking the necessary element of public benefit in the second sense [relating to the identification of the public or a section of the public]. Accordingly, if an educational institution such as we are concerned with fails to be for the public benefit because it is limited, either constitutionally or in practice, to providing benefits to the rich, this will be so because, and only because, it fails to be for the benefit of a sufficient section of the public.

We thus locate the need to include the poor within the public benefit requirement in its second sense...we therefore reach the conclusion that the schools with which we are concerned do have purposes which are for the public benefit in the first sense...

We are concerned with whether the rich (by which we mean those able to afford the school fees) are a sufficient section of the community...

We conclude from our examination of the authorities that the hypothetical school addressed in... the reference (ie where the sole object of the school is the advancement of the education of children whose families can afford to pay fees representing the cost of the provision of their education) does not have purposes which provide that element of public benefit necessary to qualify as a charity. Such a school has purposes which therefore fail to satisfy the public benefit test under the [Charities] Act. (As we note later, such a school is in practice unlikely to exist.)...

This conclusion is based on the proposition that a trust which excludes the poor from benefit cannot be a charity. There is no case which decides that point, but we consider it is right as a matter of principle, given the underlying concept of charity from early times...

It is also implicit in our conclusion that it is correct to look beyond the beneficiary concerned to see if the poor are excluded. We would expect that very few of the children who attend private schools have their own resources to pay the requisite fees. It cannot, we think, be right to focus on the children themselves in addressing this issue. Although the students themselves are the direct beneficiaries of the education, they benefit...only because their families can afford to pay. Just as in *Inland Revenue Commissioners v Educational Grants Asssociation Ltd* [1967] Ch 993 it was right to look beyond the children to their parents and so on to Metal Box in ascertaining whether there was public benefit, so too...it is right to look beyond the students to their parents or other family members paying the fees, to see whether the provision of benefit by the school is to a poor person.

It is one thing to treat a student and his family as the relevant entity for assessing whether the student is poor. It would be another thing to afford the same treatment to a student who had managed to acquire funding from a third party source. How that funding is to be brought into account in assessing whether the student is 'poor' will, in our view, depend on the source.

At one end of the scale, funding from an employer is received by the student as a purely private benefit which, we think, ought generally to be brought into account. The school could not rely on educating such students as providing a benefit to the 'poor'.

At the other end of the scale, funding from a grant-making educational charity to a child in a family which is poor by any standard is a benefit received by the student not as a private benefit but as a result of the implementation by the grant-making body of purposes which are for the public benefit. It seems to us that the school ought to be able to treat the education of that student as the provision of direct benefit to a person who is 'poor'. Of course, from the school's point of view, it makes no difference to its finances whether the fees come from the family, a third party or a charity. But that is not the point; the point is whether the school is educating poor people and, in terms of the access to schools, which is a most important consideration from the perspective of the public, a poor person in receipt of a grant is none the less poor. The contrary view could produce startling results. Some schools have large endowments out of which they are able to provide significant numbers of substantial scholarships, thus enabling them to open up their access to persons who could not otherwise afford to attend the school, including 'poor' students... It cannot be right, we consider, that the school is unable to rely on its own provision of education to poor students receiving scholarships from such endowments as a direct benefit to persons who are 'poor' in the context of its own trusts and duties...

We now turn to consider a school which, as a matter of its constitution, can admit students whatever their ability to pay, but as a matter of fact (whether because of a policy of accepting only fee-paying students or because of some financial imperative) does not do so. The first question which then arises is whether such a school is established for charitable purposes only...

Where a school is, by its constitution, open to all, we consider that, generally speaking, it is established for charitable purposes only. That such a school is charitable may be made clear expressly by its constitution, for instance by stating that its purposes may only be effected 'in a way which is for the public benefit' or some such words. But even in the absence of such words, it will often be implicit that such a school will carry out its express purposes in a way which is for the public benefit...

It is in this context of activities that indirect benefits and wider benefits... fall to be taken into account as part of the public benefit requirement. Many, and probably most although not all, schools of the type with which we are concerned provide benefits other than education to those who pay full fees. Those benefits include some or all of the following: (a) provision of scholarships and bursaries; (b) arrangements under which students from local state schools can attend classes in subjects not otherwise readily available to them; (c) sharing of teachers or teaching facilities with local state schools; (d) making available (whether on the internet or otherwise) teaching materials used in the school; (e) making available to students of local state schools other facilities such as playing fields, sports halls, swimming pools or sports grounds; (f) making those last facilities available to the community as a whole.

Category (a) is a direct benefit. Categories (b) to (e) will be direct or indirect benefits, depending on the precise constitution of the school. They might also be wider benefits.

Category (f) is not a direct benefit or an indirect benefit or even a wider benefit in the sense in which we are using those terms...

When it comes to considering whether a school which is a charity is operating for the public benefit in accordance with its charitable purposes, the primary focus must be on the direct benefits which it provides. Scholarships or other forms of direct assistance to students are therefore important. Account can certainly be taken of other direct benefits such as those described in categories (b) and (c). Account can be taken of the benefits described in category (d) since they are clearly available to the whole community; however, it must be very doubtful whether much weight can be attached to a benefit which must be comparatively easy to provide at little cost and the effect of which seems to us, on the evidence we have, very uncertain.

...we consider that the benefits described in category (e) are to be taken into account in deciding whether a school which is a charity is operating for the public benefit.

We do not, however, consider that benefits of the sort described in category (f) can be taken into account. The fact that an ancillary activity may be a good thing for the school is not enough. The ancillary activity is not itself being carried out in fulfilment of the charitable purpose, namely the advancement of education.

...we have already decided that a school which is required by its governing instrument to admit only those whose families are able to afford fees is one which excludes the poor and is not therefore for the public benefit. It might therefore be asked why the provision of a number of scholarships to poor students could ever be enough to protect its charitable status. By analogy with *Oppenheim v Tobacco Securities Trust Co Ltd* [1951] AC 297 and *Inland Revenue Commissioners v Educational Grant Association Ltd* [1967] Ch 993, it might be argued as follows: (a) a school for the rich is not charitable because the trust for that class, excluding the poor as it does, is not for the public benefit (just as the beneficiaries in *Oppenheim's* case were not a sufficient section of the community); (b) a charitable trust which in fact selects beneficiaries by reference to their membership of such a class would not be operating for the public benefit (just as in the *Educational Grants Association Ltd* case the beneficiaries were selected from a class which was too narrow and the income applied to them was not applied for charitable purposes only); and (c) the provision of scholarships to some poor students does not turn the non-charitable application of funds to the rich into a charitable application for the benefit of the public. In other words, it is not possible to turn a non-charitable operation of the school into a charitable one by providing some benefits which are for the public benefit...

Propositions (a) and (b) do have considerable force in a different context. Consider an educational grant-making institution rather than a school. Clearly, such an institution would not be a charity if its constitution required it to provide grants only to a class which excluded the poor, e g, to reimburse school fees of those well able to afford them. But suppose that its constitution allows grants to be made to all, regardless of means, so that it can as easily provide a grant to the poor as to the rich. Suppose that, in a way similar to Educational Grants Association Ltd, it gives, say, 10% of its income to the poor but gives 90% to reimburse those same school fees. It would be an almost inevitable conclusion on those facts that the selection of those to receive the 90% was being carried out not for the public benefit but for the benefit of a class which excludes the poor. It would not be a proper implementation of the institution's charitable objects.

But the schools with which we are concerned are in a very different position. Those schools cannot as easily admit one person as another. Who a school is able to admit depends on the financial state of the school, the size of its endowment and the way in which those running the school choose to prioritise expenditure—eg, on providing scholarships or keeping class sizes down by employing more staff— and the facilities which it provides. It is necessary for all of the schools to charge fees. They do not, it seems to us, choose the majority of their students because of a preference for students who have as a characteristic an ability to pay fees; they do so because they cannot afford not to choose such students. And, of course, the charging of fees does not, as we have seen, per se preclude charitable status.

These practical constraints on free selection mean that the position of schools is very different from the position of the association in the *Educational Grants Association Ltd* case. Indeed, the class of those able to pay fees is different in nature from the type of private class considered in *Oppenheim's* case and the *Educational Grants Association Ltd* case. There is no nexus at all; there is simply a shared characteristic which necessarily excludes the poor. Thus those cases do not really lend any support to the argument.

...we return to what a school has to do if it is to operate for the public benefit.... Nobody has suggested that fee-paying schools are not entitled to charitable status provided that they do enough to promote access whether by way of scholarships, bursaries or other provision, but paying regard to the need to charge fees to operate at all. Nobody complains that the schools are educating fee-paying students; the concern is that they must be seen to be doing enough for those who cannot afford fees.

This is an important distinction, because it locates the failure to act in the public benefit as being the making of inadequate provision for access by and benefits for certain sub-classes of the potential beneficiary class, the whole class being the student community at large. It may be the case that if a school which fails to meet the public benefit requirement had instead made more provision for poor students that would have meant that there was room for fewer fee-paying students, so some fee-paying students may be said to receive their education at the price of the school's failure to operate in accordance with its charitable objects. But it does not follow from that that the provision of education for the vast majority of fee-paying students is in any way beyond the school's charitable objects. In other words, even a fee-paying student would be receiving benefits not as a member of some inappropriate class but as a member of the general body of potential beneficiaries... although we have just described the inadequate provision for the 'poor' as a failure to act for the public benefit, in a sense even that is not entirely accurate. Since provision of education to fee-paying students by a school with charitable status is, of itself, for the public benefit, a school making more than de minimis or token provision, could say that the entirety of its activities were for the public benefit. But for reasons given in the next paragraph, we do not consider that to be correct. Accordingly, when we refer to a school failing to act for the public benefit, we mean that it is making inadequate provision other than the provision of education to fee-paying students.

In relation to that, there is one point of principle which we can and should resolve. There are two mutually exclusive possibilities for assessing whether the public benefit requirement is satisfied. (1) The first is that the test is satisfied if the school provides some benefit for the poor which is more than a de minimis benefit, or a token benefit for the school to be able to point at in order, as it were, to cock a snook at the Charity Commission. The justification for this approach would be that it is the de facto exclusion of the poor which prevents there being the necessary element of public benefit so that once some benefit is provided for the 'poor' however small—provided that it is more than de minimis or a token benefit—all of the school's activities, including education of fee-paying students can be taken into account as part of the public benefit provided. (2) The second approach is to apply a more fact-sensitive assessment. It is to look at what a trustee, acting in the interests of the community as a whole, would do in all the circumstance[s] of the particular school under consideration and to ask what provision should be made once the threshold of benefit going beyond the de minimis or token level had been met.

We consider that the second approach is correct. Each case must depend on its own facts. It is an approach which is not, we readily acknowledge, without difficulty of application and, of its nature, it makes it very difficult to lay down guidelines... it is necessary to look at the facts of each case and to treat the matter as one of degree: the process is one of reaching a conclusion on a general survey of the circumstances and considerations regarded as relevant rather than of making a single conclusive test.

The very nature of this approach means that it is not possible to be prescriptive about the nature of the benefits which a school must provide to the poor nor the extent of them. It is for the charity trustees of the school concerned to address and assess how their obligations might best be fulfilled in the context of their own particular circumstances.... Not all of the benefits which the school provides to those other than students paying full fees need to be for the poor. We see no reason why the provision of scholarships or bursaries to students who can pay some, but not all, of the fees should not be seen as for the public benefit. Provided that the operation of the school is seen overall as being for the public benefit, with an appropriate level of benefit for the poor, a subsidy to the not so well off is to be taken account of in the public benefit. It is certainly our view that in the right circumstances, remission of fees for an existing student who has become unable to meet any of the fees due to changed circumstances, should be seen as being not only for the public benefit but as a benefit provided to a person who has become 'poor'...

Although it is necessary that there must be more than a de minimis or token benefit for the poor, once that low threshold is reached, what the trustees decide to do in the running of the school is a matter for them, subject to acting within the range within which trustees can properly act. That is something entirely different from imposing on the trustees the view of anyone else about what is 'reasonable'. In some circumstances, it may be that the trustees would be acting properly if they provided a quite modest benefit for the poor in excess of the de minimis level. The public benefit requirement applicable to the school would then be fulfilled; and in that context, we repeat that provision of education to the full-fee-paying students is itself for the public benefit. The error of the approach of the Charity Commission as we read the guidance is to view the public benefit test as satisfied if, and only if, the provision for the poor—or as it might say, for those who cannot pay fees—is reasonable.

It follows that, whether a particular school had provided more than a mere token public benefit is a matter for the trustees to determine and will depend on the school's particular circumstances.

(c) Political purposes

An otherwise valid purpose for the advancement of education will not be charitable if it involves political propaganda masquerading as education, since the trust will not then be exclusively charitable.[147]

We have already seen that a political purpose is one that relates to a political party, or to changes in law or policy.[148] The dividing line between 'neutral' education in certain political principles and 'partisan' education in support of a political party is sometimes difficult to draw, but a trust for education about party-political principles or dogma will not be charitable. In *Re Hopkinson*,[149] a trust was declared for the 'advancement of adult education with particular reference to . . . the education of men and women of all classes (on the lines of the Labour Party's memorandum headed "A Note on Education in the Labour Party" . . .) to a higher conception of social, political and economic ideas and values and of the personal obligations of duty and service which are necessary for the realisation of an improved and enlightened social civilisation'. In holding this not to be charitable, Vaisey J said:[150]

In my judgment, there are two ways of reading the [words in the trust instrument]. They may be read, first, as equivalent to a general trust for the advancement of adult education which, standing alone, would admittedly be charitable, the super-added purpose being treated merely as a rough guide to be followed or as a hint to be taken as to the kind of adult education which the testator had in mind, the strictly educational main purpose always being adhered to, or, secondly, they may be read as indicating that the first part is to be taken as a general direction and the second part beginning with the words 'with particular reference to' as the particular direction dominating the whole of the trust. The second of these alternative views seems to me to be the right one. I think that the particular purpose is the main purpose of the trust, that is to say, while every or any kind of adult education is within the discretion reposed in the residuary legatees, the particular purpose referred to is, so to speak, the overriding and essential purpose, on the nature of which the validity of the whole trust depends.

In *Southwood v Attorney-General*,[151] a trust to advance the education of the public about disarmament was held not to be charitable because the main purpose was political, in the sense of seeking

---

[147] *Re Hopkinson* [1949] 1 All ER 346, 348 (Vaisey J).
[148] See Chapter 5.3(c)(ii), pp. 201–5.
[149] [1949] 1 All ER 346.
[150] Ibid, 348.
[151] *Southwood v AG* [2000] 3 ITELR 94.

a change in government policy, and the court was not in a position to determine whether unilateral disarmament was for the public benefit. Chadwick LJ said: [152]

> There is no objection on public benefit grounds to an educational programme which begins from the premise that peace is generally preferable to war. For my part, I would find it difficult to believe that any court would refuse to accept, as a general proposition, that it promotes public benefit for the public to be educated to an acceptance of that premise. That does not lead to the conclusion that the promotion of pacifism is necessarily charitable. The premise that peace is generally preferable to war is not to be equated with the premise that peace at any price is always preferable to any war....
>
> I would have no difficulty in accepting the proposition that it promotes public benefit for the public to be educated in the differing means of securing a state of peace and avoiding a state of war. The difficulty comes at the next stage. There are differing views as to how best to secure peace and avoid war. To give two obvious examples: on the one hand it can be contended that war is best avoided by bargaining through strength; on the other hand it can be argued, with equal passion, that peace is best secured by disarmament if necessary, by unilateral disarmament. The court is in no position to determine that promotion of the one view rather than the other is for the public benefit. Not only does the court have no material on which to make that choice; to attempt to do so would be to usurp the role of government. So the court cannot recognise as charitable a trust to educate the public to an acceptance that peace is best secured by demilitarization...Nor, conversely, could the court recognise as charitable a trust to educate the public to an acceptance that war is best avoided by collective security through the membership of a military alliance say, NATO...
>
> [The trust's] object is not to educate the public in the differing means of securing a state of peace and avoiding a state of war. [The trust's] object is to educate the public to an acceptance that peace is best secured by demilitarisation....It is because the court cannot determine whether or not it promotes the public benefit for the public to be educated to an acceptance that peace is best secured by demilitarisation that [the trust's] object cannot be recognised as charitable.

It would have been different if the trust's purpose had been more balanced and less partisan. For example, in *Re Koeppler's Will Trust*,[153] the trust sought to educate the public in the differing ways of securing peace and avoiding war, but no particular political stance was adopted, and the trust was intended to facilitate genuine discussion and the trading of ideas. Slade LJ said:[154]

> in the present case, as I have already mentioned, the activities...are not of a party-political nature. Nor, so far as the evidence shows, are they designed to procure changes in the laws or governmental policy of this or any other country: even when they touch on political matters, they constitute, so far as I can see, no more than genuine attempts in an objective manner to ascertain and disseminate the truth. In these circumstances I think that no objections to the trust arise on a political score...The trust is, in my opinion, entitled to what is sometimes called 'benignant construction', in the sense that the court is entitled to presume that the trustees will only act in a lawful and proper manner appropriate to the trustees of a charity and not, for example, by the propagation of tendentious political opinions.

The identification of political purposes has been of particular significance as regards the operation of students' unions of colleges and universities. Such unions are charities, since they have a charitable purpose connected with the advancement of education, by fostering and representing the interests of

---

[152] Ibid, 111.
[153] [1986] Ch 423.
[154] Ibid, 437.

students to further the educational purposes of the college or university. They must, however, operate for the public benefit. Consequently, such organizations must not use their funds for political purposes. There is a fine line between what is and is not acceptable political campaigning by students' unions.[155] As a basic rule, if the campaigning relates to an issue that furthers the interests of the students of that union in a way that assists in the educational aims of the university or college, then it will not be a political purpose. But a student union was restrained from making payment to a publicity campaign against the abolition of free milk for school children[156] and another was restrained from making payments to the National Student Committee to Stop War in the Gulf,[157] since, in both cases, the campaign was not related to the interests of the students of those particular unions. In the latter case, Hoffmann J said:

> The Student Union is an educational charity. Its purposes are wholly charitable and its funds can be devoted to charitable purposes only. Charitable educational purposes undoubtedly include discussion of political issues: *A-G v Ross* [1986] 1 WLR 252 at 263, per Scott J. There is, however, a clear distinction between the discussion of political matters, or the acquisition of information which may have a political content, and a campaign on a political issue. There is no doubt that campaigning, in the sense of seeking to influence public opinion on political matters, is not a charitable activity. It is, of course, something which students are, like the rest of the population, perfectly at liberty to do in their private capacities, but it is not a proper object of the expenditure of charitable money.

Funds could, however, be spent on campaigns to improve street lighting near the campus or to demonstrate against tuition fees, since this affects the interests of students as the beneficiaries of the charity.

(c) ADVANCEMENT OF RELIGION

(i) *Charitable purpose*

The recognition of the advancement of religion as a charitable purpose derives from nothing more specific than the inclusion in the Preamble to the Charitable Uses Act 1601 of 'the repair of churches'. The concept of 'advancement of religion' has been expanded dramatically since then. When considering whether a charity's purpose involves the advancement of religion it is important to consider the definition of both advancement and religion.

(a) *Religion*

Over the years, various charities relating to Christian denominations have been recognized as involving the advancement of religion, including the Church of England, non-denominational churches, the Catholic religion[158] and the Unification Church.[159] In *Thornton v Howe*,[160] a trust for the publication of the works of Joanna Southcote was considered to be for the advancement of religion, Joanna Southcote having claimed that she was with child by the Holy Ghost and would give birth to a second Messiah. A faith-healing movement has also been held to involve the advancement of religion.[161]

---

[155] See generally Chapter 5.3(c)(ii), pp. 201–5.
[156] *Baldry v Feintuck* [1972] 1 WLR 552.
[157] *Webb v O'Doherty* (1991) *The Times*, 11 February.
[158] See, e.g., *Gilmour v Coats* [1949] AC 426.
[159] Popularly known as the 'Moonies'.
[160] *Thornton v Howe* (1862) 31 Beav 14.
[161] *Funnell v Stewart* [1996] 1 WLR 288.

Other religions have been recognized as well, including charities relating to the advancement of Judaism[162] and Islam.

The interpretation of 'religion' was widened even further by the Charities Act 2011.

CHARITIES ACT 2011

3. (2) In subsection (1)—[163]

(a) in paragraph (c) 'religion' includes—

    (i) a religion which involves belief in more than one god, and

    (ii) a religion which does not involve belief in a god.

It follows that trusts for the advancement of Buddhism, Hinduism, and Sikhism clearly involve the advancement of religion.

The Charity Commission has provided guidance on the interpretation of religion.

Charity Commission Guidance on Charitable Purposes (2013)

When considering whether or not a system of belief constitutes a religion for the purposes of charity law, the courts have identified certain characteristics which describe a religious belief. These characteristics include:

- belief in a god (or gods) or goddess (or goddesses), or supreme being, or divine or transcendental being or entity or spiritual principle ('supreme being or entity') which is the object or focus of the religion

- a relationship between the believer and the supreme being or entity by showing worship of, reverence for or veneration of the supreme being or entity

- a degree of cogency, cohesion, seriousness and importance

- an identifiable positive, beneficial, moral or ethical framework.

The courts have held that certain belief systems cannot be characterized as religious. So, for example, in *Re South Place Ethical Society*,[164] the objects of the Society were 'the study and dissemination of ethical principles and the cultivation of a rational religious sentiment'. Dillon J, in holding that this was not for the advancement of religion,[165] said:[166]

In a free country...it is natural that the court should desire not to discriminate between beliefs deeply and sincerely held, whether they are beliefs in a god or in the excellence of man or in ethical principles or in Platonism or some other scheme of philosophy. But I do not see that that warrants extending the meaning of the word 'religion' so as to embrace all other beliefs and philosophies. Religion, as I see it,

---

[162] Since the Religious Disabilities Act 1846.

[163] See Chapter 5.3(c)(i), p. 190.

[164] [1980] 1 WLR 1565.

[165] In the end, the Society was held to be charitable as being for the advancement of education and for other purposes beneficial to the community.

[166] [1980] 1 WLR 1565, 1571.

is concerned with man's relations with God, and ethics are concerned with man's relations with man. The two are not the same, and are not made the same by sincere inquiry into the question: what is God? If reason leads people not to accept Christianity or any known religion, but they do believe in the excellence of qualities such as truth, beauty and love, or believe in the Platonic concept of the ideal, their beliefs may be to them the equivalent of a religion, but viewed objectively they are not religion. The ground of the opinion of the court, in the United States Supreme Court, that any belief occupying in the life of its possessor a place parallel to that occupied by belief in God in the minds of theists prompts the comment that parallels, by definition, never meet.

Although Dillon J indicated that religion required faith in a god and worship of that god, this is now inconsistent with the statutory definition of religion. But, even with the new statutory definition of religion, a trust for the advancement of ethical principles or humanism would appear not to be a trust for the advancement of religion, since there still needs to be a belief in some form of supreme being or entity that is worshipped, venerated, or revered, although other heads of charity may be relevant, such as the advancement of education.

Perhaps more contentiously, is Scientology a religion? In 1999, the Charity Commission[167] decided that the Church of Scientology should not be registered as a charity. It concluded that:

Scientology is not a religion for the purposes of English charity law. That religion for the purposes of charity law constitutes belief in a supreme being and worship of that being. That it is accepted that Scientology believes in a supreme being. However, the core practices of Scientology, being auditing[168] and training,[169] do not constitute worship as they do not display the essential characteristic of reverence or veneration for a supreme being.

In Australia, however, Scientology has been held to be a religion for tax purposes.[170] It is likely that the effect of the wider definition of religion under the Charities Act 2011 will mean that Scientology might now be classed as a religion, since there is no longer any need for a belief in a supreme being. Scientology was so characterized by the Supreme Court in *R (on the application of Hodkin) v Registrar of Births, Deaths and Marriages*,[171] for purposes of determining that a scientology chapel was a place of worship and so could be registered for weddings. Lord Toulson said:[172]

I would describe religion in summary as a spiritual or non-secular belief system, held by a group of adherents, which claims to explain mankind's place in the universe and relationship with the infinite, and to teach its adherents how they are to live their lives in conformity with the spiritual understanding associated with the belief system. By spiritual or non-secular I mean a belief system which goes beyond that which can be perceived by the senses or ascertained by the application of science. I prefer not to use the word 'supernatural' to express this element, because it is a loaded word which can carry a variety of connotations. Such a belief system may or may not involve belief in a supreme being, but it does involve a belief that there is more to be understood about mankind's nature and relationship to the universe than can be gained from the senses or from science. I emphasise that this is intended to be a description and not a definitive formula.

---

[167] *Church of Scientology (England and Wales)*, Charity Commission decision, 17 November 1999.
[168] This involves 'a series of gradient steps that Hubbard [the founder of Scientology] developed to address past painful experiences...'.
[169] This involves the intensive study of scientology scripture.
[170] *Church of the New Faith v Commissioner of Pay-Roll Tax (Victoria)* (1982) 154 CLR 120.
[171] [2013] UKSC 77; [2014] AC 610.
[172] Ibid, [57].

Even though scientology might satisfy the charitable definition of religion, it will still be necessary to establish public benefit, which was a further reason why the Charity Commission refused to register it as a charity in 1999. It still has not been registered, presumably for that reason.[173]

(b) Advancement

The advancement of religion has been defined as taking positive steps to promote or spread religious belief.[174] It was because freemasonry does not do this that it was held not to involve the advancement of religion.

United Grand Lodge of Ancient Free and Accepted Masons of England v Holborn Borough Council [1957] 1 WLR 1080, 1090 (Donovan J)

Accordingly, one cannot really begin to argue that the main object of freemasonry is to advance religion, except perhaps by saying that religion can be advanced by example as well as by precept, so that the spectacle of a man leading an upright moral life may persuade others to do likewise. The appellants did not in fact advance this argument, but even if it were accepted, it leads to no useful conclusion here. For a man may persuade his neighbour by example to lead a good life without at the same time leading him to religion. And there is nothing in the constitution, nor, apparently, in the evidence tendered to the appeals committee, to support the view that the main object of masonry is to encourage masons to go out in the world and by their example lead persons to some religion or another.

When one considers the work done by organizations which admittedly do set out to advance religion, the contrast with masonry is striking. To advance religion means to promote it, to spread its message ever wider among mankind; to take some positive steps to sustain and increase religious belief; and these things are done in a variety of ways which may be comprehensively described as pastoral and missionary. There is nothing comparable to that in masonry. This is not said by way of criticism. For masonry really does something different. It says to a man, 'whatever your religion or your mode of worship, believe in a Supreme Creator and lead a good moral life'. Laudable as this precept is, it does not appear to us to be the same thing as the advancement of religion. There is no religious instruction, no programme for the persuasion of unbelievers, no religious supervision to see that its members remain active and constant in the various religions they may profess, no holding of religious services, no pastoral or missionary work of any kind.

(ii) Public benefit

Before the enactment of the Charities Act 2011, all charitable trusts for the advancement of religion were presumed to be beneficial. Now, this has to be proven by evidence that is acceptable to the court; the faith of a particular religion that prayer and intercession will confer a benefit on the public is not sufficient.[175] It seems that the concept of public benefit under this head is similar to that in the case of education, but not identical,[176] since, whilst the pupils of a private school may form a section of the public for the purposes of education, the same is not true of the members

---

[173] See Chapter 5.4(c)(ii), p. 235.
[174] *United Grand Lodge of Ancient Free and Accepted Masons of England v Holborn Borough Council* [1957] 1 WLR 1080, 1090 (Donovan J).
[175] *Gilmour v Coats* [1949] AC 426.
[176] *Dingle v Turner* [1972] AC 601, 625 (Lord Cross of Chelsea).

of a cloistered order in the context of religion. This was recognized by the House of Lords in *Gilmour v Coats*.[177]

Gilmour v Coats [1949] AC 426

A gift was made in trust for a Carmelite Priory. The Priory was a community of strictly cloistered nuns, who devoted their lives to prayer, contemplation, penance, and self-sanctification. They engaged in no works outside the convent. It was held that the purposes of the Priory lacked the element of public benefit that was necessary to make them charitable.

Lord Simonds

It is the established belief of the Roman Catholic Church…that the prayers and other spiritual penances and exercises, in which the nuns engage for the benefit of the public, in fact benefit the public by drawing down upon them grace from God, which enables those who are not yet Christians to embrace the Christian religion and those who are already Christians to practise Christianity more fully and fruitfully, and, further that the prayers and other spiritual exercises of the nuns are the more efficacious by virtue of the fact that they devote their lives with especial devotion to the service of God. It is this benefit to all the world, arising from the value of their intercessory prayers, that the appellant puts in the forefront of her case in urging the charitable purpose of the trust.

Nor is it only on the intercessory value of prayer that the appellant relies for the element of public benefit in their lives. For it is the evidence of Cardinal Griffin—and I do not pause to ask whether it is evidence of fact or opinion—that the practice of the religious life by the Carmelite nuns and other religions is a source of great edification to other Catholics—and indeed in innumerable cases to non-Catholics—leading them to a higher estimation of spiritual things and to a greater striving after their own spiritual perfection and that the knowledge that there are men and women who are prepared to sacrifice all that the worldly in man holds dear in order to attain a greater love of God and union with Him inculcates in them a greater estimation of the value and importance of the things which are eternal than they would have if they had not these examples before them. Here then is the second element of public benefit on which the appellant relies, the edification of a wider public by the example of lives devoted to prayer.

I will reserve for final consideration an argument which was not urged in the courts below; that the trusts declared by the settlement are beneficial to the public, in that qualification for admission to the community is not limited to any private group of persons but any person being a female Roman Catholic may be accepted, and therefore those trusts provide facilities for the intensified and most complete practice of religion by those members of the public who have a vocation for it…

I turn then to the question whether, apart from this final consideration, the appellant has established that there is in the trusts which govern this community the element of public benefit which is the necessary condition of legal charity…

I need not go beyond the case of *Cocks v Manners* (1871) LR 12 Eq 574 which was decided nearly 80 years ago by Wickens V-C. In that case the testatrix left her residuary estate between a number of religious institutions, one of them being the Dominican Convent at Carisbrooke, a community not differing in any material respect from the community of nuns now under consideration. The learned

---

[177] [1949] AC 426.

judge...used these words, which I venture to repeat, though they have already been cited in the courts below (1871) LR 12 Eq 574 at 585:

'...A voluntary association of women for the purpose of working out their own salvation by religious exercises and self denial seems to me to have none of the requisites of a charitable institution, whether the word 'charitable' is used in its popular sense or in its legal sense. It is said, in some of the cases, that religious purposes are charitable, but that can only be true as to religious services tending directly or indirectly towards the instruction or the edification of the public; an annuity to an individual, so long as he spent his time in retirement and constant devotion, would not be charitable, nor would a gift to ten persons, so long as they lived together in retirement and performed acts of devotion, be charitable. Therefore the gift to the Dominican Convent is not, in my opinion, a gift on a charitable trust.'

No case, said the learned Vice-Chancellor, had been cited to compel him to come to a contrary conclusion, nor has any such case been cited to your Lordships. Nor have my own researches discovered one. But since that date the decision in *Cocks v Manners* has been accepted and approved in numerous cases...

Apart from what I have called the final argument, which I will deal with later, the contention of the appellant rests not on any change in the lives of the members of such a community as this nor, from a wider aspect, on the emergence of any new conception of the public good, but solely on the fact that for the first time certain evidence of the value of such lives to a wider public together with new arguments based upon that evidence has been presented to the court. Never before, it was urged, has the benefit to be derived from intercessory prayer and from edification been brought to the attention of the court; if it had been, the decision in *Cocks v Manners* (1871) LR 12 Eq 574 would, or at least should, have been otherwise. I have examined the records of *Cocks v Manners* which were supplied to me by the Record Office and I find that the case has been fully and accurately reported. There was no such evidence as was adduced in this case by the appellant and Cardinal Griffin. Nor, as appears from the report, was any argument addressed to this specific point nor any judgment on it. What weight is to be attributed to this, which is the mainstay of the appellant's case? To me, my Lords, despite the admirable argument of [counsel for the appellant], the weight is negligible. True it is that Wickens V-C emphasised that aspect of the religious life which is admittedly its more important aim, 'the love and contemplation of divine things' (1871) LR 12 Eq 574 at 585. But 'its secondary aim the apostolate, particularly all that pertains to our neighbour's salvation' (I use the appellant's words) is no new thing and I cannot suppose that it was absent from the learned judge's mind that those, who devote their lives to prayer, pray not for themselves alone, or that they believe that their prayers are not in vain. Nor, as I think, can he have been unaware of the effect which the example of their lives may have upon others. As I venture to think, these aspects of the case were neither insisted on in evidence or argument nor discussed by the learned judge because they do not afford any real support for the contention that there is in the purpose of the community the element of public benefit which is the condition of legal charity.

My Lords, I would speak with all respect and reverence of those who spend their lives in cloistered piety, and in this House of Lords Spiritual and Temporal, which daily commences its proceedings with intercessory prayers, how can I deny that the Divine Being may in His wisdom think fit to answer them? But, my Lords, whether I affirm or deny, whether I believe or disbelieve, what has that to do with the proof which the court demands that a particular purpose satisfies the test of benefit to the community? Here is something which is manifestly not susceptible of proof. But, then it is said, this is a matter not of proof but of belief: for the value of intercessory prayer is a tenet of the Catholic faith, therefore in such prayer there is benefit to the community. But it is just at this 'therefore' that I must pause. It is, no doubt, true that the advancement of religion is, generally speaking, one of the heads of charity. But it does not follow from this that the court must accept as proved whatever a particular church believes. The faithful must embrace their faith believing where they cannot prove; the court can act only on proof. A gift to two or ten or a hundred cloistered nuns in the belief that their prayers will benefit the world at large does not from that belief alone derive validity any more than does the belief of any other donor for any other purpose...

I turn to the second of the alleged elements of public benefit, edification by example. And I think that this argument can be dealt with very shortly. It is in my opinion sufficient to say that this is something too vague and intangible to satisfy the prescribed test. The test of public benefit has, I think, been developed in the last two centuries. To-day it is beyond doubt that that element must be present. No court would be rash enough to attempt to define precisely or exhaustively what its content must be. But it would assume a burden which it could not discharge if now for the first time it admitted into the category of public benefit something so indirect, remote, imponderable and, I would add, controversial as the benefit which may be derived by others from the example of pious lives. The appellant called in aid the use by Wickens V-C of the word 'indirectly' in the passage that I have cited from his judgment in *Cocks v Manners* (1871) LR 12 Eq 574 at 585, but I see no reason to suppose that that learned judge had in mind any such question as your Lordships have to determine....

It remains finally to deal with an argument which, as I have said, was not presented to the Court of Appeal but appears in the appellant's formal case. It is that the element of public benefit is supplied by the fact that qualification for admission to membership of the community is not limited to any group of persons but is open to any woman in the wide world who has the necessary vocation. Thus, it is said, just as the endowment of a scholarship open to public competition is a charity, so also is a gift to enable any woman (or, presumably, any man) to enter a fuller religious life a charity. To this argument which, it must be admitted, has a speciously logical appearance, the first answer is that which I have indicated earlier in this opinion. There is no novelty in the idea that a community of nuns must, if it is to continue, from time to time obtain fresh recruits from the outside world...It is a trite saying that the law is life, not logic. But it is, I think, conspicuously true of the law of charity that it has been built up not logically but empirically. It would not, therefore, be surprising to find that, while in every category of legal charity some element of public benefit must be present, the court had not adopted the same measure in regard to different categories, but had accepted one standard in regard to those gifts which are alleged to be for the advancement of education and another for those which are alleged to be for the advancement of religion, and it may be yet another in regard to the relief of poverty. To argue by a method of syllogism or analogy from the category of education to that of religion ignores the historical process of the law. Nor would there be lack of justification for the divergence of treatment which is here assumed. For there is a legislative and political background peculiar to so-called religious trusts, which has I think influenced the development of the law in this matter. Thus, even if the simple argument that, if education is a good thing, then the more education the better, may appear to be irrefutable, to repeat that argument substituting 'religion' for 'education' is to ignore the principle which I understand to be conceded that not all religious purposes are charitable purposes... Upon this final argument I would add this observation. I have stressed the empirical development of the law of charity and your Lordships may detect some inconsistency in an attempt to rationalise it. But it appears to me that it would be irrational to the point of absurdity on the one hand to deny to a community of contemplative nuns the character of a charitable institution but on the other to accept as a charitable trust a gift which had no other object than to enable it to be maintained in perpetuity by recruitment from the outside world.

Finally I would say this. I have assumed for the purpose of testing this argument that it is a valid contention that a gift for the advancement of education is necessarily charitable if it is not confined within too narrow limits. But that assumption is itself difficult to justify...if it can be imagined that it was made

> a condition of a gift for the advancement of education that its beneficiaries should lead a cloistered life and communicate to no one, and leave no record of, the fruits of their study, I do not think that the charitable character of the gift could be sustained.

This decision can usefully be contrasted with *Re Hetherington*,[178] where the testatrix had left her estate to a Roman Catholic Church for masses for her soul. In holding that this was a charitable gift, Sir Nicolas Browne-Wilkinson V-C said:[179]

> The grounds on which the trust in the present case can be attacked are that there is no express requirement that the Masses for souls which are to be celebrated are to be celebrated in public. The evidence shows that celebration in public is the invariable practice but there is no requirement of Canon law to that effect. Therefore it is said the money could be applied to saying Masses in private which would not be charitable since there would be no sufficient element of public benefit.
>
> In my judgment the cases establish the following propositions...
>
> (2) The celebration of a religious rite in public does confer a sufficient public benefit because of the edifying and improving effect of such celebration on the members of the public who attend. As Lord Reid said in *Gilmour v Coats* at 459:
>
> > 'A religion can be regarded as beneficial without it being necessary to assume that all its beliefs are true, and a religious service can be regarded as beneficial to all those who attend it without it being necessary to determine the spiritual efficacy of that service or to accept any particular belief about it.'
>
> (3) The celebration of a religious rite in private does not contain the necessary element of public benefit since any benefit by prayer or example is incapable of proof in the legal sense, and any element of edification is limited to a private, not public, class of those present at the celebration...
>
> Where there is a gift for a religious purpose which could be carried out in a way which is beneficial to the public (i.e. by public Masses) but could also be carried out in a way which would not have sufficient element of public benefit (i.e. by private masses) the gift is to be construed as a gift to be carried out only by the methods that are charitable, all non-charitable methods being excluded...
>
> Applying those principles to the present case, a gift for the saying of Masses is prima facie charitable, being for a religious purpose. In practice, those Masses will be celebrated in public which provides a sufficient element of public benefit. The provision of stipends for priests saying the Masses, by relieving the Roman Catholic Church pro tanto of the liability to provide such stipends, is a further benefit. The gift is to be construed as a gift for public Masses...private Masses not being permissible since it would not be a charitable application of the fund for a religious purpose.

Benefit was also identified in that the priests who celebrated the mass were to be paid a stipend that would relieve the Roman Catholic Church of part of its liability to pay priests, so there was a clear financial benefit to the Church that would enable its resources to be allocated elsewhere.

The interpretation of public benefit in *Gilmour v Coats* requiring engagement of the religious with the surrounding community was applied in *Neville Estates Ltd v Madden*.[180] In holding that the trustees of a Jewish synagogue in Catford held land on charitable trusts, Cross J said:[181]

---

[178] [1990] Ch 1.
[179] Ibid, 12.
[180] [1962] Ch 832.
[181] Ibid, 852.

I turn now to the argument that this is a private, not a public trust...The trust with which I am concerned resembles that in *Gilmour v Coats* [1949] AC 426 in this, that the persons immediately benefited by it are not a section of the public but the members of a private body. All persons of the Jewish faith living in or about Catford might well constitute a section of the public, but the members for the time being of the Catford Synagogue are no more a section of the public than the members for the time being of a Carmelite Priory. The two cases, however, differ from one another in that the members of the Catford Synagogue spend their lives in the world, whereas the members of a Carmelite Priory live secluded from the world. If once one refuses to pay any regard—as the courts refused to pay any regard—to the influence which these nuns living in seclusion might have on the outside world, then it must follow that no public benefit is involved in a trust to support a Carmelite Priory. As Lord Greene said in the Court of Appeal [1948] Ch 340 at 345: 'having regard to the way in which the lives of the members are spent, the benefit is a purely private one'. But the court is, I think, entitled to assume that some benefit accrues to the public from the attendance at places of worship of persons who live in this world and mix with their fellow citizens. As between different religions the law stands neutral, but it assumes that any religion is at least likely to be better than none.

But then it is said—and it is this part of the argument that has caused me the greatest difficulty: 'but this is a case of self-help'...

Generally speaking, no doubt, an association which is supported by its members for the purposes of providing benefits for themselves will not be a charity. But I do not think that this principle can apply with full force in the case of trusts for religious purposes. As Lord Simonds [in *Gilmour v Coats*] pointed out, the law of charity has been built up not logically but empirically, and there is a political background peculiar to religious trusts which may well have influenced the development of the law with regard to them.

The significance of the public benefit to trusts for the advancement of religion is especially well illustrated by the decision of the Charity Commission[182] to refuse to register the Church of Scientology as a charity. The Commission found that the public benefit requirement was not satisfied because practice of the religion was essentially private, being limited to a private class of individuals and involving private activities of auditing and training.

It is clear from these cases that both elements of public benefit need to be considered carefully, but they can often be established in the same way. Some benefit must be identified from the advancement of religion that cannot be too vague or intangible. The benefit from prayer or from edification by example will not suffice; there needs to be some direct engagement with the community. This will also satisfy the public requirement. So, for example, in *Funnell v Stewart*,[183] it was held that a trust for faith-healing work was a valid charitable trust for the advancement of religion. Public benefit was established because, although faith-healing sessions were not advertised, they were open to the public. Potential attendance by members of the public was sufficient to show public benefit. It was then assumed that such attendance would be beneficial, given the old presumption of benefit that applied under the head of charity of religion; there was no need to assess whether faith healing was effective. Since, today, public benefit can no longer be presumed, it might now be necessary to assess the efficacy of faith healing to determine whether there is a public benefit, by considering both the numbers who attended and how many had been healed, or who had at least obtained solace from attending the sessions.

---

[182] *Application for Registration as a Charity by the Church of Scientology (England and Wales)* (1999).
[183] [1996] 1 WLR 288.

(d) ADVANCEMENT OF HEALTH OR THE SAVING OF LIVES

CHARITIES ACT 2011

3(2) (b)...'the advancement of health' includes the prevention or relief of sickness, disease or human suffering;

Although advancing health and saving lives is a new head of charitable purpose, it has long been recognized as charitable. In particular, trusts for hospitals have been charitable for hundreds of years. This has included trusts for private hospitals, even though the patients had to pay fees for admission and treatment, as long as the hospital was not a commercial, profit-making concern. In *Re Resch's Will Trusts*, such a trust was held by the Privy Council to satisfy the public benefit test.

Re Resch's Will Trusts [1969] 1 AC 514

A gift was made to St Vincent's Private Hospital, which was a private non-profit-making hospital.

Lord Wilberforce:

St Vincent's Private Hospital...was established and has since 1909 been conducted by the Sisters of Charity, a voluntary association or congregation of women, governed by their constitution under which they devote themselves without reward to good works. The Sisters also conducted in 1909 and still conduct the adjacent St Vincent's Hospital which is a public hospital...The evidence shows that the reason for the establishment of the private hospital was to relieve the pressing demand of the public for admission to the general hospital which was quite inadequate to the demand upon it. Another reason was that there were many persons who needed hospital nursing and attention who were not willing to enter a public hospital but were willing and desirous of having hospital accommodation with more privacy and comfort than would be possible in the general hospital. The establishment of an adjacent private hospital would enable the honorary medical staff in the general hospital to admit for treatment under their care in the private hospital patients who were reluctant to enter the general hospital and were able and willing to pay reasonable and proper fees for admission and treatment in a private hospital. The private hospital has 82 beds as compared with over 500 in the general hospital....

A gift for the purposes of a hospital is prima facie a good charitable gift...because the provision of medical care for the sick is, in modern times, accepted as a public benefit suitable to attract the privileges given to charitable institutions...

In spite of this general proposition, there may be certain hospitals, or categories of hospitals, which are not charitable institutions...Disqualifying indicia may be either that the hospital is carried on commercially, i.e., with a view to making profits for private individuals, or that the benefits it provides are not for the public, or a sufficiently large class of the public to satisfy the necessary tests of public character. Each class of objection is taken in the present case. As regards the first, it is accepted that the private hospital is not run for the profit, in any ordinary sense, of individuals. Moreover, if the purposes of the hospital are otherwise charitable, they do not lose this character merely because charges are made to the recipients of benefits...But what is said is that surpluses are made and are used for the general purposes of the Sisters of Charity. This association, while in a broad sense philanthropic, has objects which may not be charitable in the legal sense.

...whatever the Sisters of Charity may be empowered to do with regard to their general property, as regards the share of income of the residuary estate, given to them as trustees, they are bound by the trusts declared in the will under which any money received by them must be applied exclusively for the general purposes of the private hospital as above defined. As regards these purposes, it appears, from the evidence already summarised, that the making of profits for the benefit of individuals is not among them. The most that is shown is that, on a cash basis, and without making such adjustments as would be required for commercial accounting, a net surplus is produced over the years which in fact has been applied largely, though not exclusively for hospital purposes. The share of income given by the will must be devoted entirely to the purposes of the private hospital. The character, charitable or otherwise, of the general activities of the Sisters, is not therefore a material consideration...

Their Lordships turn to the second objection. This, in substance, is that the private hospital is not carried on for purposes 'beneficial to the community' because it provides only for persons of means who are capable of paying the substantial fees required as a condition of admission.

In dealing with this objection, it is necessary first to dispose of a misapprehension. It is not a condition of validity of a trust for the relief of the sick that it should be limited to the poor sick...As early as *Income Tax Special Comrs v Pemsel* Lord Herschell was able to say [1891] AC 531 at 571:

> 'I am unable to agree with the view that the sense in which "charities" and "charitable purpose" are popularly used is so restricted as this. I certainly cannot think that they are limited to the relief of wants occasioned by lack of pecuniary means. Many examples may, I think, be given of endowments for the relief of human necessities, which would be as generally termed charities as hospitals or almshouses, where, nevertheless, the necessities to be relieved do not result from poverty in its limited sense of the lack of money.'

Similarly in *Verge v Somerville* [1924] AC 496 Lord Wrenbury, delivering the judgment of this Board on an appeal from New South Wales, pointed out that trusts for education and religion do not require any qualification of poverty to be introduced to give them validity and held generally that poverty is not a necessary qualification in trusts beneficial to the community...[The appellants] based their argument on the narrower proposition that a trust could not be charitable which excluded the poor from participation in its benefits. The purposes of the private hospital were, they said, to provide facilities for the well-to-do: an important section of the community was excluded: the trusts could not therefore be said to be for the benefit of the community. There was not sufficient 'public element'...

To support this, they appealed to some well-known authorities. [His Lordship referred to *Jones v Williams* (1767) Amb 651 and *Re Macduff* [1896] 2 Ch 451.]

Their Lordships accept the correctness of what has been said in those cases, but they must be rightly understood. It would be a wrong conclusion from them to state that a trust for the provision of medical facilities would necessarily fail to be charitable merely because by reason of expense they could only be made use of by persons of some means. To provide, in response to public need, medical treatment otherwise inaccessible but in its nature expensive, without any profit motive, might well be charitable: on the other hand to limit admission to a nursing home to the rich would not be so. The test is essentially one of public benefit, and indirect as well as direct benefit enters into the account. In the present case, the element of public benefit is strongly present. It is not disputed that a need exists to provide accommodation and medical treatment in conditions of greater privacy and relaxation than would be possible in a general hospital and as a supplement to the facilities of a general hospital. This is what the private hospital does and it does so at, approximately, cost price. The service is needed by all, not only by the well-to-do. So far as its nature permits it is open to all: the charges are not low, but the evidence shows that it cannot be said that the poor are excluded: such exclusion as there is, is of some of the poor—namely, those who have (a) not contributed sufficiently to a medical benefit scheme or (b) need to stay longer in the hospital than their benefit will cover or (c) cannot get a reduction of or exemption from the charges. The general benefit to the community of such facilities results from the beds and medical staff of the general hospital, the availability of a particular type of nursing and treatment which supplements that provided by the general hospital and the benefit to the standard of medical care in the general hospital which arises from the juxtaposition of the two institutions.

This is consistent with the Charity Commission guidance on Public Benefit,[184] which emphasizes that any private benefits must be incidental to the fulfillment of the charity's aims. It is also consistent with the analysis of incidental benefits by the Upper Tribunal in *The Independent Schools Council v The Charity Commission for England and Wales*.[185]

(e) ADVANCEMENT OF CITIZENSHIP OR COMMUNITY DEVELOPMENT

CHARITIES ACT 2011

3(2)(c)...[this] includes—

(i) rural or urban regeneration, and

(ii) the promotion of civic responsibility, volunteering, the voluntary sector or the effectiveness or efficiency of charities;

Aspects of this new head of charitable purpose were previously recognized at common law with reference to the more general head of purposes that are beneficial to the community. But, as always, it is important to satisfy the public benefit requirement and to ensure that the purposes of the trust are exclusively charitable. The significance of these requirements is illustrated by *IRC v Oldham Training and Enterprise Council*.[186] The objects of the Oldham Training and Enterprise Council ('TEC') included the promotion of vocational education, the training and retraining of the public, and the promotion of industry, commerce, and enterprise for the benefit of the public in and around Oldham. Lightman J said:[187]

It is a matter of general public utility that the unemployed should be found gainful activity and that the state should be relieved of the burden of providing them with unemployment and social security benefits...

Oldham TEC is an altruistic organisation, in the sense that no profit or benefit can be conferred on its members, and its *raison d'être* is to assist others; its objects clauses place stress on its overall objective of benefiting the public or community in or around Oldham; and it is substantially publicly funded, financed by government grants. Further, certain of its objects are indisputably charitable. The question raised is whether the remaining objects viewed in this context can and should be construed as subject to the implicit limitation 'so far as charitable'. There is of course no such express limitation. In my judgment on a careful examination of the objects clauses no such limitation can be implied or is compatible

---

[184] See Chapter 5.3(c)(ii), p. 197.
[185] [2011] UKUT 421 (TCC); [2012] Ch 214, [37]. See Chapter 5.4(b)(ii)(b), pp. 220–5.
[186] [1996] STC 1218.
[187] Ibid, 1234.

with the range of benefits and of the eligible recipients of such benefits which it is the object of Oldham TEC to provide.

To ascertain the objects of an institution such as Oldham TEC, where the objects are comprehensively set out in a document, it is necessary to refer to that document (in this case the memorandum of association) and to that alone. It is irrelevant to inquire into the motives of the founders or how they contemplated or intended that Oldham TEC should operate or how it has in fact operated. To determine whether the object, the scope of which has been ascertained by due process of construction, is a charitable purpose, it may be necessary to have regard to evidence to discover the consequences of pursuing that object (see *Incorporated Council of Law Reporting for England and Wales v A-G* [1972] Ch 73 at 99 per Buckley LJ). What the body has done in pursuance of its objects may afford graphic evidence of the potential consequences of the pursuit of its objects.

Under the unamended objects clause, the second main object, namely promoting trade, commerce and enterprise, and the ancillary object, of providing support services and advice to and for new businesses, on any fair reading must extend to enabling Oldham TEC to promote the interests of individuals engaged in trade, commerce or enterprise and provide benefits and services to them…Such efforts on the part of Oldham TEC may be intended to make the recipients more profitable and thereby, or otherwise, to improve employment prospects in Oldham. But the existence of these objects, in so far as they confer freedom to provide such private benefits, regardless of the motive or the likely beneficial consequences for employment, must disqualify Oldham TEC from having charitable status. The benefits to the community conferred by such activities are too remote.

Since the objects as a whole were not exclusively charitable,[188] it followed that the Council was not a charity.

(f) ADVANCEMENT OF THE ARTS, CULTURE, HERITAGE, OR SCIENCE

Before the Charities Act 2011 recognized this distinct head of charitable purpose, trusts for the advancement of the arts, culture, heritage, or science would be upheld as charitable only if they were considered to be for the advancement of education or for other purposes beneficial to the community. Today, such purposes do not need to be squeezed within the definition of education and are explicitly recognized as charitable purposes in their own right, but they must still satisfy the public benefit test.

When assessing the public benefit of trusts for such purposes, there must be some utility for the public in carrying out the particular purpose. So, where the trust purports to advance the arts or culture, it is necessary to consider whether there is any artistic merit in the specific purpose. For example, in *Re Delius* a trust for the promotion of the work of the famous composer Delius[189] was considered to be a charitable trust for the advancement of education. Roxburgh J said:[190]

It seems to me that in very truth the purpose [of this trust] is the spreading and establishment of knowledge and appreciation of Delius's works amongst the public of the world…and the question is whether that purpose is charitable in the eye of the law? I can do no better in this connexion than to read certain passages from the judgment of Lord Greene MR in *Royal Choral Society v IRC* [1943] 2 All

---

[188] See further Chapter 5.5, pp. 255–60.
[189] *Re Delius* [1957] Ch 299.
[190] Ibid, 305.

ER 101. There are, of course, certain points which necessarily occur to the mind in connexion with a musical composition. It might be suggested as regards some music, at any rate, that its purpose was limited to giving pleasure, and as regards all music it must be said that it gives pleasure. That is a feature about music. When I say 'all music', I mean all that can be truly called music. Indeed, a lot of pleasure is derived by some from something which can hardly be truly called music, but, at any rate, pleasure is a circumstance intimately connected with music. But that in itself does not operate to destroy the charitable character of a bequest for the advancement of the art of music. I adopt, with great satisfaction, the words of Lord Greene [1943] 2 All ER 101 at 104:

> 'Curiously enough, some people find pleasure in providing education. Still more curiously, some people find pleasure in being educated: but the element of pleasure in those processes is not the purpose of them, but what may be called a by-product which is necessarily there.'

That seems to me to be all that need be said about the aspect of pleasure connected with the music of Delius...

I do not find it necessary to consider what the position might be if the trusts were for the promotion of the works of some inadequate composer. It has been suggested that perhaps I should have no option but to give effect even to such a trust. I do not know, but I need not investigate that problem, because counsel who have argued before me have been unanimous in the view that the standard of Delius's work is so high that that question does not arise in the present case.

The point which has been made—and it is one of interest and importance—is, that first of all this trust is not a trust for the promotion of music in general but the music of a particular individual composer. That could not of itself vitiate the charitable nature of the trust, because, after all, aesthetic appreciation of music in a broad sense can only be derived from aesthetic appreciation of the works of a large number of composers. It is the aggregate of the work of a large number of composers which is the basis of the aesthetic appreciation, and, therefore, if it is charitable to promote music in general it must be charitable to promote the music of a particular composer, presupposing (as in this case I can assume) that the composer is one whose music is worth appreciating...

I cannot conceive that anybody would doubt that a trust to promote the works of Beethoven would be charitable, but the real strength of the point put in this case arises from the fact that this trust was created by the widow of Delius, and nobody would doubt that, amongst the many motives which actuated her, affection for her deceased husband was to be found. But one must be careful to distinguish motive from purpose, because motive is not relevant in these cases except in so far as it is incorporated into the purpose. Considering the purposes, it is possible to approach the purposes upon the hypothesis that their intention was...to enhance her husband's reputation.

This is, of course, rather subtle. It is a question which is the cart and which is the horse, because, of course, the more aesthetic appreciation of Delius's music is achieved the more Delius's reputation will necessarily be enhanced. The two things fit together, and there is no doubt whatever that both objects have in fact already been to a large extent achieved. But, in my judgment, it is not fair to approach the problem from that point of view. I think that there is every reason to suppose that the testatrix took the view, and was well advised to take it, that if the work of Delius was brought before the public in an efficient manner, the aesthetic appreciation of the public would grow and, inherent in that growth, would be the enhancement of Delius's reputation, which was in itself a desirable thing, and I for my part refuse to disentangle it. There is no reliable evidence on which I can disentangle it. What is quite clear to me is that these purposes would plainly be charitable if for the name 'Delius' the name 'Beethoven' were substituted and, in my judgment, they do not cease to be charitable because in this context the name is 'Delius' and not 'Beethoven'.

That there may be cases in which the art or culture is not beneficial is illustrated by *Re Pinion*.[191] The testator had provided in his will that his studio and contents, which included pictures, furniture,

---

[191] [1965] Ch 85.

china, glass, and *objets d'art* should be offered to the National Trust, kept intact in the studio, and displayed to the public. The Court of Appeal held that the trust was not for the advancement of education and was void. Harman LJ said:

> It would appear that a gift to an established museum is charitable: see *British Museum Trustees v White* (1826) 2 Sim & St 594. In *Re Holburne* (1885) 53 LT 212 a gift to trustees of objects of art to form an art museum in Bath open to the public and a fund to endow it was held a valid charitable gift as being of public utility or benefit. No question was there raised as to the merit of the collection. It must have been agreed that such merit existed, for everyone assumed it, including the judge. I conclude that a gift to found a public museum may be assumed to be charitable as of public utility if no one questions it…Where a museum is concerned and the utility of the gift is brought in question it is, in my opinion, and herein I agree with the judge, essential to know at least something of the quality of the proposed exhibits in order to judge whether they will be conducive to the education of the public. So I think with a public library, such a place if found to be devoted entirely to works of pornography or of a corrupting nature, would not be allowable. Here it is suggested that education in the fine arts is the object. For myself a reading of the will leads me rather to the view that the testator's object was not to educate anyone, but to perpetuate his own name and the repute of his family, hence perhaps the direction that the custodian should be a blood relation of his. However that may be, there is a strong body of evidence here that as a means of education this collection is worthless. The testator's own paintings, of which there are over 50, are said by competent persons to be in an academic style and 'atrociously bad' and the other pictures without exception worthless. Even the so-called 'Lely' turns out to be a 20th-century copy.
>
> Apart from pictures there is a haphazard assembly—it does not merit the name collection, for no purpose emerges, no time nor style is illustrated—of furniture and objects of so-called 'art' about which expert opinion is unanimous that nothing beyond the third-rate is to be found. Indeed one of the experts expresses his surprise that so voracious a collector should not by hazard have picked up even one meritorious object. The most that skilful cross-examination extracted from the expert witnesses was that there were a dozen chairs which might perhaps be acceptable to a minor provincial museum and perhaps another dozen not altogether worthless, but two dozen chairs do not make a museum and they must, to accord with the will, be exhibited stifled by a large number of absolutely worthless pictures and objects.
>
> It was said that this is a matter of taste…but here I agree with the judge that there is an accepted canon of taste on which the court must rely, for it has itself no judicial knowledge of such matters, and the unanimous verdict of the experts is as I have stated. The judge with great hesitation concluded that there was that scintilla of merit which was sufficient to save the rest. I find myself on the other side of the line. I can conceive of no useful object to be served in foisting upon the public this mass of junk. It has neither public utility nor educative value. I would hold that the testator's project ought not to be carried into effect and that his next-of kin is entitled to the residue of his estate.

Today it is probable that the same decision would be reached with reference to the charitable purpose relating to culture and heritage, either because it would not meet the definition of the charitable purpose as a matter of law or, more likely, because it would not satisfy the public benefit test as a matter of fact.

Even if the trust does promote culture or heritage and is regarded as beneficial, it must still be shown that the benefit is available for a sufficient section of the public and that the purposes are exclusively charitable. So, for example, in *Williams' Trustees v IRC*,[192] a trust to maintain an institute and meeting place for the benefit of Welsh people in London, with a view to creating a centre to promote the moral,

---

[192] [1947] AC 447.

social, spiritual, and educational welfare of Welsh people, was held by the House of Lords not to be charitable. Lord Simonds said:[193]

> [A] trust in order to be charitable must be of a public character. It must not be merely for the benefit of particular private individuals: if it is, it will not be in law a charity though the benefit taken by those individuals is of the very character stated in the preamble... I may however refer to a recent case in this House which in some aspects resembles the present case. In *Keren Kayemeth le Jisroel Ltd v IRC* [1932] AC 650 a company had been formed which had as its main object (to put it shortly) the purchase of land in Palestine, Syria or other parts of Turkey in Asia and the peninsula of Sinai for the purpose of settling Jews on such lands. In its memorandum it took numerous other powers which were to be exercised only in such a way as should in the opinion of the company be conducive to the attainment of the primary object. No part of the income of the company was distributable among its members. It was urged that the company was established for charitable purposes for numerous reasons, with only one of which I will trouble your Lordships, namely, that it was established for the benefit of the community or of a section of the community, namely, Jews, whether the association was for the benefit of Jews all over the world or of the Jews repatriated in the Promised Land. Lord Tomlin dealing with the argument that I have just mentioned upon the footing that, if benefit to 'a community' could be established the purpose might be charitable, proceeded to examine the problem in that aspect and sought to identify the community. He failed to do so, finding it neither in the community of all Jews throughout the world nor in that of the Jews in the region prescribed for settlement. It is perhaps unnecessary to pursue the matter. Each case must be judged on its own facts and the dividing line is not easily drawn. But the difficulty of finding the community in the present case, when the definition of 'Welsh people' in the first deed is remembered, would not I think be less than that of finding the community of Jews in Keren's case.

If the validity of this trust as a charity were to be considered today, the public benefit might be identified because the class would not, presumably, be numerically small and would not be defined with reference to a personal nexus.[194] Some of the purposes of the charity would also fall within the new head of advancing culture or heritage, especially since the trust sought to foster the study of the Welsh language, history, music, literature, and art. The problem, however, would still be that there were other purposes that were non-charitable, including providing a meeting place for 'social intercourse, study, reading, rest, recreation and refreshment'. Since these purposes are not exclusively charitable,[195] the trust would still not be treated as charitable.

(g) ADVANCEMENT OF AMATEUR SPORT

Before the enactment of the Charities Act 2011, trusts for the provision of sporting facilities or the encouragement of sport were not charitable as such. But, if the facilities or sporting activities were for pupils of schools or universities,[196] or if the game was itself of an educational nature, the trusts would be for the advancement of education. Alternatively, if the sports facilities were for the armed forces, they might be regarded as being otherwise beneficial to the community by contributing to the safety and protection of the country.[197] With the recognition of the advancement of amateur sport as a charitable purpose in its own right, such artificial interpretation of other charitable purposes is not required.

The Charities Act 2011 has clarified the meaning of sport as follows:

---

[193] Ibid, 457.
[194] See Chapter 5.3(c)(ii)(b), pp. 200–1.
[195] See Chapter 5.5, pp. 255–60.
[196] *IRC v McMullen* [1981] AC 1.
[197] *Re Gray* [1925] Ch 362.

CHARITIES ACT 2011

3. (2) (d) ...'sport' means sports or games which promote health by involving physical or mental skill or exertion;

This encompasses team sports, such as football, and solo sports, such as athletics, but it would also encompass chess, because of the mental skill involved.[198] Other games will be more borderline, such as darts, and these will involve careful assessment of the skill and exertion involved.

The public benefit requirement will apply in the normal way.

IRC v Baddeley [1955] AC 572

Playing fields were held on trust for the recreation of members of a particular Methodist church. The House of Lords held that the trust failed to meet the public benefit requirement. Viscount Simonds said:[199]

Suppose that, contrary to the view that I have expressed, the trust would be a valid charitable trust, if the beneficiaries were the community at large or a section of the community defined by some geographical limits, is it the less a valid trust if it is confined to members or potential members of a particular church within a limited geographical area? ...

Some confusion has arisen from the fact that a trust of general public utility, however general and however public, cannot be of equal utility to all and may be of immediate utility to few. A sea wall, the prototype of this class in the Preamble, is of remote, if any, utility to those who live in the heart of the Midlands. But there is no doubt that a trust for the maintenance of sea walls generally or along a particular stretch of coast is a good charitable trust. Nor, as it appears to me, is the validity of a trust affected by the fact that by its very nature only a limited number of people are likely to avail themselves, or are perhaps even capable of availing themselves, of its benefits. It is easy, for instance, to imagine a charity which has for its object some form of child welfare, of which the immediate beneficiaries could only be persons of tender age. Yet this would satisfy any test of general public utility. It may be said that it would satisfy the test because the indirect benefit of such a charity would extend far beyond its direct beneficiaries, and that aspect of the matter has probably not been out of sight. Indirect benefit is certainly an aspect which must have influenced the decision of the 'cruelty to animals' cases. But, I doubt whether this sort of rationalisation helps to explain a branch of the law which has developed empirically and by analogy upon analogy ...

In the case under appeal the intended beneficiaries are a class within a class; they are those of the inhabitants of a particular area who are members of a particular church: the area is comparatively large and populous and the members may be numerous. But, if this trust is charitable for them, does it cease to be charitable as the area narrows down and the numbers diminish? Suppose the area is confined to a single street and the beneficiaries to those whose creed commands few adherents: or suppose the class is one that is determined not by religious belief but by membership of a particular profession or by pursuit of a particular trade ...

More relevant is the case of *Verge v Somerville* [1924] AC 496. In that case, in which the issue was as to the validity of a gift 'to the trustees of the Repatriation Fund or other similar fund for the benefit of New South Wales returned soldiers', Lord Wrenbury, delivering the judgment of the Judicial Committee, said at 499 that, to be a charity, a trust must be 'for the benefit of the community or of an appreciably important class of the community. The inhabitants', he said, 'of a parish or town or any

---

[198] See *Re Dupree's Deed Trusts* [1945] Ch 16, which held that a chess tournament was educational.

[199] [1955] AC 572, 589.

particular class of such inhabitants, may, for instance, be the objects of such a gift, but private individuals, or a fluctuating body of private individuals, cannot.' Here, my Lords, are two expressions: 'an appreciably important class of the community' and 'any particular class of such inhabitants', to which in any case it is not easy to give a precise quantitative or qualitative meaning. But I think that in the consideration of them the difficulty has sometimes been increased by failing to observe the distinction, at which I hinted earlier in this opinion, between a form of relief extended to the whole community yet by its very nature advantageous only to the few and a form of relief accorded to a selected few out of a larger number equally willing and able to take advantage of it. Of the former type repatriated New South Wales soldiers would serve as a clear example. To me it would not seem arguable that they did not form an adequate class of the community for the purpose of the particular charity that was being established. It was with this type of case that Lord Wrenbury was dealing, and his words are apt to deal with it. Somewhat different considerations arise if the form, which the purporting charity takes, is something of general utility which is nevertheless made available not to the whole public but only to a selected body of the public—an important class of the public it may be. For example, a bridge which is available for all the public may undoubtedly be a charity and it is indifferent how many people use it. But confine its use to a selected number of persons, however numerous and important: it is then clearly not a charity. It is not of general public utility: for it does not serve the public purpose which its nature qualifies it to serve.

Bearing this distinction in mind, though I am well aware that in its application it may often be very difficult to draw the line between public and private purposes, I should in the present case conclude that a trust cannot qualify as a charity within the fourth class in *Income Tax Special Purposes Comrs v Pemsel* [1891] AC 531 if the beneficiaries are a class of persons not only confined to a particular area but selected from within it by reference to a particular creed.

It followed that the charity was not valid because, being a class within a class, the public benefit test was not satisfied. Whether those who are entitled to benefit can be considered to be a class within a class, so that a sufficient section of the public is not benefited, is a matter of degree and judgment.

Specific provision was made by the Recreational Charities Act 1958 to treat the provision of recreation or leisure facilities as charitable if the facilities are provided in the interests of social welfare and for the public benefit. This statute has now been consolidated in the Charities Act 2011.

CHARITIES ACT 2011

5 Recreational and similar trusts, etc.

(1) It is charitable (and is to be treated as always having been charitable) to provide, or assist in the provision of, facilities for—

    (a) recreation, or

    (b) other leisure-time occupation,

    if the facilities are provided in the interests of social welfare.

(2) The requirement that the facilities are provided in the interests of social welfare cannot be satisfied if the basic conditions are not met.

(3) The basic conditions are—

    (a) that the facilities are provided with the object of improving the conditions of life for the persons for whom the facilities are primarily intended, and

> (b) that—
>
> > (i) those persons have need of the facilities because of their youth, age, infirmity or disability, poverty, or social and economic circumstances, or
> >
> > (ii) the facilities are to be available to members of the public at large or to male, or to female, members of the public at large.
>
> (4) Subsection (1) applies in particular to—
>
> > (a) the provision of facilities at village halls, community centres and women's institutes, and
> >
> > (b) the provision and maintenance of grounds and buildings to be used for purposes of recreation or leisure-time occupation,
>
> and extends to the provision of facilities for those purposes by the organising of any activity.
>
> But this is subject to the requirement that the facilities are provided in the interests of social welfare.
>
> (5) Nothing in this section is to be treated as derogating from the public benefit requirement.

This has proved significant in treating community centres and church halls as charitable. Some of these will now be charitable by virtue of the formal recognition of the promotion of amateur sport as a charitable purpose, but, to the extent that these facilities are intended to be used for non-sporting activities, they might still be charitable by virtue of section 5 of the Charities Act 2011.

The operation of this provision is illustrated by *Guild v IRC*,[200] where the House of Lords held that a town's sports centre was charitable. The key issue was whether the facilities met the basic condition that they were 'provided with the object of improving the conditions of life for the persons for whom the facilities are primarily intended'. Lord Keith of Kinkel said:[201]

> The reason why it was said that this condition was not met was that on a proper construction it involved that the facilities should be provided with the object of meeting a need for such facilities in people who suffered from a position of relative social disadvantage...
>
> The fact is that persons in all walks of life and all kinds of circumstances may have their conditions of life improved by the provision of recreational facilities of suitable character. The proviso requiring public benefit excludes facilities of an undesirable nature... I would therefore reject the argument that the facilities are not provided in the interests of social welfare unless they are provided with the object of improving the conditions of life for persons who suffer from some form of social disadvantage. It suffices if they are provided with the object of improving the conditions of life for members of the community generally.

(h) ADVANCEMENT OF HUMAN RIGHTS

This new charitable head includes a variety of charitable purposes.

CHARITIES ACT 2011

> 3. (2) (h) the advancement of human rights, conflict resolution or reconciliation or the promotion of religious or racial harmony or equality and diversity;

---

[200] [1992] 2 AC 310.
[201] Ibid, 318.

Some of these purposes had previously been recognized as charitable either by virtue of being for the advancement of education or for other purposes beneficial to the community. In *Re Strakosch*,[202] however, a trust to appease racial feelings between the Dutch-speaking and English-speaking sections of the South African community was held not to be charitable because the scope of the gift was too wide and vague. The testator had provided a fund 'for any purpose which in [the trustees'] opinion is designed to strengthen the bonds of unity between the Union of South Africa and the Mother Country, and which incidentally will conduce to the appeasement of racial feeling between the Dutch and English speaking sections of the South African community'. Lord Greene said:[203]

> We realize the truth of the contention that the objects to which the gift is to be devoted are matters of great public concern both in the Union of South Africa and in the Mother Country. In particular the appeasement of racial feeling in the Union cannot but benefit all inhabitants of the Union, not merely the members of the two sections of the community expressly referred to. But the very wide and vague scope of the gift and the unrestricted latitude of application which its language permits make it impossible in our opinion to find that it falls within the spirit and intendment of the Preamble to the Statute of Elizabeth.

If the trust had been defined more clearly, particularly with reference to education, it might have been held valid. Similar problems as to the vagueness of the gift would arise in respect of the new charitable purpose under the Charities Act 2011.

One of the key difficulties relating to a trust for the advancement of human rights is that charities with such a purpose must not pursue political objectives, especially those that relate to seeking a change in law or policy either of this country or of a country abroad.[204] There is a fine line between pursuing political activities as a means to a charitable end and pursuing purposes that are political in their own right. This is illustrated by *McGovern v Attorney-General*,[205] which concerned whether a trust created by Amnesty International was charitable. The trust had various objects, including the relief of prisoners of conscience and procuring the abolition of torture. In holding that the trust was not charitable, since its main purpose was political, Slade J said:[206]

> I now turn to consider the status of a trust of which a main object is to secure the alteration of the laws of a foreign country. The mere fact that the trust was intended to be carried out abroad would not by itself necessarily deprive it of charitable status...
>
> I accept that the dangers of the court encroaching on the functions of the legislature or of subjecting its political impartiality to question would not be nearly so great as when similar trusts are to be executed in this country. I also accept that on occasions the court will examine and express an opinion upon the quality of a foreign law... In my judgment, however, there remain overwhelming reasons why such a trust still cannot be regarded as charitable... A fortiori the court will have no adequate means of judging whether a proposed change in the law of a foreign country will or will not be for the public benefit. Sir Raymond Evershed MR in *Camille and Henry Dreyfus Foundation Inc. v IRC* [1954] Ch 672, 684 expressed the prima facie view that the community which has to be considered in this context, even in the case of a trust to be executed abroad, is the community of the United Kingdom. Assuming that this is the right test, the court in applying it would still be bound to take account of the probable effects

---

[202] [1949] Ch 529.
[203] Ibid, 536.
[204] See Chapter 5.3(c)(ii)(c), pp. 201–5.
[205] [1982] Ch 321.
[206] Ibid, 336.

of attempts to procure the proposed legislation, or of its actual enactment, on the inhabitants of the country concerned, which would doubtless have a history and social structure quite different from that of the United Kingdom. Whatever might be its view as to the content of the relevant law from the standpoint of an English lawyer, it would, I think, have no satisfactory means of judging such probable effects upon the local community.

Furthermore, before ascribing charitable status to an English trust of which a main object was to secure the alteration of a foreign law, the court would also, I conceive, be bound to consider the consequences for this country as a matter of public policy. In a number of such cases there would arise a substantial prima facie risk that such a trust, if enforced, could prejudice the relations of this country with the foreign country concerned: compare *Habershon v Vardon* (1851) 4 De G & Sm 467. The court would have no satisfactory means of assessing the extent of such risk, which would not be capable of being readily dealt with by evidence and would be a matter more for political than for legal judgment. For all these reasons, I conclude that a trust of which a main purpose is to procure a change in the laws of a foreign country is a trust for the attainment of political objects...and is non-charitable.

Thus, far, I have been considering trusts of which a main purpose is to achieve changes in the law itself or which are of a party-political nature. Under any legal system, however, the government and its various authorities, administrative and judicial, will have wide discretionary powers vested in them, within the framework of the existing law. If a principal purpose of a trust is to procure a reversal of government policy or of particular administrative decisions of governmental authorities, does it constitute a trust for political purposes...? In my judgment it does. If a trust of this nature is to be executed in England, the court will ordinarily have no sufficient means of determining whether the desired reversal would be beneficial to the public, and in any event could not properly encroach on the functions of the executive, acting intra vires, by holding that it should be acting in some other manner. If it is a trust which is to be executed abroad, the court will not have sufficient means of satisfactorily judging, as a matter of evidence, whether the proposed reversal would be beneficial to the community in the relevant sense, after all its consequences, local and international, had been taken into account...

I therefore summarise my conclusions in relation to trusts for political purposes as follows. (1) Even if it otherwise appears to fall within the spirit and intendment of the Preamble to the Statute of Elizabeth, a trust for political purposes...can never be regarded as being for the public benefit in the manner which the law regards as charitable. (2) Trusts for political purposes falling within the spirit of this pronouncement include, *inter alia*, trusts of which a direct and principal purpose is either (i) to further the interests of a particular political party; or (ii) to procure changes in the laws of this country; or (iii) to procure changes in the laws of a foreign country; or (iv) to procure a reversal of government policy or of particular decisions of governmental authorities in this country; or (v) to procure a reversal of governmental policy or of particular decisions of governmental authorities in a foreign country.

Seeking the release of prisoners of conscience was considered to be a political purpose, since it involved demanding the reversal of administrative decisions of governmental authorities, albeit abroad. Other purposes, such as relieving the suffering of needy prisoners of conscience, were held to be charitable, but since this was one purpose amongst others that were not charitable, the trust was not wholly and exclusively charitable. Although this case was decided before what is now the Charities Act 2011 recognized the new charitable purpose of promoting human rights, it would probably be decided the same way today because the law on the definition of political purposes has not changed.[207] The significance of the recognition of the new charitable purpose is that it is now a legitimate charitable purpose

---

[207] See Chapter 5.3(c)(ii)(c), pp. 201–5.

to monitor human rights abuses, to seek redress for victims of such abuse, and to raise awareness of human rights issues, but a charity still must not cross the line and actively seek to procure changes in law or governmental policy as regards human rights issues. A consequence of the state of the law is that Amnesty International has been divided into Amnesty International, which is a registered charity with non-political purposes, and Amnesty International Ltd, which is not registered as a charity and which pursues political objectives.

(i) ADVANCEMENT OF ENVIRONMENTAL PROTECTION

This charitable purpose includes acting both for the protection and improvement of the environment.[208]

(j) RELIEF OF THOSE IN NEED

Although this is a new charitable purpose, relief of those in need used to fall within the purpose of relief of poverty. It follows from the creation of this new head that somebody can be in need even if they are not poor.

CHARITIES ACT 2011

3 (1) (j) the relief of those in need by reason of youth, age, ill health, disability, financial hardship or other disadvantage.

(2) In subsection (1)—

    (e) paragraph (j) includes relief given by the provision of accommodation or care to the persons mentioned in that paragraph . . .

The courts previously considered the meaning of being in need 'by virtue of age'.

Joseph Rowntree Memorial Trust Housing Association Ltd v Attorney-General [1983] Ch 159

A scheme to build self-contained dwellings to be let on long leases to elderly people at 70 per cent of the cost of the premises, with the remaining expense being met by a State housing grant, was held to be a charitable scheme for the relief of aged people, even though beneficiaries had to make a substantial financial contribution and, if they were to sell their lease, they could make a profit. It was held that this was a valid charitable scheme for the aged. Peter Gibson J said:[209]

the plaintiffs do not submit that the proposed schemes are charitable simply because they are for the benefit of the aged. The plaintiffs have identified a particular need for special housing to be provided for the elderly in the ways proposed and it seems to me that on any view of the matter that is a charitable purpose, unless the fundamental objections of the Charity Commissioners to which I have referred are correct. To these I now turn.

---

[208] Charities Act 2011, s. 3(1)(i).
[209] [1983] Ch 159, 174.

The first objection is...that the scheme makes provision for the aged on a contractual basis as a bargain rather than by way of bounty. This objection is sometimes expressed in the form that relief is charitable only where it is given by way of bounty and not by way of bargain...[This] does not mean that a gift cannot be charitable if it provides for the beneficiaries to contribute to the cost of the benefits they receive. There are numerous cases where beneficiaries only receive benefits from a charity by way of bargain...Another class of cases relates to fee-paying schools: see for example *Abbey Malvern Wells Ltd v Ministry of Local Government and Planning* [1951] Ch 728...It is of course crucial in all these cases that the services provided by the gift are not provided for the private profit of the individuals providing the services....

If a housing association were a co-operative under which the persons requiring the dwellings provided by the housing association had by the association's constitution contractual rights to the dwellings, that would no doubt not be charitable, but that is quite different from bodies set up like the trust and the association. The applicants for dwellings under the schemes which I am considering would have no right to any dwelling when they apply. The fact that the benefit given to them is in the form of a contract is immaterial to the charitable purpose in making the benefit available. I see nothing in this objection of the Charity Commissioners.

The second objection was that the schemes do not satisfy the requirement that the benefits they provide must be capable of being withdrawn at any time if the beneficiary ceases to qualify. No doubt charities will, so far as practical and compatible with the identified need which they seek to alleviate, try to secure that their housing stock becomes available if the circumstances of the persons occupying the premises change. But it does not seem to me to be an essential part of the charitable purpose to secure that this should always be so. The nature of some benefits may be such that it will endure for some time, if benefits in that form are required to meet the particular need that has been identified. Thus in *Re Monk* [1927] 2 Ch 197, a testatrix set up a loan fund whereby loans for up to nine years were to be made available to the poor. This was held to be charitable. No doubt the circumstances of the borrower might change whilst the loan was outstanding. If the grant of a long-term leasehold interest with the concomitant security of tenure that such an interest would give to the elderly is necessary to meet the identified needs of the elderly then in my judgment that is no objection to such a grant...

The third objection was that the schemes were for the benefit of private individuals and not for a charitable class. I cannot accept that. The schemes are for the benefit of a charitable class, that is to say the aged having certain needs requiring relief therefrom. The fact that, once the association and the trust have selected individuals to benefit from the housing, those individuals are identified private individuals does not seem to me to make the purpose in providing the housing a non-charitable one any more than a trust for the relief of poverty ceases to be a charitable purpose when individual poor recipients of bounty are selected.

The fourth objection was that the schemes were a commercial enterprise capable of producing a profit for the beneficiary. I have already discussed the cases which show that the charging of an economic consideration for a charitable service that is provided does not make the purpose in providing the service non-charitable, provided of course that no profits accrue to the provider of the service. It is true that a tenant under the schemes may recover more than he or she has put in, but that is at most incidental to the charitable purpose. It is not a primary objective. The profit—if it be right to call the increased value of the equity a profit as distinct from a mere increase avoiding the effects of inflation, as was intended—is not a profit at the expense of the charity, and indeed it might be thought improper, if there be a profit, that it should accrue to the charity which has provided no capital and not to the tenant which has provided most if not all the capital. Again, I cannot see that this objection defeats the charitable character of the schemes...

In my judgment the trustees may provide accommodation in the form of small self-contained dwellings for aged persons in need of such accommodation by granting it to them in consideration of the payment to the trustees of the whole or a substantial part of the cost or market value of such dwellings in accordance with the schemes.

If, however, housing stock is provided both to those in need and others who are not in need, this will not be an exclusively charitable purpose. This was recognized in *Helena Housing Ltd v The Commissioners for Her Majesty's Revenue and Customs.*[210]

Helena Housing Ltd v The Commissioners for Her Majesty's Revenue and Customs
[2012] EWCA Civ 569; [2012] WTLR 1519

The claimant was a company that did not trade for profit and was a registered social landlord. Its object was to provide accommodation and assistance to help house people for the benefit of the community, largely through the acquisition of a Council's former housing stock, which it then refurbished and let. Since some of the housing stock was let to people in need but some was let to people who were not in need, it was held that this was not exclusively a charitable purpose. Lloyd LJ said:[211]

The real issue is as to the balance between public benefit and benefit to individuals arising from the undertaking of all or any of Helena's objects. This type of issue has arisen in numerous previous cases, of which we were shown several. The argument was about whether or not the benefits afforded to individuals (often referred to as private benefits) were subordinate to the public benefit, so that the latter was to be seen as the real object of the relevant body.

Most charitable purposes provide particular benefits to individuals, whether to the poor person in need of support, the student in need of education, or the patient in need of treatment, to take a few obvious examples. That is the way in which the public benefit is provided.

Leaving aside the anomalous case of 'poor relations' and 'poor employees' trusts, public benefit is a prerequisite of charity, but the provision of particular benefits to particular individuals is justified as a way of providing benefits to the public by virtue of, first, the availability of the provision and, secondly, the selection of those who are to benefit on an objective basis which does not depend on any private or particular nexus of the beneficiary with the trust, the founder, the other beneficiaries or any given individual... So, in the case of Helena, the identification of those who were to occupy its accommodation would be decided (in many cases) according to the allocation policy previously used by the Council. This would not be limited to those in particular need, but there would be objective criteria of selection involving no private or personal element....

Such decided cases as there have been about the provision of housing as a charitable purpose have proceeded on the basis that it is charitable if, but not unless, it is provided by way of the relief of need, whether due to poverty, to old age or to other relevant circumstances....

Helena could not satisfy the requirements of charity. There are two reasons for this, which are separate but related.

First... the provision of housing without regard to a relevant charitable need is not in itself charitable.

An alternative way to the same conclusion is that, even accepting that there is an element, and a necessary element, of benefit to the community in the pursuit of Helena's objects, there is also a substantial element of benefit to individuals, which cannot be regarded as only subordinate to the achievement of the benefit to the community. In its nature, the benefit afforded by the provision of housing to the person who is thereby housed is of an altogether different order, as it seems to me, to the benefit afforded by the construction or maintenance of a road, a bridge or a sea-wall, or the maintenance of a fire brigade or a lifeboat service. The former provides direct benefits to the occupants of the accommodation which far outweigh the degree of indirect benefit that other members of the community may derive from the

---

[210] [2012] EWCA Civ 569; [2012] WTLR 1519.
[211] Ibid, [74].

existence of the housing stock. Accepting that it may be a good thing that a substantial housing stock in good condition should exist in the area of a community which is available for occupation by tenants, and that therefore a benefit to the community can be seen to be generated by the operations of a body such as Helena, I cannot accept that the private benefit which arises to those who occupy the accommodation is merely incidental or subsidiary to the public benefit afforded by the existence of the housing stock. It is a benefit for its own sake, not incompatible with benefit to the community, but not subordinate to it.

Of course some charitable operations…confer significant benefits on individuals. Hospitals provide one example, for the benefit of those who by reason of illness, accidental injury or otherwise, need medical treatment…I do not underestimate the importance of such benefits for the individual concerned. But it seems to me that the provision of housing accommodation for an individual or a family affords a benefit to that or those individuals of a kind which is quite different in its nature and importance from, for example, that of appropriate treatment in hospital. It is not by chance that the significance of housing to the person housed is recognised by the terms of article 8 of the European Convention on Human Rights. That seems to me to confirm my view that the provision of accommodation by way of housing confers an especially significant benefit on the person or persons so housed, and that this goes far beyond the degree of benefit that individuals may obtain from charitable operations which are justified as being within the fourth head of charity on the basis of general public utility…

I conclude that the provision of housing accommodation is, and can only be, a charitable purpose if it is justified as charitable in respect of the direct benefit provided. It can only be so justified if it is provided in order to meet a relevant need of the class eligible to occupy it.

(k) ADVANCEMENT OF ANIMAL WELFARE

Before the enactment of the Charities Act 2006, trusts for the advancement of animal welfare could be charitable only within the fourth head of *Pemsel's case*, being another purpose beneficial to the community. Now animal welfare is identified as a specific charitable head,[212] although this has not significantly altered the law as regards the definition of the charitable purpose.[213]

Animal welfare has been held to include providing for the welfare of particular types of animal, such as cats,[214] or providing for the welfare of all animals, which is the purpose of the Royal Society for the Prevention of Cruelty to Animals (RSPCA).[215] It has even included improving methods of slaughtering animals.[216] It does not include providing for the welfare of a particular animal, which might exceptionally be valid as a non-charitable purpose trust if a testamentary gift.[217]

It will still be necessary to show that there is a public benefit in advancing animal welfare. The benefit to the public has been described as indirect.[218] In *Re Wedgwood*[219] Kennedy LJ said:

A gift for the benefit and protection of animals tends to promote and encourage kindness towards them, to discourage cruelty, and to ameliorate the condition of the brute creation, and thus to stimulate humane and generous sentiments in man towards the lower animals, and by these means promote feelings of humanity and morality generally, repress brutality, and thus elevate the human race.

---

[212] Charities Act 2011, s. 3(1)(k).
[213] *Hanchett-Stamford v Attorney General* [2008] EWHC 330 (Ch); [2009] Ch 173.
[214] *Re Moss* [1949] 1 All ER 495.
[215] *Tatham v Drummond* (1864) 4 De GJ & Sm 484.
[216] *Re Wedgwood* [1915] 1 Ch 113.
[217] See Chapter 6.2(b)(i), pp. 291–2.
[218] *Hanchett-Stamford v Attorney General* [2008] EWHC 330 (Ch); [2009] Ch 173, [13] (Lewison J).
[219] *Re Wedgwood* [1915] 1 Ch 113, 122 (Kennedy LJ).

Even this indirect benefit to the public might be difficult to establish. So, for example, in *Re Grove-Grady*,[220] a trust to buy land to provide a sanctuary for all creatures so that they would be safe from molestation or destruction by man, was held not to be charitable because there was no public benefit. Russell LJ said:[221]

> So far as I know there is no decision which upholds a trust in perpetuity in favour of animals upon any other ground than this, that the execution of the trust in the manner defined by the creator of the trust must produce some benefit to mankind...
>
> [Here] the residuary estate may be applied in acquiring a tract of land, in turning it into an animal sanctuary, and keeping a staff of employees to ensure that no human being shall ever molest or destroy any of the animals there. Is that a good charitable trust within the authorities?
>
> In my opinion it is not. It is merely a trust to secure that all animals within the area shall be free from molestation or destruction by man. It is not a trust directed to ensure absence or diminution of pain or cruelty in the destruction of animal life. If this trust is carried out according to its tenor, no animal within the area may be destroyed by man no matter how necessary that destruction may be in the interests of mankind or in the interests of the other denizens of the area or in the interests of the animal itself; and no matter how painlessly such destruction may be brought about. It seems to me impossible to say that the carrying out of such a trust necessarily involves benefit to the public. Beyond perhaps hearing of the existence of the enclosure the public does not come into the matter at all. Consistently with the trust the public could be excluded from entering the area or even looking into it. All that the public need know about the matter would be that one or more areas existed in which all animals (whether good or bad from mankind's point of view) were allowed to live free from any risk of being molested or killed by man; though liable to be molested and killed by other denizens of the area. For myself I feel quite unable to say that any benefit to the community will necessarily result from applying the trust fund to the purposes indicated in the first object.

In *National Anti-Vivisection Society v IRC*,[222] a society that existed to suppress experiments on animals, was held by the House of Lords not to be charitable due to detriment to the public outweighing benefit. Lord Simonds said:[223]

> The second point is fundamental. It is at the very root of the law of charity as administered by the Court of Chancery and its successor, the Chancery Division of the High Court of Justice. It is whether the court, for the purpose of determining whether the object of the society is charitable may disregard the finding of fact that any assumed public benefit in the direction of the advancement of morals and education was far outweighed by the detriment to medical science and research and consequently to the public health which would result if the society succeeded in achieving its object, and that on balance, the object of the society, so far from being for the public benefit, was gravely injurious thereto. The society says that the court must disregard this fact, arguing that evidence of disadvantages or evils which would or might result from the stopping of vivisection is irrelevant and inadmissible.
>
> The second question raised in this appeal, which I have already tried to formulate, is of wider importance, and I must say at once that I cannot reconcile it with my conception of a court of equity that it should take under its care and administer a trust, however well-intentioned its creator, of which the consequence would be calamitous to the community...

---

[220] [1929] 1 Ch 557.
[221] Ibid, 582.
[222] [1948] AC 31. See Chapter 5.3(c)(ii)(a), p. 198.
[223] Ibid, 60.

It is to me a strange and bewildering idea that the court must look so far and no farther, must see a charitable purpose in the intention of the society to benefit animals and thus elevate the moral character of men but must shut its eyes to the injurious results to the whole human and animal creation.

(l) PROMOTION OF EFFICIENCY OF PUBLIC SERVICES

'Public services', for the purposes of this charitable head, include the armed forces, the police, fire, and rescue services, and the ambulance services.[224] Efficiency has previously been held to include physical efficiency. So, in *Re Gray*[225] it was held that a trust to establish a fund for the benefit of a regiment of the army in order to promote sport, including 'shooting, fishing, cricket, football and polo', was charitable. Romer J said:[226]

in my opinion it was not the object of the testator in the present case to encourage or promote either sport in general or any sport in particular. I think it is reasonably clear that it was his intention to benefit the officers and men of the [regiment] by giving them an opportunity of indulging in healthy sport. It is to be observed that the particular sports specified were all healthy outdoor sports, indulgence in which might reasonably be supposed to encourage physical efficiency...

But I am glad to find that there is an established principle enabling me to give effect to the gifts in the present case. This principle was established by Farwell J in *Re Good* [1905] 2 Ch 60 at 66, 67, a case that as far as I know has never been questioned in any way. In that case the testator gave his residuary personalty upon trust for the officers' mess of his regiment, to be invested and the income to be applied in maintaining a library for the officers' mess for ever, any surplus to be expended in the purchase of plate for the mess. According to the headnote of the report of that case it was held that the gift to maintain the library and to purchase plate for the officers' mess, being for a general public purpose tending to increase the efficiency of the army and aid taxation, was a good charitable bequest...

In the case before Farwell J the efficiency was mental efficiency, and the only distinction between that case and the present case is that in the present case the efficiency is physical as opposed to mental efficiency. But it is obviously for the benefit of the public that those entrusted with the defence of the realm should be not only mentally but also physically efficient, and I think I am justified in coming to the conclusion that there is no difference between mental and physical efficiency for the present purpose.

(m) OTHER BENEFICIAL PURPOSES

Other purposes will be considered to be charitable if they:[227]

(1) have been recognized under existing charity law or under section 5 of the Charities Act 2011 concerning recreational trusts; or

(2) they can reasonably be regarded as analogous to, or within the spirit of, the 12 purposes identified by the Charities Act 2011, or with the purposes recognized under existing charity law or section 5 concerning recreational trusts; or

---

[224] Charities Act 2011, s. 3(1)(l).
[225] [1925] Ch 362. See also now the purpose of advancing amateur sport. See Chapter 5.4(g), pp. 242–5.
[226] Ibid, 365.
[227] Charities Act 2011, s. 3(1)(m). See Chapter 5.3(c)(i), p. 190.

(3) they can reasonably be regarded as analogous to, or within the spirit of, the purposes that have been recognized under charity law as falling within paragraph (2) or this one.

This head operates as a safety net to ensure that charitable purposes can continue to be developed by analogy with the existing law of charity or with the heads recognized under the Charities Act itself. It is a long-standing tradition of charity law to develop charitable purposes in this way. For example, in *Incorporated Council of Law Reporting for England and Wales v Attorney-General*,[228] the Court of Appeal held that the Incorporated Council was charitable both as a trust for the advancement of education, but also under the head of for being for other purposes beneficial to the community. Russell LJ said:[229]

I come now to the question whether, if the main purpose of the council is, as I think it is, to further the sound development and administration of the law in this country, and if, as I think it is, that is a purpose beneficial to the community or of general public utility, that purpose is charitable according to the law of England and Wales.

On this point the law is rooted in the Statute of Elizabeth I, a statute the object of which was the oversight and reform of abuses in the administration of property devoted by donors to purposes which were regarded as worthy of such protection as being charitable. The Preamble to the Statute listed certain examples of purposes worthy of such protection. These were from an early stage regarded merely as examples, and have through the centuries been regarded as examples or guideposts for the courts in the differing circumstances of a developing civilisation and economy. Sometimes recourse has been had by the courts to the instances given in the Preamble in order to see whether in a given case sufficient analogy may be found with something specifically stated in the Preamble, or sufficient analogy with some decided case in which already a previous sufficient analogy has been found. Of this approach perhaps the most obvious example is the provision of crematoria by analogy with the provisions of burial grounds by analogy with the upkeep of churchyards by analogy with the repair of churches. On other occasions a decision in favour or against a purpose being charitable has been based in terms upon a more general question whether the purpose is or is not within 'the spirit and intendment' of the Statute of Elizabeth I and in particular its Preamble. Again (and at an early stage in development) whether the purpose is within 'the equity' or within 'the mischief' of the Statute. Again whether the purpose is charitable 'in the same sense' as purposes within the preview of the Statute. I have much sympathy with those who say that these phrases do little of themselves to elucidate any particular problem. 'Tell me', they say, 'what you define when you speak of spirit, intendment, equity, mischief, the same sense, and I will tell you whether a purpose is charitable according to law. But you never define. All you do is sometimes to say that a purpose is none of these things. I can understand it when you say that the preservation of sea walls is for the safety of lives and property, and therefore by analogy the voluntary provision of lifeboats and fire brigades are charitable. I can even follow you as far as crematoria. But these other generalities teach me nothing.'

I say I have much sympathy for such approach: but it seems to me to be unduly and improperly restrictive. The Statute of Elizabeth I was a statute to reform abuses: in such circumstances and in that age the courts of this country were not inclined to be restricted in their implementation of Parliament's desire for reform to particular examples given by the Statute; and they deliberately kept open their ability to intervene when they thought necessary in cases not specifically mentioned, by applying as the test whether any particular case of abuse of funds or property was within the 'mischief' or the 'equity' of the Statute.

---

[228] [1972] Ch 73. See Chapter 5.4(b)(i), p. 214.
[229] Ibid, 87.

For myself I believe that this rather vague and undefined approach is the correct one, with analogy its handmaid, and that when considering Lord Macnaghten's fourth category in *Pemsel*'s *case* [1891] AC 531 at 583 of 'other purposes beneficial to the community' . . . the courts, in consistently saying that not all such are necessarily charitable in law, are in substance accepting that if a purpose is shown to be so beneficial or of such utility it is prima facie charitable in law, but have left open a line of retreat based on the equity of the Statute in case they are faced with a purpose (e.g., a political purpose) which could not have been within the contemplation of the Statute even if the then legislators had been endowed with the gift of foresight into the circumstances of later centuries.

In a case such as the present, in which in my view the object cannot be thought otherwise than beneficial to the community and of general public utility, I believe the proper question to ask is whether there are any grounds for holding it to be outside the equity of the Statute and I think the answer to that is here in the negative. I have already touched upon its essential importance to our rule of law. If I look at the somewhat random examples in the Preamble to the Statute I find in the repair of bridges, havens, causeways, sea banks and highways examples of matters which if not looked after by private enterprise must be a proper function and responsibility of government, which would afford strong ground for a statutory expression by Parliament of anxiety to prevent misappropriation of funds voluntarily dedicated to such matters. It cannot I think be doubted that if there were not a competent and reliable set of reports of judicial decisions, it would be a proper function and responsibility of government to secure their provision for the due administration of the law. It was argued that the specific topics in the Preamble that I have mentioned are all concerned with concrete matters, and that so also is the judicially accepted opinion that the provision of a court house is a charitable purpose. But whether the search be for analogy or for the equity of the Statute this seems to me to be too narrow or refined an approach. I cannot accept that the provision, in order to facilitate the proper administration of the law, of the walls and other physical facilities of a court house is a charitable purpose, but that the dissemination by accurate and selective reporting of knowledge of a most important part of the law to be there administered is not.

Accordingly the purpose for which the association is established is exclusively charitable in the sense of Lord Macnaghten's fourth category. I would not hold that the purpose is purely the advancement of education: but in determining that the purpose is within the equity of the Statute I by no means ignore the function of the purpose in furthering knowledge in legal science.

5. EXCLUSIVELY CHARITABLE

(a) INCLUSION OF NON-CHARITABLE PURPOSES

A trust can be regarded as charitable only if all of its purposes are charitable.[230] This means that the trust cannot have a mixture of charitable and non-charitable purposes. So, for example, if the purposes of a trust are described as being 'charitable *or* benevolent', this will not be exclusively charitable, because a benevolent purpose can be wider than the legal definition of 'charitable purposes', which would mean that the trustees would be able to apply trust funds for purposes that are not necessarily charitable. If, however, the trust provides for funds to be applied for 'charitable *and* benevolent purposes', this will be charitable, because any purpose must be charitable even if it is benevolent as well. Consequently, the validity of such trusts as charities will often turn on whether the words 'or' or 'and' are used. It follows that great care must be taken when seeking to draft a charitable trust.

---

[230] Charities Act 2011, s. 1(1)(a) and s. 11.

The leading case to consider whether a trust's purposes were exclusively charitable is *Chichester Diocesan Fund and Board of Finance Incorporated v Simpson*.

Chichester Diocesan Fund and Board of Finance Incorporated v Simpson [1944] AC 341

Caleb Diplock, in his will, directed his executors to apply the residue of his estate for such charitable institutions *or* 'benevolent object or objects' as the executors in their absolute discretion should select. The House of Lords held that the gift was void. Lord Simonds said:[231]

> My Lords, the words for your consideration are 'charitable or benevolent'. The question is whether, in the context in which they are found in this will, these words give to the executors a choice of objects extending beyond that which the law recognizes as charitable. If they do not, that is the end of the matter. The trust is a good charitable trust. If they do, it appears to be conceded by counsel for the appellant institution that the trust is invalid... My Lords, of those three words your Lordships will have no doubt what the first, 'charitable', means. It is a term of art with a technical meaning and that is the meaning which the testator must be assumed to have intended. If it were not so, if in this will 'charitable' were to be given, not its legal, but some popular, meaning, it would not be possible to establish the validity of the bequest. The last of the three words 'benevolent' is not a term of art. In its ordinary meaning it has a range in some respects far less wide than legal charity, in others somewhat wider. It is, at least, clear that the two words, the one here used in its technical meaning, the other having only, and, accordingly, here used in, a popular meaning, are by no means coterminous. These two words are joined or separated by the word 'or', a particle, of which the primary function is to co-ordinate two or more words between which there is an alternative. It is, I think, the only word in our language apt to have this effect. Its primary and ordinary meaning is the same, whether or not the first alternative is preceded by the word 'either'.
>
> My Lords, averting my mind from the possible ill effects of an alternative choice between objects 'charitable' and objects 'benevolent', I cannot doubt that the plain meaning of the testator's words is that he has given this choice, and that, if he intended to give it, he could have used no words more apt to do so. Is there, then, anything in the context which narrows the area of choice by giving to the words 'or benevolent' some other meaning than that which they primarily and naturally have? And if so, what is the other meaning which is to be given to them? Let me examine the second question first. Since the test of validity depends on the area of choice not being extended beyond the bounds of legal charity, a meaning must be given to the words 'or benevolent' which retains them within these bounds. This result, it has been contended, may be reached by giving to the word 'or' not its primary disjunctive meaning but a secondary meaning which may, perhaps, be called exegetical or explanatory. Undoubtedly 'or' is capable of this meaning. So used, it is equivalent to 'alias' or 'otherwise called'. The dictionary examples of this use will generally be found to be topographical, as 'Papua or New Guinea', but, my Lords, this use of the word 'or' is only possible if the words or phrases which it joins connote the same thing and are interchangeable the one with the other. In this case the testator is assumed to use the word 'charitable' in its legal sense. I see no possible ground for supposing that he proceeds to explain it by another word which has another meaning and by no means can have that meaning. I must reject the exegetical 'or'. Then it was suggested that the words 'or benevolent' should be construed as equivalent to 'provided such objects are also of a benevolent character', that is to say, the objects must be charitable but of that order of charity which is commonly called benevolent. I think that this is only a roundabout way of saying that 'or' should be read as 'and,' that the objects of choice must have the two characteristics of charitable and benevolent.

---

[231] [1944] AC 341, 368.

It is possible that a context may justify so drastic a change as that involved in reading the disjunctive as conjunctive. I turn then to the context to see what justification it affords for reading the relevant words in any but their natural meaning. Reading and re-reading them, as your Lordships have so often done in the course of this case, I can find nothing which justifies such a departure. It is true that the word 'other' introduces the phrase 'charitable or benevolent object or objects' and to this the appellants attached some importance, suggesting that since 'other' looked back to 'charitable institution or institutions', so all that followed must be of the genus charitable. There can be no substance in this, for in the phrase so introduced the word 'charitable' is itself repeated and is followed by the alternative 'or benevolent'. Apart from this slender point it seemed that the appellants relied on what is called a general, a dominant, an overriding, charitable intention, giving charitable content to a word or phrase which might otherwise not have that quality. That such a result is possible there are cases in the books to show. Some of them have been cited to your Lordships, but here again I look in vain for any such context. On the plain reading of this will I could only come to the conclusion that the testator intended exclusively to benefit charitable objects if I excised the words 'or benevolent' which he has used. That I cannot do.

Similarly, a trust for 'charitable or philanthropic' purposes has been held not to be exclusively charitable,[232] since philanthropic purposes are not inevitably charitable. A trust for a charitable institution 'or one operating for the public good',[233] and a trust for 'worthy purposes' have been held not to be charitable.[234] A trust for charitable and deserving objects was, however, held to be exclusively charitable,[235] because the deserving objects would also have to be charitable. But it does not necessarily follow that the identification of two purposes that are connected by 'and' will be valid.[236] For example, in *Attorney-General of the Bahamas v Royal Trust Co.*,[237] a gift 'for any purposes for and/or connected with the education and welfare of Bahamian children and young people' was held to be void. 'Welfare' was considered too wide necessarily to be confined to a charitable purpose and the use of 'or', albeit as well as 'and', meant that the gift could be used for non-charitable purposes. These are harsh decisions, which are inconsistent with the general judicial attitude of benevolent construction of charitable trusts, with a view to interpret them as charitable if possible.

Although a trust for the benefit of a particular locality, including a trust for the benefit of Great Britain, would not appear to be exclusively charitable, such trusts have been held to be valid charitable trusts,[238] because they are benevolently interpreted as being confined to charitable purposes within the identified locality. In *Attorney-General of the Cayman Islands v Wahr-Hansen*,[239] Lord Browne-Wilkinson said that the 'locality cases':[240]

are cases where the gift is made, for example, to a parish (*West v Knight* (1669) 1 Cas in Ch 134) or 'for the good of' a specific county (*Attorney-General v Lord Lonsdale* (1827) 1 Sim. 105) or for 'charitable, beneficial, and public works' (*Mitford v Reynolds* (1841) 1 Ph 185) or for 'the benefit and advantage of Great Britain' (*Nightingale v Goulbourn* (1847) 5 Hare 484) or 'unto my country England': *Re Smith*

[232] *Re Macduff* [1896] 2 Ch 451.
[233] *A-G of Cayman Islands v Wahr-Hansen* [2001] 1 AC 75 (PC).
[234] *Re Atkinson's Will Trusts* [1978] 1 WLR 586.
[235] *Re Sutton* (1885) 28 Ch D 464.
[236] See e.g. *Re Eades* [1920] 2 Ch 353 ('religious, charitable and philanthropic objects' was not exclusively charitable).
[237] [1986] 1 WLR 1001.
[238] *Nightingale v Goulbourn* (1847) 5 Hare 484.
[239] [2001] 1 AC 75 (PC).
[240] Ibid, 81.

[1932] 1 Ch 153. In all these cases the gifts were held to be valid charitable trusts, even though the breadth of the words used, literally construed, would certainly have authorised the applications of the funds for non-charitable purposes in the specified locality. The courts have held that such purposes are to be impliedly limited to charitable purposes in the specified community...

There is a limited class of cases where gifts in general terms are made for the benefit of a named locality or its inhabitants. For reasons which are obscure, such cases have been benevolently construed. They are now so long established that in cases falling within the very circumscribed description of gifts for the benefit of a specified locality they remain good law. But they have been widely criticised and indeed have been said to be wrongly decided: see, for example, Michael Albery, 'Trusts for the Benefit of the Inhabitants of a Locality' (1940) 56 LQR 49. To apply the same principle to all cases where there are general statements of benevolent or philanthropic objects so as to restrict the meaning of the general words to such objects as are in law charitable would be inconsistent with the overwhelming body of authority which decides that general words are not to be artificially construed so as to be impliedly limited to charitable purposes only.

Although these are highly anomalous cases, they do exemplify the principle of benign construction of charitable gifts.[241] It is unfortunate that this same benign construction is not adopted where the gift includes non-charitable purposes so that it could be assumed that the gift would be applied only for the charitable purpose.

(b) CONSEQUENCES OF INCLUDING NON-CHARITABLE PURPOSES

Where the purposes of a trust are not exclusively charitable, the court may, on construing the language, reach one of several possible solutions.

(i) *Void trust*

The trust may be declared void, unless it can exceptionally be regarded as a valid non-charitable purpose trust.[242] If the trust is declared void, the funds will be held on resulting trust for the settlor or testator's estate.[243] A consequence of the decision in *Chichester Diocesan Fund and Board of Finance Incorporated v Simpson*,[244] that a testamentary gift to charitable institutions or benevolent objects was void, was that the testator's next of kin could claim that the executor should have given the property to the next of kin rather than disposed of it in accordance with the purported trusts, which were void. This provided the basis of a claim by the next of kin to the gifts that had been made to various charities by the executor. The nature of these claims was complex and controversial.[245]

(ii) *Incidental purposes*

If the non-charitable purpose is incidental or subsidiary to the main charitable purpose, it will not prevent the trust from being charitable.[246] This was recognized by Lord Millett in *Latimer v CIR*,[247] a

---

[241] See Chapter 5.1(a), pp. 177–8.
[242] See Chapter 6.2, pp. 289–94.
[243] See Chapter 8.3, pp. 384–99.
[244] [1944] AC 341.
[245] See Chapter 19.3(d)(i), p. 964.
[246] See generally Gravells, 'Charitable Trusts and Ancillary Purposes' [1978] Conv 92.
[247] [2004] 1 WLR 1466.

case concerning the charitable status of a trust fund for Maori claimants to pursue land claims. Lord Millett said:[248]

But the trustees are not obliged to apply the whole of the trust income as it arises. They may carry it forward and apply it in future years; and in so far as it is not wholly expended when the trust comes to an end any remaining balance is to be returned to the Crown. It follows that it cannot be said of any sum of income in the hands of the trustees that it will be applied for charitable purposes; it may be retained and ultimately become payable to the Crown. The ultimate trust in favour of the Crown is a substantial trust in its own right, and unless the Crown is a charity or holds on charitable trusts or the trust in its favour can be dismissed as merely ancillary or incidental to the primary trust to assist the Maori claimants its existence makes it impossible to contend that the trust income is applicable to exclusively charitable purposes.

Trustees of a charitable trust may be authorised to charge their own fees and expenses to the trust without causing the loss of the trust's charitable status. It cannot be said to be a purpose of the trust to enable the trustees to charge fees and expenses; such expenditure may be justified only if it helps to further the trust's charitable purpose, and may accordingly be classified as ancillary to that purpose.

Again, some trusts for charitable purposes cannot help but confer incidental benefits on individuals; they do not thereby lose their charitable status: *Royal College of Surgeons of England v National Provincial Bank Ltd* [1952] AC 631 provides a good example of this. The college was established to promote and encourage the study and practice of the art and science of surgery. The professional protection of members of the college (not a charitable purpose) was held to be 'an incidental though an important and perhaps necessary consequence of the work of the college in carrying out its main object'.

The distinction is between ends, means and consequences. The ends must be exclusively charitable. But if the non-charitable benefits are merely the means or the incidental consequences of carrying out the charitable purposes and are not ends in themselves, charitable status is not lost. The residual trust in favour of the Crown in the present case, however, is neither a means of furthering the trust's charitable purpose nor an incidental consequence of carrying out that purpose. The trust may never take effect, but if it does it will do so only after the primary trust has come to an end. It cannot be dismissed as merely ancillary or incidental to the trust's charitable purpose...

Accordingly, the critical feature of the present case is that the ultimate trust is in favour of the Crown. Their Lordships cannot accept the trustee's contention that the Crown is itself a charity, or that it holds all its funds to be applied exclusively for charitable purposes...like other public authorities...its money is applicable and is applied for numerous non-charitable purposes. It is true that these are public purposes rather than private purposes; but this means only that the government of the day considers it expedient to make public funds available for such purposes....

Governments can and do make public money available for a variety of non-charitable purposes. All charitable purposes (with well known exceptions) are public purposes; but not all public purposes are charitable purposes.

The distinction between ends and means is illustrated by *Re Coxen*,[249] where a fund was held on trust for medical charities, but provision was made for the payment of £100 for a dinner for those aldermen who attended a meeting to discuss the business of the trust; such persons would also receive a guinea each if they were to attend the whole of the meeting. This was held to be a valid charitable trust since the dinner and the payments were incidental to the main medical purpose of the trust, and might even be regarded as resulting in its better administration. In *Incorporated Council of Law Reporting for*

---

[248] Ibid, [33].
[249] [1948] Ch 747.

England and Wales v Attorney-General,[250] in holding that the activities of the Council were charitable, Buckley LJ said:[251]

> The subsidiary objects, such as printing and publishing statutes, the provision of a noting-up service and so forth, are ancillary to this primary object [of publishing law reports] and do not detract from its exclusively charitable character. Indeed, the publication of the statutes of the realm is itself, I think, a charitable purpose for reasons analogous to those applicable to reporting judicial decisions.

In *Attorney-General v Ross*,[252] a student's union was held to be a charitable trust even though one of its objects related to affiliation to the National Union of Students, a non-charitable organization, since this was an ancillary purpose that helped the charitable purpose of furthering the educational function of the institution.

(iii) *Severance*

Exceptionally, where a trust's purposes are not exclusively charitable, it may be possible to divide the fund into parts, so that some are applied to charitable purposes and the rest will either be held on a valid non-charitable purpose trust or on a resulting trust for the settlor or those entitled to a testator's residuary estate. This solution will only be possible where the language of the trust instrument can be construed as directing such a division. For example, in *Salusbury v Denton*,[253] a fund was to be used to found a school or to provide for the poor, and the remainder was to be used for the benefit of the testator's relatives. It was held that the fund was divisible into two equal parts, with the first part being used for the charitable purposes and the rest for the next of kin. Severance was possible because the will contemplated division of the estate. In *Re Coxen*,[254] Jenkins J recognized that severance will be appropriate where the amount applicable to the non-charitable purpose can be quantified, but where such quantification is not possible, the trust will fail completely.

(iv) *Retrospective validation*

In 1954, the Charitable Trusts (Validation) Act was enacted to provide that any charitable trust created before 16 December 1952 that was invalid because the fund could be used for non-charitable as well as charitable purposes, should be treated as though all the objects were charitable. Since this Act only applied retrospectively, it does not affect the general principle relating to modern trusts needing to have exclusively charitable purposes. But if the Act was able to validate old trusts despite the inclusion of non-charitable purposes, why could it not be applied prospectively? The failure to do so has been described as 'logically indefensible':[255] if the law is unjust, then it should have been changed for all trusts.

6. CY-PRÈS

Where a charitable purpose fails because, for example, it is impossible or impracticable to apply funds for the identified charitable purpose or because that purpose ceases to be charitable, it is

---

[250] [1972] Ch 73. See Chapter 5.4(m), pp. 253–4.
[251] Ibid, 103.
[252] [1986] 1 WLR 252.
[253] (1857) 3 K & J 529.
[254] [1948] Ch 747, 753.
[255] Cross, 'Some Recent Developments in the Law of Charity' (1956) 72 LQR 187, 203.

necessary to consider whether the trust should fail and the funds be returned to the creator of the trust by means of a resulting trust, or whether they might be applied for a slightly different charitable purpose by virtue of the cy-près doctrine. Where this doctrine operates it makes possible the application of funds to purposes as near as possible to those selected by the donor. The doctrine applies differently depending on whether the failure of the charitable purpose occurs before the trust commences or subsequently. Essentially, where there is an initial failure of charitable purpose, the property will be applied cy-près only if the donor can be considered to have an intention that the property should be used for the benefit of charity generally, rather than confined to the specific, particular charitable purpose that has failed. Once, however, property has been used for charitable purposes and there is a subsequent failure of those purposes, the property will be applied cy-près whether or not the donor had an intention to benefit charity generally. As Romer LJ recognized in *Re Wright*:[256]

> Once money is effectually dedicated to charity, whether in pursuance of a general or particular charitable intent, the testator's next-of-kin or residuary legatees are for ever excluded.

It follows that it is important to work out whether there has been a failure of charitable purpose and, if there has, whether it is an initial or a subsequent failure.

Where property is to be applied cy-près, the courts and the Charity Commission have the power to make schemes so that the property is applied for a similar charitable purpose.

CHARITIES ACT 2011

67 Cy-près schemes

(1) The power of the court or the Commission to make schemes for the application of property cy-près must be exercised in accordance with this section.

(2) Where any property given for charitable purposes is applicable cy-près, the court or the Commission may make a scheme providing for the property to be applied—

    (a) for such charitable purposes, and

    (b) (if the scheme provides for the property to be transferred to another charity) by or on trust for such other charity,

as it considers appropriate, having regard to the matters set out in subsection (3).

(3) The matters are—

    (a) the spirit of the original gift,

    (b) the desirability of securing that the property is applied for charitable purposes which are close to the original purposes, and

    (c) the need for the relevant charity to have purposes which are suitable and effective in the light of current social and economic circumstances.

The 'relevant charity' means the charity by or on behalf of which the property is to be applied under the scheme.

---

[256] [1954] Ch 347, 362.

(a) INITIAL FAILURE OF CHARITABLE PURPOSE

(i) *Initial failure*

To establish an initial failure of charitable purpose, it is necessary to consider whether, at the time the trust is to take effect, the identified purpose is impossible or impracticable to fulfil. Even though a particular charity no longer exists in its original form, the court may find that the charitable purpose continues elsewhere, so that it has not failed and the cy-près doctrine will not be engaged. For example, in *Re Faraker*,[257] the testatrix left £200 to 'Mrs Bailey's Charity, Rotherhithe'. A charity, known as Hannah Bayly's Charity, had been founded in 1756 by Mrs Hannah Bayly for the benefit of poor widows in Rotherhithe. In 1905, the Charity Commissioners had consolidated various local charities with the amalgamated funds being held on trust for the benefit of the poor of Rotherhithe, but no specific mention was made of widows. It was admitted that the testatrix had intended to refer to Hannah Bayly's Charity. It was held that, although Hannah Bayly's charity no longer existed, its purpose continued in the consolidated charities, so the purpose had not failed. Farwell LJ said:[258]

> In the present case there is no question of a cy-près execution. Nobody suggests that there has been a failure of poor widows in Rotherhithe, and unless and until that happy event happens there will be no case for any cy-près administration. What is said is this: the Commissioners have in fact destroyed this trust because in the scheme which they have issued dealing with the amalgamation of the several charities the objects are stated to be poor persons of good character resident in Rotherhithe, not mentioning widows in particular—not of course excluding them, but not giving them that preference which I agree with the Master of the Rolls in thinking ought to have been given. But to say that this omission has incidentally destroyed the Bayly Trust is a very strained construction of the language and one that entirely fails, because the Charity Commissioners had no jurisdiction whatever to destroy the charity. Suppose the Charity Commissioners or this Court were to declare that a particular existing charitable trust was at an end and extinct, in my opinion they would go beyond their jurisdiction in so doing. They cannot take an existing charity and destroy it; they are obliged to administer it. To say that this pardonable slip (I use the word with all respect to the draftsman) has the effect of destroying the charity appears to me extravagant. In all these cases one has to consider not so much the means to the end as the charitable end which is in view, and so long as that charitable end is well established the means are only machinery, and no alteration of the machinery can destroy the charitable trust for the benefit of which the machinery is provided.

As Cozens-Hardy MR recognized: 'Hannah Bayly's Charity is not extinct, it is not dead...it cannot die.'[259]

A charity will, however, be considered to have ceased to exist if its funds no longer remain in existence. In *Re Slatter's Will Trusts*,[260] a testatrix had left money for the work of a hospital in Australia treating tuberculosis, but the hospital had closed down before the testatrix's death because tuberculosis had been controlled in the locality. Since the hospital had not left any funds to continue this purpose, it followed that there was an initial failure of the gift. Martin[261] has criticized this decision on the grounds that the key question should not have been the continued existence of funds, but the continued existence of the charitable purpose, and presumably the purpose of eliminating tuberculosis continued elsewhere. It may have been significant, however, that the testatrix had left her estate to

---

[257] [1912] 2 Ch 488.
[258] Ibid, 495.
[259] Ibid, 493.
[260] [1964] Ch 512.
[261] 'The Construction of Charitable Gifts' (1974) 38 Conv (NS) 187, 191.

the particular hospital in Australia where her daughter had been treated for some years and had died, so that it could properly be interpreted as a gift to a particular institution. Whilst the judge found that her intention had not been to make the gift to the Red Cross Society, which ran the hospital, she may have intended her estate to be used only for the work of the particular hospital at which her daughter had been treated rather than for the purpose of treating tuberculosis generally. As always in cases of this kind, the intention of the donor is vital and must be construed very carefully.

Where a bequest is intended to be for a particular charitable institution, rather than for the institution's charitable purpose, and the institution has ceased to exist before the testator's death, there will be an initial failure of the gift.[262] This distinction between a gift to a charitable purpose and a gift to an institution is influenced by whether the intended recipient of the gift is an unincorporated or an incorporated charity. The significance of this distinction was recognized in *Re Finger's Will Trusts*.

Re Finger's Will Trusts [1972] Ch 286

A testatrix left her estate to a number of charities. One of these was the National Radium Commission, which was an unincorporated charity, and another was the National Council for Maternity and Child Welfare, which was an incorporated charity. Before the testatrix's death, both these charities ceased to exist. It was held that the gift to the unincorporated association was valid as a trust for the purpose rather than the institution, whereas the gift to the incorporated charity failed since it was a gift to the institution rather than the purpose.[263] Goff J said:[264]

> If the matter were *res integra* I would have thought that there would be much to be said for the view that the status of the donee, whether corporate or unincorporate, can make no difference to the question whether as a matter of construction a gift is absolute or on trust for purposes. Certainly drawing such a distinction produces anomalous results.
>
> In my judgment, however, on the authorities a distinction between the two is well established, at all events in this court. I refer first to *Re Vernon's Will Trusts* [1972] Ch 300n where Buckley J said at 303:
>
> > 'Every bequest to an unincorporated charity by name without more must take effect as a gift for a charitable purpose. No individual or aggregate of individuals could claim to take such a bequest beneficially. If the gift is to be permitted to take effect at all, it must be as a bequest for a purpose, *viz.*, that charitable purpose which the named charity exists to serve... A bequest to a named unincorporated charity, however, may on its true interpretation show that the testator's intention to make the gift at all was dependent upon the named charitable organisation being available at the time when the gift takes effect to serve as the instrument for applying the subject matter of the gift to the charitable purpose for which it is by inference given. If so and the named charity ceases to exist in the lifetime of the testator, the gift fails: *Re Ovey* (1885) 29 Ch D 560. A bequest to a corporate body, on the other hand, takes effect simply as a gift to that body beneficially, unless there are circumstances which show that the recipient is to take the gift as a trustee. There is no need in such a case to infer a trust for any particular purpose. The objects to which the corporate body can properly apply its funds may be restricted by its constitution, but this does not necessitate inferring as a matter of construction of the testator's will a direction that the bequest is to be held in trust to be applied for those purposes: the natural construction is that the bequest is made to the corporate

---

[262] *Re Rymer* [1895] 1 Ch 19. See further Chapter 5.6(a)(ii), pp. 265–6.

[263] Although it was applied for similar purposes by virtue of the cy-près doctrine. See Chapter 5.6(a)(iii), pp. 268–9.

[264] [1972] Ch 286, 294.

body as part of its general funds, that is to say, beneficially and without the imposition of any trust. That the testator's motive in making the bequest may have undoubtedly been to assist the work of the incorporated body would be insufficient to create a trust.'

As I read the dictum in *Re Vernon's Will Trusts*, the view of Buckley J was that in the case of an unincorporated body the gift is *per se* a purpose trust, and provided that the work is still being carried on will have effect given to it by way of scheme notwithstanding the disappearance of the donee in the lifetime of the testator, unless there is something positive to show that the continued existence of the donee was essential to the gift...

Accordingly I hold that the bequest to the National Radium Commission being a gift to an unincorporated charity is a purpose trust for the work of the commission which does not fail but is applicable under a scheme, provided (1) there is nothing in the context of the will to show—and I quote from *Re Vernon's Will Trusts*—that the testatrix's intention to make a gift at all was dependent upon the named charitable organisation being available at the time when the gift took effect to serve as the instrument for applying the subject matter of the gift to the charitable purpose for which it was by inference given; (2) that charitable purpose still survives; but that the gift to the National Council for Maternity and Child Welfare...being a gift to a corporate body fails, notwithstanding the work continues, unless there is a context in the will to show that the gift was intended to be on trust for that purpose and not an absolute gift to the corporation.

I take first the National Radium Commission and I find in this will no context whatever to make that body of the essence of the gift....

In my judgment, therefore, this is a valid gift for the purposes of the Radium Commission...and I direct that a scheme be settled for the administration of the gift.

I turn to the other gift and here I can find no context from which to imply a purpose trust. Counsel for the Attorney-General relied on *Re Meyers* [1951] Ch 534, but there the context was absolutely compelling. There were many gifts to hospitals and the case dealt only with the hospitals, and whilst hospitals are not identical, this did mean that all were of the same type and character. Moreover, not only were those gifts both to incorporated and unincorporated hospitals but in some of the corporate cases the name used by the testator was that by which the hospital was generally known to the public but was not the exact title of the corporation. In the present case there are at best three different groups of charities not one; they are not in fact grouped in the order in which they appear in the will, and the particular donees within the respective groups are not all of the same type or character. Further, and worse, two do not fit into any grouping at all, and for what it is worth they come first in the list. In my judgment, therefore, this case is not comparable with *Re Meyers* and I cannot find a context unless I am prepared—which I am not—to say that the mere fact that residue is given to a number of charities, some of which are incorporated and others not, is of itself a sufficient context to fasten a purpose trust on the corporation.

In my judgment, therefore, the bequest to the National Council for Maternity and Child Welfare fails.[265]

The reason for the distinction between incorporated and unincorporated charities is that the latter does not have a separate legal identity, so a gift to such a charity must be a gift for a charitable purpose rather than to the institution. If that purpose can still be fulfilled there has been no initial failure, unless the continued existence of the institution was essential to the gift. Where, however, a gift is to an incorporated charity, then, since such a charity has an independent legal existence, the gift will be to that body beneficially, save where it was intended to take as a trustee.[266]

---

[265] See Chapter 5.6(a)(iii), pp. 268–9 for the operation of the cy-près doctrine in this case.
[266] See *Liverpool and District Hospital for Diseases of the Heart v A-G* [1981] Ch 193.

Where a testamentary gift was made to a charitable company that entered into insolvent liquidation before the death of the testator, but, by the time the testator had died, the company had not been formally dissolved, there was no initial failure and the testamentary gift belonged to the company beneficially and so could be distributed among its creditors.[267]

(ii) *General charitable intent*

Where the charitable purpose fails before the commencement of the trust, the funds can be applied for a similar charitable purpose only if the donor had a general charitable intent. It must be shown that the donor was more concerned that the funds should be used for charitable purposes generally rather than concerned to benefit only the specific charitable purpose or institution that he or she had identified. If there is a general charitable intent the fund will be applied cy-près. If not, the fund will be held on resulting trust for the donor.

Identifying whether there was a general charitable intent requires careful construction of the trust documents and surrounding circumstances. For example, in *Re Rymer*,[268] the testator left a sum of money to the rector of St Thomas' Seminary for the education of priests in the diocese of Westminster in London. When his will was made, there was such a seminary that did educate priests in that diocese, but by the time of the testator's death, the seminary had closed and its students had been transferred to a different seminary near Birmingham. It was held that the testator did not have a general charitable intent, and so the bequest lapsed and went to the residuary legatees. Lindley LJ said:[269]

> You must construe the will and see what the real object of the language which you have to interpret is ... I cannot arrive at the conclusion at which the Appellant's counsel ask me to arrive, that this is in substance and in truth a bequest of £5,000 for the education of the priests in the diocese of Westminster. I do not think it is. It is a gift of £5,000 to a particular seminary for the purposes thereof, and I do not think it is possible to get out of that. I think the context shews it. I refer to the masses, the choice of candidates, and so on. If once you get thus far the question arises, does that seminary exist? The answer is, it does not. Then you arrive at the result that there is a lapse; and if there is a lapse, is there anything in the doctrine of cy-près to prevent the ordinary doctrine of lapse from applying? I think not. Once you arrive at the conclusion that there is a lapse, then all the authorities which are of any value shew that the residuary legatee takes the lapsed gift. We are asked to overrule that doctrine, laid down by Vice-Chancellor Kindersley in *Clark v Taylor* (1853) 1 Drew 642 and followed in *Fisk v A-G* (1867) LR 4 Eq 521. I think that the doctrine is perfectly right. There may be a difficulty in arriving at the conclusion that there is a lapse. But when once you arrive at the conclusion that a gift to a particular seminary or institution, or whatever you may call it, is 'for the purposes thereof', and for no other purpose—if you once get to that, and it is proved that the institution or seminary, or whatever it is, has ceased to exist in the lifetime of the testator, you are driven to arrive at the conclusion that there is a lapse, and then the doctrine of cy-près is inapplicable. That is in accordance with the law, and in accordance with all the cases that can be cited. I quite agree that in coming to that conclusion you have to consider whether the mode of attaining the object is only machinery, or whether the mode is not the substance of the gift. Here it appears to me the gift to the seminary is the substance of the whole thing. It is the object of the testator.

An example of a case in which a general charitable intention was identified is *Biscoe v Jackson*.[270] £10,000 was left for charitable purposes, of which £4,000 was to be applied to establish a soup kitchen

---

[267] *Re ARMS (Multiple Sclerosis Research) Ltd* [1997] 1 WLR 877.
[268] [1895] 1 Ch 19.
[269] Ibid, 34.
[270] (1887) 35 Ch D 460.

for the parish of Shoreditch and a cottage hospital adjoining it. After the testator's death, it was not possible to acquire the land to carry out the provisions in the will. The will was, however, held to show a general charitable intent to benefit the poor of Shoreditch and so the money was applied cy-près for that purpose. Cotton LJ said:[271]

> But the question which we have now to consider is this, is this to be considered as a legacy to a particular institution which cannot be carried into effect, or do we see here an expressed intention by the testator to benefit the poor of the parish of Shoreditch, pointing out a particular mode in which he desires that benefit to be effected? For if the latter be the true view, then if that particular mode cannot have effect given to it, the Court will take hold of the charitable intention to benefit the poor of the parish and will apply the legacy in the best way cy-près for their benefit.
>
> ...I think there is that general intention. It is very true that the testator leaves certain things to be done by the trustees to whom he is giving the sum of £10,000, and if that is to be considered as a gift to an existing institution, or as a gift for that purpose only, it has failed. But then, in my opinion, looking at this whole clause, we see an intention on the part of the testator to give £10,000 to the sick and poor of the parish of Shoreditch, pointing out how he desires that to be applied; and that particular mode having failed, as we must for the purposes of this appeal assume to be the case, then the intention to benefit the poor of Shoreditch, being a good charitable object, will have effect given to it according to the general principle laid down long ago by this Court, by applying it cy-près. If the will had said that the trustees must build the particular building within the parish of Shoreditch there might be some difficulty, but what the testator desires to do is to provide a particular kind of hospital and a soup kitchen for the poor of the parish of Shoreditch. To my mind that shows that he intends not that it is to be located in a particular place, though that would be a proper mode of giving effect to the particular directions contained, if a place in the parish could be found; but that it is for the benefit of the parish, that is of the poor in the parish of Shoreditch. The testator directs that this shall be done by providing them with soup in this kitchen, by providing them with relief in a cottage hospital, and then by a direction that there is to be a woman living in the hospital to look after the inmates in the hospital, and that a sum of money is to be paid to a medical man to attend to them; and then he directs his trustees 'to apply the residue of such annual income towards the necessities and for the benefit thereof, and of the patients who shall from time to time be taken into such hospital in such manner in all respects as my trustees or trustee in their or his absolute discretion think fit'. Of course we have to determine what is the effect, looking fairly at the words used by the testator, to see what his intention was. To my mind the clear result is that he intended here to provide for the benefit of the poor, which is a good charitable bequest, and to provide for that primarily in the particular way he points out.

(iii) *Defunct or non-existent charity*

Whether property can be applied cy-près following an initial failure of purpose may turn on whether the particular charity that has been identified by the donor is defunct or never existed, since this may affect whether a general charitable intent can be identified. The significance of this distinction is illustrated by *Re Harwood*,[272] in which the testatrix left bequests to the Wisbech Peace Society and the Peace Society of Belfast. The Wisbech Peace Society had existed when the will was made, but it had ceased to exist by the time of her death. The Peace Society of Belfast had never

---

[271] Ibid, 468.
[272] [1936] Ch 285.

existed. It was held that the gift to the Wisbech Peace Society could not be applied cy-près, but the other could. Farwell J said:[273]

> The first question that I have to determine is whether a gift…'to the Wisbech Peace Society, Cambridge' fails. The evidence is that this particular society ceased to exist in the testatrix's lifetime. It is said that it is being still carried on as part of the work of the Peace Committee of the Society of Friends. The onus is upon them to show that they are the persons entitled to take. The evidence in this case is so unsatisfactory that I cannot say that that onus has been discharged.
>
> That leaves the question whether there is any general charitable intent, so as to admit of the application of the cy-près doctrine. In that will there is a long list of various charitable societies including charities whose work is devoted to peace. It is said that as this is one of a long list of charitable legacies there is a general charitable intent. On the other hand, it is said that where there is a gift to a particular society, which once existed but ceased to exist before the death of the testator or testatrix, the gift lapses and there is no room for the cy-près doctrine…I do not propose to decide that it can never be possible for the Court to hold that there is a general charitable intent in a case where the charity named in the will once existed but ceased to exist before the death. Without deciding that, it is enough for me to say that, where the testator selects as the object of his bounty a particular charity and shows in the will itself some care to identify the particular society which he desires to benefit, the difficulty of finding any general charitable intent in such case if the named society once existed, but ceased to exist before the death of the testator, is very great. Here the testatrix has gone out of her way to identify the object of her bounty. In this particular case she has identified it as being 'the Wisbech Peace Society Cambridge (which is a branch of the London Peace Society)'. Under those circumstances, I do not think it is open to me to hold that there is in this case any such general charitable intent as to allow the application of the cy-près doctrine…
>
> Then there is the gift to the 'Peace Society of Belfast'.
>
> The claimant for this legacy is the Belfast Branch of the League of Nations Union. I am quite unable on the evidence to say that that was the society which this lady intended to benefit, and I doubt whether the lady herself knew exactly what society she did mean to benefit. I think she had a desire to benefit any society which was formed for the purpose of promoting peace and was connected with Belfast. Beyond that, I do not think that she had any very clear idea in her mind… At any rate I cannot say that by the description, 'the Peace Society of Belfast', the lady meant the Belfast Branch of the League of Nations Union; but there is enough in this case to enable me to say that, although there is no gift to any existing society, the gift does not fail. It is a good charitable gift and must be applied cy-près. The evidence suggests that at some time or other, possibly before the late War, there may have been a society called the Peace Society of Belfast. It is all hearsay evidence; there is nothing in the least definite about it, and it does not satisfy me that there ever was any society in existence which exactly fits the description in this case, and there being a clear intention on the part of the lady, as expressed in her will, to benefit societies whose object was the promotion of peace, and there being no such society as that named in her will, in this case there is a general charitable intent, and, accordingly, the doctrine of cy-près applies.

In drawing a distinction between defunct and non-existent charities, this decision has been described as 'remarkable'.[274] It is certainly difficult to see how the testatrix's intention can be differentiated depending on whether or not the charity that she wished to benefit had or had not existed, since in both cases she had apparently intended to benefit a particular institution. There

---

[273] Ibid, 286.
[274] *Re Finger's Will Trusts* [1972] Ch 286, 299 (Goff J).

is, however, more likely to be an intention to benefit a particular institution if the institution once existed. The significance of the distinction between an institution once existing and never existing was considered further in *Re Spence*,[275] in which a testatrix had left the residue of her estate for the benefit of the patients of the 'Old Folks Home at Hillworth Lodge Keighley'. The home had existed but had closed by the time of her death. It was held that the gift could not be applied cy-près. Megarry V-C said:[276]

> [*Re Harwood* was] concerned with gifts to institutions, rather than gifts for purposes. The case before me, on the other hand, is a gift for a purpose, namely, the benefit of the patients at a particular Old Folks Home. It therefore seems to me that I ought to consider the question, of which little or nothing was said in argument, whether the principle in *Re Harwood*, or a parallel principle, has any application to such case. In other words, is a similar distinction to be made between, on the one hand, a case in which the testator has selected a particular charitable purpose, taking some care to identify it, and before the testator dies that purpose has become impracticable or impossible of accomplishment, and on the other hand a case where the charitable purpose has never been possible or practicable?
>
> As at present advised I would answer Yes to that question. I do not think that the reasoning of the *Re Harwood* line of cases is directed to any feature of institutions as distinct from purposes. Instead, I think the essence of the distinction is in the difference between particularity and generality. If a particular institution or purpose is specified, then it is that institution or purpose, and no other, that is to be the object of the benefaction. It is difficult to envisage a testator as being suffused with a general glow of broad charity when he is labouring, and labouring successfully, to identify some particular specified institution or purpose as the object of his bounty. The specific displaces the general. It is otherwise where the testator has been unable to specify any particular charitable institution or practicable purpose, and so, although his intention of charity can be seen, he has failed to provide any way of giving effect to it. There, the absence of the specific leaves the general undisturbed...
>
> From what I have said it follows that I have been quite unable to extract from the will, construed in its context, any expression of a general charitable intention which would suffice for the moiety to be applied cy-près. Instead, in my judgment, the moiety was given for a specific charitable purpose which, though possible when the will was made, became impossible before the testatrix died. The gift of the moiety accordingly fails, and it passes as on intestacy.

Although Megarry V-C appeared to confirm the distinction between defunct and non-existent charities, his emphasis on the identification of particular and general purposes or institutions suggests that, where an institution is specifically identified to receive a bequest, there is less likely to be a general charitable intent even though the institution never existed. Certainly, in *Re Spence* itself, the identification of a specific charitable purpose meant that, since that purpose had failed, the bequest could not be applied cy-près, although that was a case where the institution had once existed.

There will, however, sometimes be circumstances under which, despite the identification of a particular charitable purpose or institution that has become defunct, the court will still be able to find a general charitable intent. This is illustrated by the unusual facts of *Re Finger's Will Trusts*,[277] in which the gift to the National Council for Maternity and Child Welfare, an incorporated charity, had failed because the charity had ceased to exist by the time of the testatrix's death. Although it was found that

---

[275] [1979] Ch 483.
[276] Ibid, 492.
[277] [1972] Ch 286. See Chapter 5.6(a)(i), pp. 263–4.

the gift was intended to be for the institution rather than for its charitable purpose, a general charitable intent was still identified. Goff J said:[278]

> Farwell J [in *Re Harwood* [1936] Ch 285] did not say that it was impossible to find a general charitable intention where there is a gift to an identifiable body which has ceased to exist but only that it would be very difficult...
>
> In the present case the circumstances are very special. First, of course...the whole estate is devoted to charity and that is, I think, somewhat emphasised by the specific dedication to charity in the preface:
>
> > 'and after payment of the said legacies my trustees shall hold the balance then remaining of my residuary estate upon trust to divide the same in equal shares between the following charitable institutions and funds.'
>
> Again, I am I think entitled to take into account the nature of the council, which as I have said was mainly, if not exclusively, a co-ordinating body. I cannot believe that this testatrix meant to benefit that organisation and that alone.
>
> Finally, I am entitled to place myself in the armchair of the testatrix and I have evidence that she regarded herself as having no relatives.
>
> Taking all these matters into account, in my judgment I can and ought to distinguish *Re Harwood* and find—as I do—a general charitable intention.

It is important to remember that the court is seeking to determine whether or not there was a general charitable intent on the part of the testator. Whilst the fact that a gift was intended to be for a particular institution is evidence that there was no general charitable intention, there may be other factors, such as those identified by Goff J, which may enable the court to identify such an intention.

(iv) *Charity by association*

Where a donor makes a number of gifts to charities with similar purposes, but one of those charities does not exist, the court will be more willing to find a general charitable intention by virtue of its association with gifts to existing charities. So, for example, in *Re Satterthwaite's Will Trusts*,[279] the testatrix left her estate to seven animal charities, an anti-vivisectionist society, and the London Animal Hospital. No such hospital existed when the will was made. It was held that the gift that was purportedly made to the hospital could be applied cy-près because the testatrix had a general charitable intent in favour of animal welfare. Harman LJ said:[280]

> If a particular donee were intended which cannot be identified, no general intent would follow. But when one looks at the whole of the residuary bequest, it seems plain that each share is intended to go to some object connected with the care or the cure of animals. That the Anti-Vivisection has been declared not to be in law a charitable object is irrelevant. The society exists to save animals from suffering.

In *Re Jenkins's Will Trusts*,[281] however, the testatrix bequeathed her residuary estate to seven institutions, one of which was the British Union for the Abolition of Vivisection, which was not a charity

---

[278] Ibid, 299.
[279] [1966] 1 WLR 277.
[280] Ibid, 284.
[281] [1966] Ch 249.

because of its political purpose.[282] The other six institutions were charities with purposes relating to animal welfare. It was held that the gift to the anti-vivisection institution failed because it was not possible to identify an intention that the gift for the non-charitable purpose should take effect as a gift for other charitable purposes simply because there were other charitable gifts, even though the non-charitable gift had a close relation to those other purposes. Buckley J said:[283]

> There are cases in which, where property has been given to some charity which cannot be identified, the court has felt able to say . . . that in the context in which the gift is found it is clear that the testator or testatrix had a charitable intention in making the particular gift and intended to benefit not a particular institution but a charitable activity . . . However, the principle of *noscitur a sociis* [interpretation by reference to context] does not in my judgment entitle one to overlook self-evident facts. If you meet seven men with black hair and one with red hair you are not entitled to say that here are eight men with black hair. Finding one gift for a non-charitable purpose among a number of gifts for charitable purposes the court cannot infer that the testator or testatrix meant the non-charitable gift to take effect as a charitable gift when in the terms it is not charitable, even though the non-charitable gift may have a close relation to the purposes for which the charitable gifts are made.
>
> In my judgment it is not possible for me in this case to come to the conclusion that the testatrix, when she made this gift to the first defendant for the express purpose of doing all that was possible to promote the passage of an Act of Parliament prohibiting vivisection, was really actuated by a charitable purpose to which the court could give effect by way of scheme.

The difference between these cases is that, in *Re Satterthwaite*, the testatrix intended to benefit an institution that did not exist, but would probably have been charitable had it existed; in *Re Jenkins*, the institution did exist, but it was not pursuing a charitable purpose. The general charitable intent was identified in *Re Satterthwaite* because of the close connection between the different charitable purposes. In *Re Jenkins*, a non-charitable purpose could not have been rendered charitable simply by virtue of its association with other charitable purposes.

The principle of construction of charity by association was analysed further in *Re Spence*,[284] where the doctrine was not applied where the testatrix had made a bequest for the benefit of old people in a particular home that no longer existed and another for blind patients in another home that did exist. Megarry V-C said:[285]

> The doctrine may for brevity be described as charity by association. If the will gives the residue among a number of charities with kindred objects, but one of the apparent charities does not in fact exist, the court will be ready to find a general charitable intention and so apply the share of the non-existent charity cy-près. I have not been referred to any explicit statement of the underlying principle, but it seems to me that in such cases the court treats the testator as having shown the general intention of giving his residue to promote charities with that type of kindred objects, and then, when he comes to dividing the residue, as casting around for particular charities with that type of objects to name as donees. If one or more of these are non-existent, then the general intention will suffice for a cy-près application. It will be observed that, as stated, the doctrine depends, at least to some extent, upon the detection of 'kindred objects' (a phrase which comes from the judgment of Luxmoore J in *In re Knox* [1937] Ch 109, 113) in the charities to which the

---

[282] See Chapter 5.3(c)(ii)(c), pp. 201–2.
[283] [1966] Ch 249, 256.
[284] [1979] Ch 483. See Chapter 5.6(a)(iii), pp. 268–9.
[285] Ibid, 494.

shares of residue are given, in this respect the charities must in some degree be *ejusdem generis* [of the same kind]...

The court is far less ready to find such an intention where the gift is to a body which existed at the date of the will but ceased to exist before the testator died, or, as I have already held, where the gift is for a purpose which, though possible and practicable at the date of the will, has ceased to be so before the testator's death. The case before me is, of course, a case in this latter category, so that [counsel] has to overcome this greater difficulty in finding a general charitable intention.

Not only does [counsel] have this greater difficulty: he also has, I think, less material with which to meet it. He has to extract the general charitable intention for the gift which fails from only one other gift: the residue, of course, was simply divided into two. In *In re Knox* and *In re Hartley* the gifts which failed were each among three other gifts, and in *In re Satterthwaite's Will Trusts* [1966] 1 WLR 277 there were seven or eight other gifts. I do not say that a general charitable intention or a genus cannot be extracted from a gift of residue equally between two: but I do say that larger numbers are likely to assist in conveying to the court a sufficient conviction both of the genus and of the generality of the charitable intention...

Where the difficulty or impossibility not only afflicts the method but also invades the concept of the alleged general charitable intention, then I think that the difficulty of establishing that the will displays any general charitable intention becomes almost insuperable.

(b) SUBSEQUENT FAILURE OF CHARITABLE PURPOSE

Once a trust fund has been dedicated to a charitable purpose, the fact that the purpose then fails cannot destroy the charitable nature of the fund. The courts will find a similar charitable purpose and the fund will be transferred to it, regardless of whether the donor had a general or particular charitable intent. The only exceptions are where the creator of the trust has expressly provided for what should happen to the fund if the purpose subsequently fails, for example by providing that the property should be returned to the settlor, or to those entitled to the testator's residuary estate, or passed to a third party.[286]

Where a testator has sought to create a charitable trust, the failure of the charitable purpose will be subsequent if it occurs after the testator's death even though it occurred before the gift was vested in the charity. So, for example, in *Re Slevin*,[287] the testator made a gift to an orphanage that was in existence at his death, but which ceased to exist soon afterwards and before the legacy was paid. It was held that the gift could be applied cy-près. Kay LJ said:[288]

In the case of a legacy to an individual, if he survived the testator it could not be argued that the legacy would fall into the residue. Even if the legatee died intestate and without next-of-kin, still the money was his, and the residuary legatee would have no right whatever against the Crown. So, if the legatee were a corporation which was dissolved after the testator's death, the residuary legatee would have no claim.

Obviously it can make no difference that the legatee ceased to exist immediately after the death of the testator. The same law must be applicable whether it was a day, or month, or year, or, as might well happen, ten years after; the legacy not having been paid either from delay occasioned by the

---

[286] *Re Peel's Release* [1921] 2 Ch 218.
[287] [1891] 2 Ch 236.
[288] Ibid, 240.

administration of the estate or owing to part of the estate not having been got in. The legacy became the property of the legatee upon the death of the testator, though he might not, for some reason, obtain the receipt of it till long after. When once it became the absolute property of the legatee, that is equivalent to saying that it must be provided for; and the residue is only what remains after making such provision. It does not for all purposes cease to be part of the testator's estate until the executors admit assets and appropriate and pay it over; but that is merely for their convenience and that of the estate. The rights as between the particular legatee and the residue are fixed at the testator's death...

In the present case we think that the Attorney-General must succeed, not on the ground that there is such a general charitable intention that the fund should be administered cy-près even if the charity had failed in the testator's lifetime, but because, as the charity existed at the testator's death, this legacy became the property of that charity, and on its ceasing to exist its property falls to be administered by the Crown, who will apply it, according to custom, for some analogous purpose of charity.

In *Re Wright*,[289] the testatrix left her residuary estate, subject to a life interest, on trust for a convalescent home. When she died in 1933, the provision of such a home was capable of being carried out, but when the life tenant died in 1942, it was no longer practicable. The Court of Appeal held that the test of practicability of charitable purpose should be applied at the date of the testatrix's death rather than when the funds became available on the death of the life tenant. This was because the former date was that on which the rights of the charity and the next of kin, who would take it if the gift to the charity failed, were ascertained. This was consequently a case of subsequent failure of the charitable purpose because the purpose had been practicable when the testatrix died and so the funds could be applied cy-près.

In *Re Tacon*,[290] the time for determining the practicability of fulfilling the charitable purpose was clarified. It was held that, where the gift is vested but liable to be defeated on the occurrence of a particular event, it is not sufficient merely to consider whether the purpose was practicable at the date of the testator's death; it is also necessary to consider whether it would be practicable at some future date. In that case, the testator had left his residuary estate to his daughter for life with remainder to her children, but, if she did not have any, part of the residuary estate was to be used to found a convalescent hospital. At the date of the testator's death, the value of the residuary estate was sufficient to establish such a hospital. His daughter died childless thirty years later, by which time the value of the residuary share had fallen significantly, so that the charitable purpose was no longer practicable. It was held that, where the gift for the charitable purpose was vested but defeasible, it should be assumed that the gift would take effect at some time in the future. In the light of that, it was considered that, had the question of practicability in the future been assessed at the time of the testator's death, the purpose would have been considered to be practicable because it would not have been anticipated that the value of money would have fallen in the meantime.

A charitable purpose will also be considered to have failed subsequently where the purpose has been fulfilled and there remains a surplus of trust funds. So, for example, in *Re King*,[291] the testatrix left the residue of her estate for a stained-glass window to be installed in a church. The residue was over £1,000 and the cost of the window was about £700. It was held that the surplus of the estate could be applied cy-près towards the installation of another window in the church.

---

[289] [1954] Ch 347.
[290] [1958] Ch 447.
[291] [1923] 1 Ch 243.

(c) ALTERATION OF ORIGINAL CHARITABLE PURPOSE

At common law, the cy-près doctrine was applicable only where the objects of the trust became impossible or inexpedient in whole or in part. Where the purpose was subject to a condition that made it impossible or impracticable to achieve the main purpose, the court could, as part of its cy-près jurisdiction, remove the condition so that the main purpose could be achieved. So, for example, in *Re Lysaght*,[292] the Royal College of Surgeons refused to accept a generous benefaction towards medical studentships because it was subject to a condition that meant that Jewish or Roman Catholic students were not eligible to receive studentships, a condition that the Royal College considered to be alien to the spirit of its work. This rendered the fulfilment of the charitable purpose impossible, because the Royal College refused to accept the gift on those terms and the testatrix wanted only the Royal College of Surgeons to be the trustee of the fund. It was held that, since the conditions relating to religious disqualification concerned the machinery of the trust and did not form an essential part of her intention to found medical studentships, a scheme was ordered whereby the Royal College held the bequest on trust, but without the offending condition. The condition that was removed was not considered to be essential to the fulfilment of the donor's dominant charitable intent.

Altering the original charitable purpose was not available, however, at common law where the fulfilment of the purpose remained possible, but the purpose was not useful or convenient. Examples include where property had been left for use as a hospital but for which purpose the site was simply not suitable,[293] or where the purpose was outmoded or was provided for from other sources. The cy-près doctrine can now be applied in such situations by statute, with the relevant provision now to be found in the Charities Act 2011, which relaxed the requirement of impracticability and impossibility.

CHARITIES ACT 2011

62 Occasions for applying property cy-près

(1) Subject to subsection (3), the circumstances in which the original purposes of a charitable gift can be altered to allow the property given or part of it to be applied cy-près are—

   (a) where the original purposes, in whole or in part—

      (i) have been as far as may be fulfilled, or

      (ii) cannot be carried out, or not according to the directions given and to the spirit of the gift,

   (b) where the original purposes provide a use for part only of the property available by virtue of the gift,[294]

   (c) where—

      (i) the property available by virtue of the gift, and

      (ii) other property applicable for similar purposes, can be more effectively used in conjunction, and to that end can suitably, regard being had to the appropriate considerations, be made applicable to common purposes,

---

[292] [1966] Ch 191.
[293] *Re Weir Hospital* [1910] 2 Ch 124.
[294] See *Re North Devon and West Somerset Relief Fund* [1953] 1 WLR 1260.

(d) where the original purposes were laid down by reference to—

    (i) an area which then was but has since ceased to be a unit for some other purpose, or

    (ii) a class of persons or an area which has for any reason since ceased to be suitable, regard being had to the appropriate considerations, or to be practical in administering the gift, or

(e) where the original purposes, in whole or in part, have, since they were laid down—

    (i) been adequately provided for by other means,

    (ii) ceased, as being useless or harmful to the community or for other reasons, to be in law charitable, or

    (iii) ceased in any other way to provide a suitable and effective method of using the property available by virtue of the gift, regard being had to the appropriate considerations.

(2) In subsection (1) 'the appropriate considerations' means—

    (a) (on the one hand) the spirit of the gift concerned, and

    (b) (on the other) the social and economic circumstances prevailing at the time of the proposed alteration of the original purposes.

Section 62 enables the original purposes of a charitable gift to be altered by the Charity Commission in certain circumstances to allow some, or all, of the donated property to be applied cy-près. The jurisdiction is significant, since it involves altering the original purposes of the gift to enable property to be applied in a different way from that intended by the donor.

The significance of section 62 is especially well illustrated by *Varsani v Jesani*.

Varsani v Jesani [1999] Ch 219

A Hindu religious sect had split into two factions in 1984; one of which recognized the divine status of the successor to the sect's founder whilst the other did not. Neither group could worship together in the charity's temple. Both factions sought a scheme to divide the charity's funds under what is now section 62, but was then section 13, of the Charities Act 1993, on the ground that the original purpose of the charity, namely to worship in the temple, had ceased to provide a suitable and effective method of using the property, having regard to the spirit of the gift. It was held that the statutory jurisdiction applied, so a scheme for the division of the charity's property between the two groups would be directed, even though the original purposes of the charity were neither impossible nor impracticable. Morritt LJ said:[295]

Now the jurisdiction to make a cy-près scheme depends on whether the case falls within one or other of the paragraphs of section 13(1). The relevant test in this case is now whether the original purpose has ceased to provide a suitable and effective method of using the property, regard being had to the spirit of the gift.

In my view that test is satisfied in this case. First, there is no doubt what the original purpose of the charity was and is. It was and is the promotion of the faith of Swaminarayan according to the teachings and tenets of Muktajivandasji. Second, until the problems disclosed by the events of 1984 arose those original purposes were both suitable and effective as a method of using the property

---

[295] Ibid, 233.

for both the majority and minority group were agreed on all relevant matters and therefore able to worship together in the temples provided by the charity. Third, the exposure of differing beliefs by the events of 1984 has produced a situation in which neither group is able to worship in the same temple as the other so that the minority group has been excluded from the facilities for the worship the charity was established to provide. Fourth, unless the impasse can be resolved as a matter of faith, so that both groups reunite to embrace the faith the charity was established to promote, the impasse will remain so long as the original purpose remains. Fifth, the impasse cannot be resolved as a matter of faith because the teachings and tenets of Muktajivandasji did not deal with whether a belief in a particular successor to Muktajivandasji or in the divine attributes of a successor were or are essential tenets of the faith...Thus the impasse and the original purpose of the charity go together. If the original purpose leads in the present circumstances to such an impasse then in my view it is self-evident that the original purpose has ceased to be a suitable and effective method of using the available property.

The court is enjoined by section 13(1)(e)(iii) of the Charities Act 1993 to have regard to the spirit of the gift...the basic intention underlying the gift or the substance of the gift rather than the form of the words used to express it or conditions imposed to effect it. It is noteworthy that the phrase is used in section 13(1) only in contexts which require the court to make a value judgment. Thus it does not appear in paragraphs (a)(i), (b), (e)(i) or (ii). Moreover, when it is used, in each case except one it appears in the context of suitability. The exception, paragraph (a)(ii), whilst not actually using the word 'suitable', requires a similar value judgment. The court is not bound to follow the spirit of the gift but it must pay regard to it when making the value judgments required by some of the provisions of section 13(1).

For my part I have no hesitation in concluding that the spirit of the gift supports the submission that the court should accept and exercise the jurisdiction conferred by section 13(1)(e)(iii), of the Charities Act 1993 by directing a scheme for the division of the property of the charity between the majority and minority groups. The choice lies between directing such a scheme for the benefit of all those who down to 1984 shared the belief for the promotion of which the charity was established and, no doubt, in many cases supported the charity financially as well, even though some of them may no longer do so, and requiring a substantial proportion of the trust property to be spent in litigation which can never finally resolve the problems which divide the two groups. I do not minimise the strength of feeling which arises in connection with disputes such as this. In such cases either or both groups often litigate in preference to permitting a benefit to be conferred on the other. But the spirit of the gift to which the court is to have regard is that which prevailed at the time of the gift when the two groups were in harmony.

Accordingly I would reject the submissions of both the minority group and the Attorney-General. First, it is not necessary to ascertain the precise limits of the purpose of the charity before deciding whether the case comes within section 13(1) of the Charities Act 1993. The purpose of this charity is clear; it is the promotion of the faith of Swaminarayan according to the teaching and tenets of Muktajivandasji. It is the expression of that purpose in the light of subsequent events which has given rise to the schism with the result that the original purpose has ceased to be a suitable and effective method of using the trust property. Second, it is not a necessary condition for the application of the section that the original purposes have become impossible or impractical, only that the circumstances come within one or other paragraph of section 13(1). Thus even if the inquiries sought were ordered and pursued and ultimately demonstrated that the minority group but not the majority group still embraced the relevant faith that does not now preclude the application of the section for the outcome of the inquiries would merely demonstrate that the original purpose was not impossible or impractical.

Chadwick LJ said:[296]

> I agree with Morritt LJ that, if the underlying question which, if either, of the views now held by the majority group and the minority group respectively do truly reflect the teachings and tenets of Muktajivandasji in the circumstances which have arisen were to be resolved in favour of one group and against the other, the position would be that the original purposes had ceased to provide a suitable and effective method of using the property available by virtue of the gift. It is not, of course, the case that the property could not be used in accordance with the original purposes. Clearly it could be so used by the group who were found, on this hypothesis, to be the followers of the true faith. But to appropriate the property to the sole use of one group, to the exclusion of the other, would not—in a case like the present—be a suitable and effective method of using that property, regard being had to the spirit of the gift.
>
> The need to have regard to the spirit of the gift requires the court to look beyond the original purposes as defined by the objects specified in the declaration of trust and to seek to identify the spirit in which the donors gave property upon trust for those purposes. That can be done, as it seems to me, with the assistance of the document as a whole and any relevant evidence as to the circumstances in which the gift was made. In the present case I have no doubt that the spirit in which property was given in 1967 was a desire to provide facilities for a small but united community of the followers of Muktajivandasji in and around Hendon to worship together in the faith of Swaminarayan. The original purposes specified in the declaration of trust—that is to say the promotion of the faith of Swaminarayan as practised in accordance with the teachings and tenets of Muktajivandasji—are no longer a suitable and effective method of using the property given in 1967, or added property held upon the same trusts, because the community is now divided and cannot worship together. Nothing that the court may decide will alter that. To hold that one group has adhered to the true faith and that the other group has not will not alter the beliefs of that other group. The position will remain that the community cannot worship together. To appropriate the use of the property to the one group to the exclusion of the other would be contrary to the spirit in which the gift was made.
>
> It follows that there would be jurisdiction to make a scheme cy-près even if the underlying question which, if either, of the views now held by the majority group and the minority group respectively do truly reflect the teachings and tenets of Muktajivandasji in the circumstances which have arisen were to be resolved in favour of one group and against the other. Given jurisdiction, it would plainly be appropriate to make a scheme. To refuse to do so would be to perpetuate a position in which the property of the charity is no longer being used in a suitable and effective manner.

The alternative to a cy-près scheme was to conduct an inquiry to determine which faction followed the true faith; that faction could then have exclusive use of the temple. This was not considered to be a suitable and effective method of using the property, having regard to the spirit in which the donors had given property on trust for the purpose of promoting the faith of the sect by the community worshipping together.

Another example of the significant jurisdiction created by section 62 is *Re Lepton's Charity*.

Re Lepton's Charity [1972] Ch 276

In 1715, the testator had left land on trust with £3 of the income each year to be paid to a Protestant dissenting minister in Pudsey, and the surplus was to be distributed to the poor and aged of the

---

[296] Ibid, 238.

town. The land was sold. The question for the court was whether what is now section 62 could be used to vary the will and raise the annual payment to the minister to £100, in the light of the fact that when the trust was established the annual income was £5 and when the case was heard the annual income was nearly £800. A scheme was ordered to vary the will on the ground that regard should be had to the charitable purposes in the trust as a whole, in particular the relative value of the payment to the minister and the residue. Pennycuick V-C said:[297]

One must next consider whether in relation to a trust for payment of a fixed annual sum out of the income of a fund to charity A and payment of the residue of that income to charity B the expression 'the original purposes of a charitable gift' in section 13(1) should be construed as referring to the trusts as a whole or must be related severally to the trust for payment of the fixed annual sum and the trust for payment of residuary income . . .

It seems to me that the words 'the original purposes of a charitable gift' are apt to apply to the trusts as a whole in such a case. Where a testator or settlor disposes of the entire income of a fund for charitable purposes, it is natural to speak of the disposition as a single charitable gift, albeit the gift is for more than one charitable purpose. Conversely, it would be rather unnatural to speak of the disposition as constituting two or more several charitable gifts each for a single purpose. Nor, I think, is there any reason why one should put this rather artificial construction on the words. The point can, so far as I can see, only arise as a practical issue in regard to a trust of the present character. A trust for division of income between charities in aliquot [proportionate] shares would give rise to different considerations, inasmuch as even if one treats it as a single gift the possibility or otherwise of carrying out the trusts of one share according to the spirit of the gift could hardly react upon the possibility or otherwise of carrying out the trusts of the other share according to the spirit of the gift. The same is true, mutatis mutandis, of trusts for charities in succession. But in a trust of the present character there is an obvious interrelation between the two trusts in that changes in the amount of the income and the value of money may completely distort the relative benefits taken under the respective trusts . . .

Once it is accepted that the words 'the original purposes of a charitable gift' bear the meaning which I have put upon them it is to my mind clear that in the circumstances of the present case the original purposes of the gift of [the land] cannot be carried out according to the spirit of the gift, or to use the words of paragraph (e)(iii) 'have ceased . . . to provide a suitable and effective method of using the property . . . regard being had to the spirit of the gift'. The intention underlying the gift was to divide a sum which, according to the values of 1715, was modest but not negligible, in such a manner that the minister took what was then a clear three-fifths of it. This intention is plainly defeated when in the conditions of today the minister takes a derisory £3 out of a total of £791.

The application of what is now section 62 in this case suggests an expansion of the statutory jurisdiction, since there was no alteration of the original charitable purpose but only of the amount that could be paid to the minister. However, the amount that would otherwise be due was so derisory that this could be regarded as defeating the original charitable purpose.

Section 62 will be engaged only if the case falls within one of the recognized conditions for that provision to apply. But, even if it does not, the court can still rely on its inherent jurisdiction to amend the terms of the charitable trust. So, for example, in *Re JW Laing Trust*,[298] in 1922 the settlor had transferred £15,000 worth of shares to be held on charitable trust, with the capital and income to be wholly distributed within ten years of his death. The settlor died in 1978. By 1982, the capital had not been distributed and was worth £24 million, with an annual income of £1.2 million. The trustee

---

[297] [1972] Ch 276, 285.
[298] [1984] Ch 143.

applied for a scheme to discharge it from the obligation of distributing within ten years of the settlor's death. The application was refused under what is now section 62, because the obligation to distribute was an administrative provision and was not an original purpose of the charitable gift that related to the charitable objects for which the gift was to be applied. However, the scheme was approved in the exercise of the court's inherent jurisdiction at common law, because the requirement as to distribution was considered to be 'inexpedient' in the altered circumstances of the charity since 1922. Peter Gibson J said:[299]

> It is necessary to identify the original purposes of the gift. I venture to suggest that, as a matter of ordinary language, those purposes in the present case should be identified as general charitable purposes and nothing further. I would regard it as an abuse of language to describe the requirement as to distribution as a purpose of the gift. Of course, that requirement was one of the provisions which the settlor intended to apply to the gift, but it would, on any natural use of language, be wrong to equate all the express provisions of a gift, which *ex hypothesi* the settlor intended to apply to the gift, with the purposes of a gift. To my mind the purposes of a charitable gift would ordinarily be understood as meaning those charitable objects on which the property given is to be applied. It is not meaningful to talk of the requirement as to distribution being either charitable or non-charitable. The purposes of a charitable gift correspond to the beneficiaries in the case of a gift by way of a private trust....
>
> I confess that from the outset I have found difficulty in accepting that it is meaningful to talk of a cy-près application of property that has from the date of the gift been devoted both as to capital and income to charitable purposes generally, albeit subject to a direction as to the timing of the capital distributions. No case remotely like the present had been drawn to my attention...
>
> In the result, despite all the arguments that have been ably advanced, I remain unpersuaded that such a gift is capable of being applied cy-près and, in particular, I am not persuaded that the requirement as to distribution is a purpose within the meaning of section 13. Rather, it seems to me to fall on the administrative side of the line, going, as it does, to the mechanics of how the property devoted to charitable purposes is to be distributed. Accordingly, I must refuse the application so far as it is based on section 13.
>
> In my judgment, the plaintiff has made out a very powerful case for the removal of the requirement as to distribution, which seems to me to be inexpedient in the very altered circumstances of the charity since that requirement was laid down 60 years ago. I take particular account of the fact that this application is one that has the support of the Attorney-General. Although the plaintiff is not fettered by the express terms of the gift as to the charitable purposes for which the charity's funds are to be applied, it is, in my view, proper for the plaintiff to wish to continue to support the causes which the settlor himself wished the charity to support from its inception, and which would suffer if that support was withdrawn as a consequence of the distribution of the charity's assets. I have no hesitation in reaching the conclusion that the court should, in the exercise of its inherent jurisdiction, approve a scheme under which the trustees for the time being of the charity will be discharged from the obligation to distribute the capital within ten years of the death of the settlor.

This reliance on the court's inherent jurisdiction can be justified on the basis that the condition did not affect the spirit of the gift and so can be distinguished from *Re Lepton's Charity*, in which the statutory jurisdiction was engaged because the amount to be paid to the minister did affect the spirit of the gift.

---

[299] Ibid, 149.

Another example of the continuing significance of the court's inherent jurisdiction is *Oldham Borough Council v Attorney-General*.[300] In that case, land had been conveyed in 1962 to the Council on trust for use as playing fields. The Council wished to sell the land to developers for a substantial sum of money and to use the proceeds to buy other playing fields with much better facilities. It was held that the court could not authorize the sale under what is now section 62, because, even though the retention of the site was part of the original purposes of the charity, none of the identified circumstances under the statute applied. It was recognized, however, that the court had an inherent jurisdiction to authorize a scheme to sell charitable property and to reinvest the proceeds on the same charitable trusts. Dillon LJ said:[301]

if the retention of a particular property is part of the 'original purposes' of a charitable trust, sale of that property would involve an alteration of the original purposes even if the proceeds of the sale were applied in acquiring an alternative property for carrying out the same charitable activities. If so, a sale of the original property could only be ordered as part of a cy-près scheme, and then only if circumstances within one or other of paragraphs (a) to (e) [of what is now section 62] are made out. The particular bearing of that in the present case is that the council accepts, and the Attorney-General agrees, that the circumstances of this charity do not fall within any of these paragraphs. If, therefore, on a true appreciation of the deed of gift and of section 13, the retention of the existing site is part of the original purposes of the charity, the court cannot authorise any sale...I have no doubt at all that the original purpose, in ordinary parlance, of the donor was, in one sense, that the particular land conveyed should be used for ever as playing fields for the benefit and enjoyment of the inhabitants of Oldham...

there are cases where the donor has imposed a condition, as part of the terms of his gift, which limits the main purpose of the charity in a way which, with the passage of time, has come to militate against the achievement of that main purpose. The condition is there part of the purpose, but the court has found itself able on the facts to cut out the condition by way of a cy-près scheme under the cy-près jurisdiction, on the ground that the subsistence of the condition made the main purpose impossible or impracticable of achievement: see *Re Dominion Students' Hall Trust* [1947] Ch 183, where a condition of a trust for the maintenance of a hostel for male students of the overseas dominions of the British Empire restricted the benefits to dominion students of European origin; and see, also *Re Robinson* [1923] 2 Ch 332, where it was a condition of the gift of an endowment for an evangelical church that the preacher should wear a black gown in the pulpit. But unlike those conditions, the intention or purpose in the present case that the actual land given should be used as playing fields is not a condition qualifying the use of that land as playing fields...

There are, of course, some cases where the qualities of the property which is the subject matter of the gift are themselves the factors which make the purposes of the gift charitable, e.g. where there is a trust to retain for the public benefit a particular house once owned by a particular historical figure or a particular building for its architectural merit or a particular area of land of outstanding natural beauty. In such cases, sale of the house, building or land would necessitate an alteration of the original charitable purposes and, therefore, a cy-près scheme because after a sale the proceeds or any property acquired with the proceeds could not possibly by applied for the original charitable purpose. But that is far away from cases such as the present, where the charitable purpose—playing fields for the benefit and enjoyment of the inhabitants of the districts of the original donees, or it might equally be a museum, school or clinic in a particular town—can be carried on on other land.

[300] [1993] Ch 210.
[301] Ibid, 219.

Consequently, where the identity of the trust property was essential to the charitable purpose, the sale of that property could only be achieved under what is now section 62, because the sale of the property would involve the alteration of the charitable purpose. Where the identity of the property was not essential to the charity's purpose, its sale could be authorized under the court's inherent jurisdiction.

(d) CHARITY COLLECTIONS

Where property has been given by a donor for a specific charitable purpose that fails initially, that property will be held on resulting trust for the donor.[302] It could not be applied cy-près because, being for a specific charitable purpose, no general charitable intent would be identifiable. Where, however, the donor cannot be identified or found or has formally disclaimed his or her right to have the property returned, the property is treated as if it were given for charitable purposes generally and can be applied cy-près.

CHARITIES ACT 2011

63. Application cy-près: donor unknown or disclaiming

(1) Property given for specific charitable purposes which fail is applicable cy-près as if given for charitable purposes generally, if it belongs—

(a) to a donor who after—

(i) the prescribed advertisements and inquiries have been published and made, and

(ii) the prescribed period beginning with the publication of those advertisements has ended,

cannot be identified or cannot be found, or

(b) to a donor who has executed a disclaimer in the prescribed form of the right to have the property returned.

(2) Where the prescribed advertisements and inquiries have been published and made by or on behalf of trustees with respect to any such property, the trustees are not liable to any person in respect of the property if no claim by that person to be interested in it is received by them before the end of the period mentioned in subsection (1)(a)(ii).

(3) Where property is applied cy-près by virtue of this section, all the donor's interest in it is treated as having been relinquished when the gift was made.

64 Donors treated as unidentifiable

(1) For the purposes of section 63 property is conclusively presumed (without any advertisement or inquiry) to belong to donors who cannot be identified, in so far as it consists of—

(a) the proceeds of cash collections made—

(i) by means of collecting boxes, or

(ii) by other means not adapted for distinguishing one gift from another, or

---

[302] See Chapter 8.3(a), pp. 384–5.

(b) the proceeds of any lottery, competition, entertainment, sale or similar money-raising activity, after allowing for property given to provide prizes or articles for sale or otherwise to enable the activity to be undertaken.

(2) The court or the Commission may by order direct that property not falling within subsection (1) is for the purposes of section 63 to be treated (without any advertisement or inquiry) as belonging to donors who cannot be identified if it appears to the court or the Commission—

(a) that it would be unreasonable, having regard to the amounts likely to be returned to the donors, to incur expense with a view to returning the property, or

(b) that it would be unreasonable, having regard to the nature, circumstances and amounts of the gifts, and to the lapse of time since the gifts were made, for the donors to expect the property to be returned.

(e) CHARITY SOLICITATIONS

Where property is donated in response to a particular charitable purpose that fails, the donor can be treated as disclaiming any interest in the property if certain conditions are satisfied.

CHARITIES ACT 2011

65 Donors treated as disclaiming

(1) This section applies to property given—

(a) for specific charitable purposes, and

(b) in response to a solicitation within subsection (2).

(2) A solicitation is within this subsection if—

(a) it is made for specific charitable purposes, and

(b) it is accompanied by a statement to the effect that property given in response to it will, in the event of those purposes failing, be applicable cy-près as if given for charitable purposes generally, unless the donor makes a relevant declaration at the time of making the gift.

(3) A relevant declaration is a declaration in writing by the donor to the effect that, in the event of the specific charitable purposes failing, the donor wishes to be given the opportunity by the trustees holding the property to request the return of the property in question (or a sum equal to its value at the time of the making of the gift).

(4) Subsections (5) and (6) apply if—

(a) a person has given property as mentioned in subsection (1),

(b) the specific charitable purposes fail, and

(c) the donor has made a relevant declaration.

(5) The trustees holding the property must take the prescribed steps for the purpose of—

(a) informing the donor of the failure of the purposes,

(b) enquiring whether the donor wishes to request the return of the property (or a sum equal to its value), and

(c) if within the prescribed period the donor makes such a request, returning the property (or such a sum) to the donor.

(6) If those trustees have taken all appropriate prescribed steps but—

(a) they have failed to find the donor, or

(b) the donor does not within the prescribed period request the return of the property (or a sum equal to its value),

Section 63(1) applies to the property as if it belonged to a donor within section 63(1)(b) (application of property where donor has disclaimed right to return of property)...

(f) SMALL CHARITIES

The Charities Act 2011 makes specific provision to enable trustees of certain small charities to determine their own cy-près application with the concurrence of the Charity Commission, as long as the charity has a gross income of less than £10,000, does not hold land on trust for charitable purposes, and is not exempt or a charitable company. The cy-près scheme might transfer all the charity's property to another charity, or replace some or all of the charity's original purposes, where they are no longer conducive to a suitable and effective application of the charity's resources.[303]

(g) CRITIQUE OF THE CY-PRÈS DOCTRINE

At the heart of the cy-près doctrine is the distinction between initial and subsequent failure of purpose. On which side of the line a particular case falls will affect whether a general charitable intent needs to be identified. The recognition that no such intent is required where there is subsequent failure involves the elevation of a rule of evidence into a rule of law.[304] This is because, in cases of subsequent failure, the old rule was that there was a presumption of general charitable intent, but this was a presumption that could be rebutted. Luxton has advocated a more rational approach to the cy-près doctrine:[305]

If the charitable purpose fails:

(a) before it has taken effect (i.e. before the property has been *applied* to that purpose)...there is a presumption of resulting trust which can be rebutted by evidence of a general charitable intention or of an intention effectually to dedicate the property to charity;...

(b) after it has taken effect but before the end of the perpetuity period...there is a presumption of effectual dedication to charity, which can be rebutted by evidence that the testator had no such intention not any general charitable intention...

At the end of the perpetuity period the property becomes effectually dedicated to charity *as a matter of law*...The charitable disposition is therefore absolute and free from determination; thus there can be no resulting trust and no claim by the next-of-kin; accordingly no general charitable intention need ever be sought for cy-près application...

The rewards to be gained from adopting this approach are rich; public policy is satisfied because the intention of the testator is important in the early years' of the trust's life but no further...All that is

---

[303] Charities Act 2011, s. 268.
[304] Luxton, 'Cy-près and the Ghost of Things that Might Have Been' [1983] Conv 107.
[305] Ibid, 117.

required is a recognition of the fact that the moment at which property becomes effectually dedicated to charity *as a matter of law* can now be shifted forward from the date of vesting in interest to the end of the perpetuity period.

QUESTION

In his will, Brian left £100,000 to be held on trust for the benefit of any of the employees of Brico Ltd who (i) suffer financial hardship; or (ii) wish to study for a vocational qualification. Brian is the chairman of Brico Ltd, a company that he founded many years ago and that has employed no more than 20 people at any one time. Brian died in 2000. Brico Ltd was wound up in 2012. The trustees of the fund seek your advice as to what should happen to the trust fund.

FURTHER READING

Charity Commission, *Guidance on charitable purposes* (2013).

Dunn, 'As "Cold as Charity"? Property, Equity and the Charitable Trust' (2000) 20 LS 222.

Garton, '*National Anti-Vivisection Society v Inland Revenue Commissioners*' Landmark Cases in Equity, (eds Mitchell and Mitchell) (Oxford: Hart, 2012) 529.

Getzler, *Morice v Bishop of Durham, Landmark Cases in Equity*, (eds Mitchell and Mitchell) (Oxford: Hart, 2012) 157.

Gravells, 'Charitable Trusts and Ancillary Purposes' [1978] Conv 92.

Luxton, 'Cy-près and the Ghost of Things that Might Have Been' [1983] Conv 107.

Luxton and Evans, 'Cogent and Cohesive? Two Recent Charity Commission Decisions on the Advancement of Religion' [2011] Conv 144.

Martin, 'The Construction of Charitable Gifts' (1974) 38 Conv (NS) 187.

Walton, '*McGovern v Attorney-General*: Constraints on Judicial Assessment of Charitable Benefit' [2014] Conv 317.

For information about the Charity Commission and details of Commission publications including recent decisions, see the website: https://www.gov.uk/government/organisations/charity-commission.

6

NON-CHARITABLE PURPOSE TRUSTS

CENTRAL ISSUES

1. Non-charitable purpose trusts are generally void because there are no ascertainable beneficiaries who are able to enforce the trust.

2. Non-charitable purpose trusts will exceptionally be valid if the purpose can be regarded as directly or indirectly benefiting ascertained individuals.

3. Testamentary trusts for certain recognized purposes, such as for animals, may exceptionally be recognized as valid. In such circumstances the trustees are not obliged to carry out the trust, but can do so if they wish.

4. There are a variety of mechanisms that can be adopted to implement a non-charitable purpose, including the use of fiduciary powers and the appointment of enforcers to enforce the trust.

5. Unincorporated associations lack legal personality to be able to hold trust property, but property is often given for the association's purposes. A trust for such a non-charitable purpose will generally not be valid, but instead the property will typically be held by an officer of the association on trust for the members of the association with the terms of that trust deriving from the association's constitution. This is known as the contract-holding theory.

6. The contract-holding explanation of how property can be held for the benefit of an association's purposes is significant in determining what should happen to any surplus property on the dissolution of the association.

1. GENERAL PRINCIPLES

(a) NON-CHARITABLE PURPOSES

Non-charitable purpose trusts are generally void for two reasons: (i) the need to establish identifiable beneficiaries; and (ii) the requirement that the purpose be certain.

(i) *Need for identifiable beneficiaries*

It is a fundamental principle of the law of trusts that the objects of the trust are people rather than purposes, because there needs to be ascertained or ascertainable beneficiaries who are in a position to enforce the trust. In *Morice v Bishop of Durham*,[1] Sir William Grant MR recognized that 'there must be somebody, in whose favour the court can decree performance'.

It follows that trusts for purposes rather than persons are generally not recognized in English law because of the absence of an ascertainable beneficiary. The recognition of charitable trusts, as we saw in Chapter 5, is a significant qualification to this principle, since these are purpose trusts that are valid, but only because they are for the benefit of the public or a section of the public. Responsibility for enforcing such trusts formally lies with the Attorney-General and practically lies with the Charity Commission. But, where the purpose is not charitable, there is typically nobody who can request such a trust to be enforced.

The leading case in which a non-charitable purpose trust was held to be void is *Re Astor's Settlement Trusts*.[2] This involved a settlement to hold the shares of a company on trust for various purposes, including the maintenance of good understanding, sympathy, and cooperation between nations, and the preservation of the independence and integrity of newspapers. The trusts were not charitable, either because they did not fall within any of the relevant heads of charity or because the purposes were political and so not for the public benefit.[3] Consequently, being for non-charitable purposes, the trusts were void, since there were no identifiable beneficiaries. Roxburgh J said:[4]

> The typical case of a trust is one in which the legal owner of property is constrained by a court of equity so to deal with it as to give effect to the equitable rights of another. These equitable rights have been hammered out in the process of litigation in which a claimant on equitable grounds has successfully asserted rights against a legal owner or other person in control of property. Prima facie therefore, a trustee would not be expected to be subject to an equitable obligation unless there was somebody who could enforce a correlative equitable right, and the nature and extent of that obligation would be worked out in proceedings for enforcement...
>
> But if the purposes are not charitable, great difficulties arise both in theory and in practice. In theory, because having regard to the historical origins of equity it is difficult to visualise the growth of equitable obligations which nobody can enforce, and in practice, because it is not possible to contemplate with equanimity the creation of large funds devoted to non-charitable purposes which no court and no department of state can control, or in the case of maladministration reform....no case has been found in the reports in which the court has ever directly enforced a non-charitable purpose against a trustee. Indeed where, as in the present case, the only beneficiaries are purposes and an at present unascertainable person, it is difficult to see who could initiate such proceedings. If the purposes are valid trusts, the settlors have retained no beneficial interest and could not initiate them. It was suggested that the trustees might proceed *ex parte* to enforce the trusts against themselves. I doubt that, but at any rate nobody could enforce the trusts against them.

It follows that a trustee will not be subject to equitable obligations unless there is somebody who could enforce a correlative equitable right. In other words, there is no duty without a corresponding right, and if there is no equitable duty, there can be no valid trust.

[1] (1804) 9 Ves 399, 405.
[2] [1952] Ch 534. See also *Bowman v Secular Society Ltd* [1917] AC 406, 441 (Lord Parker).
[3] See Chapter 5.3(c)(ii)(c), pp. 201–5.
[4] [1952] Ch 534, 541.

(ii) *Certainty of purpose*

In *Re Astor's Settlement Trusts*,[5] the non-charitable purpose trust was also held to be void because the identified purposes were considered to be too uncertain. Roxburgh J said:[6]

> The second ground upon which the relevant trusts are challenged is uncertainty. If (contrary to my view) an enumeration of purposes outside the realm of charities can take the place of an enumeration of beneficiaries, the purposes must, in my judgment, be stated in phrases which embody definite concepts and the means by which the trustees are to try to attain them must also be prescribed with a sufficient degree of certainty. The test to be applied is stated by Lord Eldon in *Morice v Bishop of Durham* (1805) 10 Ves 522 at 539 as follows:
>
> > 'As it is a maxim, that the execution of a trust shall be under the control of the court, it must be of such a nature, that it can be under that control; so that the administration of it can be reviewed by the court; or, if the trustee dies, the court itself can execute the trust: a trust therefore, which, in case of maladministration could be reformed; and a due administration directed; and then, unless the subject and the objects can be ascertained, upon principles, familiar in other cases, it must be decided, that the court can neither reform maladministration, nor direct a due administration.' ...
>
> Applying this test, I find many uncertain phrases in the enumeration of purposes, for example, 'different sections of people in any nation or community' in paragraph 1 of the third schedule, 'constructive policies' in paragraph 2, 'integrity of the press' in paragraph 3, 'combines' in paragraph 5, 'the restoration...of the independence of...writers in newspapers' in paragraph 6, and 'benevolent schemes' in paragraph 7. [Counsel] suggested that in view of the unlimited discretion bestowed upon the trustees (subject only to directions from the settlors) the trustees would be justified in excluding from their purview purposes indicated by the settlors but insufficiently defined by them. But I cannot accept this argument. The purposes must be so defined that if the trustees surrendered their discretion, the court could carry out the purposes declared, not a selection of them arrived at by eliminating those which are too uncertain to be carried out...
>
> But how in any case could I decree in what manner the trusts applicable to income were to be performed? The settlement gives no guidance at all. [Counsel] suggested that the trustees might apply to the court *ex parte* for a scheme. It is not, I think, a mere coincidence that no case has been found outside the realm of charity in which the court has yet devised a scheme of ways and means for attaining enumerated trust purposes. If it were to assume this (as I think) novel jurisdiction over public but not charitable trusts it would, I believe, necessarily require the assistance of a custodian of the public interest analogous to the Attorney-General in charity cases, who would not only help to formulate schemes but could be charged with the duty of enforcing them and preventing maladministration. There is no such person. Accordingly, in my judgment, the trusts for the application of income during 'the specified period' are also void for uncertainty.
>
> But while I have reached my decision on two separate grounds, both, I think, have their origin in a single principle, namely, that a court of equity does not recognise as valid a trust which it cannot both enforce and control. This seems to me to be good equity and good sense.

Similarly, in *Morice v Bishop of Durham*,[7] a trust for 'such objects of benevolence and liberality as the Bishop of Durham in his own discretion shall most approve of' was held to be void because the objects were uncertain and so the purpose was not clearly defined. Whereas, for charitable trusts,

---

[5] Ibid.
[6] Ibid, 547.
[7] (1804) 9 Ves 399; affirmed (1805) 10 Ves 522.

once it is clear that the settlor or testator had a charitable intent, the courts will strive to resolve any uncertainty in favour of the trust's being valid,[8] such benevolent construction will not be adopted for non-charitable purpose trusts. Consequently, even if the absence of beneficiaries to enforce the trust does not result in invalidity, and as will be seen this is sometimes the case,[9] the purpose must be defined with reference to clear concepts, and the means by which the trustees are to attain the purpose must also be prescribed with a sufficient degree of certainty.

(b) CHARITABLE PURPOSES

When considering whether a purpose trust is valid, it is always important to consider first whether the purpose is charitable and valid. Such trusts are more likely to be valid because the beneficiary principle is inapplicable to them and uncertainty in the definition of the purposes will be resolved. If it is concluded that the requirements for a charitable trust are not satisfied, its non-charitable status will generally render the trust void. So, for example, in *Re Shaw's Will Trust*,[10] George Bernard Shaw's residuary estate was left to be applied for the creation of a forty-letter alphabet. This was held not to be a charitable purpose[11] and so the trust was void as a non-charitable purpose trust. Similarly, in *Re Endacott*,[12] a gift of the testator's residuary estate to a parish council to provide some useful memorial to him was not charitable due to the absence of any public benefit, even though it purported to be a 'public trust'. The trust was, therefore, void as being for a non-charitable purpose.

Although these cases would probably be decided in the same way today, it is important to acknowledge that the gradual expansion and clarification of recognized charitable purposes, as confirmed by the Charities Act 2011, means that some purposes that were once regarded as non-charitable and void will now be valid under the law of charity, as long as the public benefit test is satisfied. So, for example, trusts for adult amateur sport were once regarded as non-charitable and void, but today this is a recognized charitable purpose.[13]

(c) CRITIQUE OF THE GENERAL INVALIDITY PRINCIPLE

Although non-charitable purpose trusts have long been regarded as generally void, it is difficult to identify any convincing rationale as to why this should be the case. If the purpose is defined clearly, the only obstacle to validity is the absence of ascertainable beneficiaries to enforce the trust. But, if the trustees are willing to perform the trust, no issue of enforceability will arise. The trustees might still fail to comply with the terms of the trust and misapply the trust property, but those who are entitled to the trust property if the trust were to fail could seek to enforce the trust if they wish to do so. This was recognized by Harman J in *Re Shaw's Will Trust*:[14]

> The principle has been recently restated by Roxburgh J in *Re Astor's Settlement* Trusts [1952] Ch 534, where the authorities are elaborately reviewed. An object cannot complain to the court, which therefore cannot control the trust, and, therefore, will not allow it to continue. I must confess that

---

[8] See Chapter 5.1(a), pp. 177–8.
[9] See Chapter 6.2, pp. 289–94.
[10] [1957] 1 WLR 729.
[11] See Chapter 5.3(c)(ii)(a), p. 198.
[12] [1960] Ch 232. See Chapter 6.2(b)(iv), pp. 293–4.
[13] See Chapter 5.4(g), pp. 242–5.
[14] [1957] 1 WLR 729, 745.

I feel some reluctance to come to this conclusion. I agree at once that, if the persons to take in remainder are unascertainable, the court is deprived of any means of controlling such a trust, but if, as here, the persons taking the ultimate residue are ascertained, I do not feel the force of this objection. They are entitled to the estate except in so far as it has been devoted to the indicated purposes, and in so far as it is not devoted to those purposes, the money being spent is the money of the residuary legatees of the ultimate remaindermen, and they can come to the court and sue the executor for a *devastavit*, or the trustee for a breach of trust, and thus, though not themselves interested in the purposes, enable the court indirectly to control them. This line of reasoning is not, I think, open to me.

Alternatively the settlor or testator could provide for the appointment of a third party to enforce the trust if necessary.[15]

Hayton, 'Developing the Obligation Characteristic of the Trust' (2001) 117 LQR 96, 98

The underlying principle, it is submitted, is that for there to be a trust obligation there needs to be some person intended by the settlor to have *locus standi* to enforce the trustee's duties...What, however, if the settlor in his trust deed expressly confers *locus standi* on an enforcer interested in the furtherance of the settlor's specific non-charitable purpose trust? Take the case of a trust to further the interests of the UK Conservative Party expressed to be enforceable by the Leader from time to time of the Conservative Party, or a trust to further the purposes of a contemplative Order of nuns expressed to be enforceable by the Head of the Order from time to time, or a trust to press for the abolition of vivisection expressed to be enforceable by the Chair from time to time of the unincorporated National Anti-Vivisection Society or a trust to further the professional interests of barristers entitled to practise in the English courts expressed to be enforceable by the Chair from time to time of the Bar Council. In each case at expiry of a valid perpetuity period the capital passes to a designated person. The trust deed clearly supplies a mechanism for the positive enforcement of the trust so that the trustees are under an obligation to account to someone in whose favour the court can decree performance...Underlying and underpinning the trust obligation is the fundamental principle that just as a car needs an engine, so a trust needs an enforcer (whether the enforcer be a beneficiary or the Attorney-General or the Charity Commissioners or some person expressly appointed by the settlor to be enforcer with *locus standi* positively to enforce the trust). Is it seriously to be suggested that the English court would invoke the orthodox beneficiary principle to refuse to give effect to a foreign non-charitable purpose trust of English assets where under the foreign governing law as a result of legislation (like that of Jersey or Bermuda or the Isle of Man or the Cayman Islands or the British Virgin Islands) such a trust is valid where the trust instrument expressly provides for an enforcer? Would the English court really hold the assets to be subject to a resulting trust for the settlor? It is submitted that, because the beneficiary principle should be regarded as the 'enforcer principle', the English court would regard the foreign trust concept neither as repugnant to the English trust concept nor contrary to English public policy, the trust being one that the English court can 'both enforce and control'.[16]...it should not matter that the settlor appoints himself the first enforcer under the terms of his trust deed as the person best fitted for the enforcement task, with provision for subsequent enforcers.

---

[15] See further Chapter 6.3(d), pp. 296–9.
[16] *Re Astor's Statement Trusts* [1952] Ch 534, 549 (Roxburgh J).

Matthews[17] has, however, argued that the beneficiary principle is not simply dependent on the beneficiaries being in a position to enforce the trust. Rather, it is the fact that the beneficiary has a proprietary right and the trustee owes him or her duties that is significant. He has said:[18]

a trust requires a beneficiary. But...the other side of this rule is the idea that the beneficiary, being the owner in equity of the trust property, may require the legal owner to convey to him or at his direction.

If this is correct, it follows that a third party enforcer of the trust who does not have a proprietary interest in trust property would not satisfy the beneficiary principle because he or she cannot require the property to be conveyed to him or her. But a third party enforcer of a non-charitable purpose trust who is not beneficially entitled to the trust property can still be regarded as having a sufficient proprietary interest in the trust property to enforce it, since he or she would be able to trace the property into the hands of a third party if it had been misappropriated and claim it, albeit not for his or her own benefit, but instead to return the property to the trust for use for the identified purpose. This has been recognized by Hayton:[19]

Such tracing process will therefore be available if trustees of a non-charitable purpose trust are regarded as legal and beneficial owners of the trust property, subject to fiduciary and equitable obligations enforceable by the enforcer designated as such in the trust instrument. Moreover, in such cases...the trust property and its traceable product is not available for claims of the trustee's private creditors, *e.g.* on the insolvency of the trustee.

Sufficient proprietary aspects therefore arise in relation to non-charitable purpose trusts to justify their existence as enforceable trusts where an enforcer is expressly appointed in the English or foreign trust instrument. The basis of the trust is the unilateral transfer of assets by a settlor to a person voluntarily undertaking the office of trustee with the benefits and burdens attaching to such office...It should make no difference whether the burdens are enforceable by the beneficiaries or by the Attorney-General or the Charity Commissioners or by the designated enforcer.

2. EXCEPTIONAL CIRCUMSTANCES IN WHICH NON-CHARITABLE PURPOSE TRUSTS ARE VALID

There are two exceptional categories of case in which non-charitable purpose trusts have been recognized as valid.

(a) DIRECT OR INDIRECT BENEFIT TO INDIVIDUALS

A trust that appears to be for non-charitable purposes might be valid as a trust for persons if the purpose can be regarded as directly or indirectly benefiting ascertained individuals. Although these individuals will not have a proprietary interest in the trust property, the benefit that they obtain from the purpose means that they, in practice, are interested in what happens to the trust property, so

---

[17] 'The New Trust: Obligations Without Rights?', in *Trends in Contemporary Trust Law* (ed. Oakley) (Oxford: Clarendon Press, 1996), ch. 1, p. 3.

[18] Ibid, p. 4.

[19] 'Developing the Obligation Characteristic of the Trust' (2001) 117 LQR 96, 102.

that they have *locus standi* to enforce the trust if necessary. This was recognized in *Re Denley's Trust Deed*.[20] In that case, trustees held land as a sports ground for the use and enjoyment of employees of a particular company for twenty-one years[21] from the death of the last survivor of a group of named individuals. The trustees also had the power to allow the facilities to be used by other people. It was held that, although the trust was expressed as a purpose, namely use and enjoyment, it directly or indirectly benefited individuals and so was valid, since such a trust did not fall within the mischief of the beneficiary principle. Goff J said:[22]

> I think there may be a purpose or object trust, the carrying out of which would benefit an individual or individuals, where that benefit is so indirect or intangible or which is otherwise so framed as not to give those persons any *locus standi* to apply to the court to enforce the trust, in which case the beneficiary principle would, as it seems to me, apply to invalidate the trust, quite apart from any question of uncertainty or perpetuity. Such cases can be considered if and when they arise. The present is not, in my judgment, of that character, and it will be seen that…the trust deed expressly states that, subject to any rules and regulations made by the trustees, the employees of the company shall be entitled to the use and enjoyment of the land. Apart from this possible exception, in my judgment the beneficiary principle…is confined to purpose or object trusts which are abstract or impersonal. The objection is not that the trust is for a purpose or object per se, but that there is no beneficiary…Where, then, the trust, though expressed as a purpose, is directly or indirectly for the benefit of an individual or individuals, it seems to me that it is in general outside the mischief of the beneficiary principle.

The observation that the trust would not have been valid had the purpose been abstract or impersonal would be relevant where, for example, the purpose had been to seek a change in the law, such as the abolition of vivisection, which had no direct or indirect benefit for particular people.

If the facts of *Re Denley* were to arise today, the trust might potentially be regarded as valid as a charitable trust, since the purpose was for the advancement of sport.[23] But the validity of this trust in the law of charity would turn on whether the public benefit test was satisfied, and this might be difficult to establish because most of those who benefited from the purpose were the employees of the same company, so that there was a personal nexus.[24] The fact, however, that the trustees had a discretion to allow people other than employees to use the facilities might have been sufficient to render the trust charitable. But, if the purpose trust is not charitable, the *Denley* principle may enable the trust to be treated as valid, although, even though *Re Denley* has been cited subsequently,[25] it has never been specifically relied on to uphold a non-charitable purpose trust.

(b) TESTAMENTARY TRUSTS OF AN IMPERFECT OBLIGATION

There are some exceptional cases in which non-charitable purpose trusts created by wills have been recognized as valid. The nature of such a trust has been summarized by Brown:[26]

---

[20] [1969] 1 Ch 373.

[21] So that the trust did not infringe the perpetuity rule. See Chapter 6.2(b), p. 291.

[22] [1969] 1 Ch 373, 383.

[23] See Chapter 5.4(g), pp. 242–5.

[24] See *Oppenheim v Tobacco Securities Trust Co. Ltd* [1951] AC 297, discussed in Chapter 5.4(b)(ii)(a), pp. 215–17.

[25] See e.g. *Re Lipinski's Will Trust* [1976] Ch 235, 248, where Oliver J considered *Re Denley* to accord with 'authority and common sense'.

[26] 'What are We to Do with Testamentary Trusts of Imperfect Obligation?' [2007] Conv 148, 157.

> If properly established within one of the relevant exceptions, such a trust is, by its nature, an imperfect obligation trust. Prima facie the trustee cannot be compelled to perform the same as there is no one in whose favour the court can decree performance. Conversely, the trustee cannot be prevented from performing the trust and will be able to make unimpeachable use of the money in applying it for one of the accepted purposes.

These trusts are difficult to justify, save as being concessions to human weakness or sentiment.[27]

The imperfect nature of the obligation was recognized in *Trimmer v Danby*,[28] where the testator had left money to erect a monument in his memory in St Paul's Cathedral. In upholding the bequest Kindersley V-C said:[29]

> I do not suppose that there would be anyone who could compel the executors to carry out this bequest and raise the monument; but if the residuary legatees or the trustees insist upon the trust being executed, my opinion is that this Court is bound to see it carried out. I think, therefore, that as the trustees insist upon the sum... being laid out according to the directions in the will, that sum must be set apart for the purpose.

Such trusts are consequently preferably analysed as powers rather than obligations.

A testamentary trust of an imperfect obligation must fall within one of the recognized categories of case in which such trusts have been treated as valid and must comply with that part of the perpetuity rule, known as the 'rule against inalienability',[30] which operates in this context to ensure that property is not bound up for non-charitable purposes indefinitely. Although the Perpetuities and Accumulations Act 2009 has reformed the law on perpetuity,[31] that Act is concerned with the remoteness of vesting of equitable interests in trust property. Since non-charitable purpose trusts do not involve the vesting of equitable interests in people, the 2009 Act expressly does not 'affect the rule of law which limits the duration of non-charitable purpose trusts'.[32] Consequently, the common law rule on the duration of such trusts still applies, namely that a trust cannot continue for longer than the life of an identified person or persons in being plus twenty-one years. If no person is identified, the trust should last for only twenty-one years.[33] If the trust might last for a longer period, it will be void from the outset,[34] save where the court is willing to construe it as lasting for no longer than the perpetuity period. In fact, no English case has upheld a non-charitable purpose trust for more than twenty-one years.[35]

(i) *Trusts for a particular animal*

A trust for the welfare of animals will be a valid charitable trust,[36] but a trust for the care of a single animal will not be charitable, presumably because the public benefit requirement will not have been satisfied since the only benefit is to the animal's owner. But such a trust will be valid even though it is for a non-charitable purpose, as long as it complies with the perpetuity rule. So, for example, in *Re*

---

[27] *Re Astor's Settlement Trusts* [1952] Ch 534, 547 (Roxburgh J).
[28] (1856) LJ Ch 424.
[29] Ibid, 417.
[30] Dawson, 'The Rule Against Inalienability—A Rule Without a Purpose' (2006) LS 414.
[31] See Chapter 3.7(a), pp. 113–16.
[32] Perpetuities and Accumulations Act 2009, s. 18.
[33] *Re Hooper* [1932] 1 Ch 38.
[34] The 'wait and see' rule under the Perpetuities and Accumulations Act 2009, s. 7, will not apply. See Chapter 3.7, p. 115.
[35] *Re Khoo Cheng Teow* [1932] Straits Settlement Reports 226.
[36] See Chapter 5.4(k), pp. 251–3.

Dean,[37] a trust for the maintenance of the testator's horses and hounds for fifty years if they lived that long was held to be valid. North J said: [38]

> The first question is as to the validity of the provision made by the testator in favour of his horses and dogs. It is said that it is not valid; because (for this is the principal ground upon which it is put) neither a horse nor a dog could enforce the trust; and there is no person who could enforce it. It is obviously not a charity, because it is intended for the benefit of the particular animals mentioned and not for the benefit of animals generally... In my opinion this provision for the particular horses and hounds referred to in the will is not, in any sense, a charity, ...
>
> Then it is said, that there is no *cestui que trust* who can enforce the trust, and that the Court will not recognise a trust unless it is capable of being enforced by some one. I do not assent to that view...
>
> Is there then anything illegal or obnoxious to the law in the nature of the provision, that is, in the fact that it is not for human beings, but for horses and dogs? It is clearly settled by authority that a charity may be established for the benefit of horses and dogs, and, therefore, the making of a provision for horses and dogs, which is not a charity, cannot of itself be obnoxious to the law, provided, of course, that it is not to last for too long a period.

Although the trust was held to be valid, it appears to have infringed the perpetuity rule, being for fifty years and without reference to the life of a specified person. The court may, however, have assumed that the horses and hounds would not have lived for longer than twenty-one years and so the trust could be declared valid. Certainly, the animals could not be used as lives in being for the purposes of the perpetuity rule: as Meredith J said in *Re Kelly*,[39] 'There can be no doubt that "lives" means lives of human beings, not animals or trees in California.'

(ii) *Trusts to erect and maintain monuments and graves*

Trusts for the erection or maintenance of tombs or monuments have long been regarded as valid, even though they are not charitable, because of the absence of any public benefit,[40] provided that they satisfy the perpetuity rule.

In *Mussett v Bingle*,[41] it was held that a testamentary bequest to erect a monument for the first husband of the testator's wife was valid since, as Hall V-C recognized, the executors 'were ready to perform, and it must be performed accordingly'. A further bequest to maintain the monument was held to be void for perpetuity. In *Re Hooper*,[42] a trust for the care and upkeep of family graves and monuments was held to be valid for twenty-one years only. After that period, it was held that any surplus money should be given to whoever was entitled to the residue of the estate.

(iii) *Trusts for the saying of private masses*

Trusts for the saying of masses that the public are entitled to attend will be charitable.[43] A trust for the saying of masses in private will not satisfy the public benefit requirement to be charitable, but will be valid as a non-charitable purpose trust if the perpetuity rule is not infringed.[44]

---

[37] (1889) 41 Ch D 552.
[38] Ibid, 556.
[39] [1932] IR 255, 260–1.
[40] *Trimmer v Danby* (1856) 25 LJ Ch 424; *Mussett v Bingle* [1876] WN 170.
[41] [1876] WN 170.
[42] [1932] 1 Ch 38.
[43] See Chapter 5.4(c)(ii), pp. 231–5.
[44] *Re Endacott* [1960] Ch 232, 246 (Lord Evershed MR).

(iv) *Trusts for other purposes*

In *Re Endacott*,[45] it was recognized by the Court of Appeal that these anomalous cases in which testamentary purpose trusts have been recognized should not be extended. The testator had left his estate to a parish council to provide 'some useful memorial' to himself. This was construed to be a trust for a non-charitable purpose that was not valid, even though it might be regarded as analogous to trusts to erect and maintain monuments and graves. Lord Evershed MR said:[46]

> I am prepared to accept, for the purposes of the argument, that it does not matter that the trusts here are attached to residue and not to a legacy; that is to say, it does not matter that the persons who would come to the court and either complain if the trusts were not being carried out, or claim the money on the footing that they had not been carried out, are next-of-kin rather than residuary legatees. Still, in my judgment, the scope of these cases . . . ought not to be extended. So to do would be to validate almost limitless heads of non-charitable trusts, even though they were not (strictly speaking) public trusts, so long only as the question of perpetuities did not arise; and, in my judgment, that result would be out of harmony with the principles of our law. No principle perhaps has greater sanction of authority behind it than the general proposition that a trust by English law, not being a charitable trust, in order to be effective, must have ascertained or ascertainable beneficiaries. These cases constitute an exception to that general rule. The general rule, having such authority as that of Lord Eldon, Lord Parker and my predecessor, Lord Greene MR, behind it, was most recently referred to in the Privy Council in *Leahy v A-G for New South Wales* [1959] AC 457.

Harman LJ said:[47]

> I cannot think that charity has anything to do with this bequest. As for establishing it without the crutch of charity, I applaud the orthodox sentiments expressed by Roxburgh J in the *Astor* case [1952] Ch 534, and I think, as I think he did, that though one knows there have been decisions at times which are not really to be satisfactorily classified, but are perhaps merely occasions when Homer has nodded, at any rate these cases stand by themselves and ought not to be increased in number, nor indeed followed, except where the one is exactly like another. Whether it would be better that some authority now should say those cases were wrong, this perhaps is not the moment to consider. At any rate, I cannot think a case of this kind, the case of providing outside a church an unspecified and unidentified memorial, is the kind of instance which should be allowed to add to those troublesome, anomalous and aberrant cases.

Reasoning by analogy, which has proved to be so significant to the development of the law of charity,[48] therefore, appears to be unavailable when considering the validity of non-charitable purpose trusts.

There have, however, been other testamentary dispositions that have been held to be valid even though they involve non-charitable purposes. So, for example, in *Re Thompson*,[49] a legacy to promote and further fox hunting was upheld as valid. Crucially this was on the basis that the recipient of the legacy had given an undertaking 'to apply the legacy when received by him towards the object expressed in the testator's will . . . and that, in case the legacy should be applied by him otherwise than towards the promotion and furthering of fox-hunting, the residuary legatees are to be at liberty to apply.' Although this was a gift rather than a trust, the requirement of the legatee giving an undertaking as to the use of the money is significant. Such undertakings by trustees could also be given in situations outside the recognized cases of testamentary trusts of imperfect obligation, such as in the circumstances of *Re Endacott*. There is consequently no reason why the recognition of such testamentary trusts of an imperfect obligation

---

[45] Ibid.
[46] Ibid, 246.
[47] Ibid, 250.
[48] See Chapter 5.3(a), pp. 187–8.
[49] [1934] Ch 342.

should be limited to these exceptional cases; any non-charitable purpose in a testamentary trust should be valid if the appropriate undertaking is given, the trust satisfies the perpetuity rule and the purpose is sufficiently certain. If the trustee does not give an undertaking to apply the fund for the non-charitable purpose, the fund should be held on resulting trust for those entitled to the testator's residuary estate.

3. OTHER MECHANISMS FOR IMPLEMENTING NON-CHARITABLE PURPOSES

There are a variety of different mechanisms that can be employed to implement a non-charitable purpose, most of which can be used without resorting to the use of a trust.

(a) FIDUCIARY POWER FOR NON-CHARITABLE PURPOSES

It is a fundamental principle that a valid power cannot be 'spelt out of an invalid trust',[50] so that what purports to be a non-charitable purpose trust cannot usually be treated as a power that the trustee may, rather than must, exercise for the non-charitable purpose,[51] save for the exceptional cases where a trust of an imperfect obligation has been recognized. In *Re Shaw*,[52] Harman J said:

> I should have wished to regard this bequest as a gift to the ultimate residuary legatees subject to a condition by which they cannot complain of income during the first 21 years after the testator's death being devoted to the alphabet project. This apparently might be the way in which the matter would be viewed in the United States, for I find in Morris and Leach's work on the Rule against Perpetuities (1956), at p. 308, the following passage quoted from the American Law Institute's Restatement of Trusts.
>
> > 'Where the owner of property transfers it upon an intended trust for a specific non-charitable purpose, and there is no definite or definitely ascertainable beneficiary designated, no trust is created; but the transferee has power to apply the property to the designated purpose, unless he is authorized so to apply the property beyond the period of the rule against perpetuities, or the purpose is capricious.'
>
> As the authors point out, this is to treat a trust of this sort as a power, for clearly there is no one who can directly enforce the trust, and if the trustees choose to pay the whole moneys to the residuary legatees, no one can complain. All that can be done is to control the trustees indirectly in the exercise of their power. In my judgment, I am not at liberty to validate this trust, by treating it as a power. (See per Jenkins LJ in *Sunnylands* case . . . [1955] Ch 20 at 36: 'We do not think that a valid power is to be spelt out of an invalid trust'. . .).

But it can still follow that it is possible to create a valid trust subject to a power for an identified non-charitable purpose to be used only within the perpetuity period. The trustee would not be required to exercise the power and, if he or she did so, this would not be a breach of trust. Since such a power need not be exercised, it might be considered not to be necessary to identify beneficiaries who could enforce it. But trustees are still required to consider the exercise of the power[53] and might exercise the power improperly, so the preferable view is that a fiduciary power to allow the property to be applied by a trustee for a non-charitable purpose would still be caught by the beneficiary principle and could be valid only if it were to fall within one of the recognized exceptions to that principle.

---

[50] *IRC v Broadway Cottages Trust* [1955] Ch 20, 36 (Jenkins LJ). See Chapter 2.6(h), pp. 51–5.
[51] *Re Endacott* [1960] Ch 232, 246 (Lord Evershed MR).
[52] [1957] 1 WLR 729, 746.
[53] See Chapter 13.2(a)(ii), p. 631.

(b) POWER ATTACHED TO GIFT WITH GIFT-OVER

A non-charitable purpose might be achieved by giving property to a person subject to a power that it should be used for a non-charitable purpose, failing which a gift-over would take effect. The donee would not be obliged to use the property for that purpose, but if he or she were to fail to do so, the gift would lapse and the gift-over would apply. This has been recognized as effective as regards charities, perhaps because of the general 'benevolence' towards charities.[54] Where a gift is made to a charity, subject to a condition that the charity perform a non-charitable purpose and with a gift-over to another charity if the condition is not fulfilled, the gift will not be caught by the perpetuity rule that generally applies to non-charitable purposes.[55] So, for example, in *Re Tyler*,[56] the testator left money to a charity, the London Missionary Society. He also committed to the care of the trustees of the charity the keys of his family vault to keep it in good repair; if the Society were to fail to so keep it, the money was to be transferred to a charitable hospital. Even though the gift had been made to a charity, the upkeep of the family vault was not a charitable purpose. It was held that both the gift and the gift-over were valid and were not caught by the perpetuity rule. Fry LJ said:[57]

> In this case the testator has given a sum of money to one charity with a gift over to another charity upon the happening of a certain event. That event, no doubt, is such as to create an inducement or motive on the part of the first donee, the London Missionary Society, to repair the family tomb of the testator. Inasmuch as both the donees of this fund, the first donee and the second, are charitable bodies, and are created for the purposes of charity, the rule of law against perpetuities has nothing whatever to do with the donees. Does the rule of law against perpetuities create any objection to the nature of the condition? If the testator had required the first donee, the London Missionary Society, to apply any portions of the fund towards the repair of the family tomb, that would, in all probability, at any rate, to the extent of the sum required, have been void as a perpetuity which was not charity. But he has done nothing of the sort. He has given the first donee no power to apply any part of the money. He has only created a condition that the sum shall go over to Christ's Hospital if the London Missionary Society do not keep the tomb in repair. Keeping the tomb in repair is not an illegal object. If it were, the condition tending to bring about an illegal act would itself be illegal; but to repair the tomb is a perfectly lawful thing. All that can be said is that it is not lawful to tie up property for that purpose. But the rule of law against perpetuities applies to property, not motives; and I know of no rule which says that you may not try to enforce a condition creating a perpetual inducement to do a thing which is lawful. That is this case.

This might be justified because the condition attached to the gift was not considered to have created an obligation on the part of the trustees to maintain the vault. Had there been such an obligation, this would have been a testamentary trust of an imperfect obligation,[58] but it would have been valid only had the perpetuity rule been satisfied. In *Re Tyler*, the charity was considered to have a power to use the fund to maintain the vault if it wished to do so, rather than to be under a duty to do so, and this was not caught by the perpetuity rule because, as Fry LJ recognized, that rule applies to property and not to motives. Where, however, a gift has been made to a charity, subject to a duty to apply the property for a non-charitable purpose, this has been held to be void, even though provision was made for the property to be transferred to another charity if the condition was not satisfied. For example, in *Re Dalziel*,[59]

---

[54] See Chapter 5.1(a), pp. 177–8.
[55] Perpetuities and Accumulations Act 2009, s. 2(3).
[56] [1891] 3 Ch 252.
[57] Ibid, 259.
[58] See Chapter 6.2(b), pp. 290–4.
[59] [1943] Ch 277.

the testatrix had left a sum of money to a hospital on condition that the income should be used for the repair of her family mausoleum, with a gift-over to another charity on the same conditions if the hospital were to fail to so repair it, but that gift-over was subject to the same conditions. It was held that the testatrix had purported to impose a duty on the hospital to maintain the mausoleum, and that this and the gift-over were void as being contrary to the perpetuity rule.

(c) MANDATE OR AGENCY

It has been recognized that a gift can be transferred to a donee who is appointed as agent for the donor and with authority to apply the gift for a non-charitable purpose.[60] If the agent were to misapply the gift, he or she would be liable for breach of fiduciary duty.[61] If he or she were to fail to apply the gift as he or she was mandated to, it would be returned to the donor except where it was agreed that the money was no longer recoverable.

(d) APPOINTMENT OF AN ENFORCER

To attract trust business a number of overseas jurisdictions have enacted statutes that provide for the possibility of creating non-charitable purpose trusts.[62] Such statutory provision is particularly important for international trust planning and business. The use of non-charitable purpose trusts is significant because, since there are no beneficiaries with equitable proprietary interests, it is possible to structure transactions and companies without needing to identify anybody who has beneficial ownership, which has the advantage of avoiding the imposition of tax liability on beneficiaries and protecting assets from creditors. For such purpose trusts to be valid, they require an enforcement mechanism, which usually involves the appointment of a person, typically known as the 'enforcer' or 'protector', to enforce the trust by application to the court if the purpose is not being carried out.[63]

Matthews in *Trends in Contemporary Trust Law* (ed. Oakley) (Oxford: Clarendon Press, 1996), p. 19

The characteristic of the true non-charitable purpose trust is that it has no beneficiaries. This means that the beneficial ownership is not in the trustees—it is after all a trust, not for their benefit—and there is no one else in whom it can be located. So—it is said—the property the subject of the trust cannot, in strict law, be said to belong beneficially to anyone. Now there are many estate-planning exercises and commercial transactions that can make good use of this phenomenon....

A curiosity is that non-charitable-purpose trust legislation in general has not purported to answer explicitly the question where the 'beneficial' ownership of the trust property lies.

But—safety in numbers—it has tended to follow a certain model. There are five main features, although it must be emphasized that not every example of such legislation makes provision for each of these features.

---

[60] *Conservative and Unionist Central Office v Burrell* [1982] 1 WLR 522.
[61] See Chapter 14, 'Fiduciary Obligations'.
[62] For example, Bermuda, British Virgin Islands, Cayman Islands, Cyprus, Isle of Man, and Jersey.
[63] See Chapter 3.6, pp. 110–12.

The five features are as follows:

1. Restrictions on the purposes for which the trust can be established; typically the legislation says that the purposes must be both workable, i.e. specific or certain and possible to carry out, and beneficial, i.e. not immoral or contrary to public policy.

2. Enforcement mechanism: typically there must be a person whose job it is to keep an eye on the trust and to enforce it. For this purpose he will have rights to information about the trust. He may be called the 'enforcer' or the 'protector', or something else, but he will have certain obligations to blow the whistle, apply to the Court, or notify an official (typically the Attorney-General) if he thinks something wrong is going on, or if there is no enforcer in office. Sometimes these duties are backed up by criminal sanctions.[64]

3. Restrictions on the trustees: it is common to provide that at least one of the trustees must be resident in the jurisdiction concerned, and/or must be a professionally qualified person or body, for example a lawyer or accountant. Also, usually a trustee may not be the enforcer.

4. Restrictions on the trust property: often such trusts are not allowed to own land in the jurisdiction concerned.

5. Duration and termination of the trust: most of the jurisdictions have perpetuity periods or maximum duration periods, and provision for what is to happen to the property at the determination of the trust...

We must see trusts—and the purpose trust in particular—in this light. It is a product, serving a commercial need. To some extent, like all law and legal institutions, it is a conjuring trick. It is a way of making another legal institution—ownership—disappear, or half-disappear. First it is refracted into legal ownership and beneficial enjoyment, and then beneficial enjoyment seems to dissolve into thin air.

There is nothing wrong in any of this, provided that we understand what we are doing, and that we are doing it deliberately. Unlike the laws of physics, the laws of man are fully mutable. But what we must not do—and we are in danger of doing it—is to misunderstand and to misuse a doctrine, to think we have achieved an object when we have not. The statutory purpose trust is, or can be, a good thing. But it is not the entirely autonomous vehicle that its promoters think. It is not the Holy Grail. There are obligations—no one doubts that—but also there are rights. If the trust has background beneficiaries, like *Re Denley*[65] then they have rights. If the trust is a sham, then again there will be real beneficiaries, able to exercise rights and—more seriously—saddled with the beneficial ownership. Even if—and it is a big if—it is a genuine, substantive purpose statutory non-charitable-purpose trust, the enforcer has rights. If there is a trust, there is a benefit. And, like the *damnosa hereditas* of the classical Roman law, the question can still be asked, to whom does it belong in the end?

If this enforcer mechanism were to be recognized in England and Wales, it would enable non-charitable purpose trusts to be treated as generally valid, since the existence of the enforcer would ensure that the trust is performed properly.

Pawlowski and Summers, 'Private purpose trusts: a reform proposal'
[2007] Conv 440, 452

An obvious way forward is the enactment of legislation validating private purpose trusts under English law. The key features of the new law should, it is submitted, comprise the following:

---

[64] See generally Waters in *Trends in Contemporary Trust Law* (ed. Oakley) (Oxford: Oxford University Press, 1996), pp. 63–122.

[65] [1969] 1 Ch 373; see Chapter 6.2(a), p. 290.

(a) Type of trust instrument

The new legislation should permit the purpose trust to be created by an *inter vivos* trust deed or by will. To avoid any difficulties in the latter case, there should be no requirement that the enforcer must be a party to the trust instrument creating the purpose trust.

(b) Definition of purpose trust

. . . the settlor/testator [should be given] the opportunity to choose a specific trust to be subject to the new legislation. The chosen trust vehicle would have to be stated within the trust instrument. This would also force the settlor/testator to consider carefully the type of trust being created.

(c) Perpetuity period

There does not appear to be any reason for a non-charitable purpose trust to be exempted from the rule against perpetuities. The new legislation could, therefore, provide for the usual . . . perpetuity period to apply to purpose trusts, but with no restriction on the accumulation of income during the trust period.

(d) Determination events

The idea of a non-charitable purpose trust being required to have a specified determination event appears sensible. The perpetuity period of 80 years is a long stop. The earlier determination should be when the purpose has been fulfilled, or if the enforcer determines that the purpose is no longer possible. This requires that the enforcer be independent of the trustees and default beneficiaries to avoid conflicts of interest.

(e) Purpose

The purpose should not be contrary to public policy, should be certain and not conflict with any existing law. An obligation could be imposed on the enforcer to satisfy himself that the purpose is legitimate— if, for example, the purpose becomes impossible to fulfil, this would be a determination event triggering the default trust provisions.

(f) Default beneficiaries

The trust instrument would have to specify how the trust assets are to be distributed on determination or at the end of the trust period . . . At the end of the trust period or on determination, it should not be possible to pass the assets into a new trust, unless it is a charitable trust that is exempt from the rule against perpetuities.

(g) Disclosure

Should the default beneficiaries be informed of their interest under the trust, so as to ensure they can enforce their rights? Some jurisdictions have taken the view that, as long as an enforcer has been appointed, there should be no reason to force disclosure onto the default beneficiaries. However, the default beneficiaries would have the right, under English law, to see trust documentation and accounts even before they were entitled to benefit. It would, therefore, seem sensible to have an obligation to inform all beneficiaries of the existence of the trust and their potential interests. The law in this area is not, however, clear, and it is hard to see why trustees of a purpose trust should have an obligation to inform beneficiaries of their rights, if trustees of non-purpose trusts do not have the same obligation . . .

(h) Enforcer

The Bermudian concept of allowing anyone with an interest to act as enforcer is attractive, but this could lead to no one acting as enforcer. An independent person (an individual rather than a company) should, it is submitted, be appointed as the enforcer. The enforcer must not be in a position of conflict and must, therefore, be independent of the trustees and beneficiaries.

Ideally, the enforcer should be appointed in the initial trust instrument. If not, there must be a mechanism in the trust instrument for the enforcer to be appointed, say by the settlor during his lifetime or by the trustees under his will. The enforcer should have a power to appoint a replacement, again with the trustees being required to appoint a new enforcer if there ceases to be an enforcer in place at any time or for any reason. As with most jurisdictions, there should be penalties to ensure that the trustees act to appoint an enforcer.

The role of the enforcer should be clearly defined as a fiduciary as opposed to personal) obligation. The court would, therefore, have the power to remove an enforcer in the event of a breach of fiduciary duty, or if the enforcer becomes incapable of fulfilling the role, in the same way as the courts can remove or appoint trustees under the Trustee Act 1925. An application to the courts could, therefore, be made if the enforcer loses capacity, becomes bankrupt, or is sentenced to prison, but it may be more practical for the enforcer to be deemed to retire automatically upon any such event occurring. The trustees would then be required to appoint a new enforcer if there is no replacement enforcer.

(i) *Trustees*

Many jurisdictions state that only designated trustees can be appointed as trustees for a purpose trust. The main difficulty with this is that in England there is no registration or licensing of trustees. This contrasts sharply with offshore jurisdictions where licensing of trustees is now commonplace. Instead, the new legislation could follow the Trustee Act 1925 approach—the purpose trust must have as trustee a trust corporation or two trustees (this could be one company and one individual). An unfit individual (e.g. a bankrupt or person of unsound mind) would not be able to act as trustee.

Hayton[66] has argued that the sort of legislation envisaged by Pawlowski and Summers is unnecessary, on the basis that the law already allows any settlor to identify expressly a person with *locus standi* to enforce the trustee's duties, which has the practical effect of allowing non-charitable purpose trusts to be treated as valid by ensuring that the beneficiary principle is satisfied. But this goes too far. The traditional attitude of the English authorities, at the very least, requires the beneficiary to be in a position to enforce the trust, save for those exceptional circumstances under which a non-charitable purpose trust is recognized. If non-charitable purpose trusts are to be expanded beyond this, legislation is required to ensure that the ambit of the trust is clearly defined, and the powers and responsibilities of the protector clearly identified.

4. UNINCORPORATED ASSOCIATIONS

The fact that trusts for non-charitable purposes are generally not valid, causes particular problems when property is transferred to an unincorporated association, which is essentially a non-commercial club or society. Such associations, unlike incorporated associations,[67] lack legal personality and so cannot own property. Yet gifts of property are regularly made to unincorporated associations and they often are colloquially considered to 'own' property, such as sports grounds. This is not possible at Law, but Equity can explain how such property can be owned and managed, by means of the trust. But, since unincorporated associations exist for purposes and because non-charitable purpose trusts are generally not valid, the trust solution may not be available.[68] Nevertheless, Equity can explain how property can be held for the purposes of unincorporated associations, although the analysis is complex and contract has a significant role to play as well. This question of property-holding is not only of theoretical significance. It can also be of real practical importance, especially when the

---

[66] 'Developing the Obligation Characteristic of the Trust' (2001) 117 LQR 96, 98.
[67] *Salomon v Salomon & Co. Ltd* [1897] AC 22.
[68] See generally *Leahy v A-G for New South Wales* [1959] AC 457, 479.

unincorporated association is dissolved, for how the property has been held will affect who is entitled to receive the property on dissolution.

(a) THE DEFINITION OF UNINCORPORATED ASSOCIATIONS

An unincorporated association was defined by Lawton LJ in *Conservative and Unionist Central Office v Burrell*[69] as:

> two or more persons bound together for one or more common purposes, not being business purposes, by mutual undertakings each having mutual duties and obligations, in an organisation which has rules which identify in whom control of it and its funds rests and on what terms and which can be joined or left at will. The bond of union between the members of an unincorporated association has to be contractual.

The key elements of this definition are that the association must be non-profit-making and that it is 'an association of persons bound together by identifiable rules and having an identifiable membership'.[70] These rules typically take the form of a constitution. A good example of an unincorporated association is an amateur football club, which is not a business and which will typically have its own constitution. In *Burrell* itself, it was held that the Conservative Party was not an unincorporated association because it consisted of a number of different components, namely local constituency parties, parliamentary parties, and Central Office, which were not contractually bound together as one association by a single constitution.

(b) PROPERTY-HOLDING FOR UNINCORPORATED ASSOCIATIONS

There are a number of different explanations as to how property can be held for the benefit of an unincorporated association. In *Neville Estates Ltd v Madden*,[71] various constructions of gifts to unincorporated associations were considered. Cross J said:[72]

> The question of the construction and effect of gifts to or in trust for unincorporated associations was recently considered by the Privy Council in *Leahy v A-G for New South Wales* [1959] AC 457.[73] The position, as I understand it, is as follows. Such a gift may take effect in one or other of three quite different ways. In the first place, it may, on its true construction, be a gift to the members of the association at the relevant date as joint tenants, so that any member can sever his share and claim it whether or not he continues to be a member of the association. Secondly, it may be a gift to the existing members not as joint tenants, but subject to their respective contractual rights and liabilities towards one another as members of the association. In such a case a member cannot sever his share. It will accrue to the other members on his death or resignation, even though such members include persons who became members after the gift took effect. If this is the effect of the gift, it will not be open to objection on the score of perpetuity or uncertainty unless there is something in its terms or circumstances or in the rules of the association which precludes the members at any given time from dividing the subject of the gift between them on the footing that they are solely entitled to it in equity.

---

[69] [1982] 1 WLR 522, 525.
[70] *Re Koeppler's Will Trust* [1986] Ch 423, 431 (Slade LJ).
[71] [1962] Ch 832.
[72] Ibid, 849.
[73] See Chapter 6.4(b)(ii), pp. 301–3.

Thirdly, the terms or circumstances of the gift or the rules of the association may show that the property in question is not to be at the disposal of the members for the time being, but is to be held in trust for or applied for the purposes of the association as a quasi-corporate entity. In this case the gift will fail unless the association is a charitable body. If the gift is of the second class, i.e., one which the members of the association for the time being are entitled to divide among themselves, then, even if the objects of the association are in themselves charitable, the gift would not, I think, be a charitable gift. If, for example, a number of persons formed themselves into an association with a charitable object—say the relief of poverty in some district—but it was part of the contract between them that, if a majority of the members so desired, the association should be dissolved and its property divided between the members at the date of dissolution, a gift to the association as part of its general funds would not, I conceive, be a charitable gift.

A particular method of property-holding might be expressly chosen by the transferor of property, but usually no method has been chosen and it is necessary to construe carefully the nature and circumstances of the transaction to determine which one is applicable on the facts. In practice, in cases of doubt, judges have a tendency to adopt the mechanism that is most likely to validate the transfer of property.

In most cases in which property is transferred to an unincorporated association, it will be vested in the treasurer or other officers of the association. Typically, the transferor will not intend the officers to receive the property beneficially, but will intend it to be used for the benefit of the association. The key question is whether this is for the benefit of the association's purposes or members and, if for the members, whether it is for the benefit of present or future members.

Five distinct methods of property-holding relating to unincorporated associations can be identified: (i) charitable trust; (ii) non-charitable purpose trust; (iii) for members at the time of the transfer; (iv) on trust for present and future members; and (v) for members subject to their existing contractual rights.

(i) *Charitable trust*

Property that is to be used for the benefit of the unincorporated association could be held on a charitable purpose trust, but only if there is a recognized charitable purpose and if the trust is for the public benefit.[74] With the recognition of the advancement of amateur sport as a distinct charitable purpose, it will be easier to treat property transferred to sports clubs as being held on trust for the charitable purposes of that club. But, as Cross J recognized in *Neville Estates Ltd v Madden*, if the association has a rule that, on dissolution, the property will be divided between the members themselves, this will negate the charitable purpose, because this will defeat the application of the cy-près doctrine.[75]

(ii) *Non-charitable purpose trust*

Unincorporated associations were once considered to be an exception to the general principle that non-charitable purpose trusts are void, but this exception was rejected by the Privy Council in *Leahy v Attorney-General for New South Wales*.[76] In that case, the testator left his property to be held on trust for an order of nuns, which was an unincorporated association. This was held to be void as a non-charitable purpose trust. Viscount Simonds said:[77]

In law a gift to [an unincorporated association] (i.e., where, to use the words of Lord Parker in *Bowman v Secular Society Ltd* [1917] AC 406 at 437, neither the circumstances of the gift nor the directions

---

[74] See Chapter 5.3, pp. 186–205.
[75] See Chapter 5.6, pp. 260–83.
[76] [1959] AC 457.
[77] Ibid, 477.

given nor the objects expressed impose on the donee the character of a trustee) is nothing else than a gift to its members at the date of the gift as joint tenants or tenants in common. It is for this reason that the prudent conveyancer provides that a receipt by the treasurer or other proper officer of the recipient society for a legacy to the society shall be a sufficient discharge to executors. If it were not so, the executors could only get a valid discharge by obtaining a receipt from every member. This must be qualified by saying that by their rules the members might have authorised one of themselves to receive a gift on behalf of them all.

It is in the light of this fundamental proposition that the statements, to which reference has been made, must be examined. What is meant when it is said that a gift is made to the individuals comprising the community and the words are added 'it is given to them for the benefit of the community'? If it is a gift to individuals, each of them is entitled to his distributive share (unless he has previously bound himself by the rules of the society that it shall be devoted to some other purpose). It is difficult to see what is added by the words 'for the benefit of the community'. If they are intended to import a trust, who are the beneficiaries? If the present members are the beneficiaries, the words add nothing and are meaningless. If some other persons or purposes are intended, the conclusion cannot be avoided that the gift is void. For it is uncertain, and beyond doubt tends to a perpetuity.

The question then appears to be whether, even if the gift to a selected Order of Nuns is prima facie a gift to the individual members of that Order, there are other considerations arising out of the terms of the will, or the nature of the society, its organisation and rules, or the subject matter of the gift which should lead the court to conclude that, though prima facie the gift is an absolute one (absolute both in quality of estate and in freedom from restriction) to individual nuns, yet it is invalid because it is in the nature of an endowment and tends to a perpetuity or for any other reason. This raises a problem which is not easy to solve ...

The prima facie validity of such a gift ... is a convenient starting point for the examination of the relevant law. For as Lord Tomlin (sitting at first instance in the Chancery Division) said in *Re Ogden* [1933] Ch 678, a gift to a voluntary association of persons for the general purposes of the association is an absolute gift and prima facie a good gift. He was echoing the words of Lord Parker in *Bowman's case* [1917] AC 406 at 442, that a gift to an unincorporated association for the attainment of its purposes 'may ... be upheld as an absolute gift to its members'. These words must receive careful consideration, for it is to be noted that it is because the gift can be upheld as a gift to the individual members that it is valid, even though it is given for the general purposes of the association. If the words 'for the general purposes of the association' were held to import a trust, the question would have to be asked, what is the trust and who are the beneficiaries? A gift can be made to persons (including a corporation) but it cannot be made to a purpose or to an object: so also, a trust may be created for the benefit of persons as *cestuis que trust* but not for a purpose or object unless the purpose or object be charitable ...

It must now be asked, then, whether in the present case there are sufficient indications to displace the *prima facie* conclusion that the gift made by ... the will is to the individual members of the selected Order of Nuns at the date of the testator's death so that they can together dispose of it as they think fit. It appears to their Lordships that such indications are ample.

In the first place, it is not altogether irrelevant that the gift is in terms upon trust for a selected Order. It is true that this can in law be regarded as a trust in favour of each and every member of the Order. But at least the form of the gift is not to the members, and it may be questioned whether the testator understood the niceties of the law. In the second place, the members of the selected Order may be numerous, very numerous perhaps, and they may be spread over the world. If the gift is to the individuals it is to all the members who were living at the death of the testator, but only to them. It is not easy to believe that the testator intended an 'immediate beneficial legacy' ... to such a body of beneficiaries. In the third place, the subject matter of the gift cannot be ignored. It appears from the evidence filed in the suit that [the property] is a grazing property of about 730 acres, with a furnished homestead containing 20 rooms and a number of outbuildings. With the greatest respect to those judges who have taken a different view, their Lordships do not find it possible to regard all the individual members of an Order as intended to become the beneficial owners of such a property. Little or no evidence has been given about the organisation and rules of the several Orders, but it is at least permissible to doubt whether it is a common feature of them, that all their members regard themselves or are to be regarded as having the capacity...to put an end to their association and distribute its assets. On the contrary, it seems reasonably clear that, however little the testator understood the effect in law of a gift to an unincorporated body of persons by their society name, his intention was to create a trust, not merely for the benefit of the existing members of the selected Order, but for its benefit as a continuing society and for the furtherance of its work...

The dominant and sufficiently expressed intention of the testator is...that 'the gift is to be an endowment of the society to be held as an endowment', and that 'as the society is according to its form perpetual' the gift must, if it is to a non- charitable body, fail.

There will, however, be circumstances under which a property might legitimately be held on trust for the purposes of the unincorporated association, even though those purposes are not charitable, if the trust can be considered to be for the direct or indirect benefit of the members of that association within the *Denley* principle.[78] In such circumstances, the members of the association will be in a position to enforce the trust since they factually benefit from the purpose. Such a trust, being a non-charitable purpose trust, must comply with the common law perpetuity rule.[79] This mechanism for property-holding by the club must be intended by the settlor, in that the settlor must intend the property to be held for the purposes of the club rather than for the members themselves.

The application of the *Denley* principle to unincorporated associations was, however, doubted by Vinelott J in *Re Grant's Will Trusts*:[80]

That case on a proper analysis, in my judgment, falls altogether outside the categories of gifts to unincorporated association and purpose trusts. I can see no distinction in principle between a trust to permit a class defined by reference to employment to use and enjoy land in accordance with rules to be made at the discretion of trustees on the one hand, and, on the other hand, a trust to distribute income at the discretion of trustees amongst a class, defined by reference to, for example, relationship to the settlor. In both cases the benefit to be taken by any member of the class is at the discretion of the trustees, but any member of the class can apply to the court to compel the trustees to administer the trust in accordance with its terms.

But there is no reason to confine the *Denley* principle in this way. In *Re Denley* itself, the discretion of the trustees was not considered to be significant and the decision was applied, amongst other mechanisms, in *Re Lipinski's Will Trust*[81] to explain how property could be used for the purposes of an unincorporated association. Despite this, the *Re Denley* principle has not been influential in explaining property holding for the benefit of unincorporated associations, with other mechanisms being much more significant in explaining both property-holding and who should benefit from the property on dissolution of the association.

---

[78] [1969] 1 Ch 373. See Chapter 6.2(a), p. 290.
[79] See Chapter 6.2(b), p. 291.
[80] [1980] 1 WLR 360, 370.
[81] [1976] Ch 235, 247 (Oliver J). See Chapter 6.4(b)(v), p. 306.

(iii) *For members at the time of the transfer*

Rather than intending to benefit the purposes of the association, the transferor may wish to benefit the members of the association at the time the property is transferred. The property may either be treated as belonging to the members absolutely, or it will be held on trust for them, with legal title in an officer such as the treasurer,[82] so that the members have equitable interests in the property.

Regardless of whether the members own the property absolutely or beneficially under a trust, their interest would be as joint tenants,[83] which means that they can sever their interest at will. Their interest in the property arises because they were members at the time of the transfer of the property, but this interest does not depend on them continuing to be members. Consequently, they would retain their interest in the property even once they had ceased to be members. They would be able to sever their share whenever they liked, even after the expiry of their membership of the association. Also, new members who join the association after the property was acquired would not have any interest in the property.

There are advantages of analysing property-holding by unincorporated associations in this way. For example, where the property is held on trust for the members, the beneficiary principle is satisfied, since the members at the time of the acquisition are the beneficiaries. Nor will the perpetuity rule be infringed, because the members are free to dispose of the income and capital when they wish.[84] But this type of mechanism is unlikely to be what the donor of the property intends, because it does not operate for the benefit of the association's purposes, but only for the benefit of the members at the time of the transfer, each of whom can sever his or her own interest for his or her own benefit at any time. Consequently, this is unlikely to be a mechanism that will be adopted by transferors. In any event, it is a mechanism that can be excluded by the rules of the association if those rules prevent members from severing their shares in the property held for the benefit of the association. As Matthews has pointed out:[85]

> The gift is to the current members of the association. But whether they may sever their shares, or whether they must retain the gift in the funds of the association and subject it to its rules, is instead a matter of construction *of the rules themselves,* and has nothing to do with the donor's intentions.

(iv) *On trust for present and future members*

To avoid the unfortunate consequences of the property being transferred for the benefit of the members at the time of the transfer, the transferor might instead wish the property to be held on trust for 'present and future members'. This would clearly satisfy the beneficiary principle, but such a trust has traditionally been regarded as void for infringing the perpetuity rule, since the property would be available indefinitely for future members, whose interests would vest outside the perpetuity period. But a trust for present and future members would presumably not now be caught by the perpetuity rule as it has been amended by statute. Under the Perpetuities and Accumulations Act 2009, the perpetuity period is 125 years, but the trust will remain valid throughout that period to see if it terminates in time.[86] If it does not, the trust will terminate automatically at the end of the period and the property will be distributed to the members at that time.

---

[82] *Re Drummond* [1914] 2 Ch 90.
[83] *Neville Estates Ltd v Madden* [1962] Ch 832, 849 (Cross J). See Chapter 6.4(b), pp. 300–1.
[84] Warburton, 'The Holding of Property by Unincorporated Associations' [1985] Conv 318, 321.
[85] Matthews, 'A Problem in the Construction of Gifts to Unincorporated Associations' [1995] Conv 302, 308.
[86] Perpetuities and Accumulations Act 2009, s. 7(2). See Chapter 3.7, p. 115.

But a trust for present and future members would still be subject to the significant limitation that each member would retain an interest in the trust property even if he or she has ceased to be a member. This is unlikely to correspond to the donor's intention.

(v) *For members subject to their existing contractual rights*

The generally preferable construction to adopt is to treat the property as either being given absolutely to an officer of the association, such as the treasurer, or held on trust for the members at the time of the transfer, but subject to their contractual rights and liabilities towards one another as members of the association.[87] These contractual rights will be derived from the association's rules or constitution, since all unincorporated associations must, by definition, have rules that bind the members[88] and that form the basis of an express or implied contract between them.[89]

This mechanism, known as the contract-holding theory, ensures that the property is available for all members, including those members who join the association in the future. The essence of property-holding according to this theory was identified by Lewison J in *Hanchett-Stamford v Attorney-General*:[90]

> The thread that runs through all [the] cases is that the property of an unincorporated association is the property of its members, but that they are contractually precluded from severing their share except in accordance with the rules of the association; and that, on its dissolution, those who are members at the time are entitled to the assets free from any such contractual restrictions. It is true that this is not a joint tenancy according to the classical model; but since any collective ownership of property must be a species of joint tenancy or tenancy in common, this kind of collective ownership must, in my judgment, be a subspecies of joint tenancy, albeit taking effect subject to any contractual restrictions applicable as between members. In some cases...those contractual restrictions may be such as to exclude any possibility of a future claim. In others they may not.

The significance of this contractual modification of the classical model of joint tenancy is that the members cannot sever the joint tenancy at will. Further, members at the time of the transfer who subsequently resign from the association will no longer have contractual rights relating to the property; the property will belong beneficially to the remaining members. Later members who join the association will be able to benefit from the property because they will have beneficial rights in the property arising from the rules of the association that they have joined.

The contract-holding theory is the mechanism of property-holding that is now most usually recognized by the courts, but it will not be available if the transferor of the property clearly intended the property to be held for the purposes of the association, or for the members at the time the property was transferred, or for present and future members. But those constructions are not usually satisfactory, because usually a trust for the purposes of the association will be void, and trusts for the members, either at the time of the transfer or present and future members, will have the unfortunate consequence, usually unintended by the donor, that a person who ceases to be a member will still have a beneficial interest in the property. Consequently, the contract-holding theory is by far the most satisfactory explanation of property-holding in respect of unincorporated associations.

---

[87] *Neville Estates Ltd v Madden* [1962] Ch 832, 849 (Cross J).
[88] See Chapter 6.4(a), p. 300.
[89] *Re Bucks Constabulary Widows' and Orphans' Fund Friendly Society (No. 2)* [1979] 1 WLR 936, 943 (Walton J).
[90] [2008] EWHC 330 (Ch); [2009] Ch 173, [47].

Whilst the members of an unincorporated association can own property without the use of a trust, in practice, where there are a significant number of members, property will most conveniently be held on trust for the members by an officer of the association.[91] The contract-holding theory will remain significant, however, since the terms of the contract between the members, in the form of the association's constitution, will be incorporated into the trust. Typically, the treasurer will hold the property on a bare trust in accordance with the rules of the association.[92] Each member will then have a beneficial interest in the property so the beneficiary principle will be satisfied, since each member can ensure that the property is applied in accordance with the rules of the association. The perpetuity rule[93] will also be satisfied, because it is a requirement of the contract-holding theory that it must be possible for the members to agree, whether unanimously or by majority depending on the rules of the association's constitution, to vary or terminate the contract between them, so that they can dispose of the property or dissolve the society.[94] Being a bare trust for persons the statutory perpetuity rule will apply and, since the trust might be terminated within 125 years of its creation, it will be valid until that time,[95] with the 'wait and see' rule applying.[96] Further, the fact that future members might benefit after the 125-year period will not invalidate the trust, since it is possible to exclude those potential members whose interests might vest outside the perpetuity period by applying the class-closing rule.[97]

That the contract-holding theory can operate within the law of trusts was recognized in *Re Lipinski's Will Trusts*.[98] The testator had left part of his estate on trust for the Hull Judeans (Maccabi) Association, an unincorporated association, to build and improve new buildings for the benefit of the association. This was held to be a valid trust for the members of the Association. Oliver J said:[99]

> At first sight, however, there appears to be a difficulty in arguing that the gift is to members of the association subject to their contractual rights *inter se* when there is a specific direction or limitation sought to be imposed upon those contractual rights as to the manner in which the subject matter of the gift is to be dealt with. This, says [counsel], is a pure 'purpose trust' and is invalid on that ground, quite apart from any question of perpetuity. I am not sure, however, that it is sufficient merely to demonstrate that a trust is a 'purpose' trust...
>
> If a valid gift may be made to an unincorporated body as a simple accretion to the funds which are the subject matter of the contract which the members have made *inter se*...I do not really see why such a gift, which specifies a purpose which is within the powers of the association and of which the members of the association are the beneficiaries, should fail. Why are not the beneficiaries able to enforce the trust or, indeed, in the exercise of their contractual rights, to terminate the trust for their own benefit? Where the donee association is itself the beneficiary of the prescribed purpose, there seems to me to be the strongest argument in common sense for saying that the gift should be construed as an absolute one within the second category[100]—the more so where, if the purpose is carried out, the members can by appropriate action vest the resulting property in themselves, for here the trustees and the beneficiaries are the same persons.

[91] *Re Bucks Constabulary Widows' and Orphans' Fund Friendly Society (No. 2)* [1979] 1 WLR 936, 939 (Walton J).

[92] *Re Horley Town Football Club* [2006] EWHC 2386 (Ch); [2006] WTLR 1817, [118] (Lawrence Collins J).

[93] See Chapter 6.2(b), p. 291.

[94] See *Re Grant's Will Trusts* [1980] 1 WLR 360. Chapter 6.4(b)(v), pp. 310–11.

[95] See Chapter 3.7(a), p. 114.

[96] Perpetuities and Accumulations Act 2009, s. 7. See Chapter 3.7, p. 115.

[97] Ibid, s. 8.

[98] [1976] Ch 235.

[99] Ibid, 246.

[100] See *Neville Estates Ltd v Madden* [1962] Ch 832, Chapter 6.4(b), pp. 300–1.

It follows that the terms of the association's constitution will be incorporated into the trust to enable the members to enforce the trust or to terminate it, by terminating the association, so that the members can then take the trust property for themselves.

Even where the property cannot be construed as intended to be held on trust, it will typically be held by the treasurer in accordance with the contractual rules of the association that bind all members.[101] This is illustrated by *Re Recher's Trusts*,[102] in which a testamentary gift was made to the London and Provincial anti-vivisection society, which was an unincorporated association with ordinary and life members and a constitution. Since the society had political objectives, the gift could not be held for charitable purposes.[103] The gift was construed as being to the members at the time of the testator's death, but subject to the contract between them. Brightman J said:[104]

> Having reached the conclusion that the gift in question is not a gift to the members of the London & Provincial Society at the date of death, as joint tenants or tenants in common, so as to entitle a member as of right to a distributive share, nor an attempted gift to present and future members beneficially, and is not a gift in trust for the purposes of the society, I must now consider how otherwise, if at all, it is capable of taking effect.
>
> As I have already mentioned, the rules of the London & Provincial Society do not purport to create any trusts except in so far as the honorary trustees are not beneficial owners of the assets of the society, but are trustees upon trust to deal with such assets according to the directions of the committee.
>
> A trust for non-charitable purposes, as distinct from a trust for individuals, is clearly void because there is no beneficiary. It does not, however, follow that persons cannot band themselves together as an association or society, pay subscriptions and validly devote their funds in pursuit of some lawful non- charitable purpose. An obvious example is a members' social club. But it is not essential that the members should only intend to secure direct personal advantages to themselves. The association may be one in which personal advantages to the members are combined with the pursuit of some outside purpose. Or the association may be one which offers no personal benefit at all to the members, the funds of the association being applied exclusively to the pursuit of some outside purpose. Such an association of persons is bound, I would think, to have some sort of constitution; that is to say, the rights and liabilities of the members of the association will inevitably depend on some form of contract *inter se*, usually evidenced by a set of rules. In the present case it appears to me clear that the life members, the ordinary members and the associate members of the London & Provincial Society were bound together by a contract *inter se*. Any such member was entitled to the rights and subject to the liabilities defined by the rules. If the committee acted contrary to the rules, an individual member would be entitled to take proceedings in the courts to compel observance of the rules or to recover damages for any loss he had suffered as a result of the breach of contract. As and when a member paid his subscription to the association, he would be subjecting his money to the disposition and expenditure thereof laid down by the rules. That is to say, the member would be bound to permit, and entitled to require, the honorary trustees and other members of the society to deal with that subscription in accordance with the lawful directions of the committee. Those directions would include the expenditure of that subscription, as part of the general funds of the association, in furthering the objects of the association. The resultant situation, on analysis, is that the London & Provincial society represented an organisation of individuals bound together by a contract under which their subscriptions became, as it were, mandated towards a certain type of expenditure as adumbrated [by the constitution]. Just as the two parties to a bi-partite bargain can vary or terminate their contract by mutual assent, so it must follow that the life members, ordinary members and associated members of the London & Provincial Society

---

[101] Warburton, 'The Holding of Property by Unincorporated Associations' [1985] Conv 318, 324.
[102] [1972] Ch 526.
[103] See Chapter 5.3(c)(ii)(c), pp. 201–5.
[104] [1972] Ch 526, 538.

could, at any moment of time, by unanimous agreement (or by majority vote, if the rules so prescribe), vary or terminate their multi-partite contract. There would be no limit to the type of variation or termination to which all might agree. There is no private trust or trust for charitable purposes or other trust to hinder the process. It follows that if all members agreed, they could decide to wind up the London & Provincial Society and divide the net assets among themselves beneficially. No one would have any *locus standi* to stop them so doing. The contract is the same as any other contract and concerns only those who are parties to it, that is to say, the members of the society.

The funds of such an association may, of course, be derived not only from the subscriptions of the contracting parties but also from donations from non-contracting parties and legacies from persons who have died. In the case of a donation which is not accompanied by any words which purport to impose a trust, it seems to me that the gift takes effect in favour of the existing members of the association as an accretion to the funds which are the subject matter of the contract which such members have made *inter se*, and falls to be dealt with in precisely the same way as the funds which the members themselves have subscribed. So, in the case of a legacy. In the absence of words which purport to impose a trust, the legacy is a gift to the members beneficially, not as joint tenants or as tenants in common so as to entitle each member to an immediate distributive share, but as an accretion to the funds which are the subject matter of the contract which the members have made *inter se*.

Unincorporated associations are of very different sizes. In smaller ones, there is likely to be only one class of member, so all members will be treated alike. Consequently, if the property that has been received for the purposes of the association is sold, the value of that property will be distributed equally between the members. But larger, unincorporated associations are likely to have different classes of member, so if property is sold, it will be necessary to determine whether all members should share in the proceeds of sale.[105] This was the key issue in *Re Horley Town Football Club*.

Re Horley Town Football Club [2006] EWHC 2386 (Ch); [2006] WTLR 1817

The members of an amateur football club wished to sell the club's football ground. The ground was held on trust for the members of the club, whose rights were determined by the club's constitution. There were, however, a number of different classes of member. It was held that, for the purposes of the contract-holding theory, a member was somebody who could vote to have the assets sold. Consequently, it was only the current full members who had a beneficial interest in the property. Lawrence Collins J said:[106]

The next question is the identity of the persons who hold the beneficial interest. I am satisfied that the beneficial ownership is in the current full members (and not the temporary or associate members), and is held on bare trust for them. The members hold subject to the current rules, and could unanimously or by AGM call for the assets to be transferred. Adult and senior members are entitled to share in distribution on per capita basis.

In *Re GKN Bolts & Nuts Ltd etc Work Sports and Social Club* [1982] 1 WLR 774 the question was whether a social club formed for the benefit of employees had ceased to exist in 1975 when, following financial difficulties, it resolved to sell the sports ground, and the basis on which there should be distribution of the assets.

---

[105] This will also be relevant where the unincorporated association is dissolved. See Chapter 6.4(c), pp. 314–23.
[106] [2006] EWHC 2386 (Ch), [2006] WTLR 1817, [118].

Sir Robert Megarry V-C said at 776:

'As is common in club cases, there are many obscurities and uncertainties, and some difficulty in the law. In such cases, the court usually has to take a broad sword to the problems, and eschew an unduly meticulous examination of the rules and regulations...I think that the courts have to be ready to allow general concepts of reasonableness, fairness and common sense to be given more than their usual weight when confronted by claims to the contrary which appear to be based on any strict interpretation and rigid application of the letter of the rules.'

He held that the club had ceased to exist. It was held that where, as in that case, there was nothing in the rules or anything else to indicate a different basis, distribution of the assets should be on the basis of equality among the members, irrespective of the length of membership or the amount of subscriptions paid. There was no possible nexus between the length of membership or the amount of subscriptions paid and the property rights of members on a dissolution. Each member was entitled to one equal share.

The club's rules provided that the club would consist of 'ordinary and honorary members and, in special cases, of temporary members as hereinafter provided'. The rules also referred to 'full members' who were the same as 'ordinary members', 'associates', 'temporary members' and spouses and children who were 'entitled to membership without voting rights'.

'Associates' were employees of a group company club having similar objects who, if they wrote their name in a book with the names of their clubs, would have the same rights as ordinary members, except that they could not vote at meetings or take away alcoholic drinks. 'Temporary members' were those invited by the committee to participate in the amenities of the club on the day of a sporting or social event. Spouses and children of members were thought by Sir Robert Megarry to fall within the same category as associates and temporary members: The object in each case was to confer the right to use the club premises and facilities without imposing the powers and responsibilities of full members, for whom alone the rule provided for the payment of subscriptions....

The result was a holding that no members except those who were properly called 'full members' or 'ordinary members' were entitled to any interest in the assets of the club.

I accept that in certain respects the distinction between 'full' members and other types of membership was somewhat clearer in *Re GKN* than it is in the present case. It appears that (with the exception of honorary members, some of whom paid a subscription but none of whom were entitled to vote or to an interest in the club's assets) in *Re GKN* there was a correspondence between members who paid subscriptions and members who were entitled to vote. In the present case, the voting rights do not correspond with the obligation to subscribe. There is a subscription for Youth Membership (under 18) and for Junior Membership (under 16), but Junior and Youth Members are not entitled to vote...

In my judgment I should adopt the same approach as Sir Robert Megarry in taking a 'broad sword' and applying fairness and common sense. In my judgment it does not make a difference that in the present case the Rules say in Rule 4 that the Club shall consist of 'members and temporary members'; or in Rule 5 provide that Associate Members will enjoy the same rights as full members except those relating to voting rights; or that Rule 15 gives a right to vote to 'independently constituted clubs enjoying Associate Membership'. I would accept that a mere inequality in voting rights would not mean that a category of members is excluded altogether from any entitlement to the surplus assets of the association upon its dissolution. But the associate members in the present case have no effective rights and it would be wholly unrealistic to treat the introduction of Associate Members by amendment of the Rules as a transfer of the Club's property to them.

The consequence would be that the beneficial ownership is held on bare trust for the members, who could either unanimously or at an AGM call for the assets to be transferred.

As regards those members who did have a beneficial interest, it was held that the proceeds of sale should be distributed amongst them equally.

It is an important feature of the contract-holding theory that the members of the association must be able to alter the association's rules to apply its funds for a new purpose, since this will show that it was a gift for them rather than for the purposes of the association. This was recognized in *Re Grant's Will Trusts*,[107] in which the testator left his estate for the benefit of the Chertsey and Walton Constituency Labour Party ('CLP'). It was held that this was not a valid gift: the contract-holding theory could not apply because the members could not change the rules. Vinelott J said:[108]

It must, as I see it, be a necessary characteristic of any gift within the second category[109] that the members of the association can by an appropriate majority, if the rules so provide, or acting unanimously if they do not, alter their rules so as to provide that the funds, or part of them, should be applied for some new purpose, or even distributed amongst the members for their own benefit. For the validity of a gift within this category rests essentially upon the fact that the testator has set out to further a purpose by making a gift to the members of an association formed for the furtherance of that purpose in the expectation that although the members at the date when the gift takes effect will be free, by a majority if the rules so provide or acting unanimously if they do not, to dispose of the fund in any way they may think fit, they and any future members of the association will not in fact do so but will employ the property in the furtherance of the purpose of the association and will honour any special condition attached to the gift...

Reading the gift in the will in the light of the rules governing the Chertsey and Walton CLP, it is, in my judgment, impossible to construe the gift as a gift made to the members of the Chertsey and Walton CLP at the date of the testator's death with the intention that it should belong to them as a collection of individuals, though in the expectation that they and any other members subsequently admitted would ensure that it was in fact used for what in broad terms has been labelled 'headquarters' purposes' of the Chertsey and Walton CLP.

I base this conclusion on two grounds. First, the members of the Chertsey and Walton CLP do not control the property, given by subscription or otherwise, to the CLP. The rules which govern the CLP are capable of being altered by an outside body which could direct an alteration under which the general committee of the CLP would be bound to transfer any property for the time being held for the benefit of the CLP to the National Labour Party for national purposes. The members of the Chertsey and Walton CLP could not alter the rules so as to make the property bequeathed by the testator applicable for some purpose other than that provided by the rules; nor could they direct that property to be divided amongst themselves beneficially...

The answer to this apparent paradox is, it seems to me, that subscriptions by members of the Chertsey and Walton CLP must be taken as made upon terms that they will be applied by the general committee in accordance with the rules for the time being including any modifications imposed by the Annual Party Conference or the National Executive Committee. In the event of the dissolution of the Chertsey and Walton CLP any remaining fund representing subscriptions would (as the rules now stand) be held on a resulting trust for the original subscribers. Thus, although the members of the CLP may not be able themselves to alter the purposes for which a fund representing subscriptions is to be used or to alter the rules so as to make such a fund divisible amongst themselves, the ultimate proprietary right of the original subscribers remains. There is, therefore, no perpetuity and no non-charitable purpose trust. But if that analysis of the terms on which subscriptions are held is correct, it is fatal to the argument that the gift in the testator's will should be construed as a gift to the members of the Chertsey

---

[107] [1980] 1 WLR 360.
[108] Ibid, 368.
[109] See Chapter 6.4(b), p. 300.

and Walton CLP at the testator's death, subject to a direction not amounting to a trust that it be used for headquarters' purposes. Equally it is in my judgment impossible, in particular having regard to the gift over to the National Labour Party, to read the gift as a gift to the members of the National Labour Party at the testator's death, with a direction not amounting to a trust, for the National Party to permit it to be used by the Chertsey and Walton CLP for headquarters' purposes.

That first ground is of itself conclusive, but there is another ground which reinforces this conclusion. The gift is not in terms a gift to the Chertsey and Walton CLP, but to the Labour Party property committee, who are to hold the property for the benefit of, that is in trust for, the Chertsey headquarters of the Chertsey and Walton CLP. The fact that a gift is a gift to trustees and not in terms of an unincorporated association, militates against construing it as a gift to the members of the association at the date when the gift takes effect, and against construing the words indicating the purposes for which the property is to be used as expressing the testator's intention or motive in making the gift and not as imposing any trust.

Whilst the contract-holding theory can be used to explain how a gift can be made for the purposes of an unincorporated association, and can be held on trust for present and future members, the use of the theory within the law of trusts does not sit easily with certain fundamental principles of the law of express trusts.

Baughen, 'Performing Animals and the Dissolution of Unincorporated Associations: The "Contract-holding theory" Vindicated' [2010] Conv 216, 225

A problem that has yet to be addressed by the judiciary is the shifting nature of the beneficiaries under the joint tenancy on which an unincorporated association's property is held. Over time members will leave the association. It is an implied term of an association's rules that a member's interest will cease in the event of their death or their ceasing to be a member of the association and their share will accrue to the remaining members. New members will also join the association and this will diminish the interest of the existing members. Both instances will involve dispositions of an 'equitable interest'... Section 53(1)(c) of the Law of Property Act 1925 ('the 1925 Act')[110] requires that such a disposition be in writing signed by the person disposing of the interest. This is unlikely to occur when an existing member leaves the association or when a new member joins it. The solution as regards former members can be derived from Cross J's dicta in *Neville Estates* that, on the death or resignation of a member, the interest of that member would accrue to the remaining members by survivorship. As regards the admission of new members, the solution probably lies in s.53(2) of the 1925 Act, which provides that '[t]his section does not affect the creation or operation of resulting, implied or constructive trusts'. It is likely that the courts would treat the alteration in the beneficial interests of existing members on the admission of new members as arising due to the operation of *Walsh v Lonsdale*,[111] with constructive trusts arising out of the network of contracts between the members.[112]

The preferable view, however, is that the departing member's interest is not transferred to the other members. Rather, it is destroyed, and the destruction of such interests does not require writing to be effective.[113]

[110] See Chapter 10.2, p. 501.

[111] (1882) LR 21 Ch D 9, CA.

[112] The constructive trust would arise under the maxim 'equity regards as done that which ought to be done' on the basis of a specifically enforceable contract. See Lord Radcliffe in *Oughtred v Inland Revenue Commissioners* [1960] AC 206 HL at 227, whose views were applied by the Court of Appeal in *Neville v Wilson* [1997] Ch 144.

[113] See Chapter 10.2(c), pp. 505–7.

(vi) *Agent for the transferor*

Rather than treating a gift of property as being a gift to the present members or as being held on trust for the members or the purposes of the association, an alternative construction is for the property to be transferred to an officer of the association as agent for the transferor, with the authority to apply the property for the transferor's intended purposes. This agency solution has proved significant where an association does not satisfy the definition of an unincorporated association, so that the contract-holding mechanism is unavailable.

Conservative and Unionist Central Office v Burrell [1982] 1 WLR 552

The Conservative Party was held not to be an unincorporated association because of the absence of a contractual link between the different components of the party. It was held that its funds were paid to the treasurer of the Party, who had title to the money as agent for the donors, so that the treasurer was only authorized to use the money for the purposes of the Party. Brightman LJ said:[114]

> The issue is whether or not the investment income of the Conservative Party Central Office funds during the relevant years was the income of an unincorporated association. The assertion is that Central Office funds are held for the purposes of an organisation known as the Conservative Party, or more fully as the Conservative and Unionist Party, that such organisation has all the necessary requirements for qualifying as an unincorporated association and that the Special Commissioners were justified in finding that it is such an association. The members of the association are said to be (i) all the persons who are members of the local constituency associations (which local associations are themselves unincorporated associations) and (ii) the members of both Houses of Parliament who accept the Conservative Party whip. The contract which is alleged to bind together the members of this unincorporated association known as the Conservative Party is said to consist of the rules forming the constitution of the National Union of Conservative and Unionist Associations, the rules regulating 'party meetings' at which the candidate chosen by the Parliamentary Conservative Party as leader of the party is presented for election as party leader and the rules forming the respective constitutions of the local constituency associations. I agree . . . that no such overall unincorporated association exists.[115]
>
> Before, however, that conclusion is accepted, I think that a critical observer is entitled to ask the question what, on that hypothesis, would be the legal relationship between a contributor to Central Office funds and the recipient of the contributions so made.
>
> Strictly speaking, this court does not have to answer that question; it has only to decide the issue whether the Special Commissioners were entitled to find that the Conservative Party is an unincorporated association. But, if no realistic legal explanation of the relationship is forthcoming except the existence of an unincorporated association, one might justifiably begin to entertain doubts as to the credibility of the hypothesis on which the question is asked. I will therefore attempt an answer . . .
>
> I will consider the hypothesis by stages. No legal problem arises if a contributor (as I will call him) hands to a friend (whom I will call the recipient) a sum of money to be applied by the recipient for political purposes indicated by the contributor, or to be chosen at the discretion of the recipient. That would be a simple case of mandate or agency. The recipient would have authority from the contributor to make use of the money, in the indicated way. So far as the money is used within the scope of the mandate,

---

[114] [1982] 1 WLR 522, 528.
[115] See Chapter 6.4(a), p. 300.

the recipient discharges himself vis-à-vis the contributor. The contributor can at any time demand the return of his money so far as not spent, unless the mandate is irrevocable, as it might be or become in certain circumstances. But once the money is spent, the contributor can demand nothing back, only an account of the manner of expenditure. No trust arises, except the fiduciary relationship inherent in the relationship of principal and agent. If, however, the recipient were to apply the money for some purpose outside the scope of the mandate, clearly the recipient would not be discharged. The recipient could be restrained, like any other agent, from a threatened misapplication of the money entrusted to him, and like any other agent could be required to replace any money misapplied.

The next stage is to suppose that the recipient is the treasurer of an organisation which receives and applies funds from multifarious sources for certain political purposes. If the contributor pays money to that treasurer, the treasurer has clear authority to add the contribution to the mixed fund (as I will call it) that he holds. At that stage I think the mandate becomes irrevocable. That is to say, the contributor has no right to demand his contribution back, once it has been mixed with other money under the authority of the contributor. The contributor has no legal right to require the mixed fund to be unscrambled for his benefit. This does not mean, however, that all contributors lose all rights once their cheques are cashed, with the absurd result that the treasurer or other officers can run off with the mixed fund with impunity. I have no doubt that any contributor has a remedy against the recipient (i.e. the treasurer, or the officials at whose direction the treasurer acts) to restrain or make good a misapplication of the mixed fund except so far as it may appear on ordinary accounting principles that the plaintiff's own contribution was spent before the threatened or actual misapplication. In the latter event the mandate given by the contributor will not have been breached. A complaining contributor might encounter problems under the law of contract after a change of the office holder to whom his mandate was originally given. Perhaps only the original recipient can be sued for the malpractices of his successors. It is not necessary to explore such procedural intricacies.

So in the present case it seems to me that the status of a contribution to the Conservative Party central funds is this. The contributor draws a cheque (for example) in favour of, or hands it to, the treasurers. The treasurers are impliedly authorised by the contributor to present the cheque for encashment and to add the contribution to Central Office funds. Central Office funds are the subject matter of a mandate which permits them to be used for the purposes of the Conservative Party as directed by the leader of the party. The contributor cannot demand his money back once it has been added to Central Office funds. He could object if Central Office funds were used or threatened to be used otherwise than in accordance with their declared purposes, unless it is correct to say, on ordinary accounting principles, that his contribution has already passed out of Central Office funds.

This discussion of mandates, and complaining contributors, is all very remote and theoretical. No contributor to Central Office funds will view his contribution in this way, or contemplate even the remotest prospect of legal action on his part. He believes he is making an out-and-out contribution or gift to a political party. And so he is in practical terms. The only justification for embarking on a close analysis of the situation is the challenge, which was thrown down by counsel for the Crown in opening, to suggest any legal framework which fits the undoubted fact that funds are held by the Central Office and are administered for the use and benefit of the Conservative Party, except the supposition that the Conservative Party is an unincorporated association.

I see no legal difficulty in the mandate theory. It is not necessary to invent an unincorporated association in order to explain the situation. The only problem which might arise in practice under the mandate theory would be the case of an attempted bequest to Central Office funds, or to the treasurers thereof, or to the Conservative Party, since no agency could be set up at the moment of death between a testator and his chosen agent. A discussion of this problem is outside the scope of this appeal and, although I think that the answer is not difficult to find, I do not wish to prejudge it.

(vii) *Estoppel*

An alternative approach to the problem of bequests for non-charitable purposes, one involving estoppel, has been suggested by Smart:[116]

> the following analysis is suggested in order to give effect to a bequest to an organisation for a non-charitable purpose: (1) trusts, contracts and mandates are not relevant; (2) there is an attempt to make a gift to an officer (usually the treasurer) of the organisation subject to the condition subsequent that the gift be used only for the relevant purpose; (3) that condition is void as repugnant, although the gift remains valid, free from the condition; (4) if the treasurer of the organisation represents that the gift is taken to be used for the relevant purpose, he will thereafter be estopped from denying the validity of the condition and enforcing his strict right to use the property for his own purposes; (5) should the treasurer make no representation and seek to take the gift for himself, then (a) the organisation might, of course, appoint a new (and willing) treasurer, or (b) the gift could be construed in favour of some other officer or individual willing to use the property for the testator's purpose; and (6) if no one can be found willing to use the gift for the intended purpose, then the gift will plainly fail.

This is an attractive explanation of how property can be held for an organization that pursues non-charitable purposes where that organization does not satisfy the definition of being an unincorporated association, primarily because of the absence of a written constitution.[117] But where the association does satisfy that definition, the contract-holding theory provides the most satisfactory explanation of property-holding for non-charitable purposes.

(c) DISSOLUTION OF UNINCORPORATED ASSOCIATIONS

Where an unincorporated association is dissolved, the disposal of any surplus assets will depend on which construction of property-holding has been recognized. Many of the difficulties previously faced can now typically be avoided through the adoption of the contract-holding theory.

(i) *Determining when the association is dissolved*

The dissolution of an unincorporated association may occur by court order, by resolution of the members according to the rules of the constitution, or, if there is no such provision, by unanimous agreement of the members. An unincorporated association will also be brought to an end if the number of members falls below two.[118] The latter point was recognized by Walton J in *Re Bucks Constabulary Widows' and Orphans' Fund Friendly Society (No. 2)*:[119]

> It may be that it will be sufficient for the society's continued existence if there are two members, but if there is only one the society as such must cease to exist. There is no association, since one can hardly associate with oneself or enjoy one's own society.

Even if the number of members of the association has not fallen below two, the association will be considered to have been dissolved if it has become moribund. This was recognized in *Re GKN Bolts &*

---

[116] 'Holding Property for Non-charitable Purposes: Mandates, Conditions and Estoppels' [1987] Conv 415, 418
[117] See Chapter 6.4(a), p. 300.
[118] *Hanchett-Stamford v Attorney-General* [2008] EWHC 330 (Ch); [2009] Ch 173.
[119] [1979] 1 WLR 936, 943.

Nuts Ltd etc. Work Sports and Social Club,[120] which concerned a social club for employees that was held to have gradually become inactive. Sir Robert Megarry V-C said:[121]

> It is plain that there never was an agreement by the entire membership that the club should be dissolved, and of course there has been no exercise by the court of its inherent jurisdiction to order a dissolution. The question therefore is whether there has been what was called in argument a spontaneous dissolution of the club.
>
> As a matter of principle I would hold that it is perfectly possible for a club to be dissolved spontaneously. I do not think that mere inactivity is enough: a club may do little or nothing for a long period, and yet continue in existence. A cataleptic trance may look like death without being death. But inactivity may be so prolonged or so circumstanced that the only reasonable inference is that the club has become dissolved. In such cases there may be difficulty in determining the *punctum temporis* of dissolution: the less activity there is, the greater the difficulty of fastening upon one date rather than another as the moment of dissolution. In such cases the court must do the best it can by picking a reasonable date somewhere between the time when the club could still be said to exist, and the time when its existence had clearly come to an end...
>
> The question is whether on the facts of the present case the society ceased to exist on December 18, 1975.
>
> On that date, the position was that the club had ceased to operate as a club for several months. The picture was not one of mere inactivity alone; there were positive acts towards the winding up of the club. The sale of the club's stock of drinks was one instance, and others were the ending of the registration for VAT, and the dismissal of the steward. The cessation of any club activities, the ending of the use of the sports ground and the abandonment of preparing accounts or issuing membership cards were all in one sense examples of inactivity; but I think that there was in all probability some element of deliberation in these matters, and not a mere inertia. In [counsel's] phrase, there was a systematic dismantling of the club and its activities.
>
> However that may be, the resolution to sell the sports ground seems to me to conclude the matter. Having taken all steps, active or passive, required to terminate the activities of the club, short of passing a formal resolution to wind it up or dissolve it, the general meeting of the club resolved to sell the club's last asset.

(ii) *Distribution of surplus asset*

When an unincorporated association is dissolved, it may have surplus assets that derive from the members through the payment of subscriptions, or from gifts from members or third parties. It is important to determine what should happen to these assets. There are three possible consequences:

  (1) the assets may be returned to the people who provided them in the first place;

  (2) the assets may be transferred to the Crown on the ground that nobody owns them—that is, they become *bona vacantia*; or

  (3) the assets may be transferred to the members at the time of the dissolution.

Which consequence applies will depend on how the assets were held in the first place.

---

[120] [1982] 1 WLR 774. See also *Keene v Wellcom London Ltd* [2014] EWHC 134 (Ch); [2014] WTLR 1011.
[121] [1982] 1 WLR 774, 779.

(a) Resulting trust for transferors of property

A resulting trust can arise when property is held on an express trust that fails.[122] In such circumstances, the property will be held on a resulting trust for the settlor. Consequently, if property has been held on trust for the purposes of the association and the association is dissolved, the property will be held on resulting trust for the people who transferred the property to the trust in shares proportionate to their contributions.[123]

Where the effect of the dissolution of the association is to terminate the express trust, the property transferred will not be held on resulting trust for the transferors of the property if they can be considered to have divested themselves of all their rights to the property. This will be the case where, for example, money was paid to the association by a member in return for contractual benefits. If the society is then dissolved, the member cannot then claim recovery of the money. This is illustrated by *Cunnack v Edwards*,[124] in which a friendly society had been formed to raise funds to provide annuities for widows of members of the society who had died. The last member died in 1879 and the last widow died in 1892, at which point there was a surplus of £1,250 that was claimed by the personal representatives of the last members. The society was held to be moribund and so had been dissolved. It was held that there was no room for a resulting trust because each member had paid their contributions without reserving any beneficial interest to himself. A L Smith LJ said:[125]

> As the member paid his money to the society, so he divested himself of all interest in this money for ever, with this one reservation, that if the member left a widow she was to be provided for during her widowhood. Except as to this he abandoned and gave up the money for ever.[126]

This principle was applied in *Re West Sussex Constabulary's Widows, Children and Benevolent (1930) Fund Trusts*.

Re West Sussex Constabulary's Widows, Children and Benevolent (1930) Fund Trusts
[1971] Ch 1

A fund had been established to provide for the widows and children of deceased members of the West Sussex police force. The funds were derived from subscriptions from members and various donations and legacies, as well as the proceeds of entertainments, raffles, and collecting boxes. The police force was amalgamated with other forces and the fund was dissolved, with a surplus. It was held that, whilst donations and legacies were held on resulting trust, the members could not recover their subscriptions because they had divested themselves of any interest in the money in return for contractual benefits. Goff J said:[127]

> Then it was argued that there is a resulting trust, with several possible consequences. If this be the right view there must be a primary division of the fund into three parts, one representing contributions from former members, another contributions from the surviving members, and the third moneys raised

---

122 See further Chapter 8.3, pp. 384–99.
123 *Re Hobourn Aero Components Ltd's Air Raid Distress Fund* [1946] Ch 194.
124 [1896] 2 Ch 679.
125 Ibid, 683.
126 Consequently the surplus passed to the Crown as *bona vacantia*. See Chapter 8.3(c)(ii), pp. 393–9.
127 [1971] Ch 1, 9.

from outside sources. The surviving members then take the second, and possibly by virtue of rule 10, the first also. That rule is as follows:

> 'Any member who voluntarily terminates his membership shall forfeit all claim against the fund, except in the case of a member transferring to a similar fund of another force, in which instance the contributions paid by the member to the West Sussex Constabulary's Widows, Children and Benevolent (1930) Fund may be paid into the fund of the force to which the member transfers.'

Alternatively, the first part may belong to the past members on the footing that rule 10 is operative so long only as the fund is a going concern, or may be *bona vacantia*. The third is distributable in whole or in part between those who provided the money, or again is *bona vacantia*.

In my judgment the doctrine of resulting trust is clearly inapplicable to the contributions of both classes. Those persons who remained members until their deaths are in any event excluded because they have had all they contracted for, either because their widows and dependants have received or are in receipt of the prescribed benefits, or because they did not have a widow or dependants. In my view that is inherent in all the speeches in the Court of Appeal in *Cunnack v Edwards* [1896] 2 Ch 679. Further, whatever the effect of the fund's rule 10 may be upon the contributions of those members who left prematurely, they and the surviving members alike are also in my judgment unable to claim under a resulting trust because they put their money on a contractual basis and not one of trust: see per Harman J in *Re Gillingham Bus Disaster Fund* [1958] Ch 300 at 314. The only case which has given me difficulty on this aspect of the matter is *Re Hobourn Aero Components Ltd's Air Raid Distress Fund* [1946] Ch 86, where in somewhat similar circumstances it was held there was a resulting trust. The argument postulated, I think, the distinction between contract and trust but in another connection, namely, whether the fund was charitable: see at 89 and 90. There was in that case a resolution to wind up but that was not, at all events as expressed, the ratio decidendi: see *per* Cohen J at 97, but, as Cohen J observed, there was no argument for *bona vacantia*. Moreover, no rules or regulations were ever made and although in fact £1 per month was paid or saved for each member serving with the forces, there was no prescribed contractual benefits. In my judgment that case is therefore distinguishable.

Accordingly, in my judgment all the contributions of both classes are *bona vacantia*, but I must make a reservation with respect to possible contractual rights. In *Cunnack v Edwards* [1895] 1 Ch 489 and *Braithwaite v A-G* [1909] 1 Ch 510 all the members had received, or provision had been made for, all the contractual benefits. Here the matter has been cut short. Those persons who died whilst still in membership cannot, I conceive, have any rights because in their case the contract has been fully worked out, and on a contractual basis I would think that members who retired would be precluded from making any claim by rule 10, although that is perhaps more arguable. The surviving members, on the other hand, may well have a right in contract on the ground of frustration or total failure of consideration, and that right may embrace contributions made by past members, though I do not see how it could apply to moneys raised from outside sources . . .

I must now turn to the moneys raised from outside sources. Counsel for the Treasury Solicitor made an overriding general submission that there cannot be a resulting trust of any of the outside moneys because in the circumstances it is impossible to identify the trust property; no doubt something could be achieved by complicated accounting, but this, he submitted, would not be identification but notional reconstruction. I cannot accept that argument. In my judgment, in a case like the present, equity will cut the Gordian knot by simply dividing the ultimate surplus in proportion to the sources from which it has arisen . . .

Then counsel divided the outside moneys into three categories, first, the proceeds of entertainments, raffles and sweepstakes; secondly, the proceeds of collecting-boxes; and, thirdly, donations, including legacies if any, and he took particular objections to each.

> I agree that there cannot be any resulting trust with respect to the first category...whatever may be the true position with regard to collecting-boxes, it appears to me to be impossible to apply the doctrine of resulting trust to the proceeds of entertainments and sweepstakes and such-like money-raising operations for two reasons: first, the relationship is one of contract and not of trust; the purchaser of a ticket may have the motive of aiding the cause or he may not; he may purchase a ticket merely because he wishes to attend the particular entertainment or to try for the prize, but whichever it be, he pays his money as the price of what is offered and what he receives; secondly, there is in such cases no direct contribution to the fund at all; it is only the profit, if any, which is ultimately received and there may even be none...
>
> And I make the following declarations: First, that the portion attributable to donations and legacies is held on a resulting trust for the donors or their estates and the estates of the respective testators; secondly, that the remainder of the fund is *bona vacantia.*

The essential feature of *Cunnack* and *West Sussex* is that, where the payer of money receives, or expects to receive, some contractual benefit in return for the payment, he or she will be considered to have given up any rights to the return of the money. The reasoning employed in *Cunnack v Edwards* has, however, been doubted on the ground that property can be held on resulting trust even though the contributor had received all of the expected contractual benefits.[128] In fact, the result in *Cunnack* can be justified for the exceptional reason that a relevant statute at the time required the rules of the association to state all the possible uses of the society's assets and no use was identified in favour of the members. In other words, a resulting trust was excluded by a statutory provision. In *Air Jamaica v Charlton*,[129] it was held that surplus funds arising from the discontinuance of a pension scheme should be held on resulting trust for the employer and the employees who had contributed to the fund, in proportion to their contributions and regardless of any benefit that they had received from the fund. This is the better view: the fact that a member had received contractual benefits from the association should not prevent a resulting trust from arising.

(b) Bona vacantia *to the Crown*

Where property is ownerless, it will be considered to be *bona vacantia* and will be transferred to the Crown. This might arise where property has been held on trust for the purposes of an unincorporated association or its present members and, once the association has been dissolved, it is not possible to identify who transferred the property to the association, such as where a member who had paid subscriptions can no longer be identified.[130]

(c) *Contractual entitlement*

The contract-holding theory is the preferable explanation of how property can be held for the purposes of an unincorporated association. The adoption of this theory has significant advantages for the analysis of what should happen to the property on dissolution of the association, since the assets will simply belong to the members at the time of the dissolution according to their contractual rights under the rules of the association. Those rules may provide for a particular method of distribution of the assets on dissolution, which would be binding on the members. But, if no such provision is made, a

---

[128] *Davis v Richards and Wallington Industries Ltd* [1990] 1 WLR 1511, 1542 (Scott J); *Air Jamaica Ltd v Charlton* [1999] 1 WLR 1399, 1412 (Lord Millett). See Chapter 8.3(c)(iii), pp. 393–9.

[129] [1999] 1 WLR 1399.

[130] See *Cunnack v Edwards* [1896] 2 Ch 679 and *Re West Sussex Constabulary's Widows, Children and Benevolent (1930) Fund Trusts* [1971] Ch 1.

term will be implied into the rules to the effect that the surplus should be distributed equally between the members at the time of the dissolution.[131]

This was considered in *Re Bucks Constabulary Widows' and Orphans' Fund Friendly Society (No. 2)*,[132] which concerned an unincorporated association that provided for the relief of widows and orphans of deceased members of the Bucks Constabulary. Its funds were derived from voluntary contributions from its members. The Constabulary amalgamated with others and the society was dissolved. The society's rules did not provide for distribution of the assets on dissolution, so a term was implied into the rules of the society that the assets should be distributed in equal shares to those people who were members at the time of the dissolution. Walton J said:[133]

> it is I think pertinent to observe that all unincorporated societies rest in contract...but there is an implied contract between all of the members *inter se* governed by the rules of the society. In default of any rule to the contrary—and it will seldom, if ever, be that there is such a rule—when a member ceases to be a member of the association he *ipso facto* ceases to have any interest in its funds...
>
> Finally, although there is at any rate one later case, for the purpose of this review there comes a case which gives me great concern, *Re West Sussex Constabulary's Widows, Children and Benevolent (1930) Fund Trusts* [1971] Ch 1. The case is indeed easily distinguishable from the present case in that what was there under consideration was a simple unincorporated association and not a friendly society ...Otherwise the facts in that case present remarkable parallels to the facts in the present case. Goff J decided that the surplus funds had become *bona vacantia*...
>
> It will be observed that the first reason given by Goff J for his decision is that he could not accept the principle of the members' clubs as applicable...If all that Goff J meant was that the purposes of the fund before him were totally different from those of a members' club then of course one must agree, but if he meant to imply that there was some totally different principle of law applicable one must ask why that should be. His second reason is that in all the cases where the surviving members had taken, the organisation existed for the benefit of the members for the time being exclusively. This may be so, so far as actual decisions go, but what is the principle? Why are the members not in control, complete control, save as to any existing contractual rights, of the assets belonging to their organisation? One could understand the position being different if valid trusts had been declared of the assets in favour of third parties, for example charities, but that this was emphatically not the case was demonstrated by the fact that Goff J recognised that the members could have altered the rules prior to dissolution and put the assets into their own pockets. If there was no obstacle to their doing this, it shows in my judgment quite clearly that the money was theirs all the time...
>
> The conclusion therefore is that, as on dissolution there were members of the society here in question in existence, its assets are held on trust for such members to the total exclusion of any claim on behalf of the Crown.

The significance of the contract-holding theory to the distribution of surplus assets on the dissolution of the unincorporated association is particularly well illustrated by *Hanchett-Stamford v Attorney-General*,[134] which concerned the Performing and Captive Animals Defence League, an

---

[131] *Re Bucks Constabulary Widows' and Orphans' Fund Friendly Society (No. 2)* [1979] 1 WLR 936. The same approach will be adopted as regards distribution of the proceeds of sale amongst members even though the association has not been dissolved: *Re Horley Town Football Club* [2006] EWHC 2386 (Ch); [2006] WTLR 1817. See Chapter 6.4(b)(v), pp. 308–10.

[132] [1979] 1 WLR 936.

[133] Ibid, 944.

[134] [2008] EWHC 330 (Ch); [2009] Ch 173.

unincorporated association that was formed in 1914 to procure a ban on the use of performing animals. Eventually, the membership dwindled to a husband and wife. When the husband died, there were substantial assets, including a property worth £675,000 and stocks and shares worth over £1.7 million. The association was held to have dissolved on the death of the penultimate member, the husband, and the survivor, the wife, was entitled to all the assets. Lewison J said:[135]

> the members for the time being of an unincorporated association are beneficially entitled to 'its' assets, subject to the contractual arrangements between them...It is important to stress that this is a form of beneficial ownership; that is to say that in some sense the property belongs to the members...
>
> There is, I think, no difficulty in accepting Walton J's ultimate conclusion [in *Re Bucks Constabulary*]. Nor is there any difficulty in accepting that the member's rights are contractual rather than equitable. Nor is there any difficulty in accepting that on a member's death he ceases to have any interest in the assets of the unincorporated association. Accretion on death is inherent in the beneficial interest in any asset being held by joint tenants in equity; and is no doubt reinforced by contractual restrictions such as the rules of an association. It, therefore, follows that the estate of a deceased member can have no claim to the assets. In *Neville Estates Ltd v Madden* [1962] Ch 832 Cross J applied the same principle to cessation of membership through resignation. This must be a facet of the contractual relations between members. Walton J also said that if there is only one member of an unincorporated association, it must cease to exist. That, too, must I think be right both for the reasons that Walton J gave; and also because if the members' rights are based in contract, a contract must cease to bind once there is no other party who can enforce it.
>
> However, what I find more difficult to accept is that a member who has a beneficial interest in an asset, albeit subject to contractual restrictions, can have that beneficial interest divested from him on the death of another member. It leads to the conclusion that if there are two members of an association which has assets of, say £2m, they can by agreement divide those assets between them and pocket £1m each, but if one of them dies before they have divided the assets, the whole pot goes to the Crown as *bona vacantia*. Since Walton J was not dealing with a case in which there was only one surviving member, his observations were obiter...
>
> The cases are united in saying that on a dissolution the members of a dissolved association have a beneficial interest in its assets, and Lord Denning MR [in *Abbatt v Treasury Solicitor* [1969] 1 WLR 1575, 1583] goes as far as to say that it is a 'beneficial equitable joint tenancy'. I cannot see why the legal principle should be any different if the reason for the dissolution is the permanent cessation of the association's activities or the fall in its membership to below two. The same principle ought also to hold if the contractual restrictions are abrogated or varied by agreement of the members. I do not find in the authorities considered by Walton J anything that binds me to hold that where there is one identifiable and living member of an unincorporated association that has ceased to exist, the assets formerly held by or for that association pass to the Crown as *bona vacantia*. In addition, article 1 of the First Protocol of the European Convention for the Protection of Human Rights and Fundamental Freedoms guarantees the peaceful enjoyment of possessions. It says: 'No one shall be deprived of his possessions except in the public interest and subject to the conditions provided for by law...'
>
> On the face of it for one of two members of an unincorporated association to be deprived of his share in the assets of the association by reason of the death of the other of them, and without any compensation, appears to be a breach of this article. It is also difficult to see what public interest is served by the appropriation by the state of that member's share in the association's assets. This, in my judgment,

---

[135] Ibid, [31].

> provides another reason why the conclusion that a sole surviving member of an unincorporated association, while still alive, cannot claim its assets is unacceptable.
>
> I therefore respectfully decline to follow Walton J's obiter dictum that a sole surviving member of an unincorporated association cannot claim the assets of the association, and that they vest in the Crown as *bona vacantia*.

Lewison J's conclusion is logical and defensible; the death of the penultimate member should not divest the final member of their entitlement to the property that had been used for the purposes of the association.

Where distribution of assets occurs by reference to the contract-holding theory, usually the assets will be distributed equally between the members at the time of the dissolution, regardless of how long they have been members or the amount of subscriptions that they have paid.[136] In *Re Bucks Constabulary Widows' and Orphans' Fund Friendly Society (No. 2)*[137] Walton J said:

> The remaining question under this head which falls now to be argued is, of course, whether they are simply held per capita, or, as suggested in some of the cases, in proportion to the contributions made by each...the interests and rights of persons who are members of any type of unincorporated association are governed exclusively by contracts; that is to say the rights between themselves and their rights to any surplus assets. I say that to make it perfectly clear that I have not overlooked the fact that the assets of the society are usually vested in trustees on trust for the members. But that is quite a separate and distinct trust bearing no relation to the claims of the members *inter se* upon the surplus funds so held upon trust for their benefit.
>
> That being the case, prima facie there can be no doubt at all but that the distribution is on the basis of equality, because, as between a number of people contractually interested in a fund, there is no other method of distribution if no other method is provided by the terms of the contract, and it is not for one moment suggested here that there is any other method of distribution provided by the contract...
>
> The members are not entitled in equity to the fund, they are entitled at law. It is a matter, so far as the members are concerned, of pure contract, and, being a matter of pure contract, it is, in my judgment, as far as distribution is concerned, completely divorced from all questions of equitable doctrines. It is a matter of simple entitlement, and that entitlement, in my judgment, at this time of day must be, and can only be, in equal shares.

This principle of equal distribution was applied by Lawrence Collins J in *Re Horley Town Football Club*:[138]

> The Rules do not specify how the Club's assets are to be distributed following dissolution. In the absence of any rule to the contrary, there is to be implied into the rules of the Club a rule to the effect that the surplus funds of the Club should be divided on a dissolution amongst the members of the Club, and this distribution will normally be per capita among the members (irrespective of length of membership or the amount of subscriptions paid) but may reflect different classes of membership.

But sometimes the terms of the contract between the members will result in a different form of distribution. For example, in *Re Sick and Funeral Society of St John's Sunday School, Golcar*,[139] a society

---

[136] *Re GKN Bolts & Nuts Ltd etc. Work Sports and Social Club* [1982] 1 WLR 774.
[137] [1979] 1 WLR 936, 952.
[138] [2006] EWHC 2386 (Ch); [2006] WTLR 1817, [129].
[139] [1973] Ch 51.

had been formed at a Sunday school to provide for sickness and death benefits for its members, who could be teachers and children. Junior members under the age of thirteen paid half the weekly subscription and received sickness benefits at half the rate. Following dissolution of the society, it was held that the effect of the rule of the association was that junior members were entitled to only a half-share of the surplus assets as compared with the ordinary members. Megarry J said:[140]

> Is each member entitled to an equal share, or is there to be a division into full shares and half-shares, with those paying ½d. a week entitled only to a half-share, and those paying 1d. a week a full share? Or is the basis of distribution to be proportionate to the amounts respectively contributed by each member? The first step, in my view, is to decide between the first two contentions on the one hand and the third on the other: is the proper basis that of division per capita, whether in full or half-shares, or that of division in proportion to the amounts contributed? In discussing this, I speak, of course, in general terms, and subject to any other basis for division that is to be discerned in the rules or any other source...
>
> It seems to me, with all respect, that much of the difficulty arises from confusing property with contract. A resulting trust is essentially a property concept: any property that a man does not effectually dispose of remains his own. If, then, there is a true resulting trust in respect of an unexpended balance of payments made to some club or association, there will be a resulting trust in respect of that unexpended balance, and the beneficiaries under that trust will be those who made the payments. If any are dead, the trusts will be for their estates; death does not deprive a man of his beneficial interest. Yet in what I may call 'the resulting trust cases', the beneficiaries who were held to be entitled were the members living at the time of the dissolution, to the exclusion of those who died or otherwise ceased to be members. If, then, there were any resulting trust, it must be a trust modified in some way, perhaps by some unexplained implied term, that distinguishes between the quick and the dead. It cannot be merely an ordinary resulting trust.
>
> On the other hand, membership of a club or association is primarily a matter of contract. The members make their payments, and in return they become entitled to the benefits of membership in accordance with the rules. The sums they pay cease to be their individual property, and so cease to be subject to any concept of resulting trust. Instead, they become the property, through the trustees of the club or association, of all the members for the time being, including themselves. A member who, by death or otherwise, ceases to be a member thereby ceases to be the part-owner of any of the club's property: those who remain continue owners. If, then, dissolution ensues, there must be a division of the property of the club or association among those alone who are owners of that property, to the exclusion of former members. In that division, I cannot see what relevance there can be in the respective amounts of the contributions. The newest member, who has made a single payment when he joined only a year ago, is as much a part-owner of the property of the club or association as a member who has been making payments for 50 years. Each has had what he has paid for: the newest member has had the benefits of membership for a year or so and the oldest member for 50 years. Why should the latter, who for his money has had the benefits of membership for 50 times as long as the former, get the further benefit of receiving 50 times as much in the winding-up?...
>
> Accordingly, I reject the basis of proportionate division in favour of equality, or division per capita. But then the second question arises, namely, whether the principle of equality prevails not only when there is no more than one class of members but when there are two or more classes. Is the proposed division into shares and half-shares sound, or ought it to be rejected in favour of equality throughout?
>
> On the footing that the rules of a club or association form the basis of the contract between all the members, I must look at the rules of the society to see whether they indicate any basis other than

---

[140] Ibid, 58.

that of equality. It seems to me that they do. Those aged from 5 to 12 years old pay contributions at half the rate (rule 9), and correspondingly their allowances (rule 12) and death benefit (rule 14) are also paid at half the rate. Where the rules have written into them the basis of inequality among different classes of members in relation to the principal contractual burdens and benefits of membership, it seems to me to follow that this inequality ought also to be applied to the surplus property of the society. A distinction between classes of members is quite different from a distinction between individual members of the same class based on the amounts contributed by each member. At any given moment one can say that the rights and liabilities of all the members of one class differ in the same way from the rights and liabilities of all the members of the other class, irrespective of the length of membership or anything else. It was indeed suggested that the words 'two classes of subscribers' in rule 9 did not mean that there were two classes of members, the word 'subscribers' being in contrast with the word 'member' used in the next sentence. But the rules are too ill-drafted for any such inferences to be drawn; and rule 5, providing for special meetings of the committee when requested by three 'subscribers', and a general meeting if required by twenty of the 'members', strongly suggests that the terms are used interchangeably. At any rate, I have heard no sensible explanations of the distinction.

In addition, it was confirmed that members who had been excluded from the association by virtue of failing to pay their subscriptions were not entitled to share in the distribution of assets, even if they had paid the arrears of their subscriptions after the association had been dissolved. They would, however, have been able to share in the distribution had they paid the arrears before dissolution, because they would then have been members at the time of the dissolution.

(iii) *Conclusions*

The rise of the contract-holding theory has had a beneficial impact on the explanation of how property can be held for the purposes of an unincorporated association whilst giving effect to the donor's intention. The contract-holding theory is also useful more generally as a mechanism for circumventing the traditional restrictions on the validity of non-charitable purpose trusts by virtue of the identification of ascertainable beneficiaries. A non-charitable purpose can, in effect, be achieved through the use of an unincorporated association.

QUESTION

Alan, in his will, left £1 million to purchase land and build a sports pavilion for the benefit of current and former employees of Alendra Ltd, a firm which Alan had created. On Alan's death in 1930, land was purchased for use as a sports ground and a pavilion was built. This was used by Alendra United FC, a football club. According to the constitution of the club, all employees of Alendra Ltd are automatically members without any obligation to pay a subscription. Other people can join the club, but only if they pay an annual subscription. No provision is made for distribution of assets on the dissolution of the club. Over the years, the number of people employed by Alendra Ltd has shrunk. Alendra United FC has eleven members, five of whom are employees or former employees. The remainder are liable to pay subscriptions, although one of them, George, has not paid his subscription for two years. The club has received an offer for the purchase of the sports ground and pavilion for £10 million for a housing development. All eleven members vote to dissolve the club. What should happen to the £10 million purchase price?

FURTHER READING

Baughen, 'Performing Animals and the Dissolution of Unincorporated Associations: The "Contract-holding Theory" Vindicated' [2010] Conv 216.

Hayton, 'Developing the Obligation Characteristic of the Trust' (2001) 117 LQR 96.

Luxton, 'Gifts to Clubs: Contract-Holding is Trumps' [2007] Conv 274.

Matthews, 'A Problem in the Construction of Gifts to Unincorporated Associations' [1995] Conv 302.

Matthews, 'The New Trust: Obligations without Rights?', in *Trends in Contemporary Trust Law* (ed. Oakley) (Oxford: Clarendon Press, 1996), ch. 1.

Pawlowski and Summers, 'Private Purpose Trusts: A Reform Proposal' [2007] Conv 440.

Warburton, 'The Holding of Property by Unincorporated Associations' [1985] Conv 318.

PART IV

NON-EXPRESS TRUSTS

7

CONSTRUCTIVE TRUSTS

CENTRAL ISSUES

1. A constructive trust arises by operation of law without regard to the intentions of the parties.

2. Most constructive trusts are triggered by the defendant's unconscionable conduct. Unconscionability can be interpreted either in a narrow subjective sense, with reference to the conscience of the particular defendant, or a wider objective sense, with reference to the conscience of a reasonable observer.

3. Exceptionally, a constructive trust will be recognized even though the defendant has not acted unconscionably, such as the constructive trust that arises once a contract to sell land has been made.

4. Some jurisdictions recognize a remedial constructive trust, whereby equitable proprietary rights arise through the exercise of judicial discretion, but such a trust is not recognized in England and Wales.

5. As with express trusts, title over particular property that is held on constructive trust is split between trustees and beneficiaries. But a constructive trustee is not subject to the same duties as an express trustee.

1. ESSENTIAL FEATURES OF CONSTRUCTIVE TRUSTS

A constructive trust is a true trust like any other, where the constructive trustee has legal title to identifiable property that is held for the benefit of the beneficiaries. But the distinctive feature of a constructive trust is that it arises by operation of law, without regard to the intentions of the parties.[1] The constructive trust differs, therefore, from an express trust, which is created by the settlor intentionally,[2] and, as will be seen, the resulting trust, which is triggered by the presumed or imputed intention of the transferor that property is to be held on trust for him or her.[3]

---

[1] *Air Jamaica v Charlton* [1999] 1 WLR 1399, 1412 (Lord Millett).
[2] See Chapter 3, 'The Requirements of an Express Trust'.
[3] See Chapter 8, 'Resulting Trusts'.

The constructive trust can arise in a wide variety of circumstances, but there is little agreement amongst the judiciary or commentators as to when and why it will be recognized. It has even been suggested by Swadling[4] that the constructive trust is a fiction:[5]

> The constructive trust is no trust at all, merely an inappropriate label to describe two species of court order...that a defendant pay the claimant a sum of money and that the defendant convey to him a particular right.

But, whilst this is undoubtedly true in some contexts where the label of 'constructive trust' has been improperly used,[6] in other contexts the term 'constructive trust' is properly employed to identify a genuine trust where legal title is held by one party and equitable title by the other, which arises by operation of law. This should legitimately be called a 'constructive trust' to distinguish it from express and resulting trusts.

Since constructive trusts arise by operation of law, there is no requirement that they be formally declared. It is for this reason that constructive trusts of land do not need to be evidenced in writing.[7] Once created, the trust functions in the same way as an express trust, save that the constructive trustee is not subject to the same obligations as an express trustee.[8] But the fact that the beneficiary of such a trust has an equitable proprietary interest in the trust property means that, if the trustee becomes insolvent, the beneficiary's claim to the trust property will rank above the claims of other unsecured creditors of the trustee.

(a) THE THEORETICAL FOUNDATIONS OF CONSTRUCTIVE TRUSTS

Identifying a single theory to explain the disparate circumstances in which constructive trusts are recognized is controversial. Sir Terence Etherton has recognized:[9]

> The search for an acceptable, universally acknowledged, principle for the establishment of a constructive trust, which gives coherence to past decisions and provides a clear guide for the future, will certainly prove elusive in relation to the many different areas of law and fact in which constructive trusts arise.

Similarly, Lord Scott[10] has recognized that 'it is impossible to prescribe exhaustively the circumstances sufficient to create a constructive trust'.

Despite this, it has sometimes been suggested that the constructive trust is a response to the defendant's unjust enrichment,[11] but the courts have recognized that there is a vital distinction between claims in unjust enrichment and claims to vindicate property rights.[12] In the 1970s, some judges, led by Lord Denning MR, used the constructive trust as a mechanism with which to create equitable property rights where justice and good conscience demanded it.[13] But this is unprincipled and uncertain. Lord Browne-Wilkinson has recognized that unconscionability on the part of the defendant is

---

[4] 'The Fiction of the Constructive Trust' (2011) CLP 399.
[5] Ibid, 400.
[6] See further Chapter 7.1(b)(iv), p. 331.
[7] Law of Property Act 1925, s. 53(2).
[8] See Chapter 7.4, pp. 358–9.
[9] 'Constructive Trusts: A New Model for Equity and Unjust Enrichment' (2008) 67 CLJ 265.
[10] In *Cobbe v Yeoman's Row Management Ltd* [2008] UKHL 55; [2008] 1 WLR 1752, [30].
[11] See Birks, *Unjust Enrichment* (2nd edn) (Oxford: Oxford University Press, 2005), p. 302.
[12] *Foskett v McKeown* [2001] 1 AC 102, 129 (Lord Millett); *Bank of Cyprus UK Ltd v Menelaou* [2015] UKSC 66; [2016] AC 176, [37] (Lord Clarke); [98] (Lord Neuberger); [108] (Lord Carnwath).
[13] *Eves v Eves* [1975] 1 WLR 1338.

the general principle that underpins the recognition of the constructive trust in all cases.[14] This was also recognized by Millett LJ in *Paragon Finance plc v DB Thakerar and Co*:[15]

> A constructive trust arises by operation of law whenever the circumstances are such that it would be unconscionable for the owner of property...to assert his own beneficial interest in the property and deny the beneficial interest of another...In these cases the plaintiff does not impugn the transaction by which the defendant obtained control of the property. He alleges that the circumstances in which the defendant obtained control make it unconscionable for him thereafter to assert a beneficial interest in the property.

Careful analysis of the different circumstances under which the constructive trust has been recognized reveals that unconscionability is indeed a significant trigger for this trust, in that the constructive trust is a response to the defendant's actual or potential unconscionable conduct. 'Unconscionability' can be interpreted in both a narrow and a wide sense, depending on the particular context. The narrow sense focuses on the conscience of the defendant and involves a subjective test relating to the defendant's knowledge or suspicion of the circumstances of receipt.[16] The wider sense involves an objective test of unconscionability and operates to ensure that the defendant does not benefit from what is considered by a reasonable observer to amount to unconscionable conduct.[17]

Unconscionability cannot, however, explain all cases where the language of the constructive trust is used, but the trusts arising in these other cases might be better analysed simply as implied trusts.[18]

Other theories have been suggested to explain constructive trusts. For example, Gardner has suggested that certain constructive trusts, which 'produce an outcome which someone intended and which would not otherwise come about',[19] operate to correct a reliance loss:[20]

> specifically, the loss that someone suffers when, acting in reasonable reliance on another's undertaking, he foregoes his opportunity to achieve the content of the undertaking in some way. If these trusts can indeed be regarded in this way, it becomes much easier to see why the law should impose them.

This thesis is used to explain the operation of certain constructive trusts,[21] but Gardner does not consider that it explains the recognition of all constructive trusts. Whilst the thesis is persuasive in its own terms, it can still be regarded as falling within a wider theory of unconscionability, for, where a party has reasonably relied on an undertaking, it is unconscionable for the party who made that undertaking to then deny it.

(b) TYPES OF CONSTRUCTIVE TRUST

Much of the complexity of the law in this area arises because the judges use the language of the constructive trust in five distinct ways.

---

[14] *Westdeutsche Landesbank Girozentrale v Islington London Borough Council* [1996] AC 669, 705.

[15] [1999] 1 All ER 400, 408.

[16] See Chapter 7.2(a), pp. 332–6.

[17] See Chapter 7.2(e), pp. 342–51.

[18] See, in particular, the trust arising from a contract to sell land, Chapter 7.2(f), pp. 351–4, and the so-called common intention constructive trust, Chapter 9.2, pp. 432–62.

[19] 'Reliance-based Constructive Trusts' in *Constructive and Resulting Trusts* (ed. Mitchell) (Oxford: Hart, 2010), p. 63.

[20] Ibid.

[21] Including secret trusts, Chapter 7.2(e)(ii), p. 346; mutual wills, Chapter 7.2(c)(iii), pp. 346–51; and proprietary estoppel, Chapter 9.4, pp. 469–80.

(i) *Institutional constructive trust*

The institutional constructive trust is the orthodox mode of analysing these trusts, which are treated as arising by operation of law on the occurrence of a certain event in which a constructive trust has previously been recognized.[22] Under this category of the constructive trust, the court simply recognizes that the trust has already arisen, without having any discretion to do otherwise.

(ii) *Remedial constructive trust*

The remedial constructive trust will be recognized where a judge, in the exercise of his or her discretion, considers that it is appropriate that the defendant should hold property on trust for the claimant. A consequence is that the creation of the equitable proprietary interest in the property that is held on trust occurs by virtue of the exercise of judicial discretion and it is this that distinguishes the remedial from the institutional constructive trust, as was recognized by Lord Browne-Wilkinson in *Westdeutsche Landesbank Girozentrale v Islington LBC*:[23]

> Under an institutional constructive trust the trust arises by operation of law as from the date of the circumstances which give rise to it: the function of the court is merely to declare that such trust has arisen in the past. The consequences that flow from such a trust having arisen (including the potentially unfair consequences to third parties who in the interim have received the trust property) are also determined by rules of law, not under a discretion. A remedial constructive trust, as I understand it, is different. It is a judicial remedy giving rise to an enforceable obligation: the extent to which it operates retrospectively to the prejudice of third parties lies in the discretion of the court.

This notion of the constructive trust has been recognized in a number of Commonwealth countries, but it has been rejected in England and Wales.[24] Whether it should be recognized in this jurisdiction will be considered later in this chapter.[25]

(iii) *Constructive trust as remedy*

Where a defendant has received property in which the claimant has an existing equitable proprietary interest, it is possible for the court to vindicate that interest by requiring the defendant to hold the property, or a share of it, on constructive trust for the claimant, regardless of whether this was the original property taken from the claimant or substitute property that can be considered to represent the original property.[26] The claimant can then call for the property to be transferred to him or her. This is different from the remedial constructive trust, because that involves the creation of an equitable proprietary interest that had not previously existed. Where the constructive trust as remedy is used, there is already an equitable proprietary interest in existence, which will typically have been created by an express trust; the constructive trust effectively operates as a conduit for the transfer of property from the defendant to the claimant. It has been suggested that, if the claimant's original equitable interest arose under an express trust, the defendant who has received the property or its substitute should hold that property on the same trust.[27] But this argument is unconvincing. The defendant

---

[22] See *Halifax Building Society v Thomas* [1996] Ch 217, 229 (Peter Gibson LJ).

[23] [1996] AC 669, 714.

[24] *FHR European Ventures LLP v Cedar Capital Partners LLC* [2014] UKSC 45; [2015] AC 250.

[25] See Chapter 7.3, pp. 355–8.

[26] See further Chapter 18.5, pp. 893–911.

[27] Lord Millett, 'Proprietary Restitution', in *Equity in Commercial Law* (eds Degeling and Edelman) (Sydney: Law Book Co., 2005), ch. 12, pp. 315–16. See also *Foskett v McKeown* [2001] 1 AC 102, 108 (Lord Browne-Wilkinson).

who has received the property will not be under the same trust obligations as the original express trustee: the defendant will not be subject to an obligation to invest the trust property, for example. The better view, therefore, is that the recipient does indeed hold the property under a distinct trust, which, because it arises by operation of law, should be characterized as a constructive trust.

(iv) *Liability to account as a constructive trustee*

Sometimes the language of the constructive trust is used even though the defendant does not hold property on trust at all, but the label 'constructive trust' is used simply as a device to hold the defendant personally liable to the claimant. So, for example, where the defendant has unconscionably received property, which has been transferred in breach of trust or fiduciary duty,[28] or where the defendant has dishonestly assisted a breach of trust or fiduciary duty,[29] the defendant will be held liable to account as though he or she were a constructive trustee. But the language of the constructive trust in this context is inappropriate because there is no property to be held on trust. The defendant's liability for both causes of action is personal, either to restore the value of any property received, or to compensate the claimant for loss suffered as a result of the defendant's assistance. The defendant holds nothing on trust for anybody. This has now been recognized in *Williams v Central Bank of Nigeria*,[30] where Lord Sumption said that this category:[31]

> ...comprises persons who never assumed and never intended to assume the status of a trustee, whether formally or informally, but have exposed themselves to equitable remedies by virtue of their participation in the unlawful misapplication of trust assets. Either they have dishonestly assisted in a misapplication of the funds by the trustee, or they have received trust assets knowing that the transfer to them was a breach of trust. In either case, they may be required by equity to account as if they were trustees or fiduciaries, although they are not. These can conveniently be called cases of ancillary liability. The intervention of equity in such cases does not reflect any pre-existing obligation but comes about solely because of the misapplication of the assets. It is purely remedial. The distinction between these two categories is not just a matter of the chronology of events leading to liability. It is fundamental. In the words of Millett LJ in *Paragon Finance plc v DB Thakerar & Co* [1999] 1 All ER 400, 413 it is 'the distinction between an institutional trust and a remedial formula—between a trust and a catch-phrase'.

(v) *Common intention constructive trust*

This is a distinct form of constructive trust, which is triggered with reference to the express, implied, or imputed intention of the parties.[32] This trust arises from an agreement or understanding of the parties as to whether they have a beneficial interest in property and, if so, what the extent of that interest might be. This is especially significant where a couple have cohabited and their home is registered either in the name of them both[33] or in the name of one of them only.[34] Although the language of the constructive trust is used in these cases, this is very different from the ordinary constructive trust, because it responds to the implied intention of the parties, rather than arising by operation of law, and so is properly described as an implied rather than a constructive trust.

---

[28] See Chapter 19.3, pp. 951–70.

[29] See Chapter 19.2, pp. 928–51.

[30] [2014] UKSC 10; [2014] AC 1189.

[31] Ibid, [9]. See also, ibid, [64] (Lord Neuberger); *Dubai Aluminium Co. Ltd v Salaam* [2002] UKHL 48; [2003] 2 AC 366, 404 (Lord Millett). See also Chapter 16.9(b)(i), pp. 784–7.

[32] See Chapter 9.2, pp. 432–62.

[33] *Stack v Dowden* [2007] UKHL 17; [2007] 2 AC 432, discussed in Chapter 9.2(c)(ii), pp. 452–4, and *Jones v Kernott* [2011] UKSC 53; [2012] 1 AC 776, discussed in Chapter 9.2(c)(iii), pp. 454–5.

[34] Chapter 9.2(c)(i), pp. 447–52.

(vi) *Conclusions*

Of the five types of constructive trust, it is the institutional constructive trust that is most significant. The remedial constructive trust is not recognized in English law. The constructive trust as remedy is relevant to equitable proprietary claims, and so is considered later.[35] Liability as a constructive trustee does not actually involve the recognition of a constructive trust of property, and the common intention constructive trust, being triggered by the intention of the parties, is clearly distinct from the core categories of the constructive trust.

2. CATEGORIES OF INSTITUTIONAL CONSTRUCTIVE TRUST

(a) UNCONSCIONABLE RETENTION

Where it is unconscionable for the defendant to retain property, he or she will hold it on constructive trust for the claimant, who is typically the person from whom the property was transferred. This category of constructive trust was recognized in *Westdeutsche Landesbank Girozentrale v Islington LBC*.

Westdeutsche Landesbank Gironzentrale v Islington LBC [1996] AC 669

The claimant bank had paid money to the defendant local authority pursuant to an interest rate swap contract that was null and void. The bank sought restitution of the money. One particular question, that was considered by Lord Browne-Wilkinson, was whether the defendant held the money it had received on a constructive trust, which was significant since it affected the type of interest that could be awarded.[36] His Lordship said:[37]

This is not a case where the bank had any equitable interest which pre-dated receipt by the local authority of the upfront payment. Therefore, in order to show that the local authority became a trustee, the bank must demonstrate circumstances which raised a trust for the first time either at the date on which the local authority received the money or at the date on which payment into the mixed account was made. Counsel for the bank specifically disavowed any claim based on a constructive trust. This was plainly right because the local authority had no relevant knowledge sufficient to raise a constructive trust at any time before the moneys, upon the bank account going into overdraft, became untraceable. Once there ceased to be an identifiable trust fund, the local authority could not become a trustee: *Re Goldcorp Exchange Ltd* [1995] 1 AC 74...

In [*Chase Manhattan Bank NA v Israel-British Bank (London) Ltd* [1981] Ch 105], a New York bank had by mistake paid the same sum twice to the credit of the defendant, a London bank. Shortly thereafter, the defendant bank went into insolvent liquidation. The question was whether Chase Manhattan had a claim *in rem* against the assets of the defendant bank to recover the second payment.

Goulding J was asked to assume that the moneys paid under a mistake were capable of being traced in the assets of the recipient bank: he was only concerned with the question whether there was a proprietary base on which the tracing remedy could be founded: at 116. He held that, where money was paid under a mistake, the receipt of such money without more constituted the recipient a trustee: he

---

[35] See Chapter 7.3, pp. 355–8.
[36] See Chapter 17.5, pp. 838–40.
[37] [1996] AC 669, 707.

said that the payer 'retains an equitable property in it and the conscience of [the recipient] is subjected to a fiduciary duty to respect his proprietary right': at 119.

It will be apparent from what I have already said that I cannot agree with this reasoning. First, it is based on a concept of retaining an equitable property in money where, prior to the payment to the recipient bank, there was no existing equitable interest. Further, I cannot understand how the recipient's 'conscience' can be affected at a time when he is not aware of any mistake. Finally, the judge found that the law of England and that of New York were in substance the same. I find this a surprising conclusion since the New York law of constructive trusts has for a long time been influenced by the concept of a remedial constructive trust, whereas hitherto English law has for the most part only recognised an institutional constructive trust: see *Metall und Rohstoff AG v Donaldson Lufkin & Jenrette Inc* [1990] 1 QB 391 at 478–480.... Thus, for the law of New York to hold that there is a remedial constructive trust where a payment has been made under a void contract gives rise to different consequences from holding that an institutional constructive trust arises in English law.

However, although I do not accept the reasoning of Goulding J, *Chase Manhattan* may well have been rightly decided. The defendant bank knew of the mistake made by the paying bank within two days of the receipt of the moneys: see at 115. The judge treated this fact as irrelevant (at 114) but in my judgment it may well provide a proper foundation for the decision. Although the mere receipt of the moneys, in ignorance of the mistake, gives rise to no trust, the retention of the moneys after the recipient bank learned of the mistake may well have given rise to a constructive trust.

Although Goulding J in *Chase Manhattan Bank* recognized that the claimant who had paid money by mistake had an equitable proprietary interest in it, he did not explain how this interest arose. In *Westdeutsche Landesbank*, Lord Browne-Wilkinson justified this on the ground that the defendant had acted unconscionably in not repaying the money after it had discovered the mistake. Constructive trusts will be triggered by this principle of unconscionable retention in other circumstances, such as where the defendant has obtained property by fraud.[38]

Lord Browne-Wilkinson's analysis of *Chase Manhattan Bank* has, however, been described by Ward LJ in *Maqsood v Mahmood*[39] as not forming part of the ratio of the case and as being tentative. Whilst this is undoubtedly true, the significance of the constructive trust in such circumstances was confirmed in *Re Farepak Food and Gifts Ltd*,[40] which recognized that claimants, who had paid in advance for goods or services, could, in principle, claim that the money was held for them on constructive trust where the defendant, at the time of receiving payment, had already decided that the goods and services would not be provided because it would cease trading, although this was not established on the facts. Presumably, the defendant's conscience should only be considered to be affected where he or she was actually aware of the claimant's mistake or the invalidity of the transaction,[41] for only then can the defendant's conduct be properly characterized as unconscionable.

Lord Browne-Wilkinson in *Westdeutsche Landesbank* went on to recognize that a thief who stole a bag of coins would similarly hold that property on a constructive trust:[42]

The argument for a resulting trust was said to be supported by the case of a thief who steals a bag of coins. At law those coins remain traceable only so long as they are kept separate: as soon as they are

---

[38] *Sinclair Investment Holdings SA v Versailles Trade Finance Ltd* [2005] EWCA Civ 722; *Campden Hill Ltd v Chakrani* [2005] EWHC 911 (Ch).

[39] [2012] EWCA Civ 251, [37].

[40] [2006] EWHC 3272 (Ch).

[41] *Westdeutsche Landesbank Girozentrale v Islington LBC* [1996] AC 669, 705 (Lord Browne-Wilkinson).

[42] [1996] AC 669, 716.

mixed with other coins or paid into a mixed bank account they cease to be traceable at law.[43] Can it really be the case, it is asked, that in such circumstances the thief cannot be required to disgorge the property which, in equity, represents the stolen coins? Moneys can only be traced in equity if there has been at some stage a breach of fiduciary duty, i.e. if either before the theft there was an equitable proprietary interest (e.g. the coins were stolen trust moneys) or such interest arises under a resulting trust at the time of the theft or the mixing of the moneys. Therefore, it is said, a resulting trust must arise either at the time of the theft or when the moneys are subsequently mixed. Unless this is the law, there will be no right to recover the assets representing the stolen moneys once the moneys have become mixed.

I agree that the stolen moneys are traceable in equity. But the proprietary interest which equity is enforcing in such circumstances arises under a constructive, not a resulting, trust. Although it is difficult to find clear authority for the proposition, when property is obtained by fraud equity imposes a constructive trust on the fraudulent recipient: the property is recoverable and traceable in equity. Thus, an infant who has obtained property by fraud is bound in equity to restore it: *Stocks v Wilson* [1913] 2 KB 235 at 244; *R Leslie Ltd v Sheill* [1914] 3 KB 607. Moneys stolen from a bank account can be traced in equity: *Bankers Trust Co v Shapira* [1980] 1 WLR 1274 at 1282: see also *McCormick v Grogan* (1869) LR 4 HL 82 at 97.

This dictum was considered by Rimer J in *Shalson v Russo*:[44]

I do not find that an easy passage. As to the first paragraph, a thief ordinarily acquires no property in what he steals and cannot give a title to it even to a good faith purchaser: both the thief and the purchaser are vulnerable to claims by the true owner to recover his property. If the thief has no title in the property, I cannot see how he can become a trustee of it for the true owner: the owner retains the legal and beneficial title. If the thief mixes stolen money with other money in a bank account, the common law cannot trace into it. Equity has traditionally been regarded as similarly incompetent unless it could first identify a relevant fiduciary relationship,[45] but in many cases of theft there will be none. The fact that, traditionally, equity can only trace into a mixed bank account if that precondition is first satisfied provides an unsatisfactory justification for any conclusion that the stolen money must necessarily be trust money so as to enable the precondition to be satisfied. It is either trust money or it is not. If it is not, it is not legitimate artificially to change its character so as to bring it within the supposed limits of equity's powers to trace: the answer is to develop those powers so as to meet the special problems raised by stolen money...

As to Lord Browne-Wilkinson's more general proposition in the second paragraph that property obtained by fraud is automatically held by the recipient on a constructive trust for the person defrauded, I respectfully regard the authorities he cites as providing less than full support for it. At any rate, they do not in my view support the proposition that property transferred under a voidable contract induced by fraud will immediately (and prior to any rescission) be held on trust for the transferor.

Rimer J's real concern with treating a thief as a constructive trustee of the stolen property is that the victim will typically have retained legal title to the stolen property so that the thief cannot be a trustee of it,[46] save where the property is mixed with other property so that it loses its identity at law.

---

[43] See Chapter 18.3(c)(i), pp. 860–4.
[44] [2003] EWHC 1637 (Ch); [2005] Ch 281, [110].
[45] See Chapter 18.3(c)(ii)(a), pp. 867–70.
[46] See also Barkehall Thomas, 'Thieves as Trustees: The Enduring Legacy of *Black v S Freedman and Co*' (2009) 3 JoE 52.

Despite this, Lord Browne-Wilkinson in *Westdeutsche Landesbank* and the High Court of Australia[47] have recognized that a thief will indeed hold property on constructive trust for the victim.[48] An explanation for this result has been suggested by Tarrant, namely that the thief holds his or her rights to possess the stolen property on trust for the victim.[49] It has been recognized that a thief does indeed have a possessory title to the stolen property, so, for example, if that property is unlawfully taken from a thief by a third party, the thief can assert his or her possessory rights against that third party.[50] It has further been recognized that the thief, or the person who obtains the stolen property from the thief, has a good title to the stolen property against anybody in the world, except for the victim of the theft.[51] The victim of theft should, therefore, be considered to have both a residuary legal title in the stolen property and an equitable proprietary interest in the thief's possessory title by virtue of the thief's unconscionable retention of the property. The victim then has a choice as to whether to rely on his or her legal property right or, instead, upon his or her equitable right to the property, when asserting a claim against the thief or a subsequent possessor of the stolen property. The advantage of relying on the equitable property right is that the remedies in Equity to vindicate property rights are much more extensive than at law,[52] and that the claimant is able to make a claim to recover the stolen property or its proceeds even though it has become mixed with other property.[53]

In *Westdeutsche* itself a constructive trust was not recognized because, once the defendant had discovered that the transaction was void, the claimant's money had ceased to be identifiable.[54] If, however, the money was identifiable when the defendant became aware that it had been paid pursuant to a void transaction, its continued retention would have been unconscionable and it would have been held on constructive trust. It has been recognized, however, in *Maqsood v Mahmood*,[55] that the recipient of money under a contract that is void because it is *ultra vires* one of the parties does not hold that money on constructive trust for the payer. Ward LJ said:[56]

> [counsel] argued…that the recipient of money under a contract under which there is a total failure of consideration, the recipient being aware at the time of payment of the facts which give rise to the failure of consideration, holds the money received on a constructive trust for the payer. This seems to me to be inconsistent with the policy recognised by the House of Lords, that it is not as a general rule desirable to introduce equitable proprietary remedies into the realm of commercial contracts, and thereby to give the counterparty under the particular contract the additional security and priority of a proprietary remedy.

It follows that the role of unconscionable conduct as a trigger for property to be held on constructive trust remains a matter of some uncertainty and controversy. But, if unconscionable conduct in not returning property to the transferor when the recipient suspects that it should not have been transferred, is to trigger a constructive trust, there is no reason why that should be confined to transfer by mistake and not apply where the underlying transaction is null and void, especially because, as will

---

[47] *Black v F S Freedman and Co.* (1910) 12 CLR 105.
[48] See also *Armstrong GmbH v Winnington Networks Ltd* [2012] EWHC 10 (Ch); [2013] Ch 156, [128] (Stephen Morris QC).
[49] 'Property Rights to Stolen Money' (2005) 32 UWALR 234, 245; Tarrant, 'Thieves as Trustees: In Defence of the Theft Principle' (2009) 3 JoE 170, 172.
[50] *Costello v Chief Constable of Derbyshire* [2001] 3 All ER 150.
[51] *Islamic Republic of Iran v Barakat Galleries Ltd* [2009] QB 22, [15] (Lord Phillips).
[52] See further Chapter 18.5, pp. 893–911.
[53] See Chapter 18.3(c)(ii)(c), pp. 870–9.
[54] [1996] AC 669, 689 (Lord Goff) and 707 (Lord Browne-Wilkinson).
[55] [2012] EWCA Civ 251.
[56] Ibid, [38].

be seen next, property can be held on constructive trust where it is transferred pursuant to a voidable contract that has been rescinded.

(b) RESCISSION OF A CONTRACT

Where a contract has been rescinded in Equity,[57] for example, for misrepresentation or undue influence, any property transferred to the defendant under the contract will be held on constructive trust for the claimant. This was recognized by Millett J in *Lonrho plc v Fayed (No. 2)*:[58]

> A contract obtained by fraudulent misrepresentation is voidable, not void, even in equity. The representee may elect to avoid it, but until he does so, the representor is not a constructive trustee of the property transferred pursuant to the contract, and no fiduciary relationship exists between him and the representee, see *Daly v Sydney Stock Exchange Ltd* (1986) 160 CLR 371 at 387–390 per Brennan J. It may well be that if the representee elects to avoid the contract and set aside a transfer of property made pursuant to it, the beneficial interest in the property will be treated as having remained vested in him throughout, at least to the extent necessary to support any tracing claim.

In *El Ajou v Dollar Land Holdings plc*,[59] however, Millett J characterized the trust that arises as an 'old-fashioned institutional resulting trust'. Characterization of the trust as resulting is not, however, consistent with the key principles relating to the law of resulting trusts, namely that such a trust arises either where there has been a failure of an express trust or where there is a voluntary transfer to the defendant.[60] Consequently, the preferable view is that the trust arising on rescission is constructive, and is justified by the defendant's unconscionable conduct in not returning the property following rescission of the underlying transaction. This was recognized by Etherton C in *The National Crime Agency v Robb*:[61]

> Millett J expressed the view in *El Ajou v Dollar Land Holdings plc* [1993] 3 All ER 717, 734 that the trust which arises on rescission for fraud is a resulting trust. Lord Browne-Wilkinson in *Westdeutsche Landesbank Girozentrale v Islington London Borough Council* [1996] AC 669 thought it was a constructive trust. Both views have academic support. I prefer that of Lord Browne-Wilkinson for the reasons given by Professor Graham Virgo in *The Principles of Equity and Trusts*, p 300. I should add, for completeness, that William Swadling is the leading academic proponent of the view that no trust of any kind arises on rescission: William Swadling, 'Rescission, Property and the Common Law' (2005) 121 LQR 123; William Swadling, 'The Fiction of the Constructive Trust' (2011) 64 Current Legal Problems 399. That, however, is not the present state of the jurisprudence binding on me.
>
> Contrary to some scholarly analysis (see Burrows, *The Law of Restitution*, 3rd ed (2011), pp 174-179 and the academic material to which he refers, including, in particular, various writings of Professor Robert Chambers), I also consider that the fact that fraud only subsequently arises in a transaction which began as a legitimate transaction is not, of itself, a bar to rescission or to a constructive trust then arising....
>
> I consider that there are good policy reasons for enabling a victim of fraud, which supervenes in a transaction, to set aside the transaction so as to pursue a proprietary claim even though that will have priority over other unsecured creditors of the fraudster or of any other person who has received traceable

---

[57] See further Chapter 20.5, pp. 1013–14.
[58] [1992] 1 WLR 1, 12.
[59] [1993] 3 All ER 717, 734.
[60] See Chapter 8.1(b), pp. 362–4.
[61] [2014] EWHC 4384 (Ch); [2015] Ch 520, [49].

proceeds. On ordinary principles, however, rescission is not possible where it would prejudice the interests of innocent third parties, or substantial restitution by both parties is not possible, or the innocent party has affirmed the transaction; and a constructive trust is no longer possible when it has ceased to be possible to identify the transferred property or its traceable proceeds in the hands of the wrongdoer. All of those bars are more likely to arise in the case of supervening fraud than where the transaction has been induced by fraud.

(c) VOLUNTARY TRANSACTIONS MADE BY MISTAKE

Although it is no longer possible to rescind a contract for mistake in Equity,[62] there is an equitable jurisdiction to set aside gifts or dispositions to trusts that have been made by mistake. Where this jurisdiction is exercised, the property that has been transferred will be held on trust for the transferor and this is preferably characterized as a constructive trust, since unconscionability is a recognized requirement for the transaction to be set aside.

The nature of this equitable jurisdiction was considered by the Supreme Court in *Pitt v Holt*.

Pitt v Holt [2013] UKSC 26; [2013] 2 AC 108

Mr Pitt had been involved in a serious road accident, for which he received compensation. His wife was appointed his receiver. She was advised to settle the compensation on trust for her husband. On his death, a substantial inheritance tax (IHT) liability was incurred. This could have been avoided by a simple restructuring of the settlement, so that half of the fund was to be applied for his benefit during his lifetime, which was how the fund was actually applied anyway. Mrs Pitt successfully sought to set the trust aside on the ground of mistake.[63]

Lord Walker:[64]

For the exercise of the equitable jurisdiction to set aside a voluntary disposition there must be (1) a mistake, which is (2) of the relevant type and (3) sufficiently serious ... That is a convenient framework against which to consider the authorities, although there is obviously some overlap between the three heads....

What is a mistake?

For present purposes a mistake must be distinguished from mere ignorance or inadvertence, and also from what scholars in the field of unjust enrichment refer to as misprediction: see Weeliem Seah, 'Mispredictions, Mistakes and the Law of Unjust Enrichment' [2007] RLR 93; the expression may have first received judicial currency in *Dextra Bank and Trust Co Ltd v Bank of Jamaica* [2002] 1 All ER (Comm) 193 ...

Forgetfulness, inadvertence or ignorance is not, as such, a mistake, but it can lead to a false belief or assumption which the law will recognise as a mistake....

---

[62] *Great Peace Shipping Ltd v Tsalviris Salvage (International) Ltd* [2002] EWCA Civ 1407; [2003] QB 679.
[63] She also sought to set the trust aside on the ground that she had breached her duty as a fiduciary. This claim failed. See Chapter 11.7(g), pp. 577–83.
[64] [2013] UKSC 26; [2013] 2 AC 108, [103].

The best-known English authority on this point is *Lady Hood of Avalon v Mackinnon* [1909] 1 Ch 476. Under a settlement Lord and Lady Hood had a joint power of appointment, and later Lady Hood as the survivor had a sole power of appointment, in favour of the children and remoter issue of their marriage. They had two daughters. In 1888 half the trust fund had been appointed (subject to the prior life interests of Lord and Lady Hood) to their elder daughter on her marriage, and had been resettled by her. In 1902 and 1904, after Lord Hood's death, Lady Hood appointed a total of £8,600 to her younger daughter. Then, wishing to achieve equality, as she thought, between her daughters, and entirely forgetting the 1888 appointment, she appointed a further £8,600 to her elder daughter (so inevitably producing inequality, unless the appointment were set aside). The elder daughter did not oppose Lady Hood's action for rescission of the last appointment, but the trustees of the resettlement (which contained an after-acquired property covenant) did oppose it. Eve J granted relief, stating, at pp 483–484:

> 'Having regard to the facts which I have stated, I must assume that Lady Hood, intending only to bring about equality between her daughters, was labouring under a mistake when she thought that equality would be brought about by the execution of the deed appointing £8,600 to her elder daughter. It was obviously a mistake, because the effect of the execution of that deed was to bring about that which Lady Hood never intended and never contemplated.'...

The fullest academic treatment of this topic is in *Goff & Jones, The Law of Unjust Enrichment*, 8th ed, paras 9-32–9–42. The editors distinguish between incorrect conscious beliefs, incorrect tacit assumptions, and true cases of mere causative ignorance ('causative' in the sense that but for his ignorance the person in question would not have acted as he did)....It may indeed be difficult to draw the line between mere causative ignorance and a mistaken conscious belief or a mistaken tacit assumption. I would hold that mere ignorance, even if causative, is insufficient, but that the court, in carrying out its task of finding the facts, should not shrink from drawing the inference of conscious belief or tacit assumption when there is evidence to support such an inference....

A misprediction relates to some possible future event, whereas a legally significant mistake normally relates to some past or present matter of fact or law....

A problem about the boundary between mistake and misprediction arose in *In re Griffiths, decd* [2009] Ch 162, a decision of Lewison J....Mr Griffiths had a valuable holding in Iota, a property company (whose shares did not attract business assets relief). He was aged 73 when, in January 2003, he and his wife took advice about tax planning. They received a lengthy report setting out various options. Most involved making potentially exempt transfers, which progressively reduce inheritance tax on qualifying gifts if the donor survives for three years, and avoid tax entirely if the donor survives for seven years after making the gift. The report recommended that seven-year term insurance cover should be obtained. Mr Griffiths decided to take various steps, the most important of which was a settlement of Iota shares worth over £2.6m. This was effected by a two-stage process which was completed in February 2004. He decided not to obtain term insurance. Unfortunately he was diagnosed with lung cancer in October 2004, and died in April 2005. Had he done nothing, the Iota shares would have formed part of his residuary estate, in which his wife took a life interest, and no inheritance tax would have been payable on his death.

In those circumstances his executor commenced proceedings asking that the dispositions should be set aside on the ground of mistake [2009] Ch 162, para 6:

> 'The relevant mistake on which they rely is that Mr Griffiths mistakenly believed, at the time of the transfers, that there was a real chance that he would survive for seven years whereas in fact at that time his state of health was such that he had no real chance of surviving that long.'

The medical evidence (in the form of letters from his general practitioner, from a consultant oncologist and from a consultant rheumatologist) was inconclusive, but the GP expressed the view that it was 'extremely unlikely' that the cancer was present in April 2003. On this evidence the judge found that in April 2003 Mr Griffiths had a life expectancy of between seven and nine years. He went on to observe (para 18):

> 'It is unfortunate that in a case involving £1m-worth of tax a proper medical report was not placed before the court and that the claimants are compelled to rely on a single sentence in a letter from [the oncologist]. Although I have hesitated about this finding, I am prepared to find, by a narrow margin that he was suffering from lung cancer on 3 February 2004; and that following the onset of lung cancer at that time his life expectancy did not exceed three years in February 2004. Had the facts been contested, I might not have felt able to make this finding.'

On the rather uncertain foundation of that finding the judge decided that the assignment of 3 February 2004 should be set aside (para 30):

> 'By that time Mr Griffiths was suffering from lung cancer about which he was unaware. He did therefore make a mistake about his state of health. Had he known in February 2004 that he was suffering from lung cancer he would also have known that his chance of surviving for three years, let alone for seven years, was remote. In those circumstances I am persuaded that he would not have acted as he did by transferring his reversionary interest in the shares to trustees.'

The judge did not say whether this was (in the *Goff & Jones* formulation) an incorrect conscious belief or an incorrect tacit assumption. The editors of that work (para 9-36) treat it as a tacit assumption but it seems close to the residual category of mere causative ignorance. Had the judge not made his hair's breadth finding about the presence of cancer in February 2004 it would have been a case of misprediction, not essentially different from a failure to predict a fatal road accident....

What type of mistake?

Some uncontroversial points can be noted briefly. It does not matter if the mistake is due to carelessness on the part of the person making the voluntary disposition, unless the circumstances are such as to show that he deliberately ran the risk, or must be taken to have run the risk, of being wrong.... Nor need the mistake be known to (still less induced by) the person or persons taking a benefit under the disposition. The fact that a unilateral mistake is sufficient (without the additional ingredient of misrepresentation or fraud) to make a gift voidable has been attributed to gifts being outside the law's special concern for the sanctity of contracts (*O'Sullivan, Elliott & Zakrzewski, The Law of Rescission* (2008), para 29.22):

> 'It is apparent from the foregoing survey that vitiated consent permits the rescission of gifts when unaccompanied by the additional factors that must be present in order to render a contract voidable. The reason is that the law's interest in protecting bargains, and in the security of contracts, is not engaged in the case of a gift, even if made by deed.'

Conversely, the fact that a purely unilateral mistake may be sufficient to found relief is arguably a good reason for the court to apply a more stringent test as to the seriousness of the mistake before granting relief....

Leaving aside for the present the degree of seriousness of the mistake, there is also controversy about its nature (or characteristics), especially as to the distinction between 'effect' and 'consequences' drawn by Millett J in *Gibbon v Mitchell* 1990] 1 WLR 1304.... I can see no reason why a mistake of law which is basic to the transaction (but is not a mistake as to the transaction's legal character or nature) should not also be included, even though such cases would probably be rare... I would provisionally conclude that the true requirement is simply for there to be a causative mistake of sufficient gravity; and, as additional guidance to judges in finding and evaluating the facts of any particular case, that the test will normally be satisfied only when there is a mistake either as to the legal character or nature of a transaction, or as to some matter of fact or law which is basic to the transaction....

The conscience test

Lindley LJ's test in *Ogilvie v Littleboy* [13 TLR 399, 400] requires the gravity of the causative mistake to be assessed in terms of injustice—or, to use equity's cumbersome but familiar term, unconscionableness....

The evaluation of what is or would be unconscionable must be objective.... The gravity of the mistake must be assessed by a close examination of the facts, whether or not they are tested by cross-examination, including the circumstances of the mistake and its consequences for the person who made the vitiated disposition. Other findings of fact may also have to be made in relation to change of position or other matters relevant to the exercise of the court's discretion.... The court cannot decide the issue of what is unconscionable by an elaborate set of rules. It must consider in the round the existence of a distinct mistake (as compared with total ignorance or disappointed expectations), its degree of centrality to the transaction in question and the seriousness of its consequences, and make an evaluative judgment whether it would be unconscionable, or unjust, to leave the mistake uncorrected. The court may and must form a judgment about the justice of the case.

Mistakes about tax

...it is still necessary to consider whether there are some types of mistake about tax which should not attract relief. Tax mitigation or tax avoidance was the motive behind almost all of the *Hastings-Bass* cases that were concerned with family trusts (as opposed to pensions trusts).[65] ... On the test proposed above, consequences (including tax consequences) are relevant to the gravity of a mistake, whether or not they are...basic to the transaction.... In some cases of artificial tax avoidance the court might think it right to refuse relief, either on the ground that such claimants, acting on supposedly expert advice, must be taken to have accepted the risk that the scheme would prove ineffective, or on the ground that discretionary relief should be refused on grounds of public policy. Since the seminal decision of the House of Lords in *WT Ramsay Ltd v Inland Revenue Comrs* [1982] AC 300 there has been an increasingly strong and general recognition that artificial tax avoidance is a social evil which puts an unfair burden on the shoulders of those who do not adopt such measures. But it is unnecessary to consider that further on these appeals.

The mistake claim in Pitt v Holt

In my opinion the test for setting aside a voluntary disposition on the ground of mistake...is satisfied in *Pitt v Holt*.

Mrs Pitt's mistake as to the tax consequences of the disposition to the trust was consequently a sufficiently serious and grave mistake to trigger the equitable jurisdiction to rescind the disposition. In reaching this decision, the fact that the disposition did not form part of an artificial or abusive tax avoidance scheme was of particular significance.[66] In *Wright v National Westminster Bank plc*[67] a trust was set aside by virtue of the settlor's mistaken belief that income from the asset which was settled on

---

[65] See Chapter 11.7(g), pp. 577–83.

[66] See also *Kennedy v Kennedy* [2014] EWHC 4129 (Ch); [2015] WTLR 837, [39] (Etherton C); *Re Pallen Trust* 2015 BCCA 222 (Court of Appeal for British Columbia).

[67] [2014] EWHC 3158 (Ch); [2015] WTLR 547. See also *Freedman v* Freedman [2015] EWHC 1457 (Ch); [2015] WTLR 1187 and *Bainbridge v Bainbridge* [2016] EWHC 898 (Ch) (settlement set aside for mistake as to tax consequences). In *Re Pallen Trust* 2015 BCCA 222 the Court of Appeal for British Columbia applied the principles recognized in *Pitt v Holt* to rescind a dividend paid to a discretionary trust on the ground that the dividend had been paid on the mistaken assumption that it would reduce a tax liability.

trust would continue to be available to him and his wife to maintain their existing standard of living. Norris J recognized:[68]

> These are the principles that I must apply in deciding whether to grant rescission of the settlement. First, in the case of a unilateral transaction such as a voluntary settlement it is uncontroversial that a unilateral mistake is sufficient (without any element of misrepresentation or fraud) to make a gift voidable. The fact that it is a unilateral mistake may be a good reason for the court to apply a more stringent test as to the seriousness of the mistake before granting relief... Second, it is clear, and was clear before *Pitt v Holt*, that it is perfectly possible for a unilateral mistake to found a proper claim for rescission of a discretionary trust.... Third, it is now clear that the relevant elements of which account must be taken in the exercise of the jurisdiction are that there must have been a causative mistake which is so grave that it would be unconscionable to refuse relief. Fourth, it is clear that the relevant mistake may be one as to the legal character or nature of the transaction or as to some matter of fact or law which was basic to the transaction. Fifth, it is clear that a causative mistake is something different from inadvertence or misprediction or ignorance. Sixth, the gravity of the mistake has to be assessed by a close examination of the facts including the circumstances of the mistake and its centrality to the transaction in question and the seriousness of its consequences. It is upon this basis that the court is required to make an evaluative judgment as to whether it would be unconscionable or unjust to leave the mistake uncorrected.

Where the equitable jurisdiction is invoked successfully, the property that had been transferred will be held on trust for the transferor. This is properly characterized as a constructive trust because the gravity of the mistake must be so serious that it is unconscionable for the donee to retain the property. This is, as Lord Walker recognized, to be determined objectively, rather than with reference to the donee's knowledge or suspicion of the mistake. Indeed, if the defendant is aware of the mistake, the constructive trust will be triggered by the ground of unconscionable retention of property, which can also operate where property has been transferred by mistake.[69]

(d) FIDUCIARIES *DE SON TORT*

Where a person has not been properly appointed as a fiduciary but does acts that are characteristic of the fiduciary office, he or she might be considered to hold property on a constructive trust. Such 'fiduciaries *de son tort*'[70] will be treated as though they have been properly appointed to the respective office and so will be subject to fiduciary duties in the ordinary way.[71] The preferable view is that a person who intermeddles with a trust is considered to be an express trustee of that trust,[72] whereas a person who acts as a fiduciary, such an executor[73] or agent,[74] will be a constructive trustee of any property they have received by acting as a fiduciary, because they cannot be considered to have intended to act as a trustee but acted unconscionably. For example, in *James v Williams*[75] a mother of three children had died intestate. The family home was to be held on trust for the children equally. Although the son, William Junior, was meant to be the administrator of the estate, he took possession of the

---

[68] [2014] EWHC 3158 (Ch); [2015] WTLR 547, [11].
[69] See Chapter 7.2(a), pp. 332–6.
[70] Perhaps better described simply as *de facto* fiduciaries. See *Dubai Aluminium Co. Ltd v Salaam* [2002] UKHL 48; [2003] 2 AC 366, 403 (Lord Millett).
[71] *Re Barney* [1892] 2 Ch 265, 273 (Kekewich J).
[72] See Chapter 11.2(i), pp. 535–6.
[73] *James v Williams* [2000] Ch 1.
[74] *Lyell v Kennedy* (1889) 14 App Cas 437.
[75] [2000] Ch 1.

property as if it were his own, even though it was established that he was aware that he was not solely entitled to the property. It was held that, by virtue of his knowledge, he was an executor *de son tort*, and so he held the property on constructive trust for himself and his two siblings. Aldous LJ said:[76]

> As a general rule a constructive trust attaches by law to property which is held by a person in circumstances where it would be inequitable to allow him to assert full beneficial ownership of the property. Is this such a case? . . .
>
> William Junior knew that he was not solely entitled to the property. He took it upon himself to take possession of the property as if he owned it and assumed responsibility for its upkeep. In my view he was under an equitable duty to hold the property for himself and his sisters . . . It would be inequitable to allow William Junior . . . to take advantage of his decision not to take out letters of administration and to act as if he was the owner with the full knowledge that he was not. This is an unusual case and, as was made clear by Mr. Hinks in his article,[77] there are many cases where executors *de son tort* could not be constructive trustees. Each case will depend upon its own facts. But, in my view, this is a case where there was a constructive trust.

(e) BREACH OF UNDERTAKING

Where the claimant has transferred property to the defendant following a legally binding undertaking from the defendant that he or she would deal with the property for the benefit of a particular person, and the defendant breaches that undertaking, Equity may intervene and require the defendant to hold the property on constructive trust for the person whom the defendant had agreed to benefit. The constructive trust can be justified because of the defendant's unconscionable conduct in reneging on the undertaking after the claimant had relied on it by transferring the property to the defendant. This type of constructive trust might arise in a variety of different circumstances.

(i) *Undertaking by purchasers*

Where a purchaser has bought land and had made an undertaking that he or she would respect the rights of a third party, that party's rights can be protected by means of a constructive trust.[78] This constructive trust has proved to be important in respect of licences over land. In *Ashburn Anstalt v Arnold*,[79] the Court of Appeal recognized that a purchaser would not normally be bound by the rights of a contractual licensee, save where the purchaser had undertaken to respect the rights of the licensee, such that the purchaser would hold the land on constructive trust for the benefit of the licensee. Fox LJ said:[80]

> In *Binions v Evans* [1972] Ch 359 the defendant's husband was employed by an estate and lived rent free in a cottage owned by the estate. The husband died when the defendant was 73. The trustees of the estate then entered into an agreement with the defendant that she could continue to live in the cottage during her lifetime as tenant at will rent free; she undertook to keep the cottage in good condition and repair. Subsequently the estate sold the cottage to the plaintiffs. The contract provided that the

---

[76] Ibid, 10.

[77] 'Executors de son tort and the Limitation of Actions' [1974] Conv 176.

[78] Alternatively the third party may have a cause of action against the purchaser by virtue of the Contracts (Rights of Third Parties) Act 1999. See Chapter 4.3(d)(i), pp. 162–3.

[79] [1989] Ch 1.

[80] Ibid, 23.

property was sold subject to the tenancy. In consequence of that provision the plaintiffs paid a reduced price for the cottage. The plaintiffs sought to eject the defendant, claiming that she was tenant at will. That claim failed. In the Court of Appeal Megaw and Stephenson LJJ decided the case on the ground that the defendant was a tenant for life under the Settled Land Act 1925. Lord Denning MR did not agree with that. He held that the plaintiffs took the property subject to a constructive trust for the defendant's benefit. In our view that is a legitimate application of the doctrine of constructive trusts. The estate would certainly have allowed the defendant to live in the house during her life in accordance with their agreement with her. They provided the plaintiffs with a copy of the agreement they made. The agreement for sale was subject to the agreement, and they accepted a lower purchase price in consequence. In the circumstances it was a proper inference that on the sale to the plaintiffs, the intention of the estate and the plaintiffs was that the plaintiffs should give effect to the tenancy agreement. If they had failed to do so, the estate would have been liable in damages to the defendant...

We come to the present case. It is said that when a person sells land and stipulates that the sale should be 'subject to' a contractual licence, the court will impose a constructive trust upon the purchaser to give effect to the licence: see *Binions v Evans* [1972] Ch 359 at 368, per Lord Denning MR. We do not feel able to accept that as a general proposition. We agree with the observations of Dillon J in *Lyus v Prowsa Developments Ltd* [1982] 1 WLR 1044 at 1051:

> 'By contrast, there are many cases in which land is expressly conveyed subject to possible incumbrances when there is no thought at all of conferring any fresh rights on third parties who may be entitled to the benefit of the incumbrances. The land is expressed to be sold subject to incumbrances to satisfy the vendor's duty to disclose all possible incumbrances known to him, and to protect the vendor against any possible claim by the purchaser... So, for instance, land may be contracted to be sold and may be expressed to be conveyed subject to the restrictive covenants contained in a conveyance some 60 or 90 years old. No one would suggest that by accepting such a form of contract or conveyance a purchaser is assuming a new liability in favour of third parties to observe the covenants if there was for any reason before the contract or conveyance no one who could make out a title as against the purchaser to the benefit of the covenants.'

The court will not impose a constructive trust unless it is satisfied that the conscience of the estate owner is affected. The mere fact that that land is expressed to be conveyed 'subject to' a contract does not necessarily imply that the grantee is to be under an obligation, not otherwise existing, to give effect to the provisions of the contract. The fact that the conveyance is expressed to be subject to the contract may often, for the reasons indicated by Dillon J, be at least as consistent with an intention merely to protect the grantor against claims by the grantee as an intention to impose an obligation on the grantee. The words 'subject to' will, of course, impose notice. But notice is not enough to impose on somebody an obligation to give effect to a contract into which he did not enter. Thus, mere notice of a restrictive covenant is not enough to impose upon the estate owner an obligation or equity to give effect to it: *London County Council v Allen* [1914] 3 KB 642...

In matters relating to the title to land, certainty is of prime importance. We do not think it desirable that constructive trusts of land should be imposed in reliance on inferences from slender materials.

There are other circumstances in which a purchaser of property has given an oral undertaking to respect the rights of another where the purchaser's attempt to renege on the undertaking is founded on fact that the informality of the undertaking means that it does not comply with statutory formalities; the purchaser may be prevented from reneging on the undertaking by virtue of the principle that 'Equity will not permit a statute to be used as an instrument of fraud.'[81] So, for example, in *Lyus*

---

[81] See Chapter 4.2(b), pp. 121–5.

v Prowsa Developments Ltd,[82] land had been purchased by the defendants expressly subject to the contractual rights of the claimant, but the defendants sought to defeat those contractual rights by relying on the provisions of the Land Registration Act 1925, by virtue of which such rights were not enforceable at law because they had not been registered. Dillon J recognized that the land was held on constructive trust to ensure that the statute was not used as an instrument of fraud. He said:[83]

> Under section 20 [of the Land Registration Act 1925], the effect of the registration of the transferee of a freehold title is to confer an absolute title subject to entries on the register and overriding interests, but, 'free from all other estates and interests whatsoever, including estates and interests of His Majesty…'
>
> It seems to me that the fraud on the part of the defendants in the present case lies not just in relying on the legal rights conferred by an Act of Parliament, but in the first defendant reneging on a positive stipulation in favour of the plaintiffs in the bargain under which the first defendant acquired the land. That makes, as it seems to me, all the difference. It has long since been held, for instance, in *Rochefoucauld v Boustead* [1897] 1 Ch 196, that the provisions of the Statute of Frauds 1677, now incorporated in certain sections of the Law of Property Act 1925, cannot be used as an instrument of fraud, and that it is fraud for a person to whom land is agreed to be conveyed as trustee for another to deny the trust and relying on the terms of the statute to claim the land for himself.

This constructive trust will, however, only be recognized where the defendant can be considered to have undertaken to respect the rights of the third party.

Chaudhary v Yaruz [2011] EWCA Civ 1314; [2013] Ch 249

The defendant had purchased a property that included a metal staircase. The claimant used this staircase to gain access to the upper floor of his property. The claimant had a right of way over the staircase, albeit one that was not registered. No express reference was made to the claimant's right in the defendant's contract of sale and, although it was obvious that the claimant needed to use the staircase to gain access to the upper floor, it was held that it was not unconscionable for the defendant to obstruct the claimant's use of the staircase. Lloyd LJ said:[84]

> Essentially [the trial judge] regarded it as equally unconscionable for the Defendant to deny a right whose existence he could have ascertained merely by inspecting the property as it was in *Lyus v Prowsa* to deny the right which was identified in the contract…
>
> With respect to the judge, I do not consider that his conclusion is correct on this point…There is nothing in the contract which seems to me to allow the court to conclude that by this contract the purchaser 'has undertaken a new obligation, not otherwise existing, to give effect to the relevant encumbrance or prior interest'. In my judgment this criterion, laid down in *Lloyd v Dugdale* [2001] EWCA Civ 1754, should be applied in a case of this kind, and if applied to these facts leads to the conclusion that the Defendant's conscience is not bound to give effect to the Claimant's asserted rights.
>
> It seems to me that the distinctions between the present case and *Lyus*…are real and significant. In that case the judge's conclusion was justified by reference to both the express provision in the contract referring in terms to the plaintiffs' contract and the fact that that contract was not binding on the bank, so that

---

[82] [1982] 1 WLR 1044.
[83] Ibid, 1054.
[84] [2011] EWCA Civ 1314; [2013] Ch 249, [57].

the reference to it in the contract between the bank and the defendant could not be explained by a need to protect the bank, nor could the plaintiffs have done anything by way of registration to protect their contract against a purchaser from the bank. Here, by contrast, the reference to the asserted right was only in general terms, within the category of incumbrances discoverable on inspection, and it was binding on the vendor so that, if it had been effective against the purchaser, the vendor needed to ensure that the contract was subject to it in order that the purchaser could not complain about it to him. Conversely, the Claimant could have ensured the protection of the right by the entry of a notice on the register.

It may be said that, on this basis, *Lyus v Prowsa* is a very unusual case, and is not likely to be followed in more than a few others. That is a fair comment, but not a fair criticism. I know of no English case in which the precedent of *Lyus* has been used successfully to make binding on a purchaser an interest which could be but was not protected on the register as against him, other than *Lloyd v Dugdale* at first instance (overturned on appeal) and the present case, also at first instance.

Since the basis of *Lyus* is showing that the conscience of the purchaser is affected, it might be argued that the apparatus of registration has no relevance to the question arising. In the *Lyus* case itself it had none, because nothing which the plaintiffs could have done could have protected their rights against the defendants. In a directly comparable case that might again be the case. But in a case such as the present, where the rights asserted are capable of protection on the register and where they are not referred to in the contract in specific but only in general terms, then it seems to me that the registration system is relevant. That is for at least two reasons. One is that, absent a specific reference in the contract, the purchaser may be thought to be entitled to rely on third parties protecting themselves in the manner provided for under the legislation. The other is that the contract provision will more readily be interpreted as intended to protect the vendor against a possible claim by the purchaser than as imposing a new personal obligation on the purchaser towards the third party.

The court invited [counsel for the Claimant] to formulate a test by which a potential purchaser's solicitor could advise him whether his conscience would be bound by some potential right, not mentioned in terms in the contract, of which signs were discoverable on inspection, but which, if it existed, could be protected by registration or an entry on the register. He sought to draw a distinction placing on one side the case of an ancient restrictive covenant properly noted on the register but which might well not be enforceable by then for lack of anyone entitled to relevant land who had the benefit of the covenant ...On the other side, as affecting the conscience of the purchaser, he would place rights actively enforceable, or in current use, as against the vendor. The third party right in *Lyus*, of course, would not have satisfied that test, since it was not enforceable against the vendor, but the licence in *Binions v Evans* was so enforceable. It does not seem to me that there could be a satisfactory test along these lines, nor on any other basis, which would put the Claimant's rights over the metal structure in a clearly defined category of rights which would be binding on the purchaser's conscience by virtue of being discoverable on inspection.

In my judgment *Lyus* is an exceptional case, and it is right that it should be...

it seems to me that, in the absence of any express reference in the contract to the rights asserted by the Claimant and an express provision requiring the purchaser to take the property subject to those rights, it is not sufficient that the metal structure was apparent on inspection of the land which was to be bought, and that it would have been apparent that it served as an access for the upper floors of both properties.

The constructive trust has been recognized where the purchaser's undertaking relates to the declaration of a trust of land in favour of the vendor or a third party, where the trust is unenforceable because it has not been evidenced in writing.[85] In such cases, it is, however, preferable to analyse the trust as

---

[85] As required by the Law of Property Act 1925, s. 53(1)(b); see Chapter 4.2(b), p. 120. See *Bannister v Bannister* [1948] 2 All ER 133.

being express rather than as arising by operation of law,[86] since a valid trust has been declared, but it is simply unenforceable because of the absence of writing.

(ii) Secret trusts

It has been seen[87] that a testator might wish to leave property to a person without making this explicit on the face of his or her will. This might be achieved by creating a secret trust under which the trustee is informed outside of the will how the property should be distributed. Once the testator has died and the trustee has received the property, he or she might decide to keep it for him or herself. According to the strict terms of the will, this appears perfectly legitimate: the will may make no reference to there being any trust at all but simply provides for an outright gift. But Equity is also concerned with the nature of the dealings between the parties. Consequently, Equity will hold the trustee to the terms of the undertaking and the property will be held on trust for those whom the testator intended to benefit.

Whether this trust is analysed as constructive or express trust has proved to be a matter of some controversy.[88] The resolution of this controversy might be considered to depend on the type of secret. A fully secret trust is one that is not apparent from the will in any way. The recipient of the property will hold the property on trust to prevent him or her from profiting from fraud.[89] This is consistent with the constructive trust being triggered by unconscionable conduct. The other type of secret trust is the half-secret trust, where reference to the trust is made in the will but the details of the trust are transmitted to the trustee separately. Here, the trust appears to be express. The classification of the secret trust as constructive or express really matters only when the subject matter of the trust is land, for then, if it is an express trust, it must be evidenced in writing.[90] In *Ottaway v Norman*,[91] a fully secret trust of land was upheld even though it was not evidenced in writing, which suggests that this was a constructive trust, although this issue was not expressly discussed. In *Re Baillie*,[92] a half-secret trust of land was required to be evidenced in writing, which suggests that it is an express trust. But, despite this apparent distinction, both fully secret and half-secret trusts are preferably analysed as being express trusts, since they are made when the testator communicates the terms of the trust to the trustee, and so operate outside the will, albeit that they are constituted only on the testator's death.[93]

(iii) Mutual wills

Where two people, such as a husband and wife, agree to make mutual wills that give the property of the first of them to die to the survivor and, after the survivor's death, to agreed legatees, the constructive trust may have a significant role to play in implementing the agreement. The key problem with mutual wills arises when the survivor has received property from the first to die and then leaves it in his or her will in a manner inconsistent with what they had previously agreed. In such circumstances, can the people who should have benefited according to the original mutual wills agreement do anything to enforce it?

One solution is contractual in that, following the enactment of the Contracts (Rights of Third Parties) Act 1999,[94] a person who is not party to a contract is able to enforce the terms of that contract in his or

---

[86] *Rochefoucauld v Boustead* [1897] 1 Ch 196, 208 (Lindley LJ), discussed in Chapter 4.2(b), pp. 122–3.
[87] See Chapter 4.2(c)(iii), pp. 127–45.
[88] See Chapter 4.2(c)(iii)(a), pp. 128–31.
[89] *McCormick v Grogan* (1869) LR 4 HL 82.
[90] Law of Property Act 1925, s. 53(1)(b). See Chapter 4.2(b), p. 120.
[91] [1972] Ch 698.
[92] (1886) 2 TLR 660.
[93] See Chapter 4.2(c)(iii)(g), p. 145.
[94] See further Chapter 4.3(d)(i), pp. 162–3.

her own right, if the contract expressly provides that the third party can enforce it or if the contract purports to confer a benefit on him or her, which may well be the case where it has been agreed that the surviving party's will should leave property to a particular person or people. An alternative solution is to recognize that the property is held on trust for those who should have received the property under the survivor's will.[95] This could be an express trust, depending on the parties' intent, but often it is best analysed as a constructive trust arising by operation of law that responds to the survivor's unconscionable conduct in not leaving the property as the parties had agreed.[96] The beneficiary of this trust can consequently enforce it even though he or she was not a party to the mutual wills contract.

The doctrine of mutual wills depends on there being a legally binding contract between the two testators not to revoke their wills.[97] It does not matter that the survivor does not receive any property under the first testator's will, since it is the existence of the agreement that is vital to the doctrine: if the survivor fails to comply with the original undertaking as to the disposition of property, the defendant's conscience will be affected and this is sufficient to trigger the constructive trust. This was recognized in *Re Dale*.

Re Dale [1994] Ch 31

A husband and wife had agreed that each would leave their estate to their son and daughter equally. The husband died first, leaving his estate of £18,500 accordingly. The wife made a new will leaving £300 to her daughter and the rest of her estate of £19,000 to her son. It was held that the son, as executor, held the estate on trust for himself and his sister equally, even though the wife had not benefited under her husband's will. Morritt J said:[98]

There is no doubt that for the doctrine [of mutual wills] to apply there must be a contract at law. It is apparent from all the cases to which I shall refer later, but in particular from *Gray v Perpetual Trustee Co Ltd* [1928] AC 391, that it is necessary to establish an agreement to make and not revoke mutual wills, some understanding or arrangement being insufficient—'without such a definite agreement there can no more be a trust in equity than a right to damages at law': see per Viscount Haldane, at 400. Thus, as the defendant submitted, it is necessary to find consideration sufficient to support a contract at law. The defendant accepted that such consideration may be executory if the promise when performed would confer a benefit on the promisee or constitute a detriment to the promisor. But, it was submitted, the promise to make and not revoke a mutual will could not constitute a detriment to the first testator because he would be leaving his property in the way that he wished and because he would be able, on giving notice to the second testator, to revoke his will and make another if he changed his mind. Accordingly, it was argued, consideration for the contract had to take the form of a benefit to the second testator.

I do not accept this submission. It is to be assumed that the first testator and the second testator had agreed to make and not to revoke the mutual wills in question. The performance of that promise by the execution of the will by the first testator is in my judgment sufficient consideration by itself. But, in addition, to determine whether a promise can constitute consideration it is necessary to consider whether its performance would have been so regarded.... Thus it is to be assumed that the first testator did not revoke the mutual will notwithstanding his legal right to do so. In my judgment, this

---

[95] *Dufour v Pereira* (1769) 1 Dick 419; *Re Hagger* [1930] 2 Ch 190.
[96] *Ollins v Walters* [2008] EWCA Civ 782; [2009] Ch 212, [37] (Mummery LJ).
[97] *Re Goodchild* [1997] 1 WLR 1216; *Ollins v Walters* [2008] EWCA Civ 782; [2009] Ch 212.
[98] [1994] Ch 31, 38.

too is sufficient detriment to the first testator to constitute consideration. Thus mutual benefit is not necessary for the purpose of the requisite contract. What is necessary to obtain a decree of specific performance of a contract in favour of a third party is not, in my judgment, a relevant question when considering the doctrine of mutual wills. A will is by its very nature revocable: cf. *Re Heys' Estate* [1914] P 192. It seems to me to be inconceivable that the court would order the second testator to execute a will in accordance with the agreement at the suit of the personal representatives of the first testator or to grant an injunction restraining the second testator from revoking it. The principles on which the court acts in imposing the trust to give effect to the agreement to make and not revoke mutual wills must be found in the cases dealing with that topic, not with those dealing with the availability of the remedy of specific performance.

The doctrine of mutual wills causes a number of conceptual and doctrinal problems, such as: when does the constructive trust arise, what property is caught by the trust, and what can the survivor do with that property? The nature and function of this trust was analysed in *Ottaway v Norman* by Brightman J,[99] who said, *obiter*, that if property is left to a person on the understanding that it would be disposed of in his or her will in favour of a particular person, a trust is created in favour of that person that is in suspense until the death of the testator, at which point the trust crystallizes on the survivor's estate, which must be dealt with as the two testators had agreed.[100] This analysis was adopted in *Re Cleaver*.

Re Cleaver [1981] 1 WLR 939

A husband and wife made wills in each other's favour, with gifts to the husband's children. On his death, the widow changed her will to leave the property to only one child. It was held that the wife held this property on constructive trust for all three children. Further, although the trust attached to her assets, she was able to enjoy the property subject to a fiduciary duty that crystallized on her death and disabled her only from voluntary dispositions that were calculated to defeat the agreement. Nourse J said:[101]

I do not find it necessary to refer to any other English case, but I have derived great assistance from the decision of the High Court of Australia in *Birmingham v Renfrew* (1937) 57 CLR 666. That was a case where the available extrinsic evidence was held to be sufficient to establish the necessary agreement between two spouses. It is chiefly of interest because both Sir John Latham CJ and more especially Dixon J examined with some care the whole nature of the legal theory on which these and other similar cases proceed. I would like to read three passages from the judgment of Dixon J which state, with all the clarity and learning for which the judgments of that most eminent judge are renowned, what I believe to be a correct analysis of the principles on which a case of enforceable mutual wills depends. The first passage reads, at 682–683:

'I think the legal result was a contract between husband and wife. The contract bound him, I think, during her lifetime not to revoke his will without notice to her. If she died without altering her will then he was bound after her death not to revoke his will at all. She on her part afforded the consideration for his promise by making her will. His obligation not to revoke his will during her life without notice to her is to be implied. For I think the express promise should be understood as meaning that if she died leaving her will unrevoked then he would not revoke his. But

---

[99] [1972] Ch 698.
[100] See Chapter 4.2(c)(iii)(c)(1), pp. 138–40.
[101] [1981] 1 WLR 939, 945.

the agreement really assumes that neither party will alter his or her will without the knowledge of the other. It has long been established that a contract between persons to make corresponding wills gives rise to equitable obligations when one acts on the faith of such an agreement and dies leaving his will unrevoked so that the other takes property under its dispositions. It operates to impose upon the survivor an obligation regarded as specifically enforceable. It is true that he cannot be compelled to make and leave unrevoked a testamentary document and if he dies leaving a last will containing provisions inconsistent with his agreement it is nevertheless valid as a testamentary act. But the doctrines of equity attach the obligation to the property. The effect is, I think, that the survivor becomes a constructive trustee and the terms of the trust are those of the will which he undertook would be his last will.'

Next, at 689:

'There is a third element which appears to me to be inherent in the nature of such a contract or agreement, although I do not think it has been expressly considered. The purpose of an agreement for corresponding wills must often be, as in this case, to enable the survivor during his life to deal as absolute owner with the property passing under the will of the party first dying. That is to say, the object of the transaction is to put the survivor in a position to enjoy for his own benefit the full ownership so that, for instance, he may convert it and expend the proceeds if he choose. But when he dies he is to bequeath what is left in the manner agreed upon. It is only by the special doctrines of equity that such a floating obligation, suspended, so to speak, during the lifetime of the survivor can descend upon the assets at his death and crystallise into a trust. No doubt gifts and settlements, *inter vivos*, if calculated to defeat the intention of the compact, could not be made by the survivor and his right of disposition, *inter vivos*, is, therefore, not unqualified. But, substantially, the purpose of the arrangement will often be to allow full enjoyment for the survivor's own benefit and advantage upon condition that at his death the residue shall pass as arranged.'

Finally, at 690:

'In *Re Oldham* [1925] Ch 75 Astbury J pointed out, in dealing with the question whether an agreement should be inferred, that in *Dufour v Pereira* (1769) 1 Dick 419 the compact was that the survivor should take a life estate only in the combined property. It was therefore, easy to fix the corpus with a trust as from the death of the survivor. But I do not see any difficulty in modern equity in attaching to the assets a constructive trust which allowed the survivor to enjoy the property subject to a fiduciary duty which, so to speak, crystallised on his death and disabled him from voluntary dispositions *inter vivos*.'

I interject to say that Dixon J was there clearly referring only to voluntary dispositions *inter vivos* which are calculated to defeat the intention of the compact. No objection could normally be taken to ordinary gifts of small value. He went on:

'On the contrary, as I have said, it seems rather to provide a reason for the intervention of equity. The objection that the intended beneficiaries could not enforce a contract is met by the fact that a constructive trust arises from the contract and the fact that testamentary dispositions made upon the faith of it have taken effect. It is the constructive trust and not the contract that they are entitled to enforce.'

It is also clear from *Birmingham v Renfrew* that these cases of mutual wills are only one example of a wider category of cases, for example secret trusts... The principle of all these cases is that a court of equity will not permit a person to whom property is transferred by way of gift, but on the faith of an agreement or clear understanding that it is to be dealt with in a particular way for the benefit of a third person, to deal with the property inconsistently with that agreement or understanding. If he attempts to do so after having received the benefit of the gift, equity will intervene by imposing a constructive trust on the property which is the subject matter of the agreement or understanding...

I would emphasise that the agreement or understanding must be such as to impose on the donee a legally binding obligation to deal with the property in the particular way and that the other two certainties, namely, those as to the subject matter of the trust and the persons intended to benefit under it, are as essential to this species of trust as they are to any other...I find it hard to see how there could be any difficulty about the second or third certainties in a case of mutual wills unless it was in the terms of the wills themselves. There, as in this case, the principal difficulty is always whether there was a legally binding obligation or merely what Lord Loughborough LC in *Lord Walpole v Lord Orford* (1797) 3 Ves 402 at 419, described as an honourable engagement.

The Court of Appeal subsequently recognized that the constructive trust actually arises on the death of the first party to die and this has significant implications for the function of the trust.

Ollins v Walters [2008] EWCA Civ 782; [2009] Ch 212

Mr Walters and his wife had made wills in almost identical terms in which they each left to the other their entire residuary estate. Ten years later, codicils were drafted to each of the wills, in which each agreed not to change his or her will without the other's consent. The wife died and the husband disputed the existence of a mutual wills contract. It was held on the facts that a contract for mutual wills had been created, and that this immediately became binding on the husband on the death of his wife. Mummery J said:[102]

The obligation on the surviving testator is equitable. It is in the nature of a trust of the property affected, so the constructive trust label is attached to it. The equitable obligation is imposed for the benefit of third parties, who were intended by the parties to benefit from it. It arises by operation of law on the death of the first testator to die so as to bind the conscience of the surviving testator in relation to the property affected.

It is a legally *sufficient* condition to establish what the judge described as 'its irreducible core'..., which he analysed as a contract between two testators, T1 and T2:

'that in return for T1 agreeing to make a will in form X and not to revoke it without notice to T2, then T2 will make a will in form Y and agree not to revoke it without notice to T1. If such facts are established then upon the death of T1 equity will impose upon T2 a form of constructive trust (shaped by the exact terms of the contract that T1 and T2 have made). The constructive trust is imposed because T1 has made a disposition of property on the faith of T2's promise to make a will in form Y, and with the object of preventing T1 from being defrauded.'

In my judgment, that is an accurate and clear statement of the equitable principles...Mr Walters would be bound by a constructive trust, but only if sufficient terms of the contract were established to raise one.

The answer to the sufficiency point is, I think, summed up in a single sentence in *Snell's Equity*, 31st ed (2005), para 22–31: 'Mutual wills provide an instance of a trust arising by operation of law to give effect to an express intention of the two testators.'

The intentions of Mr Walters and the deceased were sufficiently expressed in the contract to lay the foundations for the equitable obligations that bind the conscience of Mr Walters, as the survivor, in

---

[102] [2008] EWCA Civ 782; [2009] Ch 212, [37].

relation to the deceased's estate. The judge found all that he needed to find in order to hold that, contrary to the contentions of Mr Walters, mutual wills existed. Possible, and as yet unexplored, legal consequences of the application of the equitable principles do not negative the existence of the foundation contract or prevent a constructive trust from arising by operation of law on the death of the deceased.

It had been accepted on behalf of Mr Walters in submissions to Norris J that, if there was a valid contract for mutual wills, the doctrine operated by imposing a constructive trust on him as the survivor, because the deceased had performed her promise to leave her estate to him. In my judgment, the trust is immediately binding on him in relation to the deceased's property left to him on the basis of the contract. It is not postponed to take effect only after the death of Mr Walters when the property, or what may be left of it, comes into the hands of his personal representatives.

It followed that, on the death of the wife, the husband's conscience was bound in respect of his wife's property, which was left to him, rather than being a trust that was postponed until the death of the husband, which would only take effect when that property, or what was left of it, was received by his executors.

An important implication of the decision in *Ollins v Walters* is that, if the intended third party beneficiary dies after the death of the first party to the mutual contracts but before the death of the surviving party, then, since the constructive trust arises immediately the deceased party's property had been received by the surviving party, the death of the beneficiary of this trust will not defeat his or her beneficial interest. Consequently, that interest would pass to those entitled to his or her residuary estate, unless the beneficiary was intended only to have a life interest that would terminate on death.

(iv) *Perfecting an imperfect gift*

The constructive trust has also been used to perfect an imperfect gift, in situations where the donor has sought to make a gift of property to the donee, but has failed to transfer legal title. It has been recognized that the donor might hold the property on constructive trust for the donee where it would be unconscionable for the donor to revoke the gift.[103] This will typically involve a constructive trust being recognized for breach of an undertaking, since the donor will be considered to have acted unconscionably in seeking to revoke a gift if he or she had represented to the donee that the gift would be made and the donee had relied on this representation in some way.

(f) CONTRACTS FOR THE SALE OF LAND

All the circumstances that have been considered so far, where institutional constructive trusts are recognized, can be justified by reference to the principle that the defendant has acted unconscionably. An institutional constructive trust will, however, also be recognized where a vendor has entered into a contract to sell land, and this cannot be explained by reference to unconscionable conduct, since it is recognized even where the vendor wishes to carry out the agreement. Once the contract of sale has been concluded, the vendor holds the land on constructive trust for the purchaser until the sale is completed, at which time legal title will pass to the purchaser. The recognition of the constructive trust in this instance has usually been justified by the separate principle that 'Equity treats as done what ought to be done.'[104] Contracts for the sale of land are specifically enforceable in Equity,[105] so

---

[103] *Pennington v Waine* [2002] EWCA Civ 227; [2002] 1 WLR 2075. See Chapter 4.3(c)(ii), pp. 156–61.

[104] See Chapter 1.5(c), pp. 18–19.

[105] The principle also applies to personalty if the contract is specifically enforceable. See further Law Commission Report: *Risk of Damage after Contract for Sale* (1990) (Law Com. No. 191).

Equity is willing to treat the contract as having been performed immediately it is made, so that the vendor holds the property on trust for the purchaser by operation of law.

This is, however, an unusual form of trust. In *Lysaght v Edwards* Sir George Jessel MR said:[106]

> the position of the vendor is something between what has been called a naked or bare trustee, or a mere trustee (that is, a person without beneficial interest), and a mortgagee who is not, in equity (any more than the vendor), the owner of the estate, but is, in certain events, entitled to what the unpaid vendor is, [namely] possession of the estate and a charge upon the estate for his purchase-money.

The essential nature of the vendor–purchaser constructive trust was recognized by Lord Walker in *Jerome v Kelly*:[107]

> beneficial ownership of the land is in a sense split between the seller and the buyer on the provisional assumptions that specific performance is available and that the contract will in due course be completed...The provisional assumptions may be falsified by events, such as rescission of the contract ...If the buyer proceeds to completion the equitable interest can be viewed as passing to the buyer in stages, as title is made and accepted and as the purchase price is paid in full.

The unusual nature of this constructive trust was recognized by Lord Cairns in *Shaw v Foster*,[108] where he observed that, although the vendor is the trustee and the purchaser has a beneficial interest, the trustee also has a personal interest in the property. He said that:[109]

> The vendor was a trustee of the property for the purchaser; the purchaser was the real beneficial owner in the eye of a Court of Equity of the property subject only to this observation, that the vendor, whom I have called the trustee, was not a mere dormant trustee, he was a trustee having a personal and substantial interest in the property, a right to protect that interest, and an active right to assert that interest if anything should be done in derogation of it. The relation, therefore, of trustee and *cestui que trust* subsisted, but subsisted subject to the paramount right of the vendor and trustee to protect his own interest as vendor of the property.

Similarly, Sir George Jessel MR in *Lysaght v Edwards* recognized that:[110]

> the moment you have a valid contract for sale the vendor becomes in equity a trustee for the purchaser of the estate sold, and the beneficial ownership passes to the purchaser, the vendor having a right to the purchase-money, a charge or lien on the estate for the security of that purchase-money, and a right to retain possession of the estate until the purchase-money is paid, in the absence of express contract as to the time of delivering possession.

The limited rights of the purchaser under this constructive trust is illustrated by *Rayner v Preston*,[111] in which the vendor agreed to sell a house that he had insured. The contract did not refer to the

---

[106] (1876) 2 Ch D 499, 506.
[107] [2004] UCHL 25; [2004] 1 WLR 1409, [32].
[108] (1872) LR 5 HL 321.
[109] Ibid, 338.
[110] (1876) 2 Ch D 499, 506.
[111] (1881) 18 Ch D 1. See also *Lake v Bayliss* [1974] 1 WLR 1073; *Freevale Ltd v Metrostore (Holdings) Ltd* [1984] Ch 199; *Englewood Properties Ltd v Patel* [2005] EWHC 188 (Ch); [2005] 1 WLR 1961.

insurance. After the contract was made, but before the sale was completed, the house was damaged by fire. The insurers paid insurance money to the vendor, which the purchaser claimed. This claim failed.[112] Cotton LJ said:[113]

> It was said that the vendor is, between the time of the contract being made and being completed by conveyance, a trustee of the property for the purchaser, and that as, but for the fact of the legal ownership of the building insured being vested in him, he could not have recovered on the policy, he must be considered a trustee of the money recovered. In my opinion, this cannot be maintained. An unpaid vendor is a trustee in a qualified sense only, and is so only because he has made a contract which a Court of Equity will give effect to by transferring the property sold to the purchaser, and so far as he is a trustee he is so only in respect of the property contracted to be sold. Of this the policy is not a part. A vendor is in no way a trustee for the purchaser of rents accruing before the time fixed for completion, and here the fire occurred and the right to recover the money accrued before the day fixed for completion. The argument that the money is received in respect of property which is trust property is, in my opinion, fallacious. The money is received by virtue or in respect of the contract of insurance, and though the fact that the insured had parted with all interest in the property insured would be an answer to the claim, on the principle that the contract is one of indemnity only, this is very different from the proposition that the money is received by reason of his legal interest in the property.

The qualified nature of the constructive trust arising from the sale of land was further illustrated by the Supreme Court in *Southern Pacific Mortgages Ltd v Scott*.[114] Vendors had agreed to sell their houses to purchasers following the purchasers' promise that the vendors could remain in occupation at a low rent. The purchasers obtained mortgages and the vendors argued that they had equitable proprietary rights (to remain in occupation at a low rent) which took priority over the mortgages. This argument failed because the vendors had no equitable proprietary rights until legal title had passed to the purchasers, by which time the mortgages had been obtained and took priority. Lord Collins said:[115]

> in my judgment, the appeal should be dismissed on the principal ground that the vendors acquired no more than personal rights against the purchasers when they agreed to sell their properties on the basis of the purchasers; promises that they would be entitled to remain in occupation. Those rights would only become proprietary and capable of taking priority over a mortgage when they were fed by the purchasers' acquisition of the legal estate on completion...with the effect that the acquisition of the legal estate and the grant of the charge would be one indivisible transaction, and the vendors would not be able to assert against the lenders their interests arising only on completion.

It follows that the proprietary consequences of the constructive trust could only operate once the purchaser had acquired legal title, by which point the mortgagors' security interests trumped the vendors' rights.

Although the constructive trust of land following a contract of sale has been criticized as fictional,[116] the trust has been justified by Turner.

---

[112] It would now succeed under the Law of Property Act 1925, s. 47, which enables the purchaser to recover such sums once the conveyance has been completed.
[113] (1881)18 Ch D 1.
[114] [2014] UKSC 52; [2015] AC 385.
[115] Ibid, [79].
[116] Swadling, 'The Vendor-Purchaser Constructive Trust', in *Equity in Commercial Law* (eds Degeling and Edelman) (Sydney: Lawbook Co., 2005), pp. 475–6 and 487–8.

Turner, 'Understanding the Constructive Trust between Vendor and Purchaser' (2012) LQR 582, 602

The purpose and function of the vendor–purchaser trust are to protect the interest that the vendor and purchaser each have in the due performance of the contract...

the vendor–purchaser trust widens the class of persons against whom court orders with the relevant protective effect may be made... The vendor–purchaser trust contains two equities that (subject to defences)... further the contract's performance. One is the interest in land that a purchaser acquires upon formation of a contract of sale. This can be enforced to seek specific performance against a transferee of the land from the vendor, even though the transferee was not a contract party. The other is the vendor's lien. This equitable interest binds the relevant land both while the purchaser remains the owner, and once he has conveyed it to a third party... By enforcing the lien, the vendor procures the judicial sale of the relevant land. From the proceeds the vendor is paid the balance of the amount the purchaser promised to pay.

The purchaser's lien is the only equity comprised in the vendor–purchaser trust that furthers the protection of neither party's performance interest. The purchaser's lien protects the purchaser's right to repayment of the purchase money when the contract is not performed, provided he is not at fault. Otherwise, however, the purpose and function of the vendor–purchaser trust are to protect each party's performance interest. This protection extends beyond the protection offered at common law or by simple orders that the parties perform their respective promises.

This is a sophisticated defence of the vendor–purchaser constructive trust, but it is a defence founded on the role of Equity to support the contractual bargain, rather than by reference to unconscionability. Even on this analysis, the recognition of the 'constructive trust' is peculiar and restricted to the particular context of a specifically enforceable contract. Since the 'trust' is not triggered by unconscionability, and because it has peculiar characteristics, perhaps it should not analysed as a constructive trust at all, but simply as an equitable order.[117] In most cases this characterization will not matter, save where the property has been transferred to a third party, who was not a bona fide purchaser for value. If the property was held on a constructive trust for the purchaser of the property he or she would be able to bring a claim against the third party to recover the property; such a claim would not be available if the contract was simply considered to trigger an equitable order. As a matter of policy, it might be considered to be appropriate that the purchaser has the protection of a proprietary claim against a third party transferee, which would justify the recognition of a constructive trust.

(g) BREACH OF FIDUCIARY DUTY

In *FHR European Ventures Ltd v Cedar Capital Partners LLC*[118] the Supreme Court recognized that bribes and secret commissions received by a fiduciary in breach of fiduciary duty would be held on constructive trust for the principal. The Supreme Court adopted the following formulation of the rule as regards the liability of an agent to his or her principal:[119]

...namely that it applies to all benefits received by an agent in breach of his fiduciary duty to his principal, [and] is explained on the basis that an agent ought to account in specie to his principal for any benefit he has obtained from his agency in breach of his fiduciary duty, as the benefit should be treated

---

[117] Swadling, 'The Fiction of the Constructive Trust' (2011) CLP 399.
[118] [2014] UKSC 45; [2015] AC 250. See Chapter 14.5(b), pp. 706–14.
[119] Ibid, [30].

as the property of the principal…More subtly, it is justified on the basis that equity does not permit an agent to rely on his own wrong to justify retaining the benefit: in effect, he must accept that, as he received the benefit as a result of his agency, he acquired it for his principal.

3. REMEDIAL CONSTRUCTIVE TRUSTS

Whereas an institutional constructive trust arises by operation of law from the date of the event that gives rise to it, the remedial constructive trust arises through the exercise of the judge's discretion whenever it is considered to be just to recognize that the claimant has an equitable proprietary interest. The remedial constructive trust does not involve the vindication of some pre-existing proprietary right of the claimant. It may operate only from the date of the court order and, thus, need not affect third parties.

The remedial constructive trust is recognized in Australia,[120] New Zealand,[121] and Canada,[122] but it has never been formally recognized in England and Wales, where the orthodox interpretation is that it is institutional.[123] However, some judges have expressed willingness to recognize it. For example, Lord Browne-Wilkinson in *Westdeutsche Landesbank Girozentrale v Islington London Borough Council* said:[124]

Although the resulting trust is an unsuitable basis for developing proprietary restitutionary remedies, the remedial constructive trust, if introduced into English law, may provide a more satisfactory road forward. The court by way of remedy might impose a constructive trust on a defendant who knowingly retains property of which the plaintiff has been unjustly deprived. Since the remedy can be tailored to the circumstances of the particular case, innocent third parties would not be prejudiced and restitutionary defences, such as change of position, are capable of being given effect. However, whether English law should follow the United States and Canada by adopting the remedial constructive trust will have to be decided in some future case when the point is directly in issue.[125]

The Supreme Court has, however, confirmed that the remedial constructive trust is not recognized in England and Wales. In *FHR European Ventures LLP v Cedar Capital Partners LLC*[126] the Supreme Court stated that:

the notion…that a trust might arise once the court had given judgment for the equitable claim seems to be based on some sort of remedial constructive trust which is a concept not referred to in earlier cases, and which has authoritatively been said not to be part of English law: see per Lord Browne-Wilkinson in *Westdeutsche Landesbank Girozentrale v Islington LBC* [1996] AC 669, 714-716.

Lord Browne-Wilkinson did not reject the remedial constructive trust in that case, however, but left open whether it should be recognized.

Lord Neuberger, who delivered the judgment in *FHR*, subsequently clarified his reasons for rejecting the remedial constructive trust extra-judicially.

---

[120] *Muschinski v Dodds* (1985) 160 CLR 583; *Grimaldi v Chameleon Mining NL (No. 2)* [2012] FCAFC 6.
[121] *Powell v Thompson* [1991] 1 NZLR 597.
[122] *Pettkus v Becker* (1980) 117 DLR (3d) 257.
[123] This was implicit in the decision of the Supreme Court in *FHR European Ventures LLP v Cedar Capital Partners LLC* [2014] UKSC 45; [2015] AC 250.
[124] [1996] AC 669, 716.
[125] See also *Metall und Rohstoff AG v Donaldson Lufkin & Jenrette Inc.* [1990] 1 QB 391, 479; *Re Goldcorp Exchange Ltd* [1995] 1 AC 74, 104 (Lord Mustill); *London Allied Holdings v Lee* [2007] EWHC 2061 (Ch).
[126] [2014] UKSC 45; [2015] AC 250, [47].

Lord Neuberger, 'The remedial constructive trust – fact or fiction'[127]

There is much to be said for the notion of a remedial constructive trust displays equity at its flexible flabby worst. I will seek to show, at least arguably, that it is unprincipled, incoherent and impractical, that it renders the law unpredictable, that it is an affront to the common law view of property rights and interests, that it involves the court usurping the role of the legislature, and, as if that were not enough, that the development of the remedial constructive trust is largely unnecessary. Apart from that, it's a pretty good concept.

This concern about the courts usurping the role of the legislature was the main reason why the Court of Appeal had rejected the remedial constructive trust in *Re Polly Peck International (No. 2)*.[128] The issue in that case was whether the court had jurisdiction to hear a claim arising from the occupation of land in Cyprus by the subsidiaries of a company (PPI) that was insolvent and in administration. The claimants sought restitution of a sum received by the administrators that the claimants alleged represented the profits from the company's wrongdoing. The claimants claimed that these profits were held on a remedial constructive trust. In rejecting this claim, Mummery LJ said:[129]

In my judgment, the intervening insolvency of PPI means that under English law there is no seriously arguable case for granting the applicants a remedial constructive trust on the basis of the allegations in the draft statement of claim. PPI is a massively insolvent company subject to an administration order. The administrators are bound to distribute the assets of PPI among the creditors on the basis of insolvency. Parliament has, in such an eventuality, sanctioned a scheme for *pari passu* distribution of assets designed to achieve a fair distribution of the insolvent company's property among the unsecured creditors. This scheme, now contained in the Insolvency Act of 1986, was described by Sir Donald Nicholls Vice-Chancellor in *Re Paramount Airways Ltd* [1993] Ch 223 at 230 as 'a coherent, modernised and expanded code'.

The provisions of that code apply both to the case of an insolvent company which has gone into formal liquidation and to one in respect of which an administration order has been made. The essential characteristic of the statutory scheme is that the liquidator or administrator is bound to deal with the assets of the company as directed by statute for the benefit of all creditors who come in to prove a valid claim. There is a statutory obligation on the administrators of PPI to treat the general creditors in a particular way. A question may arise as to whether a particular asset was or was not the beneficial property of the company at the date of the commencement of the winding up (or administration). If it is established in a dispute that it is not an asset of the company then it never becomes subject of the statutory insolvency scheme: see *Chase Manhattan Bank NA v Israel-British Bank (London) Ltd* [1981] Ch 105. If, on the other hand, the asset is the absolute beneficial property of the company there is no general power in the liquidator, the administrators or the court to amend or modify the statutory scheme so as to transfer that asset or to declare it to be held for the benefit of another person. To do that would be to give a preference to another person who enjoys no preference under the statutory scheme.

In brief, the position is that there is no prospect of the court in this case granting a remedial constructive trust to the applicants in respect of the proceeds of sale of the shares held by PPI in its subsidiaries, since the effect of the statutory scheme applicable on an insolvency is to shut out a remedy which would, if available, have the effect of conferring a priority not accorded by the provisions of the

---

[127] Delivered on 10 August 2014 to the Banking Services and Finance Law Association Conference, New Zealand: https://www.supremecourt.uk/docs/speech-140810.pdf.

[128] [1998] 3 All ER 812. See also *Cobbold v Bakewell Management Ltd* [2003] EWHC 2289 (Ch), [17] (Rimer J); *Re Farepak Food and Gifts Ltd* [2006] EWHC 3272 (Ch), [38] (Mann J).

[129] [1998] 3 All ER 812, 826.

statutory insolvency scheme. In her eloquent address [counsel for the claimants] submitted that 'the law moves'. That is true. But it cannot be legitimately moved by judicial decision down a road signed 'No Entry' by Parliament. The insolvency road is blocked off to remedial constructive trusts, at least when judge-driven in a vehicle of discretion.

For those reasons alone I would refuse leave to the applicants to commence these proceedings. To a trust lawyer and, even more so to an insolvency lawyer, the prospect of a court imposing such a trust is inconceivable and, in my judgment, even the most enthusiastic student of the law of restitution would be forced to recognise that the scheme imposed by statute for a fair distribution of the assets of an insolvent company precludes the application of the equitable principles manifested in the remedial constructive trust developed by such courts as the Supreme Court of Canada.

Potter LJ agreed, but Nourse LJ went further and said that, even had the defendant been solvent, he would not have recognized a remedial constructive trust:[130]

Although...this court...in *Metall und Rohstoff AG v Donaldson, Lufkin & Jenrette Inc* [1990] 1 QB 391, Lord Mustill in *Re Goldcorp Exchange Ltd* [1995] 1 AC 74 and Lord Browne-Wilkinson in *Westdeutsche Landesbank Girozentrale v Islington London Borough Council* [1996] AC 669 have accepted the possibility that the remedial constructive trust may become part of English law, such observations, being both obiter and tentative, can only be of limited assistance when the question has to be decided, as it does here. There being no earlier decision, we must turn to principle. In doing so, we must recognise that the remedial constructive trust gives the court a discretion to vary proprietary rights. You cannot grant a proprietary right to A, who has not had one beforehand, without taking some proprietary right away from B. No English court has ever had the power to do that, except with the authority of Parliament; cf. *Chapman v Chapman* [1954] AC 429.[131] But it is said that, although that may be the law today, it may not be the law tomorrow. If the Supreme Court of Canada can develop the law so as to permit the court to vary proprietary rights without legislative authority, why cannot the House of Lords do likewise? At least, it is said, there must be a real prospect that they will, and so the applicants ought to be allowed to bring their action.

I agree with Mummery LJ that where, as here, there would be not simply a variation of proprietary rights but a variation of the manner in which the administrators are directed to deal with PPI's assets by the Insolvency Act 1986 it is not seriously arguable, even at the highest level, that a remedial constructive trust would be imposed. For myself, I would go further and hold that it would not be seriously arguable even if PPI was solvent. It is not that you need an Act of Parliament to prohibit a variation of proprietary rights. You need one to permit it; see the Variation of Trusts Act 1958 and the Matrimonial Causes Act 1973.

Despite the rejection of the remedial constructive trust in *FHR* that form of trust is recognized in other common law jurisdictions, and there remain significant arguments in favour of the trust being recognized. For example, in *London Allied Holdings v Lee*,[132] Etherton J, having referred to Birks's criticism of this form of trust as 'a nightmare trying to be a noble dream' and 'rightlessness implicit in discretionary remedialism',[133] said:[134]

An equity lawyer might observe that such language is overly emphatic, having regard, for example, to the strong discretion in the Court to decide upon the appropriate form of relief for proprietary estoppel,

---

[130] Ibid, 830.
[131] See Chapter 15.2, p. 722.
[132] [2007] EWHC 2061 (Ch).
[133] 'Property and Unjust Enrichment: Categorical Truths' [1997] NZ Law Rev 623, 641.
[134] [2007] EWHC 2061 (Ch), [274].

including whether it should be personal or proprietary and whether it should be to protect the claimant's expectations or compensate for reliance loss. Moreover, there is no English authority, including *Polly Peck International plc (No 2)* (in which Mummery LJ, with whom Potter LJ agreed, concentrated on the fact of insolvency), which is binding authority against the remedial constructive trust in principle. Nevertheless, it seems realistic to assume that an English Court will be very slow indeed to adopt the US and Canadian model. On the other hand, there still seems scope for real debate about a model more suited to English jurisprudence, borrowing from proprietary estoppel; namely a constructive trust by way of discretionary restitutionary relief, the right to which is a mere equity prior to judgment, but which will have priority over the intervening rights of third parties on established principles, such as those relating to notice, volunteers and the unconscionability on the facts of a claim by the third party to priority.

Although the recognition of the remedial constructive trust would enable the judicial creation of equitable proprietary rights, which would prejudice the rights of the defendant's creditors, being a discretionary remedy it need not be awarded if any innocent third party would suffer unacceptably,[135] or it could be determined that the remedy only operates for the time of the court order.

It is important, however, that there are clear rules as to whether or not equitable proprietary rights have been created, and the remedial constructive trust might be considered to be antithetical to such clarity and predictability.[136] Birks described the remedial constructive trust as a remedy that is 'ugly, repugnant alike to legal certainty, the sanctity of property and the rule of law'.[137]

Nevertheless, if the remedial constructive trust is to be recognized in English law, it must be triggered by a cause of action. What might that cause of action be? It could be equitable wrongdoing but, as has already been seen, the constructive trust that is exceptionally recognized where there is a breach of fiduciary duty is institutional in form, arising by operation of law rather than judicial discretion.[138] Similarly, unconscionable retention of property triggers an institutional, rather than a remedial, constructive trust. The remedial constructive trust might be considered to be an appropriate response to the defendant's unjust enrichment—indeed, Etherton J's reference to 'discretionary restitutionary relief' might suggest that this is what he was contemplating—but the fact that the defendant has been unjustly enriched at the claimant's expense is not a sufficient reason to recognize an equitable proprietary interest; the claimant should instead be confined to a personal claim against the defendant.[139] A remedy without a cause of action is meaningless and for that reason, as well as the inherent uncertainty of this unbridled judicial discretion, the remedial constructive trust should not be recognized in English law.

4. THE NATURE OF CONSTRUCTIVE TRUSTEESHIP

Although the institutional constructive trust is a real trust, it does not follow that a constructive trustee is under the same obligations as any other type of trustee. A constructive trustee will have legal title to property that is held on trust for the benefit of others and will be obliged to convey the trust property to the beneficiary, but the duties of that trustee will be less onerous than those of an express trustee.[140] For example, a constructive trustee is under no obligation to invest[141] and neither is he or

---

[135] *Grimaldi v Chameleon Mining NL (No. 2)* [2012] FCAFC 6, [510] (Finn J).
[136] Millett, 'Equity: The Road Ahead' (1995) 9 TLI 35, 42.
[137] 'Property and Unjust Enrichment: Categorical Truths' [1997] NZ Law Rev 623, 641.
[138] See Chapter 7.2(g), pp. 354–5.
[139] See further Chapter 1.4(b), pp. 13–15.
[140] Smith, 'Constructive Fiduciaries', in *Privacy and Loyalty* (ed. Birks) (Oxford: Clarendon Press, 1997), ch. 9, p. 267.
[141] *Lonrho plc v Fayed (No. 2)* [1992] 1 WLR 1, 12 (Millett J).

she required to observe the usual duty of care.[142] Since a constructive trustee may not know that he or she is a trustee,[143] it would be unreasonable to impose such obligations, including the fiduciary duty of loyalty to the beneficiaries.[144]

Smith, *Constructive Fiduciaries in Privacy and Loyalty* (ed. Birks) (Oxford: Oxford University Press, 1997), p. 267

There is an obligation on the [constructive] trustee: to convey the trust property to or to the order of the beneficiary. A breach of this obligation would create a personal liability. But the trustee cannot, without fiction, be said to have assumed obligations of the utmost selflessness. The only way to reach the contrary conclusion would be to say that this is the technique of equity: to subject trustees, even unwilling ones, to the fiduciary standard, so as to generate the corresponding liabilities. That, however, would be using the fiduciary relationship in a wholly instrumental way.

QUESTION

Alan has recently established a business selling custom-built sports cars, which he imports from China. He only enters into contracts to sell cars to customers if they pay a deposit of half the purchase price, amounting to £10,000. His business has proved to be very popular, so much so that demand outstrips supply. Unfortunately, his supplier becomes insolvent and ceases trading and Alan is unable to source his cars from anywhere else. Despite this, he accepts a deposit for a car from Brenda. Before the supplier ceased trading, Alan had also received a deposit from Clare. Alan has recently been declared bankrupt. He owes £30,000 to his unsecured creditors. He has £20,000 credited to his bank account. Brenda and Clare seek your advice as to any claims they might have in priority to Alan's other creditors.

FURTHER READING

Gardner, 'Reliance-based Constructive Trusts' in *Constructive and Resulting Trusts* (ed. Mitchell) (Oxford: Hart, 2010), ch 2.

Hopkins, 'Conscience, Discretion and the Creation of Property Rights' (2006) 4 LS 475.

McFarlane, 'Constructive Trusts Arising on a Receipt of Property Sub Conditione' (2004) 120 LQR 667.

Smith, 'Constructive Fiduciaries' in *Privacy and Loyalty* (ed. Birks) (Oxford: Oxford University Press, 1997), ch 9.

Swadling, 'The Fiction of the Constructive Trust' (2011) CLP 399.

Tarrant, 'Thieves as Trustees: In Defence of the Theft Principle' (2009) 3 JoE 170.

Turner, 'Understanding the Constructive Trust between Vendor and Purchaser' (2012) LQR 582.

---

[142] See Chapter 12.2, pp. 587–91.
[143] Compare Lord Browne-Wilkinson's assertion in *Westdeutsche Landesbank Girozentrale v Islington London Borough Council* [1996] AC 669, 705, that it is a fundamental principle of the law of trusts that a trustee must know that he or she is a trustee. Such a principle can apply only to express trusts. See Chapter 2.3, pp. 28–9.
[144] See Chapter 14, 'Fiduciary Obligations'.

8

RESULTING TRUSTS

CENTRAL ISSUES

1. Resulting trusts are a limited category of trusts that arise on certain facts where neither an express trust nor a constructive trust exists.

2. There are two principal categories of resulting trust: 'presumed' resulting trusts and 'automatic' resulting trusts.

3. Automatic resulting trusts arise where an express trust fails initially or subsequently. The property is then held by the trustee for the settlor.

4. Presumed resulting trusts arise where a person voluntarily transfers property for no consideration in return, or contributes to the purchase of property in the name of another.

5. However, the presumption of resulting trust is replaced by a presumption of advancement, or gift, if property is transferred from a father to son or from husband to wife, for example. The presumption of advancement is controversial and its future uncertain.

6. Both the presumption of resulting trust and the presumption of advancement can be rebutted by any evidence to the contrary. However, a party cannot rely upon evidence of his or her own illegal conduct, so the importance of the presumptions is most significant in the context of illegal transactions.

7. The basis of resulting trusts is controversial. The better view is that resulting trusts do not respond to unjust enrichment, but reflect a presumed intention of the transferor to have a beneficial interest in the transferred property.

8. Where property is transferred for a particular purpose and that purpose fails, the property may be held on trust, known as a *Quistclose* trust. This might be a resulting trust, but it may also be an express trust or constructive trust. The correct classification of the trust depends upon the particular circumstances of a given case.

1. INTRODUCTION

Resulting trusts operate in the space between express trusts and constructive trusts. The room for resulting trusts might, therefore, be squeezed both by more readily finding an express intention to create a trust,[1] and by a greater willingness to impose constructive trusts, particularly in the context of

---

[1] See Chapter 3.

the family home,[2] but also in more commercial contexts.[3] If the scope of express trusts and constructive trusts broadens, the role of resulting trusts will correspondingly be more limited. Nevertheless, resulting trusts are well-established, real trusts, with title to the property being divided between trustees and beneficiaries.

Resulting trusts arise where A transfers property to B, and B holds that property on trust for A. This fact-pattern is not exclusive to resulting trusts: a trustee may hold property for the settlor under both an express trust and a constructive trust as well. But whereas an express trust arises because of the express intention of the settlor, and a constructive trust does not generally[4] respond to intention but arises by operation of law,[5] a resulting trust gives effect to an intention of the settlor that has not been made express. A major difficulty lies in ascertaining the requisite intention of the settlor. There has been impetus from some commentators to expand the role of resulting trusts, relying largely on an analysis based upon unjust enrichment, based upon the contention that resulting trusts respond to the settlor's *absence* of intention that the trustee should benefit from the property.[6] The more restrictive, orthodox approach states that resulting trusts reflect the presumed, *positive* intent of the settlor to retain[7] the beneficial interest in the transferred property.

It is important to appreciate that the two approaches will often lead to similar results: a positive intention to have the beneficial interest generally corresponds to an absence of intention for anybody else to have it. But the two do not inevitably converge. So, if A gives property to B, under the mistaken belief that such money is due, but in fact A had already paid its debt to B, does B hold the money received under the second payment on resulting trust for A?[8] It might be thought that the mistake vitiates A's intention that B should benefit from the property, so the absence of intention approach could lead to a resulting trust. However, upon making the payment A did not intend to retain any beneficial interest in the property, but rather intended to transfer the beneficial interest to B; so, on the positive intention analysis no resulting trust would arise. These approaches will be explained more fully in this chapter; the preferable approach can be best assessed once the leading cases have been examined and the types of situations in which resulting trusts arise are understood.

(a) THE MEANING OF 'RESULTING'

The term 'resulting trust' comes from the Latin verb '*resalire*', which means 'to jump back': the beneficial interest is thought to 'jump back' to A. However, as Birks pointed out:[9]

> there is a continuing debate as to whether the idea of 'jumping back' in the Latin *resalire* is anything more than a misleading metaphor. It may be more accurate to say that the interest jumps up in the person beneficially entitled rather than back to him, or that it is in him from the beginning of the story and never leaves.

---

[2] See Chapter 9, 'Informal Arrangements Relating to Property'.

[3] See Chapter 7, 'Constructive Trusts'.

[4] Although see the common intention constructive trust: Chapter 9.

[5] See Chapter 7, 'Constructive Trusts'.

[6] See in particular Birks, 'Restitution and Resulting Trusts' in *Equity: Contemporary Legal Developments* (Jerusalem: Hebrew University of Jerusalem, 1992) and Chambers, *Resulting Trusts* (ed. Goldstein) (Oxford: Clarendon Press, 1997); see further Chapter 8.4, p. 399.

[7] For further discussion of whether 'retention' is the appropriate term here, see Chapter 8.1(a), pp. 361–2.

[8] Cf *Chase Manhattan Bank NA v Israel-British Bank (London) Ltd* [1981] Ch 105. See further Chapter 8.4(a), pp. 406–8.

[9] Birks, 'Restitution and Resulting Trusts' in *Equity: Contemporary Legal Developments* (ed. Goldstein) (Jerusalem: Hebrew University of Jerusalem, 1992), 360.

It might be that resulting trusts concern the transferor's retaining the beneficial interest in property.[10] Nevertheless, the transferor will generally have legal title before transferring the property to the trustee, but an equitable interest under the resulting trust; it is, therefore, difficult to consider him to be retaining an interest that he did not enjoy at the outset.[11] It might be better to view a resulting trust as creating a new equitable interest in the property transferred. But in any event, as Megarry J pointed out in *Re Vandervell (No. 2)*:[12]

> there has been a transaction which has divided the bare ownership from the beneficial interest, and whether A's beneficial interest is something that he keeps back, or whether it is something that he gets back, the result seems substantially the same.

(b) CATEGORIES OF RESULTING TRUST

The 'types' of resulting trust are often split into two categories. In *Vandervell v IRC*,[13] Lord Upjohn commented that:

> Where A transfers, or directs a trustee for him to transfer, the legal estate in property to B otherwise than for valuable consideration it is a question of the intention of A in making the transfer whether B was to take beneficially or on trust and, if the latter, on what trusts. If, as a matter of construction of the document transferring the legal estate, it is possible to discern A's intentions, that is an end of the matter and no extraneous evidence is admissible to correct and qualify his intentions so ascertained.
>
> But if, as in this case (a common form share transfer),[14] the document is silent, then there is said to arise a resulting trust in favour of A. But this is only a presumption and is easily rebutted. All the relevant facts and circumstances can be considered in order to ascertain A's intentions with a view to rebutting this presumption....
>
> But the doctrine of resulting trust plays another very important part in our law and, in my opinion, is decisive of this case.
>
> If A intends to give away all his beneficial interest in a piece of property and thinks he has done so but, by some mistake or accident or failure to comply with the requirements of the law, he has failed to do so, either wholly or partially, there will, by operation of law, be a resulting trust for him of the beneficial interest of which he had failed effectually to dispose. If the beneficial interest was in A and he fails to give it away effectively to another or others or on charitable trusts it must remain in him. Early references to Equity, like Nature, abhorring a vacuum, are delightful but unnecessary.

In *Re Vandervell (No. 2)*,[15] Megarry J emphasized this distinction:

> The distinction between the two categories of resulting trusts is important because they operate in different ways. Putting it shortly, in the first category, subject to any provisions in the instrument, the matter is one of intention, with the rebuttable presumption of a resulting trust applying if the intention

---

[10] E.g. *Godbold v Freestone* (1695) 3 Lev 406, 407 (Holt CJ).

[11] E.g. Mee, '"Automatic" Resulting Trusts: Retention, Restitution, or Reposing Trust?' in *Constructive and Resulting Trusts* (ed. Mitchell) (Oxford: Hart, 2010).

[12] [1974] Ch 269, 291.

[13] [1967] 2 AC 291, 312–13.

[14] For the facts of *Vandervell*, see Chapter 8.3(b)(i), pp. 386. See also Chapter 4, 'Creation of Express Trusts'.

[15] [1974] Ch 269, 289.

is not made manifest. For the second category, there is no mention of any expression of intention in any instrument, or of any presumption of a resulting trust: the resulting trust takes effect by operation of law, and so appears to be automatic. What a man fails effectually to dispose of remains automatically vested in him, and no question of any mere presumption can arise. The two categories are thus of presumed resulting trusts and automatic resulting trusts.

For ease of exposition, the cases will be presented in these two categories. It is important, however, to appreciate that the divide between the two is controversial. In *Westdeutsche Landesbank v Islington LBC*,[16] Lord Browne-Wilkinson recognized that there are traditionally two categories of resulting trust, but argued that *both* could be explained on the basis of presumed intentions.[17]

Under existing law a resulting trust arises in two sets of circumstances: (A) where A makes a voluntary payment to B or pays (wholly or in part) for the purchase of property which is vested either in B alone or in the joint names of A and B, there is a presumption that A did not intend to make a gift to B: the money or property is held on trust for A (if he is the sole provider of the money) or in the case of a joint purchase by A and B in shares proportionate to their contributions. It is important to stress that this is only a *presumption*, which presumption is easily rebutted either by the counter-presumption of advancement[18] or by direct evidence of A's intention to make an outright transfer... (B) Where A transfers property to B *on express trusts*, but the trusts declared do not exhaust the whole beneficial interest...Both types of resulting trust are traditionally regarded as examples of trusts giving effect to the common intention of the parties. A resulting trust is not imposed by law against the intentions of the trustee (as is a constructive trust) but gives effect to his presumed intention. Megarry J in *In Re Vandervell's Trusts (No. 2)* suggests that a resulting trust of type (B) does not depend on intention but operates automatically. I am not convinced that this is right. If the settlor has expressly, or by necessary implication, abandoned any beneficial interest in the trust property, there is in my view no resulting trust: the undisposed-of equitable interest vests in the Crown as *bona vacantia*.

For present purposes, it is important to note the general agreement that resulting trusts arise in two types of circumstances: (i) upon a voluntary conveyance, a presumed resulting trust; and (ii) where an express trust fails or does not exhaust the beneficial interest, an automatic resulting trust. It is useful to consider the cases under these two headings. Nevertheless, it may be that the same rationale—the presumed intention of the transferor—underpins both these categories; this will be considered later.[19] But it is odd that Lord Browne-Wilkinson in *Westdeutsche* referred to the intentions of both the transferor and the trustee in this context. It is preferable to focus upon the intention of the transferor alone; whether or not the trustee knew what the transferor intended should not be determinative. Seeking a common intention between the transferor and trustee is better suited to a common intention constructive trust.[20] As Lord Millett has observed:[21]

A resulting trust can also arise even if the recipient is unaware of the transfer or of the circumstances in which it was made. Indeed, this is perhaps the commonest case. The plaintiff makes a gratuitous

[16] [1996] AC 669.
[17] [1996] AC 669, 708. On *bona vacantia*, see Chapter 8.3(c)(ii), pp. 393–7.
[18] See Chapter 8.2(c), pp. 368–71.
[19] See Chapter 8.4, pp. 399–410.
[20] See Chapter 9.
[21] Millett, 'Restitution and Constructive Trusts' (1998) 114 LQR 399, 401.

transfer to the defendant. He afterwards demands the return of the property. The defendant refuses, and claims that it was a gift. The outcome depends on the plaintiff's intention at the time of the transfer, not on the defendant's understanding of his intention. This shows that the resulting trust is not merely a constructive trust which happens to be in favour of the person at whose expense the property was provided. The recipient is bound by the trust even if he honestly believed himself to be absolutely and beneficially entitled to property transferred to him by way of outright gift. His conscience may be clear. The existence of a resulting trust has never been made to depend on unconscionable conduct or notice on the part of the recipient.

2. PRESUMED RESULTING TRUSTS

It is said that Equity is generally suspicious of gifts made for no consideration in return, and will presume that a donee was expected to hold the property on trust for the donor by virtue of the so-called 'presumption of resulting trust'. In some circumstances, however, Equity will presume that a gift was intended because of the relationship between the parties, as a result of the so-called 'presumption of advancement'. The effect of these different presumptions relates to the allocation of the burden of proof:[22] where the presumption of resulting trust arises, the burden will be on the transferee to show a trust was not intended, and where the presumption of advancement applies, the burden will be on the transferor to show that he or she did not intend a gift but intended to have a beneficial interest in the property. In *Stack v Dowden*,[23] Baroness Hale said:

> The presumption of resulting trust is not a rule of law. According to Lord Diplock in *Pettit v Pettit* [1970] AC 777, 823H, the equitable presumptions of intention are 'no more than a consensus of judicial opinion disclosed by reported cases as to the most likely inference of fact to be drawn in the absence of any evidence to the contrary'. Equity, being concerned with commercial realities, presumed against gifts and other windfalls (such as survivorship). But even equity was prepared to presume a gift where the recipient was the provider's wife or child.

This passage is consistent with orthodoxy. However, it is worth highlighting that the existence of two competing 'presumptions' is controversial. It may be thought that only one is needed. So, for example, we may only need a presumption of resulting trust, and where this does not apply there is no need for any fact to be presumed and therefore no need for any 'presumption' of advancement.[24] This would be a logical approach, but the language of two different presumptions is prominent in the decided cases and so will be used in this chapter.

It is sensible first to examine the presumption of resulting trust. There are two principal categories: (i) voluntary conveyances; and (ii) resulting trusts, which arise due to a contribution of money to the purchase of property. In all events, however, it is important to remember that there is only scope for the presumptions to apply where an express intention of the transferor that the property be held on trust cannot be found. Moreover, these presumptions can be rebutted by any evidence indicating that a resulting trust was not intended.[25]

---

[22] *Russell v Scott* (1936) 55 CLR 440, 451 (Dixon and Evatt JJ).
[23] [2007] UKHL 17; [2007] 2 AC 432, [60].
[24] Swadling, 'Legislating in Vain' in *Judge and Jurist: Essays in Memory of Lord Rodger of Earlsferry* (eds Burrows, Johnston and Zimmermann) (Oxford: OUP, 2013).
[25] See Chapter 8.2(d), p. 372.

(a) VOLUNTARY CONVEYANCES

Where property is transferred for no consideration, a rebuttable presumption arises that the transferee holds on a resulting trust for the transferor.[26] In *Re Vinogradoff*,[27] Mrs Vinogradoff gratuitously transferred shares worth £800 into the joint names of herself and her granddaughter, who was four years old. On Mrs Vinogradoff's death, Farwell J held that a presumption of resulting trust arose, such that:

> The stock was not the property of the infant, but formed part of the estate of the testatrix.

The granddaughter therefore held the shares on resulting trust for her grandmother's estate. This case shows that the courts are willing to apply the presumption of resulting trust to any gift. However, the *result* in *Re Vinogradoff* appears strange, since the fact that the granddaughter was so young would suggest that she was not intended to be a trustee but the recipient of a gift, so the presumption of resulting trust might have been rebutted.[28]

The presumption of resulting trust used to apply to land in the same manner as personalty, but section 60(3) of the Law of Property Act 1925 now governs the former.

LAW OF PROPERTY ACT 1925

60. Abolition of technicalities in regard to conveyancing and deeds

> (3) In a voluntary conveyance a resulting trust for the grantor shall not be implied merely by reason that the property is not expressed to be conveyed for the use or benefit of the grantee.

The effect of this provision is that a voluntary conveyance of land takes effect as expressed, unless there is evidence of a contrary intention; in other words, there is no presumption of a resulting trust simply because the conveyance is not expressly made for the benefit of the person who receives the land. It is unclear whether such a presumption existed prior to 1925,[29] but section 60(3) has been interpreted such that any presumption of resulting trust that may once have existed does so no longer. So, although in *Hodgson v Marks*,[30] Russell LJ raised:

> the debatable question whether on a voluntary transfer of land by A to stranger B there is a presumption of a resulting trust

in *Lohia v Lohia*,[31] Nicholas Strauss QC said that:

> section 60(3) provides in effect that a voluntary conveyance means what it says; it is not necessary to use additional words to make it effective. It is likely that by 1925 the suspicion with which gifts of land were formerly viewed, which was at least one of the underlying reasons for the presumption, would

---

[26] Unless the relationship is such that a presumption of advancement arises: see Chapter 8.2(c), pp. 368–71.
[27] [1935] WN 68.
[28] For rebutting the presumption, see Chapter 8.2(d), pp. 372–83.
[29] For full discussion, see Mee, 'Resulting Trusts and Voluntary Conveyances of Land' [2012] Conv 307; cf N Jones, 'Uses and "Automatic" Resulting Trusts of Freehold' [2013] CLJ 91.
[30] [1971] Ch. 892, 933.
[31] [2001] WTLR 101, 113.

no longer have been regarded as material, and that the purpose of section 60(3) was accordingly to do away with the presumption of a resulting trust in the cases of voluntary conveyance and to make it necessary for the person seeking to establish a resulting trust to prove it.

The Court of Appeal in *Lohia* did not need to consider these comments of the trial judge,[32] but in *Khan v Ali*,[33] Morritt V-C cited the first-instance decision in *Lohia* with approval and concluded that:

Lohia v Lohia...establishes that the presumption of a resulting trust on a voluntary conveyance of land has been abolished by s.60(3) Law of Property Act 1925. It was not suggested that this proposition precludes a party to the conveyance from relying on evidence from which a resulting trust may be inferred.

Where the conveyance is of real property, there is no presumption of resulting trust simply because the conveyance does not explicitly state the transfer to be for the use or benefit of the transferee.

(b) PURCHASE-MONEY RESULTING TRUSTS

In a similar manner to voluntary conveyances, where a purchaser buys property in the name of a third party, or joins in the purchase of property with another party but in the name of that other party only, it is presumed that the property is held on resulting trust for the purchaser, proportionate to the purchaser's contribution to the purchase price. The presumption of resulting trust operates in the same manner regardless of whether the property purchased is realty or personalty: section 60(3) of the 1925 Act has no application, since the conveyance is not voluntary but given in return for the purchase of property.

As long ago as 1788, Eyre CJ was able to state in *Dyer v Dyer*[34] that:

The clear result of all the cases, without a single exception, is, that the trust of a legal estate, whether freehold, copyhold, or leasehold; whether taken in the names of the purchasers and others jointly, or in the name of others without that of the purchaser; whether in one name or several; whether jointly or successive, results to the man who advances the purchase-money. This is a general proposition supported by all the cases, and there is nothing to contradict it; and it goes on a strict analogy to the rule of the common law, that where a feoffment is made without consideration, the use results to the feoffor.

This presumption of resulting trust can still be of practical significance. For example, in *Abrahams v Trustee in Bankruptcy of Abrahams*,[35] a wife paid both her own share and that of her estranged husband in purchasing a winning National Lottery ticket. It was held that there was nothing to rebut the presumption of resulting trust, so the wife was entitled to all the winnings, which were attributable to both shares.[36]

It is important to appreciate that the resulting trust arises at the moment of purchase of the relevant property, and that the beneficial shares of the property become fixed at that point. Many cases have

---

[32] [2001] EWCA Civ 1691, [24]. See too Swadling, 'A Hard Look at *Hodgson v Marks*', in *Restitution and Equity, Vol 1: Resulting Trusts and Equitable Compensation* (eds Birks and Rose) (London: Mansfield Press, 2000), ch. 4, p. 74.

[33] [2002] EWCA Civ 974, [24].

[34] *Dyer v Dyer* (1788) 2 Cox Eq Cas 92, 93.

[35] (1999) 31 LS Gaz R 38; [1999] BPIR 637.

[36] The ticket was actually purchased on behalf of a larger syndicate. If the parties in the case were reversed so that the husband had paid for his wife's share, the presumption of advancement would have been applicable. See Chapter 8.2(c), p. 368.

concerned a party's contributing to a purchase price by taking out a mortgage; in such circumstances, the size of the mortgage facility represents the party's contribution: since the parties' shares under a resulting trust crystallize on the moment of acquisition, how the mortgage is later financed is of no consequence to the resulting trust. So, in *Curley v Parkes*,[37] Peter Gibson LJ stated that:

> The relevant principle is that the resulting trust of a property purchased in the name of another, in the absence of contrary intention, arises once and for all at the date on which the property is acquired. Because of the liability assumed by the mortgagor in a case where monies are borrowed by the mortgagor to be used on the purchase, the mortgagor is treated as having provided the proportion of the purchase price attributable to the monies so borrowed. Subsequent payments of the mortgage instalments are not part of the purchase price already paid to the vendor, but are sums paid for discharging the mortgagor's obligations under the mortgage...
>
> By reason of that principle and the modern reliance on mortgage finance the importance of the resulting trust has diminished, and instead reliance is generally placed on a constructive trust where an agreement or common intention can be found or inferred from the circumstances.

This raises an important point: resulting trusts will only arise where a constructive trust cannot be found. In the domestic context, where one party contributes money for the purchase of property in the sole name of another, the court will now prefer an analysis based upon a constructive trust to reflect the common intentions of the parties, rather than a resulting trust.[38] The same is also true regarding a purchase in the names of *both* parties. In *Jones v Kernott*,[39] Lord Walker and Baroness Hale recognized that:

> in the case of the purchase of a house or flat in joint names for joint occupation by a married or unmarried couple, where both are responsible for any mortgage, there is no presumption of a resulting trust arising from their having contributed to the deposit (or indeed the rest of the purchase) in unequal shares.

As a result of this shift in approach, many previous cases where a resulting trust was found in the domestic context should now be re-analysed as instances of a constructive trust. But where the property is purchased for *commercial* purposes, there is still scope to argue that a purchase-money resulting trust should arise. An example of this can be found in the decision of the Court of Appeal in *Laskar v Laskar*.[40] In that case, the defendant had bought her council house with her daughter. They were jointly and separately liable on the mortgage, the daughter being included because the mother could not otherwise have obtained the mortgage. The property was purchased as an investment, rather than as the family home, and rent from tenants was used to pay the mortgage instalments. A dispute arose about the beneficial ownership of the property. The Court of Appeal recognized that the presumption of resulting trust applied and, since both mother and daughter were jointly liable on the mortgage, it followed that they were deemed to have contributed the loan money equally even though there was no expectation that the daughter would actually have to pay anything. Lord Neuberger MR commented that:[41]

> It is by no means clear to me that the approach laid down by Baroness Hale of Richmond in [*Stack v Dowden*][42] intended to apply in a case such as this. In this case, although the parties were mother and

---

[37] [2004] EWCA Civ 1515, [14]–[15].
[38] *Stack v Dowden* [2007] UKHL 17; [2007] 2 AC 432. See Chapter 9, 'Informal Arrangements Relating to Property'.
[39] *Jones v Kernott* [2011] UKSC 53; [2012] 1 AC 776, [25].
[40] [2008] EWCA Civ 347; [2008] 1 WLR 2695.
[41] Ibid, [15]–[17].
[42] See Chapter 9.2(b)(iv)(c), pp. 452–4.

daughter and not in that sense in an arm's length commercial relationship, they had independent lives, and, as I have already indicated, the purchase of the property was not really for the purpose of providing a home for them. The daughter hardly lived there at the time it was purchased, and did not live there much if at all afterwards, and the mother did not live there for long. The property was purchased primarily as an investment....

It was argued that this case was midway between the cohabitation cases of co-ownership where property is bought for living in, such as *Stack*, and arm's length commercial cases of co-ownership, where property is bought for development or letting. In the latter sort of case, the reasoning in *Stack v Dowden* would not be appropriate and the resulting trust presumption still appears to apply. In this case, the primary purpose of the purchase of the property was as an investment, not as a home. In other words this was a purchase which, at least primarily, was not in 'the domestic consumer context' but in a commercial context. To my mind it would not be right to apply the reasoning in *Stack v Dowden* to such a case as this, where the parties primarily purchased the property as an investment for rental income and capital appreciation, even where their relationship is a familial one.

In some situations, however, the matrimonial home may still be held on resulting trust. This appears likely in situations where one party is seeking to use a distinct, commercial entity in order to try to hide assets. For instance, in *Prest v Petrodel Resources Ltd*,[43] a company, which was owned and controlled by Mr Prest, owned the matrimonial home of Mr and Mrs Prest, who were divorcing. The Supreme Court accepted that the company held the home on resulting trust for Mr Prest. This was because Mr Prest provided the purchase price for the property, and the company was not intended to acquire a beneficial interest in the property. There was no evidence to rebut the presumption of resulting trust, so the matrimonial home belonged beneficially to Mr Prest, and Mrs Prest could ask for the transfer of that property in proceedings for ancillary relief.[44]

(c) PRESUMPTION OF ADVANCEMENT

In *Tinsley v Milligan*,[45] Lord Browne-Wilkinson stated that:

On a transfer from a man to his wife, children or others to whom he stands *in loco parentis*, equity presumes an intention to make a gift.

An early explanation of this presumption of gift, otherwise known as the presumption of advancement, was given by Sir George Jessel MR in *Bennett v Bennett*, in which he said:[46]

The doctrine of equity as regards presumption of gifts is this, that where one person stands in such a relation to another that there is an obligation on that person to make a provision for the other, and we find either a purchase or investment in the name of the other, or in the joint names of the person and the other, of an amount which would constitute a provision for the other, the presumption arises of an intention on the part of the person to discharge the obligation to the other; and therefore, in

---

[43] [2013] UKSC 34; [2013] 2 AC 415.
[44] See Hare, 'Family Division, 0; Chancery Division, 1: piercing the corporate veil in the Supreme Court (again)' [2013] CLJ 511; see further Chapter 9.19(b)(ii), pp. 430–1.
[45] [1994] 1 AC 340, 372.
[46] (1879) 10 Ch D 474, 476.

the absence of evidence to the contrary, that purchase or investment is held to be in itself evidence of a gift.

In other words, the presumption of gift arises from the moral obligation to give.

That reconciles all the cases upon the subject but one, because nothing is better established than this, that as regards a child, a person not the father of the child may put himself in the position of one *in loco parentis* to the child, and so incur the obligation to make a provision for the child…

A person *in loco parentis* means a person taking upon himself the duty of a father of a child to make a provision for that child. It is clear that in that case the presumption can only arise from the obligation, and therefore in that case the doctrine can only have reference to the obligation of a father to provide for his child, and nothing else.

But the father is under that obligation from the mere fact of his being the father, and therefore no evidence is necessary to shew the obligation to provide for his child, because that is part of his duty. In the case of a father, you have only to prove the fact that he is the father, and when you have done that the obligation at once arises; but in the case of a person *in loco parentis* you must prove that he took upon himself the obligation.

The basis of this presumption is easily understood: when a father gives property to his child or wife, in the absence of any contrary indications, it might well be presumed that he intended a gift, rather than for him to have any beneficial interest in the property. Nevertheless, the existence of this presumption has been criticized. For example, in *Pettitt v Pettitt*,[47] Lord Reid commented that:

I do not know how this presumption first arose, but it would seem that the judges who first gave effect to it must have thought either that husbands so commonly intended to make gifts in the circumstances in which the presumption arises that it was proper to assume this where there was no evidence, or that wives' economic dependence on their husbands made it necessary as a matter of public policy to give them this advantage. I can see no other reasonable basis for the presumption. These considerations have largely lost their force under present conditions, and, unless the law has lost all flexibility so that the courts can no longer adapt it to changing conditions, the strength of the presumption must have been much diminished.

Although the necessity of wives to depend upon their husbands for economic survival has undoubtedly diminished, this does not necessarily mean that a presumption of gift is inappropriate, given the nature of the relationship between the parties. But the presumption of advancement has further been criticized because of the distinction it draws between gifts from husband to wife and from wife to husband, as well as between gifts from father to child and mother to child. So, in *Abrahams v Trustee in Bankruptcy of Abrahams*,[48] there was a presumption of resulting trust when a wife bought a lottery ticket for her husband. But, if the husband had bought a lottery ticket for his wife, there would have been the contrary presumption of advancement. Similarly, although a transfer from a father to his child raises the presumption of advancement, if the transfer is from mother to child, then the contrary presumption of resulting trust arises.[49]

Such results have rightly been criticized as discriminatory. Why should it matter whether the transferor was male or female? Indeed, it has even been suggested that the very existence of the presumption

---

[47] [1970] AC 777, 793.
[48] [2000] WTLR 593.
[49] See e.g. *Sekhon v Alissa* [1989] 2 FLR 94 (Hoffmann J). Cp *Nelson v Nelson* (1995) 132 ALR 133, in which the Australian High Court recognized a presumption of advancement between mother and child.

of advancement is contrary to human rights,[50] although the better view is that the presumption of advancement in itself is probably not contrary to the United Kingdom's obligations under the European Convention on Human Rights.[51] In any event, the distinction between male and female transferors is unsatisfactory. There appear to be two options for future reform: either abolish the presumption of advancement, or extend it so that it applies to transfers from wife to husband and mother to child, for example.

The former path was favoured in the Equality Act 2010, section 199:

EQUALITY ACT 2010

199 Abolition of presumption of advancement

(1) The presumption of advancement (by which, for example, a husband is presumed to be making a gift to his wife if he transfers property to her, or purchases property in her name) is abolished.

(2) The abolition by subsection (1) of the presumption of advancement does not have effect in relation to—

(a) anything done before the commencement of this section, or

(b) anything done pursuant to any obligation incurred before the commencement of this section.

However, despite much of the Equality Act already being implemented, section 199 is not yet in force, and there are no indications that the Government intends to bring it into force.[52] Moreover, even if section 199 is brought into force, it would not affect anything done prior to its commencement, and the courts would still need to grapple with the presumption of advancement.

There is some indication that the courts might be willing to remove the discriminatory character of the presumption of advancement by extending it to transfers made by women as well. Thus, in *Antoni v Antoni*,[53] Lord Scott, giving the advice of the Privy Council, employed gender-neutral language in describing the presumption of advancement as applying[54]

when a parent places assets in the name of a child and assumes that the parent intends to make a gift to the child.

More recently, in *Close Invoice Finance Ltd v Abaowa*, Mr Simon Picken QC, sitting as a Deputy High Court Judge, expressed a similar view.

---

[50] See e.g. Andrews, 'The Presumption of Advancement: Equity, Equality and Human Rights' [2007] Conv 340, who considers the presumption to be inconsistent with Article 14 of the European Convention on Human Rights, which prohibits discrimination on the grounds of sex, as well as Article 5 of Protocol 7 of the Convention, which provides that 'Spouses shall enjoy equality of rights and responsibilities of a private law character between them, and in their relations with their children, as to marriage, during marriage and in the event of its dissolution.'

[51] See e.g. Glister, 'Section 199 of the Equality Act 2010: How Not to Abolish the Presumption of Advancement' (2010) 73 MLR 807, who argues that Article 5 of Protocol 7 is limited to relations between spouses and their children in the context of marriage, and that the presumption of advancement is not a 'right' within the scope of Article 5. The United Kingdom has not (yet) ratified Protocol 7.

[52] For criticism of this provision, see Glister, 'Section 199 of the Equality Act 2010: How Not to Abolish the Presumption of Advancement' (2010) 73 MLR 807.

[53] [2007] UKPC 10; [2007] WTLR 1335.

[54] Ibid, [20].

Close Invoice Finance Ltd v Abaowa [2010] EWHC 1920 (QB) [93]–[94] (Mr Simon Picken QC)

I should make it clear that, had [counsel] chosen to press her original submission . . . that the presumption of advancement does not arise in a case such as the present involving a mother and a daughter, I would have had no hesitation in deciding that in the modern age the presumption of advancement should, indeed, be taken as applying between a mother and a daughter in the same way that it does as between a father and his child. The proposition that the presumption does not apply in relation to a contribution by a mother derives from the decision in *Re De Visme* (1863) 2 De GJ&SM 17, which was followed by Jessel MR (sitting as a judge of first instance) in *Bennet v Bennet* (1879) 10 Ch D 474. *De Visme*, which was not, in any event, followed by Stuart V-C in *Sayre v Hughes* (1868) LR 5 Eq 376, came before the court on an unopposed petition in lunacy. It does not appear to have been an appeal, although decided by Lords Justices. The question in the case was whether savings by a deceased mother invested in the joint names of her son (a lunatic) and her daughter (her executrix) should be transferred to the daughter as executrix. It was argued that the presumption of advancement did not apply, and the court made the order sought. No reasons were, however, given for that decision. The judges in *Sayre* and *Bennet* came to different conclusions because they had different views as to the basis for the presumption of advancement. Stuart V-C took the view that the presumption was based on affection as a motive upon which a parent will act in advancing the interests of a child and, accordingly, was at least as apposite in relation to a mother as a father (if not more so). Jessel MR was of the view that the presumption was based on the moral obligation (recognised as an equitable obligation by the Courts of Equity) of a father to provide for his children, an obligation which he said a mother did not have.

As I see it . . . the distinction between a father and a mother in relation to the presumption of advancement cannot stand today. Our society recognises fathers and mothers as having similar obligations in relation to provision for their children and recognises that, broadly speaking, fathers and mothers have similar degrees of affection for them. Transfers to children by mothers are in this day and age as likely to be gifts as are transfers by fathers. Moreover, legal policy towards the ownership of assets, by married women at least, has changed significantly since the time when *De Visme* and *Bennet* were before the court. There is now as much moral obligation on the part of a mother with money to benefit her children with it as there is in the case of a father, and it is equally likely that she will intend to confer such a benefit as a father is.

This approach seems sensible, and is likely to be adopted whilst waiting for section 199 of the Equality Act 2010 to be implemented. However, if abolishing the presumption of advancement would leave a presumption of resulting trust in its stead, it is questionable whether the implementation of section 199 would be satisfactory: where a father transfers property to his son, should it really be presumed that a gift was *not* intended?

In any event, it is important to recognize that the presumption of advancement will rarely be determinative; indeed, it is clear that it is not as strong as it once was. In *Stack v Dowden*,[55] Lord Neuberger commented that:

the presumption of advancement, as between man and wife, which was so important in the 18th and 19th centuries, has now become much weakened, although not quite to the point of disappearance.

Just like the presumption of resulting trust, the presumption of advancement is readily rebutted by contrary evidence. It is, therefore, important to consider what sort of evidence might rebut both the presumption of resulting trust and the presumption of advancement.

[55] [2007] UKHL 17; [2007] 2 AC 432, [101].

(d) REBUTTING THE PRESUMPTIONS

The presumptions are only 'long-stops' to be used in the absence of evidence to the contrary. As Lord Upjohn put it in *Vandervell*:[56]

> the so-called presumption of a resulting trust is no more than a long stop to provide the answer when the relevant facts and circumstances fail to yield a solution.

The same is undoubtedly true of the presumption of advancement. In *Pettitt v Pettitt*,[57] Lord Hodson said:

> In old days when a wife's right to property was limited, the presumption, no doubt, had great importance and today, when there are no living witnesses to a transaction and inferences have to be drawn, there may be no other guide to a decision as to property rights than by resort to the presumption of advancement. I do not think it would often happen that when evidence had been given, the presumption would today have any decisive effect.

Either presumption can be displaced by sufficient evidence to the contrary, although obviously some evidence must be introduced to the court.[58] So where a presumption of resulting trust arises, evidence that the transferor did not intend to have a beneficial interest in the property can be used to rebut the presumption. As Lord Upjohn insisted in *Vandervell*:[59]

> [the presumption of resulting trust] is only a presumption and is easily rebutted. All the relevant facts and circumstances can be considered in order to ascertain [the donor's] intentions with a view to rebutting this presumption.

A good example of the presumption of resulting trust being rebutted is *Fowkes v Pascoe*.

Fowkes v Pascoe [1875] 10 Ch App 343, 352–4

A mother, Mrs Baker, had purchased annuities in the joint names of herself and her daughter-in-law's son, Mr Pascoe. Although it was presumed that Mr Pascoe held the annuities on resulting trust, this presumption was easily rebutted in the light of the circumstances of the case, which included that Mrs Baker was wealthy, he was living in her house, and she was already providing for him financially. All this suggested that she had intended him to have a beneficial interest in the annuity.

Mellish LJ:

Now, the presumption must, beyond all question, be of very different weight in different cases. In some cases it would be very strong indeed. If, for instance, a man invested a sum of stock in the name of himself and his solicitor, the inference would be very strong indeed that it was intended solely for the purpose of trust, and the Court would require very strong evidence on the part of the solicitor to prove that it was intended as a gift; and certainly his own evidence would not be sufficient. On the other hand, a man may make an investment of stock in the name of himself and some person, although not a child or wife, yet

---

[56] [1967] 2 AC 291, 313.
[57] [1970] AC 777, 811.
[58] *Prest v Petrodel Resources Ltd* [2013] UKSC 34; [2013] 2 AC 415.
[59] [1967] 2 AC 291, 312.

in such a position to him as to make it extremely probable that the investment was intended as a gift. In such a case, although the rule of law, if there was no evidence at all, would compel the Court to say that the presumption of trust must prevail, even if the Court might not believe that the fact was in accordance with the presumption, yet, if there is evidence to rebut the presumption, then, in my opinion, the Court must go into the actual facts. And if we are to go into the actual facts, and look at the circumstances of this investment, it appears to me utterly impossible, as the Lord Justice has said, to come to any other conclusion than that the first investment was made for the purpose of gift and not for the purpose of trust. It was either for the purpose of trust or else for the purpose of gifts; and therefore evidence which shows it was not for the purpose of trust is evidence to shew that it was for the purpose of gifts. We find a lady of considerable fortune, having no nearer connections than Mr. Pascoe, who was then a young man living in her house, and for whom she was providing. We find her, manifestly out of her savings, buying a sum of £250 stock in the joint names of herself and him, and at the same time buying another sum of £250 stock, on the very same day, in the joint names of herself and a lady who was living with her as a companion. Then, applying one's common sense to that transaction, what inference is it possible to draw, except that the purchases were intended for the purpose of gifts? If they were intended for the purpose of trusts, what possible reason was there why the two sums were not invested in the same names? Besides, at the very same time the lady had a large sum of stock in her own name, and could anything be more absurd than to suppose that a lady with £4,000 or £5,000 in her own name at that time in the same stock, and having a sum of £500 to invest out of her savings, should go and invest £250 in the name of herself and a young gentleman who was living in her house, and another £250 in the name of herself and her companion, and yet intend the whole to be for herself? I cannot come to any other conclusion than that it must have been intended by the way of a present after her death.

Then, when we have once arrived at the conclusion that the first investment was intended as a gift (and the second was exactly similar), and when we find that the account was opened for the purpose of a gift, those facts appear to me to rebut the presumption altogether, because when an account is once found to be opened for the purpose of a gift there is very strong reason to suppose that everything added to that account was intended for the purpose of gift also. Assuming the testatrix to know that she had made a gift, and had invested a sum of money in stock in the joint names of herself and Pascoe for the purpose of making a present to him, it would certainly be a very extraordinary thing that she should go and add other large sums to that account, not for the purpose of making a present to him, but for the purpose of his being a trustee. I cannot help coming to the conclusion that, as a matter of fact, these investments were intended for the purpose of gift.

There were one or two facts relied on against this conclusion. It was said that Mr. Pascoe kept the matter secret for a great number of years, and never revealed it. I do not greatly rely on that. Every one who has experience knows that some persons are very reticent about their affairs, and some persons are always talking about them. You cannot form any inference as to that. If he really and bona fide believed, and had no doubt that it was intended for a gift, and for his use, I do not see that there was anything extraordinary in his not mentioning it to the persons who now say it was not mentioned to them. The only fact that in the least degree, in my opinion, went against him was his not accounting for the dividend which was due at the death of the testatrix. I think it is not at all impossible that he might have honestly believed that that was his, although I entirely agree that in point of law it was not so.

It need not necessarily be shown, however, that the transfer was by way of gift in order to rebut the presumption of resulting trust. As Lord Browne-Wilkinson recognized in *Westdeutsche*:[60]

the presumption of resulting trust is rebutted by evidence of any intention inconsistent with such a trust, not only by evidence of an intention to make a gift.

[60] [1996] AC 669, 708.

In *Westdeutsche*,[61] any presumption of resulting trust was rebutted because the payments made, pursuant to a contract that was void, were intended to discharge contractual obligations; this was inconsistent with any presumed intention to create a resulting trust, and such a conclusion was not affected by the fact that the contractual obligation was mistakenly believed to be valid. In a similar vein, if the money is advanced by way of loan, then that is also inconsistent with the argument that a resulting trust arises, since the lender does not intend to have a beneficial interest in the money lent.[62] As Browne-Wilkinson J commented in *In re Sharpe (a bankrupt)*:[63]

> if...moneys are advanced by way of loan there can be no question of the lender being entitled to an interest in the property under a resulting trust. If he were to take such an interest, he would get his money twice: once on repayment of the loan and once on taking his share of the proceeds of sale of the property.

A similar approach is taken to rebutting the presumption of advancement. Any evidence that a gift was not intended will be sufficient to rebut the presumption. However, although this presumption can be rebutted by comparatively slight evidence,[64] any declaration of a contrary intention adduced as evidence will only be admitted if it was made before, during, or immediately after the time the property was purchased or transferred. If the declaration was made after the transaction, evidence of the declaration will only be admissible either if it constituted part of the transaction, or if it operates against the interests of the person who made the declaration.[65] If subsequent declarations were admitted in favour of the person making the declaration, it might be too easy for a party to manufacture evidence to further his or her own interests. *Shephard v Cartwright* is a good illustration of this.

Shephard v Cartwright [1955] AC 431, 445–50

A father had purchased shares that were registered in the names of his children. The shares were sold and the proceeds deposited for the benefit of the children. The presumption of advancement was consequently engaged. Five years later, the father procured the written consent of the children to enable him to withdraw money from their deposit account. The children were not aware of what they had signed. The question for the court was whether this document was sufficient to rebut the presumption of advancement. Since this was evidence that did not form part of the original transaction, it could be admitted only if it was evidence of the children admitting that their father had not intended a gift, such that the evidence operated against their interests. But since the children were not aware of what they had signed, it could not be used in this way.

Viscount Simonds:

It must then be asked by what evidence can the presumption be rebutted, and it would, I think, be very unfortunate if any doubt were cast (as I think it has been by certain passages in the judgments under review) upon the well settled law on this subject. It is, I think, correctly stated in substantially the same terms in every textbook that I have consulted and supported by authority extending over a

---

[61] See further Chapter 8.4(a), pp. 401–8.
[62] Unless a '*Quistclose* trust' arises: see Chapter 8.5, p. 510.
[63] [1980] 1 WLR 219, 223.
[64] *Pettit v Pettit* [1970] AC 777, 814 (Lord Upjohn); *McGrath v Wallis* [1995] 2 FLR 114.
[65] *Shephard v Cartwright* [1955] AC 431.

long period of time. I will take, as an example, a passage from *Snell's Equity* (24th edn), p. 153, which is as follows:

> 'The acts and declarations of the parties before or at the time of the purchase, or so immediately after it as to constitute a part of the transaction, are admissible in evidence either for or against the party who did the act or made the declaration...But subsequent declarations are admissible as evidence only against the party who made them, and not in his favour.'

I do not think it necessary to review the numerous cases of high authority upon which this statement is founded. It is possible to find in some earlier judgments reference to 'subsequent' events without the qualifications contained in the textbook statement: it may even be possible to wonder in some cases how in the narration of facts certain events were admitted to consideration. But the burden of authority in favour of the broad proposition as stated in the passage I have cited is overwhelming and should not be disturbed.

But although the applicable law is not in doubt, the application of it is not always easy. There must often be room for argument whether a subsequent act is part of the same transaction as the original purchase or transfer, and equally whether subsequent acts which it is sought to adduce in evidence ought to be regarded as admissions by the party so acting, and if they are so admitted, further facts should be admitted by way of qualification of those admissions.

...

My Lords, at the outset of this opinion I said that there must often be room for argument whether subsequent events can be regarded as forming part of the original transaction so as to be admissible evidence of intention and in this case it has certainly been vigorously argued that they can. But, though I know of no universal criterion by which a link can for this purpose be established between one event and another, here I see insuperable difficulty in finding any link at all. The time factor alone of nearly five years is almost decisive, but, apart from that, the events of 1934 and 1935,[66] whether taken singly or in their sum, appear to me to be wholly independent of the original transaction. It is in fact fair to say that, so far from flowing naturally and inevitably from it, they probably never would have happened but for the phenomenal success of the enterprise. Nor can I give any weight to the argument much pressed upon us that the deceased was an honourable man and therefore could not have acted as he did, if he had in 1929 intended to give the shares outright to his children. I assume that he was an honourable man as well in the directions in regard to income tax that he gave to [his accountant] as otherwise, but I think that he may well have deemed it consistent with honourable conduct and with paternal benevolence to take back part of what he had given when the magnitude of the gift so far surpassed his expectation.

If, then, these events cannot be admitted in evidence as part of the original transaction, can they be admitted to rebut the presumption on the ground that they are admissions by the appellants against interest? I conceive it possible, and this view is supported by authority, that there might be such a course of conduct by a child after a presumed advancement as to constitute an admission by him of his parent's original intention, though such evidence should be regarded jealously. But it appears to me to be an indispensable condition of such conduct being admissible that it should be performed with knowledge of the material facts. In the present case the undisputed fact that the appellants under their father's guidance did what they were told without inquiry or knowledge precludes the admission in evidence of their conduct and, if it were admitted, would deprive it of all probative value. It is otherwise, however, with the conduct of the deceased. I have already made it clear that the respondents have failed to discharge the burden which rests on them of rebutting the presumption of advancement. The appellants, therefore, in my opinion, need no reinforcement from subsequent events. But, since inevitably in a complex case like this, either upon the footing of being examined *de bene esse* or because

---

[66] When the written consent of the children to enable the father to withdraw money from their deposit account was obtained.

they have been admitted for some other purpose than the proof of intention, all the facts relevant or irrelevant have been reviewed, I do not hesitate to say that the only conclusion which I can form about the deceased's original intention is that he meant the provision he then made for his children to be for their permanent advancement. He may well have changed his mind at a later date, but it was too late. He may have thought that, having made an absolute gift, he could yet revoke it. This is something that no one will ever know. The presumption which the law makes is not to be thus rebutted. If it were my duty to speculate upon these matters, my final question would be why the deceased should have put these several parcels of shares in six different companies into the names of his wife and three children unless he meant to make provision for them, and since counsel have not been able to suggest any, much less any plausible, reason why he should have done so, I shall conclude that the intention which the law imputes to him was in fact his intention. The reasoning which made so strong an appeal to Mellish LJ in *Fowkes v Pascoe* (1875) 10 Ch App 343 has in this case also particular weight.

Fung has criticized the 'rule' in *Shephard v Cartwright*, pointing out that:[67]

there should not be an absolute bar against the admissibility of a purchaser's subsequent acts or declarations to support a presumption of resulting trust or to rebut a presumption of advancement, particularly in view of the increasing readiness of the courts to rebut any presumption of resulting trust or presumption of advancement, and the changes in legislation regarding the admissibility of hearsay evidence in civil proceedings. The modern trend of civil litigation is to place all relevant evidence before the court and to let the court decide on the weight to be attached to it.

There is much force in this criticism. The presumption of advancement and the presumption of resulting trust are both 'long-stops'; any valuable evidence that might rebut the presumption should be available to the court. The court is then able to assess the probative weight of potentially self-serving declarations. The current approach of the courts was described by Lord Phillips MR in *Lavelle v Lavelle*:[68]

equity searches for the subjective intention of the transferor. It seems to me that it is not satisfactory to apply rigid rules of law to the evidence that is admissible to rebut the presumption of advancement. Plainly, self-serving statements or conduct of a transferor, who may long after the transaction be regretting earlier generosity, carry little or no weight. But words or conduct more proximate to the transaction itself should be given the significance that they naturally bear as part of the overall picture. Where the transferee is an adult, the words or conduct of the transferor will carry more weight if the transferee is aware of them and makes no protest or challenge to them.

In any event, where contemporaneous evidence is available, the courts have not been slow to rebut the presumption of advancement. So in *Warren v Gurney*,[69] a father had purchased a house and conveyed it to one of his daughters. The presumption of advancement was rebutted by declarations of the father, made at the time of the purchase, that a gift was not intended, and by the fact that he had retained the title deeds to the property. As Morton LJ commented:[70]

there was ample evidence to justify that conclusion of the judge [that the presumption of advancement was rebutted]. In the first place, there is the fact that the father retained the title deeds from the time

---

[67] Fung, 'The Scope of the Rule in *Shephard v Cartwright*' (2006) 122 LQR 651, 653.
[68] [2004] EWCA Civ 223; [2004] 2 FCR 418, [19].
[69] [1944] 2 All ER 472.
[70] Ibid, at 473.

> of purchase to the time of his death. I think that is a very significant fact, because title deeds, as it was said in *Coke on Littleton*, are 'sinews of the land'. One would have expected the father to have handed them over, either to the plaintiff or her husband, if he had intended the gift.

Similarly, in *McGrath v Wallis*,[71] a family home was acquired and conveyed into the name of the son since, because the father was unemployed, only the son was acceptable as the mortgagor. At the time of the transfer, a declaration of trust had been drafted indicating that the father was to have an 80 per cent beneficial interest and the son 20 per cent. This had not been signed and so it was not a valid declaration of trust, but it was sufficient to rebut the presumption of advancement.

(i) *Evidence of illegality*

There is one significant limitation upon the type of evidence that can be introduced to rebut either the presumption of resulting trust or the presumption of advancement: for reasons of public policy, a person is not allowed to rely upon evidence of his or her own illegal conduct.[72] This rule is well illustrated by the leading decision of the House of Lords in *Tinsley v Milligan*.[73]

Tinsley v Milligan [1994] 1 AC 340

Miss Tinsley and Miss Milligan were lovers. They purchased a house jointly, with both contributing to the purchase price, but agreed that it should be in the sole name of Miss Tinsley in order to facilitate false claims to housing benefit by Miss Milligan. This fraud on the Department of Social Security was carried out over several years. Subsequently, Miss Tinsley and Miss Milligan fell out and the former moved out of the house. She brought an action seeking possession and Miss Milligan counterclaimed for a declaration that Miss Tinsley held the house on trust for both parties equally, by virtue of the presumption of resulting trust. A majority of the House of Lords (Lords Jauncey of Tullichettle, Lowry, and Browne-Wilkinson) upheld the counterclaim (Lords Keith of Kinkel and Goff of Chieveley dissented). The principle upheld by the majority was that a transferor was entitled to succeed if he could establish his title without relying on his own illegality. The appellant could, therefore, rely on the presumption of resulting trust.

Lord Jauncey:

First, it is trite law that the court will not give its assistance to the enforcement of executory provisions of an unlawful contract whether the illegality is apparent *ex facie* the document or whether the illegality of purpose of what would otherwise be a lawful contract emerges during the course of the trial; *Holman v Johnson* (1775) 1 Cowp 341 at 343, per Lord Mansfield CJ...

Second, it is well established that a party is not entitled to rely on his own fraud or illegality in order to assist a claim or rebut a presumption. Thus when money or property has been transferred by a man to his wife or children for the purpose of defrauding creditors and the transferee resists his claim for recovery he cannot be heard to rely on his illegal purpose in order to rebut the presumption of advancement; *Gascoigne v Gascoigne* [1918] 1 KB 223 at 226; ... *Tinker v Tinker* [1970] P 136 at 143, per Salmon LJ.

---

[71] [1995] 2 FLR 114.
[72] *Holman v Johnson* (1775) 1 Cowp 341, 343 (Lord Mansfield).
[73] [1994] 1 AC 340.

Third, it has, however, for some years been recognised that a completely executed transfer of property or of an interest in property made in pursuance of an unlawful agreement is valid and the court will assist the transferee in the protection of his interest provided that he does not require to found on the unlawful agreement:... *Alexander v Rayson* [1936] 1 KB 169 at 184–185;... *Sajan Singh v Sardara Ali* [1960] AC 167 at 176...

I find this a very narrow question but I have come to the conclusion that the transaction whereby the claimed resulting trust in favour of the respondent was created was the agreement between the parties that, although funds were to be provided by both of them, nevertheless the title to the house was to be in the sole name of the appellant for the unlawful purpose of defrauding the Department of Social Security. So long as that agreement remained unperformed, neither party could have enforced it against the other. However, as soon as the agreement was implemented by the sale to the appellant alone she became trustee for the respondent who can now rely on the equitable proprietary interest which has thereby been presumed to have been created in her favour and has no need to rely on the illegal transaction which led to its creation.

Lord Browne-Wilkinson:

The presumption of a resulting trust is, in my view, crucial in considering the authorities. On that presumption (and on the contrary presumption of advancement) hinges the answer to the crucial question: does a plaintiff claiming under a resulting trust have to rely on the underlying illegality? Where the presumption of resulting trust applies, the plaintiff does not have to rely on the illegality. If he proves that the property is vested in the defendant alone but that the plaintiff provided part of the purchase money, or voluntarily transferred the property to the defendant, the plaintiff establishes his claim under a resulting trust unless either the contrary presumption of advancement displaces the presumption of resulting trust or the defendant leads evidence to rebut the presumption of resulting trust. Therefore, in cases where the presumption of advancement does not apply, a plaintiff can establish his equitable interest in the property without relying in any way on the underlying illegal transaction. In this case the respondent as defendant simply pleaded the common intention that the property should belong to both of them and that she contributed to the purchase price: she claimed that in consequence the property belonged to them equally. To the same effect was her evidence-in-chief. Therefore the respondent was not forced to rely on the illegality to prove her equitable interest. Only in the reply and the course of the respondent's cross-examination did such illegality emerge: it was the appellant who had to rely on that illegality.

Although the presumption of advancement does not directly arise for consideration in this case, it is important when considering the decided cases to understand its operation. On a transfer from a man to his wife, children or others to whom he stands *in loco parentis*, equity presumes an intention to make a gift. Therefore in such a case, unlike the cases where the presumption of resulting trust applies, in order to establish any claim the plaintiff has himself to lead evidence sufficient to rebut the presumption of gift and in so doing will normally have to plead, and give evidence of, the underlying illegal purpose....

The majority of cases have been those in which the presumption of advancement applied: in those authorities the rule has been stated as being that a plaintiff cannot rely on evidence of his own illegality to rebut the presumption applicable in such cases that the plaintiff intended to make a gift of the property to the transferee. Thus in *Gascoigne v Gascoigne* [1918] 1 KB 223;... *Chettiar v Chettiar* [1962] AC 294 and *Tinker v Tinker* [1970] P 136 at 141–142, the crucial point was said to be the inability of the plaintiff to lead evidence rebutting the presumption of advancement. In each case the plaintiff was claiming to recover property voluntarily transferred to, or purchased in the name of, a wife or child, for an illegal purpose. Although reference was made to Lord Eldon LC's principle,[74] none of those cases was decided on

---

[74] 'To a fraudulent plaintiff seeking relief the court would say "Let the estate lie where it falls"', *Muckleston v Brown* [1801] 6 Ves 52, 68–9.

the simple ground (if it were good law) that equity would not in any circumstances enforce a resulting trust in such circumstances. On the contrary in each case the rule was stated to be that the plaintiff could not recover because he had to rely on the illegality to rebut the presumption of advancement.

In my judgment, the explanation for this departure from Lord Eldon LC's absolute rule is that the fusion of the administration of law and equity has led the courts to adopt a single rule (applicable both at law and in equity) as to the circumstances in which the court will enforce property interests acquired in pursuance of an illegal transaction, viz. the *Bowmakers* rule: [1945] KB 65. A party to an illegality can recover by virtue of a legal or equitable property interest if, but only if, he can establish his title without relying on his own illegality. In cases where the presumption of advancement applies, the plaintiff is faced with the presumption of gift and therefore cannot claim under a resulting trust unless and until he has rebutted that presumption of gift: for those purposes the plaintiff does have to rely on the underlying illegality and therefore fails.

The majority in *Tinsley* held that Miss Milligan could rely upon her beneficial interest under a resulting trust because she had no need to rely upon her illegal conduct: she had contributed to the purchase of the property, so a resulting trust arose in her favour. She did not need to mention her defrauding the Department of Social Security to raise the presumption, so the court did not need to be influenced by it. But on only slightly different facts, the result would have been entirely different. If the case had concerned a married heterosexual couple, and the husband had contributed to the purchase of a house in the sole name of his wife, then there would have been a presumption of advancement, rather than a presumption of resulting trust. But the husband would not have been able to claim a share in the property, since he would have needed to lead evidence of illegality in order to rebut the presumption of advancement, and he would not be able to plead such evidence. Yet the merits of the two cases appear overwhelmingly similar. Although the facts of *Tinsley* would now give rise to a common intention constructive trust rather than resulting trust,[75] the reliance principle would still apply in a similar manner.[76]

Tinsley makes the 'reliance principle' crucially important: whether or not a party needs to 'rely' upon his or her illegal conduct will often be of the utmost significance. Yet, this reliance principle has been criticized as technical and arbitrary; it means that the presumptions of resulting trust and advancement are often determinative, rather than simply 'long-stops'. In *Tribe v Tribe*,[77] H.H. Judge Weeks QC at first instance found it:

difficult to see why the outcome in cases such as the present one should depend to such a large extent on arbitrary factors, such as whether the claim is brought by a father against a son, or a mother against a son, or a grandfather against a grandson.

Such concerns were reiterated in the Court of Appeal, in which Millett LJ cited the 'harshness' of the illegality defence as interpreted in *Tinsley*.[78] More recently, Black J has lamented that:[79]

[T]he courts have plainly felt uncomfortable at times with the results of the rules, which can seem sometimes to favour one of a number of parties who are all equally implicated in the illegal purpose simply by virtue of the accident of how a case has to be pleaded, but that is the way in which the law operates.

---

[75] *Stack v Dowden* [2007] UKHL 17; [2007] 2 AC 432; see Chapter 9.2, p. 432.
[76] *O'Kelly v Davies* [2014] EWCA Civ 1606; [2015] 1 WLR 2725.
[77] Cited by Nourse LJ in the Court of Appeal: [1996] Ch 107, 118.
[78] [1996] Ch 107, 133.
[79] *Q v Q* [2008] EWHC 1874 (Fam); [2009] Fam Law 17, [138].

Such unease with the operation of the 'reliance principle' seems to have been at the root of the Court of Appeal's decision in *Tribe v Tribe*.[80]

Tribe v Tribe [1996] Ch 107

A father transferred shares to his son to conceal them from his creditors. This was an illegal purpose. Once the threat from his creditors had passed, the father asked his son to return the shares to him. The son refused to do so. The son argued that, since there had been an apparent gift from father to son, the presumption of advancement applied and the father was unable to rebut this by pleading his actual unlawful purpose. This argument was consistent with *Tinsley*: the son did not need to lead evidence of any illegality to establish the presumption of advancement, but the father would need to rely on his illegal purpose in order to rebut the presumption. The Court of Appeal held that, since none of the creditors had been aware of the transfer of shares, no part of the illegal purpose had been carried into effect, so the father could withdraw from the illegal scheme as he was still within the '*locus poenitentiae*', or 'time for repentance'; the father could, therefore, plead his illegal intent in order to rebut the presumption of advancement.

Millett LJ:[81]

In my opinion the weight of the authorities supports the view that a person who seeks to recover property transferred by him for an illegal purpose can lead evidence of his dishonest intention whenever it is necessary for him to do so provided that he has withdrawn from the transaction before the illegal purpose has been carried out. It is not necessary if he can rely on an express or resulting trust in his favour; but it is necessary (i) if he brings an action at law and (ii) if he brings proceedings in equity and needs to rebut the presumption of advancement....

At heart the question for decision in the present case is one of legal policy. The primary rule which precludes the court from lending its assistance to a man who founds his cause of action on an illegal or immoral act often leads to a denial of justice. The justification for this is that the rule is not a principle of justice but a principle of policy (see the much-quoted statement of Lord Mansfield CJ in *Holman v Johnson* (1775) 1 Cowp 341 at 343).[82] The doctrine of the *locus poenitentiae* is an exception which operates to mitigate the harshness of the primary rule. It enables the court to do justice between the parties even though, in order to do so, it must allow a plaintiff to give evidence of his own dishonest intent. But he must have withdrawn from the transaction while his dishonesty still lay in intention only. The law draws the line once the intention has been wholly or partly carried into effect.

Seen in this light the doctrine of the *locus poenitentiae*, although an exception to the primary rule, is not inconsistent with the policy which underlies it. It is, of course, artificial to think that anyone would be dissuaded by the primary rule from entering into a proposed fraud, if only because such a person would be unlikely to be a studious reader of the law reports or to seek advice from a lawyer whom he has taken fully into his confidence. But if the policy which underlies the primary rule is to discourage fraud, the policy which underlies the exception must be taken to be to encourage withdrawal from a proposed fraud before it is implemented, an end which is no less desirable. And if the former objective is of such overriding importance that the primary rule must be given effect even where it leads to a

---

[80] [1996] Ch 107.
[81] [1996] Ch 107, [132]–[135].
[82] 'No Court will lend its aid to a man who founds his cause of action upon an immoral or illegal act.'

denial of justice, then in my opinion the latter objective justifies the adoption of the exception where this enables justice to be done.

To my mind these considerations are even more compelling since the decision in *Tinsley v Milligan*. One might hesitate before allowing a novel exception to a rule of legal policy, particularly a rule based on moral principles. But the primary rule, as it has emerged from that decision, does not conform to any discernible moral principle. It is procedural in nature and depends on the adventitious location of the burden of proof in any given case. Had Mr. Tribe transferred the shares to a stranger or distant relative whom he trusted, albeit for the same dishonest purpose, it cannot be doubted that he would have succeeded in his claim. He would also have succeeded if he had given them to his son and procured him to sign a declaration of trust in his favour. But he chose to transfer them to a son whom he trusted to the extent of dispensing with the precaution of obtaining a declaration of trust. If that is fatal to his claim, then the greater the betrayal, the less the power of equity to give a remedy.

In my opinion the following propositions represent the present state of the law. (1) Title to property passes both at law and in equity even if the transfer is made for an illegal purpose. The fact that title has passed to the transferee does not preclude the transferor from bringing an action for restitution. (2) The transferor's action will fail if it would be illegal for him to retain any interest in the property. (3) Subject to (2) the transferor can recover the property if he can do so without relying on the illegal purpose. This will normally be the case where the property was transferred without consideration in circumstances where the transferor can rely on an express declaration of trust or a resulting trust in his favour. (4) It will almost invariably be so where the illegal purpose has not been carried out. It may be otherwise where the illegal purpose has been carried out and the transferee can rely on the transferor's conduct as inconsistent with his retention of a beneficial interest. (5) The transferor can lead evidence of the illegal purpose whenever it is necessary for him to do so provided that he has withdrawn from the transaction before the illegal purpose has been wholly or partly carried into effect. It will be necessary for him to do so (i) if he brings an action at law or (ii) if he brings proceedings in equity and needs to rebut the presumption of advancement. (6) The only way in which a man can protect his property from his creditors is by divesting himself of all beneficial interest in it. Evidence that he transferred the property in order to protect it from his creditors, therefore, does nothing by itself to rebut the presumption of advancement; it reinforces it. To rebut the presumption it is necessary to show that he intended to retain a beneficial interest and conceal it from his creditors. (7) The court should not conclude that this was his intention without compelling circumstantial evidence to this effect. The identity of the transferee and the circumstances in which the transfer was made would be highly relevant. It is unlikely that the court would reach such a conclusion where the transfer was made in the absence of an imminent and perceived threat from known creditors.

The doctrine of the *locus poenitentiae*

...I would hold that genuine repentance is not required. Justice is not a reward for merit; restitution should not be confined to the penitent. I would also hold that voluntary withdrawal from an illegal transaction when it has ceased to be needed is sufficient.

This use of the *locus poenitentiae* is controversial. It appears that the illegal purpose of the father had been carried out, since his shares were hidden with his son for a given period, exactly as intended.[83] It is therefore not clear that the father was within the time period within which he could repent, nor that he genuinely repented.[84] The Court of Appeal suggested that the rationale of the *locus poenitentiae* was to deter illegality and encourage withdrawal, but it is very hard to understand how this

[83] Rose 'Gratuitous transfers and illegal purposes' (1996) 112 LQR 386.
[84] Cf *Bigos v Bousted* [1951] 1 All ER 92. See Samet, '*Locus poenitentiae*: Repentance, Withdrawal and Luck', in *Constructive and Resulting Trusts* (ed. Mitchell) (Oxford: Hart, 2010).

could possibly have led to the result of the case. *Tribe* seems to fall foul of the warning given by Lord Denning in *Chettiar v Chettiar*:[85]

> [H]e cannot use the process of the courts to get the best of both worlds—to achieve his fraudulent purpose and also to get his property back.

The law on illegality in this area is messy. It produces distinctions that do not seem to have solid justifications. However, *Tinsley* is binding authority from the House of Lords, and the reliance principle favoured in the case has also been applied in the context of express trusts,[86] constructive trusts,[87] and other areas of private law.[88] The Law Commission has considered reforming the illegality defence generally, and ultimately recommended statutory intervention. It proposed a statute that would abolish the 'reliance principle' as regards trusts disputes and replace it with a 'structured discretion':[89]

> ### Draft Trusts (Concealment of Interests) Bill
>
> #### Clause 5
>
> (1) In making any determinations under section 4,[90] the court may take anything which it thinks relevant into account, including (for example)—
>
> (a) the conduct of all the relevant persons;
>
> (b) the effect which the declaration or determination would have on any relevant unlawful act or purpose;
>
> (c) the fact that an offence has, or has not, been committed;
>
> (d) the value of the relevant equitable interest;
>
> (e) any deterrent effect on others;
>
> (f) the possibility that a person from whom the relevant equitable interest was to be concealed might have an interest in the value of B's [the beneficiary's] assets (for example, as a creditor of B or because of proceedings under the Matrimonial Causes Act 1973 or the Civil Partnership Act 2004).

Such a structured discretion might be welcome.[91] It would balance the desire for predictability of results with the need to ensure that the law of trusts is not used as a mechanism with which to perpetrate criminal offences. But, regardless of its merits, it appears that legislative reform is now unlikely: in March 2012 the Government stated that it had decided not to implement the Law Commission's proposals.[92]

Given the lack of legislative reform, any change in approach must come, if at all, from the Supreme Court. In other areas of private law, the Supreme Court has recently handed down a series of decisions

---

[85] [1962] AC 294, 302.

[86] *Collier v Collier* [2002] EWCA Civ 1095; [2002] BPIR 1057.

[87] *Barrett v Barrett* [2008] EWHC 1061 (Ch); [2008] 2 P & CR 17.

[88] See generally Davies, 'The Illegality Defence—Two Steps Forward, One Step Back?' [2009] Conv 182.

[89] Draft Trusts (Concealment of Interests) Bill, attached to *The Illegality Defence* Law Com. No 320 (2010).

[90] This concerns the court's discretion regarding the enforceability of an equitable interest.

[91] Davies, 'The Illegality Defence: Turning Back the Clock' [2010] Conv 282; Sheehan, 'The Law Commission on Illegality: The End (at Last) of the Saga' [2010] *LMCLQ* 543. Cf. Virgo and O'Sullivan, *Restitution and Equity Volume One: Resulting Trusts and Equitable Compensation* (eds Birks and Rose) (Oxford: Mansfield Press, 2000).

[92] *Report on the Implementation of Law Commission Proposals* HC 1900, paras 51–2.

which are difficult to reconcile,[93] and whilst some Supreme Court Justices seem to favour the strict principle of *Tinsley v Milligan*,[94] others do not.[95] None of these cases has concerned trusts, and in none has it been argued that *Tinsley* should be overruled. However, at the time of writing yet another appeal to the Supreme Court is outstanding: *Patel v Mirza*.[96] That appeal will be held in February 2016 before a panel of nine judges, and it is to be expected that the principle in *Tinsley* will be reviewed and that the law on illegality may well be altered. *Patel v Mirza* concerns the reliance principle and the *locus poenitentiae*, albeit not in the context of trusts, and it is to be hoped that the law on illegality will be somewhat clearer after the decision of the Supreme Court.

(e) NO NEED FOR THE PRESUMPTIONS?

Chambers has argued that the presumptions of resulting trust and advancement are not necessary: each case can simply be decided on the evidence available.

Chambers, 'Is There a Presumption of Resulting Trust?' in *Constructive and Resulting Trusts* (ed. Mitchell) (Oxford: Hart, 2010) p. 270

In the absence of direct evidence, courts are prepared to draw inferences of intention from the nature of the transaction and the nature of the relationship between the parties to it. If the presumptions did not exist and judges were required to determine on the balance of probabilities whether or not a gift had been intended, there would be difficult cases, but it seems likely that all of them could be decided properly. The lack of a presumption would not increase the number of cases or costs of litigation. In other words, the presumptions do not fill a necessary function.

Not only are the presumptions almost completely unnecessary, they can be undesirable as well. We are not entirely happy whenever the application of a presumption actually determines the outcome of a case.... The point is that we do not want the outcome to be determined by a presumption whenever that would differ from the outcome based on the admissible evidence. We do not need the presumptions and would be better off without them.

It is clearly the case that the presumptions are rarely determinative. Their principal role relates to the allocation of the burden of proof between the parties. So the question is: who should bear the burden of proving a trust when property is voluntarily transferred from one person to another? The presumption of resulting trust rests upon a cynical view of human relations. This may still be appropriate today. But there is a strong argument that a party does not generally intend to retain a beneficial interest in property he or she transfers to another, and that such an intention should, therefore, not be presumed; instead, the claimant should have to prove such an intention on the available evidence.[97] However, even though it might be more satisfactory simply to abolish the presumptions, it should be remembered that they are readily rebutted, and their importance is inflated only in the context of illegal transactions. Reform of the illegality defence might be a more achievable goal than wholesale reform of the well-established presumptions in the law of

---

[93] *Hounga v Allen* [2014] UKSC 47; [2014] 1 WLR 2889; *Les Laboratoires Servier v Apotex Inc* [2014] UKSC 55; [2015] AC 430; *Jetivia SA v Bilta (UK) Ltd (in liquidation)* [2015] UKSC 23; [2015] 2 WLR 1168.

[94] See, e.g. the speech of Lord Sumption in *Les Laboratoires Servier v Apotex Inc* [2014] UKSC 55; [2015] AC 430.

[95] See, e.g. the speech of Lord Toulson in *Les Laboratoires Servier v Apotex Inc* [2014] UKSC 55; [2015] AC 430.

[96] [2014] EWCA Civ 1047; [2015] Ch. 271.

[97] Cf Swadling, 'Explaining Resulting Trusts' (2008) 124 LQR 72, 84.

trusts, where those presumptions may still be considered to reflect the intention of the parties in most cases.

3. AUTOMATIC RESULTING TRUSTS

It has already been seen that resulting trusts are commonly divided into two categories: presumed resulting trusts and automatic resulting trusts. The latter arises upon the failure of an express trust: where a settlor transfers property to a trustee to hold on trust, and the express trust upon which the trustee was supposed to hold the property fails, a resulting trust will arise 'automatically'. The recognition of a resulting trust in such circumstances is a sensible outcome; after all, who else should have the beneficial interest in the transferred property? Not the trustees, who were never intended to take the property beneficially. Nor the intended beneficiaries under the express trust, since that trust has failed. The best solution is that the beneficial interest belongs to the settlor of the property him- or herself. As Lord Reid commented in *Vandervell*:[98]

> the beneficial interest must belong to or be held for somebody so if it was not to belong to the donee or be held by him in trust for somebody it must remain with the donor.

Hackney considered this to be a matter of 'proprietary arithmetic':[99]

> If I give land to trustees on trust for A for life, remainder to the first child to be born to A after the making of the gift, and A has no such child, the land will be held on trust for me after A's death. This is called a resulting trust, though... it does not spring back in any theoretical sense. This rule does not depend upon a presumption of intention, but on a simple process of proprietary arithmetic—what I once had and have not granted away, I keep.

There are a number of different ways for an express trust to fail. There are three important categories, which will be examined in turn: initial failure of the trust, invalidity of the trust, and failure of a valid trust fully to exhaust the beneficial interest of trust property.

(a) INITIAL FAILURE OF AN EXPRESS TRUST

Where an express trust is intended, but fails to be established, property that has been transferred to the putative trustee will be held on resulting trust for the settlor. The trust that fails must have been an *inter vivos* trust. If it is a testamentary trust that fails, the property will not be held on resulting trust, but will simply be distributed as part of the testator's residuary estate. If property is transferred to trustees for a charitable purpose that fails from the outset, that property may be applied cy-près for other charitable purposes if a general charitable intention can be identified.[100] If such an intention cannot be identified, then the property will be held on resulting trust for the settlor.

A good example of an automatic resulting trust arising from the initial failure of an express trust is *Re Ames' Settlement*.[101] Mr Ames and Miss Hamilton married in 1908. Ames' father transferred £10,000 to trustees to be held on the usual trusts of a marriage settlement. The parties lived together

---

[98] [1967] 2 AC 291, 308.
[99] Hackney, *Understanding Equity and Trusts* (London: Fontana Press, 1987), 153.
[100] See Chapter 5.6, p. 260.
[101] [1946] Ch 217. See too *Essery v Cowlard* (1884) 26 Ch D 191.

for a number of years in England and Kenya. In 1926, the Supreme Court of Kenya declared the marriage null and void on the ground of non-consummation. The wife surrendered all her interests under the settlement, and there were, obviously, no children. On the death of Mr Ames in 1945, the question was whether the £10,000 should be paid to those entitled under the settlement in default of there being children, or to the representatives of the settlor. Given that the father had transferred the money on the basis that there was a valid marriage, but that basis was void from the outset, Vaisey J held that the money was held on resulting trust for the father's estate. He explained:[102]

> I regard the contest as merely this: the plaintiffs hold certain funds in their hands, and they ask to which of the alternative claimants they ought to make those funds over. I think it would not be incorrect to say that the problem is really which of those parties has the better equity. The persons who constitute the hypothetical next-of-kin say 'Look at the deed of settlement. We are the persons there designated to take the fund, and there is no reason why we should not do so', and therefore claim to have the better equity. On the other hand it is said 'but that trust, with the other trusts, were all based on the consideration and contemplation of a valid marriage, and now that it has been judicially decided that there never was a marriage that trust cannot possibly form the foundation of a good equitable right'. The settlor's representatives say that theirs is the better equity because the money was only parted with by their testator on a consideration which was expressed but which in fact completely failed. It seems to me that the claim of the executors of the settlor in this case must succeed. I think that the case is, having regard to the wording of the settlement, a simple case of money paid on a consideration which failed. I do not think that that hypothetical class of next-of-kin (who were only brought in, so to speak, and given an interest in the fund on the basis and footing that there was going to be a valid marriage between John Ames and Miss Hamilton) have really any merits in equity, and I do not see how they can claim under the express terms of a document which, so far as regards the persons with whom the marriage consideration was concerned, has utterly and completely failed. If their claim be good, it is difficult to see at what precise period of time their interest became an interest in possession. But I hold that their claim is not good, and that they have not been able to establish it.

(b) INVALIDITY OF EXPRESS TRUST

A trust might be invalid for a variety of reasons. A charitable trust might fail because it is not exclusively charitable and cannot take effect as a non-charitable purpose trust, in which case the property transferred to the trustee will be held on a resulting trust for the settlor or the estate of the testator.[103] A private express trust might fail for uncertainty of objects, for example.[104] Another example is *Air Jamaica v Charlton*,[105] in which an express trust for the surplus funds of a pension scheme was held to be void, since it infringed the perpetuity rule.[106] The Privy Council held that the surplus should, therefore, be held on resulting trust for those who had contributed to the fund. Lord Millett said:[107]

> Pension schemes in Jamaica, as in England, need the approval of the Inland Revenue if they are to secure the fiscal advantages that are made available. The tax legislation in both countries places a limit on the amount which can be paid to the individual employee. Allowing the employees to enjoy any part

---

[102] [1947] Ch 217, 222–3.
[103] *Morice v Bishop of Durham* (1804) 9 Ves 399; on appeal (1805) 10 Ves 522; *Chichester Diocesan Fund and Board of Finance Inc. v Simpson* [1944] AC 341. See Chapter 5.5(b)(i), p. 258.
[104] E.g. *In re Leek* [1969] 1 Ch 563. See Chapter 3.4, p. 86.
[105] [1999] 1 WLR 1399.
[106] See Chapter 3.7, p. 112.
[107] [1999] 1 WLR 1399, 1413.

of the surplus by way of resulting trust would probably exceed those limits. This fact is not, however, in their Lordships' view a proper ground on which to reject the operation of a resulting trust in favour of the employees. The Inland Revenue had an opportunity to examine the pension plan and to withhold approval on the ground that some of its provisions were void for perpetuity. They failed to do so. There is no call to distort principle in order to meet their requirements. The resulting trust arises by operation of the general law, dehors the pension scheme and the scope of the relevant tax legislation.

Scott J[108] was impressed by the difficulty of arriving at a workable scheme for apportioning the surplus funds among the members and the executors of deceased members. This was because he thought it necessary to value the benefits that each member had received in order to ascertain his share in the surplus. On the separate settlement with mutual insurance analysis which their Lordships have adopted in the present case, however, no such process is required. The members' share of the surplus should be divided pro rata among the members and the estates of deceased members in proportion to the contributions made by each member without regard to the benefits each has received and irrespective of the dates on which the contributions were made.

(i) *The* Vandervell *litigation*

Probably the most notorious example of an automatic resulting trust arose in the *Vandervell* litigation.[109] Mr Vandervell was a wealthy man who had decided to make a gift to the Royal College of Surgeons to found a chair of pharmacology, but he wanted to do this in a tax-efficient way both for the College and for himself. Consequently, he planned to transfer a block of shares in his own private company, Vandervell Products Ltd, to the Royal College. He would then arrange for dividends to be declared on these shares, which would provide the money to found the chair. Vandervell Trustees Ltd, a trust company that acted as trustee for the Vandervell children's trust and other private trusts, would be given an option to buy these shares for £5,000. The option was included in case it might be desirable in the future to convert the company into a public company, since it would then be preferable for the shares to be under Vandervell's control or those who would act as he directed.

Although complicated, the transaction was structured in this way to ensure that the College could recover tax that had been deducted from the dividends before they were paid and that Vandervell would not be personally liable to pay any tax on the dividends because he would have no interest in the shares. Vandervell directed his bank, which held the shares on trust for him, to transfer the shares to the Royal College,[110] and the company declared £157,000 dividends, which were paid to the College. No express provision had been made for the declaration of trusts of the shares that were to be purchased by the trustee company on exercising the option. One issue was whether the option to purchase the shares, as a property right, was held on resulting trust for Vandervell. If it were, then he would be liable to pay tax on the dividends received by the Royal College, because he had a beneficial interest in the shares after all. The House of Lords considered the position prior to the exercise of the option, and rejected Vandervell's arguments that the option was held either on trust for the children's settlement or by Vandervell Trustees Ltd beneficially. Instead, their Lordships held that Vandervell had granted the option to the trust company to be held on trust, but that the objects of that trust had not been identified, so the express trust was void for want of objects and failed. As a result, Vandervell did indeed have a beneficial interest in the option under a resulting trust and was liable to pay tax on the dividends.

---

[108] In *Davis v Richards and Wallington Industries Ltd* [1990] 1 WLR 151; see Chapter 8.3(c)(ii), pp. 393–7.
[109] See further also Chapter 10.2, pp. 505–9.
[110] This was a valid transaction. See Chapter 10.2(c), p. 505.

Vandervell v Inland Revenue Commissioners [1967] 2 AC 291, 327–9 (Lord Wilberforce)

On these findings it was, in my opinion, at once clear that the appellant's contention that the option became subject to the trusts of the children's settlement of 1949 must fail, for the reason that it was not the intention of the settlor, or of his plenipotentiary, Mr. Robins, at the time the option was exercised that this should be so. I need not elaborate this point since I understand that there is no disagreement about it. This was the appellant's main (if not the sole) contention before the special commissioners and Plowman J and it remained his first contention on this appeal. The alternative which...is expressed in the printed case as being that the option was held by the trustee company in equity as well as in law as the absolute owner thereof for the purposes of its business, is, of course, one which the appellant is entitled to put forward, as a contention of law, at any stage, provided that it is consistent with the facts as found by the special commissioners. It is on that contention that the appellant ultimately fell back. For my part, I cannot find that it is so consistent...

Correspondingly, the evidence points clearly away from any conclusion that the trustee company held beneficially, or for the purpose of its business. It had no business, no function, except as a trustee; no assets, except as a trustee. The £5,000 to be paid if the option was to be exercised was, as a term of the arrangement between Mr. Vandervell and the college, part of the £150,000 benefaction; how could that come from the company's own resources? To extract from the findings a conclusion that the trustee company was to hold free from any trust but possibly subject to some understanding or gentleman's agreement seems to me, rather than even a benevolent interpretation of the evidence, a reconstruction of it. I may add that had this contention been put forward at the hearing before the special commissioners the Revenue might well have been tempted to explore, by cross-examination, the real control of the trustee company and to argue that the case came within section 415(2) of the Income Tax Act 1952.

If, then, as I think, both the first two alternatives fail, there remains only the third, which, to my mind, corresponds exactly with Mr. Robins' intentions, namely, that the option was held by the trustee company on trusts which were undefined, or in the air.

As to the consequences, there has been some difference and possibly lack of clarity below. The special commissioners held that the initially undefined trusts could be defined later in a way which might benefit the appellant, and they found the benefit to the appellant in this circumstance. The Court of Appeal, starting from the fact that the trustee company took the option as a volunteer, thought that this was a case where the presumption of a resulting trust arose and was not displaced. For my part, I prefer a slightly different and simpler approach. The transaction has been investigated on the evidence of the settlor and his agent and the facts have been found. There is no need, or room, as I see it, to invoke a presumption. The conclusion, on the facts found, is simply that the option was vested in the trustee company as a trustee on trusts, not defined at the time, possibly to be defined later. But the equitable, or beneficial interest, cannot remain in the air: the consequence in law must be that it remains in the settlor. There is no need to consider some of the more refined intellectualities of the doctrine of resulting trust, nor to speculate whether, in possible circumstances, the shares might be applicable for Mr. Vandervell's benefit: he had, as the direct result of the option and of the failure to place the beneficial interest in it securely away from him, not divested himself absolutely of the shares which it controlled.

This somewhat pragmatic approach of Lord Wilberforce is often encountered: the beneficial interest in the shares must have belonged to someone; given that the trustees were clearly not supposed to take the shares beneficially, and that Vandervell did not make clear any intention to benefit the children's trusts, the interest in the shares must have resulted to the settlor under a resulting trust. The resulting trust arose almost as a process of elimination: in the absence of evidence to the contrary, the beneficial interest in the shares was held on a resulting trust for the settlor.[111]

However, the *Vandervell* litigation resurfaced after the decision of the House of Lords. Vandervell later arranged for the trustee company to exercise the option to buy the shares. The trust company used money from the children's settlement to do so. It then treated the shares as being held on trust for the children and paid the dividends to their settlement. Vandervell eventually executed a deed transferring any interest that he might have had in the shares to the trusts of his children's settlement. Vandervell then died and a further dispute related to whether the dividends should be paid to Vandervell's estate or to the children's settlement. This was considered in *Re Vandervell's Trusts (No. 2)* and turned on whether the shares were held on resulting trust for him.[112] At first instance, Megarry J[113] held that once the option had been exercised by the trustee company, the shares were also held on resulting trust for Vandervell, even though the company had used money from the children's settlement to buy the shares. This was because, as the House of Lords had held, the option belonged to Vandervell beneficially and the purchase price simply enabled him to exercise his right to buy the shares, which belonged to him beneficially. The source of the purchase price was considered to be irrelevant to the beneficial ownership of the shares, although, since the money derived from the children's settlement, his estate was liable to repay the money to the settlement.

Re Vandervell's Trusts (No. 2) [1974] Ch 269, 294–300 (Megarry J)

It seems to me that the relevant points on resulting trusts may be put in a series of propositions which, so far as not directly supported, appear at least to be consistent with Lord Wilberforce's speech, and reconcilable with the true intent of Lord Upjohn's speech, though it may not be with all his words on a literal reading. The propositions are the broadest of generalisations, and do not purport to cover the exceptions and qualifications that doubtless exist. Nevertheless, these generalisations at least provide a starting point for the classification of a corner of equity which might benefit from some attempt at classification. The propositions are as follows.

(1) If a transaction fails to make any effective disposition of any interest it does nothing. This is so at law and in equity, and has nothing to do with resulting trusts.

(2) Normally the mere existence of some unexpressed intention in the breast of the owner of the property does nothing: there must at least be some expression of that intention before it can effect any result. To yearn is not to transfer.

(3) Before any doctrine of resulting trust can come into play, there must at least be some effective transaction which transfers or creates some interest in property.

(4) Where A effectually transfers to B (or creates in his favour) any interest in any property, whether legal or equitable, a resulting trust for A may arise in two distinct classes of case. For simplicity, I shall confine my statement to cases in which the transfer or creation is made without B providing any valuable consideration, and where no presumption of advancement can arise; and I shall state the position for transfers without specific mention of the creation of new interests.

   (a) The first class of case is where the transfer to B is not made on any trust. If, of course, it appears from the transfer that B is intended to hold on certain trusts, that will be decisive, and the case is not within this category; and similarly if it appears that B is intended to take

---

[111] For further discussion of the importance of *Vandervell* to the theoretical justifications for resulting trusts, see e.g. Chapter 8.4(b), pp. 408–10.

[112] If they were, then Vandervell's estate would have been liable to pay tax on the dividends.

[113] [1974] Ch 269.

beneficially. But in other cases there is a rebuttable presumption that B holds on a resulting trust for A. The question is not one of the automatic consequences of a dispositive failure by A, but one of presumption: the property has been carried to B, and from the absence of consideration and any presumption of advancement B is presumed not only to hold the entire interest on trust, but also to hold the beneficial interest for A absolutely. The presumption thus establishes both that B is to take on trust and also what that trust is. Such resulting trusts may be called 'presumed resulting trusts'.

(b) The second class of case is where the transfer to B is made on trusts which leave some or all of the beneficial interest undisposed-of. Here B automatically holds on a resulting trust for A to the extent that the beneficial interest has not been carried to him or others. The resulting trust here does not depend on any intentions or presumptions, but is the automatic consequence of A's failure to dispose of what is vested in him. Since ex hypothesi the transfer is on trust, the resulting trust does not establish the trust but merely carries back to A the beneficial interest that has not been disposed of. Such resulting trusts may be called 'automatic resulting trusts'.

(5) Where trustees hold property in trust for A, and it is they who, at A's direction, make the transfer to B, similar principles apply, even though on the face of the transaction the transferor appears to be the trustees and not A. If the transfer to B is on trust, B will hold any beneficial interest that has not been effectually disposed of on an automatic resulting trust for the true transferor, A. If the transfer to B is not on trust, there will be a rebuttable presumption that B holds on a resulting trust for A.

...

Now as it seems to me this passage[114] shows Lord Wilberforce as rejecting the application of what I have called the 'presumption' class of resulting trust and accepting that the case falls into what I have called the 'automatic' class. The grant of the option to the defendant company was, as he had held, on trust. There was thus no need, nor, indeed, any reason to consider whether the option was granted to the defendant company beneficially, or whether there was any presumption of a resulting trust, for that question had been foreclosed by the decision that the defendant company did not take beneficially but held on trust. The only question was whether Mr. Vandervell had ever effectually disposed of the beneficial interest that the defendant company, holding on trust, must hold on a resulting trust for him unless and until an effective trust for some other beneficiary was constituted. This had not been done, and so the defendant company continued to hold on a resulting trust for Mr. Vandervell.

If one bears in mind Lord Wilberforce's speech and the principles that I have tried to state it seems to me that when one looks again at Lord Upjohn's speech it is at least possible to read it as supporting what seems to me to be the right analysis of the case, namely, that the true grantor of the option was Mr. Vandervell, that the option was granted to the defendant company on trust, that no effective trusts were ever declared, and so the defendant company held the option on an automatic resulting trust for Mr. Vandervell. Indeed, that is what I think he was laying down. The question is whether, on the evidence before me, I ought to reach any other conclusion....

My conclusion is that there is nothing in the evidence before me that warrants any conclusion different from that reached in *Vandervell No. 1*, namely, that the option was granted to the defendant company on trust, but that no effective trusts were ever established and so the defendant company held the option on a resulting trust for Mr. Vandervell.

(3) *Effect of children's £5,000*

The third issue is that of the effect of exercising the option with £5,000 of the moneys held by the defendant company on the trusts of the children's settlement.... That issue is, in essence, whether

---

[114] From *Vandervell v Inland Revenue Commissioners* [1967] 2 AC 291, 329, which is the final paragraph in the extract at Chapter 8.3(b)(i), p. 387.

trustees who hold an option on trust for X will hold the shares obtained by exercising that option on trust for Y merely because they used Y's money in exercising the option. Authority apart, my answer would be an unhesitating No. The option belongs to X beneficially, and the money merely exercises rights which belong to X. Let the shares be worth £50,000, so that an option to purchase those shares for £5,000 is worth £45,000, and it will at once be seen what a monstrous result would be produced by allowing trustees to divert from their beneficiary X the benefits of what they hold in trust for him merely because they used Y's money instead of X's...

I need only say that the consequences of recognising any rule to the effect that trustees of more than one trust can in effect transfer the assets of one trust to another trust simply by expending the money of that other trust on improving the assets seems to me to be incalculable...I merely add that, as I have already mentioned, Mr. Balcombe has throughout accepted what he has pleaded, namely, that the plaintiff's right to the shares is subject to a lien in favour of the children's settlement for the £5,000 paid for exercising the option with interest. This in effect will restore the status quo ante as regards this payment.

This passage is a sensible approach to the difficult facts of the case, and appears to be consistent with the previous judgment of the House of Lords. However, the decision of Megarry J was overturned by the Court of Appeal, which held that even though the option had been held on resulting trust for Vandervell, the shares were not also held on resulting trust. Lord Denning MR thought that the shares were instead held on an express trust for the children's settlement, so that the dividends were properly paid to the children's settlement:[115]

In October and November 1961, the trustee company exercised the option. They paid £5,000 out of the children's settlement. The Royal College of Surgeons transferred the legal estate in the 100,000 'A' shares to the trustee company. Thereupon the trustee company became the legal owner of the shares. This was a different kind of property altogether. Whereas previously the trustee company had only a chose in action of one kind—an option—it now had a chose in action of a different kind—the actual shares. This trust property was not held by the trustee company beneficially. It was held by them on trust. On this occasion a valid trust was created at the time of the transfer. It was manifested in clear and unmistakable fashion. It was precisely defined. The shares were to be held on the trusts of the children's settlement. The evidence of intention is indisputable:

(i) The trustee company used the children's money—£5,000—with which to acquire the shares. This would be a breach of trust unless they intended the shares to be an addition to the children's settlement.

(ii) The trustee company wrote to the Revenue authorities the letter of 2 November, 1961, declaring expressly that the shares 'will henceforth be held by them upon the trusts of the [children's] settlement'.

(iii) Thenceforward all the dividends received by the trustees were paid by them to the children's settlement and treated as part of the funds of the settlement. This was all done with the full assent of Mr. Vandervell. Such being the intention, clear and manifest, at the time when the shares were conveyed to the trustee company, it is sufficient to create a trust.

Mr. Balcombe for the executors admitted that the intention of Mr. Vandervell and the trustee company was that the shares should be held on trust for the children's settlement. But he said that this intention was of no avail. He said that during the first period, Mr. Vandervell had an equitable interest in the property, namely, a resulting trust; that he never disposed of this equitable interest (because he never knew he had it): and that in any case it was the disposition of an equitable interest which, under section

[115] [1974] Ch 269, 319–20.

53 of the Law of Property Act 1925, had to be in writing, signed by him or his agent, lawfully authorised by him in writing (and there was no such writing produced)....

There is a complete fallacy in that argument. A resulting trust for the settlor is born and dies without any writing at all. It comes into existence whenever there is a gap in the beneficial ownership. It ceases to exist whenever that gap is filled by someone becoming beneficially entitled. As soon as the gap is filled by the creation or declaration of a valid trust, the resulting trust comes to an end. In this case, before the option was exercised, there was a gap in the beneficial ownership. So there was a resulting trust for Mr. Vandervell. But, as soon as the option was exercised and the shares registered in the trustees' name, there was created a valid trust of the shares in favour of the children's settlement. Not being a trust of land, it could be created without any writing. A trust of personalty can be created without any writing. Both Mr. Vandervell and the trustee company had done everything which needed to be done to make the settlement of these shares binding on them. So there was a valid trust: see *Milroy v Lord* (1862) 4 De GF & J 264 at 274,[116] per Turner LJ.

Lord Denning MR identified an intention that the trust company should hold the shares on express trust for the children's settlement from the following facts: the money used to exercise the option had been derived from that settlement, and this would have constituted a breach of trust had the trustees not intended the shares to be added to the settlement; the trust company had written to the Inland Revenue declaring that the shares were held for the children; and the dividends had been paid to the settlement. All this was done with Vandervell's assent. One major problem with this analysis is that, since the House of Lords had recognized that Vandervell had an equitable interest in the option and the children ended up with an equitable interest in the shares, there appeared to have been a transfer of a subsisting equitable interest from Vandervell to the children, and such a disposition of an equitable interest can be valid only if it is effected by writing.[117]

Further criticism might be made of some of the reasoning of Lord Denning MR. For example, there was no resolution of the board of directors of the trust company, which would have been necessary to declare an express trust of the shares. It may also be misleading to treat the option and the shares as two distinct pieces of property. As Battersby has explained:[118]

The option to purchase is not a piece of property distinct from the shares, it is merely a limited right carved out of the bundle of rights normally inherent in the shares. The trustee company, as owner of the option, had the right to become owner of the shares. Since it never had the right to exercise the option for its own benefit, both the option, prior to its exercise, and the shares, after its exercise, must be held on a resulting trust for the grantor, Vandervell, unless and until his beneficial interest is displaced by a valid creation of new trusts.

The better view is that both the option and shares were held on resulting trust for Vandervell, and that the Court of Appeal ought not to have overturned the decision of Megarry J. Indeed, one of the judges in the Court of Appeal, Stephenson LJ, expressed his reservations about the decision:[119]

I have had more doubt than Lord Denning MR and Lawton LJ whether we can overturn the judgment of Megarry J in what I have not found an easy case. Indeed, treading a (to me) dark and unfamiliar path, I had parted from both my fellow travellers and following the windings of [Counsel's] argument had

---

[116] See Chapter 4.3(b)(i), pp. 150–1.
[117] Law of Property Act 1925, s. 53(1)(c). See Chapter 10.2(d), pp. 508–9.
[118] Battersby, 'Some Thoughts on the Statute of Frauds in Relation to Trusts' (1975) 7 Ottawa LR 483, 500.
[119] [1974] Ch 269, 322–3.

nearly reached a different terminus before the light which they threw upon the journey enabled me to join them at the same conclusion.

To expound my doubts would serve no useful purpose; to state them shortly may do no harm. The cause of all the trouble is what the judge called [1974] Ch 269 at 298 'this ill-fated option' and its incorporation in a deed which was 'too short and simple' to rid Mr. Vandervell of the beneficial interest in the disputed shares, as a bare majority of the House of Lords held, not without fluctuation of mind on the part of one of them (Lord Upjohn), in *Vandervell v IRC* [1967] 2 AC 291 at 314–317. The operation of law or equity kept for Mr. Vandervell or gave him back an equitable interest which he did not want and would have thought he had disposed of if he had ever known it existed. It is therefore difficult to infer that he intended to dispose or ever did dispose of something he did not know he had until the judgment of Plowman J in *Vandervell v IRC* [1966] Ch 261 at 273, which led to the deed of 1965, enlightened him, or to find a disposition of it in the exercise by the trustee company in 1961 of its option to purchase the shares. And even if he had disposed of his interest, he did not dispose of it by any writing sufficient to comply with section 53(1)(c) of the Law of Property Act 1925.

But Lord Denning MR and Lawton LJ are able to hold that no such disposition is needed because (1) the option was held on such trusts as might thereafter be declared by the trustee company or Mr. Vandervell himself, and (2) the trustee company has declared that it holds the shares in the children's settlement. I do not doubt the first, because it was apparently the view of the majority of the House of Lords in *Vandervell v IRC* [1967] 2 AC 291. I should be more confident of the second if it had been pleaded or argued either here or below and we had had the benefit of Megarry J's views upon it. If counsel for the trustee company in the court below had thought that the evidence supported it, he would not, I think, have sought and obtained the amendment of the defence which he did to allege what the judge rejected as an unusual and improbable form of trust which was not supported by the evidence. If counsel for the trustee company in this court had accepted it, I do not think that he would have opened this appeal as he did with references to perfecting or completing the trust but none to declaring it. I see, as perhaps did counsel, difficulties in the way of a limited company declaring a trust by parole or conduct and without resolution of the board of directors, and difficulties also in the way of finding any declaration of trust by Mr. Vandervell himself in October or November 1961, or any conduct then or later which would in law or equity estop him from denying that he made one.

However, Lord Denning MR and Lawton LJ are of the opinion that these difficulties, if not imaginary, are not insuperable and that these shares went into the children's settlement in 1961 in accordance with the intention of Mr. Vandervell and the trustee company—a result with which I am happy to agree as it seems to me to be in accordance with the justice and the reality of the case.

(c) SUBSEQUENT FAILURE OF TRUST

A trust might subsequently fail, even though initially valid, because the trust becomes impossible to perform. This most commonly arises where the trust is for a valid purpose, which can no longer be fulfilled. Where a surplus remains in the trust fund, such that the express trust has failed fully to exhaust the beneficial interest in the subject matter of the trust, it needs to be determined to whom that surplus belongs. If the failed trust was a charitable trust, the property will be applied cy-près.[120] If a private trust is at issue, then the property might be held on resulting trust, but also as an absolute gift, or as *bona vacantia*.[121] These last two alternatives will be considered first, before examining situations in which a resulting trust might arise.

---

[120] See Chapter 5.6, p. 260.
[121] 'Ownerless goods'.

(i) *Absolute gift*

As a matter of construction, it might be possible that a gift for a particular purpose only does not give rise to a trust if the purpose fails, but is rather an absolute gift, and the expressed purpose was merely a motive for the gift. For example, in *Re Osoba*[122] the testator left property to his widow on trust to be used 'for her maintenance and for the training of my daughter up to university grade and for the maintenance of my aged mother'. The mother predeceased the testator, who died in 1965. His widow died in 1970, and the daughter completed her university education in 1975. There was a surplus left in the fund. This was claimed by the testator's children from a previous marriage. The Court of Appeal rejected their claim, and held that the testator's intention was to make absolute gifts to the beneficiaries: the references to maintenance and education were only expressions of motive, not requirements that the property be used for those purposes. Buckley LJ said:[123]

> If a testator has given the whole of a fund, whether of capital or income, to a beneficiary, whether directly or through the medium of a trustee, he is regarded, in the absence of any contra-indication, as having manifested an intention to benefit that person to the full extent of the subject matter, notwithstanding that he may have expressly stated that the gift is made for a particular purpose, which may prove to be impossible of performance or which may not exhaust the subject matter. This is because the testator has given the whole fund; he has not given so much of the fund as a trustee or anyone else should determine, but the whole fund. This must be reconciled with the testator's having specified the purpose for which the gift is made. This reconciliation is achieved by treating the reference to the purpose as merely a statement of the testator's motive in making the gift. Any other interpretation of the gift would frustrate the testator's expressed intention that the whole subject matter shall be applied for the benefit of the beneficiary. These considerations have, I think, added force where the subject matter is the testator's residue, so that any failure of the gift would result in intestacy. The specified purpose is regarded as of less significance than the dispositive act of the testator, which sets the measure of the extent to which the testator intends to benefit the beneficiary.

(ii) *Bona vacantia*

If property is *bona vacantia*, it means that it has no owner and will be transferred to the Crown. In some instances, it has been recognized that the surplus of a gift should properly be considered to be ownerless.[124] This was considered in the context of gifts to unincorporated associations in Chapter 6,[125] where it was concluded that money which initially belonged to somebody should not readily become ownerless.[126] However, the suggestion that the surplus of a gift should be held as *bona vacantia* has resurfaced in the context of pension fund trusts. In *Davis v Richards and Wallington Industries Ltd*,[127] a pension fund was wound up with a surplus of £3 million. The fund had been derived from contributions from employers and employees, and from funds transferred from other pension schemes. It was recognized that usually, in such circumstances, the surplus would be held on resulting trust for the employers and employees who had contributed to the fund, even though the employees would have received all that they had bargained for under their employment contract.[128] On the facts, it was held that the employer alone was entitled to the surplus, since express provision had been made for this in the trust deed. Scott

---

[122] [1979] 1 WLR 24.
[123] Ibid, 257.
[124] *Re West Sussex Constabulary's Widows, Children and Benevolent (1930) Fund Trusts* [1971] Ch 1.
[125] See Chapter 6.4(c)(ii), pp. 318–22.
[126] E.g. *Hanchett-Stamford v Attorney-General* [2008] EWHC 330 (Ch); [2009] Ch 173.
[127] [1990] 1 WLR 1511.
[128] Contradicting the reasoning in *Cunnack v Edwards* [1896] 2 Ch 679.

J held that a resulting trust could be excluded by an express or an implied term in a contract, and also went on to consider what would have been the result had the trust deed been invalid. Although normally the surplus would then have been held on resulting trust for the contributors, he concluded that it would have been paid to the Crown as *bona vacantia*, since it would not have been possible to find an intention of the employees that any surplus should be held on resulting trust for them.

Davis v Richards and Wallington Industries Ltd [1990] 1 WLR 1511, 1538–44 (Scott J)

Finally I must address myself to the arguments on resulting trust. These arguments arise only if the definitive deed was ineffective and its inefficacy cannot be remedied by the execution of the executory trust.

Mr. Charles, arguing for *bona vacantia*, has drawn a distinction between payments made under contract and payments made under a trust. He suggested that rights arising under pension schemes were, basically, rights of a contractual character rather than equitable rights arising under a trust. As I understood the argument, if the context in which the rights arise is mainly or exclusively contractual, then a resulting trust will be excluded; but, if the context is mainly or exclusively that of trust, a resulting trust may apply. Unincorporated associations, he said, were based in contract, a pension scheme was a species of unincorporated association, the contributions to pension schemes by employees and employers alike were made under contract with one another; so there was no room for any resulting trust to apply to the surplus produced by the contributions. . . .

In my opinion, the contractual origin of rights under a pension scheme, although relevant to the question whether a resulting trust applies to surplus, is not conclusive. There are a number of authorities where the courts have had to deal with the question whether the assets of a defunct association or the surplus assets of a pension scheme had become *bona vacantia* or were held on resulting trusts for the subscribers or members.

[His Lordship referred to *Re West Sussex Constabulary's Widows, Children and Benevolent (1930) Fund Trusts* and *Jones v Williams* (15 March 1988, unreported), where Knox J held that a resulting trust could be excluded by a clause in the trust deed, and continued:]

I respectfully agree with Knox J's approach. I would, however, venture one qualification. The provision in a trust deed necessary to exclude a resulting trust need not, in my opinion, be express. In the absence of an express provision it would, I think, often be very difficult for a sufficiently clear intention to exclude a resulting trust to be established. But, in general, any term that can be expressed can also, in suitable circumstances, be implied. In my opinion, a resulting trust will be excluded not only by an express provision but also if its exclusion is to be implied. If the intention of a contributor that a resulting trust should not apply is the proper conclusion, it would not be right, in my opinion, for the law to contradict that intention.

In my judgment, therefore, the fact that a payment to a fund has been made under contract and that the payer has obtained all that he or she bargained for under the contract is not necessarily a decisive argument against a resulting trust.

. . . there is a very important difference between the contractual obligation of the employees and that of the employers. The employees' contractual obligation was specific in amount, 5 per cent of salary. The employers' contractual obligation was conceptually certain but the amount was inherently uncertain. The obligation was to pay whatever was necessary to fund the scheme. The terms of rule 3 of Part II of the 1975 rules describe accurately, in my opinion, the contractual obligation of the employers:

> 'The employer will pay to the trustees such amounts as may from time to time be required to enable the trustees to maintain the benefits . . .'

In practice, the amount of the employers' contributions in respect of each employee was actuarially calculated. The calculations were based on assumptions as to the time when the benefits would become payable and as to the amount of the employee's final salary at that time. If the scheme should terminate before that time, the amount paid would be bound to have been more than needed to have been paid in order to fund the employee's benefits as at the date of termination.

Two separate questions seem to me to require to be answered. First, to what extent should the surplus, the £3 million-odd, be regarded as derived from each of these three sources?[129] One possible answer is that there should be a calculation of the total amount of employees' contributions, the total amount of funds transferred from other companies' pension schemes and the total amount of employers' contributions, and that the surplus should be regarded as derived from these three sources in the same proportions as the three totals bear to one another.

I do not accept that this is right. It ignores the different bases on which these contributions were paid. Since the employers' obligation was to pay whatever was from time to time necessary to fund the various scheme benefits and since the employees' 5 per cent contributions and the amount of the transferred funds constituted the base from which the amount of the employers' contributions would from time to time have to be assessed, it is logical, in my judgment, to treat the scheme benefits as funded first by the employees' contributions and the transferred funds, and only secondarily by the employers' contributions, and, correspondingly, to treat the surplus as provided first by the employers' contributions and only secondarily by the employees' contributions and the transferred funds.

There are two possible factual situations to be considered. It is possible (although, I think, very unlikely) that the employees' contributions and the funds transferred from the pension schemes of other companies would, without there having been any contribution at all from the employers, have been sufficient to provide in full for all the scheme benefits and, perhaps, still to have left some surplus. If that is the position, it would follow that, with the advantage of hindsight, the employers need not have made any contributions at all in order to have funded the benefits. This situation would, in my judgment, require that that surplus (which would be bound, I think, to be very small) should be regarded as derived from the employees' contributions and the transferred funds and that the balance of the surplus should be regarded as derived from the employers' contributions.

The much more likely situation is that some contribution at least was required from the employers in order to produce assets sufficient to provide all the scheme benefits to which employees became entitled on 31 July, 1982. In that event the whole of the surplus, in my judgment, should be regarded as derived from the employers' contributions. This conclusion is, to my mind, in accordance both with logic and with equity. The actuarial calculations on which the employers' actual contributions were based were themselves based upon a series of assumptions. The termination of the scheme invalidated the assumptions. The employers had, in the event, made payments exceeding the amount necessary to discharge their obligation to fund the benefits to which the employees eventually became entitled. There is a well-established equity that enables accounts drawn up under a mistake to be reopened (see Goff and Jones, *The Law of Restitution* (3rd edn, 1986), p. 199). In cases such as the present there was no mistake at the time the contributions were assessed and paid. The actuarial calculations were, I am sure, impeccable. But subsequent events having invalidated some of the assumptions underlying the calculations, the case is, in my opinion, strongly analogous to that of an account drawn up under a mistake. In my opinion, equity should treat the employers as entitled to claim the surplus, or so much of it as derived from the overpayments.

The second question is whether a resulting trust applies to the surplus, or to so much of the surplus as was derived from each of the three sources to which I have referred. As to the surplus derived from the employers' contributions, I can see no basis on which a resulting trust can be excluded. The equity to which I referred in the previous paragraph demands, in my judgment, the conclusion that the trustees hold the surplus derived from the employers' contributions upon trust for the employers. There is no express provision excluding a resulting trust and no circumstances from which, in my opinion, an

---

[129] Employees' contributions, transfers from other pension schemes, and employers' contributions.

implication to that effect could be drawn. On the other hand, in my judgment, the circumstances of the case seem to me to point firmly and clearly to the conclusion that a resulting trust in favour of the employees is excluded.

The circumstances are these.

(i) Each employee paid his or her contributions in return for specific financial benefits from the fund. The value of these benefits would be different for each employee, depending on how long he had served, how old he was when he joined and how old he was when he left. Two employees might have paid identical sums in contributions but have become entitled to benefits of a very different value. The point is particularly striking in respect of the employees, (and there were several of them), who exercised their option to a refund of contributions. How can a resulting trust work as between the various employees *inter se*? I do not think it can and I do not see why equity should impute to them an intention that would lead to an unworkable result.

(ii) The scheme was established to take advantage of the legislation relevant to an exempt approved scheme and a contracted-out scheme. The legislative requirements placed a maximum on the financial return from the fund to which each employee would become entitled. The proposed rules would have preserved the statutory requirements. A resulting trust cannot do so. In my judgment, the relevant legislative requirements prevent imputing to the employees an intention that the surplus of the fund derived from their contributions should be returned to them under a resulting trust....

Accordingly, in my judgment, if any part of the surplus has derived from employees' contributions or from the funds transferred from the pension schemes of other companies, that part of the surplus devolves as *bona vacantia*. Subject thereto, the surplus is, in my judgment, held upon trust for the employer contributors.

Scott J considered that the employees' contribution would be held as *bona vacantia* rather than on resulting trust, because it would not have been practicable to apportion the surplus with reference to the value of the benefit that each member had received, and he refused to find an intention that would lead to an unworkable result.

This approach in *Davis* has been criticized. For example, it is unclear why a settlor's (presumed) intention to retain a beneficial interest should be defeated simply because it is difficult to determine how much the contributors should receive under resulting trusts. The Court should strive to apportion the surplus in proportion to the contributors' contribution to the fund. Indeed, in *Air Jamaica v Charlton*,[130] Lord Millett, giving the advice of the Privy Council, said:

In *Davis v Richards and Wallington Industries Ltd* [1990] 1 WLR 1511 Scott J held that the fact that a party has received all that he bargained for is not necessarily a decisive argument against a resulting trust, but that in the circumstances of the case before him a resulting trust in favour of the employees was excluded. The circumstances that impressed him were two-fold. He considered that it was impossible to arrive at a workable scheme for apportioning the employees' surplus among the different classes of employees and he declined, at 1544, to 'impute to them an intention that would lead to an unworkable result'. He also considered that he was precluded by statute from 'imputing to the employees an intention' that they should receive by means of a resulting trust sums in excess of the maximum permitted by the relevant tax legislation.

These formulations also adopt the approach to intention that their Lordships have already considered to be erroneous.[131] Their Lordships would observe that, even in the ordinary case of an actuarial surplus,

---

[130] [1999] 1 WLR 1399, 1412.
[131] See Chapter 8.4(b), pp. 385–6.

> it is not obvious that, when employees are promised certain benefits under a scheme to which they have contributed more than was necessary to fund them, they should not expect to obtain a return of their excess contributions.

Lord Millett considered the resulting trust to be the preferable solution: where a claimant has contributed to the surplus of an express trust that has failed, the amount of that contribution to the surplus fund should be held on resulting trust for the claimant. However, if the value of the fund has fallen, the amount held on trust for the claimant should be reduced proportionately. But where the value of the fund has increased, this increase should be shared amongst the contributors in proportion to the amount that they contributed.

In any event, it may be that the contract-holding theory, which is so prevalent in the context of unincorporated associations,[132] should also apply to pension trusts: whereas under a resulting trust a contributor will only receive a proportionate share relative to his contributions, under the contract-holding theory the surplus funds would be distributed in full among the members at the time in accordance with the terms of the contract. Extra-judicially, Lord Browne-Wilkinson has written that:[133]

> the monies have been paid to the trustees by the members and the employer as a matter of contractual obligations between them; the doctrine of resulting trust has never been applied to contractual obligation. I would have thought that the better analysis was not under trust law but in contract. The employer, being required to pay only the balance of cost, contracted to pay the amount required them [sic] time to time by the actuary on the implied term that if the payments are excessive he is to recover the amount overpaid.

(iii) *Resulting trusts*

Any surplus of an express trust that fails may also be held on resulting trust for the settlor. This is generally to be preferred to *bona vacantia*: property should not readily become ownerless.

The resulting trust solution was clearly favoured by Lord Millett in *Air Jamaica v Charlton*[134] in the context of pension trusts. It was also applied in *Re Gillingham Bus Disaster Fund*.[135] A fund was established for the care of those injured following a bus crash, and then for other worthy causes. The public contributed £9,000 to the fund, partly from identified subscribers, but largely from street collections. There was a surplus, which Harman J found was held on resulting trust for the donors:[136]

> There arises now a further question, namely, whether, as the Treasury Solicitor claims, this surplus should be paid to the Crown as *bona vacantia*, or whether there is a resulting trust in favour of the subscribers, who are here represented by the Official Solicitor. The general principle must be that where money is held upon trust and the trusts declared do not exhaust the fund it will revert to the donor or settlor under what is called a resulting trust. The reasoning behind this is that the settlor or donor did not part with his money absolutely out and out but only *sub modo* to the intent that his wishes as declared by the declaration of trust should be carried into effect. When, therefore, this has been done any surplus still belongs to him. This doctrine does not, in my judgment, rest on any evidence of the state

---

[132] See Chapter 6.4(b)(v), pp. 305–11.
[133] Lord Browne-Wilkinson, 'Equity and its Relevance to Superannuation Schemes Today' (1992) 62 TLI 119, 124.
[134] [1999] 1 WLR 1399; see Chapter 8.3(c)(ii), pp. 396–7.
[135] [1958] Ch 300, affirmed [1959] Ch 62. See also *Re Hobourn Aero Components Air Raid Distress Fund* [1946] Ch 86.
[136] [1958] Ch 300, 310–13.

of mind of the settlor, for in the vast majority of cases no doubt he does not expect to see his money back: he has created a trust which so far as he can see will absorb the whole of it. The resulting trust arises where that expectation is for some unforeseen reason cheated of fruition, and is an inference of law based on after-knowledge of the event.

Counsel for the Crown admitted that it was for him to show that this principle did not apply to the present case....

I was referred to two cases where a claim was made to *bona vacantia* and succeeded. The first of these was *Cunnack v Edwards* [1896] 2 Ch 679. This was a case of a society formed to raise a fund by subscriptions and so forth from the members to provide for widows of deceased members. Upon the death of the last widow of a member it was found that there was a surplus. It was held by the Court of Appeal that no question of charity arose, that there was no resulting trust in favour of the subscribers, but that the surplus passed to the Crown as *bona vacantia*....

The ratio decidendi seems to have been that having regard to the constitution of the fund no interest could possibly be held to remain in the contributor who had parted with his money once and for all under a contract for the benefit of his widow. When this contract had been carried into effect the contributor had received all that he contracted to get for his money and could not ask for any more.

...

It was argued for the Crown that the subscribers to this fund must be taken to have parted with their money out and out, and that there was here, as in *Cunnack v Edwards* [1896] 2 Ch 679 and *Braithwaite v A-G* [1909] 1 Ch 510, no room for a resulting trust. But there is a difference between those cases and this in that they were cases of contract and this is not....

In my judgment the Crown has failed to show that this case should not follow the ordinary rule merely because there was a number of donors who, I will assume, are unascertainable. I see no reason myself to suppose that the small giver who is anonymous has any wider intention than the large giver who can be named. They all give for the one object. If they can be found by inquiry the resulting trust can be executed in their favour. If they cannot I do not see how the money could then, with all respect to Jenkins LJ, change its destination and become *bona vacantia*. It will be merely money held upon a trust for which no beneficiary can be found. Such cases are common and where it is known that there are beneficiaries the fact that they cannot be ascertained does not entitle the Crown to come in and claim. The trustees must pay the money into court like any other trustee who cannot find his beneficiary. I conclude, therefore, that there must be an inquiry for the subscribers to this fund.

Harman J thought that the donors parted with their money only for the purposes of the trust and, if those purposes were fulfilled, the surplus money should be held on resulting trust for them.[137] This applied both as regards the identified and anonymous donors of money. The latter were still considered to be beneficiaries of the resulting trust even though they were unascertained, and the Crown could not claim their money as *bona vacantia*. Whilst consistent with the general application of resulting trusts, this outcome did not prove to be very helpful to the settlor-beneficiaries: money was paid into court, where it was never claimed. However, nearly twenty years later, it was eventually used to pay for a memorial to the victims of the crash.[138]

Harman J relied on earlier cases which had also found a resulting trust, including *Re the Trusts of the Abbott Fund*,[139] in which money was collected for the support of two sisters who were deaf

---

[137] Cf the contract-holding theory, which is now more commonly employed in the context of unincorporated associations: Chapter 6.4(b)(v), pp. 305–11.

[138] This can be compared with a trust for charitable purposes where surplus money provided by unknown donors can be applied cy-près: Charities Act 2011 s. 63. See Chapter 5.6, p. 260.

[139] [1900] 2 Ch 326.

and dumb and had been defrauded of their inheritance. The money that had been collected for them was held on trust for their benefit, but no provision was made in the trust instrument for the disposal of the fund on the death of the survivor. When this occurred, there was a significant surplus. It was held that this should be held on resulting trust for the contributors to the fund. Stirling J said:

> The ladies are both dead, and the question is whether so far as this fund has not been applied for their benefit, there is a resulting trust of it for the subscribers. I cannot believe that it was ever intended to become the absolute property of the ladies so that they should be in a position to demand a transfer of it to themselves, or so that if they became bankrupt the trustee in the bankruptcy should be able to claim it. I believe it was intended that it should be administered by Mr. Smith,[140] or the trustees who had been nominated in pursuance of the circular. I do not think the ladies ever became absolute owners of this fund.[141] I think that the trustee or trustees were intended to have a wide discretion as to whether any, and if any what, part of the fund should be applied for the benefit of the ladies and how the application should be made. That view would not deprive them of all right in the fund, because if the trustees had not done their duty—if they either failed to exercise their discretion or exercised it improperly—the ladies might successfully have applied to the court to have the fund administered according to the terms of the circular. In the result, therefore, there must be a declaration that there is a resulting trust of the moneys remaining unapplied for the benefit of the subscribers to the Abbott fund.

4. EXPLAINING RESULTING TRUSTS

The preceding discussion in this chapter provides a descriptive account of resulting trusts, in the sense that it describes *when* resulting trusts arise. But it does not explain *why* they do so. This is a difficult issue, and to some extent can be avoided by judges, who are generally required only to apply well-established categories of resulting trust to particular cases. However, understanding the theoretical justification for resulting trusts is important to establish the reasons for their existence, and is helpful when seeking to predict the outcome of future cases that concern particularly troublesome facts.

It has already been seen that there is some controversy about whether the reasons for presumed resulting trusts are the same as those underpinning automatic resulting trusts. This is a significant issue, but can best be considered once the reasons for presumed resulting trusts are established.

(a) PRESUMED RESULTING TRUSTS

It is important to appreciate the general role of presumptions. Swadling[142] has explained that:

> Presumptions properly-so-called form part of the law of proof. Generally speaking, facts can be proved by admission, judicial notice, or evidence. In the absence of admission and judicial notice, the general rule is that facts must be proved by evidence, the burden of proving those facts lying on the party

---

[140] One of the ladies' friends who helped to raise the contributions.
[141] But the trust was valid by virtue of what is now recognized as the *Denley* principle: *Re Denley's Trust Deed* [1969] 1 Ch 373. See Chapter 6.2(a), pp. 289–90.
[142] Swadling, 'Explaining Resulting Trusts' (2008) 124 LQR 72, 74.

alleging them to have occurred. Very occasionally, however, proof by evidence of one fact, the 'basic' or 'primary' fact, gives that party to the litigation the benefit of another fact, the 'secondary' fact, without any need to adduce evidence in proof. In such cases, the fact is proved by presumption. The burden then lies on the other party to adduce evidence to rebut the presumption. If they do not, the tribunal of fact *must* find the secondary fact proved.

Thus it is not the case that a resulting trust is presumed simply because a conveyance was voluntary, for example. What is presumed appears to be a declaration of trust. It is sometimes said that what is presumed is an intention to create a trust,[143] but since the only intention effective to create a trust is one which is expressed, this might be considered to mean a declaration of trust.[144]

It is important to distinguish presumed intention from an inferred intention, which would give rise to an express trust. As Lord Neuberger has said:[145]

An inferred intention is one which is objectively deduced to be the subjective actual intention of the parties in the light of their actions and statements; it involves concluding what a party intended.

Nor is a presumed intention the same as an imputed intention, which involves 'attributing'[146] an intention to the parties. In *Jones v Kernott*,[147] Lady Hale and Lord Walker said that:

if [a court] cannot deduce exactly what shares were intended, it may have no alternative but to ask what their intentions as reasonable and just people would have been had they thought about it at the time.

Thus an imputed intention is imposed upon the settlor on the basis that that is what reasonable people would have intended. It is different from a presumed intention because it arises by operation of law; it is only employed where other types of intention fail to deliver a credible result. Being imposed by the courts, it seems that an imputed intention cannot be rebutted. It does not, therefore, correspond to the instances of presumed resulting trusts previously identified in this chapter.

Presumed resulting trusts rest upon true presumptions: the nature of the transaction gives rise to a presumption regarding the transferor's intention, and this intention triggers the resulting trust. However, the *content* of this presumption is controversial. There are two principal approaches: either the settlor is presumed to have positively intended to create a trust in his or her favour, or the settlor is presumed not to have any intention to benefit anybody else.

Early instances of resulting trusts clearly favoured the former approach: a presumed intention to create a trust was at issue. This has been demonstrated by Swadling, who concluded that:[148]

the presumption of use in the case of a conveyance without valuable consideration arose so as to reflect what was thought to be the *actual* intentions of the parties concerned. In other words, the fact of a conveyance without valuable consideration gave rise to a presumption that the transferor had in fact conveyed the land to the transferee on express trust for the transferor.

---

[143] See e.g. *Westdeutsche Landesbank Girozentrale v Islington LBC* [1996] AC 669, 708 (Lord Browne-Wilkinson).
[144] Cf Mee, 'Presumed Resulting Trusts, Intention and Declaration' [2014] CLJ 86.
[145] *Stack v Dowden* [2007] UKHL 17; [2007] 2 AC 432, [126]. See also *Jones v Kernott* [2011] UKSC 53; [2011] 3 WLR 1121, [51](3) (Lady Hale and Lord Walker).
[146] *Jones v Kernott* [2011] UKSC 53; [2011] 3 WLR 1121, [73] (Lord Kerr).
[147] Ibid, [47].
[148] 'A New Role for Resulting Trusts?' [1996] LS 110, 114. See e.g. *Cook v Fountain* (1676) 3 Swanst 585, 591.

However, with the development of the law of unjust enrichment,[149] the notion that what is really being presumed is an *absence* of intention to benefit the recipient began to evolve. Birks argued that:[150]

> The presumption of resulting trust is a presumption of non-beneficial transfer or, in other words, a presumption that the transferor did not intend the transferee to receive for his own benefit. This way of expressing the matter allows a reasonable degree of integration of the presumption into the list of 'unjust' factors upon which restitutionary plaintiffs habitually rely, such as mistake, compulsion or inequality.

The tension between a presumed positive intention to create a resulting trust and a presumed absence of intention to give the benefit of the property to the recipient was resolved, at least as a matter of authority, by the House of Lords in *Westdeutsche*.

Westdeutsche Landesbank Girozentrale v Islington London Borough Council [1996] AC 669

A local authority entered into an interest rate swaps agreement with a bank. This transaction involved an agreement between the parties by which each agreed to pay to the other an amount that was calculated by reference to the interest that would have accrued over a ten-year period from 1987, on a notional principal sum of £25 million. The rate of interest to be paid by each party was different. The bank's rate was fixed and the other was variable, being dependent on an identified fluctuating interest rate. The party that owed the highest amount of money paid the net difference to the other party every six months. In effect, this was a form of gambling on changes in the interest rate. In separate proceedings in 1990 the House of Lords held that local authorities lacked the capacity to make such contracts, which were consequently ultra vires and null and void.[151] In the present case, Westdeutsche Landesbank Girozentrale had paid more to the local authority than it had received and so it sought restitution from the local authority of the net difference. The key question for the House of Lords was whether any interest that was due was to be assessed as simple or as compound interest.

The House of Lords held that the local authority was liable to make restitution by virtue of its unjust enrichment on the ground of failure of consideration. It was liable to pay interest to the bank but this was assessed as simple interest because, other than where there is fraud, compound interest was only available in equity against a fiduciary who was accountable for profits made from breach of the fiduciary duty.[152] It was not possible to characterize the local authority as a fiduciary since it did not hold the bank's money on trust. Lord Browne-Wilkinson said:

> Although the actual question in issue on the appeal is a narrow one, on the arguments presented it is necessary to consider fundamental principles of trust law. Does the recipient of money under a contract subsequently found to be void for mistake or as being ultra vires hold the moneys received on trust even where he had no knowledge at any relevant time that the contract was void? If he does hold on trust, such trust must arise at the date of receipt or, at the latest, at the date the legal title of the payer is extinguished by mixing moneys in a bank account:[153] in the present case it does not matter at which of those dates the

---

[149] See Chapter 1.4(b), pp. 13–15.
[150] Birks, 'Restitution and Resulting Trusts' in *Equity: Contemporary Legal Developments* (ed. Goldstein) (Jerusalem: Hebrew University of Jerusalem, 1992), 346.
[151] *Hazell v Hammersmith and Fulham London Borough Council* [1992] 2 AC 1.
[152] See now *Sempra Metals Ltd v IRC* [2007] UKHL 34; [2008] 1 AC 561, where it was recognized that compound interest was generally available even if the claim was not equitable. Despite this, *Westdeutsche* remains relevant for the analysis of the resulting trust.
[153] The legal title will be extinguished because it is not possible to trace at law into a mixed bank account. See Chapter 18.3(c)(i), pp. 860–5.

legal title was extinguished. If there is a trust two consequences follow: (a) the recipient will be personally liable, regardless of fault, for any subsequent payment away of the moneys to third parties even though, at the date of such payment, the 'trustee' was still ignorant of the existence of any trust: see Burrows, 'Swaps and the Friction between Common Law and Equity' [1995] *Restitution Law Review* 15; (b) as from the date of the establishment of the trust (i.e. receipt or mixing of the moneys by the 'trustee') the original payer will have an equitable proprietary interest in the moneys so long as they are traceable into whomsoever's hands they come other than a purchaser for value of the legal interest without notice. Therefore, although in the present case the only question directly in issue is the personal liability of the local authority as a trustee, it is not possible to hold the local authority liable without imposing a trust which, in other cases, will create property rights affecting third parties because moneys received under a void contract are 'trust property'.

The practical consequences of the bank's argument

Before considering the legal merits of the submission, it is important to appreciate the practical consequences which ensue if the bank's arguments are correct. Those who suggest that a resulting trust should arise in these circumstances accept that the creation of an equitable proprietary interest under the trust can have unfortunate, and adverse, effects if the original recipient of the moneys becomes insolvent: the moneys, if traceable in the hands of the recipient, are trust moneys and not available for the creditors of the recipient. However, the creation of an equitable proprietary interest in moneys received under a void contract is capable of having adverse effects quite apart from insolvency. The proprietary interest under the unknown trust will, quite apart from insolvency, be enforceable against any recipient of the property other than the purchaser for value of a legal interest without notice.

Take the following example. T (the transferor) has entered into a commercial contract with R1 (the first recipient). Both parties believe the contract to be valid but it is in fact void. Pursuant to that contract: (i) T pays £1 million to R1 who pays it into a mixed bank account; (ii) T transfers 100 shares in X company to R1, who is registered as a shareholder. Thereafter R1 deals with the money and shares as follows: (iii) R1 pays £50,000 out of the mixed account to R2 otherwise than for value; R2 then becomes insolvent, having trade creditors who have paid for goods not delivered at the time of the insolvency; (iv) R1 charges the shares in X company to R3 by way of equitable security for a loan from R3.

If the bank's arguments are correct, R1 holds the £1 million on trust for T once the money has become mixed in R1's bank account. Similarly R1 becomes the legal owner of the shares in X company as from the date of his registration as a shareholder but holds such shares on a resulting trust for T. T therefore has an equitable proprietary interest in the moneys in the mixed account and in the shares.

T's equitable interest will enjoy absolute priority as against the creditors in the insolvency of R2 (who was not a purchaser for value) provided that the £50,000 can be traced in the assets of R2 at the date of its insolvency. Moreover, if the separation of title argument is correct, since the equitable interest is in T and the legal interest is vested in R2, R2 also holds as trustee for T. In tracing the £50,000 in the bank account of R2, R2 as trustee will be treated as having drawn out 'his own' moneys first,[154] thereby benefiting T at the expense of the secured and unsecured creditors of R2. Therefore in practice one may well reach the position where the moneys in the bank account of R2 in reality reflect the price paid by creditors for goods not delivered by R2: yet, under the tracing rules, those moneys are to be treated as belonging in equity to T.

So far as the shares in the X company are concerned, T can trace his equitable interest into the shares and will take in priority to R3, whose equitable charge to secure his loan even though granted for value will pro tanto be defeated.

All this will have occurred when no one was aware, or could have been aware, of the supposed trust because no one knew that the contract was void.

---

[154] By virtue of the rule in *Clayton's case* (1816) 1 Mer 572: see Chapter 18.3(c)(ii), p. 875.

I can see no moral or legal justification for giving such priority to the right of T to obtain restitution over third parties who have themselves not been enriched, in any real sense, at T's expense and indeed have had no dealings with T. T paid over his money and transferred the shares under a supposed valid contract. If the contract had been valid, he would have had purely personal rights against R1. Why should he be better off because the contract is void?

My Lords, wise judges have often warned against the wholesale importation into commercial law of equitable principles inconsistent with the certainty and speed which are essential requirements for the orderly conduct of business affairs: see *Barnes v Addy* (1874) LR 9 Ch App 244 at 251 and 255; *Scandinavian Trading Tanker Co AB v Flota Petrolera Ecuatoriana* [1983] 2 AC 694 at 703–704. If the bank's arguments are correct, a businessman who has entered into transactions relating to or dependent upon property rights could find that assets which apparently belong to one person in fact belong to another; that there are 'off balance sheet' liabilities of which he cannot be aware; that these property rights and liabilities arise from circumstances unknown not only to himself but also to anyone else who has been involved in the transactions. A new area of unmanageable risk will be introduced into commercial dealings. If the due application of equitable principles forced a conclusion leading to these results, your Lordships would be presented with a formidable task in reconciling legal principle with commercial common sense. But in my judgment no such conflict occurs. The resulting trust for which the bank contends is inconsistent not only with the law as it stands but with any principled development of it.

The relevant principles of trust law

(i) Equity operates on the conscience of the owner of the legal interest. In the case of a trust, the conscience of the legal owner requires him to carry out the purposes for which the property was vested in him (express or implied trust) or which the law imposes on him by reason of his unconscionable conduct (constructive trust).

(ii) Since the equitable jurisdiction to enforce trusts depends upon the conscience of the holder of the legal interest being affected, he cannot be a trustee of the property if and so long as he is ignorant of the facts alleged to affect his conscience, i.e. until he is aware that he is intended to hold the property for the benefit of others in the case of an express or implied trust, or, in the case of a constructive trust, of the factors which are alleged to affect his conscience.

(iii) In order to establish a trust there must be identifiable trust property. The only apparent exception to this rule is a constructive trust imposed on a person who dishonestly assists in a breach of trust who may come under fiduciary duties even if he does not receive identifiable trust property.[155]

(iv) Once a trust is established, as from the date of its establishment the beneficiary has, in equity, a proprietary interest in the trust property, which proprietary interest will be enforceable in equity against any subsequent holder of the property (whether the original property or substituted property into which it can be traced) other than a purchaser for value of the legal interest without notice.

These propositions are fundamental to the law of trusts and I would have thought uncontroversial. However, proposition (ii) may call for some expansion. There are cases where property has been put into the name of X without X's knowledge but in circumstances where no gift to X was intended. It has been held that such property is recoverable under a resulting trust: *Birch v Blagrave* (1755) Amb 264; *Childers v Childers* (1857) 1 De G & J 482; *Re Vinogradoff* [1935] WN 68; *Re Muller* [1953] NZLR 879. These cases are explicable on the ground that, by the time action was brought, X or his successors in title have become aware of the facts which gave rise to a resulting trust; his conscience was affected as from the time of such discovery and thereafter he held on a resulting trust under which the property was recovered from him. There is, so far as I am aware, no authority which decides that X was a trustee,

---

[155] See Chapter 19.2, p. 923.

and therefore accountable for his deeds, at any time before he was aware of the circumstances which gave rise to a resulting trust.

Those basic principles are inconsistent with the case being advanced by the bank. The latest time at which there was any possibility of identifying the 'trust property' was the date on which the moneys in the mixed bank account of the local authority ceased to be traceable when the local authority's account went into overdraft in June 1987. At that date, the local authority had no knowledge of the invalidity of the contract but regarded the moneys as its own to spend as it thought fit. There was therefore never a time at which both (a) there was defined trust property and (b) the conscience of the local authority in relation to such defined trust property was affected. The basic requirements of a trust were never satisfied.

I turn then to consider the bank's arguments in detail. They were based primarily on principle rather than on authority?...

The retention of title point

It is said that, since the bank only intended to part with its beneficial ownership of the moneys in performance of a valid contract, neither the legal nor the equitable title passed to the local authority at the date of payment. The legal title vested in the local authority by operation of law when the moneys became mixed in the bank account but, it is said, the bank 'retained' its equitable title.

I think this argument is fallacious. A person solely entitled to the full beneficial ownership of money or property, both at law and in equity, does not enjoy an equitable interest in that property. The legal title carries with it all rights. Unless and until there is a separation of the legal and equitable estates, there is no separate equitable title. Therefore to talk about the bank 'retaining' its equitable interest is meaningless. The only question is whether the circumstances under which the money was paid were such as, in equity, to impose a trust on the local authority. If so, an equitable interest arose for the first time under that trust.

[Lord Browne-Wilkinson then considered whether the bank had a pre-existing equitable interest by virtue of which the local authority would be a trustee and concluded that no such interest could be identified. He continued:]

Resulting trust

This is not a case where the bank had any equitable interest which pre-dated receipt by the local authority of the upfront payment. Therefore, in order to show that the local authority became a trustee, the bank must demonstrate circumstances which raised a trust for the first time either at the date on which the local authority received the money or at the date on which payment into the mixed account was made. Counsel for the bank specifically disavowed any claim based on a constructive trust. This was plainly right because the local authority had no relevant knowledge sufficient to raise a constructive trust at any time before the moneys, upon the bank account going into overdraft, became untraceable. Once there ceased to be an identifiable trust fund, the local authority could not become a trustee: *Re Goldcorp Exchange Ltd* [1995] 1 AC 74. Therefore, as the argument for the bank recognised, the only possible trust which could be established was a resulting trust arising from the circumstances in which the local authority received the upfront payment.

Under existing law a resulting trust arises in two sets of circumstances:

(A) Where A makes a voluntary payment to B or pays (wholly or in part) for the purchase of property which is vested either in B alone or in the joint names of A and B, there is a presumption that A did not intend to make a gift to B: the money or property is held on trust for A (if he is the sole provider of the money) or in the case of a joint purchase by A and B in shares proportionate to their contributions. It is important to stress that this is only a presumption, which presumption is easily rebutted either by the counter-presumption of advancement or by direct evidence of A's intention to make an outright transfer: see Underhill and Hayton, *Law of Trusts and Trustees*, pp. 317 et seq.; *Vandervell v*

Inland Revenue Commissioners [1967] 2 AC 291 at 312 et seq; *Re Vandervell's Trusts* (No. 2) [1974] Ch 269 at 288 et seq.

(B) Where A transfers property to B on express trusts, but the trusts declared do not exhaust the whole beneficial interest: ibid. and *Quistclose Investments Ltd v Rolls Razor Ltd* [1970] AC 567. Both types of resulting trust are traditionally regarded as examples of trusts giving effect to the common intention of the parties. A resulting trust is not imposed by law against the intentions of the trustee (as is a constructive trust) but gives effect to his presumed intention. Megarry J in *Re Vandervell's Trusts (No. 2)* [1974] Ch 269 at 289 suggests that a resulting trust of type (B) does not depend on intention but operates automatically. I am not convinced that this is right. If the settlor has expressly, or by necessary implication, abandoned any beneficial interest in the trust property, there is in my view no resulting trust: the undisposed-of equitable interest vests in the Crown as *bona vacantia*: see *Re West Sussex Constabulary's Widows, Children and Benevolent (1930) Fund Trusts* [1971] Ch 1.

Applying these conventional principles of resulting trust to the present case, the bank's claim must fail. There was no transfer of money to the local authority on express trusts: therefore a resulting trust of type (B) above could not arise. As to type (A) above, any presumption of resulting trust is rebutted since it is demonstrated that the bank paid, and the local authority received, the upfront payment with the intention that the moneys so paid should become the absolute property of the local authority. It is true that the parties were under a misapprehension that the payment was made in pursuance of a valid contract. But that does not alter the actual intentions of the parties at the date the payment was made or the moneys were mixed in the bank account. As the article by William Swadling, 'A new role for resulting trusts?' (1996) 16 LS 133 demonstrates the presumption of resulting trust is rebutted by evidence of any intention inconsistent with such a trust, not only by evidence of an intention to make a gift.

Professor Birks, 'Restitution and Resulting Trusts' (see *Equity: Contemporary Legal Developments*,[156] p. 335 at p. 360), whilst accepting that the principles I have stated represent 'a very conservative form' of definition of a resulting trust, argues from restitutionary principles that the definition should be extended so as to cover a perceived gap in the law of 'subtractive unjust enrichment' (at p. 368) so as to give a plaintiff a proprietary remedy when he has transferred value under a mistake or under a contract the consideration for which wholly fails. He suggests that a resulting trust should arise wherever the money is paid under a mistake (because such mistake vitiates the actual intention) or when money is paid on a condition which is not subsequently satisfied.

As one would expect, the argument is tightly reasoned but I am not persuaded. The search for a perceived need to strengthen the remedies of a plaintiff claiming in restitution involves, to my mind, a distortion of trust principles. First, the argument elides rights in property (which is the only proper subject matter of a trust) into rights in 'the value transferred': see p. 361. A trust can only arise where there is defined trust property: it is therefore not consistent with trust principles to say that a person is a trustee of property which cannot be defined. Second, Professor Birks's approach appears to assume (for example in the case of a transfer of value made under a contract the consideration for which subsequently fails) that the recipient will be deemed to have been a trustee from the date of his original receipt of money, i.e. the trust arises at a time when the 'trustee' does not, and cannot, know that there is going to be a total failure of consideration. This result is incompatible with the basic premise on which all trust law is built, viz. that the conscience of the trustee is affected. Unless and until the trustee is aware of the factors which give rise to the supposed trust, there is nothing which can affect his conscience. Thus neither in the case of a subsequent failure of consideration nor in the case of a payment under a contract subsequently found to be void for mistake or failure of condition will there be circumstances, at the date of receipt, which can impinge on the conscience of the recipient, thereby making him a trustee. Thirdly, Professor Birks has to impose on his wider view an arbitrary and admittedly unprincipled modification so as to ensure that a resulting trust does not arise when there has only been a failure to perform a contract, as opposed to total

---

[156] Goldstein (ed.) *Equity: Contemporary Legal Developments* (Jerusalem: Hebrew University of Jerusalem, 1992.)

failure of consideration: see pp. 356–359 and 362. Such arbitrary exclusion is designed to preserve the rights of creditors in the insolvency of the recipient. The fact that it is necessary to exclude artificially one type of case which would logically fall within the wider concept casts doubt on the validity of the concept.

If adopted, Professor Birks's wider concepts would give rise to all the practical consequences and injustices to which I have referred. I do not think it right to make an unprincipled alteration to the law of property (i.e. the law of trusts) so as to produce in the law of unjust enrichment the injustices to third parties which I have mentioned and the consequential commercial uncertainty which any extension of proprietary interests in personal property is bound to produce.

In this speech, Lord Browne-Wilkinson clearly favours the positive intent analysis of the presumed resulting trust, rather than the absence-of-intention approach favoured by Birks. However, as has already been mentioned,[157] Lord Browne-Wilkinson's references to the common intentions of the parties is misleading; resulting trusts may well arise before the trustee realizes that there is a trust. The intention of the settlor *only* should be relevant. Moreover, a trustee's conscience does not need to be affected for a resulting trust—as opposed to a constructive trust[158]—to arise. Nevertheless, if the trustee is unaware of the trust, it is unlikely that he or she will be under any fiduciary obligations.[159]

Lord Browne-Wilkinson's preference for the positive intent explanation of the presumed resulting trusts is entirely appropriate. It explains all the cases considered already under the category of 'presumed resulting trusts'. Any evidence that would contradict the presumed intention that there be a trust can be introduced to rebut that presumption. Significantly, this approach ensures that the ambit of presumed resulting trusts remains limited.

By contrast, the absence of intention approach might have led to a much more expansive role for resulting trusts. For example, a donor who transferred property whilst labouring under a mistake might have obtained a proprietary interest under a resulting trust: the transferor's intention may have been vitiated by the mistake such that he did not truly intend the transferee to receive the property beneficially. Although it is well established that a claimant might have a personal claim in unjust enrichment as a result of his or her mistake if that mistake caused the relevant transfer,[160] recognizing a resulting trust in such circumstances would extend far beyond the instances of presumed resulting trusts examined above. Nevertheless, Chambers has written that:[161]

Although the mistake cannot support an inference that the plaintiff intended to create a trust of that right, it does prove a lack of intention to benefit the defendant.

One case upon which proponents of the absence of intent analysis often rely as an example of their approach being applied by the courts is *Chase Manhattan Bank NA v Israel-British Bank (London) Ltd*.[162] In that case, the claimant bank mistakenly made the same payment twice to the defendant. Goulding J said that:[163]

a person who pays money to another under a factual mistake retains an equitable property in it and the conscience of that other is subjected to a fiduciary duty to respect his proprietary right.

---

[157] See Chapter 8.1(b), p. 363.
[158] See Chapter 7, 'Constructive Trusts'.
[159] See Chapter 14.1(b), pp. 661–3.
[160] E.g. *Barclays Bank Ltd v W J Simms Son and Cooke (Southern) Ltd* [1979] 3 All ER 522; see Chapter 1.4(b), pp. 13–15.
[161] *Resulting Trusts* (Oxford: Clarendon Press, 1997), 24–5.
[162] [1981] Ch 105. See Chapter 7.2(a), pp. 332–5.
[163] [1981] Ch 105, 119.

Chambers has pointed out that:

> Although Goulding J did not classify the trust in this situation, he reached this conclusion in reliance on Viscount Haldane LC's speech in *Sinclair v Brougham*,[164] where it was described as a 'resulting trust'.[165]

However, the argument that, because of a mistake, the claimant should be presumed not to intend the recipient to hold the property beneficially is unconvincing. In fact, there is no room for any such presumption to operate in the context of a mistaken transfer. As Swadling has explained:[166]

> The reason why such a presumption of intention is inappropriate in the case of a mistaken gift is that we are here dealing with a situation in which the actual state of mind of the transferor is known to the court; there is consequently no room for the operation of any presumption.[167] As Deane J said in *Muschinski v Dodds*, 'the presumption [of resulting trust] cannot prevail over the actual intention of that party as established by the overall evidence . . .'[168]
>
> . . . the fact that one party has been operating on defective data can in no way lead us to conclude that he or she intended the transferee to be a trustee for the transferor. An analogy might be drawn with the law relating to imperfect gifts. In the same way that evidence of a failed attempt to make an outright gift is inconsistent with an assertion that the donor intended to make himself a trustee for the donee,[169] so too the fact that a gift was mistakenly motivated will contradict any inference that the donee was intended to hold on trust for the donor.

This must be right: the donor *did* intend the donee to take the property beneficially at the moment of transfer. This is sufficient to rebut any presumption of resulting trust. The fact that the donor was mistaken is irrelevant to a proprietary claim,[170] although it may still found a personal claim in unjust enrichment. Moreover, it would be unsatisfactory for a party who has made a mistake then to obtain a proprietary right under a resulting trust; for example, why should a person who has made a mistake be protected in the event of the donee's insolvency, to the detriment of the donee's other unsecured creditors?

In *Westdeutsche*, Lord Browne-Wilkinson endorsed Swadling's analysis, and criticized the reasoning of Goulding J in *Chase Manhattan* since:[171]

> it is based on a concept of retaining an equitable property in money where, prior to the payment to the recipient bank, there was no existing equitable interest. . . .
>
> However, although I do not accept the reasoning of Goulding J., *Chase Manhattan* may well have been rightly decided. The defendant bank knew of the mistake made by the paying bank within two days of the receipt of the moneys: see at p. 115A. The judge treated this fact as irrelevant (p. 114F) but in my

---

[164] [1914] AC 398. This case recognized that property which was transferred pursuant to a void transaction would be held on resulting trust for the transferor. However, it was overruled by the House of Lords in *Westdeutsche*.

[165] *Resulting Trusts* (Oxford: Clarendon Press, 1997), 129.

[166] 'A New Role for Resulting Trusts?' [1996] LS 110, 116 (some references omitted).

[167] '. . . a resulting trust only arises where there is no other explanation of the transaction' *per* Lord Cairns LC in *Batstone v Salter* (1875) LR 10 Ch App 431, 433.

[168] (1985) 160 CLR 583, 612.

[169] *Milroy v Lord* (1862) 4 De G F & J 264; see Chapter 4.3(a), pp. 150–1.

[170] Save where the mistake was such that the claimant retained title to the property (e.g. *R v Russell* (1885) 16 QBD 190) or where the defendant was aware of the mistake and acted unconscionably (see Chapter 7.2(a), pp. 332–6; see too Chapter 7.2(c), pp. 337–41).

[171] [1996] AC 669, 714–715.

judgment it may well provide a proper foundation for the decision. Although the mere receipt of the moneys, in ignorance of the mistake, gives rise to no trust, the retention of the moneys after the recipient bank learned of the mistake may well have given rise to a constructive trust.

The discussion of the constructive trust in *Westdeutsche* is considered in Chapter 7. Significantly, the emphasis placed upon unconscionability and the apparent expansion of the constructive trust means that where property has been transferred to the defendant pursuant to a contract that is voidable, and the claimant can therefore rescind the contract in Equity, the trust on which the defendant holds the property is best analysed as a constructive trust, rather than a resulting trust. This further emphasizes the limited residual nature of resulting trusts. Lord Browne-Wilkinson in *Westdeutsche* was adamant that resulting trusts should not be allowed to expand beyond their proper scope:[172]

Those concerned with developing the law of restitution are anxious to ensure that, in certain circumstances, the plaintiff should have the right to recover property which he has unjustly lost. For that purpose they have sought to develop the law of resulting trusts so as to give the plaintiff a proprietary interest. For the reasons that I have given, in my view such development is not based on sound principle and in the name of unjust enrichment is capable of producing most unjust results. The law of resulting trusts would confer on the plaintiff a right to recover property from, or at the expense of, those who have not been unjustly enriched at his expense at all, e.g. the lender whose debt is secured by a floating charge and all other third parties who have purchased an equitable interest only, albeit in all innocence and for value.

(b) AUTOMATIC RESULTING TRUSTS

It was suggested earlier that presumed resulting trusts are best explained on the basis that the transferor is presumed positively to have intended to retain a beneficial interest under a trust in his or her own favour. But should 'automatic' resulting trusts be explained in the same way? In *Westdeutsche*, Lord Browne-Wilkinson clearly thought so. However, a major difficulty facing this approach is *Vandervell v IRC*:[173] Vandervell did not want to have any beneficial interest under any trust, yet the courts insisted that a resulting trust arose 'automatically'. This provides support to those who argue that the resulting trust in *Vandervell* arose because Vandervell did not intend the recipient to take the property beneficially.[174] Indeed, despite its rejection by Lord Browne-Wilkinson in *Westdeutsche*, the absence-of-intention approach has continued to garner support among both academics and judges. For example, Chambers has written that:[175]

The role of intention in resulting trusts is a negative one. The primary question is always whether the provider intended to benefit the recipient and not whether he or she intended to create a trust. The latter question is relevant, of course, to whether the provider has succeeded in creating an express trust, but its relevance to the resulting trust is only as an indication of a lack of intention to benefit the recipient.

---

[172] Ibid, 716.
[173] See Chapter 8.3(b)(i), p. 386.
[174] E.g. Chambers, *Resulting Trusts* (Oxford: Clarendon Press, 1997), ch. 2.
[175] Ibid, 222.

And in *Air Jamaica Ltd v Charlton*, Lord Millett, giving the advice of the Privy Council, said:[176]

> Like a constructive trust, a resulting trust arises by operation of law, though unlike a constructive trust it gives effect to intention. But it arises whether or not the transferor intended to retain a beneficial interest—he almost always does not—since it responds to the absence of any intention on his part to pass a beneficial interest to the recipient. It may arise even where the transferor positively wished to part with the beneficial interest, as in *Vandervell v Inland Revenue Commissioners* [1967] 2 AC 291. In that case the retention of a beneficial interest by the transferor destroyed the effectiveness of a tax avoidance scheme which the transferor was seeking to implement. The House of Lords affirmed the principle that a resulting trust is not defeated by evidence that the transferor intended to part with the beneficial interest if he has not in fact succeeded in doing so. As Plowman J had said in the same case at first instance [1966] Ch 261 at 275, 'As I see it, a man does not cease to own property simply by saying 'I don't want it'. If he tries to give it away the question must always be, has he succeeded in doing so or not?' Lord Upjohn [1967] 2 AC 291 at 314 expressly approved this.

However, ultimately this analysis remains unconvincing. As Swadling has noted:[177]

> even if 'transfer with no intention to benefit' was a fact susceptible of proof, there is no compelling reason why the law should respond to its 'proof' by raising a trust.... [I]f our only desire is to strip out the transferee's enrichment, a response in the nature of a personal claim for the value received serves that purpose perfectly well. Indeed, because it ensures equality of treatment between creditors in the event of the transferee's insolvency, it might be thought to do it better.

Swadling then reached the conclusion that the failure of both the positive intent and absence of intent approaches to explain the automatic resulting trust, which arises in cases such as *Vandervell*, means that:[178]

> the 'automatic' resulting trust still defies legal analysis.

It may be that 'automatic' resulting trusts arise on purely pragmatic grounds. But it is suggested that they can be explained, and that such an explanation does not need to draw a distinction with 'presumed' resulting trusts. Where an express trust fails, the law has to say what happens to the property. It is not unreasonable to presume, as a starting point, that the settlor would intend that the trustee hold the property on a resulting trust. As Mee has argued:[179]

> Looking at the question from the viewpoint of the settlor, a rule under which he becomes entitled under a resulting trust seems an entirely appropriate response to a failure in his attempt to allocate the beneficial interests; such a rule preserves the possibility of his making a renewed attempt to dispose of the beneficial interest. It seems plausible to suggest that such a rule would reflect the legal response which settlors as an abstract class would be likely to prefer.

---

[176] [1999] 1 WLR 1399, 1412.
[177] (2008) LQR 72, 101.
[178] Ibid, 102.
[179] '"Automatic" Resulting Trusts: Retention, Restitution or Reposing Trust?', in *Constructive and Resulting Trusts* (ed. Mitchell) (Oxford: Hart, 2010), p. 211.

Similarly, Rickett and Grantham have argued that:[180]

> Without evidence of actual intention, therefore, the law must fill this evidential lacuna with a presumption as to what was most likely to have been intended by the transferor. Equity's assessment is that the transferor would have intended to retain the beneficial interest. That presumption, sensible when it was formulated in the 16th century, remains eminently sensible today. The alternative presumption, that the property is to pass to the Crown, seems much less sensible in the context of our particular political economy. So the intention to which a resulting trust responds is this presumed intention, provided in that limited sense by 'operation of law'. But this is not legal make-believe. It is a judicious approach to determining the intention of the transferor or settlor. And it will give way to clear evidence of a different intention.

It might be argued that this is nevertheless inconsistent with *Vandervell*, since there was evidence that Vandervell did not intend to have any beneficial interest in the transferred property, because he wanted to structure the transaction to avoid his personal liability to pay tax. Indeed, in *Vandervell*, Lord Wilberforce said:[181]

> There is no need, or room, as I see it, to invoke a presumption. The conclusion, on the facts found, is simply that the option was vested in the trustee company as a trustee on trusts, not defined at the time, possibly to be defined later.

However, such reluctance to find scope for a presumed intention may seem to be inconsistent with Lord Browne-Wilkinson's later approach in *Westdeutsche*. In fact, a presumed positive intention to create a resulting trust might still explain *Vandervell*. It may just be that such a presumption was not rebutted by Vandervell's desire to reduce his tax liability. The presumption is particularly strong in the context of an automatic resulting trust, given that it is highly unlikely that the transferor would have even considered the possibility of the express trust failing. In *Vandervell*, there was clearly no evidence regarding who should take the property in the event of the express trust failing, and it must sensibly be presumed that a donor would rather retain a beneficial interest in transferred property than see it become *bona vacantia*. Vandervell might have sought to rebut the presumption by proving that he intended the option to be held by the trust company for the benefit of his children,[182] but it may be that the evidence was insufficient to rebut the presumption. Nevertheless, in some instances there may be a clear intention that a resulting trust should not apply, and the presumption will be rebutted.[183] This account of automatic resulting trusts being based upon the presumed intention of the settlor is theoretically justifiable, consistent with authority, and should be maintained.

5. *QUISTCLOSE* TRUSTS

(a) IDENTIFYING A *QUISTCLOSE* TRUST

Where property has been transferred for a specific purpose, and that purpose then fails, it may be that the property is held on trust for the original transferor. This situation most commonly arises

---

[180] 'Resulting Trusts: The True Nature of the Failing Trust Cases' (2000) 116 LQR 15, 17.

[181] [1967] 2 AC 291, 329.

[182] Although his children's settlement would then have borne the tax liability, which was what he was trying to avoid.

[183] This was recognized by Scott J in *Davis v Richards and Wallington* [1991] 1 WLR 1511, 1541, quoted in Chapter 8.3(c), pp. 394–6.

where one party lends money to a borrower on the understanding that the borrower can only use the money for a specified purpose. If it becomes impossible to fulfil that purpose, and the money has not been spent, then the lender might be able to enforce a proprietary interest in the money. In effect, this enables the lender to convert what would otherwise be a debt into a trust, thereby escaping the consequences of being an unsecured creditor if the borrower becomes insolvent. The trusts that arise are generally known as *Quistclose* trusts after the name of case in which the House of Lords first recognized this type of trust.[184] The most recent analysis of *Quistclose* trusts in the House of Lords in *Twinsectra Ltd v Yardley*[185] classified these trusts as resulting trusts, which is why they are considered in this chapter. However, as will be seen here, *Quistclose* trusts are not *necessarily* resulting trusts.

The essence of the *Quistclose* trust was explained by Lord Millett in *Twinsectra Ltd v Yardley*.

Twinsectra Ltd v Yardley [2002] UKHL 12; [2002] 2 AC 164, [68]–[76] (Lord Millett)

Money advanced by way of loan normally becomes the property of the borrower. He is free to apply the money as he chooses, and save to the extent to which he may have taken security for repayment the lender takes the risk of the borrower's insolvency. But it is well established that a loan to a borrower for a specific purpose where the borrower is not free to apply the money for any other purpose gives rise to fiduciary obligations on the part of the borrower which a court of equity will enforce. In the earlier cases the purpose was to enable the borrower to pay his creditors or some of them, but the principle is not limited to such cases.

Such arrangements are commonly described as creating 'a *Quistclose* trust', after the well-known decision of the House in *Quistclose Investment Ltd v Rolls Razor Ltd* [1970] AC 567 in which Lord Wilberforce confirmed the validity of such arrangements and explained their legal consequences. When the money is advanced, the lender acquires a right, enforceable in equity, to see that it is applied for the stated purpose, or more accurately to prevent its application for any other purpose. This prevents the borrower from obtaining any beneficial interest in the money, at least while the designated purpose is still capable of being carried out. Once the purpose has been carried out, the lender has his normal remedy in debt. If for any reason the purpose cannot be carried out, the question arises whether the money falls within the general fund of the borrower's assets, in which case it passes to his trustee-in-bankruptcy in the event of his insolvency and the lender is merely a loan creditor; or whether it is held on a resulting trust for the lender. This depends on the intention of the parties collected from the terms of the arrangement and the circumstances of the case....

It is unconscionable for a man to obtain money on terms as to its application and then disregard the terms on which he received it. Such conduct goes beyond a mere breach of contract. As North J explained in *Gilbert v Gonard* (1884) 54 LJ Ch 439 at 440:

> 'It is very well known law that if one person makes a payment to another for a certain purpose, and that person takes the money knowing that it is for that purpose, he must apply it to the purpose for which it was given. He may decline to take it if he likes; but if he chooses to accept the money tendered for a particular purpose, it is his duty, and there is a legal obligation on him, to apply it for that purpose.'

The duty is not contractual but fiduciary. It may exist despite the absence of any contract at all between the parties, as in *Rose v Rose* (1986) 7 NSWLR 679; and it binds third parties as in the *Quistclose* case itself. The duty is fiduciary in character because a person who makes money available on terms

---

[184] *Barclays Bank Ltd v Quistclose Investments Ltd* [1970] AC 567.
[185] [2002] UKHL 12; [2002] 2 AC 164 (Lord Millett).

that it is to be used for a particular purpose only and not for any other purpose thereby places his trust and confidence in the recipient to ensure that it is properly applied. This is a classic situation in which a fiduciary relationship arises, and since it arises in respect of a specific fund it gives rise to a trust.

This conclusion that property transferred for a specific purpose might be held on trust was first recognized by the House of Lords in *Barclays Bank Ltd v Quistclose Investments Ltd*.

Barclays Bank Ltd v Quistclose Investments Ltd [1970] AC 567

Rolls Razor Ltd had declared a dividend upon their ordinary shares. They were in serious financial difficulties and were unable to pay the dividend without a loan of £209,719 8s. 6d., which Quistclose Investments Ltd agreed to make on the condition 'that it is used to pay the forthcoming dividend due on 24 July next'. The cheque for this amount was paid into a separate account at Barclays Bank Ltd, and it was agreed that the account would 'only be used to meet the dividend due on 24 July, 1964'. Before the dividend was paid, Rolls Razor Ltd went into liquidation. The question was whether Barclays Bank Ltd could set that sum against Rolls Razor's overdraft, or whether it held it on trust for Quistclose. The House of Lords held that Barclays Bank held the money on trust for Quistclose: the fact that the transaction was a loan did not prevent there being also a trust. Lord Wilberforce said:

Two questions arise, both of which must be answered favourably to the respondents if they are to recover the money from the bank. The first is whether as between the respondents and Rolls Razor Ltd the terms upon which the loan was made were such as to impress upon the sum of £209,719 8s. 6d. a trust in their favour in the event of the dividend not being paid. The second is whether, in that event, the bank had such notice of the trust or of the circumstances giving rise to it as to make the trust binding upon them.

It is not difficult to establish precisely upon what terms the money was advanced by the respondents to Rolls Razor Ltd. There is no doubt that the loan was made specifically in order to enable Rolls Razor Ltd to pay the dividend. There is equally, in my opinion, no doubt that the loan was made only so as to enable Rolls Razor Ltd to pay the dividend and for no other purpose. This follows quite clearly from the terms of the letter of Rolls Razor Ltd to the bank of 15 July, 1964, which letter, before transmission to the bank, was sent to the respondents under open cover in order that the cheque might be (as it was) enclosed in it. The mutual intention of the respondents and of Rolls Razor Ltd, and the essence of the bargain, was that the sum advanced should not become part of the assets of Rolls Razor Ltd, but should be used exclusively for payment of a particular class of its creditors, namely, those entitled to the dividend. A necessary consequence from this, by process simply of interpretation, must be that if, for any reason, the dividend could not be paid, the money was to be returned to the respondents: the word 'only' or 'exclusively' can have no other meaning or effect.

That arrangements of this character for the payment of a person's creditors by a third person, give rise to a relationship of a fiduciary character or trust, in favour, as a primary trust, of the creditors, and secondarily, if the primary trust fails, of the third person, has been recognised in a series of cases over some 150 years.

In *Toovey v Milne* (1819) 2 B & Ald 683 part of the money advanced was, on the failure of the purpose for which it was lent (viz. to pay certain debts), repaid by the bankrupt to the person who had advanced it. On action being brought by the assignee of the bankrupt to recover it, the plaintiff was nonsuited and the nonsuit was upheld on a motion for a retrial. In his judgment Abbot CJ said, at 684:

'I thought at the trial, and still think, that the fair inference from the facts proved was that this money was advanced for a special purpose, and that being so clothed with a specific trust, no property in it passed to the assignee of the bankrupt. Then the purpose having failed, there is an implied stipulation that the money shall be repaid. That has been done in the present case; and I am of opinion that the repayment was lawful, and that the nonsuit was right.'

The basis for the decision was thus clearly stated, viz. that the money advanced for the specific purpose did not become part of the bankrupt's estate. This case has been repeatedly followed and applied: see *Edwards v Glyn* (1859) 2 E & E 29; *Re Rogers, ex p Holland and Hannen* (1891) 8 Morr 243; *Re Drucker* [1902] 2 KB 237; *Re Hooley, ex p Trustee* [1915] HBR 181. *Re Rogers* (1891) 8 Morr 243 was a decision of a strong Court of Appeal. In that case, the money provided by the third party had been paid to the creditors before the bankruptcy. Afterwards the trustee in bankruptcy sought to recover it. It was held that the money was advanced to the bankrupt for the special purpose of enabling his creditors to be paid, was impressed with a trust for the purpose and never became the property of the bankrupt. Lindley LJ decided the case on principle but said, at 248, that if authority was needed it would be found in *Toovey v Milne* (1819) 2 B & Ald 683 and other cases. Bowen LJ said at 248 that the money came to the bankrupt's hands impressed with a trust and did not become the property of the bankrupt divisible amongst his creditors, and the judgment of Kay LJ at 249 was to a similar effect.

These cases have the support of longevity, authority, consistency and, I would add, good sense. But they are not binding on your Lordships and it is necessary to consider such arguments as have been put why they should be departed from or distinguished? . . .

The second, and main, argument for the appellant was of a more sophisticated character. The transaction, it was said, between the respondents and Rolls Razor Ltd, was one of loan, giving rise to a legal action of debt. This necessarily excluded the implication of any trust, enforceable in equity, in the respondents' favour: a transaction may attract one action or the other, it could not admit of both.

My Lords, I must say that I find this argument unattractive. Let us see what it involves. It means that the law does not permit an arrangement to be made by which one person agrees to advance money to another, on terms that the money is to be used exclusively to pay debts of the latter, and if, and so far as not so used, rather than becoming a general asset of the latter available to his creditors at large, is to be returned to the lender. The lender is obliged, in such a case, because he is a lender, to accept, whatever the mutual wishes of lender and borrower may be, that the money he was willing to make available for one purpose only shall be freely available for others of the borrower's creditors for whom he has not the slightest desire to provide.

I should be surprised if an argument of this kind—so conceptualist in character—had ever been accepted. In truth it has plainly been rejected by the eminent judges who from 1819 onwards have permitted arrangements of this type to be enforced, and have approved them as being for the benefit of creditors and all concerned. There is surely no difficulty in recognising the co-existence in one transaction of legal and equitable rights and remedies: when the money is advanced, the lender acquires an equitable right to see that it is applied for the primary designated purpose (see *Re Rogers* (1891) 8 Morr 243 where both Lindley LJ and Kay LJ recognised this): when the purpose has been carried out (i.e. the debt paid) the lender has his remedy against the borrower in debt; if the primary purpose cannot be carried out, the question arises if a secondary purpose (i.e. repayment to the lender) has been agreed, expressly or by implication: if it has, the remedies of equity may be invoked to give effect to it, if it has not (and the money is intended to fall within the general fund of the debtor's assets) then there is the appropriate remedy for recovery of a loan. I can appreciate no reason why the flexible interplay of law and equity cannot let in these practical arrangements, and other variations if desired: it would be to the discredit of both systems if they could not. In the present case the intention to create a secondary trust for the benefit of the lender, to arise if the primary trust, to pay the dividend, could not be carried out, is clear and I can find no reason why the law should not give effect to it.

I pass to the second question, that of notice. I can deal with this briefly because I am in agreement with the manner in which it has been disposed of by all three members of the Court of Appeal. I am prepared, for this purpose, to accept, by way of assumption, the position most favourable to the bank, i.e. that it is necessary to show that the bank had notice of the trust or of the circumstances giving rise to the trust, at the time when they received the money, viz. on 15 July, 1964, and that notice on a later date, even though they had not in any real sense given value when they received the money or thereafter changed their position, will not do. It is common ground, and I think right, that a mere request to put the money into a separate account is not sufficient to constitute notice. But on 15 July, 1964, the bank, when it received the cheque, also received the covering letter of that date which I have set out above; previously there had been the telephone conversation between Mr. Goldbart and Mr. Parker, to which I have also referred. From these there is no doubt that the bank was told that the money had been provided on loan by a third person and was to be used only for the purpose of paying the dividend. This was sufficient to give them notice that it was trust money and not assets of Rolls Razor Ltd: the fact, if it be so, that they were unaware of the lender's identity (though the respondent's name as drawer was on the cheque) is of no significance. I may add to this, as having some bearing on the merits of the case, that it is quite apparent from earlier documents that the bank were aware that Rolls Razor Ltd could not provide the money for the dividend and that this would have to come from an outside source and that they never contemplated that the money so provided could be used to reduce the existing overdraft. They were in fact insisting that other or additional arrangements should be made for that purpose. As was appropriately said by Russell LJ, [1968] Ch 540 at 563F, it would be giving a complete windfall to the bank if they had established a right to retain the money.

Lord Wilberforce held that where the primary purpose failed, a secondary trust of the money might arise if this had been agreed either expressly or impliedly. His Lordship emphasized that money that had been paid for a particular purpose should not be available for the borrower's general creditors whom the lender had not intended to benefit.

However, it might seem somewhat generous to allow a lender a proprietary interest under a trust, rather than limiting the lender to his or her usual personal action in debt. In *Re EVTR*, Bingham LJ eventually agreed that a *Quistclose* trust arose on the facts of the case,[186] but said:[187]

My doubt has been whether the law as it stands enables effect to be given to what I can see as the common fairness of the situation.

Swadling has also questioned whether the lender should benefit from proprietary protection.

Swadling, 'Orthodoxy' in *The Quistclose Trust: Critical Essays* (ed. Swadling) (Oxford: Hart, 2004), pp. 38–9

What seems to have worried Lord Wilberforce in *Quistclose* was the thought that Barclays could exercise its right of set-off and thereby evade a Pari Passu distribution of the loan monies. This would certainly not have been possible had Rolls Razor opened a special account with a different banker, and the real question, which will not be pursued here, is whether it is correct to say

---

[186] See Chapter 8.5(a), p. 417.
[187] [1987] BCLC 646, 652.

that set-off rights operate in an insolvency in the same way as when all parties are solvent. But in seeking to avoid the application of set-off by the finding of a trust, Lord Wilberforce departed from orthodox principles of trust law. It is impossible to say that the transfer was a transfer on trust because the restriction only referred to how the rights were to be applied, not for whom they were held. And even were we able to say that a trust was intended, grave difficulties arise in identifying the objects of that trust. It could not be the creditors for a number of reasons, the most prominent of which is that it would allow them to be paid twice over. For almost identical reasons, it could not be the lender. Nor could it be the purpose, for the purpose was a private purpose and English law does not countenance trusts for private purposes. And the argument of Chambers, that there need be no primary trust,[188] does not succeed either, because it fails to explain how a personal right to see that the fund is not misapplied can bind a stranger, including the borrower's trustee in bankruptcy, to the contract which creates that right. And given that Lord Wilberforce's secondary trust depends on the validity of the primary trust, the argument that there was a consensual trust of the loan monies in favour of the lender on the failure of the purpose cannot be sustained. For the same reasons, a secondary trust arising by not-consent on the subsequent failure of the primary trust is not arguable either. In short, the House of Lords was wrong in *Quistclose* to find a trust and thereby give priority to the lender. The funds should have been held to be part of Rolls Razor's general assets and treated accordingly.

The *Quistclose* mechanism advocated by Lord Wilberforce might nonetheless be defended on policy grounds. The lender's intention that the borrower not benefit generally from the transaction should be respected, and the particular purpose imposed taken seriously. One qualm might be that recognizing that the lender has a beneficial interest under a trust may be tantamount to an unlawful preference for one creditor over another.[189] But in the context of a company on the brink of insolvency, which needs a loan for a particular purpose—such as to pay dividends—affording the lender proprietary protection might cause little prejudice, since without such protection under a trust the lender might not lend the money at all, which would increase the chances of the company becoming bankrupt—clearly, this would be disadvantageous for both the company and its unsecured creditors. Whereas if the lender were to enjoy a proprietary interest under a trust, the lender might consequently be more ready to lend money to a company suffering from financial difficulties, which would increase the chances of the company surviving and its creditors' being paid in full. This suggests that the other unsecured creditors of the company are not really worse off through the availability of *Quistclose* trusts, and fears about unlawfully preferring one creditor over another might be somewhat allayed. Admittedly, as Lord Millett recognized in *Twinsectra Ltd v Yardley*,[190] the purpose necessary for a *Quistclose* trust is not necessarily limited to a lender's enabling a borrower to pay his or her creditors, but the *Quistclose* mechanism of providing proprietary protection is clearly most necessary in the context of insolvency.

In *Twinsectra*, Lord Millett was keenly aware of the need to distinguish between a purely personal contractual obligation and a proprietary relationship. In that case, the claimant lent money to Yardley for the purchase of property. Sims, a solicitor, had given a personal undertaking to the claimant that he would retain the money that had been lent until it was applied for the purchase of the property, and that the money would not be used for any other purpose. The money was in fact used to discharge a debt owed by Sims to Yardley. Sims became bankrupt and the claimant wanted to recover the property. The only claim before the House of Lords was whether Leach, another solicitor acting for

---

[188] See especially Chambers, *Resulting Trusts* (Oxford: Clarendon Press, 1997), chapter 3.
[189] Cf. Chapter 3.2(c), pp. 73–4.
[190] [2002] UKHL 12; [2002] 2 AC 164, [68].

Yardley, was liable for dishonest assistance in a breach of trust.[191] Liability depended first on identifying that the money was held by Sims on trust. In considering the *Quistclose* trust, Lord Millett said:[192]

> A *Quistclose* trust does not necessarily arise merely because money is paid for a particular purpose. A lender will often inquire into the purpose for which a loan is sought in order to decide whether he would be justified in making it. He may be said to lend the money for the purpose in question, but this is not enough to create a trust; once lent the money is at the free disposal of the borrower. Similarly payments in advance for goods or services are paid for a particular purpose, but such payments do not ordinarily create a trust. The money is intended to be at the free disposal of the supplier and may be used as part of his cash-flow. Commercial life would be impossible if this were not the case.
>
> The question in every case is whether the parties intended the money to be at the free disposal of the recipient: *Re Goldcorp Exchange Ltd* [1995] 1 AC 74, 100, per Lord Mustill. His freedom to dispose of the money is necessarily excluded by an arrangement that the money shall be used exclusively for the stated purpose, for as Lord Wilberforce observed in the *Quistclose* case [1970] AC 567, 580:
>
>> 'a necessary consequence from this, by a process simply of interpretation, must be that if, for any reason, [the purpose could not be carried out,] the money was to be returned to [the lender]: the word 'only' or 'exclusively' can have no other meaning or effect.'
>
> [His Lordship considered the facts of the *Quistclose* case and continued:]
>
> In the present case paragraphs 1 and 2 of the undertaking are crystal clear. Mr. Sims undertook that the money would be used solely for the acquisition of property and for no other purpose; and was to be retained by his firm until so applied. It would not be held by Mr. Sims simply to Mr. Yardley's order; and it would not be at Mr. Yardley's free disposition. Any payment by Mr. Sims of the money, whether to Mr. Yardley or anyone else, otherwise than for the acquisition of property would constitute a breach of trust....
>
> In my opinion the Court of Appeal were correct to find that the terms of paragraphs 1 and 2 of the undertaking created a *Quistclose* trust. The money was never at Mr. Yardley's free disposal. It was never held to his order by Mr. Sims. The money belonged throughout to Twinsectra, subject only to Mr. Yardley's right to apply it for the acquisition of property. Twinsectra parted with the money to Mr. Sims, relying on him to ensure that the money was properly applied or returned to it.

For a *Quistclose* trust to arise, there must be a clear purpose, and the property must be transferred to be used exclusively for that purpose. It is crucial that the property is not at the free disposal of the recipient. This might be evidenced by the recipient's being required to keep the property segregated from his or her general assets.[193] As Henderson J said in *Charity Commission for England and Wales v Framjee*:[194]

> b) Where money is transferred to a recipient to be paid to a third party, and that money is not intended to be at the free disposal of the recipient, it is likely that a trust will arise: see *Twinsectra Ltd v Yardley* [2002] UKHL 12, [2002] 2 AC 164, at [68] and [73] to [74] per Lord Millett...
>
> c) Although not a pre-requisite, if there is a requirement for the money to be held by the recipient in a separate account, that will be a strong pointer in favour of the existence of a trust: see *Twinsectra* at [95], where Lord Millett referred to 'the evidential significance of a requirement that the money should be kept in a separate account'...

---

[191] See Chapter 19.2(c), pp. 938–40.
[192] [2002] UKHL 12; [2002] 2 AC 164, [73]–[103].
[193] As was the case in *Quistclose* itself. See too *Henry v Hammond* [1913] 2 KB 515, 521 (Channell J). However, segregation is not inevitably required: *Cooper v PRG Powerhouse* [2008] EWHC 498 (Ch); [2008] 2 All ER (Comm) 964.
[194] [2014] EWHC 2507; [2015] 1 WLR 16, [29].

Equally importantly, the purpose must fail. It is generally assumed that the power fails on insolvency: since one of the reasons for lending the property is commonly to avoid the borrower's insolvency, on the occurrence of this event the entire purpose of the transaction can no longer be fulfilled. However, failure of the purpose must clearly be shown. In *Re EVTR*,[195] the claimant deposited £60,000 for the sole purpose of enabling the company to buy equipment. The money was used for this purpose, but, before the equipment was delivered, the company went into receivership and the purchase was terminated. A large part of the purchase price was repaid to the company. It was held that, although the equipment had been purchased, the purpose had ultimately failed because the equipment had not been delivered, and so the money that had been repaid was held on trust for the claimant. As Bingham LJ observed:[196]

> While it is literally true that the fund which he provided was applied to the stipulated purpose, the object of the payment was not achieved and that was why the balance was repaid to the receivers.

(b) THE NATURE OF THE *QUISTCLOSE* TRUST

The common fact-pattern of *Quistclose* trusts is relatively clear: money is lent for a particular purpose, which no longer becomes possible to fulfil, usually because of the borrower's insolvency; the money could *only* be spent on that particular purpose, and on the failure of that purpose, the beneficial interest in the money lent is recognized to belong to the lender under a trust. But *why* this should be so is difficult to explain.[197] The result in *Quistclose* may have been commercially desirable, but the reason why there is a trust has provoked much debate.

In *Quistclose* itself, the House of Lords held that there were, in effect, two trusts: the primary express trust for a purpose, and then the secondary trust for the lender, which arose upon the failure of the purpose. However, this reasoning is problematic. A primary trust for identified beneficiaries would allow the beneficiaries to terminate the trust and transfer the property to themselves,[198] which is unlikely to correspond to the parties' intentions. On the other hand, a trust for a specified purpose is unlikely to be valid, since there are no objects to enforce the trust.[199] And even if the purpose trust is valid as essentially for identifiable beneficiaries,[200] this would mean that the beneficial interest in the property is in suspense until the given purpose was either fulfilled or failed. In the Court of Appeal in *Twinsectra*, Potter LJ said that:[201]

> The cases proceed on the assumption that the primary purpose trust comes to an end either when the expressed purpose is performed, in which event no question of a secondary trust arises (save in respect of any balance remaining in the hands of the borrower), or, when the purpose becomes impossible to perform (at which point the secondary trust comes into effect). Thus, in the sense, and to the extent that the lender has an equitable right to prevent the money being applied for any but its designated purpose, so long as the primary purpose trust continues, the beneficial interest in the monies lent is 'in suspense' until applied for that purpose.

---

[195] [1987] BCLC 646.
[196] Ibid, 652.
[197] Cf Swadling, 'Orthodoxy' in *The Quistclose Trust* (ed. Swadling) (Oxford: Hart, 2004): see Chapter 8.5(a), pp. 414–15.
[198] *Saunders v Vautier* (1841) 4 Beav 115. See Chapter 10.3(a), p. 519.
[199] See Chapter 5, 'Charitable Purpose Trusts'.
[200] See Chapter 6.2(a), pp. 289–90.
[201] [1999] Lloyd's Rep Bank 438, 456 [75]. See too *Carreras Rothmans Ltd v Freeman Mathews Treasure Ltd* [1985] Ch 207.

However, this approach was criticized by Peter Millett before he became a judge as 'unconventional', since:[202]

> To impute to A an intention to confer on C a right to call for property enforceable in equity but not an equitable interest in the property is to attribute to him the motivation of an antiquarian.

Subsequently, in *Twinsectra*, Lord Millett maintained that there was no need to conclude that the beneficial interest in the property was in suspense: he preferred an analysis based upon there being a resulting trust, which would account for the beneficial interest in the property at all times: the beneficial interest would remain with the transferor unless and until the purpose is fulfilled. His Lordship also rejected other attempts to explain the operation of the *Quistclose* trust.

Twinsectra Ltd v Yardley [2002] UKHL 12; [2002] 2 AC 164 (Lord Millett)

These passages [from Lord Wilberforce's speech in *Quistclose*] suggest that there are two successive trusts, a primary trust for payment to identifiable beneficiaries, such as creditors or shareholders, and a secondary trust in favour of the lender arising on the failure of the primary trust. But there are formidable difficulties in this analysis, which has little academic support. What if the primary trust is not for identifiable persons, but as in the present case to carry out an abstract purpose? Where in such a case is the beneficial interest pending the application of the money for the stated purpose or the failure of the purpose? There are four possibilities: (i) in the lender; (ii) in the borrower; (iii) in the contemplated beneficiary; or (iv) in suspense.

(i) *The lender*

In 'The *Quistclose* Trust: Who Can Enforce It?' (1985) 101 LQR 269, I argued that the beneficial interest remained throughout in the lender. This analysis has received considerable though not universal academic support: see for example Priestley J 'The Romalpa Clause and the *Quistclose* Trust' in *Equity and Commercial Transactions*, ed. Finn (1987) 217, 237; and Professor M Bridge 'The Quistclose Trust in a World of Secured Transactions' (1992) 12 OJLS 333, 352; and others. It was adopted by the New Zealand Court of Appeal in *General Communications Ltd v Development Finance Corporation of New Zealand Ltd* [1990] 3 NZLR 406 and referred to with apparent approval by Gummow J in *Re Australian Elizabethan Theatre Trust* (1991) 102 ALR 681. Gummow J saw nothing special in the *Quistclose* trust, regarding it as essentially a security device to protect the lender against other creditors of the borrower pending the application of the money for the stated purpose.

On this analysis, the *Quistclose* trust is a simple commercial arrangement akin (as Professor Bridge observes) to a retention of title clause (though with a different object) which enables the borrower to have recourse to the lender's money for a particular purpose without entrenching on the lender's property rights more than necessary to enable the purpose to be achieved. The money remains the property of the lender unless and until it is applied in accordance with his directions, and insofar as it is not so applied it must be returned to him. I am disposed, perhaps pre-disposed, to think that this is the only analysis which is consistent both with orthodox trust law and with commercial reality. Before reaching a concluded view that it should be adopted, however, I must consider the alternatives.

(ii) *The borrower*

It is plain that the beneficial interest is not vested unconditionally in the borrower so as to leave the money at his free disposal. That would defeat the whole purpose of the arrangements, which is to

---

[202] 'The *Quistclose* Trust: Who Can Enforce It?' (1985) 101 LQR 269, 282.

prevent the money from passing to the borrower's trustee-in-bankruptcy in the event of his insolvency. It would also be inconsistent with all the decided cases where the contest was between the lender and the borrower's trustee-in-bankruptcy, as well as with the *Quistclose* case itself: see in particular *Toovey v Milne* (1819) 2 B & Ald 683; *Re Rogers* (1891) 8 Morr 243.

The borrower's interest pending the application of the money for the stated purpose or its return to the lender is minimal. He must keep the money separate; he cannot apply it except for the stated purpose; unless the terms of the loan otherwise provide he must return it to the lender if demanded; he cannot refuse to return it if the stated purpose cannot be achieved; and if he becomes bankrupt it does not vest in his trustee in bankruptcy. If there is any content to beneficial ownership at all, the lender is the beneficial owner and the borrower is not...

(iii) *In the contemplated beneficiary*

In the *Quistclose* case itself [1970] AC 567, as in all the reported cases which preceded it, either the primary purpose had been carried out and the contest was between the borrower's trustee-in-bankruptcy or liquidator and the person or persons to whom the borrower had paid the money; or it was treated as having failed, and the contest was between the borrower's trustee-in-bankruptcy and the lender. It was not necessary to explore the position while the primary purpose was still capable of being carried out and Lord Wilberforce's observations must be read in that light.

The question whether the primary trust is accurately described as a trust for the creditors first arose in *Re Northern Developments Holdings Ltd* (unreported) 6 October 1978, where the contest was between the lender and the creditors. The borrower, which was not in liquidation and made no claim to the money, was the parent company of a group one of whose subsidiaries was in financial difficulty. There was a danger that if it were wound up or ceased trading it would bring down the whole group. A consortium of the group's banks agreed to put up a fund of more than £500,000 in an attempt to rescue the subsidiary. They paid the money into a special account in the name of the parent company for the express purpose of 'providing money for the subsidiary's unsecured creditors over the ensuing weeks' and for no other purpose. The banks' object was to enable the subsidiary to continue trading, though on a reduced scale; it failed when the subsidiary was put into receivership at a time when some £350,000 remained unexpended. Relying on Lord Wilberforce's observations in the passages cited above, Sir Robert Megarry V-C held that the primary trust was a purpose trust enforceable *(inter alios)* by the subsidiaries' creditors as the persons for whose benefit the trust was created.

There are several difficulties with this analysis. In the first place, Lord Wilberforce's reference to *Re Rogers* (1891) 8 Morr 243 makes it plain that the equitable right he had in mind was not a mandatory order to compel performance, but a negative injunction to restrain improper application of the money; for neither Lindley LJ nor Kay LJ recognised more than this. In the second place, the object of the arrangements was to enable the subsidiary to continue trading, and this would necessarily involve it in incurring further liabilities to trade creditors. Accordingly the application of the fund was not confined to existing creditors at the date when the fund was established. The company secretary was given to understand that the purpose of the arrangements was to keep the subsidiary trading, and that the fund was 'as good as share capital'. Thus the purpose of the arrangements was not, as in other cases, to enable the debtor to avoid bankruptcy by paying off existing creditors, but to enable the debtor to continue trading by providing it with working capital with which to incur fresh liabilities. There is a powerful argument for saying that the result of the arrangements was to vest a beneficial interest in the subsidiary from the start. If so, then this was not a *Quistclose* trust at all.

In the third place, it seems unlikely that the banks' object was to benefit the creditors (who included the Inland Revenue) except indirectly. The banks had their own commercial interests to protect by enabling the subsidiary to trade out of its difficulties. If so, then the primary trust cannot be supported as a valid non-charitable purpose trust: see *Re Grant's Will Trusts* [1980] 1 WLR 360 and cf *Re Denley's Trust Deed* [1969] 1 Ch 373.

The most serious objection to this approach is exemplified by the facts of the present case. In several of the cases the primary trust was for an abstract purpose with no one but the lender to enforce performance or restrain misapplication of the money. In *Edwards v Glyn* (1859) 2 E & E the money was advanced to a bank to enable the bank to meet a run. In *Re EVTR* [1987] BCLC 646, it was advanced 'for the sole purpose of buying new equipment'. In *General Communications Ltd v Development Finance Corporation of New Zealand Ltd* [1990] 3 NZLR 406 the money was paid to the borrower's solicitors for the express purpose of purchasing new equipment. The present case is another example. It is simply not possible to hold money on trust to acquire unspecified property from an unspecified vendor at an unspecified time. There is no reason to make an arbitrary distinction between money paid for an abstract purpose and money paid for a purpose which can be said to benefit an ascertained class of beneficiaries, and the cases rightly draw no such distinction. Any analysis of the *Quistclose* trust must be able to accommodate gifts and loans for an abstract purpose.

(iv) *In suspense*

As Peter Gibson J pointed out in *Carreras Rothmans Ltd v Freeman Mathews Treasure Ltd* [1985] Ch 207 at 223 the effect of adopting Sir Robert Megarry V-C's analysis is to leave the beneficial interest in suspense until the stated purpose is carried out or fails. The difficulty with this (apart from its unorthodoxy) is that it fails to have regard to the role which the resulting trust plays in equity's scheme of things, or to explain why the money is not simply held on a resulting trust for the lender.

Lord Browne-Wilkinson gave an authoritative explanation of the resulting trust in *Westdeutsche Landesbank Girozentrale v Islington Borough Council* [1996] AC 669 at 708 and its basis has been further illuminated by Dr R Chambers in his book *Resulting Trusts* published in 1997. Lord Browne-Wilkinson explained that a resulting trust arises in two sets of circumstances. He described the second as follows:

'Where A transfers property to B on express trusts, but the trusts declared do not exhaust the whole beneficial interest.'

The *Quistclose* case [1970] AC 567 was among the cases he cited as examples. He rejected the argument that there was a resulting trust in the case before him because, unlike the situation in the present case, there was no transfer of money on express trusts. But he also rejected the argument on a wider and, in my respectful opinion, surer ground that the money was paid and received with the intention that it should become the absolute property of the recipient.

The central thesis of Dr Chambers' book is that a resulting trust arises whenever there is a transfer of property in circumstances in which the transferor (or more accurately the person at whose expense the property was provided) did not intend to benefit the recipient. It responds to the absence of an intention on the part of the transferor to pass the entire beneficial interest, not to a positive intention to retain it. Insofar as the transfer does not exhaust the entire beneficial interest, the resulting trust is a default trust which fills the gap and leaves no room for any part to be in suspense. An analysis of the *Quistclose* trust as a resulting trust for the transferor with a mandate to the transferee to apply the money for the stated purpose sits comfortably with Dr Chambers' thesis, and it might be thought surprising that he does not adopt it.

(v) *The Court of Appeal's analysis*

The Court of Appeal were content to treat the beneficial interest as in suspense, or (following Dr Chambers' analysis) to hold that it was in the borrower, the lender having merely a contractual right enforceable by injunction to prevent misapplication. Potter LJ put it in these terms [1999] Lloyd's Rep 438 at 456, para 75:

'The purpose imposed at the time of the advance creates an enforceable restriction on the borrower's use of the money. Although the lender's right to enforce the restriction is treated as arising on the basis of a 'trust', the use of that word does not enlarge the lender's interest in the fund. The borrower is entitled to the beneficial use of the money, subject to the lender's right to prevent its misuse; the lender's limited interest in the fund is sufficient to prevent its use for other than the special purpose for which it was advanced.'

This analysis, with respect, is difficult to reconcile with the court's actual decision insofar as it granted Twinsectra a proprietary remedy against Mr. Yardley's companies as recipients of the misapplied funds. Unless the money belonged to Twinsectra immediately before its misapplication, there is no basis on which a proprietary remedy against third party recipients can be justified.

Dr Chambers' 'novel view' (as it has been described) is that the arrangements do not create a trust at all; the borrower receives the entire beneficial ownership in the money subject only to a contractual right in the lender to prevent the money being used otherwise than for the stated purpose. If the purpose fails, a resulting trust in the lender springs into being. In fact, he argues for a kind of restrictive covenant enforceable by negative injunction yet creating property rights in the money. But restrictive covenants, which began life as negative easements, are part of our land law. Contractual obligations do not run with money or a chose in action like money in a bank account.

Dr Chambers' analysis has attracted academic comment, both favourable and unfavourable. For my own part, I do not think that it can survive the criticism levelled against it by Lusina Ho and P St J Smart: 'Reinterpreting the Quistclose Trust: a Critique of Chambers' Analysis' (2001) 21 OJLS 267. It provides no solution to cases of non-contractual payment; is inconsistent with Lord Wilberforce's description of the borrower's obligation as fiduciary and not merely contractual; fails to explain the evidential significance of a requirement that the money should be kept in a separate account; cannot easily be reconciled with the availability of proprietary remedies against third parties; and while the existence of a mere equity to prevent misapplication would be sufficient to prevent the money from being available for distribution to the creditors on the borrower's insolvency (because the trustee-in-bankruptcy has no greater rights than his bankrupt) it would not prevail over secured creditors. If the bank in the *Quistclose* case [1970] AC 567 had held a floating charge (as it probably did) and had appointed a receiver, the adoption of Dr Chambers' analysis should have led to a different outcome.

Thus all the alternative solutions have their difficulties. But there are two problems which they fail to solve, but which are easily solved if the beneficial interest remains throughout in the lender. One arises from the fact, well established by the authorities, that the primary trust is enforceable by the lender. But on what basis can he enforce it? He cannot do so as the beneficiary under the secondary trust, for if the primary purpose is fulfilled there is no secondary trust: the pre-condition of his claim is destructive of his standing to make it. He cannot do so as settlor, for a settlor who retains no beneficial interest cannot enforce the trust which he has created.

Dr Chambers insists that the lender has merely a right to prevent the misapplication of the money, and attributes this to his contractual right to specific performance of a condition of the contract of loan. As I have already pointed out, this provides no solution where the arrangement is non-contractual. But Lord Wilberforce clearly based the borrower's obligation on an equitable or fiduciary basis and not a contractual one. He was concerned to justify the co-existence of equity's exclusive jurisdiction with the common law action for debt. Basing equity's intervention on its auxiliary jurisdiction to restrain a breach of contract would not have enabled the lender to succeed against the bank, which was a third party to the contract. There is only one explanation of the lender's fiduciary right to enforce the primary trust which can be reconciled with basic principle: he can do so because he is the beneficiary.

The other problem is concerned with the basis on which the primary trust is said to have failed in several of the cases, particularly *Toovey v Milne* 2 B & A 683 and the *Quistclose* case itself [1970] AC 567. Given that the money did not belong to the borrower in either case, the borrower's insolvency should not have prevented the money from being paid in the manner contemplated. A man cannot pay some only of his creditors once he has been adjudicated bankrupt, but a third party can. A company cannot pay a dividend once it has gone into liquidation, but there is nothing to stop a third party from paying the disappointed shareholders. The reason why the purpose failed in each case must be because the lender's object in making the money available was to save the borrower from bankruptcy in the one case and collapse in the other. But this in itself is not enough. a trust does not fail merely because the settlor's purpose in creating it has been frustrated: the trust must become illegal or impossible to perform. The settlor's motives must not be confused with the purpose of the trust; the frustration of the former does not by itself cause the failure of the latter. But if the borrower is treated as holding the money on a resulting trust for the lender but with power (or in some cases a duty) to carry out the lender's revocable mandate, and the lender's object in giving the mandate is frustrated, he is entitled to revoke the mandate and demand the return of money which never ceased to be his beneficially...

As Sherlock Holmes reminded Dr Watson, when you have eliminated the impossible, whatever remains, however improbable, must be the truth. I would reject all the alternative analyses, which I find unconvincing for the reasons I have endeavoured to explain, and hold the *Quistclose* trust to be an entirely orthodox example of the kind of default trust known as a resulting trust. The lender pays the money to the borrower by way of loan, but he does not part with the entire beneficial interest in the money, and insofar as he does not it is held on a resulting trust for the lender from the outset. Contrary to the opinion of the Court of Appeal, it is the borrower who has a very limited use of the money, being obliged to apply it for the stated purpose or return it. He has no beneficial interest in the money, which remains throughout in the lender subject only to the borrower's power or duty to apply the money in accordance with the lender's instructions. When the purpose fails, the money is returnable to the lender, not under some new trust in his favour which only comes into being on the failure of the purpose, but because the resulting trust in his favour is no longer subject to any power on the part of the borrower to make use of the money. Whether the borrower is obliged to apply the money for the stated purpose or merely at liberty to do so, and whether the lender can countermand the borrower's mandate while it is still capable of being carried out, must depend on the circumstances of the particular case...

When the trust in favour of the lender arises

Like all resulting trusts, the trust in favour of the lender arises when the lender parts with the money on terms which do not exhaust the beneficial interest. It is not a contingent reversionary or future interest. It does not suddenly come into being like an eighteenth-century use only when the stated purpose fails. It is a default trust which fills the gap when some part of the beneficial interest is undisposed-of and prevents it from being 'in suspense'.

Lord Millett therefore concluded that *Quistclose* trusts are resulting trusts. But what sort of resulting trust? Lord Millett insisted that there is only ever one trust—the resulting trust—which suggests that there was no express trust that has failed. Does this mean that a *Quistclose* trust is a resulting trust which responds to the settlor's presumed intention? Possibly, but difficulties might arise where it is the borrower who segregates the lender's property from his or her own general funds without being instructed to do so. If the *Quistclose* trust is a resulting trust, it might nonetheless be best explained as arising upon the failure of an express trust: the transferor is taken to intend to create a purpose trust, which is invalid as it is not charitable,[203] so the recipient instead holds the property transferred on resulting trust for the transferor. However, the recipient still has a power to use the property for the purpose for which the property was transferred at the outset, given that the transferor has consented to this.

---

[203] See Chapter 6, 'Non-charitable Purpose Trusts'.

It is important to emphasize that it is not the subjective intentions of the parties which are crucial when deciding whether a *Quistclose* trust arises. The focus is on the objective intention of the settlor. This was made clear by the Court of Appeal in *Challinor v Bellis*:[204]

> …In this respect, *Quistclose*-type trusts are no different from any other trusts. In particular, they are not presumed to exist unless a contrary intention be proved, as in the case of the traditional type of resulting trust where a person makes a gratuitous transfer of property to an apparent stranger.
>
> A person creates a trust by his words or conduct, not by his innermost thoughts. His subjective intentions are, as Lord Millett said, irrelevant. In the *Twinsectra* case, a *Quistclose* trust was established despite the transferor having no subjective intention to create a trust. But the objectivity principle works both ways. A person who does subjectively intend to create a trust may fail to do so if his words and conduct, viewed objectively, fall short of what is required. As with the interpretation of contracts, this process of interpretation is often called the ascertainment of objective intention. In the contractual context the court is looking for the objective common intention, whereas in the trust context the search is for the objective intention of the alleged settlor.
>
> Usually, the question whether the essential restrictions upon the transferee's use of the property have been imposed (so as to create a trust) turns upon the true construction of the words used by the transferor. But where, as in *Twinsectra* and indeed the present case, the transferor says or writes nothing but responds to an invitation to transfer the property on terms, then it is the true construction of the invitation which is likely to be decisive.
>
> In such cases the invitation usually comes from the transferee. In *Twinsectra* it took the form of a solicitor's written undertaking, the terms of which, as Lord Millett put it, were 'crystal clear' in restricting the use of the money transferred for the specified purpose of the acquisition of property.
>
> But I am content to assume, as the judge did in the present case, that the invitation may come from someone other than the transferee. A may say to B:
>
> > 'If you transfer money to C, it will be used solely for a specified purpose.'
>
> The proper interpretation of B's conduct in transferring money to C pursuant to that invitation is that he thereby created a *Quistclose*-type trust. Whether C will be liable for breach of that trust by using the money for some other purpose will then depend on whether C knew of the terms of A's invitation before disposing of the money.
>
> Where property is transferred on terms that do not leave it at the free disposal of the transferee then the *Quistclose*-type trust thereby established is one under which the beneficial interest in the property remains in the transferor unless and until the purposes for which it has been transferred have been fulfilled: see *Twinsectra* at paragraph 100. That beneficial interest ceases to exist if and to the extent that the property is used for the stated purposes, but not otherwise. The application of the property for the stated purpose is a power vested in the transferee, not (usually at least) a primary purpose trust.

In any event, it might be better not to try to explain *all* instances of *Quistclose* trusts in the same way. As Lord Millett himself wrote in the Foreword to a book on the *Quistclose* trust:[205]

> The so-called *Quistclose* trust probably represents the single most important application of equitable principles in commercial life. It has been well established for some two hundred years, at least in relation

---

[204] [2015] EWCA Civ 59; [2016] WTLR 43, [57]–[62].

[205] Lord Millett, 'Foreword', in *The Quistclose Trust: Critical Essays* (ed. Swadling) (Oxford: Hart, 2004). See too the chapter by Chambers in the same book, 'Restrictions on the Use of Money', as well as Glister, 'The nature of *Quistclose* trusts: classification and reconciliation' (2004) 63 CLJ 632. Compare Millett (1985) 101 LQR 269, 290, who suggested that *Quistclose* trusts might be a unique form of trust.

to insolvency, though it is now seen to be of more general application. Yet it has resisted attempts by academic lawyers to analyse it in terms of conventional equitable doctrine. Even that modern master of equity Sir Robert Megarry V-C was inclined to think that it was an aberrant creation of common law judges.

It was too much to hope that a single decision of the House of Lords would put an end to controversy. The nature of the trust and the location of the beneficial interest remain elusive and continue to be debated by distinguished academic lawyers. They demand to know whether the *Quistclose* trust is a form of express, implied, constructive or resulting trust. If the mere author of a foreword may venture to intrude in a private dispute (at the risk of exposing himself to derisive comment from all sides), I would say that it may be any of them, depending on the facts of the particular case and the boundaries between these various forms of trust, on which not everyone is agreed.

From a commercial point of view, however, the trust is simply a mechanism by which one person may allow the use of his money by another for a stated purpose without losing his right to the money more than necessary to achieve the purpose. The commercial need for such a mechanism is obvious. The problems which will face the courts are not likely to derive from any difficulty in analysing the nature of the trust, but from the need to distinguish the case where it arises from the ordinary case of the lender who naturally wishes to know why the borrower wants the money.

The nature of a *Quistclose* trust might depend upon the facts of any given case. However, it is important to appreciate that well-established principles of express, resulting, and constructive trusts should be applied.

There is a powerful argument that if a lender wishes to be protected in the event of the borrower's insolvency, that lender should make his or her intentions express. If he or she does so, then an express trust in the lender's favour could arise. Even after *Twinsectra*, this possibility has been recognized judicially by Lord Millett in *Latimer v Commissioner of Inland Revenue*.[206] In fact, the majority of the House of Lords in *Twinsectra* thought that the trust which arose was an express trust. As Lord Hoffmann commented:[207]

The terms of the trust upon which Sims held the money must be found in the undertaking which they gave to Twinsectra as a condition of payment. Clauses 1 and 2 of that undertaking made it clear that the money was not to be at the free disposal of Mr Yardley. Sims were not to part with the money to Mr Yardley or anyone else except for the purpose of enabling him to acquire property.

In my opinion the effect of the undertaking was to provide that the money in the Sims client account should remain Twinsectra's money until such time as it was applied for the acquisition of property in accordance with the undertaking. For example, if Mr Yardley went bankrupt before the money had been so applied, it would not have formed part of his estate, as it would have done if Sims had held it in trust for him absolutely. The undertaking would have ensured that Twinsectra could get it back. It follows that Sims held the money in trust for Twinsectra, but subject to a power to apply it by way of loan to Mr Yardley in accordance with the undertaking. No doubt Sims also owed fiduciary obligations to Mr Yardley in respect of the exercise of the power, but we need not concern ourselves with those obligations because in fact the money was applied wholly for Mr Yardley's benefit.

Such an express trust is factually similar to the resulting trust favoured by Lord Millett: under both approaches, the beneficial interest remains in the lender. Often, the dividing line between relying on express intentions and presumed or inferred intentions will be very thin, and not much may turn on the

---

[206] [2004] UKPC 13, [41].
[207] *Twinsectra Ltd v Yardley* [2002] UKHL 12; [2002] 2 AC 164, [12]–[13].

distinction.[208] However, it may be more satisfactory to point to a settlor's express intention in order to justify the lender's having priority over other unsecured creditors in the event of the borrower's insolvency. But for an express trust to be found, there must be sufficient certainty of intention to create a trust, and it should be noted that a consequence of this analysis is that the lender would be able to compel the use of the money for the promised purpose, or to revoke the loan and require payment immediately even though the purpose was still capable of being fulfilled, or even to require the borrower to use the money for another purpose, which might seem inconsistent with the nature of what has commonly been understood as a *Quistclose* trust. This solution is, therefore, not free from difficulty. As Payne has remarked, when considering whether this approach could explain *Quistclose* itself:[209]

> [If] the lender takes a full beneficial interest in the trust property from the start then Quistclose ought to be able to wield all of the rights normally attached to full beneficial ownership (held by a person of full age and sound mind and so on) such as the right to compel Rolls Razor to use the money for the payment of the dividend, or to revoke the loan and require immediate repayment of the money, to prevent the payment of the dividend by Rolls Razor to the shareholders while the purpose remains capable of fulfilment, or to require the borrower to use the money for some other purpose. Quistclose does not seem to have had these rights.

Although Quistclose might not appear to have had those rights, it might not be improper for them to enjoy such rights,[210] particularly if there was sufficient certainty of intention for an express trust to arise: such an express trust should not operate differently from other express trusts simply because it falls within the broad umbrella of the *Quistclose* fact-pattern. But if there is no such express intention to create a trust, then it may be that there is only a personal, contractual relationship between the parties and no trust relationship at all, unless some sort of resulting trust can be found.

(c) SUMMARY

In *Bieber v Teathers Ltd (In Liquidation)*,[211] questions again arose concerning the *Quistclose* trust. In the Court of Appeal, Patten LJ rightly emphasized that the structure of the parties' arrangements and the contractual mechanisms involved needed to be examined closely. His Lordship also accepted the utility of the summary of the key principles underpinning the current state of law regarding the *Quistclose* trust, which was provided by Norris J at first instance:[212]

> First, the question in every case is whether the payer and the recipient intended that the money passing between them was to be at the free disposal of the recipient: *Re Goldcorp Exchange* [1995] 1 AC 74 and *Twinsectra* at [74].
>
> Second, the mere fact that the payer has paid the money to the recipient for the recipient to use it in a particular way is not of itself enough. The recipient may have represented or warranted that he intends to use it in a particular way or have promised to use it in a particular way. Such an arrangement would give rise to personal obligations but would not of itself necessarily create fiduciary obligations or a trust: *Twinsectra* at [73].

---

[208] Although if the property concerned is land, only an express trust would require signed writing: see LPA 1925 s. 53(1)(b) and (2).

[209] 'Quistclose and Resulting Trusts' *Restitution and Equity, Volume 1: Resulting Trusts and Equitable Compensation* (eds Birks and Rose) (Oxford: Mansfield Press, 2000), p. 89.

[210] And presumably the lender would have such rights under a resulting trust as well.

[211] [2012] EWCA Civ 1466; [2013] 1 BCLC 248.

[212] [2012] EWHC 190 (Ch); 14 ITELR 814, [16]–[23], cited at [2012] EWCA Civ 1466, [14].

So, thirdly, it must be clear from the express terms of the transaction (properly construed) or must be objectively ascertained from the circumstances of the transaction that the mutual intention of payer and recipient (and the essence of their bargain) is that the funds transferred should not be part of the general assets of the recipient but should be used exclusively to effect particular identified payments, so that if the money cannot be so used then it is to be returned to the payer: *Toovey v Milne* (1819) 2 B&A 683 and *Quistclose Investments* at 580B.

Fourth, the mechanism by which this is achieved is a trust giving rise to fiduciary obligations on the part of the recipient which a court of equity will enforce: *Twinsectra* at [69]. Equity intervenes because it is unconscionable for the recipient to obtain money on terms as to its application and then to disregard the terms on which he received it from a payer who had placed trust and confidence in the recipient to ensure the proper application of the money paid: *Twinsectra* at [76].

Fifth, such a trust is akin to a 'retention of title' clause, enabling the recipient to have recourse to the payer's money for the particular purpose specified but without entrenching on the payer's property rights more than necessary to enable the purpose to be achieved. It is not as such a 'purpose' trust of which the recipient is a trustee, the beneficial interest in the money reverting to the payer if the purpose is incapable of achievement. It is a resulting trust in favour of the payer with a mandate granted to the recipient to apply the money paid for the purpose stated. The key feature of the arrangement is that the recipient is precluded from misapplying the money paid to him. The recipient has no beneficial interest in the money: generally the beneficial interest remains vested in the payer subject only to the recipient's power to apply the money in accordance with the stated purpose. If the stated purpose cannot be achieved then the mandate ceases to be effective, the recipient simply holds the money paid on resulting trust for the payer, and the recipient must repay it: *Twinsectra* at [81], [87], [92] and [100].

Sixth, the subjective intentions of payer and recipient as to the creation of a trust are irrelevant. If the properly construed terms upon which (or the objectively ascertained circumstances in which) payer and recipient enter into an arrangement have the effect of creating a trust, then it is not necessary that either payer or recipient should intend to create a trust: it is sufficient that they intend to enter into the relevant arrangement: *Twinsectra* at [71].

Seventh, the particular purpose must be specified in terms which enable a court to say whether a given application of the money does or does not fall within its terms: *Twinsectra* at [16].

It is in my judgment implicit in the doctrine so described in the authorities that the specified purpose is fulfilled by and at the time of the application of the money. The payer, the recipient and the ultimate beneficiary of the payment (that is, the person who benefits from the application by the recipient of the money for the particular purpose) need to know whether property has passed.

QUESTION

Fred was worried about being sued by his creditors. In order to hide his assets, he transferred his shares in Company First Ltd to his son, Steve, and gave his holiday home to his brother, Bob. Both Steve and Bob knew why Fred was giving them the shares and house. Fred's creditors are no longer looking into his affairs, but neither Steve nor Bob are willing to transfer the property back to Fred.

Fortified by the transfer of shares to his name, Steve loaned money to his sister's struggling business, Flower Power Ltd, in order to enable her to pay dividends to her shareholders. Flower Power Ltd became insolvent before the dividends were paid.

Advise Steve and Bob.

FURTHER READING

Birks, 'Restitution and Resulting Trusts' in *Equity: Contemporary Legal Developments* (ed. Goldstein) (Jerusalem: Hebrew University of Jerusalem, 1992).

Chambers, *Resulting Trusts* (Oxford: Clarendon Press, 1997), especially chapters 1–2.

Chambers, 'Is There a Presumption of Resulting Trust?', in *Constructive and Resulting Trusts* (ed. Mitchell) (Oxford: Hart, 2010).

Jones, 'Uses and "Automatic" Resulting Trusts of Freehold' [2013] CLJ 91.

Mee, '"Automatic" Resulting Trusts: Retention, Restitution, or Reposing Trust?' in *Constructive and Resulting Trusts* (ed. Mitchell) (Oxford: Hart, 2010).

Mee, 'Presumed Resulting Trusts, Intention and Declaration' [2014] CLJ 86.

Penner, 'Resulting Trusts and Unjust Enrichment: Three Controversies', in *Constructive and Resulting Trusts* (ed. Mitchell) (Oxford: Hart, 2010).

Rickett and Grantham, 'Resulting Trusts: A Rather Limited Doctrine', in *Restitution and Equity, Vol. 1* (eds Birks and Rose) (Oxford: Mansfield Press, 2000).

Swadling, 'A New Role for Resulting Trusts?' (1996) LS 110.

Swadling, 'Orthodoxy', in *The Quistclose Trust; Critical Essays* (ed. Swadling) (Oxford: Hart, 2004).

Swadling, 'Explaining Resulting Trusts' (2008) 124 LQR 72.

9

INFORMAL ARRANGEMENTS
RELATING TO LAND

CENTRAL ISSUES

1. Property transactions relating to land which fail to comply with statutory formality requirements may be rendered effective by various equitable mechanisms.

2. Where property is registered in the name of one party, another party may have an equitable interest in the property where there is a common intention that the other party should have such an interest.

3. Where property is registered in the name of two parties, it will be presumed that they have a joint beneficial interest in the property. This presumption will be rebutted by a common intention that the beneficial interest should be different.

4. Where two parties have entered into a joint venture involving the acquisition of

property by one of them, that party may be required to hold the property on constructive trust for both of them if it is unconscionable for the party acquiring the property to deny that the other has any beneficial interest in the property.

5. Where the defendant has made a representation to the claimant that the claimant will acquire an interest in specified property, and the claimant has detrimentally relied on that representation, one response of Equity is that the court may, in the exercise of its discretion, determine that the defendant holds the property on trust for the claimant. This involves the creation of an equitable proprietary right by means of the doctrine of proprietary estoppel.

---

1. GENERAL CONSIDERATIONS

(a) FORMALITIES

Trusts of land must be evidenced by signed writing to be enforceable.[1] There are also other formality requirements relating to the disposition of land.

---

[1] Law of Property Act 1925, s. 53(1)(b). See Chapter 4.2(b), p. 120.

Law of Property (Miscellaneous Provisions) Act 1989

2. Contracts for sale etc. of land to be made by signed writing.

(1) A contract for the sale or other disposition of an interest in land can only be made in writing and only by incorporating all the terms which the parties have expressly agreed in one document or, where contracts are exchanged, in each.

(2) The terms may be incorporated in a document either by being set out in it or by reference to some other document.

(3) The document incorporating the terms or, where contracts are exchanged, one of the documents incorporating them (but not necessarily the same one) must be signed by or on behalf of each party to the contract.

It follows that oral contracts for the sale of land are void.

Where parties have entered into informal arrangements relating to land, Equity may have a role to play in rendering the transaction effective. This has been recognized explicitly by statute, since the formality requirements for the creation of trusts of land[2] and contracts for the sale of land[3] do not apply to the creation or operation of resulting, constructive, or implied trusts. Consequently, these trusts have a significant role to play in validating informal arrangements relating to land, as does the doctrine of proprietary estoppel. The use of such equitable doctrines to validate informal property transactions is, however, controversial. For example, as regards estoppel, Dixon has said:[4]

> If statute requires the claimant's alleged property right to have been created with a certain type of formality, why, in the absence of such formality, can the claimant run to the back door, break in using estoppel as a jemmy, and run off with some or all of the landowner's proprietary valuables?

This is an important question, which is equally applicable to the role of trusts in this area. There is a tension between required formalities and considerations of fairness, which will be apparent throughout this chapter.

(b) EQUITABLE INTERVENTION

Difficult issues arising from informal property arrangements typically occur where property is purchased by a couple and is registered in the name of one of them only, even though they both contribute to the purchase price, either directly by payment to the vendor or indirectly by making mortgage payments. Similar problems arise where the property is registered in their joint names, but they have made different financial contributions to its purchase. In either situation, issues will arise concerning the identification of each party's rights in the property if the relationship breaks down. If the couple are married, their rights will be determined by the court's discretionary powers to grant ancillary relief.[5]

---

[2] Ibid, s. 53(2).

[3] Law of Property (Miscellaneous Provisions) Act 1989, s. 2(5).

[4] 'Confining and Defining Proprietary Estoppels: The Role of Unconscionability' (2010) 30 LS 408, 409.

[5] By virtue of the Matrimonial Causes Act 1973. A similar scheme applies for civil partners under the Civil Partnership Act 2004, Sched. 5, and marriage of same-sex couples: Marriage (Same Sex Couples) Act 2013, s. 11. Note the continuing role of the resulting trust where the parties are married: *Prest v Petrodel Resources Ltd* [2013] UKSC 34; [2013] 2 AC 415. See Chapter 8.2(b), p. 368.

But if they are unmarried, there is no statutory jurisdiction to determine their property rights. This is where Equity may have a significant role to play in determining their proprietary interests. There are six different equitable mechanisms which may assist in the determination of these interests.

(i) *Express trust*

Where land has been registered at law in the name of one or both of the parties, the beneficial interests in that property may have been determined by an express declaration of trust.[6] Such a trust will need to be evidenced in signed writing to be enforceable.[7] But, where the relationship between the parties is domestic rather than commercial, it is unlikely that they will have considered what their respective beneficial interests in the property might be, let alone prepared any written document to identify those interests. Consequently, resulting and constructive trusts are likely to be much more significant in determining what their beneficial interests are, since they do not need to be evidenced in writing.[8]

(ii) *The resulting trust*

A resulting trust may arise where one party has contributed to the purchase price of property that is registered in the name of another,[9] since it will be presumed that the payer intended the property to be held by the other party on trust for him or her. The payer's beneficial interest will be limited to the value of his or her financial contribution. The resulting trust cannot reflect other contributions, whether they are indirect financial contributions to the mortgage or non-financial contributions relating to the running of the home.[10] It has been recognized, at least in the context of a cohabiting couple who purchase a property in their joint names for their joint occupation, that the resulting trust will have no role to play in determining their beneficial interests in the family home, regardless of whether they have made a financial contribution to the acquisition of the property.[11] This is partly justified for policy reasons, since inflation in property prices means that the division of property with reference to initial financial contributions would produce an unjust result.[12]

It was, however, recognized in *Prest v Petrodel Resources Ltd*[13] that, where the home of a married couple was transferred to a company, it was appropriate to infer that the property was held on resulting trust for the spouse who owned and controlled the company. Lord Sumption said:[14]

> Whether assets legally vested in a company are beneficially owned by its controller is a highly fact-specific issue. It is not possible to give general guidance going beyond the ordinary principles and presumptions of equity, especially those relating to gifts and resulting trusts. But I venture to suggest, however tentatively, that in the case of the matrimonial home, the facts are quite likely to justify the inference that the property was held on trust for a spouse who owned and controlled the company. In many, perhaps most cases, the occupation of the company's property as the

---

[6] *Stack v Dowden* [2007] UKHL 17; [2007] 2 AC 432, [49] (Lady Hale).
[7] Law of Property Act 1925, s. 53(1)(b).
[8] Ibid, s. 53(2).
[9] See Chapter 8.2(b), pp. 366–8.
[10] *Gissing v Gissing* [1971] AC 886.
[11] *Jones v Kernott* [2011] UKSC 53; [2012] 1 AC 776, [53] (Lady Hale and Lord Walker).
[12] Ibid, [56] (Lord Collins).
[13] [2013] UKSC 34; [2013] 2 AC 415.
[14] Ibid, [52].

matrimonial home of its controller will not be easily justified in the company's interest, especially if it is gratuitous. The intention will normally be that the spouse in control of the company intends to retain a degree of control over the matrimonial home which is not consistent with the company's beneficial ownership. Of course, structures can be devised which give a different impression, and some of them will be entirely genuine. But where, say, the terms of acquisition and occupation of the matrimonial home are arranged between the husband in his personal capacity and the husband in his capacity as the sole effective agent of the company (or someone else acting at his direction), judges exercising family jurisdiction are entitled to be sceptical about whether the terms of occupation are really what they are said to be, or are simply a sham to conceal the reality of the husband's beneficial ownership.

In that case it followed that properties in which the husband had a beneficial interest could be transferred to the wife as part of a divorce settlement.

(iii) *The remedial constructive trust*

At one time, a constructive trust of the home was recognized simply on the grounds of justice and good conscience;[15] this can be characterized as a remedial constructive trust.[16] Such a trust was subsequently rejected[17] on the ground that the recognition of interests in property needs to be principled and not simply determined by reference to the exercise of judicial discretion. The remedial constructive trust has, anyway, been rejected in English law.[18]

(iv) *The institutional constructive trust*

An institutional constructive trust, which arises by operation of law where the defendant acted unconscionably,[19] may be relevant where the property has been acquired by one party and another asserts a beneficial interest in it. This is particularly significant in the commercial context, where the property has been acquired to be developed by both parties as a joint venture and the defendant who has legal title to it wishes to exclude the other from the arrangement.[20]

(v) *The common intention constructive trust*

The trust that has been of particular significance in determining beneficial interests in the family home has been the so-called 'common intention constructive trust'. This arises from an agreement or understanding of the parties as to beneficial interests in the property and what the extent of those interests might be. Being a constructive trust, the agreement or understanding is enforceable even though it is not evidenced by signed writing. Since, however, the trust is constructed by reference to the parties' common intentions rather than unconscionable conduct, this trust is distinct from an institutional constructive trust. It is preferably analysed as an implied trust.[21]

---

[15] *Heseltine v Heseltine* [1971] 1 WLR 342; *Hussey v Palmer* [1972] 1 WLR 1286; *Eves v Eves* [1975] 1 WLR 1338.
[16] See Chapter 7.3, pp. 355–8.
[17] See *Burns v Burns* [1984] Ch 317, 342 (May LJ); *Stack v Dowden* [2007] UKHL 17; [2007] 2 AC 432.
[18] *FHR European Ventures LLP v Cedar Capital Partners LLC* [2014] UKSC 45; [2015] AC 250. See Chapter 7.3, pp. 355–8.
[19] *Stack v Dowden* [2007] UKHL 17; [2007] 2 AC 432, [128] (Lord Neuberger).
[20] See Chapter 9.3, pp. 462–9.
[21] *Jones v Kernott* [2011] UKSC 53; [2012] 1 AC 776, [17] (Lady Hale and Lord Walker).

(vi) *Proprietary estoppel*

This is another equitable doctrine, which may be relevant to identify a beneficial interest in property owned at Law by another party. The essence of this doctrine is that, where the claimant has relied, to his or her detriment, on an assurance from the defendant that the claimant will acquire an interest in the defendant's property, the court may recognize that the claimant has a beneficial interest in that property.

2. COMMON INTENTION CONSTRUCTIVE TRUSTS

(a) THE BACKGROUND

The common intention constructive trust has proved to be especially significant in determining the beneficial interests in a house bought by a cohabiting couple as the family home. If their relationship ends it will be necessary to consider the extent of their respective interests in the property. If there has been an express declaration of trust in writing, this will be straightforward, but in most cases this will not have occurred and so the common intention constructive trust will become relevant.

The reasons why there are particularly acute difficulties in dealing with the problems arising from the breakdown of an unmarried couple's relationship were identified by Lord Collins in *Jones v Kernott* as relating to:[22]

> the increasing number of cohabiting couples with joint interests in their homes, and to the fact that couples (whether married or unmarried) rarely make agreements about their respective shares in their homes, and to the enormous inflation in property prices which has made the division of ownership by reference to initial financial contributions artificial and potentially productive of injustice.

The origins of the common intention constructive trust can be traced back to the decisions of the House of Lords in *Pettit v Pettit*[23] and *Gissing v Gissing*.[24] The requirements of the common intention constructive trust were identified by Lord Bridge in *Lloyds Bank plc v Rosset*, a case where the property had been registered in the name of one of the parties only.

Lloyds Bank plc v Rosset [1991] 1 AC 107, 132 (Lord Bridge)

> The first and fundamental question which must always be resolved is whether, independently of any inference to be drawn from the conduct of the parties in the course of sharing the house as their home and managing the joint affairs, there has at any time prior to acquisition, or exceptionally at some later date, been any agreement, arrangement or understanding reached between them that the property is to be shared beneficially. The finding of an agreement or arrangement to share in this sense can only, I think, be based on evidence of express discussions between partners, however imperfectly remembered and however imprecise their terms may have been. Once a finding to this effect is made it will only be necessary for the partner asserting a claim to a beneficial interest against the partner entitled to the legal estate to show that he or she has acted to his or her detriment or significantly altered his or her position in reliance on the agreement in order to give rise to a constructive trust or proprietary estoppel.
>
> In sharp contrast with this situation is the very different one where there is no evidence to support a finding of an agreement or arrangement to share, however reasonable it might have been for the parties

---

[22] Ibid, at [56].
[23] [1970] AC 777.
[24] [1971] AC 886.

to reach such an arrangement if they had applied their minds to the question, and where the court must rely entirely on the conduct of the parties both as the basis from which to infer a common intention to share the property beneficially and as the conduct relied on to give rise to a constructive trust. In this situation direct contributions to the purchase price by the partner who is not the legal owner, whether initially or by payment of mortgage instalments, will readily justify the inference necessary to the creation of a constructive trust. But, as I read the authorities, it is at least extremely doubtful whether anything less will do.

The leading cases in your Lordships' House are *Pettitt v Pettitt* [1970] AC 777 and *Gissing v Gissing* [1971] AC 886. Both demonstrate situations in the second category to which I have referred and their Lordships discuss at great length the difficulties to which these situations give rise...

Outstanding examples on the other hand of cases giving rise to situations in the first category are *Eves v Eves* [1975] 1 WLR 1338 and *Grant v Edwards* [1986] Ch 638. In both these cases, where the parties who had cohabited were unmarried, the female partner had been clearly led by the male partner to believe, when they set up home together, that the property would belong to them jointly. In *Eves v Eves* the male partner had told the female partner that the only reason why the property was to be acquired in his name alone was because she was under 21 and that, but for her age, he would have had the house put into their joint names. He admitted in evidence that this was simply an 'excuse'. Similarly, in *Grant v Edwards* the female partner was told by the male partner that the only reason for not acquiring the property in joint names was because she was involved in divorce proceedings and that, if the property were acquired jointly, this might operate to her prejudice in those proceedings. As Nourse LJ put it [1986] Ch 638 at 649:

'Just as in *Eves v Eves*, these facts appear to me to raise a clear inference that there was an understanding between plaintiff and defendant, or a common intention, that the plaintiff was to have some sort of proprietary interest in the house; otherwise no excuse for not putting her name onto the title would have been needed.'

The subsequent conduct of the female partner in each of these cases, which the court rightly held sufficient to give rise to a constructive trust or proprietary estoppel supporting her claim to an interest in the property, fell far short of such conduct as would by itself have supported the claim in the absence of an express representation by the male partner that she was to have such an interest. It is significant to note that the share to which the female partners in *Eves v Eves* and *Grant v Edwards* were held entitled were one-quarter and one-half respectively. In no sense could these shares have been regarded as proportionate to what the judge in the instant case described as a 'qualifying contribution' in terms of the indirect contributions to the acquisition or enhancement of the value of the houses made by the female partners.

Where there was an express common intention to share the beneficial interest, it was the claimant's detrimental reliance on that intention that was considered to make it unconscionable for the defendant to deny the claimant's beneficial interest in the property. The alternative approach, of inferring a common intention from contributions to the purchase price, was criticized because it failed to take into account non-financial contributions, such as to the running of the home. In *Stack v Dowden*, Lady Hale said:[25]

There is undoubtedly an argument for saying, as did the Law Commission in *Sharing Homes, A Discussion Paper*, [2002, No. 278] para 4.23, that the observations, which were strictly *obiter dicta*, of Lord Bridge of Harwich in *Lloyd's Bank plc v Rossett* [1991] 1 AC 107 have set that hurdle rather too high in certain respects.

[25] [2007] UKHL 17; [2007] 2 AC 432, [63].

In the absence of any express evidence of a common intention, there was a tendency for the courts to determine the extent of the claimant's beneficial interest by reference to what the court considered to be fair in the light of the whole course of dealing between the parties in relation to the property. In *Oxley v Hiscock*, Chadwick LJ said:[26]

> But, in a case where there is no evidence of any discussion between [the parties] as to the amount of the share which each was to have—and even in a case where the evidence is that there was no discussion on that point—the question still requires an answer. It must now be accepted that (at least in this court and below) the answer is that each is entitled to that share which the court considers fair having regard to the whole course of dealing between them in relation to the property. And, in that context, 'the whole course of dealing between them in relation to the property' includes the arrangements which they make from time to time in order to meet the outgoings (for example, mortgage contributions, council tax and utilities, repairs, insurance and housekeeping) which have to be met if they are to live in the property as their home.

This came very close to resurrecting the discredited remedial constructive trust solution.[27]

The House of Lords reconsidered the requirements for the common intention constructive trust in *Stack v Dowden*.[28] Whilst purporting to build on the old authorities, this decision has put this trust on a new footing, such that the requirements should be considered to derive from that decision and subsequent authorities.[29] All five judges in *Stack v Dowden* gave reasoned judgments, but the leading judgment was that of Lady Hale, with which three of the other judges agreed. Although Lord Neuberger agreed with the result, he adopted very different reasoning.[30] The decision in *Stack v Dowden* was subsequently clarified by the Supreme Court in *Jones v Kernott*.[31]

(b) THE KEY PRINCIPLES

When determining the nature and extent of the beneficial interests of a cohabiting couple in the family home, the relevant principles are as follows.

(i) *Express declaration of trust*

Regardless of whether the property has been conveyed into the names of one party or both of them, the beneficial interest may have been allocated by the parties expressly in writing, so that it will be held on an express trust.[32] In *Pankhania v Chandegra*,[33] Mummery LJ recognized that:

> reliance on *Stack v Dowden* and *Jones v Kernott* for inferring or imputing a different trust in this and other similar cases which have recently been before this court is misplaced where there is an express declaration of trust of the beneficial title and no valid legal grounds for going behind it.

---

[26] [2004] EWCA Civ 546; [2005] Fam 211, [69].
[27] See Chapter 9.1(b)(iii), p. 431.
[28] [2007] UKHL 17; [2007] 2 AC 432.
[29] Cf Sloan, 'Keeping up with the *Jones* case: establishing constructive trusts in the sole legal owner scenarios' (2015) 35 LS 226, 251 who argues that there is still a need for a Supreme Court decision to determine whether the law of common intention constructive trusts is finally liberated from the *Rossett* criteria. Whilst technically correct, the pronouncements of judges at all levels assumes that those criteria no longer apply.
[30] See Chapter 9.2(b)(v), pp. 444–6.
[31] [2011] UKSC 53; [2012] 1 AC 776.
[32] *Goodman v Gallant* [1986] Fam 106
[33] [2012] EWCA Civ 1438; [2013] WTLR 101, [28].

(ii) *The presumptions*

Where there is no express trust, it is to be presumed that the beneficial interest in the property mirrors the legal interest. This is consistent with maxim that 'Equity follows the Law'.[34] It follows that it is necessary to distinguish between cases of sole and joint legal ownership.[35]

(1) Where the property is registered in the name of one party only, it is to be presumed that that party has the sole beneficial interest in the property and the other party has none.[36] In *Thompson v Hurst*[37] Etherton LJ said:

> The transfer was not in fact into the joint names of the appellant and the respondent. There is, therefore, no scope for a legal presumption that the parties intended a joint tenancy both in law and equity. [Counsel's] argument amounts to a submission that there should be a legal presumption of joint beneficial ownership, not merely where the parties are indeed the joint legal owners, but where there is evidence that they would have liked to be joint legal owners but for one reason or another that was not practical or desirable. Neither *Stack* [v *Dowden*] nor *Jones* [v *Kernott*], nor any other case, is authority for such a proposition. Indeed, the proposition is neither consistent with principle nor sound policy.

Although there might have been a continuing role for a resulting trust to be presumed where the property has been registered in the name of one party only and the other has contributed to the purchase price,[38] the Privy Council in *Abbott v Abbott*[39] rejected the resulting trust even in that context, because the law has moved on in response to changing social and economic conditions.[40] It has been recognized by the Singapore Court of Appeal that the constructive trust was developed 'to mitigate the arithmetic rigour of the resulting trust when ascertaining property rights upon the breakdown of a relationship in the domestic context.'[41]

(2) Where the property is registered in the names of both parties, they both have a beneficial interest in it and it is presumed that their beneficial interests are divided equally. As Lord Neuberger said in *Stack v Dowden*:[42]

> In the absence of any relevant evidence other than the fact that the property, whether a house or a flat, acquired as a home for the legal co-owners is in joint names, the beneficial ownership will also be joint, so that it is held in equal shares. This can be said to result from the maxims that equity follows the law and equality is equity. On a less technical, and some might say more practical, approach, it can also be justified on the basis that any other solution would be arbitrary or capricious.

This has been described as the 'default option'.[43] There is no need to prove any financial contribution to the acquisition of the property for a beneficial interest to be presumed, since this simply follows from the property being conveyed into the names of both parties. It follows that this has nothing to do with the presumption of a resulting trust, since that presumption depends on a party contributing to

---

[34] See Chapter 1.5(d), p. 19.
[35] *Jones v Kernott* [2011] UKSC 53; [2012] 1 AC 776, [16] (Lady Hale and Lord Walker), [68] (Lord Kerr).
[36] *Graham-York v York* [2015] EWCA Civ 72, [25] (Tomlinson LJ).
[37] *Thompson v Hurst* [2012] EWCA Civ 1752; [2014] 1 FLR 238, [20].
[38] *Stack v Dowden* [2007] UKHL 17; [2007] 2 AC 432, [114] (Lord Neuberger).
[39] [2007] UKPC 53; [2008] 1 FLR 1451.
[40] See also *Stack v Dowden* [2007] UKHL 17; [2007] 2 AC 432, [60] (Lady Hale).
[41] *Chan Yuen Lan v See Fong Mun* [2014] SGCA 36, [95] (Rajah JA).
[42] [2007] UKHL 17; [2007] 2 AC 432, [109].
[43] *Jones v Kernott* [2011] UKSC 53; [2012] 1 AC 776, [15] (Lady Hale and Lord Walker).

the purchase price of the property.[44] It has, however, been recognized that where the cohabiting couple are also business partners there may still be a role for the presumption of resulting trust to operate.[45]

(iii) *The presumptions are rebuttable*

Both presumptions can be rebutted. In *Stack v Dowden*[46] Lady Hale said:

> The onus is upon the person seeking to show that the beneficial ownership is different from the legal ownership. So in sole ownership cases it is upon the non-owner to show that he has any interest at all. In joint ownership cases, it is upon the joint owner who claims to have other than a joint beneficial interest.

(1) Where the property is registered in the name of one party only, the other will first need to establish that there was a common intention that he or she was intended to have a beneficial interest in the property and, having done so, what proportion of the beneficial interest he or she was intended to have. In *Capehorn v Harris*,[47] Sales LJ said:

> In relation to assets acquired by unmarried co-habitees or partners, where an asset is owned in law by one person but another claims to share a beneficial interest in it a two-stage analysis is called for to determine whether a common intention constructive trust arises. First, the person claiming the beneficial interest must show that there was an agreement that he should have a beneficial interest in the property owned by his partner even if there was no agreement as to the precise extent of that interest. Secondly, if such an agreement can be shown to have been made, then absent agreement on the extent of the interest, the court may impute an intention that the person was to have a fair beneficial share in the asset and may assess the quantum of the fair share in the light of all the circumstances...
>
> There is an important difference between the approach applicable at each stage. At the first stage, an actual agreement has to be found to have been made, which may be inferred from conduct in an appropriate case. At the second stage, the court is entitled to impute an intention that each person is entitled to the share which the court considers fair having regard to the whole course of dealing between them in relation to the property. A court is not entitled to impute an intention to the parties at the first stage in the analysis.

The burden of proving a beneficial interest is a heavy one,[48] and does not involve questions of fairness; that is relevant to the second stage where the beneficial interest is quantified. It is, however, necessary to show that the claimant detrimentally relied on the common intention that he or she would have an interest in the property. This was recognized by Lewison LJ in *Curran v Collins*:[49]

> The need for detrimental reliance on the part of the claimant is an essential feature of this kind of case. Browne-Wilkinson V-C put it clearly in *Grant v Edwards*:[50]
>
> > 'If the legal estate in the joint home is vested in only one of the parties ("the legal owner") the other party ("the claimant"), in order to establish a beneficial interest, has to establish a constructive trust by showing that it would be inequitable for the legal owner to claim sole

---

[44] Ibid, [53]; (Lady Hale and Lord Walker).

[45] *Geary v Rankine* [2012] EWCA Civ 555; [2012] 2 FLR 1409, [18] (Lewison LJ).

[46] [2007] UKHL 17; [2007] 2 AC 432, [56].

[47] [2015] EWCA Civ 955; [2015] Fam Law 1347, [16].

[48] More so where the property is purchased as an investment rather than a home: *Geary v Rankine* [2012] EWCA Civ 555; [2012] 2 FLR 1409, [18] (Lewison LJ).

[49] [2015] EWCA Civ 404; [2015] Fam Law 780, [77].

[50] [1986] Ch 638, 654.

> beneficial ownership. This requires two matters to be demonstrated: (a) that there was a common intention that both should have a beneficial interest; (b) that the claimant has acted to his or her detriment on the basis of that common intention.'

This emphasis on the need for detrimental reliance has been justified by Sloan:[51]

> Detrimental reliance by the claimant was also traditionally required for a constructive trust. While this was not expressly mentioned either by the House of Lords in *Stack v Dowden*...or the Supreme Court in *Jones*, it would be difficult to justify the intervention of equity in the absence of reliance due to the need for some form of unconscionability. It must surely be a vital factor in the court's evaluation of what is 'fair' when imputing a common intention to the parties during the process of quantifying the extent of a party's interest under a constructive trust.

(2) Where the property is registered in the names of both parties, the party who claims that the beneficial interest is apportioned otherwise than equally bears the burden of proving that a different apportionment was intended. But the presumption of equal beneficial ownership is not rebutted easily. In *Jones v Kernott*,[52] Lady Hale and Lord Walker said:

> a challenge to the presumption of beneficial joint tenancy is not to be lightly embarked on...If a couple in an intimate relationship (whether married or unmarried) decide to buy a house or flat in which to live together, almost always with the help of a mortgage for which they are jointly and severally liable, that is on the face of things a strong indication of emotional and economic commitment to a joint enterprise. That is so even if the parties, for whatever reason, fail to make that clear by any overt declaration or agreement.

The existence of this joint enterprise strongly supports the presumption of equal beneficial interests in the property.

(iv) *Rebutting the presumptions*

The test for rebutting the presumptions relates to the identification of the common intention of the parties as to whether a party has a beneficial interest and, if he or she does, what the size of that interest is. This common intention was described by Lady Hale in *Stack v Dowden*[53] as follows:

> The law has indeed moved on in response to changing social and economic conditions. The search is to ascertain the parties' shared intentions, actual, inferred or imputed, with respect to the property in the light of their whole course of conduct in relation to it...
>
> The view of the Law Commission in *Sharing Homes* (2002, No. 278, para 4.27) on the quantification of beneficial entitlement [is]:
>
>> 'If the question really is one of the parties' "common intention", we believe that there is much to be said for adopting what has been called a "holistic approach" to quantification, undertaking a survey of the whole course of dealing between the parties and taking account of all conduct which throws light on the question what shares were intended.'

---

[51] Sloan, 'Keeping up with the *Jones* Case' (2015) 35 LS 226, 228.
[52] [2011] UKSC 53; [2012] 1 AC 776, [19].
[53] [2007] UKHL 17; [2007] AC 432, [59].

That may be the preferable way of expressing what is essentially the same thought, for two reasons. First, it emphasises that the search is still for the result which reflects what the parties must, in the light of their conduct, be taken to have intended. Second, therefore, it does not enable the court to abandon that search in favour of the result which the court itself considers fair.

(a) Relevant factors

The following factors were identified by Lady Hale in *Stack v Dowden* as being significant when determining whether the presumptions had been rebutted:[54]

In law, 'context is everything' and the domestic context is very different from the commercial world. Each case will turn on its own facts. Many more factors than financial contributions may be relevant to divining the parties' true intentions. These include: any advice or discussions at the time of the transfer which cast light upon their intentions then; the reasons why the home was acquired in their joint names; the reasons why (if it be the case) the survivor was authorised to give a receipt for the capital moneys; the purpose for which the home was acquired; the nature of the parties' relationship; whether they had children for whom they both had responsibility to provide a home; how the purchase was financed, both initially and subsequently; how the parties arranged their finances, whether separately or together or a bit of both; how they discharged the outgoings on the property and their other household expenses. When a couple are joint owners of the home and jointly liable for the mortgage, the inferences to be drawn from who pays for what may be very different from the inferences to be drawn when only one is owner of the home. The arithmetical calculation of how much was paid by each is also likely to be less important. It will be easier to draw the inference that they intended that each should contribute as much to the household as they reasonably could and that they would share the eventual benefit or burden equally. The parties' individual characters and personalities may also be a factor in deciding where their true intentions lay. In the cohabitation context, mercenary considerations may be more to the fore than they would be in marriage, but it should not be assumed that they always take pride of place over natural love and affection. At the end of the day, having taken all this into account, cases in which the joint legal owners are to be taken to have intended that their beneficial interests should be different from their legal interests will be very unusual.

This is not, of course, an exhaustive list. There may also be reason to conclude that, whatever the parties' intentions at the outset, these have now changed. An example might be where one party has financed (or constructed himself) an extension or substantial improvement to the property, so that what they have now is significantly different from what they had then.

These factors are very wide and the list provided by Baroness Hale is not exhaustive. It is unclear why some of these factors are relevant in deducing a common intention relating to beneficial interests,[55] such as the fact that the couple have had children. Although the factors purport to be of evidential significance, they could easily become a smokescreen behind which the court can exercise its discretion to determine an allocation of the beneficial interest that is fair and just without reference to principle, even though the court is not meant to reason in this way.[56]

(b) Express common intention

If it can be shown that the parties had an express understanding or agreement as to the apportionment of the beneficial interest in the property, this will rebut the relevant presumption, even though

---

[54] Ibid, [69].
[55] *Stack v Dowden* [2007] UKHL 17; [2007] AC 432, [106] (Lord Neuberger).
[56] See further Chapter 9.2(b)(iv)(d), pp. 441–3.

this apportionment does not correspond with the allocation of legal title to the property and does not comply with the relevant formalities required to create an enforceable express trust. This express common intention will be established on the facts, without the need to consider the factors identified by Lady Hale.

(c) Inferred common intention

If an express common intention as to the allocation of the beneficial interests cannot be established, it is then necessary to consider whether such an intention can be inferred. An inferred intent is an actual intent, albeit one that can be deduced objectively from the parties' conduct.[57] The factors identified by Lady Hale will be of particular significance in inferring a common intention.

(d) Imputed common intention

The most controversial aspect of Lady Hale's analysis of common intention is her acceptance that this intention might be imputed. The difference between inference and imputation of intention was identified by Lord Neuberger in *Stack v Dowden*:[58]

> An imputed intention is one which is attributed to the parties, even though no such actual intention can be deduced from their actions and statements, and even though they had no such intention. Imputation involves concluding what the parties would have intended, whereas inference involves concluding what they did intend.

The process of recognizing an imputed common intention could disintegrate into a determination of an allocation of the beneficial interest that the court considers to be fair. Indeed, Sir Terence Etherton has said that 'there is now a hair's breadth between the [common intention constructive trust]...and a remedial constructive trust'.[59]

The role of imputed intention was criticized by Lord Neuberger, in *Stack v Dowden*:[60]

> While an intention may be inferred as well as express, it may not, at least in my opinion, be imputed. That appears to me to be consistent both with normal principles and with the majority view of this House in *Pettit v Pettit* [1970] AC 777... The distinction between inference and imputation may appear a fine one...but it is important...
>
> I am unhappy with the formulation of Chadwick LJ in *Oxley v Hiscock* [2005] Fam 211 at paragraph 69...that the beneficial ownership should be apportioned by reference to what is 'fair having regard to the whole course of dealing between [the parties] in relation to the property'. First, fairness is not the appropriate yardstick. Secondly, the formulation appears to contemplate an imputed intention. Thirdly, 'the whole course of dealing...in relation to the property' is too imprecise, as it gives insufficient guidance as to what is primarily relevant, namely dealings which cast light on the beneficial ownership of the property, and too limited, as all aspects of the relationship could be relevant in providing the context by reference to which any alleged discussion, statement and actions must be assessed. As already explained, I also disagree with Chadwick LJ's implicit suggestion in the same paragraph that 'the arrangements which [the parties] make with regard to the outgoings' (other than mortgage

---

[57] *Jones v Kernott* [2011] UKSC 53; [2012] 1 AC 776, [51](3) (Lady Hale and Lord Walker). Cp. Lord Wilson at [88]. See further Chapter 9.2(b)(iv)(d), p. 443.

[58] [2007] UKHL 17; [2007] AC 432, [126].

[59] 'Constructive Trusts and Proprietary Estoppel: The Search for Clarity and Principle' [2009] Conv 104, 125.

[60] [2007] UKHL 17; [2007] AC 432, [125].

repayments) are likely to be of primary relevance to the issue of the ownership of the beneficial interest in the home.

I am rather more comfortable with the formulation of the Law Commission in *Sharing Homes, A Discussion Paper* (Law Com. No. 278), para 4.27, also quoted in para 61 of Baroness Hale's opinion, that the court should 'undertak[e] a survey of the whole course of dealing between the parties...taking account of all conduct which throws light on the question what shares were intended'. It is perhaps inevitable that this formulation begs the difficult questions of what conduct throws light, and what light it throws, as those questions are so fact-sensitive. 'Undertaking a survey of the whole course of dealings between the parties' should not, I think, at least normally, require much detailed or controversial evidence. That is not merely for reasons of practicality and certainty. As already indicated, I would expect almost all of 'the whole course of dealing' to be relevant only as background: it is with actions discussions and statements which relate to the parties' agreement and understanding as to the ownership of the beneficial interest in the home with which the court should, at least normally, primarily be concerned. Otherwise, the enquiry is likely to be trespassing into what I regard as the forbidden territories of imputed intention and fairness.

It was because of the continued uncertainty about the difference between inferred and imputed intention that the judges in the Supreme Court reconsidered the principles underlying the common intention constructive trust in *Jones v Kernott*.[61] Lady Hale and Lord Walker said:[62]

It is always salutary to be confronted with the ambiguities which later emerge in what seemed at the time to be comparatively clear language. The primary search must always be for what the parties actually intended, to be deduced objectively from their words and their actions. If that can be discovered, then...it is not open to a court to impose a solution upon them in contradiction to those intentions, merely because the court considers it fair to do so.

The majority in that case, consisting of Lady Hale, Lord Walker, and Lord Collins, considered that the court should primarily be concerned with searching for the parties' actual shared intentions, subject to two exceptions where an intention would be imputed. Lady Hale and Lord Walker, in a joint judgment, said:[63]

we accept that the search is primarily to ascertain the parties' actual shared intentions, whether expressed or to be inferred from their conduct. However, there are at least two exceptions. The first, which is not this case, is where the classic resulting trust presumption applies. Indeed, this would be rare in a domestic context, but might perhaps arise where domestic partners were also business partners...The second, which for reasons which will appear later is in our view also not this case but will arise much more frequently, is where it is clear that the beneficial interests are to be shared, but it is impossible to divine a common intention as to the proportions in which they are to be shared. In those two situations, the court is driven to impute an intention to the parties which they may never have had.

Lord Diplock, in *Gissing v Gissing* [1971] AC 886, 903, pointed out that, once the court was satisfied that it was the parties' common intention that the beneficial interest was to be shared in some proportion or other, the court might have to give effect to that common intention by determining what in all the circumstances was a fair share. And it is that thought which is picked up in the subsequent cases, culminating in the judgment of Chadwick LJ in *Oxley v Hiscock* [2005] Fam 211...in particular the passage in para 69 which was given qualified approval in *Stack v Dowden*: 'the answer is that each is entitled to

[61] [2011] UKSC 53; [2012] 1 AC 776.
[62] Ibid, [46].
[63] Ibid, [31].

that share which the court considers fair having regard to the whole course of dealing between them in relation to the property.'

Chadwick LJ was not there saying that fairness was the criterion for determining whether or not the property should be shared, but he was saying that the court might have to impute an intention to the parties as to the proportions in which the property would be shared. In deducing what the parties, as reasonable people, would have thought at the relevant time, regard would obviously be had to their whole course of dealing in relation to the property.

However, while the conceptual difference between inferring and imputing is clear, the difference in practice may not be so great. In this area, as in many others, the scope for inference is wide. The law recognizes that a legitimate inference may not correspond to an individual's subjective state of mind. As Lord Diplock also put it in *Gissing v Gissing* [1971] AC 886, 906:

'As in so many branches of English law in which legal rights and obligations depend upon the intentions of the parties to a transaction, the relevant intention of each party is the intention which was reasonably understood by the other party to be manifested by that party's words or conduct notwithstanding that he did not consciously formulate that intention in his own mind or even acted with some different intention which he did not communicate to the other party.'

This point has been developed by Nick Piska, 'Intention, Fairness and the Presumption of Resulting Trust after Stack v Dowden' (2008) 71 MLR 120. He observes, at pp 127–128:

'Subjective intentions can never be accessed directly, so the court must always direct itself to a consideration of the parties' objective intentions through a careful consideration of the relevant facts. The point is that the imputation/inference distinction may well be a distinction without a difference with regard to the process of determining parties' intentions. It is not that the parties' subjective intentions are irrelevant but rather that a finding as to subjective intention can only be made on an objective basis.'

Where imputation of an intention is required, the court must consider what is fair having regard to the whole course of dealing in respect of the property,[64] which will include the financial contributions made by the parties but other factors as well, including the factors identified by Lady Hale in *Stack v Dowden*. Crucially, as Lady Hale and Lord Walker recognized:[65]

In a case such as this, where the parties already share the beneficial interest, and the question is what their interests are and whether their interests have changed, the court will try to deduce what their actual intentions were at the relevant time. It cannot impose a solution upon them which is contrary to what the evidence shows that they actually intended. But if it cannot deduce exactly what shares were intended, it may have no alternative but to ask what their intentions as reasonable and just people would have been had they thought about it at the time. This is a fallback position which some courts may not welcome, but the court has a duty to come to a conclusion on the dispute put before it.

The significance of fairness was considered by Tomlinson LJ in *Graham-York v York*,[66] in respect of a claimant who was in a dysfunctional and abusive relationship with her partner:

We are concerned on this appeal with just such a case as envisaged by Lord Walker and Lady Hale in their second exception.[67] It is essential, in my judgment, to bear in mind that, in deciding in such a

---

[64] Ibid, [51](4) (Lady Hale and Lord Walker), [64] (Lord Collins).
[65] Ibid, [47].
[66] [2015] EWCA Civ 72, [22] (Tomlinson LJ).
[67] See Chapter 9.2(b)(iv)(d), p. 440.

case what shares are fair, the court is not concerned with some form of redistributive justice. Thus it is irrelevant that it may be thought a 'fair' outcome for a woman who has endured years of abusive conduct by her partner to be allotted a substantial interest in his property on his death. The plight of Miss Graham-York attracts sympathy, but it does not enable the court to redistribute property interests in a manner which right-minded people might think amounts to appropriate compensation. Miss Graham-York is 'entitled to that share which the court considers fair having regard to the whole course of dealing between them in relation to the property'. It is these last words, which I have emphasised, which supply the confines of the enquiry as to fairness.

But the approach of the majority in *Jones v Kernott* removes any rational difference between inference and imputation. That is why Lords Wilson and Kerr, whilst agreeing with the result in the case, disagreed with the approach of the other three judges. Lord Kerr said:[68]

While it may well be that the outcome in many cases will be the same, whether one infers an intention or imputes it, that does not mean that the process by which the result is arrived at is more or less the same. Indeed, it seems to me that a markedly and obviously different mode of analysis will generally be required...

It is hardly controversial to suggest that the parties' intention should be given effect to where it can be ascertained and that, although discussions between them will always be the most reliable basis on which to draw an inference as to that intention, these are not the only circumstances in which that exercise will be possible. There is a natural inclination to prefer inferring an intention to imputing one. If the parties' intention can be inferred, the court is not imposing a solution. It is, instead, deciding what the parties must be taken to have intended and where that is possible it is obviously preferable to the court's enforcing a resolution. But the conscientious quest to discover the parties' actual intention should cease when it becomes clear either that this is simply not deducible from the evidence or that no common intention exists. It would be unfortunate if the concept of inferring were to be strained so as to avoid the less immediately attractive option of imputation. In summary, therefore, I believe that the court should anxiously examine the circumstances in order, where possible, to ascertain the parties' intention but it should not be reluctant to recognise, when it is appropriate to do so, that inference of an intention is not possible and that imputation of an intention is the only course to follow.

In this context, it is important to understand what is meant by 'imputing an intention'. There are reasons to question the appropriateness of the notion of imputation in this area but, if it is correct to use this as a concept, I strongly favour the way in which it was described by Lord Neuberger in *Stack v Dowden* [2007] 2 AC 431, where he said that an imputed intention was one which was attributed to the parties, even though no such actual intention could be deduced from their actions and statements, and even though they had no such intention. This exposition draws the necessary strong demarcation line between attributing an intention to the parties and inferring what their intention was in fact.

The reason that I question the aptness of the notion of imputing an intention is that, in the final analysis, the exercise is wholly unrelated to ascertainment of the parties' views. It involves the court deciding what is fair in light of the whole course of dealing with the property. That decision has nothing to do with what the parties intended, or what might be supposed would have been their intention had they addressed that question. In many ways, it would be preferable to have a stark choice between deciding whether it is possible to deduce what their intention was and, where it is not, deciding what is fair, without elliptical references to what their intention might have—or should have—been. But imputing intention has entered the lexicon of this area of law and it is probably impossible to discard it now.

---

[68] [2011] UKSC 53; [2012] 1 AC 776, [67].

> While the dichotomy between inferring and imputing an intention remains, however, it seems to me that it is necessary that there be a well marked dividing line between the two. As soon as it is clear that inferring an intention is not possible, the focus of the court's attention should be squarely on what is fair and, as I have said, that is an obviously different examination than is involved in deciding what the parties actually intended.

Similarly, Lord Wilson said:[69]

> In the light of the continued failure of Parliament to confer upon the courts limited redistributive powers in relation to the property of each party upon the breakdown of a non-marital relationship, I warmly applaud the development of the law of equity, spear-headed by Baroness Hale of Richmond and Lord Walker of Gestingthorpe in their speeches in *Stack v Dowden* [2007] 2 AC 432, and reiterated in their judgment in the present appeal, that the common intention which impresses a constructive trust upon the legal ownership of the family home can be imputed to the parties to the relationship...
>
> Where equity is driven to impute the common intention, how can it do so other than by search for the result which the court itself considers fair?

Unlike the majority, the minority considered that the imputation of an intention had nothing to do with what the parties did intend or could be considered to have intended had they thought about it, and the key consideration was simply one of fairness.

The effect of the decision of the majority is that there should be a clear conceptual division between inferring and imputing a common intention. An inferred common intention is an actual intention, which can only be established on the evidence. If such an intention cannot be established then the court should seek to impute an intention.[70] This is an objective test which should be assessed by reference to what reasonable people would have intended had they been in the position of the parties. A wide variety of factors should be considered in establishing this, with reference to the whole course of dealings between the parties. If a common intention cannot be imputed then the relevant presumption, such as a presumption of joint tenancy where the property is registered in both names, will not have been rebutted, so the parties will share the value of the property equally.

(e) Ambulatory intention

The common intention of the parties as to the allocation of the beneficial interest might change over time. This has been called an 'ambulatory intention'. In *Stack v Dowden*[71] Lady Hale said:

> although the parties' intentions may change over the course of time, producing what my noble and learned friend, Lord Hoffmann, referred to in the course of argument as an 'ambulatory' constructive trust, at any one time their interests must be the same for all purposes. They cannot at one and the same time intend, for example, a joint tenancy with survivorship should one of them die while they are still together, a tenancy in common in equal shares should they separate on amicable terms after the children have grown up, and a tenancy in common in unequal shares should they separate on acrimonious terms while the children are still with them.

---

[69] Ibid, [78]

[70] See Pawlowski, 'Imputing a Common Intention in Single Ownership Cases' (2015) TLI 3.

[71] [2007] UKHL 17; [2007] AC 432, [62].

Compelling evidence will be required to establish a change of intention relating to the beneficial ownership. In *Stack v Dowden*[72] Lord Neuberger said:

> It seems to me that 'compelling evidence'...is required before one can infer that, subsequent to the acquisition of the home, the parties intended a change in the shares in which the beneficial ownership is held. Such evidence would normally involve discussions, statements or actions, subsequent to the acquisition, from which an agreement or common understanding as to such a change can properly be inferred.

Relevant evidence might include significant capital expenditure on the property to extend or improve it, or the separation of the parties for a substantial period of time.[73]

(v) A continuing role for the resulting trust?

In *Stack v Dowden*,[74] Lord Neuberger reached the same result as the other judges, but by a different route, which placed more emphasis on the presumption of a resulting trust:

> while the domestic context can give rise to very different factual considerations from the commercial context, I am unconvinced that this justifies a different approach in principle to the issue of the ownership of the beneficial interest in property held in joint names. In the absence of statutory provisions to the contrary, the same principles should apply to assess the apportionment of the beneficial interest as between legal co-owners, whether in a sexual, platonic, familial, amicable or commercial relationship. In each type of case, one is concerned with the issue of the ownership of the beneficial interest in property held in the names of two people, who have contributed to its acquisition, retention or value...
>
> Where the only additional relevant evidence to the fact that the property has been acquired in joint names is the extent of each party's contribution to the purchase price, the beneficial ownership at the time of acquisition will be held, in my view, in the same proportions as the contributions to the purchase price. That is the resulting trust solution. The only realistic alternative in such a case would be to adhere to the joint ownership solution. There is an argument to support the view that equal shares should still be the rule in cohabitation cases, on the basis that it may be what many parties may expect if they purchase a home in joint names, even with different contributions. However, I consider that the resulting trust solution is correct in such circumstances...
>
> There are also practical reasons for rejecting equality and supporting the resulting trust solution. The property may be bought in joint names for reasons which cast no light on the parties' intentions with regard to beneficial ownership. It may be the solicitor's decision or assumption, the lender's preference for the security of two borrowers, or the happenstance of how the initial contact with the solicitor was made...
>
> There is also an important point about consistency of approach with a case where the purchase of a home is in the name of one of the parties. As Baroness Hale observes, where there is no evidence of contributions, joint legal ownership is reflected in a presumption of joint beneficial ownership just as sole legal ownership is reflected in a presumption of sole beneficial ownership. Where there is evidence of the parties' respective contributions to the purchase price (and no other relevant evidence) and one of the parties has contributed X%, the fact that the purchase is in the sole name of the other does not prevent the former owning X% of the beneficial interest on a resulting trust basis. Indeed, it is because of the resulting trust presumption that such ownership arises. It seems to me that consistency

---

[72] Ibid, [138].
[73] *Jones v Kernott* [2011] UKSC 53; [2012] 1 AC 776. See Chapter 9.2(c)(iii), pp. 454–5.
[74] [2007] UKHL 17, [2007] AC 432, [107].

suggests that the party who contributed X% of the purchase price should be entitled to X% (no more and no less) of the beneficial interest in the same way if he is a co-purchaser. The resulting trust presumption arises because it is assumed that neither party intended a gift of any part of his own contribution to the other party. That would seem to me to apply to contributions irrespective of the name or names in which the property concerned is acquired and held, as a matter of both principle and logic...

Accordingly, in my judgment, where there are unequal contributions, the resulting trust solution is the one to be adopted. However, it is no more than a presumption, albeit an important one...

In many cases, there will, in addition to the contributions, be other relevant evidence as at the time of acquisition. Such evidence would often enable the court to deduce an agreement or understanding amounting to an intention as to the basis on which the beneficial interests would be held. Such an intention may be express (although not complying with the requisite formalities) or inferred, and must normally be supported by some detriment, to justify intervention by equity. It would be in this way that the resulting trust would become rebutted and replaced, or (conceivably) supplemented, by a constructive trust...

For instance, the fact that the parties are in a close and loving relationship would render it easier, than in a normal contractual context, to displace the resulting trust solution with, say, an equal division of the beneficial ownership. That is because a departure from the resulting trust solution normally involves a gratuitous transfer of value from one party to the other...

In other words, where the resulting trust presumption (or indeed any other basis of apportionment) applies at the date of acquisition, I am unpersuaded that (save perhaps in a most unusual case) anything other than subsequent discussions, statements or actions, which can fairly be said to imply a positive intention to depart from that apportionment, will do to justify a change in the way in which the beneficial interest is owned. To say that factors such as a long relationship, children, a joint bank account, and sharing daily outgoings of themselves are enough, or even of potential central importance, appears to me not merely wrong in principle, but a recipe for uncertainty, subjectivity, and a long and expensive examination of facts. It could also be said to be arbitrary, as, if such factors of themselves justify a departure from the original apportionment, I find it hard to see how it could be to anything other than equality. If a departure from the original apportionment was solely based on such factors, it seems to me that the judge would almost always have to reach an 'all or nothing' decision...Subject, perhaps, to exceptional cases, whose possibility it would be unrealistic not to acknowledge, an argument for an alteration in the way in which the beneficial interest is held cannot, in my opinion, succeed, unless it can be shown that there was a discussion, statement or action which, viewed in its context, namely the parties' relationship, implied an actual agreement or understanding to effect such an alteration.

So, according to Lord Neuberger, where the parties have made financial contributions to the purchase price, their beneficial interests should be presumed to be held in the same proportions as their financial contributions through the application of the presumed resulting trust. This presumption can be rebutted by a common intention that the beneficial interests were different, but this could only be established expressly or impliedly and could not be imputed.

Whilst Lord Neuberger's approach is attractive, as being consistent with the principles that underlie the resulting trust and as producing a more coherent legal regime, it is an approach that is clearly inconsistent with the approach of the other judges in *Stack v Dowden*. Lord Hope said:[75]

Where the parties have dealt with each other at arm's length it makes sense to start from the position that there is a resulting trust according to how much each party contributed...But cohabiting couples are in a different kind of relationship. The place where they live together is their home. Living together

---

[75] [2007] UKHL 17; [2007] AC 432, [3].

is an exercise in give and take, mutual co-operation and compromise. Who pays for what in regard to the home has to be seen in the wider context of their overall relationship. A more practical, down-to-earth, fact-based approach is called for in their case. The framework which the law provides should be simple, and it should be accessible.

Similarly, Lord Walker said:[76]

In a case about beneficial ownership of a matrimonial or quasi-matrimonial home (whether registered in the name of one or two legal owners) the resulting trust should not in my opinion operate as a legal presumption, although it may (in an updated form which takes account of all significant contributions, direct or indirect, in cash or in kind) happen to be reflected in the parties' common intention.

The resulting trust approach was specifically rejected by Lady Hale and Lord Walker in *Jones v Kernott*:[77]

It is not possible at one and the same time to have a presumption or starting point of joint beneficial interests and a presumption (let alone a rule) that the parties' beneficial interests are in proportion to their respective financial contributions.

In the context of the acquisition of a family home, the presumption of a resulting trust made a great deal more sense when social and economic conditions were different and when it was tempered by the presumption of advancement. The breadwinner husband who provided the money to buy a house in his wife's name, or in their joint names, was presumed to be making her a gift of it, or of a joint interest in it. That simple assumption—which was itself an exercise in imputing an intention which the parties may never have had—was thought unrealistic in the modern world by three of their Lordships in *Pettit v Pettit* [1970] AC 777. It was also discriminatory as between men and women and married and unmarried couples. That problem might have been solved had equity been able to extend the presumption of advancement to unmarried couples and remove the sex discrimination. Instead, the tool which equity has chosen to develop law is the 'common intention' constructive trust...

The time has come to make it clear, in line with *Stack v Dowden* [2008] 1 FLR 1451 (see also *Abbott v Abbott* [2008] 1 FLR 1451), that in the case of the purchase of a house or flat in joint names for joint occupation by a married or unmarried couple, where both are responsible for any mortgage, there is no presumption of a resulting trust arising from their having contributed to the deposit (or indeed the rest of the purchase) in unequal shares. The presumption is that the parties intended a joint tenancy both in law and in equity. But that presumption can of course be rebutted by evidence of a contrary intention, which may more readily be shown where the parties did not share their financial resources.

Lord Neuberger's principled resulting trust approach consequently does not reflect English law; although it remains the preferable approach to that which has actually been adopted by the courts.[78] It is an approach which has been endorsed by the Singapore Court of Appeal.[79]

---

[76] Ibid, [31].

[77] [2011] UKSC 53; [2012] 1 AC 776, [23].

[78] See further Chapter 9.2(d)(vi), pp. 460–1.

[79] *Chan Yuen Lan v See Fong Mun* [2014] SGCA 36. See Tang, 'A Dispute in Chancery Lane: re-considering the resulting and common intention constructive trust' [2015] Conv 169.

(vi) *Summary of principles*

The key principles relating to common intention constructive trusts were summarized by Lady Hale and Lord Walker in *Jones v Kernott* as follows:[80]

> In summary, therefore, the following are the principles applicable in a case such as this, where a family home is bought in the joint names of a cohabiting couple who are both responsible for any mortgage, but without any express declaration of their beneficial interests. (1) The starting point is that equity follows the law and they are joint tenants both in law and in equity. (2) That presumption can be displaced by showing (a) that the parties had a different common intention at the time when they acquired the home, or (b) that they later formed the common intention that their respective shares would change. (3) Their common intention is to be deduced objectively from their conduct: 'the relevant intention of each party is the intention which was reasonably understood by the other party to be manifested by that party's words and conduct notwithstanding that he did not consciously formulate that intention in his own mind or even acted with some different intention which he did not communicate to the other party': Lord Diplock in *Gissing v Gissing* [1971] AC 886, 906 . . . (4) In those cases where it is clear either (a) that the parties did not intend joint tenancy at the outset, or (b) had changed their original intention, but it is not possible to ascertain by direct evidence or by inference what their actual intention was as to the shares in which they would own the property, 'the answer is that each is entitled to that share which the court considers fair having regard to the whole course of dealing between them in relation to the property': Chadwick LJ in *Oxley v Hiscock* [2005] Fam 211, para 69. In our judgment, 'the whole course of dealing . . . in relation to the property' should be given a broad meaning, enabling a similar range of factors to be taken into account as may be relevant to ascertaining the parties' actual intentions. (5) Each case will turn on its own facts. Financial contributions are relevant but there are many other factors which may enable the court to decide what shares were either intended (as in case (3)) or fair (as in case (4)).
>
> This case is not concerned with a family home which is put into the name of one party only. The starting point is different. The first issue is whether it was intended that the other party have any beneficial interest in the property at all. If he does, the second issue is what that interest is. There is no presumption of joint beneficial ownership. But their common intention has once again to be deduced objectively from their conduct. If the evidence shows a common intention to share beneficial ownership but does not show what shares were intended, the court will have to proceed as at . . . (4) and (5) above.

(c) APPLICATION OF THE PRINCIPLES

When considering the operation of the principles relating to the common intention constructive trust it is still useful to distinguish between cases where the property is registered in the name of one party and where it is registered in the name of both.

(i) *Single ownership cases*

Although *Stack v Dowden* and *Jones v Kernott* were cases where the property was registered in the names of both parties, it is clear that the principles which derive from those cases are applicable where the property has been registered in the name of one party only.[81] However, as recognized in *Capehorn*

---

[80] [2011] UKSC 53; [2012] 1 AC 776, [51].
[81] See, for example, *Geary v Rankine* [2012] EWCA Civ 555, [2012] 2 FLR 1409; *Thompson v Hurst* [2012] EWCA Civ 1752, [2014] 1 FLR 238; *Graham-York v York* [2015] EWCA Civ 72; *Curran v Collins* [2015] EWCA Civ 404; *Capehorn v*

v Harris,[82] single ownership cases involve two distinct stages of inquiry: (i) identification of an actual agreement, express or inferred but not imputed, as to the sharing of the beneficial interest; (ii) quantification of the beneficial interest, which can involve imputation of an intention that each party is entitled to the share of the beneficial interest which the court considers to be fair having regard to the whole course of dealing between the parties in relation to the property. Further, it must be established that the party who is asserting a share in the beneficial interest had relied to his or her detriment on the agreement.[83] This is a requirement which does not apply in the joint ownership context, and may prove to be a significant restriction on the identification of a share of the beneficial interest in sole ownership cases. The application of these requirements will be dependent on careful analysis of the facts as illustrated by *Curran v Collins*[84] and *Geary v Rankine*.[85]

Curran v Collins [2015] EWCA Civ 404; [2015] Fam Law 780

The claimant, Ms Curran, and the defendant, Mr Collins, were in a relationship and shared a common interest in breeding dogs. The defendant had purchased various properties over a period of time in his sole name, including one in Feltham and lastly one called The Haven. Their relationship ended and the claimant sought a share in The Haven.

Arden LJ:

It is common ground that, because the properties were all held in Mr Collins' name, Ms Curran bore the legal burden of proving that she was entitled to a share. There was no express agreement. She had to show two matters. First, she had to show that she reasonably believed that the parties' common intention, to be deduced from the whole course of their conduct in relation to the properties, was that she was to have a share of the properties. Second, she had to show that she acted to her detriment on the basis of that common intention . . .

this appeal in my judgment fails. There are insuperable obstacles in Ms Curran's path: . . .

Not only did the parties have no express agreement about sharing the ownership of the properties, but also, on Mr. Collins' case, he made it expressly clear to her that the property purchases were his alone. That was sufficient to negate any reasonable belief in any common intention. However, there was one exception to this and that arose out of an episode at the time of the purchase of the Feltham house in 1986. Ms Curran raised the subject of her having a share of the property with Mr Collins and he told her that it was too expensive for her name to be on the property because it would involve paying the premia for two life insurance policies ('the Excuse'). On Ms Curran's case this statement was impliedly made on the basis that Mr Collins accepted that, but for the expense, she should be an owner of the properties. The judge rejected this argument and found that Mr Collins had made the statement to avoid any embarrassment over his refusal to make Ms Curran a co-owner and that accordingly it was sufficient to exclude any shared intention that Ms Curran should have an interest in the property. Accordingly Ms Curran's claim failed. . . .

Harris [2015] EWCA Civ 955. See generally Sloan, 'Keeping Up with the *Jones* Case: Establishing constructive trusts in sole legal owner scenarios' (2015) 35 LS 226.

[82] [2015] EWCA Civ 955, [17] (Sales LJ). See also *Geary v Rankine* [2012] EWCA Civ 555; [2012] 2 FLR 1409, [20] (Lewison LJ).

[83] *Curran v Collins* [2015] EWCA Civ 404; [2015] Fam Law 780.

[84] Ibid.

[85] [2012] EWCA Civ 555; [2012] 2 FLR 1409.

The judge found that Ms Curran did not act in any way to her detriment in reliance on the Excuse or at all. On this appeal Ms Curran does not pursue any argument either that the judge should not have made any such finding or that detrimental reliance is not required in law. . . .

Lewison LJ:

There were, potentially, two ways in which Ms Curran might have been entitled to an interest in The Haven despite the fact that it was bought by Mr Collins in his sole name and with his own money. She might have had an interest in the Feltham house which was 'rolled over' into The Haven since the proceeds of sale of the Feltham house were used in part payment for The Haven. Alternatively she might have acquired an interest in The Haven even if she did not have a pre-existing interest in the Feltham House.

The second way can be ruled out on the basis of the judge's findings of fact. The judge found at [100] and [103] that at about the time when The Haven was bought Ms Curran asked Mr Collins whether her name would be on the title deeds and he said no; and that 'the property would be owned by him alone'. In the face of that finding of fact, it is impossible to argue that Ms Curran could reasonably have been led to believe that she would acquire an interest in The Haven. Moreover, the judge's finding is entirely understandable in view of her findings about the state of the relationship between Ms Curran and Mr Collins at that time. There had been difficulties between them a year or two earlier which had led Mr Collins to ask Ms Curran to leave. But at the time when The Haven was bought the judge found at [110] that Mr Collins was prepared to 'tolerate' Ms Curran's presence:

> '. . . so long as she did not behave in a way which made it simply impossible for them to live harmoniously under the same roof, as had been growingly the case over the previous years.'

What then of the Feltham house? Once again on the basis of the judge's findings it was bought by Mr Collins in 1986 with his own money (or money that he personally borrowed) and title was in his sole name. It was not bought as a joint or family home because on the judge's findings Ms Curran and Mr Collins did not live together at that time and there was no expectation that they would. Ms Curran's life was 'anchored at her mother's house' and she did not want 'to move out to try to create some kind of family unit with [Mr Collins] with the uncertainties and risks that that would entail.' The judge also found that it was not until 2002 (some 16 years later) that Ms Curran and Mr Collins began to live together in the Feltham house. The judge also found that she made no indirect financial contribution towards the mortgage on the Feltham house, essentially because Ms Curran had no money in excess of what she spent on herself. Nor was it suggested that she had made a non-financial contribution, such as carrying out improvements, child-rearing or domestic activities.

What [Ms Curran's counsel] especially relied on was what she called a 'specious excuse' which derives from Ms Curran's evidence about what Mr Collins said about insurance. Her evidence was that when the Feltham flat was bought in 1984 it was agreed that it would be bought in Mr Collins' sole name:

> 'His reason for this, which he would later use on two further occasions and which I accepted, was that it would ultimately save money by having the property put into his sole name as only one life assurance policy would be required. He always told me that if anything were to happen to him, the property would be left to me and the insurance would pay off the mortgage.'

She said much the same about the Feltham house. The judge summarised her evidence at [44]:

> 'Her evidence is that, over the period of the Feltham house, she was, in effect, contributing directly to the mortgage in this way. She also says that this was on the basis of an agreement or understanding that she had a joint equal interest in the property with Mr. Collins, but her

name had not been put on the deeds because of a spurious excuse given to her about the costs of the insurance policy.' . . .

At [98] the judge rejected her evidence that anything was said at the time of the purchase of the Feltham flat, but accepted that something 'of this sort' was said at the time of the purchase of the Feltham house. She made her more detailed finding at [100]:

'I believe Miss Curran that something was said in the context of the acquisition of the Feltham house, at least, with regard to the costs of an insurance policy as a reason for her not being "on the title" but I am equally satisfied that this was said to forestall what Mr Collins would quite reasonably have seen as Miss Curran's getting what he would have regarded as the wrong end of the stick about the acquisition of the property. In other words I am satisfied that this was not an excuse made in the context of a pre-existing agreement arrangement or understanding that this was to be a joint purchase, of which Mr Collins was fully aware, but made in order to prevent evidence of that being recorded, but was an excuse made to forestall a confrontation arising from Miss Curran making an unjustifiable assumption as to his intention. Any such assumption would, I am satisfied, have been just such an unjustifiable assumption; I am satisfied that Mr Collins did not represent to Miss Curran that she was to have an interest in the property he was buying nor say or do anything which she could reasonably have interpreted as being intended to assure her that she did.'

In this passage the judge has clearly rejected Ms Curran's evidence that there had been an agreement or understanding that she had a joint equal interest in the property. Although she was not in a position to make a finding about exactly what it was that Mr Collins said, it cannot be right that the giving of a reason why someone is not on the title deeds inevitably leads to the inference that it must have been agreed that they would have an interest in the property. If one who is not versed in the difference between legal and beneficial ownership asks to be on the deeds and is told 'No', the more usual inference would be that they would have understood that they were not to become owners or part owners of the property. I cannot see that the result is very different if the reason given is that it is too expensive. There are, however, two cases in which a specious excuse has been held to give rise to the inference of a constructive trust. However, these cases are fact-sensitive and need to be carefully examined.

In *Eves v Eves* [1975] 1 WLR 1338 Janet and Stuart Eves were already cohabiting and had a daughter together. They were looking for a family home. It was in that context that Stuart Eves made the representation:

'He told her that it was to be their house and a home for themselves and their children. He said that, as she was under 21, it could not be in joint names and had to be in his name alone; and that, but for her age, it would have been purchased in joint names. She accepted his explanation: but he admitted in the witness-box that it was simply an "excuse." He all along was determined that it was to be in his name alone.'

There are two important parts to this representation, neither of which is present in our case. First, Stuart Eves told Janet Eves that the house was to be a home for both of them and their children. In our case Ms. Curran had no intention of moving into the Feltham house at the time it was acquired. Second, Stuart Eves told Janet Eves that the house would have been bought in both names but for her age. It is that positive assertion that it would have been bought in joint names that was capable of giving rise to an expectation that Janet Eves would acquire an interest in the house. In our case nothing of the sort was said to Ms Curran. She was simply told that she could not be on the deeds because it was too expensive.

The second case is *Grant v Edwards* [1986] Ch 638. Once again the parties were living together at the time of the purchase, and had had a child together. The exact representation that was made to Mrs. Grant is not set out verbatim, but Browne-Wilkinson V-C described it thus:

> '...the representation made by the defendant to the plaintiff [was] that the house would have been in the joint names but for the plaintiff's matrimonial disputes...'

Again there are two factors present in that case which are absent from ours. First, in that case (but not in ours) the house being acquired was acquired as a family home. Second, in that case (but not in ours) there was a positive representation that Mrs. Grant would have been a joint owner but for her matrimonial dispute.

These cases do not establish the proposition that the mere giving of a 'specious excuse' necessarily or even usually leads to an inference that the person to whom the excuse is given can reasonably regard herself as having an immediate entitlement to an interest in the property in question....

Although [Ms Curran's counsel's] skeleton argument suggested that the need for detrimental reliance had been abolished by *Stack v Dowden* and *Jones v Kernott*, she rightly abandoned that argument in the course of her oral address. The judge's finding on that point at [101] was that Ms Curran did not in any way act to her detriment in reliance on the specious excuse 'or at all'. That in itself is fatal to Ms Curran's case.

It follows that the judge's conclusion that Ms Curran had not established any interest in The Haven cannot be impeached.

Geary v Rankine [2012] EWCA Civ 555; [2012] 2 FLR 1409

The defendant, Mr Rankine, had purchased a guesthouse, Castle View, with his own money as a commercial investment. The defendant ran the business himself. The claimant, Mrs Geary, with whom the defendant had cohabited in a different property, later assisted the defendant with the business, largely by dealing with cooking and paperwork. After their relationship ended, the claimant claimed a share of the business. She asserted that, although there was no common intention that she should have a beneficial interest in the property when it was purchased by the defendant, this intention changed once she had moved in to help him run the business. Her claim was rejected by the Court of Appeal. In holding that the common intention never changed, Lewison LJ said:[86]

In a single name case of which this is one the first issue is whether it was intended that the claimant should have any beneficial interest in the property at all. If that issue is determined in the claimant's favour, the second issue is what that interest is. There is no presumption of joint beneficial ownership. But the common intention has to be deduced objectively from their conduct.

Having rejected the claim Mrs. Geary and Mr. Rankine had a common intention at the time of the purchase that Mrs. Geary should have a beneficial interest in Castle View, the judge went on to consider whether that common interest subsequently changed. It is important to stress that the object of the search is a common intention; that is, an intention common to both parties. So Mrs. Geary had to establish that despite the fact that the legal title to the property remained in Mr. Rankine's sole name, he actually intended that she should have a beneficial interest in it. As I have said that actual intention

---

[86] [2012] EWCA Civ 555; [2012] 2 FLR 1409, [20].

> may have been expressly manifested, or may be inferred from conduct; but actual intention it remains. The judge found that there was no change in Mr. Rankine's intention. He also said that there was no evidence that Mrs. Geary had taken any steps to change her own position in reliance on any assertion by Mr. Rankine that she would have an interest in the property or in reliance on any steps taken by Mr. Rankine from which she could have inferred that his intention had changed...
>
> ...in my judgment it is an impermissible leap to go from a common intention that the parties would run a business together to a conclusion that it was their common intention that the property in which the business was run, and which was bought entirely with money provided by one of them, would belong to both of them. In addition, Mrs. Geary's own evidence makes it clear to my mind that Mr. Rankine had no intention that she should have an interest in the property itself.

Where property has been registered in the name of one party to enable another to perpetrate a fraud, that other party will still be able to establish a common intention constructive trust if it is not necessary for him or her to rely on the illegal purpose to establish the common intention.[87] This was recognized in *Davies v O'Kelly*[88] where Pitchford LJ said:[89]

> ...it was not in the present case necessary for the respondent to prove the reason why the legal estate of both properties was conveyed into the appellant's sole name; it was enough that the starting point was that the legal estate was vested in the appellant alone. Subject to proof of a contrary intention, the equitable interests in the property followed the legal estate. From that starting point the judge concluded that although there was no express agreement as to disposition of the beneficial interest in [one of the properties], the common intention of the parties, inferred from their conduct throughout, was that the beneficial interest should be shared equally between them. It was not necessary for the respondent to advance his unlawful agreement in order to make good his claim to a constructive trust. ...The issue is whether public policy should intervene to prevent the respondent from enforcing his interest. The conduct identified by the judge was not the making of the unlawful agreement (which was about purpose and not about shared equitable interest) but the course of dealing between the parties relating to their financial contributions to the purchases.

(ii) *Joint ownership cases*

Stack v Dowden [2007] UKHL 17; [2007] 2 AC 432

The family home had been conveyed into the names of both parties. Two-thirds of the purchase price was contributed by the claimant, and one-third from a mortgage loan in their joint names, to which they had both contributed. On the breakdown of their relationship, the issue for the court concerned the quantification of the claimant's beneficial interest. Since the property was registered in their joint names, it was presumed that they shared the beneficial interest. Lady Hale said:[90]

> The approach to quantification in cases where the home is conveyed into joint names should certainly be no stricter than the approach to quantification in cases where it has been conveyed into the name

---

[87] By virtue of the principle recognized in *Tinsley v Milligan* [1994] 1 AC 340. See Chapter 8.2(d)(i), pp. 377–9.
[88] [2014] EWCA Civ 1606; [2015] 1 WLR 2725.
[89] Ibid, [32].
[90] [2007] UKHL 17; [2007] 2 AC 432, [66].

of one only…But the questions in a joint names case are not simply 'what is the extent of the parties' beneficial interests?' but 'did the parties intend their beneficial interests to be different from their legal interests?' and 'if they did, in what way and to what extent?' There are differences between sole and joint names cases when trying to divine the common intentions or understanding between the parties. I know of no case in which a sole legal owner (there being no declaration of trust) has been held to hold the property on a beneficial joint tenancy. But a court may well hold that joint legal owners (there being no declaration of trust) are also beneficial joint tenants. Another difference is that it will almost always have been a conscious decision to put the house into joint names. Even if the parties have not executed the transfer, they will usually, if not invariably, have executed the contract which precedes it. Committing oneself to spend large sums of money on a place to live is not normally done by accident or without giving it a moment's thought…

The burden will therefore be on the person seeking to show that the parties did intend their beneficial interests to be different from their legal interests, and in what way. This is not a task to be lightly embarked upon. In family disputes, strong feelings are aroused when couples split up. These often lead the parties, honestly but mistakenly, to reinterpret the past in self-exculpatory or vengeful terms. They also lead people to spend far more on the legal battle than is warranted by the sums actually at stake. A full examination of the facts is likely to involve disproportionate costs. In joint names cases it is also unlikely to lead to a different result unless the facts are very unusual. Nor may disputes be confined to the parties themselves. People with an interest in the deceased's estate may well wish to assert that he had a beneficial tenancy in common. It cannot be the case that all the hundreds of thousands, if not millions, of transfers into joint names using the old forms are vulnerable to challenge in the courts simply because it is likely that the owners contributed unequally to their purchase.

It was held that this was one of the exceptional cases in which the proportion of the beneficial interest was intended to be different from the legal interest, so that the claimant had a 65 per cent interest and the defendant 35 per cent. Lord Hope said:[91]

In a case such as this, where the parties had already been living together for about eighteen years and had four children when [the property] was purchased in joint names and payments on the mortgage secured on that property were in effect contributed to by each of them equally, there would have been much to be said for adhering to the presumption of English law that the beneficial interests were divided between them equally. But I do not think that it is possible to ignore the fact that the contributions which they made to the purchase of that property were not equal. The relative extent of those contributions provides the best guide as to where their beneficial interests lay, in the absence of compelling evidence that by the end of their relationship they did indeed intend to share the beneficial interests equally. The evidence does not go that far. On the contrary, while they pooled their resources in the running of the household, in larger matters they maintained their financial independence from each other throughout their relationship…

I think that indirect contributions, such as making improvements which added significant value to the property, or a complete pooling of resources in both time and money so that it did not matter who paid for what during their relationship, ought to be taken into account as well as financial contributions made directly towards the purchase of the property. I would endorse Chadwick LJ's view in *Oxley v Hiscock* [2005] Fam 211, para 69 that regard should be had to the whole course of dealing between them in relation to the property. But the evidence in this case shows that there never was a stage when both

---

[91] Ibid, [11].

parties intended that their beneficial interests in the property should be shared equally. Taking a broad view of the matter, therefore, I agree that the order that the Court of Appeal provides the fairest result that can be achieved in the circumstances.

It is not clear whether the House of Lords held that the common intention was implied or imputed, although the nature of the factors identified might suggest an imputed intent. Subsequently, however, in *Jones v Kernott*,[92] Lady Hale and Lord Walker emphasized that the relevant intention in *Stack v Dowden* had been inferred. In fact, the same result could have been achieved by the straightforward application of the presumption of resulting trust, which was how Lord Neuberger reached the same conclusion as the other judges. The claimant had contributed 65 per cent of the purchase price and on that basis, he said, she was entitled to a 65 per cent share of the beneficial interest.

(iii) *Ambulatory intent*

Whether an initial common intention as regards the allocation of the beneficial interest can be considered to have changed over time was considered in *Jones v Kernott*.

Jones v Kernott [2011] UKSC 53; [2012] 1 AC 776

A couple had purchased a house in 1985, which was conveyed into their joint names. They separated in 1993. It was accepted that, at that time, they held the property beneficially in equal shares, there being insufficient evidence to rebut the presumption that their beneficial interests followed the legal title. The claimant continued to live in the house with their children, whilst the defendant had acquired alternative accommodation and made no further contribution towards the acquisition of the property. The claimant assumed sole responsibility for paying the mortgage, and for repairs and improvements to the property. The defendant severed the joint tenancy in 2008, at which point the claimant asserted that their beneficial interests were no longer equal. The Supreme Court held that, after their separation, the common intention of the parties had changed. Lady Hale and Lord Walker said:[93]

In this case, there is no need to impute an intention that the parties' beneficial interests would change, because the judge made a finding that the intentions of the parties did in fact change. At the outset, their intention was to provide a home for themselves and their progeny. But thereafter their intentions did change significantly...They separated in October 1993. No doubt in many such cases, there is a period of uncertainty about where the parties will live and what they will do about the home which they used to share. This home was put on the market in late 1995 but failed to sell. Around that time a new plan was formed. The life insurance policy was cashed in and [the defendant] was able to buy a new home for himself. He would not have been able to do this had he still had to contribute towards the mortgage, endowment policy and other outgoings on [the family home]. The logical inference is that they intended that his interest in [the family home] should crystallise then. Just as he would have the sole benefit of any capital gain in his own home, [the claimant] would have the sole benefit of any capital gain in [the family home]. In so far as the judge did not in so many words infer that this was their intention, it is clearly the intention which reasonable people would have had had they thought about it at the time. But in our view it is an intention which he both could and should have inferred from their conduct.

---

[92] [2011] UKSC 53; [2012] 1 AC 776, [30].
[93] Ibid, [48].

Whilst all the judges recognized that the parties' initial common intention as to the allocation of the beneficial interest had changed over time, there was a clear division of opinion as to how this ambulatory intention was to be ascertained. Lady Hale and Lords Walker and Collins accepted that the intention could be inferred, because the trial judge had found that the common intention of the parties as to the extent of their beneficial interest had changed on their separation. This was supported by the fact that the defendant no longer contributed to payment of the mortgage loan but acquired a new property for himself. Lords Kerr and Wilson, on the other hand, considered that a changed common intention could not be inferred on the facts, but could only be imputed. They agreed with the other judges as to the appropriate division of the value of the property, but only because this was the fair solution. Lord Collins recognized that this distinction between inference and imputation is a fine one:[94]

> I agree, therefore, that authority justifies the conceptual approach of Lord Walker and Baroness Hale JJSC that, in joint names cases, the common intention to displace the presumption of equality can, in the absence of express agreement, be inferred (rather than imputed...) from their conduct, and where, in such a case, it is not possible to ascertain or infer what share was intended, each will be entitled to a fair share in the light of the whole course of dealing between them in relation to the property.
>
> That said, it is my view that in the present context the difference between inference and imputation will hardly ever matter (as Lord Walker and Baroness Hale JJSC recognise...), and that what is one person's inference will be another person's imputation...
>
> Nor will it matter in practice that at the first stage, of ascertaining the common intention as to the beneficial ownership, the search is not, at least in theory, for what is fair. It would be difficult (and, perhaps, absurd) to imagine a scenario involving circumstances from which, in the absence of express agreement, the court will infer a shared or common intention which is unfair. The courts are courts of law, but they are also courts of justice.

(iv) *Application beyond cohabitating couple cases*

The common intention constructive trust has been extended beyond cohabiting couples to other personal relationships in which the purchased property is the parties' home, described as the 'domestic consumer context'.[95] So, for example, it has been applied where a house was purchased by a mother and son in joint names as a home for them both.[96] But, because of the very unusual circumstances of the case, it was held that they did not share the beneficial interest equally. These circumstances included that the property had been purchased by the mother from a local authority at a substantial discount, and she could not have funded the mortgage without the assistance of her son, who also lived in the property. That explained why the property was purchased in their joint names. However, the primary purpose of the acquisition was to provide a home for the mother and the judge concluded that there was no intent that their interests in the property should be equal. The discount obtained by the mother was more than 50 per cent of the purchase price and the son's financial contribution was significantly less. Consequently, the son was held to have a one-third share of the beneficial interest.

The common intention constructive trust will not, however, be engaged where the property is purchased as an investment rather than as a family home. So, for example, in *Laskar v Laskar*,[97] the defendant was a council tenant who had bought her house from the council as an investment. She used her right-to-buy discount as a statutory tenant, which reduced the purchase price of the property of

---

[94] Ibid, [64].
[95] *Stack v Dowden* [2007] UKHL 17; [2007] AC 432, [58] (Lady Hale).
[96] *Adekunle v Ritchie* [2007] WTLR 1505. See also *Gallarotti v Sebastianelli* [2012] EWCA Civ 865, [2012] WTLR 1509.
[97] [2008] EWCA Civ 347; [2008] 1 WLR 2695. See Chapter 8.2(b), pp. 367–8.

£79,000 by £29,000. The defendant needed to borrow the remaining amount from her bank. Legal title to the property was registered in the name of the defendant and her daughter, the claimant. They were jointly liable on the mortgage, but payments were actually derived from rent obtained by letting the property. The claimant and the defendant paid the remaining balance of £7,000 between them. Their relationship broke down and the daughter claimed an equal share of the beneficial interest, reflecting her joint legal interest with her mother. It was held that the *Stack v Dowden* presumption was not applicable because the property had been purchased primarily as an investment. Lord Neuberger preferred to employ the presumption of resulting trust and said:[98]

> It is by no means clear to me that the approach laid down by Baroness Hale of Richmond in [*Stack v Dowden*] was intended to apply in a case such as this.... although the parties were mother and daughter and not in that sense in an arm's length commercial relationship, they had independent lives, and, as I have already indicated, the purchase of the property was not really for the purpose of providing a home for them. The daughter hardly lived there at the time it was purchased, and did not live there much if at all afterwards, and the mother did not live there for long. The property was purchased primarily as an investment.
>
> It was argued that this case was midway between the cohabitation cases of co-ownership where property is bought for living in, such as *Stack*, and arm's length commercial cases of co-ownership, where property is bought for development or letting. In the latter sort of case, the reasoning in *Stack v Dowden* would not be appropriate and the resulting trust presumption still appears to apply. In this case, the primary purpose of the purchase of the property was as an investment, not as a home. In other words this was a purchase which, at least primarily, was not in 'the domestic consumer context' but in a commercial context. To my mind it would not be right to apply the reasoning in *Stack v Dowden* to such a case as this, where the parties primarily purchased the property as an investment for rental income and capital appreciation, even where their relationship is a familial one.
>
> If, however, the presumption in *Stack* would apply here, then I consider that it would have been rebutted anyway. On the facts in *Stack* there was a departure from the presumption of equality, and the outcome was that the shares of the beneficial interest were substantially proportionate to the financial contributions of the parties. This, in my opinion, would be a stronger case for departing from the presumption of equality even if it does apply.

Consequently, because of the daughter's contribution to the acquisition of the property through her liability on the mortgage and direct contribution to the purchase price, she was entitled to a one-third beneficial interest. This reliance on the presumption of the resulting trust is defensible and consistent with fundamental principles of the law of trusts.

(d) DOCTRINAL FOUNDATIONS

The difficulty with the law following *Stack v Dowden* and *Jones v Kernott* concerns the recognition that it is possible to impute a common intention to the parties concerning the quantification of their beneficial interest. This does not purport to be a real intention on their part, but one that is imposed on the basis that, had the parties considered the matter, this is what the court considers they would have intended, and with reference to a variety of factors the significance of which is difficult to assess. Can this resort to imputed intention be justified? Various doctrinal mechanisms can be identified to explain why a common intention constructive trust is recognized and why an imputed intent might be sufficient to establish a common intent.

---

[98] Ibid, [15].

(i) *Discretionary remedialism*

If the imputed common intention is simply a smokescreen to enable the court to achieve what it considers to be a fair result, it would be preferable to state this explicitly, as Lords Kerr and Wilson did in *Jones v Kernott*,[99] and it would not then be necessary to search for any doctrinal foundation for the trust, since it would be blatantly remedial and discretionary. But this discretionary approach to imputed intention was explicitly rejected in *Stack v Dowden* and is inconsistent with the approach of the majority in *Jones v Kernott*.[100]

(ii) *Unconscionability*

The imputation of intention might instead respond to the defendant's unconscionable conduct,[101] so that the so-called 'common intention constructive trust' would be properly characterized as an orthodox institutional constructive trust.[102] But it has never been a requirement of the common intention constructive trust that the defendant's conduct needs to be be characterized as unconscionable. The key principles underpinning the common intention constructive trust focus on the identification of an agreement or understanding as to the allocation of the beneficial interest between the parties.

(iii) *Unjust enrichment*

An alternative way to justify the imputed intention is by reference to the law of unjust enrichment. Indeed, all aspects of the common intention constructive trust might be analysed in this way.[103] If it can be shown that the defendant has been unjustly enriched at the expense of the claimant, the defendant will be liable to make restitution to the claimant to the extent of that enrichment.[104] Sir Terence Etherton has suggested that the defendant's unjust enrichment would justify the recognition of a beneficial interest in the family home.[105]

> My conclusion will be that, although not presented as such in the speeches, *Stack* is, on analysis, a radical departure from previous authority in its use of the constructive trust as proprietary restitutionary relief for unjust enrichment rather than the declaration of a pre-existing trust on traditional lines. It is an example of the grant of discretionary relief by way of a remedial constructive trust, and it marks the creation, for policy reasons, of a new ground of restitution for autonomous or subtractive unjust enrichment. I will also conclude that this analysis helps us to understand the clear difference between the roles and spheres of the common intention constructive trust to be found in the cohabitation cases, on the one hand, and proprietary estoppel, on the other hand. Further, it provides a basis for identifying the policy ground for not extending the *Stack* approach to other areas of joint acquisition of property, especially in the commercial field.

---

[99] See Chapter 9.2(b)(iv)(d), pp. 442–3.

[100] It is, however, consistent with reform proposals of the Law Commission. See Chapter 9.2(e), pp. 461–2.

[101] As in Australia: *Muschinski v Dodds* (1985) 160 CLR 583.

[102] See Chapter 7.1(b)(i), p. 330.

[103] As occurs in Canada: *Kerr v Baranow* 2011 SCC 10; (2011) 328 DLR (4th) 577. See McInnes, 'Cohabitation, Trusts and Unjust Enrichment in the Supreme Court of Canada' (2011) 127 LQR 339. Also in Scotland: see *Satchwell v McIntosh* 2006 SLT 117; *McKensie v Nutter* 2007 SLT 17.

[104] See Chapter 1.4(b), pp. 14–15.

[105] 'Constructive Trusts: A New Model for Equity and Unjust Enrichment' (2008) 67 CLJ 265, 266. See also Gardner, 'Family Property Today' (2008) 124 LQR 422, 437.

He explained the result in *Stack v Dowden* with reference to unjust enrichment as follows:[106]

> I suggest that the relief in *Stack* was in response to unjust enrichment. There was an enrichment of Mr. Stack, at the expense of Ms. Dowden since he was the joint owner of the property but she contributed financially more than half of the purchase price of the property. On the later approach of Professor Birks, that is to say, all enrichments are unjust unless there is some juristic reason for the retention of the enrichment, the enrichment of Mr. Stack was plainly unjust. On the facts, Ms. Dowden did not intend to make a gift to Mr. Stack of the benefit of her contributions. On the other, more traditional approach . . . the following specific unjust factor or factors may be identified from the *Pettitt* to *Stack* case law. Mr. Stack, relying on his joint legal title, sought to retain the financial benefit of the disproportionately large contributions by Ms. Dowden which she never intended should enure for his financial benefit on sale. Mr. Stack relied on the absence of a valid and enforceable contract or a valid express trust adjusting the parties' beneficial interests to reflect the disproportionate contributions of Ms. Dowden. Mr. Stack thereby acted unconscionably . . . since the intimate nature of their relationship was both the cause of Ms. Dowden's contributions and the reason why she never sought or acted on legal advice in relation to them to protect her interests. The key to the decision, therefore, is the intimacy of the personal relationship between the parties . . .
>
> It is at this point that issues of policy intervene. It is well established that the categories of unjust enrichment are not closed . . .
>
> The constructive trust imposed in *Stack*, not being an institutional trust, is a discretionary remedial trust. It need not be seen, and it should not be seen, however, as the full-blown retrospective remedial constructive trust of the US and Canadian model . . . That would be inconsistent with our jurisprudence and, in particular, our settled rules defining priorities between property interests. There is no difficulty, however, in a model analogous to the power of the court to award a property interest for proprietary estoppel. In that case, the right to the relief is a mere equity prior to judgment, which will take its priority in relation to other property interests in accordance with settled law and statute.

If this explanation of the common intention constructive trust is accepted it would mean that, if the family home of a cohabiting couple is registered in the name of the defendant and the claimant has contributed to the purchase price, paid for utilities, and has decorated the property, the claimant would have a beneficial interest in the house to the extent that the defendant has been enriched by his or her contributions, including the services that the claimant has provided.

This reliance on the law of unjust enrichment to explain the common intention constructive trust is inappropriate for three reasons. First, to establish unjust enrichment, it must be shown that the case falls within one of the recognized grounds of restitution, such as mistake or total failure of basis.[107] But, where a cohabiting party has contributed to the purchase price, for example, it will be difficult to establish that he or she has been mistaken or expected to receive something in return that is not forthcoming. Sir Terence Etherton suggest that a new ground of restitution should be recognized for policy reasons, namely unconscionability. But there is no authority for this and unconscionability is too vague to be recognized as a ground of restitution in its own right. Gardner has argued that it is sufficient that there was an absence of basis for the enrichment.[108] But this too is not supported by authority. Secondly, the law of unjust enrichment cannot be used to create proprietary interests.[109] Thirdly, the remedial constructive trust has been rejected by the Supreme Court.[110] It follows that unjust enrichment cannot be used to explain the common intention constructive trust.

---

[106] (2008) 67 CLJ 265, 280.
[107] See Chapter 1.4(b), p. 14.
[108] Gardner, 'Family Property Today' (2008) LQR 422, 438.
[109] *Foskett v McKeown* [2001] 1 AC 102; *Bank of Cyprus (UK) Ltd v Menelaou* [2015] UKSC 66; [2016] AC 176.
[110] *FHR European Ventures LLP v Cedar Capital Partners LLC* [2014] UKSC 45; [2015] AC 250.

(iv) *Proprietary estoppel*

Before *Stack v Dowden*,[111] the generally accepted view was that proprietary estoppel and the common intention constructive trust were similar, if not identical,[112] because both depended on the claimant's detrimental reliance. In *Stack v Dowden* Lord Walker considered that proprietary estoppel and the common intention constructive trust should not be assimilated:[113]

> I add a brief comment as to proprietary estoppel. In paragraphs 70 and 71 of his judgment in *Oxley v Hiscock* [2005] Fam 211 Chadwick LJ considered the conceptual basis of the developing law in this area, and briefly discussed proprietary estoppel, a suggestion first put forward by Sir Nicolas Browne-Wilkinson V-C in *Grant v Edwards* [1986] Ch 638, 656. I have myself given some encouragement to this approach (*Yaxley v Gotts* [2000] Ch 162, 177) but I have to say that I am now rather less enthusiastic about the notion that proprietary estoppel and 'common-interest' constructive trusts can or should be completely assimilated. Proprietary estoppel typically consists of asserting an equitable claim against the conscience of the 'true' owner. The claim is a 'mere equity'. It is to be satisfied by the minimum award necessary to do justice (*Crabb v Arun District Council* [1976] Ch 179, 198), which may sometimes lead to no more than a monetary award. A 'common-intention' constructive trust, by contrast, is identifying the true beneficial owner or owners, and the size of their beneficial interests.

Recent decisions have, however, affirmed that detrimental reliance does constitute a key requirement of the common intention constructive trust, at least in sole name cases.[114] It may follow that the debate about the assimilation of proprietary estoppel and the common intention constructive trust will be renewed, although the better view is that such assimilation would not be appropriate because the common intention constructive trust and proprietary estoppel have different functions and requirements.[115]

(v) *The relationship of the parties*

Gardner has suggested that the operation of the common intention constructive trust will turn on whether the parties have a 'materially communal relationship':[116]

> Essentially, the common intention imputed to parties having a materially communal relationship will give them equal shares in the house, as in *Abbott v Abbott*; while that imputed to parties not having such a relationship, as in *Stack v Dowden*, will give them shares proportionate to their individual contributions to the acquisition of the house, though indirect contributions will count as much as direct ones.
>
> A 'materially communal' relationship is one in which C and D in practical terms...pool all their material resources (including money, other assets, and labour), rather than keeping separate tallies. The presence of a joint bank account will strongly, almost conclusively, suggest a materially communal relationship, but its absence will not particularly prove the opposite. The parties' having, or not having, a sexual relationship will prove nothing either way; likewise even their having children together, though in this

---

[111] [2007] UKHL 17, [2007] AC 432.

[112] *Yaxley v Gotts* [2000] Ch 162, 177 (Robert Walker LJ); *Oxley v Hiscock* [2004] EWCA Civ 546; [2005] Fam 211, [66] (Chadwick LJ).

[113] [2007] UKHL 17; [2007] AC 432, [37].

[114] See especially *Curran v Collins* [2015] EWCA Civ 404; [2015] Fam Law 780. See Chapter 9.2(c)(i), pp. 448–51.

[115] See Chapter 9.4, pp. 469–80.

[116] 'Family Property Today' (2008) 124 LQR 422, 431. See also Gardner, 'Rethinking Family Property' (1993) 109 LQR 263.

event it is probably commoner for their relationship to be materially communal. If they are married or civil partners, their relationship will necessarily be regarded as materially communal, regardless of the nature and scale of their contributions to the family economy... But an unmarried couple could operate likewise, once again regardless of their contributions to the family economy; though if D is the sole wage-earner, while C keeps house and perhaps looks after their children, it is hard to see their relationship otherwise than as materially communal...

A non-materially communal relationship is one without this profile. That is not to say that it may not be close in other respects; the parties may even pool their material resources in one or more areas, as where a couple both shop for groceries or maybe even buy a car together; but it lacks the key characteristic of a practical pooling of their material resources across the board... For present purposes, however, the parties must at least both contribute to the acquisition of the house (albeit that their contributions may be indirect, as where C meets the household bills while D pays off the mortgage): for in the case of a non-materially communal relationship, it is these contributions that generate the imputed common intention, giving the parties shares in the house in proportion to them.

This analysis is consistent with *Abbott v Abbott*,[117] in which equal beneficial interests were recognized where the parties shared a bank account, and *Stack v Dowden*,[118] in which differing beneficial interests were recognized where the couple's financial affairs were kept separate. It is also consistent with *Jones v Kernott*,[119] where the earlier separation of the parties meant that it was appropriate for differential beneficial interests to be recognized. But Gardner's analysis cannot be used to explain the relevance of the holistic approach, by virtue of which all factors are to be taken into account when assessing the common intention, such as whether the couple had children. Further, if such a test were applied to determine the operation of the common intention constructive trust, this would produce unacceptable uncertainty, especially as regards the structure of negotiations between the parties following the breakdown of their relationship. There is a need for legal certainty to enable legal advisers to advise their clients clearly and to prevent the dispute from being litigated.

(vi) *Rejection of imputed intention*

The continued relevance of imputed intention makes a mockery of the purported aim of seeking out the common intention of the parties. The quest to identify a common intention has previously been described as a myth,[120] and it continues to be so after the decisions in *Stack v Dowden* and *Jones v Kernott*. The real danger of the willingness to impute a common intention is that the courts are actually seeking to redistribute the beneficial interests in property to achieve a just result, but without the benefit of any clear principles. The justification for imputing a common intention cannot be satisfactorily explained and should be rejected. If it is appropriate to recognize the common intention constructive trust, then that common intention should be established only by reference to an express or inferred agreement or understanding as to the existence and quantification of beneficial interests; there should be no role for an imputed intent.

The preferable solution, however, would be to bring the presumption of the resulting trust back into the picture, as advocated by Lord Neuberger in *Stack v Dowden*. Beneficial interests in the family home should, first, be presumed to follow the legal interest, or, secondly, be presumed to be determined by the financial contribution to the acquisition of the property. In both cases, the presumption

---

[117] [2007] UKPC 53; [2008] 1 FLR 1451.
[118] [2007] UKHL 17; [2007] 2 AC 432. See Chapter 9.2(c)(ii), pp. 452–4.
[119] *Jones v Kernott* [2011] UKSC 53; [2012] 1 AC 776: see Chapter 9.2(c)(iii), pp. 454–5.
[120] Glover and Todd, 'The Myth of Common Intention' (1996) 16 LS 325.

could be rebutted by the parties' express or inferred common intention, but only where such an intention can be clearly proved. Beyond this, the law of trusts should not go. This 'trusts approach' would have the added advantage of removing the distinction that has emerged between allocation of the beneficial interest in domestic and commercial contexts. Even in the commercial context, it would be appropriate for the presumption of resulting trust to be rebutted by the common intention of the parties that the beneficial interest should be apportioned differently, although it would be more likely that the presumption would be rebutted in the domestic context.

(e) REFORM OF THE LAW

Despite the best efforts of the judges in the House of Lords and Supreme Court, there remains much uncertainty as to when the presumption that the beneficial interests should follow the legal interests will be rebutted. Although the presumption is meant to be rebutted only in exceptional circumstances, this has occurred in a significant number of the reported cases, including *Stack v Dowden* and *Jones v Kernott*. But it is unclear what makes a case exceptional and so permits the application of the holistic inquiry by reference to a myriad of factors, the significance of those factors being uncertain.

The real problem with the use of the common intention constructive trust to determine beneficial interests in the family home is that the courts have essentially been seeking to redistribute the beneficial interest in property, but are restricted by the use of the trust device that operates within the law of property. The law of property demands certainty of principle, and does not commend itself to the exercise of poorly defined discretion and manipulation of the law and evidence to obtain what is considered to be a fair result. As Deane J recognized in the Australian case of *Muschinksi v Dodds*:[121]

> proprietary rights fall to be governed by principles of law and not by some mix of judicial discretion, subjective views about which party 'ought to win' and the 'formless void' of individual moral opinion.

If the trust law solution is considered to be too restrictive the only alternative solution is a statutory one, to give the courts explicit discretion to redistribute the beneficial interest in the family home to achieve fairer results. Such statutory intervention has occurred in other jurisdictions.[122] It has been recommended by the English Law Commission,[123] and is available where the parties are married. After conducting a comprehensive review of the law and its application in practice, the Law Commission recommended that a new statutory scheme should be created, which would apply to cohabiting couples who separate. The scheme would apply, unless it was specifically disapplied by the couple, where two key conditions were satisfied:

(1) the couple had a child together or had lived together as a couple in a joint household for a specified minimum period (possibly between two and five years); and

(2) the party who was seeking relief had made 'qualifying contributions to the relationship giving rise to certain enduring consequences at the point of separation'.[124]

If these conditions were satisfied, the court would be given a structured discretion to order adjustment of the beneficial interests in the property.

---

[121] (1985) 160 CLR 583, 616.
[122] See, e.g, the New South Wales De Facto Relationships Act 1984.
[123] *Cohabitation: The Financial Consequences of Relationship Breakdown*, Law Com. No. 307 (London: HMSO, 2007).
[124] Ibid, 3.

Law Commission, *Cohabitation: The Financial Consequences of Relationship Breakdown*
(Law Com. No. 307, 2007), 1.19

In broad terms, the scheme would seek to ensure that the pluses and minuses of the relationship were shared between the couple. The applicant would have to show that the respondent retained a benefit, or that the applicant had a continuing economic disadvantage, as a result of contributions made to the relationship. The value of any award would depend on the extent of the retained benefit or continuing economic disadvantage. The court would have discretion to grant such financial relief as might be appropriate to deal with these matters, and in doing so would be required to give first consideration to the welfare of any dependent children.

The court would be given wide powers to ensure that the relief was appropriate, such as by making a financial award, transferring property, or creating a settlement of the property. If this scheme were to apply, the law of implied trusts, estoppels, and contract would be excluded.

Such a scheme would be explicitly redistributive in approach, and would enable the judge to obtain what is considered to be the just and fair result. But the scheme would not be comprehensive: it could be excluded by the parties; it would not cover cohabitants whose relationship was not intimate, such as parent and child; and it would not deal with disputes involving a third party, such as a bank, claiming an interest in the family home. It follows that, even if this statutory scheme were adopted, there would be a continuing role for the common intention constructive trust. The Government responded cautiously to the Law Commission's recommendations and stated that it had no immediate plans to implement them. Attempts in 2013 and 2014 to implement the recommendations by means of a Private Member's Bill[125] failed. The Bill was introduced in the 2015/16 Parliamentary session, but, without Government support, has little chance of being enacted. Consequently, the trust will continue to have a vital role in determining beneficial interests in the family home. The failure to legislate is unfortunate, and may lead to further distortion of the law of property in order to satisfy wider concerns of fairness. But judges cannot simply jettison the law of trusts in favour of a broad discretion without the authority of Parliament. Legislative reform is required.

3. JOINT VENTURE CONSTRUCTIVE TRUSTS

Where two parties have entered into an arrangement involving the acquisition of property by one of them, that party may be required to hold the property on constructive trust for both of them if it is unconscionable for the party acquiring the property to deny that the other has any beneficial interest in it. This is sometimes described as the '*Pallant v Morgan* equity' after a case of that name which recognized this form of trust.[126] In *Pallant v Morgan*,[127] the agents of two neighbouring landowners agreed in an auction room just before an auction of land that the claimant's agent would refrain from bidding and that, if the defendant's agent were successful in his bid, the land would be divided between them. The defendant's bid was successful, but he then denied that the claimant had any interest in the property. The agreement was not sufficiently certain to be specifically enforceable, but the court

---

[125] Cohabitation Rights Bill.

[126] But note Hopkins, 'The *Pallant v Morgan* Equity' [2002] Conv 35, who considers this doctrine to have been created by the Court of Appeal in *Banner Homes Group plc v Luff Developments Ltd* [2000] Ch 371, discussed in Chapter 9.3(a), pp. 463–4, because *Pallant v Morgan* turned on the application of the law of agency. See also *Crossco No. 4 Unlimited v Jolan Ltd* [2011] EWCA Civ 1619, [2012] 1 P and CR 16, [88] (Etherton LJ), [128] (Arden LJ).

[127] [1953] Ch 43.

decided that the defendant held the property on trust for both of them in equal shares, because the claimant had been kept out of the bidding process by a promise, that if the claimant did not bid, an agreement as to the division of the property would be reached.

(a) REQUIREMENTS FOR THE JOINT VENTURE CONSTRUCTIVE TRUST

The requirements for the joint venture constructive trust were identified by Chadwick LJ in *Banner Homes Group plc v Luff Developments Ltd*.

Banner Homes Group plc v Luff Developments Ltd [2000] Ch 371 (Chadwick LJ)

The present appeal provides the first opportunity, so far as I am aware, for this court to consider the basis and scope of what may be called the *Pallant v Morgan* equity in a case in which reliance has to be placed upon it by the appellant. In my view there is no doubt that such an equity does exist and is firmly based. It is an example of the wider equity to which Millett J referred in *Lonrho plc v Fayed (No 2)* [1992] 1 WLR 1 at 9–10:

'Equity will intervene by way of constructive trust, not only to compel the defendant to re-store the plaintiff's property to him, but also to require the defendant to disgorge property which he should have acquired, if at all, for the plaintiff. In the latter category of case, the defendant's wrong lies not in the acquisition of the property, which may or may not have been lawful, but in his subsequent denial of the plaintiff's beneficial interest. For such to be the case, however, the defendant must either have acquired property which but for his wrongdo-ing would have belonged to the plaintiff, or he must have acquired property in circumstances in which he cannot conscientiously retain it as against the plaintiff.'

Or, as the same judge was to say in this court, in the passage in *Paragon Finance plc v D B Thakerar & Co* [1999] 1 All ER 400 at 408–409. . . .:

'His [the defendant's] possession of the property is coloured from the first by the trust and confidence by means of which he obtained it, and his subsequent appropriation of the prop-erty to his own use is a breach of that trust.'

It is important, however, to identify the features which will give rise to a *Pallant v Morgan* equity and to define its scope; while keeping in mind that it is undesirable to attempt anything in the nature of an exhaustive classification. As Millett J pointed out in *Lonrho plc v Fayed (No 2)* [1992] 1 WLR 1 at 9, in a reference to the work of distinguished Australian commentators, equity must retain its 'inherent flex-ibility and capacity to adjust to new situations by reference to mainsprings of the equitable jurisdiction'. Equity must never be deterred by the absence of a precise analogy, provided that the principle invoked is sound. Mindful of this caution, it is, nevertheless, possible to advance the following propositions.

(1) A *Pallant v Morgan* equity may arise where the arrangement or understanding on which it is based precedes the acquisition of the relevant property by one of those parties to that arrangement. It is the pre-acquisition arrangement which colours the subsequent acquisition by the defendant and leads to his being treated as a trustee if he seeks to act inconsistently with it. Where the arrangement or understanding is reached in relation to property already owned by one of the parties, he may (if the arrangement is of sufficient certainty to be enforced specifically) thereby constitute himself trustee on the basis that 'equity looks on that as done which ought to be done'; or an equity may arise under the principles developed in the proprietary estoppel cases...

(2) It is unnecessary that the arrangement or understanding should be contractually enforceable. Indeed, if there is an agreement which is enforceable as a contract, there is unlikely to be any need to

invoke the *Pallant v Morgan* equity; equity can act through the remedy of specific performance and will recognise the existence of a corresponding trust.... In particular, it is no bar to a *Pallant v Morgan* equity that the pre-acquisition arrangement is too uncertain to be enforced as a contract—see *Pallant v Morgan* itself...

(3) It is necessary that the pre-acquisition arrangement or understanding should contemplate that one party (the acquiring party) will take steps to acquire the relevant property; and that, if he does so, the other party (the non-acquiring party) will obtain some interest in that property. Further, it is necessary that (whatever private reservations the acquiring party may have) he has not informed the non-acquiring party before the acquisition (or, more accurately, before it is too late for the parties to be restored to a position of no advantage/no detriment) that he no longer intends to honour the arrangement or understanding.

(4) It is necessary that, in reliance on the arrangement or understanding, the non-acquiring party should do (or omit to do) something which confers an advantage on the acquiring party in relation to the acquisition of the property; or is detrimental to the ability of the non-acquiring party to acquire the property on equal terms. It is the existence of the advantage to the one, or detriment to the other, gained or suffered as a consequence of the arrangement or understanding, which leads to the conclusion that it would be inequitable or unconscionable to allow the acquiring party to retain the property for himself, in a manner inconsistent with the arrangement or understanding which enabled him to acquire it.... In many cases the advantage/detriment will be found in the agreement of the non-acquiring party to keep out of the market. That will usually be both to the advantage of the acquiring party—in that he can bid without competition from the non-acquiring party—and to the detriment of the non-acquiring party—in that he loses the opportunity to acquire the property for himself. But there may be advantage to the one without corresponding detriment to the other.

(5) That leads, I think, to the further conclusions: (i) that, although, in many cases, the advantage/detriment will be found in the agreement of the non-acquiring party to keep out of the market, that is not a necessary feature; and (ii) that, although there will usually be advantage to the one and co-relative disadvantage to the other, the existence of both advantage and detriment is not essential—either will do. What is essential is that the circumstances make it inequitable for the acquiring party to retain the property for himself in a manner inconsistent with the arrangement or understanding on which the non-acquiring party has acted. Those circumstances may arise where the non-acquiring party was never 'in the market' for the whole of the property to be acquired; but (on the faith of an arrangement or understanding that he shall have a part of that property) provides support in relation to the acquisition of the whole which is of advantage to the acquiring party. They may arise where the assistance provided to the acquiring party (in pursuance of the arrangement or understanding) involves no detriment to the non-acquiring party; or where the non-acquiring party acts to his detriment (in pursuance of the arrangement or understanding) without the acquiring party obtaining any advantage therefrom.

The fact that the claimant's reliance on the joint venture need not be detrimental is one factor that distinguishes the joint venture constructive trust from proprietary estoppel.[128]

The requirements of the joint venture constructive trust were elegantly summarized by Lord Scott in *Cobbe v Yeoman's Row Management Ltd*:[129]

A particular factual situation where a constructive trust has been held to have been created arises out of joint ventures relating to property, typically land. If two or more persons agree to embark on a joint venture which involves the acquisition of an identified piece of land and a subsequent exploitation of,

[128] See further Chapter 9.4, pp. 469–80.
[129] [2008] UKHL 55; [2008] 1 WLR 1752, [30].

or dealing with, the land for the purposes of the joint venture, and one of the joint venturers, with the agreement of the others who believe him to be acting for their joint purposes, makes the acquisition in his own name but subsequently seeks to retain the land for his own benefit, the court will regard him as holding the land on trust for the joint venturers. This would be either an implied trust or a constructive trust arising from the circumstances and if, as would be likely from the facts as described, the joint venturers have not agreed and cannot agree about what is to be done with the land, the land would have to be resold and, after discharging the expenses of its purchase and any other necessary expenses of the abortive joint venture, the net proceeds of sale divided equally between the joint venturers.

(b) THE NATURE OF THE JOINT VENTURE CONSTRUCTIVE TRUST

Since this is a trust that responds to the defendant's unconscionability, it follows that the trust should properly be characterized as an institutional constructive trust rather than a common intention constructive trust, and properly forms part of the category of unconscionability arising from breach of an undertaking.[130] In *Crossco No. 4 Unlimited v Jolan Ltd*,[131] however, a majority of the Court of Appeal characterized the 'joint venture constructive trust' as a common intention constructive trust. The case arose from a demerger of a family-owned group of companies involving a split into trading and property businesses. It appeared to have been agreed that a particular building would be transferred to the property company, but the trading company would be able to trade from the ground floor. The trading company asserted an equity to have a lease of the ground floor. This was rejected. Arden LJ, with whom McFarlane LJ agreed, characterized the trust as a form of common intention constructive trust. She said:[132]

the reasoning in *Banner Homes v Luff Developments Ltd* [2000] Ch 372...makes it clear that the ratio of that case is firmly based on a common intention constructive trust. By common intention constructive trust, I mean a constructive trust of the kind enunciated in *Gissing v Gissing* [1971] Ch 162. [This] analysis of *Banner Homes*...was accepted by Lord Scott in *Cobbe v Yeoman's Row Management Ltd* [2008] 1 WLR 1752. The speech of Lord Walker in *Stack v Dowden* [2077] 2 AC 432 and the joint judgment of Lady Hale and Lord Walker in *Jones v Kernott* [2011] UKSC 53 may mean that common intention constructive trusts may be limited in the future to family cases, but I do not consider that that position is so clear as to make it possible at this stage for this court to hold that *Banner Homes* cannot stand with decisions of the House of Lords and Supreme Court, and to treat the ratio of *Banner Homes* as not binding on it.

In those circumstances, it is not open to the court to determine this appeal on the basis that the case can be treated as having some other ratio. Applying the requirements for a constructive trust of this kind...the critical question in the constructive trust claim on this appeal is, therefore, whether the conduct of the [defendant] was unconscionable.

A common intention constructive trust was not recognized on the facts because the defendant was not considered to have acted unconscionably; rather, the claimant had acted under a mistake of which the defendant was not aware. But Arden LJ's emphasis on the need to establish unconscionability

---

[130] McFarlane, 'Constructive Trusts on a Receipt of Property Sub Coditione' (2004) 120 LQR 667. See Chapter 7.2(e), pp. 342–51. See also Gardner, 'Reliance-Based Constructive Trusts' in *Constructive and Resulting Trusts* (ed. Mitchell) (2010), pp. 72–4.

[131] [2011] EWCA Civ 1619; [2012] 1 P and CR 16. See Hopkins, 'The *Pallant v Morgan* "Equity"—Again' [2012] Conv 327. See also *Cobbe v Yeoman's Row Management Ltd* [2008] UKHL 55; [2008] 1 WLR 1752, [31] (Lord Scott).

[132] [2011] EWCA Civ 1619; [2012] 1 P and CR 16, [129].

suggests that this constructive trust is very different from that recognized in *Stack v Dowden*, where unconscionability is not required. Etherton LJ was not convinced that the joint venture constructive trust is a common intention constructive trust. He suggested an alternative explanation:[133]

> The passage of time and developments in the law have, in my judgment, shown the connection between the common intention constructive trust and the *Pallant v Morgan* equity as explained and applied in *Banner Homes* to be untenable. In a commercial context, it is to be expected that the parties will normally take legal advice about their respective rights and interests and will normally reduce their agreements to writing and will not expect to be bound until a contract has been made…They do not expect their rights to be determined in an 'ambulatory' manner by retrospective examination of their conduct and words over the entire period of their relationship. They do not expect the court to determine their respective property rights and interests by the imputation of intentions which they did not have but which the court considers they would have had if they had acted justly and reasonably and thought about the point.
>
> It is not necessary to resort to the common intention constructive trust to provide an explanation for the cases in which the *Pallant v Morgan* equity was, or is said to have been, applied. They can all be explained, and, in my judgment, ought to be explained in wholly conventional terms by the existence and breach of fiduciary duty.…In the absence of agency or partnership, it would require particular and special features for such fiduciary duties to arise between commercial co-venturers. It is clear, however, that in special circumstances they can arise.…
>
> If the cases in which the *Pallant v Morgan* equity has been applied are interpreted as I suggest, then they can be seen as cases in which the Court is, pursuant to the constructive trust, depriving the defendant of the advantage obtained in breach of trust. The irrelevance of lack of complete agreement, whether documented or not, is then easily explained, as is the latitude with which the Court devises the best way to deprive the defendant of the unconscionable advantage.

Etherton LJ concluded that, since the trial judge had held that the defendant did not owe the claimant any fiduciary duty, the claim must fail.

Although Arden LJ did not endorse Etherton LJ's analysis of the joint venture constructive trust for reasons of precedent, she was attracted by his analysis, if only because it would restrict the operation of the joint venture constructive trust. Etherton LJ's characterization of the trust is also consistent with the general tenor of the decision of the Supreme Court in *FHR European Ventures LLP v Cedar Capital Partners LLC*,[134] that profits obtained in breach of fiduciary duty are held on constructive trust.

Rather than relating the joint venture constructive trust to the need to identify a breach of fiduciary duty, the preferable analysis of the joint venture constructive trust is that it arises where property has been obtained by the defendant under an arrangement with the claimant that it is unconscionable for the defendant to ignore following the claimant's reliance on the arrangement. As Lord Neuberger said extra-judicially:[135]

> But the essential point seems to me to be that, in order to give rise to a constructive trust, the property in question must have been acquired by one party under an agreement with the other party, so that it can be said that equity is simply giving effect to an underlying agreement.

---

[133] Ibid, [87].

[134] [2014] UKSC 45; [2015] AC 250. See Chapter 7.2(g), pp. 354–5.

[135] Lord Neuberger, 'The Stuffing of Minerva's Owl? Taxonomy and Taxidermy in Equity' (2009) 68 CLJ 537, 549. Man Yip, 'The *Pallant v Morgan* Equity Reconsidered' (2013) 33 LS 549 does not consider *Pallant v Morgan* to have created a new doctrine of constructive trust but, rather, an orthodox constructive trust which derives from the agency relationship.

Since such an arrangement relates to the sale of land it should be in writing,[136] but it is appropriate to give effect to the informal arrangement in Equity because of the defendant's unconscionable conduct and the claimant's reliance, even though that reliance is not necessarily detrimental.

(c) OPERATION OF THE JOINT VENTURE CONSTRUCTIVE TRUST

The significance of the joint venture constructive trust is particularly well illustrated by *Banner Homes Group plc v Luff Developments Ltd*.

Banner Homes Group plc v Luff Development Ltd [2000] Ch 372

The claimant, Banner, and the defendant, Luff, had formed a joint venture to purchase a site for development. They reached an agreement in principle to acquire a site through a company, which they would incorporate and own equally. The defendant incorporated the company and owned all its shares. The company then acquired the site with funds provided by the defendant. The defendant had second thoughts about pursuing the joint venture with the claimant and, without informing the claimant, started to look for another partner. The defendant did not inform the claimant because it feared that the claimant might acquire the site for itself. The defendant then told the claimant that it was withdrawing from the joint venture. It was held that the defendant held the shares in the company on constructive trust for the claimant and the defendant equally. Chadwick LJ said:[137]

> The judge was referred—as we have been—to a number of cases at first instance which illustrate the circumstances in which equity will impose a constructive trust on property acquired by one person, say A, in furtherance of some pre-acquisition arrangement or understanding with another, say B, that, upon the acquisition of the property by A in circumstances in which B kept out of the market, B would be granted some interest in the property; notwithstanding that the arrangement or understanding falls short of creating contractual obligations enforceable at law . . .
>
> In my view the judge misunderstood the principles upon which equity intervenes in cases of this nature when he held that 'Banner's hope and expectation, however much Luff may have encouraged it, that a formal agreement would be entered into following which Banner would discharge the obligations and take the benefits arising under the joint venture' could not 'give rise to the common arrangement or understanding which is a necessary foundation for the establishment of the equity'. He was wrong to reject the constructive trust claim on the grounds that Banner was seeking to invoke the assistance of equity in order to 'turn a common arrangement or understanding, which is implicitly qualified by the right of either side to withdraw, into an unqualified arrangement or undertaking which denied any such right'. The *Pallant v Morgan* equity does not seek to give effect to the parties' bargain—still less to make for them some bargain which they have not themselves made—as the cases to which I have referred make clear. The equity is invoked where the defendant has acquired property in circumstances where it would be inequitable to allow him to treat it as his own; and where, because it would be inequitable to allow him to treat the property as his own, it is necessary to impose on him the obligations of a trustee in relation to it. It is invoked because there is no bargain which is capable of being enforced. If there were an enforceable bargain there would have been no need for equity to intervene in the way that it has done in the cases to which I have referred.

---

[136] Law of Property (Miscellaneous Provisions) Act 1989, s. 2(1).
[137] [2000] Ch 372, [8].

I am satisfied, also, that the judge was wrong to reject the constructive trust claim on the grounds that Banner had failed to show that it had acted to its detriment in reliance on the arrangement agreed on 14 July, 1995. There was evidence, to which I have referred, that the existence of the arrangement led Banner to regard the site as 'out of play'; that is to say, the existence of the arrangement made it unnecessary, and inappropriate, for Banner to consider the site as a potential acquisition for its own commercial portfolio. But, as the judge himself recognised, one of the reasons why Luff wanted Banner kept 'on board'—and so did not disclose its own doubts as to the future of the joint venture—was that, 'if dropped, Banner might emerge as a rival for the site'. In other words, Luff saw it as an advantage that Banner's belief that the site was out of play should be maintained. Luff wanted to keep Banner out of the market. In those circumstances, it does not lie easily in Luff's mouth to say that Banner suffered no detriment. But whether or not Banner suffered detriment from the fact that it never regarded itself as free to consider the site as a potential acquisition of its own does not seem to me conclusive. Luff obtained the advantage which it sought. Further, Luff obtained the advantage of knowing that it had Banner's support, as a potential joint venturer whose commitment was not in doubt, in an acquisition on which it had not been willing to embark on its own.

As I have sought to show, the *Pallant v Morgan* equity is invoked where it would be inequitable to allow the defendant to treat the property acquired in furtherance of the arrangement or understanding as his own. It may be just as inequitable to allow the defendant to treat the property as his own when it has been acquired by the use of some advantage which he has obtained under the arrangement or understanding as it is to allow him to treat the property as his own when the plaintiff has suffered some detriment under the arrangement or understanding. That, as it seems to me, is this case.

A significant limitation on the operation of the joint venture constructive trust was recognized by the House of Lords in *Cobbe v Yeoman's Row Management Ltd*.[138] In that case the claimant had entered into an oral agreement with Mrs Lisle-Mainwaring, on behalf of the defendant, to purchase flats that belonged to the defendant, and with a view to redeveloping the property and sharing the profits between the claimant and the defendant, the claimant having obtained planning permission for the development at his own expense. Relying upon this oral agreement that the property would be sold to him; the claimant obtained the necessary planning permission, but the defendant then withdrew from the agreement. The claimant was not able to sue on the agreement because it was not in writing.[139] Since writing is not required if the property is held on constructive trust, the claimant argued that it was held on a joint venture constructive trust. This argument failed because the defendant already owned the property. Lord Scott said:[140]

The constructive trust in these failed joint venture cases cannot, in my opinion, be recognised or imposed in the present case. The Yeoman's Row property was owned by the defendant company some years before Mrs. Lisle-Mainwaring began her joint venture discussions (for such in effect they were) with Mr. Cobbe. In the *Banner Homes* case [2000] Ch 372, 397 Chadwick LJ commented on how the situation might appear in such a case:

'Where the arrangement or understanding is reached in relation to property already owned by one of the parties, he may (if the arrangement is of sufficient certainty to be enforced specifically) thereby constitute himself trustee on the basis that 'equity looks on that as done which ought to be done'....'

---

[138] [2008] UKHL 55; [2008] 1 WLR 1752.
[139] Law of Property (Miscellaneous Provisions) Act 1989, s. 2(1).
[140] [2008] UKHL 55; [2008] 1 WLR 1752, [33].

... 'if the arrangement is of sufficient certainty to be enforced specifically' there would be a straight-forward contractual remedy, with no need to resort to trusts. But the point underlying Chadwick LJ's comment is a valid one. If the property that is to be the subject of the joint venture is owned by one of the parties before the joint venture has been embarked upon (as opposed to being acquired as part of the joint venture itself), on what basis, short of a contractually complete agreement for the joint venture, can it be right to regard the owner as having subjected the property to a trust and granted a beneficial interest to the other joint venturers? As Chadwick LJ observed in the *Banner Homes* case, at p 400: 'The [*Pallant v Morgan*] equity is invoked where the defendant has acquired property in circumstances where it would be inequitable to allow him to treat it as his own.' ...

The circumstances of the present case are that the property in question was owned by the defendant company before any negotiations for a joint venture agreement had commenced. The interest in the property that Mr. Cobbe was expecting to acquire was an interest pursuant to a formal written agreement some of the terms of which remained still to be agreed and that never came into existence. Mr. Cobbe expended his time and money in making the planning application in the knowledge that the defendant company was not legally bound. Despite the unconscionability of the defendant company's behaviour in withdrawing from the inchoate agreement immediately planning permission had been obtained, this seems to me a wholly inadequate basis for imposing a constructive trust over the property in order to provide Mr. Cobbe with a remedy for his disappointed expectations. This property was never joint venture property and I can see no justification for treating it as though it was.

Instead, a personal claim founded on unjust enrichment succeeded as regards the value of the claimant's services in obtaining planning permission for the benefit of the defendant.

4. PROPRIETARY ESTOPPEL

Proprietary estoppel is an independent cause of action which enables the court to create property rights in land. The essence of proprietary estoppel was recognized by Lord Scott in *Cobbe v Yeoman's Row Management Ltd*:[141]

An 'estoppel' bars the object of it from asserting some fact or facts, or, sometimes, something that is a mixture of fact and law, that stands in the way of some right claimed by the person entitled to the benefit of the estoppel. The estoppel becomes a 'proprietary' estoppel ... if the right claimed is a proprietary right, usually a right to or over land but, in principle, equally available in relation to chattels or choses in action.

Where the defendant has made a representation that the claimant will acquire an interest in specified property and the claimant has detrimentally relied on that representation, the claimant may have a mere equity entitling him or her to equitable relief. This equity is satisfied by the minimum necessary to do justice, which may be no more than a monetary award,[142] but might involve the court, in the exercise of its discretion, deciding that the defendant holds property on trust for the claimant. This trust can be characterized as constructive, because unconscionability is a key component of proprietary estoppel. The trust is, however, truly remedial and exists only from the date of the court order.

Proprietary estoppel has operated in a wide range of circumstances. Examples include where a gift of property was made imperfectly,[143] where there was a common expectation that property would be

---

[141] [2008] UKHL 55; [2008] 1 WLR 1752, [14].
[142] *Crabb v Arun District Council* [1976] Ch 179, 198 (Scarman LJ).
[143] *Dillwyn v Llewellyn* (1862) 4 De G F and J 517.

acquired by the claimant,[144] or where the claimant made a unilateral mistake that the property belonged to him or her in circumstances where the defendant was aware of the mistake and did nothing to explain the true situation.[145]

The different contexts in which proprietary estoppel arises has been usefully identified by McFarlane and Sales.

McFarlane and Sales, 'Promises, Detriment and Liability: Lessons from Proprietary Estoppel' (2015) 1341 LQR 610, 611

The law of proprietary estoppel has developed rapidly in the last 50 years. The 'classic example' of the doctrine, depending on A's standing by whilst B builds on A's land, believing that land to be B's own, was well-established long before the term 'proprietary estoppel' came into use... As noted by Lord Neuberger in *Fisher v Brooker*,[146] the principle applying in such a case 'can be characterized as acquiescence'. This acquiescence principle applies where B adopts a particular course of conduct in reliance on a mistaken belief as to B's current rights and A, knowing both of B's belief and the existence of A's own inconsistent right, fails to take a reasonably available opportunity to assert that right against B... The requirement that A be aware of the true state of affairs is 'addressed to and limited to cases where the party is alleged to be estopped by acquiescence' and so does not apply to cases of 'estoppel by representation'.[147] In the latter case, A may be prevented from denying the truth of a representation made as to matter of fact, or of mixed fact and law, where B has acted on the basis of the truth of that representation....

If it consisted only of the application to the proprietary context of the long-established acquiescence and representation-based principles, proprietary estoppel would have nothing to contribute to the debate about the legal effect of promises. The key development in the law of proprietary estoppel over the last fifty or so years, however, has been the emergence of a distinct, third strand... In contrast to either the acquiescence or representation-based strands, this form of the doctrine can assist B where B has simply relied on a belief as to A's future conduct, rather than on a mistaken view of B's current rights, or of a matter of fact or mixed fact and law... This third form of proprietary estoppel may therefore protect B where, for example, B has acted in a particular way in reliance on A's promise that A will leave particular land to B on A's death.... In addition to confirming the existence of this strand of proprietary estoppel, the decision of the House of Lords in *Thorner v Major* made clear that such protection for B can arise only if A committed him or herself to that future conduct by making an express or implied promise to B.

(a) REQUIREMENTS FOR PROPRIETARY ESTOPPEL

In *Thorner v Major*, Lord Walker identified the requirements for proprietary estoppel as follows:[148]

most scholars agree that the doctrine is based on three main elements, although they express them in slightly different terms: a representation or assurance made to the claimant; reliance on it by the claimant; and detriment to the claimant in consequence of his (reasonable) reliance.

---

[144] *Plimmer v Wellington Corporation* (1884) 9 App Cas 669.
[145] *Willmot v Barber* (1880) 15 Ch D 96.
[146] [2009] 1 WLR 1764, [62].
[147] *Hopgood v Brown* [1955] 1 WLR 213, 233 CA (Lord Evershed MR).
[148] [2009] UKHL 18; [2009] 1 WLR 776, [29].

The representation made to the claimant must be a promise or assurance that the claimant has, or will have, a proprietary interest in identified property.[149] The representation must be sufficiently clear and unequivocal in its context.[150] This means that, where the representation relates to the acquisition of a proprietary interest in the future, it can be reasonably understood by the claimant to constitute a commitment or assurance by the defendant as to the defendant's future conduct.[151] It is not necessary to show that the defendant actually intended the representation to be relied on.[152]

The operation of the doctrine of proprietary estoppel as a mechanism for the informal creation of property rights is illustrated by *Thorner v Major* itself.

Thorner v Major [2009] UKHL 18; [2009] 1 WLR 776

The claimant, David, had worked on the farm of Peter, a relative, for nearly thirty years without payment, but with the expectation, encouraged by Peter, that David would inherit the farm on Peter's death. Peter died intestate. The House of Lords held that David's estate was estopped from denying that the claimant had acquired a beneficial interest in the farm. Lord Hoffmann said:[153]

A distinctive feature of this case, as Lloyd LJ remarked in the Court of Appeal...was that the representation was never made expressly but was 'a matter of implication and inference from indirect statements and conduct.' It consisted of such matters as handing over to David in 1990 an insurance policy bonus notice with the words 'that's for my death duties' and other oblique remarks on subsequent occasions which indicated that Peter intended David to inherit the farm. As Lloyd LJ observed...such conduct and language might have been consistent with a current intention rather than a definite assurance. But the judge found as a fact that these words and acts were reasonably understood by David as an assurance that he would inherit the farm and that Peter intended them to be so understood.

The Court of Appeal said, correctly, that the fact that Peter had actually intended David to inherit the farm was irrelevant. The question was whether his words and acts would reasonably have conveyed to David an assurance that he would do so. But Lloyd LJ accepted...that the finding as to what Peter would reasonably have been understood to mean by his words and acts was a finding of fact which was not open to challenge. That must be right. The fact that he spoke in oblique and allusive terms does not matter if it was reasonable for David, given his knowledge of Peter and the background circumstances, to have understood him to mean not merely that his present intention was to leave David the farm but that he definitely would do so.

However, the Court of Appeal allowed the appeal on the ground that the judge had not found that the assurance was intended to be relied upon and that there was no material upon which he could have made such a finding. The judge had found that David had relied upon the assurance by not pursuing other opportunities but not, said Lloyd LJ, that Peter had known about these opportunities or intended to discourage David from pursuing them.

At that point, it seems to me, the Court of Appeal departed from their previously objective examination of the meaning which Peter's words and acts would reasonably have conveyed and required proof of his subjective understanding of the effect which those words would have upon David. In my opinion it

---

[149] Ibid, [2] (Lord Hoffmann). The representation can be made by silence or inaction. This is defended by Samet, 'Proprietary Estoppel and Responsibility for Omissions' (2015) MLR 85.
[150] [2009] UKHL 18; [2009] 1 WLR 776, [56] (Lord Walker).
[151] Ibid, [5] (Lord Hoffmann), [17] (Lord Scott), [60] (Lord Walker), [77] (Lord Neuberger).
[152] *Thorner v Major* [2009] UKHL 18; [2009] 1 WLR 776.
[153] Ibid, [2].

did not matter whether Peter knew of any specific alternatives which David might be contemplating. It was enough that the meaning he conveyed would reasonably have been understood as intended to be taken seriously as an assurance which could be relied upon. If David did then rely upon it to his detriment, the necessary element of the estoppel is in my opinion established. It is not necessary that Peter should have known or foreseen the particular act of reliance.

The judge found . . . not only that it was reasonable for David to have understood Peter's words and acts to mean that 'he would be Peter's successor to [the farm]' but that it was reasonable for him to rely upon them. These findings of fact were in my opinion sufficient to support the judge's decision.

It was irrelevant that what constituted the farm varied over time, as the farmer had bought and sold land, since the assurance clearly related to the farm as it existed at the farmer's death.

Although there are three requirements to establish proprietary estoppel, there is a further consideration, namely that of unconscionability. The role of unconscionability was identified by Lord Walker in *Cobbe v Yeoman's Row Management Ltd*:[154]

Here [unconscionability] is being used (as in my opinion it should always be used) as an objective value judgment on *behaviour* (regardless of the state of mind of the individual in question). As such it does in my opinion play a very important part in the doctrine of equitable estoppel, in unifying and confirming, as it were, the other elements. If the other elements appear to be present but the result does not shock the conscience of the court, the analysis needs to be looked at again. In this case Mrs. Lisle-Mainwaring's conduct was unattractive. She chose to stand on her rights rather than respecting her non-binding assurances, while Mr. Cobbe continued to spend time and effort, between Christmas 2003 and March 2004, in obtaining planning permission. But Mr. Cobbe knew that she was bound in honour only, and so in the eyes of equity her conduct, although unattractive, was not unconscionable.

Unconscionability, therefore, involves an objective value judgment of the nature of the defendant's conduct in the light of his or her representation and the claimant's detrimental reliance. It follows that proprietary estoppel will not be established just because the defendant's conduct is unattractive; something more will be required.

The requirements for proprietary estoppel, following the decision in *Thorner v Major*, were usefully summarized by McFarlane and Robertson:[155]

As to the details of the test for proprietary estoppel, the speeches in *Thorner* direct attention to three questions: (1) whether A can reasonably be understood to have made a commitment or promise (as opposed to a mere expression of intention); (2) whether reliance by B could reasonably be taken to have been intended by A; and (3) whether B's actual reliance can be regarded as reasonable in the circumstances. *Thorner* suggests that these questions are very closely connected, and indeed that a positive answer to the third question assumes positive answers to the first and second. It must be emphasised that an objective test applies to each of the questions: for example, in a case where B cares for A following A's promise that she will leave her land to B, it may be that A had no actual intention of leaving her land to B, nor even to influence B's conduct by making the promise. Nonetheless, A's promise will amount to an assurance sufficient to found a proprietary estoppel claim as it can reasonably be understood by B to have constituted a commitment by A as to A's future conduct. The test looks to B's reasonable understanding of A's conduct, not that of a hypothetical stranger, and is thus sensitive to the particular context of A and B's relationship.

---

[154] [2008] UKHL 55; [2008] 1 WLR 1752, [92]. For the facts, see Chapter 9.4(c), p. 475.
[155] 'Apocalypse Averted: Proprietary Estoppel in the House of Lords' (2009) 125 LQR 535, 539.

(b) THE NATURE OF THE RELIEF

Once the requirements of proprietary estoppel have been satisfied, the court has a discretion to award the claimant appropriate relief in the light of all relevant circumstances. For example, this may mean that the court decides that the claimant should not obtain any relief, or that the benefits that he or she had already received are sufficient to satisfy the estoppel.[156] Or it may be that the claimant should receive only some of the assets promised by the defendant,[157] or that the claimant should acquire a beneficial interest in the property, which will be held on constructive trust for the claimant.[158]

If the defendant has made a representation that the claimant relies on to his or her detriment and the defendant subsequently changes his or her mind, this should be taken into account by the court when determining the appropriate relief. But there will be circumstances under which the nature of the claimant's detrimental reliance is such that the defendant should not be able to revoke the representation or assurance. So, for example, in *Thorner v Major*, where Peter had assured David that he would leave his farm to David in his will, if Peter had subsequently changed his mind and left his farm to somebody else, the court might have concluded that, because of David's detrimental reliance on Peter's assurance, the farm could not be left to anybody else, unless Peter's alteration of his will was justified by a change in circumstances. As Lord Neuberger recognized:[159]

> even if Peter's 'implicit statement' may have been revocable, as the Court of Appeal thought, I should not be taken as accepting that it would necessarily follow that, once the statement had been maintained by Peter and acted on by David for a substantial period, it would have been open to Peter freely to go back on it. It may be that he could not have done so, at least without paying David appropriate compensation, unless the change of mind was attributable to, and could be justified by, a change of circumstances. It seems to me that it would be arguable that, even assuming that the 'implicit statement' was not irrevocable, if, say in 2004, Peter had changed his mind, David would nonetheless have been entitled to equitable relief, in the light of his fourteen or more years of unpaid work on the farm.

Lord Scott would have dealt with this problem of the defendant acting contrary to his representation by restricting proprietary estoppel to representations about present property interests and leaving representations about future property interests to be dealt with by means of a remedial constructive trust:[160]

> These reflections invite some thought about the relationship between proprietary estoppel and constructive trust and their respective roles in providing remedies where representations about future property interests have been made and relied on. There are many cases in which the representations relied on relate to the acquisition by the representee of an immediate, or more or less immediate, interest in the property in question. In these cases a proprietary estoppel is the obvious remedy. The representor is estopped from denying that the representee has the proprietary interest that was promised by the representation in question. *Crabb v Arun District Council* [1976] Ch 179 seems to me a clear example of such a case. The Council had represented that Mr. Crabb would be entitled to have access to the private road at gateway B and had confirmed that representation by erecting gateposts and a gate across the gateway. Once Mr. Crabb, in reliance on that representation, had acted to his

---

[156] *Sledmore v Dalby* (1996) 72 P & CR 196.
[157] *Jennings v Rice* [2002] EWCA Civ 159; [2003] 1 P & CR 100.
[158] *Thorner v Major* [2009] UKHL 18; [2009] 1 WLR 776.
[159] Ibid, [89] (Lord Neuberger).
[160] Ibid, [20].

detriment in selling off a portion of his land so that his only means of access to and egress from his retained land was via gateway B, it was too late for the Council to change its mind. The Council was estopped from denying that Mr. Crabb had the necessary access rights... In cases where the owner of land stands by and allows a neighbour to build over the mutual boundary, representing either expressly or impliedly that the building owner is entitled to do so, the owner may be estopped from subsequently asserting his title to the encroached upon land. This, too, seems to me straightforward proprietary estoppel. There are many other examples of decided cases where representations acted on by the representee have led to the representor being estopped from denying that the represen-tee had the proprietary interest in the representor's land that the representation had suggested. Constructive trust, in my opinion, has nothing to offer to cases of this sort. But cases where the relevant representation has related to inheritance prospects seem to me difficult, for the reasons I have given, to square with the principles of proprietary estoppel established by the... *Crabb v Arun District Council* line of cases and, for my part, I find them made easier to understand as constructive trust cases. The possibility of a remedial constructive trust over property, created by the common intention or understanding of the parties regarding the property on the basis of which the claimant has acted to his detriment, has been recognised at least since *Gissing v Gissing* [1971] AC 886... The 'inheritance' cases... are, to my mind, more comfortably viewed as constructive trust cases... For my part I would prefer to keep proprietary estoppel and constructive trust as distinct and separate remedies, to confine proprietary estoppel to cases where the representation, whether express or implied, on which the claimant has acted is unconditional and to address the cases where the repre-sentations are of future benefits, and subject to qualification on account of unforeseen future events, via the principles of remedial constructive trusts.

But, bearing in mind the discretion judges have in determining the relief for proprietary estoppel, nothing is to be gained by distinguishing between proprietary estoppel and the remedial constructive trust in this way. In either case, the court will have a discretion to determine the appropriate relief, but it is far better to do this having satisfied the requirements of proprietary estoppel, rather than to leave the claim and remedy to be determined by the exercise of judicial discretion in imposing a remedial constructive trust. Anyway, the remedial constructive trust has since been rejected by the Supreme Court in *FHR European Ventures LLP v Cedar Capital Partners LLC*.[161]

Even though the claim for proprietary estoppel is structured, the discretion to determine the ap-propriate relief can be criticized. The operation of this discretion lacks transparency in providing reasons for the chosen outcome and fails to take into account the aim of proprietary estoppel, which is to redress the unconscionability that arises where the claimant detrimentally relies on an expectation induced by the defendant. As Gardner has said:[162]

overall, this discretion cannot be sufficiently reconciled with the Rule of Law: it involves an unaccep-table degree of rule by men (the individual judges), not laws. The reasons for this are, however, fully capable of repair. A clearer perception of the jurisdiction's aim is readily attainable, as is a practice of greater transparency in the justification of chosen outcomes, and a sharper focus in appraising the apt-ness of these justifications.

Gardner correctly concludes that the aim of the jurisdiction is to respond to the defendant's unconscionability and rightly considers that, if the focus of the discretion is on that aim, it is defensible.

---

[161] [2014] UKSC 45; [2015] AC 250.
[162] 'The Remedial Discretion in Proprietary Estoppel: Again' (2006) 122 LQR 492, 512.

(c) LIMITATIONS ON PROPRIETARY ESTOPPEL

Following the decision of the House of Lords in *Cobbe v Yeoman's Row Management Ltd*,[163] there are three potentially significant restrictions on the application of the doctrine of proprietary estoppel. In *Cobbe*, although the claimant was aware that the sale of the property depended on a formal agreement being made, and the negotiations relating to that agreement were still continuing, he was encouraged by the defendant's representative, Mrs Lisle-Mainwaring, to believe that a formal, written contract would be forthcoming. In reliance on such representations by Mrs Lisle-Mainwaring, the claimant spent time and money obtaining planning permission. Once planning permission had been obtained the defendant withdrew from the negotiations. The claimant was unable to sue the defendant for breach of contract because the oral contract was unenforceable. He sought to assert a right in the property by virtue of proprietary estoppel, but was unable to do so. Lords Scott[164] and Walker[165] suggested different reasons for this.

(i) *Evidential function of estoppel*

Lord Scott said:[166]

> The terms that had already been agreed were regarded by the parties as being 'binding in honour', but it follows that the parties knew they were not legally binding. So what is it that the defendant company is estopped from asserting or from denying? It cannot be said to be estopped from asserting that the second agreement was unenforceable for want of writing, for Mr. Cobbe does not claim that it was enforceable; nor from denying that the second agreement covered all the terms that needed to be agreed between the parties, for Mr. Cobbe does not claim that it did; nor from denying that, pre-18 March 2004, Mr. Cobbe had acquired any proprietary interest in the property, for he has never alleged that he had. And what proprietary claim was Mr. Cobbe making that an estoppel was necessary to protect? His originally pleaded claim to specific performance of the second agreement was abandoned at a very early stage in the trial...and the proprietary claims that remained were claims that the defendant company held the property on trust for itself and Mr. Cobbe. These remaining proprietary claims were presumably based on the proposition that a constructive trust of the property, with appropriate beneficial interests for the defendant company and Mr. Cobbe, should, by reason of the unconscionable conduct of Mrs. Lisle-Mainwaring, be imposed on the property. I must examine that proposition when dealing with constructive trust as a possible means of providing Mr. Cobbe with a remedy, but the proposition is not one that requires or depends upon any estoppels...

> unconscionability of conduct may well lead to a remedy but, in my opinion, proprietary estoppel cannot be the route to it unless the ingredients for a proprietary estoppel are present. These ingredients should include, in principle, a proprietary claim made by a claimant and an answer to that claim based on some fact, or some point of mixed fact and law, that the person against whom the claim is made can be estopped from asserting. To treat a 'proprietary estoppel equity' as requiring neither a proprietary claim by the claimant nor an estoppel against the defendant but simply unconscionable behaviour is, in my respectful opinion, a recipe for confusion.

> The problem is that when [Mr. Cobbe] made the planning application his expectation was, for proprietary estoppel purposes, the wrong sort of expectation. It was not an expectation that he would, if the planning application succeeded, become entitled to 'a certain interest in land'. His expectation was

---

[163] [2008] UKHL 55; [2008] 1 WLR 1752.
[164] With whose judgment Lords Hoffmann, Brown, and Mance agreed.
[165] With whose judgment Lords Scott and Brown agreed.
[166] [2008] UKHL 55; [2008] 1 WLR 1752, [15].

that he and Mrs. Lisle-Mainwaring, or their respective legal advisers, would sit down and agree the outstanding contractual terms to be incorporated into the formal written agreement, which he justifiably believed would include the already agreed core financial terms, and that his purchase, and subsequently his development of the property, in accordance with that written agreement would follow...

Let it be supposed that Mrs. Lisle-Mainwaring were to be held estopped from denying that the core financial terms of the second agreement were the financial terms on which Mr. Cobbe was entitled to purchase the property. How would that help Mr. Cobbe? He still would not have a complete agreement. Suppose Mrs. Lisle-Mainwaring had simply said she had changed her mind and did not want the property to be sold after all. What would she be estopped from denying? Proprietary estoppel requires, in my opinion, clarity as to what it is that the object of the estoppel is to be estopped from denying, or asserting, and clarity as to the interest in the property in question that that denial, or assertion, would otherwise defeat. If these requirements are not recognised, proprietary estoppel will lose contact with its roots and risk becoming unprincipled and therefore unpredictable, if it has not already become so. This is not, in my opinion, a case in which a remedy can be granted to Mr. Cobbe on the basis of proprietary estoppel.

Lord Scott was correct to assert that the defendant could not be estopped from asserting that the oral contract was unenforceable for want of writing, because the claimant had not claimed that the contract was enforceable. But the conclusion that the defendant could not be estopped from asserting that the claimant did not have a proprietary interest is incorrect, and betrays a misunderstanding about the role of proprietary estoppel. That doctrine does not simply have an evidential function to prevent the defendant from asserting the truth. Rather, proprietary estoppel is a cause of action in its own right that can generate property rights. This has been recognized by McFarlane and Robertson:[167]

a curtailment [of proprietary estoppel] would be inconsistent with the results of a number of Court of Appeal decisions in which a proprietary estoppel claim has been successfully based on an assurance that land will be left to B on the death of A (see, e.g. *Gillett v Holt* [2001] Ch. 210 CA and *Jennings v Rice* [2002] EWCA Civ 159; [2003] 1 FCR 501). It seems Lord Scott retains that narrow view of proprietary estoppel; for that reason, his Lordship's preferred explanation of the result in *Thorner* is that David acquired a right under a common intention constructive trust, rather than through proprietary estoppel (at [20]). However, the reasoning of the other members of the panel in *Thorner* does rest on proprietary estoppel and so is consistent only with the rejection of Lord Scott's narrow interpretation of the doctrine. Indeed, in a postscript to his speech in *Thorner* (at [67]), Lord Walker admitted to having some difficulty with Lord Scott's characterisation of proprietary estoppel in *Yeoman's Row*.

(ii) *Commercial or domestic context*

Lord Walker in *Cobbe*, with whose judgment Lords Scott and Brown agreed, rejected the operation of proprietary estoppel for a different reason. He said:[168]

Mr. Cobbe's case seems to me to fail on the simple but fundamental point that, as persons experienced in the property world, both parties knew that there was no legally binding contract, and that either was therefore free to discontinue the negotiations without legal liability—that is, liability in equity as well as at law... Mr. Cobbe was therefore running a risk, but he stood to make a handsome profit if the deal

---

[167] 'Apocalypse Averted: Proprietary Estoppel in the House of Lords' (2009) 125 LQR 535, 537.
[168] [2008] UKHL 55; [2008] 1 WLR 1752, [91].

went ahead, and the market stayed favourable. He may have thought that any attempt to get Mrs. Lisle-Mainwaring to enter into a written contract before the grant of planning permission would be counter-productive. Whatever his reasons for doing so, the fact is that he ran a commercial risk, with his eyes open, and the outcome has proved unfortunate for him.

It follows that proprietary estoppel could be established only where the claimant believed that the defendant was legally bound to transfer the proprietary interest to the claimant. This is a more convincing explanation as to why proprietary estoppel failed on the facts of *Cobbe*, but it does not explain many of the earlier cases where proprietary estoppel succeeded even though the claimant was not led to believe that the defendant was legally bound to transfer property to the claimant, such as where the defendant represented that he would leave property to the claimant in his will.

Lord Walker's approach to proprietary estoppel appears to be inconsistent with the later decision of the House of Lords in *Thorner v Major*,[169] where Lord Walker gave the leading speech. In *Thorner*, David's claim succeeded even though he had not been not led to believe that he had a legally enforceable claim for the farm. The reason for the difference between *Cobbe* and *Thorner* was identified by Lord Neuberger in *Thorner* itself:[170]

There are two fundamental differences between [*Cobbe*] and this case. First, the nature of the uncertainty in the two cases is entirely different...In that case, there was no doubt about the physical identity of the property. However, there was total uncertainty as to the nature or terms of any benefit (property interest, contractual right, or money), and, if a property interest, as to the nature of that interest (freehold, leasehold, or charge), to be accorded to Mr. Cobbe.

In this case, the extent of the farm might change, but, on the Deputy Judge's analysis, there is, as I see it, no doubt as to what was the subject of the assurance, namely the farm as it existed from time to time. Accordingly, the nature of the interest to be received by David was clear: it was the farm as it existed on Peter's death. As in the case of a very different equitable concept, namely a floating charge, the property the subject of the equity could be conceptually identified from the moment the equity came into existence, but its precise extent fell to be determined when the equity crystallised, namely on Peter's death.

Secondly, the analysis of the law in *Cobbe*...was against the background of very different facts. The relationship between the parties in that case was entirely arm's length and commercial, and the person raising the estoppel was a highly experienced businessman. The circumstances were such that the parties could well have been expected to enter into a contract, however, although they discussed contractual terms, they had consciously chosen not to do so. They had intentionally left their legal relationship to be negotiated, and each of them knew that neither of them was legally bound...

In this case, by contrast, the relationship between Peter and David was familial and personal, and neither of them, least of all David, had much commercial experience. Further, at no time had either of them even started to contemplate entering into a formal contract as to the ownership of the farm after Peter's death. Nor could such a contract have been reasonably expected even to be discussed between them. On the Deputy Judge's findings, it was a relatively straightforward case: Peter made what were, in the circumstances, clear and unambiguous assurances that he would leave his farm to David, and David reasonably relied on, and reasonably acted to his detriment on the basis of, those assurances, over a long period.

---

[169] [2009] UKHL 18; [2009] 1 WLR 776.
[170] Ibid, [92].

It follows that, in the commercial context, if the claimant takes the risk that a contract to sell land will be made, this should be sufficient to defeat proprietary estoppel. In the domestic context, however, the parties would not normally enter into a contract, so there is a role for Equity to assist the claimant. This distinction was advocated extra-judicially by Lord Neuberger:[171]

I suggest that, before he can establish a proprietary estoppel claim, a claimant must show that he acted in the belief that he has something which can be characterised as a legal right—at least in a commercial arm's length context.

I add that qualification, because it is perhaps in this connection that the difference between commercial and domestic cases (which Lord Walker discussed in *Cobbe* at paragraphs 66–8, and which I also touched on in *Thorner* v. *Major* at paragraphs 96–7) comes into focus. The notion that a claimant takes his chance, where he knows that he has no legally enforceable right, is easier to accept in the context of a commercial and arm's length relationship than in a domestic or familial context. In a commercial situation, the absence of a contractual relationship normally arises from the parties, with easy access to legal advice, considering themselves better off, or at least choosing to take a risk, rather than being bound. Maybe Mr. Cobbe wanted to be free to walk away, rather than being committed to paying £12m. and developing the property, if the market went the wrong way. Maybe he thought that he might be able to negotiate a better deal once planning permission was obtained. But, whatever his reason for not having a contract, he faced no emotional or social impediment to insisting on some form of legally binding protection before he went ahead with seeking planning permission. Why should equity assist him, when [the defendant] decided to negotiate a better deal?

But it is much easier to see why David Thorner should have been able to invoke proprietary estoppel. His older, gruff and taciturn cousin led him to believe that, if he continued to provide work and companionship, he would inherit the farm. The notion that David could or should have asked for a commitment in writing, in the context of an informal family relationship, seems somewhat unreal. It would have risked harming the relationship with Peter, and the only solicitor he knew would no doubt have been advising Peter. Unlike in *Cobbe*, formal contractual rights and obligations were simply not the stuff of the relationship between Peter and David Thorner . . .

at least in many domestic cases, it would be inappropriate to require strict adherence to a rule that the claimant must have believed that he had a legally enforceable right. But that is not inconsistent with the decision in a commercial case such as *Cobbe*. Where parties can reasonably be expected to regulate their relationship by a binding contract if they want to do so, equity should fear to tread. Not so where the relationship between the parties is such that they cannot be expected to have recourse to contracts.

The limited role of proprietary estoppel in the commercial context was emphasized by Arden LJ in *Crossco No. 4 Unlimited v Jolan Ltd*:[172]

The House of Lords made it clear that where parties have been dealing on the basis that their negotiations are 'subject to contract', proprietary estoppel will not ordinarily be available: see *Cobbe v Yeoman's Row Management Ltd* [2008] 1 WLR 1752. The result is not unconscionable because the disappointed party will always have known that that was the position. This may be contrasted with the decision of this court in *Herbert v Doyle* [2010] EWCA Civ 1095, where the trial judge had made a clear finding that the parties had agreed to the adjustment of their interests in a site on a basis that was not subject to contract. For the law in general to provide scope for claims in respect of unsuccessful

---

[171] 'The Stuffing of Minerva's Owl? Taxonomy and Taxidermy in Equity' (2009) 68 CLJ 537, 542.
[172] [2011] EWCA Civ 1619; [2012] 1 P and CR 16, [133].

negotiations that do not result in legally enforceable contracts would, in my judgment, be likely to inhibit the efficient pursuit of commercial negotiations, which is a necessary part of proper entrepreneurial activity.

(iii) *Enforcing a void contract*

In *Cobbe v Yeoman's Row Management Ltd* the oral contract of sale was void because it did not comply with the requisite formalities.[173] An interest in the property could, however, be obtained if it were held on implied, resulting, or constructive trust for the claimant.[174] This exception does not mention proprietary estoppel, so Lord Scott in *Cobbe* held that proprietary estoppel cannot render enforceable an agreement that the statute has already declared to be void:[175]

The question arises, therefore, whether a complete agreement for the acquisition of an interest in land that does not comply with the section 2 prescribed formalities, but would be specifically enforceable if it did can become enforceable via the route of proprietary estoppel. It is not necessary in the present case to answer this question, for the second agreement was not a complete agreement and, for that reason, would not have been specifically enforceable so long as it remained incomplete. My present view, however, is that proprietary estoppel cannot be prayed in aid in order to render enforceable an agreement that statute has declared to be void. The proposition that an owner of land can be estopped from asserting that an agreement is void for want of compliance with the requirements of section 2 is, in my opinion, unacceptable. The assertion is no more than the statute provides. Equity can surely not contradict the statute.

If this is correct, it constitutes a significant limitation on the operation of proprietary estoppel, since it would mean that there is no scope for the doctrine to create beneficial interests in property by means of informal arrangements. Lord Scott's conclusion can be avoided by two different arguments. First, where the relief awarded by the court is to recognize that the claimant has a beneficial interest in the relevant property, that property should be considered to be held on constructive trust for the claimant and this constructive trust will fall within the statutory exception. Secondly, proprietary estoppel does not enforce the void contract between the claimant and the defendant, so the policy behind the relevant statutory formality is not engaged. This was recognized by Lord Neuberger, extra-judicially:[176]

Consider the facts in... *Thorner v Major*. As in the great majority of proprietary estoppel cases, the defendant made a statement or gave an indication, which was relied on by the claimant as meaning that he would be granted an interest in land. If Lord Scott's approach is right, there are two possibilities. First, as section 2 [of the Law of Property Miscellaneous Provisions Act 1989] would prevent the claimant from mounting a claim in contract, every proprietary estoppel claim must fail, as the statutory formalities were not complied with. Alternatively, section 2 presents no problem where the statement or indication is so imprecise that we are not near contractual territory. Either alternative is unpalatable. The first would mean that any proprietary estoppel claim based on an indication or promise that the

---

[173] Law of Property (Miscellaneous Provisions) Act 1989, s. 2(1).
[174] Ibid, s. 2(5).
[175] [2008] UKHL 55; [2008] 1 WLR 1752, [29]. In *Pearson v Lehman Brothers Finance SA* [2010] EWHC 2914 (Ch), Briggs J left open whether the dictum of Lord Scott extended to the need to use writing to dispose of an equitable beneficial interest under s. 53(1)(c) of the Law of Property Act 1925. See Chapter 10.2, p. 501.
[176] 'The Stuffing of Minerva's Owl? Taxonomy and Taxidermy in Equity' (2009) 68 CLJ 537, 546.

claimant will get an interest in land will fall foul of section 2, unless the claimant happens to be able to erect a constructive trust out of the arrangement…The second would mean that the clearer and more precise the defendant's indication or promise, and therefore the stronger the claimant's case in principle, the more likely it is that section 2 will scotch any proprietary estoppel claim…

I suggest that section 2 has nothing to do with the matter. In cases such as… *Thorner v. Major*, the estoppel rests on the finding that it would be inequitable for the defendant to insist on his strict legal rights. So the fact that, if there was a contract, it would be void is irrelevant: indeed the very reason for mounting the proprietary estoppel claim is that there is no enforceable contract. I accept of course that it is not open to a claimant to take the unvarnished point that it is inequitable for a defendant to rely on the argument that an apparent contract is void for not complying with the requirements of section 2. But where there is the superadded fact that the claimant, with the conscious encouragement of the defendant, has acted in the belief that there is a valid contract, I suggest that section 2 offers no bar to a claim based in equity.

Crucially, proprietary estoppel is a distinct cause of action in its own right, so that any proprietary rights that arise derive from the estoppel rather than the contract.[177]

QUESTION

Alan and Brenda are an unmarried couple who, before they met, each owned their own house. In 1995, they decided to live together and agreed to sell their houses and pool their resources to buy a new house as the family home. They sold their houses for £200,000 each. They decided to buy a new house, Blackacre, for £400,000. Having obtained financial advice, they decided to contribute £100,000 each to the purchase of Blackacre and obtain a mortgage loan from a bank for the remainder of the purchase price. Blackacre was registered in the name of both Alan and Brenda and became the family home. They each contributed a further £100,000 to purchase Whiteacre as an investment opportunity. Whiteacre was purchased for £400,000 and they obtained a mortgage loan of £200,000 to purchase that property. Whiteacre was registered in the name of Alan only. Monthly rent from Whiteacre was used to pay the mortgage. Alan and Brenda jointly made monthly mortgage payments in respect of Blackacre. In 2005, Alan was injured at work and lost his job. Brenda then became solely responsible for the mortgage payments. In 2015, Alan and Brenda separated. Alan moved out of Blackacre. Both properties have significantly increased in value and Alan seeks your advice as to the beneficial ownership of both Whiteacre and Blackacre.

FURTHER READING

Dixon, 'The Never-Ending Story—Co-ownership After *Stack v Dowden*' [2007] Conv 456.

Dixon, 'Confining and Defining Proprietary Estoppels: The Role of Unconscionability' (2010) 30 LS 408.

Etherton, 'Constructive Trusts and Proprietary Estoppel: The Search for Clarity and Principle' [2009] Conv 104.

Gardner, 'The Remedial Discretion in Proprietary Estoppel: Again' (2006) 122 LQR 492.

Gardner, 'Family Property Today' (2008) 124 LQR 422.

---

[177] McFarlane, 'Proprietary Estoppel and Failed Contractual Negotiations' [2005] Conv 501.

Hopkins, 'The *Pallant v Morgan* Equity' [2002] Conv 35.

Hopkins, 'The *Pallant v Morgan* "Equity"—Again' [2012] Conv 327.

Lord Neuberger, 'The Stuffing of Minerva's Owl? Taxonomy and Taxidermy in Equity' (2009) 68 CLJ 537.

McFarlane and Robertson, 'Apocalypse Averted: Proprietary Estoppel in the House of Lords' (2009) 125 LQR 535.

McFarlane and Sales, 'Promises, Detriment, and Liability: Lessons from Proprietary Estoppel' (2015) 131 LQR 610.

Sloan, 'Keeping Up with the *Jones* Case: Establishing Constructive Trusts in the Sole Legal Owner Scenarios' (2015) 35 LS 226.

Swadling, 'The Common Intention Constructive Trust in the House of Lords: An Opportunity Missed' (2007) 123 LQR 511.

PART V

BENEFICIARIES

10

BENEFICIARIES

CENTRAL ISSUES

1. The beneficiary of a trust has a variety of equitable rights arising from the trust. The nature of these rights will depend on the type of trust that has been created.

2. Beneficiaries of a fixed trust have proprietary rights in the trust property and also a variety of personal rights, including the right to ensure the proper administration of the trust and the right to be informed of an entitlement to trust property.

3. Objects of a discretionary trust do not have any proprietary rights to trust property but they have a variety of personal rights,

including the right to ensure the proper administration of the trust.

4. Beneficiaries do not have a right to inspect trust documents, but disclosure of such documents can be ordered through the exercise of judicial discretion.

5. The disposition of subsisting equitable interests must be effected by signed writing.

6. Adult beneficiaries can unanimously agree to terminate the trust if between them they are absolutely entitled to the beneficial interest.

---

1. NATURE OF A BENEFICIARY'S RIGHTS

Once a private trust has been validly created and constituted, the beneficiary acquires equitable rights, which may be both proprietary and personal. All beneficiaries can enforce these rights against the trustee. In *Armitage v Nurse*,[1] Millett LJ said:

> there is an irreducible core of obligations owed by the trustees to the beneficiaries and enforceable by them which is fundamental to the concept of a trust. If the beneficiaries have no rights enforceable against the trustees there are no trusts.

The nature of the right that is enforceable by the beneficiary will depend on the nature of the trust that has been established, although some rights are common to all beneficiaries, namely the right to have trustees perform the trusts honestly and in good faith for the benefit of the beneficiaries.[2]

---

[1] [1998] Ch 241, 253.
[2] Ibid (Millett LJ).

In particular, the rights of beneficiaries under resulting and constructive trusts are limited, by virtue of the limited responsibilities of the trustees of such trusts.[3]

The beneficiaries can disclaim their beneficial interest by declining it.[4] The right to disclaim exists because nobody is required to accept a gift if he or she does not wish to do so. But it is presumed that, once a beneficiary is aware of the beneficial interest, he or she will not wish to disclaim it; silence is treated as tacit acceptance.[5] If a beneficiary does wish to disclaim his or her interest, he or she must do so actively, within a reasonable time, and show unequivocally that he or she rejects it.[6] In *Lady Naas v Westminster Bank Ltd*,[7] Lord Wright recognized that:

> Disclaimer of a deed has been rightly described as a solemn irrevocable act. If it is alleged, the court must be satisfied that it is fully proved by the party alleging it, who must also establish that it was made with full knowledge and with full intention. In this case, I can find no evidence that the first appellant ever intended or desired to disclaim.

A disclaimer operates retrospectively and the interest disclaimed then passes to the other beneficiaries.[8]

(a) FIXED TRUSTS

(i) *Proprietary rights*

In *Westdeutsche Landesbank Girozentrale v Islington LBC*,[9] Lord Browne-Wilkinson recognized that:

> Once a trust is established, as from the date of its establishment the beneficiary has, in equity, a proprietary interest in the trust property, which proprietary interest will be enforceable in equity against any subsequent holder of the property (whether the original property or substituted property into which it can be traced) other than a purchaser for value of the legal interest without notice.

The nature of a beneficiary's proprietary rights has been identified by Nolan:[10]

> A beneficiary's proprietary rights under a trust consist principally in the beneficiary's primary, negative, right to exclude non-beneficiaries from the enjoyment of trust assets. Infringement of this primary right will generate secondary rights by which a beneficiary may also prevent (or at least restrict) access to assets by non-beneficiaries. In short, these secondary rights are to claim misapplied trust assets (together with their fruits, and any other assets to the extent they can be treated as representing original trust assets), subject to applicable defences, and to have the assets resulting from that claim (or their proceeds) vested in their proper owner. ... In short, equitable proprietary interests under a trust are characterised by consistent exclusionary rights, enforceable against a wide category of people, coupled with highly variable positive rights, enforceable against a very limited number of

---

[3] See Chapter 7.4, pp. 358–9; Chapter 14.1(c), p. 663.

[4] A disclaimer can be made verbally rather than by writing: *Re Paradise Motor Co. Ltd* [1968] 1 WLR 1125. See Chapter 10.2(h), p. 519.

[5] *Standing v Bowring* (1885) 31 Ch D 282.

[6] *Re Paradise Motor Co.* [1968] 1 WLR 1125, 1141 (Danckwerts LJ).

[7] [1940] AC 366, 396.

[8] *JW Broomhead (Vic) Pty Ltd v JW Broomhead Pty Ltd* [1985] VR 891, 934 (McGarvie J).

[9] [1996] AC 669, 705.

[10] 'Equitable property' (2006) 122 LQR 232, 236.

persons. This means that the key proprietary features of a beneficiary's interest under a trust are his primary negative right to exclude non-beneficiaries from enjoyment of trust assets and secondary rights to vindicate that primary right if it is infringed.

One consequence of the beneficiary having a proprietary interest in the trust property is that, if the trustee becomes insolvent, the property will not be available to the trustee's creditors, but will continue to be held on trust for the beneficiaries, whose proprietary rights will consequently prevail over those of the trustee's creditors even though the trustee owns the fund at Law. Further, if trust property is misappropriated by the trustee and is transferred to a third party, the beneficiaries will be able to bring a proprietary claim to recover the property even though the third party is unaware of the beneficiary's interest,[11] save if such a third party had provided value for the property.

The beneficiary's equitable proprietary interest might be overreached,[12] and so extinguished, if the property is transferred from the trust pursuant to an authorized transaction.

Lord Millett in *Equity in Commercial Law* (eds Degeling and Edelman) (Sydney: Lawbook Co., 2005), p. 315

The beneficiaries' interests in a trust fund are proprietary interests in the assets from time to time comprised in the fund subject to the trustees' overriding powers of managing and alienating the trust assets and substituting others. On an authorised sale of a trust investment, the beneficiaries' proprietary interests in the investment are overreached; that is to say, they are automatically transferred from the investment which is sold to the proceeds of sale and any new investment acquired with them. This is the 'fiction of persistence', except that it is not a fiction. The beneficiaries' interests in the new investment are exactly the same as their interest in the old. They have a continuing beneficial interest which persists in the substitute.

Now suppose that the disposal is unauthorised. The trustee sells a trust investment in breach of trust and uses the proceeds to buy shares for himself. The beneficiaries have a continuing proprietary interest in the original investment but they cannot recover it from the purchaser if he is a bona fide purchaser of the legal title without notice of the breach. But they can instead claim a proprietary interest in the shares which the trustee bought for himself …

The only difference between an unauthorised substitution of trust property and an authorised one is one of timing. If the substitution is authorised the beneficiaries' interest in the substituted property is automatically and fully vested at the moment of acquisition. If the substitution is unauthorised, their interest is inchoate, for they may reject it. Their interest in the substitute does not crystallise fully until they elect to accept it. Their right to accept it is a right given to them by the law of property. It is an incident of their property rights in the original asset. Unjust enrichment does not come into it.

Whether an equitable proprietary interest has been overreached will depend on whether the transaction was authorized. If it was not authorized, the beneficiary will retain his or her equitable proprietary interests, save where the property, or its substitute, has been acquired by a bona fide purchaser for value.

The peculiar position of testamentary trusts needs to be emphasized as regards when equitable proprietary rights arise. On the death of the testator, his or her estate passes to the executor, who has

---

[11] See further Chapter 18.4, pp. 889–93.
[12] Fox, 'Overreaching', in *Breach of Trust* (eds Birks and Pretto) (Oxford: Hart, 2002), ch. 4. See further Chapter 2.7(d), pp. 56–7.

full ownership of it. The executor owes fiduciary duties to the beneficiaries to administer the estate and to implement any trusts created by the will, which can be enforced by the beneficiaries. But, until the estate has been administered by the executor, the intended beneficiaries do not have a proprietary interest in the property.[13]

(ii) *Personal rights*

Beneficiaries of fixed trusts also have a variety of personal rights.

(a) *Rights to ensure proper administration of the trust*

The beneficiaries have a right to compel the trustees to administer the trust properly. Beneficiaries can apply to the court if the trustees fail to take the necessary action to preserve trust property.[14] The court can direct the trustees to enforce a claim against third parties or allow the beneficiary to sue a third party for the benefit of the trust.[15] Beneficiaries cannot, however, order a trustee to depart from the terms of the trust.[16]

(b) *Right to be informed*

The beneficiaries have a right to be informed that they have a right to the trust property once they have become entitled to the property, such as on attaining a specified age.[17]

(c) *Rights following breach of trust*

If the trustees have breached the trust, the beneficiaries can sue them for that breach.[18] If the trust is still subsisting, then the effect of the remedy will be to restore value to the trust. But where the trust is no longer subsisting, the remedy will be awarded to the beneficiaries directly. This was recognized by Lord Browne-Wilkinson in *Target Holdings Ltd v Redferns*:[19]

> The equitable rules of compensation for breach of trust have been largely developed in relation to such traditional trusts, where the only way in which all the beneficiaries' rights can be protected is to restore to the trust fund what ought to be there. In such a case the basic rule is that a trustee in breach of trust must restore or pay to the trust estate either the assets which have been lost to the estate by reason of the breach or compensation for such loss. … If specific restitution of the trust property is not possible, then the liability of the trustee is to pay sufficient compensation to the trust estate to put it back to what it would have been had the breach not been committed … Hitherto I have been considering the rights of beneficiaries under traditional trusts where the trusts are still subsisting and therefore the right of each beneficiary, and his only right, is to have the trust fund reconstituted as it should be. But what if at the time of the action claiming compensation for breach of trust those trusts have come to an end? Take as an example again the trust for A for life with remainder to B. During A's lifetime B's only right is to have the trust duly administered and, in the event of a breach, to have the trust fund restored. After A's death, B becomes absolutely entitled. He of course has the right to

---

[13] *Commissioner for Stamp Duties v Livingston* [1965] AC 694. See Chapter 2.6(g), pp. 50–1.
[14] *Fletcher v Fletcher* (1844) 4 Hare 67.
[15] See *Foley v Burnell* (1783) 1 Bro CC 274.
[16] *Re Brockbank* [1948] Ch 206.
[17] *Hawkesley v May* [1956] 1 QB 304, 322 (Havers J). See further Chapter 13.3(a), p. 639.
[18] See Chapter 17.1(a), pp. 798–800.
[19] [1996] AC 421, 435. See further Chapter 17.3, pp. 809–21.

have the trust assets retained by the trustees until they have fully accounted for them to him. But if the trustees commit a breach of trust, there is no reason for compensating the breach of trust by way of an order for restitution and compensation to the trust fund as opposed to the beneficiary himself. The beneficiary's right is no longer simply to have the trust duly administered: he is, in equity, the sole owner of the trust estate. Nor, for the same reason, is restitution to the trust fund necessary to protect other beneficiaries. Therefore, although I do not wholly rule out the possibility that even in those circumstances an order to reconstitute the fund may be appropriate, in the ordinary case where a beneficiary becomes absolutely entitled to the trust fund the court orders, not restitution to the trust estate, but the payment of compensation directly to the beneficiary.

This was amplified by Lord Reed in *AIB Group (UK) plc v Redler*:[20]

The pecuniary remedy for a breach of trust affecting the trust fund cannot involve a payment to a particular beneficiary, unless the beneficiary is absolutely entitled to the fund. Absent such entitlement, the only way to ensure that each beneficiary is appropriately compensated is for the payment to be made into the trust fund, to be held in accordance with the terms of the trust. This is accomplished by adding the appropriate amount to the fund, so that the fund is restored or replenished. Where, on the other hand, the trust is no longer subsisting, compensation for the breach of trust can be paid directly to the beneficiary absolutely entitled. As Lord Browne-Wilkinson explained, the measure of compensation is the same as if there had been an accounting and execution of the trust: in other words, the difference between what the beneficiary ought to have received and what he has in fact received as a result of the diminution in the trust fund.

(d) Rights against third parties

If a third party has received property in which the beneficiaries have a proprietary interest, but the third party no longer has that property, the beneficiaries may have a personal claim against the third party in the action known as 'unconscionable receipt'.[21] Beneficiaries also have rights against third parties who dishonestly assist a breach of trust.[22]

(e) Tortious rights

Where the trust property has been stolen, the beneficiary usually has no direct personal claim in conversion against the thief, because conversion cannot be used to protect the beneficiary's equitable property rights.[23] If, however, the beneficiary was in possession of the trust property at the time of the theft, he or she would have a claim in conversion, but based on his or her possessory right rather than an equitable property right.[24] Similar principles underpin claims in negligence. Where a third party has negligently damaged the trust property, the beneficiary has no direct claim against the tortfeasor for economic loss since the beneficiary has no legal or possessory title to the property.[25] The trustees will have a direct claim against the tortfeasor, although any damages will be held on trust for the beneficiary.[26] If the trustee refuses to sue the tortfeasor, the beneficiary could sue the

---

[20] [2014] UKSC 58; [2015] AC 1503, [100]. See further Chapter 17.3, pp. 821–31.
[21] See Chapter 19.3, pp. 928–51.
[22] See Chapter 19.2, pp. 951–70.
[23] *MCC Proceeds Inc. v Lehman Bros International (Europe)* [1994] 4 All ER 675.
[24] *Healey v Healey* [1915] 1 KB 938.
[25] *Leigh and Sillivan Ltd v Aliakmon Shipping Co. Ltd* [1986] AC 785, 812 (Lord Brandon).
[26] Similarly, where the trustee has a direct claim against a third party for breach of contract that caused loss to the beneficiary: *Pan Atlantic Insurance Co. Ltd v Pine Top Insurance Co. Ltd* [1989] 2 Lloyd's Rep 568.

trustee for breach of trust, or sue the tortfeasor him or herself, but only by making the trustee a party to the proceedings,[27] since the trustee's legal title to the property can be used to establish the property tort claims as these are Common Law claims that are based on interference with legal property rights. This ability to name the trustee as a defendant to enable the beneficiary to bring proceedings against a third party is known as the '*Vandepitte* procedure',[28] and its application is not confined to tort claims, but has been recognized as regards claims for losses sustained by the beneficiaries consequent upon a third party breaching a contract with the trustee.[29] This is a shortcut procedure to avoid two claims, one involving the beneficiary applying to the court to require the trustee to sue and the other involving the trustee suing the third party.[30]

Justifications for this procedure were provided by Lord Collins in *Roberts v Gill and Co.*:[31]

> Consequently it has been the consistent practice ... for almost 300 years that, where a beneficiary brings an action in his own name to recover trust property, the trustees should be joined as defendants. *Daniell's Chancery Practice*, 7th ed 1901, p. 176 states: '....such an action cannot, however, be maintained without the personal representative being a party'. To put it differently, it would be 'procedurally improper to continue without the addition ... which is proposed': McGee, *Limitation Periods*, 5th ed 2006, para 23.025. The purpose of joinder has been said to ensure that they are bound by any judgment and to avoid the risk of multiplicity of actions: Lewin, *Trusts*, 18th ed 2008, para 43-05. But joinder also has a substantive basis, since the beneficiary has no personal right to sue, and is suing on behalf of the estate, or more accurately, the trustee.

(f) Rights to inspect trust documents

If the beneficiaries are to monitor the trustees' performance of their duties, it is important that they have access to documents relating to the management and administration of the trust, and the powers of the trustee to distribute trust assets. Whether the beneficiaries have rights to such documents has proved controversial. It was at one time thought that the beneficiaries had a proprietary right to trust documents because they belonged to the trust and so belonged in Equity to the beneficiaries who consequently had a right to see all such documents. In *O'Rourke v Darbishire*,[32] Lord Wrenbury said:

> The beneficiary is entitled to see all trust documents because they are trust documents and because he is a beneficiary. They are in this sense his own. Action or no action, he is entitled to access to them. This has nothing to do with discovery. The right to discovery is a right to see someone else's documents. The proprietary right is a right to access to documents which are your own.

It has since been recognized that the beneficiaries have no right to inspect trust documents but the court has discretion to disclose such documents as part of its supervisory jurisdiction to administer trusts.[33]

---

[27] *Shell UK Ltd v Total UK Ltd* [2010] EWCA Civ 180; [2011] QB 86. See Chapter 2.7(e)(i), pp. 57–8.
[28] After *Vandepitte v Preferred Accident Insurance Corporation of New York* [1933] AC 70, 79 (PC) (Lord Wright).
[29] *Vandepitte v Preferred Accident Insurance Corporation of New York*, ibid; *The Alabzero* [1977] AC 744.
[30] *Barbados Trust Co. Ltd v Bank of Zambia* [2007] EWCA Civ 148; [2007] 2 All ER (Comm) 445, [45] (Waller LJ).
[31] [2010] UKSC 22; [2011] 1 AC 240, [62].
[32] [1920] AC 581, 626. See also *Re Londonderry's Settlement* [1965] Ch 918.
[33] *Schmidt v Rosewood Trust Ltd* [2003] UKPC 26; [2003] 2 AC 709; *Breakspear v Ackland* [2008] EWHC 220 (Ch); [2009] Ch 32.

Schmidt v Rosewood Trust Ltd [2003] UKPC; [2003] 2 AC 709

The petitioner sought the disclosure of documents relating to two trusts of which his father had been co-settlor. The petitioner claimed discretionary interests under the trusts. He was also the administrator of his father's estate. The trustees opposed disclosure because the petitioner was not a beneficiary under the trust and his father was only an object of a power and so had no entitlement to gain access to trust documents. The Privy Council held that the court could order the documents to be disclosed, but this did not depend on whether the beneficiary had a proprietary right to disclosure.

Lord Walker:

Much of the debate before the Board addressed the question whether a beneficiary's right or claim to disclosure of trust documents should be regarded as a proprietary right. [Counsel for the trustees] argued that it should be classified in that way, and from that starting point he argued that no object of a mere power could have any right or claim to disclosure, because he had no proprietary interest in the trust property. [Counsel for the Trustees] submitted that this point has been conclusively settled by the decision of the House of Lords in *O'Rourke v Darbishire* [1920] AC 581 …

The Board does not find it surprising that Lord Wrenbury's observations [in *O'Rourke*] have been so often cited, since they are a vivid expression of the basic distinction between the right of a beneficiary arising under the law of trusts (which most would regard as part of the law of property) and the right of a litigant to disclosure of his opponent's documents (which is part of the law of procedure and evidence). But the Board cannot regard it as a reasoned or binding decision that a beneficiary's right or claim to disclosure of trust documents or information must always have the proprietary basis of a transmissible interest in trust property. That was not an issue in *O'Rourke v Darbishire*.

Their Lordships consider that the more principled and correct approach is to regard the right to seek disclosure of trust documents as one aspect of the court's inherent jurisdiction to supervise, and if necessary to intervene in, the administration of trusts. The right to seek the court's intervention does not depend on entitlement to a fixed and transmissible beneficial interest. The object of a discretion (including a mere power) may also be entitled to protection from a court of equity, although the circumstances in which he may seek protection, and the nature of the protection he may expect to obtain, will depend on the court's discretion … [Counsel for the Trustees'] submission to the contrary effect tends to prove too much, since he would regard the object of a discretionary trust as having a proprietary interest even though it is not transmissible (except in the special case of collective action taken unanimously by all the members of a closed class).

Their Lordships are therefore in general agreement with the approach adopted in the judgments of Kirby P and Sheller JA in the Court of Appeal of New South Wales in *Hartigan Nominees Pty Ltd v Rydge* [1992] 29 NSWLR 405. That was a case concerned with disclosure of a memorandum of wishes addressed to the trustees by Sir Norman Rydge (who was in substance, but not nominally, the settlor). Kirby P said, at pp 421–422:

> 'I do not consider that it is imperative to determine whether that document is a "trust document" (as I think it is) or whether the respondent, as a beneficiary, has a proprietary interest in it (as I am also inclined to think he does). Much of the law on the subject of access to documents has conventionally been expressed in terms of the "proprietary interest" in the document of the party seeking access to it. Thus, it has been held that a cestui que trust has a "proprietary right" to seek all documents relating to the trust: see *O'Rourke v Darbishire* [1920] AC 581, 601, 603. This approach is unsatisfactory. Access should not be limited to documents in which a proprietary right may be established. Such rights may be sufficient; but

they are not necessary to a right of access which the courts will enforce to uphold the *cestui que trust's* entitlement to a reasonable assurance of the manifest integrity of the administration of the trust by the trustees. I agree with Professor HAJ Ford's comment, in his book (with Mr W A Lee) *Principles of the Law of Trusts*, 2nd ed (1990) Sydney, Law Book Co, p 425, that the equation of rights of inspection of trust documents with the beneficiaries' equitable rights of property in the trust assets "gives rise to far more problems than it solves" (at p 425): "The legal title and rights to possession are in the trustees: all the beneficiary has are equitable rights against the trustees ... The beneficiary's rights to inspect trust documents are founded therefore not upon any equitable proprietary right which he or she may have in respect of those documents but upon the trustee's fiduciary duty to keep the beneficiary informed and to render accounts. It is the extent of that duty that is in issue. The equation of the right to inspect trust documents with the beneficiary's equitable proprietary rights gives rise to unnecessary and undesirable consequences. It results in the drawing of virtually incomprehensible distinctions between documents which are trust documents and those which are not; it casts doubts upon the rights of beneficiaries who cannot claim to have an equitable proprietary interest in the trust assets, such as the beneficiaries of discretionary trusts; and it may give trustees too great a degree of protection in the case of documents, artificially classified as not being trust documents, and beneficiaries too great a right to inspect the activities of trustees in the case of documents which are, equally artificially, classified as trust documents."'

Mahoney JA, at p 435, favoured the proprietary basis but recognised that it extended to information of a non-documentary kind. Sheller JA, at p 444, considered that inquiry as to an applicant's proprietary interest was 'if not a false, an unhelpful trail'. All three members of the court expressed reservations about the reasoning and conclusions in *Re Londonderry's Settlement* [1965] Ch 918.

It will be observed that Kirby P said that for an applicant to have a proprietary right might be sufficient, but was not necessary. In the Board's view it is neither sufficient nor necessary. Since *Re Cowin* 33 Ch D 179 well over a century ago the court has made clear that there may be circumstances (especially of confidentiality) in which even a vested and transmissible beneficial interest is not a sufficient basis for requiring disclosure of trust documents; and *Re Londonderry's Settlement* and more recent cases have begun to work out in some detail the way in which the court should exercise its discretion in such cases. There are three such areas in which the court may have to form a discretionary judgment: whether a discretionary object (or some other beneficiary with only a remote or wholly defeasible interest) should be granted relief at all; what classes of documents should be disclosed, either completely or in a redacted form; and what safeguards should be imposed (whether by undertakings to the court, arrangements for professional inspection, or otherwise) to limit the use which may be made of documents or information disclosed under the order of the court. ...

Their Lordships have already indicated their view that a beneficiary's right to seek disclosure of trust documents, although sometimes not inappropriately described as a proprietary right, is best approached as one aspect of the court's inherent jurisdiction to supervise, and where appropriate intervene in, the administration of trusts. There is therefore in their Lordships' view no reason to draw any bright dividing line either between transmissible and non-transmissible (that is, discretionary) interests, or between the rights of an object of a discretionary trust and those of the object of a mere power (of a fiduciary character). The differences in this context between trusts and powers are (as Lord Wilberforce demonstrated in *Re Baden* [1971] AC 424, 448–449) a good deal less significant than the similarities. The tide of Commonwealth authority, although not entirely uniform, appears to be flowing in that direction.

However, the recent cases also confirm (as had been stated as long ago as *Re Cowin* 33 Ch D 179 in 1886) that no beneficiary (and least of all a discretionary object) has any entitlement as of right to disclosure of anything which can plausibly be described as a trust document. Especially when there are issues as to personal or commercial confidentiality, the court may have to balance the competing interests of different beneficiaries, the trustees themselves, and third parties. Disclosure may have to be limited and safeguards may have to be put in place. Evaluation of the claims of a beneficiary (and especially of a discretionary object) may be an important part of the balancing exercise which the court has to perform on the materials placed before it. In many cases the court may have no difficulty in concluding that an applicant with no more than a theoretical possibility of benefit ought not to be granted any relief.

Whilst replacing the old test of a proprietary right to disclosure of trust documents with a judicial discretion to disclose might be considered to introduce too much uncertainty, the modern approach to disclosure is clearer and more principled, because the court is no longer required to speculate as to whether a particular document is or is not a trust document. Rather, the judge has a discretion to determine, in the light of all relevant circumstances, whether it is appropriate to authorize disclosure.

(b) DISCRETIONARY TRUSTS

(i) *Proprietary rights*

A discretionary trust is a trust for distribution amongst members of a class of objects that the trustees have a discretion to select. The objects of such trusts do not have a proprietary right to trust property. This was made clear by Lord Wilberforce in *Gartside v IRC*,[34] when considering whether the interests of objects is proprietary and so taxable:

No doubt in a certain sense a beneficiary under a discretionary trust has an 'interest': the nature of it may, sufficiently for the purpose, be spelt out by saying that he has a right to be considered as a potential recipient of benefit by the trustees and a right to have his interest protected by a court of equity. Certainly that is so, and when it is said that he has a right to have the trustees exercise their discretion 'fairly' or 'reasonably' or 'properly' that indicates clearly enough that some objective consideration (not stated explicitly in declaring the discretionary trust, but latent in it) must be applied by the trustees and that the right is more than a mere spes [a hope]. But that does not mean that he has an interest which is capable of being taxed by reference to its extent in the trust fund's income: it may be a right, with some degree of concreteness or solidity, one which attracts the protection of a court of equity, yet it may still lack the necessary quality of definable extent which must exist before it can be taxed.

It follows that the objects have no proprietary interest in the trust fund itself, because nobody knows whether an object will benefit under the trust until the trustees have exercised their discretion to distribute the trust property to members of the class. As Ungoed-Thomas J recognized in *Sainsbury v IRC*:[35]

The only right which any object has in an exhaustive, as in a non-exhaustive, trust is to have the trustees exercise their discretion and to be protected by the court in that right. True, the trustees' discretion does not extend in the case of an exhaustive trust, as in a non-exhaustive trust, to deciding whether to make distributions to objects, but only whether the distribution that must be made shall be made to one or more of them and if more than one, in what proportion. But, since, in an exhaustive as in a non-exhaustive trust, it cannot be said before distribution that an object is entitled to any defined part of the income, this difference between them does not make the right of any individual object quantifiable.

---

[34] [1968] AC 553, 617.
[35] [1970] Ch 712, 724.

Although objects of a discretionary trust do have rights, these are not proprietary because they are not transmissible interests,[36] although the objects can claim against third parties who have misappropriated trust assets, which is one of the characteristics of a proprietary right.[37] They can, however, seek only the return of the misappropriated property to the trust and cannot obtain the misappropriated property for themselves, since the distribution of the property will still be determined by the exercise of the trustee's discretion.

(ii) *Personal rights*

Objects under a discretionary trust have a fundamental right to ensure that the trust is administered properly, in the sense that the trustees consider the exercise of their power of appointment and exercise that power in a reasonable time. Beneficiaries have a number of specific personal rights relating to this fundamental right to ensure proper administration of the trust.

(a) *Application to court*

If the trustees fail to exercise their discretion, the objects can apply to the court. The court has a variety of options open to it,[38] including directing the trustees to exercise their discretion, appointing new trustees, authorizing a scheme of distribution, or directing the trustees to distribute the trust assets.

(b) *Rights arising from breach of trust*

If the trustees' power of appointment is exercised in breach of trust, the beneficiaries can apply to the court to have the appointment set aside.

(c) *Right to be informed*

Since the objects have a right to put their case to the trustees for the exercise of their discretion,[39] it follows that the objects should have a right to be informed that they are objects.[40]

(d) *Rights to trust documents*

In the same way as beneficiaries of a fixed trust can request to see trust documents,[41] so too can the objects of a discretionary trust. Under the old theory of proprietary rights in trust documents, the objects would not have been able to see the documents, since they were not considered to have any proprietary rights in trust property. But with the recognition by the Privy Council in *Schmidt v Rosewood Trust Ltd*[42] that the court has a discretion to disclose documents to beneficiaries, and that this does not depend on the assertion of any proprietary rights but follows instead from the shift of emphasis to the court's inherent jurisdiction to supervise the proper administration of the trust, it follows that objects of a discretionary trust can request disclosure of trust documents. This was specifically recognized in *Schmidt* itself. But the court will be less likely to exercise its discretion to disclose trust documents in

---

[36] *Schmidt v Rosewood Trust Ltd* [2003] UKPC 26; [2003] 2 AC 709, [51] and [54].

[37] See further Chapter 1.4(a), pp. 11–13. See Nolan, 'Equitable Property' (2006) 122 LQR 232, 257.

[38] *McPhail v Doulton* [1971] AC 424, 456–7 (Lord Wilberforce). See Chapter 13.2(b)(i), pp. 632–4.

[39] *Murphy v Murphy* [1999] 1 WLR 282.

[40] Hayton, 'The Irreducible Core Content of Trusteeship', in *Trends in Contemporary Trust Law* (ed. Oakley) (Oxford: Clarendon Press, 1996), p. 49.

[41] See Chapter 10.1(a)(ii)(f), pp. 490–3.

[42] [2003] UKPC 26; [2003] 2 AC 709. See Chapter 10.1(a)(ii)(f), pp. 491–3.

favour of an object under a discretionary trust,[43] since the objects have only a theoretical possibility of benefiting under the trust.

The operation of this judicial discretion to discretionary trusts was considered in *Breakspear v Ackland*.

Breakspear v Ackland [2008] EWHC 220 (Ch); [2009] Ch 32

The beneficiaries sought the disclosure of a 'wish letter', which had been written to the trustees by Basil, the settlor, as well as disclosure of oral communications from Basil to the trustees. Briggs J said:[44]

The essential characteristic of a wish letter (to which Basil's is no exception) is that it is a mechanism for the communication by a settlor to trustees of the settlement of non-binding requests by him to take stated matters into account when exercising their discretionary powers. Typically, wish letters are concerned with the exercise of dispositive discretions, but they may include wishes in relation to the exercise of powers of investment, or of other purely administrative powers. For present purposes I am concerned with a wish letter which is substantially contemporaneous with the settlement itself. The question whether later wish letters have the same status is beyond the scope of this judgment.

The large increase in the use of wish letters has gone hand in hand with the rise in the popularity of discretionary trusts, in preference to the more detailed fixed interest trust. The combination of a broad discretionary trust accompanied by a wish letter may be said to have two particular advantages. The first, an advantage which it enjoys over the old-fashioned fixed interest trust, is that it preserves flexibility for the trustees in responding to changes in the beneficiaries' circumstances which are not or cannot be foreseen by the settlor. The second advantage, which stems from the placing of the trusts affecting the property and the settlor's non-binding wishes into separate documents, is that the settlor may make use of a confidential wish letter as the medium for the written expression of facts, beliefs, expectations, concerns and (occasionally) prejudices about the beneficiaries which it would or might be hurtful, impolitic or simply undesirable for him to include in a document which the beneficiaries had a right to inspect. That advantage may be summarised in the word confidentiality, so long as it is appreciated that the word has both a subjective and an objective connotation. Confidentiality may serve a purely selfish desire of the settlor to keep his wishes, beliefs and the communication of certain facts secret from the family. Objectively speaking, that secrecy may in many cases be thoroughly beneficial, since it may tend to preserve family harmony and mutual respect, while enabling trustees to be briefed as to matters relevant to the exercise of their discretionary powers, rather than kept in ignorance of them.

The use and advantages of wish letters in conjunction with broad discretionary trusts is not confined to family trusts. For example, the advantage of flexibility may be equally applicable to an employee trust. None the less, the advantage of confidentiality is at its most obvious in relation to a family trust, and it is in the effect upon that advantage which any uncertainty or change in the law relating to disclosure of wish letters at the request of beneficiaries is at its most acute. Plainly, if the law is that, generally, wish letters are not disclosable, settlors will be encouraged to use them as the medium for the communication of valuable but confidential information relevant to the exercise of the trustees' discretionary powers. If by contrast wish letters are generally disclosable, that potential advantage is likely to be wholly closed off for the future, and the disclosure of genuinely confidential information in existing wish letters at the request of beneficiaries is likely to risk causing precisely the harm which led to that

---

[43] Ibid, [54].
[44] [2008] EWHC 220 (Ch); [2009] Ch 32, 36.

information being included in a wish letter in the first place, and to defeat what may to date have been real expectations of confidentiality in the minds both of settlors and trustees.

Since few would argue that clearly and rationally expressed wishes and relevant information included by settlors in wish letters could be treated by trustees as wholly irrelevant to the exercise of their discretionary powers, it is inescapable that their content will potentially be relevant, both to beneficiaries in monitoring the performance by trustees of their fiduciary obligations, and to the court in enforcing that performance where necessary and appropriate. Furthermore, the contents of a relevant wish letter may make all the difference to a beneficiary in understanding, in the context of an otherwise broadly drafted discretionary trust, what are or may be his or her expectations of benefit from the assets of a family settlement. While such expectations may on occasion be damaging, in particular to young beneficiaries, a broad knowledge of their prospects may be of significant advantage to them in planning both their own lives, and the education and maintenance of their children and other dependants. It is incidentally for this latter purpose that the claimants say that they have made their claim to disclosure.

There is therefore an inevitable tension between on the one hand the advantages of confidentiality, and on the other hand, the advantages of disclosure, in relation to wish letters. ... It is tempting to say that the infinitely variable weight to be given to those competing considerations in any particular case is best resolved by the exercise of discretion by the judge resorted to for the resolution of the impasse, rather than by the laying down of rules or even guidelines. But in my judgment this superficially attractive solution has real disadvantages. The first is that unless the principles are generally understood, settlors are likely to treat the uncertainty as to the general confidentiality of wish letters as a disincentive to their beneficial use. The second is that the uncertainty is likely to lead to more rather than less applications to court to resolve questions of disclosure, and will therefore be a recipe for litigation. In the context of the likely asset base of even wealthy families, the attendant cost should be avoided if at all possible ...

The first question is whether it is either permissible or appropriate in the light of *O'Rourke v Darbishire* [1920] AC 581 and the *Londonderry* case [1965] Ch 918 for me to decide at first instance that the basis upon which trustees and the court should approach a request for disclosure of a wish letter (or of any other document in the possession of trustees in their capacity as such) is one calling for the exercise of discretion rather than the adjudication upon a proprietary right. In my judgment it is both permissible and appropriate to answer that question in the affirmative ... Furthermore, ... even the Court of Appeal in the *Londonderry* case itself found the proprietary analysis to be both inconclusive and unsatisfactory, by comparison with the recognition of a clear, principled basis for refusing disclosure even in cases where there appeared to be a prima facie proprietary right to disclosure.

On that basis, the second question is whether the *Londonderry* principle[45] remains good law, at least in England. In my opinion, it is still good law and, in any event, law by which a first instance judge remains bound, unless and until released by some higher judicial or parliamentary authority.

At the heart of the *Londonderry* principle is the unanimous conclusion (most clearly expressed by Danckwerts LJ) that it is in the interests of beneficiaries of family discretionary trusts, and advantageous to the due administration of such trusts, that the exercise by trustees of their dispositive discretionary powers be regarded, from start to finish, as an essentially confidential process. It is in the interests of the beneficiaries because it enables the trustees to make discreet but thorough inquiries as to their competing claims for consideration for benefit without fear or risk that those inquiries will come to the beneficiaries' knowledge. They may include, for example, inquiries as to the existence of some life-threatening illness of which it is appropriate that the beneficiary in question be kept ignorant. Such confidentiality serves the due administration of family trusts both because it tends to reduce the scope for litigation about the rationality of the exercise by trustees of their discretions, and because it is likely to encourage suitable trustees to accept office, undeterred by a perception that their discretionary

---

[45] Which held that trustees need not disclose reasons for their decision. See Chapter 11.7(b), pp. 566–8.

deliberations will be subjected to scrutiny by disappointed or hostile beneficiaries, and to potentially expensive litigation in the courts.

I recognise the force of the contrary proposition ... that the conferral of a general confidentiality upon the exercise by trustees of their discretionary powers may in particular cases reduce the practical extent to which they can be held to account. Trustees undoubtedly are accountable for the exercise of those powers, but it seems to me quite wrong to suppose that the courts have been mindless of the existence of that core principle of accountability, during the period of more than 150 years when the law has been that it is better for confidentiality to be afforded. ...

Nor can I see any persuasive basis for thinking that the reasoning which led the English courts to think it appropriate in the interests of beneficiaries, and in the administration of trusts, to confer confidentiality on the exercise by family trustees of their discretionary dispositive powers has ceased to hold good. It is not obvious that the potentially disastrous consequences of a resort to civil litigation about the administration of family trust property, in terms of the expenditure of time and cost, are much less of a potential evil than they were in the 19th century. Nor is there any less need today than there always has been to avoid deterring suitable family trustees from accepting an arduous unpaid office. Of course there is a risk that the conferral of such confidentiality may enable unworthy trustees to use it as a shield for the concealment of their culpable inadequacies, but this risk cannot have been ignored in the 19th century, and now that it is recognised that the general principle of confidentiality is subject to being overridden as a matter of discretion by the court, it may fairly be supposed that the risk has if anything become more rather than less manageable.

My reason for concluding that, regardless of my own opinion, I am bound to continue to treat the *Londonderry* principle as still being good law is simply because it formed part of the ratio of that decision, it has never been overruled, and because, if anything, it received a general endorsement rather than criticism in *Schmidt v Rosewood Trust Ltd* [2003] 2 AC 709.

I turn therefore to the question whether, and if so in what way, the *Londonderry* principle applies to wish letters. In that context I am content to limit myself to wish letters arising in the context of family discretionary trusts, rather than employee trusts, pension trusts or other business trusts, leaving for another occasion the manner in which the *Londonderry* principle is applicable to them. The defining characteristic of a wish letter is that it contains material which the settlor desires that the trustees should take into account when exercising their (usually dispositive) discretionary powers. It is therefore brought into existence for the sole purpose of serving and facilitating an inherently confidential process. It seems to me axiomatic that a document brought into existence for the sole or predominant purpose of being used in furtherance of an inherently confidential process is itself properly to be regarded as confidential, to substantially the same extent and effect as the process which it is intended to serve ...

While in a sense a wish letter is the companion of the trust deed, it by no means follows that it therefore needs or ought to be afforded similar treatment in the hands of the trustees. The trust deed is a document which confers and identifies the trustees' powers. There is in principle nothing confidential about the existence and precise boundaries of those powers. By contrast, the wish letter, operating exclusively within those boundaries and purely in furtherance of the trustees' confidential exercise of discretionary powers, may properly be afforded a status of confidentiality which the trust deed itself entirely lacks ...

Generally, the confidence which ordinarily attaches to a wish letter is such that, for the better discharge of their confidential functions, the trustees need not disclose it to beneficiaries merely because they request it unless, in their view, disclosure is in the interests of the sound administration of the trust, and the discharge of their powers and discretions ...

Before applying those principles to the facts of the present case, I shall briefly summarise what I consider to be their practical effect in relation to family discretionary trusts, separately in relation to each of the three stages in which the issue may typically arise. First, trustees should in general regard a wish letter (that is a document from the settlor the sole or predominant purpose of which is or appears to be to assist them in the exercise of their discretionary powers) as invested with a confidentiality designed to be maintained, relaxed, or if necessary abandoned, as they judge best serves the interests of the beneficiaries and the due administration of the trust. This discretion to maintain, relax or abandon confidence arises regardless of a request for disclosure by a beneficiary, and persists regardless of the incapacity, death or change of heart on the part of the settlor.

Where a beneficiary makes a request for disclosure, that in my judgment merely triggers an occasion upon which the trustees need to exercise (or reconsider the exercise of) that discretion, giving such weight to the making of and reasons for that request as they think fit. Having made their decision the trustees are not obliged to give reasons for it,[46] any more than in relation to any other exercise of their discretionary powers. In a difficult case the trustees may, as always, seek the directions of the court on the question whether to disclose but, bearing in mind the inevitable cost associated with doing so, the trustees will need to think twice before concluding that the difficulty of the question justifies the expenditure. It is by no means a matter for criticism (of the type levelled against the trustees in this case) that trustees do not either give reasons or apply to the court for directions, if minded not to accede to a beneficiary's request for disclosure …

Before leaving this general legal analysis, I emphasise that the application of the *Londonderry* principle to wish letters in the way in which I have sought to explain them is not to be taken as something akin to a statutory code. The question begins and ends, both for trustees and for the court, a question of discretion, or of the review of the exercise of discretion. There are no fixed rules, and the trustees need not approach the question with any pre-disposition towards disclosure or non-disclosure. All relevant circumstances must be taken into account, and in all cases other than those limited to a strict review of the negative exercise of a discretion, both the trustees and the court have a range of alternative responses, not limited to the black and white question of disclosure or non-disclosure. The responses … may include, in an appropriate case, a private reading of the wish letter by the judge to himself.

Briggs J decided that the wish letter should be disclosed. This was because the risk of family division following disclosure was outweighed by the fact that the trustees would be seeking the approval of the court to a scheme of distribution of the trust fund. In seeking this approval the trustees would have surrendered the protection of confidentiality since, in order to sanction the scheme, it would be necessary for the court to consider the reasons for the exercise of the trustees' discretion, which would, in turn, require the court to see the wish letter. Had the trustees not been seeking court sanction of the scheme, the letter would not have been disclosed.

(e) Access to information

The objects of a discretionary trust may ask the settlors and trustees for information about various matters relating to the trust. This was recognized in *Murphy v Murphy*.[47] The claimant sought disclosure of the names and addresses of the trustees of a discretionary trust, known as the 1965 settlement, from the defendant, his father, who was the settlor of the trust. Neuberger J said:[48]

If all the discretionary beneficiaries wished, for good reasons, to know the identity of the trustees of a settlement, and the settlor (who reserved the power of appointment of trustees) refused to tell them, it would be surprising—indeed, I suggest, remarkable—if the court had no power to compel him to

---

[46] See further Chapter 11.7(b), pp. 566–8.
[47] [1999] 1 WLR 282.
[48] Ibid, 290.

do so. Similarly, if all but one or two of the beneficiaries wished to know, particularly if the one or two were receiving all the income. If that is right, it would seem to follow that one would expect the court at least to have jurisdiction to require a settlor in such circumstances to give the information to a single discretionary beneficiary.

It appears on the plaintiff's evidence (not denied by the defendant in his affidavit) that there is a settlement with assets, in respect of which the plaintiff is within the class of discretionary beneficiaries. The plaintiff says, through his counsel, that he is seeking both to find out what has happened to the trust funds, and to make out a case as to why he should receive some of those funds. His bona fides is not challenged in this regard. While there is no question of any wrongdoing so far as the defendant or the trustees of his 1965 settlement are concerned, I would, in light of the above discussions require authority or established principle to support the proposition that a discretionary beneficiary was never entitled to seek such information before I was prepared so to hold.

The question which therefore has to be considered in relation to the defendant's 1965 settlement is whether it is appropriate to grant the relief sought by the plaintiff in all the circumstances. In this connection, it should be emphasised that the mere fact that the court has jurisdiction to make the order cannot in my view mean that the court has no discretion as to whether to make such an order. The very reasoning which leads me to the conclusion that there is power to make such an order, namely the wide and flexible jurisdiction of the court of equity, must carry with it a broad discretion …

That, then, brings me to the question of whether, in all the circumstances, I should order the defendant to disclose the names and addresses of the [trustees of the] defendant's 1965 settlement to the plaintiff. I have reached the conclusion that such an order ought to be made, subject to the question of whether the defendant should have a limited opportunity of putting in any further facts on which he wishes to rely. First, it is not as if the plaintiff is, as it were, something of a remote beneficiary, or one beneficiary among a great many. The number of potential discretionary beneficiaries is pretty limited …

It appears to me that it would be most undesirable for this court to make orders which would be likely to result in trustees of discretionary private trusts being badgered with claims by many beneficiaries for consideration to be given to their claims for trust moneys, or for accounts as to how trust moneys have been spent: the duties of a trustee are, it may fairly be said, quite onerous enough without such added problems. On the other hand, when accepting the appointment as a trustee of a discretionary trust, a person must appreciate that he will have duties, about which he should have been advised … Above all, each case must be judged on its merits. Bearing in mind the specific factors to which I have made reference, I do not see how it could seriously be argued that discretionary trustees would run a risk of a flood of applications of this sort, if I allowed the plaintiff the relief he seeks so far as the trustees of the defendant's 1965 settlement are concerned.

The court exercised its discretion to disclose the identity of the trustees both because the beneficiary was one of the settlor's children and so not a remote object and because he was not well off, suggesting that he was more likely to receive a distribution from the trust fund.

(c) FIDUCIARY POWER

(i) *Proprietary rights*

Where a trustee has a fiduciary power to distribute trust property to the objects, he or she is not obliged to exercise it but need only consider its exercise.[49] It follows that the objects who might benefit

---

[49] See Chapter 13.2(a)(ii), pp. 631–2.

from the exercise of the power cannot be considered to have any proprietary interest in the trust fund, because they do not know whether they will receive any part of that fund. They do not even have a right to be considered. Until the power is exercised, those who take the property in default of its exercise have an equitable proprietary interest in the property. If the power is exercised in favour of certain objects, then this will defeat the equitable interest of those who take in default.

(ii) *Personal rights*

(a) *Release of the power*

An object of a power can 'release the power' before it is exercised. This means that the object can no longer receive property in the exercise of the trustee's power of appointment.

(b) *Application to court*

Whether the objects of a fiduciary power can apply to the court to ensure the proper operation of the power was considered in *Re Manisty's Settlement*.[50] Templeman J said:[51]

> The court cannot insist on any particular consideration being given by the trustees to the exercise of the power. If a settlor creates a power exercisable in favour of his issue, his relations and the employees of his company, the trustees may in practice for many years hold regular meetings, study the terms of the power and the other provisions of the settlement, examine the accounts and either decide not to exercise the power or to exercise it only in favour, for example, of the children of the settlor. During that period the existence of the power may not be disclosed to any relation or employee and the trustees may not seek or receive any information concerning the circumstances of any relation or employee. In my judgment it cannot be said that the trustees in those circumstances have committed a breach of trust and that they ought to have advertised the power or looked beyond the persons who are most likely to be the objects of the bounty of the settlor. The trustees are, of course, at liberty to make further inquiries, but cannot be compelled to do so at the behest of any beneficiary. The court cannot judge the adequacy of the consideration given by the trustees to the exercise of the power, and it cannot insist on the trustees applying a particular principle or any principle in reaching a decision.
>
> If a person within the ambit of the power is aware of its existence he can require the trustees to consider exercising the power and in particular to consider a request on his part for the power to be exercised in his favour. The trustees must consider this request, and if they decline to do so or can be proved to have omitted to do so, then the aggrieved person may apply to the court which may remove the trustees and appoint others in their place. This, as I understand it, is the only right and only remedy of any object of the power.

In *Mettoy Pension Trustees Ltd v Evans*,[52] however, it was recognized that the court has similar powers of intervention in respect of fiduciary powers as those that exist for discretionary trusts.[53] But since the donees of fiduciary powers are required only to consider the exercise of the power and are not required to exercise it, it is difficult to see why it is appropriate that all the weapons in the judicial armoury that are available regarding discretionary trusts, should be equally available where a trustee has not considered exercising the power, which he or she is not obligated to exercise, within

---

[50] [1974] Ch 17.
[51] Ibid, 25.
[52] [1990] 1 WLR 1587. See Chapter 13.2(b)(ii), pp. 634–6.
[53] See Chapter 13.2(b)(i), pp. 632–4.

a reasonable time. For example, failure to exercise a fiduciary power should not result in the creation of a scheme of arrangement or an order directing the trustees to distribute trust assets. It should be sufficient either for the court to direct the trustees to consider whether the power should be exercised or to replace the trustees if they refuse to consider the exercise of the power.

(c) Trust documents

The court has a discretion to order the release of trust documents to the object of a fiduciary power, as was specifically recognized by the Privy Council in *Schmidt v Rosewood Trust Ltd*,[54] which concerned in part a claim by the object of a fiduciary power to see a trust document.

(d) Right to information

There is no reason why the discretion of the court recognized in *Murphy v Murphy*[55] to release information about the trust and trustees cannot be exercised in favour of objects of a fiduciary power, especially since trust documents might be released to them.

2. DISPOSITION OF AN EQUITABLE INTEREST

Where a beneficiary seeks to dispose of a subsisting equitable interest, section 53(1)(c) of the Law of Property Act 1925 applies, such that signed writing is required.

LAW OF PROPERTY ACT 1925

53. Instruments required to be in writing

(1) Subject to the provisions hereinafter contained with respect to the creation of interests in land by parol—

    (c) a disposition of an equitable interest or trust subsisting at the time of the disposition, must be in writing signed by the person disposing of the same, or by his agent thereunto lawfully authorised in writing or by will.

For section 53(1)(c) to be applicable there must be an equitable interest or trust that is *already* subsisting at the time of the disposition.[56] Consequently, the provision will not apply to a declaration of trust that *creates* an equitable interest.

The rationale behind this provision was encapsulated by Lord Upjohn in *Vandervell v IRC*,[57] who stated that:

the object of the section, as was the object of the old Statute of Frauds, is to prevent hidden oral transactions in equitable interests in fraud of those truly entitled, and making it difficult, if not impossible, for the trustees to ascertain who are in truth his beneficiaries.

---

[54] [2003] UKPC 26; [2003] 2 AC 709.
[55] [1999] 1 WLR 282, 290 (Neuberger J). See Chapter 10.1(b)(ii)(e), pp. 498–9.
[56] *Kinane v Mackie-Conteh* [2005] EWCA Civ 45.
[57] [1967] 2 AC 291, 311.

Thus section 53(1)(c) ensures there is evidence that can be relied upon to prove various dealings with subsisting equitable interests. This is important because the ease with which equitable interests can be hidden behind a trust means that they are particularly vulnerable to instances of fraud.

In this section, various types of transaction will be considered. In each situation it must be decided whether or not section 53(1)(c) is engaged such that signed writing is required. Essentially, a distinction needs to be drawn between the *disposition* of a subsisting equitable interest and its *dissipation*. Signed writing is required for the former, but not the latter. It is helpful to compare Figures 10.1 and 10.2.

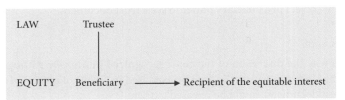

Figure 10.1 Signed writing required under section 53(1)(c)

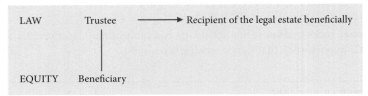

Figure 10.2 Signed writing not required under section 53(1)(c)

Signed writing is required in Figure 10.1 but not in Figure 10.2. This is because in Figure 10.1 there is a subsisting equitable interest at the start and at the end. There has, therefore, been a disposition of a subsisting equitable interest and so signed writing is required. On the other hand, in Figure 10.2 there is a subsisting equitable interest at the start but no subsisting equitable interest at the end. That interest has been dissipated in the transfer of the property to a third party absolutely, which does not count as a disposition for the purposes of section 53(1)(c), so signed writing is not required. The reasons why, and how this has been developed by the case law, will be discussed in this section.

(a) ASSIGNMENT OF EQUITABLE INTEREST

An assignment of an equitable interest clearly falls within the scope of section 53(1)(c) so that writing is required to effect the assignment. An assignment can be represented by Figure 10.3. This is the same structure as in Figure 10.1. Signed writing is required. This was the result reached in *Re Danish Bacon Co. Ltd Staff Pension Fund Trusts*.[58] In that case, an employee had the right to nominate a person to receive benefits due under the company's pension fund. The employee had nominated his wife in the approved form, which was duly signed and witnessed. He then changed the nomination by letter to the company. Since the employee had a subsisting equitable interest as regards payment of the pension, section 53(1)(c) was engaged and so writing was required to effect the assignment. Megarry J

---

[58] [1971] 1 WLR 248.

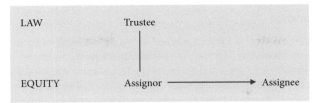

Figure 10.3 Assignment of an equitable interest

found that the signed writing requirement might be fulfilled across two or more documents, rather than necessarily in only one document.[59]

> I have been referred to no authority on the point relating to the words in section 53(1)(c) which run 'a disposition ... must be in writing ...'; indeed, despite the riches of authority on this point under section 40,[60] section 53(1)(c) appears to be wholly barren. However, if a statutory requirement that a 'memorandum' shall be 'in writing' may be satisfied by two or more documents, I do not see why two or more documents should not satisfy the requirement that a 'disposition' shall be 'in writing'. True, section 40(1) is merely directed to providing written evidence of a transaction, whereas under section 53(1)(c) (unlike section 53(1)(b))[61] the matter is one not merely of evidence but of the disposition itself. Yet two documents are used in constituting a strict settlement of land or establishing a trust for sale of land, and there are well-established rules for the incorporation of documents in a will; and if two or more documents, when read together, dispose of an equitable interest, I do not see why the court should insist on separating them and subjecting each separately to the test of section 53(1)(c).

(b) DIRECTION TO TRUSTEE TO HOLD ON TRUST FOR ANOTHER

The leading case on whether an instruction by a beneficiary to the trustees to hold upon different trusts constitutes a disposition of a subsisting equitable interest within section 53(1)(c) is the decision of the House of Lord in *Grey v Inland Revenue Commissioners*.

Grey v Inland Revenue Commissioners [1960] AC 1

The settlor, Mr Hunter, had made six settlements in favour of his grandchildren. He later transferred substantial blocks of shares to the trustees, which they held on trust for him. Then he orally instructed the trustees to hold the shares upon the trusts of the six settlements. Finally, documents were executed in confirmation of the oral declaration, and these were executed by Mr Hunter. The question was whether the trusts of the shares had been created by the oral declaration or by the later documents. The House of Lords held that there had been a disposition of subsisting equitable interests, which was effected by signed writing.

---

[59] Ibid, 254. See too *Crowden v Aldridge* [1993] 1 WLR 433.

[60] Law of Property Act 1925, s. 40, which required contracts for the sale or other disposition of land to be made in writing. See now Law of Property (Miscellaneous Provisions) Act 1989, s. 2.

[61] See Chapter 4.2(b), p. 120.

Viscount Simmonds:

If the word 'disposition' [in section 53(1)(c)] is given its natural meaning, it cannot, I think, be denied that a direction given by Mr. Hunter, whereby the beneficial interest in the shares theretofore vested in him became vested in another or others, is a disposition. But it is contended by the appellants that the word 'disposition' is to be given a narrower meaning and (so far as relates to *inter vivos* transactions) be read as if it were synonymous with 'grants and assignments' and that, given this meaning, it does not cover such a direction as was given in this case. As I am clearly of the opinion, which I understand to be shared by your Lordships, that there is no justification for giving the word 'disposition' a narrower meaning than it ordinarily bears, it will be unnecessary to discuss the interesting problem that would otherwise arise.

Viscount Simmonds was concerned with 'grants and assignments' as this was the language used in section 9 of the Statute of Frauds 1677. However, the House of Lords was clear that the Law of Property Act 1925 had the same effect as the Statute of Frauds 1677.

Whether the trust of the shares was created by the oral instruction or written documents mattered because it affected liability to pay stamp duty. Stamp duty was payable *ad valorem*[62] upon a 'conveyance on sale', which included 'every instrument … whereby any property, or any estate or interest in any property, upon the sale thereof is transferred to or vested in a purchaser, or any other person on his behalf or by his direction'.[63] Thus in *IRC v Angus*,[64] Lord Esher said:

the thing which is made liable to the duty is an 'instrument'. If a contract of purchase and sale, or conveyance by way of purchase and sale, can be, or is carried out without an instrument, the case is not within the section, and no tax is imposed. It is not the transaction of purchase and sale which is struck at; it is the instrument whereby the purchase and sale are effected which is struck at.

Whether the trusts of the shares in *Grey v IRC* were effected by the oral direction or by the later documents depended on whether the oral declaration was valid. Had the oral declaration created a trust of the shares, it would have been valid. However, the House of Lords held that the trusts were already in existence and Mr Hunter was seeking to transfer his subsisting equitable interest to the beneficiaries. This involved a disposition and so the passing of the interest could only be effected by an instrument in writing, and that document was liable to stamp duty.[65]

The transaction in *Grey* can be illustrated by Figure 10.4, which is the same as Figure 10.1.

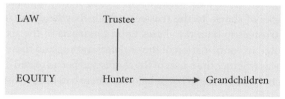

Figure 10.4 *Grey v IRC*

---

[62] Meaning a tax assessed by the value of the land.
[63] Stamp Act 1891, s. 54, now repealed by Finance Act (FA)1999, s. 139, Sch. 20, Pt V (2).
[64] (1889) 23 QBD 579, 589.
[65] See too *Baird v Baird* [1990] 2 AC 548 (PC).

(c) CONVEYANCE OF LEGAL ESTATE BY NOMINEE

Grey v IRC was distinguished in *Vandervell v Inland Revenue Commissioners*,[66] where the transfer was not of the beneficial interest only, but rather of the legal estate absolutely. As a result, the House of Lords held that signed writing in accordance with section 53(1)(c) was not required. The reasons given by the Law Lords are unsatisfactory, but the decision is commercially sensible and principles not considered by the House of Lords can be used to explain the result.

Vandervell v Inland Revenue Commissioners [1967] 2 AC 291, 311

Vandervell decided to give to the Royal College of Surgeons sufficient money to endow a Chair of Pharmacology. This was to be done by transferring a holding of shares in Vandervell Products Ltd, which were vested in the National Provincial Bank Ltd on trust for Vandervell, to the Royal College, and then declaring dividends on the shares, for which the Royal College would be free of liability to pay tax because it is a charity. An option to repurchase the shares for £5,000 was given to Vandervell Trustees Ltd, a company that acted as trustee for the Vandervell family trusts. The bank transferred the shares to the Royal College, and the dividends were declared.

The Revenue assessed Vandervell to Surtax on the dividends on the ground that he had not divested himself absolutely of all his interest in the shares. This was upheld by the House of Lords because Vandervell Trustees Ltd held the option on a resulting trust for Vandervell.[67] One argument for the Revenue was that the bank had conveyed only the legal estate in the shares to the Royal College of Surgeons; the equitable interest remained in Vandervell because he had failed to effect its disposition in writing as required by section 53(1)(c). This argument was rejected.

Lord Upjohn:

[Section 53(1)(c) was] applied in *Grey*[68] and *Oughtred*[69] to cases where the legal estate remained outstanding in a trustee and the beneficial owner was dealing and dealing only with the equitable estate. That is understandable; the object of the section, as was the object of the old Statute of Frauds, is to prevent hidden oral transactions in equitable interests in fraud of those truly entitled, and making it difficult, if not impossible, for the trustees to ascertain who are in truth his beneficiaries. But when the beneficial owner owns the whole beneficial estate and is in a position to give directions to his bare trustee with regard to the legal as well as the equitable estate there can be no possible ground for invoking the section where the beneficial owner wants to deal with the legal estate as well as the equitable estate …

[I]f the intention of the beneficial owner in directing the trustee to transfer the legal estate to X is that X should be the beneficial owner I can see no reason for any further document or further words in the document assigning the legal estate also expressly transferring the beneficial interest; the greater includes the less. …

Counsel for the Crown admitted that where the legal and beneficial estate was vested in the legal owner and he desired to transfer the whole legal and beneficial estate to another he did not have to do more than transfer the legal estate and he did not have to comply with section 53(1)(c); and I can see no relevant difference between that case and this.

---

[66] [1967] 2 AC 291.
[67] See Chapter 8, 'Resulting Trusts'.
[68] [1960] AC 1; see Chapter 10.2(b), pp. 503–4.
[69] [1960] AC 206.

There is no doubt that the result in *Vandervell* was commercially desirable. Shares are often bought and sold by nominees on the oral instructions of beneficiaries, and it would be very inconvenient to demand signed writing before nominees could act, particularly given that shares are now often transferred electronically under the CREST system. However, the reasoning in the House of Lords is problematic. Although Lord Upjohn stated that a transfer of the greater legal estate includes a transfer of the lesser equitable estate, this does not explain whether section 53(1)(c) is engaged such that signed writing is required.[70] Nevertheless, the reasoning of Lord Upjohn is preferable to that of the other judges. For example, Lord Wilberforce stated:[71]

> The case should then be regarded as one in which the appellant himself has, with the intention to make a gift, put the college in a position to become the legal owner of the shares, which the college in fact became.
>
> If the appellant had died before the college had obtained registration it is clear on the principle of *In re Rose*[72] that the gift would have been complete, on the basis that he had done everything in his power to transfer the legal interest, with an intention to give, to the college.

Such reasoning is unsatisfactory and circular. Vandervell had only done everything in his power to give the shares to the college if signed writing was not required. But this was the very issue the House of Lords was supposed to be deciding.

Figure 10.5 illustrates the facts of *Vandervell*. This is the same as Figure 10.2. The result of *Vandervell* means that signed writing is unnecessary in this situation. But this may be surprising. After all, Vandervell had a subsisting equitable interest at the beginning, which no longer existed at the end, so it might be thought that he had disposed of that subsisting equitable interest and section 53(1)(c) should apply. An explanation as to why writing was not required has been provided by Nolan, writing over thirty years after the case was decided. This explanation rests upon the doctrine of overreaching.[73]

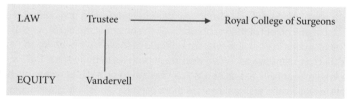

Figure 10.5 *Vandervell v IRC*

Nolan, '*Vandervell v IRC*: a case of overreaching' (2002) 61 CLJ 169, 188

> The doctrine of overreaching can be used to explain and justify their Lordships' decision in *Vandervell* that the Royal College of Surgeons got good legal title to 100,000 'A' shares in Vandervell Products Ltd., free of Vandervell's prior equitable interest in them, even though Vandervell had not transferred

---

[70] Nor is it obvious that there was really scope for Lord Upjohn to rely upon the purpose of section 53(1)(c) when the words of the statute seem relatively clear and unambiguous.

[71] [1967] 2 AC 291, 330.

[72] [1949] Ch 78. See Chapter 4.3(c)(i), pp. 153–5.

[73] See Chapter 2.7(d), pp. 56–7.

that interest to the Royal College in accordance with section 53(l)(c) of the Law of Property Act 1925. Vandervell, without any need for formality, instructed National Provincial Bank Ltd. to give away its legal title to the shares, free of his equitable interest in them. The shares were transferred to the Royal College, and re-registered in its name, so it acquired good legal title to them. The gift of the shares also overreached Vandervell's equitable interest in them. Consequently, the Royal College acquired the shares free of that interest. No aspect of these transactions amounted to the disposition of a subsisting equitable interest, within section 53(1)(c).

This explanation of their Lordships' decision relies on a well understood and well accepted doctrine, overreaching, which is very commonly encountered in the administration of trusts: it does not relegate a case so practically important as *Vandervell* to the status of a useful 'anomaly' or 'exception'. Understanding their Lordships' decision in terms of such a familiar, well known, doctrine has another major benefit. The substantial body of law relating to overreaching can be used to establish the limits within which *Vandervell* should properly be applied: it can be used to establish the consequences which may follow in a variety of circumstances when a nominee, acting on instructions from his beneficiary, deals with an asset he holds for that beneficiary.

Whilst this overreaching analysis was not employed by the House of Lords, it is consistent with the result. It was crucial that the trustees were not acting in breach of trust. If they were, overreaching could not have occurred.

Nolan considers how an analysis based upon overreaching might work in a variety of situations. The most difficult scenario is perhaps where the beneficiary instructs his trustee to transfer legal title to shares to another person to hold on trust for a different party.

Nolan, '*Vandervell v IRC*: A Case of Overreaching' (2002) 61 CLJ 169, 186–7

The next set of facts to be considered is, perhaps, the most difficult. What if the Bank, at Vandervell's direction, had given the shares to the trustees of another settlement which Vandervell himself had established? There is no single answer to this question.

So long as the court was satisfied that Vandervell had done two distinct things—that he had first created a settlement, and that he had then directed the Bank to transfer the shares to the trustees of that settlement—the result should be [that there was no disposition]. Vandervell's initial establishment of one settlement should not affect the correct legal interpretation of his subsequent, and independent, direction to the Bank as trustee of another settlement.

The question would be more difficult to answer had the two events taken place at the same time. In such a case, the precise facts at issue would be vitally important, because the court could reach one of two very different conclusions. On the one hand, the court could take the view that there were still two separate transactions, a transfer of the shares coupled with a declaration of new trusts over them, neither of which amounted to a disposition of Vandervell's subsisting equitable interest, within section 53(1)(*c*) of the Law of Property Act 1925. On the other hand, the court might hold that the creation of the new settlement, and the direction to transfer the shares to the trustees of that settlement, were merely parts of a single scheme, by which Vandervell tried to substitute another person for himself as beneficiary of the shares; and in the light of *Grey v IRC*, that scheme would surely involve a disposition of *Vandervell's* equitable interest in the shares. Such a disposition would fall squarely within section 53(1)(*c*) of the Law of Property Act 1925 and would therefore only be valid if embodied in duly signed writing. The limits of the *Vandervell* principle would have been crossed.

(d) CONSTITUTION OF TRUST FOLLOWING RESULTING TRUST

Vandervell's problems did not end with the decision of the House of Lords. This is because when the trustees later exercised the option, it needed to be determined who, if anyone, had an equitable interest in the option and shares, and whether there had been a disposition of a subsisting equitable interest.

Re Vandervell's Trusts (No. 2) [1974] Ch 269

In 1961 Vandervell Trustees Ltd exercised the option, taking £5,000 from the Vandervell children's settlement for the purpose. The Royal College of Surgeons transferred the shares to Vandervell Trustees Ltd. The Revenue made a further claim that tax was due on the ground that Vandervell Trustees Ltd had held the shares on trust for Vandervell. In 1965, Vandervell executed a deed, formally transferring to the children's settlement any right or interest that he might still have in the shares. Vandervell died and his estate sued Vandervell Trustees Ltd for the return of the dividends paid on the shares since 1961. They succeeded before Megarry J, but failed in the Court of Appeal.

Lord Denning addressed the issue of what had happened to the equitable interest which Vandervell had previously enjoyed in the option.[74]

> [Counsel] for the executors admitted that the intention of Mr. Vandervell and the trustee company was that the shares should be held on trust for the children's settlement. But he said that this intention was of no avail. He said that during the first period, Mr. Vandervell had an equitable interest in the property, namely, a resulting trust; that he never disposed of this equitable interest (because he never knew he had it): and that in any case it was the disposition of an equitable interest which, under section 53 of the Law of Property Act 1925, had to be in writing, signed by him or his agent, lawfully authorised by him in writing (and there was no such writing produced). He cited *Grey v IRC* [1960] AC 1 and *Oughtred v IRC* [1960] AC 206.
>
> There is a complete fallacy in that argument. A resulting trust for the settlor is born and dies without any writing at all. It comes into existence whenever there is a gap in the beneficial ownership. It ceases to exist whenever that gap is filled by someone becoming beneficially entitled. As soon as the gap is filled by the creation or declaration of a valid trust, the resulting trust comes to an end. In this case, before the option was exercised, there was a gap in the beneficial ownership. So there was a resulting trust for Mr. Vandervell. But, as soon as the option was exercised and the shares registered in the trustees' name, there was created a valid trust of the shares in favour of the children's settlement. Not being a trust of land, it could be created without any writing. A trust of personalty can be created without writing. Both Mr. Vandervell and the trustee company had done everything which needed to be done to make the settlement of these shares binding on them. So, there was a valid trust: see *Milroy v Lord* (1862) 4 De GF & J 264 at 274,[75] per Turner LJ.

The reasoning of Lord Denning MR is difficult to follow. Whilst it is clear from section 53(2) of the Law of Property Act 1925 that a resulting trust is born without the need for any formalities, it is not clear why it should be thought to die in the same manner. Once the resulting trust existed, Vandervell

---

[74] [1974] Ch 269, 320.
[75] See Chapter 4.3(b)(i), pp. 150–1.

had a real, subsisting equitable interest under the trust. As such, to dispose of it needed signed writing in accordance with section 53(1)(c). This point was recognized by Stephenson LJ in the Court of Appeal, although ultimately he did not dissent:[76]

> To expound my doubts would serve no useful purpose; to state them shortly may do no harm. The cause of all the trouble is what the judge called [1974] Ch 269 at 298, 'this ill-fated option' and its incorporation in a deed which was 'too short and simple' to rid Mr. Vandervell of the beneficial interest in the disputed shares, as a bare majority of the House of Lords held, not without fluctuation of mind on the part of one of them (Lord Upjohn), in *Vandervell v IRC* [1967] 2 AC 291 at 314–317. The operation of law or equity kept for Mr. Vandervell or gave him back an equitable interest which he did not want and would have thought he had disposed of if he had ever known it existed. It is therefore difficult to infer that he intended to dispose or ever did dispose of something he did not know he had until the judgment of Plowman J in *Vandervell v IRC* [1966] Ch 261 at 273, which led to the deed of 1965, enlightened him, or to find a disposition of it in the exercise by the trustee company in 1961 of its option to purchase the shares. And even if he had disposed of his interest, he did not dispose of it by any writing sufficient to comply with section 53(1)(c) of the Law of Property Act 1925.

The analysis of Stephenson LJ seems convincing. The transaction can be represented in Figure 10.6. This looks remarkably like Figure 10.1. It is difficult to explain why there was not a disposition of a subsisting equitable interest from Vandervell to the Children's Settlement. Lord Denning thought that the resulting trust simply died when the express trust in favour of the children was created. But why? Perhaps it was important that the subject matter of the resulting trust was the option, and the subject matter of the different express trust was shares. But it is not clear why this would be so.

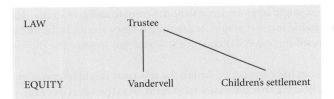

Figure 10.6 *Re Vandervell's Trusts (No. 2)*

Ultimately, *Vandervell (No. 2)* is a very hard decision to explain. It is notable that Nolan's explanation of *Grey* and *Vandervell* does not encompass *Vandervell (No. 2)*. This might be because the judges in *Vandervell (No. 2)* were simply confused. However, it is difficult not to have sympathy with the result on the particular facts of the case: Vandervell had sought to have nothing to do with the option or the shares, and had already suffered a heavy financial blow by the previous decision of the House of Lords that he enjoyed an equitable interest under a resulting trust, despite that being not at all what he wanted. Indeed, this is why Stephenson LJ declined to dissent, finding that the case reached:[77]

> a result with which I am happy to agree as it seems to me to be in accordance with the justice and the reality of the case.

---

[76] [1974] Ch 269, 332.
[77] Ibid, 323.

(e) DECLARATION BY BENEFICIARY AS TRUSTEE

The beneficiary might declare him- or herself to be a trustee. This creates a sub-trust, as it operates 'below' the main trust. So, if A hold shares on trust for B, who then declares him, or herself to be holding on trust for C, B becomes the trustee of a sub-trust and C the beneficiary of that sub-trust (see Figure 10.7).

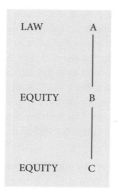

Figure 10.7 Sub-trust

It is important to consider whether the creation of the sub-trust requires signed writing in accordance with section 53(1)(c). A distinction between 'passive' and 'active' sub-trusts is often drawn. Under an 'active' sub-trust, B would be required to perform certain duties of a trustee, such as exercising a discretion to select beneficiaries, and so could not simply 'drop out' of the picture.[78] As a result, C's interest might be considered to be different from B's interest. Thus B, in declaring the sub-trust of the equitable interest would be creating a new interest in favour of C, and this would fall outside the scope of section 53(1)(c), since it would not involve the disposition of an existing interest.

However, if B does not have any active duties, the sub-trust might be considered to be 'passive'. For example, A might be holding shares on bare trust for B, who then declares him- or herself to be holding all those shares on bare trust for C. In such an event, B would simply 'drop out' of the picture. This was the result in *Grainge v Wilberforce*,[79] in which Chitty J held that:

> where A was trustee for B, who was trustee for C, A held in trust for C, and must convey as C directed. B ... might therefore be left out.

This analysis derives further support from *Re Lashmar*,[80] in which Lindley LJ held that it would be possible to 'look through [B] as nobody'. Such a situation might be represented by Figure 10.8.

If B does drop out of the picture, it would leave A holding for C. Figure 10.8 might be redrawn as in Figure 10.9.

This is the same as Figure 10.1. Signed writing in accordance with section 53(1)(c) is required, since the effect of the transaction is to dispose of an existing equitable interest.

---

[78] *Re Lashmar* [1891] 1 Ch 258, 269 (Fry LJ).
[79] (1889) 5 TLR 436, 437.
[80] [1891] 1 Ch 258, 268.

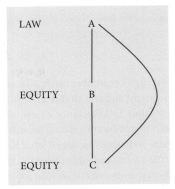

Figure 10.8 'Passive' sub-trusts: the sub-trustee 'drops out' of the picture

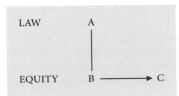

Figure 10.9 The effect of the sub-trustee 'dropping out'

However, this analysis based upon a sub-trustee dropping out of the picture has been questioned by the Court of Appeal in *Nelson v Greening and Sykes (Builders) Ltd.*[81] The case itself concerned the validity of a charging order, rather than formalities, but Lawrence Collins LJ said:

> [There is an argument on] the principle that if A holds a beneficial interest upon trust for B who in turn holds it on trust for Mr Nelson, B falls out of the equation and A holds the beneficial interest directly upon trust for Mr Nelson …
>
> In my judgment, the argument fails. …
>
> It is also true that in *Grey v IRC* [1958] Ch 690 (affirmed [1960] AC 1) at 715, Lord Evershed MR (dissenting, but not on this point) said that where a person who is the owner beneficially of property (and the legal estate is vested in another as trustee for him) makes a declaration of trust the practical effect would seem, in common sense, to amount, or be capable of amounting, to the 'getting rid of' a trust or equitable interest then subsisting. It is said in Snell, *Equity* (31st ed. McGhee, 2005), para 19–11 that 'where property is transferred to T 'on trust for B absolutely' [i]f B in turn becomes a bare trustee of his equitable interest for C, T will hold directly in trust for C …', citing *Head v Lord Teynham* (1783) 1 Cox Eq. 57 (which only holds that where trustees and the beneficiary are before the court, an intermediate trustee of the equitable interest need not be made a party).
>
> These authorities do not bind this court to hold that as a matter of law an intermediate trustee ceases to be a trustee. I accept the submission for G&S that saying (as Lord Evershed MR said) that the practical effect would seem to amount to or be capable of amounting to the 'getting rid' of the trust of the equitable interest then subsisting, is not the same as saying that as a matter of law it does get rid of

---

[81] [2007] EWCA Civ 1358; [2008] 8 EG 158.

the intermediate trust. What he was saying was that in the case of a trust and sub-trust of personal property the trustees may decide that as a matter of practicality it is more convenient to deal directly with the beneficiary of the sub-trust.

On this approach of Lawrence Collins LJ, B's equitable interest is, as a matter of law, not inevitably lost, even if the sub-trust is passive. This might suggest that declarations of sub-trusts will never require signed writing in accordance with section 53(1)(c), since a new interest will always be created under the sub-trust. However, this approach might be considered to be less than satisfactory. After all, if the purpose of section 53(1)(c) is to require written evidence of what happens to equitable interests, which might be hidden beneath the legal title and susceptible to fraudulent activities, it would be preferable to insist upon signed writing and the requirements of section 53(1)(c) for any sub-trust, active or passive. This argument has been made by Green.

Green, '*Grey, Oughtred and Vandervell*: A Contextual Reappraisal' (1984) 47 MLR 385, 398–9

If one abandons the notion of declarants who have constituted themselves bare trustees of subsisting equitable interests 'dropping out of the picture', the question of whether a declaration of trust over a subsisting equitable interest needs to comply with section 53(1)(c) admits of a uniform answer whatever the complexities of the trusts declared. The orthodoxy is that such declarations are outside section 53(1)(c), but there is no authority which directly supports that view, and in its absence this writer would make the following plea on behalf of the contrary position. It has already been noted that the characteristic which makes a subsisting equitable interest worthy of protection is the beneficial interest attached to it. When looked at in this way, it will readily be seen that assignments and declarations of trust, both of which have the effect of extinguishing the beneficial interest in the owner of a hitherto subsisting equitable interest, are equally deserving of formal protection. And both should be caught by section 53(1)(c) by adopting the notion of a declaration of trust working a 'part-disposal' of a subsisting equitable interest, a disposal of the beneficial part of hitherto subsisting equitable rights. (In this connection, one might enlist Viscount Simmonds' judgment in *Grey* as supportive of the view that it is to dispositions of beneficial interests that section 53(1)(c) is addressed.) Adopting this view, one would escape the absurd suggestion that a declaration of trust shifting beneficial ownership lies outside section 53(1)(c), whilst a subsequent assignment of the declarant's outstanding valueless equitable right falls within it; and one would have the satisfaction of treating like transactions in a like manner, finally jettisoning the incoherent formal distinction adopted by the draftsman in 1677.

(f) ORAL CONTRACT FOR THE SALE OF SHARES

An agreement to sell shares in a *private* company may be specifically enforceable. This is because damages may not be an adequate remedy if the agreement to sell the shares is breached; unlike a *public* company, damages cannot enable the purchaser to acquire equivalent shares. As the contract is specifically enforceable, a constructive trust may arise: since Equity will specifically enforce the agreement, Equity will 'treat as done that which ought to be done',[82] and find that equitable title has already passed to the purchaser.[83] However, legal title would remain with the vendor, who would hold the shares on constructive trust. Such a trust may arise without requiring

---

[82] See Chapter 1.5(c), pp. 18–19.
[83] For further discussion concerning the constructive trust that arises upon the conclusion of a specifically enforceable contract for the sale of property, see Chapter 7.2(f), pp. 351–4.

signed writing.[84] Where, however, the vendor is selling a subsisting equitable interest, it has been suggested that signed writing in accordance with section 53(1)(c) is required. Indeed, this was the decision of a majority of the House of Lords in *Oughtred v IRC*.[85]

Oughtred v Inland Revenue Commissioners [1960] AC 206

100,000 preference shares and 100,000 ordinary shares in William Jackson and Son Ltd were held on trust for Mrs Oughtred for life and after her death on trust for her son Peter absolutely. Mrs Oughtred also held 72,700 shares absolutely. On Mrs Oughtred's death, estate duty would be payable on the settled property and her own free estate. In order to reduce the tax liability, Mrs Oughtred and Peter orally agreed that she would transfer to him her 72,700 shares, and Peter would release to his mother his remainder interest in the 200,000 preference and ordinary shares. Subsequently, documents covering these transfers were executed. The Revenue claimed stamp duty on the transfer of Peter's interest in the 200,000 shares. The key issue for the court was whether the oral contract had been effective to transfer the property in the shares. If it had been effective, then stamp duty was not payable.

The House of Lords held that the oral contract had not been effective. The shares were transferred by the documents and so stamp duty was payable.

Lord Jenkins:

It is said further that in the present case the disputed transfer transferred nothing beyond a bare legal estate, because, in accordance with the well-settled principle applicable to contracts of sale, between contract and completion the appellant became under the oral agreement beneficially entitled in equity to the settled shares, subject to the due satisfaction by her of the purchase consideration, and accordingly the entire beneficial interest in the settled shares had already passed to her at the time of the execution of the disputed transfer, and there was nothing left upon which the disputed transfer could operate except the bare legal estate.

The Commissioners of Inland Revenue seek to meet this argument by reference to section 53(1)(c) of the Law of Property Act, 1925. They contend that as the agreement of 18 June, 1956, was an oral agreement it could not, in view of section 53(1)(c), effect a disposition of a subsisting equitable interest or trust, and accordingly that Peter's subsisting equitable interest under the trusts of the settlement, in the shape of his reversionary interest, remained vested in him until the execution of the disputed transfer, which in these circumstances operated as a transfer on sale to the appellant of Peter's reversionary interest and additionally as a transfer not on sale to the appellant of the legal interest in the settled shares. It was by this process of reasoning that the Commissioners arrived at the opinion expressed in the case stated that the disputed transfer attracted both the ad valorem duty exigible on a transfer on sale of the reversionary interest and also the fixed duty of 10s ...

I find it unnecessary to decide whether section 53(2) has the effect of excluding the present transaction from the operation of section 53(1)(c), for, assuming in the appellant's favour that the oral contract did have the effect in equity of raising a constructive trust of the settled shares for her untouched by section 53(1)(c), I am unable to accept the conclusion that the disputed transfer was prevented from being a transfer of the shares to the appellant on sale because the entire beneficial interest in the settled shares was already vested in the appellant under the constructive trust, and there was accordingly nothing left for the disputed transfer to pass to the appellant except the bare legal estate. The constructive trust in favour of a purchaser which arises on the conclusion of a contract for sale is founded upon the purchaser's right to

---

[84] Law of Property Act 1925, s. 53(2).
[85] Followed in *Parinv (Hatfield) Ltd v Inland Revenue Commissioners* [1998] STC 305.

enforce the contract in proceedings for specific performance. In other words, he is treated in equity as entitled by virtue of the contract to the property which the vendor is bound under the contract to convey to him. This interest under the contract is no doubt a proprietary interest of a sort, which arises, so to speak, in anticipation of the execution of the transfer for which the purchaser is entitled to call. But its existence has never (so far as I know) been held to prevent a subsequent transfer, in performance of the contract, of the property contracted to be sold from constituting for Stamp Duty purposes a transfer on sale of the property in question. Take the simple case of a contract for the sale of land. In such a case a constructive trust in favour of the purchaser arises on the conclusion of the contract for sale, but (so far as I know) it has never been held on this account that a conveyance subsequently executed in performance of the contract is not stampable ad valorem as a transfer on sale. Similarly, in a case like the present one, but uncomplicated by the existence of successive interests, a transfer to a purchaser of the investments comprised in a trust fund could not, in my judgment, be prevented from constituting a transfer on sale for the purposes of Stamp Duty by reason of the fact that the actual transfer had been preceded by an oral agreement for sale.

In truth, the title secured by a purchaser by means of an actual transfer is different in kind from, and may well be far superior to, the special form of proprietary interest which equity confers on a purchaser in anticipation of such transfer.

This difference is of particular importance in the case of property such as shares in a limited company. Under the contract the purchaser is no doubt entitled in equity as between himself and the vendor to the beneficial interest in the shares, and (subject to due payment of the purchase consideration) to call for a transfer of them from the vendor as trustee for him. But it is only on the execution of the actual transfer that he becomes entitled to be registered as a member, to attend and vote at meetings, to effect transfers on the register, or to receive dividends otherwise than through the vendor as his trustee.

This approach received the support of a majority of the judges. Since the transaction was concluded by means of a written document, stamp duty became payable on that document. However, Viscount Radcliffe, dissenting, was persuaded that the oral contract created a constructive trust, and section 53(1)(c), therefore, did not apply. He said:

Viscount Radcliffe (dissenting):

The reason of the whole matter, as I see it, is as follows: On 18 June, 1956, the son owned an equitable reversionary interest in the settled shares: by his oral agreement of that date he created in his mother an equitable interest in his reversion, since the subject matter of the agreement was property of which specific performance would normally be decreed by the court. He thus became a trustee for her of that interest *sub modo*:[86] having regard to subsection (2) of section 53 of the Law of Property Act, 1925, subsection (1) of that section did not operate to prevent that trusteeship arising by operation of law. On 26 June Mrs. Oughtred transferred to her son the shares which were the consideration for her acquisition of his equitable interest: upon this transfer he became in a full sense and without more the trustee of his interest for her. She was the effective owner of all outstanding equitable interests. It was thus correct to recite in the deed of release to the trustees of the settlement, which was to wind up their trust, that the trust fund was by then held upon trust for her absolutely. There was, in fact, no equity to the shares that could be asserted against her, and it was open to her, if she so wished, to let the matter rest without calling for a written assignment from her son. Given that the trustees were apprised of the making of the oral agreement and of Mrs. Oughtred's satisfaction of the consideration to be given by her, the trustees had no more to do than to transfer their legal title to her or as she might direct. This and no more is what they did.

It follows that, in my view, this transfer cannot be treated as a conveyance of the son's equitable reversion at all. The trustees had not got it: he never transferred or released it to them: how then could they

---

[86] Meaning 'within limits'.

convey it? With all respect to those who think otherwise, it is incorrect to say that the trustees' transfer was made either with his authority or at his discretion. If the recital as to Mrs. Oughtred's rights was correct, as I think that it was, he had no remaining authority to give or direction to issue. A release is, after all, the normal instrument for winding up a trust when all the equitable rights are vested and the legal estate is called for from the trustees who hold it. What the release gave the trustees from him was acquittance for the trust administration and accounts to date, and the fact that he gave it in consideration of the legal interest in the shares being vested in his mother adds nothing on this point. Nor does it, with respect, advance the matter to say, correctly, that at the end of the day Mrs. Oughtred was the absolute owner of the shares, legal and equitable. I think that she was: but that is description, not analysis. The question that is relevant for the purpose of this appeal is how she came to occupy that position; a position which, under English law, could be reached by more than one road.

Viscount Radcliffe held that, due to the constructive trust arising under a specifically enforceable agreement, albeit an oral agreement, the equitable interest in the shares had already passed from Peter to Mrs Oughtred. Thus, when the written document was executed, Peter no longer had a subsisting equitable interest, since it had already been transferred to his mother, and section 53(1)(c) was not engaged.

The speeches in *Oughtred* are not easy to interpret, and do not deal with many of the difficult points head-on. The Court of Appeal in *Neville v Wilson*,[87] therefore, felt able to look at this area in the round. Ultimately, the dissenting sentiments of Viscount Radcliffe were approved.

Neville v Wilson [1997] Ch 144 (Nourse LJ)

Shareholders of a company ('J.E.N.') had entered into an oral agreement with one another in 1969 for the informal liquidation of the company. Part of this agreement was to the effect that the company's equitable interest in the shares of another company should be divided amongst the shareholders according to their existing shareholdings. The issue for the court was whether this agreement was effective to dispose of the company's interest in its shares. The House of Lords held that the effect of the agreement was to constitute each shareholder a constructive trustee of the shares so that section 53(2) LPA 1925 applied.

Nourse LJ:

The effect of the agreement, more closely analysed, was that each shareholder agreed to assign his interest in the other shares of J.E.N.'s equitable interest in exchange for the assignment by the other shareholders of their interests in his own aliquot share.[88] Each individual agreement having been a disposition of a subsisting equitable interest not made in writing, there then arises the question whether it was rendered ineffectual by section 53 of the Law of Property Act 1925 …

The simple view of the present case is that the effect of each individual agreement was to constitute the shareholder an implied or constructive trustee for the other shareholders, so that the requirement for writing contained in subsection (1)(c) of section 53 was dispensed with by subsection (2). That was the view taken by Upjohn J [1958] Ch 383 at first instance and by Lord Radcliffe in the House of Lords in *Oughtred v Inland Revenue Commissioners*. In order to see whether it is open to us to adopt it in this court, we must give careful consideration to those views and to the other speeches in the House of Lords …

---

[87] [1997] Ch 144.
[88] Meaning 'a part of a larger holding'.

The views of their Lordships as to the effect of section 53 can be summarised as follows. Lord Radcliffe, agreeing with Upjohn J, thought that subsection (2) applied. He gave reasons for that view. Lord Cohen and Lord Denning thought that it did not. Although neither of them gave reasons, they may be taken to have accepted the submissions of Mr. Wilberforce at 220–222. Lord Keith and Lord Jenkins expressed no view either way. We should add that when the case was in this court Lord Evershed MR, in delivering the judgment of himself, Morris and Ormerod LJJ said [1958] Ch 678 at 687:

> 'In this court the case for the Crown has, we think, been somewhat differently presented, and in the end of all, the question under section 53 of the Law of Property Act 1925, does not, in our judgment, strictly call for a decision. We are not, however, with all respect to the judge, prepared to accept, as we understand it, his conclusions upon the effect of section 53 of the Law of Property Act 1925.'

The basis of this court's decision was the same as that adopted by the majority of the House of Lords.

We do not think that there is anything in the speeches in the House of Lords which prevents us from holding that the effect of each individual agreement was to constitute the shareholder an implied or constructive trustee for the other shareholders. In this respect we are of the opinion that the analysis of Lord Radcliffe, based on the proposition that a specifically enforceable agreement to assign an interest in property creates an equitable interest in the assignee, was unquestionably correct; cf. *London and South Western Railway Co v Gomm* (1882) 20 Ch D 562, 581, per Sir George Jessel MR. A greater difficulty is caused by Lord Denning's outright rejection of the application of section 53(2), with which Lord Cohen appears to have agreed.

So far as it is material to the present case, what subsection (2) says is that subsection (1)(c) does not affect the creation or operation of implied or constructive trusts. Just as in *Oughtred v Inland Revenue Commissioners* the son's oral agreement created a constructive trust in favour of the mother, so here each shareholder's oral or implied agreement created an implied or constructive trust in favour of the other shareholders. Why then should subsection (2) not apply? No convincing reason was suggested in argument and none has occurred to us since. Moreover, to deny its application in this case would be to restrict the effect of general words when no restriction is called for, and to lay the ground for fine distinctions in the future. With all the respect which is due to those who have thought to the contrary, we hold that subsection (2) applies to an agreement such as we have in this case.

For these reasons we have come to the conclusion that the agreement entered into by the shareholders of J.E.N. in about April 1969 was not rendered ineffectual by section 53 of the Act of 1925.

The decision in *Neville* appears to decide that a constructive trust does arise under a specifically enforceable contract without the need for signed writing. This approach is consistent with *Chinn v Collins*,[89] in which Lord Wilberforce recognized, in the context of a tax avoidance scheme, that, where legal title to shares was held by a nominee, an agreement to sell the shares would be effective to pass the equitable interest in them once the purchase price had been paid without the need to satisfy any formalities, regardless of whether the agreement was specifically enforceable.

However, that such transactions fall outside the scope of section 53(1)(c) has not been welcomed by all. For example, in *United Bank of Kuwait plc v Sahib*, Chadwick J said:[90]

> I should, perhaps, add (without seeking to decide the point) that I am far from persuaded that section 53(2) of the Law of Property Act 1925 can have any application in a case where it is sought to avoid the

---

[89] [1981] AC 533, 548.
[90] [1997] Ch 107, 129.

effect of section 53(1)(c) by relying on an oral contract to make the disposition which section 53(1)(c) requires to be in writing. The point arose in *Oughtred v Inland Revenue Commissioners* [1960] AC 206. It was put, succinctly, by counsel for the Inland Revenue (Mr. Wilberforce QC) in argument, at 221: 'it cannot be right that an oral contract can transfer property when an oral disposition cannot.' Lord Denning, at 233 accepted the point. So also, I think, did Lord Cohen, at 230. Lord Radcliffe did not accept it, at 227. Lord Jenkins, with whose judgment Lord Keith of Avonholm agreed, found it unnecessary to decide the point, at 239. I am happy to be able to take the same course. It is unnecessary to decide that point in the present case.[91]

Such criticism has been echoed by academics.

Nolan, 'The Triumph of Technicality' (1996) 55 CLJ 436, 438

[*Neville v Wilson*] illustrates the extreme technicality and artificiality of the case law which has grown up around the Law of Property Act 1925 section 53(1)(c). If a person directs his trustees that the assets they hold for him are now to be held for someone else, then this amounts to a disposition of that person's subsisting equitable interest, within section 53(1)(c) (*Grey v IRC* [1960] AC 1). Yet according to *Neville v Wilson*, if a person does not unilaterally tell his trustees what to do, but instead contracts for value to dispose of his beneficial interest, that is not a disposition of a subsisting equitable interest within section 53(1)(c), because technically what is involved is the creation of a new equitable interest in the purchaser, coupled with destruction of the 'old' equitable interest in the hands of the vendor; and this is so, even though that 'new' interest is logically identical to the 'old' (cp. *Grey v IRC* [1958] Ch 375 at 382, per Upjohn J; [1958] Ch 690 at 715, per Lord Evershed MR).

Such criticisms have some force, and it may be that the approach of the majority in *Oughtred* will come back into fashion. However, for now the law seems to be that which was set out in *Neville*.[92] Nevertheless, it might be possible to reconcile the two cases on the basis that the former involved an executory transaction, whereas the latter involved an executed transaction.

Thompson, 'Mere formalities' [1996] Conv 366, 370–1

Perhaps the way of rationalising the cases dealing with this difficult area is to consider the types of contract involved and, particularly, whether they are executory or executed. If one takes the case of a contract for the sale of land, it is generally accepted that because it is specifically enforceable, the purchaser becomes the beneficial owner of the property. Nevertheless, until the purchase price has been paid, it is equally clear that the vendor also retains a valuable interest in the property. He would only become a bare trustee for the purchaser once the purchase price is paid in full. This, of course, does not normally happen until completion of the purchase. Consequently the conveyance and payment of the purchase price does operate to transfer to the purchaser at least some equitable interest in the property in addition to the legal estate. Applying this to *Oughtred,* when the contract was still executory, it could be argued that, despite the acquisition of a beneficial interest under a constructive trust, the nature of this trust is so unusual that mother and son still retained a beneficial interest in their

---

[91] This aspect of the case was not considered on appeal to the Court of Appeal: [1997] Ch 107.
[92] It was followed in *Slater v Simm* [2007] EWHC 951 (Ch); [2007] WTLR 143, [24]. See also *Halloran v Minister Administering National Parks and Wildlife Act 1974* [2006] HCA 3, noted by Turner [2006] Conv 390.

respective shares pending completion of the transaction. As a result writing was necessary to transfer that interest. In *Neville v. Wilson,* on the other hand, the consideration involved was the agreement to liquidate a company. This had been done so that, on one side, the contract had been completed. In principle, therefore, it would seem right to say that the entire beneficial interest in the shares had passed without the need for separate writing.

This reasoning may not, of course, be found to be totally convincing. The problems that occur in areas such as this arise principally when contracts which are specifically enforceable are still to be completed. This causes some kind of equitable interest to vest in the purchaser with all the attendant problems that this creates. Once the contract has been completed on one side, there should be no further difficulty in holding the vendor to be a trustee of the property, the nature of that trust being entirely orthodox. The decision of the Court of Appeal in *Neville v Wilson* seems therefore, with respect, to be entirely right.

(g) NOMINATION OF FUTURE BENEFITS

Where a person nominates another to receive a benefit in the future, section 53(1)(c) cannot apply. This is because a *future* equitable interest is involved. At the time of the nomination, there was no *subsisting* equitable interest sufficient to engage the requirement of signed writing. This approach was favoured, albeit tentatively and *obiter*, by Megarry J in *Re Danish Bacon Co. Ltd Staff Pension Fund Trusts*:[93]

Whether section 53(1)(c) does apply is a matter upon which I am by no means clear ... What I am concerned with is a transaction whereby the deceased dealt with something which *ex hypothesi* could never be his. He was not disposing of his pension, nor of his right to the contributions and interest if he left the company's service. He was dealing merely with a state of affairs that would arise if he died while in the company's pensionable service, or after he had left it without becoming entitled to a pension. If he did this, then the contributions and interest would, by force of the rules, go either to his nominee, if he had made a valid nomination, or to his personal representatives, if he had not. If he made a nomination, it was revocable at any time before his death.

The question is thus whether an instrument with this selective, contingent and defeasible quality, which takes effect only on the death of the person signing it, can fairly be said to be 'a disposition of an equitable interest or trust subsisting at the time of the disposition'.

[Counsel] put much emphasis on the word 'subsisting': however wide the word 'disposition' might be in its meaning, there was no disposition of a subsisting equity, he said. I should hesitate to describe an instrument which has a mere possibility of becoming a 'disposition' as being in itself a disposition *ab initio*; and I agree that the word 'subsisting' also seems to point against the nomination falling within section 53(1)(c) ... I very much doubt whether the nomination falls within section 53(1)(c); but as I have indicated, I do not have to decide that point, and I do not do so.

Stronger support for this approach may be found in *Gold v Hill*,[94] in which the deceased had nominated a solicitor as the beneficiary of a life insurance policy. During an informal conversation the deceased had informed the solicitor of the nomination and of his desire that the solicitor should use the proceeds of the policy for the benefit of the woman with whom the deceased was living. One question considered by Carnwath J was whether this nomination in the form of a trust was valid, since it had not been made in writing. His Lordship referred to *Re Danish Bacon* and held that the nomination

---

[93] [1971] 1 WLR 248, 255.
[94] [1999] 1 FLR 54.

did not have to be made in writing because it did not involve the disposition of a subsisting equitable interest, and it was irrelevant that the nomination was made in the form of a trust. He said:[95]

> The true view is that the trust did not crystallise until the sum became payable upon death. Until then, there is no subsisting equitable interest capable of being disposed of within the meaning of section 53.

(h) DISCLAIMER OF BENEFICIAL INTEREST

It has been held that a disclaimer does not need to satisfy the requirements of section 53(1)(c): after a disclaimer any subsisting equitable interest dissipates or disappears, so it does not involve a disposition of an interest from one party to another so that the interest continues. This was recognized by Danckwerts LJ in *Re Paradise Motor Co. Ltd*:[96]

> The … argument was that there could here be no disclaimer of the beneficial interest in the shares because a disclaimer would, by re-transfer, be a disposition of an equitable interest in property, and neither of the suggested disclaimers was in writing signed by [the disclaimant]: see the Law of Property Act, 1925, section 53(2). We think that the short answer to this is that a disclaimer operates by way of avoidance and not by way of disposition.

3. TERMINATION OF THE TRUST BY THE BENEFICIARIES

(a) THE RULE IN *SAUNDERS V VAUTIER*

The rule in *Saunders v Vautier*[97] states that an adult beneficiary of a trust, who is of sound mind and is entitled to the whole beneficial interest, can direct the trustees to transfer the trust property to him or her. The consequence of this transfer will be the termination of the trust.

Saunders v Vautier (1841) 4 Beav 115

A testator left shares in his will to trustees on trust to accumulate the dividends until Vautier should attain the age of 25, and then to transfer the capital and accumulated dividends to him. Vautier, having attained the age of 21,[98] successfully claimed that he was entitled to have the whole fund transferred to him.

Lord Langdale MR:

I think that principle has been repeatedly acted upon; and where a legacy is directed to accumulate for a certain period, or where the payment is postponed, the legatee, if he has an absolute indefeasible interest in the legacy, is not bound to wait until the expiration of that period, but may require payment the moment he is competent to give a valid discharge.

---

[95] Ibid, 65.
[96] [1968] 1 WLR 1125, 1143.
[97] (1841) 4 Beav 115.
[98] Which was then the age of majority. It is now 18: Family Law Reform Act 1969, s. 1.

On a subsequent hearing before Lord Cottenham LC,[99] it was argued on behalf of the testator's residuary legatees that Vautier's interest was contingent on his attaining the age of twenty-five and, therefore, this rule did not apply. The Lord Chancellor held that the interest was vested,[100] but that the enjoyment of it was merely postponed, so that the enjoyment of the interest was not contingent upon him attaining the age of twenty-five. It follows that the trust must be carefully construed to determine whether the beneficiary's interest is vested or is contingent upon a particular condition. If it is contingent, then the rule in *Saunders v Vautier* will not be applicable;[101] because if the contingency is not subsequently satisfied, somebody else would be entitled to the property, and it would not be appropriate for the person with the contingent interest to terminate the trust and obtain the benefit of the trust property absolutely. So, for example, if Vautier's interest was contingent on the death of a person with a life interest, it would not have been possible for Vautier by himself to demand the transfer of the fund until the person with the life interest had died.

The rule has been extended to include cases where there are two or more beneficiaries,[102] and even where there are beneficiaries entitled in succession,[103] such as where there is trust for A for life with remainder to B. In both these cases all the beneficiaries must be of full age and of sound mind and must together be entitled to the whole beneficial interest. Also, all the beneficiaries must unanimously concur in the direction to the trustees.

The essence of the rule in *Saunders v Vautier* is that all those who are entitled to the whole of the beneficial interest can direct the trustees in how the trust fund should be dealt with, as long as they are all of full capacity and as long as they all agree. Although the rule applies even if the settlor purports to exclude it,[104] it is not possible to rely on the rule in *Saunders v Vautier* to override the terms of an existing trust and still keep that trust in operation. In *Stephenson v Barclays Bank Trust Co. Ltd*,[105] Walton J said:

> Now it is trite law that the persons who between them hold the entirety of the beneficial interests in any particular trust fund are as a body entitled to direct the trustees how that trust fund is to be dealt with … However, in view of the arguments advanced to me by Mr. Lawton, and more particularly that advanced by him on the basis of the decision of Vaisey J in *Re Brockbank* [1948] Ch 206, I think it may be desirable to state what I conceive to be certain elementary principles.
>
> (1) In a case where the persons who between them hold the entirety of the beneficial interests in any particular trust fund are all *sui juris* and acting together, ('the beneficial interest holders'), they are entitled to direct the trustees how the trust fund may be dealt with.
>
> (2) This does not mean, however, that they can at one and the same time override the pre-existing trusts and keep them in existence. Thus, in *Re Brockbank* itself the beneficial interest holders were entitled to override the pre-existing trusts by, for example, directing the trustees to transfer the trust fund to X and Y, whether X and Y were the trustees of some other trust or not, but they were not entitled to direct the existing trustee to appoint their own nominee as a new trustee of the existing trust. By so doing they would be pursuing inconsistent rights.
>
> (3) Nor, I think, are the beneficial interest holders entitled to direct the trustees as to the particular investment they should make of the trust fund. I think this follows for the same reasons as the above. Moreover, it appears to me that once the beneficial interest holders have determined to end the trust they are not entitled, unless by agreement, to the further services of the trustees. Those

---

[99] (1841) Cr & Ph 240.
[100] See Chapter 1.4(a)(iv), p. 13.
[101] *Re Couturier* [1907] 1 Ch 470, 473 (Joyce J).
[102] *Re Sandeman's Will Trusts* [1937] 1 All ER 368; *Lloyd's Bank plc v Duker* [1987] 1 WLR 1324.
[103] *Anson v Potter* (1879) 13 Ch D 141; *Re White* [1901] 1 Ch 570.
[104] *Stokes v Cheek* (1860) 28 Beav 620.
[105] [1975] 1 WLR 882, 889.

trustees can of course be compelled to hand over the entire trust assets to any person or persons selected by the beneficiaries against a proper discharge, but they cannot be compelled, unless they are in fact willing to comply with the directions, to do anything else with the trust fund which they are not in fact willing to do.

The effect of the rule in *Stephenson* is that the operation of the rule in *Saunders v Vautier* always results in the termination of the trust, and cannot be used to vary the trust. If the beneficiaries do wish to vary the trust, they will need to terminate the trust under the rule in *Saunders v Vautier* so that legal title will be transferred to them. They can resettle the property on a new trust if they wish.[106] This will not require writing, because it will not involve the disposition of an equitable interest, since the equitable interest will be destroyed on the termination of the trust.[107]

The rule in *Saunders v Vautier* is of vital significance to the law of trusts, since it implicitly acknowledges that the property that is held on trust for the beneficiaries is their property in Equity. As a result, the beneficiaries should be able to decide what they do with it.

Matthews, 'The comparative importance of the rule in *Saunders v Vautier*' (2006) 122 LQR 266, 273

Why does this rule matter? First, it illustrates and exemplifies the idea of beneficial (or 'equitable') ownership or property. But we must be careful what we mean by this. It is true that the rights of trust beneficiaries are good against many—if not in practice most—third parties. They fail only when the asset concerned ... reaches the hands of a bona fide purchaser for value without notice ...

However, it is not this aspect of 'property' that the rule in *Saunders v Vautier* illustrates ... Instead, it is the idea of *exclusive decision-making*. If I give something to you, then the 'property' idea should mean that it is yours to deal with as you please. 'Property' means—indeed, etymologically, has to mean—that *you* decide. I should not be able, consistently with the idea of property, to make something your 'property', and then *tell you how to deal with it* ... *Saunders v Vautier* is in one sense merely an application of the same principle: if there is only one beneficiary of a particular trust, that beneficiary must be entitled to take the property subject to the trust and decide what he wishes to do with it ... The same is true if two or more persons are interested, and they are agreed on what should happen.[108] In English law the settlor cannot oust this principle even by express declaration.[109] ... Whatever the subject-matter of the trust, it no longer belongs to the settlor or (obviously) the testator, and the decision whether to enjoy it or destroy it is no longer one for him. Instead it is ultimately a decision for those who benefit from the trust.

The strongest argument against the rule in *Saunders v Vautier* is that the operation of the rule means that the settlor's or testator's intention can be defeated, as occurred in *Saunders v Vautier* itself, since the beneficiary obtained the benefit of the trust property before he attained the age of twenty-five. But why should the will of the creator of the trust prevail once the trust has been validly created? Given that the property belongs to the beneficiary in Equity, and the rule requires that the beneficiary must be of full capacity so that he or she does not need to be protected by Equity by virtue of age or mental incapacity, it is suggested that it is right that the beneficiary be free to control what happens to the property to which he or she is beneficially entitled.

---

[106] See further Chapter 15.1, p. 722.
[107] See Chapter 10.2(c), pp. 505–7.
[108] *Barton v Briscoe* (1822) Jac 603; *Re Bowes* [1896] 1 Ch 507.
[109] *Stokes v Cheek* (1860) 28 Beav 620.

(b) DISCRETIONARY TRUSTS

Although the objects of a discretionary trust do not have a proprietary interest in the trust fund,[110] the rule in *Saunders v Vautier* is also applicable to such trusts.[111]

Re Smith [1928] Ch 915

A fund was held by trustees on trust to apply income and capital for the maintenance and benefit of Lilian Aspinall. Provision was made for the accumulation of any surplus. The accumulations and remainder after her death were to be held on trust for any of her sons who attained the age of twenty-one and any of her daughters who attained that age or who were married. She had three children. All reached the age of twenty-one, but one subsequently died. At this point, Lillian Aspinall was past the age of child-bearing. She joined together with her two surviving children and the legal representatives of her deceased child, and they all mortgaged their interests to the Legal and General Assurance Co. The issue for the court was whether the mortgage was valid. In holding that it was, Romer J said:[112]

> The question I have to determine is whether the Legal and General Assurance Company are now entitled to call upon the trustees to pay the whole of the income to them. It will be observed from what I have said that the whole of this share is now held by the trustees upon trusts under which they are bound to apply the whole income and eventually pay over or apply the whole capital to Mrs. Aspinall and the three children or some or one of them. So far as the income is concerned they are obliged to pay it or apply it for her benefit or to pay it or apply it for the benefit of the children. So far as regards the capital they have a discretion to pay it and to apply it for her benefit and subject to that, they must hold it upon trust for the children. Mrs. Aspinall, the two surviving children and the representatives of the deceased child are between them entitled to the whole fund. In those circumstances it appears to me, notwithstanding the discretion which is reposed in the trustees, under which discretion they could select one or more of the people I have mentioned as recipients of the income, and might apply part of the capital for the benefit of Mrs. Aspinall and so take it away from the children, that the four of them, if they were all living, could come to the Court and say to the trustees: 'hand over the fund to us'. It appears to me that that is in accordance with the decision of the Court of Appeal in a case of *Re Nelson* [1928] Ch 920n, of which a transcript of the judgments has been handed to me, and is in accordance with principle. What is the principle? As I understand it is this. Where there is a trust under which trustees have a discretion as to applying the whole or part of a fund to or for the benefit of a particular person, that particular person cannot come to the trustees and demand the fund; for the whole fund has not been given to him but only so much as the trustees think fit to let him have. But when the trustees have no discretion as to the amount of the fund to be applied, the fact that the trustees have a discretion as to the method in which the whole of the fund shall be applied for the benefit of the particular person does not prevent that particular person from coming and saying: 'hand over the fund to me'. That appears to be the result of the two cases which were cited to me: *Green v Spicer* (1830) 1 Russ & M 395 and *Younghusband v Gisborne* (1844) 1 Coll 400.
>
> Now this third case arises. What is to happen where the trustees have a discretion whether they will apply the whole or only a portion of the fund for the benefit of one person, but are obliged to apply the

---

[110] See Chapter 10.1(b)(i), p. 493.
[111] *Re Smith* [1928] Ch 915. See also *Schmidt v Rosewood Trust Ltd* [2003] UKPC 26; [2003] 2 AC 709, [40].
[112] [1928] Ch 915, 917.

rest of the fund, so far as not applied for the benefit of the first named person, to or for the benefit of a second named person? There, two people together are the sole objects of the discretionary trust and, between them, are entitled to have the whole fund applied to them or for their benefit. It has been laid down by the Court of Appeal in the case to which I have referred that, in such a case as that you treat all the people put together just as though they formed one person, for whose benefit the trustees were directed to apply the whole of a particular fund. The case before the Court of Appeal was this: a testator had directed his trustees to stand possessed of one-third of his residuary estate upon trust during the lifetime of the testator's son Arthur Hector Nelson: 'to apply the income thereof for the benefit of himself and his wife and child or children or of any such persons to the exclusion of the others or other of them as my trustees shall think fit'. What happened was something very similar to what happened in the case before me. Hector Nelson, his wife and the only existing child of the marriage joined together in asking the trustees to hand over the income to them, and it was held by the Court of Appeal that the trustees were obliged to comply with the request, in other words, to treat all those persons who were the only members of the class for whose benefit the income could be applied as forming together an individual for whose benefit a fund has to be applied by the trustees without any discretion as to the amount so to be applied.

It follows that, where the trustees are required to distribute the whole of the fund, but they have a discretion as to which object will benefit and by how much, it is possible to treat all of the objects as though they were one person,[113] who are then able to request the trustees to transfer the property to them. This will work, however, only if all the objects have capacity to do so, namely if they are adults and of sound mind, if they all agree, and also only where all the objects are readily identifiable.

(c) FIDUCIARY POWERS

The rule in *Saunders v Vautier* extends to objects of a fiduciary power of appointment.

Matthews, 'The comparative importance of the rule in *Saunders v Vautier*' (2006) 122 LQR 266, 269

Even if the trust only creates powers of appointment with a gift over in default of appointment, the rule still applies. Suppose that there is a trust for such of A, B, C and D, as the trustee may select, but in default of appointment for E absolutely. A, B, C and D between them do not have the entire beneficial interest, for the property will go to E if no appointment is made. Nor does E have the entire beneficial ownership, for it would be perfectly lawful for the property to be appointed to one of A, B C and D.[114] But, if all of A to E join together, they must all account for the entire equitable interest. So each of the possible objects, even the objects of the power, A to D, must join in for the rule in *Saunders v Vautier* to apply.[115] Thus even a modern pension trust may be terminated by the exercise of the *Saunders v Vautier* power, provided *all* the possible persons to benefit join in the direction to the trustee.[116]

---

[113] *Re Nelson* [1928] Ch 920n.
[114] *Re Sharp's ST* [1973] Ch 331, 338.
[115] *Schmidt v Rosewood Trust* [2003] UKPC 26; [2003] 2 AC 709, [41].
[116] *Buschau v Rogers Communications Inc* (2004) 236 DLR (4th) 18; 6 ITELR 919, [11], [41]–[55].

QUESTION

By his will, Fred, who died in 2015, left £10,000 to be held on discretionary trust by Alan and Brenda for Fred's three children from his second marriage, Charles, Debbie, and Eric, to assist with the costs of their education. Fred made no provision for Georgina, a child of his first marriage. Alan and Brenda have failed to make any payments to Charles, Debbie, and Eric, despite repeated requests for financial assistance with their education. Charles, Debbie, and Fred, who are now aged twenty, eighteen, and seventeen respectively, seek your advice about the following matters:

(i) They wish to be paid £1,000 each for the benefit of their education.

(ii) They suspect that Fred wrote to Alan and Brenda giving them instructions about payments from the trust fund. Despite repeated attempts to get information from Alan and Brenda, they have heard nothing.

(iii) They would like financial assistance from the trust fund to be given to Georgina to help her with the costs of her education.

FURTHER READING

Green, '*Grey, Oughtred and Vandervell*: A Contextual Reappraisal' (1984) 47 MLR 385.

Fox, 'Overreaching', in *Breach of Trust* (eds Birks and Pretto) (Oxford: Hart, 2002), ch. 4.

Ho, 'Trustees' Duties to Provide Information', in *Exploring Private Law* (eds Bant and Harding) (Cambridge: Cambridge University Press, 2010), ch. 15.

Honoré, 'Trusts: The Inessentials' in *Rationalizing Property, Equity and Trusts: Essays in Honour of Edward Burn* (ed. Getzler) (Oxford: Oxford University Press, 2003) pp. 17–20.

Matthews, 'The Comparative Importance of the Rule in *Saunders v Vautier*' (2006) 122 LQR 266.

Nolan, '*Vandervell v IRC*: A Case of Overreaching' (2002) 61 CLJ 169.

Nolan, 'Equitable Property' (2006) 122 LQR 232.

Nolan, 'Understanding the Limits of Equitable Property' (2006) 1 JoE 18.

Thompson, 'Mere Formalities' [1996] Conv 366.

Waters, 'The Nature of the Trust Beneficiary's Interest' (1967) 45 Canadian Bar Review 219.

PART VI

TRUSTEES

GENERAL PRINCIPLES
RELATING TO TRUSTEES

CENTRAL ISSUES

1. All trusts need trustees, but the nature of trusteeship varies according to the type of trust.

2. There are a number of different types of trustee and a variety of rules relating to their appointment, retirement, and removal.

3. Although trustees are not generally paid for fulfilling their responsibilities in administering the trust, in some circumstances they can receive payment to reimburse them for expenses or to pay for their services.

4. Once appointed, trustees have a wide variety of powers. Misuse of these powers will constitute breach of trust, but the determination of when the exercise of powers can be characterized as invalid and the consequences of misusing a power raise significant issues of both theoretical and practical importance, particularly whether the exercise of the power should be treated as void or voidable.

1.   THE ESSENCE OF TRUSTEESHIP

A trustee holds an office that involves significant responsibility and onerous duties. This was recognized by Lord Hardwicke LC in *Knight v Earl of Plymouth*:[1]

> a trust is an office necessary in the concerns between man and man and ... if faithfully discharged, attended with no small degree of trouble and anxiety ... it is an act of great kindness in any one to accept it.

The office of trustee has a number of significant features.

(a)   HOLDING PROPERTY FOR ANOTHER

Trustees have the primary rights of ownership in trust property, but are not able to exploit the beneficial incidents of this ownership for themselves in their capacity as trustees. It is possible for a trustee

---

[1] (1747) Dick 120, 126.

also to be a beneficiary of the trust, but there must be at least one other beneficiary; the trustee cannot hold the property for him- or herself alone. The trustees will usually have legal title to the property vested in them, although it is possible to declare a trust over an equitable interest, which means that the trustees will have equitable title to the property but still hold it for at least one other person on a sub-trust.[2] If a trustee does not have legal or equitable title to the property vested in him or her, it has been recognized that they can still be considered to be a trustee if they have sufficient control of the property so that they can simply require the property be vested in them.[3]

(b) JOINT TENANCY

Where there is more than one trustee, the trustees hold the property as joint tenants. It follows that none of them has a distinct interest or share in the property. Consequently, if one of the trustees dies, no part of the trust property will pass to the deceased trustee's estate, but it will remain vested in the surviving trustees.[4] If a sole trustee dies, the trust property will pass to his or her personal representative, but subject to the trust, so the personal representative will be responsible as trustee for the property[5] until new trustees can be appointed.

TRUSTEE ACT 1925

18. Devolution of powers of trusts

(1) Where a power or trust is given to or imposed on two or more trustees jointly, the same may be exercised or performed by the survivors or survivor of them for the time being.

(2) Until the appointment of new trustees, the personal representatives or representative for the time being of a sole trustee, or, where there were two or more trustees of the last surviving or continuing trustee, shall be capable of exercising or performing any power or trust which was given to, or capable of being exercised by, the sole or last surviving or continuing trustee, or other trustees or trustee for the time being of the trust.

(c) IRREDUCIBLE CORE OF TRUST OBLIGATIONS

A trustee owes an irreducible core of obligations to the beneficiaries that are enforceable by the beneficiaries against the trustee.[6] The fundamental duty of all trustees is to perform the trust honestly and in good faith for the benefit of the beneficiaries.

(d) VOLUNTARY ASSUMPTION OF RESPONSIBILITY

It is generally not possible to impose trusteeship on a person without his or her consent; a trustee must accept the demands of the office voluntarily.[7] In *Westdeutsche Landesbank Girozentrale v Islington LBC*,[8] Lord Browne-Wilkinson said:

---

[2] See Chapter 10.2(e), pp. 510–12.

[3] *Re Barney* [1892] 2 Ch 265, 273 (Kekewich J).

[4] Trustee Act 1925, s. 18(1).

[5] Ibid, s. 18(2). If the trustee dies intestate, the trust property will vest in the Public Trustee until the grant of administration: Administration of Estates Act 1925, s. 9. See Chapter 11.2(g), p. 534.

[6] *Armitage v Nurse* [1998] Ch 241, 253 (Millett LJ). See Chapter 16.2, p. 744.

[7] As with any fiduciary. See Chapter 14.1, pp. 660–3.

[8] [1996] AC 669, 705.

> The equitable jurisdiction to enforce trusts depends upon the conscience of the holder of the legal interest being affected. He cannot be a trustee ... until he is aware that he is intended to hold the property for the benefit of others in the case of an express or implied trust or, in the case of a constructive trust, of the factors which are alleged to affect his conscience.

This is correct and uncontroversial as regards express trustees. As regards constructive trusts, they can be recognized even though the defendant was unaware of factors that affect his or her conscience.[9] But it is as regards the resulting trust, which Lord Browne-Wilkinson called an 'implied trust', that his dictum is most controversial in suggesting that a resulting trustee must be aware that he or she is intended to hold the property for the benefit of somebody else. This is not consistent with the preferable analysis of the resulting trust, namely that it arises by operation of law where the claimant can be presumed to have intended that the property was held on trust for him or her,[10] and this does not require the defendant's conscience to be affected in any way or the defendant to have any awareness that a resulting trust has been presumed.[11] The preferable view is that the notion of voluntary assumption of responsibility is key to the imposition of fiduciary obligations and the personal liability of trustees, but not to as whether or not a trust exists.

(e) TRUST WILL GENERALLY NOT FAIL FOR WANT OF A TRUSTEE

If no trustee accepts appointment, the trust will not fail for want of a trustee and the court will make an appropriate appointment, unless the settlor or testator made the validity of the trust dependent on the acceptance of appointment by a particular trustee.[12] In *Re Lysaght*,[13] for example, the testatrix had left money to the Royal College of Surgeons to establish a charitable trust for the provision of studentships for trainee surgeons, except for those of 'Jewish or Roman Catholic' faiths. The Royal College said that it was unable to accept such a gift, since the religious discrimination was invidious and alien to its work. It was held that, normally, if a trustee felt unable to accept the trust, he or she should simply make way for one who would accept it. Buckley J said:[14]

> Obviously a trustee will not normally be permitted to modify the terms of his trust on the ground that his own opinions or convictions conflict with them. If his conscience will not allow him to carry out the trust faithfully in accordance with its terms, he must make way for a trustee who can and will do so.

Where, as in *Re Lysaght* itself, the identity of the trustee is essential to the testator, the trust might fail for want of a trustee. But, on the facts, the trust was saved by deleting the offending term because this was considered to be an inessential part of the testatrix's paramount charitable intent to establish the studentships.[15]

---

[9] See Chapter 7.1(a), pp. 328–9.
[10] See Chapter 8.4, pp. 399–410.
[11] Although, where an automatic resulting trust arises following the initial or subsequent failure of an express trust, the trustee will have been aware that he or she was expected to hold the property for the benefit of others, albeit not necessarily for the settlor of the trust. See Chapter 8.3, pp. 384–99.
[12] *Re Lysaght* [1966] Ch 191.
[13] Ibid.
[14] Ibid, 206–7.
[15] See Chapter 5.6(c), p. 273.

(f) INABILITY TO CHALLENGE TRUST DEED

In *Khaira v Shergill*[16] the Supreme Court recognized that trustees who have been appointed under the terms of a trust are not able to challenge the validity of the trust deed. Lords Neuberger, Sumption and Hodge said:[17]

> trustees who have been appointed under the terms of a trust deed cannot challenge the validity of the deed. That would presumably be justified on the ground that the only basis on which they have any title to involve themselves in the affairs of the trust is as trustees, and they cannot therefore impugn the very document under which they achieved that status. [That] would be almost tantamount to denying their own title.

2. TYPES OF TRUSTEE

We have already seen three different types of trustee, namely the express trustee appointed by a settlor or a testator,[18] the resulting trustee,[19] and the constructive trustee.[20] There are a number of other categories and types of trustee, some of which overlap.

(a) AMATEUR TRUSTEE

Although this is not a specific legal category of trustee,[21] if trustees are not paid then less will be expected of them in fulfilling their duties when compared to professional trustees. Amateur trustees are more likely to be relieved of liability for breach of trust.[22]

(b) PROFESSIONAL TRUSTEE

A 'professional trustee' has been defined for the purposes of the Trustee Act 2000 as somebody who 'acts in the course of a profession or a business which consists of or includes the provision of services in connection with the management or administration of trusts'.[23] Professional trustees are likely to be banks or solicitors. Higher standards of care will be expected from them than from amateur trustees.[24]

---

[16] [2014] UKSC 33; [2015] AC 359.
[17] Ibid, [26].
[18] See Chapter 3, 'The Requirements of an Express Trust'.
[19] See Chapter 8, 'Resulting Trusts'.
[20] See Chapter 7, 'Constructive Trusts'.
[21] Although the 'lay trustee' is recognized in the context of remuneration for services: Trustee Act 2000, s. 28(2). See Chapter 11.6(c)(i), p. 559. The fact that a trustee is a professional rather than an amateur is also relevant when determining the duty of care to be expected of trustees: Trustee Act 2000, s. 1. See Chapter 12.2(b), p. 589.
[22] See Chapter 16.2(b)(iii), pp. 749–52.
[23] Trustee Act 2000, s. 28(5).
[24] *Re Waterman's Will Trusts* [1952] 2 All ER 1054, 1055 (Harman J). See also the Trustee Act 2000, s. 1(1), discussed in Chapter 12.2(b), p. 589.

(c) PENSION TRUSTEE

Trustees of pension funds are subject to the usual responsibilities of trustees of private trusts, but provision is made for additional responsibilities by the Pensions Act 1995 as regards, for example, powers of investment and delegation.[25] The duties of such trustees may sometimes differ from those of a trustee of a private trust. So, for example, trustees of a pension trust cannot delegate any of their investment functions.[26]

(d) CHARITY TRUSTEE

'Charity trustees' have the general control and management of the administration of a charity.[27] It does not follow that such people are necessarily 'trustees of a charity', because the vehicle for the creation of a charity need not be a trust; it could be a company. In such a case, the directors of the company are charity trustees for purposes of the Charities Act 2011, but are not trustees of the charity.[28] This is generally a distinction of only technical significance, since charity trustees are still subject to fiduciary duties and have administrative responsibilities in just the same way as they would if they were trustees of a trust.

(e) JUDICIAL TRUSTEE

Where the administration of a trust by the trustees has broken down, the settlor, trustees, or beneficiaries may apply to the court to have a judicial trustee appointed under the Judicial Trustees Act 1896, either to help the existing trustees to administer the trust, or to replace the trustees and take sole responsibility for the administration of the trust.

JUDICIAL TRUSTEES ACT 1896

1. Power of court on application to appoint judicial trustee

(1) Where application is made to the court by or on behalf of the person creating or intending to create a trust, or by or on behalf of a trustee or beneficiary, the court may, in its discretion, appoint a person (in this Act called a judicial trustee) to be a trustee of that trust, either jointly with any other person or as sole trustee, and, if sufficient cause is shown, in place of all or any existing trustees.

(2) The administration of the property of a deceased person, whether a testator or intestate, shall be a trust, and the executor or administrator a trustee, within the meaning of this Act.

(3) Any fit and proper person nominated for the purpose in the application may be appointed a judicial trustee, and, in the absence of such nomination, or if the court is not satisfied of the fitness of a person so nominated, an official of the court may be appointed, and in any case a judicial trustee shall be subject to the control and supervision of the court as an officer thereof.

---

[25] Pensions Act 1995, s. 34.
[26] Trustee Act 2000, s. 36(5). See further Chapter 12.4, pp. 593–611.
[27] Charities Act 2011, s. 177.
[28] *Re French Protestant Hospital* [1951] Ch 567.

(4) The court may, either on request or without request, give to a judicial trustee any general or special directions in regard to the trust or the administration thereof.

(5) There may be paid to a judicial trustee out of the trust property such remuneration, not exceeding the prescribed limits, as the court may assign in each case, subject to any rules under this Act respecting the application of such remuneration where the judicial trustee is an official of the court, and the remuneration so assigned to any judicial trustee shall, save as the court may for special reasons otherwise order, cover all his work and personal outlay.

(6) In any case where the court shall so direct, an inquiry into the administration by a judicial trustee of any trust, or into any dealing or transaction of a judicial trustee, shall be made in the prescribed manner.

The judicial trustee is able to exercise the discretionary powers of a trustee, such as the power to compromise disputes, without obtaining directions from the court. This was recognized in *Re Ridsdel*.

Re Ridsdel [1947] Ch 597, 605 (Jenkins J)

the object of the Judicial Trustees Act 1896, as I understand it, was to provide a middle course in cases where the administration of the estate by the ordinary trustees had broken down and it was not desired to put the estate to the expense of a full administration. In those circumstances, a solution was found in the appointment of a judicial trustee, who acts in close concert with the court and under conditions enabling the court to supervise his transactions. I cannot think that it was intended to complicate the matter by prohibiting such a trustee from exercising any discretion without first going to the court and asking for directions. That … involves this, that whenever the trustee wanted to exercise some discretion, such as the power of compromise under section 15 of the Trustee Act 1925,[29] he would perforce have to come to the court for directions; but (to give only one instance) the court would give no directions without summoning before it all persons interested in the exercise of the discretion in order that the matter might be argued and decided in the presence of all parties. One would thus reduce the administration of an estate by a judicial trustee to very much the same position as where an estate is being administered by the court and every step has to be taken in pursuance of the court's directions. It does not seem to me to be right or necessary to construe the Judicial Trustee Rules 1897,[30] as having any such effect.

(f) CUSTODIAN TRUSTEE

A custodian trustee is a corporate trustee that is authorized by statute to be appointed to have custody of trust property and related documents.[31] Such a trustee does not have general responsibility for the administration of the trust, since it has no discretion as to what to do with the trust property and must give effect to the decisions of the other trustees (known as 'managing trustees') relating, for example, to the investment of trust property. But custodian trustees are real trustees, since they hold the trust property and income derived from it on trust for the beneficiaries according to the terms of the trust instrument, they cannot benefit from the property themselves, and they owe duties to the beneficiaries not to misapply the trust property and to avoid a conflict between

---

[29] See Chapter 12.9, pp. 626–7.
[30] Which supplement the Judicial Trustees Act 1896.
[31] Public Trustee Act 1906, s. 4.

personal interest and duty;[32] they are subject to the irreducible core of trust obligations that are a prerequisite to establish trusteeship.

Re Brooke Bond & Co. Ltd's Trust Deed [1963] Ch 357

The Welfare Insurance Co. Ltd was a custodian trustee under a trust deed that secured the pension fund of the employees of Brooke Bond & Co. Ltd. The fund's managing trustees had powers to take out a group insurance policy and they desired to take it out with Welfare Insurance Co. Ltd. The question was whether, without leave of the court, the custodian trustee could enter into the policy with the managing trustees, and retain for their own benefit any profit that they might make. Cross J held that they could not:[33]

It is apparent that the duties of a custodian trustee differ substantially from those of an ordinary trustee. If the trust instrument or the general law gives the trustee power to do this, that or the other, it is not for the custodian trustee to consider whether it should be done. The exercise of powers or discretions is a matter for the managing trustees with which the custodian trustee has no concern, and he is bound to deal with the trust property so as to give effect to the decisions and actions taken by the managing trustees unless what he is requested to do by them would be a breach of trust or would involve him in personal liability. On the other hand, it is plain that he is a trustee holding the trust property and its income on trust for the beneficiaries according to the terms of the trust instrument and he is prima facie liable to the beneficiaries for any dealing with capital or income which is a breach of trust. In practice this liability may be considerably qualified as regards income by the provisions of [the Public Trustee Act 1906, s.2] subsection (2)(e) and as regards capital or income by the provisions of subsection (2)(h); but subject to the protection provided by those subsections the custodian trustee, as I understand the matter, is as liable as an ordinary trustee to be sued by a beneficiary for the misapplication of the trust property. His position is quite unlike that of a third party—a bailee of the trust property, for instance—who is in contractual relationship with the trustee but owes no duty to the beneficiaries.

It is, however, argued that the fact that a custodian trustee is not concerned with the management of the trust makes the rule that a trustee may not make a profit out of his trust inapplicable to him. If trustees have power to sell or lease the trust property or to invest it in some way, the custodian trustee is not concerned with the question whether the power should be exercised and is not concerned with any negotiations which take place between the managing trustees and the other contracting parties. All the custodian trustee is concerned to do is to be satisfied that the managing trustees have the power to enter into the transaction which they call on him to carry out.

That being the position, it is said how can there be any conflict between his interest and duty if he himself is the other contracting party? He must indeed satisfy himself that the proposed transaction is one which the managing trustees have power to enter into just as he would have to do if they had contracted with a third party, but once he is satisfied as to that, his duty in the matter is at an end and he can properly look only to his own interests in negotiating the terms of the contract in question with the managing trustees.

This argument is ingenious but in my judgment it is unsound. In the first place, it presupposes that a hard and fast line can always be drawn between the power to enter into a contract of a certain character

---

[32] *Re Brooke Bond and Co. Ltd's Trust Deed* [1963] Ch 357. See also *Forster v Williams Deacon's Bank Ltd* [1935] Ch 359 (bank may not be appointed both managing trustee and custodian trustee in order to allow it to charge fees as custodian trustee).

[33] [1963] Ch 357, 363.

and the terms of the contract. I do not think that this is always the case. For example, the managing trustees may have power to lease the trust property but only on the terms that they obtain the best rent reasonably obtainable. In such a case if the proposal was to grant a lease to a nominee of the custodian trustee, the custodian trustee would be under a duty to see that the best rent was obtained so that no breach of trust was committed, but it would be to his interest as the prospective lessee to have the rent fixed at as low a figure as possible. Again it is prima facie the duty of a trustee to place at the disposal of the beneficiaries any special knowledge he has of the value of the trust property or of any advantages or disadvantages of any contract which is in contemplation with regard to it. It may be that if the contract is being made by the managing trustees with a third party, a custodian trustee is under no positive duty to communicate any such knowledge which he may have to the managing trustees. I do not say whether that is so or not, but assuming it is so it does not follow by any means that if the custodian trustee was himself the other contracting party he could properly refrain from disclosing any such special knowledge to the managing trustees as a third party would be entitled to refrain from disclosing it. I appreciate that it may well be that the chances of there being a conflict between interest and duty are less in the case of transactions between a custodian trustee and managing trustees than they are in the case of transactions between an ordinary trustee and his co-trustees. But the possibility of conflict is still there and the rule, as Lord Herschell pointed out in *Bray v Ford* [1896] AC 44, is an inflexible one unless the trust instrument provides for a profit being made by the trustees or the court makes a special order in a particular case.

For the reasons I have tried to give, I can see no sound reason for saying that the rule does not apply to a custodian trustee as much as to an ordinary trustee.

There are a number of advantages in appointing a custodian trustee, which are more significant where the trust fund is large and the trust is expected to last for some time.[34] First, where the trust property is vested in a custodian trustee, it is not necessary to vest the property in the managing trustees each time a new one is appointed. If there are a number of trustees who are likely to change over time, this is a significant advantage. Secondly, having the property vested in a custodian trustee makes the selection and review of investments easier to implement. Finally, having a professional trustee to manage the trust property may reduce the possibility of a breach of trust.

(g) PUBLIC TRUSTEE

The Public Trustee is a corporation that is an officer appointed by the Lord Chancellor under the Public Trustee Act 1906. The functions of the Public Trustee are much more limited today than they used to be and, essentially, the office has a residuary function to act as a trustee where nobody else is suitable, able, and willing to act.

(h) TRUST CORPORATION

A trust corporation is a special kind of trustee which is the Public Trustee; is specifically appointed by the court to be a trustee; or is entitled to be a custodian trustee.[35] Having a trust corporation is significant to the administration of the trust, since it can often act alone when two trustees would otherwise be required. So, for example, a trust corporation alone can give a valid receipt for the

---

[34] Maurice, 'The Office of Custodian Trustee' (1960) 24 Conv 196.
[35] Trustee Act 1925, s. 68(18). See also Law of Property (Amendment) Act 1926, s. 3.

proceeds of sale under a trust for land, whereas at least two individual trustees would be required to give a valid receipt.[36]

(i) *TRUSTEE* DE SON TORT

In some circumstances, a person who has not been appointed as a trustee will be treated as though he or she were an actual trustee,[37] where that person took it upon him or herself to do acts that are characteristic of a trustee.[38] This is called a trustee *de son tort*, meaning a 'trustee of his own wrong'. The key feature of a trustee *de son tort* was recognized in *Mara v Browne*[39] as being that the trustee has intermeddled with the trust in some way and becomes responsible as a trustee for that intermeddling.

A person will be treated as a trustee *de son tort* in two situations:

(1) where they assumed the position of a trustee in fact, even though they had not been properly appointed, and they intended to act as trustee;[40]

(2) where a person has obtained such command or control of trust property that he or she can call for title to the property to be vested in him or her.[41]

In each case the trustee is properly characterized as an express trustee,[42] because he or she has inter-meddled with an existing trust and is simply deemed to have been appointed as a trustee to that trust. In *Dubai Aluminium Co. Ltd v Salaam*,[43] Lord Millett considered *Mara v Browne*.[44]

The case concerned a marriage settlement. The first defendant, whom I shall call HB, was a solicitor. He advised the persons who were acting as trustees, though not yet formally appointed as such. He suggested a series of investments for the trust funds. They were not proper investments for trustees to make. The money was to be lent on building property of a speculative character and the margin was unsatisfactory. The investments were made and the money was lost. Lord Herschell considered that, if the claimants had charged HB with negligence as a solicitor and brought the action in time, they might well have succeeded, in which case both HB and his partner would have been liable. But any such action was barred by the Statute of Limitations. Accordingly the claimants alleged that HB had intermeddled with the trust and was liable as a trustee *de son tort*. They alleged that he had laid out the trust moneys at a time when there were no trustees, and therefore must be taken to have acted as a principal in the matter and not as a mere agent for the trustees. Such a claim was not statute-barred. The judge agreed with this analysis and held that both HB and his partner were liable.

The Court of Appeal took a different view of the facts. They held that it was not correct to say that at the relevant dates there were no trustees. But even if there had been none HB would not have been liable. He did not intend or purport to act as a trustee, and no one supposed that he was so acting. He

---

[36] Trustee Act 1925, s. 14(2).
[37] *Taylor v Davies* [1920] AC 636, 651 (Viscount Cave).
[38] *Dubai Aluminium Co. Ltd v Salaam* [2002] UKHL 48; [2003] 2 AC 366, [138] (Lord Millett).
[39] [1896] 1 Ch 199, 209 (AL Smith LJ).
[40] Ibid.
[41] *Re Barney* [1892] 2 Ch 265, 273 (Kekewich J); *Soar v Ashwell* [1893] 2 QB 390, 394 (Lord Esher MR).
[42] *Soar v Ashwell* [1893] 2 QB 390, 394 (Lord Esher MR). Compare Kay LJ, 405, who described the trustee *de son tort* as a constructive trustee.
[43] [2002] UKHL 48; [2003] 2 AC 36, [136].
[44] [1896] 1 Ch 199.

purported to act throughout only as solicitor to the trustees and was understood by all concerned to be acting as such.

This summary is sufficient to show what Lord Herschell and Rigby LJ in *Mara v Browne* meant by 'constructive trustee'. They meant 'trustee *de son tort*'; that is to say, a person who, though not appointed to be a trustee, nevertheless takes it upon himself to act as such and to discharge the duties of a trustee on behalf of others. In *Taylor v Davies* [1920] AC 636, 651, Viscount Cave described such persons as follows:

'though not originally trustees, [they] had taken upon themselves the custody and administration of property on behalf of others; and though sometimes referred to as constructive trustees, they were, in fact, actual trustees, though not so named.'

Substituting dog Latin for bastard French, we would do better today to describe such persons as *de facto* trustees. In their relations with the beneficiaries they are treated in every respect as if they had been duly appointed. They are true trustees and are fully subject to fiduciary obligations. Their liability is strict; it does not depend on dishonesty. Like express trustees they could not plead the Limitation Acts as a defence to a claim for breach of trust. Indeed, for the purposes of the relevant provision (section 25(3) of the Supreme Court of Judicature Act 1873...), which distinguished between property held on express trusts and other trusts, they were treated by the courts as express trustees. That is why the action in *Mara v Browne* was not statute-barred.

3. APPOINTMENT OF TRUSTEES

(a) NUMBER OF TRUSTEES

For all trusts, it is sufficient to have only one trustee. The only significant restriction on the maximum number of trustees appointed arises where the subject matter of the trust is land and the trust is not charitable: for such a trust, the maximum number of trustees is limited to four.

TRUSTEE ACT 1925

34. Limitation of the number of trustees

(2) In the case of settlements and dispositions creating trusts of land made or coming into operation after the commencement of this Act—

  (a) the number of trustees thereof shall not in any case exceed four, and where more than four persons are named as such trustees, the four first named (who are able and willing to act) shall alone be the trustees, and the other persons named shall not be trustees unless appointed on the occurrence of a vacancy;

  (b) the number of the trustees shall not be increased beyond four.

(3) This section only applies to settlements and dispositions of land, and the restrictions imposed on the number of trustees do not apply—

  (a) in the case of land vested in trustees for charitable, ecclesiastical, or public purposes; or

  (b) where the net proceeds of the sale of the land are held for like purposes; or

  (c) to the trustees of a term of years absolute limited by a settlement on trusts for raising money, or of a like term created under the statutory remedies relating to annual sums charged on land.

(b) BY THE SETTLOR

The settlor can choose anybody whom he or she likes to be a trustee, except that a child cannot act as trustee of any trust.[45] It is even possible for a settlor to appoint him or herself as a trustee. Where this happens, and the settlor already owns the property to be held on trust, the trust will be immediately constituted, since the settlor will already have the legal title vested.[46] If another person is appointed as trustee, the trust will only be properly constituted once title to the property is vested in the trustee.[47]

The selection of the right trustees is a matter of the greatest importance. Modern settlements usually give many discretionary powers to the trustees. In selecting the original trustees, the settlor will select persons who can be relied on to exercise these powers in a manner of which he or she would him or herself approve. The settlor cannot, however, control the trustees in the exercise of their powers and discretions. Once the settlor has appointed trustees, he or she cannot determine subsequent appointments of trustees, save where the settlor has reserved the power in the trust instrument to make such appointments.[48]

(c) BY THE TESTATOR

Similar rules about the appointment of trustees apply where a trust is declared in a will. The testator can choose whomever he or she likes to be the trustee, other than a child. It is possible for the testator to choose the same person to be both executor and trustee. If different people are chosen as trustee and executor, the executors will hold the property in the testator's estate immediately on the testator's death until the property is vested in the trustees appointed by the will. If all the trustees chosen by the testator have predeceased the testator, the testator's personal representatives will hold the property on trust until trustees are appointed.[49]

(d) BY TRUSTEES OR THOSE WITH POWER TO APPOINT

The trust instrument may give an express power to a particular person to appoint new trustees. Additionally, there are specific statutory powers to appoint new trustees, although these powers may be excluded by the trust instrument.[50]

(i) General statutory power of appointment

TRUSTEE ACT 1925

36. Power of appointing new or additional trustees

(1) Where a trustee, either original or substituted, and whether appointed by a court or otherwise, is dead, or remains out of the United Kingdom for more than twelve months, or desires to be discharged from all or any of the trusts or powers reposed in or conferred on him, or refuses or is

---

[45] Law of Property Act 1925, s. 20. Although it has been recognized that a child can hold personalty on a resulting trust: *Re Vinogradoff* [1935] WN 68. See Chapter 8.2(a), p. 465.

[46] See Chapter 4.3(a), pp. 145–9.

[47] See Chapter 4.3(b), pp. 149–51.

[48] See Chapter 11.3(d)(i), pp. 537–8.

[49] *Re Smirthwaite's Trust* (1871) LR 11 Eq 251.

[50] Trustee Act 1925, s. 69(2).

unfit to act therein, or is incapable of acting therein, or is an infant, then, subject to the restrictions imposed by this Act on the number of trustees,—

(a) the person or persons nominated for the purpose of appointing new trustees by the instrument, if any, creating the trust; or

(b) if there is no such person, or no such person able and willing to act, then the surviving or continuing trustees or trustee for the time being, or the personal representatives of the last surviving or continuing trustee,[51]

may, by writing, appoint one or more other persons (whether or not being the persons exercising the power) to be a trustee or trustees in the place of the trustee so deceased, remaining out of the United Kingdom, desiring to be discharged, refusing, or being unfit or being incapable, or being an infant, as aforesaid.

(7) Every new trustee appointed under this section as well before as after all the trust property becomes by law, or by assurance, or otherwise, vested in him, shall have the same powers, authorities, and discretions, and may in all respects act as if he had been originally appointed a trustee by the instrument, if any, creating the trust.

This general statutory power of appointment applies where the trust instrument nominates particular people to appoint trustees. It also applies if no such people have been identified, or if they have been identified, but are not able and willing to act, since the surviving or continuing trustees may appoint a new trustee.[52] The nominated people or trustees can appoint a new trustee by writing, but only in the particular circumstances identified in section 36.

The question of whether a person has been nominated to make an appointment may raise some subtle issues of interpretation. For example, in *Re Wheeler and De Rochow*[53] a marriage settlement gave to the husband and wife, or the survivor of them, the power to appoint new trustees in certain specified circumstances, including that of a trustee becoming 'incapable' of acting. One of the trustees became bankrupt and absconded. This rendered him 'unfit' but not 'incapable'. The question was whether a new trustee should be appointed by the husband (as the survivor), under paragraph (a) of section 36(1), or by the continuing trustees under paragraph (b). Kekewich J held that the husband and wife (or the survivor) were the 'persons nominated for the purpose of appointing new trustees by the instrument' only in the circumstances specified in the settlement. No such circumstances had occurred, so the new trustee needed to be appointed by the continuing trustees with reference to the general statutory power to make an appointment on the ground that one of the existing trustees was unfit.

(ii) *Replacement of trustees*

TRUSTEE ACT 1925

36 (2) Where a trustee has been removed under a power contained in the instrument creating the trust, a new trustee or new trustees may be appointed in the place of the trustee who is removed, as if he

---

[51] Or the executor of a deceased sole trustee: *Re Shafto's Trusts* (1885) 29 Ch D 247. A personal representative may exercise the power without having obtained probate: *Re Crowhurst Park* [1974] 1 WLR 583; but a trustee so appointed will be unable to prove his or her title unless a grant is obtained. Apart from the circumstances covered by the sub-paragraph, executors do not have power to appoint new trustees; see *Re King's Will Trusts* [1964] Ch 542.

[52] Trustee Act 1925, s. 36(1).

[53] [1896] 1 Ch 315.

were dead, or, in the case of a corporation, as if the corporation desired to be discharged from the trust, and the provisions of this section shall apply accordingly, but subject to the restrictions imposed by this Act on the number of trustees.

Where a trustee has been removed under a power in the trust instrument,[54] the nominated people with the power to appoint or the other trustees will be able to exercise their general statutory power of appointment. If, once a trustee has been removed, there is a single trustee left who is not a trust corporation,[55] the trustee who had been removed must be replaced, save where only one trustee was originally appointed.[56]

(iii) *Additional trustees*

TRUSTEE ACT 1925

36 (6) Where, in the case of any trust, there are not more than three trustees—

  (a) the person or persons nominated for the purpose of appointing new trustees by the instrument, if any, creating the trust; or

  (b) if there is no such person, or no such person able and willing to act, then the trustee or trustees for the time being;

may, by writing appoint another person or other persons to be an additional trustee or additional trustees, but it shall not be obligatory to appoint any additional trustee, unless the instrument, if any, creating the trust, or any statutory enactment provides to the contrary, nor shall the number of trustees be increased beyond four by virtue of any such appointment.

Under this provision, unlike the general statutory power of appointment, the person with the power of appointment cannot appoint him- or herself as trustee.

(iv) *Selecting trustees*

The people exercising the statutory power of appointment have a free choice as to whom they can appoint. They can often even appoint themselves.[57] They can also choose to appoint foreign trustees to administer the trust.[58]

Richard v The Hon A.B. Mackay [2008] WTLR 1667[59]

The English trustees of a settlement made in 1965 by Lord Tanlaw, on trusts governed by English law, sought a declaration that transfer of part of the trust fund to a new settlement to be established

---

[54] See Chapter 11.5(a), p. 549.
[55] *Jasmine Trustees Ltd v Wells and Hind* [2007] EWHC 38 (Ch); [2008] Ch 194.
[56] Trustee Act 1925, s. 37(1)(c). In *Mettoy Pension Trustees Ltd v Evans* [1990] 1 WLR 1587, 1607, Warner J doubted whether the express terms of the settlement can override these provisions.
[57] Trustee Act 1925, s. 36(1). Cp s. 36(6).
[58] *Re Smith's Trusts* (1872) 26 LT 820; *Richard v The Hon AB Mackay* [2008] WTLR 1667.
[59] Decided 4 March 1987.

in Bermuda was valid. The beneficiaries under the proposed new settlement were the infant children of Lord Tanlaw, and, although the family had international connections, Lord Tanlaw was domiciled and resident in the United Kingdom. Millett J held that the transfer was valid.

In *Re Whitehead's Will Trusts* [1971] 1 WLR 833 Sir John Pennycuick, the Vice-Chancellor, was asked to declare that an appointment of foreign trustees of an English trust was effective to discharge the English trustees.

At 837, he said:

> '... the law has been quite well established for upwards of a century that there is no absolute bar to the appointment of persons resident abroad as trustees of an English trust. I say "no absolute bar", in the sense that such an appointment would be prohibited by law and would consequently be invalid. On the other hand, apart from exceptional circumstances, it is not proper to make such an appointment, that is to say, the court would not, apart from exceptional circumstances, make such an appointment; nor would it be right for the donees of the power to make such an appointment out of court. If they did, presumably the court would be likely to interfere at the instance of the beneficiaries. There do, however, exist exceptional circumstances in which such an appointment can properly be made. The most obvious exceptional circumstances are those in which the beneficiaries have settled permanently in some country outside the United Kingdom and what is proposed to be done is to appoint new trustees in that country. In those exceptional circumstances it has, I believe, almost uniformly been accepted as the law that trustees in the country where the beneficiaries have settled can properly be appointed.'

At 838, the learned Vice-Chancellor added:

> ' ... It cannot, I think, make any difference whether the court is asked under the Variation of Trusts Act 1958 to transfer a fund to a new settlement in a foreign country or whether one is concerned merely with the appointment of new trustees of the existing settlement.'

This is not a case where the family concerned or the beneficiaries have become resident abroad. The settlor and his two children live in England. Nor is it a case where the proposed new settlement is to be formed in the country where the beneficiaries reside or may be expected to reside in the future. The possibility which is envisaged is that they may well wish to live in the Far East, whereas the seat of the proposed settlement is to be Bermuda.

But in my judgment the language of Sir John Pennycuick, which is narrowly drawn, is too restrictive for the circumstances of the present day if, at least, it is intended to lay down any rule of practice. Nor in my view is it accurate to equate the approach that the court adopts to exercise its own discretion with the approach it adopts when asked to authorise the trustees to exercise theirs.

Where the court is invited to exercise an original discretion of its own, whether by appointing trustees under the Trustee Act 1925 or by approving a scheme under the Variation of Trust Act 1958,[60] or where the trustees surrender their discretion to the court, the court will require to be satisfied that the discretion should be exercised in the manner proposed. The applicants must make out a positive case for the exercise of the discretion, and the court is unlikely to assist them where the scheme is nothing more than a device to avoid tax and has no other advantages of any kind.

Where, however, the transaction is proposed to be carried out by the trustees in exercise of their own discretion, entirely out of court, the trustees retaining their discretion and merely seeking the authorisation of the court for their own protection, then in my judgment the question that the court asks itself

---

[60] See further Chapter 15.3(b), pp. 724–39.

is quite different. It is concerned to ensure that the proposed exercise of the trustees' power is lawful and within the power and that it does not infringe the trustees' duty to act as ordinary, reasonable and prudent trustees might act, but it requires only to be satisfied that the trustees can properly form the view that the proposed transaction is for the benefit of beneficiaries or the trust estate ...

Certainly in the conditions of today, when one can have an international family with international interests, and where they are as likely to make their home in one country as in another and as likely to choose one jurisdiction as another for the investment of their capital, I doubt that the language of Sir John Pennycuick is really in tune with the times. In my judgment, where the trustees retain their discretion, as they do in the present case, the court should need to be satisfied only that the proposed transaction is not so inappropriate that no reasonable trustee could entertain it.

I have evidence before me that the proposed trustee is the leading trustee corporation in Bermuda, that the trust law of Bermuda is similar to and based upon and derived from English law, and that there are no restrictions upon the free movement of capital. I think I can take judicial notice of the fact that Bermuda has a stable regime within the United States' sphere of influence and that many wealthy families, acting in their own interests and in a businesslike way, have been in the habit in recent years of entrusting substantial portions of their fortunes to trustees in that jurisdiction.

There are obvious potential advantages in diversification. What is proposed is only the removal from the jurisdiction of 25 per cent of a very substantial fund. There is great force in the submission that what is proposed is positively a prudent step, and I have no doubt at all that it cannot possibly be stigmatised as imprudent or unreasonable ...

Accordingly I consider that there is no reason why the trustees should not take the view that the proposed transaction is for the benefit of the principal beneficiaries, and I will give the direction sought.

There may be a variety of reasons why trustees would wish to appoint foreign trustees, including that the beneficiaries live abroad permanently, the trust property is located abroad, or the trust should be relocated to avoid a tax liability.[61] In *Re Beatty's WT (No. 2)*,[62] executors and trustees wished to appoint Jersey resident trustees, since having overseas trustees would avoid capital gains tax on a trust estate that had included Van Gogh's *Sunflowers*, which had just been sold at auction for the then record price of £22.5 million. There were three principal beneficiaries of the trust. One was resident in Australia, one was about to emigrate to Spain, and the third was resident in the United Kingdom. Vinelott J said:[63]

Turning again to the instant case, there are, in my judgment, clearly circumstances which the executors can properly regard as justifying the appointment of the proposed new trustees as trustees of the will. Lord Brooke is and Lady Charlotte is about to become resident outside the United Kingdom. It is impractical to appropriate the whole residuary estate into one-third shares and impractical, therefore, to appoint trustees resident in and to administer the trusts in a single jurisdiction where all the beneficiaries are domiciled and resident. Mrs. Thompson-Jones is herself willing that trustees resident outside the United Kingdom should be appointed, and she is the only beneficiary now ascertainable who is resident in the United Kingdom. It would, I think, be unjust to the non-resident beneficiaries that because Mrs. Thompson-Jones is resident here they should be exposed to heavy fiscal liabilities which will not arise if non-resident trustees are appointed.

---

[61] *Re Beatty's WT (No. 2)* (4 March 1987) (1997) 11 TLI 77.
[62] Ibid.
[63] Ibid, 80.

> There can be no question but that the proposed individual new trustees are responsible persons and the proposed corporate trustee is a well-established and well-known trust corporation.
>
> The trustees all reside in a stable jurisdiction in which many English trusts are now administered and in which the assets and the future administration of the trusts will be fully safeguarded.
>
> In these circumstances, I have no hesitation in giving the direction and making the order sought.

(v) Continuing trustees

The general statutory power of appointment of trustees may be exercised by a 'continuing trustee'. This is defined to include 'a refusing or retiring trustee, if willing to act in the execution of the provisions of' section 36 of the Trustee Act 1925.[64] It follows that a retiring sole trustee or group of trustees is able to appoint successors. But it has been held that a retiring or refusing trustee can participate in the exercise of the power of appointment only if he or she is competent, and ready and willing to act. For example, in *Re Coates to Parsons*[65] the title to a chapel was vested in eleven trustees. One died, and another, Dearlove, remained out of the United Kingdom for twelve months. The nine remaining trustees purported to replace him, acting under the statutory power. A purchaser under a contract for sale of the land by the trustees objected to the title, one of the grounds being that Dearlove had not participated in the appointment of new trustees. North J nevertheless upheld the appointment, saying:[66]

> I hold, therefore, that under the terms of the Act the nine trustees, who were clearly continuing trustees were competent to make the appointment, unless it was shewn that the person who had been absent for so long, and in whose place there was a clear right to substitute a new trustee, was willing and competent to act. This has not been shewn, and it seems to me, therefore, that the first objection, viz. that WR Dearlove ought to have concurred in making the appointment, is not established.

Where two trustees wish to retire, it is not possible for them to appoint one trustee to replace them unless it is a trust corporation, because, where there were originally two trustees, it is not possible to reduce the overall number of trustees.[67] Further, when replacing a trustee who has been abroad for over a year, it is not necessary for that trustee to participate in the exercise of the power of appointment, because that trustee is being removed rather than retiring or refusing to act. This was recognized in *Re Stoneham's ST*[68] in which one trustee, Stoneham, had absented himself from the United Kingdom for over twelve months. His co-trustee, intending to retire, appointed two others in place of Stoneham and himself. Stoneham wished to continue to act as a trustee. Danckwerts J nevertheless held that the appointments made by the co-trustee as a retiring trustee were valid and that Stoneham's participation was not necessary:

> I come to the conclusion quite plainly that a trustee who is removed against his will is not a refusing or retiring trustee, not, at any rate, in the case of a trustee removed because of his absence outside the United Kingdom for consecutive periods of more than 12 months.

---

[64] Trustee Act 1925, s. 36(8).
[65] (1886) 34 Ch D 370.
[66] Ibid, 377.
[67] Trustee Act 1925, s. 37(1)(c). See *Adam and Co. International Trustees Ltd v Theodore Goddard* [2000] WTLR 349.
[68] [1953] Ch 59.

(e) AT THE DIRECTION OF THE BENEFICIARIES

The rule in *Saunders v Vautier*[69] gives a power to the adult beneficiaries of a trust who are between them absolutely entitled to the beneficial interest in the trust property to terminate the trust, and to direct the trustees to transfer the property to them if they are of full capacity and agree to the termination of the trust. It has been held, however, that this is an all-or-nothing power: it does not enable the beneficiaries to interfere with the administration of the trust, whilst keeping the trust on foot.

Re Brockbank [1948] Ch 206, 209 (Vaisey J)

It seems to me that the beneficiaries must choose between two alternatives: Either they must keep the trusts of the will on foot, in which case those trusts must continue to be executed by trustees duly appointed pursuant either to the original instrument or to the powers of s. 36 of the Trustee Act 1925, and not by trustees arbitrarily selected by themselves; or they must, by mutual agreement, extinguish and put an end to the trusts …

The claim of the beneficiaries to control the exercise of the defendant's fiduciary power of making or compelling an appointment of the trustees is, in my judgment, untenable. The court itself regards such a power as deserving of the greatest respect and as one with which it will not interfere …

If the court, as a matter of practice and principle, refuses to interfere with the legal power of appointment of new trustees, it is, in my judgment, *a fortiori* not open to the beneficiaries to do so. As I have said, they can put an end to the trust if they like; nobody doubts that; but they are not entitled, in my judgment, to arrogate to themselves a power which the court itself disclaims possessing, and to change trustees whenever they think fit at their whim or fancy—for it follows from Mr. Cross' argument for the present plaintiffs … that whenever the beneficiaries choose to say that they do not like their trustee, they can order him to retire and order him to appoint anyone they like to succeed him. That seems to me to show a complete disregard of the true position. As I have said, as long as the trust subsists, the trust must be executed by persons duly, properly and regularly appointed to the office.

There is, however, a statutory mechanism that enables the beneficiaries to secure the appointment of their nominated trustees without terminating the trust.

TRUSTS OF LAND AND APPOINTMENT OF TRUSTEES ACT 1996

19. Appointment and retirement of trustee at instance of beneficiaries[70]

(1) This section applies in the case of a trust where—

    (a) there is no person nominated for the purpose of appointing new trustees by the instrument, if any, creating the trust, and

    (b) the beneficiaries under the trust are of full age and capacity and (taken together) are absolutely entitled to the property subject to the trust.

---

[69] (1841) 4 Beav 115. See Chapter 10.3, pp. 519–23.

[70] A similar power of direction is available to the beneficiaries where the trustee is incapable of acting because he or she lacks capacity to act: Trusts of Land and Appointment of Trustees Act 1996, s. 20.

(2) The beneficiaries may give a direction or directions of either or both of the following descriptions—

   (a) a written direction to a trustee or trustees to retire from the trust, and

   (b) a written direction to the trustees or trustee for the time being, (or, if there are none, to the personal representative of the last person who was a trustee) to appoint by writing to be a trustee or trustees the person or persons specified in the direction.[71]

(5) This section has effect subject to the restrictions imposed by the Trustee Act 1925 on the number of trustees.

The existence of this statutory power has been criticized by Keppel-Palmer[72] on the ground that:

> To allow beneficiaries the whip hand over trustees, by threatening to and replacing them on a whim, surely undermines the basis of trusteeship, especially in its stakeholding between the interests of the beneficiaries. With so many of the powers of trustees being discretionary, are we going to discover that the concept of trusteeship is under attack. As Vaisey J articulated:[73] 'a discretionary power ... in my opinion is no longer exercisable and, indeed, can no longer exist if it has become one of which the exercise can be dictated by others'.

Against this, the existence of this power of the beneficiaries to appoint trustees can be considered to be an important power to give the beneficiaries significant indirect influence over the management of the trust property, since they are not restricted in the choice of people whom they can direct the trustees to appoint and can, therefore, choose people whom they might consider will look after their own interests more appropriately.

(f) BY THE COURT

A trust will not fail for want of a trustee.[74] Consequently, if the trustees or other people with the power to appoint a trustee fail to do so, the court will intervene and appoint a trustee.

TRUSTEE ACT 1925

41. Power of court to appoint new trustees[75]

(1) The court may, whenever it is expedient to appoint a new trustee or new trustees, and it is found inexpedient difficult or impracticable so to do without the assistance of the court, make an order appointing a new trustee or new trustees either in substitution for or in addition to any existing trustee or trustees, or although there is no existing trustee.In particular and without prejudice to the generality of the foregoing provision, the court may make an order appointing a new trustee in substitution for a trustee who lacks capacity to exercise his functions as trustee or is a bankrupt, or is a corporation which is in liquidation or has been dissolved.

---

[71] For sub-ss (3) and (4) see Chapter 11.4(b), p. 549.
[72] (1996) 146 NLJ 1779, 1786.
[73] *Re Brockbank* [1948] Ch 206, 208. See Chapter 11.3(e), p. 543.
[74] *Re Lysaght* [1966] Ch 191. See Chapter 11.1(e), p. 529.
[75] Trustee Act 1925, s. 41(1). This power extends to the Charity Commission to appoint charity trustees: Charities Act 2011, s. 69(1)(b).

43. Powers of new trustee appointed by the court

Every trustee appointed by a court of competent jurisdiction shall, as well before as after the trust property becomes by law, or by assurance, or otherwise, vested in him, have the same powers, authorities, and discretions, and may in all respects act as if he had been originally appointed a trustee by the instrument, if any, creating the trust.

This power of the court to make an appointment may be relevant in a wide variety of circumstances, including where a sole trustee has died intestate or where the donee of a power to appoint cannot exercise it because he or she is underage.[76] This power of appointment will be relevant only where there is no other authorized person who is willing and able to make an appointment.[77] So, for example, in *Re May's Will Trusts*,[78] although one of the trustees was in Belgium at the time of the German invasion of that country during the Second World War, there was no evidence that she was incapable of exercising the power of appointment, and so the court was unable to exercise its statutory power of appointment.

When the court is selecting an appropriate trustee, it should have regard to a number of principles that were identified in the important case of *Re Tempest*.

Re Tempest [1866] 1 Ch App 485 (CA in Ch)

A family settlement was created by the will of Sir Charles Tempest, appointing Stoner and Fleming as trustees. Stoner predeceased the testator. The persons to whom the power of appointing new trustees was given were unable to agree upon a selection. A petition was presented, asking the court to appoint Petre. One beneficiary opposed this, on the ground that Petre was connected with, and proposed by, a branch of the family with which the testator was not on friendly terms, and which he had excluded from participation in the management of his property. The Master of the Rolls appointed Petre and Lord Camoys 'hoping to satisfy both parties'.

It was held that Petre was not a person whom the Court would appoint.

Turner LJ:

There are two questions raised by this appeal. First, whether the order of the Master of the Rolls ought to be reversed in so far as it appoints Mr. Petre to be a trustee of the testator's will; and secondly, whether assuming that the order ought to be reversed in this respect, Lord Camoys ought to be appointed the trustee. The first of these questions has not seemed to me to be altogether free from difficulty, and in my view of this case it is by no means an unimportant question. It involves, as I think, to no inconsiderable extent the principles on which this Court ought to act in the appointment of new trustees.

It was said in argument, and has been frequently said, that in making such appointments the Court acts upon and exercises its discretion; and this, no doubt, is generally true; but the discretion which the Court has and exercises in making such appointments, is not, as I conceive, a mere arbitrary discretion, but a discretion in the exercise of which the Court is, and ought to be, guided by some general rules and principles, and, in my opinion, the difficulty which the Court has to encounter in these cases lies not so

---

[76] *Re Parsons* [1940] Ch 973.
[77] *Re Gibbon's Trusts* (1882) 30 WR 287.
[78] [1941] Ch 109.

much in ascertaining the rules and principles by which it ought to be guided, as in applying those rules and principles to the varying circumstances of each particular case. The following rules and principles may, I think, safely be laid down as applying to all cases of appointments by the Court of new trustees.

First, the Court will have regard to the wishes of the persons by whom the trust has been created, if expressed in the instrument creating the trust, or clearly to be collected from it. I think this rule may be safely laid down, because if the author of the trust has in terms declared that a particular person, or a person filling a particular character, should not be a trustee of the instrument, there cannot, as I apprehend, be the least doubt that the Court would not appoint to the office a person whose appointment was so prohibited, and I do not think that upon a question of this description any distinction can be drawn between express declarations and demonstrated intention. The analogy of the course which the Court pursues in the appointment of guardians affords, I think, some support to this rule. The Court in those cases attends to the wishes of the parents, however informally they may be expressed.

Another rule which may, I think, safely be laid down is this—that the Court will not appoint a person to be trustee with a view to the interest of some of the persons interested under the trust, in opposition either to the wishes of the testator or to the interests of others of the *cestui que trusts*. I think so for this reason, that it is of the essence of the duty of every trustee to hold an even hand between the parties interested under the trust. Every trustee is in duty bound to look to the interests of all, and not of any particular member or class of members of his *cestui que trusts*.

A third rule which, I think, may safely be laid down is,—that the Court in appointing a trustee will have regard to the question, whether his appointment will promote or impede the execution of the trust, for the very purpose of the appointment is that the trust may be better carried into execution.

These are the principles by which, in my judgment, we ought to be guided in determining whether Mr. Petre ought to be appointed to be a trustee of this will, and, in my opinion, there are substantial objections to his appointment on each of the three grounds to which I have referred. There is not, of course, and cannot be, any possible objection to Mr. Petre in point of character, position, or ability, and I desire most anxiously to be understood as not intending, in disapproving his appointment, to cast the slightest possible reflection upon him. I have not for one moment doubted that he is a gentleman of most unexceptionable character, and well qualified in every respect to fill the office of trustee; but I think that the principles to which I have referred are opposed to his appointment.

First, as to the wishes of this testator, it is impossible, I think, to read this will without being fully satisfied that the great object and purpose of the testator was to exclude Mr. Charles Henry Tempest not only from all interest in, but from all connection with his estate. A more complete exclusion of him, both from any interest in and from any power over the estate, could not, as it seems to me, have been devised. Is it then consistent with this purpose of the testator that a trustee should be appointed who, upon the evidence before us, I cannot doubt is the nominee of Mr. Charles Henry Tempest, and is proposed for the purpose of carrying into effect his wishes and intentions? The facts, I think, prove that this is the position of Mr. Petre. He is proposed by Mr. Washington Hibbert, the father-in-law of Mr. CH Tempest, and the very person the connection with whom led to the making of this will, by which he was excluded. He is supported, and I desire not to be understood as saying, in any other than a legal sense, improperly, by Mr. AC Tempest his brother, who it appears upon the evidence declined to attend the testator's funeral on account of the dispositions of the will; and one of the principal witnesses in support of his appointment, and the person most active in these proceedings is Mr. Broadbent, the solicitor of Sir CH Tempest, under whose advice we find that Mr. Petre adopted that most unfortunate and, I must say, ill-advised step of declining to meet his co-trustees. Looking to all these circumstances, and to the whole of the evidence before us, I have as little doubt as to what led to the proposal of Mr. Petre as I have as to the intentions of this testator, and upon this ground, therefore, I think that Mr. Petre ought not to be appointed to be a trustee of this will.

It was said for the respondents, that the testator's dispositions were captious and absurd, and ought not therefore to be regarded, but much as we may regret that such dispositions were made, we cannot disregard them.

Then, as to the second ground, the objection to the appointment of Mr. Petre seems to me to be still more decisive. The evidence, in my opinion, very plainly shews that Mr. Petre has been proposed as a trustee, and has accepted that office, with a view to his acting in the trust in the interests of some only of the objects of it, and in opposition to the wishes of the testator, and not with a view to his acting as an independent trustee for the benefit of all the objects of the trusts, and I do not hesitate to say that, in my opinion, this fact is alone sufficient to prevent us from confirming his appointment. It was objected on the part of the respondents, that the proof of this fact rests upon evidence of what has occurred since the order under appeal was pronounced, and ought not, therefore, to be attended to; but this is a rehearing of the Petition under which Mr. Petre has been appointed. The question before us, therefore, is, whether he ought now to be appointed or not—a question of his present fitness or unfitness—and I am aware of no rule which precludes us from receiving upon such a question evidence of what has occurred since the original hearing. Supposing, however, that there was any difficulty upon that point, I apprehend there can be no doubt that the evidence of what has so occurred ought to be looked at as shewing the purpose for which he was proposed, and that it was not proper that he should be appointed at the time when the order appointing him was made.

It was also argued on the part of the respondents, that their interests ought to be considered in the appointment to be made by the Court, and there would have been great force in this argument, if it could have been considered that Mr. Petre was proposed as an independent trustee to act on behalf of, and with a view to, the interests of all the *cestui que trusts*; but when the purpose for which he is proposed is seen, this argument loses all weight and cannot be attended to. It is the appointment of a trustee for the benefit of all, and not with a view to the interests of some, that the wishes of *cestui que trusts* are to be consulted, for the trustee to be appointed must represent and consult the interests of all, and not of some only of the *cestui que trusts*. It was indeed with this view, that in the course of the argument I suggested to the parties the expediency of their agreeing upon the appointment of an independent trustee.

The third and remaining ground of objection to the appointment of Mr. Petre is, I think, open to more difficulty. On the one hand, there cannot, I think, be any doubt that the Court ought not to appoint a trustee whose appointment will impede the due execution of the trust; but, on the other hand, if the continuing or surviving trustee refuses to act with a trustee who may be proposed to be appointed—and I make this observation with reference to what appears to have been said by Mr. Fleming, as to Mr. Petre having come forward in opposition to his wishes—I think it would be going too far to say that the Court ought, on that ground alone, to refuse to appoint the proposed trustee; for this would, as suggested in the argument, be to give the continuing or surviving trustee a veto upon the appointment of the new trustee. In such a case, I think it must be the duty of the Court to inquire and ascertain whether the objection of the surviving or continuing trustee is well founded or not, and to act or refuse to act upon it accordingly. If the surviving or continuing trustee has improperly refused to act with the proposed trustee, it might be a ground for removing him from the trust. Upon the facts of this case, however, it seems to me that the objections taken by Mr. Fleming to the appointment of Mr. Petre were and are well founded, and upon the whole case, therefore, my opinion is, that the order under appeal, so far as it appoints Mr. Petre, ought to be discharged. …

The order upon this appeal should, I think, be to discharge the order at the Rolls, to appoint Lord Camoys to be the trustee in the place of Mr. Stoner, and to vest the estate in him and Mr. Fleming.

It follows that there are three key considerations that the court should bear in mind when determining how it should exercise its discretion in selecting trustees: (1) the wishes of the settlor or testator; (2) the wishes of beneficiaries; and (3) the proper administration of the trust. In *Polly Peck International plc v Henry*,[79] Buckley J refused to appoint a new trustee to a pension trust under section 41 because the proposed trustee lacked expertise and the appointment would not have been cost-effective for the trust.

Positive reasons must be identified for the court to appoint foreign trustees. A common reason for wishing to appoint such trustees is to avoid tax, but this is unlikely to be regarded as a legitimate reason for the court to make such an appointment.[80]

(g) BY THE CHARITY COMMISSION

In charitable trusts, the Charity Commission can appoint a person to act as a trustee for a variety of reasons, including the need to replace a trustee removed by the Commission or because one or more existing trustees is unfit, incapable, or absent.[81]

4. RETIREMENT OF TRUSTEES

(a) VOLUNTARY RETIREMENT

A trustee can voluntarily retire from the trust by deed.

TRUSTEE ACT 1925

39. Retirement of trustee without a new appointment

(1) Where a trustee is desirous of being discharged from the trust, and after his discharge there will be either a trust corporation or at least two persons to act as trustees to perform the trust, then, if such trustee as aforesaid by deed declares that he is desirous of being discharged from the trust, and if his co-trustees and such other person, if any, as is empowered to appoint trustees, by deed consent to the discharge of the trustee, and to the vesting in the co-trustees alone of the trust property, the trustee desirous of being discharged shall be deemed to have retired from the trust, and shall, by the deed, be discharged therefrom under this Act, without any new trustee being appointed in his place.

A trustee who retires from the trust should, normally, obtain a formal discharge of liability from the beneficiaries. But, even if such a discharge is not obtained, the retired trustee will not be liable for breaches of trust that occur after his or her retirement, except where the trustee resigned in order to facilitate a breach of trust.[82] A trustee who has resigned will, however, remain liable for breaches of trust that occurred before the resignation. A trustee who purports to retire, but fails to comply with the statutory requirements, will continue in office.[83]

---

[79] [1999] 1 BCLC 407.

[80] *Re Beatty's WT (No. 2)* (4 March 1987) (1997) 11 TLI 77. Compare where the trustees wish the court to approve the exercise of their discretion in favour of such an appointment: see Chapter 11.3(d)(iv), pp. 539–42.

[81] Charities Act 2011, s. 80(2).

[82] *Head v Gould* [1898] 2 Ch 250, 272. See further Chapter 16.8, p. 780.

[83] *Jasmine Trustees Ltd v Wells and Hind (a firm)* [2007] EWHC 38 (Ch); [2008] Ch 194.

(b) BY DIRECTION OF THE BENEFICIARIES

The beneficiaries can unanimously compel a trustee to retire from office.

TRUSTS OF LAND AND APPOINTMENT OF TRUSTEES ACT 1996

19 (3) Where—

   (a) a trustee has been given a direction under subsection (2)(a),[84]

   (b) reasonable arrangements have been made for the protection of any rights of his in connection with the trust,

   (c) after he has retired there will be either a trust corporation or at least two persons to act as trustees to perform the trust, and

   (d) either another person is to be appointed to be a new trustee on his retirement (whether in compliance with a direction under subsection (2) (b) or otherwise) or the continuing trustees by deed consent to his retirement,

he shall make a deed declaring his retirement and shall be deemed to have retired and be discharged from the trust.[85]

(4) Where a trustee retires under subsection (3) he and the continuing trustees (together with any new trustee) shall (subject to any arrangements for the protection of his rights) do anything necessary to vest the trust property in the continuing trustees (or the continuing and new trustees).

This power will not be available if the instrument nominates somebody to make trustee appointments. This power of the beneficiaries to compel retirement is a significant one, especially when coupled with the power to force an appointment of a new or replacement trustee.[86] But it can be regarded as a logical extension of the beneficiaries' power to terminate a trust under the rule in *Saunders v Vautier*, and it is a power that has a number of safeguards against abuse, including the need for reasonable arrangements to be in place to protect the retiring trustee's rights. It certainly has the potential to affect the dynamics between the trustees and beneficiaries in a small trust where the beneficiaries are absolutely entitled to trust property.

5. REMOVAL OF TRUSTEES

(a) BY THE TRUST INSTRUMENT

The trust instrument may provide for the removal of a trustee. Where such a power to remove has been exercised, the trustee will be treated as having died, so that either a person with the power to appoint trustees or the remaining trustees may appoint a new trustee.[87]

---

[84] A written direction by the beneficiaries to a trustee or trustees to retire from the trust. See Chapter 11.3(e), p. 544.

[85] It is not clear what would happen if the trustee refused to retire. One consequence may be that the beneficiaries would terminate the trust under the rule in *Saunders v Vautier* (1841) 4 Beav 115, see Chapter 10.3(a), pp. 519–21.

[86] See Chapter 11.3(e), p. 544.

[87] Trustee Act 1925, s. 36(2). See Chapter 11.3(d)(ii), pp. 538–9.

(b) GENERAL STATUTORY POWER

The donee of a power to appoint trustees or the trustees themselves may remove one trustee and replace him or her with a new trustee on the specific grounds recognized by the Trustee Act 1925,[88] such as where the trustee has been abroad for over a year, is a child, or is incapable or unwilling to act as a trustee.

(c) BY THE CHARITY COMMISSION

Where the Charity Commission has conducted an inquiry with regard to a charity[89] and concludes that there has been misconduct or mismanagement in the administration of the charity, the Commission can remove any charity trustee who has been involved in the misconduct or mismanagement.[90] The Commission also has the power to remove a charity trustee who has been declared bankrupt in the last five years, is incapable of acting because of a mental disorder, or is absent or refuses to act and this is impeding the proper administration of the charity.[91]

(d) BY THE COURT

The court has a statutory power to remove a trustee and appoint a new trustee in his or her place.[92] In particular, the court can appoint a new trustee in substitution for an existing one on the grounds of incapacity to exercise the functions of a trustee, bankruptcy, or insolvency.[93]

The court also has an inherent jurisdiction to remove a trustee from the trust, but only where cogent grounds are established.[94]

Letterstedt v Broers [1894] 9 App Cas 371

The Privy Council had to consider whether, independently of statute, it should remove the Board of Executors of Cape Town, the sole surviving executors and trustees of the will of Mr Letterstedt, against whom a beneficiary had made allegations of misconduct in the administration of the trust. The Board was removed; but the allegations were not substantiated, and no costs were awarded. Lord Blackburn[95] described the principles upon which the court's discretion should be exercised:

The whole case has been argued here, and, as far as their Lordships can perceive, in the Court below, as depending on the principles which should guide an English Court of Equity when called upon to remove old trustees and substitute new ones. It is not disputed that there is a jurisdiction 'in cases requiring such a remedy', as is said in *Story's Equity Jurisprudence*, s.1287, but there is very little to be

---

[88] Ibid, s. 36(1). See Chapter 11.3(d)(i), pp. 537–8.
[89] By virtue of Charities Act 2011, s. 46. See Chapter 5.2(b)(iii), p. 182.
[90] Ibid, s. 18(2).
[91] Ibid, s. 18(4).
[92] Trustee Act 1925, s. 41(1). See Chapter 11.3(e), p. 544. This power extends to the Charity Commission to remove charity trustees: Charities Act 2011, s. 69(1)(b).
[93] Trustee Act 1925, s. 41(1).
[94] *Re Edwards' Will Trusts* [1982] Ch 30, 42 (Buckley J).
[95] [1884] 9 App Cas 371, 385.

found to guide us in saying what are the cases requiring such a remedy; so little that their Lordships are compelled to have recourse to general principles.

Story says, s.1289, 'But in cases of positive misconduct, Courts of Equity have no difficulty in interposing to remove trustees who have abused their trust; it is not indeed every mistake or neglect of duty, or inaccuracy of conduct of trustees, which will induce Courts of Equity to adopt such a course. But the acts or omissions must be such as to endanger the trust property or to shew a want of honesty, or a want of proper capacity to execute the duties, or a want of reasonable fidelity'.

It seems to their Lordships that the jurisdiction which a Court of Equity has no difficulty in exercising under the circumstances indicated by Story is merely ancillary to its principal duty, to see that the trusts are properly executed. This duty is constantly being performed by the substitution of new trustees in the place of original trustees for a variety of reasons in non-contentious cases. And therefore, though it should appear that the charges of misconduct were either not made out, or were greatly exaggerated, so that the trustee was justified in resisting them, and the Court might consider that in awarding costs, yet if satisfied that the continuance of the trustee would prevent the trusts being properly executed, the trustee might be removed. It must always be borne in mind that trustees exist for the benefit of those to whom the creator of the trust has given the trust estate.

The reason why there is so little to be found in the books on this subject is probably that suggested by Mr. Davey in his argument. As soon as all questions of character are as far settled as the nature of the case admits, if it appears clear that the continuance of the trustee would be detrimental to the execution of the trusts, even if for no other reason than that human infirmity would prevent those beneficially interested, or those who act for them, from working in harmony with the trustee, and if there is no reason to the contrary from the intentions of the framer of the trust to give this trustee a benefit or otherwise, the trustee is always advised by his own counsel to resign, and does so. If, without any reasonable ground, he refused to do so, it seems to their Lordships that the Court might think it proper to remove him; but cases involving the necessity of deciding this, if they ever arise, do so without getting reported. It is to be lamented that the case was not considered in this light by the parties in the Court below, for, as far as their Lordships can see, the Board would have little or no profit from continuing to be trustees, and as such coming into continual conflict with the appellant and her legal advisers, and would probably have been glad to resign, and get out of an onerous and disagreeable position. But the case was not so treated.

In exercising so delicate a jurisdiction as that of removing trustees, their Lordships do not venture to lay down any general rule beyond the very broad principle above enunciated, that their main guide must be the welfare of the beneficiaries. Probably it is not possible to lay down any more definite rule in a matter so essentially dependent on details often of great nicety. But they proceed to look carefully into the circumstances of the case …

It is quite true that friction or hostility between trustees and the immediate possessor of the trust estate is not of itself a reason for the removal of the trustees. But where the hostility is grounded on the mode in which the trust has been administered, where it has been caused wholly or partially by substantial overcharges against the trust estate, it is certainly not to be disregarded.

Looking therefore at the whole circumstances of this very peculiar case, the complete change of position, the unfortunate hostility that has arisen, and the difficult and delicate duties that may yet have to be performed, their Lordships can come to no other conclusion than that it is necessary, for the welfare of the beneficiaries, that the Board should no longer be trustees.

Probably if it had been put in this way below they would have consented. But for the benefit of the trust they should cease to be trustees, whether they consent or not.

Their Lordships think therefore that the portion of the final judgment which is, 'that the prayer for removal of the executors be refused', should be reversed, and that in lieu of it the Court below should be directed to remove the Board from the further execution of the trusts created by the will, and to take all necessary and proper proceedings for the appointment of other and proper persons to execute such trusts in future, and to transfer to them the trust property in so far as it remains vested in the Board. The rest of the judgment should stand.

The fundamental principle relating to the exercise of the court's jurisdiction to remove trustees concerns the welfare of the beneficiaries and the preservation of the trust property. The application of this principle was considered in *Re Wrightson*,[96] where the trustees had committed a breach of trust and the court had to consider whether the trustees should be removed. Warrington J said:[97]

[Counsel for the plaintiffs] as one argument, or as one reason for the removal of the trustees, said, in effect, 'we do not like to have these persons who have been charged with a breach of trust and have admitted it, and who have made that statement which is set out in the pleadings, in custody of our trust estate'. That is not enough, especially when there are other *cestuis que trust* entitled. A somewhat similar question arose in the case of *Forster v Davies* (1861) 4 De GF & J 133 at 139, in which Turner LJ expressed the view, which I have just expressed, that disagreement between the *cestuis que trust* and the trustees, or the disinclination on the part of the *cestuis que trust* to have the trust property remain in the hands of a particular individual, is not a sufficient ground for the removal of the trustees. You must find something which induces the court to think either that the trust property will not be safe, or that the trust will not be properly executed in the interests of the beneficiaries. Is that so here, and is it for the welfare of the trust generally, and not merely of the plaintiffs, that these trustees should be removed? I think it is not. The trustees were undoubtedly guilty of a breach of trust, and they undoubtedly in the statement to which I have referred expressed views which have occasioned the blame which has been attached to the trustees both by Buckley J and myself, but, having regard to the fact that the Court has now the power of seeing that the trust is properly executed, to the fact that a large proportion of the beneficiaries do not require the trustees to be removed, and further (and this is of great importance), to the extra expense and loss to the trust estate which must be occasioned by the change of trustees, I think it would not be for the welfare of the *cestuis que trust* generally, or necessary for the protection of the trust estate, that these trustees should be removed. I must therefore refuse the application for their removal as well as the application for the further accounts and inquiries.

One of the most extreme examples of the application of these principles is in *Thomas and Agnes Carvel Foundation v Carvel* which, although it concerned the removal of an executor, involved exactly the same principles as for removal of a trustee.

Agnes Carvel Foundation v Carvel [2007] EWHC 1314; [2008] Ch 395

An American businessman, who made his money as one of the biggest sellers of ice cream in the United States, and his wife, Agnes, made mutual wills[98] whereby they mutually agreed that the first to die would leave his or her money to the other and, on the death of that person, to a named foundation. The husband died first. A few years later, Agnes changed her will to leave her estate to a corporation that was incorporated in her own name and that of her niece, Pamela, who was also the executor. On the death of Agnes, Pamela sought to transfer the estate to the corporation.

---

[96] [1908] 1 Ch 789.
[97] Ibid, 800.
[98] See Chapter 7.2(e)(iii), pp. 346–51.

It was held that, since Pamela had a clear conflict of interest and was either dishonest, or at the very least did not understand her responsibilities as an executor, she should be removed. Lewison J said:[99]

The foundation's application to remove Pamela is mainly based on her conduct of proceedings thus far. It is a striking fact that after the surrogate [Court in New York] had ruled that the foundation was entitled to receive Agnes's residuary estate (a decision that Pamela knew about) she issued proceedings in the High Court in England in which she was both claimant and defendant, seeking payment of moneys from the estate without notifying the foundation. She pursued those proceedings until the Chancery order was made, still without notifying the foundation. As I have said, the claim was based on three categories of expense: (i) sums which Pamela said she had incurred on behalf of Agnes during her lifetime; (ii) debts which Agnes had contracted but had not paid; and (iii) sums which Pamela had incurred as Agnes's personal representative and in respect of which she claimed to be entitled to indemnity from the estate.

The first of these categories was a claim as creditor of the estate against the estate. In other words, this was Pamela's personal claim against the estate. The second category is more obscure, but seems also to have been Pamela's personal claim against the estate. The third was a claim in her representative capacity (in effect against the beneficiaries). A pause for thought ought to have led Pamela to realise that there was an obvious conflict of interest between her personal claims and her duties as personal representative. The procedural nonsense of a claim to which she was both claimant and sole defendant ought to have been obvious too. [Counsel for Pamela] pointed out that Pamela was acting as a litigant in person. However, Pamela is an experienced litigant. I do not regard the fact that she was a litigant in person as an excuse. If anything, it counts against her, because a responsible personal representative, with the interests of the estate at heart, would have consulted a lawyer …

Even after all the criticism that has been levelled at Pamela for taking this course, both by the foundation and Judge Andrews, she still says that she believes that it was appropriate for her to have obtained the Chancery order and that there was no need to inform the foundation either that she had applied for it or that it had been granted. [Counsel for Pamela] submitted, and I agree, that I should not on a summary application infer that Pamela has acted dishonestly or with deliberate disregard of her duties. But if I do not draw that inference, what is left? The only alternative conclusion that I can draw from this is that Pamela does not understand her responsibilities, and is not willing to learn them. There is no prospect of Pamela's position being any better after a trial …

It is plain that there is intense hostility between Pamela and the foundation. Pamela is partisan as between the foundation on the one hand and Carvel-Florida on the other. So far as the foundation is concerned, the hostility is, in my judgment, grounded on the way in which the trusts have been administered.

Lord Blackburn [in *Letterstedt v Broers*] cited as the guiding principle to the jurisdiction to remove trustees as being 'the welfare of the beneficiaries'. [Counsel for the foundation] submitted:

'Pamela has wholly disregarded this principle. Her every act has been calculated to promote her own personal interests and to prejudice those of the foundation. She is in a position of irreconcilable conflict with the principal beneficiary of Agnes's estate and her hostility to the foundation renders it quite impossible for her to fulfil her fiduciary duties. Her position as personal representative is untenable. She should be removed.'

I agree. I will order Pamela to be removed as personal representative.

[99] [2007] EWHC 1314 (Ch); [2008] Ch 395, 409.

6. PAYMENT TO TRUSTEES

The office of trustee is voluntary and generally gratuitous,[100] meaning that a trustee should not be paid for administering the trust;[101] as Lord Hardwicke LC recognized in *Knight v Earl of Plymouth*,[102] it is an 'act of great kindness' for anyone to become a trustee. This is consistent with one of the core duties of trustees, which is that they should not profit from their position as trustees.[103] There are, however, certain situations in which trustees have either a right or a legitimate expectation to receive payment in respect of their administration of the trust.

(a) REIMBURSEMENT OF EXPENSES

Where trustees have incurred reasonable expenditure in administering the trust, they have a right to be reimbursed either from the trust fund or, sometimes, from the beneficiaries themselves.

(i) *From the trust*

TRUSTEE ACT 2000

31. Trustees' expenses

(1) A trustee—

    (a) is entitled to be reimbursed from the trust funds, or

    (b) may pay out of the trust funds,

expenses properly incurred by him when acting on behalf of the trust.

(2) This section applies to a trustee who has been authorised under a power conferred by Part IV[104] or any other enactment or any provision of subordinate legislation, or by the trust instrument—

    (a) to exercise functions as an agent of the trustees, or

    (b) to act as a nominee or custodian,

as it applies to any other trustee.

The trustees are not bound to make any payment to the beneficiaries until their expenses have been reimbursed[105] and they have a lien on the trust property to secure their right to be reimbursed.[106]

Whether expenses were properly incurred was considered in *Re Chapman*,[107] where a barrister trustee had been paying income from the trust to a life tenant. He began to think that the life tenant was dead and he had been paying the income to an imposter. He incurred expense in investigating

---

[100] *Re Duke of Norfolk's Settlement Trust* [1982] Ch 61, 79 (Fox LJ).
[101] *Robinson v Pett* (1724) 3 P Wms 249, 250 (Lord Talbot LC).
[102] (1747) Dick 120, 126. See Chapter 11.1, p. 527.
[103] See Chapter 14.4, pp. 682–704.
[104] See Chapter 12.7, pp. 620–6.
[105] *Stott v Milne* (1884) 25 Ch D 710.
[106] *Alsop Wilkinson (a firm) v Neary* [1996] 1 WLR 1220, 1224 (Lightman J).
[107] (1894) 72 LT 66.

whether this was the case. The court held that there was no foundation for his suspicions and nobody else would have displayed such 'phenomenal scepticism'. As Lord Herschell recognized:[108]

> I think that a trustee is bound to act reasonably. I do not dissent from the defendant's proposition that what is reasonable must be measured by the responsibility which the law imposes on a trustee. I do not think that a trustee is bound to run any risks. I think that he is entitled to satisfy himself by all reasonable inquiry and investigation, because, if he pays money to any person who is not properly entitled to receive it, he may be held liable. But if he sees risk where none in fact exists, and if he refuses to be satisfied by evidence which would satisfy all reasonable men, then I think that he must bear all the expenses which his conduct causes, and cannot throw that expense upon any particular beneficiary or the trust estate.

Consequently, the expenses were considered to be so unreasonable as to be vexatious, oppressive, and wholly unjustifiable. His claim for reimbursement failed. In *Foster v Spencer*,[109] however, it was recognized that business-class air travel from Malaysia to attend to trust matters in England was a reasonable expense on the particular facts of the case.

If trustees are uncertain whether they have a right to be reimbursed from the trust, they should apply to the court for directions. It has been held that the right to be reimbursed from the trust fund enables the trustee simply to retain part of that fund so that they do not have a cause of action in debt or for damages against the fund.[110] This is significant because it means that the trustees are unable to claim interest on the reimbursement that they retain. As Judge Paul Baker QC recognized in *Foster v Spencer*: [111]

> These proceedings are not proceedings for the recovery of a debt or damages. No party can be ordered to pay them. The trustees are entitled to the expenses out of the trust estate, and only out of the trust estate. They come to court simply to gain approval of their exercise of their right of retainer so as to forestall any future allegations of breach of trust.

(ii) *From the beneficiaries*

If the trust fund is not sufficient to reimburse the trustee, he or she may look to the beneficiaries for reimbursement of expenses. If the trustee has incurred expenses by virtue of holding the trust property, he or she can be indemnified by the beneficiaries who are between them absolutely entitled to the property. In *Hardoon v Belilios*,[112] the claimant was employed by a firm of share brokers. In order to assist a syndicate speculating in shares, shares in a bank were placed in his name. The defendant was the absolute beneficial owner of the shares. On the liquidation of the bank, the liquidator claimed £400 from the claimant. The Privy Council held that the defendant was personally liable to reimburse the claimant's expenses. Lord Lindley said:[113]

> Where the only *cestui que trust* is a person *sui juris*, the right of the trustee to indemnity by him against liabilities incurred by the trustee by his retention of the trust property has never been limited to the trust property; it extends further, and imposes upon the *cestui que trust* a personal obligation enforceable in equity to indemnify his trustee. This is no new principle, but is as old as trusts themselves.

---

[108] Ibid, 67.
[109] [1996] 2 All ER 672.
[110] *Foster v Spencer* [1996] 2 All ER 672.
[111] Ibid, 678.
[112] [1901] AC 118.
[113] Ibid, 124.

It follows that the beneficiaries can be liable to indemnify the trustees even if the expense exceeds the value of the trust property. This is because, as Lord Lindley recognized:[114]

> [t]he plainest principles of justice require that the [beneficiary] who gets all the benefit of the property should bear its burden unless he can show some good reason why his trustee should bear them himself.

The liability of beneficiaries to indemnify the trustee is the corollary of the rule in *Saunders v Vautier*.[115] As a result there will be no such liability to indemnify the trustee if the conditions for that rule are not satisfied.[116] This will be the case if one of the beneficiaries is a child, since they are not then all of full capacity.

If a trustee has incurred liability when not acting on behalf of the trust, the beneficiaries may still be liable to indemnify the trustee, if they requested that this liability be incurred. So, in *Bush v Higham*,[117] a trustee was entitled to be indemnified by the beneficiary for interest payments when he had borrowed money at the beneficiary's request.

(b) REIMBURSEMENT OF THE COSTS OF LITIGATION

A related problem is whether the trustees can recover the costs of litigation. Where trustees have incurred a liability to pay for the costs of litigation relating to the trust, this will constitute an expense that might be reimbursed from the trust fund under section 31 of the Trustee Act 2000. Trustees may incur litigation costs either in suing somebody or in defending proceedings. In either case, it is necessary to consider whether the costs were properly incurred for the benefit of the trust.[118]

Re Beddoe [1893] 1 Ch 547, 562 (Bowen LJ)

The principle of law to be applied appears unmistakably clear. A trustee can only be indemnified out of the pockets of his *cestuis que trust* against costs, charges, and expenses properly incurred for the benefit of the trust—a proposition in which the word 'property' means reasonably as well as honestly incurred. While I agree that the trustees ought not to be visited with personal loss on account of mere errors in judgment, which fall short of negligence or unreasonableness, it is on the other hand essential to recollect that mere bona fides is not the test, and that it is no answer in the mouth of a trustee who has embarked in idle litigation to say that he honestly believed what his solicitor told him, if his solicitor has been wrong-headed and perverse. Costs, charges, and expenses which in fact have been unreasonably incurred, do not assume in the eye of the law the character of reasonableness simply because the solicitor is the person who was in fault. No more disastrous or delusive doctrine could be invented in a Court of Equity than the dangerous idea that a trustee himself might recover over from his own *cestuis que trust* costs which his own solicitor has unreasonably and perversely incurred merely because he had acted as his solicitor told him.

---

[114] Ibid, 123.
[115] (1841) Cr & Ph 240. See Chapter 10.3(a), pp. 519–21.
[116] See Hughes, 'The Right of a Trustee to a Personal Indemnity from Beneficiaries' (1990) 64 ALJ 567.
[117] (1728) 2 P Wms 453.
[118] Trustee Act 2000, s. 31. See also *Holding and Management Ltd v Property Holding and Investment Trust plc* [1989] 1 WLR 1313, 1324 (Nicholls LJ).

If there be one consideration again more than another which ought to be present to the mind of a trustee, especially the trustee of a small and easily dissipated fund, it is that all litigation should be avoided, unless there is such a chance of success as to render it desirable in the interests of the estate that the necessary risk should be incurred.

In assessing whether the costs of litigation were properly incurred, it is useful to distinguish between three types of dispute involving the trust,[119] which were identified by Lightman J in *Alsop Wilkinson (a firm) v Neary*.

Alsop Wilkinson (a firm) v Neary [1996] 1 WLR 1220, 1223 (Lightman J)

Trustees may be involved in three kinds of dispute.

(1) The first (which I shall call 'a trust dispute') is a dispute as to the trusts on which they hold the subject matter of the settlement. This may be 'friendly' litigation involving e.g. the true construction of the trust instrument or some other question arising in the course of the administration of the trust: or 'hostile' litigation e.g. a challenge in whole or in part to the validity of the settlement by the settlor on grounds of undue influence or by a trustee in bankruptcy or a defrauded creditor of the settlor, in which case the claim is that the trustees hold the trust funds as trustees for the settlor, the trustee in bankruptcy or creditor in place of or in addition to the beneficiaries specified in the settlement. The line between friendly and hostile litigation, which is relevant as to the incidence of costs, is not always easy to draw: see *Re Buckton* [1907] 2 Ch 406.

(2) The second (which I shall call a 'beneficiaries dispute') is a dispute with one or more of the beneficiaries as to the propriety of any action which the trustees have taken or omitted to take or may or may not take in the future. This may take the form of proceedings by a beneficiary alleging breach of trust by the trustees and seeking removal of the trustees and/or damages for breach of trust.

(3) The third (which I shall call 'a third-party dispute') is a dispute with persons, otherwise than in the capacity of beneficiaries, in respect of rights and liabilities e.g. in contract or tort assumed by the trustees as such in the course of administration of the trust.

Trustees (express and constructive) are entitled to an indemnity against all costs, expenses and liabilities properly incurred in administering the trust and have a lien on the trust assets to secure such indemnity. Trustees have a duty to protect and preserve the trust estate for the benefit of the beneficiaries and accordingly to represent the trust in a third-party dispute. Accordingly their right to an indemnity and lien extends in the case of a third-party dispute to the costs of proceedings properly brought or defended for the benefit of the trust estate. Views may vary whether proceedings are properly brought or defended, and to avoid the risk of a challenge to their entitlement to the indemnity, (a beneficiary dispute), trustees are well advised to seek court authorisation before they sue or defend. The right to an indemnity and lien will ordinarily extend to the costs of such an application. The form of application is a separate action to which all the beneficiaries are parties (either in person or by a representative defendant). With the benefit of their views the judge thereupon exercising his discretion determines what course the interests of justice require to be taken in the proceedings: see *Evans v Evans* [1986] 1 WLR 101, considered by Hoffmann LJ in *McDonald v Horn* [1995] ICR 685. So long as the trustees make full disclosure of the strengths and weaknesses of their case, if the trustees act as authorised by the court, their entitlement to an indemnity and lien is secure.

---

[119] *Re Buckton* [1907] 2 Ch 406, 414–15 (Kekewich J).

A beneficiaries dispute is regarded as ordinary hostile litigation in which costs follow the event and do not come out of the trust estate: see *per* Hoffmann LJ in *McDonald v Horn* [1995] ICR 685 at 696.

The role of trustees in case of a trust dispute was considered by Kekewich J in two cases.

[His Lordship considered *Merry v Pownall* [1898] 1 Ch 306 and *Ideal Bedding Co Ltd v Holland* [1907] 2 Ch 157, and continued:] I do not think that the view expressed by Kekewich J in the *Ideal Bedding* case that in case of a trust dispute (as was the dispute in that case) a trustee has a duty to defend the trust is correct or in accordance with modern authority. In a case where the dispute is between rival claimants to a beneficial interest in the subject matter of the trust, rather the duty of the trustee is to remain neutral and (in the absence of any court direction to the contrary and substantially as happened in *Merry's* case [1898] 1 Ch 306) offer to submit to the court's directions leaving it to the rivals to fight their battles. If this stance is adopted, in respect of the costs necessarily and properly incurred e.g. in serving a defence agreeing to submit to the courts direction and in making discovery, the trustees will be entitled to an indemnity and lien. If the trustees do actively defend the trust and succeed, e.g. in challenging a claim by the settlor to set aside for undue influence, they may be entitled to their costs out of the trust, for they have preserved the interests of the beneficiaries under the trust: consider *Re Holden, ex p Official Receiver* (1887) 20 QBD 43. But if they fail, then in particular in the case of hostile litigation although in an exceptional case the court may consider that the trustees should have their costs (see *Bullock v Lloyds Bank Ltd* [1955] Ch 317) ordinarily the trustees will not be entitled to any indemnity, for they have incurred expenditure and liabilities in an unsuccessful effort to prefer one class of beneficiaries e.g. the express beneficiaries specified in the trust instrument, over another e.g. the trustees in bankruptcy or creditors, and so have acted unreasonably and otherwise than for the benefit of the trust estate ...

The nature of a 'trust dispute' was considered further in *Spencer v Fielder*,[120] where Etherton C said:[121]

There are obvious types of case in which trustees will not usually be entitled to be indemnified in respect of their costs under [section 31 of the Trustee Act 2000]. One is if they are successfully sued for compensation for past breaches of trust. Another is where they take an unsuccessful partisan position in hostile litigation between rival claimants to a beneficial interest in the subject matter of the trust. ... They are to be contrasted with cases where, whatever the form, the substance of the litigation is to clarify some matter of uncertainty in the administration of the trust or the conduct of the trustees in the litigation is otherwise in the best interests of the beneficiaries as a body rather than for the personal benefit of the trustees themselves ....

I have emphasised that what matters is whether, in substance, trustees who are parties to litigation are acting in the best interests of the trust rather than for their own benefit. It is clear, for example, that, depending on the precise facts, trustees may be entitled to an indemnity for costs even though incidentally they will secure a personal benefit from a successful claim or defence or where there are allegations of breach of trust ...

Since it may not be clear whether the proceedings are proper in a particular case, it is preferable for trustees to seek court authorization before they sue or defend proceedings, especially in respect of third party disputes, and the trustee will be indemnified the cost of this application.[122] The directions given by the court are called a '*Beddoe*' order. If the court directs the action to be taken, the trustees

---

[120] [2014] EWHC 2768 (Ch); [2015] 1 WLR 2786.
[121] Ibid, [26].
[122] *Re Beddoe* [1893] 1 Ch 547.

will be reimbursed their costs even if they lose, unless the trustees failed to make full and proper disclosure to the court when seeking directions.[123] There is no breach of trust simply in commencing litigation without first obtaining a *Beddoe* order,[124] but the failure to obtain such an order means that the trustees will take the risk of having to pay the costs of the litigation personally if they lose and it cannot be shown that bringing or defending the proceedings was reasonable.

(c) REMUNERATION FOR SERVICES PROVIDED

Although, generally, trustees will not be paid for services provided to the trust, there are some particular situations in which a trustee can be remunerated for what he or she has done for the trust.

(i) *Authorized by trust instrument*

The trust instrument can provide for payment out of the trust fund for the services of a trustee.

TRUSTEE ACT 2000

28. Trustees' entitlement to payment under trust instrument

(1) Except to the extent (if any) to which the trust instrument makes inconsistent provisions, subsections (2) to (4) apply to a trustee if—

(a) there is a provision in the trust instrument entitling him to receive payment out of trust funds in respect of services provided by him to or on behalf of the trust, and

(b) the trustee is a trust corporation or is acting in a professional capacity.

(2) The trustee is to be treated as entitled under the trust instrument to receive payment in respect of services even if they are services which are capable of being provided by a lay trustee.

(3) Subsection (2) applies to a trustee of a charitable trust who is not a trust corporation only—

(a) if he is not a sole trustee, and

(b) to the extent that a majority of the other trustees have agreed that it should apply to him.

(4) For the purposes of this Part, a trustee acts in a professional capacity if he acts in the course of a profession or business which consists of or includes the provision of services in connection with—

(a) the management or administration of trusts generally or a particular kind of trust, or

(b) any particular aspect of the management or administration of trusts generally or a particular kind of trust,

and the services he provides to or on behalf of the trust fall within that description.

…

(6) For the purposes of this Part, a person acts as a lay trustee if he—

(a) is not a trust corporation, and

(b) does not act in a professional capacity.

---

[123] *McDonald v Horn* [1995] 1 All ER 961.
[124] *Bonham v Blake Lapthorn Linnell* [2007] WTLR 189.

The provision for payment in the trust instrument may take the form given in *Encyclopedia of Forms and Precedents*.

Encyclopedia of Forms and Precedents (5th edn) (ed. Lord Millett) (London: LexisNexis) vol. 40 (1), p. 443

Any trustee other than the settlor and any spouse of the settlor being a solicitor or other person engaged in any profession or business shall be entitled to charge and be paid all usual professional or other charges for business done by him or his firm in relation to the trusts of this settlement and also his reasonable charges in addition to disbursements for all other work and business done and all time spent by him or his firm in connection with matters arising in the premises including matters which might or should have been attended to in person by a trustee not being a solicitor or other person so engaged but which such a Trustee might reasonably require to be done by a solicitor or other person so engaged.

(ii) *Authorized by statute*

Where no provision is made by the trust instrument or any other statute for remuneration, the Trustee Act 2000 authorizes reasonable remuneration to be made from the trust fund for services provided by certain trustees.

TRUSTEE ACT 2000

29. Remuneration of certain trustees

(1) Subject to subsection (5), a trustee who—

    (a) is a trust corporation, but

    (b) is not a trustee of a charitable trust,

    is entitled to receive reasonable remuneration out of the trust funds for any services that the trust corporation provides to or on behalf of the trust.

(2) Subject to subsection (5), a trustee who—

    (a) acts in a professional capacity, but

    (b) is not a trust corporation, a trustee of a charitable trust or a sole trustee,

    is entitled to receive reasonable remuneration out of the trust funds for any services that he provides to or on behalf of the trust if each other trustee has agreed in writing that he may be remunerated for the services.

(3) 'Reasonable remuneration' means, in relation to the provision of services by a trustee, such remuneration as is reasonable in the circumstances for the provision of those services to or on behalf of that trust by that trustee and for the purposes of subsection (1) includes, in relation to the provision of services by a trustee who is an authorised institution under the Banking Act 1987 and provides the services in that capacity, the institution's reasonable charges for the provision of such services.

(4) A trustee is entitled to remuneration under this section even if the services in question are capable of being provided by a lay trustee.

(5) A trustee is not entitled to remuneration under this section if any provision about his entitlement to remuneration has been made—

    (a) by the trust instrument, or

    (b) by any enactment or any provision of subordinate legislation.

(6) This section applies to a trustee who has been authorised under a power conferred by Part IV[125] or the trust instrument—

    (a) to exercise functions as an agent of the trustees, or

    (b) to act as a nominee or custodian,

as it applies to any other trustee.

32. Remuneration and expenses of agents, nominees and custodians

(1) This section applies if, under a power conferred by Part IV[126] or any other enactment or any provision of subordinate legislation, or by the trust instrument, a person other than a trustee has been—

    (a) authorised to exercise functions as an agent of the trustees, or

    (b) appointed to act as a nominee or custodian.

(2) The trustees may remunerate the agent, nominee or custodian out of the trust funds for services if—

    (a) he is engaged on terms entitling him to be remunerated for those services, and

    (b) the amount does not exceed such remuneration as is reasonable in the circumstances for the provision of those services by him to or on behalf of that trust.

(3) The trustees may reimburse the agent, nominee or custodian out of the trust funds for any expenses properly incurred by him in exercising functions as an agent, nominee or custodian.

Specific provision is made for the remuneration of charity trustees from charity funds where services are provided to the charity.[127] Such remuneration is tightly controlled and subject to a number of conditions, including that the maximum amount of remuneration is set out in a written agreement and is no more than is reasonable for the provision of the service by the trustee. Also, the other charity trustees must be satisfied that the provision of the service by that person is in the best interests of the charity.

(iii) *Authorized by the court*

The court has a residual jurisdiction to authorize payment to be retained by a trustee for services provided to the trust. There are two particular situations in which this jurisdiction might be exercised. First, where a trustee has been found liable for breach of fiduciary duty, it is possible for the court to award what is known as the 'equitable allowance' to reflect the value of the work done by the trustee despite the breach of duty.[128]

Secondly, the court has a residual jurisdiction to authorize remuneration, which will be relevant where no provision has been made in the trust instrument for payment and the statutory power is not engaged, such as where the trustee is not a professional.

---

[125] See Chapter 12.7, pp. 620–6.

[126] Ibid.

[127] Charities Act 2011, s. 185. See Charity Commission, *Trustee Expenses and Payments*, CC11 (London: HMSO, 2012), for published guidance on best practice as regards paying charity trustees.

[128] See Chapter 14.4(d)(iv), p. 698.

Re Duke of Norfolk's Settlement Trusts [1982] Ch 61

A trustee company was entitled under a settlement made in 1958 to remuneration in accordance with its usual scale of fees then in force. In 1966 further property was added to the settlement, involving the trustee company in exceptionally burdensome work in connection with its development; this was entirely outside anything that could reasonably have been foreseen when the trustee company accepted office. The introduction of Capital Transfer Tax in 1975 also involved further work. The trustee company sought extra remuneration for this additional work done, and also a general review of its fees for the future.

At first instance,[129] Walton J awarded the company additional remuneration in respect of the development, but not in respect of Capital Transfer Tax. He further held that the court had no inherent jurisdiction to authorize any general increase in fees for the future. The Court of Appeal reversed the latter part of Walton J's decision. Brightman LJ said:[130]

In this appeal we are concerned with the power of the High Court to authorise a trust corporation, which has been in office for some 20 years, to charge fees for its future services in excess of those laid down in the trust instrument. In his admirable submissions in the unwelcome role of *advocatus diaboli* [Devil's advocate] which this court imposed upon him, Mr. Romer confined himself to that narrow issue. He did not dispute that the High Court can, in the exercise of its inherent jurisdiction, authorise a trustee to retain remuneration where none is provided by the terms of the trust. What the court has no jurisdiction to do, he submitted, was to authorise an increase in the general level of remuneration of a paid trustee by way of addition to the remuneration which is allowed by the trust, once the trust has been unconditionally accepted.

Where the court appoints a trust corporation to be a trustee, it has a statutory power to authorise it to charge remuneration: Trustee Act 1925, section 42. The inherent power of the court to authorise a prospective trustee to charge remuneration is exemplified by such cases as *Re Freeman's Settlement Trusts* (1887) 37 Ch D 148. The inherent power to authorise an unpaid trustee to charge remuneration, notwithstanding prior acceptance of the unpaid office, was regarded by Lord Langdale MR in *Bainbrigge v Blair* (1845) 8 Beav 588 as undoubted.

If the court has an inherent power to authorise a prospective trustee to take remuneration for future services, and has a similar power in relation to an unpaid trustee who has already accepted office and embarked upon his fiduciary duties on a voluntary basis, I have some difficulty in appreciating the logic of the principle that the court has no power to increase or otherwise vary the future remuneration of a trustee who has already accepted office. It would mean that, if the remuneration specified in the trust instrument were lower than was acceptable to the incumbent trustee or any substitute who could be found, the court would have jurisdiction to authorise a substitute to charge an acceptable level of remuneration, but would have no jurisdiction to authorise the incumbent to charge precisely the same level of remuneration. Such a result appears to me bizarre, and to call in question the validity of the principle upon which it is supposedly based.

Two foundations for the principle are suggested. One is that the right to remuneration is based upon contract, and the court has no power to vary the terms of a contract. The contractual conception suffers from the difficulties explained in the judgment of Fox LJ.[131] It also seems to me, in the context of

---

[129] [1979] Ch 37.

[130] [1982] Ch 61, 80.

[131] Fox LJ considered the contractual analysis to be artificial, since it would often be unclear with whom the trustee was contracting and often the trustee knows nothing of the terms of the settlement until the settlor is dead: [1982] Ch 61, 76.

the present debate, to give little weight to the fact that a trustee, whether paid or unpaid, is under no obligation, contractual or otherwise, to provide future services to the trust. He can at any time express his desire to be discharged from the trust and in that case a new trustee will in due course be appointed under section 36 or section 41 of the Trustee Act 1925.[132] The practical effect therefore of increasing the remuneration of the trustee (if the contractual conception is correct) will merely be to amend for the future, in favour of a trustee, the terms of a contract which the trustee has a unilateral right to determine. The interference of the court in such circumstances can hardly be said, in any real sense, to derogate from the contractual rights of the settlor or the beneficiaries if he or they are to be regarded as entitled to the benefit of the contract.

The other foundation suggested for the supposed principle is that the remuneration allowed to a trustee under the terms of the trust is a beneficial interest, and the court has no inherent jurisdiction to vary that beneficial interest save in special circumstances not here material: see *Chapman v Chapman* [1954] AC 429.[133] I agree that the remuneration given to a trustee by a will is an interest within the meaning of section 15 of the Wills Act 1837; that it is a gift upon a condition for the purposes of the legislation which formerly charged legacy duty upon testamentary gifts; and that an executor or trustee remunerated by the will cannot retain such remuneration against creditors if the estate turns out to be insolvent. There are obvious arguments why a testator should not be able to circumvent the provisions of the Wills Act, or avoid legacy duty, or defeat his creditors, by the award of remuneration to his executors or trustees. It does not follow that a remunerated trustee is to be considered as a *cestui que trust* for the purposes of the principles laid down in the *Chapman* case. If he were it is difficult, as Fox LJ says, to see what right the court would have to authorise remuneration to be charged by a prospective trustee, since such authority will have the inevitable effect of adding a new beneficiary to the trust at the expense of the existing beneficiaries.

These principles were considered further in *Foster v Spencer*,[134] where remuneration was awarded to the trustees of a cricket club for their past, but not future, services.[135] Paul Baker QC said:[136]

Where, as in this case, there were no funds out of which to pay remuneration at the time of their appointment, nor was a true appreciation of the extent of the task possible, a prospective application would be impracticable, if not impossible. The refusal of remuneration ... would result in the beneficiaries being unjustly enriched at the expense of the trustees.

The right of the trustee to remuneration for past services cannot depend upon the circumstances that at the time he seeks it, his services are further required so that he is in a position to demand remuneration for the past as a condition of continuing in office.

The services rendered by the trustees were wholly outside their contemplation when appointed. They were appointed as trustees of a cricket club which had its own ground. They found themselves obliged by unforeseen circumstances to dispose of the ground. This proved far more difficult than would normally be expected and made great demands on the expertise of Mr. Sealy and of Mr. Foster [the trustees], and on the time of all of them. I have no doubt that if they had realised what they were in for, they would have declined to act unless remunerated in some way.

The authorities provide little or no guidance on the issue of quantum. As might be expected, it is left to the discretion of the court. The size of the trust fund is one obvious factor. The cost of engaging outside

---

[132] See Chapter 11.3(d)(i), pp. 537–8; Chapter 11.3(f), p. 544.
[133] See Chapter 15.2, p. 722.
[134] [1996] 2 All ER 672.
[135] The trustees were also reimbursed for past expenses. See Chapter 11.6(a), p. 555.
[136] [1996] 2 All ER 672, 681.

professional help, the amount of time spent are all relevant. In the end, however, the judge must try to assess what is reasonable in all the circumstances …

Finally I come to the application for future remuneration, which is sought on behalf of all three trustees. The suggestion here is that I should make an order in the form of the normal wide professional charging clause.

I am unable to do that. The present position is that owing to the efforts of the trustees, the trust assets are now in the form of cash and deposits. The tasks remaining are quite different from those leading to the disposal of the ground. They consist of restoring the originating summons to determine the beneficial interests. I do not see that that calls for any special expertise on the part of the trustees. They have said that they are not willing to continue if not allowed to charge. It was submitted in reply that the experience of the trustees is very important and difficult to replace with anybody who would not charge. I am not persuaded of this. It may be that the knowledge of the trustees is important for the purpose of placing evidence before the court in determining the beneficial interest, but the duties of the trustees at this stage would not appear to be onerous. The burden will fall on solicitors who will be paid. There may be other beneficiaries who could be persuaded to take over if the plaintiffs insist on resigning. I do not say that if the burden proves too onerous than at present seems likely, a further application would be excluded. But as things stand, I cannot say that the continued services of these trustees is necessary for the good administration of the trusts, whether these take the form of a distribution among the contributors or the refounding of the cricket club elsewhere.

Judge Baker QC's analysis of the court's jurisdiction to award remuneration with reference to unjust enrichment is open to two possible objections.

(1) The assessment of the value of the services should not lie in the discretion of the court, as he suggested. The focus should simply be on what the beneficiaries saved by not having to employ somebody to provide the service. The additional factors to which he referred, such as the size of the trust fund and the amount of time the trustees actually spent on the work, are not relevant to a claim in unjust enrichment, since the focus of the claim should be placed only on the value of the benefit to the defendant.

(2) A claim in unjust enrichment creates a right to be paid if the elements of the claim are satisfied,[137] whereas the traditional approach to the court's jurisdiction is that the availability and amount of any remuneration lies completely within the court's discretion. *Foster v Spencer* illustrates starkly the consequences of shifting legal analysis from a judicial discretion to a legal right to payment. Equity lawyers might prefer the former analysis as being consistent with the distinct and ancient equitable jurisdiction that is founded on the court's responsibility for ensuring the good administration of trusts.[138] But, as we have already seen,[139] the divide between Common Law and Equity is narrowing. The law of unjust enrichment explains numerous long-standing Common Law claims, so there is no reason why it should not be used to explain claims in Equity too. And surely the unjust enrichment analysis is preferable. It means that a claim to remuneration is much clearer and predictable and that, where unjust enrichment can be established, the remedy reflects the value of the defendant's enrichment. Where the services are necessary, as in *Foster v Spencer*, trustees will be able to obtain remuneration for services provided to the trust without the need to seek authorization from the court. But, if in doubt, trustees should still apply to court to seek authorization for the money to be paid.

---

[137] See Chapter 1.4(b), pp. 13–15.
[138] *Re Duke of Norfolk's Settlement Trusts* [1982] Ch 61, 79 (Fox LJ).
[139] See Chapter 1.2, pp. 8–10.

7. EXERCISE OF POWERS

Trustees typically have a number of powers that they may exercise relating to the administration of the trust[140] or the disposition of the trust estate to beneficiaries.[141] A number of rules and principles of general application have been developed relating to the exercise of these powers.

(a) UNANIMITY OF DECISION-MAKING

As a general rule, trustees must be unanimous in exercising any powers vested in them. In *Re Allen-Meyrick's Will Trusts*,[142] Buckley J said:

> It is true that the reason why they have accumulated that fund is that they have not been able to agree how their discretion should be exercised; but that discretion if exercised at all must be exercised by the trustees unanimously. If they have not succeeded in being unanimous, they have not succeeded in exercising their discretion.

Consequently a decision of a majority binds neither the minority nor the trust estate.[143] Trustees of charities[144] and pension trusts[145] can, however, act by a majority. For all other trusts, a majority decision will be effective only if it is authorized by the trust instrument.[146]

The significance of the general rule requiring unanimity of decision-making is illustrated by *Re Mayo*,[147] in which the trustees were under a duty to sell the trust property, but had a power to postpone sale if they so wished. One of the three trustees wished to sell, but the other two wished to postpone. Since there was no unanimity of decision, it was held that the duty trumped the power and they were obliged to sell. They could have postponed the sale only if they had all agreed to do so.

The fact that trustees of most private trusts must make their decisions unanimously, whereas trustees of charitable and pension trusts are bound by a majority decision, is inconsistent and difficult to justify.[148] One possible explanation is that charitable trusts are more likely to have a larger number of trustees, making a unanimity requirement more difficult to implement. But the fact that charity trustees do have a larger number of trustees may, in fact, be a consequence of the rule that majority decision-making is sufficient in charities. If the unanimity rule were abolished for private trusts, there might be a greater incentive to increase the number of trustees appointed in private trusts. The preferable view is that the majority rule should be extended to all trusts. The strongest argument against this is that it would mean that a minority trustee would be bound by the decision of the majority. Since the liability of trustees is joint and several,[149] it would follow that, if the decision of the majority involves the trustees in committing a breach of trust, any trustee could be liable for this, even the minority trustee who did not vote in favour. But this could be dealt with sensibly

---

[140] See further Chapter 12, 'The Administration of Trusts'.
[141] See further Chapter 13, 'Dispositive Powers and Duties'.
[142] [1966] 1 WLR 499, 505.
[143] *Luke v South Kensington Hotel Co* (1879) 11 Ch D 121.
[144] *Re Whiteley* [1910] 1 Ch 600, 608 (Eve J).
[145] Pension Act 1995, s. 32(1).
[146] *Re Butlin's WT* [1976] Ch 251, in which the trust instrument was rectified to allow for majority decision-making as regards all decisions of the trustees. See further Chapter 20.4, pp. 1010–13.
[147] [1943] Ch 302.
[148] See Jaconelli, 'Decision-taking by Private and Charitable Trustees' [1991] Conv 30.
[149] See Chapter 16.5(b), pp. 775.

by the exercise of the court's statutory discretion to relieve a trustee of liability where he or she had acted honestly and reasonably.[150]

Jaconelli, 'Decision-taking by Private and Charitable Trustees' [1991] Conv 30, 34

Rule by majority is the practice in regard to the day-to-day operational decisions of many different types of bodies, in contrast to organic or constitutional decisions which tend to require the attainment of a higher figure (unanimity, for example). Indications of such a dichotomy are already to be found in aspects of trust law. At the one extreme is the duty of trustees for sale to consult those beneficially entitled in possession with a view to the possible execution of the trust and to 'give effect to the wishes of such persons, or, in the case of dispute, of the majority (according to the value of their combined interests) of such persons.'[151] At the other is the unanimous decision required of the beneficiaries before they may terminate the trust under the rule in *Saunders* v. *Vautier*.[152] It is suggested that this approach be taken further and that decision-taking by majority be established as the norm in the management of private trusts.[153] Such a rule might be considered unduly harsh, in that a trustee could be held liable together with his colleagues in respect of a trust management decision to which he has voiced a reasoned dissent. However, there exist means of dealing with this difficulty. The U.S. Uniform Trustees' Powers Act 1964 exempts from liability the dissenting trustee who has communicated his dissent in writing to his fellow trustees.[154] And there is surely scope for relieving his English equivalent from liability by virtue of the provisions of the Trustee Act 1925, s.61, on the ground that he 'has acted honestly and reasonably, and ought fairly to be excused for the breach of trust.'

(b) PROVISION OF REASONS

Trustees are not required to give reasons to the beneficiaries for their decisions as to whether or not to exercise a power.[155] In *Re Londonderry's Settlement*, Salmon LJ justified this rule as follows:[156]

The settlement gave the absolute discretion to appoint to the trustees and not to the courts. So long as the trustees exercise this power with the consent of persons called appointors under the settlement and exercise it bona fide with no improper motive, their exercise of the power cannot be challenged in the courts—and their reasons for acting as they did are, accordingly, immaterial. This is one of the grounds for the rule that trustees are not obliged to disclose to beneficiaries their reasons for exercising a discretionary power. Another ground for this rule is that it would not be for the good of

---

[150] Trustee Act 1925, s. 61. See Chapter 16.3, pp. 760–9.
[151] Law of Property Act 1925, s. 26(3).
[152] (1841) 4 Beav 115.
[153] Such a change would necessitate a sub-rule to deal with the possibility of a tie in the trustees' votes. It is suggested, in line with the general practice, that in such a situation the existing state of affairs in regard to the trust should remain unchanged.
[154] The text of section 6(a) reads: 'Any power vested in three or more trustees may be exercised by a majority, but a trustee who has not joined in exercising a power is not liable to the beneficiaries or to others for the consequences of the exercise; and a dissenting trustee is not liable for the consequences of an act in which he joins at the direction of the majority of the trustees, if he expressed his dissent in writing to any of his co-trustees at or before the time of the joinder.'
[155] *Re Londonderry's Settlement* [1965] Ch 918. The same rule applies to trustees of a pension trust: *Wilson v Law Debenture Trust Court plc* [1995] 2 All ER 337.
[156] [1965] Ch 918, 936.

the beneficiaries as a whole, and yet another that it might make the lives of trustees intolerable should such an obligation rest upon them… Nothing would be more likely to embitter family feelings and the relationship between the trustees and members of the family, were trustees obliged to state their reasons for the exercise of the powers entrusted to them. It might indeed well be difficult to persuade any persons to act as trustees were a duty to disclose their reasons, with all the embarrassment, arguments and quarrels that might ensue, added to their present not inconsiderable burdens.

The operation of this rule is illustrated by *Re Beloved Wilkes' Charity*.

Re Beloved Wilkes' Charity (1851) 3 Mac and G 440

Trustees of a charitable trust were to select a boy to be educated at Oxford in preparation for him to become an Anglican priest. Preference was to be given to boys from four named parishes if, in the judgment of the trustees, a fit and proper candidate from one of those parishes could be found. In 1848, the trustees selected Charles Joyce, who did not come from one of the four parishes. They gave no reasons for their choice, but stated that they had considered the candidates impartially. It appeared, however, that Joyce's brother was a Minister, who had sought to influence the trustees. The court was asked to set aside the selection, and to select William Gale, whose father was a respectable farmer residing in one of the specified parishes.

The Court held that, in the absence of evidence that the trustees had exercised their discretion unfairly or dishonestly, it would not interfere.

Lord Truro LC:

The question, therefore, is, whether it was the duty of the trustees to enter into particulars, or whether the law is not, that trustees who are appointed to execute a trust according to discretion, that discretion to be influenced by a variety of circumstances (as, in this instance, by those particular circumstances which should be connected with the fitness of a lad to be brought up as a minister of the Church of England), are not bound to go into a detail of the grounds upon which they come to their conclusion, their duty being satisfied by shewing that they have considered the circumstances of the case, and have come to their conclusion accordingly. Without occupying time by going into a lengthened examination of the decisions, the result of them appears to me so clear and reasonable, that it will be sufficient to state my conclusion in point of law to be, that in such cases as I have mentioned it is to the discretion of the trustees that the execution of the trust is confided, that discretion being exercised with an entire absence of indirect motive, with honesty of intention, and with a fair consideration of the subject. The duty of supervision on the part of this Court will thus be confined to the question of the honesty, integrity, and fairness with which the deliberation has been conducted, and will not be extended to the accuracy of the conclusion arrived at, except in particular cases. If, however, as stated by Lord Ellenborough in *The King v Archbishop of Canterbury* (1812) 15 East 117, trustees think fit to state a reason, and the reason is one which does not justify their conclusion, then the Court may say that they have acted by mistake and in error, and that it will correct their decision; but if, without entering into details, they simply state, as in many cases it would be most prudent and judicious for them to do, that they have met and considered and come to a conclusion, the Court has then no means of saying that they have failed in their duty, or to consider the accuracy of their conclusion. It seems, therefore, to me, that having in the present case to look to the motives of the trustees as developed in the affidavits, no ground exists for imputing bad motives. The Petitioners, indeed, candidly state, on the face of their petition, that they do not impute such motives, they merely charge the trustees with a miscarriage as regards the duty which they had to perform. I cannot, therefore, deal with the case as if the petition had contained a statement of a different kind, and if I could, still I should say, having read the affidavits, that I see nothing whatever which can lay the foundation for any judicial conclusion that the trustees intentionally and from bad motives failed in their duty, if they failed at all.

It is important, therefore, for the courts to determine whether the trustees had exercised their discretion honestly and fairly; if they have, the court will not intervene. If trustees do give reasons for their decision, the court will look at the adequacy of those reasons; if they are found wanting, this may result in the decision being set aside.[157] Consequently, it is preferable for the trustees simply to state that they have met and reached a decision, without providing reasons, since it is not then possible to challenge their decision,[158] unless there is additional evidence of bad faith or error in making the decision.

The justification for the general rule that there is no duty to provide reasons is that the effective administration of the trust would be undermined if the trustees were subject to investigation as to whether they had exercised their powers or fulfilled their duties in the best possible manner. Further, the rule is meant to avoid litigation and disputes within the family,[159] although it is just as likely that it creates an atmosphere of suspicion that could be resolved simply by the trustees providing some explanation for their decisions.[160] Crucially, however, as Hayton has recognized: 'the beneficiaries' rights to enforce the trust and make the trustees account for their conduct with the correlative duties of the trustees to the beneficiaries are at the core of the trust'.[161] But the enforcement of these irreducible core duties becomes much more difficult if trustees do not give reasons for their decisions, so if the focus is placed on the irreducible core of trust duties then a duty to give reasons should be recognized.

(c) SURRENDER OF POWERS TO COURT

The court will be willing to give directions on specific matters relating to the exercise of a power, but it is not possible for trustees to surrender their powers to the court completely in the expectation that the court will make all subsequent decisions on behalf of the trustees. This principle is illustrated by *Re Allen-Meyrick's Will Trusts*,[162] in which trustees held property on trust, with a power to apply the income for the maintenance of the testator's husband as they, in their absolute discretion, thought fit. The trustees had made some payments to the husband, but had not been able to agree on making any more once he had become bankrupt. Once it had become clear that they were not able to reach agreement as to whether any further payments should be made to the husband, they sought to surrender their discretion completely to the court. It was held that the court would not accept the surrender of such a discretionary power prospectively and absolutely where that power was to be exercised over a period of time. As Buckley J said:[163]

I see great force in the submission that the court ought not to accept a surrender of such a discretion as this of a kind which would relieve the trustees of their obligations to consider from time to time how the power ought to be exercised. And I do not think that it would be right for the court to accept any sort of

[157] *Klug v Klug* [1918] 2 Ch 67.
[158] See *Re Londonderry's Settlement* [1965] Ch 918.
[159] *Hartigan Nominees Pty Ltd v Ridge* (1992) 29 NSWLR 405.
[160] Ibid, 420 (Kirby P).
[161] 'The Irreducible Core Content of Trusteeship' in *Trends in Contemporary Trust Law* (ed. Oakley), p. 47.
[162] [1966] 1 WLR 499.
[163] Ibid, 503.

surrender of a discretion which would relieve the trustees of their obligation from time to time to apply their minds to the problem and to inform the court, if they cannot themselves arrive at a satisfactory answer, of the relevant circumstances and seek the court's direction from time to time. This is a discretion of a kind which essentially depends upon circumstances which will change or may change from year to year or from period to period, and if the court were to attempt to undertake the exercise of this discretion, the court itself would have to be informed from time to time of the changing circumstances … But that does not mean that they are not entitled to come to the court and say:

> 'We are in doubt as to how we ought to exercise this discretion in respect of a particular fund of income which we have now got in hand, and in the particular circumstances which at present exist.'

It seems to me to be immaterial whether, in approaching the court, they place before the court a particular proposal as a basis for discussion. If they desired to surrender their existing discretion in respect of existing funds in relation to existing circumstances, I see no reason why they should not be permitted to do so, or why the court should not, in the light of the information placed before it by trustees, say what the court considers to be the right thing to do in relation to that fund and to those circumstances.

Where the trustees legitimately surrender their discretion, the court has an unfettered discretion to determine what should be done in the best interests of the trust and of the beneficiaries. To enable the court to assess this, the parties are obliged to put before the court all of the available material to enable the discretion to be exercised.

RSPCA v Attorney-General
[2002] 1 WLR 448, 462 (Lightman J)

There is a stream of authority to the effect there is a distinction between cases where trustees seek the approval by the court of a proposed exercise by them of their discretion and where they surrender their discretion to the court (see e.g. *Re Allen-Meyrick's Will Trusts*, [1966] 1 WLR 499 at 503). In cases where there is a surrender, the court starts with a clean sheet and has an unfettered discretion to decide what it considers should be done in the best interests of the trust. In cases where there is no surrender, the primary focus of the court's attention must be on the views of the trustees and the exercise of discretion proposed by the trustees. Though not fettered by those views, the court is bound to lend weight to them unless tested and found wanting and it will not, without good reason, substitute its own view for those of the trustees. Mr. Henderson, for the Attorney-General, however, submitted that there is no difference between the two situations and that, in both cases, the court is vested with the discretion previously vested in the trustees. In support of this proposition he relies on the speech of Lord Oliver in *Marley v Mutual Security Merchant Bank and Trust Co Ltd* [1991] 3 All ER 198. In that case the trustees entered into a contract for sale whose binding effect was made conditional upon obtaining the prior approval of the court. The question raised for judicial guidance was, rather, the question of fact whether the price agreed was the best price reasonably obtainable than how a discretion should be exercised. Lord Oliver (giving the opinion of the Privy Council) held that, in that case, the trustees had surrendered their discretion to the court and that the court in such a situation was engaged solely in considering what ought to be done in the best interests of the trust and the beneficiaries, and that for that purpose the parties were obliged to put before the court all the material appropriate to enable it to exercise that discretion. By the terms of the contract, the trustees reposed in the court the decision whether the price was such that the contract should become unconditional and be completed. No question arose as to the distinction between a case where there was a surrender of discretion (as was held to have occurred in that case) and a case where there is no such surrender. My view that Lord Oliver's speech lends no support to Mr. Henderson's proposition accords with that expressed by Hart J in *Public Trustees v Cooper*.

Rather than seeking directions from the court as to how the discretion should be exercised, the trustees may instead simply seek the approval of the court as to the proposed exercise of their powers or ask the court to construe the ambit of the powers.[164] Where the trustees seek court approval of a proposed exercise of a power, the court is concerned only to determine whether the proposed exercise is lawful, is within the scope of the power, and is a decision that would be made by a reasonable trustee.[165] A consequence of the court authorizing the exercise of a power is that the beneficiaries cannot then allege a breach of trust and seek a remedy for loss suffered as a result of the power being exercised.

As a last resort, trustees or beneficiaries can apply for the court to administer the trust, but the court will make an administration order only if the issues cannot be resolved in any other way,[166] such as by surrendering a discretion on a one-off basis, seeking directions, or replacing the trustees.[167]

(d) SURRENDER OF POWERS TO A THIRD PARTY

Although it might be considered to be part of the irreducible core of a trustee's obligations[168] that he or she should exercise a discretion for him or herself, it was recognized in *Citibank v MBIA Assurance*[169] that a third party can legitimately instruct the trustees as to the exercise of their discretion and that the trustees will not be liable for breach of trust if they follow those instructions. This was regarded as legitimate because the trustees remained subject to a duty of good faith and continued to have a real discretion to exercise.[170] The better view, however, is that such a surrender of a discretion to a third party contravenes fundamental principles of the law of trusts, especially the obligation of the trustees to exercise their powers for the benefit of the beneficiaries rather than for the benefit of the trustees or the third party.[171]

(e) RELEASE OF POWERS

Where trustees are obliged to exercise the power, such as a power of appointment under a discretionary trust, it cannot be released, in the sense of the trustee determining not to exercise the power, because otherwise the trustee would commit a breach of trust.[172] Even where the trustee has a fiduciary power, which he or she need not exercise, but the exercise of which he or she must consider,[173] that power cannot be released by the trustee determining not to consider the exercise of the power.[174]

---

[164] See *Public Trustee v Cooper* [2001] WTLR 901, 924 (Hart J).
[165] *RSPCA v Attorney-General* [2002] 1 WLR 448.
[166] Civil Procedure Rules 1998, Pt 64.
[167] See Chapter 11.3(f), pp. 544–8.
[168] See *Armitage v Nurse* [1998] Ch 241, 253 (Millett LJ).
[169] [2007] EWCA Civ 11; [2007] 1 All ER (Comm) 475.
[170] Ibid, [82] (Arden LJ).
[171] Trukhtanov, 'The Irreducible Core of Trust Obligations' (2007) 123 LQR 342, 344. Failure to exercise a power for the benefit of the beneficiaries could also constitute fraud on the power. See Chapter 11.7(f)(vii), pp. 575–7.
[172] *Re Mills* [1930] 1 Ch 654, 661 (Lord Hanworth MR).
[173] See Chapter 13.2(a)(ii), pp. 631–2.
[174] *Mettoy Pension Trustees Ltd v Evans* [1990] 1 WLR 1587.

(f) INVALID EXECUTION OF POWERS

Although the court will compel a trustee to carry out a specific duty, where the trustees have agreed to the exercise of a discretionary power, the courts will not interfere as long as the power is exercised in good faith and within the limits with which it has been given to them.[175]

Tempest v Lord Camoys [1882] 21 Ch D 571

Under the will of Sir Charles Robert Tempest, the trustees, James Fleming and Wilfred Tempest, had the power to raise money by mortgage to purchase property for the trust. Some of the family wished to purchase Bracewell Hall for £60,000, using £30,000 of available money, and raising the balance by mortgage. Tempest supported the purchase, but Fleming was opposed to it. Tempest asked that the purchase should be ordered.

The Court held that it would not interfere with the bona fide exercise of a trustee's discretion, and since the trustees needed to act unanimously or not at all, Tempest alone could not sanction the purchase.

Jessel MR:

It is very important that the law of the Court on this subject should be understood. It is settled law that when a testator has given a pure discretion to trustees as to the exercise of a power, the Court does not enforce the exercise of the power against the wish of the trustees, but it does prevent them from exercising it improperly. The Court says that the power, if exercised at all, is to be properly exercised. This may be illustrated by the case of persons having a power of appointing new trustees. Even after a decree in a suit for administering the trusts has been made they may still exercise the power, but the Court will see that they do not appoint improper persons.

But in all cases where there is a trust or duty coupled with the power the Court will then compel the trustees to carry it out in a proper manner and within a reasonable time. In the present case there was a power which amounts to a trust to invest the fund in question in the purchase of land. The trustees would not be allowed by the Court to disregard that trust, and if Mr. Fleming had refused to invest the money in land at all the Court would have found no difficulty in interfering. But that is a very different thing from saying that the Court ought to take from the trustees their uncontrolled discretion as to the particular time for the investment and the particular property which should be purchased. In this particular case it appears to me that the testator in his will has carefully distinguished between what is to be at the discretion of his trustees and what is obligatory on them.

There is another difficulty in this case. The estate proposed to be purchased will cost £60,000, and only £30,000 is available for the purchase, and the trustees will have to borrow the remaining £30,000. There is power to raise money by mortgage at the absolute discretion of the trustees, and assuming that such a transaction as this is within the power, and that the trustees can mortgage the estate before they have actually bought it, there is no trust to mortgage, it is purely discretionary. The Court cannot force Mr. Fleming to take the view that it is proper to mortgage the estate in this way; he may very well have a different opinion from the other trustee. Here again the Court cannot interfere with his discretion.

---

[175] *Re Beloved Wilkes' Charity* (1851) 3 Mac & G 440, see Chapter 11.7(b), pp. 567–8. See generally Nolan, 'Controlling fiduciary power' (2009) 68 CLJ 293.

There will, however, be certain circumstances under which the exercise of a discretionary power by trustees will be held to be invalid and void. This may occur for a variety of reasons.

(i) *Formal defects*

If there are formal or procedural defects, the exercise of the power will be ineffective, for example if the trustees fail to use a required formality, such as a deed, or to obtain a required consent for a transaction.

(ii) *Unauthorized exercise*

Where the trustees purport to exercise the power in a way that is not authorized,[176] such as where they seek to delegate to an agent where the power of delegation has been excluded by the trust instrument[177] or seek to make an appointment to somebody who does not fall within the class of objects in a discretionary trust, the exercise of the power will be invalid.

(iii) *Unlawful exercise of the power*

The exercise of the power may be invalid because it infringes the law, such as the rule against perpetuities.[178] This is illustrated by *Re Hastings-Bass*,[179] in which funds from a trust in which Captain Hastings-Bass had a protected life interest were advanced[180] to his son to be held on other trusts in an attempt to save estate duty. But these trusts were void for perpetuity. The question for the Court of Appeal was whether the trustees had validly exercised their discretion to exercise the power of advancement. It was held that the advancement was effective to create a life interest in favour of the son, since that was not caught by the perpetuity rule, but the beneficial interests in the capital were void because of the perpetuity rule. Therefore, as regards the capital, the exercise of the power of advancement was invalid. The ratio of the case was considered by Lord Walker in *Pitt v Holt*:[181]

> Buckley LJ's own statement of the principle of the decision in *Hastings-Bass* seems to be the passage at p 41 which has often been cited in later cases:
>
> > 'To sum up the preceding observations, in our judgment, where by the terms of a trust ... a trustee is given a discretion as to some matter under which he acts in good faith, the court should not interfere with his action notwithstanding that it does not have the full effect which he intended, unless (1) what he has achieved is unauthorised by the power conferred upon him, or (2) it is clear that he would not have acted as he did (a) had he not taken into account considerations which he should not have taken into account, or (b) had he not failed to take into account considerations which he ought to have taken into account.'
>
> Lloyd LJ [in the Court of Appeal in *Pitt v Holt*][182] did not accept that as the true ratio. He thought that the Court of Appeal had already decided the case on the ground that the advancement, so far as not

---

[176] *Re Hastings-Bass* [1975] Ch 25, 41 (Buckley LJ).
[177] See further Chapter 12.1, p. 586.
[178] See Chapter 3.7, pp. 112–16.
[179] [1975] Ch 25.
[180] See Chapter 13.5, pp. 651–9, for consideration of the power of advancement.
[181] [2013] UKSC 26; [2013] 2 AC 108, [24].
[182] [2011] EWCA Civ 197; [2012] Ch 132.

struck down by the rule against perpetuities, must stand unless it could not, in that attenuated form, reasonably be regarded as beneficial to the advancee. That is an objective test which does not call for an inquiry into the actual states of mind of the trustees.

Lloyd LJ expanded this line of thought in para 66:

'If the problem to be resolved is what is the effect on an operation such as an advancement of the failure of some of the intended provisions, because of external factors such as perpetuity, it is not useful to ask what the trustees would have thought and done if they had known about the problem. The answer to that question is almost certainly that they would have done something different, which would not have run into the perpetuity or other difficulty. It is for that reason that the test has to be objective, by reference to whether that which was done, with all its defects and consequent limitations, is capable of being regarded as beneficial to the intended object, or not. If it is so capable, then it satisfies the requirement of the power that it should be for that person's benefit. Otherwise it does not satisfy that requirement. In the latter case it would follow that it is outside the scope of the power, it is not an exercise of the power at all, and it cannot take effect under that power.'

On this analysis, limb (1) of Buckley LJ's statement of principle covers the whole ground, and limb (2) adds nothing. I respectfully agree with Lloyd LJ's criticism of the statement of principle. I think it is also open to criticism for the generality of its reference to unintended consequences ('notwithstanding that it does not have the full effect which he intended').

(iv) *Excessive exercise*

Where an appointment is partly good and partly bad, the court will seek to sever the good from the bad so that the good exercise remains valid.[183] So, for example, if the trustee were to exercise a power of appointment in favour of two people, one of whom was an object within the power and the other not, the appointment to the former could be severed[184] and will be valid. Similarly, in *Re Hastings-Bass*,[185] the exercise of the power of advancement was valid to the extent that it did not infringe the perpetuity rule. The case simply involved the 'severance of good from bad',[186] so the exercise of the power was valid to the extent that it was capable of taking effect.

(v) *Failure to exercise discretion*

The trustees may have been unaware that they had any discretion to exercise before acting and so will not be considered to have made a decision. This is illustrated by the exceptional case of *Turner v Turner*,[187] in which appointments made under fiduciary powers were held to be void because the trustees had failed to apply their minds to the exercise of the discretion that had been entrusted to them. They were described as 'ciphers', who simply signed the deeds of appointment as they were requested to do by the settlor, who was not a trustee, without realizing that they had any discretion to exercise and without reading or understanding the documents. This vitiated the exercise of the power of appointment and so the purported appointment was a nullity.

---

[183] *Re Oliphant* (1917) 86 LJ Ch 452.
[184] *Price v Williams-Wynn* [2006] WTLR 1633.
[185] [1975] Ch 25.
[186] Lord Walker, 'The Limits of the Principals in *Re Hastings-Bass*' (2002) 13 King's College LJ 173, 176.
[187] [1984] Ch 100.

(vi) *Bad faith*

Where a power is exercised in bad faith, the exercise will be void. Bad faith has been equated with equitable fraud and dishonesty.[188] In *Armitage v Nurse*,[189] Millett LJ defined dishonesty subjectively as connoting:

> 'at the minimum an intention on the part of the trustee to pursue a particular course of action, either knowing that it is contrary to the interests of the beneficiaries or being recklessly indifferent whether it is contrary to their interests or not.'

> It is the duty of a trustee to manage the trust property and deal with it in the interests of the beneficiaries. If he acts in a way which he does not honestly believe is in their interests then he is acting dishonestly. It does not matter whether he stands or thinks he stands to gain personally from his actions. A trustee who acts with the intention of benefiting persons who are not the objects of the trust is not the less dishonest because he does not intend to benefit himself.

Trustees would not be acting in bad faith if they believed themselves to be acting in the best interests of the beneficiaries, even if the exercise of the power had adverse consequences for the beneficiaries. If, however, the trustees are professional trustees, they would be considered to have acted dishonestly, and so presumably in bad faith, even if they considered that the exercise of the power was in the best interests of the beneficiaries, if the belief was so unreasonable that no reasonable trustee in that profession would have shared that belief.

In *Walker v Stones*,[190] Sir Christopher Slade recognized that:

> At least in the case of a solicitor-trustee, a qualification must in my opinion be necessary to take account of the case where the trustee's so-called 'honest belief', though actually held, is so unreasonable that, by any objective standard, no reasonable solicitor-trustee could have thought that what he did or agreed to do was for the benefit of the beneficiaries.

Although this was decided in the context of the operation of exemption clauses to exclude trustee's liability for breach of duty, and Sir Christopher Slade limited his decision to solicitor-trustees, there is no reason why this test should not be applied generally to determine whether the actual exercise of a power by a professional trustee was valid. In *Fattal v Walbrook Trustees (Jersey) Ltd*,[191] Lewison J said:

> Although Sir Christopher limited his observations to the case of a solicitor-trustee, I did not understand [counsel] to argue that a different principle was applicable to a professional trustee. Based on this common ground, therefore, what is required to show dishonesty in the case of a professional trustee is:
>
> i) A deliberate breach of trust;
>
> ii) Committed by a professional trustee:
>
>   a) Who knows that the deliberate breach is contrary to the interests of the beneficiaries; or
>
>   b) Who is recklessly indifferent whether the deliberate breach is contrary to their interests or not; or

---

[188] *Armitage v Nurse* [1998] Ch 241, 254 (Millett LJ).

[189] Ibid, 251.

[190] [2001] QB 902, 939, discussed in Chapter 16.2(b)(iii)(a), pp. 750–2. See also *Barnes v Tomlinson* [2006] EWHC 3115 (Ch), [79] (Kitchin J).

[191] [2010] EWHC 2767 (Ch), [81]

c) Whose belief that the deliberate breach is not contrary to the interests of the beneficiaries is so unreasonable that, by any objective standard, no reasonable professional trustee could have thought that what he did or agreed to do was for the benefit of the beneficiaries.

It follows that bad faith may be determined objectively where the trustee is a professional. This can be justified by the need to hold professional trustees to a higher standard of acceptable conduct.

(vii) *Fraud on the power*

If the power is exercised for an improper purpose, it will be invalid by virtue of the doctrine of fraud on the power. In *Vatcher v Paull*,[192] Lord Parker said:

The term fraud in connection with frauds on a power does not necessarily denote any conduct on the part of the appointor amounting to fraud in the common law meaning of the term or any conduct which could be properly termed dishonest or immoral. It merely means that the power has been exercised for a purpose, or with an intention, beyond the scope of or not justified by the instrument creating the power. Perhaps the most common instance of this is where the exercise is due to some bargain between the appointor and appointee, whereby the appointor, or some other person not an object of the power, is to derive a benefit. But such a bargain is not essential. It is enough that the appointor's purpose and intention is to secure a benefit for himself, or some other person not an object of the power. In such a case the appointment is invalid, unless the Court can clearly distinguish between the quantum of the benefit bona fide intended to be conferred on the appointee and the quantum of the benefit intended to be derived by the appointor or to be conferred on a stranger.

The nature of this doctrine of fraud on the power was considered by the Supreme Court in *Pitt v Holt; Futter v Futter*.[193] Lord Walker considered the approach of Lloyd LJ[194] in the Court of Appeal and said:[195]

Lloyd LJ then addressed the difficult question of how a fraudulent appointment (that is, an appointment ostensibly within the scope of a power, but made for an improper purpose) is to be fitted into the classification. The exercise of an equitable power may be fraudulent in this sense whether or not the person exercising it is a fiduciary. A well-known example of trustees exercising a power for an improper purpose is provided by *In re Pauling's Settlement Trusts* [1964] Ch 303, in which a power ostensibly exercisable for the benefit of young adult beneficiaries was used to distribute trust capital to be frittered away on their improvident parents' living expenses.

There is Court of Appeal authority that a fraudulent appointment is void rather than voidable: *Clouette v Storey* [1911] 1 Ch 18. In that case the appointee under an improper appointment had charged his equitable interest as security for a loan (and in doing so made two false statutory declarations as to the genuineness of the appointment). It was held that the lender had no security, even though it had no notice of the equitable fraud. ... Lightman J in *Abacus Trust Co (Isle of Man) v Barr* [2003] Ch 409, para 31 found the judgment of Farwell LJ problematic and Lloyd LJ shared

---

[192] [1915] AC 372, 378.
[193] [2013] UKSC 26; [2013] 2 AC 108.
[194] [2011] EWCA Civ 197; [2012] Ch 132, [97].
[195] [2013] UKSC 26; [2013] 2 AC 108, [61].

his reservations [2012] Ch 132, para 98. So do I. It is hard to know what to make of Farwell LJ's observations [1911] 1 Ch 18, 31:

'If an appointment is void at law, no title at law can be founded on it; but this is not so in equity: the mere fact that the appointment is void does not prevent a Court of Equity from having regard to it: eg, an appointment under a limited power to a stranger is void, but equity may cause effect to be given to it by means of the doctrine of election.'

The decision in *Cloutte v Storey* may have to be revisited one day. For present purposes it is sufficient to note that a fraudulent appointment (that is, one shown to have been made for a positively improper purpose) may need a separate pigeon-hole somewhere between the categories of excessive execution and inadequate deliberation.

The advantage of the doctrine rendering the exercise of the power voidable, at least from the perspective of the third party, is that the bars on rescinding transactions will apply,[196] one of which is that rescission will be barred if a third party has acquired a legal interest in property transferred for value and without notice of the defect that renders the transaction voidable. If the doctrine of fraud on the power is to render a transaction voidable rather than void, the trustee must be considered to have acted within the scope of the power but in breach of duty in doing so.[197] That is consistent with the interpretation of fraud for the purposes of the doctrine, since it simply involves the power being exercised for an improper purpose.[198] This encompasses an exercising of a power for a purpose that is collateral to the purpose for which the power was created,[199] or the exercise of the power wantonly or capriciously.[200] A 'capricious decision' has been described as one that is 'irrational, perverse or irrelevant to any sensible expectations of the settlor'.[201] But, since trustees are not required to give reasons for the exercise of their discretion,[202] it will be difficult to show that the exercise was capricious. In *Hillsdown Holdings plc v Pensions Ombudsman*,[203] a pension fund had a surplus, but its rules prevented the trustees from paying this to the employer. The trustees transferred the fund to another pension scheme, which was able to pay the surplus to the employer. Even though the employer had agreed to increase the members' benefits under the new pension scheme in return for receiving the surplus, it was held that the transfer of the funds to this other pension scheme constituted fraud on the power, because the transfer was motivated by the collateral purpose of benefiting the employer and so was held to be void. But, rather than treating the exercise of the power to be void, it would have been preferable to consider the trustees as having acted within the scope of the power but in breach of duty, so that the exercise of the power was voidable.

It is not, however, necessarily fraud on the power that the trustee or a third party benefits indirectly from the exercise of the power.[204] So, for example, if a father exercises a power of appointment in favour of his infant child and that child dies before attaining the age of majority, the father will receive the property as next of kin, but this will not invalidate the exercise of the power, except if the trustee intended to benefit from the appointment. In short, a trustee or third party can benefit from

---

[196] See Chapter 20.5, p. 1013.
[197] See further Chapter 11.7(g), pp. 577–83.
[198] *Vatcher v Paull* [1915] AC 372, 378 (Lord Parker of Waddington).
[199] *Hillsdown Holdings plc v Pensions Ombudsman* [1997] 1 All ER 862, 883 (Knox J).
[200] *Pilkington v IRC* [1964] AC 612, 641 (Viscount Radcliffe).
[201] *Re Manisty* [1974] 1 Ch 17, 23 (Templeman J). See further Chapter 3.4(c), pp. 106–8.
[202] See Chapter 11.7(b), pp. 566–8.
[203] [1997] 1 All ER 862.
[204] *Vatcher v Paull* [1915] AC 372, 379 (Lord Parker of Waddington).

the exercise of a power without the doctrine of fraud on the power being engaged, if the purpose of the trustee in exercising the power is not considered to be improper.

(g) INADEQUATE DELIBERATION

Where trustees make a decision that has an adverse effect on the trust or the beneficiaries, the trustees may apply to the court to have the decision set aside on the ground that they have taken into account an irrelevant consideration or ignored a relevant consideration. This became known as the 'rule in *Hastings-Bass*'.[205] Following the decision of the Supreme Court in *Pitt v Holt; Futter v Futter*[206] the 'rule in *Hastings-Bass*' still exists, but its operation is now significantly different from earlier interpretations.

As we have already seen,[207] *Re Hastings-Bass* itself actually involved the exercise of a power that was partially void because it infringed the perpetuity rule. In that case, Buckley LJ stated that the court would not interfere with the discretion of a trustee unless he or she would not have acted as he or she did had he or she not taken into account considerations that he or she should not have taken into account or had ignored considerations that he or she ought to have taken into account. This dictum was taken out of context in *Mettoy Pension Trustees Ltd v Evans*,[208] in which it was formulated in positive terms as the 'rule in *Hastings-Bass*'. It was subsequently invoked in a series of first-instance cases, including a decision of Lloyd LJ[209] in *Sieff v Fox*, in which it was formulated as follows:[210]

> Where trustees act under a discretion given to them by the terms of the trust, in circumstances in which they are free to decide whether or not to exercise that discretion, but the effect of the exercise is different from that which they intended, the court will interfere with their action if it is clear that they would not have acted as they did had they not failed to take into account considerations which they ought to have taken into account, or taken into account considerations which they ought not have taken into account.

In that case, trustees of a settlement, having received professional advice concerning potential tax liability, exercised their power of appointment in favour of a beneficiary. The tax advice was incorrect and the beneficiary was liable to pay over £1 million of capital gains tax. The trustees successfully applied to have the appointment set aside on the ground that, had they known of the true tax position, they would not have made the appointment.

The rule in *Hastings-Bass* has been reformulated by Lord Walker in *Pitt v Holt; Futter v Futter*.

Pitt v Holt; Futter v Futter [2013] UKSC 26, [2013] 2 AC 108[211]

Mr Pitt was injured in a road accident for which he received significant compensation. His wife, who was his appointed receiver, obtained professional financial advice and put the

---

[205] [1975] Ch 25.
[206] [2013] UKSC 26; [2013] 2 AC 108.
[207] See Chapter 11.7(f)(iii), pp. 572–3.
[208] [1990] 1 WLR 1587.
[209] Sitting as a first-instance judge.
[210] [2005] EWHC 1312(Ch); [2005] 1 WLR 3811, [119].
[211] See Davies and Virgo, 'Relieving Trustee's Mistakes' [2013] RLR 73.

compensation into a discretionary trust for the benefit of her husband, herself, and their children. On Mr Pitt's death, his estate was liable to inheritance tax on the sum held on trust. This tax liability could have been avoided by the inclusion of a clause in the trust that half of the fund was to be applied for his benefit during his lifetime. Mrs Pitt sought a declaration that the settlement could be set aside, both on the ground that a relevant consideration had been ignored and by reason of mistake. In the second appeal, *Futter v Futter*, the trustees had exercised powers of advancement under two discretionary trusts in order to avoid capital gains tax, having obtained advice from a firm of solicitors. But, in giving this advice, the solicitors had ignored a statutory provision which meant that the tax was not avoided. The trustees sought a declaration that the exercise of the power was ineffective on the ground that a relevant consideration had been ignored.

Lord Walker:

It is now generally recognised that the label 'the rule in *Hastings-Bass*' is a misnomer. The decision of the Court of Appeal in *In re Hastings-Bass, decd* [1975] Ch 25 can be seen, on analysis, to be concerned with a different category of the techniques by which trust law controls the exercise of fiduciary powers. That decision is concerned with the scope of the power itself, rather than with the nature of the decision-making process which led to its being exercised in a particular way: see R C Nolan, 'Controlling Fiduciary Power' [2009] CLJ 293, especially pp 294–295, 306–309. The rule would be more aptly called 'the rule in *Mettoy*', from the decision of Warner J in *Mettoy Pension Trustees Ltd v Evans* [1990] 1 WLR 1587. But the misnomer is by now so familiar that it is best to continue to use it, inapposite though it is.

As *Mettoy*'s case illustrates, the rule is concerned with trustees who make decisions without having given proper consideration to relevant matters which they ought to have taken into consideration. It has also been applied to other fiduciaries (in *Pitt v Holt* Mrs. Pitt was acting as a receiver appointed by the Court of Protection). *Mettoy*'s case was concerned with the rules of an occupational pension scheme, as are some other cases on the rule. But since the turn of the century there have been several cases concerned with family trusts, and in particular with tax-planning arrangements involving trusts, where the arrangements have for one reason or another proved unexpectedly disadvantageous, and the court has been asked to restore the status quo ante under the *Hastings-Bass* rule.

In the Court of Appeal [2012] Ch 132, para 227 Longmore LJ described the appeals as

> 'examples of that comparatively rare instance of the law taking a seriously wrong turn, of that wrong turn being not infrequently acted on over a 20-year period but this court being able to reverse that error and put the law back on the right course.'

If the law did take a seriously wrong turning it was because a number of first instance judges were persuaded that three separate strands of legal doctrine, all largely associated with practice in the Chancery Division, should be spun or plaited together so as to produce a new rule.

The first strand of legal doctrine starts with the entirely familiar proposition that trustees, in the exercise of their fiduciary discretions, are under constraints which do not apply to adult individuals disposing of their own property. ...

The second strand is that a voluntary disposition (typically a gift, outright or in settlement) may be set aside on the ground of mistake ... this branch of equitable jurisdiction is distinct from the *Hastings-Bass* rule, but similar issues arise as to the nature and gravity of the relevant error or inadvertence, and in practice they sometimes overlap. ...

The third strand of legal doctrine, and the most abstruse one, is concerned with the partial validity of an instrument which cannot be entirely valid because it infringes some general rule of law. ...

Lord Walker then went on to consider how the rule in *Hastings-Bass* should be interpreted. He examined the decision of Lightman J in *Abacus Trust Co (Isle of Man) v Barr*,[212] and continued:

> … Lightman J decided, correctly in my view, that a fundamental mistake was not necessary. A fundamental, or at least serious mistake may be necessary for rescission on the ground of mistake (that is relevant to the second ground of appeal in *Pitt v Holt*),[213] but for the rule which Abacus was invoking (para 21):
>
>> 'the rule does not require that the relevant consideration unconsidered by the trustee should make a fundamental difference between the facts as perceived by the trustee and the facts as they should have been perceived. All that is required in this regard is that the unconsidered relevant considerations would or might have affected the trustee's decision, and in a case such as the present that the trustee would or might have made a different appointment or no appointment at all.'
>
> But … it must be sufficiently serious as to amount to a breach of duty.
>
> … Lightman J held that a breach of duty on the part of the trustee is essential to the application of the rule (para 23):
>
>> 'What has to be established is that the trustee in making his decision has, in the language of Warner J in *Mettoy Pension Trustees Ltd v Evans* [1990] 1 WLR 1587, 1625, failed to consider what he was under a duty to consider. If the trustee has in accordance with his duty identified the relevant considerations and used all proper care and diligence in obtaining the relevant information and advice relating to those considerations, the trustee can be in no breach of duty and its decision cannot be impugned merely because in fact that information turns out to be partial or incorrect.'
>
> That is in my view a correct statement of the law, and an important step towards correcting the tendency of some of the earlier first instance decisions. If in exercising a fiduciary power trustees have been given, and have acted on, information or advice from an apparently trustworthy source, and what the trustees purport to do is within the scope of their power, the only direct remedy available (either to the trustees themselves, or to a disadvantaged beneficiary) must be based on mistake (there may be an indirect remedy in the form of a claim against one or more advisers for damages for breach of professional duties of care). …
>
> Lightman J held that in cases where the rule applies … it makes the trustees' disposition voidable, not void. The Court of Appeal agreed with his analysis, and so do I. The rule, properly understood, depends on breach of duty in the performance of something that is within the scope of the trustees' powers, not in the trustees doing something that they had no power to do at all. Beneficiaries may lose their right to complain of a breach of trust by complicity, by laches or acquiescence or in other ways. …
>
> In the core of his judgment [in this case in the Court of Appeal] Lloyd LJ correctly spelled out the very important distinction between an error by trustees in going beyond the scope of a power (for which I shall use the traditional term 'excessive execution') and an error in failing to give proper consideration to relevant matters in making a decision which is within the scope of the relevant power (which I shall term 'inadequate deliberation'). *Hastings-Bass* and *Mettoy* were, as he rightly observed, cases in quite different categories. The former was a case of excessive execution and the latter might have been, but in the end was not, a case of inadequate deliberation. …
>
> Lloyd LJ [2012] Ch 132, para 115 reaffirmed the view that he had expressed in *Sieff v Fox* [2005] 1 WLR 3811, para 86, that 'fiscal consequences may be relevant considerations which the trustees ought to

---

[212] [2003] EWHC 114 (Ch), [2003] Ch 409.
[213] See Chapter 7.2(c), pp. 337–41.

take into account'. I agree. In the private client world trusts are mostly established by and for wealthy families for whom taxes (whether on capital, capital gains or income) are a constant preoccupation. It might be said, especially by those who still regard family trusts as potentially beneficial to society as a whole, that the greater danger is not of trustees thinking too little about tax, but of tax and tax avoidance driving out consideration of other relevant matters.

That is particularly true of offshore trusts. They are usually run by corporate trustees whose officers and staff (especially if they change with any frequency) may know relatively little about the settlor, and even less about the settlor's family. The settlor's wishes are always a material consideration in the exercise of fiduciary discretions. But if they were to displace all independent judgment on the part of the trustees themselves (or in the case of a corporate trustee, by its responsible officers and staff) the decision-making process would be open to serious question. …

Lightman J [in *Abacus Trust Co (Isle of Man) v Barr* [2003] EWHC 114 Ch, [2003] Ch 409] was in my view right to decide that when the vitiating error is inadequate deliberation on relevant matters (rather than mistake) the inadequacy must be sufficiently serious as to amount to a breach of duty … It would set the bar too high (or too low, depending on the spectator's point of view) to apply the *Hastings-Bass* rule whenever trustees fall short of the highest standards of mature deliberation and judgment. …

It is a striking feature of the development of the *Hastings-Bass* rule that it has led to trustees asserting and relying on their own failings, or those of their advisers, in seeking the assistance of the court. … There may be cases in which there is for practical purposes no other suitable person to bring the matter before the court, but I agree with Lloyd LJ's observation (para 130) that in general it would be inappropriate for trustees to take the initiative in commencing proceedings of this nature. They should not regard them as uncontroversial proceedings in which they can confidently expect to recover their costs out of the trust fund.

Lloyd LJ stated the correct principle, as he saw it, at para 127:

> 'It seems to me that the principled and correct approach to these cases is, first, that the trustees' act is not void, but that it may be voidable. It will be voidable if, and only if, it can be shown to have been done in breach of fiduciary duty on the part of the trustees. If it is voidable, then it may be capable of being set aside at the suit of a beneficiary, but this would be subject to equitable defences and to the court's discretion. The trustees' duty to take relevant matters into account is a fiduciary duty, so an act done as a result of a breach of that duty is voidable. Fiscal considerations will often be among the relevant matters which ought to be taken into account. However, if the trustees seek advice (in general or in specific terms) from apparently competent advisers as to the implications of the course they are taking, and follow the advice so obtained, then, in the absence of any other basis for a challenge, I would hold that the trustees are not in breach of their fiduciary duty for failure to have regard to relevant matters if the failure occurs because it turns out that the advice given to them was materially wrong. Accordingly, in such a case I would not regard the trustees' act, done in reliance on that advice, as being vitiated by the error and therefore voidable.' …

In my view Lightman J [in *Abacus Trust Co (Isle of Man) v Barr* [2003] EWHC 114 Ch, [2003] Ch 409] was right to hold that for the rule to apply the inadequate deliberation on the part of the trustees must be sufficiently serious as to amount to a breach of fiduciary duty. Breach of duty is essential (in the full sense of that word) because it is only a breach of duty on the part of the trustees that entitles the court to intervene … It is not enough to show that the trustees' deliberations have fallen short of the highest possible standards, or that the court would, on a surrender of discretion by the trustees, have acted in a different way. Apart from exceptional circumstances (such as an impasse reached by honest and reasonable trustees) only breach of fiduciary duty justifies judicial intervention. …

It is undoubtedly correct that trustees may be liable for breach of trust even though they have acted in accordance with skilled professional advice. Such advice cannot protect trustees from potential liability for a loss to the trust fund resulting from a decision that is, judged objectively, beyond the trustees' powers and detrimental to the trust (though professional advice may lead to their obtaining relief under section 61 of the Trustee Act 1925[214]).

Trustees may be liable, even if they have obtained apparently competent professional advice, if they act outside the scope of their powers (excessive execution), or contrary to the general law ... That can be seen as a form of strict liability in that it is imposed regardless of personal fault. Trustees may also be in breach of duty in failing to give proper consideration to the exercise of their discretionary powers, and a failure to take professional advice may amount to, or contribute to, a flawed decision-making process. But it would be contrary to principle and authority to impose a form of strict liability on trustees who conscientiously obtain and follow, in making a decision which is within the scope of their powers, apparently competent professional advice which turns out to be wrong. ...

Finally, on this part of the case, there is the submission that the trustees' duty to take account of relevant considerations is to be interpreted as a duty to act on advice only if it is correct—in effect, a duty to come to the right conclusion in every case. I have left this submission until the end because it is to my mind truly a last-ditch argument. It involves taking the principle of strict liability for ultra vires acts ... out of context and applying it in a different area, so as to require trustees to show infallibility of judgment. Such a requirement is quite unrealistic. It would tip the balance much too far in making beneficiaries a special favoured class, at the expense of both legal certainty and fairness. It is contrary to the well-known saying of Lord Truro LC in *In re Beloved Wilkes's Charity* (1851) 3 Mac and G 440, 448:

> 'that in such cases as I have mentioned it is to the discretion of the trustees that the execution of the trust is confided, that discretion being exercised with an entire absence of indirect motive, with honesty of intention, and with a fair consideration of the subject. The duty of supervision on the part of this court will thus be confined to the question of the honesty, integrity, and fairness with which the deliberation has been conducted, and will not be extended to the accuracy of the conclusion arrived at, except in particular cases.'

The trustees' duty does not extend to being right ('the accuracy of the conclusion arrived at') on every occasion.

Lord Walker applied these principles to the facts of the two cases. In *Futter*, the Supreme Court concluded that the transactions were valid because, although the trustees had ignored a relevant consideration as regards the fiscal consequences of the transaction as they had been given the wrong advice by the solicitors, the trustees had not breached their fiduciary duty in following that advice. In *Pitt* too the Supreme Court held that the settlement could not be avoided by virtue of the rule in *Hastings-Bass*, because, although Mrs Pitt as receiver was in a fiduciary position (albeit not a trustee), she had not breached her duty in creating the trust, since she had reasonably relied on the advice of her advisers. An alternative claim lay for negligence against the professional advisers, although the settlement was instead set aside on the ground of mistake.[215]

Lord Walker also considered some other controversial issues relating to the operation of the rule in *Hastings-Bass*. The first of these was whether, had the trustees ignored the irrelevant consideration or taken into account the relevant consideration, it would or might have affected the decision they made. Lord Walker said:[216]

---

[214] See further Chapter 16.3, pp. 760–9.
[215] See Chapter 7.2(c), pp. 337–41.
[216] [2013] UKSC 26; [2013] 2 AC 108, [91].

> In his statement of the correct principle ... Lloyd LJ did not provide an answer to the 'would or might?' debate. That was not, I think, an oversight. The *Hastings-Bass* rule is centred on the failure of trustees to perform their decision-making function. It is that which founds the court's jurisdiction to intervene if it thinks fit to do so. Whether the court will intervene is another matter. ...
>
> It has been suggested ... that 'would not' is the appropriate test for family trusts, but that a different 'might not' test (stricter from the point of view of the trustees, less demanding for the beneficiaries) is appropriate for pensions trusts, since members of a pension scheme are not volunteers, but have contractual rights. That is an ingenious suggestion, and in practice the court may sometimes think it right to proceed in that way. But as a matter of principle there must be a high degree of flexibility in the range of the court's possible responses. It is common ground that relief can be granted on terms. In some cases the court may wish to know what further disposition the trustees would be minded to make, if relief is granted, and to require an undertaking to that effect. ... To lay down a rigid rule of either 'would not' or 'might not' would inhibit the court in seeking the best practical solution in the application of the rule in a variety of different factual situations.

The preferable view is that the 'might not' test should be applicable regardless of the type of trust. If a beneficiary has established that the trustees breached their duty, it would be a very difficult hurdle also to have to prove that the trustees *would* have acted differently had they not breached their duty. If the beneficiaries can establish that the trustees *might* have acted differently had there not been a breach of duty, the court should be able to set aside the disposition.

Lord Walker also considered whether the operation of the rule in *Hastings-Bass* should render a disposition void or voidable. He said:[217]

> Counsel on both sides readily admitted that they had hesitated over this point, but in the end they were all in agreement that Lloyd LJ was right in holding (para 99) that,
>
>> 'if an exercise by trustees of a discretionary power is within the terms of the power, but the trustees have in some way breached their duties in respect of that exercise, then (unless it is a case of a fraud on the power) the trustees' act is not void but it may be voidable at the instance of a beneficiary who is adversely affected.'
>
> In my judgment that is plainly right, and in the absence of further argument on the point it is unnecessary to add much to it. The issue has been clouded, in the past, by the difficult case *Clouette v Storey* [1911] 1 Ch 18,[218] a case on appointments that are fraudulent in the equitable sense, that is made for a positively improper purpose. Here we are concerned not with equitable fraud, nor with dispositions which exceed the scope of the power, or infringe the general law (such as the rule against perpetuity). We are in an area in which the court has an equitable jurisdiction of a discretionary nature, although the discretion is not at large, but must be exercised in accordance with well-settled principles.

It follows from the decision of the Supreme Court that the rule in *Hastings-Bass* applies to cases of inadequate deliberation, but only where the trustees had breached a duty. Although Lord Walker referred to breach of fiduciary duty, he presumably did not intend to restrict this to fiduciary duty which is restrictively defined,[219] but intended it to encompass any breach of a trustee's duties, including the duty of care.[220] The trustees will have breached their duty if they failed to take into account a relevant matter or took into account an irrelevant matter when deciding to exercise their discretion. But the

---

[217] Ibid, [93].
[218] See Chapter 11.7(f)(vii), pp. 575–7.
[219] *Bristol and West Building Society v Mothew* [1998] Ch 1, 18 (Millett LJ). See Chapter 14.1(a), pp. 660–1.
[220] See Chapter 12.2, pp. 587–91.

Supreme Court recognized that trustees who act upon professional advice in making authorized dispositions will not generally commit any breach of duty; this was the case in both *Pitt* and *Futter*.

The fact that trustees failed to take into account the fiscal consequences of their power being exercised may constitute a breach of duty, but not if the trustees sought and acted on professional advice from a proper source, since then they will have complied with their duty to act with reasonable skill and care.[221] It follows that, if the trustees did act reasonably in obtaining and relying on professional advice, it is much less likely that the transaction will be set aside where it has adverse fiscal consequences, whereas, if the trustees acted unreasonably in not obtaining or relying on professional advice, the transaction might be set aside because the trustees will have breached their duty.[222] This is an inevitable consequence of *Pitt v Holt* requiring proof of breach of duty, but it does not follow that the trustees and beneficiaries are without remedy where the trustees reasonably relied on the professional advice, because, if that advice was negligent, the trustees and beneficiaries will have a claim in tort against the advisers. One result of the decision in *Pitt v Holt* will be to shift potential liability on to the negligent advisers, which is entirely appropriate.

Whether a particular matter that has been taken into account or that has been ignored can be considered to be a relevant matter so as to amount to a breach of duty will depend on careful consideration of the facts of the case. Particular matters that should be taken into account might include the wishes of the settlor,[223] and the wishes, circumstances, and needs of the beneficiaries. The trustees' personal disapproval of a beneficiary should not be taken into account, as illustrated in a case where a trustee declined to make an appointment to her daughter because the daughter had married without her mother's consent.[224]

The rationalization of the rule in *Hastings-Bass* by recognizing that there are two distinct rules, which depend on whether the trustee has acted outside or within the scope of the power, is to be welcomed. Whether the exercise of a discretionary power by a trustee or another fiduciary is void, voidable, or valid will depend on the circumstances in which the power is exercised. If the trustee acts outside the scope of the power, the exercise of the power will be void. If the trustee acts within the scope of the power, it is valid, unless the trustee can be considered to have acted in breach of duty in doing so. But the exercise of a discretionary power can only be considered to be inappropriate where it involves a breach of duty.

QUESTION

Alan and Brenda hold £10,000 on discretionary trust for the benefit of Charles and Debbie. Alan has never been interested in the trust and leaves all the administration to Brenda. Charles informs Brenda that he has just lost his job and that he is very short of money. Brenda is unable to contact Alan, who is travelling abroad, and so she decides to transfer £9,000 from the trust fund to Charles, without checking on Charles's financial circumstances. In fact, he had quickly obtained another, better paid job. Brenda cannot stand Debbie and would never have given her a penny from the trust fund.

Brenda seeks your advice as to whether the £9,000 can be recovered from Charles. Brenda also seeks your advice about what she can do about Alan's lack of interest in the trust.

---

[221] See further Chapter 12.2(b), pp. 589–90.
[222] See, for example Trustee Act 2000, s. 5, Chapter 12.4(b)(iii), pp. 596–7.
[223] *Abacus Trust Co. (Isle of Man) v Barr* [2003] EWHC 114; [2003] Ch 409.
[224] *Klug v Klug* [1918] 2 Ch 67.

FURTHER READING

Barlow, 'The Appointment of Trustees: A Disappointing Decision' [2003] Conv 15.

Davies and Virgo, 'Relieving Trustee's Mistakes' [2013] RLR 73.

Hayton, 'The Irreducible Core Content of Trusteeship' in *Trends in Contemporary Trust Law* (ed. Oakley), (Oxford: Clarendon Press, 1996) ch. 3.

Jaconelli, 'Decision-taking by Private and Charitable Trustees' [1991] Conv 30.

Nolan, 'Controlling Fiduciary Power' (2009) 68 CLJ 293.

Trukhantov, 'The Irreducible Core of Trust Obligations' (2007) 123 LQR 342.

12

THE ADMINISTRATION OF TRUSTS

CENTRAL ISSUES

1. Trustees are responsible for the administration of the trust. They are subject to certain duties, which must be performed, and have a number of powers, which may be exercised, relating to trust administration.

2. Trustees are required to perform their administrative responsibilities diligently, and are subject to a duty to comply with the standard of skill and care expected of all trustees.

3. Trustees are responsible for safeguarding the trust assets for the benefit of the beneficiaries.

4. Trustees have a duty to invest trust assets in the best interests of present and future beneficiaries.

5. It is the duty of a trustee to act in the interests of all the beneficiaries. It follows that trustees are under a duty to maintain a fair balance between beneficiaries and not to prefer one beneficiary or class of beneficiary over another.

6. Trustees have a variety of significant powers and duties relating to the management of trust property.

7. To assist with the administration of the trust, it is possible for trustees collectively and individually to delegate certain functions to others.

8. Trustees must keep accounts of the trust and are required to disclose them to beneficiaries if they so request.

9. Trustees have various powers to settle any claims relating to the trust or to enter into a compromise agreement.

1. DUTIES AND POWERS

Trustees are responsible for the administration of the trust. They are subject to certain duties, which must be performed, and have a number of powers, which may be exercised, relating to trust administration. The nature of these duties and powers are examined in this chapter. The range of trustees' duties was helpfully identified by Lord Toulson in *AIB Group (UK) plc v Redler*:[1]

> The range of duties owed by a trustee include: (1) a custodial stewardship duty, that is, a duty to preserve the assets of the trust except in so far as the terms of the trust permit the trustee to do otherwise; (2) a management stewardship duty, that is, a duty to manage the trust property with proper care; (3) a

---

[1] [2014] UKSC 58; [2015] AC 1503, [51].

duty of undivided loyalty, which prohibits the trustee from taking any advantage from his position without the fully informed consent of the beneficiary or beneficiaries.

The custodial and management stewardship duties are considered in this chapter. The duty of undivided loyalty is a fiduciary duty which is considered in Chapter 14.

Trustees' duties are imperative; Equity requires strict compliance. Failure to comply with their duties may render trustees liable for breach of trust,[2] even though they thought that what they were doing or failing to do was in the best interests of the trust and would benefit the beneficiaries. However onerous the duties of a trustee may be, a clause can be inserted in the trust instrument that may be effective to exempt a trustee from liability,[3] and section 61 of the Trustee Act 1925 gives the court a discretion to excuse a trustee from liability for breach of trust where the trustee has acted honestly and reasonably and ought fairly to be excused from liability.[4]

Trustees have such powers as are given to them by statute or by the trust instrument. Most of the duties or powers can be expanded, modified, or even excluded by the trust instrument, as regards the statutory powers conferred by the Trustee Act 1925:

TRUSTEE ACT 1925

69. Application of Act

(2) The powers conferred by this Act on trustees are in addition to the powers conferred by the instrument, if any, creating the trust, but those powers, unless otherwise stated, apply if and so far only as a contrary intention is not expressed in the instrument, if any, creating the trust, and have effect subject to the terms of that instrument.

Similarly, as regards the powers conferred by the Trustee Act 2000:

TRUSTEE ACT 2000

Sched 1, para. 7 Exclusion of duty of care

The duty of care does not apply if or in so far as it appears from the trust instrument that the duty is not meant to apply.

It follows that the creator of a trust has significant discretion as to the nature and extent of the trustee's administrative duties and powers. The judge-made rules of Equity, together with the various statutes, provide a menu as to what duties and powers might be available. If the creator of the trust does not want the trustee to be subject to these duties or have these powers, they can be excluded or modified; alternatively, the creator of the trust may wish to expand them, save exceptionally if the statute says that the duty or power applies regardless of what the trust instrument states.[5]

---

[2] See Chapter 16, 'Liability for Breach'.
[3] See Chapter 16.2, pp. 744–60.
[4] See Chapter 16.3, pp. 760–9.
[5] See, e.g. the power to raise money by selling or mortgaging trust property: Trustee Act 1925, s. 16(2). See Chapter 12.6(c), pp. 618–19.

In what follows, it will be assumed that the trustee whose administrative duties and powers are being considered is an express trustee. The Trustee Act 1925 does, however, define a trustee to include 'implied and constructive trustees',[6] and so the statutory powers and duties are considered to be of general application to all trustees, although it is unclear whether the same is true of powers and duties created by the Trustee Act 2000, since that statute does not define what is meant by 'trustee'.

2. THE DUTY OF CARE

Trustees are required to perform their administrative responsibilities diligently, and are subject to a duty to comply with the standard of skill and care expected of all trustees. There are two distinct tests of the duty of care: one at common law and the other statutory.

(a) COMMON LAW DUTY OF CARE

At common law trustees are expected to exercise the same standard of diligence and care as an ordinary prudent person of business would exercise in the management of his or her own affairs.[7] As Lord Blackburn said in *Speight v Gaunt*:[8]

> as a general rule a trustee sufficiently discharges his duty if he takes in managing trust affairs all those precautions which an ordinary prudent man of business would take in managing similar affairs of his own.

What constitutes the 'own affairs' of a business-person has sometimes been interpreted to mean his or her private affairs,[9] or his or her own business.[10] In many cases, there will be no difference between the standard adopted for one's private affairs and one's business affairs, although a higher standard of care might sometimes be expected when acting in business than in private matters.

The application of the common law test is particularly well illustrated by *Speight v Gaunt*.

Speight v Gaunt (1883) 9 App Cas 1

A trustee was instructed by the beneficiaries of the trust to invest the bulk of the trust assets in securities. On the advice of the beneficiaries, the trustee selected a stockbroker, not realizing that he was nearly insolvent. The stockbroker showed the trustee a forged note as evidence that the securities had been purchased. The trustee transferred the trust funds to him and the stockbroker then absconded with the money. The beneficiaries sued the trustee for imprudently choosing and relying on a dishonest agent. It was held that the trustee had not breached his duty of care because he had complied with the standards of business practice

---

[6] Trustee Act 1925, s. 68(17).
[7] Getzler, 'Duty of Care' in *Breach of Trust* (eds Birks and Pretto) (Oxford: Hart, 2002), p. 41.
[8] (1883) 9 App Cas 1, 19.
[9] *Learoyd v Whiteley* (1887) 12 App Cas 727, 733 (Lord Watson).
[10] *Speight v Gaunt* (1883) 22 Ch D 727, 730 (Jessel MR).

at the time, namely to transfer the payment before the securities were executed. As Lord Blackburn said:[11]

> Judges and lawyers who see brought before them the cases in which losses have been incurred, and do not see the infinitely more numerous cases in which expense and trouble and inconvenience are avoided, are apt to think men of business rash. I think that the principle ... is that, while the course is usual, a trustee is not to be blamed if he honestly, and without knowing anything that makes it exceptionally risky in his case, pursues that usual course. ... It would be both unreasonable and inexpedient to make a trustee responsible for not being more prudent than ordinary men of business are.

This standard of the ordinary prudent business-person is an objective test that pays no regard to the absence of skills or experience of the trustee to lower the standard of care. This is illustrated by *Re Vickery*,[12] in which the defendant trustee, who had been a missionary in London and who was completely ignorant of business affairs, was judged against the standard of the reasonable trustee, rather than the reasonable missionary. The trustee was, however, still found not to have breached his duty of care when he chose a local solicitor to administer the trust, even though that solicitor, Jennens, had in fact previously been suspended from practice and later absconded with the trust property. As Maugham J emphasized:[13]

> It is essential in this case to guard oneself against judging the conduct of the defendant in the light of subsequent events. To have employed a new solicitor as soon as the defendant became aware that HH Jennens was a person with a tarnished reputation for honesty would certainly have meant further costs. It might have proved quite unnecessary even on the supposition that Jennens was a rogue. Even a man of the world might have thought that the sum involved—the sum of [£300] or thereabouts—was far too small to make it probable that the solicitor would be likely—unless, indeed, in the case of stern necessity—for such a sum to expose himself to the orders of the Court and to the action of the Law Society.

If, however, the trustee is a paid professional, the standard of care will be raised to the standard that such a professional would be expected to exhibit. In *Bartlett v Barclays Bank Trust Co. Ltd*,[14] Brightman J said:

> So far, I have applied the test of the ordinary prudent man of business. Although I am not aware that the point has previously been considered, except briefly in *In re Waterman's Will Trusts* [1952] 2 All ER 1054, I am of opinion that a higher duty of care is plainly due from someone like a trust corporation which carries on a specialised business of trust management. A trust corporation holds itself out in its advertising literature as being above ordinary mortals. With a specialist staff of trained trust officers and managers, with ready access to financial information and professional advice, dealing with and solving trust problems day after day, the trust corporation holds itself out, and rightly, as capable of providing an expertise which it would be unrealistic to expect and unjust to demand from the ordinary prudent man or woman who accepts, probably unpaid and sometimes reluctantly from a sense of family duty, the burdens of a trusteeship. Just as, under the law of contract, a professional person possessed

---

[11] (1883) 9 App Cas 1, 20.
[12] [1931] 1 Ch 572.
[13] Ibid, 584.
[14] [1980] Ch 515, 534.

> of a particular skill is liable for breach of contract if he neglects to use the skill and experience which he professes, so I think that a professional corporate trustee is liable for breach of trust if loss is caused to the trust fund because it neglects to exercise the special care and skill which it professes to have.

The prudent business-person test involves a hypothetical figure against which the standard of the trustee's performance can be objectively measured. This is an equivalent standard to that which is adopted for the tort of negligence; in fact, the equitable duty of care can be regarded as having now been assimilated into the Common Law tort of negligence and outside the exclusive jurisdiction of Equity.[15] It follows that liability for breach of this duty of care is subject to the same rules and remedies as the tort of negligence, including, for example, that the trustee's liability will be subject to the defence of contributory negligence.[16]

Even if the trustees have apparently not satisfied the standard of skill and care, it does not follow that they will be liable to the beneficiaries, since the beneficiaries also need to show that, had the trustees complied with the relevant standard of skill and care, they would have acted differently.[17] This is a difficult burden to satisfy. So, for example, in *Nestlé v National Westminster Bank plc*,[18] the trustee bank breached its duty of care in its management of the trust's investments, but it was not liable to the beneficiaries because it could not be shown that the trust would have benefited financially had there been better management of the investments.

(b) STATUTORY DUTY OF CARE

The Trustee Act 2000 created a statutory duty of care, which is applicable to the exercise of those powers and duties that are provided for under the 2000 Act, other statutory provisions, and many powers created by the trust instrument. The common law duty of care remains relevant in respect of other powers and duties, most notably to the dispositive powers of appointment of trust property to beneficiaries[19] and the powers of maintenance[20] and advancement.[21] It appears, however, that there is no difference between the common law and statutory duties of care.[22]

TRUSTEE ACT 2000

1. The duty of care

(1) Whenever the duty under this subsection applies to a trustee, he must exercise such care and skill as is reasonable in the circumstances, having regard in particular—

  (a) to any special knowledge or experience that he has or holds himself out as having, and

---

[15] *Henderson v Merrett Syndicates Ltd* [1995] 2 AC 145; *Bristol and West Building Society v Mothew* [1998] Ch 1; *Swindle v Harrison* [1997] 4 All ER 705. See Getzler, 'Duty of Care' in Breach of Trust (eds Birks and Pretto) (2002), p. 71.
[16] See Chapter 17.3(a)(ii)(c), pp. 833–4.
[17] It must also be shown that the loss arose from the breach of duty. See Chapter 17.3(a)(ii)(a), pp. 831–2.
[18] [1993] 1 WLR 1260. See further Chapter 12.5(a), pp. 611–14.
[19] See Chapter 13.2, pp. 630–8.
[20] See Chapter 13.4, pp. 647–50.
[21] See Chapter 13.5, pp. 651–9.
[22] *Pitt v Holt; Futter v Futter* [2011] EWCA Civ 197; [2012] Ch 132, [107] (Lloyd LJ). This was not considered in the Supreme Court. See Chapter 12.2(c), p. 591.

(b) if he acts as trustee in the course of a business or profession, to any special knowledge or experience that it is reasonable to expect of a person acting in the course of that kind of business or profession.

(2) In this Act the duty under subsection (1) is called 'the duty of care'.

2. Application of duty of care

Schedule 1 makes provision about when the duty of care applies to a trustee.

This schedule applies the statutory duty of care to all powers of investment, whether conferred by statute[23] or the trust instrument;[24] any power to acquire land, however conferred;[25] when appointing agents, nominees, or custodians,[26] however conferred; any power to compound liability[27] and any power to insure property.[28] But in all cases the duty of care can be excluded by the trust instrument.[29]

The statutory duty of care requires all trustees to comply with the standard of the reasonable trustee, even those trustees who are plainly incompetent and unsuited to the task. Although reasonableness is assessed with regard to what is reasonable 'in the circumstances', the defendant's circumstances should not be taken into account to reduce the standard of care below that of the reasonable trustee.[30] But the standard of care expected of trustees can be raised if the trustee possesses particular knowledge or experience or is acting in the course of a business or profession. What is reasonable in the circumstances should be influenced by factors such as the size of the trust fund and the complexity of the trust.

Breach of the statutory duty of care should be regarded as a tort of breach of duty rather than breach of trust. This is significant, since it will affect the application of particular rules such as those relating to causation, remoteness, remedies, and limitation periods.[31]

(c) THE RELATIONSHIP BETWEEN THE COMMON LAW AND STATUTORY TESTS

The creation of a statutory duty of care based on reasonableness in the circumstances had been proposed by the Law Commission,[32] which rejected the common law language of the 'prudent person of business'. A number of reasons were identified for this decision, including that adopting a prudent business-person test would simply involve a restatement of the common law test, that the statutory standard has explicit regard to the particular skills of the trustee, that the standard of care must be

---

[23] See Chapter 12.4(b), pp. 594–600.

[24] See Chapter 12.4(b)(i), pp. 594–5.

[25] See Chapter 12.4(b)(v), pp. 597–8.

[26] See Chapter 12.7, pp. 620–6.

[27] See Chapter 12.9, pp. 626–7.

[28] See Chapter 12.6(d), p. 619.

[29] Trustee Act 2000, Sched. 1(7). But note the Pension Act 1995, s. 33, which prevents the exclusion or restriction of the duty of care as regards the exercise of investment powers in pension trusts.

[30] Although the defendant's circumstances may be relevant when determining whether the trustee's breach might be excused. See Chapter 16.3(c), pp. 766–8.

[31] See Chapter 16.9(a), pp. 781–4.

[32] Law Commission, *Trustees' Powers and Duties*, Law Com. No. 260 (1999).

robust and demanding, and that there may, in fact, be little difference between the two alternatives. Indeed, the Law Commission stated that the:[33]

> statutory duty of care probably represents no more than a codification of the existing common law duty.

This is the preferable view, and was endorsed by Lloyd LJ in *Pitt v Holt*:[34]

> trustees are under a duty of care, obliging them to exercise such skill and care as is reasonable in the circumstances, under section 1 of the Trustee Act 2000. This puts into statutory form (in relation to specific functions of the trustees) the duty recognised in *Speight v Gaunt* (1883) 22 Ch D 727 and (1883) 9 App Cas 1, which continues to apply to cases where the statutory duty does not.

Both the common law and statutory tests involve an objective core, whether that is described with reference to the prudent business-person or the reasonable person. The standard of care for both tests is higher where the particular trustee is a professional. Although the statutory test qualifies the objective test where the trustee has particular skills or experience, this would presumably be true of the common law test too, since the justification for raising the standard of care expected from professional trustees is that they hold themselves out as having specific skills or experience. Presumably any trustee with particular skills or experience should comply with a higher standard of care at common law, even if he or she were not a professional. Consequently, it should not matter whether the common law or statutory test applies; the same rules on determining the standard of care will operate.

3. DUTY TO SAFEGUARD TRUST ASSETS

The trustees are responsible for safeguarding the trust assets for the benefit of the beneficiaries. This means, for example, that, on appointment, a trustee must ensure that the trust funds are properly invested and that trust assets, such as securities and chattels, are kept securely.[35] This duty also means that if money is owed to the trust, the trustees must take all reasonable steps to ensure that the debt is discharged.

Re Brogden [1888] 38 Ch D 546

By his will, Mr Brogden covenanted to pay £10,000 to the trustees of his daughter's marriage settlement within five years of his death. This money was to be paid from his partnership with his sons. Budgett was one of the trustees of the marriage settlement. He pressed Brogden's sons on many occasions for payment of the money, both before and after the expiry of the five-year period. On several occasions security for the payment was given, one of these being in response to an action started by Budgett for the administration of the estate. Throughout, Budgett was trying to avoid disturbance within the family, and any crisis that would upset the solvency of the firm since the Brogden partnership was becoming less prosperous. Eventually the partnership became

---

[33] Ibid, 25.
[34] [2011] EWCA Civ 197; [2012] Ch 132, [107]. This was not considered by the Supreme Court on appeal.
[35] *Re Miller's Deed Trust* (1978) 75 LS Gaz 454.

insolvent and the securities worthless. The question was whether Budgett was liable to the beneficiary of the marriage settlement for breach of trust.

The Court of Appeal held that Budgett was liable, as he had not taken all possible steps to obtain payment of the £10,000.

Cotton LJ:

Now what was the duty of the trustee, Mr. Budgett? It was his duty, in my opinion, at the expiration of five years, to call for payment and to take reasonable means of enforcing payment if the executors did not pay the debt and the legacy. And there having been a postponed period during which no steps were to be taken against the partners or against the executors, it was the more his duty at the expiration of that period to assume that the executors had done what it was their duty to do by preparing for paying the debts and paying the legacies of the testator. ... And, in my opinion, in the case here, it became the duty of Mr. Budgett to take active measures immediately after the expiration of the five years—that is immediately the legacy became payable and immediately the debt became payable.

We must therefore consider what he did. The five years expired in the beginning of December, 1874. I do not suggest that during the remainder of that month of December he should have taken any legal proceedings. That would hardly be expected, but what in my opinion he ought to have done, if not in December, 1874, early in the year 1875, was to have demanded payment, and if payment was not made, then he ought to have taken effectual proceedings in order to recover payment both of the legacy and of the debt. I do not say it was his duty to recover them, because that assumes that he could have done so: but in my opinion it was his duty to demand payment of them, and to take effectual proceedings for the purpose of recovering them ...

In my opinion it is not for the *cestuis que trust* seeking to make the trustee liable, to shew that if he had done his duty he would have got the money for which they are seeking to make him answerable. It is the trustee who is seeking to excuse himself for the consequences of his breach of duty. It was his duty to take active proceedings if necessary earlier—to take active proceedings by way of action at law, if necessary; and if the trustee is to excuse himself, it is for him to shew that if he had taken proceedings no good would have resulted from it ...

I have therefore come to the conclusion that the decision of Mr. Justice North must be affirmed. It is an unfortunate position no doubt for Mr. Budgett, and I quite think that he believed that the firm were perfectly solvent, and that he was incurring no risk in letting the money remain with them. He ought not to have trusted them; as he did that and his expectations and those of the family have turned out to be wrong, and he has not shewn that no good would have resulted from his performing his duty by pressing for payment, and if necessary by taking proceedings to enforce payment, he must be held liable.

It does not necessarily follow that trustees must sue for money that is owed to the trust in every case. Other courses of action might be more appropriate. For example, in *Re Ezekiel's Settlement Trust*,[36] it was held to be appropriate for a trustee to enter into a compromise[37] as regards money that was owed to the trust, even though the beneficiary wanted the full amount due to be recovered through litigation. Resorting to litigation was not a reasonable course of action since there was an unacceptable risk that the trust might suffer a loss as the result of bearing the costs of the litigation. Similarly, in *Ward v Ward*,[38] a trustee was held not to have committed a breach of trust by failing to call for money owed to the trust by a beneficiary, since this would have resulted in the bankruptcy of the beneficiary.

[36] [1942] Ch 230.
[37] By virtue of the power to compound liabilities under the Trustee Act 1925, s. 15. See Chapter 12.9, pp. 626–7.
[38] (1843) 2 HL Cas 777n.

4. DUTY TO INVEST

(a) GENERAL PRINCIPLES

Trustees have a duty to invest trust assets in the best interests of present and future beneficiaries.[39] There are two significant, and potentially conflicting, principles that arise from this duty.[40]

(1) Trustees must safeguard the trust fund by preserving the capital value of that trust fund. This principle encourages trustees to adopt a conservative investment policy, which seeks to avoid taking significant risks with the investment by speculating with the trust funds.[41] In *Nestlé v National Westminster Bank plc*,[42] Leggatt LJ said:

> When trusts came into their own in Victorian times they were no doubt intended to preserve capital while assuring beneficiaries of a steady, if conservative, income. Little was demanded of a trustee beyond the safeguarding of the trust fund by refraining from improvident investment. This process was no doubt also intended to save beneficiaries from trouble and anxiety, or what is now called 'hassle' … The importance of preservation of a trust fund will always outweigh success in its advancement. Inevitably, a trustee in the bank's position wears a complacent air, because the virtue of safety will in practice put a premium on inactivity. Until the 1950s active management of the portfolio might have been seen as speculative, and even in these days such dealing would have to be notably successful before the expense would be justified.

(2) A more modern approach to investment policy is to recognize that trustees must maximize returns for the benefit of the beneficiaries. In *Re Wragg*,[43] PO Lawrence J defined 'investment' as meaning:

> to apply money in the purchase of some property from which interest or profit is expected and which property is purchased in order to be held for the sake of the income which it will yield.

This principle encourages trustees to speculate with the trust fund, so as to obtain a good income from investments and to ensure that the capital value of the fund increases. This principle requires trustees to have the widest possible investment powers, so that they can invest the trust assets in the most appropriate way for the benefit of the trust.

Usually trustees are given wide powers of investment in the trust instrument. Otherwise those powers are derived from Part II of the Trustee Act 2000. The purpose of this Part of the Act was to create wide investment powers for trustees through a regime that is consistent with modern investment practice, known as 'portfolio theory', by virtue of which trustees should have regard to the composition of their investments as a whole, known as the 'portfolio', to determine whether they are balanced and suit the needs of the particular trust.

Thornton, 'Ethical Investments: A Case of Disjointed Thinking' (2008) CLJ 396, 399

> However, investors do not consider individual assets in isolation. By holding a combination of assets known as a portfolio they are able to spread, and thus minimise, the risk to which the fund is exposed.

---

[39] *Cowan v Scargill* [1985] Ch 270, 286–7 (Sir Robert Megarry V-C).
[40] See Law Commission, *Trustee's Powers and Duties* (Law Com. No. 260, 1999), p. 18.
[41] *Learoyd v Whiteley* (1887) 12 App Cas 727, 733 (Lord Watson).
[42] [1993] 1 WLR 1260, 1281.
[43] [1919] 2 Ch 58, 65.

This can be demonstrated statistically, since the variance of a group of assets will tend to be less than the average of the variance of the individual assets themselves. … As Lord Nicholls of Birkenhead has pointed out, the traditional prohibition upon selecting investments 'attended with hazard' must be read in the context of a strategy whereby risk is managed across a balanced portfolio, incorporating a prudent mixture of low and higher risk assets.[44] Diversification cannot, of course, eliminate all risk; it cannot remove 'systematic' or market risk but only 'non-systematic' or firm-specific risk.[45]

Some combinations of assets will be more effective than others in reducing the overall risk on the portfolio. To take a very simple example, if two assets are likely to perform well under opposite market conditions or at different times, then dividing the fund between these two would substantially reduce the degree of risk; on the other hand, dividing the fund between two investments which will tend to track each other and perform well under similar conditions would be less effective at reducing overall risk. To adopt Emma Ford's colourful example, 'the risk in owning stock in an umbrella manufacturer is lower if the investor also owns stock in a suntan lotion manufacturer'.[46] …

In theory, if a portfolio contains a sufficient number of independent assets then, whatever the variance of the individual assets within the portfolio, the average variance of the portfolio as a whole always approaches zero. In real life, unfortunately, things are not that simple. In most markets, assets tend not to perform independently, but to move up and down in an interrelated manner. Thus by increasing the number of assets in the investment portfolio and by ensuring that they are as independent as possible, the variance or risk can be minimised but never reduced entirely to zero. As the size of the portfolio increases, the addition of any new asset will have a smaller and smaller effect—though always, in theory, some effect—in terms of the reduction of overall risk.

The significance of portfolio theory to the management of risk is that the emphasis is placed on the risk level of the entire portfolio rather than the risk being attached to each investment in isolation.[47] Consequently, a high-risk investment might be justified when considered in conjunction with other less risky investments, even though such an investment might have been considered to be too risky for the trust and, therefore, a breach of trust if considered in isolation.

(b) INVESTMENT POWERS

(i) *General power of investment*

TRUSTEE ACT 2000

3. General power of investment

(1) Subject to the provisions of this Part, a trustee may make any kind of investment that he could make if he were absolutely entitled to the assets of the trust.

(2) In this Act the power under subsection (1) is called 'the general power of investment'.

---

[44] 'Trustees and their Broader Community: Where Duty, Morality and Ethics Converge' (1995) 9(3) Trust Law International 71, 76.
[45] Bodie, Kane, and Marcus, *Investments* (6th edn) (Boston, 2005), p. 224.
[46] 'Trustee Investment and Modern Portfolio Theory' (1996) 10(4) Trust Law International.
[47] *Nestlé v National Westminster Bank plc* (1996) 10 TLI 113, 115 (Hoffmann J).

(3) The general power of investment does not permit a trustee to make investments in land other than in loans secured on land (but see also section 8).[48]

(4) A person invests in a loan secured on land if he has rights under any contract under which—

    (a) one person provides another with credit, and

    (b) the obligation of the borrower to repay is secured on land.

(5) 'Credit' includes any cash loan or other financial accommodation.

(6) 'Cash' includes money in any form.

6. Restriction or exclusion of this Part etc.

(1) The general power of investment is—

    (a) in addition to powers conferred on trustees otherwise than by this Act, but

    (b) subject to any restriction or exclusion imposed by the trust instrument or by any enactment or any provision of subordinate legislation.

Schedule 1

1   The duty of care[49] applies to a trustee—

    (a) when exercising the general power of investment or any other power of investment, however conferred;

    (b) when carrying out a duty to which he is subject under section 4 or 5[50] (duties relating to the exercise of a power of investment or to the review of investments).

The notes to the Trustee Act 2000, which are not binding, indicate that trustees are permitted to invest in assets that are expected to produce either an income return *or* a capital return, so investment in assets that will not yield an income can still count as legitimate investment.

The general power of investment applies to most trusts, even those that were settled before 2001 when the Trustee Act came into force,[51] although the general power can be expanded, restricted, or excluded by the trust instrument.[52] The general power of investment does not apply to trustees of pension schemes,[53] or authorized unit trusts,[54] or to charitable trustees who are managing common investment,[55] since alternative statutory provision is made for these trustees.

(ii) *Standard investment criteria*

In exercising the general power of investment or any power of investment, such as one created by the trust instrument, or when reviewing the investments, the trustee is under a duty to have regard to the 'standard investment criteria'.

---

[48] See Chapter 12.4(b)(v), pp. 597–8.
[49] See Chapter 12.2(b), pp. 589–90.
[50] See Chapter 12.4(b)(ii), pp. 595–6.
[51] Trustee Act 2000, s. 7.
[52] Ibid, s. 6(1).
[53] Ibid, s. 36(3).
[54] Ibid, s. 37(1).
[55] Ibid, s. 38. See Chapter 12.4(b)(iv), p. 598.

TRUSTEE ACT 2000

4. Standard investment criteria

(1) In exercising any power of investment, whether arising under this Part or otherwise, a trustee must have regard to the standard investment criteria.

(2) A trustee must from time to time review the investments of the trust and consider whether, having regard to the standard investment criteria, they should be varied.

(3) The standard investment criteria, in relation to a trust, are—

    (a) the suitability to the trust of investments of the same kind as any particular investment proposed to be made or retained and of that particular investment as an investment of that kind, and

    (b) the need for diversification of investments of the trust, in so far as is appropriate to the circumstances of the trust.

These two criteria reflect portfolio theory. As regards the second criterion of diversification, in *Cowan v Scargill*[56] Megarry V-C found that:

'circumstances of the trust' plainly includes matters such as the size of the trust funds: the degree of diversification that is practicable and desirable for a large fund may plainly be impracticable or undesirable (or both) in the case of a small fund.

(iii) *Duty to obtain advice*

TRUSTEE ACT 2000

5. Advice

(1) Before exercising any power of investment, whether arising under this Part or otherwise, a trustee must (unless the exception applies) obtain and consider proper advice about the way in which, having regard to the standard investment criteria, the power should be exercised.

(2) When reviewing the investments of the trust, a trustee must (unless the exception applies) obtain and consider proper advice about whether, having regard to the standard investment criteria, the investments should be varied.

(3) The exception is that a trustee need not obtain such advice if he reasonably concludes that in all the circumstances it is unnecessary or inappropriate to do so.

(4) Proper advice is the advice of a person who is reasonably believed by the trustee to be qualified to give it by his ability in and practical experience of financial and other matters relating to the proposed investment.

A trustee might reasonably conclude that it is not necessary to obtain such advice where, for example, the fund is relatively small so that the cost of obtaining the advice might be more than the value of

---

[56] [1985] Ch 270, 289.

the fund. The trustee is not required to follow the advice obtained, but it must be reasonable to decide not to do so. As Megarry V-C commented in *Cowan v Scargill*:[57]

> although a trustee who takes advice on investments is not bound to accept and act on that advice, he is not entitled to reject it merely because he sincerely disagrees with it, unless in addition to being sincere he is acting as an ordinary prudent man would act.

(iv) *Delegation of investment powers*

Investment powers can be delegated to an agent,[58] who will be bound by any restrictions on the exercise of those powers in the same way as would the trustee.[59] So, for example, an agent who is authorized to exercise the general power of investment must also have regard to the standard investment criteria. An agent is not, however, required to obtain investment advice if he or she is the kind of person from whom it would have been proper for the trustees to obtain such advice,[60] such as a financial adviser.

(v) *Purchase of land*

Part III of the Trustee Act 2000 provides for powers to acquire land.

TRUSTEE ACT 2000

8. Power to acquire freehold and leasehold land

(1) A trustee may acquire freehold or leasehold land in the United Kingdom—

    (a) as an investment,

    (b) for occupation by a beneficiary, or

    (c) for any other reason.

(2) 'Freehold or leasehold land' means—

    (a) in relation to England and Wales, a legal estate in land …

(3) For the purpose of exercising his functions as a trustee, a trustee who acquires land under this section has all the powers of an absolute owner in relation to the land.

9. Restriction or exclusion of this Part etc.

The powers conferred by this Part are—

    (a) in addition to powers conferred on trustees otherwise than by this Part, but

    (b) subject to any restriction or exclusion imposed by the trust instrument or by any enactment or any provision of subordinate legislation.

---

[57] Ibid.
[58] Trustee Act 2000, Pt IV. See Chapter 12.7, pp. 620–6.
[59] Ibid, s. 13(1).
[60] Ibid, s. 13(2).

Schedule 1

2   The duty of care[61] applies to a trustee—

   (a) when exercising the power under section 8 to acquire land;

   (b) when exercising any other power to acquire land, however conferred;

   (c) when exercising any power in relation to land acquired under a power mentioned in sub-paragraph (a) or (b).

The statutory power only relates to the acquisition of land in the United Kingdom, so trustees do not have a statutory power to acquire land abroad, although such a power can be included in the trust instrument. A default power to buy land abroad was not included in the Trustee Act 2000 because trusts are not universally recognized abroad and the purchase of land for a trust in a country that does not recognize the trust might cause difficulties.

(vi) *Common investment funds for charities*

Provision is made for the establishment of common investment schemes for charities, which provide a useful mechanism for participating charitable trusts collectively to get the benefit of expert investment experience.

CHARITIES ACT 2011

96. Schemes to establish common investment funds

(1) The court or the Commission may by order make and bring into effect schemes (in this section referred to as 'common investment schemes') for the establishment of common investment funds under trusts which provide—

   (a) for property transferred to the fund by or on behalf of a charity participating in the scheme to be invested under the control of trustees appointed to manage the fund; and

   (b) for the participating charities to be entitled (subject to the provisions of the scheme) to the capital and income of the fund in shares determined by reference to the amount or value of the property transferred to it by or on behalf of each of them and to the value of the fund at the time of the transfers.

(2) The court or the Commission may make a common investment scheme on the application of any two or more charities.

(3) A common investment scheme may be made in terms admitting any charity to participate, or the scheme may restrict the right to participate in any manner.

(vii) *Duty to obtain the best price*

When trustees are buying or selling trust property, they are under a duty to obtain the best price and must not be influenced by ethical or moral considerations. There will even be circumstances under which trustees may have to act dishonourably for the benefit of the trust.[62] So, even where trustees

---

[61] Ibid, s. 1. See Chapter 12.2 (b), pp. 589–90.
[62] *Cowan v Scargill* [1985] Ch 270, 288 (Sir Robert Megarry V-C).

have accepted an offer to sell property subject to contract, if they subsequently receive a better offer, they should typically renege on the first offer and accept the second. In other words, there is a duty to 'gazump'. But each case will turn on its facts in assessing whether it is reasonable to gazump: if there is a risk that the higher offer will not result in a sale, or a speedy transaction is of the essence, it might then be reasonable to proceed with the sale as initially agreed.

Buttle v Saunders [1950] 2 All ER 193

Trustees had orally agreed to sell trust land to Mrs Simpson for £6,142. After all the documents had been prepared for the sale to Mrs Simpson, but before the contract was signed, one of the beneficiaries, Canon Buttle, offered £6,500 since he wished to purchase the land for a charity. The trustees felt that they had reached a stage in the negotiations with Mrs Simpson from which they could not honourably withdraw. Canon Buttle brought an action to restrain the trustees from selling for any price below that which he had offered. Wynn-Parry J held that the trustees must accept Canon Buttle's offer:[63]

It has been argued on behalf of the trustees that they were justified in the circumstances in not pursuing the offer made by Canon Buttle and in deciding to go forward with the transaction with Mrs. Simpson. It is true that persons who are not in the position of trustees are entitled, if they so desire, to accept a lesser price than that which they might obtain on the sale of property, and not infrequently a vendor, who has gone some lengths in negotiating with a prospective purchaser, decides to close the deal with that purchaser, notwithstanding that he is presented with a higher offer. It redounds to the credit of a man who acts like that in such circumstances. Trustees, however, are not vested with such complete freedom. They have an overriding duty to obtain the best price which they can for their beneficiaries. It would, however, be an unfortunate simplification of the problem if one were to take the view that the mere production of an increased offer at any stage, however late in the negotiations, should throw on the trustees a duty to accept the higher offer and resile from the existing offer. For myself, I think that trustees have such a discretion in the matter as will allow them to act with proper prudence. I can see no reason why trustees should not pray in aid the common-sense rule underlying the old proverb: 'a bird in the hand is worth two in the bush'. I can imagine cases where trustees could properly refuse a higher offer and proceed with a lower offer. Each case must, of necessity, depend on its own facts. In regard to the case now before me, my view is that the trustees and their solicitors acted on an incorrect principle. The only consideration which was present to their minds was that they had gone so far in the negotiations with Mrs. Simpson that they could not properly, from the point of view of commercial morality, resile from those negotiations. That being so, they did not, to any extent, probe Canon Buttle's offer as, in my view, they should have done. It was urged on me that, by pausing to probe his offer, they ran the risk of losing the contract with Mrs. Simpson. On the view of the facts which I take, I do not consider that that was much of a risk. Mrs. Simpson had bought the leasehold term, which was nearing its end, and she was a very anxious purchaser. Equally, Canon Buttle had demonstrated beyond a peradventure that he was a very anxious buyer, and, as it seems to me, the least the trustees should have done would have been to have said to him: 'You have come on the scene at a late stage. You have made this offer well past the eleventh hour. We have advanced negotiations with Mrs. Simpson which can be concluded within a matter of hours. If you are really serious in your offer, you must submit in the circumstances to somewhat stringent terms, and you must be prepared to bind yourself at once to purchase the property for the sum of £6,500 on the terms, so far as applicable, of

---

[63] [1950] 2 All ER 193, 195.

the draft contract which otherwise would be entered into with Mrs. Simpson.' I have not the slightest doubt but that in the circumstances Canon Buttle would have agreed to those stringent terms and that the matter would have been carried out.[64]

(c) SELECTING INVESTMENTS

(i) *General duty*

When trustees select investments, they must have regard to the principles of portfolio theory, as embodied in the standard investment criteria.[65] A number of distinct principles can be identified to assist in the selection of investments.

(1) Trustees must ensure that the investments chosen are permitted by the terms of the trust.[66]

(2) The investments should be diversified, so that the trustees do not, for example, invest all the funds in the shares of one particular company.

(3) Trustees should avoid investments that are particularly risky,[67] although this is now subject to modern investment practice in the light of the recognition of the portfolio theory.

In *Cowan v Scargill*,[68] Megarry V-C recognized that:

The starting point is the duty of the trustees to exercise their powers in the best interests of the present and future beneficiaries of the trust, holding the scales impartially between different classes of beneficiaries. This duty of the trustees towards their beneficiaries is paramount. They must, of course, obey the law; but subject to that, they must put the interests of their beneficiaries first. When the purpose of the trusts is to provide financial benefits for the beneficiaries, as is usually the case, the best interests of the beneficiaries are normally their best financial interests. In the case of a power of investment, as in the present case, the power must be exercised so as to yield the best return for the beneficiaries, judged in relation to the risks of the investments in question; and the prospects of the yield of income and capital appreciation both have to be considered in judging the return from the investment.

(4) Trustees should maintain a fair balance between beneficiaries when selecting investments, since different beneficiaries will benefit from different types of investment.[69] For example, a beneficiary with a life interest will benefit from investments with stronger income returns, whereas a beneficiary entitled to the remainder would benefit from investments with greater capital growth. The operation of this obligation is considered later in respect of the distinct duty to maintain balance.[70]

(5) Trustees are not generally required to consult the beneficiaries on the selection of investments, unless this is required by the trust instrument, and are not bound to act on the wishes of

---

[64] The property was subsequently ordered to be sold to Mrs Simpson for £6,600.
[65] See Chapter 12.4(b)(ii), pp. 595–6.
[66] *Speight v Gaunt* (1883) 9 App Cas 1, 19 (Lord Blackburn).
[67] *Learoyd v Whiteley* (1887) 12 App Cas 727, 733 (Lord Watson).
[68] [1985] Ch 270, 287.
[69] *Nestlé v National Westminster Bank plc* [1993] 1 WLR 1261. See Chapter 12.5(a), pp. 611–14.
[70] See Chapter 12.5, pp. 611–18.

beneficiaries. Where, however, the beneficiaries do make comments, the trustees should consider them. In *X v A*,[71] Arden LJ said:

> Counsel told me that, in this case, the trustee was not happy at the idea of putting itself in a position where it was obliged to do what the beneficiaries asked unless it could think of a good reason not to do so. The investment decisions might be complex, the beneficiaries might disagree and in the immediate future the trustee's lien would take priority. I accept the trustee should not be bound in any way to act on the wishes of the beneficiaries. ... On the other hand, I regard it as implicit in the direction sought that the trustee should consider any comments which the beneficiaries make, and take them into account to the extent appropriate.

(ii) *Ethical considerations*

The extent to which trustees can take into account ethical considerations when selecting investments has proved to be a matter of particular controversy.

Cowan v Scargill [1985] Ch 270

A mineworkers' pension fund, with assets of over £3,000 million and very wide powers of investment, was managed by a committee of ten trustees, of whom five were appointed by the National Coal Board (NCB) and five, including the defendant, by the National Union of Mineworkers (NUM). Prior to 1982 the plan for investment included overseas investment and investment in oil and gas. In 1982, when a revised plan was considered, the five union trustees, on the basis of union policy determined at the annual conference, refused to accept the revised plan, unless it was amended so that there would be no increase in overseas investment, overseas investment already made would be withdrawn at an opportune time, and there would be no investment in energies competing with coal. The NCB trustees applied to the court for directions as to whether it was appropriate to take ethical considerations into account when selecting investments.

The Court held that the NUM trustees committed a breach of trust in refusing to concur in adopting the revised plan for investment due to taking into account ethical considerations.

Sir Robert Megarry V-C:

In considering what investments to make trustees must put on one side their own personal interests and views. Trustees may have strongly held social or political views. They may be firmly opposed to any investment in South Africa[72] or other countries, or they may object to any form of investment in companies concerned with alcohol, tobacco, armaments or many other things. In the conduct of their own affairs, of course, they are free to abstain from making any such investments. Yet under a trust, if investments of this type would be more beneficial to the beneficiaries than other investments, the trustees must not refrain from making the investments by reason of the views that they hold.

Trustees may even have to act dishonourably (though not illegally) if the interests of their beneficiaries require it. Thus where trustees for sale had struck a bargain for the sale of trust property but had not bound themselves by a legally enforceable contract, they were held to be under a duty to consider

---

[71] [2000] 1 All ER 490, 496.
[72] This was during the period of Apartheid in South Africa.

and explore a better offer that they received, and not to carry through the bargain to which they felt in honour bound: *Buttle v Saunders* [1950] 2 All ER 193.[73] In other words, the duty of trustees to their beneficiaries may include a duty to 'gazump', however honourable the trustees. As Wynn-Parry J said at 195, trustees 'have an overriding duty to obtain the best price which they can for their beneficiaries'. In applying this to an official receiver in *Re Wyvern Developments Ltd* [1974] 1 WLR 1097 at 1106, Templeman J said that he 'must do his best by his creditors and contributories. He is in a fiduciary capacity and cannot make moral gestures, nor can the court authorise him to do so.' In the words of Sir James Wigram V-C in *Balls v Strutt* (1841) 1 Hare 146 at 149:

> 'It is a principle in this court, that a trustee shall not be permitted to use the powers which the trust may confer upon him at law, except for the legitimate purposes of his trust; ... '

Powers must be exercised fairly and honestly for the purposes for which they are given and not so as to accomplish any ulterior purpose, whether for the benefit of the trustees or otherwise: see *Duke of Portland v Lady Topham* (1864) 11 HL Cas 32, a case on a power of appointment that must apply *a fortiori* to a power to trustees as such.

Thirdly, by way of caveat I should say that I am not asserting that the benefit of the beneficiaries which a trustee must make his paramount concern inevitably and solely means their financial benefit, even if the only object of the trust is to provide financial benefits. Thus if the only actual or potential beneficiaries of a trust are all adults with very strict views on moral and social matters, condemning all forms of alcohol, tobacco and popular entertainment, as well as armaments, I can well understand that it might not be for the 'benefit' of such beneficiaries to know that they are obtaining rather larger financial returns under the trust by reason of investments in those activities than they would have received if the trustees had invested the trust funds in other investments. The beneficiaries might well consider that it was far better to receive less than to receive more money from what they consider to be evil and tainted sources. 'Benefit' is a word with a very wide meaning, and there are circumstances in which arrangements which work to the financial disadvantage of a beneficiary may yet be for his benefit: see, for example, *Re T's Settlement Trusts* [1964] Ch 158 and *Re CL* [1969] 1 Ch 587.[74] But I would emphasise that such cases are likely to be very rare, and in any case I think that under a trust for the provision of financial benefits the burden would rest, and rest heavily, on him who asserts that it is for the benefit of the beneficiaries as a whole to receive less by reason of the exclusion of some of the possibly more profitable forms of investment. Plainly the present case is not one of this rare type of cases. Subject to such matters, under a trust for the provision of financial benefits, the paramount duty of the trustees is to provide the greatest financial benefits for the present and future beneficiaries.

Fourth, the standard required of a trustee in exercising his powers of investment is that he must

> 'take such care as an ordinary prudent man would take if he were minded to make an investment for the benefit of other people for whom he felt morally bound to provide:'

per Lindley LJ in *Re Whiteley* (1886) 33 Ch D 347 at 355; see also at 350, 358; and see *Learoyd v Whiteley* (1887) 12 App Cas 727.[75] That duty includes the duty to seek advice on matters which the trustee does not understand, such as the making of investments, and on receiving that advice to act with the same degree of prudence. This requirement is not discharged merely by showing that the trustee has acted in good faith and with sincerity. Honesty and sincerity are not the same as prudence and reasonableness. Some of the most sincere people are the most unreasonable; and Mr. Scargill told me that he had met quite a few of them. Accordingly, although a trustee who takes advice on investments is not bound to accept and act on that advice, he is not entitled to reject it merely because he sincerely disagrees with it, unless in addition to being sincere he is acting as an ordinary prudent man would act.

---

[73] See Chapter 12.4(b)(vii), pp. 598–600.
[74] See Chapter 15.3(b)(iii)(c), p. 731.
[75] Now see the statutory duty of care, Chapter 12.2(b), pp. 589–90.

Fifth, trustees have a duty to consider the need for diversification of investments. ... In the case before me, it is not in issue that there ought to be diversification of the investments held by the fund. The contention of the defendants, put very shortly, is that there can be a sufficient degree of diversification without any investment overseas or in oil, and that in any case there is no need to increase the level of overseas investments beyond the existing level. Other pension funds got on well enough without overseas investments, it was said, and in particular the NUM's own scheme had, in 1982, produced better results than the scheme here in question. This was not so, said Mr. Jenkins, if you compared like with like, and excluded investments in property, which figure substantially in the mineworkers' scheme but not at all in the NUM scheme: and in any case the latter scheme was much smaller, being of the order of £7 million.

I shall not pursue this matter. Even if other funds in one particular year, or in many years, had done better than the scheme which is before me, that does not begin to show that it is beneficial to this scheme to be shorn of the ability to invest overseas. ...

Sixth, there is the question whether the principles that I have been stating apply, with or without modification, to trusts of pension funds ... I can see no reason for holding that different principles apply to pension fund trusts from those which apply to other trusts. Of course, there are many provisions in pension schemes which are not to be found in private trusts, and to these the general law of trusts will be subordinated. But subject to that, I think that the trusts of pension funds are subject to the same rules as other trusts. The large size of pension funds emphasises the need for diversification, rather than lessening it, and the fact that much of the fund has been contributed by the members of the scheme seems to me to make even more important that the trustees should exercise their powers in the best interests of the beneficiaries. In a private trust, most, if not all, of the beneficiaries are the recipients of the bounty of the settlor, whereas under the trusts of a pension fund many (though not all) of the beneficiaries are those who, as members, contributed to the funds so that in due time they would receive pensions. It is thus all the more important that the interests of the beneficiaries should be paramount, so that they may receive the benefits which in part they have paid for. I can see no justification for holding that the benefits to them should run the risk of being lessened because the trustees were pursuing an investment policy intended to assist the industry that the pensioners have left, or their union ...

I can see no escape from the conclusion that the NUM trustees were attempting to impose the prohibitions in order to carry out union policy; and mere assertions that their sole consideration was the benefit of the beneficiaries do not alter that conclusion. If the NUM trustees were thinking only of the benefit of the beneficiaries, why all the references to union policy instead of proper explanations of how and why the prohibitions would bring benefits to the beneficiaries? No doubt some trustees with strong feelings find it irksome to be forced to submerge those feelings and genuinely put the interests of the beneficiaries first. Indeed, there are some who are temperamentally unsuited to being trustees, and are more fitted for campaigning for changes in the law. This, of course, they are free to do; but if they choose to become trustees they must accept that the rules of equity will bind them in all they do as trustees.

It follows that trustees should put aside their personal interests and views when selecting investments. So, for example, if a trustee is personally opposed to the tobacco industry or the trade in armaments, the trust should still invest in such industries if they give a better financial return.

The operation of this principle when selecting investments is particularly well illustrated by a decision of the Scottish courts in *Martin v City of Edinburgh DC*,[76] where the District Council was a trustee that had withdrawn trust investments in South Africa as a protest against that country's apartheid

[76] [1988] SLT 329.

policy. It was held that this constituted a breach of trust, since the councillors had not considered the effect of the investment policy on the interests of the trust. Lord Murray said:[77]

> A trustee cannot be expected to divest himself of political beliefs or all moral, religious or other conscientiously held principles. He should recognise that he has preferences and do his best to exercise fair and impartial judgment on the issues before him.

Sir Robert Megarry V-C[78] suggested in *Cowan v Scargill* that, where the beneficiaries are all adults with full legal capacity who are absolutely entitled to the trust property, it is legitimate for the trustees to have regard to ethical considerations when selecting investments if all of the beneficiaries have strict views on such matters, effectively involving an application of the principle in *Saunders v Vautier*.[79] But, whereas that principle normally operates to terminate the trust,[80] here it apparently operates to qualify the normal rules on selecting investments.

The settlor or testator can exclude certain investments from the power of investment on ethical grounds or may explicitly require the trustees to have regard to ethical considerations when selecting investments.[81] This will involve a reduction of the general investment powers of trustees, but it is possible to do this by the trust instrument.[82] If a pension trust has an ethical investment policy, this must be explicit.[83]

The general principles relating to the selection of investments apply to charity trustees as well, but there is greater scope for such trustees to have regard to ethical considerations.

Harries v Church Commissioners for England [1992] 1 WLR 1241

The Bishop of Oxford claimed that the Church Commissioners, whose purpose is to promote the Christian faith through the Church of England, should not select investments in a manner incompatible with that purpose, even if this involved a risk of significant financial detriment. Sir Donald Nicholls V-C held that ethical considerations could be taken into account only in so far as the profitability of investments was not jeopardized.[84]

> For some time there have been voices in the Church of England expressing disquiet at the investment policy of the Commissioners. They do not question either the good faith or the investment expertise of the Commissioners. Their concern is not that the Commissioners have failed to get the best financial return from their property and investments. Their concern is that, in making investment decisions, the Commissioners are guided too rigorously by purely financial considerations, and that the Commissioners give insufficient weight to what are now called 'ethical' considerations. They contend, moreover, that the Commissioners have fallen into legal error. The Commissioners attach overriding importance to financial considerations, and that is a misapprehension of the approach they ought properly to adopt when making investment decisions. The Commissioners ought to have in mind that the

---

[77] Ibid, 334.
[78] [1985] Ch 270, 288.
[79] (1841) Cr & Ph 240. See Chapter 10.3(a), pp. 519–21.
[80] See Chapter 15.1, p. 722.
[81] *Harries v Church Commissioners for England* [1992] 1 WLR 1241, 1247 (Sir Donald Nicholls V-C).
[82] Trustee Act 2000, s. 6(1). See Chapter 12.4(b)(i), p. 595.
[83] Pension Act 1995, s. 35.
[84] [1992] 1 WLR 1241, 1244.

underlying purpose for which they hold their assets is the promotion of the Christian faith through the Church of England. The Commissioners should not exercise their investment functions in a manner which would be incompatible with that purpose even if that involves a risk of incurring significant financial detriment....

Before going further into the criticism made of the Commissioners I will consider the general principles applicable to the exercise of powers of investment by charity trustees. It is axiomatic that charity trustees, in common with all other trustees, are concerned to further the purposes of the trust of which they have accepted the office of trustee. That is their duty. To enable them the better to discharge that duty, trustees have powers vested in them. Those powers must be exercised for the purpose for which they have been given: to further the purposes of the trust. That is the guiding principle applicable to the issues in these proceedings. Everything which follows is no more than the reasoned application of that principle in particular contexts.

Broadly speaking, property held by charitable trustees falls into two categories. First, there is property held by trustees for what may be called functional purposes. The National Trust owns historic houses and open spaces. The Salvation Army owns hostels for the destitute. And many charities need office accommodation in which to carry out essential administrative work. Second, there is property held by trustees for the purpose of generating money, whether from income or capital growth, with which to further the work of the trust. In other words, property held by trustees as an investment. Where property is so held, prima facie the purposes of the trust will be best served by the trustees seeking to obtain therefrom the maximum return, whether by way of income or capital growth, which is consistent with commercial prudence. That is the starting point for all charity trustees when considering the exercise of their investment powers. Most charities need money; and the more of it there is available, the more the trustees can seek to accomplish.

In most cases this prima facie position will govern the trustees' conduct. In most cases the best interests of the charity require that the trustees' choice of investments should be made solely on the basis of well-established investment criteria, having taken expert advice where appropriate and having due regard to such matters as the need to diversify, the need to balance income against capital growth, and the need to balance risk against return.

In a minority of cases the position will not be so straightforward. There will be some cases, I suspect comparatively rare, when the objects of the charity are such that investments of a particular type would conflict with the aims of the charity. Much-cited examples are those of cancer research companies and tobacco shares, trustees of temperance charities and brewery and distillery shares, and trustees of charities of the Society of Friends and shares in companies engaged in production of armaments. If, as would be likely in those examples, trustees were satisfied that investing in a company engaged in a particular type of business would conflict with the very objects their charity is seeking to achieve, they should not so invest. Carried to its logical conclusion the trustees should take this course even if it would be likely to result in significant financial detriment to the charity. The logical conclusion, whilst sound as a matter of legal analysis, is unlikely to arise in practice. It is not easy to think of an instance where in practice the exclusion for this reason of one or more companies or sectors from the whole range of investments open to trustees would be likely to leave them without an adequately wide range of investments from which to choose a properly diversified portfolio.

There will also be some cases, again I suspect comparatively rare, when trustees' holdings of particular investments might hamper a charity's work either by making potential recipients of aid unwilling to be helped because of the source of the charity's money, or by alienating some of those who support the charity financially. In these cases, the trustees will need to balance the difficulties they would encounter, or likely financial loss they would sustain, if they were to hold the investments against the risk of financial detriment if those investments were excluded from their portfolio. The greater the risk of financial detriment, the more certain the trustees should be of countervailing disadvantages to the charity before they incur that risk. Another circumstance where trustees would be entitled, or even required, to take into account non-financial criteria would be where the trust deed so provides.

No doubt there will be other cases where trustees are justified in departing from what should always be their starting point. The instances I have given are not comprehensive. But I must emphasise that of their very nature, and by definition, investments are held by trustees to aid the work of the charity in a particular way: by generating money. That is the purpose for which they are held. That is their *raison d'être*. Trustees cannot properly use assets held as an investment for other, *viz.*, non-investment, purposes. To the extent that they do they are not properly exercising their powers of investment. This is not to say that trustees who own land may not act as responsible landlords or those who own shares may not act as responsible shareholders. They may. The law is not so cynical as to require trustees to behave in a fashion which would bring them or their charity into disrepute (although their consciences must not be too tender: see *Buttle v Saunders* [1950] 2 All ER 193). On the other hand, trustees must act prudently. They must not use property held by them for investment purposes as a means for making moral statements at the expense of the charity of which they are trustees. Those who wish may do so with their own property, but that is not a proper function of trustees with trust assets held as an investment.

I should mention one other particular situation. There will be instances today when those who support or benefit from a charity take widely different views on a particular type of investment, some saying that on moral grounds it conflicts with the aims of the charity, others saying the opposite. One example is the holding of arms-industry shares by a religious charity. There is a real difficulty here. To many questions raising moral issues there are no certain answers. On moral questions widely differing views are held by well-meaning, responsible people. This is not always so. But frequently, when questions of the morality of conduct are being canvassed, there is no identifiable yardstick which can be applied to a set of facts so as to yield one answer which can be seen to be 'right' and the other 'wrong'. If that situation confronts trustees of a charity, the law does not require them to find an answer to the unanswerable. Trustees may, if they wish, accommodate the views of those who consider that on moral grounds a particular investment would be in conflict with the objects of the charity, so long as the trustees are satisfied that course would not involve a risk of significant financial detriment. But when they are not so satisfied trustees should not make investment decisions on the basis of preferring one view of whether on moral grounds an investment conflicts with the objects of the charity over another. This is so even when one view is more widely supported than the other.

I have sought above to consider charity trustees' duties in relation to investment as a matter of basic principle. I was referred to no authority bearing directly on these matters. My attention was drawn to *Cowan v Scargill* [1985] Ch 270, a case concerning a pension fund. I believe the views I have set out accord with those expressed by Sir Robert Megarry V-C in that case, bearing in mind that he was considering trusts for the provision of financial benefits for individuals. In this case I am concerned with trusts of charities, whose purposes are multifarious.

[His Lordship considered the Commissioners' objects and their investment policy, and continued:] The statement of policy records that the Commissioners do not invest in companies whose main business is in armaments, gambling, alcohol, tobacco or newspapers. Of these, newspapers fall into a category of their own. The Commissioners' policy regarding newspapers is based on the fact that many newspapers are associated, to a greater or lesser extent, with a particular political party or political view. Leaving aside newspapers, the underlying rationale of the Commissioners' policy on these items is that there is a body of members of the Church of England opposed to the businesses in question on religious or moral grounds. There are members who believe these business activities are morally wrong, and that they are in conflict with Christian teaching and its moral values. But this list has only to be read for it to be obvious that many committed members of the Church of England take the contrary view. To say that not all members of the Church of England eschew gambling, alcohol or tobacco would be an understatement. As to armaments, the morality of war, and the concepts of a 'just war', are issues which have been debated for centuries. These are moral questions on which no single view can be shown to be 'right' and the others 'wrong'. As I understand the position, the Commissioners have felt able to exclude these items from their investments despite the conflicting views on the morality of holding these items as investments because there has remained open to the Commissioners an adequate width of alternative investments.

I have already indicated that at the heart of the plaintiffs' case is a contention that the Commissioners' policy is erroneous in law in that the Commissioners are only prepared to take non-financial considerations into account to the extent that such considerations do not significantly jeopardise or interfere with accepted investment principles. I think it is implicit, if not explicit, in the Commissioners' evidence that they do regard themselves as constrained in this way. So far as I have been able to see, this is the only issue identifiable as an issue of law raised in these proceedings. In my view this self-constraint applied by the Commissioners is not one which in practice has led to any error of law on their part, nor is it likely to do so. I have already indicated that the circumstances in which charity trustees are bound or entitled to make a financially disadvantageous investment decision for ethical reasons are extremely limited. I have noted that it is not easy to think of a practical example of such a circumstance. There is no evidence before me to suggest that any such circumstance exists here. ...

I add only this. In bringing these proceedings the Bishop of Oxford and his colleagues are actuated by the highest moral concern. But, as I have sought to show, the approach they wish the Commissioners to adopt to investment decisions would involve a departure by the Commissioners from their legal obligations. Whether such a departure would or would not be desirable is, of course, not an issue in these proceedings. That is a matter to be pursued, if at all, elsewhere than in this court.

This decision has been criticized for being unnecessarily restrictive on charity investment.

Nobles, 'Charities and Ethical Investment' [1992] Conv 115, 116

This decision seems very peculiar. Charitable trustees can give money away in pursuit of their charity's purposes. In so doing, they are not required to limit their bounty to such as all persons would agree were within their objects. Charities can be somewhat more controversial and radical than this. They can undertake any work which can reasonably come within their objects and, by the same token, must avoid activities which cannot reasonably be said to come within their objects. What can reasonably come within a charity's purposes and what must be considered to conflict with a charity's purposes, is ultimately a matter for the courts. There has never been any suggestion that the courts could not control charities within these broad limits, and there is no suggestion in this case that the bounty of a charity should be controlled on any other basis. Why should investment be made subject to stricter controls? ... The ordinary business of a pension scheme is to provide financial benefits to individuals and, in the ordinary course of events, the best way to achieve this is to have the largest possible fund. The same logic applies to private family trusts. If the courts abandon the criteria of best financial interests they have no standard by which to control the trustees' investment policies other than the purely subjective one of whether they agree with the morals or politics of the trustees. But charitable trusts do provide criteria, other than financial interests, by which to assess their investment policies. They exist to further charitable purposes. The grant of bounty has to be assessed by reference to such purposes, and so should the investment policy. If trustees cannot make, or cannot be allowed to make, controversial moral judgments on the extent to which their investments give effect to their charity's purposes then they should not be able to make the same judgments when giving away its property. Conversely, if they can be trusted to make these judgments when giving away the charity's property, they can be trusted to make its investments on the same basis.

However, a distinction needs to be drawn between direct and indirect fulfilment of the charity's purposes. When making distributions, trustees are directly benefiting the objects and have a free discretion as to whom or what they will benefit, subject to the restrictions of the trust instrument. But when making investment decisions that have indirect effects on the fulfilment of the charity's objectives, the ultimate aim is to maximize the financial return for the furtherance of those purposes, and so restrictions are properly imposed on what the trustees can and cannot take into account when determining their investment policies. In other words, the distinction is between administrative and dispositive decisions, a distinction that is just as relevant to charitable trusts as it is to private trusts. Determining investment policy is an administrative matter and raises different considerations from making appointments of trust property.

(d) TRUSTEES HOLDING CONTROLLING INTEREST IN A COMPANY

Where the trustees own sufficient shares in a company to give them a controlling interest of that company, they will be subject to additional obligations to safeguard the trust's investment in the company because, through their majority control, they are able to become actively involved in the management of the company.

Bartlett v Barclays Bank Trust Co. Ltd (No. 1) [1980] Ch 515

Barclays Bank was trustee of the Bartlett Trust, of which the sole asset was a holding of 99.8 per cent of shares in a private property company. The beneficiaries were the settlor's family. No beneficiary was on the board of the company, and none of the directors was a nominee of the bank. The board wished the company to invest in property development. The bank agreed to this so long as the beneficiaries were not left short of income. The company invested in two projects without consulting the bank, one at Guildford, which was successful, and the other, opposite the Old Bailey, which was not, because planning permission could not be obtained. A substantial loss was suffered. The bank was not aware of the hazardous nature of the projects and did not intervene to prevent them. The bank had been content simply to rely upon information issued at annual general meetings, which would have been available to any ordinary shareholder. The beneficiaries sued the bank for breach of trust.

It was held that the bank had breached the trust and was liable for the loss.

Brightman J:

I turn to the question, what was the duty of the bank as the holder of shares? ...The bank, as trustee, was bound to act in relation to the shares and to the controlling position which they conferred, in the same manner as a prudent man of business. The prudent man of business will act in such manner as is necessary to safeguard his investment. He will do this in two ways. If facts come to his knowledge which tell him that the company's affairs are not being conducted as they should be, or which put him on inquiry, he will take appropriate action. Appropriate action will no doubt consist in the first instance of inquiry of and consultation with the directors, and in the last but most unlikely resort, the convening of a general meeting to replace one or more directors. What the prudent man of business will not do is to content himself with the receipt of such information on the affairs of the company as a shareholder ordinarily receives at annual general meetings. Since he has the power to do so, he will go further and see that he has sufficient information to enable him to make a responsible decision from time to time either to let matters proceed as they are proceeding, or to intervene if he is dissatisfied. This topic was considered by Cross J in *Re Lucking's Will Trusts* … [1967] 3 All ER 726. In that case nearly 70 per cent of the shares in the company were held by two trustees, L and B, as part of the estate of a deceased; about 29 per cent belonged to L in his own right, and 1 per cent belonged to L's wife. The directors in 1954 were Mr. and Mrs. L and D, who was the manager of the business. In 1956 B was appointed trustee to act jointly with L. The company was engaged in the manufacture and sale of shoe accessories. It had a small factory employing about twenty people, and one or two travellers. It also had an agency in France. D wrongfully drew some £15,000 from the company's bank account in excess of his remuneration, and later became bankrupt. The money was lost. Cross J said, at 874:

> 'The conduct of the defendant trustees is, I think, to be judged by the standard applied in *Speight v Gaunt* (1883) 9 App Cas 1, namely, that a trustee is only bound to conduct the business of the trust in such a way as an ordinary prudent man would conduct a business of his own. Now what steps, if any, does a reasonably prudent man who finds himself a majority shareholder in a private company take with regard to the management of the company's affairs? He does not, I think, content himself with such information as to the management of the company's affairs as he is entitled to as shareholder, but ensures that he is represented on the board. He may be prepared to run the business himself as managing director or, at least, to become a non-executive director while having the business managed by someone else. Alternatively, he may find someone who will act as his nominee on the board and report to him from time to time as to the company's affairs. In the same way, as it seems to me, trustees holding a controlling interest ought to ensure so far as they can that they have such information as to the progress of the company's affairs as directors would have. If they sit back and allow the company to be run by the minority shareholder and receive no more information than shareholders are entitled to, they do so at their risk if things go wrong.'

I do not understand Cross J to have been saying that in every case where trustees have a controlling interest in a company it is their duty to ensure that one of their number is a director or that they have a nominee on the board who will report from time to time on the affairs of the company. He was merely outlining convenient methods by which a prudent man of business (as also a trustee) with a controlling interest in a private company, can place himself in a position to make an informed decision whether any action is appropriate to be taken for the protection of his asset. Other methods may be equally satisfactory and convenient, depending upon the circumstances of the individual case. Alternatives which spring to mind are the receipt of copies of the agenda and minutes of board meetings if regularly held, the receipt of monthly management accounts in the case of a trading concern, or quarterly reports. Every case will depend on its own facts. The possibilities are endless. It would be useless, indeed misleading, to seek to lay down a general rule. The purpose to be achieved is not that of monitoring every move of the directors, but of making it reasonably probable, so far as circumstances permit, that the trustee or (as in the *Lucking* case) one of them will receive an adequate flow of information in time to enable the trustees to make use of their controlling interest should this be necessary for the protection of their trust asset, namely, the shareholding. The obtaining of information is not an end in itself, but merely a means of enabling the trustees to safeguard the interests of their beneficiaries. …

It was not proper for the bank to confine itself to the receipt of the annual balance sheet and profit and loss account, detailed annual financial statements and the chairman's report and statement, and to attendance at the annual general meetings and the luncheons that followed, which were the limits of the bank's regular sources of information. Had the bank been in receipt of more frequent information it would have been able to step in and stop, and ought to have stopped, the board embarking on the Old Bailey project. That project was imprudent and hazardous and wholly unsuitable for a trust whether undertaken by the bank direct or through the medium of its wholly-owned company. Even without the regular flow of information which the bank ought to have had, it knew enough to put it upon inquiry. There were enough obvious points at which the bank should have intervened and asked questions.

The bank had breached the trust because it had failed to safeguard the investment in the company. As a controlling shareholder it should have ensured that it received sufficient information to enable it to make an informed decision as to what action was necessary to protect the investment, and it should then have taken that action. Options open to the trustee who is a controlling shareholder might include convening a general meeting to remove and replace one or more of the directors,[85] either with a nominee or with the trustee itself.

(e)   ENLARGEMENT OF INVESTMENT POWERS BY THE COURT

Although the statutory powers of investment are wide, there may be exceptional circumstances where the trustees wish to have the powers widened by the courts either under the Trustee Act 1925[86] or the Variation of Trusts Act 1958.[87] Similarly, the powers of investment under the trust instrument may be restrictive and the trustees might wish to have the restriction removed.

The courts were, at one stage, willing to extend investment powers only in special circumstances,[88] but in *Trustees of the British Museum v Attorney-General*,[89] the court broadened the range of circumstances under which it was willing to widen investment powers, primarily because investment powers at the time were considered to be too restrictive and outdated. In that case, the court approved a scheme to give the trustees of the British Museum wide powers of investment of charitable funds to enable investment abroad. The court was influenced by a number of factors in reaching this decision, including the common practice at the time for trust instruments to give wider investment powers than the statutory powers of investment, the fact that the trustees were eminent, responsible, and willing to obtain independent financial advice, and that the fund was large, being worth over £5 million, and so was more like a pension trust with wider powers of investment. Sir Robert Megarry V-C said:[90]

The size of the fund in question may be very material. A fund that is very large may well justify a latitude of investment that would be denied to a more modest fund; for the spread of investments possible for a larger fund may justify the greater risks that wider powers will permit to be taken.

The object of the trust may be very material. In the present case, the desirability of having an increase of capital value which will make possible the purchase of desirable acquisitions for the museum despite soaring prices does something to justify the greater risks whereby capital appreciation may be obtained.

Since that decision, statutory powers of investment have been modernized and expanded through the enactment of the Trustee Act 2000. Consequently, there will be much less need for applications to be made to court to widen investment powers, although there will still be situations in which trustees might wish to have their investment powers enlarged, such as where the trustees wish to invest in land

---

[85] Companies Act 2006, s. 168.
[86] Section 57. See Chapter 15.3(a), p. 723.
[87] See Chapter 15.3(b), p. 725.
[88] *Re Kolb's Will Trusts* [1962] Ch 531; *Mason v Farbrother* [1983] 2 All ER 1078.
[89] [1984] 1 WLR 418. See also *Steel v Wellcome Custodian Trustees Ltd* [1988] 1 WLR 167.
[90] [1984] 1 WLR 418, 424.

abroad, which is not permitted by the general statutory powers of investment, or to remove restrictions on investment powers in the trust instrument that are now out of line with the wide investment powers under the Trustee Act 2000. This will involve overturning the wishes of the settlor or testator and, therefore, raise sensitive issues that will be examined in Chapter 15.

5. DUTY TO MAINTAIN A FAIR BALANCE BETWEEN BENEFICIARIES

(a) GENERAL PRINCIPLES

It is the duty of a trustee to act in the interests of all the beneficiaries. It follows that trustees are under a duty to maintain a fair balance between beneficiaries and not to prefer one beneficiary or class of beneficiary over another.[91] The duty to maintain a fair balance between different classes of beneficiary is particularly important where there are beneficiaries with a life interest and others with an interest in remainder, since those interests will potentially conflict. Life tenants are entitled to receive income receipts and those entitled to an interest in remainder will eventually get the benefit of capital receipts. The beneficiaries with a life interest (the 'income beneficiaries') will prefer investments that will produce the highest possible income, but will not be especially concerned by poor capital growth. The beneficiaries with the remainder interest (the 'capital beneficiaries') will prefer investments that will preserve the capital value of the trust property and will have a good prospect of substantial future growth.

Nestlé v National Westminster Bank plc [1993] 1 WLR 1261

The claimant's grandfather died in 1922 and appointed what became the National Westminster Bank plc as his executor and trustee. Under his will, his widow had a life interest in the family home. On her death, their two sons, George and John (the claimant's uncle and father), each had a half-interest in the residue. When they died, their shares went to their children. In 1986 the claimant, who had become absolutely entitled to the capital, claimed that the trust fund, which was then valued at £269,203, should have been worth £1.8 million. She brought an action against the trustee bank for default in the management of the fund. It was held that, although the bank had failed to maintain balance between beneficiaries, it could not be established that this had caused loss to the claimant.

Leggatt LJ:

... during the 64 years for which the trust set up by the plaintiff's grandfather endured, the contentment of his descendants declined. The plaintiff's uncle and father conducted with the respondent bank vigorous campaigns designed to improve their respective incomes, which, if the bank had not resisted them, would have worked to the ultimate detriment of the plaintiff, while the plaintiff herself is now locked in mortal financial combat with the bank.

George and John Nestlé saw the bank, or said they saw the bank, as unfairly looking out for the plaintiff at their expense. In fact John turns out to have had a fortune of his own, which was invested in equities. So to the extent that he was successful in getting the bank to invest in gilts he was achieving a balance

---

[91] *Nestlé v National Westminster Bank plc* [1993] 1 WLR 1261.

between his funds. The plaintiff, on the other hand, with whom her father was latterly at odds, has become obsessed with the idea that the bank over the years has failed to look after her interests. She claims that the sum of £269,203 which she inherited should have been larger than it was. ...

The plaintiff alleges that the bank is in breach of trust because over the years since her grandfather set up the trust the bank has supposed that its power of investment was more limited than it was; has failed to carry out periodic reviews of the portfolio, and to maintain a proper balance between equities and gilts, and to diversify the equity investments; and has unduly favoured the interests of her father and her uncle as life-tenants at the expense of her own interest as remainderman. She says that in consequence the trust fund was worth less in 1986 than it should have been.

The essence of the bank's duty was to take such steps as a prudent businessman would have taken to maintain and increase the value of the trust fund. Unless it failed to do so, it was not in breach of trust. A breach of duty will not be actionable, and therefore will be immaterial, if it does not cause loss. In this context I would endorse the concession of Mr. Nugee for the bank that 'loss' will be incurred by a trust fund when it makes a gain less than would have been made by a prudent businessman. A claimant will therefore fail who cannot prove a loss in this sense caused by breach of duty. So here in order to make a case for an inquiry, the plaintiff must show that loss was caused by breach of duty on the part of the bank.

On the plaintiff's behalf Mr. Lyndon-Stanford seeks to rely on a presumption against a wrongdoing trustee. He invokes Brightman J's dictum in *Bartlett v Barclays Bank Trust Co Ltd (No 2)* [1980] Ch 515 at 545 that: 'the trustee's obligation is to restore to the trust estate the assets of which he has deprived it'. But that presupposes deprivation.

The plaintiff alleges, and I am content to assume, that the bank was at all material times under a misapprehension about the meaning of the investment clause in the will, with the result that the bank believed that the scope of its powers of investment was more confined than it was. I also regard it as unlikely that the bank conducted any reviews of the portfolio between 1922 and 1959. If any were conducted, they were unplanned, sporadic and indecisive. Mr. Lyndon-Stanford argues that it should be presumed that, had there been a better balance between gilts and equities and had the equity investment been more diversified, the fund would ultimately have been worth more than it was. The fallacy is that it does not follow from the fact that a wider power of investment was available to the bank than it realised either that it would have been exercised or that, if it had been, the exercise of it would have produced a result more beneficial to the bank than actually was produced. Loss cannot be presumed, if none would necessarily have resulted. Until it was proved that there was a loss, no attempt could be made to assess the amount of it ...

In my judgment either there was a loss in the present case or there was not. Unless there was a loss, there was no cause of action. It was for the plaintiff to prove on balance of probabilities that there was, or must have been, a loss. If proved, the court would then have had to assess the amount of it, and for the purpose of doing so might have had recourse to presumptions against the bank. In short, if it were shown that a loss was caused by breach of trust, such a presumption might avail the plaintiff in quantifying the loss. The plaintiff's difficulty is in reaching that stage ...

No testator, in the light of this example, would choose this bank for the effective management of his investment. But the bank's engagement was as a trustee; and as such, it is to be judged not so much by success as by absence of proven default ... The very process of attempting to achieve a balance, or (if that be old-fashioned) fairness, as between the interests of life tenants and those of a remainderman inevitably means that each can complain of being less well served than he or she ought to have been. But by the undemanding standard of prudence the bank is not shown to have committed any breach of trust resulting in loss.

Although the claimant failed to recover any compensation, this was only because she was unable to prove that she had suffered loss as a result of the bank's investment policy. If it could have been shown that, had the trustees adopted a different investment policy, the value of the fund would have increased, the trustee bank might have been liable to compensate the fund.

The nature of the duty to maintain a fair balance between beneficiaries was considered further by Staughton LJ:[92]

> The obligation of a trustee is to administer the trust fund impartially, or fairly (I can see no significant difference), having regard to the different interests of beneficiaries. Wilberforce J said in *Re Pauling's Settlement Trusts (No 2)* [1963] Ch 576, 586:
>
> > 'The new trustees would be under the normal duty of preserving an equitable balance, and if at any time it was shown they were inclining one way or the other, it would not be a difficult matter to bring them to account.'
>
> At times it will not be easy to decide what is an equitable balance. A life tenant may be anxious to receive the highest possible income, whilst the remainderman will wish the real value of the trust fund to be preserved. If the life tenant is living in penury and the remainderman already has ample wealth, common sense suggests that a trustee should be able to take that into account, not necessarily by seeking the highest possible income at the expense of capital but by inclining in that direction. However, before adopting that course a trustee should, I think, require some verification of the facts ...
>
> Similarly I would not regard it as a breach of trust for the trustees to pay some regard to the relationship between Mr. George Nestlé and the plaintiff. He was merely her uncle, and she would have received nothing from his share of the fund if he had fathered a child who survived him. The trustees would be entitled, in my view, to incline towards income during his life tenancy and that of his widow, on that ground. Again common sense suggests to me that such a course might be appropriate, and I do not think that it would be a breach of the duty to act fairly, or impartially ...
>
> A trustee should also bear in mind, as the trustees did, that Estate Duty or Capital Transfer Tax is likely to be reduced in such a case if part of the fund is invested in tax-exempt gilts. That may provide a compensating benefit for the remainderman. Of course it is by no means certain that the benefit will materialise; the life tenant may return to this country, as happened in the case of Mrs. Elsie Nestlé. It has been said that nothing in this world is certain except death and taxes. But even the tax benefit was imponderable, since it could not be forecast what rate of tax would be applicable on the death of a life tenant.

It follows that, when trustees are administering the trust, they should have regard to the effects of their decisions on both those entitled to the life interest and those entitled to an interest in remainder, and ensure that both are treated even-handedly. So, for example, in *Nestlé*, a relevant consideration when selecting investments concerned the adverse tax consequences of focusing on capital or income returns, which might justify the trustees in shifting the balance towards whichever of income or capital would result in a lower tax liability.

The duty to ensure balance has been described as preserving 'an equitable balance'[93] between the different classes of beneficiary. But Hoffmann J in *Nestlé v National Westminster Bank plc*,[94] had preferred the language of fairness to that of balance:

> the trustee must act fairly in making investment decisions which may have different consequences for different classes of beneficiaries. There are two reasons why I prefer this formulation to the traditional

[92] *Nestlé v National Westminster Bank plc* [1993] 1 WLR 1260, 1279.
[93] *Re Pauling's Settlement Trusts (No. 2)* [1963] Ch 576, 586 (Wilberforce J). See also *Cowan v Scargill* [1985] Ch 270, 286 (Sir Robert Megarry V-C), Chapter 12.4(c)(ii), pp. 601–3.
[94] 29 June, 1988; [2000] WTLR 795, 803.

image of holding the scales equally between tenant for life and remainderman. The first is that the image of the scales suggests a weighing of known quantities whereas investment decisions are concerned with predictions of the future. Investments will carry current expectations of their future income yield and capital appreciation and these expectations will be reflected in their current market price, but there is always a greater or lesser risk that the outcome will deviate from those expectations. A judgment on the fairness of the choices made by the trustees must have regard to these imponderables. The second reason is that the image of the scales suggests a more mechanistic process than I believe the law requires. The trustees have in my judgment a wide discretion. They are for example entitled to take into account the income needs of the tenant for life or the fact that the tenant for life was a person known to the settlor or a stranger. Of course these cannot be allowed to become the overriding considerations but the concept of fairness between classes of beneficiaries does not require them to be excluded. It would be an inhuman law which required trustees to adhere to some mechanical rule for preserving the real value of the capital when the tenant for life was the testator's widow who had fallen upon hard times and the remainderman was young and well-off.

Whether the emphasis is placed on fairness or maintaining an equitable balance probably makes no difference in practice; the duty is essentially one to maintain a fair balance between beneficiaries. This duty can be expressly or implicitly excluded by the trust instrument, as will be the case where the trustees are given a power to choose between different beneficiaries or classes of beneficiary when exercising a power of appointment.[95]

(b) CLASSIFICATION OF INCOME AND CAPITAL

An important feature of the duty to maintain balance between beneficiaries concerns the allocation of receipts and expenses to income and capital.

(i) *Receipts*

The classification and allocation of receipts as income or capital is significant to the duty to maintain a fair balance in determining which receipts benefit beneficiaries with a life interest and which benefit the beneficiaries entitled to the remainder. A useful metaphor to apply is that of trees and fruit, with the growth of a tree representing capital and the fruits representing income. In many cases, the fruits of property will be treated as income, whereas other gains will be capital. So, for example, if a trust has a leasehold interest in a property, the rent that the trustees receive will be income and money received on selling the lease to a third party will be capital. In other cases, a receipt will simply be apportioned fairly between the life tenant and person with an interest in remainder. In *Jaffray v Marshall*,[96] Nicholas Stewart QC considered the classification of interest on compensation payable to a trust fund:

The only remaining issue is apportionment of that interest as between the life and remainder interests ... It is accepted that the high rates of interest in modern times contain a large element which merely preserves capital values. In principle that element should belong to the capital or remainder beneficiaries ... I take account of the fact that the period since 1989 has not been a period of the very high level of inflation that has been seen at times in fairly recent years. Accordingly, the rate of

---

[95] *Edge v Pensions Ombudsman* [2000] Ch 602.
[96] [1993] 1 WLR 1285, 1294.

> return needed to preserve capital is not as high as it has been in the past, which is only another way of saying the same thing. I stress the broadness of that view and no expert evidence has been adduced on these matters. In my view a fair apportionment of the interest in this case is that half should go to income and half to capital.

Classification of income and capital used not to be intuitive as regards distributions from companies. Although dividends paid on shares are treated as income and the distribution of bonus shares are treated as capital,[97] in more complicated transactions the classification of income and capital in company law was applied in trust law, such that most distributions were treated as income.[98] This rule was changed by section 2 of the Trusts (Capital and Income) Act 2012, by virtue of which all distributions of corporate assets to a trust are to be treated as a receipt of capital, subject to any contrary intention in the trust instrument. This reform makes classification of income and capital more intuitive and less artificial.

(ii) *Expenses*

Classification is also significant as regards trust expenses, since it is necessary to ascertain whether these are to be charged to income or to capital. A trust expense may relate to administrative matters, such as paying for professional fees or remunerating the trustees,[99] or may relate to the maintenance of the trust property, such as the cost of repairing a house.

Express provision may be made for the classification of trust expenses in the trust instrument, or the trustees may be given an express power to allocate expenses to income or capital. But, if no such provision is made, the law of trusts provides a default rule, as recognized by Lord Templeman in *Carver v Duncan*: [100]

> Trustees are entitled to be indemnified out of the capital and income of their trust fund against all obligations incurred by the trustees in the due performance of their duties and the due exercise of their powers. The trustees must then debit each item of expenditure either against income or against capital. The general rule is that income must bear all ordinary outgoings of a recurrent nature, such as rates and taxes, and interest on charges and incumbrances. Capital must bear all costs, charges and expenses incurred for the benefit of the whole estate.

The meaning of expenses being incurred for the benefit of the whole estate was considered by Sir John Chadwick in *Revenue and Customs Commissioners v Trustees of the Peter Clay Discretionary Trust*:[101]

> it is, I think, beyond argument that an expense is incurred 'for the benefit of the whole estate' in the present context when the purpose or object for which that expense is incurred is to confer benefit both on the income beneficiaries and on those entitled to capital on the determination of the income trusts. ... expenses which are of that nature are to be charged against capital. ... under the general law, expenses incurred for the benefit of both the income and capital beneficiaries must be charged against capital. It is only those expenses which are incurred exclusively for the benefit of the income beneficiaries that may be charged against income.

---

[97] *Bouch v Sproule* (1887) LR 12 App Cas 385.
[98] *Rae (Inspector of Taxes) v Lazard Investment Co. Ltd* [1963] 1 WLR 555, 565 (Lord Reid).
[99] See Chapter 11.6(a), pp. 554–6.
[100] [1985] AC 1082, 1120.
[101] [2008] EWCA Civ 1441; [2009] Ch 296, [28].

So, for example, the cost of repairing trust property, insurance premiums, and payments to professional advisers, are classified as capital. It is, however, possible to apportion an expense between income and capital if part of the expense can be shown to relate to work carried out for the benefit of the income beneficiary alone. Whilst this apportionment must be based on evidence rather than on the trustees' view of what is a fair balance as between income and capital beneficiaries, it can still be regarded as founded on the principle of ensuring a fair balance between beneficiaries, since it is fair that the burden of the expense should be borne by the beneficiary who benefits from it.[102]

(c) TOTAL RETURN INVESTMENT POLICY

One method for implementing the duty to ensure a balance between beneficiaries in respect of the selection of investments would be to adopt what is known as a 'total return' investment policy, which enables trustees to select investments on the basis of expected returns from the investment regardless of whether the return is classified as income or capital. Trustees would then have the discretion to allocate the investment returns to the beneficiaries entitled to the life interest and the remainder according to what they might expect to enjoy in the light of their respective interests in the fund, and in that way the trustees might maintain a balance between the two interests. The essence of a total return investment policy is that the trustees can select their investments without regard to the duty to balance the interests of income and capital beneficiaries; the duty to balance arises only subsequently, when receipts are received that can then be allocated to income or capital. The aim of such an investment policy is simply to increase the investment return across the whole of the investment portfolio.

Although a total investment return policy would benefit trusts and beneficiaries, generally it cannot be adopted because it is inconsistent with the duty to maintain balance between the interests of beneficiaries when selecting investments. In other words, the effect of the present law is to concentrate the trustees' minds on the form of the return, whether it is income or capital, rather than the substantive issue of maximizing the return of the whole portfolio regardless of how the fruits of the investments are classified. In private trusts, trustees are able to adopt such an investment policy only if the terms of the trust enable them to select investments without regard to the form of likely receipts, and then allocate receipts to income and capital subsequently.

The Law Commission considered whether trustees should be given a power to allocate receipts, and also expenses, to capital or income as the trustees consider appropriate. In its Consultation Paper on the classification of capital and income in trusts, the Law Commission provisionally recommended creating a statutory power of allocation.[103] However, in its final report,[104] the Law Commission reluctantly admitted that it was unable to maintain this recommendation because of the significant tax implications of giving trustees discretion to classify receipts. But, since charities usually do not pay tax,[105] section 104A of the Charities Act 2011[106] has been enacted which creates a general statutory power for charities with an endowment fund (under which not all property is available to be expended for charitable purposes) to adopt a total return investment policy, without requiring prior sanction of the Charity Commission.

---

[102] Law Com. No. 315, *Capital and Income in Trusts: Classification and Apportionment* (2009), para. 7.53.
[103] *Capital and Income in Trusts: Classification and Apportionment*, CP No. 175 (2004).
[104] Law Com. No. 315, op. cit.
[105] See Chapter 5.1(a), p. 178.
[106] Inserted by Trusts (Capital and Income) Act 2013, s. 4.

CHARITIES ACT 2011

104A Investment of endowment fund on total return basis

(1) This section applies to any available endowment fund of a charity.

(2) If the condition in subsection (3) is met in relation to the charity, the charity trustees may resolve that the fund, or a portion of it –

    (a) should be invested without the need to maintain a balance between capital and income returns, and

    (b) accordingly, should be freed from the restrictions with respect to expenditure of capital that apply to it.

(3) The condition is that the charity trustees are satisfied that it is in the interests of the charity that regulations under section 104B(1)(b) should apply in place of the restrictions mentioned in subsection 2(b).

(d) RULES TO RESTORE BALANCE

Various rules were developed in Equity to maintain or restore balance between income and capital beneficiaries, involving a duty either to sell and reinvest unauthorized trust property, called conversion, or to apportion capital or income between beneficiaries. Most of these rules were based on the presumed intention of the settlor or testator that the income and capital beneficiaries should enjoy the benefits of the trust equally.[107] For example, if personal property was left by will to one person for life, with remainder to another person, and there was a significant risk that the property would fall in value, this would affect the interest of the person entitled to the remainder, since the capital value of the property would have fallen by the time he or she was entitled to the property. Consequently, the trustees would be under a duty to convert such property into authorized investments,[108] which would give the life tenant an income, for example in the form of dividends, and the beneficiary entitled to the remainder would obtain the benefit of the capital value of the investment. These complex rules to restore balance became increasingly insignificant in practice, both because the rules were usually excluded by the trust instrument and because an investment is highly unlikely to be unauthorized today due to the wide investment powers under the Trustee Act 2000.[109] With the recognition of portfolio theory, wasting or hazardous investments are more likely to be appropriate because they can be balanced by purchasing less risky investments and also because the obligation to select and review investments according to the standard investment criteria[110] provides sufficient protection to all classes of beneficiary against the effect of such investments. Consequently, the rules to restore balance were abolished for new trusts by section 1(2) of the Trusts (Capital and Income) Act 2013, save if the trust instrument makes specific provision for their operation.

(e) DUTY TO ACCUMULATE INCOME

Where the trustees have a power or duty to accumulate income by adding it to capital rather than distributing it to the beneficiaries, there used to be statutory restrictions on the length of time of such accumulation.[111] Section 13 of the Perpetuities and Accumulations Act 2009 removed these restrictions

---

[107] Law Com. No. 315, *Capital and Income in Trusts: Classification and Apportionment* (2009), para. 6.10.
[108] This was called the first rule in *Howe v Lord Dartmouth* (1802) 7 Ves 137.
[109] See Chapter 12.4(b), pp. 594–600.
[110] Trustee Act 2000, s. 3(1). See Chapter 12.4(b)(ii), pp. 595–6.
[111] Law of Property Act 1925, s. 164.

for all trusts other than for charitable trusts, under which income can be accumulated for no more than twenty-one years.[112] The exception for charities is sensible, since money held by a charitable trust should regularly be spent in order to further the trust's charitable purposes.

6. POWERS AND DUTIES RELATING TO PROPERTY

Trustees have a variety of powers and duties relating to the administration of trust property.

(a) POWERS OVER LAND

Trustees of land have all of the powers of an absolute owner in respect of the land,[113] but they must have regard to the rights of the beneficiaries;[114] they have a duty to consult adult beneficiaries who have an interest in possession,[115] and they are subject to the statutory duty of care.[116] Trustees can convey land to the beneficiaries who are of full age and capacity, and who are absolutely entitled to the property, even if the beneficiaries have not requested the conveyance.[117]

The most significant power arising from trustees being in the position of absolute owners of the land is that they have a power to sell the land. Where trustees sell land that has been held on trust, they are able to give a valid written receipt only if the purchase money is received by two trustees or a trust corporation;[118] if it is not, the purchaser might be liable for loss or misapplication of the purchase money and the interests of the beneficiaries will not be overreached.

(b) POWERS RELATING TO PERSONAL PROPERTY

Where property other than land, such as chattels or shares, is held on trust, there may be an express power to sell the property. Written receipt of payment by one trustee is sufficient to discharge the purchaser, so that he or she will not be liable for loss or misapplication of the purchase money.[119]

(c) POWER TO RAISE CAPITAL MONEY

Where trustees, other than charitable trustees, are authorized to pay or apply capital money for any purpose, they have the power to raise the money by mortgaging property.

TRUSTEE ACT 1925

16. Power to raise money by sale, mortgage, &c

(1) Where trustees are authorised by the instrument, if any, creating the trust or by law to pay or apply capital money subject to the trust for any purpose or in any manner, they shall have and shall be

[112] Perpetuities and Accumulations Act 2009, s. 14.
[113] Trusts of Land and Appointment of Trustees Act 1996, s. 6.
[114] Ibid, s. 6(5).
[115] Ibid, s. 11(1).
[116] Ibid, s. 6(9).
[117] Ibid, s. 6(2).
[118] Trustee Act 1925, s. 14(2).
[119] Trustee Act 1925, s. 14(1).

> deemed always to have had power to raise the money required by sale, conversion, calling in, or mortgage of all or any part of the trust property for the time being in possession.
>
> (2) This section applies notwithstanding anything to the contrary contained in the instrument, if any, creating the trust, but does not apply to trustees of property held for charitable purposes, or to trustees of a settlement for the purposes of the Settled Land Act, 1925, not being also the statutory owners.

But this does not authorize trustees to raise money by charging existing investments in order to purchase others.[120]

(d) POWER TO INSURE

Trustees may insure trust property and pay the premiums from trust funds.

TRUSTEE ACT 1925

19. Power to insure

(1) A trustee may—

    (a) insure any property which is subject to the trust against risks of loss or damage due to any event, and

    (b) pay the premiums out of the trust funds.

(2) In the case of property held on a bare trust, the power to insure is subject to any direction given by the beneficiary or each of the beneficiaries—

    (a) that any property specified in the direction is not to be insured;

    (b) that any property specified in the direction is not to be insured except on such conditions as may be so specified.

(3) Property is held on a bare trust if it is held on trust for—

    (a) a beneficiary who is of full age and capacity and absolutely entitled to the property subject to the trust, or

    (b) beneficiaries each of whom is of full age and capacity and who (taken together) are absolutely entitled to the property subject to the trust.

(5) In this section 'trust funds' means any income or capital funds of the trust.

Any insurance money that is paid in respect of loss or damage to the property should be treated as capital money under the trust rather than income,[121] and it may be used to reinstate the property.[122]

(e) POWER OF COURT TO AUTHORIZE DEALINGS WITH TRUST PROPERTY

Where the trust instrument or any statute does not create a power for the trustees to deal with trust property, such as a power to sell the property, it is possible for the trustees or beneficiaries

---

[120] *Re Suenson-Taylor's Settlement Trusts* [1974] 1 WLR 1280.

[121] Trustee Act 1925, s. 20(1). For the relevance of this classification, see Chapter 12.5(b), pp. 614–16.

[122] Ibid, s. 20(4).

to apply to the court for the power to be conferred on the trustees, either for a specific transaction or generally.

TRUSTEE ACT 1925

57. Power of court to authorise dealings with trust property

Where in the management or administration of any property vested in trustees, any sale, lease, mortgage, surrender, release, or other disposition, or any purchase, investment, acquisition, expenditure, or other transaction, is in the opinion of the court expedient, but the same cannot be effected by reason of the absence of any power for that purpose vested in the trustees by the trust instrument, if any, or by law, the court may by order confer upon the trustees, either generally or in any particular instance, the necessary power for the purpose, on such terms, and subject to such provisions and conditions, if any, as the court may think fit and may direct in what manner any money authorised to be expended, and the costs of any transaction, are to be paid or borne as between capital and income.

(1) The court may, from time to time, rescind or vary any order made under this section, or may make any new or further order.

(2) An application to the court under this section may be made by the trustees, or by any of them, or by any person beneficially interested under the trust.

7. POWERS OF DELEGATION

Originally, a trustee was expected to perform all of his or her duties personally. In reality, this has proved to be impracticable, especially as the size of trust funds have increased, and over the years it has become possible for trustees collectively to delegate certain functions to other people. Initially this was the result of judicial development, but there is now a relevant statutory regime to be found in Part IV of the Trustee Act 2000.

(a) DELEGATION TO AGENTS

Trustees have a statutory power collectively to appoint an agent with the authority to exercise any or all of the trustees' delegable functions.

(i) *Power to appoint agents*

TRUSTEE ACT 2000

11. Power to employ agents

(1) Subject to the provisions of this Part, the trustees of a trust may authorise any person to exercise any or all of their delegable functions as their agent.

(2) In the case of a trust other than a charitable trust, the trustees' delegable functions consist of any function other than—

(a) any function relating to whether or in what way any assets of the trust should be distributed,[123]

(b) any power to decide whether any fees or other payment due to be made out of the trust funds should be made out of income or capital,[124]

(c) any power to appoint a person to be a trustee of the trust,[125] or

(d) any power conferred by any other enactment or the trust instrument which permits the trustees to delegate any of their functions or to appoint a person to act as a nominee or custodian.[126]

(3) In the case of a charitable trust, the trustees' delegable functions are—

(a) any function consisting of carrying out a decision that the trustees have taken;

(b) any function relating to the investment of assets subject to the trust (including, in the case of land held as an investment, managing the land and creating or disposing of an interest in the land);

(c) any function relating to the raising of funds for the trust otherwise than by means of profits of a trade which is an integral part of carrying out the trust's charitable purpose;

(d) any other function prescribed by an order made by the Secretary of State.[127]

(4) For the purposes of subsection (3)(c) a trade is an integral part of carrying out a trust's charitable purpose if, whether carried on in the United Kingdom or elsewhere, the profits are applied solely to the purposes of the trust and either—

(a) the trade is exercised in the course of the actual carrying out of a primary purpose of the trust, or

(b) the work in connection with the trade is mainly carried out by beneficiaries of the trust.

(ii) *People who may act as agents*

Trustees may authorize one or more of their number to exercise delegable functions as an agent on behalf of all of the trustees,[128] but they cannot appoint a beneficiary as an agent even if the beneficiary is also a trustee.[129] The powers to appoint agents can be restricted or excluded by the trust instrument.[130]

(iii) *Linked functions*

The person who is appointed as an agent to exercise a particular function is subject to the specific duties or restrictions that attach to that function.[131] So, for example, an agent who is authorized to exercise the general power of investment is bound to consider the standard investment criteria.[132]

---

[123] See Chapter 13.2, pp. 630–8.

[124] See Chapter 12.5(b), pp. 614–16.

[125] See Chapter 11.3(d), pp. 537–48.

[126] See Chapter 12.7(e), pp. 625–6.

[127] The Secretary of State has not done so and there are no plans to do so.

[128] Trustee Act 2000, s. 12(1).

[129] Ibid, s. 12(3).

[130] Ibid, s. 26.

[131] Ibid, s. 13(1).

[132] See Chapter 12.4(b)(ii), pp. 595–6.

(iv) *Terms of appointment*

The appointment of an agent can generally be on such terms as the trustees determine.

TRUSTEE ACT 2000

14. Terms of agency

(1) Subject to subsection (2) and sections 15(2)[133] and 29 to 32,[134] the trustees may authorise a person to exercise functions as their agent on such terms as to remuneration and other matters as they may determine.

(2) The trustees may not authorise a person to exercise functions as their agent on any of the terms mentioned in subsection (3) unless it is reasonably necessary for them to do so.

(3) The terms are—

(a) a term permitting the agent to appoint a substitute;

(b) a term restricting the liability of the agent or his substitute to the trustees or any beneficiary;

(c) a term permitting the agent to act in circumstances capable of giving rise to a conflict of interest.

If an agent incurs expenses when acting on behalf of the trust[135] or exercising the functions of an agent,[136] he or she can be reimbursed from the trust fund. There is also a statutory power to remunerate agents for services provided to the trust if the agent was engaged on terms that entitled him or her to be remunerated and the amount paid does not exceed what is reasonable in the circumstances for the provision of that particular service.[137]

There are particular restrictions on the delegation of trustees' asset management functions, which include investing trust assets, and acquiring and managing trust property.[138] Such functions must be delegated by an agreement that is in writing or is evidenced in writing;[139] a written policy statement must be prepared that gives guidance as to how the delegated functions should be exercised in the best interests of the trust, such as any ethical considerations that should be borne in mind; and the agreement must include a term that the agent will comply with the policy statement.[140] Trustees have a duty to assess whether the policy statement is being complied with and a duty to consider whether it needs to be revised or replaced, and, if they decide that it does, they are under a duty to so revise or replace it.[141]

(b) APPOINTMENT OF NOMINEES AND CUSTODIANS

Trustees also have the power to appoint a nominee in respect of particular trust assets, such as shares, which are then vested in the nominated person who can exercise rights on behalf of the trustees, such as the right to vote. Trustees also have the power to appoint a custodian of particular trust assets to manage those assets. Appointments of nominees or custodians must be made in writing or be evidenced in writing.

---

[133] Delegation of asset management functions.
[134] See Chapter 11.6, pp. 554–61.
[135] Trustee Act 2000, s. 31(2).
[136] Ibid, s. 32(3).
[137] Ibid, s. 32(1).
[138] Ibid, s. 15(5).
[139] Ibid, s. 15(1).
[140] Ibid, s. 15(2).
[141] Ibid. s. 22(2).

TRUSTEE ACT 2000

16. Power to appoint nominees

(1) Subject to the provisions of this Part, the trustees of a trust may—

    (a) appoint a person to act as their nominee in relation to such of the assets of the trust as they determine (other than settled land), and

    (b) take such steps as are necessary to secure that those assets are vested in a person so appointed.

17. Power to appoint custodians

(1) Subject to the provisions of this Part, the trustees of a trust may appoint a person to act as a custodian in relation to such of the assets of the trust as they may determine.

(2) For the purposes of this Act a person is a custodian in relation to assets if he undertakes the safe custody of the assets or of any documents or records concerning the assets.

A person can be appointed as a nominee or custodian only if he or she is a professional nominee or custodian, or is a company controlled by the trustees.[142] The powers to appoint nominees or custodians can be restricted or excluded by the trust instrument.[143] The nominee or custodian can be reimbursed expenses[144] and can be remunerated for reasonable services provided.[145]

The power to appoint nominees might be considered to be controversial, since it appears to contradict one of the key characteristics of a trustee, namely that trust property is vested in the trustee who has control of it.[146] Where a nominee is appointed, the trust property will be vested in the nominee, who then acquires legal title to it. But this is for the better administration of the trust and is, therefore, an appropriate power, especially because the trustee remains responsible for reviewing the arrangements, so can still be regarded as retaining control over the property.

(c) REVIEWING DELEGATION ARRANGEMENTS

Where trustees have appointed an agent, custodian, or nominee, the trustees are under a duty to keep the arrangements under review.

TRUSTEE ACT 2000

22. Review of agents, nominees and custodians etc.

(1) While the agent, nominee or custodian continues to act for the trust, the trustees—

    (a) must keep under review the arrangements under which the agent, nominee or custodian acts and how those arrangements are being put into effect,

---

[142] Ibid, s. 19(2).
[143] Ibid, s. 26.
[144] Ibid, s. 32(3).
[145] Ibid, s. 32(1).
[146] *Webb v Jonas* (1888) 39 Ch D 660. See Chapter 11.1(a), pp. 527–8.

  (b) if circumstances make it appropriate to do so, must consider whether there is a need to exercise any power of intervention that they have, and

  (c) if they consider that there is a need to exercise such a power, must do so.

  (4) 'Power of intervention' includes—

  (a) a power to give directions to the agent, nominee or custodian;

  (b) a power to revoke the authorisation or appointment.

(d) LIABILITY OF TRUSTEES

TRUSTEE ACT 2000

23. Liability for agents, nominees and custodians etc.

  (1) A trustee is not liable for any act or default of the agent, nominee or custodian unless he has failed to comply with the duty of care applicable to him, under paragraph 3 of Schedule 1—[147]

  (a) when entering into the arrangements under which the person acts as agent, nominee or custodian, or

  (b) when carrying out his duties under section 22.

  (2) If a trustee has agreed a term under which the agent, nominee or custodian is permitted to appoint a substitute, the trustee is not liable for any act or default of the substitute unless he has failed to comply with the duty of care applicable to him, under paragraph 3 of Schedule 1—

  (a) when agreeing that term, or

  (b) when carrying out his duties under section 22 in so far as they relate to the use of the substitute.

The effect of this provision is that, if the trustees have exercised such skill and care as is reasonable in the circumstances as regards the appointment of the agent, nominee, or custodian, and in reviewing the arrangements, they will not be vicariously liable if the agent, nominee or custodian has caused loss by acting negligently.

If a trustee exceeds the statutory powers in authorizing a person to exercise functions as an agent or in appointing a nominee or custodian, the authorization or appointment is not invalidated.[148] Consequently, any action of the agent, nominee, or custodian that is within the scope of his or her own authority will be effective and binding on the trust.

The statutory duty of care under the Trustee Act 2000 applies to trustees as regards appointment and reviewing arrangements.

TRUSTEE ACT 2000

Schedule 1

3 (1) The duty of care applies to a trustee—

  (a) when entering into arrangements under which a person is authorised under section 11 to exercise functions as an agent;

---

[147] See Chapter 12.2(b), pp. 589–90.
[148] Trustee Act 2000, s. 24.

(b) when entering into arrangements under which a person is appointed under section 16 to act as a nominee;

(c) when entering into arrangements under which a person is appointed under section 17 or 18 to act as a custodian;

(d) when entering into arrangements under which, under any other power, however conferred, a person is authorised to exercise functions as an agent or is appointed to act as a nominee or custodian;

(e) when carrying out his duties under section 22 (review of agent, nominee or custodian, etc).

(2) For the purposes of sub-paragraph (1), entering into arrangements under which a person is authorised to exercise functions or is appointed to act as a nominee or custodian includes, in particular—

(a) selecting the person who is to act,

(b) determining any terms on which he is to act, and

(c) if the person is being authorised to exercise asset management functions, the preparation of a policy statement under section 15.

(e) SPECIFIC POWERS OF DELEGATION

Various statutes make provision for specific powers of delegation. So, for example, it is possible for an individual trustee to delegate the execution or exercise of trusts, powers, or discretions.

TRUSTEE ACT 1925

25. Delegation of trustee's functions by power of attorney.

(1) Notwithstanding any rule of law or equity to the contrary, a trustee may, by power of attorney, delegate the execution or exercise of all or any of the trusts, powers and discretions vested in him as trustee either alone or jointly with any other person or persons.

(2) A delegation under this section—

(a) commences as provided by the instrument creating the power or, if the instrument makes no provision as to the commencement of the delegation, with the date of the execution of the instrument by the donor; and

(b) continues for a period of twelve months or any shorter period provided by the instrument creating the power.

(4) Before or within seven days after giving a power of attorney under this section the donor shall give written notice of it (specifying the date on which the power comes into operation and its duration, the donee of the power, the reason why the power is given and, where some only are delegated, the trusts, powers and discretions delegated) to—

(a) each person (other than himself), if any, who under any instrument creating the trust has power (whether alone or jointly) to appoint a new trustee; and

(b) each of the other trustees, if any;

but failure to comply with this subsection shall not, in favour of a person dealing with the donee of the power, invalidate any act done or instrument executed by the donee.

(7) The donor of a power of attorney given under this section shall be liable for the acts or defaults of the donee in the same manner as if they were the acts or defaults of the donor.

This provision operates differently from the powers of delegation under the Trustee Act 2000, since that Act concerns delegation of functions by the trustees collectively, whereas the power under the 1925 Act enables an individual trustee to delegate his or her functions for a limited period of time. Under the 1925 Act it is possible for a trustee to delegate functions to a beneficiary, in contrast to the regime under the 2000 Act. Moreover, the trustee who appoints an agent under the 1925 Act remains liable for the acts and omissions of the agent as if they were the acts and omissions of the trustee, whereas trustees who have delegated under the 2000 Act are not vicariously liable, but are personally liable only for failing to comply with the statutory duty of skill and care.

Another specific power of delegation relates to trustees of land who can collectively delegate to one or more beneficiary, who is of full age and beneficially entitled to an interest in possession in land that is subject to the trust, any of the trustees' functions relating to that land for any period or indefinitely.[149]

8. DUTY TO KEEP ACCOUNTS

Trustees must keep accounts of the trust and are required to disclose them to beneficiaries if they so request.[150] Trustees have the power, rather than a duty, to have the trust accounts audited.

TRUSTEE ACT 1925

22. (4) Trustees may, in their absolute discretion, from time to time, but not more than once in every three years unless the nature of the trust or any special dealings with the trust property make a more frequent exercise of the right reasonable, cause the accounts of the trust property to be examined or audited by an independent accountant, and shall, for that purpose, produce such vouchers and give such information to him as he may require; and the costs of such examination or audit, including the fee of the auditor, shall be paid out of the capital or income of the trust property, or partly in one way and partly in the other, as the trustees, in their absolute discretion, think fit, but, in default of any direction by the trustees to the contrary in any special case, costs attributable to capital shall be borne by capital and those attributable to income by income.

9. POWERS TO COMPOUND LIABILITIES AND TO SETTLE CLAIMS

Trustees have various powers to settle any claims relating to the trust or to enter into a compromise,[151] or they can extend the time of payment of money owed to the trust.[152] The trustees are not liable for

---

[149] Trusts of Land and Appointment of Trustees Act 1996, s. 9(1) and (5). Under the Trustee Delegation Act 1999, s. 1, trustees of land who are also beneficiaries can delegate all trustee functions relating to the land.

[150] *Pearse v Green* (1819) 1 Jac & W 135, 140 (Plumer MR).

[151] See *Re Earl of Strafford* [1980] Ch 28.

[152] Trustee Act 1925, s. 15.

any losses that arise from the exercise of these powers if they have complied with the statutory duty of care.[153]

TRUSTEE ACT 1925

15. Power to compound liabilities

A personal representative, or two or more trustees acting together, or, subject to the restrictions imposed in regard to receipts by a sole trustee not being a trust corporation, a sole acting trustee where by the instrument, if any, creating the trust, or by statute, a sole trustee is authorised to execute the trusts and powers reposed in him, may if and as he or they think fit—

(a) accept any property, real or personal, before the time at which it is made transferable or payable; or

(b) sever and apportion any blended trust funds or property; or

(c) pay or allow any debt or claim on any evidence that he or they think sufficient; or

(d) accept any composition or any security, real or personal, for any debt or for any property, real or personal, claimed; or

(e) allow any time of payment of any debt; or

(f) compromise, compound, abandon, submit to arbitration, or otherwise settle any debt, account, claim, or thing whatever relating to the testator's or intestate's estate or to the trust;

and for any of those purposes may enter into, give, execute, and do such agreements, instruments of composition or arrangement, releases, and other things as to him or them seem expedient, without being responsible for any loss occasioned by any act or thing so done by him or them if he has or they have discharged the duty of care set out in section 1(1) of the Trustee Act 2000.[154]

In *Alsop Wilkinson v Neary*,[155] it was held that a trustee, against whom hostile litigation had been brought challenging the validity of a settlement, was not under a duty to defend the trust, but should remain neutral, leaving it to the rival claimants to the beneficial interest to fight their own battles.

QUESTION

Alan and Brenda hold £100,000 on discretionary trust for Charles and Debbie, who are both eighteen years old. Alan and Brenda have no experience of financial matters. Brenda speaks to her next-door neighbour, Edward, about the best way to invest the trust fund. Edward, who is a solicitor, advises Brenda to invest half the money in a new high-tech company, IT Ltd, which he is helping to set up, and the remainder of the money in Fag Ltd, a highly profitable company, which manufactures and sells cigarettes. Knowing that the grandmother of Charles and Debbie died from lung cancer, Alan and Brenda decide not to invest in Fag Ltd, but they do invest £50,000 of the trust fund in IT Ltd. Alan and Brenda do not know what to do with the remaining £50,000 of the trust fund, so they give the money to Edward, telling him to 'invest it wisely'. Edward invests the money in IT Ltd. IT Ltd has been an unmitigated failure. Its shares are now worthless.

Consider the potential liability of Alan and Brenda.

---

[153] See Chapter 12.2(b), pp. 589–90.
[154] Ibid.
[155] [1996] 1 WLR 220. See Chapter 11.6(b), pp. 556–9.

FURTHER READING

Ford, 'Trustee Investment and Modern Portfolio Theory' (1996) 10(4) TLI 102.

Getzler, 'Duty of Care' in *Breach of Trust* (eds Birks and Pretto) (Oxford: Hart, 2002), p. 41.

Nicholls of Birkenhead, Lord, 'Trustees and Their Broader Community: Where Duty, Morality and Ethics Converge' (1995) 9(3) TLI 71.

Nobles, 'Charities and Ethical Investment' [1992] Conv 115.

Thornton, 'Ethical Investments: A Case of Disjointed Thinking' (2008) CLJ 396.

13

DISPOSITIVE POWERS AND DUTIES

CENTRAL ISSUES

1. Dispositive powers and duties relate to the distribution of trust property to beneficiaries or objects.

2. Trustees may have various powers relating to the appointment of trust property to beneficiaries. These powers relate to whether an appointment should be made and, if so, in whose favour it should be exercised and what should be appointed.

3. There are various consequences of a dispositive power not being exercised, including liability for breach of trust and the court's exercising the power instead. Sometimes the trustees may be authorized by the court to exercise the power late.

4. Where beneficiaries of an express trust have a right to receive a distribution, the trustees are under a duty to find the beneficiaries

and to make distributions, without any demand for payment first being required from the beneficiaries.

5. Where there is doubt as to a beneficiary's entitlement, or the identity or location of possible beneficiaries, there are various mechanisms to enable distributions to be made without the trustees incurring liability for breach of trust.

6. Trustees have a statutory power of maintenance to pay income to a beneficiary even though that beneficiary is not yet entitled to receive the income under the terms of the trust instrument.

7. Trustees have a statutory power of advancement to pay capital from the trust for the advancement or benefit of a beneficiary before that beneficiary has a right to receive the capital.

1. NATURE OF DISPOSITIVE POWERS AND DUTIES

Dispositive powers and duties relate to the distribution of trust property to beneficiaries or objects. They are sometimes known as 'beneficial' powers and duties. The distinction between administrative and dispositive powers and duties may be difficult to draw,[1] but it is a distinction that needs to be made because different rules relate to administrative and dispositive powers and duties.

(1) The decision whether to exercise a dispositive power is a matter for the trustees to determine and is not subject to the duty of care,[2] either at common law or under the Trustee Act 2000. But,

[1] *Re Butlin's Will Trust* [1976] Ch 251, 263 (Brightman J).
[2] See Chapter 12.2, pp. 587–91.

once trustees have decided to exercise a discretionary power, the manner in which they exercise that power or exercise any dispositive duty will be assessed against the reasonable standard of care. The statutory duty of care under the Trustee Act 2000 applies only to administrative functions, so only the common law duty of care will apply to the exercise of dispositive functions, although, as was seen in Chapter 12,[3] the preferable view is that there is no difference between statutory and common law duties of care.

(2) Whereas many administrative functions can be delegated, it is not possible to delegate any dispositive function that relates to whether and in what way any of the trust assets should be distributed.[4] In other words, all decisions about the exercise of dispositive functions must be made by the trustees rather than delegated to an agent.

(3) Trustees are not permitted to release their dispositive powers.[5] Trustees must exercise their dispositive powers validly, so, for example, the powers must be exercised for a proper purpose and not capriciously. In other words, the doctrine of fraud on the power applies.[6] If the trustees breach a duty in the exercise of the power, that exercise is voidable following the decision in *Pitt v Holt*.[7]

2. POWERS OF APPOINTMENT

Trustees may have various powers relating to the appointment of trust property to beneficiaries, including the power to decide whether to make an appointment of trust property at all and, if an appointment is to be made, to whom it is to be made and in what proportion. The nature of a power of appointment will turn on whether it is a trust power, which must be exercised, or a fiduciary power, which may be exercised.[8]

(a) EXERCISING POWERS OF APPOINTMENT

(i) *Trust power*

The method of exercising a trust power of appointment was considered by Lord Wilberforce in *McPhail v Doulton*:[9]

> a trustee with a duty to distribute, particularly among a potentially very large class, would surely never require the preparation of a complete list of names, which anyhow would tell him little that he needs to know. He would examine the field, by class and category; might indeed make diligent and careful inquiries, depending on how much money he had to give away and the means at his disposal, as to the composition and needs of particular categories and of individuals within them; decide upon certain priorities or proportions, and then select individuals according to their needs or qualifications. If he acts in this manner, can it really be said that he is not carrying out the trust? ...

---

[3] See Chapter 12.2(c), pp. 590–1.
[4] Trustee Act 2000, s. 11(2). A general non-fiduciary power of appointment can be delegated, but such a power is, by definition, not held by a trustee: *Re Triffitt's Settlement* [1958] Ch 852, 861 (Upjohn J).
[5] See Chapter 11.7(e), p. 570.
[6] See Chapter 11.7(f)(vii), pp. 575–7.
[7] [2013] UKSC 26; [2013] 2 AC 108. See Chapter 11.7(g), pp. 577–83.
[8] See Chapter 2.6(h), pp. 51–5.
[9] [1971] AC 424, 457.

Then, as to the trustees' duty of inquiry or ascertainment, in each case the trustees ought to make such a survey of the range of objects or possible beneficiaries as will enable them to carry out their fiduciary duty ... A wider and more comprehensive range of inquiry is called for in the case of trust powers than in the case of powers.

It has been recognized that, in very large discretionary trusts, the trustee must assess the size of the class in a business-like way,[10] this being the language of the common law duty of care, which still applies to the exercise of powers of appointment.[11] If the trustees make a distribution to the objects without conducting a reasonable survey of the class, and of the needs of particular categories and individuals, the trustees will be liable for breach of trust.

If a trustee exercises the trust power improperly, for example, by distributing outside the range of objects as defined by the trust instrument, or by exercising the power capriciously,[12] the exercise of the power will be void.[13]

(ii) *Fiduciary power*

Where the trustees have a fiduciary power of appointment, they are subject to a duty to consider the exercise of the power periodically, but they are not required to exercise it.

Re Hay's Settlement Trusts [1982] 1 WLR 202, 209 (Megarry V-C)

In the case of a trust, of course, the trustee is bound to execute it, and if he does not, the court will see to its execution. A mere power is very different. Normally the trustee is not bound to exercise it, and the court will not compel him to do so. That, however, does not mean that he can simply fold his hands and ignore it, for normally he must from time to time consider whether or not to exercise the power, and the court may direct him to do this.

When he does exercise the power, he must, of course (as in the case of all trusts and powers) confine himself to what is authorised, and not go beyond it. But that is not the only restriction. Whereas a person who is not in a fiduciary position is free to exercise the power in any way that he wishes, un-hampered by any fiduciary duties, a trustee to whom, as such, a power is given is bound by the duties of his office in exercising that power to do so in a responsible manner according to its purpose. It is not enough for him to refrain from acting capriciously; he must do more. He must 'make such a survey of the range of objects or possible beneficiaries ...' as will enable him to carry out his fiduciary duty. He must find out 'the permissible area of selection and then consider responsibly, in individual cases, whether a contemplated beneficiary was within the power and whether, in relation to other possible claimants, a particular grant was appropriate': *In re Baden (No. 1)* [1971] AC 424, 449, 457 *per* Lord Wilberforce ... The last proposition, relating to the survey and consideration, at first sight gives rise to some difficulty. It is now well settled that no mere power is invalidated by it being impossible to ascertain every object of the power; provided the language is clear enough to make it possible to say whether any given individual is an object of the power, it need not be possible to compile a complete list of every object: see *In re Gestetner Settlement* [1953] Ch 672, 688; *In re Gulbenkian's Settlements* [1970] AC 508; *In re Baden (No. 1)* [1971] AC 424. As Harman J said in the *Gestetner* case [1953] 1 Ch

---

[10] *Re Baden's Deed Trusts (No. 2)* [1973] Ch 9, 20 (Sachs LJ).
[11] See Chapter 12.2(a), pp. 587–9.
[12] *Re Manisty's Settlement* [1974] Ch 17. See Chapter 3.4(c), pp. 105–9.
[13] See Chapter 11.7(f), pp. 571–7.

> 672, 688, the trustees need not 'worry their heads to survey the world from China to Peru, when there are perfectly good objects of the class in England.'
>
> That brings me to the third point. How is the duty of making a responsible survey and selection to be carried out in the absence of any complete list of objects? This question was considered by the Court of Appeal in *In re Baden (No. 2)* [1973] Ch 9. ... The trustee must not simply proceed to exercise the power in favour of such of the objects as happen to be at hand or claim his attention. He must first consider what persons or classes of persons are objects of the power within the definition in the settlement or will. In doing this, there is no need to compile a complete list of the objects, or even to make an accurate assessment of the number of them: what is needed is an appreciation of the width of the field, and thus whether a selection is to be made merely from a dozen or, instead, from thousands or millions ... Only when the trustee has applied his mind to the size of the problem 'should he then consider in individual cases whether, in relation to other possible claimants, a particular grant is appropriate. In doing this, no doubt he should not prefer the undeserving to the deserving; but he is not required to make an exact calculation whether, as between deserving claimants, A is more deserving than B: see *In re Gestetner Settlement* [1953] Ch 672, 688, approved in *In re Baden (No. 1)* [1971] AC 424, 453.
>
> If I am right in these views, the duties of a trustee which are specific to a mere power seem to be threefold. Apart from the obvious duty of obeying the trust instrument, and in particular of making no appointment that is not authorised by it, the trustee must, first, consider periodically whether or not he should exercise the power; second, consider the range of objects of the power; and third, consider the appropriateness of individual appointments. I do not assert that this list is exhaustive; but as the authorities stand it seems to me to include the essentials, so far as relevant to the case before me.

It follows that, whilst a fiduciary power need not be exercised, the trustees must at least consider its exercise.

(b) CONSEQUENCES OF A FAILURE TO EXERCISE A DISPOSITIVE POWER

Where a trustee fails to exercise a trust power within a reasonable time, he or she will be liable for breach of trust by virtue of failing to make an appointment. Similarly, the trustees will be liable for breach of trust if they fail to consider whether or not to exercise a fiduciary power in a reasonable time. But, where trustees fail to make an appointment under a fiduciary power, they will not be liable, since they are not under any duty to make an appointment.

In addition to potential liability for breach of trust, there may be other consequences should trustees fail to exercise a power of appointment.

(i) *Trust power*

If a trustee fails to exercise a trust power, the court will endeavour to fulfil the settlor's or testator's intent by securing execution of the power. In *McPhail v Doulton*,[14] Lord Wilberforce said:

> But in the case of a trust power, if the trustees do not exercise it, the court will ... I would venture to amplify this by saying that the court, if called upon to execute the trust power, will do so in the manner best calculated to give effect to the settlor's or testator's intentions. It may do so by appointing new

---

[14] [1971] AC 424, 457.

trustees,[15] or by authorising or directing representative persons of the classes of beneficiaries to prepare a scheme of distribution, or even, should the proper basis for distribution appear by itself directing the trustees so to distribute.

In addition, the court may direct the trustees to exercise their discretion. In *Tempest v Lord Camoys*,[16] Jessel MR recognized that:

in all cases where there is a trust or duty coupled with the power the Court will then compel the trustees to carry it out in a proper manner and within a reasonable time.

Re Locker's Settlement [1977] 1 WLR 1323

Trustees held property on a discretionary trust with a duty to apply all the income to the objects of the trust, but they accumulated the income for a number of years. Goulding J held that, since they had failed to distribute the income within a reasonable time, the trustees had breached their trust, but the trustees were authorized to exercise their discretion out of time.[17]

A court of equity, where trustees have failed to discharge their duty of prompt discretionary distribution of income, is concerned to make them as owners of the trust assets at law dispose of them in accordance with the requirements of conscience; that is, to give benefits to the *cestuis que trust* in accordance with the confidence that the settlor reposed in them, the trustees. In a case such as the present, where the trustees desire to repair their breach of duty, and to make restitution by doing late what they ought to have done early, and where they are in no way disabled from doing so, the court should, in my judgment, permit and encourage them to take that course. A tardy distribution at the discretion of the trustees is, after all, nearer to prompt distribution at the discretion of the trustees, which is what the settlor intended, than tardy distribution by the trustees at the discretion of someone else. There are, no doubt, cases where a manifestation of obstinacy or bias on the part of the trustees, or of hostility and suspicion (even unjustified hostility and suspicion) on the part of the potential *cestuis que trust*, or some other circumstance, must make such a solution of the problem inadvisable. The court may readily listen to the misgivings of potential beneficiaries who have been unable to get the trustees to exercise their discretion after repeated requests and are hoping themselves, if they have the *locus standi* to do so, to invoke the court's jurisdiction. The other solutions recommended by Lord Wilberforce [in *McPhail v Doulton*][18] are then available to the court. ...

It has been argued by Mr. Blackburne, on behalf of some of the objects of the trust, that once a reasonable time for the distribution of a particular item of income has elapsed, the trustees' discretion over that income is extinguished and either cannot be revived, or ought not to be revived, by the court. That submission is founded on *In re Allen-Meyrick's Will Trusts* [1966] 1 WLR 499[19] and *In re Gulbenkian's Settlements (No 2)* [1970] Ch 408. They, however, concerned permissive, as distinct from obligatory, discretionary powers, and in each case the trust instrument contained a subsisting trust to take effect in default of exercise of the power. The discretion of the trustees ought to be exercised promptly, if at all, where its exercise is optional, just as it ought to be exercised promptly in every case where its

---

[15] See Chapter 11.3(f), pp. 544–8.
[16] (1882) 21 Ch D 571, 578.
[17] [1977] 1 WLR 1323, 1325.
[18] [1971] AC 424.
[19] See Chapter 13.2(b)(ii), pp. 636–7.

exercise is obligatory. But the consequences of non-exercise are to my mind quite different in the two situations. In the cases cited, failure to exercise the permissive power within the proper limits of time left the default trust standing. In the case of an obligatory power (in other words, a compelling trust to distribute), the failure to execute the trust promptly is an unfulfilled duty still in existence. Therefore, as it seems to me, the *Allen-Meyrick* and *Gulbenkian* cases do not carry me any further. It follows from Lord Wilberforce's observations in [*McPhail v Doulton*], that if the court appoints new trustees to remedy their predecessors' default, they, the new trustees, can execute the neglected discretionary trust (being one of a mandatory character). *A fortiori*, it seems to me, the court can permit the existing trustees, if willing and competent to do so, to repair their own inaction.

This late exercise of the power of appointment by the trustees is preferable to the discretion being exercised by somebody else, because the settlor had intended the trustees to exercise the discretion,[20] and it is better that the discretion be exercised late rather than never exercised at all.

(ii) *Fiduciary power*

It has been assumed that, if a trustee fails to exercise a fiduciary power of appointment within a reasonable time, the power will simply lapse and the court will not compel performance,[21] unless there was an improper purpose behind the failure to exercise the power,[22] although the court might still be willing to compel the trustee to consider whether or not the power should be exercised.[23] However, in *Mettoy Pension Trustees Ltd v Evans*,[24] it was recognized that the court has similar powers of intervention for failure to exercise a fiduciary power as apply to the failure to exercise a trust power of appointment, including appointing replacement trustees, ordering a scheme of distribution to be prepared by the objects of the power, or even directing the exercise of the power itself.

Mettoy Pension Trustees Ltd v Evans [1990] 1 WLR 1587

Mettoy Co. plc had been wound up with a surplus in its pension fund. The company had a power of appointment in favour of the pensioners, with any surplus not appointed to them going to the company. The liquidator wished to release the company's power of appointment and pay the surplus from the pension fund to the company's creditors. The company's power of appointment was characterized as a fiduciary power. Being such it was held that the power could not simply be released; the donee of the power had a duty to consider its exercise. But the original donee of the power was the company, which could not exercise it because it had gone into liquidation. The liquidator could not properly exercise the power, because he had a conflict of interest between his duty to the creditors of the company and his duty to the pensioners to consider whether it was appropriate to consider the exercise of the power. Warner J said:[25]

The question then arises, if the discretion is a fiduciary power which cannot be exercised either by the receivers or by the liquidator, who is to exercise it? ... The discretion cannot be exercised by the

---

[20] *Re Locker's Settlement* [1977] 1 WLR 1323, 1325 (Goulding J).
[21] *McPhail v Doulton* [1971] AC 424, 456 (Lord Wilberforce).
[22] *Klug v Klug* [1908] 2 Ch 67.
[23] *Re Hay's ST* [1982] 1 WLR 202, 209 (Sir Robert Megarry V-C).
[24] [1990] 1 WLR 1587.
[25] Ibid, 1617.

directors of the company, because on the appointment of the liquidator all the powers of the directors ceased. I was referred to a number of authorities on the circumstances in which the court may interfere with or give directions as to the exercise of discretions vested in trustees, namely *Gisborne v Gisborne* (1877) 2 App.Cas. 300; *In re Hodges* (1878) 7 Ch. D 754; *Tabor v Brooks* (1878) 10 Ch D 273; *Klug v Klug* [1918] 2 Ch 67; *In re Allen-Meyrick's Will Trusts* [1966] 1 WLR 499; *In re Baden's Deed Trusts* [1971] AC 424; *In re Manisty's Settlement* [1974] Ch 17, 25–26 and *In re Locker's Settlement* [1977] 1 WLR 1323. None of those cases deals directly with a situation in which a fiduciary power is left with no one to exercise it. They point however to the conclusion that in that situation the court must step in. [Having quoted from the judgment of Lord Wilberforce in *McPhail v Doulton*,[26] he continued:] In that latter part he was indicating how the court might give effect to a discretionary trust when called on to execute it. It seems to me however that the methods he indicated could be equally appropriate in a case where the court was called on to intervene in the exercise of a discretion in category 2 [fiduciary power]. In saying that, I do not overlook that, in *In re Manisty's Settlement* [1974] Ch 17, 25, Templeman J expressed the view that the only right and the only remedy of an object of the power who was aggrieved by the trustees' conduct would be to apply to the court to remove the trustees and appoint others in their place. However, the earlier authorities to which I was referred, such as *In re Hodges*, (1878) 7 Ch D 754 and *Klug v Klug* [1918] 2 Ch 67, had not been cited to Templeman J. I conclude that, in a situation such as this, it is open to the court to adopt whichever of the methods indicated by Lord Wilberforce appears most appropriate in the circumstances.

Since there was nobody else who could exercise the power, it was held that the court would be willing to exercise the power according to a scheme of distribution that would need to be approved subsequently.

The decision in *Mettoy Pension Trustees* is potentially significant in its apparent assimilation of the judicial responses where there is a failure to exercise a trust power and a fiduciary power, although it might be confined in its operation to the particular context of pension trusts.[27]

Gardner, 'Fiduciary Powers in Toytown' (1991) 107 LQR 214, 216

For a long time, however, the fact that a power might be fiduciary was largely academic, because the remedies available to the objects for actually securing the performance of the donees' duty to consider it were very undeveloped. In *Re Wills' Trust Deeds* [1964] Ch 219 at p. 236, it was said that the only remedy for breach of the duty to the objects is to activate the gift over to the takers in default. A pyrrhic victory indeed. *Re Hay's Settlement Trusts* [1982] 1 WLR 202 at p. 209 did a little better for objects by stating that the court might direct donees to carry out their duty, and *Re Gestetner* [1953] Ch 672 at p. 688 and *Re Manisty's Settlement* [1974] Ch 17 at p. 25 said that new trustees might be appointed to do so. Even this response, however, was only possible where the time allowed for exercising the power had not yet expired (*Turner v Turner* [1984] Ch 100); where it had been allowed to expire, even by the wrongful inactivity of the donees, the gift over automatically took effect (*Re Allen-Meyrick's Will Trusts* [1966] 1 WLR 499 at p. 505). By contrast, in discretionary trusts, as well as ordering the trustees themselves to carry out their duty and appointing new ones to do so—even when the discretion is out of time (*Re Locker's Settlement Trusts* [1977] 1 WLR 1323)— it is possible to approve a scheme devised by the beneficiaries themselves, or, in the last resort, for the judge to exercise the discretion (*McPhail v Doulton* [1971] AC 424 at pp. 456-457). But given that powers of appointment may involve a duty to

---

[26] See Chapter 13.2(b)(i), pp. 632–3.
[27] See Chapter 2.4(b)(ix), pp. 33–6.

the objects, there seems to be no essential difference so far as the nature of that duty is concerned between them and discretionary trusts. The fact that such powers have a gift over in default simply means that there is an additional option in the discretion, rather than affecting its nature. In principle, then, the remedial needs of fully fiduciary powers of appointment are the same as those of discretionary trusts. The fact that the authorities on powers lagged in this way behind those on discretionary trusts seemed to indicate that the courts were still finding it difficult entirely to free themselves of the notion that such powers cannot be truly fiduciary.

In the *Mettoy* case, however, the established remedies for powers of appointment were of no help. It would have been impossible to leave the existing donee to exercise the discretion, because that was the Mettoy company itself, which was now represented by its liquidators. As donee, the liquidators would have been under a duty to give proper consideration to exercising the power in favour of the pensioners; but this conflicted with the duty they inherently owed the company's creditors, which would have impelled them to exercise the power in the company's own favour as taker in default. Nor (perhaps slightly puzzlingly) had there been a request for new trustees. So on the authorities as they stood for powers, there was an impasse. But Warner J now decided … that all the remedies available in discretionary trusts are equally available in fully fiduciary powers. He was therefore able to approve or dictate a scheme himself …

This adoption of discretionary trust remedies for fully fiduciary powers of appointment is of considerable doctrinal importance. *Ubi remedium, ibi jus.*[28] The idea of such powers involving duties to their objects no longer rests even partly on statements about these duties in the abstract: the new position on remedies means that they have now been given the most comprehensive available concrete form.

Despite this, it remains necessary to distinguish between trust powers and fiduciary powers, where the power of appointment is not exercised. If a fiduciary power is not exercised within a reasonable time, the power will lapse if the trust instrument provides for a gift-over to another person to take effect in such circumstances. In *Re Allen-Meyrick's Will Trust*,[29] the trustees had a power to distribute income for the maintenance of the testatrix's husband in their absolute discretion, and, subject to that power, to hold the trust property on trust for her godchildren in equal shares absolutely. The trustees failed to reach a decision as to whether to exercise the power for the benefit of the husband (the first defendant), who was an undischarged bankrupt. It was held that, after a reasonable time had elapsed from the receipt of the income, the trustees' discretion to apply it for the benefit of the husband terminated, and the income was held for the godchildren (the second and third defendants). Buckley J said:[30]

it is incumbent upon the trustees to make up their minds as income becomes distributable from time to time to what extent they will apply it for the maintenance of the first defendant, and to the extent that they do not decide so to apply it the trust for the benefit of the second and third defendants attaches to the fund and it becomes theirs.

As I have said, the trustees have been making certain payments for the benefit of the first defendant and have accumulated in their hands a certain fund of undistributed income. So far as a reasonable period after receipt of any part of that accumulated fund has elapsed, I think that the trustees' discretion in respect thereof must be treated as being at an end. It is true that the reason why they have accumulated that fund is that they have not been able to agree how their discretion should be exercised; but that discretion if exercised at all must be exercised by the trustees unanimously. If they have not succeeded in being unanimous, they have not succeeded in exercising their discretion.

[28] 'Where there is a remedy, there is a right.'
[29] [1966] 1 WLR 499.
[30] Ibid, 505.

Another key difference between trust powers and fiduciary powers that have not been exercised is that, where the exercise of the power is specifically time-limited, then, as regards trust powers, the court may be willing to allow trustees to exercise the power late,[31] but it has been held that a fiduciary power cannot be exercised late.

Breadner v Granville-Grossman [2001] Ch 523

A fixed trust had been established for the testator's cousins, subject to the trustees' exercising a fiduciary power of appointment before a particular date. The trustees exercised the power of appointment a day late and sought the confirmation of the court that the exercise of the power was valid. Park J held that the power could not be exercised late.[32]

The 1976 power expired at midnight on 1 August 1989 and had not been exercised. Until then the cousins' beneficial property rights, which had been vested in them by the 1976 appointment, were defeasible by an exercise of the 1976 power. At the precise point in time when the 1976 power expired the possibility of the cousins' property rights being defeated disappeared. Their rights were no longer vested but defeasible. They were vested indefeasibly. [Counsel's] argument amounts to saying that I have an equitable jurisdiction to deprive trust beneficiaries of indefeasibly vested interests. That would be a very strong thing for a court to do and I do not accept that I have the power to do it.

At the time when I am writing this judgment there exists a fund of money and investments, the legal ownership of which is vested in the trustees. Who owns the fund beneficially? Certainly not the trustees, so how do I find out who does? The answer is: from the terms of the trust instruments ...

It is trite law that there is a distinction between two kinds of dispositive discretion which may be vested in trustees. There are discretions which the trustees have a duty to exercise (sometimes called 'trust powers') and discretions which the trustees may exercise but have no duty to exercise (sometimes called 'mere powers'). The distinction is most familiar in the context of discretions to distribute income. In cases of trust powers the trustees are bound to distribute the income, but have a discretion as to how it should be divided between the beneficiaries. In cases of mere powers the trustees have two discretions: first, a discretion whether to distribute the income or not; and second, if they decide that they will exercise the first discretion, a further discretion as to how to divide the income between the beneficiaries. In the latter kind of case there will usually be a default trust which deals with the income if the trustees do not exercise their discretion to distribute it. Typically the default trust will provide for the undistributed income to be accumulated or to be paid as of right to a beneficiary whose interest in it is vested but defeasible by the trustees exercising their discretion to distribute....

Sometimes the distinction does not matter, but there is an important difference between the two kinds of case if the trustees do not exercise the discretion to distribute income within the normal time for exercising it. That time is usually 'a reasonable time'. If there is a trust power and, although the trustees are required to exercise it within a reasonable time, they do not do so, the discretion still exists. If the trustees are willing to exercise it, albeit later than they should have done, the court will permit them to do so. That is what happened in *In re Locker's Settlement*.[33] Alternatively the court will exercise the discretion itself. But if the discretion to distribute is a mere power, and the trustees do not exercise it within a reasonable time of the receipt of an item of income, the discretion no longer exists as respects

---

[31] See Chapter 13.2(b)(i), pp. 633–4.
[32] [2001] Ch 523, 540.
[33] See Chapter 13.2(b)(i), pp. 633–4.

that income. The default trusts take effect indefeasibly. That is what happened in *In re Allen-Meyrick's Will Trusts*.

The distinction between trust powers and mere powers is, as I have said, most commonly encountered in connection with powers to distribute income. But the distinction also exists in connection with other kinds of dispositive powers, including powers of appointment ...

Given that the 1976 power was a mere power which the trustees did not have to exercise, it ceased to be exercisable on 1 August 1989, and the fact that the trustees had failed to perform their duty to consider whether or not to exercise it cannot mean that it continued to be exercisable after all. The power had still expired, and it did not exist on 2 August 1989, when the trustees purported to exercise it. [Counsel] says that the duty to consider whether to exercise the power was ancillary to the power, and cannot have an independent and continuing existence apart from the power itself. I agree with him. The trustees' failure to consider whether to exercise the power may give rise to consequences between themselves and Jonathan, but it cannot mean that the interests of the cousins under the 1976 appointment continued to be defeasible after 1 August 1989 ...

I think the cousins are fortunate in the way that things worked out for them and I am sorry for Jonathan [the settlor's son], but my conscience does not impel me to say that the cousins must not be allowed to retain the interests which the deliberate actions of the settlor and the trustees have conferred upon them. Jonathan may or may not be able to recover what he has effectively lost through an action against the trustees. I accept that it will not be plain sailing for him, since apart from anything else there is a trustee-exoneration clause in the settlement. But any possibility of redress for Jonathan lies, if at all, in a claim against the trustees, and not in an attempt to take the cousins' property rights away from them.

The general tenor of *Breadner v Granville-Grossman* is inconsistent with the approach of the court in *Re Locker's Settlement*,[34] in which the court authorized a tardy exercise of a trust power, and with *Mettoy Pension Fund*, in which judicial responses to failure to exercise a trust power and a fiduciary power were assimilated, although that decision might be confined in its application to pension fund trusts. Perhaps the explanation for the approach in *Breadner* was that the power was specifically time-limited, so that the power had lapsed by the passage of time according to the clear words of the trust instrument, whereas in *Re Locker's Settlement* the terms of the trust instrument did not expressly limit the time for performance. Or perhaps the distinction simply reflects the essential nature of trust powers and fiduciary powers: a trust power does not lapse even if it has not been exercised within a reasonable time, whereas fiduciary powers do. It is also significant that, in *Breadner*, the default trust came into effect and it would not have been appropriate to deprive the trust beneficiaries of their rights by resurrecting the lapsed fiduciary power. It follows that, although the approach in *Breadner* appears to be inconsistent with that of *Locker* and *Mettoy*, it is possible to reconcile the decisions.

3. DUTY TO DISTRIBUTE

(a) DUTY TO INFORM BENEFICIARIES AND OBJECTS OF THEIR RIGHTS

Where beneficiaries of an express trust have a right to receive payment of income or capital, or both, the trustees are under a duty to find the beneficiaries and to make distributions to them as the money becomes due, without any demand for payment first being required from the beneficiaries.

---

[34] [1977] 1 WLR 1323.

Hawkesley v May

[1956] 1 QB 305, 322 (Havers J)

So far as an executor is concerned, I am bound by the decision of the Court of Appeal in *In re Lewis*[35] to hold that there is no legal duty upon him to give notice of the terms of the legacy to the legatee. I see no reason, however, to extend this doctrine, which has no attraction for me on the merits, to a trustee under an express trust. The position of an executor and a trustee, although now, for many purposes, assimilated under the Law of Property Act, 1925, is still not identical, and there is a distinction between a will, which is a public document in the sense that anybody can go to Somerset House and see it, and a trust deed, which is a private document to which the *cestui que trust* has no access. In the absence of any authority to the contrary I decline to extend this doctrine to trustees under an express trust.

I hold, therefore, that there was a duty upon the defendants Tidy and Collins, as trustees of the Musgrave settlement, to inform the plaintiff on attaining 21 that he had an interest in the capital and income of the trust funds of the Musgrave settlement. *A fortiori*, if the trustees did not hand over to the plaintiff on attaining 21 income to which he was entitled, it would be their duty to explain to him that he was entitled to call for and have the interest paid to him …

I hold that there was no duty on the trustees to give the plaintiff legal advice or to inform him of his right to sever, though they would be bound, in my opinion, to disclose on demand any document relating to the trust …

As to the third question, no authority was cited to me by any of the defendants in support of their proposition that the obligation on the trustees was to pay income, if income was payable to the plaintiff on attaining 21 (as I hold it was), only on demand. It seems to me that the passage which I have cited in *Low v Bouverie*[36] is contrary to that view, and no authority has been cited in support of the defendants' proposition … I hold that it was the duty of the trustees to pay the income of his share to the plaintiff on attaining the age of 21 without any demand by him; and also to pay the capital to the plaintiff and his sister as joint tenants upon the sister attaining 21 without any demand by them

The obligation of trustees to inform beneficiaries of their rights is a product of the fundamental principle of trustee accountability: trustees cannot be held accountable if beneficiaries are unaware of their right to receive trust property.[37]

As regards the objects of a discretionary trust, since they have a right to put their case to the trustees for the exercise of their discretion,[38] it follows that the trustees should be under a duty to take reasonable steps to draw this right to the objects' attention.[39] What constitutes reasonable steps will depend on the size of the class: trustees will not be expected to search for all possible objects where the class is very large.[40]

As regards fiduciary powers of appointment, the objects of the power have no right to be informed that they are objects.[41]

---

[35] [1904] 2 Ch 646.

[36] [1891] 3 Ch 82, 99.

[37] Fox, 'The Irreducible Core for a Valid Trust' (2011) 17 T&T 16, 20.

[38] *Murphy v Murphy* [1999] 1 WLR 282.

[39] Hayton, 'The Irreducible Core Content of Trusteeship', in *Trends in Contemporary Trust Law* (ed. Oakley) (Oxford: Clarendon Press, 1996), ch. 3.

[40] *Hartigan Nominees Pty Ltd v Rydge* (1992) 29 NSWLR 405, 432 (Mahoney JA).

[41] *Re Manisty's Settlement* [1974] Ch 17, 25 (Templeman J).

(b) TRUSTEE PROTECTION AGAINST LIABILITY
FOR OVERPAYMENT

Where there is doubt as to the beneficiary's entitlement, or known or suspected beneficiaries cannot be found, there are various steps that the trustees can take to ensure that the duty to distribute is fulfilled without breach of trust. This is particularly significant where the trustees wish to distribute all the trust assets so that there would be no trust property left to meet the claims of beneficiaries who subsequently come forward.

(i) *Directions from the court*

The trustees can apply to the court for directions[42] as to the claims of the beneficiaries and what they should do if an identified beneficiary cannot be found. If the trustees comply with the directions of the court, they cannot be liable to the beneficiary who did not receive any distribution or to creditors who come forward subsequently.[43]

(ii) *Advertisement for beneficiaries*

Trustees may advertise for unknown beneficiaries.

TRUSTEE ACT 1925

27. Protection by means of advertisements

(1) With a view to the conveyance to or distribution among the persons entitled to any real or personal property, the trustees of a settlement, trustees of land, trustees for sale of personal property or personal representatives may give notice by advertisement in the Gazette,[44] and in a newspaper circulating in the district in which the land is situated, and such other like notices, including notices elsewhere than in England and Wales, as would, in any special case, have been directed by a court of competent jurisdiction in an action for administration, of their intention to make such conveyance or distribution as aforesaid, and requiring any person interested to send to the trustees or personal representatives within the time, not being less than two months, fixed in the notice or, where more than one notice is given, in the last of the notices, particulars of his claim in respect of the property or any part thereof to which the notice relates.

(2) At the expiration of the time fixed by the notice the trustees or personal representatives may convey or distribute the property or any part thereof to which the notice relates, to or among the persons entitled thereto, having regard only to the claims, whether formal or not, of which the trustees or personal representatives then had notice and shall not, as respects the property so conveyed or distributed, be liable to any person of whose claim the trustees or personal representatives have not had notice at the time of conveyance or distribution; but nothing in this section—

    (a) prejudices the right of any person to follow the property, or any property representing the same, into the hands of any person, other than a purchaser, who may have received it; or

---

[42] Under the Civil Procedure Rules, Pt 64 and Practice Direction 64A.
[43] *Re Yorke* [1997] 4 All ER 907, 921 (Lindsay J).
[44] 'The Official Newspaper of Record', known as the *London Gazette*. It was first published in 1665 and claims to be the first newspaper in English.

(b) frees the trustees or personal representatives from any obligation to make searches or obtain official certificates of search similar to those which an intending purchaser would be advised to make or obtain.

(3) This section applies notwithstanding anything to the contrary in the will or other instrument, if any, creating the trust.

The effect of this provision is that, after the expiration of the time fixed by the advertisement, the trustees can make the distribution to those people who have claims of which the trustees had notice, and the trustees will not be personally liable to anybody of whose claim they did not have notice. But this provision does not prevent those who were entitled, but who did not come forward, from bringing a proprietary claim against the person who has received the property to which they were entitled, save where that property was received by a bona fide purchaser for value.[45]

The advertisement will protect the trustees from liability only if they have no notice of the beneficiaries' claims.

MCP Pension Trustees Ltd v Aon Pension Trustees Ltd [2010] EWCA Civ 377; [2012] Ch 1

A pension scheme was administered by the defendant on behalf of the claimant trustee. The claimant knew that some new members, known as 'the D and R transferees', had been transferred into the scheme from a different scheme. The defendant failed to maintain the scheme records properly, so that the names of the new members were removed from the relevant documents. The claimant sought to wind up the scheme and placed an advert requesting anybody with claims against the assets to make contact. Nobody came forward. The claimant distributed the assets, and then became aware of the claims of the new members, having forgotten about them, and settled a number of these claims. The claimant sued the defendant for damages for negligently maintaining the records. The defendant's liability turned on whether the claimant was protected from liability by placing the advert: if it were protected, the claimant would not have suffered any loss for which the defendant would be liable. In other words, the claimant was arguing that it was not protected from liability by placing the advert because it did have notice of the claims of the new members. It was held that, although the claimant had forgotten about the new members, it still had notice of the claims and so it was not protected by the advertisement. Elias J said:[46]

I turn to consider the section. The purpose is clear. If there was the possibility that beneficiaries or potential beneficiaries may emerge from the woodwork and make claims on the funds of a trust after the distribution, trustees would be unwilling to distribute because of the risk of personal liability to such claimants. This section therefore sets out a procedure which, if properly followed, relieves trustees of that risk.

There are three points to note about the drafting of the section and they are not in dispute. First, the section relieves the trustees from liability only with respect to claims of which they did not have notice at the time of distribution. If they did have notice they must honour the claim, even though the claimant does not reply to the advertisement made in pursuance of section 27 …

Second, there is no definition in the section or indeed elsewhere in the Act of what constitutes notice. Third, having regard to general concepts of equity, notice means actual or constructive notice and the

---

[45] See further Chapter 18.6(a), pp. 911–16.
[46] [2010] EWCA Civ 377; [2012] Ch 1, 26.

trustee may have constructive notice of a claim even though he does not have actual knowledge of it. As Lord Esher MR observed in *English and Scottish Mercantile Investment Co Ltd v Brunton* [1892] 2 QB 700, 708, constructive notice is 'wholly founded on the assumption that a man does not know the facts'. ...

In my judgment, this case can be resolved simply by focusing on the concept of actual notice ...

Since the assumption for the purposes of the preliminary hearing is that the D & R transferees did transfer to the works scheme, it is conceded, for the purposes at least in the preliminary issue, that the trustees did know of the transfers at the time of transfer and did accordingly have actual notice at that time that the D & R transferees were beneficiaries of the scheme. However, the defendant alleges that this does not constitute effective notice within the meaning of section 27 because the trustees had genuinely forgotten that they were beneficiaries by the time the funds were distributed. The submission is that once they had forgotten this fact they ceased to have knowledge of it; and that once they ceased to have knowledge of it, they ceased to have notice of it. It follows in my view that the only real issue which the court has to decide is whether a trustee who once had actual knowledge for [sic] the particular person as a beneficiary but who by the time of distribution of the funds has genuinely forgotten that fact can escape liability to that beneficiary by virtue of section 27.

The fundamental premise underlying the defendant's argument is that, at least for the purpose of identifying actual notice, knowledge and notice are the same thing. Once knowledge is lost notice ceases. This is linked with the submission that there is a temporal dimension to the question whether the trustees have notice. Section 27(2) provides in terms that the trustees are not liable to any person 'of whose claim the trustees ... have not had notice at the time of ... distribution'. The argument is that the trustees do not have notice at the time of distribution that someone is a beneficiary of the trust if they genuinely forget that fact, even though they had such notice at an earlier time. It is said that this does not create any injustice because the trustees have to prove, the onus being on them, that they have genuinely forgotten that fact and this would in practice be difficult to establish. However, if they can prove it, it is submitted that it is just that they should not be liable simply because their memory has failed them ...

Jeremy Cousins QC, sitting as a deputy judge of the Chancery Division ... held that section 27 merely requires that notice must have been given by the time of distribution. However, notice is not to be equated with knowledge and, even if the trustees forget that notice has been given, that does not cause the notice to lapse or otherwise negate the notice.

I agree with the conclusion reached by the judge. The trustees had actual notice of the interests of the beneficiaries, notwithstanding that the transferees did not reply to the advertisement ... The fact that the trustees had forgotten that they had notice is immaterial. I agree with the judge that knowledge and notice are different things and that, even on the assumption that forgetting something involves no longer having knowledge of it (itself an interesting philosophical point), the fact that the trustees may have forgotten that they had received notice by the time of distribution is quite irrelevant. Section 27 is only concerned with whether the notice has been received by the time funds are distributed. Once actual notice is given, then in general it will persist and remain notice at the time of distribution.

(iii) Benjamin *order*

A *Benjamin* order is made by a court to authorize the trustees to distribute all of the trust property or all of the assets of a deceased's estate even though, after all practical inquiries have taken place, the whereabouts, or even the continued existence, of all of the beneficiaries is not known.

In *Re Benjamin*,[47] Philip Benjamin was entitled, if still alive on the date of his father's death, to a share in his father's estate. His father died in June 1893, but Philip had disappeared in September 1892, and enquiries had failed to trace him. Joyce J said:[48]

> I think in this case that Philip David Benjamin must be presumed to be dead … The question is as to when he died. If he is to be presumed to be dead, I think the case of *Re Walker* (1871) 7 Ch App 120 distinctly applies, and the onus of proof is on his administrator. He has failed to adduce any evidence to shew that PD Benjamin survived the testator. I myself consider it highly probable that he died on 1 September, 1892, or at all events shortly after. I am clearly of opinion that the onus is on those claiming under him to prove that he survived the testator. In my opinion, therefore, the trustees are at liberty to distribute. I am anxious, however, not to do anything which would prevent his representative from making any claim if evidence of his death at any other time should be subsequently forthcoming. I shall not, therefore, declare that he is dead, but I will make an order in the following form:—
>
> > 'In the absence of any evidence that the said PD Benjamin survived the testator, let the trustees of the testator's will be at liberty to divide the share of the testator's estate devised and bequeathed in favour of the said PD Benjamin, his wife and children, upon the footing that PD Benjamin was unmarried and did not survive the testator.'

The purpose of the *Benjamin* order is to protect the trustees from liability if those beneficiaries who did not receive anything under the distribution subsequently come forward.

The potential reach of a *Benjamin* order was expanded in *Re Green's Will Trusts*.[49] The testatrix, Mrs Green, made her will in 1972 and left all her property to her son, Barry, with it going to charity if he did not claim it by 2020. Barry had not been heard of since 1943, when he was in a plane that disappeared over Berlin on a wartime bombing raid. Neither the plane nor the crew were ever found. The Air Ministry certified that all members of the crew were presumed dead. Barry's mother was convinced that her son had survived. She died in 1976. It was held that, since it was virtually certain that Barry was dead (and the evidence of death in this case was considered to be much stronger than in *Re Benjamin*), a *Benjamin* order would be made so that the executors of the will could distribute the estate on that assumption, even though this order conflicted with the testatrix's clear intention as expressed in the will. Nourse J[50] justified this decision as follows:

> The true view is that a *Re Benjamin* order does not vary or destroy beneficial interests. It merely enables trust property to be distributed in accordance with the practical probabilities, and it must be open to the court to take a view of those probabilities entirely different from that entertained by the testator.

The result of this case has been criticized due to the lack of respect afforded to the testator's wishes.

Luxton, 'Eluding the Dead Hand: A Live Issue?' [1986] Conv 138

> The decision is disturbing because the testatrix's express directions were avowedly disregarded. Nourse J did not accept that Mrs. Green's intention was determinative of what the court ought to do. He

---

[47] [1902] 1 Ch 723.
[48] Ibid, 725.
[49] [1985] 3 All ER 455.
[50] Ibid, 462.

said he could see 'emotional force' in such submission, but he did not think it could withstand 'the test of rational analysis.' …This is, with respect, a somewhat paternalistic attitude; and given the fact that the court made an order ignoring her express directions, the tribute to Mrs. Green's 'marvellous and enduring faith' sounds hollow, even patronising. Why, it must be asked, was adherence to those directions not a practical probability? Compliance with the express terms of the trust was surely perfectly practicable. Furthermore, in its use of a *Benjamin* order, *Re Green* does not extend, but on the contrary runs counter to, the principle (established in previous cases) underlying the use of such orders. This principle can be described as fidelity to testators' intentions. Thus, in none of the previous reported cases in which a *Benjamin* order has been made, has there been any conflict with the terms of the trust; rather the court has been faced with a situation which the testator either never envisaged or at least did not provide for. What the previous cases reveal instead is that, in facilitating the earlier distribution of the estate, the *Benjamin* order is at the very least not inconsistent with the testator's intentions (or what it may be presumed the testator would have intended if faced with the particular circumstances before the court).

The principle that a *Benjamin* order should not run roughshod over testators' intentions is seen most clearly in cases where the eventuality is not even foreseen, as in *Re Benjamin* itself, where the execution of the will preceded Phillip's disappearance. But the principle is equally applicable to cases in which the eventuality is merely not provided for, as where the will is made after the beneficiary's disappearance but contains no specific provision dealing with the consequent problem of the beneficiary's remaining hidden at the time the estate falls to be distributed …

Departure from the terms of Mrs. Green's will might not be of great significance if Nourse J's statement that the *Benjamin* order did not destroy beneficial interests could be accepted fully. Yet whilst this statement is true in theory, in practice a beneficiary tracing assets at a later date might well find his action of limited (or of no) value: the equitable tracing rules require the property to be identifiable, and there is no right to trace against a bona fide purchaser.[51] A recipient of trust property distributed under a *Benjamin* order is presumably an innocent volunteer; and, whilst a recipient of property wrongly distributed under a will is liable in a personal action to the beneficiary (*Re Diplock*),[52] there is no precedent for holding personally liable an innocent volunteer who has received property distributed under a *Benjamin* order. The order itself, of course, exempts the trustees from any liability. No comfort here then, for the missing beneficiary unable to trace.

It is difficult to resist the conclusion that the making of the *Benjamin* order in *Re Green* reflects a basic hostility to dispositions which the court does not consider that a reasonable testator would make …

Given the already stringent limitations on private trusts, it would be most regrettable if the courts were now to facilitate, by the subterfuge of a *Benjamin* order, distributions that could effectively destroy both the testator's express directions and a beneficiary's interest under a perfectly valid trust. Supported by the principle of fidelity to testator's intentions, the juridical basis of the *Benjamin* order is strong: set in conflict with those intentions, the juridical basis (now the mere convenience of facilitating an immediate distribution) is not merely weak, it is overthrown. In its disregard of testamentary intentions, the decision in *Re Green* is, in the final analysis, indefensible.

Although the decision does undermine the testator's wishes, since it was tolerably clear that the son was dead, this could be considered to be a case where delaying the distribution of the estate would have served no useful purpose.

If the beneficiary does eventually come forward, he or she cannot sue the trustee for breach of trust, because the trustee will be protected by the *Benjamin* order. The beneficiary will instead need to bring a proprietary claim in respect of the property that was transferred or a personal claim against the recipient of the trust property, although, as Luxton pointed out, this may well be fruitless. But the key

---

[51] See *MCP Pension Trustees Ltd v Aon Pension Trustees Ltd*.
[52] [1948] Ch 465, affd. sub. nom. *Ministry of Health v Simpson* [1951] AC 251.

benefit of the *Benjamin* order is that it allows trust property to be distributed whilst leaving open the possibility of the lost beneficiary coming forward and claiming what is rightfully his or hers if all the trust property has not yet been distributed.

(iv) *Insurance*

Another solution to the problem of a beneficiary appearing after the trust fund has been distributed is to take out a missing beneficiary insurance policy, which provides a fund to meet the claim of a missing beneficiary without imposing liability on the trustee or depriving the overpaid beneficiary of what he or she has received.

In *Re Evans*,[53] the defendant had been appointed the administrator of her deceased father's estate, which was held on trust for herself and her brother, the claimant. The defendant had not heard from her brother for thirty years and assumed that he was dead. She consequently distributed the estate to herself once she had taken out a missing beneficiary insurance policy. Her brother reappeared and issued proceedings in respect of certain matters concerning the administration of the estate, including the purchase of the insurance policy. Richard McCombe QC said:[54]

> In my view, personal representatives, particularly of small estates, should not be discouraged from seeking practical solutions to difficult administration problems, without the expense of resort to the court. Further, in small intestate administrations, where frequently the representative will have a personal interest, sizeable sums should not have to be tied up indefinitely for fear of the re-emergence of a long-lost beneficiary. The missing beneficiary policy does provide, at relatively small cost, a practical answer to such problems. Such a policy provides a fund to meet the claim of such a beneficiary in exoneration of the representative and of the overpaid beneficiary. The policy is to the advantage of all and is to some extent more effective than the limited protection provided by the more costly application to court for a *Benjamin* order. I am disinclined, therefore, to draw a distinction in this case between cases where the personal representative is beneficially entitled and those where he or she is not. It may be that circumstances will differ in future cases, but in my view the defendant was advised to take a practical course in circumstances where the beneficiary had been unheard of for nearly thirty years and to my mind the premium was a sensible and proper expense of this administration.

(v) *Retention of a fund*

The trustees may decide to make a distribution to the beneficiaries, but set aside a sum of money in a fund to be used to discharge any subsequent liabilities arising from overpaying beneficiaries. This fund may be used to satisfy claims from unpaid beneficiaries or creditors who subsequently come forward.[55] Specific provision is made by statute for the creation of such a fund to meet liabilities arising under a lease and then for the trustees to distribute the rest of the trust assets to those who are entitled to them.[56]

(vi) *Payment into court*

Trustees may pay the trust money into court if they can establish genuine doubt as to the identity and location of the beneficiaries, for example.

---

[53] [1999] 2 All ER 777.
[54] Ibid, 785.
[55] See *Re Yorke* [1997] 4 All ER 907, 921 (Lindsay J).
[56] Trustee Act 1925, s. 26(1).

TRUSTEE ACT 1925

63. Payment into court by trustees

(1) Trustees, or the majority of trustees, having in their hands or under their control money or securities belonging to a trust, may pay the same into court.

(2) The receipt or certificate of the proper officer shall be a sufficient discharge to trustees for the money or securities so paid into court.

(3) Where money or securities are vested in any persons as trustees, and the majority are desirous of paying the same into court, but the concurrence of the other or others cannot be obtained, the court may order the payment into court to be made by the majority without the concurrence of the other or others.

(4) Where any such money or securities are deposited with any banker, broker, or other depositary, the court may order payment or delivery of the money or securities to the majority of the trustees for the purpose of payment into court.

(5) Every transfer payment and delivery made in pursuance of any such order shall be valid and take effect as if the same had been made on the authority or by the act of all the persons entitled to the money and securities so transferred, paid, or delivered.

The effect of such payment into court is that the trustees retire from the trust.[57] The trustees will be discharged from their obligations to administer the funds[58] and their discretionary powers will be terminated.[59] They will, however, remain liable for past breaches[60] and responsible for any money intended for them as trustees that comes into their hands subsequently, but they will not be liable otherwise for anything that happens after they have paid money into the court.

(vii) Lawyer's opinion

Distribution in reliance on the opinion of an appropriately qualified lawyer may absolve trustees from liability in respect of the distribution, but only if the opinion is presented to the High Court and a judge agrees to sanction the distribution.

ADMINISTRATION OF JUSTICE ACT 1985

48. Power of High Court to authorise action to be taken in reliance on counsel's opinion

(1) Where—

(a) any question of construction has arisen out of the terms of a will or a trust; and

(b) an opinion in writing given by a person who has a 10 year High Court qualification... has been obtained on that question by the personal representatives or trustees under the will or trust,

---

[57] *Re Williams' Settlement* (1858) 4 K & J 87.
[58] *Re Lloyd's Trust* (1854) 2 WR 371.
[59] *Re Nettlefold's Trusts* (1888) 59 LT 315.
[60] *Barker v Peile* (1865) 2 Drew & Sm 340.

> the High Court may, on the application of the personal representatives or trustees and without hearing argument, make an order authorising those persons to take such steps in reliance on the said opinion as are specified in the order.
>
> (2) The High Court shall not make an order under subsection (1) if it appears to the court that a dispute exists which would make it inappropriate for the court to make the order without hearing argument.

(c) WRONGFUL DISTRIBUTION

Where trustees have transferred trust property to the wrong beneficiary or have transferred too much property to one beneficiary, the trustees could bring a restitutionary claim against the recipient of the property. There are two potential claims that are open to the trustees in such circumstances.

(i) *Proprietary claim*

The trustee may seek to recover the property, or its identifiable substitute, that has been mistakenly transferred to the beneficiary, on the ground that the trustee has a continuing proprietary interest in that property.[61] This can be established by resorting to the equitable jurisdiction to set aside voluntary dispositions for mistake.[62]

(ii) *Personal claim*

Alternatively, the trustee may have a personal claim to recover the value of the property that has been transferred to the wrong person. Such a claim would arise within the law of unjust enrichment[63] and would probably be founded on mistake.[64] Since the exercise of a trustee's dispositive powers involves a voluntary disposition of property, the equitable jurisdiction for setting aside mistaken voluntary dispositions would be engaged, so that restitution will only be awarded where the mistake was of such gravity that it would be unconscionable for the recipient to retain the property.[65]

4. POWER OF MAINTENANCE

(a) NATURE OF THE POWER

Where a beneficiary is a minor, he or she will typically not be entitled to receive any income from the trust until attaining the age of majority at eighteen. But it may be useful for the minor to receive income from the trust before that age, to pay for his or her education, for example, rather than have to wait until he or she is old enough to have a right to receive it. Similarly, an adult beneficiary may not yet be entitled to income under the trust, since he or she has a contingent interest, but might benefit from receiving some income now. In both circumstances the trustees might wish to exercise their statutory power of maintenance to pay income to the beneficiary, even though that beneficiary is not yet entitled to receive it under the terms of the trust instrument. The statutory power of maintenance was amended, following recommendations of the Law Commission.[66]

---

[61] See further Chapter 18.5(b), pp. 893–911.
[62] *Pitt v Holt* [2013] UKSC 26; [2013] 2 AC 108. See Chapter 7.2(c), pp. 337–41.
[63] See Chapter 1.4(b), pp. 14–15.
[64] See Chapter 1.4(b), p. 14.
[65] *Pitt v Holt* [2013] UKSC 26; [2013] 2 AC 108. See Chapter 7.2(c), pp. 337–41.
[66] *Intestacy and Family Provision Claims on Death* (Law Com. No. 331, 2011).

TRUSTEE ACT 1925

31. Power to apply income for maintenance and to accumulate surplus income during a minority

(1) Where any property is held by trustees in trust for any person for any interest whatsoever, whether vested or contingent, then, subject to any prior interests or charges affecting that property—

   (i) during the infancy of any such person, if his interest so long continues, the trustees may, at their sole discretion, pay to his parent or guardian, if any, or otherwise apply for or towards his maintenance, education, or benefit, the whole or such part, if any, of the income of that property as the trustees may think fit, whether or not there is—

      (a) any other fund applicable to the same purpose; or

      (b) any person bound by law to provide for his maintenance or education; and

   (ii) if such person on attaining the age of eighteen years has not a vested interest in such income, the trustees shall thenceforth pay the income of that property and of any accretion thereto under subsection (2) of this section to him, until he either attains a vested interest therein or dies, or until failure of his interest.

The effect of this power is that, as regards minors, the trustees can apply income from the trust for their maintenance, education, and benefit. As regards adult beneficiaries who are contingently entitled to the capital on the happening of a future event, the trustees have the power to apply income for their benefit before the occurrence of the event. The statutory power is to be read into every trust instrument in the absence of contrary intention either to modify or exclude it.[67]

In *Re Vestey's Settlement*,[68] Sir Raymond Evershed MR said:

> The language of s. 31 is by no means easy to follow, nor does it seem to me that the section has been put together in a manner to make the task of apprehending its effect easy.

(b) MINORS

As regards minors, the trustees have the power to pay income from the property to the child's parent or guardian, or to apply income for the child's maintenance, education, or benefit, as the trustees think fit.[69] This power can be exercised even though there is another fund available for the same purpose and even though somebody else is bound by law to provide for the maintenance or education of the child. Under the statute as originally enacted, the exercise of the trustees' discretion was subject to a proviso, as a result of which they had to consider various matters, such as the age of the child and his or her requirements, and a restriction was imposed on the amount of income which could be paid out. This proviso was removed by section 8(b) of the Inheritance and Trustees' Powers Act 2014, meaning that the trustees can consider all relevant matters in exercising their discretion

---

[67] Trustee Act 1925, s. 69(2). See further Chapter 12.1, p. 586.

[68] [1951] Ch 209, 216.

[69] Under section 31 of the Trustee Act 1925 as originally enacted, the trustee's discretion was restricted by an objective standard of reasonableness. The provision was amended by section 8(a) of the Inheritance and Trustees' Powers Act 2014, to give the trustees an unfettered discretion. As the Explanatory Note to the Act states, however, the 'general law on trustees' decision-making applies; the decision must be taken in good faith after due consideration of the circumstances.'

and pay out as much income as they consider appropriate. The trustees can legitimately exercise the power even though this indirectly benefits one of the parents of the child, but they cannot set out to benefit the parent.[70]

(c) TRUSTS THAT CARRY THE INTERMEDIATE INCOME

The power of maintenance applies to all minors with a vested[71] interest, namely an interest that does not depend on a prior condition being satisfied, such as reaching a specified age. If the minor has a contingent interest, the power will apply only if the trust 'carries the intermediate income'.[72] The precise meaning of this phrase is obscure. Essentially such trusts arise where the beneficiary is entitled to the income from the date of the gift, such as on the death of the testator, until the property vests. The phrase generally applies to all testamentary gifts except for contingent pecuniary legacies or where such trusts are excluded by the will.[73] The power cannot be exercised in favour of an object of a discretionary trust because he or she has no right to the income.[74]

The power of maintenance can also be exercised for the benefit of adult beneficiaries who have a contingent interest in trust property, but, again, only if the trust carries the intermediate income.[75] Where an adult beneficiary has a vested interest in trust property, there is no need for the power of maintenance to be exercised, since he or she is already entitled to the income.

(d) DUTY TO ACCUMULATE INCOME

TRUSTEE ACT 1925

31 (2) During the infancy of any such person, if his interest so long continues, the trustees shall accumulate all the residue of that income by investing it, and any profits from so investing it from time to time in authorised investments, and shall hold those accumulations as follows:—

(i) If any such person—

   (a) attains the age of eighteen years, or marries under that age or forms a civil partnership under that age, and his interest in such income during his infancy or until his marriage or his formation of a civil partnership is a vested interest; or

   (b) on attaining the age of eighteen years or on marriage or formation of a civil partnership under that age becomes entitled to the property from which such income arose in fee simple, absolute or determinable, or absolutely, or for an entailed interest;

   the trustees shall hold the accumulations in trust for such person absolutely, but without prejudice to any provision with respect thereto contained in any settlement by him made under any statutory powers during his infancy, and so that the receipt of such person after marriage or the formation of a civil partnership, and though still an infant, shall be a good discharge; and

---

[70] *Fuller v Evans* [2000] 1 All ER 636.
[71] See Chapter 1.4(a)(iv), p. 13.
[72] Trustee Act 1925, s. 31(3).
[73] Ker, 'Trustees' Power of Maintenance' (1953) 17 Conv 273, 275–9.
[74] *Re Vestey's Settlement* [1951] Ch 209.
[75] Ibid.

> (ii) In any other case the trustees shall, notwithstanding that such person had a vested interest in such income, hold the accumulations as an accretion to the capital of the property from which such accumulations arose, and as one fund with such capital for all purposes, and so that, if such property is settled land, such accumulations shall be held upon the same trusts as if the same were capital money arising therefrom; but the trustees may, at any time during the infancy of such person if his interest so long continues, apply those accumulations, or any part thereof, as if they were income arising in the then current year.

During the infancy of the child, any surplus of the income that has not been applied for the maintenance of that child must be accumulated by investing it, and the accumulated income is treated as an accretion to the capital of the trust property to which the child is entitled when he or she reaches the age of eighteen. The income from these investments can be used for the maintenance of the child.

(e) EXCLUSION OF THE STATUTORY POWER

The power of maintenance will be excluded if a contrary intention is expressed in the trust instrument.[76] The significance of this is illustrated by *Re Turner's Will Trust*,[77] in which the testator had created a trust for those of his grandchildren who attained the age of twenty-eight. The will contained an express power of maintenance and instructed the trustees to accumulate the surplus income. It was held that the direction to accumulate excluded the statutory power of maintenance. Romer LJ said:[78]

> The fact that section 31 contains provisions that are directory is immaterial. Powers of maintenance, in the comprehensive meaning of that term, usually do. Nothing is more common, for instance, than a direction to trustees to accumulate during the minority income not applied in maintenance. Such a direction is merely ancillary to the power of maintenance strictly so called, and may well be regarded as a part of the power of maintenance in its comprehensive sense. Such a direction is indeed contained in sub-section 2 of section 31 of the Trustee Act, 1925, and is an essential part of the statutory power of maintenance conferred upon trustees by the section. In the same way the direction contained in cl. (ii) of subsection 1 can be regarded as being merely an essential part of the new statutory power. This statutory power of maintenance, that is to say, the totality of the provisions to be found in section 31 of the Act, is, in our opinion, one of the 'powers conferred by this Act' within the meaning of section 69, sub-section 2, and therefore only applies if and so far as a contrary intention is not expressed in the instrument creating the trust and has effect subject to the terms of that instrument.

The duty to accumulate income can also be excluded by a contrary intention in the trust instrument.[79] So, in *Re Delamere's Settlement Trust*,[80] the trustees had appointed income to the beneficiaries 'absolutely'. This was held to exclude the duty to accumulate.

---

[76] Trustee Act 1925, s. 69(2).
[77] [1937] Ch 15.
[78] Ibid, 27.
[79] Trustee Act 1925, s. 69(2).
[80] [1984] 1 WLR 813.

5. POWER OF ADVANCEMENT

(a) NATURE OF THE POWER

Whereas the power of maintenance relates to income, the statutory power of advancement relates to the payment of capital from the trust for the advancement or benefit of a beneficiary whose interest is only contingent on the occurrence of a particular event, so does not yet have a right to receive the capital.

TRUSTEE ACT 1925

32. Power of advancement[81]

(1) Trustees may at any time or times pay or apply any capital money subject to a trust, or transfer or apply any other property forming part of the capital of the trust property, for the advancement or benefit, in such manner as they may, in their absolute discretion, think fit, of any person entitled to the capital of the trust property or of any share thereof, whether absolutely or contingently on his attaining any specified age or on the occurrence of any other event, or subject to a gift over on his death under any specified age or on the occurrence of any other event, and whether in possession or in remainder or reversion, and such payment, transfer or application may be made notwithstanding that the interest of such person is liable to be defeated by the exercise of a power of appointment or revocation, or to be diminished by the increase of the class to which he belongs:

Provided that—

(a) property (including any money) so paid, transferred or applied for the advancement or benefit of any person must not, altogether, represent more than the presumptive or vested share or interest of that person in the trust property; and

(b) if that person is or becomes absolutely and indefeasibly entitled to a share in the trust property the money or other property so paid, transferred or applied shall be brought into account as part of such share; and

(c) no such payment, transfer or application shall be made so as to prejudice any person entitled to any prior life or other interest, whether vested or contingent, or other property paid, transferred or applied unless such person is in existence and of full age and consents in writing to such payment, transfer or application.

(1A) In exercise of the foregoing power trustees may pay, transfer or apply money or other property on the basis (express or implied) that it shall be treated as a proportionate part of the capital out of which it was paid, transferred or applied, for the purpose of bringing it into account in accordance with proviso (b) to subsection (1) of this section.

This statutory power of advancement is to be read into every trust instrument in the absence of a contrary intention.[82] It gives the trustees a power to pay capital money or transfer other trust capital to the beneficiary directly, or to apply the capital money or other trust property for the advancement or benefit of the beneficiary.

---

[81] As amended by the Inheritance and Trustees' Powers Act 2014, s. 9.
[82] Trustee Act 1925, s. 69(2).

(b) RESTRICTIONS ON THE EXERCISE OF THE POWER

As section 32 makes clear, the exercise of the power of advancement is subject to certain restrictions.

(i) *Amount paid*

The money paid should not exceed the presumptive or vested share of the beneficiary.[83]

(ii) *Subsequent absolute entitlement*

If the person to whom money has been paid becomes absolutely and indefeasibly entitled to a share in the property, the money or property that has been paid, transferred or applied must be taken into account as part of his or her share.[84]

(iii) *Avoiding prejudice to others*

The payment, transfer or application of property should not be made if it prejudices any person who is entitled to another interest in the money or property, such as a life interest, unless that person is of full age and consents in writing to the advancement.[85]

(iv) *Exclusion of the power*

The power may be excluded by express or implied contrary intent in the trust instrument that it is not applicable.[86] The existence of an express power of advancement in the trust instrument does not necessarily exclude the statutory power, save where they are incompatible, such as where the trust instrument limits the amount of money or property that can be paid, transferred or applied.[87] In practice, the power is rarely excluded.

(v) *Proper exercise*

The power of advancement, like any power, must be exercised for the proper purpose and not capriciously. So, for example, in *Klug v Klug*,[88] one of the trustees was willing to exercise the power of advancement in favour of the beneficiary, but the other trustee, who was the beneficiary's mother, refused to exercise the power because the claimant had married without her approval. It was held that the mother had failed to exercise her discretion at all and the court directed that the power of advancement out of capital should be made. It would have been different had the mother determined that the power should not be exercised because, for example, it would not have been in the claimant's best interest for the advancement to be made out of capital.

(c) ADVANCEMENT OR BENEFIT

The key consideration when deciding whether the power should be exercised is whether it is for the advancement or benefit of the beneficiary. The use of the word 'advancement' concerns the improvement

---

[83] Ibid, s. 32(1)(a).
[84] Trustee Act 1925, s. 32(1)(b).
[85] Ibid, s. 32(1)(c).
[86] Ibid, s. 69(2).
[87] *Re Evans' Settlement* [1967] 1 WLR 1294.
[88] [1918] 2 Ch 67.

of the beneficiary's condition, and does not relate to the act of advancing money or property from the trust. 'Advancement or benefit' has traditionally encompassed the making of payments that contribute to the establishment in life of the beneficiary, such as by assisting him or her in training, or obtaining a professional qualification.[89] The use of the power has since been expanded to encompass providing a more immediate financial benefit to beneficiaries.

Pilkington v Inland Revenue Commissioners [1964] AC 612

Mr Pilkington died in February 1935. In his will, dated 14 December 1934, he left the income of his residuary estate on trust for his nephews and nieces in equal shares. The capital was to be held upon trust for the children of each beneficiary in such shares as the trustees should appoint, and in default of appointment in equal shares. Richard Pilkington was one of the beneficiaries. He was married and had three children, one of whom, Penelope, was two years old. The trustees decided, with Richard's consent, to advance one-half of Penelope's expectant share in the trust, and to pay it to the trustees of a new trust that was being set up for Penelope's benefit. The main object of the trustees was to avoid a tax liability, which would be payable on that part of the fund on Richard's death. The terms of the new trust were that the income should be applied for Penelope's maintenance, education, and benefit until she attained the age of twenty-one and the surplus should be accumulated; on Penelope's attaining the age of twenty-one, the income should be paid to her; and the capital should be paid to her on attaining the age of thirty. The question for the House of Lords was whether the trustees could properly exercise the power of advancement in this way.

Held: This exercise was within the terms of the statutory power as being for Penelope's benefit, but the particular exercise was void for perpetuity. The transfer of property to the new trust was an exercise of a power under the original trust, so the period of vesting started with the creation of the first trust: since the daughter was not able to take under the new trust until she attained the age of 30, this was held to be too remote as a period of vesting.[90]

Viscount Radcliffe:

The word 'advancement' itself meant in this context the establishment in life of the beneficiary who was the object of the power or at any rate some step that would contribute to the furtherance of his establishment ... Typical instances of expenditure for such purposes under the social conditions of the nineteenth century were an apprenticeship or the purchase of a commission in the army or of an interest in business. In the case of a girl there could be advancement on marriage (*Lloyd v Cocker* (1860) 27 Beav 645). Advancement had, however, to some extent a limited range of meaning, since it was thought to convey the idea of some step in life of permanent significance, and accordingly, to prevent uncertainties about the permitted range of objects for which moneys could be raised and made available, such words as 'or otherwise for his or her benefit' were often added to the word 'advancement'. This wide construction of the range of the power, which evidently did not stand upon niceties of distinction provided that the proposed application could fairly be regarded as for the benefit of the beneficiary who was the object of the power, must have been carried into the statutory power created by section 32, since it adopts without qualification the accustomed wording 'for the advancement or benefit in such manner as they may in their absolute discretion think fit'.

---

[89] *Re Pauling's Settlement Trusts* [1964] Ch 303.
[90] See now the Perpetuities and Accumulations Act 2009, discussed in in Chapter 3.7, pp. 113–16.

So much for 'advancement', which I now use for brevity to cover the combined phrase 'advancement or benefit'. It means any use of the money which will improve the material situation of the beneficiary. It is important, however, not to confuse the idea of 'advancement' with the idea of advancing the money out of the beneficiary's expectant interest. The two things have only a casual connection with each other. The one refers to the operation of finding money by way of anticipation of an interest not yet absolutely vested in possession or, if so vested, belonging to an infant: the other refers to the status of the beneficiary and the improvement of his situation. The power to carry out the operation of anticipating an interest is not conferred by the word 'advancement' but by those other words of the section which expressly authorise the payment or application of capital money for the benefit of a person entitled ...

I think, with all respect to the Commissioners [who were contesting the exercise of the power], a good deal of their argument is infected with some of this confusion. To say, for instance, that there cannot be a valid exercise of a power of advancement that results in a deferment of the vesting of the beneficiary's absolute title (Miss Penelope, it will be remembered, is to take at 30 under the proposed settlement instead of at 21 under the will) is in my opinion to play upon words. The element of anticipation consists in the raising of money for her now before she has any right to receive anything under the existing trusts: the advancement consists in the application of that money to form a trust fund, the provisions of which are thought to be for her benefit ...

I have not been able to find in the words of section 32, to which I have now referred, anything which in terms or by implication restricts the width of the manner or purpose of advancement. It is true that, if this settlement is made, Miss Penelope's children, who are not objects of the power, are given a possible interest in the event of her dying under 30 leaving surviving issue. But if the disposition itself, by which I mean the whole provision made, is for her benefit, it is no objection to the exercise of the power that other persons benefit incidentally as a result of the exercise. Thus a man's creditors may in certain cases get the most immediate advantage from an advancement made for the purpose of paying them off, as in *Lowther v Bentinck* (1874) LR 19 Eq 166, and a power to raise money for the advancement of a wife may cover a payment made direct to her husband in order to set him up in business: *Re Kershaw's Trusts* (1868) LR 6 Eq 322. The exercise will not be bad therefore on this ground.

Nor in my opinion will it be bad merely because the moneys are to be tied up in the proposed settlement. If it could be said that the payment or application permitted by section 32 cannot take the form of a settlement in any form but must somehow pass direct into or through the hands of the object of the power, I could appreciate the principle upon which the Commissioners' objection was founded. But can that principle be asserted? Anyone can see, I think, that there can be circumstances in which, while it is very desirable that some money should be raised at once for the benefit of an owner of an expectant or contingent interest, it would be very undesirable that the money should not be secured to him under some arrangement that will prevent him having the absolute disposition of it. I find it very difficult to think that there is something at the back of section 32 which makes an advancement impossible. Certainly neither Danckwerts J nor the members of the Court of Appeal in this case took that view. Both Lord Evershed MR and Upjohn LJ [1961] Ch 466 at 481, 486 explicitly accept the possibility of a settlement being made in exercise of a power of advancement. ...

The Commissioners' objections seem to be concentrated upon such propositions as that the proposed transaction is 'nothing less than a resettlement' and that a power of advancement cannot be used so as to alter or vary the trusts created by the settlement from which it is derived. Such a transaction, they say, amounts to using the power of advancement as a way of appointing or declaring new trusts different from those of the settlement. The reason why I do not find that these propositions have any compulsive effect upon my mind is that they seem to me merely vivid ways of describing the substantial effect of that which is proposed to be done and they do not in themselves amount to convincing arguments against doing it. Of course, whenever money is raised for advancement on terms that it is to be settled on the beneficiary, the money only passes from one settlement to be caught up in the other. It is therefore the same thing as a resettlement. But, unless one is to say that such moneys can never be applied by way of settlement, an argument which, as I have shown, has few supporters and is contrary to authority, it merely describes the inevitable effect of such an advancement to say that it is nothing less than a resettlement. Similarly, if it is part of the trusts and powers created by one settlement that the trustees of it should have power to raise money and make it available for a beneficiary upon new trusts approved by them, then they are in substance given power to free the money from one trust and to subject it to another. So be it: but, unless they cannot require a settlement of it at all, the transaction they carry out is the same thing in effect as an appointment of new trusts.

In the same way I am unconvinced by the argument that the trustees would be improperly delegating their trust by allowing the money raised to pass over to new trustees under a settlement conferring new powers on the latter. In fact I think that the whole issue of delegation is here beside the mark. The law is not that trustees cannot delegate: it is that trustees cannot delegate unless they have authority to do so. If the power of advancement which they possess is so read as to allow them to raise money for the purpose of having it settled, then they do have the necessary authority to let the money pass out of the old settlement into the new trusts. No question of delegation of their powers or trusts arises …

I ought to note for the record (1) that the transaction envisaged does not actually involve the raising of money, since the trustees propose to appropriate a block of shares in the family's private limited company as the trust investment, and (2) there will not be any actual transfer, since the trustees of the proposed settlement and the will trustees are the same persons. As I have already said, I do not attach any importance to these factors nor, I think, do the Commissioners. To transfer or appropriate outright is only to do by short cut what could be done in a more roundabout way by selling the shares to a consenting party, paying the money over to the new settlement with appropriate instructions and arranging for it to be used in buying back the shares as the trust investment. It cannot make any difference to follow the course taken in *Re Collard's Will Trusts* [1961] Ch 293 and deal with the property direct. On the other point, so long as there are separate trusts, the property effectually passes out of the old settlement into the new one, and it is of no relevance that, at any rate for the time being, the persons administering the new trust are the same individuals.

I have not yet referred to the ground which was taken by the Court of Appeal as their reason for saying that the proposed settlement was not permissible. To put it shortly, they held that the statutory power of advancement could not be exercised unless the benefit to be conferred was 'personal to the person concerned, in the sense of being related to his or her own real or personal needs' [1961] Ch 466 at 481. Or, to use other words of the learned Master of the Rolls at 484, the exercise of the power 'must be an exercise done to meet the circumstances as they present themselves in regard to a person within the scope of the section, whose circumstances call for that to be done which the trustees think fit to do'. Upjohn LJ at 487 expressed himself in virtually the same terms.

My Lords, I differ with reluctance from the views of judges so learned and experienced in matters of this sort: but I do not find it possible to import such restrictions into the words of the statutory power which itself does not contain them. First, the suggested qualification, that the considerations or circumstances must be 'personal' to the beneficiary, seems to me uncontrollably vague as a guide to general administration. What distinguishes a personal need from any other need to which the trustees in their discretion think it right to attend in the beneficiary's interest? And, if the advantage of preserving the funds of a beneficiary from the incidence of death duty is not an advantage personal to that beneficiary, I do not see what is. Death duty is a present risk that attaches to the settled property in which Miss Penelope has her expectant interest, and even accepting the validity of the supposed limitation, I would not have supposed that there was anything either impersonal or unduly remote in the advantage to be conferred upon her of some exemption from that risk. I do not think, therefore, that I can support the interpretation of the power of advancement that has commended itself to the Court of Appeal, and, with great respect, I think that the judgments really

amount to little more than a decision that in the opinion of the members of that court this was not a case in which there was any occasion to exercise the power. That would be a proper answer from a court to which trustees had referred their discretion with a request for its directions; but it does not really solve any question where, as here, they retain their discretion and merely ask whether it is impossible for them to exercise it.

To conclude, therefore, on this issue, I am of opinion that there is no maintainable reason for introducing into the statutory power of advancement a qualification that would exclude the exercise in the case now before us. It would not be candid to omit to say that, though I think that that is what the law requires, I am uneasy at some of the possible applications of this liberty, when advancements are made for the purposes of settlement or on terms that there is to be a settlement. It is quite true, as the Commissioners have pointed out, that you might have really extravagant cases of resettlements being forced on beneficiaries in the name of advancement, even a few months before an absolute vesting in possession would have destroyed the power. I have tried to give due weight to such possibilities, but when all is said I do not think that they ought to compel us to introduce a limitation of which no one, with all respect, can produce a satisfactory definition. First, I do not believe that it is wise to try to cut down an admittedly wide and discretionary power, enacted for general use, through fear of its being abused in certain hypothetical instances. And moreover, as regards this fear, I think that it must be remembered that we are speaking of a power intended to be in the hands of trustees chosen by a settlor because of his confidence in their discretion and good sense and subject to the external check that no exercise can take place without the consent of a prior life tenant; and that there does remain at all times a residual power in the court to restrain or correct any purported exercise that can be shown to be merely wanton or capricious and not to be attributable to a genuine discretion. I think, therefore, that, although extravagant possibilities exist, they may be more menacing in argument than in real life.

The other issue on which this case depends, that relating to the application of the rule against perpetuities, does not seem to me to present much difficulty. It is not in dispute that, if the limitations of the proposed settlement are to be treated as if they had been made by the testator's will and as coming into operation at the date of his death, there are trusts in it which would be void *ab initio* as violating the perpetuity rule. They postpone final vesting by too long a date. It is also a familiar rule of law in this field that, whereas appointments made under a general power of appointment conferred by will or deed are held as taking effect from the date of the exercise of the power, trusts declared by a special power of appointment, the distinguishing feature of which is that it can allocate property among a limited class of persons only, are treated as coming into operation at the date of the instrument that creates the power. The question therefore resolves itself into asking whether the exercise of a power of advancement which takes the form of a settlement should be looked upon as more closely analogous to a general or to a special power of appointment.

On this issue I am in full agreement with the views of Upjohn LJ in the Court of Appeal [1961] Ch 466 at 488. Indeed, much of the reasoning that has led me to my conclusion on the first issue that I have been considering leads me to think that for this purpose there is an effective analogy between powers of advancement and special powers of appointment. When one asks what person can be regarded as the settlor of Miss Penelope's proposed settlement, I do not see how it is possible to say that she is herself or that the trustees are. She is the passive recipient of the benefit extracted for her from the original trusts; the trustees are merely exercising a fiduciary power in arranging for the desired limitations. It is not their property that constitutes the funds of Miss Penelope's settlement; it is the property subjected to trusts by the will of the testator and passed over into the new settlement through the instrumentality of a power which by statute is made appendant to those trusts. I do not think, therefore, that it is important to this issue that money raised under a power of advancement passes entirely out of the reach of the existing trusts and makes, as it were, a new start under fresh limitations, the kind of thing that happened under the old form of family resettlement when the tenant in tail in remainder barred the entail with the consent of the protector of the settlement. I think that the important point for the purpose of the rule against perpetuities is that the new settlement is only effected by the operation of a fiduciary power which itself 'belongs' to the old settlement.

In the conclusion, therefore, there are legal objections to the proposed settlement which the trustees have placed before the court.

In *Re Clore's Settlement Trusts*,[91] the court held that the exercise of the power of advancement to enable payment to be made to a specific charity could be considered to be for the material benefit of a rich minor who felt that he had a moral obligation to make appropriate donations to charity. This is an even more extreme interpretation of 'benefit', since it involves a financial loss being caused to the beneficiary, albeit with the advantage of an improved moral well-being.

A more restrictive interpretation of benefit was adopted in *X v A*,[92] in which it was held that a purported exercise of the power to pay capital to the beneficiary to spend on charitable purposes did not improve her material situation.

X v A [2005] EWHC 2706 (Ch); [2006] 1 WLR 741, 752

The trust had been settled by a vicar, who had inherited his wealth from the family company. His strongly held view, shared by his wife, was that inherited wealth brought with it many disadvantages. His wife had a life interest in the property and she asked her trustees to transfer capital from the trust fund for her to use it for charitable purposes. Hart J directed the trustees not to exercise the power of advancement in this way:

[Counsel] submitted that the only questions to be answered were whether the wife was reasonably entitled to regard herself as being under a moral obligation to make or procure the making of the proposed gift to charity and whether she did in fact recognise the obligation. As to the latter it was plain on the evidence (he submitted) that she did recognise the obligation and, as to the former, that it was not for the trustees or the court to decide whether they would take the same view. It was enough, he submitted, that the wife's view was one she could reasonably take. It could not be said that her view of her moral obligations was unreasonable. Accordingly, the proposed transaction was capable of being viewed as being for her benefit within the meaning of the authorities, and the preconditions for the exercise of the power were therefore fulfilled. The question of the quantum of the proposed exercise of the power only arose, on this submission, at the second stage of the inquiry, namely as to whether the court should give its blessing to the particular exercise of the power which was proposed.

In my judgment these submissions place a greater weight on the personal views of the beneficiary than is justified by the authorities. In *In re Clore's Settlement Trusts* itself the references made in the judgment to the sense of obligation felt by the beneficiary himself are made with the view of imposing a requirement additional to the initial requirement that there should be an existing moral obligation capable of being recognised by the court. In *In re Clore's Settlement Trusts* the court acknowledged that earlier examples of charitable gifts had been on a very different scale from that proposed before it ... but said that the question of the size of the particular gift must depend on 'all the circumstances, including the

---

position in life of the beneficiary, the amount of the fund and the amount of his other resources' and added [1966] 1 WLR 955, 958:

> 'If the obligation is not to be met out of the capital of the trust fund, he would have to meet it out of his own pocket, if at all. Accordingly, the discharge of the obligation out of the capital of the trust fund does improve his material situation.'

That passage emphasised the potentially limiting effect of the requirement (from which none of the authorities have departed) that there be some sense in which the beneficiary's material situation can be said to be improved by the situation ... In the present case I find it impossible to see how this requirement can be satisfied. It cannot be said that the proposed advance is relieving the wife of an obligation she would otherwise have to discharge out of her own resources if only because the amount proposed to be advanced exceeds the amount of her own free resources. In any event the court has no reason to suppose that, in relation to her free assets, she will regard the advance as having discharged her moral obligation. The moral imperative informing her request to the trustees might logically be thought to apply to her own assets regardless of whether or not an advance is made out of the trust fund.

I entirely accept that in distinguishing between the objective existence of a moral obligation on the one hand and the beneficiary's own recognition of it on the other there is a danger of the court being cast adrift in an open sea. How, as [counsel] asked rhetorically, can the court assess the validity and nature of a moral obligation otherwise than by reference to the beneficiary's own views on the subject? That is certainly not a question to which the court can give an abstract answer, whether by reference to the Bible or to Bentham, to Kant or the Koran. The answer has to be found in the concrete examples provided by the decided cases and the reliance placed in them on generally accepted norms applicable in the context of dealings with settled wealth. No such case goes anywhere near recognising the existence of a moral obligation of the extent in question here.

For those reasons I do not think that I can conclude that it is open to the trustees to make the proposed advance. ... Lest there be any doubt on the subject my answer to the question whether the power can in principle (i e as a matter of construction) be exercised by advancing money to or for the benefit of the wife so that she may discharge a moral obligation to charity my answer is affirmative. To the question whether the exercise actually proposed can properly be said to be for her benefit the answer is negative.

It follows that, whilst the beneficiary's belief as to benefit is relevant, ultimately the question of benefit is to be assessed objectively, and the size of the proposed gift is a particularly significant factor.

(d) APPLICATION OF THE MONEY

In *Re Pauling's Settlement Trusts*,[93] it was recognized that once the power of advancement had been exercised, the trustees were obliged to check that the money had been applied for the purpose for which it was advanced. Willmer J said: [94]

> Furthermore, it is clear that the power ... may be exercised, if the circumstances warrant it, either by making an out-and-out payment to the person to be advanced, or for a particular purpose specified by the trustees. Thus in argument an example was given that when George [one of the beneficiaries] was called to the Bar the trustees might have quite properly advanced to him a sum of capital quite

---

[93] [1964] Ch 303.
[94] Ibid, 334.

generally for his living expenses to support him while starting to practice, provided they thought that this was a reasonable thing to do, and that he was a type of person who could reasonably be trusted to make proper use of the money. On the other hand, if the trustees make the advance for a particular purpose which they state, they can quite properly pay it over to the advancee if they reasonably think they can trust him or her to carry out the prescribed purpose. What they cannot do is to prescribe a particular purpose, and then raise and pay the money over to the advancee leaving him or her entirely free, legally and morally, to apply it for that purpose or to spend it in any way he or she chooses, without any responsibility on the trustees even to inquire as to its application.

QUESTION

Alan and Brenda hold property on discretionary trust for Charles, Debbie, and Edward. According to the terms of the trust Charles, Debbie, and Edward are entitled to the capital in equal shares when they attain the age of twenty-five. Charles is thirty, Debbie is twenty-six, and Edward is seventeen. Charles went travelling ten years ago and has not been heard from since. Debbie wants money to pay a deposit on a house. Edward would like some money from the trust to buy a car and to pay for piano lessons. Alan and Brenda seek your advice as to their dispositive powers.

FURTHER READING

Gardner, 'Fiduciary Powers in Toytown' (1991) 107 LQR 214.

Ker, 'Trustees' Power of Maintenance' [1953] Conv 273.

Luxton, 'Eluding the Dead Hand: A Live Issue?' [1986] Conv 138.

14

FIDUCIARY OBLIGATIONS

CENTRAL ISSUES

1. A fiduciary owes a duty of loyalty to his or her principal. The fiduciary must always act in the best interests of the principal.

2. Fiduciary relationships are voluntary. Some relationships, such as solicitor–client, are well recognized as fiduciary in nature, but fiduciary relationships can arise in a wide variety of situations.

3. Not every breach of duty by a fiduciary is a breach of fiduciary duty: the duty breached may be contractual or tortious, for example. However, only a fiduciary can breach a fiduciary duty.

4. Fiduciary duties are proscriptive: they tell the fiduciary what he or she must not do. The fiduciary must not profit from his or her position as a fiduciary or place him- or herself in a position where the fiduciary's personal interests might conflict with the duties owed to his or her principal, unless he or she has obtained the prior fully informed consent of the principal.

5. Fiduciary obligations are strict, and any profits made by the fiduciary in breach must be disgorged to his or her principal. Such profits are held on constructive trust for the principal.

1. FIDUCIARY RELATIONSHIPS

Fiduciary relationships have been described by Sir Anthony Mason, a retired judge of the High Court of Australia, as a 'concept in search of a principle'.[1] It remains difficult to state exactly *what* a fiduciary relationship is, and *when* a person will be considered to be a fiduciary.

(a) WHAT IS A FIDUCIARY RELATIONSHIP?

In *Bristol and West Building Society v Mothew*, Millett LJ identified the essential characteristics of a fiduciary as follows:[2]

---

[1] 'Themes and Prospects', in *Essays in Equity* (ed. Finn) (Sydney: Law Book Co., 1985), ch. 12, p. 246.
[2] [1998] Ch 1, 18.

A fiduciary is someone who has undertaken to act for or on behalf of another in a particular matter in circumstances which give rise to a relationship of trust and confidence. The distinguishing obligation of a fiduciary is the obligation of loyalty. The principal is entitled to the single-minded loyalty of his fiduciary. This core liability has several facets. A fiduciary must act in good faith; he must not make a profit out of his trust; he must not place himself in a position where his duty and his interest may conflict; he may not act for his own benefit or the benefit of a third person without the informed consent of his principal. This is not intended to be an exhaustive list, but it is sufficient to indicate the nature of fiduciary obligations. They are the defining characteristics of the fiduciary. As Dr. Finn pointed out in his classic work *Fiduciary Obligations* (1977), p. 2, he is not subject to fiduciary obligations because he is a fiduciary; it is because he is subject to them that he is a fiduciary.

The reliance on Finn's work is important: a person is only a fiduciary *if* fiduciary obligations are owed. Finn later wrote that:[3]

A person will be a fiduciary in his relationship with another when and in so far as that other is entitled to expect that he will act in that other's interests or (as in a partnership) in their joint interests, to the exclusion of his own several interest.

Put crudely, the central idea is service of another's interests. And the consequential obligation a fiduciary finding attracts is itself one designed essentially to procure loyalty in service.

These extracts suggest that the crucial element is *loyalty* owed by the fiduciary to his or her principal. This requires the fiduciary to prioritize the interests of the principal over his or her own. As suggested by Millett LJ, this means that the fiduciary must not profit from his or her position as a fiduciary, and not place him- or herself in a position where the fiduciary's own interests or duties conflict with those of his or her principal. Such duties may be onerous, and require a fiduciary to forsake an opportunity that could be exploited by all others. It is therefore important to consider exactly *when* a person will be subject to such duties.

(b) WHEN DO FIDUCIARY RELATIONSHIPS ARISE?

A trustee–beneficiary relationship under an express trust is often said to be the epitome of a fiduciary relationship; the types of relationships that have been classified as fiduciary have grown incrementally by analogy with trustees of an express trust.[4] For example, it is now clear that agents,[5] solicitors,[6] company directors,[7] and partners[8] owe fiduciary duties: in each case the principal is entitled to expect that the fiduciary will act in the principal's best interests.

---

[3] 'Fiduciary Law and the Modern Commercial World' in *Commercial Aspects of Trusts and Fiduciary Obligations* (ed. McKendrick) (Oxford: Clarendon Press, 1992), p. 9.

[4] For some attempts to state when a fiduciary relationship will arise, see e.g. Scott, 'The Fiduciary Principle' (1949) 37 California Law Review 539; Sealy, 'Fiduciary Relationships' (1962) 20 CLJ 69; Weinrib, 'The Fiduciary Obligation' (1975) 25 University of Toronto Law Journal 1.

[5] *De Bussche v Alt* (1878) 8 Ch D 286.

[6] *Brown v IRC* [1965] AC 244; *Hilton v Barker Booth and Eastwood (a firm)* [2005] UKHL 8; [2005] 1 WLR 567.

[7] *Regal (Hastings) Ltd v Gulliver* [1967] 2 AC 134n. The duty is owed to the company and not to the shareholders: *Percival v Wright* [1902] 2 Ch 421. But note *Peskin v Anderson* [2001] 1 BCLC 372, 379 (Mummery LJ) (exceptionally a separate fiduciary duty might be owed to shareholders). Directors duties must now be considered in light of the Companies Act 2006: see Chapter 14.2(f), pp. 469–72.

[8] *Featherstonhaugh v Fenwick* (1810) 17 Ves 298; *Clegg v Fishwick* (1849) 1 Mac & G 294.

It is also possible for fiduciary relationships to arise in the context of other, specific relationships. It is not always easy to determine when such an *ad hoc* fiduciary relationship exists. Birks has commented that:[9]

> It is manifestly impossible to predict whether a relationship will or will not be accounted fiduciary when a case comes to court. In many of the leading cases distinguished judges have been almost equally divided as to whether or not a relationship was fiduciary. The necessary elements can be spelled out: a fiduciary is one who has discretion, and therefore, power, in the management of another's affairs, in circumstances in which that one cannot reasonably be expected to monitor him or take other precautions to protect his own interests. But it turns out that this has a very low predictive yield.

It is undoubtedly true that issues about whether or not a relationship should be classified as fiduciary can be much disputed. But the pessimism of Birks might be allayed somewhat by emphasizing that fiduciary relationships should be considered to be *voluntary* in nature. As a result, fiduciary obligations should only arise where the fiduciary has expressly or impliedly *agreed* to be bound by those obligations. As Cromwell J observed in *Galambos v Perez*, a decision of the Canadian Supreme Court:[10]

> I note that ... this Court [has previously] considered competing bases for the imposition of *ad hoc* fiduciary duties, opposing to a certain extent mutual understanding and reasonable expectations of the alleged beneficiary ... [W]hat is required in all cases of *ad hoc* fiduciary obligations is that there be an undertaking on the part of the fiduciary to exercise a discretionary power in the interests of that other party. To repeat what was said by McLachlin J. in *Norberg*, 'fiduciary relationships ... are always dependent on the fiduciary's undertaking to act in the beneficiary's interests'.[11] As Dickson J. put it in *Guerin*, fiduciary duties may arise where 'by statute, agreement, or perhaps by unilateral undertaking, one party has an obligation to act for the benefit of another'.[12]
>
> The fiduciary's undertaking may be the result of the exercise of statutory powers, the express or implied terms of an agreement or, perhaps, simply an undertaking to act in this way. In cases of *per se* fiduciary relationships, this undertaking will be found in the nature of the category of relationship in issue. The critical point is that in both *per se* and *ad hoc* fiduciary relationships, there will be some undertaking on the part of the fiduciary to act with loyalty.

This analysis provides a satisfactory basis for fiduciary relationships. The close connection with contractual relationships in this context has been pointed out by Edelman:[13]

> if we persist in seeing fiduciary obligations as imposed by law, and dependent upon conceptions of status, the quest to understand and explain why different fiduciaries owe different duties will remain an impossible task. In contrast, by understanding fiduciary duties as terms which are expressed or implied into manifested undertakings to another, it is much easier to understand why the nature of fiduciary duties will always depend upon the circumstances. This explanation illuminates the reason why exactly the same analysis is undertaken by courts when determining, on the one hand, whether fiduciary duties have arisen and, on the other hand, in determining whether such duties should be implied into contracts or other voluntary undertakings. The analyses are the same because fiduciary duties *are* terms expressed or implied in voluntary undertakings.

[9] 'Equity in the Modern Law: An Exercise in Taxonomy' (1996) 26 University of Western Australia Law Review 1, 18.
[10] *Galambos v Perez* 2009 SCR 48; [2009] 3 SCR 247, [76]–[77].
[11] *Norberg v Wynrib* [1992] 2 SCR 226, 273.
[12] *Guerin v The Queen*, [1984] 2 SCR 335, 384.
[13] 'When Do Fiduciary Duties Arise?' (2010) LQR 302, 326.

The strict and sometimes onerous nature of fiduciary obligations can be more readily accepted if it is understood that the fiduciary has voluntarily accepted these obligations. Moreover, this strengthens the ability to predict whether a relationship should be characterized as fiduciary, since the focus of inquiry is upon whether a person voluntarily undertook fiduciary obligations. Even if there is no express undertaking, principles governing implied terms are well-known,[14] and can be used in this area. However, this explanation for when fiduciary obligations arise is not without its critics. For example, Conaglen has written:[15]

> Fiduciary duties have been held to arise where it is legitimate to expect that one party will act in the interests of the other to the exclusion of his own several interests. An undertaking is an important way of generating that kind of expectation, but given the undertaking can be implied as well as express — and it is very rarely express — the idea that fiduciary doctrine is fundamentally concerned with undertakings does not advance our understanding of that doctrine very far. It does usefully highlight that the expectation ought to be based on conduct of the putative fiduciary, rather than the conduct of others, but it does not mean that fiduciary doctrine is simply a part of contract law or the law of 'voluntary undertakings', whatever the latter might entail.

(c) DO ALL TRUSTEES OWE FIDUCIARY OBLIGATIONS?

Considering fiduciary obligations to be voluntarily assumed also helps us to decide whether *all* trustees should be thought to be in a fiduciary relationship. Clearly, express trustees have voluntarily undertaken fiduciary obligations, but the same is not clearly the case for trusts imposed by law. A constructive trustee has not voluntarily assumed any fiduciary obligations; even if a constructive trust arises due to unconscionability, fiduciary obligations cannot necessarily be implied, because the constructive trustee will not have knowingly subjected him- or herself to fiduciary obligations.[16] Similarly, a resulting trustee may have no idea that he or she is a trustee, and it might, therefore, be unduly intrusive to impose fiduciary obligations upon him or her. But if the resulting trust arises because of a failure of an express trust, then the trustee *would* have assumed a position as a fiduciary under the intended express trust, and fiduciary obligations should follow.[17]

2. NATURE OF FIDUCIARY DUTIES

Fiduciary duties are often said to be *proscriptive*: they are negative in the sense that they tell a fiduciary what he or she must *not* do. In *Bray v Ford*, Lord Herschell insisted that:[18]

> It is an inflexible rule of a Court of Equity that a person in a fiduciary position … is not, unless otherwise expressly provided, entitled to make a profit; he is not allowed to put himself in a position where his interest and duty conflict.

---

[14] See e.g. McKendrick, *Contract Law: Text, Cases and Materials* (5th edn) (Oxford: Oxford University Press, 2012), 337–69.

[15] Conaglen, 'Fiduciary Duties and Voluntary Undertakings' (2013) 7 Journal of Equity 105, 126–127. See too Smith, 'Fiduciary Relationships: Ensuring the Loyal Exercise of Judgement on Behalf of Another' (2014) 130 LQR 608.

[16] Millett, 'Restitution and Constructive Trusts' (1998) 114 LQR 399, 405. Cf *Independent Trustee Services Ltd v GP Noble Trustees Ltd* [2012] EWCA Civ 195; [2012] 3 All ER 210, [80] (Lloyd LJ).

[17] See Chambers, *Resulting Trusts* (Oxford: Clarendon Press, 1997), pp. 196–200.

[18] [1896] AC 44, 50.

It is not totally clear whether the 'no-profit' and 'no-conflict' rules are distinct. It has been suggested that the former is merely an example of the latter. For example, in *Boardman v Phipps*, Lord Upjohn commented that the rule that a fiduciary:[19]

> must not make a profit out of his trust ... is part of the wider rule that a trustee must not place himself in a position where his duty and his interest may conflict.

By contrast, in *Chan v Zacharia* Deane J reviewed *Boardman v Phipps* and concluded that:[20]

> the two themes, while overlapping, are distinct.

The latter approach might better reflect the current state of English law. Decisions such as *Regal (Hastings) v Gulliver*,[21] and indeed *Boardman v Phipps*,[22] which are discussed in detail later,[23] seem to suggest that a fiduciary may have to account for the profits gained from his or her position even where it may be difficult to establish a breach of the no-conflict rule. Conaglen has justified the separate existence of the no-profit rule since:[24]

> the profit principle is a prophylactic application of the conflict principle: the likelihood of there being a conflict in such circumstances is treated as sufficient justification for equity to prohibit all unauthorised profits, without requiring strict proof in every case that there was a conflict.

Although this chapter will consider the cases under two discrete headings of 'no conflict' and 'no profit', it should be remembered that there is a large degree of overlap between the two, and a decision which infringes the no-profit rule might equally be analysed as a 'no-conflict' case.

(a) BEYOND PROSCRIPTIVE DUTIES?

The no-conflict and no-profit principles are very clearly proscriptive and in accordance with traditional understanding of the nature of fiduciary duties. However, it is sometimes suggested that a fiduciary may be under a *positive* duty to disclose information to his or her principal.[25] In some situations, this is undoubtedly true: for example, if a fiduciary acts for two principals whose interests conflict, then if the fiduciary receives information from one principal that would be beneficial to the other, the fiduciary must disclose that information.[26] But this is entirely consistent with the proscriptive nature of fiduciary duties: the fiduciary must not place him- or herself in a position where his or her duty to one principal might conflict with his or her duty to another principal, so the fiduciary must disclose information to avoid such a conflict. In order to act for two principals whose interests might conflict,

---

[19] [1967] 2 AC 46, 123.
[20] [1984] HCA 36; (1984) 154 CLR 178, [24].
[21] [1967] 2 AC 134n.
[22] [1967] 2 AC 46.
[23] See Chapter 14.4(d), pp. 687–98.
[24] *Fiduciary Loyalty* (Oxford: Hart, 2010), pp. 120–1.
[25] See e.g. Lee, 'Rethinking the Content of the Fiduciary Obligation' [2009] Conv 236.
[26] *Hilton v Barker Booth and Eastwood* [2005] 1 WLR 567.

the fully informed consent of both should be obtained. Obtaining prior authorization from a principal is often crucial for a fiduciary to avoid breaching a duty.[27]

Item Software UK Ltd v Fassihi[28] is sometimes considered to be an example of a fiduciary being under a *positive* obligation to disclose information, such that non-disclosure itself might be a breach of fiduciary duty.[29] In that case, Arden LJ held that a director had to disclose an intention to compete with his principal; failure to do so would be evidence of disloyalty.[30] Yet, even this decision does not seem to alter radically the nature of fiduciary duties. In *Shepherds Investments Ltd v Walters*, Etherton J analysed *Fassihi* and insisted that:[31]

> There is no separate and independent duty of disclosure.... There is a breach because the director's conflict between his personal interest and his duty to the company has not been authorised after full disclosure to, and informed consent by, the company.... Those are straightforward applications of ordinary principles of equity concerning fiduciary duties.

Etherton J's interpretation of *Fassihi* maintains the idea that fiduciary duties are proscriptive only. Admittedly, the Court of Appeal in *Fassihi* did not clearly adopt this analysis, but it is the preferable approach and consistent with orthodoxy.

(b) NOT ALL DUTIES OWED BY A FIDUCIARY ARE FIDUCIARY DUTIES

Fassihi also raises the issue of whether a positive duty on a director to disclose misconduct should be analysed as fiduciary in nature at all. Not every breach by a fiduciary is a breach of fiduciary duty. This point was clearly made by Millett LJ in *Mothew*:[32]

> The expression 'fiduciary duty' is properly confined to those duties which are peculiar to fiduciaries and the breach of which attracts legal consequences differing from those consequent upon breach of other duties. Unless the expression is so limited it is lacking in practical utility. In this sense it is obvious that not every breach of duty by a fiduciary is a breach of fiduciary duty.

This is an important passage. A fiduciary will only breach a *fiduciary* duty if that duty was owed by a fiduciary *alone*. Thus, if a solicitor acts incompetently, he or she might be sued in negligence: this would not be a breach of fiduciary duty since all such professionals owe a duty to act with reasonable skill and care, and this is not peculiar to a fiduciary relationship.[33] There is no breach of the obligation of loyalty. Such an analysis might help to explain *Fassihi*: the duty to disclose misconduct

---

[27] See Chapter 14.3(b), pp. 680–2.
[28] [2004] EWCA (Civ) 1244; [2005] 2 BCLC 91.
[29] See e.g. Lee, 'Rethinking the Content of the Fiduciary Obligation' [2009] Conv 236.
[30] [2004] EWCA (Civ) 1244; [2005] 2 BCLC 91, [63]–[68].
[31] [2006] EWHC 836 (Ch); [2007] 2 BCLC 202, [132]. See too *Customer Systems plc v Ranson* [2012] EWCA Civ 841; [2012] IRLR 769.
[32] *Bristol & West Building Society v Mothew* [1998] Ch 1, 16.
[33] *Bristol & West Building Society v Mothew* [1998] Ch 1; *Hilton v Barker, Booth and Eastwood* [2005] UKHL 8; [2005] 1 WLR 567. It is true that in some instances 'fiduciary duty' is used in a looser sense (e.g. *Pitt v Holt; Futter v Futter* [2013] UKSC 26; [2013] 2 AC 108, discussed in Chapter 11.7(g), pp. 577–83) but generally the approach in *Mothew* has been very well accepted. For criticism, see e.g. Getzler, 'Am I My Beneficiary's Keeper? Fusion and Loss-Based Fiduciary Remedies' in Degeling and Edelman, *Equity in Commercial Law* (Sydney: Lawbook Co, 2005).

is common to all employees[34] and is not particular to fiduciaries. It should not be analysed as a fiduciary duty.

In *Fassihi*, it was not crucial to the outcome of the case whether the duty to disclose was classified as fiduciary. But in many situations it will be. This is because, as Millett LJ observed, the *remedies* available for breach of fiduciary duty are different and often more extensive than those available for other breaches.

(c) THE STRICTNESS OF FIDUCIARY DOCTRINE

The remedies available for breach of fiduciary duty are considered in greater detail in Section 5 of this chapter. But it is important to appreciate that the *prima facie* remedy for breach of fiduciary duty is an account of profits. By this measure, the fiduciary will have to give up any gains made as a result of the breach, regardless of whether or not the principal suffered any loss, and even if he or she acted in good faith.[35] In some situations, a constructive trust will be imposed upon the profits made.[36] Such gain-based, or restitutionary, remedies are largely justified on the basis that they *deter* the fiduciary from breaching his or her fiduciary duties.[37] There is no incentive to breach a fiduciary duty if the fiduciary will not be able to gain from the breach.[38]

Conaglen, 'The Nature and Function of Fiduciary Loyalty' (2005) 121 LQR 452, 453

[F]iduciary duties serve a function which differs from that served by other legal duties. The concept of fiduciary 'loyalty' is an encapsulation of a subsidiary and prophylactic form of protection for non-fiduciary duties which enhances the chance that those non-fiduciary duties will be properly performed. The primary means by which this notion of loyalty is given effect is a range of fiduciary duties which seek to insulate fiduciaries from influences that are likely to distract from such proper performance. It is often observed that fiduciary doctrine is applied in a prophylactic manner, although frequently without much clarification of [what] that means ... fiduciary doctrine's prophylactic aspect is more than merely the strictness of its application; the argument presented here is that fiduciary doctrine is prophylactic in its very nature, as it is designed to avert breaches of non-fiduciary duties by seeking to neutralise influences likely to sway the fiduciary away from properly performing those non-fiduciary duties. This understanding of fiduciary loyalty provides a theoretical underpinning for a number of tenets of fiduciary doctrine that are acknowledged in the case law but are otherwise unexplained.

Fiduciary doctrine is frequently conceptualised as exhorting more moral behaviour from fiduciaries. Properly understood, the doctrine is far more cynical, functional and instrumentalist in outlook, focusing on lessening the danger that a fiduciary's undertaking will not be properly performed.

This prophylactic approach explains why the remedies available are so strict: it is imperative that fiduciary duties are carried out properly. This might be thought to be more important in the equitable context than the purely contractual, for example, since a contracting party would generally be aware of a need to protect his or her own interests, whereas a principal in a fiduciary relationship might expect to be able to trust and rely upon his or her principal without taking any further action.

---

[34] *Fassihi* [2004] EWCA (Civ) 1244; [2005] 2 BCLC 91, [55]–[60].
[35] E.g. *Boardman v Phipps* [1967] 2 AC 46, see further Chapter 14.4(d), pp. 687–98.
[36] See Chapter 14.5(b), p. 706.
[37] See e.g. Edelman, *Gain-Based Damages* (Oxford: Hart, 2002), p. 216.
[38] Although he or she may be entitled to an allowance for his or her contributions to the gain made: see Chapter 14.5(e), p. 716.

(d) SCOPE OF FIDUCIARY DUTIES

Before considering the content of the no-conflict and no-profit rules, it is important to appreciate that fiduciary duties are not of unlimited scope. As Lord Upjohn commented in *Boardman v Phipps*:[39]

> Once it is established that there is [a fiduciary] relationship, that relationship must be examined to see what duties are thereby imposed upon the agent, to see what is the scope and ambit of the duties charged upon him. Having defined the scope of those duties one must see whether he has committed some breach thereof.

Different fiduciary relationships are of different scope.[40] Care needs to be taken in assessing the extent of the voluntarily undertaken fiduciary duties.[41]

In the commercial context, the courts are especially wary about imposing fiduciary duties, as this might disturb the normal commercial allocation of risk. For example, in *Re Goldcorp Exchange Ltd*[42] the claimants argued that the defendants had breached fiduciary duties in not allocating purchased gold bullion to them. But this was readily rejected by the Privy Council, who could only identify contractual obligations. Lord Mustill pointedly remarked that:[43]

> high expectations do not necessarily lead to equitable remedies.

In a similar vein, Lord Millett has warned that:[44]

> It is of the first importance not to impose fiduciary obligations on parties to a purely commercial relationship who deal with each other at arms' length and can be expected to look after their own interests.

It is clearly important that fiduciary relationships do not intrude excessively in the affairs of commercial parties. Sometimes a fiduciary relationship will genuinely exist,[45] but this must be justified by reference to the voluntary undertakings of the parties.

(e) FIDUCIARY RELATIONSHIPS CAN END: INSTANCES OF RETIREMENT

Fiduciary obligations do not necessarily continue forever. A relationship can be terminated by agreement. Some difficulties have arisen regarding the retirement of fiduciaries. If a fiduciary resigns or retires in good faith, and an opportunity only later arises that might have conflicted with the fiduciary

---

[39] *Boardman v Phipps* [1967] 2 AC 46, 127.

[40] Millett, 'Equity's Place in the Law of Commerce' (1998) 114 LQR 214.

[41] In the American case of *Securities and Exchange Commission v Chenery Corporation* (1943) 318 US 80 at 85–6, Frankfurter J said: 'To say that a man is a fiduciary only begins the analysis: it gives direction to further inquiry. To whom is he a fiduciary? What obligation does he owe as a fiduciary? In what respects has he failed to discharge these obligations? And what are the consequences of his deviation from duty?' (1943) 318 US 80, 85–6.

[42] [1995] 1 AC 74 (PC): see Chapter 3.3(c), p. 78.

[43] Ibid, 98.

[44] Millett, 'Equity's Place in the Law of Commerce' (1998) 114 LQR 214, 217–18.

[45] See e.g. the recent discussion of the Law Commission, *Fiduciary Duties of Investment Intermediaries* (Law Com No 350, 2014).

relationship that has ended, then there will be no breach of fiduciary duty. In *Attorney-General v Blake*, Scott V-C recognized that:[46]

> The law would not impose a duty that represented an unreasonable restraint on the ability of the ex-[fiduciary] to earn his living by exploiting the experience and knowledge acquired during his years of service.

Scott V-C consequently held that a spy who had left the intelligence services no longer owed fiduciary duties not to exploit the expertise he or she had gained.[47] In a similar vein, in *Island Export Finance Ltd v Umunna*, Hutchinson J said that:[48]

> It would, it seems to me, be surprising to find that directors alone, because of the fiduciary nature of their relationship with the company, were restrained from exploiting after they had ceased to be such any opportunity of which they had acquired knowledge while directors. Directors, no less than employees, acquire a general fund of knowledge and expertise in the course of their work, and it is plainly in the public interest that they should be free to exploit it in a new position.

Because in *Umunna* the defendant had consistently acted in good faith and had not been disloyal, he was allowed to exploit an opportunity *after* he had resigned, which he would not have been able to exploit had he still been a director of the company.

However, a fiduciary cannot simply retire *in order to* exploit an opportunity which would place him or her in conflict with his or her fiduciary obligations. This was made clear in *Industrial Development Consultants v Cooley*.[49] In that case, the defendant, who was the managing director of a company, had been negotiating for a new business opportunity on behalf of the company. He then resigned in order to exploit that opportunity himself. Roskill J had no difficulty in deciding that he had breached his fiduciary obligations, despite no longer being a director at the time he made the profit. Similar conclusions have been reached in other cases where the resignation of a fiduciary was in bad faith.[50] A good explanation of this approach has been given in *Foster Bryant Surveying Ltd v Bryant* by Rix LJ, who thought that these cases are:[51]

> not saying that the fiduciary duty survived the end of the relationship as director, but that the lack of good faith with which the future exploitation was planned while still a director, and the resignation which was part of that dishonest plan, meant that there was already then a breach of fiduciary duty, which resulted in the liability to account for the profits which, albeit subsequently, but causally connected with that earlier fiduciary breach, were obtained from the diversion of the company's business property to the defendant's new enterprise.

Thus, it is not the case that the fiduciary obligation *continues* after resignation, although some other duties—notably confidentiality—may well do so. Rather, the fiduciary obligation is breached whilst the person is *still* a fiduciary, since the disloyalty occurs prior to resignation.

---

[46] [1997] Ch 84, 93.
[47] And although a duty of confidence might continue, the information at issue was no longer confidential.
[48] [1986] BCLC 460, 482.
[49] [1972] 1 WLR 443.
[50] *CMS Dolphin Ltd v Simonet* [2001] EWHC 415 (Ch); [2001] 2 BCLC 704; *In Plus Group Ltd v Pyke* [2002] EWCA Civ 370; [2002] 2 BCLC 201.
[51] [2007] EWCA Civ 200; [2007] 2 BCLC 239, [69].

The rationale here appears to be straightforward: only bad faith whilst still a fiduciary should be sanctioned. But ultimately, as Rix LJ concluded in *Foster Bryant*:[52]

> The jurisprudence also demonstrates, to my mind, that in the present context of retiring directors, where the critical line between a defendant being or not being a director becomes hard to police, the courts have adopted pragmatic solutions based on a common-sense and merits based approach.

(f) LIMITING THE COMMON LAW OF FIDUCIARY OBLIGATIONS: A STATUTORY FRAMEWORK FOR COMPANY DIRECTORS

Fiduciary obligations generally arise at Common Law. However, caution should be exercised when dealing with company directors: the duties of such directors are now to be found in the Companies Act 2006, ss. 170–1. Reference should therefore be made to the statutory duties, rather than the Common Law, although these statutory duties are derived from those that have been developed by the courts.

Companies Act 2006

170 Scope and nature of general duties

(1) The general duties specified in sections 171 to 177 are owed by a director of a company to the company.

(2) A person who ceases to be a director continues to be subject—

    (a) to the duty in section 175 (duty to avoid conflicts of interest) as regards the exploitation of any property, information or opportunity of which he became aware at a time when he was a director, and

    (b) to the duty in section 176 (duty not to accept benefits from third parties) as regards things done or omitted by him before he ceased to be a director.

To that extent those duties apply to a former director as to a director, subject to any necessary adaptations.

(3) The general duties are based on certain common law rules and equitable principles as they apply in relation to directors and have effect in place of those rules and principles as regards the duties owed to a company by a director.

(4) The general duties shall be interpreted and applied in the same way as common law rules or equitable principles, and regard shall be had to the corresponding common law rules and equitable principles in interpreting and applying the general duties.

(5) The general duties apply to shadow directors where, and to the extent that, the corresponding common law rules or equitable principles so apply.

The general duties

171 Duty to act within powers

A director of a company must—

(a) act in accordance with the company's constitution, and

(b) only exercise powers for the purposes for which they are conferred.

---

[52] Ibid, [76].

172 Duty to promote the success of the company

(1) A director of a company must act in the way he considers, in good faith, would be most likely to promote the success of the company for the benefit of its members as a whole ...

173 Duty to exercise independent judgment

(1) A director of a company must exercise independent judgment ...

174 Duty to exercise reasonable care, skill and diligence

(1) A director of a company must exercise reasonable care, skill and diligence.

(2) This means the care, skill and diligence that would be exercised by a reasonably diligent person with—

  (a) the general knowledge, skill and experience that may reasonably be expected of a person carrying out the functions carried out by the director in relation to the company, and

  (b) the general knowledge, skill and experience that the director has.

175 Duty to avoid conflicts of interest

(1) A director of a company must avoid a situation in which he has, or can have, a direct or indirect interest that conflicts, or possibly may conflict, with the interests of the company.

(2) This applies in particular to the exploitation of any property, information or opportunity (and it is immaterial whether the company could take advantage of the property, information or opportunity).

(3) This duty does not apply to a conflict of interest arising in relation to a transaction or arrangement with the company.

(4) This duty is not infringed—

  (a) if the situation cannot reasonably be regarded as likely to give rise to a conflict of interest; or

  (b) if the matter has been authorised by the directors.

(5) Authorisation may be given by the directors—

  (a) where the company is a private company and nothing in the company's constitution invalidates such authorisation, by the matter being proposed to and authorised by the directors; or

  (b) where the company is a public company and its constitution includes provision enabling the directors to authorise the matter, by the matter being proposed to and authorised by them in accordance with the constitution.

(6) The authorisation is effective only if—

  (a) any requirement as to the quorum at the meeting at which the matter is considered is met without counting the director in question or any other interested director, and

  (b) the matter was agreed to without their voting or would have been agreed to if their votes had not been counted.

(7) Any reference in this section to a conflict of interest includes a conflict of interest and duty and a conflict of duties.

176 Duty not to accept benefits from third parties

(1) A director of a company must not accept a benefit from a third party conferred by reason of—

  (a) his being a director, or

  (b) his doing (or not doing) anything as director.

(2) A "third party" means a person other than the company, an associated body corporate or a person acting on behalf of the company or an associated body corporate.

(3) Benefits received by a director from a person by whom his services (as a director or otherwise) are provided to the company are not regarded as conferred by a third party.

(4) This duty is not infringed if the acceptance of the benefit cannot reasonably be regarded as likely to give rise to a conflict of interest.

(5) Any reference in this section to a conflict of interest includes a conflict of interest and duty and a conflict of duties.

177 Duty to declare interest in proposed transaction or arrangement

(1) If a director of a company is in any way, directly or indirectly, interested in a proposed transaction or arrangement with the company, he must declare the nature and extent of that interest to the other directors.

...

(5) This section does not require a declaration of an interest of which the director is not aware or where the director is not aware of the transaction or arrangement in question.

For this purpose a director is treated as being aware of matters of which he ought reasonably to be aware.

(6) A director need not declare an interest—

(a) if it cannot reasonably be regarded as likely to give rise to a conflict of interest;

(b) if, or to the extent that, the other directors are already aware of it (and for this purpose the other directors are treated as aware of anything of which they ought reasonably to be aware); or

(c) if, or to the extent that, it concerns terms of his service contract that have been or are to be considered—

(i) by a meeting of the directors, or

(ii) by a committee of the directors appointed for the purpose under the company's constitution.

Supplementary provisions

178 Civil consequences of breach of general duties

(1) The consequences of breach (or threatened breach) of sections 171 to 177 are the same as would apply if the corresponding common law rule or equitable principle applied.

(2) The duties in those sections (with the exception of section 174 (duty to exercise reasonable care, skill and diligence) are, accordingly, enforceable in the same way as any other fiduciary duty owed to a company by its directors.

179 Cases within more than one of the general duties

Except as otherwise provided, more than one of the general duties may apply in any given case.

180 Consent, approval or authorisation by members

(1) In a case where—

(a) section 175 (duty to avoid conflicts of interest) is complied with by authorisation by the directors, or

(b) section 177 (duty to declare interest in proposed transaction or arrangement) is complied with, the transaction or arrangement is not liable to be set aside by virtue of any common law rule or equitable principle requiring the consent or approval of the members of the company.

This is without prejudice to any enactment, or provision of the company's constitution, requiring such consent or approval.

...

These provisions show that the statutory provisions replace the Common Law regarding company directors, but it is clear that directors' duties are based upon the Common Law; how the law has developed at Common Law is clearly relevant to interpreting the statutory duties. The remedies for breach of duty are the same as at Common Law,[53] and the no-conflict[54] and no-profit[55] rules are also included in the statute. The general principles underpinning fiduciaries, therefore, remain important in the context of directors, although a thorough investigation of the statutory duties is beyond the scope of this book.[56]

3. THE NO-CONFLICT PRINCIPLE

It has already been seen that the no-conflict principle is a fundamental aspect of fiduciary obligations. Consistent with the prophylactic nature of fiduciary doctrine, it only needs to be shown that there is a *potential* for conflict, rather than actual conflict. In considering this aspect of the no-conflict principle in *Boardman v Phipps*, Lord Upjohn said:[57]

In my view it means that the reasonable man looking at the relevant facts and circumstances of the particular case would think that there was a real sensible possibility of conflict; not that you could imagine some situation arising which might, in some conceivable possibility in events not contemplated as real sensible possibilities by any reasonable person, result in a conflict.

There are various ways in which the no-conflict rule can be engaged. For example, a fiduciary's personal interests might conflict with his or her duty to his or her principal, or the fiduciary's duty to one principal might conflict with his or her duty to another principal. These situations will be considered in turn.

(a) CONFLICT BETWEEN INTEREST AND DUTY

(i) *The dealing rules*

During the administration of a trust, a trustee may wish to purchase either the trust property itself or a beneficiary's interest under the trust. Equity has evolved two rules to resolve the conflict which

---

[53] s. 178.

[54] s. 175.

[55] s. 176, although a conflict must still be likely: s. 176(4).

[56] See e.g. Lim, 'Directors' Fiduciary Duties: A New Analytical Framework' (2013) 129 LQR 129; Davies and Worthington, *Gower and Davies' Principles of Modern Company Law* (9th edn) (London: Sweet & Maxwell, 2012), ch. 16.

[57] [1967] 2 AC 46, 124. Lord Upjohn was considering the previous comments of Lord Cranworth LC in *Aberdeen Rail Co. v Blaikie Brothers* (1854) 1 Macq 461, 471: 'And it is a rule of universal application, that no one, having such duties to discharge, shall be allowed to enter into engagements in which he has, or can have, a personal interest conflicting, or which possibly may conflict with the interests of those whom he is bound to protect.'

may arise in such circumstances between the trustee's duty to the beneficiaries and his or her personal interest. The first, called the 'self-dealing rule', provides that a trustee may not sell trust property to him- or herself, and renders the transaction voidable at the option of the beneficiaries, regardless of how fair the transaction is. The second, known as the 'fair-dealing rule', is that if a trustee purchases a beneficiary's interest, the transaction will generally be voidable as a result of the breach of the 'no-conflict' rule, but the transaction is not voidable as of right by the beneficiary, and will not be set aside if the trustee has behaved fairly. However, there is some debate about whether the two rules should be considered to be distinct, and this will be considered once the application of the two rules has been illustrated.[58]

(a) Self-dealing

The rationale behind the self-dealing rule is clear: if a fiduciary deals on behalf of him- or herself and the principal in the same transaction, there is a clear conflict between the interests of the fiduciary and the principal.[59] So, if a fiduciary seeks to purchase property belonging to the principal to which the fiduciary has legal title, the principal's interest in gaining the highest price possible conflicts with the fiduciary's interest in paying the lowest price possible. Such conflict renders the transaction voidable, and the principal can rescind it without having to prove it was unfair. As Megarry V-C said in *Tito v Waddell (No. 2)*:[60]

> The self-dealing rule is (to put it very shortly) that if a trustee sells the trust property to himself, the sale is voidable by any beneficiary *ex debito justitiae*,[61] however fair the transaction.

In *Wright v Morgan*,[62] a testator left land on trust for sale, and provided that it should be offered to one of his sons at a price to be fixed by valuers. Although the son was also a trustee, he was clearly able to purchase the land because this was explicitly provided for in the will.[63] That son did not purchase the land but instead assigned the option to purchase to his brother, who later became a trustee but was not explicitly authorized to buy the land by the terms of the will. The brother did subsequently purchase the land, but the court held that this transaction could be set aside because of the self-dealing rule: the brother's duties as a trustee conflicted with his interests as a purchaser. The court insisted that the transaction was voidable even though the price was fair, having been set by an independent valuer.

A more difficult application of the self-dealing rule can be found in the following case.

Holder v Holder [1968] Ch 353 (CA)

The testator was the owner of two farms in Gloucestershire. His third son, Victor, the defendant, was tenant of part of one farm. As his father became advanced in years, Victor also undertook responsibility for the farming of the remainder of the land, making annual payments to his father.

The testator died, having appointed his widow, a daughter, and Victor his executors. His will provided that the estate should be divided equally between the widow and all the children. The executors took preliminary steps towards the administration of the estate. Victor subsequently

---

[58] See Chapter 14.3(c), pp. 677–8.
[59] *Wright v Morgan* [1926] AC 788, 797 (Lord Dunedin).
[60] [1977] Ch 106, 241.
[61] 'as of right'.
[62] [1926] AC 788.
[63] Cf *Sargeant v National Westminster Bank plc* (1990) 61 P & CR 518.

purchased the farms at a fair price at an auction, and the money was paid to the beneficiaries under the will. One of the children, Frank, later sought to set the transaction aside.

The Court of Appeal held that (i) in the special circumstances of the case, Victor, although an executor, was not precluded from purchasing; (ii) Frank, by receiving his share of the purchase money, had precluded himself from relief.

Harman LJ:[64]

The cross-appeal raises far more difficult questions and they are broadly three. First, whether the actions of Victor before probate made his renunciation ineffective. Secondly, whether on that footing he was disentitled from bidding at the sale. Thirdly, whether the plaintiff is disentitled from taking this point because of his acquiescence.

It was admitted at the bar in the court below that the acts of Victor were enough to constitute intermeddling with the estate and that his renunciation was ineffective. On this footing he remained a personal representative, even after probate had been granted to his co-executors, and could have been obliged by a creditor or a beneficiary to re-assume the duties of an executor. The judge decided in favour of the plaintiff on this point because Victor at the time of the sale was himself still in a fiduciary position and like any other trustee could not purchase the trust property. I feel the force of this argument, but doubt its validity in the very special circumstances of this case. The reason for the rule is that a man may not be both vendor and purchaser; but Victor was never in that position here. He took no part in instructing the valuer who fixed the reserves or in the preparations for the auction. Everyone in the family knew that he was not a seller but a buyer. In this case Victor never assumed the duties of an executor. It is true that he concurred in signing a few cheques for trivial sums and endorsing a few insurance policies, but he never, so far as appears, interfered in any way with the administration of the estate. It is true he managed the farms, but he did that as tenant and not as executor. He acquired no special knowledge as executor. What he knew he knew as tenant of the farms.

Another reason lying behind the rule is that there must never be a conflict of duty and interest, but in fact there was none here in the case of Victor, who made no secret throughout that he intended to buy. …

… [Victor's] interference with the administration of the estate was of a minimal character and the last cheque he signed was in August before he executed the deed of renunciation. He took no part in the instructions for probate, nor in the valuations or fixing of the reserves. Everyone concerned knew of the renunciation and of the reason for it, namely, that he wished to be a purchaser. Equally, everyone, including the three firms of solicitors engaged, assumed that the renunciation was effective and entitled Victor to bid. I feel great doubt whether the admission made at the bar was correct, as did the judge, but assuming it was right, the acts were only technically acts of intermeddling and I find no case where the circumstances are parallel. Of course, I feel the force of the judge's reasoning that if Victor remained an executor he is within the rule, but in a case where the reasons behind the rule do not exist I do not feel bound to apply it. My reasons are that the beneficiaries never looked to Victor to protect their interests. They all knew he was in the market as purchaser; that the price paid was a good one and probably higher than anyone not a sitting tenant would give. Further, the first two defendants alone acted as executors and sellers; they alone could convey: they were not influenced by Victor in connection with the sales.

I hold, therefore, that the rule does not apply in order to disentitle Victor to bid at the auction, as he did. If I be wrong on this point and the rule applies so as to disentitle Victor to purchase, there arises a further defence, namely, that of acquiescence …

---

[64] [1968] Ch 353, 391–5.

On the whole I am of opinion that in the circumstances of this case it would not be right to allow the plaintiff to assert his right (assuming he has one) because with full knowledge of the facts he affirmed the sale. He has had £2,000 as a result. He has caused [Victor] to embark on liabilities which he cannot recoup. There can in fact be no restitutio in integrum, which is a necessary element in rescission.

Some of the reasoning here is very difficult to explain. Victor was an executor, and as such owed fiduciary duties, which clearly conflicted with his personal interest in purchasing property from the estate he was administering. This would seem to be a clear breach of the self-dealing rule. It may be that the concession that Victor had failed effectively to renounce his executorship was improperly made, and the court might have been influenced by this in seeking to avoid the strict nature of the self-dealing rule. But fiduciary obligations are strict and it is suggested that the self-dealing rule should have applied given that Victor continued to be a fiduciary.

However, upholding the transaction because the claimant had affirmed the sale seems entirely orthodox and principled. After all, the self-dealing rule only renders a transaction voidable rather than void, and it is well-established that affirmation can bar a right to rescind.[65]

The result in *Holder* has also been defended by Vinelott J in *Re Thompson's Settlement*,[66] on the basis that Victor never accepted a duty to act in the interests of the beneficiaries through his limited acts as an executor. *Re Thompson's Settlement* concerned not the sale of property, but the assignment of leases. The self-dealing rule applied because the assignees of the leases were also trustees of the land that was leased, and the consent of all the trustees was necessary for the assignment. In effectively assigning the leases to themselves, there was a clear conflict of interest and duty.[67]

Re Thompson's Settlement [1986] Ch 99 (Vinelott J)

[Counsel's] other and more radical submission founded upon *Holder v Holder* [1968] Ch 353 was that the self-dealing rule only applies to a sale by trustees to one of their number, alone or jointly with others, or to a purchase by trustees from one of their number, alone or jointly with others, and to analogous dealings with trust property or trust moneys such as the grant of a lease by or to trustees. He founded that submission upon the statement by Harman LJ, at p. 391, that 'the reason for the rule is that a man may not be both vendor and purchaser ... ' He submitted that in the instant case the only dealings analogous to the sale of property were the assignments or purported assignments of the leases which were never themselves trust property. He submitted that in such a case the fair-dealing rule applies (because it is founded on the principle that a man must not put himself in a position where his duty and interest conflict and because in relation to the trustees it was their duty to consider whether to consent to the assignments) but not the self-dealing rule which only applies if there is a sale or purchase by trustees or something analogous to it. I do not think that the self-dealing rule can be so confined. ... The principle is applied stringently in cases where a trustee concurs in a transaction which cannot be carried into effect without his concurrence and who also has an interest in or owes a fiduciary duty to another in relation to the same transaction. ...

The decision of the Court of Appeal in *Holder v Holder* does not in my judgment assist [Counsel]. The reason why, in the words of Harman LJ, the rule did not apply was that Victor, though he might technically have been made an executor notwithstanding the purported renunciation, had never acted as executor in a way which could be taken to amount to acceptance of a duty to act in the interests of the beneficiaries under his father's will.

---

[65] *Peyman v Lanjani* [1985] Ch 457; see Chapter 20.5, p. 1013.
[66] [1986] Ch 99.
[67] Ibid, 115–16.

It is sensible for the self-dealing rule not to be limited to the sale and purchase of trust property. Indeed, in *Kane v Radley-Kane*[68] it was held that the self-dealing rule applied to a personal representative who had appropriated property to satisfy a legacy to herself without the sanction of the court or the consent of the beneficiaries. It followed that the appropriation was voidable at the suit of a beneficiary.

One final aspect of *Holder* should be mentioned, namely the following suggestion of Danckwerts LJ:[69]

> It is said that it makes no difference [to the application of the self-dealing rule], even though the sale may be fair and honest and may be made at a public auction: see *Snell's Equity*, 26th Edn, 1966 p. 260. But the court may sanction such a purchase, and if the court can do that (see *Snell's Equity*, p. 219), there can be no more than a practice that the court should not allow a trustee to bid. In my view it is a matter for the discretion of the judge.

That the court may have a discretion to sanction a transaction that would otherwise be voidable due to the self-dealing rule has received some judicial support.[70] Nevertheless, it should be treated with great caution: recognizing judicial discretion in this area risks undermining the strict nature of fiduciary obligations, and seems out of kilter with the consistently strict application of fiduciary doctrine in other areas.[71]

(b) Fair-dealing

If the fiduciary does not also control the property he or she purchases, then the transaction will not *inevitably* be voidable. So, if the fiduciary purchases his or her beneficiary's interest in trust property, then the transaction will not always be set aside. As Megarry V-C put it in *Tito v Waddell (No. 2)*: [72]

> The fair-dealing rule is ... that if a trustee purchases the beneficial interest of any of his beneficiaries, the transaction is not voidable ex debito justitiae,[73] but can be set aside by the beneficiary unless the trustee can show that he has taken no advantage of his position and has made full disclosure to the beneficiary, and that the transaction is fair and honest.

This echoes what Lord Eldon LC had said in *Coles v Tecothick*:[74]

> As to the objection to a purchase by the trustee, the answer is, that a trustee may buy from the cestui que trust, provided there is a distinct and clear contract, ascertained to be such after a jealous and scrupulous examination of all the circumstances, proving, that the cestui que trust intended, the trustee should buy; and there is no fraud, no concealment, no advantage taken, by the trustee of information, acquired by him in the character of trustee. I admit, it is a difficult case to make out, wherever it is contended, that the exception prevails.

The last line of this passage undoubtedly still holds true. The Court will not be easily persuaded that the transaction is substantively fair, and a fiduciary should always remain wary about the consequences of

---

[68] [1999] Ch 274 (Sir Richard Scott V-C).
[69] [1968] Ch 353, 398.
[70] *Hillsdown Holdings plc v Pensions Ombudsman* [1997] 1 All ER 862, 895 (Knox J).
[71] See e.g. Chapter 14.4(d), pp. 687–98.
[72] [1977] Ch 106, 241.
[73] 'As a matter of right'.
[74] (1804) 9 Ves 234, 247.

dealing with his or her principal. It is important to note that this rule applies to fiduciaries who are not trustees. For example, a solicitor may not purchase property from his or her client if their relationship concerns that property, unless the client provides his or her fully informed consent.[75]

However, Conaglen has argued that substantive fairness is not really at issue in the context of the fair-dealing rule, and that the crucial issue is whether the principal has given his or her fully informed consent.

Conaglen, 'A Re-appraisal of the Fiduciary Self-dealing and Fair-dealing Rules' (2006) 64 CLJ 366, 380–1, 384

the fundamental concern at which the fair-dealing rule seeks to strike is the need to ensure that the principal gave fully informed consent when agreeing to enter into a transaction with his fiduciary. Such consent is required because of the conflict which arises when a fiduciary enters into a transaction with his client where the subject-matter of the transaction is the subject of the fiduciary relationship: in such a situation the fiduciary normally owes duties to his principal in respect of the subject-matter of the transaction and those duties will generally be in conflict with his personal interest in the transaction.

…

The fairness of a transaction can be relevant in applying the fair-dealing rule as it provides *evidence* as to whether the fiduciary made full disclosure of all material facts. In other words, the fairness or otherwise of the transaction assists the court in determining whether the principal's apparent consent to the transaction was fully informed, because the substantive content of the transaction can support inferences about whether the fiduciary disclosed all material information to the principal.

(c) Are the dealing rules distinct?

The fair-dealing and self-dealing rules have often been considered to be distinct. For example, in *Tito v Waddell*, Megarry V-C insisted that:[76]

I can well see that both rules, or both limbs, have a common origin in that equity is astute to prevent a trustee from abusing his position or profiting from his trust: the shepherd must not become a wolf. But subject to that, it seems to me that for all practical purposes there are two rules: the consequences are different, and the property and the transactions which invoke the rules are different. I see no merit in attempting a forced union which has to be expressed in terms of disunity. I shall accordingly treat the rules as being in essence two distinct though allied rules.

A desire to keep the two rules separate is understandable. Where the self-dealing rule applies, there is only really one party to the transaction, since the fiduciary is dealing with him- or herself. By contrast, where the fair-dealing rule applies, there are two parties to the transaction, since the fiduciary is dealing with the principal. Given that the principal is an independent party in the latter transaction, it might seem appropriate to be less stringent and to allow the fiduciary to prove that the transaction is fair and should not be set aside.

---

[75] *Gibson v Jeyes* (1801) 6 Ves 266 (31 E.R. 1044); *Moody v Cox & Hatt* [1917] 2 Ch 71; *Demerara Bauxite Co. Ltd v Hubbard* [1923] AC 673.
[76] [1977] Ch 106, 241.

However, regardless of which rule applies, it is likely that the fiduciary is in a stronger position than the principal, and that the fundamental concern in both scenarios is the prevention of a conflict of interest and duty.

Conaglen, 'A Re-appraisal of the Fiduciary Self-dealing and Fair-dealing Rules' (2006) 64 CLJ 366, 392

It is suggested ... that the fiduciary dealing rules can just as well be understood as a single doctrine, emanating directly from the fundamental fiduciary conflict principle, which requires the fiduciary to prove two things before he can maintain a transaction which falls within either of the two fiduciary dealing rules: (a) the *existence* of the principal's consent to the fiduciary's involvement in the transaction; and (b) that the consent was of a *high quality*, which requires full disclosure of the nature of the fiduciary's interest in the transaction and which can involve reference to the fairness (or otherwise) of the transaction as evidence from which full disclosure (or a lack thereof) can potentially be inferred.

This approach should be preferred. Conaglen's detailed analysis shows that, traditionally, the courts are much more concerned with the fully informed consent of the principal than the substantive fairness of the transaction. It seems better for the court to focus on the former, given the inevitable difficulties involved in analysing the substantive fairness of transactions between autonomous parties.[77] Considering the fair-dealing and self-dealing rules to be aligned in this way avoids an artificial distinction between some transactions, which are fair and still voidable, and others, which are fair and cannot be set aside; this would be the consequence of a rigid and substantive divide between 'self-dealing' and 'fair-dealing'.

(ii) *Remuneration*

It is generally expected that a trustee will not receive remuneration unless this has been explicitly authorized by the trust deed. This was well recognized at Common Law, and Lord Herschell's comments in *Bray v Ford*—that a fiduciary 'is not, unless otherwise expressly provided, entitled to make a profit'[78]—were often cited. This approach has now been recognized by section 28 of the Trustee Act 2000. Moreover, under certain circumstances a trustee will be able to claim reasonable remuneration under the authority of section 29—notably if the trustee is a trust corporation or a professional trustee.

TRUSTEE ACT 2000

28 Trustee's entitlement to payment under trust instrument

(1) Except to the extent (if any) to which the trust instrument makes inconsistent provision, subsections (2) to (4) apply to a trustee if—

(a) there is a provision in the trust instrument entitling him to receive payment out of trust funds in respect of services provided by him to or on behalf of the trust, and

(b) the trustee is a trust corporation or is acting in a professional capacity.

---

[77] Courts are traditionally reluctant to examine the substantive fairness of a transaction; for example, the court will not enquire as to the adequacy of consideration provided to create a binding contract: e.g. *Bainbridge v Firmstone* (1838) 8 A&E 743.
[78] [1896] AC 44 at 51, quoted in Chapter 14.2, p. 663.

(2) The trustee is to be treated as entitled under the trust instrument to receive payment in respect of services even if they are services which are capable of being provided by a lay trustee....

(5) For the purposes of this Part, a trustee acts in a professional capacity if he acts in the course of a profession or business which consists of or includes the provision of services in connection with—

    (a) the management or administration of trusts generally or a particular kind of trust, or

    (b) any particular aspect of the management or administration of trusts generally or a particular kind of trust,

and the services he provides to or on behalf of the trust fall within that description.

(6) For the purposes of this Part, a person acts as a lay trustee if he—

    (a) is not a trust corporation, and

    (b) does not act in a professional capacity.

29 Remuneration of certain trustees

(1) Subject to subsection (5), a trustee who—

    (a) is a trust corporation, but

    (b) is not a trustee of a charitable trust,

is entitled to receive reasonable remuneration out of the trust funds for any services that the trust corporation provides to or on behalf of the trust.

(2) Subject to subsection (5), a trustee who—

    (a) acts in a professional capacity, but

    (b) is not a trust corporation, a trustee of a charitable trust or a sole trustee,

is entitled to receive reasonable remuneration out of the trust funds for any services that he provides to or on behalf of the trust if each other trustee has agreed in writing that he may be remunerated for the services....

(5) A trustee is not entitled to remuneration under this section if any provision about his entitlement to remuneration has been made—

    (a) by the trust instrument, or

    (b) by any enactment or any provision of subordinate legislation.

...

Similar principles apply to directors. In *Guinness plc v Saunders*, Lord Goff observed that:[79]

the directors of a company, like other fiduciaries, must not put themselves in a position where there is a conflict between their personal interests and their duties as fiduciaries, and are for that reason precluded from contracting with the company for their services except in circumstances authorised by the articles of association.

The basis of this prohibition is clear: if a fiduciary is paid, there is a potential conflict between his or her financial interest and the interests of the principal.[80] But if payment has been authorized by the principal beforehand—either expressly or impliedly—then any objection the principal may have had rings hollow. Indeed, the court may, in some circumstances, hold that the fiduciary should be

---

[79] *Guinness plc v Saunders* [1990] 2 AC 663, 700.
[80] This may also be seen as breach of the 'no-profit' rule: see Chapter 14.4, p. 682.

remunerated even where this was not explicitly authorized beforehand. For example, in *Re Duke of Norfolk's Settlement Trusts*,[81] trustees were allowed to keep their remuneration since they had shown exceptional skill and expertise in administering a trust and carrying out substantial, unforeseen work on a redevelopment project for the trust. In the Court of Appeal, Fox LJ commented that:[82]

> the court has an inherent jurisdiction to authorise the payment of remuneration of trustees and that that jurisdiction extends to increasing the remuneration authorised by the trust instrument. In exercising that jurisdiction the court has to balance two influences which are to some extent in conflict. The first is that the office of trustee is, as such, gratuitous; the court will accordingly be careful to protect the interests of the beneficiaries against claims by the trustees. The second is that it is of great importance to the beneficiaries that the trust should be well administered. If therefore the court concludes, having regard to the nature of the trust, the experience and skill of a particular trustee and to the amounts which he seeks to charge when compared with what other trustees might require to be paid for their services and to all the other circumstances of the case, that it would be in the interests of the beneficiaries to increase the remuneration, then the court may properly do so.

A similar discretion applies to other fiduciaries; in the context of company directors, Lord Goff observed in *Guinness v Saunders* that:[83]

> the exercise of the jurisdiction is restricted to those cases where it cannot have the effect of encouraging trustees in any way to put themselves in a position where their interests conflict with their duties as trustees.

In *Re Macadam*,[84] the articles of a company provided that the trustees of the testator's will may 'appoint two persons ... to be directors of the company' in which the trust owned shares. The trustees appointed themselves. It was held that they were accountable to the trust for the fees received as directors because of the conflict that arose between their personal interests and those of the trust. However, had the trustees been explicitly authorized by the will, then their appointment as trustees would have been valid and they would have been able to keep the remuneration.[85]

(b) CONFLICT BETWEEN DUTY AND DUTY

The no-conflict principle might be engaged not only by a conflict between the fiduciary's personal interest and his or her duty to his principal, but also by a conflict between his or her duty to one principal and a conflicting duty owed to another principal.[86] This might happen where a fiduciary—such as a solicitor or agent—acts for both parties to a transaction; for example, there may be a potential conflict between the duty owed to the purchaser and the duty owed to the vendor. As Lord Cozens-Hardy MR observed in *Moody v Cox*:[87]

> A solicitor may have a duty on one side and a duty on the other, ... but if he chooses to put himself in that position it does not lie in his mouth to say to the client, 'I have not discharged that which the law

---

[81] [1982] 1 Ch 61.

[82] Ibid, 79 (Fox LJ).

[83] *Guinness plc v Saunders* [1990] 2 AC 663, 701.

[84] [1946] Ch 73 (Ch D, Cohen J).

[85] *Re Keeler's Settlement Trusts* [1981] Ch 156.

[86] See Conaglen, 'Fiduciary Regulation of Conflicts between Duties' (2009) 125 LQR 111.

[87] [1971] 2 Ch 71, 81.

says is my duty towards you, my client, because I owe a duty to the beneficiaries on the other side.' The answer is that if a solicitor involves himself in that dilemma it is his own fault. He ought before putting himself in that position to inform the client of his conflicting duties, and either obtain from that client an agreement that he should not perform his full duties of disclosure or say—which would be much better—'I cannot accept this business.'

However, such situations are not uncommon, and Lord Cozens-Hardy's suggestion that solicitors should refuse business is often circumvented by the consent of both opposing principals. As long as both principals are fully informed of the situation and agree to the fiduciary's acting for both sides, then it seems sensible to allow the fiduciary to do so. Indeed, in some circumstances it is often quicker and more efficient for both parties to instruct a sole solicitor rather than for both parties to have separate solicitors; a good example might be a routine conveyance in which one solicitor acts not only for the purchaser, but also for the bank providing a mortgage. However, it is important that the consent of both parties be genuine. In *Clarke Boyce v Mouat*, Lord Jauncey said:[88]

Informed consent means consent given in the knowledge that there is a conflict between the parties and that as a result the solicitor may be disabled from disclosing to each party the full knowledge which he possesses as to the transaction or may be disabled from giving advice to one party which conflicts with the interests of the other. If the parties are content to proceed upon this basis the solicitor may properly act.

This issue returned to the House of Lords in *Hilton v Barker Booth and Eastwood (a firm)*.[89] In that case, Bromage had persuaded Hilton to purchase a property, develop it, and then sell it back to Bromage. Bromage paid a deposit but then failed to complete the sale, so Hilton rescinded the transaction. The same firm—Barker Booth and Eastwood—had acted for both parties in the transaction. Hilton sued the firm because it had made Bromage seem creditworthy when in fact he had been made bankrupt and convicted for fraud. The failure to disclose Bromage's background was a breach of duty. The House of Lords actually held that there had been a breach of contract, but the same result could have been reached on the basis of breach of fiduciary duty.[90] The fiduciary's duty to Bromage clearly conflicted with the duty owed to Hilton, and Hilton had not given its fully informed consent to the fiduciary's acting for both parties: indeed, had it been fully informed of all the material facts, it is highly unlikely that Hilton would have allowed the fiduciary so to act. Lord Walker recognized that:[91]

the fact that [a solicitor] has chosen to put himself in an impossible position does not exonerate him from liability.

It has been suggested that even if a fiduciary has the fully informed consent of both principals, he or she may commit a breach of fiduciary duty if he or she intentionally favours one principal over another. This would be evidence of disloyalty. This argument was formulated by Millett LJ in *Mothew*, as follows:[92]

Even if a fiduciary is properly acting for two principals with potentially conflicting interests he must act in good faith in the interests of each and must not act with the intention of furthering the interests

[88] [1994] 1 AC 428, 435.
[89] [2005] UKHL 8; [2005] 1 WLR 567.
[90] See Conaglen, 'Conflicting Duties Owed by Solicitors Acting for Multiple Clients' (2005) 64 CLJ 291.
[91] [2005] UKHL 8; [2005] 1 WLR 567, [44].
[92] [1998] Ch 1, 19.

of one principal to the prejudice of those of the other ... I shall call this 'the duty of good faith.' But it goes further than this. He must not allow the performance of his obligations to one principal to be influenced by his relationship with the other. He must serve each as faithfully and loyally as if he were his only principal.

4. THE NO-PROFIT PRINCIPLE

A fiduciary must not profit from his or her position as a fiduciary without the fully informed prior consent of his or her principal. There is a close relationship with the no-conflict rule, and the no-profit principle has been explained on the basis that the very fact of profiting from a fiduciary position is so likely to involve a conflict of interest and duty that the court will not demand strict proof of a conflict. Whether this rationale is sufficient to merit its separate existence and application can be considered once the leading cases have been highlighted.

It is impossible to discuss every situation in which the no-profit rule can apply. As Lord Young observed in *Huntington Copper and Sulphur Co Ltd v Henderson*:[93]

Whenever it can be shewn that the trustee has so arranged matters as to obtain an advantage, whether in money or money's worth, to himself personally through the execution of his trust, he will not be permitted to retain it, but be compelled to make it over to his constituent.

There is a vast array of possibilities through which a fiduciary may profit from his or her position as a fiduciary. The crucial principles can be gleaned from the leading cases.

(a) LEASES HELD ON TRUST

(i) *Renewal of a lease*

The no-profit rule is often thought to derive from the following case.

Keech v Sandford (1726) Sel Cas Ch 61

The lessee of the profits of Romford market left his estate to a trustee (Sandford) on trust for an infant (Keech). Prior to the expiration of the lease, Sandford applied to the lessor for a renewal of the lease for the benefit of the infant. The lessor refused: because the lease was of the profits only and not of the land, if the rent was not paid the lessor did not have the remedy of distress available, so would have been forced to sue upon the contract, by which an infant would not be bound. After Sandford failed to renew the lease for the benefit of the infant, Sandford took the lease for himself. Keech later sued Sandford for the profits he had made from the lease. His claim succeeded: the Court held that the lease should be assigned to Keech, and that Sandford was holding the profits made from the lease on a constructive trust for Keech.

---

[93] (1877) 4 R 294, 308.

King LC:

I must consider this as a trust for the infant; for I very well see, if a trustee, on the refusal to renew, might have a lease to himself, few trust estates would be renewed to cestui que use; though I do not say there is a fraud in this case, yet he should rather have let it run out, than to have had the lease to himself. This may seem hard, that the trustee is the only person of all mankind who might not have the lease; but it is very proper that the rule should be strictly pursued, and not in the least relaxed; for it is very obvious what would be the consequences of letting trustees have the lease, on refusal to renew to cestui que use.

The result in this case was very hard on Sandford. The lessor would absolutely not have allowed the beneficiary of the trust to take the lease, so why prevent Sandford from renewing the lease himself? Why force him simply to let it run out? Clearly, being a fiduciary requires sacrifice: a fiduciary may be the only person in the whole world unable to exploit an opportunity. In *Keech*, the *potential* risk of conflict between Sandford's personal interests and duty to Keech was sufficient for the court to impugn the transaction—even though Keech was never going to be able to renew the lease and his interest in the transaction might, therefore, be considered to have lapsed.[94]

In analysing the decision in *Keech v Sandford*, Smith has argued that this supports the idea that the no-profit rule is distinct from the no-conflict rule:[95]

In order to see the case as an example of the rules against conflicts, one must first take a very wide view of what is a conflict, so that it encompasses all profit-making. One must then say that the rules against conflicts, when they are breached, not only allow the exercise of fiduciary powers to be retroactively set aside; they also allow the recovery of profits. Such a wide understanding necessarily swallows up the no-profit rule. But it is hardly necessary to say that the rules against conflicts also allow the recovery of profits, given that this is clearly the business of the no-profit rule. Moreover, viewing them as separate norms means that it is not necessary to identify any conflict in order for the no-profit rule to be activated. This makes sense of the wide range and scope of the no-profit rule that is revealed by the cases.

Keech is therefore better seen as a simple application of the no-profit rule. The separate remedies for the two rules—avoidance of legal acts, for the no-conflict rules, and profit-stripping for the no-profit rule—help us to see that there are indeed two separate norms. This is reinforced when we notice that there are a number of other situations which, like *Keech*, can and do activate the no-profit rule even though there is no conflict in relation to the exercise of fiduciary powers.

The rule in *Keech v Sandford* was considered in *Re Biss*.[96] Mr Biss had carried on a profitable business as a common lodging-house keeper on premises let to him under a seven-year lease. On its expiry, he continued as a yearly tenant. He died, leaving a widow and three children, one of whom was an infant. The widow, who was his administratrix, and an adult son continued the business, and they applied for a renewal of the lease. This was refused, but a new three-year lease was then granted to the adult son. The question was whether he should be compelled to hold the lease upon trust. The Court

---

[94] See Hicks, 'The Remedial Principle in *Keech v Sandford* Reconsidered' (2010) 69 CLJ 285.

[95] Smith, 'Fiduciary Relationships: Ensuring the Loyal Exercise of Judgement on Behalf of Another' (2014) 130 LQR 608, 626.

[96] [1903] 2 Ch 40.

of Appeal decided that he could hold it beneficially. The son, in obtaining the lease, was not in breach of any fiduciary duty.

> **Collins MR:**
>
> In the present case the appellant is simply one of the next-of-kin of the former tenant, and had, as such, a possible interest in the term. He was not, as such, a trustee for the others interested, nor was he in possession. The administratrix represented the estate and alone had the right to renew incident thereto, and she unquestionably could renew only for the benefit of the estate. But is the appellant in the same category? Or is he entitled to go into the facts to shew that he has not, in point of fact, abused his position, or in any sense intercepted an advantage coming by way of accretion to the estate? He did not take under a will or a settlement with interests coming after his own, but simply got a possible share upon an intestacy in case there was a surplus of assets over debts. It seems to me that his obligation cannot be put higher than that of any other tenant in common against whom it would have to be established, not as a presumption of law but as an inference of fact, that he had abused his position. If he is not under a personal incapacity to take a benefit, he is entitled to shew that the renewal was not in fact an accretion to the original term, and that it was not until there had been an absolute refusal on the part of the lessor, and after full opportunity to the administratrix to procure it for the estate if she could, that he accepted a proposal of renewal made to him by the lessor. These questions cannot be considered or discussed when the party is by his position debarred from keeping a personal advantage derived directly or indirectly out of his fiduciary or quasi-fiduciary position; but when he is not so debarred I think it becomes a question of fact whether that which he has received was in his hands an accretion to the interest of the deceased, or whether the connection between the estate and the renewal had not been wholly severed by the action of the lessor before the appellant accepted a new lease. This consideration seems to get rid of any difficulty that one of the next of kin was an infant. The right or hope of renewal incident to the estate was determined before the plaintiff intervened.

This result seems straightforward and satisfactory. The son was not a fiduciary, and therefore fell outside the scope of the principle in *Keech*. Moreover, he had not abused his position, so there was no reason to interfere with the completed transaction. However, the Master of the Rolls considered that whereas trustees—such as in *Keech*—could never renew a lease for their own benefit, given their clear status as fiduciaries, there was only a 'rebuttable presumption of fact' for mortgagees, joint tenants, and partners.[97] The last category is odd: partners are fiduciaries and therefore different from mortgagees and joint tenants, who are not. But it is not obvious that any distinction should be drawn between different classes of fiduciary at all. Indeed, Cretney has argued that it would be sensible for *all* persons not to be subject to an automatic, absolute exclusionary rule:[98]

> It is difficult to see the logic of this distinction [between persons in a fiduciary capacity and others] … It may be justifiable to have a special onus for trustees, but why should it be contrary to public policy to allow a trustee to rebut a presumption of misbehaviour?

Cretney argued against the decision in *Keech*, and for the ambit of its application to be narrowed: a fiduciary should be able to show that he always acted loyally and in the best interests of his principal, and thereby avoid liability. However, this argument has failed to convince English courts. In fact, the principle of *Keech* has even been extended to apply to the purchase of the *reversion* of a lease.

---

[97] *Re Biss* [1903] 2 Ch 40, 56.
[98] Cretney, 'The Rationale of *Keech v Sandford*' [1969] Conv 161, 176.

(ii) *Purchase of the reversion*

Sanctioning the renewal of the lease itself in *Keech* might perhaps be justified on the basis that the trustee is dealing with trust property. However, the same is not true where the trustee merely purchases the reversion of the lease:[99] this never belonged to the trust, and, where the lease was not renewable by custom,[100] the trust never had any expectation of obtaining the reversion and would not be prejudiced by the trustee's purchase of it. Thus at first instance in *Boardman v Phipps* Wilberforce J was able to state:[101]

> whereas in the case of a renewal the trustee is in effect buying a part of the trust property, in the case of a reversion this is not so; it is a separate item altogether, and therefore the trustee may purchase it unless, in so doing, he is in effect destroying part of the trust property.

However, the principle of *Keech* was thought to apply to the purchase of the reversion of a lease by the Court of Appeal in *Protheroe v Protheroe*.[102] A husband held a lease on trust for himself and his wife. After they separated, the husband purchased the reversion. The court held that the freehold was also purchased on trust for the husband and wife. Lord Denning MR boldly stated that:[103]

> There is a long established rule of equity from *Keech v. Sandford*, downwards that if a trustee, who owns the leasehold, gets in the freehold, that freehold belongs to the trust and he cannot take the property for himself. On that principle when the husband got in the freehold, it attached to and became part of the trust property.

This assertion is surprising: the principle given by Lord Denning does not accord with *Keech*, or the clear understanding of the law as illustrated by Wilberforce J in *Boardman*. It is unclear why a fiduciary should be unable to purchase the reversion of a lease held on trust where there is no conflict with the interests of the trust. Nevertheless, there is little doubt that *Protheroe* is good law. In *Thompson's Trustee in Bankruptcy v Heaton*, Pennycuick V-C cited *Protheroe* and held that:[104]

> this decision, like the rule in *Keech v Sandford*, is really in modern terms an application of the broad principle that a trustee must not make a profit out of the trust estate.

This approach has received the support of the Court of Appeal in *Don King Productions Inc. v Warren*.[105] Both *Thompson* and *Don King* concerned partnerships rather than trusts. However, the courts were satisfied that the same principles applied to partners given their position as fiduciaries. In *Thompson*, the judge insisted that:[106]

> The fiduciary relation here arises not from a trust of property but from the duty of good faith which each partner owes to the other. It is immaterial for this purpose in which partner the legal estate in the leasehold interest concerned is vested.

---

[99] Generally the freehold interest held by the owner of the property.
[100] *Phillips v Phillips* (1885) 29 Ch D 673.
[101] [1964] 1 WLR 993, 1009.
[102] [1968] 1 WLR 519.
[103] Ibid, 521.
[104] [1974] 1 WLR 605, 606.
[105] [2000] Ch 291, 340. This case did not concern the renewal of a lease but of management and promotion agreements entered into by a partner for the benefit of a partnership, to which similar principles applied.
[106] *Thompson's Trustee in Bankruptcy v Heaton* [1974] 1 WLR 605, 613.

This, at least, is a sensible approach, which emphasizes that although *Keech* is concerned with a breach of trust, the breach was of a fiduciary duty. As such, the principles from the case ought to apply to all fiduciaries. This stands in contrast to what was said in *Re Biss*,[107] but is much to be preferred.

(b) PROFITING FROM THE PRINCIPAL'S PROPERTY

It is straightforward that if a fiduciary makes a profit from the principal's property, then he or she will have to give up the gains made. This principle was succinctly stated by Lord Reid in *Brown v Inland Revenue Commissioners*:[108]

> The general principle is well settled. A solicitor has a fiduciary duty to his clients and any person who has such a duty 'shall not take any secret remuneration or any financial benefit not authorized by the law, or by his contract, or by the trust deed under which he acts, as the case may be' (*per* Lord Normand in *Dale v. Inland Revenue Commissioners*).[109] If the person in a fiduciary position does gain or receive any financial benefit arising out of the use of the property of the beneficiary he cannot keep it unless he can show such authority.

This is sensible: a fiduciary must not be allowed to use his or her principal's property without prior authorization. The conflict between the fiduciary's interest and duty is obvious. In *Sinclair v Versailles*, Lord Neuberger MR observed that:[110]

> it is possible to regard *Keech* ... as an example of a trustee acquiring an asset through seizing for his own benefit an opportunity which was effectively owned by the trust. As explained by Hicks[111] ... the opportunity to renew a tenancy, although not strictly a legal right, was effectively recognised as such by the courts in the 18th century. Thus, King LC himself in *Addis v Clement*[112] ... referred to a church lease as being 'always renewable' and therefore possible to regard as 'a perpetual estate'. Viewed in this way, *Keech* ... can be said to be an orthodox, if rather strict, application of the principle that where a trustee takes advantage of an opportunity, which is really owned by the beneficiary, he holds the consequent proceeds for the beneficiary.

This principle appears to extend to situations where the fiduciary makes a profit using property that did not *actually* belong to the principal, but *would have* belonged to the principal had the fiduciary not acted as he or she did. In other words, if the fiduciary *intercepts* property that was destined for the principal, such property will be considered properly to belong to the principal. This seems satisfactory: a fiduciary who deprives the principal of property cannot complain if the principal argues that the property rightfully belongs to him or her. In *Cook v Deeks*,[113] the Privy Council insisted that directors could not exploit their majority shareholding to divert a contract originally negotiated for the benefit of the company to the directors' own private shareholding. The contract was a corporate asset, and all profits made on the contract were to belong to the company. The directors could not

---

[107] Chapter 14.4(a)(i), pp. 683–4.
[108] [1965] AC 244, 256.
[109] [1954] AC 11.
[110] *Sinclair Investments (UK) Ltd v Versailles Trade Finance Ltd (In Administration)* [2011] EWCA Civ 347; [2012] Ch 453, [58]: this aspect of the decision survives the departure from a key aspect of *Sinclair* in *FHR European Ventures LLP v Mankarious* [2014] UKSC 45; [2015] AC 250; see further Chapter 14.5(b), pp. 706–11.
[111] Hicks, 'The Remedial Principle in *Keech v Sandford* Reconsidered' (2010) 69 CLJ 285, 295–8.
[112] (1728) 2 P Wms 456, 459.
[113] [1916] 1 AC 554.

keep the profits for themselves given the breach of fiduciary duty in using the principal's property for their personal gain.

(c) BRIBES

It is clear that a fiduciary should not be allowed to profit from his or her position by accepting a bribe to act disloyally towards his or her principal.[114] This is clearly prejudicial to the principal's interests. Since the fiduciary would not have been offered a bribe if he or she were not a fiduciary, it is sensible for the fiduciary to have to account for the profits made through accepting the bribe. A good example is *Reading v Attorney-General*,[115] in which the defendant, who was a sergeant in the British Army serving in Egypt, received bribes to sit on lorries whilst wearing military uniform, so that the police would not stop the lorries, which were illegally transporting alcohol. Lord Porter insisted that:[116]

> he is not acting in the course of his employment, he is taking advantage of the position which his employment gives him and for reward so gained he is answerable to his master none the less ... though the obtaining of the money is a criminal act.

Thus the Crown was able to strip the sergeant of the profits he received in breach of fiduciary duty. The rationale is clear: accepting bribes is a criminal act and corrupts the fiduciary. This should be deterred. Requiring restitution of the gain helps to achieve this goal.

It should be noted that the principles that apply to bribes are equally pertinent when considering secret commissions. So, in *Daryadan Holdings Ltd v Solland International Ltd*,[117] where an agent received a secret commission of 10 per cent of the contract price in exchange for contracts between his principal and a third party, Lawrence Collins J relied upon cases concerning bribery and said:[118]

> An agent or other fiduciary who makes a secret profit is accountable to his or her principal or cestui que trust....
>
> Any surreptitious dealing between one principal to a transaction and the agent of the other is a fraud on the other principal.

(d) EXPLOITATION OF OPPORTUNITIES

A fiduciary cannot exploit an opportunity that arises because of his or her position as a fiduciary.[119] However, care must be taken to ensure that the fiduciary does indeed owe fiduciary duties in respect of the opportunity offered. As noted already, it is important to consider precisely what fiduciary obligations are owed to whom when considering whether someone is a fiduciary.[120]

Many of the leading cases concerning exploitation of opportunities involve directors. Such cases must today be considered using the Companies Act 2006, which insists on the need for a conflict of interest before a breach of fiduciary duty will be found.[121] Caution should be exercised before

---

[114] Accepting a bribe also clearly breaches the no-conflict principle.
[115] [1951] AC 507.
[116] Ibid, 516.
[117] [2004] EWHC 622 (Ch); [2005] Ch 119.
[118] Ibid, at [51]–[52].
[119] At least not without the fully informed consent of his principal.
[120] See Chapter 14.2(d), p. 667.
[121] s. 176(4): see Chapter 14.2(f), pp. 669–72.

applying previous decisions to cases arising since the Companies Act 2006. Nevertheless, previous cases are clearly still helpful: the Act does not alter the fiduciary principles for any fiduciary other than directors.

Following *Keech v Sandford*, the courts have consistently held that the principle that fiduciaries should not profit from their position is strict. It can, therefore, apply even when the fiduciary has acted in good faith, and the principal is not disadvantaged in any way; indeed, in some of the cases the principal's position has actually been *improved* by the actions of the wrongdoing fiduciary. A good example of this is the following case.

Regal (Hastings) v Gulliver [1967] 2 AC 134n (1942) HL[122]

Regal owned a cinema in Hastings, and set up a subsidiary company, known as 'Amalgamated', in order to acquire the leases of two further cinemas. Amalgamated had a share capital of 5,000 made up of 5,000 £1 shares. The owner of the cinemas was only willing to lease them if the shares of Amalgamated were completely subscribed for. This posed a problem for Regal, which had resources to subscribe for only 2,000 of the 5,000 shares. In order to make sure the acquisition still went ahead, four of the directors and the company solicitor subscribed for 500 shares each, and the fifth director found others to subscribe for the remaining 500 shares. This enabled the leases to be purchased. The shares in Amalgamated were later sold for a substantial profit, and a new board of directors of Regal brought a claim against the solicitor and directors for the profits they had made from their positions as fiduciaries.

All members of the House of Lords agreed that the directors who had benefited from purchasing the shares in Amalgamated would have to give up those gains. The reasoning was squarely based upon *Keech v Sandford*. For example, Lord Russell said:[123]

> The rule of equity which insists on those, who by use of a fiduciary position make a profit, being liable to account for that profit, in no way depends on fraud, or absence of bona fides; or upon such questions or considerations as whether the profit would or should otherwise have gone to the plaintiff, or whether the profiteer was under a duty to obtain the source of the profit for the plaintiff, or whether he took a risk or acted as he did for the benefit of the plaintiff, or whether the plaintiff has in fact been damaged or benefited by his action. The liability arises from the mere fact of a profit having, in the stated circumstances, been made. The profiteer, however honest and well-intentioned, cannot escape the risk of being called upon to account.
>
> The leading case of *Keech v. Sandford* is an illustration of the strictness of this rule of equity in this regard, and of how far the rule is independent of these outside considerations. ...
>
> I am of opinion that the directors standing in a fiduciary relationship to Regal in regard to the exercise of their powers as directors, and having obtained these shares by reason and only by reason of the fact that they were directors of Regal and in the course of the execution of that office, are accountable for the profits which they have made out of them. The equitable rule laid down in *Keech v. Sandford* and *Ex parte James*[124] and similar authorities applies to them in full force. It was contended that these cases were distinguishable by reason of the fact that it was impossible for Regal to get the shares owing to

---

[122] Nolan, '*Regal (Hastings) Ltd v Gulliver* (1942)' in *Landmark Cases in Equity* (eds Mitchell and Mitchell) (Oxford: Hart, 2012).

[123] [1967] 2 AC 134n, 144–5, and 149–50. See too e.g. Viscount Sankey (137–8), Lord Wright (155), Lord Porter (1580).

[124] (1803) 8 Ves 337.

lack of funds, and that the directors in taking the shares were really acting as members of the public. I cannot accept this argument. It was impossible for the cestui que trust in *Keech v. Sandford* to obtain the lease, nevertheless the trustee was accountable. The suggestion that the directors were applying simply as members of the public is a travesty of the facts.

The claim against the director who had not subscribed for any shares failed: he had not made any profit to disgorge. The claim against the solicitor also failed, since the board of directors of Regal had consented to his purchasing the shares: given the fully informed consent of his principal, the solicitor could not later be sued for breach of fiduciary duty.

That the other directors had to account for their profits may seem harsh. After all, without the contributions of those directors, Amalgamated would have been unable to acquire the leases and the company would have made no money at all. To that extent, it may seem as if Regal received an 'unexpected windfall'[125] from suing its former directors.[126] So what should the directors have done? Viscount Sankey thought that liability was appropriate because:

At all material times they were directors and in a fiduciary position, and they used and acted upon their exclusive knowledge acquired as such directors. They framed resolutions by which they made a profit for themselves. They sought no authority from the company to do so.

But what if the directors had sought authority to purchase the shares themselves? Who could have given such authority? The consent of the board of directors was sufficient to absolve the solicitor of liability, but should the board be able to consent to the directors' actions? This is obviously more tricky because the board was controlled by the wrongdoing directors. It seems odd to say that the directors as board members could have consented to the directors as individuals purchasing shares in the company's subsidiary. Lord Russell stated that:[127]

They could, had they wished, have protected themselves by a resolution (either antecedent or subsequent) of the Regal shareholders in general meeting. In default of such approval, the liability to account must remain.

Requiring a resolution of the shareholders may appear logical. After all, it is ultimately the shareholders who will suffer if the directors act badly, so the shareholders' fully informed authorization should negate any liability that may fall upon the fiduciaries. However, in *Cook v Deeks* such resolution of the shareholders was thought to be ineffective.[128] That decision might be distinguished on the basis that the fiduciaries in *Cook* clearly acted badly,[129] whereas in *Regal* they did not.[130] More persuasively, perhaps, in *Prudential Assurance Co. v Newman Industries (No. 2)* Vinelott J reconciled the two cases on the basis that in *Cook* the directors controlled the majority shareholding, whereas this was not the case in *Regal*.[131] Thus, if the shareholders had sanctioned the acts of the directors in *Regal*, there would have been no claim for breach of fiduciary duty.

---

[125] [1967] 2 AC 134n, 157 (Lord Porter).
[126] See Prentice, 'Corporate Opportunity—Windfall Profits' (1979) 42 MLR 215.
[127] [1967] 2 AC 134n, 150. See too Lord Wright at 157.
[128] See [1916] 1 AC 554; see Chapter 14.4(b), p. 686.
[129] Perhaps thereby negating fully informed consent.
[130] But see Nolan, '*Regal (Hastings) Ltd v Gulliver* (1942)' in *Landmark Cases in Equity* (eds Mitchell and Mitchell) (Oxford: Hart, 2012).
[131] [1981] Ch 257, 308. Although the Editorial Note of *Regal* at [1942] 1 All ER 378, 379 appears to assume that the directors in *Regal* also controlled the majority of the shareholding in the company, Vinelott J thought differently.

There is an important question to be raised about when a fiduciary's exploitation of an opportunity is properly sanctioned by his or her principal. This will be considered further when analysing whether the approach of the English courts is too strict. However, it is significant to note that in *Regal*, the decision that Regal did not have the necessary financial resources to subscribe for all the shares in Amalgamated was made by the directors, who were the very persons who benefited from this decision. It might, therefore, be thought that there was a conflict between the interests of the directors and the company, and that the directors should rightly be stripped of their profits.

The strict nature of the English approach is perhaps best now exemplified by the decision of the House of Lords in the following case.

Boardman v Phipps [1967] 2 AC 46 (HL, Viscount Dilhorne, Lord Cohen, Lord Hodson, Lord Guest, and Lord Upjohn)[132]

Mr Phipps left his residuary estate, which included 27 per cent of the shares in Lester and Harris Ltd, on trust for his widow for life and after her death for his four children. The trustees in 1955 were his widow (the life tenant), Mrs Noble (his daughter), and Mr Fox (a professional trustee and an accountant).

In 1956, Tom Phipps, a son of the testator and one of the beneficiaries, and Mr Boardman, the solicitor to the trust, were dissatisfied with the way in which the business of Lester and Harris Ltd was conducted. They unsuccessfully sought to effect change at the company's annual general meeting, and then encouraged the trust to invest in the company in order to improve its performance. Mrs Noble and Mr Fox insisted that the trust was in no position to buy the remaining shares in the company, and would not consider doing so under any circumstances. The trustees were not authorized to purchase the shares and would have had to apply to the court for permission to do so; the active trustees refused to do this. The third trustee, the testator's widow, was senile and not consulted. Whilst acting on behalf of the trust in dealing with the company, Mr Boardman obtained valuable information, which he thought he could exploit to make the business more profitable. He wrote to the testator's four children to ask for their consent to his negotiating for his own personal interest, and assumed that silence meant that consent had tacitly been given. Ultimately, Mr Boardman and Tom Phipps purchased all the shares in Lester and Harris Ltd other than those owned by the trust. They reorganized the business, and greatly improved the fortunes of the company. This clearly benefited Boardman, Phipps, and indeed the trust, which maintained a large shareholding in the company.

On this summary it would appear as if everybody was a winner: the fortunes of the company improved, the trust's shareholding improved, and Boardman and Phipps also made a profit. Nevertheless, John Phipps, one of the testator's sons and one of the beneficiaries under the trust, sued Boardman for breach of fiduciary duty, as well as Tom Phipps.

The *result* of the case is clear: by a 3:2 majority, the House of Lords insisted that the defendants had breached their fiduciary duties and had to account for their profits. However, Boardman was granted a liberal allowance for the work he had done to turn around the fortunes of the company. This 'equitable allowance' will be analysed later.[133] But of greater interest at present is *why* Boardman and Phipps were liable to account for their profits at all.

---

[132] See Bryan, '*Boardman v Phipps* (1967)' in *Landmark Cases in Equity* (eds Mitchell and Mitchell) (Oxford: Hart, 2012).

[133] See Chapter 14.5(e), pp. 716–17.

The *reasoning* of the majority is difficult to pin down. Indeed, there are many difficult aspects of the case. The more important factors will be considered in turn.

(i) *What fiduciary obligations were at issue?*

As has already been shown, it is insufficient simply to assert that because Boardman was a solicitor he was a fiduciary. It is crucial to determine to whom he owed such duties: to the trustees, or to the beneficiaries? As a solicitor advising the trust, it might be expected that he owed fiduciary obligations to the trustees as principals. This was the view of the dissenting judges, Viscount Dilhorne[134] and Lord Upjohn; the latter expressed his unease with the idea of a solicitor permanently, or constantly, owing fiduciary duties:[135]

> A solicitor who acts for a client from time to time is no doubt rightly described throughout as being in a fiduciary capacity to him but that means fundamentally no more than this, that if he has dealings with his client, e.g. accepts a present from him or buys property from him, there is a presumption of undue influence and the onus is on the solicitor to justify the present or purchase ... That principle has no relevance to the present case. There is no such thing as an office of being solicitor to a trust ... It is perfectly clear that a solicitor can if he so desires act against his clients in any matter in which he has not been retained by them provided, of course, that in acting for them generally he has not learnt information or placed himself in a position which would make it improper for him to act against them. This is an obvious application of the rule that he must not place himself in a position where his duty and his interest conflict. So in general a solicitor can deal in shares in a company in which the client is a shareholder, subject always to the general rule that the solicitor must never place himself in a position where his interest and his duty conflict.

Lord Upjohn's comments are a reminder that the *scope* of fiduciary obligations must always be established. But his conclusion that Boardman owed fiduciary obligations chimes well with Lord Guest in the majority, who said:[136]

> I take the view that from first to last Boardman was acting in a fiduciary capacity to the trustees.

This approach is odd: if Boardman owed fiduciary obligations to the trustees, why was John Phipps—a beneficiary under the trust—able to sue Boardman for breach of fiduciary duty? Surely the claim should have been brought by the trustees as principals? This important question is not well addressed in their Lordships' speeches. For example, Lord Upjohn commented that:[137]

> Whether [Boardman] was ever in a fiduciary capacity to the respondent was not debated before your Lordships and I do not think it matters.

But clearly it *does* matter. It is imperative to determine to whom fiduciary obligations are owed and thus whether John Phipps as a beneficiary under the trust had a valid claim on the facts. There is some

---

[134] [1967] 2 AC 46, 87, 94.
[135] Ibid, 126.
[136] Ibid, 115.
[137] Ibid, 125–6.

suggestion that fiduciary obligations were properly owed to John Phipps. For example, Lord Hodson said that:[138]

> there was a potential conflict between Boardman's position as solicitor to the trustees and his own interest in applying for the shares. He was in a fiduciary position vis-a-vis the trustees and through them vis-a-vis the beneficiaries.

However, it is not clear why owing fiduciary obligations to the trustees extends to the beneficiaries of the trust. Perhaps this is because the obligations owed to the trustees are held for the benefit of the beneficiaries. In any event, Lord Cohen also appeared to approach the question on similar lines, since he insisted that: [139]

> the appellants could not purchase the shares on their own behalf without the informed consent of the beneficiaries: it is now admitted that they did not obtain that consent. They are therefore, in my opinion, accountable to the respondent for his share of the net profits they derived from the transaction.

If Boardman had needed to obtain the informed consent of the beneficiaries of the trust, this would suggest that fiduciary obligations were owed to them. But why? Although not articulated in the case itself, it might be that by participating in the negotiations with the company, and acting as an agent of the trust, Boardman somehow owed fiduciary obligations not only to the trustees, but also to the beneficiaries of the trust. In any event, this point does not seem to have been argued or caused much concern.

Another difficult issue, which was not fully argued, was whether Tom Phipps owed the same fiduciary obligations as Boardman. This was because Tom Phipps accepted that he did, and refused the Court of Appeal's offer to sever himself from Boardman.[140] However, Lord Cohen did say:[141]

> Tom Phipps was only a beneficiary and was not as such debarred from bidding for the shares, but no attempt was made in the courts below to differentiate between them. Had such an attempt been made it would very likely have failed as Tom Phipps left the negotiations largely to Mr. Boardman and it might well be held that if Mr. Boardman was disqualified from bidding Tom Phipps could not be in a better position.

This might be because undertaking the negotiations as an agent of the trust gives rise to a fiduciary relationship to the trust and the beneficiaries on the particular facts at issue. The preferable view is that Tom Phipps was an intermeddler who assumed the authority of an agent that he did not have, such that he was an agent *de son tort*[142] and, therefore, accountable as a fiduciary to those for whom he purported to act.[143] In any event, the judges were happy to associate Tom Phipps with Boardman; to simplify our discussion we will focus on Boardman's liability, although on the facts of the case this also meant that Tom Phipps was liable.

---

[138] Ibid, 112.
[139] Ibid, 104.
[140] Ibid, 125–6 (Lord Upjohn); 106 (Lord Hodson).
[141] Ibid, 104.
[142] See Chapter 11.2(h)(i), pp. 535–6.
[143] See Bryan, 'Boardman v Phipps (1967)' in *Landmark Cases in Equity* (eds Mitchell and Mitchell) (Oxford: Hart, 2012), pp. 586–9.

(ii) *Information as property*

It would obviously be appropriate for Boardman to have to account for his gains if he had exploited trust property: the profits made from trust property clearly belong to the trust. But what property of the trust had he used in order to make his profits? There is some suggestion in the judgments that the information Boardman obtained whilst negotiating with the company on behalf of the trust should be considered to be trust property. This view was put forward by both Lord Hodson and Lord Guest, in the majority:

Lord Hodson:

As to this it is said on behalf of the appellants that information as such is not necessarily property and it is only trust property which is relevant. I agree, but it is nothing to the point to say that in these times corporate trustees, e.g., the Public Trustee and others, necessarily acquire a mass of information in their capacity of trustees for a particular trust and cannot be held liable to account if knowledge so acquired enables them to operate to their own advantage, or to that of other trusts. Each case must depend on its own facts and I dissent from the view that information is of its nature something which is not properly to be described as property. We are aware that what is called 'know-how' in the commercial sense is property which may be very valuable as an asset. I agree with the learned judge and with the Court of Appeal that the confidential information acquired in this case which was capable of being and was turned to account can be properly regarded as the property of the trust. It was obtained by Mr. Boardman by reason of the opportunity which he was given as solicitor acting for the trustees in the negotiations with the chairman of the company, as the correspondence demonstrates. The end result was that out of the special position in which they were standing in the course of the negotiations the appellants got the opportunity to make a profit and the knowledge that it was there to be made.[144]

Lord Guest:

If Boardman was acting on behalf of the trust, then all the information he obtained … became trust property. The weapon which he used to obtain this information was the trust holding and I see no reason why information and knowledge cannot be trust property.[145]

However, the third member of the majority, Lord Cohen, was more cautious about such reasoning:[146]

the appellants obtained both the information which satisfied them that the purchase of the shares would be a good investment and the opportunity of acquiring them as a result of acting for certain purposes on behalf of the trustees. Information is, of course, not property in the strict sense of that word and, as I have already stated, it does not necessarily follow that because an agent acquired information and opportunity while acting in a fiduciary capacity he is accountable to his principals for any profit that comes his way as the result of the use he makes of that information and opportunity. His liability to account must depend on the facts of the case. In the present case much of the information came the appellants' way when Mr. Boardman was acting on behalf of the trustees on the instructions of Mr. Fox and the opportunity of bidding for the shares came because he purported for all purposes except

---

[144] [1967] 2 AC 46, 107.
[145] Ibid, at 115.
[146] Ibid, at 102–3.

for making the bid to be acting on behalf of the owners of the 8,000 shares in the company. In these circumstances it seems to me that the principle of the *Regal* case applies and that the courts below came to the right conclusion.

Lord Cohen's approach relies upon Boardman's profiting from his position as a fiduciary, and he considered this to be consistent with *Regal*. This aspect of the decision will be discussed in Section (iii) below, but it is suggested that he was correct in rejecting the proposition that the information gained was the property of the trust. This was certainly the view of the two minority judges as well. The reason for this was well expressed by Lord Upjohn:[147]

> In general, information is not property at all. It is normally open to all who have eyes to read and ears to hear. The true test is to determine in what circumstances the information has been acquired. If it has been acquired in such circumstances that it would be a breach of confidence to disclose it to another then courts of equity will restrain the recipient from communicating it to another. In such cases such confidential information is often and for many years has been described as the property of the donor, the books of authority are full of such references; knowledge of secret processes, 'know-how,' confidential information as to the prospects of a company or of someone's intention or the expected results of some horse race based on stable or other confidential information. But in the end the real truth is that it is not property in any normal sense but equity will restrain its transmission to another if in breach of some confidential relationship.
>
> ....
>
> There is, in my view, and I know of no authority to the contrary, no general rule that information learnt by a trustee during the course of his duties is property of the trust and cannot be used by him. If that were to be the rule it would put the Public Trustee and other corporate trustees out of business and make it difficult for private trustees to be trustees of more than one trust. This would be the greatest possible pity for corporate trustees and others may have much information which they may initially acquire in connection with some particular trust but without prejudice to that trust can make it readily available to other trusts to the great advantage of those other trusts.
>
> The real rule is, in my view, that knowledge learnt by a trustee in the course of his duties as such is not in the least property of the trust and in general may be used by him for his own benefit or for the benefit of other trusts unless it is confidential information which is given to him (1) in circumstances which, regardless of his position as a trustee, would make it a breach of confidence for him to communicate to anyone for it has been given to him expressly or impliedly as confidential, or (2) in a fiduciary capacity, and its use would place him in a position where his duty and his interest might possibly conflict.

A similar approach was taken by Viscount Dilhorne.[148] Thus Lord Cohen, in the majority, and the two dissenting judges did not agree that the information constituted trust property. Given that only two judges in the House of Lords considered information to be trust property, this should be rejected as the basis of the decision. Information is best protected by the equitable doctrine of breach of a relationship of confidence. It is consequently unnecessary to consider information to be proprietary. Nevertheless, some references to information as property can still be found.[149] These should not be followed.

---

[147] Ibid, at 127–9.
[148] Ibid, at 89, 91.
[149] E.g. *Quarter Master UK Ltd v Pyke* [2005] 1 BCLC 245, [71] (Paul Morgan QC).

(iii) *Profit from position*

The majority decision is better explained on the basis of a strict application of the principle that a fiduciary should not profit from his or her position as a fiduciary. Indeed, all members of the majority relied on the previous decision of the House of Lords in *Regal*. In fact, *Regal* was only reported in the official reports *after Boardman v Phipps*, because it was so heavily relied upon in the later case!

Lord Cohen's reliance on *Regal* has already been shown. On this issue, he was joined by both Lord Hodson and Lord Guest.

Lord Hodson:

As *Keech v Sandford* shows, the inability of the trust to purchase makes no difference to the liability of the appellants, if liability otherwise exists. The distinction on the facts as to intention to purchase shares between this case and *Regal (Hastings) Ltd v Gulliver* is not relevant. The company (Regal) had not the money to apply for the shares upon which the profit was made. The directors took the opportunity which they had presented to them to buy the shares with their own money and were held accountable. Mr. Fox's refusal as one of the trustees [in *Phipps*] to take any part in the matter on behalf of the trust, so far as he was concerned, can make no difference. Nothing short of fully informed consent which the learned judge found not to have been obtained could enable the appellants in the position which they occupied having taken the opportunity provided by that position to make a profit for themselves.[150]

Lord Guest:

Boardman and Tom Phipps … placed themselves in a special position which was of a fiduciary character in relation to the negotiations with the directors of Lester & Harris relating to the trust shares. Out of such special position and in the course of such negotiations they obtained the opportunity to make a profit out of the shares and knowledge that the profit was there to be made. A profit was made and they are accountable accordingly.[151]

This is a strict version of the no-profit principle since it appears all-encompassing: *any* profits derived from the position of being a fiduciary must be accounted for. This appeared harsh to the minority, who thought that the no-profit rule was simply part of the wider no-conflict principle, and that there was no real conflict of interest here, given that the trust was never going to invest in the company. This is a crucial and controversial issue, and deserves full consideration.

(iv) *No conflict*

The minority's view that no conflict existed can be found in the following extracts:

Viscount Dilhorne:

On the facts of this case there was not, in my opinion, any conflict or possibility of a conflict between the personal interests of the appellants and those of the trust. There was no possibility so long as Mr. Fox was opposed to the trust buying any of the shares of any conflict of interest arising through the purchase of the shares by the appellants.[152]

---

[150] [1967] 2 AC 46, 109.
[151] Ibid, 118.
[152] Ibid, at 88.

Lord Upjohn:

It is perhaps stated most highly against trustees or directors in the celebrated speech of Lord Cranworth L.C. in *Aberdeen Railway v. Blaikie*, where he said:

> 'And it is a rule of universal application, that no one, having such duties to discharge, shall be allowed to enter into engagements in which he has, or can have, a personal interest conflicting, or which possibly may conflict, with the interests of those whom he is bound to protect.'

The phrase 'possibly may conflict' requires consideration. In my view it means that the reasonable man looking at the relevant facts and circumstances of the particular case would think that there was a real sensible possibility of conflict; not that you could imagine some situation arising which might, in some conceivable possibility in events not contemplated as real sensible possibilities by any reasonable person, result in a conflict.

...

My Lords, I believe the only conflict between the duty and interest of the appellants that can be suggested is that having learnt so much about the company and realised that in the hands of experts like Tom the shares were a good buy at more than £3 a share they should have communicated this fact to the trustees and suggested that they ought to consider a purchase and an application to the court for that purpose.

This, so far as I can ascertain, was suggested for the first time in the judgment of Lord Denning M.R [in the Court of Appeal].

Had this been an issue in the action this might have been a very difficult matter, but it never was. There is no sign of any such case made in the pleadings; but what is much more important is that from start to finish in all three courts there was no suggestion of this in argument on behalf of the respondent; and what is most important of all, there is no suggestion in cross-examination of either of the trustees or of the appellants that the latter were under any such obligation.[153]

This last point of Lord Upjohn was of potential importance but simply not argued. Once Boardman and Tom Phipps knew that they would be buying the shares at a very advantageous, low price, perhaps they ought to have informed the trust of this and allowed the trust the option of making the most of this opportunity. However, it is not clear how realistic it is to expect parties to do this during the course of confidential and protracted negotiations.[154]

The test identified by Lord Upjohn has been cited with approval many times since.[155] It is crucial to identify whether 'the reasonable man looking at the relevant facts and circumstances of the particular case would think that there was a real sensible possibility of conflict'.[156] However, Lord Upjohn's approach might be contrasted with the opinion of Lord Cohen:[157]

Mr. Boardman and Tom Phipps were not general agents of the trustees but they were their agents for certain limited purposes. The information they had obtained and the opportunity to purchase the

---

[153] Ibid, at 124, 131.

[154] Particularly since the trust would still have needed to apply to the court in order to obtain permission to purchase shares in the company.

[155] E.g. *Queensland Mines v Hudson* (1978) 18 ALR 1, 3 (Lord Scarman); *Bhullar v Bhullar* [2003] EWCA Civ 424; [2003] 2 BCLC 241, [272].

[156] Compare the test of the High Court of Australia in *Howard v Commissioner of Taxation* [2014] HCA 21, [37]: 'If there is no possible conflict between personal interest and fiduciary duty, and if the gain or benefit is not obtained by use or by reason of the fiduciary position, the fiduciary is not liable to account for the gain or benefit.'

[157] [1967] 2 AC 46, 103–4, 106, 111, 112.

21,986 shares afforded them by their relations with the directors of the company—an opportunity they got as the result of their introduction to the directors by Mr. Fox—were not property in the strict sense but that information and that opportunity they owed to their representing themselves as agents for the holders of the 8,000 shares held by the trustees. In these circumstances they could not, I think, use that information and that opportunity to purchase the shares for themselves if there was any possibility that the trustees might wish to acquire them for the trust. Mr. Boardman was the solicitor whom the trustees were in the habit of consulting if they wanted legal advice. Granted that he would not be bound to advise on any point unless he is consulted, he would still be the person they would consult if they wanted advice. He would clearly have advised them that they had no power to invest in shares of the company without the sanction of the court. In the first phase he would also have had to advise on the evidence then available that the court would be unlikely to give such sanction: but the appellants learnt much more during the [negotiations] … It may well be that … the answer of the court would have been the same but, in my opinion, Mr. Boardman would not have been able to give unprejudiced advice if he had been consulted by the trustees and was at the same time negotiating for the purchase of the shares on behalf of himself and Tom Phipps. In other words, there was, in my opinion, at the crucial date, a possibility of a conflict between his interest and his duty.

…

Mr. Boardman's fiduciary position arose from the fact that he was at all material times solicitor to the trustees of the will of Mr. Phipps senior. This is admitted, although counsel for the appellants has argued, and argued correctly, that there is no such post as solicitor to trustees. The trustees either employ a solicitor or they do not in a particular case and there is no suggestion that they were under any contractual or other duty to employ Mr. Boardman or his firm. Nevertheless as a historical fact they did employ him and look to him for advice at all material times and this is admitted. It was as solicitor to the trustees that he obtained the information.

…

No doubt it was but a remote possibility that Mr. Boardman would ever be asked by the trustees to advise on the desirability of an application to the court in order that the trustees might avail themselves of the information obtained. Nevertheless, even if the possibility of conflict is present between personal interest and the fiduciary position the rule of equity must be applied.

….

… there was a potential conflict between Boardman's position as solicitor to the trustees and his own interest in applying for the shares. He was in a fiduciary position vis-a-vis the trustees and through them vis-a-vis the beneficiaries.

Lord Cohen was of the view that even a remote possibility of conflict was sufficient to engage the no-conflict principle. It is not clear whether this also constitutes a 'real sensible possibility': it might be suggested that even a remote possibility can be real and sensible. Given the frequency with which Lord Upjohn's test is cited and applied, it might be best to conclude that Lord Upjohn was not dissenting on the nature of the legal test to be employed, but only on the *application* of the test to the facts of the case.[158] Whereas the majority thought that there was a conflict, the minority did not.

The decision in *Phipps* is very hard on Boardman, who might reasonably have thought no conflict existed. A strict rule might be justified on the basis that it is always possible for the fiduciary in such a situation to obtain the fully informed consent of his principal. As Lord Guest insisted:[159]

---

[158] E.g. Lord Scarman in *Queensland Mines v Hudson* (1978) 18 ALR 1, 3: 'Lord Upjohn, who dissented on the facts but not on the law'.

[159] [1967] 2 AC 46, 117.

> The only defence available to a person in such a fiduciary position is that he made the profits with the knowledge and assent of the trustees. It is not contended that the trustees had such knowledge or gave such consent.

However, one of the trustees was senile, and in the midst of important negotiations, obtaining the consent of all the trustees may have been difficult and time-consuming. The consent of all the active trustees may have seemed sufficient. Yet, as discussed already it might be that Boardman should also have obtained the consent of the *beneficiaries*, not only that of the trustees.[160]

The actual impact of the decision on Boardman was mitigated by allowing him to keep an equitable allowance for his skill and work, which was assessed on a 'liberal scale'.[161] This aspect of the decision will be examined later,[162] but such an allowance would be unnecessary if the rules of Equity were relaxed a little to allow a fiduciary to act and retain any profits made where his principal clearly will not exploit the opportunity and has suffered no loss. In *Phipps*, the solicitor had risked losing his own money by attempting to revive the fortunes of the company, so it might seem fair for him to keep those profits if he proved to be successful and thereby also increased the wealth of the trust fund. It is important to consider whether English law is too strict in this area.

(e) A MORE RELAXED APPROACH?

As soon as *Phipps* was decided, it was the subject of academic criticism. For example, Professor Jones wrote:[163]

> To say that the fiduciaries' profit was made solely through the use of property (the information) received qua fiduciaries, when the trust could not have utilised it and when the negotiations would have failed but for Boardman's business acumen and Boardman and Phipps' financial intervention, offends legal as well as common sense. …
>
> The main ground of the decision was that there was a conflict between Boardman and Phipps' self-interest and their fiduciary duty; they had made a profit out of their special position of trust. It is difficult to accept, however, that any reasonable person could conclude on these facts that there was any real (as distinct from a hypothetical) conflict of interest. In our view the reasoning of the dissenting law lords is convincing. Lord Upjohn's realistic, commonsense approach is that of Justice Clark in the *Becker* case.[164] Both judges refused to apply blindly a rule of equity. In neither *Becker's case* nor *Phipps v Boardman* had the profit been made at the expense of the fiduciary's principal. In both cases the fiduciary's actions had benefited the principal: the purchase of the debentures in the Becker case encouraged public confidence in a company which was in a parlous financial position; in *Phipps v Boardman* the long negotiations conducted with considerable skill by Boardman, and the purchase of the outstanding shares by Boardman and Tom Phipps, had resulted in great financial benefit to the trust.

It is interesting to note Professor Jones' reference to the American case of *Becker*. There have been strong calls for reform of the strict application of the no-profit rule in cases such as *Phipps* by some American scholars, partly influenced by reasoning from an economic perspective. For example, had

---

[160] Chapter 14.4(d)(i), pp. 691–2.
[161] [1967] 2 AC 46, 104 (Cohen); 112 (Hodson).
[162] Chapter 14.5(e), pp. 716–17.
[163] 'Unjust Enrichment and the Fiduciary's Duty of Loyalty' (1968) 84 LQR 472, 483–502.
[164] *Manufacturers Trust Co. v Becker* 338 US 304, 70 Sup Ct 127 (1949).

Boardman sought but failed to obtain the consent of his principals, then he would not have been able to invest in the company, so the company would probably have continued to be unprofitable, and as a result the shareholding of the trust fund would not have made the gains it did. It might seem odd for the law to demand this: the stultification of economically advantageous conduct would appear to be the result. This sort of reasoning has prompted Professor Langbein to argue:[165]

> The underlying purpose of the duty of loyalty ... is to advance the best interest of the beneficiaries.... a transaction prudently undertaken to advance the best interest of the beneficiaries best serves the purpose of the duty of loyalty, even if the trustee also does or might derive some benefit. A transaction in which there has been conflict or overlap of interest should be sustained if the trustee can prove that the transaction was prudently undertaken in the best interest of the beneficiaries. In such a case, inquiry into the merits is better than 'no further inquiry.'
>
> ... In *Boardman v. Phipps* the sole interest rule was applied in a manner that created rather than prevented unjust enrichment, by transferring to the beneficiaries of the trust a gain that the defendant fiduciaries earned on their own property in the course of maximizing the interests of the trust.
>
> The House of Lords's message to trustees is: Thou shalt not create value for thy trust beneficiary in circumstances in which there may be actual or potential benefit to thyself. In such cases, the deterrent effect of the sole interest rule contravenes the purpose of the rule, which is to benefit the beneficiary.

It would certainly be possible to adopt a more relaxed approach to breach of fiduciary duty, and allow a fiduciary to justify his actions where he acted prudently and in the principal's best interests. Such conduct could still be considered to be loyal. In fact, some other jurisdictions do not seem to take as strict an approach as the English courts. For example, in *Peso-Silver Mines Ltd v Cropper*,[166] the Supreme Court of Canada held that an account of profits would not be awarded where the fiduciary exploited an opportunity that had previously been declined by the principal.[167] Cartwright J considered *Regal* but ultimately concluded that the fiduciary could keep the profits made, observing that:

> There are affirmative findings of fact that [the fiduciary] and his co-directors acted in good faith, solely in the interests of the appellant and with sound business reasons in rejecting the offer. There is no suggestion in the evidence that the offer to the appellant was accompanied by any confidential information unavailable to any prospective purchaser or that the respondent as director had access to any such information by reason of his office.

In that case the fact that the board rejected the opportunity meant that the fiduciary was free to exploit it. It is important to note that the fiduciary disclosed all relevant information, so the principal's consent could be considered to be fully informed. However, given that the fiduciary was also on the board of the company, this might cause unease amongst some.[168] But the Court considered that an unequivocal rejection of the opportunity by the principal meant that the fiduciary was not subsequently under a duty to seek permission to exploit the opportunity at a later date. It could reasonably be assumed that such permission would be granted.

The Privy Council decision in the Australian case of *Queensland Mines v Hudson*[169] is in a similar vein. The managing director of a company (Mr Hudson) obtained licences to develop a mine. He did

---

[165] 'Questioning the Trust Law Duty of Loyalty: Sole Interest or Best Interest?' (2005) 114 Yale LJ 929, 932, 955.
[166] [1966] SCR 673.
[167] For a similar approach in Australia, see *Consul Development v DPC Estates* (1975) 132 CLR 373.
[168] Cf. Companies Act 2006, s. 175. See Chapter 14.2(f), pp. 669–72.
[169] [1978] 52 ALJR 379.

this for the benefit of the company (Queensland Mines), but the company was unable to carry out further work on the project due to financial difficulties. With the full consent of the board of the company, the managing director resigned and exploited the mine himself. The Privy Council held that he was able to keep the profits gained. Lord Scarman insisted that there was:[170]

> no real, sensible possibility of a conflict of interest between Mr Hudson and Queensland Mines, and that Queensland Mines were fully informed of the facts and assented to Mr Hudson's exploitation of the mining exploration licence in his own name, for his own gain, and at his own risk and expense.
>
> …the opportunity to earn these royalties arose initially from the use made by Mr Hudson of his position as managing director … He must, therefore, account to that company unless he can show that, fully informed as to the circumstances, Queensland Mines renounced its interest and assented to Mr Hudson 'going it alone', ie at his own and expense and for his own benefit.
>
> …The board of the company knew the facts, decided to renounce the company's interest … and assented to Mr Hudson doing what he could with the licences at his own risk and for his own benefit.

Repeated references to Mr Hudson's personally taking on the risk clearly emphasize where the Privy Council thought the merits lay. Mr Hudson was not speculating with the property of his principal, but with his *own* money. In such ventures, it would have been very possible to lose everything. Indeed, the principal company could not get financing for this venture, partly because of the risks involved. *Hudson* might show a reluctance to sanction a fiduciary who takes on such risks in good faith when the principal will not avail itself of the opportunity. Of course, this does not sit entirely comfortably with the decision in *Boardman v Phipps*.

Decisions such as *Peso* and *Hudson* are controversial: can a board of directors really authorize and consent to a fellow director's exploiting an opportunity?[171] Even if the other directors genuinely have no interest in a particular case, it might be advantageous for them to ensure that consent to that *type* of venture is readily given, in order to facilitate any future opportunity that they might make the most of. As Sullivan has concluded:[172]

> *Queensland Mines v Hudson* suggests that many … breaches can now be forestalled or condoned by the simple expedient of obtaining the consent of boardroom colleagues who are often little more than ciphers. This is an unwelcome prospect.

However, English law has now clearly decided that directors are able to authorize such conduct by section 175 of the Companies Act 2006.[173]

Suggestions that English law should perhaps step back from the generally applicable strict approach shown in *Boardman v Phipps* have been made judicially. For example, in *Murad v Al-Saraj*[174] the defendant breached his fiduciary duties by failing to disclose to his partners in a joint venture how he was financing his contribution to the purchase of a property and the commission he was to receive. Arden LJ went out of her way to suggest that a more liberal approach was possible, citing as examples *Peso Silver Mines* and *Hudson*.

---

[170] Ibid, at 5, 8, 9–10.
[171] Cf. *Regal (Hastings) Ltd v Gulliver* [1967] 2 AC 134n.
[172] Sullivan, 'Going It Alone—Queensland Mines v Hudson' (1979) 42 MLR 711, 715.
[173] See Chapter 14.2(f), pp. 669–72.
[174] [2005] EWCA Civ 959; [2005] WTLR 1573.

Murad v Al-Saraj

[2005] EWCA Civ 959; [2005] WTLR 1573 (Arden LJ)

Now, in a case like the *Regal* case, if the rule of equity under which the defendants were held liable to account for secret profits were not inflexible, the crucial issue of fact would be: what the company would have done if the opportunity to subscribe for shares in its subsidiary had been offered to it? In the passage just cited,[175] as I have said, Lord Wright makes the point that it is very difficult to investigate that issue. However, while that may have been so in the past in the days of Lord Eldon and Lord King, that would not be the case today. The court has very extensive powers under the Civil Procedure Rules for instance to require information to be given as to a party's case. ... It may be that the time has come when the court should revisit the operation of the inflexible rule of equity in harsh circumstances, as where the trustee has acted in perfect good faith and without any deception or concealment, and in the belief that he was acting in the best interests of the beneficiary. I need only say this: it would not be in the least impossible for a court in a future case, to determine as a question of fact whether the beneficiary would not have wanted to exploit the profit himself, or would have wanted the trustee to have acted other than in the way that the trustee in fact did act. Moreover, it would not be impossible for a modern court to conclude as a matter of policy that, without losing the deterrent effect of the rule, the harshness of it should be tempered in some circumstances. In addition, in such cases, the courts can provide a significant measure of protection for the beneficiaries by imposing on the defaulting trustee the affirmative burden of showing that those circumstances prevailed. Certainly the Canadian courts have modified the effect of equity's inflexible rule (see *Peso Silver Mines Ltd v Cropper* (1966) 58 DLR (2d) 1; see also the decision of the Privy Council on appeal from Australia in *Queensland Mines v Hudson* (1978) 52 AJLR 399), though I express no view as to the circumstances in which there should be any relaxation of the rule in this jurisdiction. That sort of question must be left to another court.

In short, it may be appropriate for a higher court one day to revisit the rule on secret profits and to make it less inflexible in appropriate circumstances, where the unqualified operation of the rule operates particularly harshly and where the result is not compatible with the desire of modern courts to ensure that remedies are proportionate to the justice of the case where this does not conflict with some other overriding policy objective of the rule in question.[176]

These comments were also supported by Parker LJ, who observed that:[177]

there can be little doubt that the inflexibility of the 'no conflict' rule may, depending on the facts of any given case, work harshly so far as the fiduciary is concerned. It may be said with force that that is the inevitable and intended consequence of the deterrent nature of the rule. On the other hand, it may be said that commercial conduct which in 1874 was thought to imperil the safety of mankind may not necessarily be regarded nowadays with the same depth of concern.

However, the Court of Appeal recognized that the strict application of the rule should not be relaxed in *Murad*: the fiduciary had acted in bad faith by fraudulently misrepresenting his position to his partners. He clearly did not merit lenient treatment. Given that there was little chance of the Court showing a benevolent approach in *Murad*, it is, perhaps, even more significant that two members of the Court of Appeal saw fit to suggest a change of approach, even though no change was actually made.

---

[175] *Regal (Hastings) Ltd v Gulliver*, [1967] 2 AC 134n, 154.
[176] [2005] EWCA Civ 959; [2005] WTLR 1573, [82]–[83].
[177] Ibid, [121].

Nevertheless, the English courts have consistently taken a strict approach to breach of fiduciary obligations, stretching back to *Keech v Sandford* and *Caffrey v Darby*;[178] the latter, as Arden LJ noted in *Murad*:[179]

> makes it clear that equity imposes stringent liability on a fiduciary as a deterrent— *pour encourager les autres.*

Indeed, a strict approach is the *ratio* of both *Murad* and the slightly earlier decision of the Court of Appeal in *Bhullar v Bhullar*.[180] A director of a company was held liable to the company for the profits that he obtained from the acquisition of a property that was situated next to that of the company, even though the director discovered the property as a passer-by rather than as director. The opportunity did not come to him in a fiduciary position, yet he was still liable to account for his profits. This case might best be explained on the basis that there was a conflict of interest: the director's interest in purchasing the property for himself conflicted with the company's interest in purchasing the property. This suggests that a conflict might arise not only where an opportunity is proximite to the *commercial* interests of a principal, but also where the proximity is *geographic*.[181]

Part of the difficulty in analyzing some of the cases might arise because of an idea that the no-conflict and no-profit rules are linked—in other words, that a fiduciary should only have to give up a profit where there was also a conflict of interest. But the independent existence of a no-profit rule, which seems apparent from cases such as *Keech v Sandford* and *Boardman v Phipps*, has recently been defended in a sophisticated analysis by Smith:[182]

> I propose an understanding of the no-profit rule as a rule of primary attribution. By this, I mean that when a profit is acquired in the relevant circumstances, the fiduciary immediately comes under a primary duty to render the profit to the beneficiary. This understanding is different from that which appears in almost all of the literature, because the near-universal assumption is that the rule creates a secondary obligation; disgorgement of profits is a remedy that arises in response to wrongdoing. My argument is that the beneficiary's right to the profit in question is primary: it arises out of the nature of the fiduciary relationship, not out of wrongful conduct. Even though the fiduciary might have breached a duty, the beneficiary's right to the profit does not depend on the proof of any such breach. On this approach, while it is necessary to explain why the profit rightly belongs to the beneficiary at the moment it is acquired by the fiduciary, it is not necessary to provide an explanation that is couched in terms of a remedy for a wrongful act.
>
> How can this approach be justified? My understanding of the no-conflict rules is based directly on the need to ensure that the fiduciary exercises judgement loyally. The no-conflict rules forbid the fiduciary from exercising judgement that is subject to a requirement of loyalty, where a conflicting motivational pressure would render it impossible for the fiduciary to be sure of complying with the requirement of loyalty. I would propose a quite different justification for the no-profit rule. The fiduciary relationship is characterized by the acquisition by the fiduciary of part of the autonomy—part of the choice-making ability—of the beneficiary. Our autonomy belongs to us, in a non-legal sense. The law seeks, so far as it can, to give effect to this. Thus, when the fiduciary, through the use of the levers of control that he

---

[178] (1801) 6 Ves 488.

[179] [2005] EWCA Civ 959; [2005] WTLR 1573, [74].

[180] [2003] EWCA Civ 424; [2003] 2 BCLC 241.

[181] Armour, 'Corporate Opportunities: If in Doubt, Disclose (But How?)' (2004) CLJ 33.

[182] Smith, 'Fiduciary Relationships: Ensuring the Loyal Exercise of Judgement on Behalf of Another' (2014) 130 LQR 608, 628–629.

holds over the beneficiary's autonomy, is able to extract some wealth or value, the law ascribes it to the beneficiary as a matter of primary right. Expressed as a legal test, and as one that makes no reference to conflicts, the question is simply whether the profit in question was acquired 'by use of a fiduciary position'. If it was, then '[t]he liability arises from the mere fact of a profit having been made'. The asset in question may have been acquired by the fiduciary; but as between the fiduciary and the beneficiary, the law attributes the asset to the beneficiary, from the moment it is acquired. In other words, the effect of the no-profit rule is not, as is generally supposed, 'if you wrongfully profit, a remedy of disgorgement will be imposed'. Rather, it is 'you cannot profit from this relationship, because anything you try to extract from it will not belong to you'.

Ultimately, there is tension between allowing a fiduciary to act prudently in the best interests of a principal, even where this would place the fiduciary in breach, and adopting a consistently strict approach in order always to protect the duties a fiduciary owes. The latter is clearly English law; it operates to encourage fiduciaries to make full disclosure to their principals,[183] and to give fiduciaries an incentive to obtain the fully informed consent of their principals prior to acting. Unduly harsh results might be alleviated by granting an equitable allowance.

Conaglen, 'Strict Liability and Account of Profits' (2005) CLJ 278, 280–1[184]

Langbein argues that the fiduciary conflict principle imposes too high a cost as it prohibits transactions which are beneficial to the fiduciary's principal as well as non-beneficial transactions.

This argument is not compelling and should be rejected in favour of the longstanding orthodoxy. Fiduciary doctrine is prophylactic, both in nature and in methodology, because 'human nature being what it is, there is danger … of the person holding the fiduciary position being swayed by interest rather than by duty': *Bray v. Ford* [1896] A.C. 44 at p. 51 … In cost–benefit terms, therefore, the benefit is the protection against temptation that fiduciary doctrine provides. The courts refuse to consider whether the transaction has caused any loss, or whether the principal could have earned the profit for itself, or whether … the principal would have consented to the profit being made, because the possibility that courts might countenance such arguments can do nothing to reduce the fiduciary's temptation.

To understand the cost side of the cost–benefit analysis, it must be borne in mind that fiduciary doctrine is not punitive in the protection it affords. A fiduciary is liable to account only for profits 'acquired in consequence of the fiduciary's breach of duty': *Warman International Ltd. v. Dwyer* (1995) 182 C.L.R. 544 at p. 565; *Murad* at [85], [112], [115]–[116]. The court can grant the fiduciary an allowance to reflect his skill and effort in obtaining the profit … And crucially, in terms of a cost–benefit analysis, the fiduciary can immunise himself against any liability to account by seeking authorisation for the profit-making, in the trust instrument or equivalent, from a court, or by obtaining the fully informed consent of his principal. The courts risk undermining the internal logic and the protective function of fiduciary doctrine if they allow a fiduciary to seek to avoid liability by arguing that the impugned transaction was nonetheless in the best interests of the beneficiaries. In particular, the very fact that a fiduciary perceives a transaction involving a conflict to be justified, but has nonetheless chosen not to seek authorisation either from the court or from his principal, raises serious questions as to the wisdom of sustaining it—all too often '[s]ecrecy is the badge of fraud': *Agip (Africa) Ltd. v. Jackson* [1990] Ch. 265 at p. 294 … Only in a minuscule number of cases will obtaining one or other of those

---

[183]   See too *Sharma v Sharma* [2013] EWCA Civ 1287; [2014] BCC 73, [43] (Jackson LJ).
[184]   This is an extract from a note on *Murad*. For fuller discussion of Langbein's approach, see Conaglen, 'The Extent of Fiduciary Accounting and the Importance of Authorisation Mechanisms' (2011) CLJ 548; see too Leslie, 'In Defense of the No Further Inquiry Rule: A Response to Professor Langbein' (2005) 47 William and Mary L Rev 541; Flannigan, 'The Strict Character of Fiduciary Liability' [2006] NZ L Rev 209.

forms of authorisation present any form of difficulty for an honest fiduciary, in which cases all the fiduciary need do is abstain. The cost involved in abstention in that small number of cases is minute when compared with the benefit of the prophylactic protection that fiduciary doctrine has successfully provided for hundreds of years.

5. REMEDIES

Various remedies may be available following a breach of fiduciary duty. The transaction itself will be voidable where the no-conflict or no-profit principle has been breached, and can, therefore, be rescinded by the principal. However, rescission will not be available where the principal has affirmed the transaction, or it is impossible to put the parties back into their original positions. An injunction may also be available to restrain future breaches.[185] Such general equitable remedies will be discussed in Chapter 20. In this chapter, we will concentrate upon situations where neither of those remedies is available or desired. Instead, the principal will seek either an account of profits, or a constructive trust, or equitable compensation. The principal might sue for all the above, but ultimately may have to choose the most advantageous.[186]

(a) PERSONAL LIABILITY—ACCOUNT OF PROFITS

Making a fiduciary give up the *value* of the gains he has made from the breach is the prima facie remedy for breach of fiduciary duty. Because the fiduciary does not have to account for the *specific* profits, but only their value, this is a personal remedy. The process of taking an account involves determining the profits made and then deducting expenses properly incurred in order to reach a net figure for the profits made. In *CMS Dolphin Ltd v Simonet*, Lawrence Collins J put it as follows:[187]

The fiduciary is liable for the whole of the profit. There are no firm rules for determining which is the relevant profit ... the fiduciary should be accountable for the profits properly attributable to the breach of fiduciary duty, taking into account the expenses connected with those profits and a reasonable allowance for overheads (but not necessarily salary for the wrongdoer), together with a sum to take account of other benefits derived from those contracts. For example, other contracts might not have been won, or profits made on them, without (e.g.) the opportunity or cash flow benefit which flowed from contracts unlawfully obtained. There must, however, be some reasonable connection between the breach of duty and the profits for which the fiduciary is accountable.

It is sensible to demand a reasonable connection between the breach and the profits made. However, a 'but for' causal link does not seem to be required. This can be seen from *Murad*, the facts of which have already been outlined.[188] The wrongdoing fiduciary sought to reduce the amount of profits for

---

[185] *Marks and Spencer plc v Freshfields Bruckhaus Deringer (a firm)* [2004] EWHC 1337 (Ch); [2004] 1 WLR 2331, [26] (Lawrence Collins J).

[186] See Chapter 14.5(d), p. 715.

[187] [2001] 2 BCLC 704, [97].

[188] Chapter 14.4(e), p. 701.

which he had to account on the basis that he would have made some of those profits even if he had *not* committed any breach, so there was no causal link between *all* the profits and his breach: 'but for' his breach, he would *still* have made some of his profits. This was accepted by his principals, who agreed that even if Al-Saraj had not lied about the transaction, they would still have continued with the joint venture, although they would have demanded a greater share of the profits. Nevertheless, the majority of the Court of Appeal[189] was clear that Al-Saraj had to account for all his profits.

Arden LJ:

To test [counsel's] argument on the extent of the liability to account, in my judgment it is necessary to go back to first principle. It has long been the law that equitable remedies for the wrongful conduct of a fiduciary differ from those available at common law. ... Equity recognises that there are legal wrongs for which damages are not the appropriate remedy. In some situations therefore, as in this case, a court of equity instead awards an account of profits. As with an award of interest (as to which see *Wallersteiner v Moir (No 2)* [1975] QB 373),[190] the purpose of the account is to strip a defaulting fiduciary of his profit. ...

Furthermore, a loss to the person to whom a fiduciary duty is owed is not the other side of the coin from the profit which the person having the fiduciary duty has made: that person may have to account for a profit even if the beneficiary has suffered no loss.

I would highlight two well-established points about the reach of the equitable remedies:

(1) the liability of a fiduciary to account does not depend on whether the person to whom the fiduciary duty was owed could himself have made the profit.

(2) when awarding equitable compensation, the court does not apply the common law principles of causation. ...

The fact that the fiduciary can show that that party would not have made a loss is, on the authority of the *Regal* case, an irrelevant consideration so far as an account of profits is concerned. Likewise, it follows in my judgment from the *Regal* case that it is no defence for a fiduciary to say that he would have made the profit even if there had been no breach of fiduciary duty.

In my judgment it is not enough for the wrongdoer to show that, if he had not been fraudulent, he could have got the consent of the party to whom he owed the fiduciary duty to allow him to retain the profit. The point is that the profit here was in fact wholly unauthorised at the time it was made and has so remained. To obtain a valid consent, there would have to have been full and frank disclosure by Mr. Al-Saraj to the Murads of all relevant matters. It is only actual consent which obviates the liability to account.

... in the interests of efficiency and to provide an incentive to fiduciaries to resist the temptation to misconduct themselves, the law imposes exacting standards on fiduciaries and an extensive liability to account. ...

For policy reasons, the courts decline to investigate hypothetical situations as to what would have happened if the fiduciary had performed his duty ...

Again, for the policy reasons, on the taking of an account, the court lays the burden on the defaulting fiduciary to show that the profit is not one for which he should account: see, for example, *Manley v Sartori* [1927] Ch 157. This shifting of the onus of proof is consistent with the deterrent nature of the fiduciary's liability. The liability of the fiduciary becomes the default rule.[191]

---

[189] Clarke LJ dissented.
[190] Chapter 17.5, pp. 838–40.
[191] [2005] EWCA Civ 959; [2005] WTLR 1573, [56]–[77].

This decision is tough on the fiduciary. On the facts of *Murad*, the defendant was a deliberate wrong-doer, and may garner little sympathy. But not all wrongdoing fiduciaries will elicit such condemnation. Although it is understandable that the claimant should be able to strip a wrongdoing fiduciary of profits made in breach of duty, why should the claimant have any claim over profits which the fiduciary would have received regardless of his or her breach of duty? It may be preferable to require a 'but for' causal link between the breach of duty and gain made in order to ensure that the determination of the profits for which the defendant should be accountable is both straightforward and clear. Such a 'but for' test of causation is employed in the context of equitable compensation,[192] and has been favoured as regards gain-based remedies in the context of dishonest assistance,[193] and could be generally applied to the remedy of an account of profits.[194] However, current orthodoxy remains the decision in *Murad*. As the Court of Appeal has recently pointed out:[195]

> A fiduciary's liability to account for a secret profit does not depend on any notion of causation. It is sufficient that the profit falls within the scope of his duty of loyalty to the beneficiary.

(b) PROPRIETARY CLAIMS

A claimant might prefer a proprietary claim to a personal claim where the wrongdoing fiduciary is insolvent or where he or she wishes to trace through the profits into other property.[196] If the fiduciary receives assets from his or her wrongdoing, which (are likely to) rise in value, then a proprietary claim could also be advantageous.[197]

Deciding when a proprietary claim arises after a breach of fiduciary duty was a controversial issue for a long time. However, the decision of the Supreme Court in *FHR European Ventures LLP v Mankarious*[198] provides overdue and welcome clarity: any profits a fiduciary makes in breach of duty will be held on constructive trust for his principal.

The sole judgment of the panel of seven Supreme Court Justices in *FHR* was given by Lord Neuberger PSC. In that judgment, his Lordship departed from what Lord Neuberger MR had said only a few years previously in the Court of Appeal in *Sinclair v Versailles*.[199] The very different approach can be explained, at least partly, by the fact that the Supreme Court was not bound by precedent in the same way as the Court of Appeal, and indeed the Supreme Court thought it appropriate to disapprove an earlier decision of the House of Lords, *Tyrrell v Bank of London*.[200]

FHR European Ventures LLP v Mankarious [2014] UKSC 45; [2015] AC 250[201]

FHR purchased a long lease of the Monte Carlo Grand Hotel in Monaco for €211.5 million. The sellers agreed to pay €10 million to an agent ('Cedar') who was acting for the purchasers. This was

---

[192] *Swindle v Harrison* [1997] 4 All ER 705; see Chapter 14.5(c), p. 714.
[193] E.g. *Novoship (UK) Ltd v Mikhaylyuk* [2014] EWCA Civ 908; [2015] QB 499.
[194] Cf. *Warman International Ltd v Dwyer* (1995) 182 CLR 544, [40].
[195] *Novoship (UK) Ltd v Mikhaylyuk* [2014] EWCA Civ 908; [2015] QB 499, [96].
[196] See e.g. *A-G for Hong Kong v Reid* [1994] 1 AC 324, discussed later. On tracing, see Chapter 18.
[197] See Chapter 1.4(a)(i), p. 11 and Chapter 18.
[198] [2014] UKSC 45; [2015] AC 250.
[199] [2011] EWCA Civ 347; [2012] Ch 453.
[200] (1862) 10 HL Cas 26.
[201] See Gummow, 'Bribes and Constructive Trusts' (2015) 131 LQR 21; Conaglen, 'Proprietary Remedies for Breach of Fiduciary Duty' [2014] CLJ 490.

held to be a secret commission. The Supreme Court held that Cedar held the money on constructive trust for Investment Group.

Lord Neuberger PSC:

This is the judgment of the Court on the issue of whether a bribe or secret commission received by an agent is held by the agent on trust for his principal, or whether the principal merely has a claim for equitable compensation in a sum equal to the value of the bribe or commission. The answer to this rather technical sounding question, which has produced inconsistent judicial decisions over the past 200 years, as well as a great deal of more recent academic controversy, is important in practical terms. If the bribe or commission is held on trust, the principal has a proprietary claim to it, whereas if the principal merely has a claim for equitable compensation, the claim is not proprietary. The distinction is significant for two main reasons. First, if the agent becomes insolvent, a proprietary claim would effectively give the principal priority over the agent's unsecured creditors, whereas the principal would rank pari passu, ie equally, with other unsecured creditors if he only has a claim for compensation. Secondly, if the principal has a proprietary claim to the bribe or commission, he can trace and follow it in equity, whereas (unless we develop the law of equitable tracing beyond its current boundaries) a principal with a right only to equitable compensation would have no such equitable right to trace or follow.

The principal's right to seek an account undoubtedly gives him a right to equitable compensation in respect of the bribe or secret commission, which is the quantum of that bribe or commission (subject to any permissible deduction in favour of the agent – eg for expenses incurred). That is because where an agent acquires a benefit in breach of his fiduciary duty, the relief accorded by equity is, again to quote Millett LJ in *Mothew* at p 18, 'primarily restitutionary or restorative rather than compensatory'. The agent's duty to account for the bribe or secret commission represents a personal remedy for the principal against the agent. However, the centrally relevant point for present purposes is that, at least in some cases where an agent acquires a benefit which came to his notice as a result of his fiduciary position, or pursuant to an opportunity which results from his fiduciary position, the equitable rule ('the Rule') is that he is to be treated as having acquired the benefit on behalf of his principal, so that it is beneficially owned by the principal. In such cases, the principal has a proprietary remedy in addition to his personal remedy against the agent, and the principal can elect between the two remedies.

...

Legal Principle and Academic Articles

The respondents' formulation of the Rule, namely that it applies to all benefits received by an agent in breach of his fiduciary duty to his principal, is explained on the basis that an agent ought to account in specie to his principal for any benefit he has obtained from his agency in breach of his fiduciary duty, as the benefit should be treated as the property of the principal, as supported by many judicial dicta ... More subtly, it is justified on the basis that equity does not permit an agent to rely on his own wrong to justify retaining the benefit: in effect, he must accept that, as he received the benefit as a result of his agency, he acquired it for his principal....

The appellant's formulation of the Rule, namely that it has a more limited reach, and does not apply to bribes and secret commissions, has ... various different formulations and justifications. Thus, it is said that, given that it is a proprietary principle, the Rule should not apply to benefits which were not derived from assets which are or should be the property of the principal, a view supported by the reasoning of Lord Westbury in *Tyrrell*. It has also been suggested that the Rule should not apply to benefits which could not have been intended for the principal and were, rightly or wrongly, the property of the agent, which seems to have been the basis of Cotton LJ's judgment in *Heiron*[202] at p 325 and *Lister*[203] at p 12. In *Sinclair*, it was suggested that the effect of the authorities was that the Rule should not apply to a benefit which the agent had obtained by taking advantage of an opportunity which arose as a result of the agency, unless the opportunity 'was properly that of the [principal]' – para 88. Professor Worthington's subsequent formulation[204] ... is very similar but subtly different (and probably more satisfactory).

Each of the formulations set out ... above have their supporters and detractors. In the end, it is not possible to identify any plainly right or plainly wrong answer to the issue of the extent of the Rule, as a matter of pure legal authority. There can clearly be different views as to what requirements have to be satisfied before a proprietary interest is created. More broadly, it is fair to say that the concept of equitable proprietary rights is in some respects somewhat paradoxical. Equity, unlike the common law, classically acts in personam (see eg Maitland, *Equity*, p 9); yet equity is far more ready to accord proprietary claims than common law. Further, two general rules which law students learn early on are that common law legal rights prevail over equitable rights, and that where there are competing equitable rights the first in time prevails; yet, given that equity is far more ready to recognise proprietary rights than common law, the effect of having an equitable right is often to give priority over common law claims – sometimes even those which may have preceded the equitable right. Given that equity developed at least in part to mitigate the rigours of the common law, this is perhaps scarcely surprising. However, it underlines the point that it would be unrealistic to expect complete consistency from the cases over the past 300 years. It is therefore appropriate to turn to the arguments based on principle and practicality, and then to address the issue, in the light of those arguments as well as the judicial decisions discussed above.

Arguments based on principle and practicality

The position adopted by the respondents, namely that the Rule applies to all unauthorised benefits which an agent receives, is consistent with the fundamental principles of the law of agency. The agent owes a duty of undivided loyalty to the principal, unless the latter has given his informed consent to some less demanding standard of duty. The principal is thus entitled to the entire benefit of the agent's acts in the course of his agency. This principle is wholly unaffected by the fact that the agent may have exceeded his authority. The principal is entitled to the benefit of the agent's unauthorised acts in the course of his agency, in just the same way as, at law, an employer is vicariously liable to bear the burden of an employee's unauthorised breaches of duty in the course of his employment. The agent's duty is accordingly to deliver up to his principal the benefit which he has obtained, and not simply to pay compensation for having obtained it in excess of his authority. The only way that legal effect can be given to an obligation to deliver up specific property to the principal is by treating the principal as specifically entitled to it.

On the other hand, there is some force in the notion advanced by the appellant that the Rule should not apply to a bribe or secret commission paid to an agent, as such a benefit is different in quality from a secret profit he makes on a transaction on which he is acting for his principal, or a profit he makes from an otherwise proper transaction which he enters into as a result of some knowledge or opportunity he has as a result of his agency. Both types of secret profit can be said to be benefits which the agent should have obtained for the principal, whereas the same cannot be said about a bribe or secret commission which the agent receives from a third party.

---

[202] *Metropolitan Bank v Heiron* (1880) 5 Ex D 319.
[203] *Lister & Co v Stubbs* (1890) 45 Ch D 1.
[204] Worthington, 'Fiduciary Duties and Proprietary Remedies: Addressing the Failure of Equitable Formulae' (2013) 72 CLJ 720.

The respondents' formulation of the Rule has the merit of simplicity: any benefit acquired by an agent as a result of his agency and in breach of his fiduciary duty is held on trust for the principal. On the other hand, the appellant's position is more likely to result in uncertainty. Thus, there is more than one way in which one can identify the possible exceptions to the normal rule, which results in a bribe or commission being excluded from the Rule ... Clarity and simplicity are highly desirable qualities in the law. Subtle distinctions are sometimes inevitable, but in the present case, as mentioned above, there is no plainly right answer, and, accordingly, in the absence of any other good reason, it would seem right to opt for the simple answer.

A further advantage of the respondents' position is that it aligns the circumstances in which an agent is obliged to account for any benefit received in breach of his fiduciary duty and those in which his principal can claim the beneficial ownership of the benefit. Sir George Jessel MR in *Pearson's Case*[205] at p 341 referred in a passage cited above to the agent in such a case having 'to account either for the value ... or ... for the thing itself ...'. The expression equitable accounting can encompass both proprietary and non-proprietary claims. However, if equity considers that in all cases where an agent acquires a benefit in breach of his fiduciary duty to his principal, he must account for that benefit to his principal, it could be said to be somewhat inconsistent for equity also to hold that only in some such cases could the principal claim the benefit as his own property. ....

The notion that the Rule should not apply to a bribe or secret commission received by an agent because it could not have been received by, or on behalf of, the principal seems unattractive. The whole reason that the agent should not have accepted the bribe or commission is that it puts him in conflict with his duty to his principal. Further, in terms of elementary economics, there must be a strong possibility that the bribe has disadvantaged the principal. Take the facts of this case: if the vendor was prepared to sell for €211.5m, on the basis that it was paying a secret commission of €10m, it must be quite likely that, in the absence of such commission, the vendor would have been prepared to sell for less than €211.5m, possibly €201.5m. While Simon J was not prepared to make such an assumption without further evidence, it accords with common sense that it should often, even normally, be correct; indeed, in some cases, it has been assumed by judges that the price payable for the transaction in which the agent was acting was influenced pro rata to account for the bribe – see eg *Fawcett*[206] at p 136.

...

The respondents are also able to point to a paradox if the appellant is right and a principal has no proprietary right to his agent's bribe or secret commission. If the principal has a proprietary right, then he is better off, and the agent is worse off, than if the principal merely has a claim for equitable compensation. It would be curious, as [counsel] frankly conceded, if a principal whose agent wrongly receives a bribe or secret commission is worse off than a principal whose agent obtains a benefit in far less opprobrious circumstances, eg the benefit obtained by the trustees' agents in Boardman. Yet that is the effect if the Rule does not apply to bribes or secret commissions.

Wider policy considerations also support the respondents' case that bribes and secret commissions received by an agent should be treated as the property of his principal, rather than merely giving rise to a claim for equitable compensation. As Lord Templeman said giving the decision of the *Privy Council in Attorney General for Hong Kong v Reid* [1994] 1 AC 324, 330H, '[b]ribery is an evil practice which threatens the foundations of any civilised society'. Secret commissions are also objectionable as they inevitably tend to undermine trust in the commercial world. That has always been true, but concern about bribery and corruption generally has never been greater than it is now – see for instance, internationally, the OECD Convention on Combating Bribery of Foreign Public Officials in International Business Transactions 1999 and the United Nations Convention against Corruption 2003, and, nationally, the

---

[205] *In re Caerphilly Colliery Co, Pearson's Case* (1877) 5 Ch D 336.
[206] *Fawcett v Whitehouse* (1829) 1 Russ & M 132.

Bribery Acts 2010 and 2012. Accordingly, one would expect the law to be particularly stringent in relation to a claim against an agent who has received a bribe or secret commission.

On the other hand, a point frequently emphasised by those who seek to justify restricting the ambit of the Rule is that the wide application for which the respondents contend will tend to prejudice the agent's unsecured creditors, as it will serve to reduce the estate of the agent if he becomes insolvent. This was seen as a good reason in *Sinclair* for not following *Reid* – see at [2012] Ch 453, para 83. While the point has considerable force in some contexts, it appears to us to have limited force in the context of a bribe or secret commission. In the first place, the proceeds of a bribe or secret commission consists of property which should not be in the agent's estate at all, as Lawrence Collins J pointed out in *Daraydan*,[207] para 78 (although it is fair to add that insolvent estates not infrequently include assets which would not be there if the insolvent had honoured his obligations). Secondly, as discussed in para 37 above, at any rate in many cases, the bribe or commission will very often have reduced the benefit from the relevant transaction which the principal will have obtained, and therefore can fairly be said to be his property.

Nonetheless, the appellant's argument based on potential prejudice to the agent's unsecured creditors has some force, but it is, as we see it, balanced by the fact that it appears to be just that a principal whose agent has obtained a bribe or secret commission should be able to trace the proceeds of the bribe or commission into other assets and to follow them into the hands of knowing recipients (as in *Reid*). Yet, as [counsel] rightly accepts, tracing or following in equity would not be possible, at least as the law is currently understood, unless the person seeking to trace or follow can claim a proprietary interest. Common law tracing is, of course, possible without a proprietary interest, but it is much more limited than equitable tracing. Lindley LJ in *Lister* at p 15 appears to have found it offensive that a principal should be entitled to trace a bribe, but he did not explain why, and we prefer the reaction of Lord Templeman in *Reid*, namely that a principal ought to have the right to trace and to follow a bribe or secret commission.

Finally, on this aspect, it appears that other common law jurisdictions have adopted the view that the Rule applies to all benefits which are obtained by a fiduciary in breach of his duties. In the High Court of Australia, Deane J said in *Chan v Zacharia* (1984) 154 CLR 178, 199 that any benefit obtained 'in circumstances where a conflict .... existed ... or ... by reason of his fiduciary position or of opportunity or knowledge resulting from it ... is held by the fiduciary as constructive trustee'. More recently, the Full Federal Court of Australia has decided not to follow *Sinclair*: see *Grimaldi*, where the decision in *Reid* was preferred – see the discussion at paras 569–584. Although the Australian courts recognise the remedial constructive trust, that was only one of the reasons for not following *Sinclair*. As Finn J who gave the judgment of the court said at para 582 (after describing *Heiron* and *Lister* as 'imposing an anomalous limitation ... on the reach of *Keech v Sandford*' at para 569), 'Australian law' in this connection 'matches that of New Zealand ..., Singapore, United States jurisdictions ... and Canada'. As overseas countries secede from the jurisdiction of the Privy Council, it is inevitable that inconsistencies in the common law will develop between different jurisdictions. However, it seems to us highly desirable for all those jurisdictions to learn from each other, and at least to lean in favour of harmonising the development of the common law round the world.

...

Conclusions

...

Were it not for the decision in *Tyrrell*, we consider that it would be plainly appropriate for this Court to conclude that the courts took a wrong turn in *Heiron* and *Lister*, and to restate the law as being as the

---

[207] *Daraydan Holdings Ltd v Solland International Ltd* [2005] Ch 119.

respondents contend. Although the fact that the House of Lords decided *Tyrrell* in the way they did gives us pause for thought, we consider that it would be right to uphold the respondents' argument and disapprove the decision in *Tyrrell*. In the first place, *Tyrrell* is inconsistent with a wealth of cases decided before and after it was decided. Secondly, although *Fawcett* was cited in argument at p 38, it was not considered in any of the three opinions in *Tyrrell*; indeed, no previous decision was referred to in the opinions, and, although the opinions were expressed with a confidence familiar to those who read 19th century judgments, they contained no reasoning, merely assertion. Thirdly, the decision in *Tyrrell* may be explicable by reference to the fact that the solicitor was not actually acting for the client at the time when he acquired his interest in the adjoining land – hence the reference in Lord Westbury's opinion to 'the limit of the agency' and the absence of 'privity [or] obligation' ... In other words, it may be that their Lordships thought that the principal should not have a proprietary interest in circumstances where the benefit received by the agent was obtained before the agency began and did not relate to the property the subject of the agency.

Quite apart from these three points, we consider that, the many decisions and the practical and policy considerations which favour the wider application of the Rule and are discussed above justify our disapproving *Tyrrell*. In our judgment, therefore, the decision in *Tyrrell* should not stand in the way of the conclusion that the law took a wrong turn in *Heiron* and *Lister*, and that those decisions, and any subsequent decisions (*Powell & Thomas*,[208] *Attorney-General's Reference (No 1 of 1985)*[209] and *Sinclair*, at least in so far as they relied on or followed *Heiron* and *Lister*, should be treated as overruled.

This is a helpful decision in that it clarifies what has long been a difficult area of the law. Any profits a fiduciary makes from a breach of fiduciary duty will be held by the fiduciary on constructive trust for his or her principal. As the Supreme Court recognized, this was in fact the order that Wilberforce J made at first instance in *Boardman v Phipps*,[210] and if an 'innocent' fiduciary such as Mr Boardman has to hold his profits on trust for his principals, so should a dishonest fiduciary who receives a bribe have to hold that property on constructive trust. As Lord Neuberger pointed out in his judgment, this has the advantage of simplicity and avoiding fine distinctions between different types of breach of fiduciary duty.

It is important to note that the principal can still choose to pursue a personal claim rather than a proprietary claim against the fiduciary.[211] Lord Neuberger called this 'equitable compensation', but this may be misleading if compensation is understood as a loss-based remedy. The personal claim that the fiduciary should account for the value of profits made from the breach of duty may be advantageous if the value of property received by the fiduciary has fallen since the moment of receipt. And it follows from *Boardman v Phipps* that an equitable allowance may be granted to the fiduciary, even if the claim of the principal is proprietary in nature.

As Lord Neuberger observed, a huge amount had been written on whether the fiduciary should hold illicit gains on trust. It might therefore be a little frustrating that the reasoning in *FHR* does not deeply engage in some of the more thorny aspects of principle and policy. But it is suggested that this may be expecting too much. The Supreme Court was surely right to observe that there was no obvious answer to this issue, and a proprietary remedy is most effective in providing a civil remedy for bribery, as it allows a wronged principal to trace into substitute assets and ensures there is no prospect at all of a fiduciary gaining any advantage from receiving a bribe. This might be illustrated by the following example.

---

[208] *Powell & Thomas v Evan Jones & Co* [1905] 1 KB 11.
[209] [1986] QB 491.
[210] [1964] 1 WLR 993 (affirmed [1965] Ch 992, and [1967] 2 AC 46. See Hicks, 'Proprietary relief and the order in *Boardman v Phipps*' [2013] Conv 232.
[211] [2014] UKSC 45; [2015] AC 250, [7].

Imagine that, in breach of fiduciary duty, the fiduciary receives a diamond ring as a bribe. The ring is worth £100,000. The principal then sues the fiduciary. Should the fiduciary have a choice whether to give the principal the actual ring or £100,000? It seems preferable to give the choice to the principal, since the principal is innocent and the fiduciary not. If the principal is able to ask for the specific property received as a bribe, then this explains the proprietary remedy afforded by a constructive trust.

FHR followed a wealth of Commonwealth authority, and a significant decision of the Privy Council in *Attorney-General for Hong Kong v Reid*.[212] In that case, Mr Reid was Acting Director of Public Prosecutions in Hong Kong. In breach of his fiduciary duty to the Crown, he accepted bribes of NZ$2.5 million as an inducement to exploit his official position by obstructing the prosecution of certain criminals. Mr Reid used the bribes to purchase three freehold properties in New Zealand, two for himself and his wife, and one for his solicitor. Neither his wife nor his solicitor could establish that they were bona fide purchasers for value without notice. The Attorney-General for Hong Kong therefore sought to trace an interest into the freehold properties. In order to do so, the Attorney-General had to establish a proprietary interest in the bribe money under a trust.[213] The Privy Council held that this was possible.

The decision in *Reid* was criticized by some commentators.[214] Partly this was because of the reasoning of Lord Templeman in the Privy Council. The bribe originates with the briber, and not the principal, so how does the principal obtain any proprietary interest in the bribe itself? His Lordship relied upon the maxim, 'Equity regards as done that which ought to be done', and concluded that because *at the moment of receipt* of the bribe, the fiduciary should account to his principal, Equity will assume that this has already been done and that therefore the bribe belongs to the principal: it would be unconscionable for the fiduciary to deny this, and a constructive trust is appropriate. But the problem with such reasoning is that it does not tell us precisely *what* ought to be done: is the fiduciary under an obligation to give that particular bribe *in specie* to his principal, or is he merely under a personal obligation to account for the value of the bribe received?

Moreover, it was argued that the result in *Reid* was too hard on a fiduciary's creditors. Often, the reason why a proprietary remedy is desired is because it gives the principal better protection in the event of the fiduciary's insolvency. But this has a corresponding adverse effect upon the fiduciary's creditors who have given value for their rights. This was thought to be problematic in *Lister and Co. v Stubbs*.[215] The claimant company (Lister) employed the defendant (Stubbs) to purchase supplies for the firm. Stubbs bought goods from another company, Varley & Co., having received secret commissions of over £5,000 to induce him to place orders with that company. Stubbs used the secret profits to invest in land, and Lister sought to establish that Stubbs held the profits on constructive trust for Lister, which gave Lister a proprietary base to trace into the purchased land.[216] The Court of Appeal held that the bribes were not held on constructive trust.[217]

Lindley LJ:

Then comes the question, as between *Lister & Co.* and *Stubbs*, whether *Stubbs* can keep the money he has received without accounting for it? Obviously not. I apprehend that he is liable to account for it the moment that he gets it. It is an obligation to pay and account to Messrs. *Lister & Co.*, with or

---

[212] [1994] 1 AC 324.

[213] See further Chapter 18.3, p. 851.

[214] See e.g. Goode, 'Proprietary Liability for Secret Profits—A Reply' (2011) 127 LQR 493, criticizing Hayton, 'Proprietary Liability for Secret Profits' (2011) 127 LQR 487.

[215] (1890) 45 Ch D 1.

[216] For tracing, see Chapter 18.3, p. 851.

[217] (1890) 45 Ch D 1, 15–16.

without interest, as the case may be. I say nothing at all about that. But the relation between them is that of debtor and creditor; it is not that of trustee and *cestui que trust*. We are asked to hold that it is—which would involve consequences which, I confess, startle me. One consequence, of course, would be that, if *Stubbs* were to become bankrupt, this property acquired by him with the money paid to him by Messrs. *Varley* would be withdrawn from the mass of his creditors and be handed over bodily to Lister & Co. Can that be right? Another consequence would be that, if the Appellants are right, *Lister & Co.* could compel *Stubbs* to account to them, not only for the money with interest, but for all the profits which he might have made by embarking in trade with it. Can that be right? It appears to me that those consequences shew that there is some flaw in the argument. If by logical reasoning from the premises conclusions are arrived at which are opposed to good sense, it is necessary to go back and look again at the premises and see if they are sound. I am satisfied that they are not sound—the unsoundness consisting in confounding ownership with obligation. It appears to me that ... we should be doing what I conceive to be very great mischief if we were to stretch a sound principle to the extent to which the Appellants ask us to stretch it, tempting as it is to do so as between the Plaintiffs and *Stubbs*.

Lindley LJ was concerned with the impact a constructive trust would have upon creditors. Affording the principal a proprietary interest in the profits would mean that the profits would not be available to the mass of creditors on insolvency.[218]

The concern for unsecured creditors is understandable, but *FHR* decides that it is misplaced. This has long been the position of Lord Millett:

Millett, 'Bribes and Secret Commission' [1993] RLR 7, 16–17

the fundamental question can be squarely faced: should a proprietary remedy be available at all to a plaintiff who is not merely seeking to recover his own property? ... It is the writer's contention that the relevant policy issue has been settled for over two hundred years. The rule of equity is that a fiduciary must not place himself in a position where his interest may conflict with his duty, and must not make a profit for himself out of his position without his principal's consent; *and a fiduciary will not be allowed to retain any advantage acquired in violation of the rule*.[219] ... The rule is laid down 'pour encourager les autres'.[220] The principal is given a remedy because this is considered necessary to enforce the high standards which equity demands of a fiduciary. A fiduciary who fails to observe them must be stripped of every advantage which he has obtained thereby; better that the principal should receive a windfall than that the fiduciary (or his creditors) should benefit.[221] This applies to every secret profit made by the fiduciary; a bribe is *a fortiori*.

However, this requires that a proprietary remedy should be available if necessary. In the absence of such a remedy, a fiduciary who receives a bribe and invests it at a profit will retain an advantage....

Considerations of policy lead to the same result where the fiduciary is insolvent. Unless a proprietary remedy is available, the creditors of an insolvent fiduciary who has received a bribe will benefit.

---

[218] See Chapter 1.4(a)(i), p. 11.
[219] *Hamilton v Wright* (1842) 9 Cl & F 111, 124.
[220] Voltaire, *Candide*, Ch. 23.
[221] See the judgment of Denning J in *Reading v A-G* [1948] 1 KB 268, 275, cited with approval by Lord Porter [1951] AC [515]: 'It is money which the servant ought not to be allowed to keep, and the law says it shall be taken from him and given to his master'.

> Sympathy for their plight is misplaced. Allowing a proprietary remedy merely withdraws from the insolvent's estate an asset which it was never meant to have....Neither the fiduciary himself nor his creditors can be allowed to derive any advantage from his violation of his fiduciary duty. Better that the principal receive a windfall than that the creditors should obtain any benefit from an asset which ought never to have formed part of their debtor's estate.

This approach may well be preferable. After all, the insolvency regime operates in order to protect proprietary rights which have already been acquired prior to the insolvency. It is therefore important first to decide whether or not a constructive trust arises before any question of insolvency is addressed.

Although *FHR* provides clarity, it should not be thought that this is an area where the issues are easy to resolve. As Nolan has written, when contemplating a decision of the Supreme Court in the future:[222]

> And it would be useful to have a judgment in English law which is right because it is final: there is precious little prospect of agreement on a judgment that is final because it is right.

The judgment in *FHR* is right because it is final. The law in this area is now clear: a fiduciary holds secret profits on a constructive trust for his or her principal.

(c) EQUITABLE COMPENSATION

It should be noted that the fact that an account of profits is available does not mean that a compensatory remedy is unavailable. As Prentice and Nolan have observed:[223]

> an award of losses caused by the breach may be necessary to achieve these objectives [of deterring and controlling disloyalty] if the fiduciary makes no profit through the breach, or the profit is small, or is difficult to ascertain: in such circumstances, stripping profits will do little to deter or control disloyalty. More importantly still, once deterrence and control have failed, and disloyalty has caused harm, there should be compensation for that harm.

In *Swindle v Harrison*,[224] the Court of Appeal clearly accepted that a solicitor who breached his or her fiduciary duty might have to compensate the principal for loss suffered. *Swindle* concerned a loan from the fiduciary to the principal, but the former breached his fiduciary obligations by failing to disclose that he personally would make a profit from the loan. The principal sued the solicitor (called Mr Swindle!) for compensation for her loss. The Court held that a compensatory award was available in principle, but no such remedy was available on the facts, because even if the fiduciary had not breached his duty and had disclosed his profits, the principal would still have taken the loan. *Swindle*, therefore, highlights that a causal link between the breach and the loss is required.[225] This is important: there was contrary Privy Council authority to suggest a causal link between the breach and loss was not required,[226] but this is clearly inconsistent with both *Swindle* and the approach to equitable

---

[222] Nolan, 'Bribes: A Reprise' (2011) 127 LQR 19, 23.
[223] 'The Issue of Shares—Compensating the Company for Loss' (2002) 118 LQR 180, 185.
[224] [1997] 4 All ER 705. See also *Nocton v Lord Ashburton* [1914] AC 932, 956–7.
[225] See further Conaglen, 'Equitable Compensation for Breach of Fiduciary Fair Dealing Rules' (2003) 119 LQR 46, 267–9.
[226] *Brickenden v London Loan & Savings Co* [1934] 3 DLR 465, 469 (PC) (Lord Thankerton).

compensation taken more generally for breach of trust.[227] This is analysed further in Chapter 17.[228] However, it is important to note that there may be differences between common law and equitable claims. For instance, contributory negligence does not seem to be a defence to claims for breach of fiduciary duty.[229]

(d) CHOOSING BETWEEN ALTERNATIVE REMEDIES

Although equitable compensation is available to a principal, he or she cannot recover *both* for his or her loss *and* for the fiduciary's gain where this would lead to double recovery. As Lord Nicholls observed in the Privy Council case of *Tang Man Sit v Capacious Investments Ltd*:[230]

> Sometimes the two remedies are alternative and inconsistent. The classic example, indeed, is (1) an account of profits made by a defendant in breach of his fiduciary obligations and (2) damages for the loss suffered by the plaintiff by reason of the same breach. The former is measured by the wrongdoer's gain, the latter by the injured party's loss. [...]
>
> Faced with alternative and inconsistent remedies a plaintiff must choose, or elect, between them. He cannot have both.

This principle of election helps to prevent double recovery. Yet, it should be observed that the two remedies will not *inevitably* be inconsistent. A principal may sue for an account of profits even when he or she suffers no loss. So if the principal has *also* suffered loss, it would seem logical for him or her to be able to recover that loss in addition to the fiduciary's gains, which would have been available in any event.[231] Claiming one should not necessarily preclude the other. Such arguments led the Law Commission to conclude that:[232]

> ultimately the law is requiring an 'election' where it is not really necessary; the two remedies are not inevitably inconsistent. The 'principled' approach would be to recognize this, to remove any mandatory requirement of election, to allow a plaintiff to claim compensation and restitution, and for the court to resolve the problem of double recovery at the stage of assessing quantum.

However, the language of election continues to be used. In the recent decision of *Ramzan v Brookwide Ltd*, the Court of Appeal cited *Tang Man Sit* and held that the claimant had to elect between a claim for damages for breach of trust and a claim for loss of profit, because otherwise damages for the same wrong would be measured both by the claimant's loss and by the defendant's gain. In such circumstances, Arden LJ insisted that:[233]

> The court must treat [the claimant] as having elected to receive the larger award.

---

[227] *AIB Group (UK) Plc v Mark Redler & Co* [2014] UKSC 58; [2015] AC 1503.
[228] Chapter 17.3, p. 809.
[229] At least where the breach is deliberate: *Nationwide Building Society v Balmer Radmore (A Firm)* [1999] PNLR 606.
[230] [1996] 1 AC 514, 521.
[231] Birks, 'Inconsistency Between Compensation and Restitution' (1996) 112 LQR 375.
[232] Law Com. No. 247, *Aggravated, Exemplary and Restitutionary Damages* (1997), [3.71].
[233] [2011] EWCA Civ 985, [60].

(e) EQUITABLE ALLOWANCE

The court may, in appropriate cases, authorize remuneration in favour of fiduciaries who have breached their fiduciary duty, even though they would ordinarily have to account for all profits made. A good example of this can be found in *Boardman v Phipps*, in which all members of the House of Lords were in agreement that the solicitor, Boardman, should receive an allowance calculated on a 'liberal scale' for his skill and work in making profits by improving the fortunes of the purchased company.[234] This allowance is of long-standing.[235] In *O'Sullivan v Management Agency and Music Ltd*,[236] the Court of Appeal thought that an element of profit might even be included in the allowance.

However, the award of an equitable allowance is not automatic; for example, in *Guinness plc v Saunders*,[237] the House of Lords refused remuneration to a company director who was assumed to have acted bona fide but in circumstances that involved a clear conflict of interest and duty. Lord Goff said:

> It will be observed that the decision [in *Boardman v Phipps*] to make the allowance was founded upon the simple proposition that it would be inequitable now for the beneficiaries to step in and take the profit without paying for the skill and labour which has produced it. ... The inequity was found in the simple proposition that the beneficiaries were taking the profit although, if Mr. Boardman (the solicitor) had not done the work, they would have had to employ an expert to do the work for them in order to earn that profit.
>
> The decision has to be reconciled with the fundamental principle that a trustee is not entitled to remuneration for services rendered by him to the trust except as expressly provided in the trust deed. Strictly speaking, it is irreconcilable with the rule as so stated. It seems to me therefore that it can only be reconciled with it to the extent that the exercise of the equitable jurisdiction does not conflict with the policy underlying the rule. And, as I see it, such a conflict will only be avoided if the exercise of the jurisdiction is restricted to those cases where it cannot have the effect of encouraging trustees in any way to put themselves in a position where their interests conflict with their duties as trustees.
>
> Not only was the equity underlying Mr. Boardman's claim in *Boardman v Phipps* clear and, indeed, overwhelming; but the exercise of the jurisdiction to award an allowance in the unusual circumstances of that case could not provide any encouragement to trustees to put themselves in a position where their duties as trustees conflicted with their interests.

Clearly, a court must be satisfied that awarding an allowance will not reduce the deterrence function of the restitutionary remedy of stripping a fiduciary of wrongly obtained profits. Yet Lord Goff did recognize that sometimes the allowance must be granted, because without the work of the fiduciary the profit would never have been made. This might be explained on the basis that not all the profits were caused by the breach of fiduciary duty, but rather by the work of the fiduciary. As the High Court of Australia commented in *Warman International Ltd v Dwyer*:[238]

> when it appears that a significant proportion of an increase in profits has been generated by the skill, efforts, property and resources of the fiduciary, the capital which he has introduced and the

---

[234] See Chapter 14.4(d), p. 687.
[235] Eg *Brown v Litton* (1711) 1 P Wms 140.
[236] [1985] QB 428.
[237] [1990] 2 AC 663.
[238] (1995) 182 CLR 544, [33]. Cited in *Murad* [2005] EWCA Civ 959; [2005] WTLR 1573, [114] (Jonathan Parker LJ).

risks he has taken, so long as they are not risks to which the principal's property has been exposed. Then it may be said that the relevant proportion of the increased profits is not the product or consequence of the plaintiff's property but the product of the fiduciary's skill, efforts, property and resources.

Warman is also important since the High Court of Australia suggested that a defendant may only be liable to account for profits over a specified period of time, rather than in perpetuity. This recognition of a principle of remoteness is sensible, and, received the support of Jonathan Parker LJ in *Murad*.[239]

QUESTION

Pete wanted to expand his business. He appointed Fred as his agent to find a nearby property for Pete's company. Brian then offered Fred £50,000 to persuade Pete to buy Brian's property for £50,000 more than its fair market value. Fred agreed, and discharged a mortgage on his own house with the money Brian paid him.

Pete bought Brian's property, but is now disappointed with the premises Fred had encouraged him to buy. Pete therefore, hires Sandy to act as his agent in purchasing new offices. Dragon Ltd approach Sandy and offer him the opportunity to buy nearby offices, which would be perfect for both Sandy and Pete. Sandy tells Pete about the proposition from Dragon Ltd, but Pete does not want to be rushed into a decision and asks Sandy to keep looking for other alternatives. Sandy then falls ill, and Pete and Sandy agree to end their working relationship. Soon after, Dragon Ltd offer the offices to Sandy once more, and this time Sandy accepts the offer. It has proved to be a good investment, and the value of the property has risen by 25 per cent in one year.

Pete seeks your advice regarding any claims he may have against Fred and Sandy.

FURTHER READING

Bryan, '*Boardman v Phipps* (1967)' in *Landmark Cases in Equity* (eds Mitchell and Mitchell) (Oxford: Hart, 2012).

Conaglen, *Fiduciary Loyalty* (Oxford: Hart, 2010).

Conaglen, 'The Extent of Fiduciary Accounting and the Importance of Authorisation Mechanisms' (2011) CLJ 548.

Edelman, 'When Do Fiduciary Duties Arise?' (2010) LQR 302.

Finn, *Fiduciary Obligations* (Sydney: Law Book Company, 1977).

Hicks, 'The Remedial Principle in *Keech v Sandford* reconsidered' (2010) 69 CLJ 285.

Langbein, 'Questioning the Trust Law Duty of Loyalty: Sole Interest or Best Interest?' (2005) 114 Yale LJ 929.

Lee, 'Rethinking the Content of the Fiduciary Obligation' [2009] Conv 236.

---

[239] [2005] EWCA Civ 959; [2005] WTLR 1573, [115]. See further Virgo, 'Restitutionary Remedies for Wrongs: Causation and Remoteness' in *Justifying Private Law Remedies* (ed. Rickett) (Oxford: Hart, 2008).

Millett, 'Bribes and Secret Commission' (1993) RLR 7.

Nolan, '*Regal (Hastings) Ltd v Gulliver* (1942)' in *Landmark Cases in Equity* (eds Mitchell and Mitchell) (Oxford: Hart, 2012).

Smith, 'Fiduciary Relationships: Ensuring the Loyal Exercise of Judgement on Behalf of Another' (2014) 130 LQR 608.

PART VII

VARIATION

15

VARIATION OF TRUSTS

CENTRAL ISSUES

1. Where all the beneficiaries of a trust are of full age, under no disability, and all agree, they can terminate the trust and resettle the trust property on a new trust. This has the practical effect of varying the original trust.

2. The court has an exceptional inherent jurisdiction to vary a trust in cases of necessity.

3. Where the court considers a particular transaction to be expedient in the management or administration of trust property, but the trust instrument or the law does not give the trustee the power to undertake that transaction, the court can confer such a power on the trustee.

4. The Variation of Trusts Act 1958 enables the court to consent to the variation of a trust on behalf of certain actual or potential beneficiaries who are unable to consent to the variation.

5. In most cases, the court will only consent to a variation of the trust where it is for the benefit of the beneficiaries on whose behalf the court is consenting. Benefit can include non-financial benefit.

6. It is a matter of some controversy as to whether the intention of the settlor or testator in establishing the trust can be taken into account when the court determines whether to approve the variation of trust.

7. The Act enables the revocation of an existing trust and establishment of a new trust, but only where the new trust can be regarded in substance as similar to the old trust.

A trustee must administer the trust in accordance with its terms, otherwise he or she will commit a breach of trust.[1] Sometimes, however, the observance of the terms of the trust will be detrimental to the interests of the beneficiaries. In particular, the structure of the trust may have adverse tax consequences for the beneficiaries. The question then arises as to whether it is possible to vary the terms of the trust. There are a variety of mechanisms for doing so. One of these is where the trust instrument makes specific provision for variation of the terms of the trust by the trustees.[2] If no such provision is made there are three other mechanisms for trust variation.

---

[1] See Chapter 16.1, pp. 743–4.
[2] *Society of Lloyd's v Robinson* [1999] 1 WLR 756.

1. TERMINATION OF THE TRUST

Where all the beneficiaries of the trust are of full age, under no disability, and all agree, they can terminate the trust by virtue of the rule in *Saunders v Vautier*.[3] This enables the beneficiaries either to distribute the trust assets amongst themselves or to agree to resettle the trust property on other trusts. Resettlement will have the practical effect of varying the original trust, although technically that original trust will have been destroyed and replaced by a new one. But termination of the trust under the rule in *Saunders v Vautier* will not be available where there are beneficiaries who are minors, who are not yet born, who lack capacity, or who are not ascertained.

2. INHERENT JURISDICTION OF THE COURT

The court has an inherent jurisdiction to authorize trustees to do certain administrative acts that are beyond their powers, with the consequence of varying the trust temporarily and *ad hoc*, even though not all the beneficiaries can consent to it because of incapacity or because they are not yet born. The exercise of this jurisdiction is exceptional and must clearly be for the benefit of all of the beneficiaries. The exercise of the jurisdiction is confined to cases of necessity, such as where there is a need to postpone the sale of property for a reasonable time, and does not operate simply because a particular action would be of benefit to the beneficiaries.[4] The court does not otherwise have an inherent jurisdiction to vary trusts.[5] The one narrow exception to this arises where there is a dispute between the beneficiaries, which the beneficiaries are prepared to compromise. In such circumstances the court can sanction the compromise on behalf of child and unborn beneficiaries.[6] This inherent jurisdiction cannot be invoked where the administration of the trust is not in dispute.

3. STATUTORY PROVISIONS

There are two statutory provisions that give the courts the power to vary the trust. Although the most significant of these is Variation of Trusts Act 1958, the other, the Trustee Act 1925, will be considered briefly first.

(a) POWER TO AUTHORIZE DEALINGS WITH TRUST PROPERTY

Where the court considers a particular transaction to be expedient in the management or administration of trust property, but the trust instrument or the law does not give the trustee the power to undertake that transaction, the court can confer the power on the trustee.

---

[3] (1841) 4 Beav 115. See Chapter 10.3(a), pp. 519–20.
[4] *Re New* [1901] 2 Ch 534; *Re Tollemache* [1903] 1 Ch 955.
[5] *Chapman v Chapman* [1954] AC 429.
[6] Ibid.

TRUSTEE ACT 1925

57. Power of court to authorise dealings with trust property

(1) Where in the management or administration of any property vested in trustees, any sale, lease, mortgage, surrender, release, or other disposition, or any purchase, investment, acquisition, expenditure or other transaction, is in the opinion of the court expedient, but the same cannot be effected by reason of the absence of any power for that purpose vested in the trustees by the trust instrument, if any, or by law, the court may by order confer upon the trustees, either generally or in any particular instance, the necessary power for the purpose, on such terms, and subject to such provisions and conditions, if any, as the court may think fit and may direct in what manner any money authorized to be expended, and the costs of any transaction, are to be paid or borne as between capital and income.

(2) The court may, from time to time, rescind or vary any order made under this section, or may make any new or further order.

(3) An application to the court under this section may be made by the trustees, or by any of them, or by any person beneficially interested under the trust.

This provision can be used to give the trustees the power to sell, lease, or purchase trust property, or to expand the trustees' powers of investment,[7] although this is less significant following the expansion of investment powers by the Trustee Act 2000.[8] It may remain useful, however, where the statutory powers of investment have been restricted by the trust deed, although it is unclear when, if ever, the courts would consider it to be expedient to vary the powers of investment.

Section 57 of the Trustee Act 1925 only concerns the conferral of powers relating to the administration or management of trust property and cannot be used to alter beneficial interests under the trust. The conferral of such administrative powers on the trustees can also be undertaken under the Variation of Trusts Act 1958,[9] but section 57 has certain advantages, including that it is not necessary to obtain the consent of all adult beneficiaries for the variation to take effect. This was recognized in *Anker-Petersen v Anker-Petersen*,[10] where it was held that both section 57 of the Trustee Act 1925 and the Variation of Trusts Act 1958 could be used to extend investment powers but, where there was no alteration of the beneficial interests, section 57 was preferable. Judge Paul Baker QC said:[11]

> Where, however, no alteration of the beneficial interests [is] contemplated it appears to me more convenient to use section 57. In the first place the Trustees are the natural persons to make the applications and they are the normal applicants under section 57 (see sub-section (3)) but only exceptionally are they applicants under the Act of 1958: see *Re Druce's Settlement Trusts* [1962] 1 WLR 363. Secondly, it is not essential to obtain the consent of every adult beneficiary under section 57 as it is under the Variation of Trusts Act 1958. Thirdly, the court is not required to give consent on behalf of

---

[7] *Mason v Farbrother* [1983] 2 All ER 1078.
[8] See Chapter 12.4(b), pp. 594–600.
[9] See Chapter 15.3(b), p. 725.
[10] (1990) 6 December, reported (1998) 12 TLI 166.
[11] Ibid, 170.

> every category of beneficiary separately but, more realistically, would consider their interests collectively in income on the one hand and in capital on the other.
>
> These points lead to a less costly application without, in my judgment, imperilling the legitimate interests of the beneficiaries. It is also claimed that section 57 applications are cheaper and more convenient because they are taken in chambers whereas applications under the Act of 1958 are taken in open court. This is not something which is dictated by the statutory provisions, but rests in the practice of the court.

(b) VARIATION OF TRUSTS ACT 1958

Whilst the rule in *Saunders v Vautier* enables beneficiaries to terminate a trust and resettle trust property, it only applies where the beneficiaries are adults, of full capacity, fully entitled to the trust property, and all consent. If any of the beneficiaries are incapable of consenting because, for example, they are infants or not yet born, the rule in *Saunders v Vautier* will not apply. This is why the Variation of Trusts Act 1958 was needed: it gives the court the power to approve a variation on behalf of particular categories of people who are not in a position to consent to it. This function of the 1958 Act was identified by Mummery LJ in *Goulding v James*.[12]

> First, what varies the trust is not the court, but the agreement or consensus of the beneficiaries. Secondly, there is no real difference in principle in the rearrangement of the trusts between the case where the court is exercising its jurisdiction on behalf of the specified class under the 1958 Act and the case where the resettlement is made by virtue of the doctrine in *Saunders v Vautier* (1841) 4 Beav 115, and by all the adult beneficiaries joining together. Thirdly, the court is merely contributing on behalf of infants and unborn and unascertained persons the binding assents to the arrangement which they, unlike an adult beneficiary, cannot give. The 1958 Act has thus been viewed by the courts as a statutory extension of the consent principle embodied in the rule in *Saunders v Vautier*. The principle recognises the rights of beneficiaries, who are *sui juris* and together absolutely entitled to the trust property, to exercise their proprietary rights to overbear and defeat the intention of a testator or settlor to subject property to the continuing trusts, powers and limitations of a will or trust instrument.

When the court approves the variation on behalf of these beneficiaries, the approval binds the beneficiaries.[13] It does not, however, bind the adult beneficiaries who are capable of consenting and who must consent in their own right for the variation to be effective. In the same way that settlors or testators cannot exclude the operation of the rule in *Saunders v Vautier*, so too they cannot exclude the application of the Variation of Trusts Act 1958.[14]

The Variation of Trusts Act 1958 gives the court the power to approve an arrangement that revokes or varies a trust or enlarges the powers of the trustees to manage or administer the trust property.[15] Although the Act covers some of the ground provided for by section 57 of the Trustee Act 1925, and

---

[12] [1997] 2 All ER 239, 247.
[13] *Inland Revenue Commissioners v Holmden* [1968] AC 685, 701 (Lord Reid).
[14] *Goulding v James* [1997] 2 All ER 239, 251 (Mummery LJ).
[15] Variation of Trusts Act 1958, s. 1(1). It has also been applied to trusts arising on the death of a testator: *Re Bernstein* [2008] EWHC 3454 (Ch); [2010] WTLR 559.

has also been used to vary investment powers,[16] it is significantly wider since it also enables beneficial interests to be varied.

VARIATION OF TRUSTS ACT 1958

1. Jurisdiction of courts to vary trusts

(1) Where property, whether real or personal, is held on trusts arising, whether before or after the passing of this Act, under any will, settlement or other disposition, the court may if it thinks fit by order approve on behalf of—

(a) any person having, directly or indirectly, an interest, whether vested or contingent, under the trusts who by reason of infancy or other incapacity is incapable of assenting, or

(b) any person (whether ascertained or not) who may become entitled, directly or indirectly, to an interest under the trusts as being at a future date or on the happening of a future event a person of any specified description or a member of any specified class of persons, so however that this paragraph shall not include any person who would be of that description, or a member of that class, as the case may be, if the said date had fallen or the said event had happened at the date of the application to the court, or

(c) any person unborn, or

(d) any person in respect of any discretionary interest of his under protective trusts where the interest of the principal beneficiary has not failed or determined.

any arrangement (by whomsoever proposed, and whether or not there is any other person beneficially interested who is capable of assenting thereto) varying or revoking all or any of the trusts, or enlarging the powers of the trustees of managing or administering any of the property subject to the trusts:

Provided that except by virtue of paragraph (d) of this subsection the court shall not approve an arrangement on behalf of any person unless the carrying out thereof would be for the benefit of that person.

There have been very few reported cases on the interpretation of this legislation. Evans has suggested a reason for this:[17]

One of the reasons why reported cases on the VTA [Variation of Trusts Act] 1958 have come along relatively infrequently is, it is suggested, because such applications are expensive. The procedure is invariably High Court, all adults with a beneficial interest must be a party to the application and separately represented, and the hearing is usually in open court. Whilst there have been applications under the Act which have considered moral and social benefits, and the general welfare of beneficiaries … in practice the majority of applications which have been made to the court under VTA 1958 have involved restructuring of beneficial interests or administrative provisions which have the effect of saving significant amounts of tax. This financial incentive is the main inducement to incur the expense of an application.

---

[16] *British Museum (Trustees) v Attorney-General* [1984] 1 All ER 337. See Chapter 12.4(e), pp. 610–11.
[17] 'Variation Clarification' [2011] Conv 151, 152.

(i) *Variation and resettlement*

The 1958 Act only makes specific reference to the court approval of an arrangement that varies or revokes a trust or enlarges the administrative powers of the trustees; no reference is made to a power to authorize the revocation and then resettlement of the trust. This would suggest that, if beneficiaries were to want to revoke and resettle the trust, they could not do so under the statute;[18] they would have to resort to the rule in *Saunders v Vautier*, which would be inapplicable if any of the beneficiaries lacked capacity or were unascertained. The 1958 Act has, however, been interpreted as extending to the authorization of an arrangement that revokes an existing trust and establishes a new trust, but only where the new trust can be regarded in substance as similar to the old trust.[19] Consequently, although the form adopted is revocation and resettlement, this is effectively a variation under which the new trust is recognizable as the old. Whether the court will authorize such revocation of the original trust and resettlement on a new trust will depend on whether the 'substratum' of the original trust can be identified in the new trust. This appears to be a very easy test to satisfy.

Re Ball's Settlement Trusts [1968] 1 WLR 899, 903 (Megarry J)

… while there is plainly jurisdiction to approve the arrangement in so far as it revokes the trusts, in my view there is equally plainly no jurisdiction to approve the arrangement as regards 'resettling' the property, at any rate *eo nomine* ['by that name']. In this connection, I bear in mind the words of Wilberforce J in *Re T's Settlement Trusts* [1964] Ch 158. He there said at 162:

> 'I have no desire to cut down the very useful jurisdiction which this Act has conferred upon the court. But I am satisfied that the proposal as originally made to me falls outside it. Though presented as "a variation" it is in truth a complete new resettlement. The former trust funds were to be got in from the former trustees and held upon wholly new trusts such as might be made by an absolute owner of the funds. I do not think that the court can approve this.' …

But it does not follow that merely because an arrangement can correctly be described as effecting a revocation and resettlement, it cannot also be correctly described as effecting a variation of the trusts. The question then is whether the arrangement in this case can be so described. In the course of argument I indicated that it seemed desirable for the summons to be amended by substituting the words 'varying' for the word 'revoking' and deleting the reference to 'resettling', and that I would give leave for this amendment to be made. On the summons as so amended the question is thus whether the arrangement can fairly be said to be covered by the word 'varying' so that the court has power to approve it.

There was some discussion of the ambit of this word in *Re Holt's Settlement* [1969] 1 Ch 100. It was there held that if in substance the new trusts were recognizable as the former trusts, though with variations, the change was comprehended within the word 'varying', even if it had been achieved by a process of revocation and new declaration. In that case, the new trusts were plainly recognizable as the old trusts with variations. In the present case, the new trusts are very different from the old. The settlor's life interest vanishes; so does the power of appointment, though that will now be released. In place of the provision in default of appointment for absolute interests for the two sons if they survive the settlor, and if not, for their issue stirpitally,[20] there is now a life interest for each son, and vested absolute interests for the children of the sons born before 1 October, 1977. There is a clean sweep of the somewhat exiguous administrative provisions and an equally exiguous new set in their place. …All

---

[18] See *Re Towler's Settlement Trust* [1964] Ch 158, 162 (Wilberforce J).

[19] *Re Holt's Settlement* [1969] 1 Ch 100.

[20] Meaning a line of descendants from an ancestor.

that remains of the old trusts are what I may call the general drift or purport, namely, that a moiety of the trust fund is to be held on certain trusts for each son and certain of his issue. Is the word 'varying' wide enough to embrace so categorical a change? ...

If an arrangement changes the whole substratum of the trust, then it may well be that it cannot be regarded merely as varying that trust. But if an arrangement, while leaving the substratum, effectuates the purpose of the original trust by other means, it may still be possible to regard that arrangement as merely varying the original trusts, even though the means employed are wholly different and even though the form is completely changed.

I am, of course, well aware that this view carries me a good deal farther than I went in *Re Holt's Settlement* [1969] 1 Ch 100. I have felt some hesitation in the matter, but on the whole I consider that this is a proper step to take. The jurisdiction of the Act is beneficial and, in my judgment, the court should construe it widely and not be astute to confine its beneficent operation. I must remember that in essence the court is merely contributing on behalf of infants and unborn and unascertained persons the binding assents to the arrangement which they, unlike an adult beneficiary, cannot give. So far as is proper, the power of the court to give that assent should be assimilated to the wide powers which the ascertained adults have.

In this case, it seems to me that the substratum of the original trusts remains. True, the settlor's life interest disappears; but the remaining trusts are still in essence trusts of half of the fund for each of the two named sons and their families, with defined interests for the sons and their children in place of the former provisions for a power of appointment among the sons and their children and grandchildren and for the sons to take absolutely in default of appointment. In the events which are likely to occur, the differences between the old provision and the new may, I think, fairly be said to lie in detail rather than in substance. Accordingly, in my judgment, the arrangement here proposed, with the various revisions to it made in the course of argument, can properly be described as varying the trusts of the settlement.

This wide construction of the 1958 Act is consistent with the court's general attitude to the legislation, namely that the jurisdiction is beneficial and the court is only providing consent on behalf of those who cannot give it, so there is no harm in adopting a wide interpretation.

(ii) *People on whose behalf approval may be given*

The 1958 Act identifies four categories of people who are unable to consent to the variation of trust and on whose behalf the court is able to consent: those who are unable to consent due to infancy or incapacity, which includes mental incapacity;[21] any person unborn; anybody with a discretionary interest under a protective trust;[22] and anybody who may become entitled to an interest under the trust in the future.

The rationale behind this last category is that the court is able to consent to a variation on behalf of people who cannot consent because they belong to a class that is only ascertainable in the future, and so their membership of that class cannot be ascertained at the time when consent to the variation is required.[23] This category only includes those who have a hope of an interest in the future, such as the next of kin of a life tenant or a possible spouse, and does not include somebody who is already entitled to an interest under the trust. So, in *Knocker v Youle*,[24] income was held on trust for the settlor's daughter for life with remainder to those appointed under her will. In default of appointment there

---

[21] *Re CL* [1969] 1 Ch 587.
[22] Under the Trustee Act 1925, s. 33. See Chapter 2.4(b)(viii), pp. 31–3.
[23] Harris, 'Ten Years of Variation Trusts' (1969) 33 Conv 113, 116.
[24] [1986] 1 WLR 934.

was a gift over to the settlor's son or, if he was dead, to the settlor's four sisters or, if they were dead, to their issue who had attained the age of 21 (the cousins of the settlor's son and daughter). The settlor's son and daughter sought a variation of the trust. The issue for the court was whether, since the settlor's four sisters were dead, the court had jurisdiction to consent to the variation on behalf of the sisters' children under section (1)(1)(b), on the ground that they might be entitled to an interest under the trust in the future. In holding that the court did not have jurisdiction to approve the variation on their behalf, Warner J said:[25]

> it is not strictly accurate to describe the cousins as persons 'who may become entitled ... to an interest under the trusts'. There is no doubt of course that they are members of a 'specified class'. Each of them is, however, entitled now to an interest under the trusts, albeit a contingent one ... and albeit also that it is an interest that is defeasible on the exercise of the general testamentary powers of appointment vested in [the settlor's son and daughter]. Nonetheless, it is properly described in legal language as an interest, and it seems to me plain that in this Act the word 'interest' is used in its technical, legal sense. Otherwise, the words 'whether vested or contingent' in section 1(1)(a) would be out of place.
>
> What counsel invited me to do was in effect to interpret the word 'interest' in section 1(1) loosely, as a layman might, so as not to include an interest that was remote. I was referred to two authorities: *Re Moncrieff's Settlement Trusts (Practice Note)* [1962] 1 WLR 1344, and the earlier case, *Re Suffert's Settlement* [1961] Ch 1. In both those cases, however, the class in question was a class of prospective next-of-kin, and of course it is trite law that the prospective or presumptive next-of-kin of a living person do not have an interest. They have only a *spes successionis*, a hope of succeeding, and quite certainly they are the typical category of persons who fall within section 1(1)(b). Another familiar example of a person falling within that provision is a potential future spouse. It seems to me, however, that a person who has an actual interest directly conferred upon him or her by a settlement, albeit a remote interest, cannot properly be described as one who 'may become' entitled to an interest.

Section 1(1)(b) is subject to a proviso, the effect of which is that the court cannot consent on behalf of a person who would become entitled to an interest under the trust either if: (i) his or her entitlement depended on a future date; or (ii) an event that had happened at the time of the application to the court to approve the variation of the trust. This proviso aims to draw a distinction between a person who is nowhere in sight, such as a future spouse, and someone who is easily identifiable, such as a next of kin.[26] The court can approve the variation on behalf of the former, but not the latter.

This is illustrated by *Re Suffert's Settlement*,[27] where the beneficiary sought a variation of a trust so that the bulk of the fund was transferred to her. She had a life interest in the fund, and if she were to die without leaving any children, the fund would be held on trust for her statutory next of kin. When the application for approval of the variation was made, she was unmarried and her nearest relatives were three adult cousins. It was held that the court could approve the variation on behalf of her unborn children,[28] but not on behalf of the cousins. This was because their prospective interest under the trust was conditional on the occurrence of a particular event, namely the beneficiary's death. If it was assumed that she had died by the time the application for approval of the variation

---

[25] Ibid, 937.
[26] Ibid.
[27] [1961] Ch 1.
[28] By virtue of the Variation of Trusts Act 1958, s. 1(1)(c).

was made, the cousins would be members of the specified class. Consequently, the cousins needed to decide for themselves whether or not to agree to the variation; the court could not agree to the variation on their behalf.

This was confirmed in *Knocker v Youle* where some of the cousins had attained the age of twenty-one.

Knocker v Youle [1986] 1 WLR 934, 937 (Warner J)

The second difficulty … is that there are … 17 cousins who, if the failure or determination of the earlier trusts declared by the settlement had occurred at the date of the application to the court, would have been members of the specified class, in that they were then living and over 21. Therefore, they are prima facie excluded from section 1(1)(b) by what has been conveniently called the proviso to it, that is to say the part beginning 'so however that this paragraph shall not include …' They are in the same boat, if I may express it in that way, as the first cousins in *Re Suffert's Settlement* and the adopted son in *Re Moncrieff's Settlement Trusts (Practice Note)*. The court cannot approve the arrangement on their behalf; only they themselves can do so.

[Counsel] suggested that I could distinguish *Re Suffert's Settlement* and *Re Moncrieff's Settlement Trusts (Practice Note)* in that respect for two reasons. First, he suggested, that the proviso applied only if there was a single event on the happening of which one could ascertain the class. Here, he said, both [the settlor's son and daughter] must die without exercising their general testamentary powers of appointment to the full before any of the cousins could take anything. But it seems to me that what the proviso is referring to is the event on which the class becomes ascertainable, and that that is a single event. It is, in this case, the death of the survivor of [the settlor's son and daughter], neither of them having exercised the power to the full …

The second reason suggested by [counsel] why I should distinguish the earlier authorities was that the event hypothesised in the proviso was the death of the survivor of [the settlor's son and daughter] on the date when the originating summonses were issued, that is to say on 6 January, 1984. There is evidence that on that day there were in existence wills of both of them exercising their testamentary powers to the full. The difficulty about that is that the proviso does not say 'so however that this paragraph shall not include any person who would have become entitled if the said event had happened at the date of the application to the court'. It says 'so however that this paragraph shall not include any person who would be of that description, or a member of that class, as the case may be, if the said date had fallen or the said event had happened at the date of the application to the court'. So the proviso is designed to identify the presumptive members of the class at the date of the application to the court and does not advert to the question whether at that date they would or would not have become entitled.

I was reminded by counsel of the principle that one must construe Acts of Parliament having regard to their purpose, and it was suggested that the purpose here was to exclude the need to join as parties to applications under the Variation of Trusts Act 1958 people whose interests were remote. In my view, however, that principle does not enable me to take the sort of liberty with the language of this statute that I was invited to take. It is noteworthy that remoteness does not seem to be the test if one thinks in terms of presumptive statutory next-of-kin. The healthy issue of an elderly widow who is on her death bed, and who has not made a will, have an expectation of succeeding to her estate; that could hardly be described as remote. Yet they are a category of persons on whose behalf the court could, subject of course to the proviso, approve an arrangement under this Act. On the other hand, people in the position of the cousins in this case have an interest that is extremely remote. Nonetheless, it is an interest, and the distinction between an expectation and an interest is one which I do not think that I am entitled to blur. So, with regret, having regard to the particular circumstances of this case, I have to say that I do not think that I have jurisdiction to approve these arrangements on behalf of the cousins.

The notion of an 'interest under a trust' in section 1(1)(a) of the Variation of Trusts Act 1958 has been interpreted to include interests under a discretionary trust or an implied trust arising on the death of a testator. In *Bernstein v Jacobson*,[29] Blackburne J said:

the fact that during the period of administration of an estate the beneficiaries, whether legatees or otherwise, have no legal or equitable interest in the assets comprised in the estate, but have no more than a right to require the deceased's estate to be duly administered, does not mean that even if it can be said that the property comprised in the estate is held on trusts arising under a will, settlement or other disposition, the legatees cannot establish an interest under those trusts so as to come within section 1(1)(a). It is clear that the reference to 'interest' in that paragraph is not so confined. It is not in dispute that the 1958 Act authorises the court to give its approval on behalf of beneficiaries of a discretionary trust, notwithstanding that they have no fixed proprietary entitlement but only a right to be considered. That section 1(1)(a) extends to such an interest is confirmed by the fact that section 1(1)(d) applies to 'any person in respect of any discretionary interest of his under protective trusts where the interest of the principal beneficiary has not failed or determined'. It would be perverse if the Act extended to the beneficiaries of a discretionary trust under protective trusts where the interest to the principal beneficiary had not yet failed or determined, but not to those beneficiaries where the principal beneficiary's interest had failed or determined.

(iii) *Principles applicable to the exercise of the court's discretion*

The court has a discretion to approve the variation of the trust if 'it thinks fit'.[30] Where approval is sought on behalf of a person who lacks capacity, who is unborn, or who is not yet ascertained, the court can approve the variation only if it is for the benefit of that person. The only exception to this principle is where the person on whose behalf the approval is given is a person who would be entitled under a protective trust if it that trust had failed or determined.

Various principles can be identified to assist the determination of whether the variation is for the benefit of those who are unable to consent to the variation.

(a) *Tax-saving*

The court may be willing to approve the variation of a trust even if its sole objective is to make a significant saving of tax. In *Bernstein v Jacobson*,[31] approval of a variation of trust on behalf of infant grandchildren was sought in order to reduce the burden of inheritance tax, which would thereby increase the value of the legacies given to the grandchildren significantly. This pecuniary advantage was considered to outweigh any potential disadvantages, such as the children obtaining a benefit of substantial sums of money at an early age, which might not necessarily be considered to be for their benefit. The significance of this has been recognized by Evans:[32]

---

[29] [2008] EWHC 3454 (Ch); [2010] WTLR 559, [29].
[30] Variation of Trusts Act 1958, s. 1(1).
[31] [2008] EWHC 3454 (Ch); [2010] WTLR 559.
[32] 'Variation Clarification' [2011] Conv 151, 154.

Blackburne J [in *Bernstein*] was completely happy that a scheme which had as its sole objective a significant saving of [inheritance tax] was for the benefit of the step-grandchildren. This of itself was not ground-breaking. Considerable authority had built up for variations having been authorised purely to effect [savings of inheritance tax and capital gains tax] and savings of income tax ... it emerges from the decision that the benefit to be gained by savings of [inheritance tax] can outweigh the perceived disadvantages of young persons becoming entitled to absolute vested interests in substantial sums of money at too young an age. There had previously been occasions where courts had regarded increasing the age at which young persons receive their funds as for their benefit in the belief that they are likely to be more responsible at, for example, the age of 25.[33]

(b) Risk-taking

In determining whether the variation is likely to benefit the people who are unable to consent themselves, the court should be willing to take the same risk as a reasonable adult would take in approving the scheme.[34] Consequently, the scheme should be approved if it is highly likely to benefit the relevant people, even though there might be a small chance that the scheme might prove to be prejudicial. This was recognized by Megarry J in *Re Holt's Settlement*,[35] in respect of the approval of an arrangement on behalf of an unborn child, which would disadvantage the child if the child's mother died in child birth or shortly thereafter. He accepted that:

although there was the chance that its mother would die immediately afterwards, there was also the alternative chance that its mother would survive its birth for a substantial period of time. In the latter event, which was the more probable, the advantages of the arrangement would accrue to the infant ... Such an unborn person falls ... into the category of unborn persons on whose behalf the court should be prepared to take a risk if the arrangement appears on the whole to be for their benefit.

(c) Non-pecuniary benefit

In *Re Holt's Settlement*,[36] Megarry J recognized that:

The word 'benefit' is, I think, plainly not confined to financial benefit, but may extend to moral or social benefit.

There have even been cases in which the variation was to the clear financial detriment of the beneficiary, but the variation was still approved because the beneficiary would have consented to the variation if he or she had had the capacity to do so. For example, in *Re CL*,[37] the court approved a variation whereby the beneficiary gave up her life interest in a trust fund to her adopted daughters; the beneficiary lacked the mental capacity to consent to the transaction, but she would have done so had she not been incapacitated.

---

[33] See *Towler's Settlement Trusts, Re* [1964] Ch 158, where the contingency age was increased from twenty-one to twenty-five.

[34] *Re Cohen's Settlement Trust* [1959] 1 WLR 965.

[35] [1969] 1 Ch 100, 121.

[36] Ibid, at 121. Note also the meaning of 'benefit' for the purposes of the exercise of the power of advancement: Chapter 13.5(c), pp. 652–8.

[37] [1969] 1 Ch 587.

The significance of non-pecuniary considerations was emphasized in *Re Weston's Settlements*, which concerned an application to vary two settlements that the settlor had made in favour of his sons.

Re Weston's Settlements [1969] 1 Ch 223, 245

The settlor and his sons had moved to Jersey, and the settlor applied to the court to approve an arrangement under the 1958 Act to insert a power for the trustees to discharge the property from the trusts of the English settlements and to subject it to identical trusts of a Jersey settlement. This was to avoid capital gains tax and to save estate duty, so there was an obvious financial benefit to the sons. Despite this, the variation was not considered to be for the benefit of the sons. Lord Denning said:[38]

> Two propositions are clear: (i) in exercising its discretion, the function of the court is to protect those who cannot protect themselves. It must do what is truly for their benefit. (ii) It can give its consent to a scheme to avoid death duties or other taxes. Nearly every variation that has come before the court has tax avoidance for its principal object: and no one has ever suggested that this is undesirable or contrary to public policy.
>
> But I think it necessary to add this third proposition: (iii) the court should not consider merely the financial benefit to the infants or unborn children, but also their educational and social benefit. There are many things in life more worthwhile than money. One of these things is to be brought up in this our England, which is still 'the envy of less happier lands'. I do not believe it is for the benefit of children to be uprooted from England and transported to another country simply to avoid tax ... here the family had only been in Jersey three months when they presented this scheme to the court. The inference is irresistible: the underlying purpose was to go there in order to avoid tax. I do not think that this will be all to the good for the children. I should imagine that, even if they had stayed in this country, they would have had a very considerable fortune at their disposal, even after paying tax. The only thing that Jersey can do for them is to give them an even greater fortune. Many a child has been ruined by being given too much. The avoidance of tax may be lawful, but it is not yet a virtue. The Court of Chancery should not encourage or support it—it should not give its approval to it—if by so doing it would imperil the true welfare of the children, already born or yet to be born.
>
> There is one thing more. I cannot help wondering how long these young people will stay in Jersey. It may be to their financial interest at present to make their home there permanently. But will they remain there once the capital gains are safely in hand, clear of tax? They may well change their minds and come back to enjoy their untaxed gains. Is such a prospect really for the benefit of the children? Are they to be wanderers over the face of the earth, moving from this country to that, according to where they can best avoid tax? I cannot believe that to be right. Children are like trees: they grow stronger with firm roots.
>
> The long and short of it is, as the judge said, that the exodus of this family to Jersey is done to avoid British taxation. Having made great wealth here, they want to quit without paying the taxes and duties which are imposed on those who stay. So be it. If it really be for the benefit of the children, let it be done. Let them go, taking their money with them. But, if it be not truly for their benefit, the court should not countenance it. It should not give the scheme its blessing. The judge refused his approval. So would I. I would dismiss this appeal.

---

[38] [1969] 1 Ch 223, 245.

It does not, however, follow that the 1958 Act cannot be used to vary a trust to enable it to be moved to a foreign country, but this is only likely to be authorized where there is a genuine and permanent connection with that country.[39]

(d) Family harmony

Another form of non-pecuniary benefit that might arise from the variation of trust is that the variation may contribute to family harmony.

Re Remnant's Settlement Trust [1970] Ch 560

A family trust fund was subject to forfeiture in respect of any one of the children of two sisters who practised Roman Catholicism or who was married to a Roman Catholic, with the forfeited portion accruing in favour of the other beneficiaries. One sister, Mrs Hooper, and her children were Protestants, and the other sister, Mrs Crosthwaite, and her children were Roman Catholics. Both sisters made an application to the court to approve an arrangement that deleted the forfeiture provision. This was approved, even though it was not for the financial benefit of the children of the Protestant sister, who would have benefited from the forfeiture of the interests of the other sister and her children. Pennycuick J said:[40]

The three considerations set out by Mrs. Crosthwaite, and elaborated by counsel, are these: first, that the forfeiture provisions represent a deterrent to each of the Hooper children from adopting the Roman Catholic faith should she be minded to do so; secondly, that they operate as a deterrent to each of the Hooper children in the selection of a husband when the time comes; and thirdly, that the forfeiture provisions represent a source of possible family dissension. I am not sure that there is very much weight in the first of those considerations because there is no reason to suppose that any of these children has any particular concern with the Roman Catholic faith. On the other hand, I do think there is very real weight in the second and in the third considerations. Obviously a forfeiture provision of this kind might well cause very serious dissension between the families of the two sisters. On the best consideration I can give it I think that the deletion of the forfeiture provisions on the terms contained in the arrangement ... should be regarded as for the benefit of the three Hooper children.

I have not found this an easy point, but I think I am entitled to take a broad view of what is meant by 'benefit', and so taking it, I think this arrangement can fairly be said to be for their benefit ...

It remains to consider whether the arrangement is a fair and proper one. As far as I can see, there is no reason for saying otherwise, except that the arrangement defeats this testator's intention. That is a serious but by no means conclusive consideration. I have reached the clear conclusion that these forfeiture provisions are undesirable in themselves in the circumstances of this case and that an arrangement involving their deletion is a fair and proper one. I propose accordingly to approve the arrangement with one or two modifications which are not material to this judgment.

I would only like to add this word of caution. The effect of any particular forfeiture provision must depend on the nature of the provision itself and upon the circumstances in which it is likely to operate. A forfeiture provision is by no means always intrinsically undesirable. Again, you may have the position that a forfeiture provision benefits exclusively one or the other party concerned, and in that case it might be very difficult to say that the deletion of the provision was for the benefit of that party, unless there was the fullest financial compensation. However, I am not concerned to go further into those

---

[39] *Re Windeatt's Will Trusts* [1969] 1 WLR 692.
[40] [1970] Ch 560, 566.

> matters. It is sufficient for me to say that on the facts of this particular case the deletion of the forfeiture provisions, upon the terms of the arrangement, is for the benefit of everyone concerned and that the arrangement is a fair and proper one.

The prevention of conflict and dissension within the family is, however, only one factor to be taken into account when considering whether or not to approve a scheme of variation; the scheme might not be approved even though it would remove a source of conflict if other factors outweigh this consideration.[41]

(e) Considerations other than benefit

Even if the variation is for the benefit of the beneficiaries on whose behalf the court is asked to consent, it does not follow that the court will approve the scheme of variation.[42] It has been recognized that, because the court will approve the variation only if it thinks fit, it is appropriate to consider the arrangement as a whole to determine whether it is in its nature fair and proper.[43] This involves 'a practical and business-like consideration of the arrangement, including the total amounts of the advantages which the various parties obtain, and their bargaining strength'.[44]

One factor that will prevent the court from approving a variation is fraud on the power. As Sir Ralph Gibson said in *Goulding v James*:[45]

> If, of course, it can be shown that the arrangement put forward constitutes, for example, a dishonest or inequitable or otherwise improper act on the part of one or more of the beneficiaries, then such evidence would clearly be relevant to the question whether the court would 'think fit' to approve it on behalf of minor or unborn persons.

Another more controversial consideration relates to the relevance of the intention of the settlor or testator when the trust was established.

Goulding v James [1997] 2 All ER 239

Mrs Froud had created a trust under her will in which her daughter had a life interest and her grandson would take absolutely on attaining the age of forty. The reason why the testatrix structured the trust in this way was because she did not want her daughter, June, to have access to the capital of the fund, since she did not trust her daughter's husband, and she considered her grandson, Marcus, to be a 'free spirit' and likely to waste the money whilst he was young. June and Marcus sought to vary the trust, so that each had 45 per cent of the residuary estate, with the remaining 10 per cent held on trusts for the benefit of the unborn great-grandchildren of the testatrix. The court was required to approve the scheme of variation only on behalf of the unborn great-grandchildren, under section 1(1)(c). The trial judge had refused to vary the trust, since it was considered to be contrary to the intention of the testatrix. The Court of Appeal

---

[41] *Re Tinker's Settlement* [1960] 1 WLR 1011.
[42] *Goulding v James* [1997] 2 All ER 239, 249 (Mummery LJ).
[43] *Re Remnant's Settlement Trusts* [1970] Ch 560, 565 (Pennycuick J).
[44] *Re Van Gruisen's Will Trusts* [1964] 1 WLR 449, 450 (Ungoed-Thomas J).
[45] [1997] 2 All ER 239, 252.

reversed this decision because the scheme would benefit the unborn great-grandchildren. Mummery J said:[46]

The role of the court is not to stand in as, or for, a settlor in varying the trusts ... the court acts 'on behalf of' the specified class and, in appropriate cases, supplies consent for persons incapable of consenting. The court does not ... simply approve an arrangement; it approves an arrangement 'on behalf of' a specified class. ... in so acting, the court has a discretion. The court may, if it thinks fit, by order, approve on behalf of the specified beneficiaries. [Counsel] pointed, however, to the proviso in section 1(1) of the 1958 Act, which highlights 'benefit' as a mandatory factor in the exercise of discretion ... Although [counsel] accepted that in some cases, such as *Re Steed's Will Trusts*,[47] the intentions, wishes and motives of the settlor or testator may be relevant and weighty, in this case he contended that they are not relevant, because they do not relate to the class of persons for whom the court approves the arrangement. Alternatively, if they are relevant, it is not a proper exercise of the discretion in this case to allow extrinsic evidence of Mrs. Froud's wishes to outweigh the undoubted benefit to be conferred on her great-grandchildren, on whose behalf the court is empowered to act ...

In my judgment, the legal position is as follows.

(1) The court has a discretion whether or not to approve a proposed arrangement.

(2) That discretion is fettered by only one express restriction. The proviso to section 1 prohibits the court from approving an arrangement which is not for the benefit of the classes referred to in (a), (b) or (c). The approval of this arrangement is not prevented by that proviso, since it is plainly the case that it is greatly for the benefit of the class specified in section 1(1)(c).

(3) It does not follow from the fact of benefit to unborns that the arrangement must be approved. In *Re Van Gruisen's Will Trusts* [1964] 1 WLR 449 at 450, Ungoed-Thomas J said:

'It is shown that actuarially the provisions for the infants and unborn persons are more beneficial for them under the arrangement than under the present trusts of the will. That, however, does not conclude the case. The court is not merely concerned with this actuarial calculation, even assuming that it satisfies the statutory requirement that the arrangement must be for the benefit of the infants and unborn persons. The court is also concerned whether the arrangement as a whole, in all the circumstances, is such that it is proper to approve it. The court's concern involves, *inter alia*, a practical and business-like consideration of the arrangement, including the total amounts of the advantages which the various parties obtain, and their bargaining strength.'

(4) That overall discretion described by Ungoed-Thomas J is to be exercised with regard to all relevant factors properly considered in the statutory context. The context is that the court is empowered to approve an arrangement 'on behalf of' the members of a specified class. As Lord Denning MR said in *Re Weston's Settlements* [1969] 1 Ch 223 at 245, 'in exercising its discretion, the function of the court is to protect those who cannot protect themselves' ...

(5) Viewed in that context, an important factor in this case is that Mrs. June Goulding and Mr. Marcus Goulding are *sui juris* and Mrs. Froud's intentions and wishes related to their beneficial interests under the testamentary trusts rather than to the contingent interests of her unborn great-grandchildren whom the court is concerned to protect. [Counsel] did not dispute that Mrs. June Goulding and Mr. Marcus Goulding are legally entitled to do what they want with their beneficial

[46] [1997] 2 All ER 239, 247.
[47] [1960] Ch 407. See Chapter 15.3(b)(iii)(e), p. 737.

interests in the residuary estate. Mrs. June Goulding, for example, is entitled, contrary to the firmest of intentions expressed by her late mother, to assign her life interest to her husband or to dispose of it for a capital sum and give that capital sum to her husband. Mrs. Froud's contrary non-testamentary wishes could not inhibit Mrs. June Goulding's proprietary rights, as a person beneficially entitled to the life interest in residue.

(6) In these circumstances the critical question is what relevance, if any, can Mrs. Froud's intentions and wishes with regard to the interests in residue taken under the will by her daughter and grandson and with regard to the exclusion of her son-in-law from direct or indirect benefit, have to the exercise of the court's jurisdiction on behalf of unborn great-grandchildren of Mrs. Froud? On this crucial question the judge was impressed by [counsel's] submission that Mrs. Froud's intentions and wishes are important and should be taken into account on the authority of the Court of Appeal decision in *Re Steed's Will Trusts*. I do not accept [counsel's] submission that the Court of Appeal in that case laid down any rule, principle or guideline of general application on the importance of the intentions and wishes of a settlor or testator to applications to approve arrangements under the 1958 Act ...

To sum up. The flaw in the judge's refusal to approve the arrangement is that, in reliance on the supposed scope of the decision in *Re Steed's Will Trusts*, he allowed extrinsic evidence of the subjective wishes of Mrs. Froud as regards her daughter, son-in-law and grandson to outweigh considerations of objective and substantial benefit to the class on whose behalf the court is empowered to act. If the judge had adopted the correct approach to the exercise of his discretion, he could only have come to the conclusion that the intentions and wishes of Mrs. Froud, expressed externally to her will in relation to the adult beneficiaries and an adult non-beneficiary, had little, if any, relevance or weight to the issue of approval on behalf of the future unborn great-grandchildren, whose interest in residue was multiplied five-fold under the proposed arrangement.

This decision has been criticized by Luxton on the ground that it interferes unacceptably with the exercise of judicial discretion.

Luxton, 'Variation of Trusts: Settlors' Intention and the Consent Principle in *Saunders v Vautier*' (1997) 60 MLR 719, 725

Although several earlier cases have, in discussing the Variation of Trusts Act 1958, drawn an analogy with the doctrine of *Saunders v Vautier*, they have all done so in the context of an analysis either of jurisdiction, or of the effect of a variation (so that an arrangement under the Act is treated as substituting new trusts for old). It does not follow from such cases that the analogy should be pressed into service to restrict the manner in which the court may exercise the discretion which the statute confers upon it. This is, however, precisely what the Court of Appeal has done in *Goulding v James*. It did not, however, draw such analogy to its logical conclusion, which would have resulted in the court, in the exercise of its overall discretion, having to exclude any consideration of the settlor's intentions, even if they related to the person on whose behalf the court was asked to give its consent. As it was bound by its earlier decision in *Re Steed*, the Court of Appeal chose to steer a middle course; but it has in so doing sought to lay down rules in an area which is essentially one of discretion. The essence of its reasoning can, perhaps, be expressed in the words of Laddie J[48] at first instance, summing up the applicants' argument that he went on to reject: namely, 'that the intentions of the settlor should always be taken into account and then always dismissed as being insufficiently weighty'. Earlier cases have indicated that

---

[48] [1996] 4 All ER 865, 869.

the discretion is a wide one, and judges have previously avoided laying down rules of law respecting its exercise, no doubt because they felt that such rules would undesirably fetter the judicial discretion in ways not laid down in the Act itself. It is to be hoped that *Goulding v James* does not represent the beginning of a trend in the opposite direction.

In *Goulding v James*, repeated reference was made to the earlier decision of the Court of Appeal in *Re Steed's Will Trusts*,[49] where the court did explicitly consider the intention of the testator to determine whether to approve a scheme of variation. In that case, a farm was held on a protective trust[50] for the testator's housekeeper for life. The testator had expressed a wish that the housekeeper should have the use and enjoyment of the capital value during her life, and that if the property was sold, the capital value should be applied for her benefit. The trustees wished to sell the farm, and the housekeeper sought to restrain the sale. She brought a summons under the 1958 Act asking the court to approve an arrangement under which the trustees would hold the farm on trust for her absolutely rather than on a protective trust. The court refused to approve the variation on behalf of a future husband of the housekeeper, particularly because it would undermine the testator's intention that the housekeeper should be provided for throughout her life and would not be tempted to part with the money in favour of her brother, who the testator thought might 'sponge' off his sister. Lord Evershed MR said:[51]

the court must regard the proposal as a whole, and so regarding it, then ask itself whether in the exercise of its jurisdiction it should approve that proposal on behalf of the person who cannot give a consent, because he is not in a position to do so. If that is a right premise, then it follows that the court is bound to look at the scheme as a whole, and when it does so, to consider, as surely it must, what really was the intention of the benefactor ... the court must, albeit that it is performing its duty on behalf of some person who cannot consent on his or her own part, regard the proposal in the light of the purpose of the trust as shown by the evidence of the will or settlement itself, and of any other relevant evidence available.

But although the testator's intention was decisive in that case, it was a very different case from that of *Goulding v James*, as Mummery LJ identified:[52]

A close examination of the facts and reasoning in *Re Steed's Will Trusts* reveals two significant special features of that case.

The applicant in that case, unlike Mrs. June Goulding, had only a protected life interest held on the protective trusts in section 33 of the Trustee Act 1925. After exercising a power of appointment the protected life tenant applied to the court to lift the protective trusts, so that she would become absolutely entitled to a farm and legacy settled on those trusts. The applicant in that case did not have the same beneficial rights as Mrs. June Goulding has in relation to her life interest. Very different considerations affected the court's discretion in *Re Steed's Will Trusts*. The court was asked to approve the arrangement proposed by the protected life tenant on behalf of the person or persons specified in section 1(1)(d) of the 1958 Act, that is 'any person in respect of any discretionary interest of his under protective trusts where the interest of the principal beneficiary has not failed or determined'. The proviso as regards benefit does not apply to that paragraph, so that the court may approve an arrangement, the

---

[49] [1960] Ch 407.
[50] Trustee Act 1925, s. 33. See Chapter 2.4(b)(viii), pp. 31–3.
[51] [1960] Ch 407, 421.
[52] [1997] 2 All ER 239, 250.

carrying-out of which would not be for the benefit of that person. The court may consider whether or not there is benefit as a discretionary factor, but lack of benefit for such a person is no barrier to the approval of the court. The relevant paragraph (d) person in *Re Steed's Will Trusts*, where the applicant was unmarried and past the age of child-bearing, was the applicant's 'spectral husband', as he was described. In deciding whether or not to approve on his behalf, the court was not in the position (which exists here) of having to balance mandatory benefit to a specified paragraph (c) class against other discretionary factors, such as the intentions and wishes of the testator.

It follows that, whilst the intention of the settlor or testator in creating the trust cannot be dismissed as irrelevant, it is more likely to be relevant in a protective trusts case, where benefit of the variation to those on whose behalf the court is consenting is not relevant. In all other cases, benefit is essential and this is unlikely to be trumped by the court respecting the original intention of the testator or settlor.

More generally, since the court is consenting only on behalf of those beneficiaries who are incapable of consenting to the variation, it is difficult to see why considerations other than the benefit to those beneficiaries should be relevant, save where there is evidence that those seeking the variation are wishing to perpetrate a fraud on the power, in which case the court should not associate itself with such unconscionable conduct. If the beneficiaries were capable of consenting to the variation, their only concern would be the benefit arising to them from the variation, whether it be pecuniary or non-pecuniary. Similarly, this should be the prime consideration for the court when determining whether the variation should be approved. Such an approach was advocated by Sir Ralph Gibson in *Goulding v James*:[53]

Where there is an application under the [1958 Act] for approval of an arrangement agreed by the beneficiaries, capable of giving assent, it is not clear to me why evidence of the intention of the testator can be of any relevance whatever if it does no more than explain why the testator gave the interests set out in the will and the nature and degree of feeling with which such provisions were selected. If the arrangement agreed by the beneficiaries is to do no more with their interests than the beneficiaries are able in law to do in accordance with the provisions of the will, I can see no relevance in evidence which shows no more than the original intention or motivation of the testator. The fact that a testator would not have approved or would have disapproved very strongly does not alter the fact that the beneficiaries are entitled in law to do it and, if it be proved, that the arrangement is for the benefit of the unborn.

(iv) *Effect of court approval*

Since the function of the court's approval of the scheme of variation is merely to provide consent on behalf of those who cannot consent themselves, it follows that the approval of the scheme by the court does not make it effective automatically. Rather, the scheme only becomes effective through the agreement or consensus of all of the beneficiaries.[54] This was recognized by Lord Reid in *IRC v Holmden*:[55]

Each beneficiary is bound because he has consented to the variation. If he was not of full age when the arrangement was made he is bound because the court was authorised by the Act to approve it on his behalf and did so by making an order ... So the arrangement must be regarded as an arrangement made by the beneficiaries themselves. The court merely acted on behalf of or as representing those beneficiaries who were not in a position to give their own consent and approval.

---

[53] [1997] 2 All ER 239, 252.
[54] *Goulding v James* [1997] 2 All ER 239, 247 (Mummery LJ).
[55] [1968] AC 685, 701.

This is significant where a consequence of the scheme is the disposal of a beneficial interest in property, since such a disposition requires signed writing.[56] Such writing can be provided by those adult beneficiaries who consent to the scheme of variation. It is not required as regards the consent provided by the court. It was held in *Re Holt's Settlement*[57] that the 1958 Act constitutes an exception from the need for writing to dispose of an equitable interest.

Re Holt's Settlement [1969] Ch 100, 109 (Megarry J)

the basic issue is whether an order under the Act of 1958 by itself varies the terms of the trust. Put rather differently, the question is whether the Act does no more than empower the court to supply on behalf of the infants, unborn persons and others mentioned in section 1(1) that binding approval which they cannot give, leaving the other beneficiaries to provide their own approvals in some other document which will bind them ...

[Counsel] for the trustees, went back to the words of section 1(1), and emphasized that the power of the court was a power exercisable 'by order' and that that power was a power to approve an arrangement 'varying or revoking' all or any of the trusts. In emphasizing those phrases, he said that the right way to read the section was to say that the power of the court was merely a power to make an order approving an arrangement which in fact varied or revoked the trusts, and not an arrangement which failed to do any such thing. When the adults by their counsel assented to the arrangement, and the court on behalf of the infants by order approved the arrangement, then there was an arrangement which varied or revoked the trusts. So the order of the court both conferred jurisdiction and exercised it. His escape from section 53(1)(c) had a similar dexterity about it: by conferring an express power on the court to do something by order, Parliament in the Act of 1958 had provided by necessary implication an exception from section 53(1)(c). ... Rather than read into the Act words that are not there ... one should construe the Act as authorizing an order which is efficacious to achieve its avowed object. [Counsel] pointed to the long title of the Act which reads: 'An Act to extend the jurisdiction of courts of law to vary trusts in the interests of beneficiaries and sanction dealings with trust property'.

... I did not find his argument compelling. Indeed, at times I think it tended to circularity. But I find it tempting; and I yield. It is not a construction which I think the most natural. But it is not an impossible construction; it accords with the long title; it accords with the practice which has been relied upon for many years in some thousands of cases; and it accords with considerations of convenience. The point is technical, and I do not think that I am doing more than straining a little at the wording in the interests of legislative efficacy.

Bearing in mind that the court does not amend or vary the trusts of the original settlement—this occurring instead by the consent of the beneficiaries—the conclusion in *Re Holt's Settlement*, that writing is not required to dispose of an equitable interest where it is effected by court order, is difficult to defend as a matter of principle. An alternative route to effect a disposition of the equitable interest without signed writing is available where an agreement to vary the trust is specifically enforceable, for then a constructive trust arises as soon as the agreement is made, which will effect the disposition of the equitable interest without the need for writing.[58]

---

[56] Law of Property Act 1925, s. 53(1)(c). See Chapter 10.2, p. 501.
[57] [1969] 1 Ch 100.
[58] Law of Property Act 1925, s. 53(2). See Chapter 10.2(f), pp. 512–18.

> **QUESTION**
>
> In his will, Alan left £10,000 for Brenda and Colin to hold on a discretionary trust for the benefit of Alan's children, Debbie and Elizabeth, and Alan's grandchildren, except for Elizabeth's son, Fred, who Alan described as a 'drug-addled idiot'. Alan died in 2015. Debbie has one child, George, who is four years old, and she is expecting another child next year. Elizabeth has two children: Fred, who is twenty, and Harriet, who is sixteen. Fred has been addicted to drugs for some time, but has recently been to a rehabilitation clinic and is now clean. Debbie and Elizabeth both want the trust to be varied to remove the disqualification of Fred as an object of the trust. They seek your advice.

FURTHER READING

Evans, 'Variation Clarification' [2011] Conv 151.

Harris, 'Ten Years of Variation of Trusts' (1969) 33 Conv 113.

Harris, *Variation of Trusts* (London: Sweet and Maxwell, 1975).

Luxton, 'Variation of Trusts: Settlors' Intention and the Consent Principle in *Saunders v Vautier*' (1997) 60 MLR 719.

PART VIII

BREACH

16

LIABILITY FOR BREACH

CENTRAL ISSUES

1. A trustee is personally liable for a breach of trust. Such liability is strict.

2. Trustees may seek to escape liability by relying on an exclusion clause in the trust instrument. Such clauses might exclude certain duties owed by the trustees, or exempt the trustees from liability for a breach of trust.

3. Exemption clauses must not infringe the 'irreducible core' of obligations owed by a trustee, which consists of the duty to perform the trust honestly and in good faith for the benefit of the beneficiaries.

4. The court might excuse a breach of trust where trustees have acted honestly, reasonably, and it is fair to do so.

5. A beneficiary who has consented to a breach of trust may be prevented from bringing a claim against the trustee.

6. The liability of trustees for a breach of trust is joint and several: a beneficiary may sue only one trustee for all the loss suffered. That trustee may then seek contribution from others who are responsible for the same damage.

7. Claims for breach of trust may be barred if a limitation period has expired.

1. THE NATURE OF BREACH OF TRUST

The duties of trustees were explained in Part VI. Failure to comply with those duties will constitute a breach of trust. There is a wide variety of different types of breach of trust. In *Armitage v Nurse*, Millett LJ said:[1]

> Breaches of trust are of many different kinds. A breach of trust may be deliberate or inadvertent; it may consist of an actual misappropriation or misapplication of the trust property or merely of an investment or other dealing which is outside the trustees' powers; it may consist of a failure to carry out a positive obligation of the trustees or merely of a want of skill and care on their part in the management of the trust property; it may be injurious to the interests of the beneficiaries or be actually to their benefit.

---

[1] [1998] Ch 241.

Generally, a breach of trust will involve the trustees doing what they were not authorized to do, not doing what they were under a duty to do, or carrying out their duties badly. The chapters in this Part will consider the remedies that might flow from a breach of trust, or from a breach of fiduciary duty, the nature of which was considered in Chapter 14. This chapter will concentrate upon whether the trustee might be able to escape or reduce any liability, primarily by virtue of a defence.

2. EXEMPTION CLAUSES

The liability of trustees might be excluded or limited by a clause in the trust instrument. Such clauses have been considered under a variety of names, including exemption clauses, exoneration clauses, exclusion clauses, and exculpatory clauses. There is little significant difference between these terms. However, there are essentially two principal types of exemption clause. These have been identified by Matthews:[2]

> The most common is that which *excludes liabilities, e.g.* that a trustee is not to be liable for losses occurring such and such a way. Often, but not always, such liabilities are expressed to be liabilities for breach of trust ... A quite different type of provision is that which *excludes duties, e.g.* that a trustee is to be under no duty to supervise activities of any company in which it holds shares. This type may operate either by negating *positive* duties that would otherwise arise ... or by permitting acts that would otherwise be prohibited.

These two types of exclusion clause operate in a similar manner, but are distinct. The latter indicates that the trustee does nothing wrong in failing to comply with an ordinarily applicable duty if it has been excluded in the trust instrument. The former provides that, although the trustee is considered to have breached an applicable duty, he or she might be relieved from the consequences or liabilities that flow from that breach. However, the operation of both types of clause has been greatly influenced by the decision of the Court of Appeal in *Armitage v Nurse*. This decision will be discussed in more detail later,[3] but of particular significance was the identification by Millett LJ of an 'irreducible core' of a trust:[4]

> there is an irreducible core of obligations owed by the trustees to the beneficiaries and enforceable by them which is fundamental to the concept of a trust. If the beneficiaries have no rights enforceable against the trustees there are no trusts. But I do not accept the further submission that these core obligations include the duties of skill and care, prudence and diligence. The duty of the trustees to perform the trusts honestly and in good faith for the benefit of the beneficiaries is the minimum necessary to give substance to the trusts.

This passage sets out the irreducible core of obligations necessary for there to be a trust. Its meaning and ambit is significant for both types of exemption clauses. It might also be noted that similar principles apply in situations concerning fiduciaries who are not trustees: although liability can generally be excluded, there are some core duties of fiduciaries that are so fundamental to

[2] 'The Efficacy of Trustee Exemption Clauses in English Law' [1989] Conv 42, 43.
[3] E.g. Chapter 16.2(b)(iii), pp. 749–59.
[4] [1998] Ch 241, 253.

the fiduciary relationship that it would not be appropriate to exclude liability for breach of such duties.[5]

(a) EXCLUDING DUTIES

The irreducible core highlighted by Millett LJ clearly suggests that it is impossible to exclude:

> the duty of the trustees to perform the trusts honestly and in good faith for the benefit of the beneficiaries.

However, the decision of the Court of Appeal in *Citibank v MBIA Assurance*[6] does not fit comfortably with this approach. In *Citibank*, the trust deed stated that a guarantor, MBIA, had the right to instruct the trustees as to the exercise of their discretion and that the trustees would not be liable for breach of trust if they followed these instructions. Arden LJ held that such a term could legitimately operate to exempt the trustees from liability if they did follow the guarantor's instructions:[7]

> [Counsel] submits that the effect of the structure which enables a direction to be given to the trustee by MBIA is to reduce the trustee's obligations below the irreducible minimum identified by Millet LJ in *Armitage v Nurse*. In my judgment this is not correct. The trustee continues at all times to have an obligation of good faith, and in addition … there are other clauses in the trust deed where the trustee has a real discretion to exercise, for example in clause 8 of the trust deed which also confers a discretion on the trustee to give authorisations or waivers. In my judgment, while it is correct that it would be a surprising interpretation of the documentation, against which the court should lean, if the powers of the trustee were so reduced that it ceases to be a trustee at all, that point has not been reached in the present case and therefore there is no risk of recharacterising the office of trustee as something else.

This conclusion is, perhaps, surprising. The effect of the clause was that, when the guarantor told the trustee what to do, the trustee simply had to do it, regardless of the interests of the beneficiaries. This seems to contradict a core element of a trust; as Millett LJ highlighted in *Armitage v Nurse*, the trustees' duties must be performed *for the benefit of the beneficiaries*. As Trukhtanov has pointed out:[8]

> the *Armitage* test does not begin to be met since there is no one who could be subject to the 'core' duties.

Acting for the benefit of the guarantor, without considering the interests of the beneficiaries, seems unsatisfactory. Indeed, an analogy might be made between the type of control the guarantor had over the trustee in *Citibank* and that of a settlor of a trust who retains effective control over his 'trustee'. In such instances, the trust may well be declared to be a sham and not enforced.[9] It is suggested that the preferable approach in *Citibank* may have been either not to recognize the validity of such a clause in

---

[5] See Edelman, 'Four Fiduciary Puzzles', in *Exploring Private Law* (eds Bant and Harding) (Cambridge: Cambridge University Press, 2010), ch. 13, p. 305, who recognizes that those fiduciary duties that are imposed by law, such as the duty of honesty, cannot be excluded.

[6] [2007] EWCA Civ 11; [2007] 1 All ER (Comm) 475.

[7] Ibid, [82].

[8] 'The Irreducible Core of Trust Obligations' (2007) 123 LQR 342, 344.

[9] See Chapter 3.2(b), pp. 69–73.

the context of a trust relationship, or to conclude that what was created was not a trust. As Kenny has argued in a slightly different context:[10]

> Instead of analysing the issue within the context of the trust relationship, a more satisfactory approach would have been to consider whether the trust relationship is the appropriate vehicle for conducting what, in the case of paid trustees, is a business activity. It is time to reconsider and look at this purely in the context of what is permissible within a business relationship, and to define the parties' rights and obligations accordingly.

It may be that the relationships in which 'trustees' do not have to consider the best interests of their 'beneficiaries' could better be analysed using doctrines such as agency, for example, rather than trust. However, cases such as *Citibank* serve to highlight:[11]

> the practical reality which is that the only element of the traditional concept of trust that commercial providers of finance really care about is the beneficial proprietary interest in the fund which secures their credit risk; rules governing the trustee/beneficiary relationship that would otherwise arise where the device of trust is employed are discarded and replaced by purely contractual arrangements.

Nevertheless, there is more to a trust than merely locating the beneficial proprietary interest in assets; the willingness in *Citibank* to recognize a broader range of duties that may be excluded by the trust deed might seem unfortunate. But in any event, exemption clauses should not be permitted to extend to exclude the fiduciary obligations of an express trustee to act loyally, in the best interests of the beneficiaries and without regard to his or her own personal interest; these are of paramount importance and must invariably be fulfilled. Only the non-fiduciary duties of a trustee can be excluded by the trust instrument. That it must be possible to exclude some such duties has been recognized in the Trustee Act 2000, which permits the exclusion of the non-fiduciary duty of care owed by trustees.

TRUSTEE ACT 2000

Schedule 1, paragraph 7

The duty of care does not apply if or in so far as it appears from the trust instrument that the duty is not meant to apply.

(b) EXCLUDING LIABILITIES

It is well established that the settlor can exempt the trustee from liability in the case of some breaches of trust. This seems to have developed from a desire not to deter people from becoming trustees. However, the nature and scope of such clauses have proved to be somewhat controversial.

(i) *No exclusion of liability?*

It is worth contemplating why clauses that relieve trustees from personal liability in instances where they have committed a breach of trust have been allowed by the courts. Such clauses are regularly

---

[10] 'The Good, the Bad and the Law Commission' [2007] Conv 103, 108 (considering the Law Commission's report on exclusion clauses, discussed further in Chapter 16.2(b)(iv), pp. 752–9).

[11] Trukhantov, 'The Irreducible Core of Trust Obligations' (2007) 123 LQR 342, 346.

upheld by the courts, so the issue is largely resolved as a matter of precedent. But on a strong proprietary model of the trust, it might be thought anomalous for personal promises made by the settlor to bind subsequent property.

Penner, 'Exemptions', in *Breach of Trust* (eds Birks and Pretto) (Oxford: Hart, 2002), 262–3

... because the trust terms are not a matter of agreement between a settlor and any particular individual, but are rather terms which 'run' with the property binding successors in title and because relief from liability can only be given to particular individuals qua individuals, a trustee exemption clause cannot operate to relieve a trustee of liability. Trustee exemption clauses are not exactly repugnant to the trust; they are ineffective because they purport to do that which is simply conceptually impossible.

... from the proprietary perspective, the trustee is not like a 'contracting party', but is rather the *grantee* of a property which is burdened in a particular way, and so the incidents of the property he is granted must be incidents which can run with the property, and personal rights like the benefit of an exclusion clause cannot.

... By taking title to trust property, a trustee does not undertake any personal commitments to a settlor; he undertakes personal commitments to the beneficiaries, whom he need never personally have met, much less come to any agreements with by which they might have conferred personal rights upon him. His personal obligations to the beneficiaries flow entirely from the fact that he takes title to property which is beneficially theirs. All of the obligations of the trust, from keeping the property separate and keeping the trust accounts to disposing of the property according to the trust terms and the general fiduciary obligation are all obligations imposed by the law, ie, are default terms, which over the history of the trust the law has found important to impose, but impose purely as a function of giving effect to the fact that the property belong beneficially not to the trustee, but to the beneficiaries.

This might suggest that trustees should only be able to rely on terms in trust instruments against their beneficiaries if their right to do so is itself proprietary. However, the benefit of an exclusion clause might be considered to be a *personal* right, and as such may not extend to third parties, including the beneficiaries. Such an approach has recently been identified by Lord Clarke in the Privy Council decision in *Spread Trustee Co. Ltd v Hutcheson*:[12]

If, as is common ground, the essential obligation is to act as a prudent trustee would act, namely with reasonable care and skill, it can be said with force that the core obligation of a person acting en bon père de famille[13] includes a duty to act with reasonable care and skill and thus without negligence. In these circumstances there might be much to be said for saying, as a matter of policy, that it is not permissible to exclude liability for any breach of that duty.

Admittedly, Lord Clarke was considering the law of Guernsey, but the requirement of acting '*en bon père de famille*' broadly equates to acting as a fiduciary. It may be argued that given how important it is to ensure that trustees act reasonably, it would be perverse to exclude the duty to act reasonably. However, as Lord Clarke immediately went on to recognize in *Spread Trustee*:[14]

Yet it is common ground that ordinary negligence, that is a failure to act with reasonable care and skill, can lawfully be excluded under both Guernsey customary law and English law.

---

[12] [2011] UKPC 13; [2012] 2 AC 194.
[13] Literally, 'as a good father'; this is the standard expected of trustees in Guernsey law.
[14] [2011] UKPC 13; [2012] 2 AC 194, [63].

The 'strong' proprietary model does not represent the approach of the courts to trusts in general, and certainly not to exclusion clauses. Settlors clearly are able to exclude the liability of trustees, and this may derive theoretical support from the 'obligational' theory of trusts.[15]

(ii) *Development of exclusion clauses*

An inability to protect trustees from the consequences of their own actions may have made many settlors uncomfortable in choosing friends and relatives to act as their trustees. And, conversely, many potential trustees may have been unwilling to act for fear of incurring heavy liabilities if they performed their tasks badly. Inserting appropriate exclusion clauses into the trust instrument became a straightforward way to circumvent these problems and ensure that the office of trustee was not too burdensome.

However, it might be noted that the duties of a trustee are not inevitably as onerous as is sometimes portrayed. After all, the principal duty of a trustee involves acting reasonably and honestly. This does not seem to be too onerous, although at times trusteeship might be time-consuming. Moreover, a person cannot be forced to assume the functions of a trustee of an express trust against his or her will.[16]

Nevertheless, the development of exclusion clauses was a largely pragmatic development, which enabled family trusts to thrive. In fact, recognizing the possibility of relieving trustees from the consequences of their breach of duty in the trust instrument might parallel the courts' ability to excuse such breaches. For example, section 61 of the Trustee Act 1925 allows the court to excuse a trustee's breach of duty if the trustee acted honestly and reasonably and it would be fair to do so.[17] If such relief can be obtained *ex post facto*, then it seems appropriate for it also to be available *ex ante* in the trust instrument, if that accords with the wishes of the settlor. Indeed, this is a more efficient and less expensive way to ensure that trustees do not incur liability for honest and reasonable breaches of their duty, and avoids some of the hazards inherent in relying upon the equitable discretion of a court.

Recognizing the validity of such exclusion clauses is consistent with the notion that some breaches of duty might actually be a good thing. In *Armitage v Nurse*, Millett LJ cited:[18]

> the remark famously attributed to Selwyn LJ by Sir Nathaniel Lindley MR in the course of argument in *Perrins v Bellamy* [1899] 1 Ch. 797, 798: 'My old master, the late Selwyn LJ, used to say, "The main duty of a trustee is to commit *judicious* breaches of trust." '

For example, a term in the trust deed might have become antiquated, and perhaps limits the range of possible investments a trustee might make.[19] Where the trustee is certain that such an investment would be in the best interests of the beneficiaries, then it *might* be understood why a trustee would make such an investment. But if the trustee has to rely on the court's equitable discretion subsequently to excuse the breach of duty, the trustee may be less willing to take actions that, although clearly advantageous for the beneficiaries, would represent a breach of duty. However, the meaning of a 'judicious' breach is notoriously unclear, and it would seem preferable for trustees not to commit a deliberate breach of trust without the prior consent of the beneficiaries[20] or approval of the court.[21]

---

[15] Cf. Chapter 2.7(e), p. 59.
[16] See Chapter 11.1(d), pp. 528–9.
[17] See Chapter 16.3, p. 760.
[18] [1998] Ch 241, 251.
[19] Although it may be possible to vary that term: see Chapter 15, 'Variation of Trusts'.
[20] Which in some circumstances may not be straightforward: see Chapter 14.4(d), pp. 691–2.
[21] See Chapter 11.7(c), p. 570.

Admittedly, this is potentially expensive and time-consuming, so it might appear easier and more straightforward for the trust instrument to exclude liability, if this corresponds with the wishes of the settlor.

(iii) *Setting the level of fault*

In principle, excluding liability for some types of breach of trust seems acceptable. But in *Armitage v Nurse*,[22] the Court of Appeal insisted that the 'irreducible core' of a trust needed to be respected, so it is not possible for the trust instrument to exclude liability for *all* breaches of trust, regardless of the nature of the trustee's level of fault. In *Armitage v Nurse*, a beneficiary of the trust, Paula, brought a claim against the trustee for breach of trust. The trustee relied upon Clause 15 of the trust instrument, which provided that:

> No trustee shall be liable for any loss or damage which may happen to Paula's fund or any part thereof or the income thereof at any time or from any cause whatsoever unless such loss or damage shall be caused by his own actual fraud.

One of the questions for the court to consider was the validity of this exemption clause. Millett LJ said:[23]

> In my judgment, the meaning of the clause is plain and unambiguous. No trustee can be made liable for loss or damage to the capital or income of the trust property caused otherwise than by his own actual fraud. 'Actual fraud' means what it says. It does not mean 'constructive fraud' or 'equitable fraud'. The word 'actual' is deliberately chosen to exclude them ...
>
> The expression 'actual fraud' in clause 15 is not used to describe the common law tort of deceit. As the judge appreciated it simply means dishonesty. I accept the formulation put forward by [counsel] on behalf of the respondents which (as I have slightly modified it) is that it:
>
> > 'connotes at the minimum an intention on the part of the trustee to pursue a particular course of action, either knowing that it is contrary to the interests of the beneficiaries or being recklessly indifferent whether it is contrary to their interests or not.'
>
> It is the duty of a trustee to manage the trust property and deal with it in the interests of the beneficiaries. If he acts in a way which he does not honestly believe is in their interests then he is acting dishonestly. It does not matter whether he stands or thinks he stands to gain personally from his actions. A trustee who acts with the intention of benefiting persons who are not the objects of the trust is not the less dishonest because he does not intend to benefit himself.
>
> In my judgment clause 15 exempts the trustee from liability for loss or damage to the trust property no matter how indolent, imprudent, lacking in diligence, negligent or wilful he may have been, so long as he has not acted dishonestly.

This is more extensive than the related jurisdiction to excuse a breach of trust under section 61 of the Trustee Act 1925: for that provision to apply, a trustee must have acted not only honestly but also reasonably.[24] But this passage shows that a trustee might have been indolent and wilful, and yet still be able to rely upon an exclusion clause. Millett LJ held that, once it is recognized that liability for

---

[22] [1998] Ch 241.
[23] Ibid, 250–1.
[24] See Chapter 16.3(b), pp. 761–5.

negligent actions can be excluded by the trust deed, this must also extend to grossly negligent acts, since English law does not draw a sharp distinction between types of negligence:[25]

It is, of course, far too late to suggest that the exclusion in a contract of liability for ordinary negligence or want of care is contrary to public policy. What is true of a contract must be equally true of a settlement. It would be very surprising if our law drew the line between liability for ordinary negligence and liability for gross negligence. In this respect English law differs from civil law systems, for it has always drawn a sharp distinction between negligence, however gross, on the one hand and fraud, bad faith and wilful misconduct on the other. The doctrine of the common law is that: 'Gross negligence may be evidence of mala fides, but it is not the same thing': see *Goodman v Harvey* (1836) 4 Ad & El 870 at 876, *per* Lord Denman CJ. But while we regard the difference between fraud on the one hand and mere negligence, however gross, on the other as a difference in kind, we regard the difference between negligence and gross negligence as merely one of degree. English lawyers have always had a healthy disrespect for the latter distinction. In *Hinton v Dibbin* (1842) 2 QB 646 Lord Denman CJ doubted whether any intelligible distinction exists; while in *Grill v General Iron Screw Collier Co* (1866) LR 1 CP 600 at 612 Willes J famously observed that gross negligence is ordinary negligence with a vituperative epithet.

Excluding liability for gross negligence may be palatable where the trustee is a lay person acting entirely gratuitously. But it seems more difficult to defend where the trustee is a paid professional. This aspect of the decision in *Armitage* is very controversial, and will be analysed later. However, it is important first to appreciate that, as regards professional trustees, a slightly different standard of fault might apply.

(a) Professional trustees

In *Armitage v Nurse*, the Court of Appeal held that the irreducible core meant that any trustee could not rely on an exemption clause if he or she had acted dishonestly. The meaning of dishonesty was examined again in *Walker v Stones*.[26] The professional trustees of a discretionary trust were also partners in a firm of solicitors. Clause 15 of the so-called Bacchus trust deed exempted trustees from all liability other than 'wilful fraud or dishonesty'. The Court of Appeal considered there to be no material difference between the exemption clause in this case and that in *Armitage v Nurse*. The beneficiaries of the trust alleged that the trustees had acted in breach of trust by acting for the benefit of people who were not objects of the trust, and the trustees sought to rely upon the exclusion clause. In considering the appropriate test for dishonesty, Sir Christopher Slade said:[27]

At least in the case of a solicitor-trustee, a qualification must in my opinion be necessary to take account of the case where the trustee's so-called 'honest belief', though actually held, is so unreasonable that, by any objective standard, no reasonable solicitor-trustee could have thought that what he did or agreed to do was for the benefit of the beneficiaries. I limit this proposition to the case of a solicitor-trustee, first, because on the facts before us we are concerned only with solicitor-trustees and, secondly, because I accept that the test of honesty may vary from case to case, depending on, among other things, the role and calling of the trustee: compare *Twinsectra Ltd v Yardley* [1999] Lloyd's Rep Bank 438, at 464, *per* Potter LJ.[28] ...

The word 'honest' at first sight points exclusively to a state of mind. But, as the *Twinsectra* case illustrates, its scope cannot be so limited. A person may in some cases act dishonestly, according to the ordinary use

---

[25] [1998] Ch 241, 254.
[26] [2001] QB 902.
[27] Ibid, 939.
[28] See now *Twinsectra Ltd v Yardley* [2002] 2 AC 164; see Chapter 19.2(c), pp. 935–40.

of language, even though he genuinely believes that his action is morally justified. The penniless thief, for example, who picks the pocket of the multi-millionaire is dishonest even though he genuinely considers the theft is morally justified as a fair redistribution of wealth and that he is not therefore being dishonest.

This objective approach to dishonesty in *Walker v Stones* does not seem to correspond precisely with the more subjective stance adopted in *Armitage v Nurse*, in which Millett LJ said:[29]

By consciously acting beyond their powers (as, for example, by making an investment which they know to be unauthorised) the trustees may deliberately commit a breach of trust; but if they do so in good faith and in the honest belief that they are acting in the interest of the beneficiaries their conduct is not fraudulent.

This passage does not sit well with Sir Christopher Slade's conclusion in *Walker v Stones*[30] that the exemption clause:

would not exempt the trustees from liability for breaches of trust, even if committed in the genuine belief that the course taken by them was in the interests of the beneficiaries, if such belief was so unreasonable that no reasonable solicitor-trustee could have held that belief.

Perhaps the different approaches can be explained by Sir Christopher Slade's exclusive focus upon professional trustees. He justified an objective approach by referring to the test of dishonesty employed by the Privy Council in *Royal Brunei Airlines Sdn Bhd v Tan*[31] in the context of accessory liability, which is discussed in Chapter 19.[32] Essentially, this test provides that dishonesty is to be assessed at the standard of a reasonable person in light of what the defendant knew. Having outlined this test, Sir Christopher Slade went on to say:[33]

There is an obvious difference of emphasis between the judgments in *Royal Brunei Airlines Sdn Bhd v Tan* and *Armitage v Nurse* [1998] Ch 241 so far as they relate to the concept of dishonesty and it has been suggested that they may be irreconcilable. I do not think they are. The decision in *Royal Brunei Airlines Sdn Bhd v Tan* was cited to the Court of Appeal in *Armitage v Nurse*. Millett LJ did not purport to distinguish *Royal Brunei Airlines Sdn Bhd v Tan*, either on the grounds that it related to the liability of accessories or on any other grounds. As already stated, I can see no grounds for applying a different test of honesty in the context of a trustee exemption clause, such as clause 15 of the Bacchus trust deed, from that applicable to the liability of an accessory in a breach of trust. It would be surprising if the court in *Armitage v Nurse* had regarded itself as differing from *Royal Brunei Airlines Sdn Bhd v Tan* without saying so or explaining why. I think that in the relevant passage from his judgment quoted above at 250–251[34] and in particular in saying that if trustees deliberately commit a breach of trust they are not dishonest provided that 'they may do so in good faith and in the honest belief that they are acting in the interests of the beneficiaries'—Millett LJ was directing his mind to the not uncommon case of what Selwyn LJ had once described as 'judicious breaches of trust'. I think it most unlikely that he would have intended this dictum to apply in a case where a solicitor-trustee's perception of the interests of

---

[29] [1998] Ch 241, 251.
[30] [2001] QB 902, 941.
[31] [1995] 2 AC 378.
[32] See Chapter 19.2(c), p. 931.
[33] [2001] QB 902, 941.
[34] See Chapter 16.2(b)(iii), p. 749.

> the beneficiaries was so unreasonable that no reasonable solicitor-trustee could have held such belief. Indeed in my opinion such a construction of the clause could well render it inconsistent with the very existence of an effective trust.

This decision is welcome: it would be odd for a trustee who is well remunerated for his work not to be liable for a breach of duty that no reasonable trustee would have made. However, this is tantamount to finding that a professional trustee who is grossly negligent will not be able to rely upon the protection afforded by an exemption clause.[35] Yet in *Armitage*, the Court of Appeal was explicit in deciding that a term in the trust instrument can legitimately exclude liability for all negligent acts of the trustee, including those that are grossly negligent.

So, can *Armitage* and *Walker* be reconciled? On their facts, they certainly can. *Walker* concerned a solicitor-trustee, and its impact might not extend beyond that particular context. There may be sound policy reasons for holding solicitor-trustees to a higher standard. However, it is suggested that the logic underpinning *Walker* may be equally applicable to all professional trustees who are paid to undertake the duties of trustees; relieving such trustees from liability for breaches of duty, which no reasonable trustee would have made, could be considered to be inappropriate. Nevertheless, incorporating this approach within 'dishonesty' expands the scope of the irreducible core identified by Millett LJ, and limits the potential effectiveness of exclusion clauses. The decision in *Armitage* was, therefore, more trustee-friendly.[36]

(iv) *Assessing exclusion clauses and potential reform*

The appropriate range of breaches of duty for which liability might be excluded is a controversial issue. The focus of attention largely concerns the level of fault displayed by a professional trustee: can liability for (gross) negligence be legitimately excluded? The leading decision remains *Armitage v Nurse*,[37] which decided that only liability for fraudulent acts cannot be excluded.

Although *Armitage* is binding at the level of the Court of Appeal, the persuasiveness of some of the reasoning has been doubted. For example, although Millett LJ thought that the difference between negligence and gross negligence is simply a matter of degree in English law, in some areas gross negligence has been considered to be a different type of fault. Gross negligence, but not mere negligence, can lead to liability for the criminal offence of manslaughter.[38] And in the context of bailment, a gratuitous bailee is only liable for gross negligence. As Lord Clarke said in *Spread Trustee v Hutcheson*:[39]

> English law does distinguish between simple negligence and gross negligence. Some examples will suffice. A gratuitous bailee is only liable for gross negligence. … The concept of gross negligence also appears in section 2 of the Libel Act 1843. Finally, gross negligence is one of the bases upon which a person can be convicted of manslaughter: *R v Adomako* [1995] 1 AC 171.
>
> Those examples simply show that English law does recognise gross negligence in some contexts. They also show that English law recognises the difference in legal principle between negligence and

---

[35] Although it may be that a trustee who did not even realise that he or she was committing a breach of trust could not be characterized as dishonest: for further discussion of dishonesty, see Chapter 19.2(c), p. 931.

[36] In *Armitage*, at the material time the trustees consisted of one professional man and two distant relatives: see [1998] Ch 241, 263.

[37] E.g. *Spread Trustee v Hutcheson* [2011] UKPC 13; [2012] 2 AC 194, [52] (Lord Clarke).

[38] *Simester and Sullivan's Criminal Law: Theory and Doctrine* (5th edn) (eds Simester, Spencer, Sullivan, and Virgo) (Oxford: Hart, 2013), p. 407.

[39] [2011] UKPC 13; [2012] 2 AC 194, [50]–[51].

> gross negligence and between those types of negligence and fraud. To describe negligence as gross does not change its nature so as to make it fraudulent or wilful misconduct.

Similarly, Millett LJ's analysis of Scots law in *Armitage* fails entirely to convince. Lord Clarke observed in *Spread Trustee* that:[40]

> Millett LJ considered the relevant Scots law in some detail. He analysed a number of cases and concluded that they were all decided as a matter of construction of the particular clause. The Board has already indicated that, at any rate for the purposes of this appeal, it accepts the submission made on behalf of the parties that Scots law was not based solely on the construction of particular clauses but that there is a rule of Scots law or policy to the effect that gross negligence cannot be excluded because in Scots law culpa lata dolo aequiparatur.[41] It follows that Millett LJ was wrong to say that the submission that it is contrary to public policy to exclude the liability of a trustee for gross negligence is not supported by any Scottish authority.

Indeed, prior to *Armitage*, the English authorities regarding what types of breach were excludable were far from clear. As Millett LJ himself recognized in *Armitage*,[42] the Law Commission had considered this issue in a Consultation Paper entitled 'Fiduciary Duties and Regulatory'[43] and concluded that:[44]

> trustees and fiduciaries cannot exempt themselves from liability for fraud, bad faith and wilful default. It is not, however, clear whether the prohibition on exclusion of liability for 'fraud' in this context only prohibits the exclusion of common law fraud or extends to the much broader doctrine of equitable fraud. It is also not altogether clear whether the prohibition on the exclusion of liability for 'wilful default' also prohibits exclusion of liability for gross negligence although we incline to the view that it does.

Although the decision in *Armitage v Nurse* has some potential weaknesses, this does not mean that it is necessarily unsatisfactory for grossly negligent breaches of trust to be excluded in the trust instrument. Whether or not such breaches should be excludable is a question of policy. Millett LJ was not averse to the notion that reform of this area might be desirable, and said:[45]

> At the same time, it must be acknowledged that the view is widely held that these [exemption] clauses have gone too far, and that trustees who charge for their services and who, as professional men, would not dream of excluding liability for ordinary professional negligence should not be able to rely on a trustee exemption clause excluding liability for gross negligence. Jersey introduced a law in 1989 which denies effect to a trustee exemption clause which purports to absolve a trustee from liability for his own 'fraud, wilful misconduct or gross negligence.' The subject is presently under consideration in this country by the Trust Law Committee ... If clauses such as clause 15 of the settlement are to be denied effect, then in my opinion this should be done by Parliament, which will have the advantage of wide consultation with interested bodies and the advice of the Trust Law Committee.

---

[40] Ibid, [48].
[41] 'Gross negligence is equal to fraud.'
[42] [1998] Ch 241, 252.
[43] Law Com. CP No. 124 (1992).
[44] Ibid, [3.3.41].
[45] [1998] Ch 241, 256.

These comments did prompt a closer look at exclusion clauses. The Trust Law Committee was first to publish a Consultation Paper, in which it provisionally favoured a statutory provision to the effect that:[46]

> a trustee remunerated for his services as trustee (but not an executor-trustee who received a legacy as a token of the testator's affection or esteem, being of a significant lesser value than the amount of remuneration that might reasonably be expected to be paid for the services as executor-trustee) may not rely on an exemption clause excluding liability for breach of trust arising from negligence.

Soon after, the Law Commission was tasked with investigating this area. This was largely because the Government was challenged about the inclusion of a provision in the Trustee Act 2000, which would allow the trust instrument to exclude the statutory duty of care.[47] As the Bill was passing through Parliament, Lord Goodhart argued that paid professional trustees, and trust companies providing trustee services as part of their business, should only be entitled to rely on an exemption clause if it were reasonable in all the circumstances so to do.[48] In its initial Consultation Paper, the Law Commission agreed and provisionally recommended reform similar to that proposed by the Trust Law Committee.

Law Commission, 'Executive Summary' to *Trustee Exemption Clauses: A Consultation Paper* (2003) Law Com. CP No. 171, pp. iii–iv

The Law Commission does not believe that an absolute prohibition on all trustee exemption clauses is justifiable at present. One of the advantages of the trust is its flexibility and its adaptability to different factual circumstances and to different kinds of relationship. To deny settlors all power to modify or to restrict the extent of the obligations and liabilities of the trustee would have a very significant impact on the nature of the trust relationship. The trust would inevitably become more inflexible. We are particularly concerned that excessive regulation of trustee exemption clauses may deter lay trustees from assuming the responsibility of trusteeship in the first place.

At the same time, the Law Commission does believe that there is a very strong case for some regulation of trustee exemption clauses. Their increased use in recent years has without doubt reduced the protection afforded to beneficiaries in the event of breach of trust. While there is a need to maintain a balance between the respective interests of settlor, trustee and beneficiary, we believe that the current law is too deferential to trustees, in particular professional trustees who hold themselves out as having special knowledge skills and experience, charge for the services they provide and insure themselves against the risk of liability for breach of trust.

We therefore propose to draw a distinction between the professional trustee and the lay trustee. 'Professional' trustees would comprise trust corporations and any other trustees acting in a professional capacity. All others would be 'lay' trustees. As a matter of good practice, the draftsman of a trust should always bring the presence of a trustee exemption clause to the attention of the settlor, explain clearly its implications and discuss the alternatives which may be available for the protection of those who may be acting as trustees.

We make several provisional proposals which would require legislation:

- All trustees should be given power to make payments out of the trust fund to purchase indemnity insurance to cover their liability for breach of trust.

---

[46] Trust Law Committee, 'Consultation Paper on Trustee Exemption Clauses' (1999) [7.7].
[47] Schedule 1, para. 7: see Chapter 16.2(a), p. 746.
[48] As described by Baroness Hale in *Spread Trustee v Hutcheson* [2011] UKPC 13; [2012] 2 AC 194, [136].

- Professional trustees should not be able to rely on clauses which exclude their liability for breach of trust arising from negligence.
- In so far as professional trustees may not exclude liability for breach of trust they should not be permitted to claim indemnity from the trust fund.
- In determining whether professional trustees have been negligent, the court should have power to disapply duty exclusion clauses or extended powers clauses where reliance on such clauses would be inconsistent with the overall purposes of the trust and it would be unreasonable in the circumstances for the trustee to be exempted from liability.

These proposals of the Law Commission are sensible. After all, the main reason why a professional is chosen to act as trustee is to ensure a certain level of skill and expertise. The settlor is prepared to pay for the trustee's skills and experience, but that decision is undermined if the trustee is able to act negligently without fear of incurring any liability. Moreover, professional trustees may well be expected to have liability insurance; this strengthens the contention that any losses suffered by a professional trustee's negligently carrying out his or her duties ought to be borne by that negligent trustee rather than a beneficiary, given that only the former but not the latter is likely to be insured. However, where trustees are not at fault in breaching their duties, it is unobjectionable for them to rely upon a valid exclusion clause.

Such reform would have been similar to, but not the same as, that which has occurred in the contractual sphere. The Unfair Contract Terms Act 1977 allows the court to strike down certain types of exclusion clauses in a contract if they are unreasonable.[49] However, the proposals of the Law Commission regarding trust instruments would not assess the reasonableness of the clause itself, but rather the reasonableness of the trustee's actions. The difference can be explained due to the importance of protecting the beneficiaries' proprietary interest in the trust fund, which is irrelevant in the contractual context, and the fact that a trust may often be expected to last for much longer than a contractual relationship. As the Law Commission observed:[50]

while it must be conceded that there are some similarities between a contract and a trust, the contract derives its enforceability from the vital factors of agreement and consideration, whereas the trust is based firmly on the grant of property. Although the terms of the trust may in certain circumstances be negotiated and agreed between the settlor and the trustees, and the trustees may be remunerated for the services which they provide, these are not necessary components of the trust relationship.

Moreover, the trust has a proprietary impact which transcends the ordinary principles of contract law. This can indeed be exemplified by reference to the trustee exemption clause which is intended to benefit not only those persons who assume the obligation of trusteeship immediately following execution of the trust, but also their successors.

The Unfair Contract Terms Act 1977 is inapplicable in the trust context.[51] Any agreement that there may be is made between the settlor and trustee,[52] but it is not the settlor who can sue the trustee for breach of trust. Any claim is brought by the beneficiary. Even where the settlor is also the beneficiary under the trust that is created, it is uncertain whether he or she should be able to rely upon the 1977 Act since the positions of settlor and beneficiary are distinct and should remain separate.

[49] See e.g. s. 3. For further discussion, see McKendrick, *Contract Law: Text, Cases and Materials*, (5th edn) (Oxford: Oxford University Press, 2012), pp. 421–56.
[50] *Trustee Exemption Clauses: A Consultation Paper* (2003) Law Com. CP No. 171, [2.60]–[2.61].
[51] *Baker v JE Clark and Co.* [2006] EWCA Civ 464.
[52] But, typically, the trust is a voluntary instrument: cf. *Re Butlin's Settlement Trusts* [1976] Ch 251, 360 (Brightman J).

However, the proposals of the Law Commission met strong opposition. Most significantly, professional trustees were unhappy to see any possible extension regarding their possible liabilities, and feared their insurance premiums being raised. They highlighted the possibility of many trusts being taken off-shore to supposedly more 'generous' jurisdictions, which did not subject exemption clauses to such tight scrutiny and restrictions. This latter argument was unconvincing to the Law Commission initially, and may continue to fail to persuade: in 1989 Jersey recognized that liability for fraud, wilful misconduct, and gross negligence could not be excluded,[53] as did Guernsey in 1990,[54] and this seems to be less generous to trustees than *Armitage v Nurse*. Nevertheless, in its final report the Law Commission thought legislative reform to be inappropriate.

Law Commission, 'Executive Summary' to *Trustee Exemption Clauses* (2006) Law Com. No. 301, pp. 3–4

It is clear that restricting the use of exemption clauses in the manner provisionally proposed by the [Consultation Paper] would have a significant impact on the trusts system as a whole. Exemption clauses operate to control risk and to keep costs down, thereby encouraging a sufficient number of trustees to operate in the market. There is no clear alternative protection available to trustees. We accept in the light of consultation responses that trustee indemnity insurance is not capable of filling the role. ...

Consultation has shown that there is, among reputable trustees, a strongly-held belief that trustee exemption clauses should not be included in a trust without the full knowledge and consent of the settlor. We consider the current state of affairs in which many settlors appear to be unaware of the existence or the effect of trustee exemption clauses unacceptable. It undermines the argument that settlors may autonomously decide to grant their trustees the protection of exemption. It also challenges the view that exemption clauses operate in a properly functioning market; the asymmetry of information between the trustee and the settlor has the effect of conferring on the former the benefit of a protection not appreciated by the latter.

We are of the view that trustees should be required to ensure that the settlors are aware of any trustee exemption clauses in their trust deeds. ...

We have considered the option, discussed in the [Consultation Paper], of introducing a statutory requirement that trustees must disclose to the settlor any exemption clause on which they wish to be able to rely. We have rejected this approach on the grounds that it would be likely to give rise to delay and additional cost when setting up a trust and to uncertainty as to the validity of the clause thereafter. It is also unclear how such a statutory requirement could adequately frame the regulation of duty modification clauses.

We have concluded that a practice-based approach, rather than legislation, is the better means to bring about reform of the conduct of trustees. The Report therefore recommends a rule of practice that:

> Any paid trustee who causes a settlor to include a clause in a trust instrument which has the effect of excluding or limiting liability for negligence must before the creation of the trust take such steps as are reasonable to ensure that the settlor is aware of the meaning and effect of the clause.

From this, it can be seen that a 'soft law' approach was ultimately preferred by the Law Commission: as long as professional trustees ensure that settlors have fully understood the import and effect of an exclusion clause at the time the trust instrument is created, trustees who have not committed fraud will later be able to rely upon that exclusion clause, even if they have been grossly negligent.

---

[53] Trusts (Jersey) Law 1984, art. 26(9), as amended by Trusts (Amendment) (Jersey) Law 1989, art. 8.
[54] See now Trusts (Guernsey) Law 2007, s. 39(7)(a).

This about-turn from the Law Commission was very warmly welcomed by professional trustees, and professional bodies sensibly began to implement codes of conduct.[55] But professional bodies regulating the conduct of their members clearly lack the sanctions that are available to courts of law, and may be of little help to beneficiaries seeking redress. Indeed, it will not inevitably be the case that a trustee is a member of a regulatory body, or even that all regulatory bodies will have a code. And even if a code is in place, the strength of the relevant organization will determine how effective any sanctions it can impose may be.

The stance taken in *Armitage* and, ultimately, by the Law Commission places great emphasis upon the settlor's freedom to choose the terms on which he creates a trust. Such 'settlor autonomy' stresses the importance of the obligations underpinning a trust. If the trust is seen as a mechanism by which the settlor can give property to others, then the beneficiaries—as volunteers and recipients of that gift—simply have to accept the gift with the strings the settlor attaches to it. If the settlor deliberately chooses not to grant the beneficiaries any remedy if the trustees act negligently, that wish should be respected.

However, such reasoning was previously criticized by Penner,[56] who observed that *Armitage v Nurse*:

> Endorses a strong version of 'freedom of trust', akin to a strong version of freedom of contract: so long as the legal arrangement of rights and duties voluntarily undertaken by the parties has some kind of workable legal effect, the law should give effect to it; it is not the role of the law to require parties to a legal arrangement to accept a standard 'package' of terms, unless there is some sufficiently weighty countervailing public policy consideration. Distinguished from any strand linking it to the notion of fiduciary obligations *per se*, Millett LJ's essential core duty of loyalty and good faith reduces to the irremovable duty of the trustee not to commit a fraud on the beneficiaries, wherein fraud encompasses either intentional wrongdoing or reckless disregard of the beneficiaries' interests, thus dishonesty to some substantial degree. Thus the core duty of a trustee is determined according to a *standard of fault*, not a kind of duty. The essence of trusteeship accordingly concerns the *way* in which a trustee acquits or fails to acquit whatever duties the trust terms impose, dishonestly rather than negligently or innocently, not some minimum or essential *kinds of duty* which give the trust substance, such as the duty to keep the trust property separate from his won, or the keep the trust accounts, etc. With respect, it is submitted that this is misguided, and confuses the nature of duty with the nature of liability.

In any event, the existence of some codes of conduct clearly does not eliminate the possibility that settlors will continue to agree to such clauses without being fully aware of their effects. It is unsurprising to find that the Law Commission received much criticism for its complete reversal between the consultation paper and report. Kenny described it as an:[57]

> astonishing result ... It is incomprehensible that it is still permissible to have paid trustees, chosen for their reliability and expertise, who do not have to assume responsibility for their own misconduct, and in fact will still be entitled to payment. ... The possibility of non-compliance remains, and there is no sanction for this. Years later, when a clause is being relied on, how will it be possible to know what the settlor was told or understood? Far more fundamentally, the question of why a professional should be able to rely on such clauses has not been answered. The consultation process has produced an explanation but this explanation is far from convincing.

---

[55] E.g. the Society of Trust and Estate Practitioners issued a Practice Rule that its members should disclose clauses exempting trustees and executors from liability: *Trustee Exemption Clauses: STEP Practice Rule* (2006).

[56] 'Exemptions', in *Breach of Trust* (eds Birks and Pretto) (Oxford: Hart, 2002), p. 250.

[57] 'The Good, the Bad and the Law Commission' [2007] Conv 103.

Behind such misgivings lies a suspicion that the wealthy might of professional trustees in the City of London managed to force the Law Commission to back away from reform. However, reform was always likely to be controversial; any legislative provision would no doubt have been difficult to draft, and there is a sound argument that the autonomy of the settlor deserves to be respected.

Given the lack of legislative reform, some solace for critics of the Law Commission might be found in the broader definition of dishonesty enunciated in *Walker v Stones*. After all, if professional trustees cannot rely upon exclusion clauses if they acted in a manner in which no other trustee would have acted, that comes close to removing the possibility of excluding liability for gross negligence.[58] However, some may feel that this still gives trustees too much leeway: they are still able to rely upon exclusion clauses if merely negligent, and courts may be somewhat hesitant to use the label of 'dishonesty' since branding a professional person dishonest can have seriously deleterious effects, and may seem inappropriate where he or she did not actually realize that he or she was committing a breach of duty.[59] Negligence is the more appropriate nomenclature.

In any event, it is not unlikely that this issue will be revisited by the courts. Indeed, it reached the Privy Council in *Spread Trustee Co. Ltd v Hutcheson*, but that decision cannot be the final word: the actual decision concerns the previous customary law in Guernsey, not English law, and there was no full discussion of arguments concerning principle and policy. However, some of the *dicta* in the case may be significant. For example, Lord Clarke said that:[60]

> The critical point is that *Armitage v Nurse* correctly states English law as it stands at present.

Armitage is, therefore, considered currently to be authoritative, but it only has that status 'at present'. It may well be subject to review. Indeed, Baroness Hale[61] expressly pointed out that:

> the Supreme Court of the United Kingdom has never had an opportunity to consider whether that case was rightly decided.

Her Ladyship went on to cast doubt upon English law's allowing the trust deed to exclude liability for gross negligence, and said:[62]

> I suspect that even an English lawyer would regard it as unacceptable that a guardian of the estate of a minor might be excused liability for gross negligence.

In a similar vein, Lord Kerr revealed some discomfort with *Armitage*, concluding with the following comments:[63]

> If, as I suggested at the beginning of this judgment, the placing of reliance on a responsible person to manage property so as to promote the interests of the beneficiaries of a trust is central to the concept of trusteeship, denying trustees the opportunity to avoid liability for their gross negligence seems to be entirely in keeping with that essential aim.

---

[58] Although it is unclear whether a trustee would be dishonest under the definition in *Walker v Stones* if the trustee did not know that he or she was committing a breach of trust: see Chapter 16.2(b)(iii)(a), pp. 750–2.

[59] Cf. *Twinsectra Ltd v Yardley* [2002] 2 AC 164 (Lord Hutton), Chapter 19.2(c), p. 937.

[60] [2011] UKPC 13; [2012] 2 AC 194, [52].

[61] Ibid, [129].

[62] Ibid, [139].

[63] Ibid, [180].

Such comments are sure to fuel future litigation. The fact that two members of the Supreme Court—Baroness Hale and Lord Kerr—expressed doubts about *Armitage* and dissented in the Privy Council suggests that a definitive pronouncement from the Supreme Court would be desirable. It may well be that the Supreme Court would welcome such a case: leave to appeal in *Walker v Stones* was granted, but the case was compromised before the appeal was heard. Any reform now seems to be dependent upon the judiciary.

(c) INTERPRETING EXCLUSION CLAUSES

Even in the absence of reform, courts have sought to restrict the relief that might be available to a professional trustee through interpreting exclusion clauses narrowly. For example, in *Walker v Stones*, Sir Christopher Slade commented that:[64]

> Millett LJ analysed the permitted scope of trustee exemption clauses in *Armitage v Nurse* at 251–256. His analysis in my judgment clearly illustrates the need, as a matter of policy, for the courts to construe clauses of this nature no more widely than their language on a fair reading requires. I cannot believe it would be the intention of the draftsmen of clauses such as clause 15 of the Bacchus trust deed to exempt trustees from liability for a breach of trust in a case such as that postulated at the end of the immediately preceding paragraph.

Thus, as a matter of interpretation, the relevant exclusion clause may not cover the nature of the particular breach in question. Indeed, in *Spread Trustee*, Lord Mance[65] stated that:

> English law will construe exempting provisions strictly. ... in a chapter in *Trends in Contemporary Trust Law* ed A J Oakley (1996), 'The Irreducible Core Content of Trusteeship,' ... Professor David Hayton endorsed the same view, referring in a footnote to *Knox v Mackinnon* and *Rae v Meek* with the comment that 'in context the wording of some exemption clauses may be construed contra proferentem as not extending to omissions considered to be gross negligence'.

This is a sensible approach for the courts to adopt. Where the exclusion clause clearly and unambiguously covers the situation at issue, then the clause must be given effect to the extent that it does not interfere with the irreducible core. But where the clause is not so clear, and competing interpretations of the trust instrument are equally viable, the court should prefer the interpretation that favours the beneficiaries, rather than professional trustees who seek to rely on a clause that they probably drafted. Restricting the ambit of exclusion clauses in this way helps to ensure that the irreducible core is not undermined and that the protection of the beneficiaries' rights is strengthened.

In *Wight v Olswang*,[66] the Court of Appeal held that a clause that exempted solicitor-trustees of liability had to be interpreted restrictively. Consequently, when one clause exempted them from all liability and another exempted only the liability of unpaid trustees, it was held that the latter prevailed. This narrow approach to construction should be applied to all types of exclusion clause.[67] In *Citibank*

---

[64] [2001] QB 902, 941. The immediately preceeding paragraph concerned the test of dishonesty and is quoted in Chapter 16.2(b)(iii)(a), p. 751.

[65] [2011] UKPC 13; [2012] 2 AC 194, [106].

[66] [1999] 1 ITELR 783.

[67] In *Bogg v Raper* [1998] EWCA Civ 661; [1998] 1 ITELR 267 the Court of Appeal had to construe an exemption clause inserted into a trust deed by a solicitor-trustee. The court held that the interpretation could cover the acts of the trustee, but that he could only rely on it if he had drawn the testator's attention to the clause and explained its effect.

v MBIA, Arden LJ recognized that a clause which restricts the duties owed by a trustee might be interpreted narrowly in order to ensure the integrity of the irreducible core of obligations a trustee owes:[68]

> it is correct that it would be a surprising interpretation of the documentation, against which the court should lean, if the powers of the trustee were so reduced that it ceases to be a trustee at all.

(d) EFFECT OF EXCLUSION CLAUSES

It is clear that a trustee cannot rely upon an exclusion clause if he or she has been fraudulent. But what if the trustee has only been negligent, and seeks to rely upon an exclusion clause that purports also to exclude any liability for the trustee's fraudulent conduct: does the clause fail in its entirety, and not exclude liability for the trustee's negligent acts, or is the clause only invalid to the extent that it undermined the irreducible core of the obligations owed by a trustee, and can be relied upon by a trustee who has only been negligent? There is no clear answer to this question, and the appropriate solution might depend upon the precise facts of a case. General principles of severance might apply. If the settlor's intention to relieve the trustee of liability for any breach of duty can be clearly established, then it seems sensible to allow the trustee to rely upon the clause if he has been negligent and this does not offend the 'irreducible core'. The offensive words could be severed from the otherwise valid exclusion clause. But if the settlor failed to appreciate the clause's effect, then it is not so obvious that severing the invalid part of the clause would help to promote the settlor's true intentions, and as a result the court might decide that the entire clause should fail.

3. RELIEF BY THE COURT

A trustee might escape personal liability for breach of trust not only through an exclusion clause in the trust instrument, but also through section 61 of the Trustee Act 1925.

TRUSTEE ACT 1925

61. Power to relieve trustee from personal liability

If it appears to the court that a trustee, whether appointed by the court or otherwise, is or may be personally liable for any breach of trust, whether the transaction alleged to be a breach of trust occurred before or after the commencement of this Act, but has acted honestly and reasonably, and ought fairly to be excused for the breach of trust and for omitting to obtain the directions of the court in the matter in which he committed such breach, then the court may relieve him either wholly or partly from personal liability for the same.

Clearly, there are three requirements that need to be satisfied for the court to grant any relief: honesty, reasonableness, and fairness. These will be examined in turn. It is important to note that this provision is potentially applicable in respect of any breach of trust, including where the trustee makes an unauthorized investment or distributes assets to the wrong objects.[69] Section 61 does not apply to

---

[68] [2007] EWCA Civ 11; [2007] 1 All ER (Comm) 475, [82].
[69] *Re Stuart* [1897] 2 Ch 583.

future breaches, and only covers past events, since only then may there be liability from which relief can be granted. However, it is not necessary for the trustee first to establish that there has definitely been a breach of trust.[70] The burden of proof naturally lies on the wrongdoing trustee, who must show that he or she deserves the 'dubious prerogative of mercy'[71] vested in the court.

(a) HONESTY

For the purposes of section 61, honesty essentially equates to good faith. The appropriate test for dishonesty probably mirrors that adopted in the context of trustee exclusion clauses. If the trustee is a lay trustee, a subjective standard is used,[72] whereas, for a professional trustee, an objective test is preferred.[73] So, if the trustee genuinely believed he or she was acting in the best interests of the beneficiary, then the court might still decide that the trustee was dishonest if the trustee was a professional and no reasonable professional trustee would have held that belief. It is worth emphasizing that the burden lies squarely upon the trustee to prove that he or she acted honestly. As Nicholas Davidson QC, sitting as a Deputy High Court Judge in *Ikbal v Sterling Law*, rightly observed, the fact that dishonesty may not be alleged:[74]

> does not dispose of the issue: it is for the trustee affirmatively to prove honesty, and the fact that those acting for the beneficiary may not have enough material to justify alleging dishonesty in a Statement of Case does not relieve the trustee of that task.

(b) REASONABLENESS

Reasonableness is assessed objectively. An important factor is whether or not the trustees took legal advice. This may be particularly significant given that it would also have been possible for the trustees to seek directions from the court before breaching their duties.[75] However, even if a trustee follows legal advice, it seems that the court will not necessarily relieve the trustee from liability: if the advice was wrong, the trustee could sue the advisor for negligence, and thereby ensure that the trust suffers no loss; failing to take such steps is unlikely to be excused.[76] Yet the claim against the advisor will succeed only if the advisor was negligent, and the possibility of a claim does not necessarily ensure a satisfactory remedy. It is suggested that only in very rare cases should the court decide that an honest trustee who has followed legal advice has not acted reasonably: what else was the trustee supposed to do?

Although it might be thought that the requirement of reasonableness means that a trustee who has breached the duty of care has inevitably failed to act reasonably, the court may still be prepared to apply section 61. So, in *Re Smith*,[77] the trustee was a widow who lived in the country and employed a firm of solicitors to act as her agents. The solicitor's clerk fraudulently obtained the trustee's signature on certain cheques and induced her to initial alterations to the cheques. He then absconded with the money. The trustee was held to have breached the trust, but her liability was excused because she had

---

[70] *Re Smith* (1902) 86 LT 401 (Ch D) (Kekewich J).
[71] Maugham, 'Excusable Breaches of Trust' (1898) 14 LQR 159.
[72] Cf *Armitage v Nurse* [1998] Ch 241: see Chapter 16.2(b)(iii), pp. 749–50.
[73] Cf *Walker v Stones* [2001] QB 902: see Chapter 16.2(b)(iii)(a), pp. 750–2.
[74] *Ikbal v Sterling Law* [2013] EWHC 3291 (Ch); [2014] PNLR 9, [226].
[75] See Chapter 11.7(c), p. 568.
[76] *National Trustees Company of Australasia Ltd v General Finance Company of Australasia Ltd* [1905] AC 373.
[77] (1902) 86 LT 401.

acted honestly and reasonably, even though she had not taken all the precautions against fraud that a reasonable trustee would have taken. It does not follow, however, that trustees will be relieved of liability in all cases of negligence. In fact, where a trustee falls below the expected standard of prudence, he or she will generally not be relieved of liability. *Re Smith* might be distinguished because of the peculiar position of the trustee, who had committed what might be considered to be a morally innocent breach of trust. Nevertheless, the trustee did commit a breach of trust, and the relief granted under section 61 was personal to that trustee; if the beneficiary had sued the solicitor's clerk for dishonestly assisting a breach of trust, for example, that claim would surely have succeeded since the solicitor's clerk would not be able to rely upon section 61.[78]

Re Smith might be contrasted with *Re Stuart*, where Stirling J refused to grant relief under section 61 when the trustee had breached his duty in making improper investments.

Re Stuart [1897] Ch 583, 590 (Stirling J)

A jurisdiction is given to the Court under special circumstances, the Court being satisfied as to the several matters mentioned in the section, to relieve the trustee of the consequences of a breach of trust as regards his personal liability. But the Court must first be satisfied that the trustee has acted honestly and reasonably. As to the honesty of the trustee in this case there is no question; but that is not the only condition to be satisfied, and the question arises whether the other conditions are satisfied. I quite agree that this section applies to a trustee making an improper investment of the trust funds as well as to any other breach of trust. This matter has been considered by Byrne J in *Re Turner* [1897] 1 Ch 536 at 542, where he says this:

> 'I think that the section relied on is meant to be acted upon freely and fairly in the exercise of judicial discretion, but I think that the Court ought to be satisfied, before exercising the very large powers conferred upon it, by sufficient evidence, that the trustee acted reasonably. I do not think that I have sufficient evidence in this case that he so acted; in fact, it does not appear from the letters that Mr. Turner acted in respect of this mortgage as he would probably have acted had it been a transaction of his own. I think that if he was—and he well may have been—a businesslike man, he would not, before lending his money, have been satisfied without some further inquiry as to the means of the mortgagor and as to the nature and value of the property upon which he was about to advance his money.'

That has since been approved by the Court of Appeal; and I willingly adopt what is there laid down as a guide to me in this matter. In my opinion the burden lies on the trustee who asks the Court to exercise the jurisdiction conferred by this section to shew that he has acted reasonably; and, certainly, it is fair in dealing with such a question to consider whether [the trustee] would have acted with reference to these investments as he did if he had been lending money of his own.

Whether or not a trustee has acted reasonably will depend very much upon the facts of any particular case. A particular area of controversy at the moment concerns claims for breach of trust in the context of conveyancing transactions. There have been high-profile examples where the Court of Appeal has seen fit to overturn the decision of a trial judge regarding the reasonableness of a trustee's conduct for the purposes of relief under section 61.[79] These cases have helped to develop clearer guidance concerning relief under section 61.

---

[78] See further Chapter 19.2, p. 928.

[79] E.g. *Nationwide Building Society v Davisons* [2012] EWCA Civ 1626, [2013] PNLR 12; *Santander UK Plc v RA Legal Solicitors* [2014] EWCA Civ 183, [2014] PNLR 20.

Lloyds TSB Bank plc v Markandan & Uddin [2012] EWCA Civ 65; [2012] 2 All ER 884

The defendant was a firm of solicitors ('M&U') which was acting for the claimant lender on a mortgage loan. The lender transferred £742,500 to M&U, which the latter held on trust with instructions to advance the money to the vendors upon completion of the purchase of the particular property in return for a first legal charge in favour of the lender. Unfortunately, M&U was the victim of a fraud: it transferred the money to what it believed to be a firm of solicitors acting for the vendors, thought to be called Deen Solicitors, but in fact M&U transferred the money to fraudsters who made off with it. Although there was a genuine firm of solicitors called Deen Solicitors in Luton, the fraudsters purported to be acting from a branch office in London which did not in fact exist.

M&U had therefore transferred the mortgage funds in breach of trust: there was no completion of the transaction and therefore no authority to part with the money. M&U sought relief under section 61. This was unsuccessful. Although M&U had acted honestly, it had not acted reasonably. In particular, M&U had failed to check that Deen Solicitors actually had an office at the address given in London, and failed to take adequate steps to verify the transaction after the bogus solicitors had breached certain undertakings. Rimer LJ said:

> Whilst it is impossible not to have sympathy for M&U in becoming enmeshed in the fraud, the judge's conclusion was that, by these two shortcomings, they brought their misfortune upon themselves. If they had instead performed their role as solicitors with exemplary professional care and efficiency, but had still parted with the loan money in circumstances that were objectively reasonable, the decision on the section 61 application might have been different.
>
> It is, therefore, the discretionary power under section 61 that provides the key to the claimed unfairness of holding a solicitor liable for breach of trust in circumstances such as the present. The careful, conscientious and thorough solicitor, who conducts the transaction by the book and acts honestly and reasonably in relation to it in all respects but still does not discover the fraud, may still be held to have been in breach of trust for innocently parting with the loan money to a fraudster. He is, however, likely to be treated mercifully by the court on his section 61 application. M&U's conduct of the transaction was, however, found to fall short of the standard that merited such mercy.

The test laid down in *Markandan & Uddin* by the Court of Appeal seems quite strict. It was quickly recognized as laying down binding propositions of law, although in the Court of Appeal decision in *Nationwide Building Society v Davisons*,[80] the facts of which were similar to *Markandan & Uddin*, Morritt C appeared to favour a somewhat less stringent approach in insisting that:[81]

> [section 61] only requires [the trustee] to have acted reasonably. That does not, in my view, predicate that he has necessarily complied with best practice in all respects. The relevant action must at least be connected with the loss for which relief is sought and the requisite standard is that of reasonableness not of perfection.
>
> ... The lapse from best practice, if any, did not cause the loss to Nationwide. Given that [the trustee] acted both honestly and reasonably I can see no ground on which Davisons should be denied relief from all liability.

---

[80] [2012] EWCA Civ 1626; [2013] PNLR 12.
[81] Ibid, [48]–[50].

This seems to a much more generous approach to trustees: even if they have failed to comply with best practice, the court may still grant relief under section 61 if such failure does not cause any loss to the beneficiary. This was applied in *Ikbal v Sterling Law*,[82] where the judge found that even though the solicitors had acted 'very unreasonably indeed' in some respects, there was a 'lack of causal connection between the defendant's behaviour and the loss'.[83] Somewhat reluctantly, the judge thought that this meant that the solicitors were entitled to relief under section 61.

These cases were reviewed by the Court of Appeal in *Santander UK v RA Legal Solicitors*, which is now the leading decision in this area.

Santander UK Plc v RA Legal Solicitors [2014] EWCA Civ 183; [2014] PNLR 20

RA Legal was a firm of solicitors acting for both the purchaser and claimant lender in the purchase of a residential property. RA Legal transferred the purchase monies—£150,000 from the mortgage lender and £50,000 from the purchaser—to Sovereign Chambers LLP, a firm of solicitors who purported to act on behalf of the vendor. Sovereign was a firm in good standing with the Law Society, but was nonetheless a fraudster: it had no authority to sell the property on behalf of the vendor. The lender sued RA Legal for breach of trust in paying away the mortgage monies otherwise than upon completion. The trial judge excused RA Legal from liability under section 61. This was overturned by the Court of Appeal, which seemed in substance to inch away from the analysis on causation in *Davisons*.

Briggs LJ:

...it seems to me that some element of causative connection will usually have to be shown, and that conduct (even if unreasonable) which is completely irrelevant or immaterial to the loss will usually fall outside the court's purview under section 61. ... I would, finally, caution against an over-mechanistic application of the requirement to show the necessary connection between the conduct complained of and the lender's loss. There may be highly unreasonable conduct which lies at the fringe of materiality in terms of causation, and only slightly unreasonable conduct which goes to the heart of a causation analysis. It would be wrong in my view to allow this purely mechanistic application of a causation-based test for the identification of relevant conduct to exclude the former from any consideration under section 61.

Briggs LJ thought that RA Legal acted unreasonably in providing a Certificate of Title certifying that it had investigated title when that investigation was incomplete. His Lordship was unimpressed by the fact that such conduct was not uncommon amongst solicitors in order to encourage lenders to transfer the mortgage funds in good time and to avoid delays. Briggs LJ thought that:[84]

The pretence that the investigation of title has been completed when it has not is a method of dealing with that difficulty which borders on dishonesty. It is nothing to the point that, if subsequently revealed defects are properly addressed, it causes the lender no loss. On the contrary, [counsel's] submission that unqualified certificates are frequently given prematurely involves the implicit admission that this is done deliberately, rather than by accident. If so, it simply makes the misconduct all the more serious.

Nonetheless, Briggs LJ was prepared to accept that the premature Certificate of Title was irrelevant to the claimant's loss, since there was 'an insufficient type of connection, being purely historical and

---

[82] [2013] EWHC 3291 (Ch); [2014] PNLR 9.
[83] Ibid, [237].
[84] [2014] EWCA Civ 183; [2014] PNLR 20, [60].

entirely irrelevant to the risk of a subsequent fraud'.[85] But his Lordship thought that RA Legal's departure from best practice by making inadequate requisitions and accepting inadequate replies to them was in fact serious and consequential. Briggs LJ concluded:[86]

> The question whether a trustee has acted reasonably in respect of matters connected with the beneficiary's loss is not in my judgment to be resolved purely by considering each specific complaint separately. The question is whether the trustee's relevant conduct was reasonable, taken as a whole. Looking at the matter in the round, I have been driven to the conclusion that the judge took an altogether too lenient view of the seriousness of R.A. Legal's numerous departures from best practice...
>
> [RA Legal's actions] represent departures from a sophisticated regime, worked out over many years, whereby risks of loss to lenders and lay clients are minimised, even if not wholly eradicated. Where solicitors fail, in serious respects, to play their part in that structure, and at the same time are swindled into transferring and then releasing trust money to a fraudster without authority, they cannot expect to persuade the court that it is fair to excuse them from liability, upon the basis that they have demonstrated that they have in all respects connected with that loss, acted reasonably.

Although Briggs LJ said that he did not mean to cast any doubt upon the decision in *Davisons*, it seems clear that the decision in *RA Legal* restricts the circumstances where relief under section 61 will be granted: after all, unreasonable conduct that is not connected with the loss seems potentially relevant under the scheme of Briggs LJ. Any significant departure from best practice committed by the solicitor-trustee appears likely to prevent reliance upon section 61. This approach was endorsed by Etherton C, who said:[87]

> ... section 61 must be interpreted consistently with equity's high expectation of a trustee discharging fiduciary obligations.
>
> It seems clear, against that background, that the object of section 61 is not to introduce a particular causation test which is distinct from and negates the normal rules for fixing liability for personal liability for breach of trust. It is not a statutory gloss intended to introduce familiar causation concepts, such as a 'but for test' or an 'effective cause' test. It is an exceptional statutory jurisdiction to relieve a trustee from liability despite equity's stringent duties imposed on trustees. I agree with Briggs LJ, therefore, that the test is not one of strict causation. On the other hand, it seems equally clear that the court's jurisdiction to grant relief under section 61 is not precluded by conduct of the trustee which, although unreasonable, played absolutely no part in the occasioning of the loss.

It is suggested that the guidance provided in *RA Legal* is welcome. Whilst entirely irrelevant conduct should be disregarded,[88] the court should be slow to find a lack of a causal link between unreasonable conduct and the losses suffered. The fact that the fraudulent scheme would have succeeded anyway is not sufficient for a trustee to gain the protection of section 61. Any unreasonable conduct that increases the risk of there being a breach of trust should generally lead to a refusal to grant relief under section 61. Codes of practice have evolved in order to minimize the risks of transactions going wrong, so departures from such codes should lead to the court's being reluctant to exercise its discretion under section 61.

---

[85] Ibid, [61]. See too Etherton C at [110].

[86] [2014] EWCA Civ 183; [2014] PNLR 20, [96]–[99].

[87] Ibid, [108]–[109]

[88] Charlwood has suggested the example of failing to carry out a coal mining search which would have come back negative anyway: Charlwood, 'Conveyancing Solicitors' Liability for Breach of Trust' (2014) 30 PN 102, 106.

(c) FAIRNESS

Where the trustee has acted honestly and reasonably then it will generally be fair to excuse the trustee for his breach of duty. However, fairness does not inevitably follow from the first two requirements.

Perrins v Bellamy [1898] 2 Ch 521, 527–9

Trustees held certain properties on trust. They were advised by solicitors that they had a power of sale over the properties, and a surveyor recommended that the properties be sold. The trustees, therefore, sold the properties, but it transpired that this was in breach of trust and that the advice received from their solicitors was incorrect. The beneficiaries argued that it would not be fair to relieve the trustees from liability for the breach, because the trustees had failed to seek the directions of the court. This argument was rejected.

Kekewich J:

The Legislature has made the absence of all dishonesty a condition precedent to the relief of the trustee from liability. But that is not the grit of the section. The grit is in the words 'reasonably, and ought fairly to be excused for the breach of trust'. How much the latter words add to the force of the word 'reasonably' I am not at present prepared to say. I suppose, however, that in the view of the Legislature there might be cases in which a trustee, though he had acted reasonably, ought not fairly to be excused for the breach of trust. Indeed, I am not sure that some of the evidence adduced in this case was not addressed to a view of that kind, as, for instance, the evidence by which it was attempted to shew that these trustees, though they acted reasonably in selling the property, ought not fairly to be excused because the plaintiff Mrs. Perrins objected to their selling, and her objection was brought to their notice. In the section the copulative 'and' is used, and it may well be argued that in order to bring a case within the section it must be shewn not merely that the trustee has acted 'reasonably', but also that he ought 'fairly' to be excused for the breach of trust. I venture, however, to think that, in general and in the absence of special circumstances, a trustee who has acted 'reasonably' ought to be relieved, and that it is not incumbent on the Court to consider whether he ought 'fairly' to be excused, unless there is evidence of a special character shewing that the provisions of the section ought not to be applied in his favour. I need not pursue that subject further, because in the present case I find no ground whatever for saying that these trustees, if they acted reasonably, ought not to be excused. The question, and the only question, is whether they acted reasonably. In saying that, I am not unmindful of the words of the section which follow, and which require that it should be shewn that the trustee ought 'fairly' to be excused, not only 'for the breach of trust', but also 'for omitting to obtain the directions of the Court in the matter in which he committed such breach of trust'. I find it difficult to follow that. I do not see how the trustee can be excused for the breach of trust without being also excused for the omission referred to, or how he can be excused for the omission without also being excused for the breach of trust. If I am at liberty to guess, I should suppose that these words were added by way of amendment, and crept into the statute without due regard being had to the meaning of the context. The fact that a trustee has omitted to obtain the directions of the Court has never been held to be a ground for holding him personally liable, though it may be a reason guiding the Court in the matter of costs, or in deciding whether he has acted reasonably or otherwise, and especially so in these days when questions of difficulty, even as regards the legal estate, can be decided economically and expeditiously on originating summons. But if the Court comes to the conclusion that a trustee has acted reasonably, I cannot see how it can usefully proceed to consider, as an independent matter, the question whether he has or has not omitted to obtain the directions of the Court.

Kekewich J emphasized that, although the wording of the statute clearly contemplates a situation where the trustees have acted reasonably but still might not fairly be excused, in practice, fairness adds little to reasonableness in the vast majority of cases. However, this analysis might be limited to situations involving lay trustees, particularly since Kekewich J appears to have taken a broader approach to 'reasonableness' than has been adopted in more recent cases.

In any event, the courts tend to be more reluctant to find that professional trustees ought fairly to be excused. As Lowry and Edmunds[89] have observed, the primary concern of the Victorian drafters of section 61 and its predecessors was not to jeopardize the supply of competent lay trustees by exposing them to the risk of liability for honest and reasonable breaches. The same rationale does not necessarily apply to professional trustees:[90]

> Throughout the twentieth, and into the present century, there has been a discernible shift towards an increasing professionalisation of trusteeship. Section 61 may continue to provide a residual safeguard for the honest and reasonable lay trustee. However, it does not automatically follow that such relief fulfils any valuable role in respect of a professional trustee of a commercial trust.

In *Re Pauling's Settlement Trusts*,[91] a power of advancement had been exercised improperly by the trustee, which was a bank. The breach of trust arose from the bank being improperly advised by its solicitors. It was held that more is expected from professional trustees than amateurs and, without more, it would not be possible to relieve them of liability, even though they had acted honestly and reasonably. Willmer LJ explained that:[92]

> The bank also rely for relief from the consequences of any breach of trust upon section 61 of the Trustee Act, 1925. At this stage all we propose to say is that it would be a misconstruction of the section to say it does not apply to professional trustees, but, as was pointed out in the Judicial Committee of the Privy Council in *National Trustees Company of Australasia Ltd v General Finance Company of Australasia Ltd* [1905] AC 373 at 381 ' … without saying that the remedial provisions of the section should never be applied to a trustee in the position of the appellants, their Lordships think it is a circumstance to be taken into account … ' Where a banker undertakes to act as a paid trustee of a settlement created by a customer, and so deliberately places itself in a position where its duty as trustee conflicts with its interest as a banker, we think that the court should be very slow to relieve such a trustee under the provisions of the section.

Nevertheless, the court ultimately did relieve the bank of liability because an additional factor was identified that made it fair to excuse the bank: the beneficiaries had consented in writing to the exercise of the power.[93]

Of course, the court is able to exercise its discretion under section 61 to relieve a professional trustee from liability. Fairness is 'essentially a matter within the discretion of the judge'.[94] A range of factors can therefore be relevant. One which might be significant is the identity of the beneficiary. It is clear that courts should have regard to the effect of the grant of relief on the beneficiary.[95] The court might

---

[89] 'Excuses', in *Breach of Trust* (eds Birks and Pretto) (Oxford: Hart, 2002).
[90] Ibid, p. 271.
[91] [1964] Ch 303.
[92] Ibid, 338–9.
[93] For consent, see Chapter 16.4, pp. 769–74.
[94] *Marsden v Regan* [1954] 1 WLR 423, 435 (Evershed MR).
[95] *RA Legal* [2014] EWCA Civ 183; [2014] PNLR 20, [33] (Briggs LJ); *Marsden v Regan* [1954] 1 WLR 423, 434 (Evershed MR); *Bartlett v Barclays Trust Co. (No.1)* [1980] Ch 515, 538 (Brightman J).

therefore generally be more prepared to grant relief to a professional trustee where the beneficiary is also a commercial entity who is insured and can be expected to absorb its loss. On the other hand, if the beneficiary is a private individual without the benefit of adequate insurance, granting relief to the trustee under section 61 could have particularly hard consequences on the beneficiary and may not be fair. As Briggs LJ said in *RA Legal*:[96]

> An institutional lender may well be insured (or effectively self-insured) for the consequences of third party fraud. But an innocent purchaser may have contributed his life's savings to the purchase and have no recourse at all other than against his insured solicitor, where for example the fraudster is a pure interloper, rather than a dishonest solicitor in respect of whose fraud the losers may have recourse against the Solicitors' Compensation Fund.

Although the identity of the beneficiary might be relevant, it should be noted that it is unlikely that section 61 will avail a trustee who wishes to assert a defence of contributory negligence. At first instance in *Markandan & Uddin*,[97] Roger Wyand QC, sitting as a Deputy High Court Judge, noted that there was nothing in *Vesta v Butcher*[98] which indicated that contributory negligence should be extended to instances of breach of trust. The judge then went on to state that:[99]

> [section 61] could have provided for the conduct of the beneficiary to be taken into account as the Defendant here wishes. It did not and it is not for the Court to extend the law in a way that was not done by the legislature.

The judge's conclusions on contributory negligence were not pursued on appeal,[100] and should be supported: the focus of section 61 is firmly placed on the trustee who has committed the breach of trust, not the beneficiary. It might further be argued that a beneficiary should not be expected to take steps to protect his position against a trustee's breach of trust.[101]

(d) ASSESSING SECTION 61

Although in the recent decision of the Supreme Court in *AIB Group (UK) Plc v Mark Redler & Co*, Lord Toulson thought that section 61 might be invoked as a '*deus ex machina*',[102] this appears to be unsatisfactory. Section 61 remains a useful provision: it seems appropriate for the court to be able to excuse some breaches of trust. Some trusts are complex, and trust duties may be strict and difficult to comply with; technical breaches of trust can be committed entirely innocently. The significance of section 61 is particularly pronounced in situations where there is no exclusion clause in the trust instrument. A distinction between lay and professional trustees has been drawn in the context of exemption clauses, and seems equally sensible in this context. This explains why the courts appear to be more willing to apply section 61 where the breach of trust has been committed by a lay trustee rather than a professional trustee. In any event, section 61 is important in striking a balance between

---

[96] [2014] EWCA Civ 183; [2014] PNLR 20, [33].
[97] [2010] EWHC 2517 (Ch); [2011] PNLR 6, [42].
[98] [1989] AC 852 (HL).
[99] [2010] EWHC 2517 (Ch); [2011] PNLR 6, [42].
[100] *Markandan & Uddin* [2012] EWCA Civ 65; [2012] 2 All ER 884, [7].
[101] For further discussion of contributory negligence in the context of claims for breach of fiduciary duty, see *Nationwide Building Society v Balmer Radmore* [1999] PNLR 606, 672–677 (Blackburne J).
[102] [2014] UKSC 58; [2014] 3 WLR 1367, [69] (Lord Toulson). See Davies, 'Section 61 of the Trustee Act 1925: *Deus ex Machina*?' [2015] Conv 375.

protecting beneficiaries and avoiding the imposition of too harsh liabilities upon trustees. However, settlors and beneficiaries are entitled to expect professional, paid trustees to comply with the duties imposed by the trust, and very rarely will such persons have acted reasonably in breaching their duties and it be fair to excuse that breach. Trustees should have to work very hard to prove that they acted honestly, reasonably and ought fairly to be excused.

4. CONSENT

(a) GENERAL PRINCIPLES

A beneficiary who consents to a breach of duty cannot then complain if the trustee commits the breach of duty for which consent was obtained. In *Walker v Symonds*,[103] Lord Eldon explained:

> It is established by all the cases, that if the *cestui que trust* joins with the trustees in that which is a breach of trust, knowing the circumstances, such a *cestui que trust* can never complain of such a breach of trust. I go further, and agree that either concurrence in the act, or acquiescence without original concurrence, will release the trustees: but that is only a general rule, and the Court must inquire into the circumstances which induced concurrence or acquiescence; recollecting in the conduct of that inquiry, how important it is on the one hand, to secure the property of the *cestui que trust*; and on the other, not to deter men from undertaking trusts, from the performance of which they seldom obtain either satisfaction or gratitude.

A beneficiary who consents to acts which involve a breach of trust is considered to join with the trustees and cannot then complain about the breach. However, the consent of one beneficiary will not provide a trustee with a defence to claims by other beneficiaries: consent operates to bar only the claim of the particular claimant who consents.

At first instance in *Re Pauling's Settlement Trusts*, Wilberforce J said:[104]

> the court has to consider all the circumstances in which the concurrence of the *cestui que trust* was given with a view to seeing whether it is fair and equitable that, having given his concurrence, he should afterwards turn round and sue the trustees: that, subject to this, it is not necessary that he should know that what he is concurring in is a breach of trust, provided that he fully understands what he is concurring in, and that it is not necessary that he should himself have directly benefited by the breach of trust.

The equitable discretion is therefore broad. The consenting beneficiary must be of full age and sound mind, and the consent freely given. The beneficiary must be fully informed, in that he or she must know of all the key facts and relevant surrounding circumstances concerning what the trustee seeks to do. It is not always necessary for the claimant to realize that there would be a breach of trust or for the claimant to benefit from the breach, but as Payne has commented:[105]

> The issue of the beneficiary's state of knowledge should be applied flexibly in the light of the facts of each case and of the overarching concepts of fairness and equity. In some cases ... the individual ought

---

[103] (1818) 3 Swans 1, 64.
[104] [1962] 1 WLR 86, 108. This was accepted by counsel in the Court of Appeal: [1964] Ch 303, 339.
[105] 'Consent', in *Breach of Trust* (eds Birks and Pretto) (Oxford: Hart, 2002), p. 319.

not to be denied a subsequent remedy against the wrongdoer without being shown to have known not only of the circumstances which give rise to the breach, but also that those circumstances do, in fact, amount to a breach of trust or fiduciary duty.

Precisely what level of knowledge will be sufficient to establish consent will depend upon the precise facts of the case. There was further discussion of this issue in *Re Pauling's Settlement Trusts*.

Re Pauling's Settlement Trusts [1964] Ch 303, 347–8

Commander and Mrs Younghusband were married in 1919; clause 11 of their marriage settlement contained a power of advancement for the trustee, which was a bank, Coutts & Co., to advance property to the children of the marriage. Between 1948 and 1954 the trustees made a number of advancements to the children, who sometimes received independent legal advice as to their rights under the settlement, but not on every occasion. In 1954, as a result of a scheme of one son's for avoiding estate duty on his mother's death, the children first became aware that the advancements might have been in breach of trust. In 1958 they brought an action against the trustees claiming £29,160, on the ground that this sum had been improperly paid out by way of advancement to beneficiaries who were presumed to be subject to undue influence and who were not emancipated from parental control. Other aspects of this decision will be considered later,[106] but on the issue of consent, Upjohn LJ was clear:

At the time of this advance the son George was 23 years old. He had done his military service, and was up at Cambridge. The judge thought him an exceptionally able young man, well acquainted with his rights, and able to take care of himself. He had no separate advice about this £2,000 advance, but he had been advised about the Hodson loan transaction, and in the course of receiving the explanations then offered he must have realised what the power was which the trustees were purporting to exercise. Indeed, the fatal opinion of counsel advising on the possibility of using clause 11 to purchase a house in the Isle of Man was, on the evidence, familiar not only to George, but to Ann [his sister]. The judge held that he was emancipated from parental control, and well enough acquainted with his position to make his consent to this advance binding upon him, and this court cannot reverse that finding, depending, as it does, so much upon the demeanour of the witness.

The case of the other son, Francis, is quite different. He was at this time 28 years old, and was apparently living for the most part with his grandmother, so that he was removed from immediate parental control. On the other hand, we now know that he was a schizophrenic. This diagnosis had been made in 1940 when he found one day of life in the Royal Air Force altogether too much for him, and was repeated by a doctor who saw him in 1951. He was not called by either side, it being agreed that his memory was not at all to be trusted. Consent to this, as to other transactions in which he was involved, was written out and sent to him by his father. There is no letter from him anywhere in the correspondence. No representative of the bank ever saw him. He was obviously left purposely in the background. On the other hand, he was capable of teaching in a boys school, which he did for two years towards the end of the war, and was accepted for entry to Edinburgh University after the war, where also he continued for two years as a student. Further, when he went with his brother to be advised over the Hodson loan, the partner in Farrer & Co who saw him thought him capable of understanding the transaction. Moreover, it has never been alleged that he was at any material time incapacitated from contracting

---

[106] See Chapter 16.4(b), pp. 772–3.

or conducting business affairs by reason of his mental health, though we cannot think that if the bank had known of his history of ill-health they would have acted on the consents he returned signed to his father. But the bank did not know the facts. We have considered anxiously whether, before making an advance, they should have made some inquiry into his circumstances. It is alleged in the particulars of the statement of claim (paragraph 10) that the law presumes undue influence to exist between a person suffering from mental ill-health and the person with whom he resides; but in the end [counsel] rightly abandoned this plea, for there is no such presumption though actual undue influence may not be difficult to prove. The presumption exists only as to the medical adviser. On the whole, we do not feel able to say that the presumption of undue influence must be held to exist between Francis and his parents having regard to his age and his absence from home, and we conclude that the bank were not bound to make inquiries as to his state of mind or fitness as an object of the power they were affecting to exercise. Accordingly, though this was the plainest breach of trust, we agree with the judge that the bank have a good defence, for they obtained consents from the two children concerned, and they were emancipated.

Clearly, a range of factors will be considered when determining whether or not the consent provided by the beneficiary is sufficient to bar a claim against the trustee. Whether or not such 'consent' was provided in the context of a relationship of undue influence might be particularly important; indeed, the consent of the daughter in *Re Pauling's Settlement Trusts* was ineffective for this very reason.

Consent might be further justified as a bar to the beneficiary's claim against the trustee on the basis of an agreement between the parties that no claim will be brought for that breach of duty. However, this rationale is best placed to explain consent given *prior* to the breach of trust. Consent may be given after the breach of trust has occurred in order to release the trustee from liability, but this would create a compromise agreement so should only be effective if consideration has been provided for the release.[107] A different explanation for the defence of consent is based upon estoppel, which should be available to a trustee who has detrimentally relied on the representation not to sue.

(b) IMPOUNDING A BENEFICIARY'S INTEREST

The consent of a beneficiary to a trustee's breach of duty may not only bar a claim, but also result in the beneficiary's losing his or her beneficial interest.

TRUSTEE ACT 1925

62. Power to make beneficiary indemnify for breach of trust

Where a trustee commits a breach of trust at the instigation or request or with the consent in writing of a beneficiary, the court may, if it thinks fit, make such order as to the court seems just, for impounding all or any part of the interest of the beneficiary in the trust estate by way of indemnity to the trustee or persons claiming through him.

The effect of section 62 is to indemnify the trustee: compensation for breach of trust will be provided from the beneficiary's share of the trust fund rather than by the trustee. Obviously, the most that can

---

[107] *Stackhouse v Barnston* (1805) 10 Ves 453, 466 (Sir William Grant MR); *De Bussche v Alt* (1878) 8 Ch D 286, 314 (Thesiger LJ). Actual consent is needed; it is insufficient that a beneficiary only would have consented to the trustee's actions if aware of the circumstances: cf *Murad v Al-Saraj* [2005] EWCA Civ 959, discussed in Chapter 14.5(a), pp. 704–6.

be impounded is the value of the beneficiary's interest; beyond that, section 62 can offer no relief. The nature of this provision was discussed by Wilberforce J in *Re Pauling's Settlement Trusts (No. 2)*.[108]

Re Pauling's Settlement Trusts (No. 2) [1963] Ch 576, 583

Coutts and Co., the trustees of a family trust, were held liable for breach of trust in respect of a number of advances of capital made to the children of the life tenant, Mrs Younghusband. The bank claimed to be entitled to impound the life interest of Mrs Younghusband. The beneficiaries instituted proceedings because they sought the appointment of two new trustees in the place of the bank, which opposed this on the ground that such an appointment might negate their right to impound. Wilberforce J agreed to appoint new trustees, but held that this would not imperil the defendants' right to impound under section 62.

Wilberforce J:

Next I come to a separate series of objections which raise some difficult questions of law. The defendants, as I have already mentioned, have a claim to impound the life interest of Mrs. Younghusband now vested in the Guardian Assurance Co Ltd in order to recoup themselves against any money which they may be ordered to repay. What is said by the defendants is that that right to impound would be prejudiced if new trustees were appointed now and the trust fund handed over to them. That involves a consideration as to what is the nature of the right to impound which exists in favour of a trustee who has committed a breach of trust at the instigation of a beneficiary. I have to consider both the ordinary right which exists in equity apart from statute and also the further statutory right which has been conferred by section 62 of the Trustee Act, 1925, both of which are invoked by the defendants as plaintiffs in the Chancery action now pending. It seems to me that it is not possible to maintain, as is the defendants' contention here, that a trustee, having committed a breach of trust, is entitled to remain as a trustee until it has exercised its right to impound the income of the beneficiary in order to recoup itself. That seems to me an impossible proposition. It is quite true that, in the reported authorities, there is no case where the right to impound has been exercised by a former trustee as distinct from an existing trustee, but it seems to me in principle that it is impossible to contend that the right to impound is limited to the case where the trustee seeking the right is an actual trustee. The nature of the right to impound seems to me to turn on two things: first, that the money paid back to capital is in its origin the money of the trustee, and that when it comes to considering who should get the income of it, the trustee who has provided the money has a better right to it than the tenant for life who has instigated the breach of trust. The alternative way of putting the matter is that the trustee in breach of trust is in some way subrogated to the rights of the beneficiary. He stands in his position in order that he may be indemnified. That seems to me the way in which it was put by the Lords Justices in *Raby v Ridehalgh* (1855) 7 De GM & G 104. It does not seem to me that there is any support in authority or in principle for saying that the right depends upon the actual possession of the trust fund, and it appears to me that the analogy which has been sought to be drawn with the executor's right to retain is a false one and does not apply to this case. So much for the equitable right to impound as opposed to the statutory right.

As regards the statutory right, that depends on the language of section 62 of the Trustee Act, 1925, and at first sight it might look as if that right only exists in favour of a person who is actually a trustee. But, on consideration, that seems to me to be a misconstruction of the section. In the first place, the same objection against limiting the right in that way applies to the statutory jurisdiction. It seems to me an absurdity that it is required as a condition of exercising the right to obtain an impounding order, that

---

[108] For the first stage of this litigation, see Chapter 16.3(a), pp. 770–1.

the trustee who, *ex hypothesi*, is in breach of trust, must remain the trustee in order to acquire a right of indemnity. Further, it seems to me on the authorities, and, indeed, on the very terms of the section, that the section is giving an additional right, among other things, to deal with the case of a married woman beneficiary; that the statutory right is extending the equitable right and not limiting it, and that it is not right to read the section so as to apply only to a person who was formerly a trustee. The section begins with the words: 'where a trustee commits a breach of trust', thereby indicating that at the time the breach of trust is committed the person in question must be a trustee. Then further down in the section there is a reference to a trustee and that appears to me to be merely a reference back to the same person as the person who committed the breach of trust and not as an indication that the person in question must be a trustee at the date of the order. I would add to that, that here the writ which has been issued in the Chancery Division was issued at a time when the defendants were trustees, and, therefore, at the date of the writ the requirement of being a trustee was fulfilled. So that, although I entirely appreciate that the defendants may be anxious not to lose their right to impound the income of the tenant for life, that right could not, in my view, be prejudiced by appointing new trustees at this stage.

Importantly, the court has a broad discretion when deciding whether or not to impound a beneficial interest. However, absent an instigation or request from the beneficiary, the trustee will need to have the beneficiary's consent in signed writing in order not only to have a defence to that beneficiary's claim, but also to go further and impound his or her interest.

A good example of the court's exercising its discretion can be found in *Re Somerset*.[109] The trustees of a marriage settlement lent an excessive sum upon mortgage. They lent the money at the instigation, request, and consent in writing of the tenant for life, Mr Somerset. When the security proved to be inadequate, Mr Somerset and his infant children sued the trustees for breach of trust. Liability to the children was admitted, but the defendant trustees claimed that they were entitled to impound Somerset's life interest for the purposes of meeting the claim. However, the Court of Appeal refused to impound the beneficiary's interest. Although Mr Somerset approved the investment, he had not intended to be a party to a breach of trust, and in effect left the trustees to determine whether the investment was a proper one for the sum advanced. Lindley MR said:[110]

Did the trustees commit the breach of trust for which they have been made liable at the instigation or request, or with the consent in writing of the Appellant? The section is intended to protect trustees, and ought to be construed so as to carry out that intention. But the section ought not, in my opinion, to be construed as if the word 'investment' had been inserted instead of 'breach of trust'. An enactment to that effect would produce great injustice in many cases. In order to bring a case within this section the *cestui que trust* must instigate, or request, or consent in writing to some act or omission which is itself a breach of trust, and not to some act or omission which only becomes a breach of trust by reason of want of care on the part of the trustees. If a *cestui que trust* instigates, requests, or consents in writing to an investment not in terms authorized by the power of investment, he clearly falls within the section; and in such a case his ignorance or forgetfulness of the terms of the power would not, I think, protect him—at all events, not unless he could give some good reason why it should, e.g., that it was caused by the trustee. But if all that a *cestui que trust* does is to instigate, request, or consent in writing to an investment which is authorized by the terms of the power, the case is, I think, very different. He has a right to expect that the trustees will act with proper care in making the investment, and if they do not they cannot throw the consequences on him unless they can shew that he instigated, requested, or consented in writing to their non-performance of their duty in this respect.

[109] [1894] 1 Ch 231.
[110] Ibid, 265.

Since the beneficiary had only consented to an authorized loan, but not to its exceeding the authorized limit, the court decided it would be inappropriate to impound the beneficiary's interest. Beneficiaries are entitled to assume that trustees carry out requests in accordance with the terms of the trust.

(c) RULE IN *RE DACRE*

Related to section 62 is the so-called 'rule in *Re Dacre*'. This rule is engaged where a trustee is also beneficially entitled to trust property and misappropriates part of the trust property. In such circumstances, the trustee is considered to have acted properly and already to have received his or her share of the trust property as beneficiary, so that the trustee, or anybody claiming through the trustee, is not entitled to receive any more property when the trust assets are distributed.

Re Dacre [1916] 1 Ch 344, 346–7 (Lord Cozens-Hardy MR)

It has been settled by a long series of authorities, which are binding upon us, that a defaulting trustee cannot claim a share in the estate unless and until he has made good his default, and the true principle, I think, is that which is laid down by Sir George Jessel in *Jacubs v. Rylance*,[111] and which is again affirmed by Stirling J. in the case of *Doering v. Doering*,[112] and lastly emphatically affirmed by Parker J. in *In re Towndrow*,[113] where during the course of the argument he said this: 'The real principle is that where there is an aggregate fund in which the trustee is beneficially interested and to which he owes something, he must be taken to have paid himself that amount on account of his share.' That principle he lays down again in the same judgment, where, quoting the words of Stirling J., he says: 'The theory on which that rule is based is that the Court treats the trustee as having received his share by anticipation, and the answer to any claim made by the trustee is this: 'You have already received your share; you have it in your own hands.' That doctrine has been applied not merely as against the defaulting trustee, but against his assignees for value. It has been applied against the defaulting trustee and his assignees although the default was after the date of the assignment. I cannot see any ground for holding that the persons claiming in right of the insolvent estate of Henry Dacre can be in any better position than the assignee for value of this particular property.

---

5. LIABILITY BETWEEN TRUSTEES

(a) NATURE OF LIABILITY

A trustee's liability to compensate a beneficiary for loss suffered from a breach of trust is personal. It is important to appreciate that it is not vicarious: a trustee is not vicariously liable for the acts of his or her co-trustees.[114] But trustees are required to act jointly: one trustee cannot escape liability by leaving his or her co-trustees to do all the work.[115] All trustees need to participate in the decision-making process. Given the personal nature of liability, it is common for professional trustees to seek to insert an exclusion clause into the trust instrument,[116] and to protect

[111] LR 17 Eq. 341.
[112] 42 Ch D 203.
[113] [1911] 1 Ch 662, 666, 668.
[114] E.g. *Townley v Sherborne* (1633) J Bridg 35, [37]–[38].
[115] *Bahin v Hughes* (1886) 31 Ch D 390.
[116] See Chapter 16.2, p. 744.

themselves by taking out indemnity insurance to cover their liability for breach of trust, either to the beneficiaries or third parties; it is possible for insurance premiums to be paid from the trust fund.[117]

(b) JOINT AND SEVERAL LIABILITY

The personal liability of trustees is joint and several. This means that a claimant can sue the trustees either together (jointly) or separately (severally). If only one trustee is sued, that trustee will be liable to compensate in full for the loss suffered due to the breach of trust. The claimant's choice whether to sue the trustees together or separately will be influenced by how easy it is to issue proceeding against the trustees, and particularly by their ability to pay and satisfy the claim.

A trustee who has been sued by a claimant may legitimately seek to pass on any liability to his or her co-trustees. There are two mechanisms for ensuring this distribution of liability: contribution and indemnity.

(i) *Contribution*

Where a trustee is liable for a breach of trust, it is possible for that trustee to apply to the court to require other trustees who were liable for the same breach to make a contribution towards the remedy. Before 1979, the equitable rules of contribution provided that the liability was to be shared equally between co-trustees, even where one of them was more to blame than another.[118] These rules were superseded by the Civil Liability (Contribution) Act 1978.

CIVIL LIABILITY (CONTRIBUTION) ACT 1978

1. Entitlement to contribution

(1) Subject to the following provisions of this section, any person liable in respect of any damage suffered by another person may recover contribution from any other person liable in respect of the same damage (whether jointly with him or otherwise).

2. Assessment of contribution

(1) Subject to subsection (3) below,[119] in any proceedings for contribution under section 1 above the amount of the contribution recoverable from any person shall be such as may be found by the court to be just and equitable having regard to the extent of that person's responsibility for the damage in question.

(2) Subject to subsection (3) below, the court shall have power in any such proceedings to exempt any person from liability to make contribution, or to direct that the contribution to be recovered from any person shall amount to a complete indemnity.

...

---

[117] Specific provision is made for such insurance cover being obtained by charity trustees: Charities Act 2011, s. 189.
[118] See e.g. *Bahin v Hughes* (1886) 31 Ch D 390.
[119] Subsection (3) limits liability to make a contribution where there has been prior agreement for an upper limit or statutory reduction of damages.

6. Interpretation

(1) A person is liable in respect of any damage for the purposes of this Act if the person who suffered it (or anyone representing his estate or dependants) is entitled to recover compensation from him in respect of that damage (whatever the legal basis of his liability, whether tort, breach of contract, breach of trust or otherwise).

The statutory contribution regime clearly departs from previous authority, since the court now has a broad discretion when determining how to apportion liability between the parties. The court simply has to achieve a 'just and equitable' result. Assessing the appropriate contribution each party should make is therefore a difficult exercise; the court has to form a view about how much responsibility for the losses each party should bear, and attribute liability accordingly.

Determining whether the parties are liable for the 'same damage' has raised some interesting issues. Where both parties are co-trustees and sued by a beneficiary for losses caused by a single breach of trust, establishing the 'same damage' is straightforward. But the Act can apply in more complicated scenarios, and is clearly not limited to claims involving two trustees. For example, in *Friends' Provident Life Office v Hillier Parker May and Rowden*,[120] Hillier Parker had recommended that Friends' Provident make payments of interest to developers. But due to Hillier Parker's advice, Friends' Provident actually overpaid. Friends' Provident sued Hillier Parker for negligence and breach of contract. Hillier Parker then claimed a contribution from the developers: Hiller Parker argued that the developers had received the money as a result of a mistake, and should therefore be holding the money on trust.[121] In spending the money, rather than making restitution of the money to Friends' Provident, Hillier Parker claimed that the developers had committed a breach of trust, and contributed to the 'same damage' suffered by Friends' Provident as that caused by Hillier Parker's breach of duty. The Court of Appeal held that this claim was arguable, and that contribution might be payable. Auld LJ said:[122]

> Here, Hillier Parker's case is that the developers were in breach of trust in dissipating the money, in failing to pay it back when asked to do so, and in denying Friends' Provident's entitlement to repayment. In my view, and in the light of my construction of sections 1(1) and 6(1) of the Act of 1978 under the heading of quasi-contract, whatever the precise form of remedy Friends' Provident might have in respect of that money, whether restitutionary or in damages, it is for compensation for damage it has suffered by its loss in the sense referred to by Viscount Haldane LC in *Nocton v Lord Ashburton* [1914] AC 932 and in the words of the Act.
>
> Accordingly, assuming that the developers are trustees for Friends' Provident of all or some of the notional interest the subject of this action and are in breach of that trust by paying the money away for their own use, or in not repaying it on demand by Friends' Provident or in asserting that they, not Friends' Provident, were entitled to it, then, subject to any successful defence of estoppel, I would hold that section 1(1) of the Act of 1978 applies to a claim for restitutionary compensation based on such liability.

This might appear strange at first sight; 'restitution' involves gain-based remedies, whereas 'compensation' concerns losses, so Auld LJ's reference to 'restitutionary compensation' seems odd. However, in the context of a claim in contribution, it seems defensible on policy grounds: both restitutionary and compensatory claims might be squeezed into the Act's language of 'same damage' in order to ensure

---

[120] [1997] QB 85.

[121] For consideration of when a trust might arise in response to a mistaken payment, see *Westdeutsche Landesbank Girozentrale v Islington London Borough Council* [1996] AC 669, discussed in Chapter 7.2(a), pp. 332–6.

[122] [1997] QB 85, 108.

that neither the person who wrongly makes the gain, nor the person who inflicts the loss, is necessarily liable to the claimant in full.[123] However, a liability to make contribution should operate only to the extent that the value of the claimant's loss corresponds to the value of the defendant's gain,[124] for only then can the parties be considered to be liable for the same damage.

(ii) *Indemnity*

Although the Civil Liability (Contribution) Act 1978 excluded the courts' inherent equitable jurisdiction to order a contribution, it does not exclude any right to an indemnity. One trustee will be required to indemnify another where the former bears the full liability for the breach of trust. The liability of one trustee fully to indemnify another is recognized only in very exceptional circumstances.

(a) *Benefit of breach*

Where two trustees have breached the trust, but one of them obtained the benefit of the breach, that trustee will be liable to indemnify the other. This may typically arise where the trustee is also a beneficiary of the trust. For example, in *Chillingworth v Chambers*,[125] the claimant, Chillingworth, and defendant, Chambers, were trustees of a testamentary trust. Chillingworth was married to one of the beneficiaries, and, on her death, became himself a beneficiary. The trustees made an unauthorized investment in mortgages of leasehold property, and the losses suffered by the trust were made good out of Chillingworth's interest as a beneficiary. Chillingworth then sought contribution from his co-trustee, Chambers, but the court refused to grant him any relief. Kay LJ said:[126]

> On the whole, I think that the weight of authority is in favour of holding that a trustee who, being also *cestui que trust*, has received, as between himself and his co-trustee, an exclusive benefit by the breach of trust, must indemnify his co-trustee to the extent of his interest in the trust fund, and not merely to the extent of the benefit which he has received. I think that the plaintiff must be treated as having received such an exclusive benefit.

AL Smith LJ agreed, observing that:[127]

> I do not doubt, had the plaintiff in the present case not been a co-trustee with the defendant, but only a *cestui que trust* of the estate of which the defendant was trustee, that, inasmuch as the plaintiff had authorized and consented to the breach of trust which is now complained of, he could not have claimed contribution from the defendant to make good the loss he had sustained; and, what is more, that the defendant would have been entitled to impound the plaintiff's interest in his one-fifth share to exonerate him from any loss he might have been called upon to make good by reason of the breach of trust.

This approach helps to ensure that a trustee-beneficiary cannot benefit from his or her breach of duty, and that the trustee's beneficial interest is first exhausted in satisfying a claim.

---

[123] A similar approach was adopted in *City Index Ltd v Gawler* [2007] EWCA Civ 1382; [2008] Ch 313, in which the Court of Appeal held that receipt-based restitutionary liability could involve the 'same damage' as liability for breach of trust. This is discussed in further detail in Chapter 19.3(e), pp. 969–70.

[124] Goymour, 'A Contribution to Knowing Receipt Liability? (*City Index v Gawler*)' [2008] RLR 113, 118. See further Chapter 19, 'Third Party Liability'.

[125] [1896] 1 Ch 685.

[126] Ibid, 707.

[127] Ibid, 709.

The principle that a trustee may be indemnified by another when only the latter has benefited from the breach is not limited to situations where the trustee is also a beneficiary. In *Bahin v Hughes*, Cotton LJ said:[128]

> Now I think it wrong to lay down any limitation of the circumstances under which one trustee would be held liable to the other for indemnity, both having been held liable to the *cestui que trust*; but so far as cases have gone at present, relief has only been granted against a trustee who has himself got the benefit of the breach of trust, or between whom and his co-trustees there has existed a relation, which will justify the Court in treating him as solely liable for the breach of trust.

(b) Sole responsibility of one trustee

Where only one trustee was responsible for the breach of trust, that trustee will be liable to indemnify the other trustees. This can be seen from the *dicta* of Cotton LJ quoted immediately above: if there is a certain relationship between the trustees, then that relationship might justify one trustee's indemnifying the other if the influence of the former was such that the latter was effectively unable to exercise an independent judgment. So, where one of the trustees is a solicitor, and a non-lawyer relies upon the solicitor co-trustee for guidance, the solicitor will generally have to indemnify his lay co-trustee for any breach of trust.

A good illustration of this is *Re Partington*.[129] The trustees of a fund were Mr Allen, a solicitor, and Mrs Partington, the widow of the testator. Mr Allen undertook the whole administration of the trust. A breach of trust was committed, and the widow was entitled to a full indemnity from the solicitor. Stirling J held that Mr Allen had not communicated sufficiently to Mrs Partington concerning the affairs of the trust. As a result, Mrs Partington was unable to exercise a judgment upon the unauthorized investment. Stanley J said:

> The trustee, Mrs. Partington, appears to me to have been misled by her co-trustee by reason of his not giving her full information as to the nature of the investments which he was asking her to advance the money upon, and I think he has been guilty of negligence also in his duty as a solicitor.

This result seems appropriate: given Mr Allen's actions, the widow's reliance on his skill and expertise was reasonable. However, it should not be thought that an indemnity will inevitably be awarded against solicitor-trustees. It still needs to be established that the solicitor-trustee actually had a controlling influence over the other trustees. In *Head v Gould*,[130] for example, an attempt to obtain an indemnity against a solicitor-trustee failed. Kekewich J said:[131]

> True it is that the defendant Gould is a solicitor, and that he was appointed trustee for that very reason. True no doubt, also, that the legal business was managed by him, and I do not propose to absolve him from any responsibility attaching to him on that ground; but I do not myself think that Byrne J,[132] or any other judge ever intended to hold that a man is bound to indemnify his co-trustee against loss merely because he was a solicitor, when that co-trustee was an active participator in the breach of trust complained of, and is not proved to have participated merely in consequence of the advice and control of the solicitor

---

[128] (1886) 31 Ch D 390, 395–6.
[129] (1887) 57 LT 654.
[130] [1898] 2 Ch 250.
[131] Ibid, 265.
[132] In *Re Turner* [1897] 1 Ch 536. See also *Lockhart v Reilly* (1856) 25 LJ Ch 697.

Moreover, not all solicitors should inevitably be treated the same way. A solicitor practising exclusively in criminal law would not be expected to bring the same sort of expertise to the office of trustee as would a practitioner specializing in chancery work.

6. LIABILITY OF TRUSTEES TO CREDITORS

Where a trustee is liable to a third party creditor, either for breach of a contract entered into on behalf of the trust or in tort arising from the operation of the trust, the trustee will be personally liable to the third party creditor.[133] However, the trustee may be indemnified from the trust fund:

TRUSTEE ACT 2000

Section 31

(1) A trustee—

    (a) is entitled to be reimbursed from the trust funds, or

    (b) may pay out of the trust funds,

expenses properly incurred by him when acting on behalf of the trust.

But in some situations the trustee will not be able to be indemnified from the trust fund. For example, the trust fund may be insufficient, or the trustee may have acted in breach of duty. If the trustee does not have sufficient funds to discharge his or her liability, the creditors may be left unsatisfied: even though the creditors may be subrogated to a trustee's right to an indemnity from the trust fund, if the trustee would not be indemnified due to his or her breach of duty, then the subrogated creditors will find themselves facing the same problem.[134] Nor can the creditors seek payment from the trust assets: the trust is not a legal entity in its own right so cannot be sued. As the Trust Law Committee has observed:[135]

> Because a trust is not a legal entity like a company, it cannot be a principal and so cannot have an agent. Moreover, since it is not an artificial person like a company, no *ultra vires* rules can apply to it nor can rules analogous to company law rules enabling third parties to assume that internal procedures have been complied with or that particular persons have ostensible or apparent authority.
>
> Instead, the individual or company that is trustee is personally liable to the full extent of his, her or its private wealth unless in the contract with the creditor there is a provision limiting liability e.g. to the extent that there are trust assets out of which the trustee can be indemnified. The contract cannot be *ultra vires* an individual who is trustee because individuals have the full capacity of natural persons to enter into contracts.

The Trust Law Committee went on to conclude that such rules are unfair. After all, the trustee will have been acting for the benefit of the beneficiaries and, as between the beneficiaries and the creditor, is it really appropriate that the creditor bear the risk of the trustee's insolvency? The Trust Law

---

[133] See e.g. *Perring v Draper* [1997] EGCS 109.

[134] *Re Johnson* (1880) 15 Ch D 548. On subrogation generally, see Chapter 18.5(b)(ii)(c), p. 900.

[135] *Rights of Creditors against Trustees and Trust Funds* (London: HMSO, 1999), [2.2]–[2.3].

Committee suggested the creditor should still have a right of indemnity out of the trust fund even where the trustee was in breach of his equitable duties, the major exception being where the trustee had acted dishonestly. However, reform in this area is no longer on the Law Commission's agenda, so any change in approach will have to be developed by the courts. This does not appear to be imminent, especially because sensible arguments can be made in favour of the status quo. For example, if the creditor had entered into a contract to sell goods to a trustee who was not acting in his capacity as trustee, the creditor would take the risk of insolvency in the normal way. This does not seem inappropriate, and any reforms would have to be careful not to undermine this result. Indeed, since the trust fund cannot be used to compensate the third party creditor, the current law can be considered to strengthen the protection afforded to beneficiaries in the event of a breach of trust. This is also consistent with the fundamental principle that trust property is not regarded as belonging to the trustee absolutely, so that he or she cannot use it to defray all liabilities. Nevertheless, favouring the beneficiaries over the trustee's creditors where the trustee was acting for the beneficiaries is very generous to beneficiaries, and particularly hard on innocent creditors who provided value for their rights.

7. LIABILITY PRIOR TO APPOINTMENT

A trustee will not be liable for breach of trust where the breach occurred before the trustee was appointed.[136] On appointment, if a trustee discovers that a breach of trust previously occurred, he or she should commence proceedings against the former trustee; if the new trustee fails to do so, he or she may be liable for this breach of trust in his or her own right.

8. LIABILITY AFTER RETIREMENT

A trustee remains liable for breaches of trust committed whilst a trustee, even though he or she has retired from the trust. But a trustee will not be liable for breaches of trust that occurred after the trustee retired, except if the trustee retired in order to facilitate a breach of trust,[137] or if the trustee in retiring parts with the trust property without due regard to it, so that loss is suffered in the transfer of the property to the new trustees.[138] This can be explained on the basis that the trustee commits a breach of duty whilst still a trustee, and is examined more fully in the context of fiduciary obligations in Chapter 14.[139]

9. LIMITATION

If a claim is not brought within a certain period, the defendant may be able to rely upon the defence of limitation. Imposing limitation periods means that, after a given length of time, potential defendants can continue their affairs without fear of a claim from the past disrupting them. Limitation periods provide finality and certainty. As Best CJ noted in *A'Court v Cross*:[140]

> Long dormant claims have often more of cruelty than of justice in them.

---

[136] *Re Strahan* [1856] 8 De GM & G 291.
[137] *Head v Gould* [1898] 2 Ch 250, 272 (Kekewich J).
[138] Ibid, 269 (Kekewich J).
[139] Chapter 14.2(e), pp. 667–9.
[140] (1825) 3 Bing 329, 332–3.

There is a general public interest in the spectre of litigation not hovering over the parties for an unduly long period of time. Moreover, if a claim is brought long after the events in question, the evidence produced is likely to be unreliable. In *Birkett v James*, Lord Salmon said that:[141]

> When cases (as they often do) depend predominantly on the recollection of witnesses delay can often be most prejudicial to defendants and to plaintiffs also. Witnesses' recollections grow dim with the passage of time and the evidence of honest men differs sharply on the relevant facts. In some cases it is sometimes impossible for justice to be done because of the extreme difficulty in deciding which version of the facts is to be preferred.

Limitation periods are important throughout the law, and Equity is no different. Swadling has stated that:[142]

> to discover whether in any given case a claim in equity is time-barred, a three-stage process must be gone through, in which it is asked:
>
> i)   Is this an action to which there is an express statutory time limit on the bringing of claims?
>
> ii) If not, is this an action to which a court will apply a statutory limit 'by analogy'?
>
> iii) If not, is this an action nevertheless barred by the doctrine of laches?

This methodical approach should ensure that questions of limitation are addressed in a comprehensive manner. All three questions need to be analysed in turn, although there is some debate about how distinct the latter two questions are.[143] In any event, the second question highlights Equity's sensible tendency to follow the Common Law guidelines. As Lord Redesdale commented in *Hovenden v Lord Annesley*:[144]

> Courts of Equity have constantly guided themselves by the principle that, wherever the legislature has limited a period for law proceedings, equity will, in analogous cases, consider the equitable rights as bound by the same limitation.

(a) STATUTORY LIMITATION PERIODS

The Limitation Act 1980 establishes limitation periods for various types of claim.

LIMITATION ACT 1980

2. Time limit for actions founded on tort

An action founded on tort shall not be brought after the expiration of six years from the date on which the cause of action accrued.

---

[141] [1978] AC 297, 327.
[142] 'Limitation' in *Breach of Trust* (eds Birks and Pretto) (Oxford: Hart, 2002), pp. 319–20.
[143] See e.g. Watt, 'Laches, Estoppel and Election' in *Breach of Trust* (eds Birks and Pretto) (Oxford: Hart, 2002).
[144] (1806) 2 Sch & Lef 607, 632. See also *Knox v Gye*, quoted in *Coulthard v Disco Mix Club Ltd*: see Chapter 16.9(b)(ii), pp. 787–8.

5. Time limit for actions founded on simple contract

An action founded on simple contract shall not be brought after the expiration of six years from the date on which the cause of action accrued.

21. Time limit for actions in respect of trust property

(1) No period of limitation prescribed by this Act shall apply to an action by a beneficiary under a trust, being an action—

    (a) in respect of any fraud or fraudulent breach of trust to which the trustee was a party or privy; or

    (b) to recover from the trustee trust property or the proceeds of trust property in the possession of the trustee, or previously received by the trustee and converted to his use.

(2) Where a trustee who is also a beneficiary under the trust receives or retains trust property or its proceeds as his share on a distribution of trust property under the trust, his liability in any action brought by virtue of subsection (1)(b) above to recover that property or its proceeds after the expiration of the period of limitation prescribed by this Act for bringing an action to recover trust property shall be limited to the excess over his proper share.

    This subsection only applies if the trustee acted honestly and reasonably in making the distribution.

(3) Subject to the preceding provisions of this section, an action by a beneficiary to recover trust property or in respect of any breach of trust, not being an action for which a period of limitation is prescribed by any other provision of this Act, shall not be brought after the expiration of six years from the date on which the right of action accrued.

    For the purposes of this subsection, the right of action shall not be treated as having accrued to any beneficiary entitled to a future interest in the trust property until the interest fell into possession.

(4) No beneficiary as against whom there would be a good defence under this Act shall derive any greater or other benefit from a judgment or order obtained by any other beneficiary than he could have obtained if he had brought the action and this Act had been pleaded in defence.

The general limitation period is six years for breach of contract, tort, and also for a claim by a beneficiary[145] to recover trust property or for breach of trust. For the purposes of the Limitation Act 1980, the term 'trustee' extends to trustees of implied and constructive trusts, as well as personal representatives.[146]

However, as section 21 itself makes clear, the general period of six years may not apply in some instances. For example, section 21(3) provides that where a beneficiary is entitled to a future interest in property, the cause of action will not accrue until the interest has fallen into possession. As Millett LJ explained in *Armitage v Nurse*:[147]

> The rationale of section 21(3) … is not that a beneficiary with a future interest has not the means of discovery, but that he should not be compelled to litigate (at considerable personal expense) in respect of an injury to an interest which he may never live to enjoy. Similar reasoning would apply to exclude a person who is merely the object of a discretionary trust or power which may never be exercised in his favour.

---

[145] Or by a trustee on behalf of a beneficiary: *Cattley v Pollard* [2006] EWHC 3130 (Ch); [2007] Ch 353, 377 (Richard Sheldon QC).

[146] Limitation Act 1980, s. 38(1).

[147] [1998] Ch 241, 251.

The normal limitation period of six years will also be displaced where the breach of trust was fraudulent: a fraudulent trustee should not be able to defeat a beneficiary's claim simply through the lapse of time. Similarly, no time limit is prescribed by the Act for claims to recover trust property or the proceeds of such property that is in the possession of a trustee. Nor does section 21 apply to an action brought by the Attorney-General to enforce a charitable trust: the Attorney-General sues on behalf of the public at large, who cannot be considered to be beneficiaries because they do not have a right to property either present or future.[148]

The normal limitation period of six years is also qualified by other provisions in the 1980 Act. For example, claims relating to the personal estate of a deceased person are subject to a twelve-year limitation period.[149]

LIMITATION ACT 1980

22. Time limit for actions claiming personal estate of a deceased person

Subject to section 21 (1) and (2) of this Act—

(a) no action in respect of any claim to the personal estate of a deceased person or to any share or interest in any such estate (whether under a will or on intestacy) shall be brought after the expiration of twelve years from the date on which the right to receive the share or interest accrued; and

(b) no action to recover arrears of interest in respect of any legacy, or damages in respect of such arrears, shall be brought after the expiration of six years from the date on which the interest became due.

However, where the claim is for an account the limitation period will be the same as that for the claim itself.

LIMITATION ACT 1980

23. Time limit in respect of actions for an account

An action for an account shall not be brought after the expiration of any time limit under the Act which is applicable to the claim which is the basis of the duty to account.

So, for example, where the liability of an agent to account is contractual, the contractual limitation period of six years applies. And where the liability to account is not referable to a contract, the court will determine the limitation period by analogy with the statute and will apply a six-year limitation period. But where the liability to account arises from a trust, such as where an agent holds property as trustee, no statutory limitation period will apply, and no analogy with contract is appropriate.

It should also be noted that the general statutory limitation period does not apply to claims for equitable relief.

---

[148] *A-G v Cocke* [1988] Ch 414 (Harman J).
[149] See e.g. *Re Loftus* [2005] 2 All ER 700.

LIMITATION ACT 1980

36. Equitable jurisdiction and remedies

(1) The following time limits under this Act, that is to say—

    (a) the time limit under section 2 for actions founded on tort;

    (b) the time limit under section 5 for actions founded on simple contract;

shall not apply to any claim for specific performance of a contract or for an injunction or for any other equitable relief, except in so far as any such time limit may be applied by the court by analogy in like manner as the corresponding time limit under any enactment repealed by the Limitation Act 1939 was applied before 1st July 1940.

(2) Nothing in this Act shall affect any equitable jurisdiction to refuse relief on the ground of acquiescence or otherwise.

This provision is controversial: it is unclear why equitable relief should not be governed by a statutory limitation period and only be subject to the equitable doctrine of laches. Possible reform of this provision, and of the law of limitation more generally, will be considered later.[150]

(b) AMBIT OF THE STATUTORY PROVISIONS

The scope of the statutory provisions has proved to be particularly controversial regarding claims involving constructive trusts and breach of fiduciary duty.

(i) *Constructive trusts*

Part of the difficulty in determining the limitation period applicable to constructive trusts arises from the fact that the label 'constructive trust' is used to describe a wide variety of situations, and that this label is sometimes inaccurate and unhelpful.[151] In *Paragon Finance v D B Thakerar and Co.*,[152] Millett LJ helpfully distinguished between two types of constructive trust. The first arises where the defendant, although not expressly appointed as a trustee, assumed the duties of one. In this instance, the defendant would be a real trustee, albeit under a constructive trust, and would be treated like an express trustee. The second category of 'constructive trust' arises where the defendant is personally liable for being implicated in wrongdoing, such as where he or she has unconscionably received property in breach of trust or fiduciary duty.[153] But here the language of 'constructive trustee' is simply a formula for relief and there is no trust at issue.[154] For a long time the law in this area was very confused, but has now been made clear by the decision of the Supreme Court in *Central Bank of Nigeria v Williams*.[155]

Central Bank of Nigeria v Williams [2014] UKSC 10; [2014] AC 1189[156]

Dr Williams was a Nigerian national resident in England. He claimed to have been the victim of a fraud instigated by the Nigerian State Security Services in 1986. He was induced to serve

---

[150] See Chapter 16.9(e), pp. 792–3.
[151] See Chapter 7, 'Constructive Trusts'.
[152] [1999] 1 All ER 400.
[153] See Chapter 19.3, p. 951.
[154] See Chapter 19.1(c), p. 927.
[155] [2014] UKSC 10; [2014] AC 1189.
[156] Davies, 'Limitation in Equity' [2014] LMCLQ 313.

as a guarantor of a bogus transaction for importation of foodstuffs into Nigeria. As part of that transaction, Dr Williams paid over $6.5 million to his English solicitor, Mr Gale, to hold on trust for him. Dr Williams contended that Mr Gale then fraudulently paid out over $6 million to the Central Bank of Nigeria ('the Bank'), and pocketed the rest of the money. In 2010, Dr Williams commenced proceedings against the Bank for both dishonest assistance in a breach of trust[157] and knowing receipt of trust property.[158] The Bank argued that these claims were time barred. A bare majority of the Supreme Court overturned the decision of the Court of Appeal and held that the limitation period for the claims against the Bank had expired.

Lord Sumption:

The problem is that in this all-embracing sense the phrase 'constructive trust' refers to two different things to which very different legal considerations apply. The first comprises persons who have lawfully assumed fiduciary obligations in relation to trust property, but without a formal appointment. They may be trustees de son tort, who without having been properly appointed, assume to act in the administration of the trusts as if they had been; or trustees under trusts implied from the common intention to be inferred from the conduct of the parties, but never formally created as such. These people can conveniently be called de facto trustees. They intended to act as trustees, if only as a matter of objective construction of their acts. They are true trustees, and if the assets are not applied in accordance with the trust, equity will enforce the obligations that they have assumed by virtue of their status exactly as if they had been appointed by deed. Others, such as company directors, are by virtue of their status fiduciaries with very similar obligations. In its second meaning, the phrase 'constructive trustee' refers to something else. It comprises persons who never assumed and never intended to assume the status of a trustee, whether formally or informally, but have exposed themselves to equitable remedies by virtue of their participation in the unlawful misapplication of trust assets. Either they have dishonestly assisted in a misapplication of the funds by the trustee, or they have received trust assets knowing that the transfer to them was a breach of trust. In either case, they may be required by equity to account as if they were trustees or fiduciaries, although they are not. These can conveniently be called cases of ancillary liability. The intervention of equity in such cases does not reflect any pre-existing obligation but comes about solely because of the misapplication of the assets. It is purely remedial. The distinction between these two categories is not just a matter of the chronology of events leading to liability. It is fundamental. In the words of Millett LJ in *Paragon Finance plc v DB Thakerar & Co* [1999] 1 All ER 400, 413, it is 'the distinction between an institutional trust and a remedial formula—between a trust and a catch-phrase'.

Selangor United Rubber Estates Ltd v Cradock (No 3) [1968] 1 WLR 1555, is a decision of Ungoed-Thomas J about the elements of ancillary liability. It has been much criticised for drawing the net of liability too wide, and for making excessively fine distinctions between different mental states. But it contains a clear and entirely orthodox statement of the different categories of constructive trustee. The judge observed, at p 1579:

'It is essential at the outset to distinguish two very different kinds of so-called constructive trustees: (1) Those who, though not appointed trustees, take on themselves to act as such and to possess and administer trust property for the beneficiaries, such as trustees de son tort. Distinguishing features for present purposes are (a) they do not claim to act in their own right but for the beneficiaries, and (b) their assumption to act is not of itself a ground of liability (save in the sense of course of liability to account and for any failure in the duty so assumed), and so their status as trustees precedes the occurrence which may be the subject of claim against them. (2) Those whom a court of equity will treat as trustees by reason of their action, of which complaint is made. Distinguishing features are (a) that such trustees claim to act

---

in their own right and not for beneficiaries, and (b) no trusteeship arises before, but only by reason of, the action complained of.'

Later in his judgment, at p 1582, the judge expanded on the characteristics of his category (2):

It seems to me imperative to grasp and keep constantly in mind that the second category of constructive trusteeship (which is the only category with which we are concerned) is nothing more than a formula for equitable relief. The court of equity says that the defendant shall be liable in equity, as though he were a trustee. He is made liable in equity as trustee by the imposition or construction of the court of equity. This is done because in accordance with equitable principles applied by the court of equity it is equitable that he should be held liable as though he were a trustee.'

The same point was made in very similar language by Millett LJ in the *Paragon case* [1999] 1 All ER 400, 408–409:

'Regrettably, however, the expressions "constructive trust" and "constructive trustee" have been used by equity lawyers to describe two entirely different situations. The first covers those cases already mentioned, where the defendant, though not expressly appointed as trustee, has assumed the duties of a trustee by a lawful transaction which was independent of and preceded the breach of trust and is not impeached by the plaintiff. The second covers those cases where the trust obligation arises as a direct consequence of the unlawful transaction which is impeached by the plaintiff.

A constructive trust arises by operation of law whenever the circumstances are such that it would be unconscionable for the owner of property (usually but not necessarily the legal estate) to assert his own beneficial interest in the property and deny the beneficial interest of another. In the first class of case, however, the constructive trustee really is a trustee. He does not receive the trust property in his own right but by a transaction by which both parties intend to create a trust from the outset and which is not impugned by the plaintiff. His possession of the property is coloured from the first by the trust and confidence by means of which he obtained it, and his subsequent appropriation of the property to his own use is a breach of that trust … In these cases the plaintiff does not impugn the transaction by which the defendant obtained control of the property. He alleges that the circumstances in which the defendant obtained control make it unconscionable for him thereafter to assert a beneficial interest in the property.

The second class of case is different. It arises when the defendant is implicated in a fraud. Equity has always given relief against fraud by making any person sufficiently implicated in the fraud accountable in equity. In such a case he is traditionally though I think unfortunately described as a constructive trustee and said to be "liable to account as constructive trustee". Such a person is not in fact a trustee at all, even though he may be liable to account as if he were. He never assumes the position of a trustee, and if he receives the trust property at all it is adversely to the plaintiff by an unlawful transaction which is impugned by the plaintiff. In such a case the expressions "constructive trust" and "constructive trustee" are misleading, for there is no trust and usually no possibility of a proprietary remedy; they are "nothing more than a formula for equitable relief".'

Consistent with this approach, the majority of the Supreme Court held that section 21(1)(a) of the Limitation Act 1980 only applied to fraudulent breaches of already existing trusts, including the first category of constructive trusts. This is a real trust, because the trustee holds property on trust for a beneficiary. However, the second category of 'constructive trust' does not really involve a true trust: the defendant does not hold any property for the benefit of another. Thus a defendant liable as a 'constructive trustee' for unconscionable receipt may no longer still have the property received in breach of trust, and a person liable as a 'constructive trustee' for dishonest assistance in a breach of trust may never receive any trust property at all.[159] As a result, section 21(1)(a) would not prevent such defendants from relying upon a statutory limitation period.

The decision in *Williams* is useful in emphasizing that the wrongs of dishonest assistance and knowing receipt are different from the wrongs of breach of trust and breach of fiduciary duty, and that as a result it is not surprising that different limitation periods might apply.[160] The bare majority of the Supreme Court also dismissed the argument, favoured by the dissenting judges, that even though the Bank was not a trustee for the purposes of section 21(1)(a), it was nonetheless sued 'in respect of any fraud or fraudulent breach of trust to which the trustee was a party or privy'. On the face of the legislative provision, this may be considered to be somewhat controversial, but is nevertheless welcome for policy reasons in providing clarity to the law. Any other approach would create an unfortunate divide between cases concerning fraudulent and innocent breaches of trust: a defendant who dishonestly assists an innocent breach of trust would fall outside the scope of section 21(1)(a), yet a defendant who dishonestly assists a fraudulent breach of trust would fall within section 21(1)(a). But why should the quality of the primary breach of trust alter the limitation period against the accessory? The Supreme Court has authoritatively decided that section 21(1)(a) does not apply to dishonest assistance or knowing receipt; instead, the normal limitation period of six years applies.[161]

(ii) Breach of fiduciary duty

Where the defendant is liable for breach of fiduciary duty, the appropriate limitation period depends upon the nature of the claim. If it is a claim to recover property that the fiduciary holds as trustee, the usual considerations concerning trustees will apply, and there will be no statutory limitation period. By contrast, if the fiduciary has breached a non-fiduciary duty, then he or she might be sued in contract or tort, so the normal six-year limitation period would apply.

If the fiduciary is liable for a deliberate and dishonest breach of fiduciary duty, then no statutory limitation period will apply. But the appropriate limitation period will still be six years, by analogy with the Common Law tort of deceit. This point was also made in the following case.

Coulthard v Disco Mix Club Ltd [2000] 1 WLR (Jules Sher QC)

[The issue is] whether the time limits under the 1980 Act would be applied by analogy by virtue of section 36 of the 1980 Act to the claims in breach of fiduciary duty pleaded in this case. That section provides that the statutory time limits (for example, the six years for breach of contract) shall not apply to equitable relief except in so far as they may be applied by the court by analogy 'in like manner as the corresponding time limit under any enactment repealed by the Limitation Act 1939 was applied before 1st July 1940'.

The best description of the circumstances in which the court of equity acted by analogy to the statute is, I think, contained in the speech of Lord Westbury in *Knox v Gye* (1872) LR 5 HL 656 at 674–675:

'The general principle was laid down as early as the case of *Lockey v Lockey* (1719) Prec Ch 518, where it was held that where a Court of Equity assumes a concurrent jurisdiction with Courts

---

[159] See further Chapter 19.2, p. 928.

[160] See further Chapter 19.1, p. 923.

[161] It was accepted by counsel and all the Justices that section 21(3) of the Limitation Act applies to dishonest assisters and knowing recipients. But compare Swadling, 'Limitation' in *Breach of Trust* (eds Birks and Pretto) (Oxford: Hart, 2002) 341–342, who argues that, since section 21(3) was only ever designed to cover express trustees, no limitation period, and only laches, applies to dishonest assisters and knowing recipients.

of Law no account will be given after the legal limit of six years, if the statute be pleaded. If it could be doubted whether the executor of a deceased partner can, at Common Law, have an action of account against the surviving partner, the result will still be the same because a Court of Equity, in affording such a remedy and giving such an account, would act by analogy to the Statute of Limitations. For where the remedy in Equity is correspondent to the remedy at Law, and the latter is subject to a limit in point of time by the Statute of Limitations, a Court of Equity acts by analogy to the statute, and imposes on the remedy it affords the same limitation. This is the meaning of the common phrase, that a Court of Equity acts by analogy to the Statute of Limitations, the meaning being, that where the suit in Equity corresponds with an action at Law which is included in the words of the statute, a Court of Equity adopts the enactment of the statute as its own rule of procedure. But if any proceeding in Equity be included within the words of the statute, there a Court of Equity, like a Court of Law, acts in obedience to the statute … Where a Court of Equity frames its remedy upon the basis of the Common Law, and supplements the Common Law by extending the remedy to parties who cannot have an action at Common Law, there the Court of Equity acts in analogy to the statute; that is, it adopts the statute as the rule of procedure regulating the remedy it affords.'

Two things emerge from these passages. First, where the court of equity was simply exercising a concurrent jurisdiction giving the same relief as was available in a court of law the statute of limitation would be applied. But, secondly, even if the relief afforded by the court of equity was wider than that available at law the court of equity would apply the statute by analogy where there was 'correspondence' between the remedies available at law or in equity.

Now, in my judgment, the true breaches of fiduciary duty, i.e. the allegations of deliberate and dishonest under-accounting, are based on the same factual allegations as the common law claims of fraud. The breaches of fiduciary duty are thus no more than the equitable counterparts of the claims at Common Law. The court of equity, in granting relief for such breaches would be exercising a concurrent jurisdiction with that of the common law. I have little doubt but that to such a claim the statute would have been applied.

… one could scarcely imagine a more correspondent set of remedies as damages for fraudulent breach of contract and equitable compensation for breach of fiduciary duty in relation to the same factual situation, namely, the deliberate withholding of money due by a manager to his artist. It would have been a blot on our jurisprudence if those selfsame facts gave rise to a time bar in the common law courts but none in the court of equity.

I should note in closing on this aspect that, of course, if there was any allegation of fraud or deliberate concealment which had not been discovered by Mr. Coulthard before the inception of the period of six years before action, the matter would be wholly different. There is no such allegation here. On his own evidence Mr. Coulthard had discovered, more than six years before action, the facts giving rise to the alleged dishonesty.

Similarly, where the relief sought is equitable compensation for a fiduciary's failure to act in the best interests of the principal, it has been held that the six-year statutory limitation period that applies to tort claims will apply by analogy. This was the result in *Cia de Seguros Imperio v Health (REBX) Ltd.*

Cia de Seguros Imperio v Heath (REBX) Ltd [2001] 1 WLR 112, 124 (Clarke LJ)

the outcome of the appeal turns on the correct application of section 36(1) of the Limitation Act 1980 to the facts of this case. The time limits in sections 2 and 5 of the Act do not apply directly. The claim with which the appeal is concerned is based on alleged breaches of fiduciary duty on the part of the defendant to act in what it honestly believed to be the best interests of the plaintiff. It was originally described in the prayer to the points of claim as a claim for damages. Detailed analysis of the position has revealed that the basis of the claim is equitable and that the claim is one for compensation. It was, however, no doubt described as a claim for damages because that is what, in truth, it is. As Waller LJ has put it, the reality of the claim is that it is a claim for damages which would be assessed in the same way as a claim for damages at common law. As I see it, it is a claim for equitable compensation, but not the kind of equitable compensation which may be awarded in lieu of rescission or specific restitution.

As a claim for equitable relief, it falls within the expression 'other equitable relief' in section 36(1) of the 1980 Act, which thus provides, so far as relevant, that the time limits in sections 2 and 5 shall not apply—'except in so far as any such time limit may be applied by the court by analogy in like manner as the corresponding time limit under any enactment repealed by the Limitation Act 1939 was applied before 1 July 1940'.

It is not in dispute that the Limitation Act 1939 repealed statutes which contained similar provisions to sections 2 and 5 of the Act of 1980. It follows, as I see it, that those time limits may be applied by analogy 'in like manner' as those time limits were applied.

I agree with Waller LJ that that cannot mean that it is necessary to find an identical case decided before 1940 in which a court of equity in fact applied a previous statute by analogy. The section cannot, to my mind, have been intended to be read so narrowly. It must mean that the court is to have power to apply sections 2 and 5 by analogy in the kind of case in which equity would have done the same. In such a case the court will be applying the provision by analogy 'in like manner as the corresponding time limit … was applied before 1 July, 1940'. The correct approach is to identify if possible the principle which the courts of equity adopted and to apply a similar principle now.

I would certainly have expected a court of equity to apply the common law time limits by analogy on the facts of this case. As Waller LJ has pointed out, and as the judge demonstrated by a detailed analysis of the points of claim, the essential nature of the pleaded case is the same whether it is put as damages for breach of contract, damages for breach of duty or damages (or compensation) for breach of fiduciary duty. The only additional element is the defendant's alleged intention, which on the facts here adds nothing of substance to the claim for damages. Indeed it would be quite unnecessary to include this claim if it were not thought necessary to do so in order to advance the time-bar argument …

… there is a sufficient close similarity between the exclusive equitable right in question, namely the claim for compensation for breach of fiduciary duty, and the legal rights to which the statute applies—namely the claim for damages for breach of contract founded on simple contract and the claim in tort for damages for breach of duty—that a court of equity would (and will) ordinarily act on the statute of limitation by analogy. There is nothing in the particular circumstances of the case to make it unjust to do so. On the contrary, it is just to do so because there is no reason why, if the claims for damages for breach of contract and tort are time-barred, the claim for damages for breach of fiduciary duty should not be time-barred also.

A limitation period of six years is appropriate, but the reasoning of Clarke LJ might not be entirely convincing. A fiduciary's duty to act in the principal's best interests is not obviously a fiduciary duty;[162] as a result, the contractual and tortious limitation periods might have applied directly rather than merely by analogy. By contrast, where there is liability for breaching the fundamental, proscriptive, fiduciary obligation of loyalty, as illustrated in particular by the no-conflict and no-profit rules, different considerations apply. Such claims are not analogous to any claim at Common Law, so no

---

[162] It may be considered to impose a positive duty to act: see further Chapter 14.2(a), pp. 664–5.

statutory limitation period will apply, even by analogy.[163] Claims might be barred due to lapse of time only if laches is established.[164]

(c) EXTENSION OF LIMITATION PERIOD

The limitation period may be extended if the person who has a right of action is under a disability: that person generally has six years to bring a claim, but the time only begins to run once the person ceases to be under a disability or dies.

LIMITATION ACT 1980

28. Extension of limitation period in case of disability

(1) Subject to the following provisions of this section, if on the date when any right of action accrued for which a period of limitation is prescribed by this Act, the person to whom it accrued was under a disability, the action may be brought at any time before the expiration of six years from the date when he ceased to be under a disability or died (whichever first occurred) notwithstanding that the period of limitation has expired.

(2) This section shall not affect any case where the right of action first accrued to some person (not under a disability) through whom the person under a disability claims.

(3) When a right of action which has accrued to a person under a disability accrues, on the death of that person while still under a disability, to another person under a disability, no further extension of time shall be allowed by reason of the disability of the second person.

(4) No action to recover land or money charged on land shall be brought by virtue of this section by any person after the expiration of thirty years from the date on which the right of action accrued to that person or some person through whom he claims.

(d) POSTPONEMENT OF LIMITATION PERIOD

The limitation period may be postponed in the event of fraud, concealment, or mistake.

LIMITATION ACT 1980

32. Postponement of limitation period in case of fraud, concealment or mistake

(1) Subject to subsection (3) below, where in the case of any action for which a period of limitation is prescribed by this Act, either—

   (a) the action is based upon the fraud of the defendant;[165] or

---

[163] *Tito v Waddell (No. 2)* [1977] Ch 106, 248–50 (Megarry V-C); *A-G v Cocke* [1988] Ch 414, 421 (Harman J).
[164] See Chapter 16.10(a), p. 793.
[165] *Cattley v Pollard* [2006] EWHC 3130 (Ch); [2007] Ch 353.

(b) any fact relevant to the plaintiff's right of action has been deliberately concealed from him by the defendant;[166] or

(c) the action is for relief from the consequences of a mistake;

the period of limitation shall not begin to run until the plaintiff has discovered the fraud, concealment or mistake (as the case may be) or could with reasonable diligence have discovered it.[167]

References in this subsection to the defendant include references to the defendant's agent and to any person through whom the defendant claims and his agent.

(2) For the purposes of subsection (1) above, deliberate commission of a breach of duty in circumstances in which it is unlikely to be discovered for some time amounts to deliberate concealment of the facts involved in that breach of duty.

(3) Nothing in this section shall enable any action—

(a) to recover, or recover the value of, any property, or

(b) to enforce any charge against, or set aside any transaction affecting, any property;

to be brought against the purchaser of the property or any person claiming through him in any case where the property has been purchased for valuable consideration by an innocent third party since the fraud or concealment or (as the case may be) the transaction in which the mistake was made took place.

(4) A purchaser is an innocent third party for the purposes of this section—

(a) in the case of fraud or concealment of any fact relevant to the plaintiff's right of action, if he was not a party to the fraud or (as the case may be) to the concealment of that fact and did not at the time of the purchase know or have reason to believe that the fraud or concealment had taken place; and

(b) in the case of mistake, if he did not at the time of the purchase know or have reason to believe that the mistake had been made.

This provision makes it clear that the limitation period might be postponed such that time does not start to run until the claimant has discovered the fraud, concealment, or mistake, or at least could have discovered it with 'reasonable diligence'. The meaning of this latter requirement was considered by Millett LJ in *Paragon Finance v D B Thakerar & Co.*:[168]

The question is not whether the plaintiffs should have discovered the fraud sooner; but whether they could with reasonable diligence have done so. The burden of proof is on them. They must establish that they could not have discovered the fraud without exceptional measures which they could not reasonably have been expected to take. In this context the length of the applicable period of limitation is irrelevant. In the course of argument May LJ observed that reasonable diligence must be measured against some standard, but that the six-year limitation period did not provide the relevant standard. He suggested that the test was how a person carrying on a business of the relevant kind would act if he had adequate but not unlimited staff and resources and were motivated by a reasonable but not excessive sense of urgency. I respectfully agree.

---

[166] In *Bartlett v Barclays Bank Trust Co. Ltd* [1980] Ch 515, the trustee unsuccessfully pleaded the forerunner of paragraph (b) (Limitation Act 1939, s. 26(b)); Brightman J found, at 537, that 'there was no cover-up by the bank. The bank had no inkling that it was acting in breach of trust'.

[167] See *Peco Arts Inc v Hazlitt Gallery Ltd* [1983] 1 WLR 1315.

[168] [1999] 1 All ER 400, [418].

(e) REFORM

The law of limitation has been criticized as being unnecessarily complex, unfair, and outdated. For example, in *Cia de Seguros Imperio v Heath (REBX) Ltd*, Sir Christopher Staughton complained:[169]

> It seems to me unfortunate that the claimant, an insurance company in Portugal, should have to endure a prolonged and expensive contest as to the rules of equity as they were 60 years ago and more. And all that for the purpose of determining whether claims that arose before September 1989 are time-barred.
>
> It is not obvious to me why it is still necessary to have special rules for the limitation of claims for specific performance, or an injunction, or other equitable relief. And if it is still necessary to do so, I do not see any merit in continuing to define the circumstances where a particular claim will be time-barred by reference to what happened, or might have happened, more than 60 years ago. If a distinction still has to be drawn between common law and equitable claims for limitation purposes, I would hope that a revised statute will enact with some precision where that distinction should be drawn, rather than leave it to the product of researches into cases decided long ago.

Such complaints seem well-founded, particularly as regards the distinction between the approaches at Common Law and Equity. The Law Commission considered reform of the law on limitation periods, and recommended that there should be a primary limitation period that would run from the date of the claimant's actual or constructive knowledge of the facts giving rise to the claim, rather than from the date on which the cause of action accrued. This primary limitation period would be three years, but would be subject to an absolute maximum of ten years. Such a reform would specifically apply to claims for breach of trust. This would be a welcome development, and make the law in this area more consistent, clear, and easy to understand. However, although the Government accepted the Law Commission's proposals in principle, legislative reform has not been pursued.

Law Commission, *Limitation of Actions* (2001) No. 270, pp. 201–12

(1) The primary limitation period should start to run from the 'date of knowledge' rather than, for example, the date the cause of action accrues.

(2) The date of knowledge (which is when the primary limitation period should start to run) should be the date when the claimant has (actual or constructive) knowledge of the following facts:—

   (a) the facts which give rise to the cause of action;

   (b) the identity of the defendant; and

   (c) where injury, loss or damage has occurred or a benefit has been received, that the injury, loss, damage or benefit are significant.

(3) For the purposes of the definition of the date of knowledge, a claimant will be deemed to know that the injury, loss, damage or benefit is significant if

   (a) the claimant knows the full extent of the injury, loss, damage suffered by the claimant (or any other relevant person), or (in relation to a claim for restitution) of any benefit obtained by the defendant (or any other relevant person); or

   (b) a reasonable person would think that, on the assumption that the defendant does not dispute liability and is able to satisfy a judgment, a civil claim was worth making in respect of the injury, loss, damage or benefit concerned. …

---

[169] [2001] 1 WLR 112, 124.

(5) 'Actual knowledge' should not be defined in the proposed legislation and should be treated as a straightforward issue of fact which does not require elaboration.

(6) The claimant should be considered to have constructive knowledge of the relevant facts when the claimant in his or her circumstances and with his or her abilities ought reasonably to have known of the relevant facts.

(7) Unless the claimant has acted unreasonably in not seeking advice from an expert, the claimant should not be treated as having constructive knowledge of any fact which an expert might have acquired. Where an expert has been consulted, the claimant will not be deemed to have constructive knowledge of any information which the expert either acquired, but failed to communicate to the claimant, or failed to acquire. ...

(15) The primary limitation period applying under the core regime should be three years.

(16) A claim, other than in respect of a personal injury, should be subject to a long-stop limitation period of ten years. ...

(54) Subject to our recommendations in paragraph 56 below all claims for breach of trust should be subject to the core regime.

(55) Claims to recover trust property should be subject to the core regime; but in the case of a claim for the recovery of trust property held on a bare trust, the cause of action shall not accrue unless and until the trustee acts in breach of trust.

(56) Legislation should provide that where a claim by one beneficiary has become time-barred, that beneficiary should not be permitted to benefit from a successful claim by another beneficiary whose claim is not time-barred.

Pursuant to the application of the core regime, there is no need to provide a trustee with protection equivalent to that which is currently found in Limitation Act 1980, section 21(2).[170]

Neither the primary limitation period nor the long-stop limitation period should apply to claims for breach of trust or to recover trust property which are brought by either the Attorney-General or the Charity Commissioners.

(57) Neither the primary limitation period nor the long-stop limitation period in respect of a claim for breach of trust or to recover trust property by a beneficiary with a future or contingent interest will start until that interest has fallen into possession.

(58) The core regime should apply to claims in respect of the personal estate of a deceased person (including any claims in respect of a claim to arrears of interest on legacies).

10. LACHES AND ACQUIESCENCE[171]

LIMITATION ACT 1980

36. Acquiescence

Nothing in this Act shall affect any equitable jurisdiction to refuse relief on the ground of acquiescence or otherwise.

---

[170] See Chapter 14.9(a), p. 782.
[171] See e.g. Watt, 'Laches, Estoppel and Election' in *Breach of Trust* (eds Birks and Pretto) (Oxford: Hart, 2002), pp. 353–77.

This provision explicitly preserves the equitable doctrine of acquiescence. The term 'otherwise' has been interpreted to encompass laches.[172]

(a) LACHES

Laches is a judge-made equitable doctrine that defeats a claim where there has been an unreasonable delay before the claim is brought. Laches will be available where there is no prescribed limitation period under the Limitation Act 1980, such as where the trustee is sued for a fraudulent breach of trust, or where the claimant seeks to recover trust property.[173] However, there is no scope for laches if the statute does prescribe a limitation period to govern the claim.[174]

The rationale underpinning laches is that Equity will not assist a claimant who has acted unreasonably in failing to bring a claim promptly. In *Lindsay Petroleum Co. v Hurd*, Sir Barnes Peacock commented that:[175]

> the doctrine of laches in Courts of Equity is not an arbitrary or a technical doctrine. Where it would be practically unjust to give a remedy, either because the party has, by his conduct, done that which might fairly be regarded as equivalent to a waiver of it, or where by his conduct and neglect he has, though perhaps not waiving that remedy, yet put the other party in a situation in which it would not be reasonable to place him if the remedy were afterwards to be asserted, in either of these cases, lapse of time and delay are most material. But in every case, if an argument against relief, which otherwise would be just, is founded upon mere delay, that delay of course not amounting to a bar by any statute of limitations, the validity of that defence must be tried upon principles substantially equitable. Two circumstances, always important in such cases, are, the length of the delay and the nature of the acts done during the interval, which might affect either party and cause a balance of justice or injustice in taking the one course or the other, so far as relates to the remedy.

These factors undoubtedly remain important. Indeed, in *Fisher v Brooker* Lord Neuberger relied upon this decision to say, *obiter*, that although he:[176]

> would not suggest that it is an immutable requirement, some sort of detrimental reliance is usually an essential ingredient of laches.

The modern approach tends to frame the inquiry as one of unconscionability. So, in *Frawley v Neill*, Aldous LJ said:[177]

> In my view the more modern approach should not require an inquiry as to whether the circumstances can be fitted within the confines of a preconceived formula derived from earlier cases. The inquiry should require a broad approach, directed to ascertaining whether it would in all the circumstances be unconscionable for a party to be permitted to assert his beneficial right. No doubt the circumstances which gave rise to a particular result in the decided cases are relevant to the question whether or not it would be conscionable or unconscionable for the relief to be asserted, but each case has to be decided on its facts applying the broad approach.

---

[172] *Re Loftus (deceased)* [2006] EWCA Civ 1124; [2007] 1 WLR 591, [33] (Chadwick LJ).
[173] Ibid, [41] (Chadwick LJ).
[174] *Re Pauling's Settlement Trusts* [1964] Ch 303.
[175] (1874) LR 5 PC 221, 239–40. See too *Erlanger v New Sombrero Phosphate Co.* (1878) 3 App Cas 1218, 1279 (Lord Blackburn).
[176] *Fisher v Brooker* [2009] UKHL 41; [2009] 1 WLR 1764, [64].
[177] [2000] CP Reports 20, but otherwise unreported, 1 March 1999; cited with approval by Chadwick LJ in *Re Loftus (deceased)* [2006] EWCA Civ 1124; [2007] 1 WLR 591, [42].

The operation of the defence of laches can be seen in *Nelson v Rye*.[178] The claimant in that case was a musician, who claimed that his manager had breached his fiduciary duty in receiving money on behalf of the claimant, but not accounting to the claimant for it. Laddie J said:[179]

> It can be misleading to approach the equitable defences of laches and acquiescence as if they consisted of a series of precisely defined hurdles over each of which a litigant must struggle before the defence is made out.
>
> … So here, these defences are not technical or arbitrary. The courts have indicated over the years some of the factors which must be taken into consideration in deciding whether the defence runs. Those factors include the period of the delay, the extent to which the defendant's position has been prejudiced by the delay, and the extent to which that prejudice was caused by the actions of the plaintiff. I accept that mere delay alone will almost never suffice, but the court has to look at all the circumstances, including in particular those factors set out above, and then decide whether the balance of justice or injustice is in favour of granting the remedy or withholding it. If substantial prejudice will be suffered by the defendant, it is not necessary for the defendant to prove that it was caused by the delay. On the other hand, the plaintiff's knowledge that the delay will cause such prejudice is a factor to be taken into account. With these considerations in mind, I turn to the facts.

On the facts, his Lordship held that the defences succeeded, largely due to the claimant's wilful refusal to involve himself in his financial affairs. In addition, the defendant had destroyed most of the relevant paperwork, and the oral evidence was unreliable; the delay had caused prejudice to the defendant.

(b) ACQUIESCENCE

As can be seen from Laddie J's remarks in *Nelson v Rye*, acquiescence and laches are closely related. However, the two are distinct. Acquiescence requires conduct that shows the claimant has waived his or her rights and is thereby estopped from later asserting those rights, but does not inevitably involve any delay.[180] Laches, on the other hand, simply requires delay and not necessarily acquiescence.[181] Acquiescence can also be distinguished from consent: the former may be passive, whereas active steps are required to establish the latter.

For acquiescence to be established, the claimant must know, or ought to know, of his or her rights against the defendant. Thus, in *Re Pauling's Settlement*[182] the defence of acquiescence failed because the claimant beneficiaries were only informed of their rights regarding a breach of trust after any purported acquiescence. Upjohn LJ said:[183]

> As to acquiescence, we think that this must be looked at rather broadly. We were, of course, pressed with the leading case of *Allcard v Skinner* (1887) 36 Ch D 145, but in that case the plaintiff had her rights fully explained to her by a brother, who was a barrister, and by her solicitor, and yet she took no steps until five or six years later. Even that gave rise to a difference of opinion in a very strong Court of Appeal.

---

[178] [1996] 1 WLR 1378. This decision was subsequently overruled in *Paragon Finance v D B Thakerar & Co.* [1999] 1 All ER 400 but only on the different point regarding whether the Limitation Act 1980 applied to a claim founded on a breach of fiduciary duty. The discussion of laches in *Nelson* remains apposite.

[179] [1996] 1 WLR 1378, 1382.

[180] *Duke of Leeds v Earl of Amherst* (1846) 2 Ph. 117, 123.

[181] For further consideration of the relationship between the two doctrines, see *Lester v Woodgate* [2010] EWCA Civ 199; [2010] 2 P & CRDG 14, quoted in Chapter 20.1(a), pp. 976–7. Cf *Fisher v Brooker* [2009] UKHL 41; [2009] 1 WLR 1764, [62] (Lord Neuberger).

[182] [1964] Ch 303. For a summary of the facts, see Chapter 16.4(a), p. 770.

[183] [1964] Ch 303, 353.

In this case it would be wrong, we feel, to place any disability upon the beneficiaries because it so happened that George[, one of the beneficiaries,] was a member of the Bar, and had been in well-known chambers. He had not been in Chancery chambers where it may be said that these things are better understood; but the real truth of the matter is that a party cannot be held to have acquiesced unless he knew, or ought to have known, what his rights were. On the facts of this case we cannot criticise any of the plaintiffs for failing to appreciate their rights until another junior counsel, whom they consulted on a far-fetched and futile scheme of George's for avoiding Estate Duty on his mother's death, advised that the advances might be improper. That was in 1954, and thereupon the family, headed, of course, by George, took immediate steps to explore this matter. This is a most complicated action, and many matters had to be explored before an action for breach of trust could properly be mounted. The writ was issued in 1958, and we do not think it right to hold that the plaintiffs were debarred by acquiescence from bringing an action which otherwise, to the extent we have indicated, is justified.

QUESTION

Steve created a trust in favour of his children, Alan, Brian, and Charles. The trustees of the trust were Peter, Leona, and Charles. Peter is a solicitor, Leona a dentist, and Charles a struggling musician. The terms of the trust instrument prohibit investment in land: however, Alan wanted the trust to purchase a freehold property, which he was sure would be an excellent rental investment. Charles agreed, whilst Peter and Leona were happy simply to follow the lead of Alan and Charles. The property was purchased in 2006. However, the previous owners of the property are now known to have committed a series of murders in the property, and it is impossible to find tenants to live there. Moreover, a crash in the property market means that the value of the property is less than half what the trustees paid.

Advise the beneficiaries of any claims they may have against the trustees.

FURTHER READING

Davies, 'Section 61 of the Trustee Act 1925: *Deus ex Machina*?' [2015] Conv 375.

Kenny, 'The Good, the Bad and the Law Commission' [2007] Conv 103.

Law Commission, *Limitation of Actions* (2001) No. 270, particularly pp. 127–35.

Law Commission, *Trustee Exemption Clauses: A Consultation Paper* (2003) Law Com. CP No. 171, particularly pp. 9–31.

Law Commission, *Trustee Exemption Clauses* (2006) Law Com. No. 301, particularly pp. 9–34.

Lowry and Edmunds, 'Excuses', in *Breach of Trust* (eds Birks and Pretto) (Oxford: Hart, 2002).

Payne, 'Consent', in *Breach of Trust* (eds Birks and Pretto) (Oxford: Hart, 2002).

Penner, 'Exemptions', in *Breach of Trust* (eds Birks and Pretto) (Oxford: Hart, 2002).

Swadling, 'Limitation' in *Breach of Trust* (eds Birks and Pretto) (Oxford: Hart, 2002).

Trukhantov, 'The Irreducible Core of Trust Obligations' (2007) 123 LQR 342.

Watt, 'Laches, Estoppel and Election' in *Breach of Trust* (eds Birks and Pretto) (Oxford: Hart, 2002).

17

PERSONAL CLAIMS AND REMEDIES

CENTRAL ISSUES

1. Beneficiaries may always take an account of the state of the trust fund. This is consistent with the duty of the trustees to provide information to the beneficiaries.

2. The traditional approach, when taking an account, is to say that an unauthorized disbursement may be falsified; the trustees then need to restore the misapplied property or its equivalent value. On the other hand, where trustees have failed properly to safeguard the value of the fund, the account may be surcharged and the trustees required to compensate the trust fund for losses suffered. However, modern cases tend to focus upon the concept of 'equitable causation' in all instances, concentrating upon whether the breach of trust has caused any loss.

3. A breach of trust does not 'stop the clock', and the wrongdoing trustee continues to hold the office of trusteeship. The valuation of any claim against the trustee occurs at the date of judgment.

4. A trustee cannot set off any gains made from one unauthorized investment against losses suffered from another, unless both investments were part of a single transaction or scheme.

5. Trustees may have to pay interest upon any monetary award made against them. The court has a discretion to award compound interest.

6. Trustees may also have to account for any profits made from their breach of duty.

7. Punitive damages for equitable wrongdoing are not available.

---

1. INTRODUCTION

This chapter considers the personal liability of trustees for breach of trust. Proprietary claims and remedies are examined in Chapter 18. Proprietary remedies involve the claimant's recovering particular property from the defendant, or obtaining a security interest in the defendant's property. A crucial advantage of proprietary remedies is that they provide the claimant with priority over other creditors in the event of the defendant's insolvency.[1] Personal claims, by contrast, do not enjoy such

---

[1] See Chapter 1.4(a)(i), p. 11. There may also be other advantages of proprietary remedies; e.g. the claimant might be able to gain the benefit of an increase in the value of the property.

priority over the claims of others. However, where the defendant is solvent and the property in question has fallen in value, a personal remedy for the *value* of the claimant's loss or defendant's gain may be preferable to a proprietary remedy. Personal remedies are also to be preferred when the property in which the claimant had a proprietary interest has been dissipated, because in such circumstances no proprietary remedy will be possible.[2]

(a) PRIMARY AND SECONDARY OBLIGATIONS DISTINGUISHED

When considering liability for breach of trust, it is helpful to distinguish primary and secondary obligations. Primary obligations concern the duties imposed directly by the law of trusts. A breach of a primary obligation can give rise to a secondary obligation, such as the obligation to compensate the claimant for loss suffered or to account for any profits made. The difference is potentially important: for example, whereas considerations such as remoteness may be relevant to secondary obligations, and affect the monetary remedy awarded to the claimant, the enforcement of the primary obligations owed by trustees will not be affected by such concerns. It can never be too remote to enforce the primary obligations that a trustee has undertaken.

Chambers has written that:[3]

> The direct enforcement of trust duties is different from all other consequences of breach of trust. The duties enforced (and corresponding rights to enforce those duties) are the primary duties (and rights) that arose when the trust was created. Although a breach of trust is the reason for seeking the court's help to enforce a particular duty, the duty exists independently of the breach. In contrast, the other consequences of breach of trust are secondary duties (and rights) created by the breach.

Equity is more willing to enforce primary duties than the Common Law. This stems from Equity's insistence that the trustee acts as a good person who must be taken to observe the highest standards of behaviour, which contrasts with the Common Law's general tolerance of breach of contract, for example, as simply a common incident of commercial life.[4] Indeed, in *Target Holdings Ltd v Redferns*,[5] Lord Browne-Wilkinson explained that:[6]

> The basic right of a beneficiary is to have the trust duly administered in accordance with the provisions of the trust instrument, if any, and the general law.

The court might enforce the trustees' primary duties in a number of ways, such as by compelling distribution of trust property to the beneficiaries,[7] preventing trustees from distributing trust property improperly,[8] or requiring the sale of unauthorized investments and reinvestment in authorized ones. The court might also issue a declaration that a trustee should not act in a particular way. For example, in *Cowan v Scargill*,[9] the court clarified the law on the considerations that trustees can take into

---

[2] E.g. Chapter 18.1(a)(i), p. 847.

[3] 'Liability', in *Breach of Trust* (eds Birks and Pretto) (Oxford: Hart, 2002), p. 5.

[4] Albeit one that can trigger secondary obligations: see eg *Photo Production Ltd v Securicor Transport Ltd* [1980] 1 All ER 556, 567–8 (Lord Diplock).

[5] [1996] 1 AC 421.

[6] Ibid, 434.

[7] *Re Locker's Settlement Trust* [1977] 1 WLR 1323.

[8] *Fox v Fox* (1870) LR 11 Eq 142.

[9] [1985] Ch 270. See Chapter 12.4(c)(ii), pp. 601–4.

account when objecting to the trust's investment policy. There was disagreement among the trustees about what course of action to take, and what considerations were relevant; one group of trustees sought directions from the court. Megarry V-C said:[10]

> The summons is cast in the form of asking the court to give directions; but I doubt whether this is the most appropriate remedy. I think that at this stage it would be more appropriate for me to make declarations, and leave it to the defendants to carry out their duties as trustees in accordance with those declarations. I am ready to assume that they will comply with the law once the court has declared what it is. ... I shall not assume that the defendants intend to demonstrate their unfitness to continue as trustees by refusing to comply with the law as declared by the court. Accordingly, subject to what may be said when I have concluded this judgment, I propose to make suitable declarations, and to give liberty to apply for directions or other appropriate relief if the declarations are not duly acted upon. It is important to get this large trust back on the rails; and it may help to do this if at this stage the court refrains from giving directions or making any coercive orders, whether under the inherent jurisdiction or otherwise, and remains in the background while the normal operation of the scheme is being re-established. It is very much to be hoped that there will be no need to consider the exercise of the court's inherent power to remove trustees.

Although a declaration is much less coercive than other options available to a court, having confidence that trustees will comply with declarations of the court is both appropriate and realistic. The trustees are better placed than the courts to run the trust, so a declaration might well be preferred to the court's issuing directions and effectively usurping the powers of the trustees: the court's jurisdiction is mainly supervisory.

Another possibility, raised by the quotation from *Cowan v Scargill*, is for the court to replace trustees. It is difficult to ascertain whether such replacement arises in response to a primary or secondary obligation. As was seen in Chapter 11,[11] there is no need for a breach of trust before trustees can be replaced, but often the reason why a trustee is replaced is because he or she has not carried out the duties of a trustee satisfactorily. Chambers has noted the difficulty of classifying this option of the courts:[12]

> When used as a response to breach of trust, the replacement of trustees is designed to prevent future breaches. Decisions to replace trustees in breach are based on the likelihood that they will breach their trusts in the future. In this context, the goal of replacement is linked directly to the breach.
>
> The goal of replacing trustees in breach is the proper performance of the trust. Although replacement is not a form of direct enforcement (since it is not one of the trustee's primary duties), it is used to increase the likelihood that the primary trust duties will be performed. On the other hand, replacement of trustees is not a form of substitute performance (since the new trustees will carry out the original trust). However, in one sense, the purpose of replacing a trustee (which is proper performance of the trust by another person) is similar to the purpose of paying damages for breach of contract (which enables the claimant to make a new contract and thereby obtain the expected benefits of the broken contract from another person).
>
> The replacement of trustees illustrates the problem of identifying (or at least labelling) the goals of the miscellaneous consequences of breach of trust. It is neither direct enforcement of a primary duty nor substitutive performance, but something in between needed because of the nature of the

---

[10] [1985] Ch 270, 296–7.
[11] See Chapter 11.5, p. 549.
[12] 'Liability', in *Breach of Trust* (eds Birks and Pretto) (Oxford: Hart, 2002), pp. 38–9.

> trust relationship. It serves two purposes: first, the removal of actual or potential impediments to the proper performance of the trust and, secondly, the preservation of trust assets from loss through misuse.

The replacement of trustees is governed by statute. Another difficult area, the classification of which might have greater practical significance, concerns the taking of an account. As Chambers has observed:[13]

> Normally, it is fairly easy to tell whether a trust duty is a primary duty created by the settlor or a secondary duty created as a consequence of an unexcused breach of trust. However, this distinction can be difficult to make, especially in relation to the trustees' duty to account.

The duty to account needs to be analysed carefully. Whether primary or secondary obligations are involved, and why this may be important, can be better explained once the various aspects of the account have been introduced. However, it is important to note that the importance and continuing vitality of the account as a remedy is currently unclear as a result of the recent decision of the Supreme Court in *AIB Group (UK) Plc v Mark Redler & Co.*[14] But this decision is best assessed once the traditional orthodoxy is understood.

2. TAKING AN ACCOUNT

The taking of an account is not really a remedy at all.[15] As Lord Millett pointed out in the Hong Kong decision in *Hall* v *Libertarian Investments Ltd*:[16]

> It is often said that the primary remedy for breach of trust or fiduciary duty is an order for an account, but this is an abbreviated and potentially misleading statement of the true position. In the first place an account is not a remedy for wrong. Trustees and most fiduciaries are accounting parties, and their beneficiaries or principals do not have to prove that there has been a breach of trust or fiduciary duty in order to obtain an order for account. Once the trust or fiduciary relationship is established or conceded the beneficiary or principal is entitled to an account as of right. Although like all equitable remedies an order for an account is discretionary, in making the order the court is not granting a remedy for wrong but enforcing performance of an obligation.

Taking an account is simply a process that can be employed in order to assess the state of the trust fund.[17] In this respect, the taking of an account can enforce the trustees' primary duty to provide information to the beneficiaries and keep accurate accounts of the trust. All express trustees owe a primary duty to account for their administration of the trust fund, including all receipts, investments, and distributions. Taking an account may lead to the enforcement of primary or secondary obligations, both of which will be examined in this chapter.

---

[13] Chambers, 'Liability', in *Breach of Trust* (eds Birks and Pretto) (Oxford: Hart, 2002), p. 6.

[14] [2014] UKSC 58, [57].

[15] For the development of the trustee's duty to account from the Common Law taking of an account, see Stoljar, 'The Transformations of Account' (1964) 80 LQR 203.

[16] [2013] HKCFA 93; [2014] 1 HKC 368, [167].

[17] Getzler, 'Equitable Compensation and the Regulation of Fiduciary Relationships' in *Restitution and Equity: Resulting Trusts and Equitable Compensation, volume one* (eds Birks and Rose) (Oxford: Mansfield Press, 2000), p. 250.

An account will also be available where a fiduciary who is not a trustee is responsible for managing the principal's property as a steward of it, such as where a fiduciary holds property as an executor or receiver.[18] But not all fiduciaries are responsible for property; in such circumstances, no account can be taken. Given that the vast majority of fiduciaries who hold property for their principal will be trustees, this chapter will focus upon trustees.

Where the account shows that the trust fund has suffered a loss, a claim may be brought against the trustees to restore the fund to the position it would have been in had there been no breach of duty. Such a claim is most commonly brought by a beneficiary, but other trustees who are not responsible for the breach of trust may also sue on behalf of the trust. If the trust is a charitable trust, the Charity Commission and Attorney-General both have standing to sue.[19]

When an account is taken, two principal problems may be revealed: the trustees may have misappropriated assets from the trust fund, for example by making unauthorized investments; or, alternatively, the trustees may have breached their duty in failing appropriately to safeguard the value of the fund, which will be the case, for example, where they have negligently failed to diversify the types of assets held by the trust.[20] In the first situation, a beneficiary might *falsify* the unauthorized disbursement; in the second, the account might be *surcharged* to bring its value up to the appropriate level. Significantly, the trustee will be liable to compensate the trust fund from his or her own resources whether the account is falsified or surcharged. These two facets of taking an account will now be examined in turn.

(a) FALSIFICATION

Where a disbursement of trust assets has been made in breach of trust, that disbursement can be falsified when taking an account. The operation of falsification was explained by Lord Millett.

Millett, 'Equity's Place in the Law of Commerce' (1998) 114 LQR 214, 226–7

Where the beneficiary complains that the trustee has misapplied trust money, he falsifies the account, that is to say, he asks for the disbursement to be disallowed. If, for example, the trustee lays out trust money in an unauthorised investment which falls in value, the beneficiary will falsify the account by asking the court to disallow both the disbursement and the corresponding asset on the other side of the account. The unauthorised investment will then be treated as having been bought with the trustee's own money and on his own behalf. He will be required to account to the trust estate for the full amount of the disbursement—not for the amount of the loss. That is what is meant by saying that the trustee is liable to restore the trust property; and why common law rules of causation and remoteness of damage are out of place. …

Where the beneficiary elects to falsify the account, the unauthorised investment is not shown as an asset, the disbursement is disallowed, and the trustee is accountable in every respect as if he had not disbursed the money. He is liable to restore the money to the trust estate; as notionally restored it remains subject to all the trusts powers and provisions of the trust as if it had never been disbursed; and the account is taken accordingly.

So, if the trust instrument prevents the trustees from investing in land, but the trustees in breach of trust purchase land for the trust, the beneficiaries would be entitled to falsify that investment upon

[18] Ibid.
[19] See Chapter 5.2, p. 179.
[20] See e.g. *Nestlé v National Westminster Bank plc* [1993] 1 WLR 1260; see Chapter 12.5(a), pp. 611–14.

taking an account of the trust. As a result, the trustees would be assumed to have purchased the land with their own money, and would have to use their own resources to restore the money missing from the trust fund, which was used to purchase the land. This process is independent of considerations of remoteness: even if the losses suffered were unforeseeable, for example, they could still be recovered through the process of falsification. The trustees are simply liable to reconstitute the fund, which will never be too remote; that is, the relevant loss can never be too remote.[21]

Falsification is particularly important following the purchase of unauthorized investments or the improper sale of authorized investments. Both these situations will be analysed in turn.

(i) *Purchase of unauthorized investments*

In *Knott v Cottee*,[22] the testator, who died in 1844, bequeathed his personal estate to be held on trust and invested in 'the public or Government Stocks or Funds of Great Britain, or upon real security in England or Wales'. In breach of trust, the executor invested in foreign stocks and Exchequer bills. In a suit by the beneficiaries, he was required to deposit the Exchequer bills in court, and in 1846 they were sold, under an order of the court, at a loss. The court made a decree in 1848 declaring the investments to be unauthorized. By that time, the price of the bills had risen; if they had been sold then, there would have been a profit.

The unauthorized investments could be falsified; the executor was personally liable for the breach of trust. One issue for the court was whether the executor should be credited with the proceeds of the Exchequer bills as sold in 1846, or with their (increased) value in 1848, when they were declared to be unauthorized. Romilly MR held that the executor should be charged with the amount improperly invested, and credited with the proceeds actually received on their sale:[23]

> As to the mode of charging the executor in respect of the Exchequer bills, I treat the laying out in Exchequer bills in this way: the persons interested were entitled to ear-mark them, as being bought with the testator's assets, in the same manner as if the executor had bought a house with the trust funds; and though they do not recognize the investment, they had a right to make it available for what was due; and though part of the property of the executor, it was specifically applicable to the payment. When the Exchequer bills were sold and produced £3,955, the Court must consider the produce as a sum of money refunded by the executor to the testator's estate on that day; and on taking the account, the Master must give credit for this amount as on the day on which the Exchequer bills were sold.

This approach is sensible: to fail to give credit for the amount actually raised through the sale of the bills would have been to ignore the reality of the state of the trust fund. However, the account must be taken with regard to what actually happened; there was therefore no scope to contemplate what the bills would have been worth if sold later.

(ii) *Improper sale of authorized investments*

In *Re Massingberd's Settlement*,[24] the trustees of a settlement had the power to invest in Consols.[25] In 1875 they sold Consols and reinvested in certain unauthorized mortgages. The mortgages were called

---

[21] See Elliott, 'Remoteness Criteria in Equity' (2002) 65 MLR 588.
[22] (1852) 16 Beav 77.
[23] Ibid, 81.
[24] (1890) 63 LT 296.
[25] Consols are a form of government bonds; the name 'consol' was originally short for 'consolidated annuities'.

in and the whole of the money invested was recovered. Proceedings later began in 1887, at which time Consols stood higher than they had done in 1875. The unauthorized sale of the Consols was falsified, and the Court of Appeal held that the trustees must produce either the Consols sold or their present money equivalent. The value of assets sold in breach of trust should be assessed at the date of judgment, or, exceptionally, at the later date when they would have been properly sold.[26] But such valuation does not occur on the date at which the claim is brought.

This suggests that trustees must 'restore'[27] the trust fund to the position it would have been in had the unauthorized investments in the mortgages not occurred: the trust fund would, at the date of judgment, still have had the Consols, so it was incumbent upon the trustees either to purchase the Consols for the trust or to give the trust sufficient money to purchase the Consols.

An influential illustration of this principle was provided by Street J in *In re Dawson (dec'd)*,[28] a decision of the Supreme Court of New South Wales. In 1939, a trustee paid away NZ£4,700 in breach of trust. At the time of the improper disbursement, there was parity between the New Zealand pound and Australian pound. However, by the time the claim was made against the trustee to restore the trust estate, NZ£4,700 was worth nearly A£6,000. Street J held that the defaulting trustee was under a strict liability to make good the trust fund. In order to restore the trust fund to the position it would have been in had the money not wrongly been paid away, the trustee was required to pay A£6,000. Street J held that previous authorities:

> ... demonstrate that the obligation to make restitution, which courts of equity have from very early times imposed on defaulting trustees and other fiduciaries is of a more absolute nature than the common law obligation to pay damages for tort or breach of contract. ... Increases in market values between the date of the breach and the date of recoupment are for the trustee's account: the effect of such increases would, at common law, be excluded from the computation of damages; but in equity a defaulting trustee must make good the loss by restoring to the estate the assets of which he deprived it notwithstanding that market values may have increased in the meantime. The obligation to restore to the estate the assets of which he deprived it necessarily connotes that, where a monetary compensation is to be paid in lieu of restoring assets, that compensation is to be assessed by reference to the value of the assets at the date of restoration and not at the date of deprivation.

The judge explicitly said that '[c]onsiderations of causation, foreseeability and remoteness do not readily enter the matter'.[29] In effect, the wrongdoing trustee in *Re Dawson* was taken to have paid away his own monies rather than the monies of the trust fund, since equity would not countenance the possibility that the trustee acted badly when it could insist that the trustee acted properly. The trustee was held up to his primary obligation to act as a reasonable and honest trustee. The trustee was still under a primary obligation to account for NZ£4,700 to the trust fund, and the trustee could still do this. Upon the beneficiary's falsifying the account to delete the unauthorized disbursement, the trustee had the option of making good the state of the fund either by restoring the relevant trust property in specie (in other words, by restoring the particular monies paid away) or by paying a monetary substitute out of the trustee's own funds.

[26] *Re Bell's Indenture* [1980] 1 WLR 1217 at 1233.
[27] For further consideration of appropriate language in this area, see Chapter 17.2(a)(iv), p. 805.
[28] [1966] NSWR 211.
[29] Ibid, 215.

(iii) *Adoption*

The mere fact that an investment is unauthorized does not mean that the beneficiary necessarily has to falsify the relevant disbursement. The trustee might have committed what is sometimes called a 'judicious' breach of trust,[30] and the unauthorized investment may have increased in value. In such circumstances, it is often said that the beneficiary can choose to 'adopt' the unauthorized investment. However, as Millett has explained, this may be something of a misnomer:[31]

> If the unauthorised investment has appreciated in value, then the beneficiary will be content with it. He is not obliged to falsify the account which the trustee renders; he can always accept it. … Where the beneficiary accepts the unauthorised investment, he is often said to affirm or adopt the transaction. That is not wholly accurate. The beneficiary has a right to elect, but it is merely a right to decide whether to complain or not.

But whilst this approach may appropriately cover instances where the beneficiary seeks either to accept or falsify the investment absolutely, the situation is more complicated where the beneficiary wants to 'adopt' an unauthorized investment as *partial* satisfaction of any claim he or she may have: if the value of the unauthorized investment is still less than the purchase price, should the beneficiary be able *both* to accept the investment as part of the trust's assets *and* sue the trustees for the difference between the value of the investment and the value that the trust fund should have?

In *Thornton v Stokill*,[32] the court held that a beneficiary had a stark choice between adopting the investment or falsifying the disbursement. In that case, £400 of trust money had been invested in houses in breach of trust. The court insisted that the beneficiaries could not claim the houses *and* the difference in value between the houses and the misapplied £400.

On the other hand, in *Re Lake*[33] the contrary approach was favoured. Solicitors acting for a trust invested £5,500 in a contributory mortgage. The mortgagor later sought to set aside the mortgage for fraud, and the trustees agreed to compromise the claim in return for a payment of £500. Wright J held that by entering into the compromise agreement, the trustees had adopted the mortgages. However, he also found that it was still possible to recover the difference between the £5,500 lost through the unauthorized investment and the £500 recovered by adopting the mortgage.

Which approach is to be preferred? *Thornton v Stokill* is more consistent with the proprietary nature of the beneficiary's interest. As Penner has written:[34]

> a beneficiary cannot logically adopt an asset as trust property and at the same time falsify the account so as to make the trustee personally liable. The beneficiary has an *election* either to adopt the transaction in any form he chooses or to falsify the account, but elect he must; he cannot have it both ways.

This is rigidly logical: if the beneficiary adopts the investment as trust property, then there is nothing to falsify and no further claim against the trustee. However, it seems very generous to a trustee, and leaves the beneficiary in an unenviable position. Falsification leads only to a

---

[30] E.g. *Target Holdings Ltd v Redferns* [1996] AC 421, 433; see further Chapter 17.3(a), p. 811.
[31] Millett, 'Equity's Place in the Law of Commerce' (1998) 114 LQR 214, 226.
[32] (1855) 1 Jur (NS) 751.
[33] [1903] 1 KB 439.
[34] 'Duty and Liability in Respect of Funds' in *Commercial Law: Perspectives and Practice* (eds Lowry and Mistelis) (London: LexisNexis Butterworths, 2006), p. 219.

personal remedy against the trustee; if the investment is adopted as *partial* satisfaction in respect of the shortfall in the trust fund, the position of the beneficiaries is not quite so precarious, and the value of the trust fund is necessarily higher than it would otherwise be when a personal claim against the trustee is launched.[35] But obviously, the beneficiaries would still be in a worse position than if the investment had simply not been made. It is therefore understandable why a court might wish to allow a beneficiary to adopt an investment as partial satisfaction of the personal liability of a trustee.

(iv) *Terminology*

A recurring problem in this area is that different language has been used to describe the liability of the trustees. It has been said already that the trustees have to 'restore' the trust fund; for example, in *In re Dawson (dec'd)*, Street J said that:[36]

> The form of relief is couched in terms appropriate to require the defaulting trustee to restore to the estate the assets of which he deprived it.

However, Street J also used the language of 'restitution':[37]

> The obligation of a defaulting trustee is essentially one of effecting a restitution to the estate.

Both the language of 'restitution' and 'restoration' have been used in subsequent cases.[38] Provided it is clear that the trustees have to put the trust fund in the position it would have been in had there not been a breach of trust, no difficulties may arise. However, it has been argued that such language may be liable to confuse.[39] Certainly, the trustees are not required to make 'restitution' in the sense of giving back the gains they have made: the trustees might not have made any gains. As a result of falsification, the trustees simply have to compensate the trust fund. It might, therefore, be preferable to speak of the trustees' 'restoring' the fund to its original position, even though the trustees do not generally restore what they initially took but rather replace it with money instead. This might also be considered to represent a 'reconstitution' of the fund.[40] Nevertheless, Edelman and Elliott consider the language of 'substitutive compensation' to be more accurate, since 'the compensation is given as a substitute for the property the trustee was bound to maintain and apply'.[41]

Regardless of the choice of language used, it is crucial to appreciate that, although falsification is generally a response to a breach of trust, the remedy that arises is not secondary and different from the primary obligation of the trustee. Falsification compels the performance of the primary obligation to maintain the proper state of the trust fund, essentially through restoring the trust to its previous position. If property has been disposed of in breach of trust, then the trustee must either return the very property disbursed or its monetary equivalent, both of which correspond to the primary obligations imposed upon trustees.

---

[35] See Fox, 'Overreaching' in *Breach of Trust* (eds Birks and Pretto) (Oxford: Hart, 2002) p. 108.
[36] [1966] NSWR 211, 216.
[37] Ibid, 214.
[38] E.g. *Target, Holdings Ltd v Redferns* [1996] AC 421: see Chapter 17.3(a), p. 809.
[39] Edelman and Elliott, 'Money Remedies against Trustees' (2004) 18 TLI 116, 117–18.
[40] See e.g. *Target, Holdings Ltd v Redferns* [1996] AC 421, 433: see Chapter 17.3(a), p. 809.
[41] 'Money Remedies against Trustees' (2004) 18 TLI 116, 118.

(b) SURCHARGE

If the trustee has failed properly to safeguard the value of the trust fund, then the trust fund will have suffered loss through not being worth as much as it ought to be worth. This may simply be through failing properly to diversify the assets held on trust.[42] In such circumstances, there is no disbursement to falsify. However, the beneficiary is able to surcharge the account to bring it up to its appropriate value. This was explained by Lord Millett as follows:[43]

> If the beneficiary is dissatisfied with the way in which the trustee has carried out his trust—if, for example, he considers that the trustee has negligently failed to obtain all that he should have done for the benefit of the trust estate, then he may surcharge the account. He does this by requiring the account to be taken on the footing of wilful default. In this context 'wilful default' bears a special and unusual meaning; it means merely lack of ordinary prudence or due diligence.[44] The trustee is made to account, not only for what he has in fact received, but also for what he might with due diligence have received. Since the trustee is, in effect, charged with negligence, and the amount by which the account is surcharged is measured by the loss occasioned by his want of skill and care, the analogy with common law damages for negligence is almost exact.[45] Although he is a fiduciary, his duty of care is not a fiduciary duty.[46] In this context it must be right to adopt the common law rules of causation and remoteness of damage to their fullest extent. The trustee's liability is enforced in the course of taking the trust account rather than by an action for damages, but the obligation of skill and care is identical to the common law duty of care.

Surcharging the account does not 'reconstitute' the fund in the same way that falsification does: there is nothing to reconstitute, since nothing has been taken out of the fund. Edelman and Elliott have explained that:[47]

> This remedy is not given by way of substitutively enforcing the performance of the trustee's primary duties. Rather, compensatory damages require the trustee to make good losses occasioned by his breach of trust. The compensation is reparative rather than substitutive in nature.

It is sensible that such 'reparative compensation', unlike 'substitutive compensation', be subject to rules of causation and remoteness; the goal of remedying the loss suffered by the fund is comparable to the object of compensation at Common Law. However, it is obviously difficult to refer simply to 'common law' rules of causation and remoteness, since there is no single set of such common law rules: the rules on remoteness, for example, vary between contract and tort, and indeed between different torts. Nevertheless, Elliott has argued that:[48]

> The progress of the law is towards treating reparation claims for breach of trust in two broad compartments that correspond to the two major compartments discernable in tort law. The first includes claims arising from unintentional and judicious breaches of trust; here the principal remoteness test

---

[42] E.g. *Nestlé v National Westminster Bank plc* [1993] 1 WLR 1260. See Chapter 12.5(a), pp. 611–14.

[43] *Equity's Place in the Law of Commerce* (1998) 114 LQR 214, 225–6.

[44] See, e.g. *Re Chapman* [1896] 2 Ch 763.

[45] See *Henderson v Merrett Syndicates Ltd* [1995] 2 AC 145, p. 205 (Lord Browne-Wilkinson).

[46] See *Permanent Building Society v Wheeler* (1994) 14 ACSR 109, 157–8 (Ipp J) approved in *Bristol & West Building Society v Mothew* [1997] 2 WLR 436, 448–9.

[47] 'Money Remedies against Trustees' (2004) 18 TLI 116, 118.

[48] 'Remoteness Criteria in Equity' (2002) 65 MLR 588, 597.

should be reasonable foreseeability of the kind of loss. The second includes claims arising from intentional disloyalty; here unforeseeable losses should be recoverable so long as they are the direct result of the breach.

The extent to which the remedy available after surcharging the account should resemble an award of damages pursuant to a common law wrong is, however, controversial. In *Bristol & West Building Society v Mothew*,[49] Millett LJ repeated his view that:

Equitable compensation for breach of the duty of skill and care resembles common law damages in that it is awarded by way of compensation to the plaintiff for his loss. There is no reason in principle why the common law rules of causation, remoteness of damage and measure of damages should not be applied by analogy in such a case.

But in *AIB v Redler*, Lord Reid noted that this:[50]

dictum has been questioned, or given a restrictive application, in a number of other jurisdictions.

The extent to which the remedies in this area should be 'fused' will be revisited when examining *AIB v Redler* in further detail later in this chapter.

A good example of surcharging the account is provided by *Fry v Fry*.[51] A testator, who died in 1834, provided by his will that the Langford Inn should be sold 'as soon as convenient after [his] decease … either by auction or private sale, and for the most money that could be reasonably obtained for the same'. However, the trustees had some difficulty in selling. In 1836 they advertised and offered to sell for £1,000. They refused an offer of £900. In 1843, a new railway line opened, which deprived the Inn of much of its passing business and made it difficult to sell. It was again advertised in 1854, but no offer was received. Romilly MR held the trustees liable for breach of trust in consequence of their negligence for so many years in not selling the property. The trustees would therefore be liable for the difference between the amount eventually received and £900.

When assessing the loss suffered by the trust fund, it is important to establish what value the fund should have at the date of judgment rather than at the date of breach;[52] the burden rests upon the claimants to establish what would be the value of the fund had there been no breach of trust. For example, in *Nestlé v National Westminster Bank plc*,[53] a bank had acted in breach of trust in failing either to review the trust investments or to take legal advice on the scope of its powers, and was also in breach of trust because it did not properly diversify the investments of the fund. When the beneficiary took an account of the trust, she was therefore entitled to surcharge the account. However, the beneficiary's claim for reparative compensation failed because she had not shown the extent of the trust's loss, and the onus was upon her to do so. As Dillon LJ remarked:[54]

The starting point must, in my judgment, be that, as the plaintiff is claiming compensation, the onus is on her to prove that she has suffered loss because from 1922 to 1960 the equities in the annuity

---

[49] [1998] Ch 1, 17.
[50] [2014] UKSC 58, [119].
[51] (1859) 27 Beav 144.
[52] See Chapter 17.3(a)(ii), p. 818.
[53] [1993] 1 WLR 1260. See Chapter 12.5(a), pp. 611–14.
[54] Ibid, 1269.

fund were not diversified ... in the present case, if the annuity fund had been invested wholly in fixed interest securities, it would have been relatively easy to prove, even though the event never happened, that the annuity fund would have been worth much more if a substantial part had been invested in equities. Consequently fair compensation could have been assessed. Equally it would have been possible, even though more difficult and much more expensive, to prove, if it be the fact, that the equities in the annuity fund would have performed even better if diversified than they did as concentrated in bank and insurance shares. But the plaintiff has not provided any such proof. She has not even provided any material which would enable the court to assess the strength of, or value, the chance which she claims she has lost. Therefore her claim for compensation or damages in respect of the investment of the annuity fund from 1922 to 1960 must, in my judgment, fail.

Had steps been taken to establish the shortfall in the fund, the claimant should have sought to ascertain the difference between the fund's current value and what it would have been worth had it been handled by a prudent trustee. As Staughton LJ said:[55]

I would be inclined to prefer a comparison with what a prudent trustee was likely to have achieved — in other words, the average performance of ordinary shares during the period.

(c) CLASSIFYING THE ACCOUNT

There does not need to be any breach of trust for an account to be taken. It is possible to insist that the purpose of the account is to enforce the primary obligation of a trustee to account for the administration of the trust.

Lord Millett, 'Equity's Place in the Law of Commerce' (1998) 114 LQR 214, 225

Lord Diplock has said that a contracting party is under a primary obligation to perform his contract and a secondary obligation to pay damages if he does not. It is tempting, but wrong, to assume that a trustee is likewise under a primary obligation to perform the trust and a secondary obligation to pay equitable compensation if he does not. The primary obligation of a trustee is to account for his stewardship. The primary remedy of the beneficiary—any beneficiary no matter how limited his interest—is to have the account taken, to surcharge and falsify the account, and to require the trustee to restore to the trust estate any deficiency which may appear when the account is taken. The liability is strict.

However, a breach of trust will often be the reason the beneficiary seeks an account, and explains why the trustee has to make up for any shortfall in the trust fund. It might therefore be possible to view the breach of trust as triggering a secondary obligation to remedy the wrong, albeit hidden behind the beneficiaries' primary right to ensure that the trustee is accountable for the administration of the trust. But as has been seen already, Edelman and Elliott have argued that a distinction might be drawn between falsification, or substitutive compensation, which concerns the enforcement of primary duties, and surcharging, or reparative compensation, which involves the enforcement of a secondary obligation flowing from the breach of trust.[56] This distinction might also help to explain

---

[55] Ibid, at 1280.
[56] 'Money Remedies against Trustees' (2004) 18 TLI 116.

why the rules of remoteness, for example, are, traditionally, at least, relevant only to the latter, and not to the former.[57]

It is now important to examine whether this traditional understanding of the law has been undermined by more recent decisions at the highest level in England and Wales. Both the House of Lords in *Target Holdings Ltd v Redferns* and the Supreme Court in *AIB v Redler* appeared to favour an approach based on compensation for the beneficiary's loss in cases which could have been analysed as raising issues of falsification, albeit in the context of bare, commercial trusts.

3. MOVING TOWARDS EQUITABLE COMPENSATION

(a) *TARGET HOLDINGS LTD V REDFERNS*

Target Holdings Ltd v Redferns [1996] AC 421

Mirage Properties Ltd, the owners of a commercial property in Birmingham, agreed to sell it to Crowngate Developments Ltd for £775,000. Crowngate applied for a loan from Target Holdings Ltd; the loan application form stated that the property was valued at £2 million. On this basis, Target agreed to lend Crowngate a total of £1,706,000 on the security of the property. This was all part of a mortgage fraud perpetrated by Crowngate and Mirage in order to inflate the price of the property artificially. Target was unaware of this fraudulent scheme.

Redferns was a firm of solicitors acting for both Crowngate and Target. Redferns held the mortgage advance on a bare trust for Target, with authority to release the money to Crowngate only upon receipt of the executed conveyances and mortgage of the property. However, Redferns released the money before the documents were executed. It was admitted that this was a breach of trust. The property was in due course found to be worth only £500,000.

It is apparent from the judgments at all levels in the case that Redferns was probably involved in the fraudulent scheme, and could therefore have been sued by Target in the tort of deceit. However, this would have required Target to establish all the elements necessary for such a claim, including an intentional representation that Redferns knew to be false, or at least that Redferns was recklessly indifferent regarding the truth of the representation made.[58] Target instead sought summary judgment for breach of trust, which it perceived to be much more straightforward. Target asked Redferns to reconstitute the trust fund by paying the difference between the value of the property and the money advanced to Crowngate. This argument succeeded in the Court of Appeal,[59] which held that, as soon as the money had been transferred in breach of trust, the claimant had a right to have the trust fund reconstituted, even though the claimant had later received the security that it was intending to obtain and regardless of the fact that that security was worth much less than anticipated, since Common Law principles of causation did not apply to a claim for breach of trust.

The decision of the Court of Appeal was unanimously overturned by the House of Lords. Lord Browne-Wilkinson gave the leading speech, with which all the other members of the House of Lords agreed.

---

[57] See further Elliott, 'Remoteness Criteria in Equity' (2002) 65 MLR 588.
[58] *Derry v Peek* (1888) LR 14 App Cas 337.
[59] [1994] 1 WLR 1089.

Lord Browne-Wilkinson:

Before considering the technical issues of law which arise, it is appropriate to look at the case more generally. Target allege, and it is probably the case, that they were defrauded by third parties (Mr. Kohli and Mr. Musafir and possibly their associates) to advance money on the security of the property. If there had been no breach by Redferns of their instructions and the transaction had gone through, Target would have suffered a loss in round figures of £1.2 million (i.e. £1.7 million advanced less £500,000 recovered on the realisation of the security). Such loss would have been wholly caused by the fraud of the third parties. The breach of trust committed by Redferns left Target in exactly the same position as it would have been if there had been no such breach: Target advanced the same amount of money, obtained the same security and received the same amount on the realisation of that security. In any ordinary use of words, the breach of trust by Redferns cannot be said to have caused the actual loss ultimately suffered by Target unless it can be shown that, but for the breach of trust, the transaction would not have gone through, … if the transaction had not gone through, Target would not have advanced the money at all and therefore Target would not have suffered any loss. But the Court of Appeal[60] decided (see Ralph Gibson LJ at 1100; Peter Gibson LJ at 1104) and it is common ground before your Lordships that there is a triable issue as to whether, had it not been for the breach of trust, the transaction would have gone through. Therefore the decision of the Court of Appeal in this case can only be maintained on the basis that, even if there is no causal link between the breach of trust and the actual loss eventually suffered by Target (i.e. the sum advanced less the sum recovered) the trustee in breach is liable to bear (at least in part) the loss suffered by Target.

The transaction in the present case is redolent of fraud and negligence. But, in considering the principles involved, suspicions of such wrongdoing must be put on one side. If the law as stated by the Court of Appeal is correct, it applies to cases where the breach of trust involves no suspicion of fraud or negligence. For example, say an advance is made by a lender to an honest borrower in reliance on an entirely honest and accurate valuation. The sum to be advanced is paid into the client account of the lender's solicitors. Due to an honest and non-negligent error (e.g. an unforeseeable failure in the solicitors' computer) the moneys in client account are transferred by the solicitors to the borrower one day before the mortgage is executed. That is a breach of trust. Then the property market collapses and when the lender realises his security by sale he recovers only half the sum advanced. As I understand the Court of Appeal decision, the solicitors would bear the loss flowing from the collapse in the market value: subject to the court's discretionary power to relieve a trustee from liability under section 61 of the Trustee Act 1925,[61] the solicitors would be bound to repay the total amount wrongly paid out of the client account in breach of trust receiving credit only for the sum received on the sale of the security.

To my mind in the case of an unimpeachable transaction this would be an unjust and surprising conclusion. At common law there are two principles fundamental to the award of damages. First, that the defendant's wrongful act must cause the damage complained of. Second, that the plaintiff is to be put 'in the same position as he would have been in if he had not sustained the wrong for which he is now getting his compensation or reparation': *Livingstone v. Rawyards Coal Company* (1880) 5 App. Cas. 25. 39. *per* Lord Blackburn. Although, as will appear, in many ways equity approaches liability for making good a breach of trust from a different starting point, in my judgment those two principles are applicable as much in equity as at common law. Under both systems liability is fault based: the defendant is only liable for the consequences of the legal wrong he has done to the plaintiff and to make good the damage caused by such wrong. He is not responsible for damage not caused by his wrong or to pay by way of compensation more than the loss suffered from such wrong. The detailed rules of equity as to causation and the quantification of loss differ, at least ostensibly, from those applicable at common

---

[60] Ibid.
[61] See Chapter 16.3, p. 760.

law. But the principles underlying both systems are the same. On the assumptions that had to be made in the present case until the factual issues are resolved (i.e. that the transaction would have gone through even if there had been no breach of trust), the result reached by the Court of Appeal does not accord with those principles. Redferns as trustees have been held liable to compensate Target for a loss caused otherwise than by the breach of trust. I approach the consideration of the relevant rules of equity with a strong predisposition against such a conclusion.

The considerations urged before your Lordships, although presented as a single argument leading to the conclusion that the views of the majority in the Court of Appeal are correct, on analysis comprise two separate lines of reasoning, viz.

1. an argument developed by Mr. Patten (but not reflected in the reasons of the Court of Appeal) that Target is now (i.e. at the date of judgment) entitled to have the 'trust fund' restored by an order that Redferns reconstitute the trust fund by paying back into client account the moneys paid away in breach of trust. Once the trust fund is so reconstituted, Redferns as bare trustee for Target will have no answer to a claim by Target for the payment over of the moneys in the reconstituted 'trust fund'. Therefore, Mr. Patten says, it is proper now to order payment direct to Target of the whole sum improperly paid away, less the sum which Target has received on the sale of property;

2. the argument accepted by the majority of the Court of Appeal that, because immediately after the moneys were paid away by Redferns in breach of trust there was an immediate right to have the 'trust fund' reconstituted, there was then an immediate loss to the trust fund for which loss Redferns are now liable to compensate Target direct.

The critical distinction between the two arguments is that argument (A) depends upon Target being entitled now to an order for restitution to the trust fund whereas argument (B) quantifies the compensation payable to Target as beneficiary by reference to a right to restitution to the trust fund at an earlier date and is not dependent upon Target having any right to have the client account reconstituted now.

Before dealing with these two lines of argument, it is desirable to say something about the approach to the principles under discussion. The argument both before the Court of Appeal and your Lordships concentrated on the equitable rules establishing the extent and quantification of the compensation payable by a trustee who is in breach of trust. In my judgment this approach is liable to lead to the wrong conclusions in the present case because it ignores an earlier and crucial question, viz., is the trustee who has committed a breach under any liability at all to the beneficiary complaining of the breach? There can be cases where, although there is an undoubted breach of trust, the trustee is under no liability at all to a beneficiary. For example, if a trustee commits a breach of trust with the acquiescence of one beneficiary, that beneficiary has no right to complain and an action for breach of trust brought by him would fail completely. Again there may be cases where the breach gives rise to no right to compensation. Say, as often occurs, a trustee commits a judicious breach of trust by investing in an unauthorised investment which proves to be very profitable to the trust. A carping beneficiary could insist that the unauthorised investment be sold and the proceeds invested in authorised investments: but the trustee would be under no liability to pay compensation either to the trust fund or to the beneficiary because the breach has caused no loss to the trust fund. Therefore, in each case the first question is to ask what are the rights of the beneficiary: only if some relevant right has been infringed so as to give rise to a loss is it necessary to consider the extent of the trustee's liability to compensate for such loss.

The basic right of a beneficiary is to have the trust duly administered in accordance with the provisions of the trust instrument, if any, and the general law. Thus, in relation to a traditional trust where the fund is held in trust for a number of beneficiaries having different, usually successive, equitable interests, (e.g. A for life with remainder to B), the right of each beneficiary is to have the whole fund vested in the trustees so as to be available to satisfy his equitable interest when, and if, it falls into possession. Accordingly, in the case of a breach of such a trust involving the wrongful paying away of trust assets, the liability of the trustee is to restore to the trust fund, often called 'the trust estate', what ought to have been there.

The equitable rules of compensation for breach of trust have been largely developed in relation to such traditional trusts, where the only way in which all the beneficiaries' rights can be protected is to restore to the trust fund what ought to be there. In such a case the basic rule is that a trustee in breach of trust must restore or pay to the trust estate either the assets which have been lost to the estate by reason of the breach or compensation for such loss. Courts of Equity did not award damages but, acting in personam, ordered the defaulting trustee to restore the trust estate: see *Nocton v. Lord Ashburton* [1914] A.C. 932, 952, 958, *per* Viscount Haldane L.C. If specific restitution of the trust property is not possible, then the liability of the trustee is to pay sufficient compensation to the trust estate to put it back to what it would have been had the breach not been committed: *Caffrey v. Darby* (1801) 6 Ves. 488; *Clough v. Bond* (1838) 3 My. and Cr. 490. Even if the immediate cause of the loss is the dishonesty or failure of a third party, the trustee is liable to make good that loss to the trust estate if, but for the breach, such loss would not have occurred: see *Underhill and Hayton, Law of Trusts and Trustees* 14th ed. (1987) pp. 734-736; *In re Dawson decd.; Union Fidelity Trustee Co. Ltd. v. Perpetual Trustee Co. Ltd.* [1966] 2 N.S.W.R. 211; *Bartlett v. Barclays Bank Trust Co. Ltd. (Nos. 1 and 2)* [1980] Ch. 515. Thus the common law rules of remoteness of damage and causation do not apply. However there does have to be some causal connection between the breach of trust and the loss to the trust estate for which compensation is recoverable viz. the fact that the loss would not have occurred but for the breach: see also *In re Miller's Deed Trusts* (1978) 75 L.S.G. 454; *Nestle v. National Westminster Bank Plc.* [1993] 1 W.L.R. 1260.

Hitherto I have been considering the rights of beneficiaries under traditional trusts where the trusts are still subsisting and therefore the right of each beneficiary, and his only right, is to have the trust fund reconstituted as it should be. But what if at the time of the action claiming compensation for breach of trust those trusts have come to an end. Take as an example again the trust for A for life with remainder to B. During A's lifetime B's only right is to have the trust duly administered and, in the event of a breach, to have the trust fund restored. After A's death, B becomes absolutely entitled. He of course has the right to have the trust assets retained by the trustees until they have fully accounted for them to him. But if the trustees commit a breach of trust, there is no reason for compensating the breach of trust by way of an order for restitution and compensation to the trust fund as opposed to the beneficiary himself. The beneficiary's right is no longer simply to have the trust duly administered: he is, in equity, the sole owner of the trust estate. Nor, for the same reason, is restitution to the trust fund necessary to protect other beneficiaries. Therefore, although I do not wholly rule out the possibility that even in those circumstances an order to reconstitute the fund may be appropriate, in the ordinary case where a beneficiary becomes absolutely entitled to the trust fund the court orders, not restitution to the trust estate, but the payment of compensation directly to the beneficiary. The measure of such compensation is the same i.e. the difference between what the beneficiary has in fact received and the amount he would have received but for the breach of trust.

...

Argument A

As I have said, the critical step in this argument is that Target is now entitled to an order for reconstitution of the trust fund by the repayment into client account of the moneys wrongly paid away, so that Target can now demand immediate repayment of the whole of such moneys without regard to the real loss it has suffered by reason of the breach.

Even if the equitable rules developed in relation to traditional trusts were directly applicable to such a case as this, as I have sought to show a beneficiary becoming absolutely entitled to a trust fund has no automatic right to have the fund reconstituted in all circumstances. Thus, even applying the strict rules so developed in relation to tradition trusts, it seems to me very doubtful whether Target is now entitled to have the trust fund reconstituted. But in my judgment it is in any event wrong to lift wholesale the detailed rules developed in the context of traditional trusts and then seek to apply them to trusts of quite a different kind. In the modern world the trust has become a valuable device in commercial and financial dealings. The fundamental principles of equity apply as much to such trusts as they do to the traditional trusts in relation to which those principles were originally formulated. But in my judgment it is important, if the trust is not to be rendered commercially useless, to distinguish between the basic principles of trust law and those specialist rules developed in relation to traditional trusts which are applicable only to such trusts and the rationale of which has no application to trusts of quite a different kind.

This case is concerned with a trust which has at all times been a bare trust. Bare trusts arise in a number of different contexts: e.g. by the ultimate vesting of the property under a traditional trust, nominee shareholdings and, as in the present case, as but one incident of a wider commercial transaction involving agency. In the case of moneys paid to a solicitor by a client as part of a conveyancing transaction, the purpose of that transaction is to achieve the commercial objective of the client, be it the acquisition of property or the lending of money on security. The depositing of money with the solicitor is but one aspect of the arrangements between the parties, such arrangements being for the most part contractual. Thus, the circumstances under which the solicitor can part with money from client account are regulated by the instructions given by the client: they are not part of the trusts on which the property is held. I do not intend to cast any doubt on the fact that moneys held by solicitors on client account are trust moneys or that the basic equitable principles apply to any breach of such trust by solicitors. But the basic equitable principle applicable to breach of trust is that the beneficiary is entitled to be compensated for any loss he would not have suffered but for the breach. I have no doubt that, until the underlying commercial transaction has been completed, the solicitor can be required to restore to client account moneys wrongly paid away. But to import into such trust an obligation to restore the trust fund once the transaction has been completed would be entirely artificial. The obligation to reconstitute the trust fund applicable in the case of traditional trusts reflects the fact that no one beneficiary is entitled to the trust property and the need to compensate all beneficiaries for the breach. That rationale has no application to a case such as the present. To impose such an obligation in order to enable the beneficiary solely entitled (i.e. the client) to recover from the solicitor more than the client has in fact lost flies in the face of common sense and is in direct conflict with the basic principles of equitable compensation. In my judgment, once a conveyancing transaction has been completed the client has no right to have the solicitor's client account reconstituted as a 'trust fund'.

Argument B

The key point in the reasoning of the Court of Appeal is that where moneys are paid away to a stranger in breach of trust, an immediate loss is suffered by the trust estate: as a result, subsequent events reducing that loss are irrelevant. They drew a distinction between the case in which the breach of trust consisted of some failure in the administration of the trust and the case where a trustee has actually paid away trust moneys to a stranger. There is no doubt that in the former case, one waits to see what loss is in fact suffered by reason of the breach i.e. the restitution or compensation payable is assessed at the date of trial, not of breach. However, the Court of Appeal considered that where the breach consisted of paying away the trust moneys to a stranger it made no sense to wait: it seemed to Peter Gibson L.J. [1994] 1 W.L.R. 1089, 1103G-H obvious that in such a case 'there is an immediate loss, placing the trustee under an immediate duty to restore the moneys to the trust fund'. The majority of the Court of Appeal therefore considered that subsequent events which diminished the loss in fact suffered were irrelevant, save for imposing on the compensated beneficiary an obligation to give credit for any benefit he subsequently received. In effect, in the view of the Court of Appeal one 'stops the clock' at the date the moneys are paid away: events which occur between the date of breach and the date of trial are irrelevant in assessing the loss suffered by reason of the breach.

A trustee who wrongly pays away trust money, like a trustee who makes an unauthorised investment, commits a breach of trust and comes under an immediate duty to remedy such breach. If immediate proceedings are brought, the court will make an immediate order requiring restoration to the trust fund of the assets wrongly distributed or, in the case of an unauthorised investment, will order the sale of the unauthorised investment and the payment of compensation for any loss suffered. But the fact that there is an accrued cause of action as soon as the breach is committed does not in my judgment mean that the quantum of the compensation payable is ultimately fixed as at the date when the breach occurred. The quantum is fixed at the date of judgment at which date, according to the circumstances then pertaining, the compensation is assessed at the figure then necessary to put the trust estate or the beneficiary back into the position it would have been in had there been no breach. I can see no justification for 'stopping the clock' immediately in some cases but not in others: to do so may, as in this case, lead to compensating the trust estate or the beneficiary for a loss which, on the facts known at trial, it has never suffered.

…

In *Canson Enterprises Ltd. v. Boughton and Co.* (1991) 85 D.L.R. (4th) 129 the plaintiffs had bought some property in a transaction in which they were advised by the defendant, a solicitor. To the knowledge of the solicitor, but not of the plaintiffs, there was an improper profit being made by the vendors. If the plaintiffs had known that fact, they would not have completed the purchase. The defendant's solicitor was in breach of his fiduciary duties to the plaintiffs. After completion the plaintiffs built a warehouse on the property, which due to the negligence of engineers and builders, was defective. The question was whether the defendant solicitor was liable to compensate the plaintiffs for the defective building, the plaintiffs contending that 'but for' the defendant's breach of fiduciary duty they would not have bought the property and therefore would not have built the warehouse. Although the Supreme Court of Canada were unanimous in dismissing the claim, they reached their conclusions by two differing routes. The majority considered that damages for breach of fiduciary duty fell to be measured by analogy with common law rules of remoteness, whereas the minority considered that the equitable principles of compensation applied. Your Lordships are not required to choose between those two views. But the judgment of McLachlin J. (expressing the minority view) contains an illuminating exposition of the rules applicable to equitable compensation for breach of trust. Although the whole judgment deserves study, I extract the following statements (at pp. 160C, 162E and 163E):

> 'While foreseeability of loss does not enter into the calculation of compensation for breach of fiduciary duty, liability is not unlimited. Just as restitution in specie is limited to the property under the trustee's control, so equitable compensation must be limited to loss flowing from the trustee's acts in relation to the interest he undertook to protect. Thus, Davidson states "It is imperative to ascertain the loss resulting from breach of the relevant equitable duty"' (at p. 354, emphasis added)

…

> 'A related question which must be addressed is the time of assessment of the loss. In this area tort and contract law are of little help…. The basis of compensation at equity, by contrast, is the restoration of the actual value of the thing lost through the breach. The foreseeable value of the items is not in issue. As a result, the losses are to be assessed as at the time of trial, using the full benefit of hindsight.' (emphasis added).

…

> 'In summary, compensation is an equitable monetary remedy which is available when the equitable remedies of restitution and account are not appropriate. By analogy with restitution, it attempts to restore to the plaintiff what has been lost as a result of the breach, i.e., the plaintiffs loss of opportunity. The plaintiffs actual loss as a consequence of the breach is to be assessed with the full benefit of hindsight. Foreseeability is not a concern in assessing

> compensation, but it is essential that the losses made good are only those which, on a common sense view of causation, were caused by the breach.' (emphasis added).
>
> In my view this is good law. Equitable compensation for breach of trust is designed to achieve exactly what the word compensation suggests: to make good a loss in fact suffered by the beneficiaries and which, using hindsight and common sense, can be seen to have been caused by the breach.

The judgment in *Target* is very significant, and there is much of interest in the long extract given above. In overturning the decision of the Court of Appeal, the House of Lords placed great emphasis upon whether or not the trustee's breach of duty had caused the beneficiary any loss. Some important aspects and criticisms of the reasoning of Lord Browne-Wilkinson will now be addressed.

(i) Traditional and commercial trusts

Lord Browne-Wilkinson distinguished 'traditional' trusts and 'commercial' trusts in his speech. His Lordship saw the force in requiring the trustees to restore the fund of a 'traditional' trust where there are a number of beneficiaries and the trust continues to exist. But for bare trusts arising in a commercial context, Lord Browne-Wilkinson did not think that the same approach should necessarily apply: once the underlying commercial transaction has been completed, there is no longer any need to reconstitute the trust fund because the trust has ended, and the trustee is only under an obligation to compensate the beneficiary for any losses suffered.

This distinction between traditional and commercial trusts was described by Nolan as:[62]

> novel, though not unreasonable: there are arguments for and against. One might say that those engaged in commerce, who vest property in a nominee so that the nominee can deal with it on behalf of the beneficial owner, should not necessarily be able to look to the nominee as, in effect, a guarantor of the integrity of the fund. If the nominee and his beneficiary actually intend such onerous duties to fall on the nominee, there is no reason why the law should not give effect to their wishes. If, though, the arrangement between the parties is silent on the matter, then the law is not so wrong to treat the arrangement as being in substance, if not in form, more akin to agency than to other instances of trusteeship, so that the duties of a nominee are more like those of an agent than those of an active trustee. In reply, however, it might be argued that, if a person has seen fit to vest an asset in a nominee, he should have the same protection as any other beneficiary of a trust. Furthermore, where the trusts of a settlement have become exhausted, leaving one person beneficially entitled to a trust fund, why should his rights, and so also the duties of his trustee, suddenly become different from those subsisting before the fund vested in him absolutely?

This last point raised is, perhaps, telling. Indeed, Lord Millett has, extra-judicially, been emphatic that the distinction drawn between 'traditional' and 'commercial' trusts is unhelpful.

Lord Millett, 'Equity's Place in the Law of Commerce' (1998) 114 LQR 224, 225

> It is impossible to dissent from the proposition that equity is flexible and that circumstances alter cases. It is also true that, as Lord Browne-Wilkinson pointed out, the circumstances in which the solicitor was entitled to part with his client's money were regulated by the client's instructions and were not part of

---

[62] 'A Targeted Degree of Liability' [1996] LMCLQ 161, 162.

the trusts on which the money was held. This is plainly correct. The only trust was a bare trust for the client; its instructions were superimposed on that trust. It was a form of *Quistclose* trust.[63] But nothing turns on this, except that it made the instructions revocable. Application of trust money in such circumstances otherwise than in accordance with the unrevoked instructions of the beneficial owner is still a breach of trust. Likewise trustee investment powers are not part of the trusts on which trust money is held, but an unauthorised investment of trust money is still a breach of trust.

But what is the specialist rule applicable only to family trusts which excludes the principle limiting the amount of recoverable compensation to the loss actually occasioned by the breach? If there is such a rule it must be of general application. Is it seriously to be supposed that the result in *Target Holdings Ltd v Redferns* would have been different if the trust in question had been a traditional trust? Suppose trustees of a family settlement with power to invest on mortgage decide to do so, but negligently part with the trust money without obtaining the executed mortgage and title deeds in exchange. Suppose, too, that a few days later they do obtain the necessary documents. And suppose that the property has been overvalued and the investment proves to be a bad one. Is it seriously suggested that the trustees are to be held liable for anything more than a few days' loss of interest?

It is unclear why the equitable principles should differ to any significant degree between so-called 'traditional' trusts and 'commercial' trusts. It is suggested that this distinction is artificial and unhelpful. Indeed, in *Youyang Pty Ltd v Minter Ellison Morris Fletcher*,[64] the High Court of Australia suggested that such a divide was unnecessary. The case was similar to *Target*: Minters were solicitors who held money on trust for Youyang, but in breach of trust released money to a company called ECCCL before obtaining the stipulated bearer deposit certificate. The High Court said that:[65]

the creation of the trust in favour of Youyang was not an end in itself; the terms of the trust which bound Minters were concerned with the application of the trust moneys in completion of a larger commercial transaction with Youyang and Minters' client, ECCCL, as the principal actors. To acknowledge that situation is not necessarily to embrace any theory of reductionism whereby, notwithstanding the rigour of the rule requiring observance of the terms of the trust, in certain events 'commercial' trusts do not provide for their beneficiaries the full panoply of personal and proprietary rights and remedies designed by equity: cf Austin, 'Moulding the Content of Fiduciary Duties', in Oakley (ed), *Trends in Contemporary Trust Law*, (1996) 153 at 167–168. Rather, it emphasises that, in the administration of the pecuniary remedy Youyang seeks for misapplication of its funds by Minters, regard should be had to the scope and purpose of the trust which bound Minters.

It is right not to deprive all beneficiaries under 'commercial' trusts of the full range of rights and remedies afforded by Equity in the context of trust relationships. Concentrating upon the scope and purpose of the trust seems preferable. On this basis, if a commercial trust continues to exist and the fund is held for the benefit of beneficiaries, then the fact that it is 'commercial' rather than 'traditional' should not prevent the beneficiaries from seeking the reconstitution of the trust fund. And conversely, where a 'traditional' trust has come to an end—for example, because the beneficiary is absolutely entitled to the property and the trustee ceases to manage the fund—the same consequences should ensue as where a 'commercial' trust ceases to exist because the commercial transaction has occurred.

In this latter scenario, the decision in *Target* suggests that the appropriate claim is for equitable compensation: the trustee should compensate the beneficiary for any loss suffered. This is because

---

[63] See Chapter 8.5, p. 410.
[64] (2003) 196 ALR 482.
[65] Ibid, [49].

there no longer exists a trust the fund of which can be reconstituted. However, the fact that there is no longer property in a trust fund might not *necessarily* mean that the taking of an account should be impossible. After all, it seems sensible for a beneficiary to be able to take an account of a trust that previously existed in order to ascertain that there was no impropriety regarding the management of the trust fund; past breaches should not be remedied any differently simply because the trustees no longer have stewardship over the fund. Subsequent falsification (or surcharge) might, therefore, ensure that, in effect, the trust was always administered properly.

In *AIB v Redler*, Lord Toulson explained the relevance of 'commercial' and 'traditional' trusts as follows:[66]

> As to the criticism of the passage in *Target Holdings* where Lord Browne-Wilkinson said that it would be 'wrong to lift wholesale the detailed rules developed in the context of traditional trusts' and apply them to a bare trust which was 'but one incident of a wider commercial transaction involving agency', it is a fact that a commercial trust differs from a typical traditional trust in that it arises out of a contract rather than the transfer of property by way of gift. The contract defines the parameters of the trust. Trusts are now commonly part of the machinery used in many commercial transactions, for example across the spectrum of wholesale financial markets, where they serve a useful bridging role between the parties involved. Commercial trusts may differ widely in their purpose and content, but they have in common that the trustee's duties are likely to be closely defined and may be of limited duration. Lord Browne-Wilkinson did not suggest that the principles of equity differ according to the nature of the trust, but rather that the scope and purpose of the trust may vary, and this may have a bearing on the appropriate relief in the event of a breach. Specifically, Lord Browne-Wilkinson stated that he did not cast doubt on the fact that monies held by solicitors on client account are trust monies, or that basic equitable principles apply to any breach of such trust by solicitors. What he did was to identify the basic equitable principles. In their application, the terms of the contract may be highly relevant to the question of fact whether there has been a loss applying a 'but for' test, that is, by reference to what the solicitors were instructed to do. If the answer is negative, the solicitors should not be required to pay restitutive monetary compensation when there has in fact been no loss resulting from their breach. That is not because special rules apply to solicitors, but because proper performance of the trustee's obligations to the beneficiary would have produced the same end result.
>
> I agree with the view of Professor David Hayton, in his chapter 'Unique Rules for the Unique Institution, the Trust' in Degeling & Edelman (eds), *Equity in Commercial Law* (2005), pp 279-308, that in circumstances such as those in *Target Holdings* the extent of equitable compensation should be the same as if damages for breach of contract were sought at common law. That is not because there should be a departure in such a case from the basic equitable principles applicable to a breach of trust, whether by a solicitor or anyone else. (If there were a conflict between the rules of equity and the rules of the common law, the rules of equity would prevail by reason of section 49(1) of the Senior Courts Act 1981, derived from the provisions of the Judicature Act 1875.) Rather, the fact that the trust was part of the machinery for the performance of a contract is relevant as a fact in looking at what loss the bank suffered by reason of the breach of trust, because it would be artificial and unreal to look at the trust in isolation from the obligations for which it was brought into being. I do not believe that this requires any departure from proper principles.

Similarly, Lord Reed said:[67]

> That is not to say that there is a categorical distinction between trusts in commercial and non-commercial relationships, or to assert that there are trusts to which the fundamental principles of equity do

---

[66] [2014] UKSC 58; [2015] AC 1503, [70]–[71].
[67] Ibid, [102].

> not apply. It is, on the other hand, to recognise that the duties and liabilities of trustees may depend, in some respects, upon the terms of the trust in question and the relationship between the relevant parties

This highlights the importance of the contract which creates a trust in these instances of 'commercial' bare trust. The contract appears to influence the scope of the trustee's obligations, but this does not mean that the remedies should differ as between traditional and commercial trusts, however they are defined. This will be further examined later when considering the impact of the decision in *AIB*.[68]

(ii) *Compensation for breach of trust*

In *Target*, the House of Lords disagreed with the Court of Appeal's conclusion that where a trustee commits a breach of duty the claim for compensation crystallizes and can be quantified straight away. Lord Browne-Wilkinson explained that the breach of trust does not 'stop the clock'.

Indeed, this is an important difference between the general approach adopted at Common Law: damages at Common Law are generally assessed at the date of breach.[69] Moreover, whilst a breach of contract may well terminate a contractual relationship between the parties,[70] a breach of trust cannot simply put an end to the defendant's role as trustee. Equity insists that the trustee acts as a 'good person' and in the best interests of the beneficiaries. Since the trustee cannot walk away from the trust, there is no reason to 'stop the clock' at the date of breach.

The fact that the clock does not stop has two very important consequences. First, it means that the defendant continues to exercise the powers and duties of a trustee. So, in *Target*, this meant that when Redferns later received the mortgage documents, it was able to accept them on behalf of and for the benefit of the beneficiary, Target. But such an analysis suggests that the trust did not simply end upon the advancement of the mortgage monies and may be inconsistent with parts of Lord Browne-Wilkinson's analysis. Secondly, it means that any losses that form the subject of a claim need to be assessed at the date of judgment rather than the date of breach. Since the value of the claim is assessed at the date of judgment, it is at that point that the claimant must be able to establish loss. If the claimant is unable to show any loss, then he or she will not be able to recover equitable compensation. However, it should be remembered that even if the beneficiary has suffered no loss, a gains-based remedy may still be available against a trustee who has personally profited from a breach of duty.[71]

Lord Browne-Wilkinson appeared to require a 'but-for' test of causation for loss, and drew upon Common Law ideas in support. Lord Millett was critical of this approach, commenting that Lord Browne-Wilkinson:[72]

> proceeds to speak exclusively in terms of causation, introducing the 'but for' test while at the same time rejecting other tests of causation and remoteness of damage which have been adopted by the common law. This fails to explain why the trustee's liability is strict, or why equity should not adopt the common law rules of causation and remoteness *in toto*.

---

[68] Chapter 17.3(a)(ii), immediately below.

[69] With some exceptions: see the discussion in *Golden Strait Corporation v Nippon Yusen KK (The Golden Victory)* [2007] UKHL 12; [2007] 2 AC 353.

[70] For termination, see generally McKendrick, *Contract Law: Text, Cases and Materials* (5th edn) (Oxford: Oxford University Press, 2012), ch. 22.

[71] See Chapter 14.5, p. 704.

[72] 'Equity's Place in the Law of Commerce' (1998) 114 LQR 214, 225.

Where the trustee has breached a non-fiduciary duty of care and the claimants seek to recover losses flowing from the breach (in the context of surcharge), it might seem sensible to draw upon rules on causation and remoteness developed at Common Law. However, the distinction drawn above in the context of the taking of an account seems important: where the beneficiary seeks to enforce the performance of the trustees' primary duties through 'falsification', issues of remoteness simply do not arise; but remoteness is relevant to claims for 'surcharge'.[73]

The approach of Lord Browne-Wilkinson has given rise to much controversy and discussion. The utility of such a 'fusionist' approach in this area was brought to the fore in the decision of the Supreme Court in *AIB v Redler*, examined immediately below. However, it is important to note that some of the stepping-stones used in the reasoning of Lord Browne-Wilkinson are perhaps somewhat shaky. For example, his Lordship did not even mention the word 'falsify', and instead relied upon cases concerned with surcharge[74] or breach of fiduciary duty[75] in support of his conclusion that the only remedy open to Target was 'equitable compensation'.[76] This seems to be a significant departure from the traditional approach, and if correct should preferably have been explicitly made as a conscious choice. Indeed, although Lord Browne-Wilkinson cited the decision of the Supreme Court of Canada in *Canson Enterprises Ltd v Boughton and Co.*[77] in support of a single concept of 'equitable compensation', this may have been based upon a misreading of *Canson*. Edelman and Elliott[78] have shown that:

> both the majority and concurring judges in *Canson Enterprises* began with the idea that equitable compensation in a case of misapplied trust property is substitutive in nature, but differed in their characterisation of equitable compensation in a case that does not involve trust property. It is for this reason an irony of Lord Browne-Wilkinson's speech in *Target Holdings Ltd v Redferns* that he took *Canson Enterprises* as his authority for the proposition that equitable compensation in a case of misapplied trust property is reparative in nature.

However, such difficulties do not necessarily mean that the result in *Target* is incorrect. Indeed, the same result might be reached by applying the principles of falsification, without invoking difficult concepts such as 'equitable compensation'.

This appears to have been recognized by the majority of the Court of Appeal in *Target*. For example, Peter Gibson LJ said:[79]

> It is not in dispute or in doubt that the obligation of a trustee who commits a breach of trust is to account for and restore to the trust fund that which has thereby been lost to it. The remedy afforded to the beneficiary by equity is compensation in the form of restitution of that which has been lost to the trust estate, not damages.

However, the majority of the Court of Appeal used this approach to justify the beneficiary's recovering over £1 million, because it decided that the value of the claim crystallized at the date of breach. This was incorrect, since the value of a claim should only be assessed at the date of judgment.[80] At this later

---

[73] See e.g. Elliott, 'Remoteness Criteria in Equity' (2002) 65 MLR 588.

[74] Eg *Nestlé v National Westminster Bank Plc* [1993] 1 WLR 1260; *Bartlett* v *Barclays Bank Trust Co. Ltd. (Nos. 1 and 2)* [1980] Ch 515.

[75] Notably *Canson Enterprises Ltd* v *Boughton & Co* (1991) 85 DLR (4th) 129.

[76] See e.g. Mitchell 'Equitable Compensation for Breach of Fiduciary Duty' (2013) 66 CLP 307, 323–327.

[77] (1991) 85 DLR (4th) 129.

[78] 'Money Remedies Against Trustees' (2004) 18 TLI 116, 124.

[79] [1994] 1 WLR 1089, 1101. Admittedly, the language of 'compensation' in the form of restitution is difficult: see Chapter 1.4(b), p. 13.

[80] Chapter 17.3(a)(ii), p. 818.

date, it could not be established that any loss had arisen from the breach. The taking of an account may therefore still provide an entirely satisfactory route to the result achieved by the House of Lords in *Target*. As Lord Millett has explained subsequently:[81]

> The solicitor held the plaintiff's money in trust for the plaintiff but with its authority to lay it out in exchange for an executed mortgage and the documents of title. He paid it away without obtaining these documents. This was an unauthorised application of trust money which entitled the plaintiff to falsify the account. The disbursement must be disallowed and the solicitor treated as accountable as if the money were still in his client account and available to be laid out in the manner directed. It was later so laid out. The plaintiff could not object to the acquisition of the mortgage or the disbursement by which it was obtained; it was an authorised application of what must be treated as trust money notionally restored to the trust estate on the taking of the account. To put the point another way; the trustee's obligation to restore the trust property is not an obligation to restore it in the very form in which he disbursed it, but an obligation to restore it in any form authorised by the trust.

This analysis is both important and convincing. Given that there was no stopping of the clock, Redferns continued to be able to act on behalf of Target. So, when Redferns received the mortgage documents, it did so for the benefit of Target as beneficiary of the trust. This meant that when Target later came to take an account, there was nothing that could meaningfully be falsified: at the date of judgment, the account showed the trust fund to be in its intended position. This is because the fund would be expected to contain either the money to be loaned, or the mortgage documents. Target had authorized Redferns to hold either. Target had no claim against Redferns, because the latter had already legitimately restored the trust fund to its appropriate position, and, since Target had not revoked its instructions, it could not demand that the trust comprise of the money itself rather than the mortgage documents.

This reasoning has been criticized by Edelman:[82]

> Lord Millett's rationalisation is not a satisfactory basis for justifying the result in *Target Holdings* on equity's traditional approach. The trust money was paid out in an unauthorised manner. When the mortgage was later acquired this did not retrospectively turn an unauthorised application of funds into an authorised one. At least, it could not do so without ratification or waiver by Target Holdings. The moment Redferns paid out the money without having first obtained the mortgage they came under a duty to reimburse the trust fund. When they later obtained the mortgage, Target Holdings could have refused to accept the mortgage. Any explanation of the result in *Target* needs to acknowledge that the unauthorised transaction had not been immediately cured.

However, it is suggested that such criticism is insufficient to undermine Lord Millett's analysis. Edelman focuses only on the initial disbursement of the money in breach of duty, and not on the subsequent receipt of the mortgage documents for which the trustee still had authority. As Conaglen has explained in defence of Lord Millett's explanation for *Target*, and in response to Edelman's objections:[83]

> The original disbursement was unauthorised when it was made, and remained so when the parties came to court. The point is not that the disbursement was ever authorised, but rather that the trustee's conduct subsequent to that unauthorised disbursement was itself authorised and therefore

---

[81] 'Equity's Place in the Law of Commerce' (1998) 114 LQR 214, 227.
[82] 'Money Awards of the Cost of Performance' (2010) 4 JoE 122, 128.
[83] 'Explaining *Target Holdings v Redferns*' (2010) 4 JoE 288, 300.

> needed to be reflected in the accounts. The trust accounts are an account of the trustee's stewardship of the entire fund, rather than the tale of a specific breach of trust. The earlier disbursement of funds without receipt of the mortgage documents could still be falsified when the accounts were taken, because it was made without authority. But the important point is that the receipt of the mortgage charges could not be falsified unless it too was made without authority, which was not the case in *Target Holdings*. Further, there was no basis on which the beneficiary could expect the trustee to receive the mortgages without releasing the mortgage funds to the mortgagor. Thus, if the receipt of the mortgages could not be falsified, then the trust beneficiaries would have to accept the trust accounts being drawn as if the mortgage funds had been released to the mortgagor at the time when the mortgages were received.

Thus the initial disbursement was never anything other than unauthorized, but its effect was neutralized by the subsequent, authorized receipt of the mortgage certificates.

Nevertheless, favouring the approach of Lord Millett does not necessarily mean that other interpretations might not lead to the same result. For example, as suggested in the short extract given earlier, Edelman has argued that waiver might explain the result in *Target*. It may be that Target waived its strict rights against Redferns, and was thereby prevented from later changing its mind and seeking substantial relief. However, this explanation was not raised by the House of Lords in the case itself, and it is unclear whether Target really waived its rights once it knew of the breach of trust.[84] Nevertheless, it is certainly appropriate to consider waiver wherever it arises.

Be that as it may, Lord Millett's traditional analysis was rejected by the Supreme Court in *AIB v Redler*, which upheld the key pillars of the reasoning in *Target*.

(b) AIB GROUP (UK) PLC V MARK REDLER & CO

AIB Group (UK) Plc v Mark Redler & Co [2014] UKSC 58; [2015] AC 1503

Mark Redler & Co ('Redler') is a firm of solicitors which was retained to act for both the Sondhi family and AIB, a Bank, on the re-mortgage of the Sondhis' family home. AIB advanced £3.3 million to Redler for this purpose. The letter of instruction incorporated the Council of Mortgage Lenders' Handbook for England and Wales,[85] by virtue of which the mortgage lender required a fully enforceable first charge over the property and for all existing charges to be redeemed on or before completion. The handbook also stated: 'You [Redler] must hold the loan on trust for us [AIB] until completion. If completion is delayed, you must return it to us when and how we tell you'.

The Sondhis' property was already subject to a charge in favour of Barclays Bank Plc ('Barclays'). The Barclays charge secured borrowings of about £1.5 million on two accounts. Unfortunately, Redler only paid to Barclays enough money to pay off one of the two accounts (about £1.2 million), which was insufficient to redeem the Barclays charge. Just over £300,000 remained outstanding, and Barclays refused to release its charge unless the debt was paid in full. The borrowers, who had received the balance of the £3.3 million, initially promised to do so, but never did. Redler tried to resolve its error without involving AIB, but eventually told the bank of the breach of duty; AIB then negotiated directly with Barclays, and AIB's charge was registered as a second charge.

[84] There does not seem to have been any delay after the beneficiary became aware of the breach of trust, which would have been necessary for any equitable doctrine of delay to bar a claim. See further Chapter 16.10, pp. 793–6.
[85] http://www.cml.org.uk/cml/handbook.

The Sondhis subsequently defaulted on the loan and declared bankruptcy. The property was sold by Barclays for £1.2 million. AIB as second chargee received £867, 697.

By paying away the mortgage monies without obtaining a first legal charge over the property, Redler acted in breach of trust.[86] AIB argued that completion had not yet occurred, so Redler remained under a duty to hold the mortgage advance on trust for AIB; AIB therefore sought £3.3 million in order to reconstitute the trust fund.[87] Redler, on the other hand, argued that its liability should be limited to the difference in value of the bank's security caused by Redler's failure to pay off the entirety of the Barclays charge: this was only around £300,000 (the sum received by Barclays as first chargee).

Redler's argument succeeded at every level. A unanimous Supreme Court[88] insisted that a causal link between Redler's breach of duty and AIB's loss needed to be established, regardless of whether the claim was brought at Common Law or in Equity.

Lord Toulson:

The debate which has followed *Target Holdings* is part of a wider debate, or series of debates, about equitable doctrines and remedies and their inter-relationship with common law principles and remedies, particularly in a commercial context. The parties have provided the court with nearly 900 pages of academic writing. Much of it has been helpful, but to attempt even to summarise the many threads of argument which run through it, acknowledging the individual authors, would be a lengthy task and, more importantly, would not improve the clarity of the judgment. Nor is it necessary to set out a full historical account of all the case law cited in the literature reaching back to *Caffrey v Darby* (1801) 6 Ves Jun 488.

In the present case the solicitors owed a compendium of duties to the bank. Their relationship was governed by a contract but they held the money advanced by the bank on trust for the purpose of performing their contractual obligations. They broke their contract and acted in breach of trust when they released to the borrowers the money advanced by the bank, less a part of the sum required to redeem the Barclays mortgage, when they should have paid to Barclays the full amount required for that purpose, in return for an undertaking to issue a redemption certificate, and should have released the diminished balance to the borrowers.

The determination of this appeal involves two essential questions. The more important question in the appeal is whether Lord Browne-Wilkinson's statement in *Target Holdings* of the fundamental principles which guided him in that case should be affirmed, qualified or (as the bank would put it) reinterpreted. Depending on the answer to that question, the second is whether the Court of Appeal properly applied the correct principles to the facts of the case.

Two main criticisms have been made of Lord Browne-Wilkinson's approach. They have been made by a number of scholars, most recently by Professor Charles Mitchell in a lecture on 'Stewardship of Property and Liability to Account' delivered to the Chancery Bar Association on 17 January 2014, in which he described the Court of Appeal's reasoning in this case as incoherent. He expressed the hope that 'if the case reaches the Supreme Court their Lordships will recognise that Lord Browne-Wilkinson took a false step in *Target* when he introduced an inapt causation requirement into the law governing … substitutive performance claims.' He added that if it is thought too harsh to fix the solicitors in this case with liability to restore the full amount of the loan (subject only to a deduction for the amount received by the sale of the property), the best way to achieve this is 'not to bend the rules governing substitutive performance claims out of shape', but to use the Trustee Act 1925, section 61, to relieve them from some or all of their liability.

---

[86] Lord Reed was attracted ([2014] UKSC 58; [2015] AC 1503, [140]) by the idea that the breach of trust only involved the misapplication of the £309,000 paid to the Sondhis rather than Barclays, but this had been rejected by the Court of Appeal and was not challenged in the Supreme Court: the breach of trust was paying away the entire £3.3 million.

[87] Strictly the claim was for £3.3 million minus the £867,697 actually received from the sale of the property.

[88] Lord Toulson and Lord Reed gave reasoned speeches; Lord Neuberger, Lady Hale, and Lord Wilson agreed with both speeches.

The primary criticism is that Lord Browne-Wilkinson failed to recognise the proper distinctions between different obligations owed by a trustee and the remedies available in respect of them. The range of duties owed by a trustee include:

(1) a custodial stewardship duty, that is, a duty to preserve the assets of the trust except insofar as the terms of the trust permit the trustee to do otherwise;

(2) a management stewardship duty, that is, a duty to manage the trust property with proper care;

(3) a duty of undivided loyalty, which prohibits the trustee from taking any advantage from his position without the fully informed consent of the beneficiary or beneficiaries.

Historically the remedies took the form of orders made after a process of accounting. The basis of the accounting would reflect the nature of the obligation. The operation of the process involved the court having a power, where appropriate, to 'falsify' and to 'surcharge'.

According to legal scholars whose scholarship I have no reason to doubt, in the case of a breach of the custodial stewardship duty, through the process of an account of administration in common form, the court would disallow (or falsify) the unauthorised disposal and either require the trust fund to be reconstituted in specie or order the trustee to make good the loss in monetary terms. The term 'substitutive compensation' " has come to be used by some to refer to a claim for the value of a trust asset dissipated without authority. (See the erudite judgment in *Agricultural Land Management Ltd v Jackson (No 2)* [2014] WASC 102 of Edelman J, who attributes authorship of the term to Dr Steven Elliott.)

In a case of breach of a trustee's management stewardship duty, through the process of an action on the basis of wilful default, a court could similarly falsify or surcharge so as to require the trustee to make good the loss resulting from the breach. The phrase 'wilful default' is misleading because, as Brightman LJ explained in *Bartlett v Barclays Bank Trust Co Ltd (Nos 1 and 2)* [1980] Ch 515, 546, conscious wrongdoing is not required. In this type of case the order for payment by the trustee of the amount of loss is referred to by some as 'reparative compensation', to differentiate it from 'substitutive compensation', although in a practical sense both are reparative compensation.

In a case of breach of the duty of undivided loyalty, there are possible alternative remedies. If the trustee has benefited from it, the court will order him to account for it on the application of the beneficiary. In *Bristol and West Building Society v Mothew* [1998] Ch 1 Millett LJ described such relief as 'primarily restitutionary or restorative rather than compensatory'. Alternatively, the beneficiary may seek compensation in respect of his loss.

The history of the account of profits is more complex than this summary might suggest, and the whole concept of equitable compensation has developed and become far more prominent in the law since *Nocton v Lord Ashburton*. However, what I have said is sufficient to identify the main criticism advanced against Lord Browne-Wilkinson's approach in *Target Holdings*. It is said that he treated equitable compensation in too broad-brush a fashion, muddling claims for restitutive compensation with claims for reparative compensation.

The relevant principle, it is suggested, in a case of unauthorised dissipation of trust funds is that 'the amount of the award is measured by the objective value of the property lost, determined at the date when the account is taken and with the benefit of hindsight', per Millett NPJ in *Libertarian Investments Ltd v Hall* [2014] 1 HKC 368, para 168. In determining the value of what has been lost, the court must take into account any offsetting benefits received, but it is not relevant to consider what the trustee ought to have done. The court is concerned only with the net value of the lost asset.

This argument has the approval of Edelman J in *Agricultural Land Management Ltd v Jackson (No2)*, and there are statements in the authorities cited by him which support that approach, for example, by Lord Halsbury LC in *Magnus v Queensland National Bank* (1888) 37 Ch D, at paras 466, 472, although the issue in that case was different. The defendant advanced an argument which Bowen LJ, at para

480, likened to a case where 'A man knocks me down in Pall Mall, and when I complain that my purse has been taken, the man says, "Oh, but if I had handed it back again, you would have been robbed over again by somebody else in the adjoining street."' It is good sense and good law that if a trustee makes an unauthorised disbursement of trust funds, it is no defence to a claim by the beneficiary for the trustee to say that if he had not misapplied the funds they would have been stolen by a stranger. In such a case the actual loss has been caused by the trustee. The hypothetical loss which would have otherwise have occurred through the stranger's intervention would have been a differently caused loss, for which that other person would have been liable. Bowen LJ's example is far removed in terms of causation of loss from the present case, where the loan agreement involved the bank taking the risk of the borrowers defaulting, and the fault of the solicitors lay in releasing the funds without ensuring that the bank received the full security which it required, with the consequence that the amount of the bank's exposure was greater than it should have been.

In *Bank of New Zealand v New Zealand Guardian Trust Co Ltd* [1999] 1 NZLR 664 Tipping J rightly observed that while historically the law has tended to place emphasis on the legal characterisation of the relationship between the parties in delineating the remedies available for breach of an obligation, the nature of the duty which has been breached can often be more important, when considering issues of causation and remoteness, than the classification or historical source of the obligation.

Tipping J identified three broad categories of breach by a trustee. First, there are breaches of duty leading directly to damage or to loss of trust property. Secondly, there are breaches involving an element of infidelity. Thirdly, there are breaches involving a lack of appropriate skill and care. He continued at para 687:

> 'In the first kind of case the allegation is that a breach of duty by a trustee has directly caused loss of or damage to the trust property. The relief sought by the beneficiary is usually in such circumstances of a restitutionary kind. The trustee is asked to restore the trust estate, either in specie or by value. The policy of the law in these circumstances is generally to hold the trustee responsible if, but for the breach, the loss or damage would not have occurred. This approach is designed to encourage trustees to observe to the full their duties in relation to trust property by imposing on them a stringent concept of causation [i.e. a test by which a 'but for' connection is sufficient]. Questions of foreseeability and remoteness do not come into such an assessment.'

According to the bank's argument, the responsibility of the solicitors is still more stringent. It seeks to hold them responsible for loss which it would have suffered on the judge's findings if they had done what they were instructed to do. This involves effectively treating the unauthorised application of trust funds as creating an immediate debt between the trustee and the beneficiary, rather than conduct meriting equitable compensation for any loss thereby caused. I recognise that there are statements in the authorities which use that language to describe the trustee's liability. For example, in *Ex p Adamson; In re Collie* (1878) 8 Ch D 807, at paras 807, 819, James and Baggallay LJJ said that the Court of Chancery never entertained a suit for damages occasioned by fraudulent conduct or for breach of trust, and that the suit was always for 'an equitable debt, or liability in the nature of a debt'. This was long before the expression 'equitable compensation' entered the vocabulary. Equitable monetary compensation for what in that case was straightforward fraud was clothed by the court in the literary costume of equitable debt, the debt being for the amount of the loss caused by the fraud. Whatever label is used, the question of substance is what gives rise to or is the measure of the 'equitable debt or liability in the nature of a debt', or entitlement to monetary compensation, and what kind of 'but for' test is involved. It is one thing to speak of an 'equitable debt or liability in the nature of a debt' in a case where a breach of trust has caused a loss; it is another thing for equity to impose or recognise an equitable debt in circumstances where the financial position of the beneficiaries, actual or potential, would have been the same if the trustee had properly performed its duties.

Conclusion

There are arguments to be made both ways, as the continuing debate among scholars has shown, but absent fraud, which might give rise to other public policy considerations that are not present in this case, it would not in my opinion be right to impose or maintain a rule that gives redress to a beneficiary for loss which would have been suffered if the trustee had properly performed its duties.

The same view was expressed by Professor Andrew Burrows in Burrows and Peel (eds.), *Commercial Remedies*, 2003, pp 46-47, where he applauded *Target Holdings* for impliedly rejecting older cases that may have supported the view that the accounting remedy can operate differently from the remedy of equitable compensation. Despite the powerful arguments advanced by Lord Millett and others, I consider that it would be a backward step for this court to depart from Lord Browne-Wilkinson's fundamental analysis in *Target Holdings* or to 're-interpret' the decision in the manner for which the bank contends.

All agree that the basic right of a beneficiary is to have the trust duly administered in accordance with the provisions of the trust instrument, if any, and the general law. Where there has been a breach of that duty, the basic purpose of any remedy will be either to put the beneficiary in the same position as if the breach had not occurred or to vest in the beneficiary any profit which the trustee may have made by reason of the breach (and which ought therefore properly to be held on behalf of the beneficiary). Placing the beneficiary in the same position as he would have been in but for the breach may involve restoring the value of something lost by the breach or making good financial damage caused by the breach. But a monetary award which reflected neither loss caused nor profit gained by the wrongdoer would be penal.

The purpose of a restitutionary order is to replace a loss to the trust fund which the trustee has brought about. To say that there has been a loss to the trust fund in the present case of £2.5m by reason of the solicitors' conduct, when most of that sum would have been lost if the solicitors had applied the trust fund in the way that the bank had instructed them to do, is to adopt an artificial and unrealistic view of the facts.

I would reiterate Lord Browne-Wilkinson's statement, echoing McLachlin J's judgment in *Canson*, about the object of an equitable monetary remedy for breach of trust, whether it be sub-classified as substitutive or reparative. As the beneficiary is entitled to have the trust properly administered, so he is entitled to have made good any loss suffered by reason of a breach of the duty.

A traditional trust will typically govern the ownership-management of property for a group of potential beneficiaries over a lengthy number of years. If the trustee makes an unauthorised disposal of the trust property, the obvious remedy is to require him to restore the assets or their monetary value. It is likely to be the only way to put the beneficiaries in the same position as if the breach had not occurred. It is a real loss which is being made good. By contrast, in *Target Holdings* the finance company was seeking to be put in a better position on the facts (as agreed or assumed for the purposes of the summary judgment claim) than if the solicitors had done as they ought to have done.

Other considerations reinforce my view that the House of Lords did not take a wrong step in *Target Holdings*.

Most critics accept that on the assumed facts of *Target Holdings* the solicitors should have escaped liability. But if causation of loss was not required for them to be liable, some other way had to be found for exonerating them from liability (unless the court was to use section 61 of the 1925 Act as a *deus ex machina*). The solution suggested by the bank is that the solicitors in *Target Holdings* should be treated as if the moneys which had been wrongly paid out had remained in or been restored to the solicitors' client account and had then been properly applied after the solicitors had obtained the necessary paperwork. There is something wrong with a state of the law which makes it necessary to create fairy tales.

As to the criticism of the passage in *Target Holdings* where Lord Browne-Wilkinson said that it would be 'wrong to lift wholesale the detailed rules developed in the context of traditional trusts' and apply them to a bare trust which was 'but one incident of a wider commercial transaction involving agency', it is a fact that a commercial trust differs from a typical traditional trust in that it arises out of a contract rather than the transfer of property by way of gift. The contract defines the parameters of the trust. Trusts are now commonly part of the machinery used in many commercial transactions, for example across the spectrum of wholesale financial markets, where they serve a useful bridging role between the parties involved. Commercial trusts may differ widely in their purpose and content, but they have in common that the trustee's duties are likely to be closely defined and may be of limited duration. Lord Browne-Wilkinson did not suggest that the principles of equity differ according to the nature of the trust, but rather that the scope and purpose of the trust may vary, and this may have a bearing on the appropriate relief in the event of a breach. Specifically, Lord Browne-Wilkinson stated that he did not cast doubt on the fact that monies held by solicitors on client account are trust monies, or that basic equitable principles apply to any breach of such trust by solicitors. What he did was to identify the basic equitable principles. In their application, the terms of the contract may be highly relevant to the question of fact whether there has been a loss applying a 'but for' test, that is, by reference to what the solicitors were instructed to do. If the answer is negative, the solicitors should not be required to pay restitutive monetary compensation when there has in fact been no loss resulting from their breach. That is not because special rules apply to solicitors, but because proper performance of the trustee's obligations to the beneficiary would have produced the same end result.

I agree with the view of Professor David Hayton, in his chapter 'Unique Rules for the Unique Institution, the Trust' in Degeling & Edelman (eds), *Equity in Commercial Law* (2005), pp 279-308, that in circumstances such as those in *Target Holdings* the extent of equitable compensation should be the same as if damages for breach of contract were sought at common law. That is not because there should be a departure in such a case from the basic equitable principles applicable to a breach of trust, whether by a solicitor or anyone else. (If there were a conflict between the rules of equity and the rules of the common law, the rules of equity would prevail by reason of section 49(1) of the Senior Courts Act 1981, derived from the provisions of the Judicature Act 1875.) Rather, the fact that the trust was part of the machinery for the performance of a contract is relevant as a fact in looking at what loss the bank suffered by reason of the breach of trust, because it would be artificial and unreal to look at the trust in isolation from the obligations for which it was brought into being. I do not believe that this requires any departure from proper principles.

There remains the question whether the Court of Appeal properly applied the reasoning in *Target Holdings* to the facts of the present case. It was argued on behalf of the bank that this case falls within Lord Browne-Wilkinson's statement that '[u]ntil the underlying commercial transaction has been completed, the solicitor can be required to restore to the client account monies wrongly paid away.'

This argument constricts too narrowly Lord Browne-Wilkinson's essential reasoning. Monetary compensation, whether classified as restitutive or reparative, is intended to make good a loss. The basic equitable principle applicable to breach of trust, as Lord Browne-Wilkinson stated, is that the beneficiary is entitled to be compensated for any loss he would not have suffered but for the breach. In this case, proper performance of the obligations of which the trust formed part would have resulted in the solicitors paying to Barclays the full amount required to redeem the Barclays mortgage, and, as Patten LJ said, the bank would have had security for an extra £300,000 or thereabouts of its loan.

When Lord Browne-Wilkinson spoke of completion he was talking about a commercial transaction. The solicitors did not 'complete' the transaction in compliance with the requirements of the CML Handbook. But as a commercial matter the transaction was executed or 'completed' when the loan monies were released to the borrowers. At that moment the relationship between the borrowers and the bank became one of contractual borrower and lender, and that was a fait accompli. The Court of Appeal was right in the present case to understand and apply the reasoning in *Target Holdings* as it did.

The further argument advanced on behalf of the bank in this court about the Solicitors' Accounts Rules takes matters no further, for the reasons which Mr McPherson gave in his response to it. The solicitors were at fault in not reporting to the bank what they had done and in failing at that stage to remedy their breach of trust by ensuring that the shortfall was paid to Barclays. Their failure to do so was a breach of the rules, which could have disciplinary consequences but it does not affect the outcome in the present appeal. There is, as Mr McPherson submitted, no satisfactory logical reason why the question of the solicitors' liability to provide redress to the bank for a loss which it would have suffered in any event should turn on their compliance or non-compliance with their obligations under rule 7.

My analysis accords with the reasoning of Lord Reed and with his general conclusions at paragraphs 133 to 138. Equitable compensation and common law damages are remedies based on separate legal obligations. What has to be identified in each case is the content of any relevant obligation and the consequences of its breach. On the facts of the present case, the cost of restoring what the bank lost as a result of the solicitors' breach of trust comes to the same as the loss caused by the solicitors' breach of contract and negligence.

Lord Reed:

Notwithstanding some differences, there appears to be a broad measure of consensus across a number of common law jurisdictions that the correct general approach to the assessment of equitable compensation for breach of trust is that described by McLachlin J in *Canson Enterprises* and endorsed by Lord Browne-Wilkinson in *Target Holdings*. In Canada itself, McLachin J's approach appears to have gained greater acceptance in the more recent case law, and it is common ground that equitable compensation and damages for tort or breach of contract may differ where different policy objectives are applicable.

Following that approach, which I have discussed more fully at paras 90-94, the model of equitable compensation, where trust property has been misapplied, is to require the trustee to restore the trust fund to the position it would have been in if the trustee had performed his obligation. If the trust has come to an end, the trustee can be ordered to compensate the beneficiary directly. In that situation the compensation is assessed on the same basis, since it is equivalent in substance to a distribution of the trust fund. If the trust fund has been diminished as a result of some other breach of trust, the same approach ordinarily applies, mutatis mutandis.

The measure of compensation should therefore normally be assessed at the date of trial, with the benefit of hindsight. The foreseeability of loss is generally irrelevant, but the loss must be caused by the breach of trust, in the sense that it must flow directly from it. Losses resulting from unreasonable behaviour on the part of the claimant will be adjudged to flow from that behaviour, and not from the breach. The requirement that the loss should flow directly from the breach is also the key to determining whether causation has been interrupted by the acts of third parties. The point is illustrated by the contrast between *Caffrey v Darby*, where the trustee's neglect enabled a third party to default on payments due to the trust, and *Canson Enterprises*, where the wrongful conduct by the third parties occurred after the plaintiff had taken control of the property, and was unrelated to the defendants' earlier breach of fiduciary duty.

It follows that the liability of a trustee for breach of trust, even where the trust arises in the context of a commercial transaction which is otherwise regulated by contract, is not generally the same as a liability in damages for tort or breach of contract. Of course, the aim of equitable compensation is to compensate: that is to say, to provide a monetary equivalent of what has been lost as a result of a breach of duty. At that level of generality, it has the same aim as most awards of damages for tort or breach of contract. Equally, since the concept of loss necessarily involves the concept of causation, and that concept in turn inevitably involves a consideration of the necessary connection between the breach of duty and a postulated consequence (and therefore of such questions as whether a consequence flows 'directly' from the breach of duty, and whether loss should be attributed to the conduct of third parties, or to the conduct of the person to whom the duty was owed), there are some structural similarities between the assessment of equitable compensation and the assessment of common law damages.

Those structural similarities do not however entail that the relevant rules are identical: as in mathematics, isomorphism is not the same as equality. As courts around the world have accepted, a trust imposes different obligations from a contractual or tortious relationship, in the setting of a different kind of relationship. The law responds to those differences by allowing a measure of compensation for breach of trust causing loss to the trust fund which reflects the nature of the obligation breached and the relationship between the parties. In particular, as Lord Toulson explains at para 71, where a trust is part of the machinery for the performance of a contract, that fact will be relevant in considering what loss has been suffered by reason of a breach of the trust.

This does not mean that the law is clinging atavistically to differences which are explicable only in terms of the historical origin of the relevant rules. The classification of claims as arising in equity or at common law generally reflects the nature of the relationship between the parties and their respective rights and obligations, and is therefore of more than merely historical significance. As the case law on equitable compensation develops, however, the reasoning supporting the assessment of compensation can be seen more clearly to reflect an analysis of the characteristics of the particular obligation breached. This increase in transparency permits greater scope for developing rules which are coherent with those adopted in the common law. To the extent that the same underlying principles apply, the rules should be consistent. To the extent that the underlying principles are different, the rules should be understandably different.

The present case

In the present case, AIB transmitted £3.3m to Redler for the purpose of discharging the Sondhis' debt to Barclays, discharging the related charge which Barclays held over their property, paying the balance of the money to the Sondhis and obtaining a first charge over the property. If Redler had performed their trust, they would on completion have held a registrable first charge which secured a debt of £3.3m. In the event, on completion they held a second charge in respect of that debt; but Barclays continued to hold a first charge in respect of an undischarged debt of £309,000, and AIB's charge could not be registered because Barclays' charge included a covenant against the registration of other charges. Following negotiations between AIB and Barclays, it was agreed during 2008 that AIB's charge could be registered and that Barclays' priority would be limited to £273,777.42, with the consequence that AIB's interest was worth £273,777.42 less than it should have been. That proved to be the position in 2011, when the security was enforced and these proceedings were begun: the proceeds of sale were insufficient to meet the Sondhis' liabilities to both Barclays and AIB, and in consequence AIB received £273,777.42 less than they would have done if Redler had fulfilled their instructions.

AIB argue that they are entitled to payment of the entire £3.3m, less the £867,697.78 which they received on the sale of the property, on the basis that Redler's liability for their breach of trust is unlimited by causation or remoteness. In my opinion that argument is based on three fallacies, each of which is fatal to AIB's claim. First, it assumes that Redler misapplied the entire £3.3m, whereas in my opinion all that was misapplied was the £309,000 which was paid to the Sondhis rather than Barclays. Since the Court of Appeal's decision to the contrary was not challenged, however, it is necessary to consider the appeal on the basis on which it was argued by both parties, namely that the breach of trust involved the misapplication of the entire £3.3m. On that premise, the appeal fails because it rests on the remaining fallacies. The second fallacy in AIB's argument is that it assumes that the measure of Redler's liability was fixed as at the date of the breach of trust: a proposition which was rejected in *Target Holdings* and in the Commonwealth authorities which I have cited. The third fallacy is that the argument assumes that liability does not depend on a causal link between the breach of trust and the loss: Redler is sought to be made liable for the consequences of the hopeless inadequacy of the security accepted by AIB before Redler's involvement, despite the fact that Redler's breach of trust did not affect that security except to the extent, initially, of £309,000, and finally of £273,777.42. That proposition also was rejected in *Target Holdings* and in the Commonwealth cases.

In these circumstances, applying the approach to the assessment of equitable compensation which I have explained, it appears to me that the loss to the trust estate as a result of Redler's breach of trust proved to be £273,777.42: that amount proved to be the pecuniary value of the difference between a first ranking security and one which was postponed to Barclays'. That was also the loss to AIB, who were absolutely entitled to the trust estate. The trust no longer being on foot, the appropriate order is for Redler to pay AIB £273,777.42 plus interest from 2011.

On one level, the decision of the Supreme Court in *AIB* settles the controversy following *Target*: the focus of the court's analysis should now be upon compensating the beneficiary for loss caused by the trustee's breach of duty. Indeed, *AIB* is a stronger case than *Target* in many respects. After all, in *Target*, the relevant mortgage documents were subsequently executed and received by Redferns. In *AIB*, Redler *never* obtained a first legal charge over the property in favour of AIB. This meant that AIB could argue that the transaction had not been completed, distinguishing *Target*. But the Supreme Court took a very generous approach to completion, since:[89]

as a commercial matter the transaction was executed or 'completed' when the loan monies were released to the borrowers. At that moment the relationship between the borrowers and the bank became one of contractual borrower and lender.

This pragmatic approach is perhaps understandable given the context of the dispute in question: AIB was 'anxious' to push through the Sondhis' remortgage of the property, which was 'driven by the need to facilitate business lending which the bank was very keen to make'.[90] The Supreme Court was prepared to find that there was completion upon satisfaction of the 'commercial purpose', but this is less certain than insisting upon compliance with the terms of the solicitor's instructions: Redler's breach of trust meant that there was no completion in accordance with the requirements of Redler's instructions. Moreover, it would seem that AIB did not simply seek the relationship of lender-borrower; AIB wanted to be a secured lender with priority over other chargees. This purpose was not fulfilled.

It is important to appreciate why *AIB* escalated to the Supreme Court. In *Target*, the lender (Target) was entitled to see *either* £1.5 million *or* the mortgage documents in the trust fund upon taking an account. The latter was present, so there was no defect in the fund. But in *AIB*, the bank would have expected to see *either* £3.3 million in the trust fund, *or* the first legal charge over the Sondhis' property. Neither was present. But the Supreme Court nonetheless held that AIB was only entitled to recover the losses it suffered as a result of Redler's breach of duty. *AIB* entrenches a decisive shift in focus away from the primary obligations of a trustee towards the trustee's secondary obligations to compensate the beneficiary after a breach of trust. The elision between falsification and surcharge—clearly rejected by earlier cases—that began with Lord Browne-Wilkinson's judgment in *Target* was compounded by Lord Toulson's remark that 'in a practical sense both are reparative compensation'.[91]

Clearly, the result in *AIB* is consistent with the Common Law remedies available for breach of contract and in negligence. That was obviously attractive to the Supreme Court, although it may have been preferable to consider the breach of trust only to relate to the £309,000 which was not properly

[89] [2014] UKSC 58; [2015] AC 1503, [74].
[90] Ibid, [14].
[91] Ibid, [54].

paid to Barclays in order to reach that result (as Lord Reed suggested in his conclusion; unfortunately, this point was not argued in the Supreme Court). In any event, the decision has been welcomed by some commentators as providing clarity and certainty in the remedial context.[92] However, some concerns may remain.

First, some of the reasoning in *AIB* is itself somewhat unconvincing. For example, Lord Toulson's dismissal of falsification as resting upon 'fairy tales' is evocative rhetoric, but greater explanation would have been helpful when departing from long-standing orthodoxy. Indeed, as Lord Sumption had recently explained in *Williams v Central Bank of Nigeria*:[93]

> [i]f the trustee misapplied the assets, equity would ignore the misapplication and simply hold him to account for the assets as if he had acted in accordance with his trust.

Fundamentally, it seems important to hold trustees to a high standard. As McLachlin J insisted in *Canson*, the relationship at issue has:[94]

> trust, not self-interest, at its core, and when the breach occurs, the balance favours the person wronged.

Given the control the trustee has over the beneficiary's property, leading to a sense of 'vulnerability' about the beneficiary, there are strong arguments in favour of stricter rules in Equity which might be employed in order to protect the beneficiary. As Lord Millett has pointed out:[95]

> If a trustee or fiduciary has committed a breach of trust or fiduciary duty, Equity makes him account as if he had not done so... This is a radically different approach [to the Common Law]; indeed it is the converse approach. It does not treat the defendant as a wrongdoer; it disregards his wrongdoing, makes him account as if he has acted properly throughout, and does not permit him to deny that he has done so.

Moreover, although Lord Toulson deprecated the language of 'equitable debt' as a 'literary costume', it is clear that earlier authorities do refer to 'an equitable debt, or liability in the nature of a debt'.[96] Debt claims enforce the primary obligations of the trustee rather than any secondary obligations that arise upon breach. Yet Lord Toulson rejected any analysis based upon an obligation to pay a debt and said that 'a monetary award which reflected neither loss caused nor profit gained by the wrongdoer would be penal'.[97] This would mean that all debt claims—even those brought at Common Law[98]—should be considered to be penal. That would be a startling conclusion. It is not penal to hold a party—particularly a trustee—up to the duties to which he or she voluntarily assented.[99]

---

[92] E.g. Ho, 'Equitable compensation on the road to Damascus?' (2015) 131 LQR 213.

[93] [2014] UKSC 10; [2014] AC 1189, [13]. See Chapter 16.9(b)(i), pp. 784–7.

[94] (1991) 85 DLR (4th) 129, 543.

[95] 'Proprietary Restitution' in *Equity in Commercial Law* (eds Degeling and Edelman) (Sydney: Lawbook Co., 2005) 309, 310.

[96] [2014] UKSC 58; [2015] AC 1503, [61], citing *Ex p Adamson; In re Collie* (1878) 8 Ch D 807, 819 (James and Baggallay LJJ). See too *In re Smith, Fleming & Co* (1879) 11 Ch D 306, 311 (James LJ); *Webb v Stenton* (1883) 11 QBD 518, 530 (Fry LJ).

[97] [2014] UKSC 58; [2015] AC 1503, [64].

[98] Common Law claims are not at all uncommon: see, notoriously, *White & Carter (Councils) Ltd v McGregor* [1962] AC 413.

[99] Thus the remedies of specific performance and injunction—which similarly enforce the primary obligations owed—should also not be considered to be penal.

Furthermore, it is unclear how consistent the views across the Commonwealth on this issue really are. Although Lord Reed thought that there was much support, the cases cited would generally not be understood to be falsification cases.[100] And the leading decision of the High Court of Australia on this issue, *Youyang Pty Ltd v Minter Ellison Morris Fletcher*,[101] appears instead to maintain a traditional approach to falsification, rather than accepting the language of 'equitable compensation'. Imagine that, in breach of trust, a trustee purchased a second-hand car rather than a brand new car. Has the transaction been completed? On the approach of the Supreme Court in *AIB*, it might be tempting to conclude that, since the trustee has purchased a car, the beneficiary should simply sue for the difference in value between the second-hand car he now has rather than the brand new car he was entitled to under the terms of the trust. Yet it seems unsatisfactory for the wrong type of car to be the beneficiary's problem, rather than the trustee's problem. The traditional approach would allow the beneficiary to falsify the wrongful disbursement, and insist that the wrongdoing trustee either obtain the brand new car for the beneficiary, or provide a monetary substitute.

These issues mean that there continues to be debate about the rationale, meaning, and scope of *AIB v Redler* across the common law world. Be that as it may, *AIB v Redler* is clearly the leading decision in this jurisdiction. Of course, the facts of the case concern a bare trust in a commercial context, but it is suggested that the thrust of the reasoning applies to all trusts. Indeed, it would be odd if the remedies available against a lay trustee were more extensive than those available against a professional trustee. The focus is therefore likely to be on the principles of compensation that should apply to claims for breach of trust. Some of the key issues will now be highlighted, but the analysis is necessarily speculative: it remains to be seen how *AIB v Redler* will be applied by the courts.

(i) *Causation*

AIB appears to demand the familiar 'but for' test,[102] and this seems sensible when focusing on a trustee's responsibility for loss. It is clearly insufficient that the wrongdoing trustee simply provided an opportunity for the loss to occur; the trustee must cause the loss.[103] However, as in *AIB*, this may lead to different outcomes from the traditional approach. Ho has given the example of a trustee who wrongfully disposes of a seaside bungalow shortly before a tsunami would have destroyed it in any event.[104] Traditionally, a beneficiary would still be able to falsify the wrongful misapplication of trust property. Yet it is difficult to see how the wrongful act of the trustee causes the beneficiary's loss, when that loss would have been suffered in any event. Admittedly, Ho recognizes that it might not be desirable to leave the beneficiary with no remedy, and suggests that 'the court will need to adjust the causal test to deal with multiple sufficient causes such as these'. It is not clear how this should be done, and given the complexities of causation at common law it is suggested, sadly, that it is unlikely that causation in equity will prove to be simple.

In *Libertarian*, Ribeiro PJ held that:[105]

[w]here the plaintiff provides evidence of loss flowing from the relevant breach of duty, the onus lies on a defaulting fiduciary to disprove the apparent causal connection between the breach of duty and the loss (or particular aspects of the loss) apparently flowing therefrom.

---

[100] Davies, 'Remedies for Breach of Trust' (2015) 78 MLR 681, 689–690.
[101] [2003] HCA 15; (2003) 212 CLR 484.
[102] E.g. *AIB* [2014] UKSC 58; [2015] AC 1503, [73] (Lord Toulson); [132] (Lord Reed). See too *Target* [1996] AC 421, 431.
[103] *Swindle v Harrison* [1997] 4 All ER 705, 727 (Hobhouse LJ).
[104] Ho, 'Equitable compensation on the road to Damascus?' (2015) 131 LQR 213, 217.
[105] *AIB*, [93].

Given the control over the trust property that the trustee enjoys, and the consequent difficulties that a beneficiary faces when seeking to establish and prove a breach of duty, it seems entirely appropriate to put the onus on the trustee to disprove an apparent causal connection.[106] However, it will not be sufficient for a trustee to show that if he had not committed a breach of trust the same loss would have been caused by some other third party's dishonest conduct.[107] Moreover, it is difficult to see much scope for the principle of *novus actus interveniens* in the context of equitable compensation, since rarely will anything happen to trust property which is truly independent of a breach of the duty to safeguard it. For instance, imagine that one trustee carelessly allows trust property to come exclusively under the control of another trustee. The latter then misappropriates the trust assets. The first trustee, who only breached a duty of care, is nonetheless liable for all losses suffered, even though the immediate cause of the loss is the latter trustee's misappropriation of the trust assets.

(ii) *Remoteness*

Compensation requires some rules of remoteness. Whilst issues of remoteness are irrelevant to actions for the agreed sum,[108] equitable compensation must establish principles of remoteness. If 'the relentless contractualisation of trust law'[109] continues apace, and the principles of equitable compensation mirror the contractual principles, then contract cases on remoteness such as *Hadley v Baxendale*[110] and *The Achilleas*[111] might be thought to be relevant in Equity. But that is surely misguided. The point of the contractual rules is that there exists an agreement between the parties, and when making that agreement each party could bring the risk of certain losses to the other party's attention. Yet in the context of trusts, the beneficiary may not always have a contract with the trustee, and the trustee at the time of the dispute may not be the same person that originally agreed to the terms of the trust instrument. In most commercial trusts, admittedly, there will be a concurrent contractual claim, but that contractual claim should stand apart. It may be that the contractual claim should trump the equitable claim, but the equitable claim—and certainly any free-standing equitable claim—should not adopt the contractual principles of remoteness. Not least because under the contractual approach foreseeability is assessed at the date of entering into the contract.[112] But given the higher standard expected of trustees, and the different situations that can evolve over the course of a trust relationship, it is surely more appropriate for any foreseeability requirement to be assessed at the date of breach.

If an analogy is to be drawn to the Common Law, it would be more sensible to look across to tort law. But there is a split between the 'reasonable foreseeability' approach of *The Wagon Mound*[113] in the tort of negligence and the 'direct consequences' approach[114] adopted in the context of the intentional torts, such as deceit.[115] It would be possible for equity similarly to adopt different approaches depending on whether or not the breach of duty was deliberate, and this differentiation may be evolving in the context of breach of fiduciary duty.[116] However, given the higher standards demanded in equity,

---

[106] See too *Re Brogden* (1888) 38 Ch D 546, 567–568, 572–573.

[107] [2014] UKSC 58; [2015] AC 1503, [58] (Lord Toulson).

[108] *In re Dawson (dec'd)* [1966] NSWR 211, 215 (Street J).

[109] Getzler, 'Equitable Compensation and the Regulation of Fiduciary Relationships' in *Restitution and Equity Volume 1: Resulting Trusts and Equitable Compensation* (eds Birks and Rose) (London: Mansfield Press, 2000) 257.

[110] (1854) 9 Exch 341.

[111] *Transfield Shipping Inc v Mercator Shipping Inc (The Achilleas)* [2008] UKHL 48; [2009] 1 AC 61.

[112] E.g. *Jackson v Royal Bank of Scotland* [2005] UKHL 3; [2005] 1 WLR 377.

[113] [1961] AC 388.

[114] *Re Polemis & Furness, Withy & Co Ltd* [1921] 3 KB 560.

[115] *Smith New Court Securities Ltd v Citibank NA* [1997] AC 254.

[116] See the differing judgments in *Swindle v Harrison* [1997] 4 All ER 705. For a common law analogy in the tort of conversion, see *Kuwait Airlines Corp v Iraqi Airways Co (Nos 4 and 5)* [2002] UKHL 19; [2002] 2 AC 122, [100]–[104] (Lord Nicholls).

there is a strong argument for a stricter approach to be taken for all breaches of equitable duty.[117] As McLachlin J commented in *Canson*:[118]

> In negligence we wish to protect reasonable freedom of action of the defendant, and the reasonable-ness of his or her action may be judged by what consequences can be foreseen. In the case of a breach of fiduciary duty, as in deceit, we do not have to look to the consequences to judge the reasonable-ness of the actions. A breach of fiduciary duty is a wrong in itself, regardless of whether a loss can be foreseen. Moreover the high duty assumed and the difficulty of detecting such breaches makes it fair and practical to adopt a measure of compensation calculated to ensure that fiduciaries are kept 'up to their duty'.

This passage was cited with approval in *Libertarian*,[119] and surely applies equally to breach of trust. Indeed, *Canson* was a case where the claim failed because the losses suffered were too remote from the breach of fiduciary duty on any test.[120]

In *AIB*, Lord Reed said that 'the foreseeability of loss is generally irrelevant, but the loss must be caused by the breach of trust, in the sense that it must flow directly from it'.[121] It is suggested that foreseeability of loss should be irrelevant in the context of misapplication of trust property.[122] The risk of unforeseeable consequential loss should be visited upon the wrongdoing fiduciary rather than the vulnerable beneficiary.[123] Perhaps foreseeability may be relevant where a duty to take reasonable care has been breached such that—in traditional language—the account could be surcharged,[124] and this may explain the qualification of 'generally' in Lord Reed's statement. This depends upon how the nature of the trustee's obligation is explained. If it is akin to a duty to take care in tort, then foreseeability should be relevant. But if a higher standard is demanded of the trustee as a fiduciary, then foreseeability should not limit the recoverable losses.

(iii) *Mitigation and contributory fault*

If compensation in Equity were to operate along similar lines to compensation at Common Law, then it might be expected that the claimant's failure to act reasonably in mitigating his or her losses should reduce the amount the claimant could recover. Moreover, if the claimant was at fault in causing his or her own loss, then the trustee might have a defence of contributory negligence. Yet here again it has been said that Equity differs from the Common Law. For example, in *Corporación Nacional del Cobre de Chile v Sogemin Metals Ltd*,[125] Carnwath J said:

> Also of assistance in this context is the decision of the Canadian Supreme Court in *Canson Enterprises Ltd. v Boughton & Co.* (1991) 85 DLR (4th) 129. The judgment of McLachlin J. in that case was cited with

---

[117] Cf Elliott, 'Remoteness Criteria in Equity', (2002) 65 MLR 588.
[118] (1991) 85 DLR (4th) 129, 553.
[119] [2013] HKCFA 93; [2014] 1 HKC 368, [80]
[120] (1991) 85 DLR (4th) 129, 590 (Stevenson J).
[121] [2014] UKSC 58; [2015] AC 1503, [135].
[122] *Clough v Bond* (1838) 3 My & C 490, 496 (Cottenham LC); *In re Dawson (dec'd)* [1966] NSWR 211, 215 (Street J); *Canson Enterprises Ltd v Boughton & Co* [1991] 3 SCR 534, 555–556 (McLachlin J); *Target* 438-439 (Lord Browne-Wilkinson); *Bank of New Zealand v New Zealand Guardian Trust Co Ltd* [1999] 1 NZLR 664, 687 (Tipping J).
[123] Cf *Smith New Court Securities Ltd v Citibank NA* [1997] AC 254.
[124] See e.g. *Bristol & West Building Society v Mothew* [1998] Ch 1, 17 (Millett LJ); cf *Youyang Pty Ltd v Minter Ellison Morris Fletcher* [2003] HCA 15; (2003) 212 CLR 484, [39]. See further Getzler, 'Am I My Beneficiary's Keeper? Fusion and Loss-Based Fiduciary Remedies' in Degeling and Edelman, *Equity in Commercial Law* (Sydney, Lawbook Co., 2005).
[125] [1997] 1 WLR 1396, 1403.

approval by Lord Browne-Wilkinson in *Target Holdings Ltd. v Redferns* [1996] AC 421. McLachlin J. ... went on to say, at pp. 161–162:

'The thrust of these dicta is that while the plaintiff will not be required to act in as reasonable and prudent a manner as might be required in negligence or contract, losses stemming from the plaintiff's unreasonable actions will be barred. This is also sound policy in the law of fiduciary duty. In negligence and contract the law limits the actions of the parties who are expected to pursue their own best interest. Each is expected to continue to look after their own interests after a breach of tort, and so a duty of mitigation is imposed. In contrast, the hallmark of fiduciary relationship is that the fiduciary, at least within a certain scope, is expected to pursue the best interest of the client. It may not be fair to allow the fiduciary to complain when the client fails forthwith to shoulder the fiduciary's burden. This approach to mitigation accords with the basic rule of equitable compensation that the injured party will be reimbursed for all losses flowing directly from a breach. When a plaintiff, after due notice and opportunity, fails to take the most obvious steps to alleviate his or her losses, then we may rightly say that the plaintiff has been "the author of his own misfortune." At this point the plaintiff's failure to mitigate may become so egregious that it is no longer sensible to say that the losses which followed were caused by the fiduciary's breach. But until that point, mitigation will not be required.'

This seems sensible. Beneficiaries under a trust do not expect to have to protect themselves against breach of trust, and nor should they. Any contrary approach would be inconsistent with Equity's insistence that the trustees act as good persons. So, unless the acts of the beneficiaries are so unreasonable that they can be said to be the cause of the loss suffered, the trustee should not be able to use the beneficiary's conduct as a defence to reduce his or her liability. Of course, this does resemble mitigation in the context of damages at common law, but this threshold seems to be very high: in *Magnus v Queensland National Bank*,[126] it was held that a trustee bank was liable where it had paid money to the wrong person, even though the beneficiaries were aware of this and had not taken steps to recover it from the recipient.[127] This failure to intervene did not break the chain of causation. Such an approach may, admittedly, sometimes seem somewhat harsh on a trustee, but it should be remembered that there is a strong interest in trustees being held to a very high standard, and if the trustee has acted honestly and reasonably the court might excuse his or her liability if it would be fair to do so.[128]

(iv) *Quantifying the loss: cost of cure*

An interesting question arises about whether the principles of equitable compensation require the trustee to compensate the trust fund (or possibly the beneficiary) for the diminution in value suffered as a result of the breach of duty or for the cost of cure in repairing the breach. In *Brudenell-Bruce v Moore & Cotton*,[129] Newey J held that the answer to this question should reflect that given at common law. *Brudenell-Bruce* concerned the estate of the Earl of Cardigan. Lord Cardigan is the beneficiary of a bare trust administered by professional trustees. Lord Cardigan claimed that the trustees failed to maintain the Stable Block of Tottenham House, the seat of the Cardigan family. On the facts, the judge rejected the claim that the trustees had acted in breach of trust, but nevertheless went on to consider what the appropriate remedy would have been had there been a breach of trust.

---

[126] (1888) 37 Ch D 466.
[127] Although note that the defence of acquiescence may be available: see Chapter 20.1(a), pp. 976–7.
[128] Trustee Act 1925, s. 61; see Chapter 16.3, p. 760.
[129] [2014] EWHC 3679 (Ch); [2015] WTLR 373.

The beneficiary argued that the full cost of repair should be awarded, contending that even if 'it is going to cost £5 million to restore the Stable Block but fully restored it is only going to be worth £4 million, that is just the price that the trustees pay for allowing this collapse to have occurred in the first place'.[130] Newey J rejected that argument:[131]

It is [counsel's] contention that trust law is different. He argues that the principles applicable to the calculation of damages in contract and tort do not apply to the assessment of equitable compensation. Whatever, however, may be the case where equitable compensation is awarded as a substitute for performance of a trustee's obligation to deliver up trust assets in specie, I can see no reason why the Courts should be more willing to award compensation based on cost of reinstatement in circumstances such as those in the present case than they would be to measure damages in that way for breach of contract or a tort.

...

In *AIB*, Lord Reed explained that equitable compensation for breach of trust 'aims to provide the pecuniary equivalent of performance of the trust' (paragraph 93) and that the measure of compensation for a breach of trust 'will generally be based upon the diminution in the value of the fund caused by the trustee's default' (paragraph 94). The present case is, in my view, plainly one where, had a relevant breach of trust been established, it would have been appropriate to measure compensation by the resulting "diminution in the value of the fund", not by the cost of reinstating the Stable Block.

Newey J relied upon common law decisions such as *Ruxley Electronics and Construction Ltd v Forsyth*[132] and *In Southampton Container Terminals Ltd v Schiffahrtsgesellschaft 'Hansa Australia' GmbH (The 'Maersk Colombo')*[133] to conclude that the full cost of cure measure should not be awarded where that would be unreasonable.

Equitable awards should not be unreasonable. But it is not obvious that this is an area where equity should 'follow the law'. The restrictions on the full cost of cure remedy in English law are controversial, and have not been followed in Australia, for example.[134] If what the claimant really wants is performance of the 'bargain' or 'transaction', why should the courts not protect that performance interest?[135] This question might be thought to be particularly difficult to answer in the context of breach of trust. After all, it is important that Equity hold trustees up to their primary obligations to perform the trust properly, which would suggest that the cost of reinstatement be the prima facie remedy available. Indeed, it is not clear whether *AIB* fully supports the restrictions on the cost of cure remedy favoured by Newey J. Equitable compensation will 'generally' be for the diminution in value, because this will generally also equate to the cost of cure remedy. But where the two measures differ— as in, for example, *Ruxley* and *Brudenell-Bruce*—then a choice has to be made, and Lord Reed's insistence on 'the pecuniary equivalent of performance' might favour a cost of cure award. It is suggested that the cost of cure remedy has been unduly restricted at common law, and that equity should not be bound to follow suit.[136]

---

[130] Ibid, [146].
[131] Ibid, [151], [155].
[132] [1996] AC 344.
[133] [2001] EWCA Civ 717; [2001] 2 Lloyd's Rep. 275.
[134] *Tabcorp Holdings Ltd v Bowen Investments Pty Ltd* [2009] HCA 8; (2009) 236 CLR 272.
[135] See generally Edelman, 'Money Awards for the Cost of Performance' (2010) J Eq 122.
[136] See e.g. *Elder's Trustee and Executor Co v Higgins* (1963) 113 CLR 426, 473.

(v) Conclusions

Remedies for breach of trust has been a difficult subject for some time. It may be that *AIB v Redler* now provides greater clarity when seeking to apply the law: a compensatory view should be taken. But it is important to appreciate that this is controversial and appears to be a shift away from the traditional approach. Indeed, it remains to be seen whether *AIB* will be followed elsewhere in the Commonwealth, and its scope remains unclear: is the decision limited to the narrow context of bare, commercial trusts, such that the traditional approach to the account and falsification continues to apply in other contexts? Or does *AIB* govern all claims for breach of trust, such that the accounting process may become virtually redundant?

At the very start of his judgment in *AIB,* Lord Toulson said that:[137]

> 140 years after the Judicature Act 1873, the stitching together of equity and the common law continues to cause problems at the seams.

Even though the Judicature Act 1873 was only concerned with the 'fusion' of the administration of common law and equity, rather than the 'fusion' of the substantive rules of each jurisdiction,[138] it is clearly now important to understand further the principles underpinning equitable compensation. The need to hold trustees up to a high standard suggests that a strict approach to causation and remoteness, for example, will generally be appropriate, especially given the difficulties beneficiaries face in discovering breaches of trust.[139]

4. SET-OFF

Upon the taking of an account the beneficiary might be able to falsify or surcharge and thereby demand that the trustee pay money to the trust fund. However, the trustee may seek to rely upon gains made through another investment entered into on behalf of the trust in order to reduce the amount he or she has to pay. Whether or not the trustee is able to set off such gains against losses suffered has raised some difficult issues.

There is long-standing authority that there is no right to set-off where the gains made are entirely distinct from the losses caused. For example, in *Dimes v Scott,*[140] a testator, who died in 1802, left his estate upon trust for his widow for her life, and after her death upon trust for the claimant. The estate included an investment in an East India Company loan bearing interest at 10 per cent. The retention of this investment was not authorized by the will. Instead of selling this unauthorized investment within a year of the testator's death, the trustees retained it, and paid the whole income to the widow. This was a breach of trust. However, in 1813 the loan was repaid, and the proceeds were invested in Consols with a yield of 3 per cent. The price of Consols was lower than it had been a year after the testator's death, and the trustees were able to purchase more Consols than they would have been able to purchase if they had made the switch a year after the testator's death.

Lord Lyndhurst LC held that the trustees were liable for breach of trust in paying the whole income to the widow, and that they could not set off against that liability the extra Consols, which the delay had enabled them to purchase.

---

[137] [2014] UKSC 58; [2015] AC 1503, [1].
[138] See Chapter 1.2, pp. 8–10.
[139] See e.g. *Santander UK v RA Legal Solicitors* [2014] EWCA Civ 183; [2014] PNLR 20, [112] (Etherton C).
[140] (1828) 4 Russ 195.

Dimes v Scott [1828] 4 Russ 195 (Lord Lyndhurst LC)

This testator left his property to trustees, who were directed to convert it into money, and to invest the proceeds in government or real securities; and he gave the interest of the money so to be invested to his widow for life, with remainder to the lady who is one of the present Plaintiffs. Part of his property consisted of a sum which he had subscribed to what is called the decennial loan. The trustees did not convert his share of this loan into money; but, suffering it to remain as they found it, paid the interest, which was £10 per cent, to the tenant for life. Was that a proper performance of their duty?

The directions of the will were most distinct; and, according to the case of _Howe v Lord Dartmouth_ (1802) 7 Ves 137 and the principles of this Court, it was the duty of the trustees to have sold the property within the usual period after the testator's death.

If they neglected to sell it, still, so far as regarded the tenant for life, the property was to be considered as if it had been duly converted. Had the conversion taken place, and the proceeds been invested in that which is considered in this Court as the fit and proper security, namely, £3 per cent stock, the tenant for life would not have been entitled to more than the interest which would have resulted from such stock. The executor is therefore chargeable with the difference between the interest which the fund, if so converted, would have yielded, and the £10 per cent which was actually produced by the fund, and was paid over by him to the tenant for life.

It is said, that, if the subscription to the decennial loan had been sold, and the produce invested in stock at the end of a year from the testator's death, the sale would have been much less advantageous to the estate than the course which has been actually followed; and that, if the executor is to be charged for not having made the conversion at the proper time, he ought on the other hand, to have the benefit of the advantage which has accrued from his course of conduct. The answer is this: with respect to the principal sum, at whatever period the subscription to the decennial loan was sold, the estate must have the whole amount of the stock that was bought; and if it was sold at a later period than the rules of the Court require, the executor is not entitled to any accidental advantage thence arising. As to the payments to the tenant for life, the executors are entitled to have credit only for sums I have adverted to, namely, the dividends on so much £3 per cent stock as would have been purchased with the proceeds of the subscription to the decennial loan, if the conversion had taken place at the proper time. On the other hand, he is chargeable with the whole of the difference between the amount of those dividends and the amount of the sums which have been received in respect of interest on the money which was continued in the decennial loan. I think, therefore, that the judgment of the Master of the Rolls must be affirmed.

Where, however, a gain is made and a loss suffered in the course of the same transaction, the gain can be set off against the loss. So, in _Fletcher v Green_,[141] trustees made a secured loan to a firm of which one of the trustees was a partner. The security was sold at a loss, and the proceeds were paid into court and invested in shares that increased in value. It was held that this gain could be set off against the loss suffered from the sale of the security, presumably because this all formed part of the same transaction.

It may sometimes be difficult to identify whether the gain and loss arise from one single or two distinct transactions. A helpful example is _Bartlett v Barclays Bank Trust Co. Ltd (Nos 1 and 2)_.[142] The trustee was a bank that had failed to oversee the actions of a company in which the trust held a majority of the shares. The directors of that company invested in two building developments, one of which, in Guildford, was profitable, but the other, around the Old Bailey in London, caused a huge loss to

---

[141] (1864) 33 Beav 426.
[142] [1980] Ch 515.

the company. Brightman J allowed the gains made from the Guildford project to be set off against the losses suffered through the Old Bailey project and said:[143]

> The general rule as stated in all the textbooks, with some reservations, is that where a trustee is liable in respect of distinct breaches of trust, one of which has resulted in a loss and the other in a gain, he is not entitled to set off the gain against the loss, unless they arise in the same transaction. The relevant cases are, however, not altogether easy to reconcile. All are centenarians and none is quite like the present. The Guildford development stemmed from exactly the same policy and (to a lesser degree because it proceeded less far) exemplified the same folly as the Old Bailey project. Part of the profit was in fact used to finance the Old Bailey disaster. By sheer luck the gamble paid off handsomely, on capital account. I think it would be unjust to deprive the bank of this element of salvage in the course of assessing the cost of the shipwreck. My order will therefore reflect the bank's right to an appropriate set-off.

The two projects may at first appear to be distinct, but in fact they can be considered to be part of a single breach of failing to supervise speculative property developments. The same breach resulted in both projects, so it was only fair to set the gains of one off against the losses of the other.

Two principal reasons are invoked to justify the general rule that gains cannot be set off against losses. First, trustees should not be allowed to benefit from the good luck that a gain might counteract a loss: otherwise, trustees might be tempted to speculate in risky investments in order to seek future gains to offset any losses, and the principle that we expect the highest standards from trustees may be undermined. Secondly, and more convincingly, the general rule seems logical as a matter of causation. Where the gain and the loss arise from the same transaction, they can be considered to be causally connected to a single breach, and so it is appropriate to set off the gain against the loss. But where the loss and gain arise from two distinct decisions made by the trustee, they cannot be considered to be causally connected to the same breach of trust, and so no right to set-off should exist.

5. INTEREST

It is clear that the defendant trustee may have to pay interest on any money award made against him or her.[144] The reasons for the payment of interest were identified by Lord Cranworth in *Attorney-General v Alford*:[145]

> What the Court ought to do, I think, is to charge him only with the interest which he has received, or which it is justly entitled to say he ought to have received, or which it is so fairly to be presumed that he did receive that he is estopped from saying that he did not receive it.

The first two situations identified by Lord Cranworth effectively mean that defendants have to give up any gains they made, or ought to have made, from the breach of duty. The third situation, on the other hand may be seen as compensatory. As Elliott has explained:[146]

> Trustees and certain other fiduciaries are often required to invest the money productively, and if they fail to do so then they may be charged with the interest the fund would have earned if they had done their duty. Interest of this third type is given by way of compensation.

---

[143] Ibid, 538.
[144] See generally Elliott, 'Rethinking Interest on Withheld and Misapplied Trust Money' [2001] Conv 313.
[145] (1855) 4 De GM & G 843, 851.
[146] Elliott, 'Rethinking Interest on Withheld and Misapplied Trust Money' [2001] Conv 313, 317.

In *Alford* itself, the court held that interest should be charged at the ordinary, simple rate. Judges have a discretion to award simple interest by virtue of the Supreme Court Act 1981, section 35A. But there is also an equitable jurisdiction to award compound interest.

Westdeutsche Landesbank Girozentrale v Islington London Borough Council [1996] AC 669 (Lord Goff)

In cases of misconduct which benefits the executor, however, the court may fairly infer that he used the money in speculation, and may, on the principle in *odium spoliatoris omnia praesumuntur*,[147] assume that he made a higher rate, if that was a reasonable conclusion.

Likewise in *Burdick v Garrick* (1870) 5 Ch App 233, where a fiduciary agent held money of his principal and simply paid it into his bank account, it was held that he should be charged with simple interest only. Lord Hatherley LC, at 241–242, applied the principle laid down in *A-G v Alford*, namely that:

> 'the court does not proceed against an accounting party by way of punishing him for making use of the plaintiff's money by directing rests, or payment of compound interest, but proceeds upon this principle, either that he has made, or has put himself in such a position that he is to be presumed to have made, 5 per cent, or compound interest, as the case may be. If the court finds … that the money received has been invested in an ordinary trade, the whole course of decision has tended to this, that the court presumes that the party against whom relief is sought has made that amount of profit which persons ordinarily do make in trade, and in those cases the court directs rests to be made.'

For a more recent case in which the equitable jurisdiction was invoked, see *Wallersteiner v Moir (No 2)* [1975] QB 373.

From these cases it can be seen that compound interest may be awarded in cases where the defendant has wrongfully profited, or may be presumed to have so profited, from having the use of another person's money. The power to award compound interest is therefore available to achieve justice in a limited area of what is now seen as the law of restitution, viz. where the defendant has acquired a benefit through his wrongful act.

Compound interest differs from simple interest since it is calculated not only with reference to the sum owed by the defendant, but also with reference to the interest that has already accrued. As a result, compound interest will increase the value of the remedy afforded to the claimant. It is important to note that, since the decision of the House of Lords in *Sempra Metals v IRC*,[148] compound interest is now generally available regardless of whether the claim is brought in Equity or at Common Law. Compound interest may often be appropriate where the claimant would have earned interest on already accrued interest had the money been in the claimant's account from the outset.

However, as the above passage from *Westdeutsche* indicates, compound interest will not be awarded simply to punish a defendant. Nevertheless, there can be little doubt that, in practice, the conduct of the defendant may well influence the court when deciding whether or not to award compound interest. In fact, not awarding compound interest may actually allow a defendant to profit from his or her wrong, so interest awards may have a disgorgement, rather than a penal, function. Certainly, where the defendant is in business and would be expected to invest money and actually to make use of the interest accruing, compound interest will generally be awarded. For example, in *Wallersteiner v Moir (No. 2)*,[149] the defendant was a company director and international financier who was shown to have

---

[147] 'Everything can be presumed against a wrongdoer.'
[148] [2007] UKHL 34; [2008] 1 AC 561. See Ridge, 'Pre-judgment Compound Interest' (2010) LQR 279.
[149] [1975] QB 373.

improperly used company funds for his own benefit in breach of fiduciary duty. He was held liable to pay compound interest at the rate of 1 per cent over the minimum lending rate. Scarman LJ said:[150]

> Dr. Wallersteiner was at all material times engaged in the business of finance. Through a complex structure of companies he conducted financial operations with a view to profit. The quarter-million pounds assistance which he obtained from the two companies in order to finance the acquisition of the shares meant that he was in a position to employ the money or its capital equivalent in those operations. Though the truth is unlikely ever to be fully known, shrouded as it is by the elaborate corporate structure within which Dr. Wallersteiner chose to operate, one may safely presume that the use of the money (or the capital it enabled him to acquire) was worth to him the equivalent of compound interest at commercial rates with yearly rests, if not more. I, therefore, agree that he should be ordered to pay compound interest at the rates, and with the rests, proposed by Lord Denning MR and Buckley LJ.

The courts also enjoy some discretion regarding the rate at which interest is to be awarded. In *Bartlett v Barclays Bank Trust Co. Ltd (No. 2)*, Brightman LJ said:[151]

> In my judgment, a proper rate of interest to be awarded, in the absence of special circumstances, to compensate beneficiaries and trust funds for non-receipt from a trustee of money that ought to have been received is that allowed from time to time on the courts' short-term investment account, established under section 6(1) of the Administration of Justice Act 1965.[152] To some extent the high interest rates payable on money lent reflect and compensate for the continual erosion in the value of money by reason of galloping inflation. It seems to me arguable, therefore, that if a high rate of interest is payable in such circumstances, a proportion of that interest should be added to capital in order to help maintain the value of the corpus of the trust estate. It may be, therefore, that there will have to be some adjustment as between life tenant and remaindermen. I do not decide this point and I express no view upon it.

6. GAIN-BASED REMEDIES

Most trustees will owe fiduciary duties.[153] Significantly, this means that a trustee may have to disgorge any profits he or she makes from a breach of fiduciary duty. The remedy of an account of profits was discussed in Chapter 14.[154] It deters fiduciaries from breaching their obligations, and operates to ensure that they cannot profit from their breach. Indeed, where a trustee breaches a non-fiduciary duty, he or she should still have to give up any gains made from his or her breach of duty:[155] a trustee is always to act in the best interests of the trust, so it should be assumed that any profits flowing from the breach of duty are made for the benefit of the trust. However, the trust's loss will often correspond to the trustee's gain, so the choice between the appropriate measure of the remedy is unlikely often to be significant. Nevertheless, the claimant should not be able to recover for both the trust's loss and the trustee's gain where this would lead to double recovery.[156]

---

[150] Ibid, 406.
[151] [1980] Ch 515, 547.
[152] See now Court Funds Rules 1987, r. 26.
[153] See generally, Chapter 14, 'Fiduciary Obligations'.
[154] Chapter 14.5(a), p. 704.
[155] Unless there is a defence, such as consent: see Chapter 16.4, p. 769.
[156] See *Tang Man Sit v Capacious Investments Ltd* [1996] 1 AC 514; see further Chapter 14.5(d), p. 715.

7. PUNITIVE AWARDS

An account of profits might deter a trustee from breaching his or her obligations: if the trustee has to give up any gains he or she might make to the beneficiary, then there is no real incentive to commit the breach. However, the trustee would be no *worse* off if the only remedy awarded were gain-based. As Lord Diplock observed in *Cassell v Broome*,[157] albeit in the tortious context:[158]

> to restrict the damages recoverable to the actual gain made by the defendant if it exceeded the loss caused to the plaintiff, would leave a defendant contemplating an unlawful act with the certainty that he had nothing to lose to balance against the chance that the plaintiff might never sue him or, if he did, might fail in the hazards of litigation. It is only if there is a prospect that the damages may exceed the defendant's gain that the social purpose of this category is achieved—to teach a wrongdoer that tort does not pay.

Damages that exceed the defendant's gain and claimant's loss are generally known as 'punitive damages', or 'exemplary damages'.[159] These are able to work in tandem with restitutionary awards in order to ensure not only that the defendant does not profit from his or her wrong, but also that he or she is punished for the wrongdoing.

However, as Lord Diplock made clear, punitive damages will only be appropriate in the rare instances where it is necessary to teach a wrongdoer that the wrong will not pay. Punitive damages may be awarded in response to any tort,[160] but not, apparently, to breaches of contract.[161] Orthodoxy suggests that punitive awards are not available in England for equitable wrongdoing either. For example, in *Vyse v Foster*,[162] James LJ said:

> This Court [of Equity] is not a Court of penal jurisdiction. It compels restitution of property unconscientiously withheld; it gives full compensation for any loss or damage through failure of some equitable duty; but it has no power of punishing anyone.

However, this approach has not been mirrored in Canada[163] and New Zealand,[164] where punitive awards are possible. Indeed, the Law Commission of England and Wales has recommended that punitive damages for equitable wrongdoing should be available where the defendant has deliberately and outrageously disregarded the claimant's rights and other remedies are inadequate:[165]

> we can ultimately see no reason of principle or practicality for excluding equitable wrongs from any rational statutory expansion of the law of exemplary damages. We consider it unsatisfactory to perpetuate the historical divide between common law and equity, unless there is very good reason to do so. Professor Waddams argues,

---

[157] [1972] AC 1027.

[158] Ibid, 1130.

[159] See generally, Law Commission, *Aggravated, Exemplary and Restitutionary Damages*, Law Com No. 247 (London: HMSO, 1997).

[160] *Kuddus v Chief Constable of Leicestershire Constabulary* [2001] UKHL 29; [2002] 2 AC 122.

[161] *Addis v Gramophone Co. Ltd* [1909] AC 488.

[162] (1872) 8 Ch App 309, 333.

[163] *Huff v Price* [1990] 76 DLR (4th) 138; *Whiten v Pilot Insurance Co.* [2002] 1 SCR 595 (Supreme Court of Canada).

[164] *Aqualculture Corporation v New Zealand Green Mussels Ltd* [1990] 3 NZLR 299.

[165] *Aggravated, Exemplary and Restitutionary Damages*, Law Com. No. 247 (London: HMSO, 1997), [5.55].

> '... the availability of exemplary damages should not be determined by classification of the wrong as a common law tort or as a breach of an equitable obligation ...'[166]
>
> Indeed, we can see good reason for allowing punitive damages to be recovered against, for example, the dishonest trustee who acts in breach of his fiduciary duty or the person who dishonestly abuses another's confidence. Thus if, as we propose, punitive damages are awardable in respect of the (common law) tort of deceit, it would be anomalous if analogously wrongful conduct could not also give rise to an award, just because the cause of action originated in equity. Moreover, 'deterrence' is an aim that is not alien to courts of equity. For example, it is a clear aim of the commonplace equitable remedy of an account of profits awarded for breach of fiduciary duty or breach of confidence. To the extent that such remedies already achieve the aims of a punitive damages award in full or in part, and intentionally or incidentally, this will be a legitimate reason for refusing to make an award under the 'last resort' test, or for making a lower award than would otherwise be necessary.

Allowing punitive damages in Equity would be consistent with their availability in tort. However, it has been countered that it might produce a divide between Equity and Contract, since punitive awards are not clearly available for the latter.[167]

This issue was considered by the New South Wales Court of Appeal in *Harris v Digital Pulse Pty Ltd*.[168] The case actually concerned a breach of duty by two employees of a company who diverted their employer's business to their own, rival company. But much of the Court's decision concentrated upon whether punitive awards are available in Equity. Spigelman CJ and Heydon JA, in the majority, ruled that a punitive award was inappropriate. The former largely restricted his judgment to the particular nature of the case at issue, but the latter was more expansive and said:[169]

> That exemplary damages should be recoverable in tort is not surprising, for as Windeyer J pointed out in *Uren v John Fairfax & Sons Pty Ltd* (1966) 117 CLR 118 at 149 in a passage referred to with approval by the High Court in *Gray v Motor Accident Commission* (1998) 196 CLR 1 at [16], 'the roots of tort and crime' are 'greatly intermingled'. Common law crimes are usually crimes involving mens rea, and in a practical sense issues of motivation, intention to injure, and malign purposes such as dishonesty commonly arise. These mental states overlap with those relevant to the grant of exemplary damages. But equitable duties do not, in standard forms of their operation, turn on those mental states. There is no strong reason to import exemplary damages from one field into so different a field.

By contrast, Mason P dissented and supported the decision of the trial judge to award punitive damages:[170]

---

[166] Waddams, *The Law of Damages* (2nd edn) (Toronto: Canada Law Book, 1990), [11.240], criticizing an Ontario Court of Appeal decision that exemplary damages should not be available for breach of fiduciary duty, because the action was equitable, not tortious.

[167] Although the Canadian Supreme Court has awarded punitive damages for breach of contract: see e.g. *Whiten v Pilot Insurance Co.* [2002] 1 SCR 595 (Supreme Court of Canada).

[168] (2003) 197 ALR 626. See Edelman, 'A "Fusion Fallacy" Fallacy?' (2003) 119 LQR 375 and Burrows, 'Remedial Coherence and Punitive Damages in Equity', in *Equity in Commercial Law* (eds Degeling and Edelman) (Sydney: Lawbook Co., 2005).

[169] (2003) 197 ALR 626, [399].

[170] Ibid, [195], [199].

Palmer J was correct in holding that it was illogical and unprincipled to confine the remedy of exemplary damages to tortious causes of action. As his Honour observed, the availability of exemplary damages should be coextensive with the rationale of the remedy. That rationale is the composite goal of punishing, deterring and vindicating a person who is the victim of wrongdoing clearly proscribed. In that context, it is, as Palmer J observed, absurd to think that a plaintiff whose life savings were stolen by a solicitor would have any different sense of outrage depending upon whether the defendant was sued at common law for deceit or in equity for breach of fiduciary duty. The defendant will have been given advance particulars of the basis of the claim (see Supreme Court Rules Part 15 r5A). Assuming that the plaintiff is able to establish the breach of fiduciary duty plus the additional elements of conscious wrongdoing necessary to trigger an award of exemplary damages, a disinterested observer would be bemused to learn that the law would say that exemplary damages should be withheld, whereas they would have been awarded if the *identical* facts were established had the case been pleaded in tort. ...

In its auxiliary jurisdiction, equity has embraced the role of supplementing the inadequacies of 'common law' remedies. It has always claimed a right of intervention if appropriate to achieve a just result. Discretion and flexibility ensure that equity will not be forced to act where proprietary remedies such as a constructive trust or lien would be inappropriate or disproportionate. How strange therefore that equity should stand back coyly, keeping its hands clean by washing them like Caesar, even if the criteria for the exceptional, discretionary remedy of exemplary damages are met.

In any event, even if the availability of punitive damages were to be recognized in principle, they would never be available as of right, and the court would always have a discretion whether or not to award a punitive remedy. It might be expected that punitive damages would only be granted in response to exceptional instances of particularly egregious wrongdoing.

QUESTION

Bob died in 1980, and in his will left £20,000 to Colin and Anna to hold on trust for his children. Colin and Anna have never sought professional advice regarding the range of investments held by the trust. The fund is now worth £22,000. If it had been properly managed, the children think the value of the trust fund would be around £75,000.

The terms of the trust deed prevent the trustees from investing in foreign currency funds. Nevertheless, in 2010 Colin and Anna invested £1,000 in Japanese Yen and £1,000 in Swiss Francs. The investment in Japanese Yen is now worth only £500, but the investment in Swiss Francs is worth £2,000.

Colin and Anna also decided to invest some of the trust fund in a film project run by Likely Pictures. For this purpose, Colin and Anna transferred £8,000 to their solicitor, Barry. Barry was under instructions to hold this money on trust for Colin and Anna, and to release the money to Likely Pictures only upon receiving written confirmation from Steve, an award-winning director, that he had agreed to work on the project. Barry transferred the money to Likely Pictures before receiving this confirmation. Soon after receiving the money, Likely Pictures went into insolvent liquidation. Barry received written confirmation from Steve that he had agreed to work on the project after he had paid the money to Likely Pictures, but before Likely Pictures became insolvent.

Advise Bob's children.

FURTHER READING

Chambers, 'Liability', in *Breach of Trust* (eds Birks and Pretto) (Oxford: Hart, 2002).

Davies, 'Remedies for Breach of Trust' (2015) 78 MLR 681.

Elliott, 'Rethinking Interest on Withheld and Misapplied Trust Money' [2001] Conv 313.

Elliott, 'Remoteness Criteria in Equity' (2002) 65 MLR 588.

Millett, 'Equity's Place in the Law of Commerce' (1998) 114 LQR 214.

18

PROPRIETARY CLAIMS AND REMEDIES

CENTRAL ISSUES

1. Proprietary claims are based upon a claimant's property rights. Proprietary claims might lead to personal remedies, considered in Chapter 19, or proprietary remedies, considered in this chapter.

2. Proprietary claims may be brought at Common Law or in Equity, depending on whether the property right upon which the claim is based is recognized at Common Law or in Equity. The source of the right may affect the remedy that is awarded and the defences available.

3. Proprietary claims require the claimant to have a right that can be identified in property in the defendant's hands either through the process of following or that of tracing.

4. Following is the process by which the original item of property is identified in the hands of another. Tracing is the process by which a claimant's property right is identified in a substitute of that original item of property.

5. Whereas Equity can trace into and through a mixture of property from different sources,

orthodoxy suggests that the Common Law cannot.

6. Where property in which the claimant has an equitable proprietary interest has been mixed with property belonging to another person, various presumptions apply relating to whom the mixed fund and any subsequently acquired assets belong. Generally, everything is presumed against a wrongdoing fiduciary and in favour of an innocent claimant. But where the claimant and defendant are both innocent, they usually share the mixed fund in proportion to their original contributions.

7. Equitable proprietary remedies include the constructive trust, a charge or lien, and subrogation.

8. A claimant can generally elect between available proprietary remedies. However, the defendant may be able to establish the defence of bona fide purchaser for value without notice, or, possibly, change of position.

1. INTRODUCTION

Where a breach of trust or fiduciary duty has involved the transfer of property in which the beneficiary or principal has an equitable proprietary interest, the beneficiary or principal may wish to bring a claim to assert his or her proprietary interest in assets that are now in the hands of another person. Such claims are founded on the beneficiary's equitable interest in the property, and so are properly characterized as proprietary claims. But, although the *claim* is founded on the beneficiary's proprietary rights, the *remedy* awarded is not necessarily a proprietary one. There are two different types of remedy which are available in respect of equitable proprietary claims:

a) *Proprietary remedies*, which enable claimants to assert rights against particular property which is still in the hands of the defendant.

b) *Personal remedies*, which enable claimants to sue the defendant personally for the *value* of the property which has been received by the defendant but has not necessarily been retained.

This distinction between claims and remedies has been consistently emphasized by Lord Millett. For example, in *Trustee of the Property of FC Jones and Sons (a firm) v Jones*, a case considered more fully later,[1] he said that the claimant:[2]

> has no proprietary *remedy*. But it does not follow that he has no proprietary *claim*.

The essence of an equitable proprietary claim lies in establishing that another person has received property in which the claimant has a proprietary interest recognized in Equity. The property received may be the original property, in which case the claimant can *follow* his property into the hands of another, or substitute property, in which case the claimant will need to *trace* the value of his property into the substitute asset. The rules of tracing will be considered in detail later,[3] but it is important to appreciate that tracing is simply an evidential process to support a proprietary claim, but is neither a claim nor a remedy in itself.

Boscawen v Bajwa [1996] 1 WLR 328, 334 (Millett LJ)

> Equity lawyers habitually use the expressions 'the tracing claim' and 'the tracing remedy' to describe the proprietary claim and the proprietary remedy which equity makes available to the beneficial owner who seeks to recover his property in specie from those into whose hands it has come. Tracing properly so-called, however, is neither a claim nor a remedy but a process. Moreover, it is not confined to the case where the plaintiff seeks a proprietary remedy; it is equally necessary where he seeks a personal remedy against the knowing recipient or knowing assistant.[4] It is the process by which the plaintiff traces what has happened to his property, identifies the persons who have handled or received it, and justifies his claim that the money which they handled or received (and, if necessary, which they still retain) can properly be regarded as representing his property.

---

[1] Chapter 18.3(c)(i), pp. 864–5.
[2] *Jones v Jones* [1997] Ch 159, 168 (as Millett LJ). See also e.g. *Foskett v McKeown* [2001] 1 AC 102, 128 (Lord Millett).
[3] See Chapter 18.3(b), p. 854.
[4] These claims are considered in Chapter 19, 'Third Party Liability'.

This chapter will focus upon proprietary claims and proprietary remedies. Personal remedies, the most significant of which is unconscionable receipt, will be considered in Chapter 19. However, it is important to understand how the two types of remedy overlap and interrelate.

(a) TYPES OF PROPRIETARY REMEDY

There are two principal categories of proprietary remedy:

i) Allowing the claimant to recover the property transferred or substitute property. This is often effected by imposing a constructive trust upon the defendant to hold the property for the claimant. Depending on the circumstances, a claimant might only recover a share of the property rather than the property in its entirety.

ii) Recognizing the value of the claimant's proprietary interest through a security interest in the property, normally a charge or lien, which gives the claimant priority over unsecured creditors of the defendant.

The first type of remedy will be preferred by a claimant if the property in question has risen in value, since the claimant will benefit from an appropriate share of the increase in value. But if the property has fallen in value, then a charge or lien will be preferred, as this will secure the value of the claimant's original proprietary interest if the defendant becomes insolvent, and is unaffected by any fluctuating value of the property.[5]

(i) *Advantages of personal remedy over proprietary remedy*

If the property in the defendant's hands has fallen in value below the level of the claimant's original interest, a proprietary remedy may not be advantageous. For example, if a defendant has £10,000 of the claimant's money, but spends it all on a luxurious holiday, there will be no property left upon which a proprietary remedy can attach. By contrast, a personal claim for the full £10,000 might still succeed.

Boscawen v Bajwa [1996] 1 WLR 328, 334 (Millett LJ)

> The plaintiff will generally be entitled to a personal remedy; if he seeks a proprietary remedy he must usually prove that the property to which he lays claim is still in the ownership of the defendant.

(ii) *Advantages of proprietary remedy over personal remedy*

Where the property still exists and is of sufficient value to satisfy the claim, a proprietary remedy will often be preferred. This is because it affords the claimant protection upon the defendant's insolvency: the claim is against the *property* itself, rather than only against the defendant personally. Moreover, the personal claim is not usually able to give the claimant the benefit of any increase in the value of the property.[6]

---

[5] Although if the value of the property falls *below* the value of the claimant's security interest, the claimant will only have a proprietary remedy to the extent of the current value of the property, and will need to pursue a personal claim against the defendant for the deficit.

[6] See Chapter 1.4(a)(i), p. 11.

(b) ANALYSING PROPRIETARY CLAIMS

Proprietary claims can seem very complicated at first. However, identifying a clear framework will be useful when analysing difficult cases. The preferable framework requires the following elements to be identified in turn, each of which will be considered more fully in the rest of the chapter.

(i) *The proprietary base*

The claimant must show that he or she has a legal or an equitable proprietary interest in the misappropiated property.

(ii) *Following and tracing*

The claimant must be able either to follow that property into the hands of the defendant, or trace its value into a substitute asset received and retained by the defendant. This establishes the claimant's proprietary interest in the relevant property held by the defendant. The nature of the tracing rules will depend on whether the claimant has a legal or an equitable proprietary interest.

(iii) *Claiming*

Once the claimant has identified assets in which he or she has a proprietary interest, the claimant can then assert his or her rights in those assets. The nature of the claimant's claim will be influenced by the nature of his or her proprietary base. A legal property right at the outset will lead to a legal claim; an equitable right to an equitable claim. The nature of the claim cannot exceed the original interest: if the claimant had a security interest in the original property, he or she will only be able to assert a security interest in the subsequent property.[7]

(iv) *Identification of the remedy*

Once the claim is established, a remedy should be granted to vindicate the claimant's proprietary right. This may be proprietary or personal, and the claimant is able to choose between the two. As Lord Millett said of an equitable proprietary claim in *Foskett v McKeown*:[8]

> In such a case the beneficiary is entitled *at his option* either to assert his beneficial ownership ... or to bring a personal claim ... He will normally exercise the option in the way most advantageous to himself.

(v) *Defences*

The most significant defence is that a claimant's equitable right will be defeated if the defendant purchased the property for value in good faith and without notice of the claimant's right. Whether a defendant who has relied upon his or her receipt of the property by doing something he or she would not ordinarily have done is able to avail him or herself of a defence of change of position is more controversial.

---

[7] *Foskett v McKeown* [2001] AC 102, 127. See Chapter 18.4, pp. 889–90.
[8] Ibid, 130.

2. THE PROPRIETARY BASE

Christopher Clarke J has reiterated that:[9]

> In order to be able successfully to trace property it is necessary for the claimant, firstly, to identify property of his, which has been unlawfully taken from him ('a proprietary base').

The claimant may have retained legal title to the property. In such circumstances, he or she will be able to pursue a legal proprietary claim, and follow or trace the property or its value at Common Law. However, as will be explored in this chapter,[10] equitable claims are often preferred as they are more flexible than their Common Law counterparts: if the claimant's property has been mixed with another's property then it might lose its identity at Law, making it impossible to trace through a mixture at Common Law,[11] but not necessarily in Equity. Also, proprietary remedies are generally not available at Common Law.

In order to ground an equitable proprietary claim, an equitable proprietary base is required. A beneficiary under an express,[12] resulting,[13] or constructive[14] trust clearly has an equitable proprietary right. But an equitable proprietary base may also arise under other circumstances, such as proprietary estoppel.[15]

Difficult situations arise where the claimant's property has been stolen. A thief does not obtain legal title to property simply by stealing it. So, for example, I do not lose legal title to my watch if you steal it from me. I can sue you in the tort of conversion, and if you swap my watch for a necklace, then I can either trace my proprietary interest at Common Law into the necklace, or follow my watch into the hands of a third party. In both scenarios, I would be relying upon legal title. Indeed, in the latter instance, a legal claim might be preferable to an equitable claim: if the third party was a bona fide purchaser for value without notice that would defeat an equitable claim but not a legal claim, since the rule of 'nemo dat quod non habet' operates at Common Law and means that the thief cannot give better title than he or she had. Since the thief did not obtain title, the third party cannot get good title either. However, the victim is unlikely to recover the watch itself; although section 3 of the Torts (Interference with Goods) Act 1977 allows for this possibility, this provision has been interpreted such that an order for delivery of the watch itself will only be made at the court's discretion where damages would be an inadequate remedy.

Torts (Interference with Goods) Act 1977

Section 3

(1) In proceedings for wrongful interference against a person who is in possession or in control of the goods relief may be given in accordance with this section, so far as appropriate.

(2) The relief is—

    (a) an order for delivery of the goods, and for payment of any consequential damages, or

---

[9] *OJSC Oil Company Yugraneft (in liquidation) v Abramovich* [2008] EWHC 2613 (Comm), [349].
[10] See Chapter 18.3(c), p. 860.
[11] At least, this is the traditional approach. For criticism and recent developments, see Chapter 18.3(c)(i), pp. 862–3.
[12] Chapter 3, 'The Requirements of An Express Trust'.
[13] Chapter 8, 'Resulting Trusts'.
[14] Chapter 7, 'Constructive Trusts'.
[15] *Thorner v Majors* [2009] UKHL 18; [2009] 1 WLR 776. See Chapter 9.4, p. 469.

(b) an order for delivery of the goods, but giving the defendant the alternative of paying damages by reference to the value of the goods, together in either alternative with payment of any consequential damages, or

(c) damages.

(3) Subject to rules of court—

(a) relief shall be given under only one of paragraphs (a), (b) and (c) of subsection (2),

(b) relief under paragraph (a) of subsection (2) is at the discretion of the court, and the claimant may choose between the others.

The example of a thief was discussed by Lord Browne-Wilkinson in *Westdeutsche Landesbank Girozentrale v Islington London Borough Council*.[16] His Lordship thought that:[17]

Although it is difficult to find clear authority for the proposition, when property is obtained by fraud equity imposes a constructive trust on the fraudulent recipient: the property is recoverable and traceable in equity.

This statement seems contrary to the analysis provided above. Indeed, in *Shalson v Russo*, Rimer J insisted that:[18]

a thief ordinarily acquires no property in what he steals and cannot give a title to it even to a good faith purchaser: both the thief and the purchaser are vulnerable to claims by the true owner to recover his property. If the thief has no title in the property, I cannot see how he can become a trustee of it for the true owner: the owner retains the legal and beneficial title.

The two statements might be reconciled in situations where the claimant's property is mixed with other property. For example, if the thief were to steal my watch, sell it, and then put the proceeds of the sale in his bank account in which he already had money, the mixing of funds would be sufficient to defeat my legal claim. But in such circumstances I would obtain an equitable proprietary base: legal title to the money would pass to the thief, but it would be unconscionable for him to deny that a proportion of the money in his account properly belongs to me, so he will be found to hold the money on constructive trust.[19]

The more difficult scenario does not involve mixing. What if my solicitor steals my money from my bank account, and does not mix the money with his own funds? The initial analysis, supported by Rimer J in *Shalson v Russo*, suggests that legal title remains with me and that I should pursue a legal claim. By contrast, Lord Browne-Wilkinson's approach would allow an equitable claim. Establishing which claim is to be preferred might be important: if the fiduciary has become insolvent, only the equitable claim might fully protect my proprietary interest, by virtue of the stronger equitable proprietary remedies. Perhaps the best theoretical explanation for the existence of a constructive trust in such circumstances has been provided by Tarant:[20]

after a theft ... stolen money is subject to two legal property rights. The first property right is the true owner's right to possession. The second property right is the thief's newly acquired property right of

---

[16] [1996] AC 669, 715.

[17] [1996] AC 669, 716.

[18] [2003] EWHC 1637 (Ch); [2005] Ch 281, [110].

[19] For discussion of constructive trusts and the decision in *Westdeutsche*, see Chapter 7.2(a), pp. 332–6.

[20] 'Property Rights to Stolen Money' (2005) 32 UWALR 234, 245. See too Tarant, 'Thieves as Trustees: In Defence of the Theft Principle' (2009) 3 JoE 170. Compare S Barkehall-Thomas, 'Thieves as Trustees: The Enduring Legacy of *Black v S Freedman & Co Ltd*' (2009) 3 JoE 52.

> possession. ... The trust property is the thief's legal property right of possession of the money; the money itself is not trust property.

On this basis, the thief is not holding legal title on trust. Rather, he is holding possessory title to the money on trust. This may seem odd, since it means that the legal owner of the money is also the beneficiary under the constructive trust. But it is explicable once it is understood that there are many different types of proprietary rights, and that titles to property are relative to one another. So the thief obtains a Common Law possessory title, which is good against third parties who cannot prove a stronger title to the money than that of the thief, and the thief holds this title on trust for the beneficiary.[21]

Nevertheless, some might remain uncomfortable with the legal owner of property being the beneficiary of a trust when legal title to the property remains with himself, not the thief. But as Fox has observed:[22]

> The reason for recognizing the trust is entirely pragmatic: it is anomalous that a person who has a distinct equitable title to the money before it is misapplied, such as the principal in a fiduciary relationship, should have standing to follow or trace the money in equity, whereas a person with an undivided legal and beneficial title should be left to rely on the vagaries of the common law rules of identification to recover it.

This is undoubtedly right; it is important that the claimant be able to trace after a thief misappropriates his property. But it is unclear why, if such intricacies are necessary to establish an equitable property base in order to protect the claimant in the event of the thief's insolvency, the same priority should not simply be afforded to a legal owner whose property has been stolen.[23]

The difficulties inherent in the complicated case law highlight the artificiality of having distinct rules for tracing at Common Law and Equity.[24] In the fight against modern, large-scale fraud, it would be preferable to have only one set of tracing rules, and the more generous equitable jurisdiction should be preferred. Indeed, steps may be being taken to move in this direction.[25]

3. FOLLOWING AND TRACING

Both following and tracing are that which are employed in order to identify the claimant's proprietary rights in assets held by the defendant. However, the two processes are distinct. In *Foskett v McKeown*, Lord Millett said:[26]

> The process of ascertaining what happened to the plaintiffs' money involves both tracing and following. These are both exercises in locating assets which are or may be taken to represent an asset belonging to the plaintiffs and to which they assert ownership. The processes of following and tracing are,

---

[21] This analysis seems to accord with that in *Armstrong DLW GmbH v Winnington Networks Ltd* [2012] EWHC 10 (Ch); [2012] 3 WLR 835, [127] (Stephen Morris QC).

[22] Fox, *Property Rights in Money* (Oxford: Oxford University Press, 2008), p. 140.

[23] In *Transfer of the Property of Jones & Sons v Jones* [1997] CL 159, 168, Millett LJ suggested that priority might be given to the owner. For further consideration of the perceived historical restrictions of tracing and proprietary remedies at Common Law, see e.g. Chapter 18.3(c)(i), p. 860.

[24] Difficulties do not only arise at the stage of establishing the proprietary base. Another supposed requirement for tracing in Equity is that there be a fiduciary relationship, which is also difficult to find in the case of a thief: see Chapter 18.3(c)(ii)(a), pp. 867–70. But an important difference arises regarding the remedy: proprietary remedies are not well recognized at Common Law. See Chapter 18.5, p. 893.

[25] See Chapter 18.3(c)(i), pp. 862–3.

[26] [2001] 1 AC 102, 127.

> however, distinct. Following is the process of following the same asset as it moves from hand to hand. Tracing is the process of identifying a new asset as the substitute for the old. Where one asset is exchanged for another, a claimant can elect whether to follow the original asset into the hands of the new owner or to trace its value into the new asset in the hands of the same owner. In practice his choice is often dictated by the circumstances.

Thus if a car is stolen by a fiduciary and sold to a third party, then the claimant will have a choice between following the car into the hands of the third party, or tracing into the money received by the fiduciary. It is sensible to allow the innocent claimant who is the victim of the misappropriation to choose between following and tracing. If the car is worth more than the purchase money received by the fiduciary, the claimant would prefer to follow the car. But if the car has fallen in value and the fiduciary received more than the car is currently worth, it would be advantageous for the claimant to trace instead.

This election analysis explains why the claimant cannot assert a proprietary interest against *both* the original asset *and* a substitute asset. However, it is unclear precisely *when* a right in the substitute asset arises. If the original asset is dissipated, it seems sensible for a right in the substitute asset to arise automatically. The situation is more complicated where both the original asset and substitute asset still exist: there is authority for the proposition that the claimant immediately obtains a proprietary interest in the new asset upon the wrongful misappropriation,[27] but also for the proposition that the claimant has a power to crystallize his or her interest in that new asset.[28] The latter seems more consistent with an approach based on election, but may lead to the difficult conclusion that a claimant will no longer be able to crystallize his or her proprietary interest once the defendant who holds the substitute asset is insolvent; this would mean that the claimant will not have priority over the defendant's other creditors, whose interests also need protection.

(a) FOLLOWING

Following generally relates to the identification of tangible things and involves a practical investigation of what has happened to a physical object. It is focussed upon the original thing held by the claimant, and follows that thing into the hands of a 'new' person. By contrast, tracing is concerned with 'new' substitute assets.

When trying to follow something into the hands of another, difficulties might arise where it is disputed whether or not the thing still exists. For example, sometimes the original thing might be followed into a mixture. Where the mixture is readily divisible, such that the original thing can easily be separated, then following is straightforward. But this will not always be the case: for example, in *Spence v Union Marine Insurance Co.*,[29] the claimant's cotton was mixed with other cotton. Bovill CJ said:[30]

> when goods of different owners become by accident so mixed together as to be undistinguishable, the owners of the goods so mixed become tenants in common of the whole, in the proportions which they have severally contributed to it. ...

---

[27] *Cave v Cave* (1880) 15 Ch D 639 (Fry J); *Re Diplock's Estate* [1948] Ch 465; *Foskett* 134 (Lord Millett).

[28] *Foskett v McKeown* [2001] 1 AC 102, 127 (Lord Millett, quoted immediately above); see also *Lipkin Gorman v Karpnale Ltd* [1991] 2 AC 548, 573 (Lord Goff).

[29] (1868) LR 3 CP 427.

[30] Ibid, 437–8.

> The goods being before they are mixed the separate property of the several owners, unless, which is absurd, they cease to be property by reason of the accidental mixture, when they would not so cease if the mixture were designed, must continue to be the property of the original owners; and, as there would be no means of distinguishing the goods of each, the several owners seem necessarily to become jointly interested, as tenants in common, in the bulk.

Finding a tenancy in common allows each owner to take back their original share, but whereas normally the consent of all tenants, or a court order, is necessary to sever a tenancy in common, Bovill CJ suggested that each contributor has a right to take his or her portion from the mixture. Smith has called this a tenancy in common 'of an unusual sort',[31] but in any event it appears possible to follow into such a mixture and for the contents of the mixture to be attributed to the original owners rateably, in proportion to their contributions.[32]

Bovill CJ limited his comments to accidental mixing. He thought a different approach is taken where one party wrongfully mixes his property with property belonging to another. This follows the views of Blackstone, who wrote that:[33]

> if one wilfully intermixes his money, corn or hay, with that of another man, without his approbation or knowledge, … our law, to guard against fraud, gives the entire property, without any account, to him whose original dominion is invaded, and endeavoured to be rendered uncertain, without his own consent.

In *Jones v De Marchant*,[34] a husband made a fur coat out of twenty-two beaver skins, eighteen of which were his and four of which belonged to his wife but were misappropriated by the husband. He gave the coat to his mistress. The Canadian court insisted that the coat belonged to his wife. This result was supported by Lord Millett in *Foskett v McKeown*, who emphasized that:[35]

> The determinative factor was that the mixing was the act of the wrongdoer through whom the mistress acquired the coat otherwise than for value.

So in *Jones v De Marchant* it appears that the wife could follow her skins into the coat, even though the coat was a new asset, and it was impossible to separate and identify the original thing.[36] It seems right that the new product belonged to the innocent party (the wife) rather than the wrongdoer (the husband). As a result, the husband did not enjoy good title to pass on to his mistress, a third party donee.

However, it may be that *Jones* will no longer be followed where the property in question is fungible. *Indian Oil Corporation v Greenstone Shipping Co.* concerned the mixing of crude oil. Staughton J held that:[37]

> where B wrongfully mixes the goods of A with goods of his own, which are substantially of the same nature and quality, and they cannot in practice be separated, the mixture is held in common and A is

---

[31] Smith, *The Law of Tracing*, (Oxford: Clarendon Press, 1987), p. 75.

[32] For further discussion of accidental mixing, see Hickey, 'Dazed and Confused: Accidental Mixtures of Goods and the Theory of Acquisition of Title' (2003) 66 MLR 368.

[33] *Commentaries on the Laws of England* (Oxford: Clarendon Press, 1766) Vol. 2, 405.

[34] (1916) 28 DLR 561.

[35] [2001] 1 AC 102, 133.

[36] Although tracing might have been a viable alternative; see Chapter 18.3(b), p. 854.

[37] [1988] QB 345, 370–1. This passage received the support of Moore-Bick J in *Glencore International AG v Metro Trading International Inc. (formerly Metro Bunkering and Trading Co.) v Ors* [2001] 1 All ER (Comm) 103, [158]–[159].

entitled to receive out of it a quantity equal to that of his goods which went into the mixture, any doubt as to that quantity being resolved in favour of A. He is also entitled to claim damages from B in respect of any loss he may have suffered, in respect of quality or otherwise, by reason of the admixture.

Whether the same rule would apply when the goods of A and B are not substantially of the same nature and quality must be left to another case. It does not arise here.

It may at times be difficult to decide whether or not the original thing still exists such that it can be followed. Obviously, where it has been destroyed, there is no longer anything to follow. But there are other ways for the thing to lose its original identity. For example, it might become inextricably attached to something else, and thereby lose its separate identity. Or it may be so altered that it becomes a different type of thing. Both these examples involve difficult questions of judgment and degree.

Where one thing becomes attached to another such that it is impossible to separate, then it is often said that the 'subsidiary' thing 'accedes' to the 'principal' item.[38] Determining which is the 'principal' item may sometimes be difficult, but generally it will be the more dominant thing. So a link would accede to a chain, for example;[39] the chain would continue to exist, but the link would be submerged in the chain. However, in some situations neither item may be subsidiary to the other; indeed both might be identical. For example, two floating docks might be joined together to form a new entity.[40] In that event, the preferable view is that neither dock can be followed, and that both are submerged in the new, larger dock. It is no longer possible to identify the original thing.

Where the original thing is only slightly altered, it might still be identified and followed; but if it has changed so radically that it is a different thing then that will prevent following. This is known as 'specification'. This again involves difficult questions of degree. Where a car has been scrapped and the metal used to make various tools, it is impossible to follow the car.[41] But where a car has simply been painted, it will not have radically changed and is still identifiable.

Perhaps the most common form of misappropriated property is money. Although money is a thing which, in principle, can be followed, the difficulty is that money has no earmark: it is often impossible to identify certain coins or banknotes as originally belonging to the claimant.[42] For example, it would require the claimant to make a note of the series numbers of banknotes in order to follow them. Where money is mixed, tracing is to be preferred to following.

(b) TRACING

In *Shalson v Russo*, Rimer J described tracing:[43]

as the process by which a claimant seeks to show that an interest he had in an asset has become represented by an interest in a different asset.

---

[38] See generally Smith, *The Law of Tracing* (Oxford: Clarendon Press, 1987), pp. 104ff.

[39] *Pulcifer v Page* (1851) 32 Me 404.

[40] Smith, *The Law of Tracing* (Oxford: Clarendon Press, 1987), p. 106, based on *Wylie v Mitchell* (1870) 8 M 552 (Ct Sess).

[41] Although tracing might be possible; see Chapter 18.3(b), p. 841.

[42] See *Core's case* (1537) 1 Dyer 20a; *Isaac v Clark* (1615) 2 Bulst 306. Cf. Fox, 'Identification of Money at Common Law' (2010) 69 CLJ 28.

[43] [2003] EWHC 1637 (Ch); [2005] Ch 281, [102].

It is a process in the same manner as following, but whereas following concerns the physical thing, tracing is focussed upon the *value* inherent in property. This value can pass from one asset to another, as determined by the rules of tracing. In *Foskett v McKeown*, Lord Millett said:[44]

> We also speak of tracing one asset into another, but this too is inaccurate. The original asset still exists in the hands of the new owner, or it may have become untraceable. The claimant claims the new asset because it was acquired in whole or in part with the original asset. What he traces, therefore, is not the physical asset itself but the value inherent in it.

Foskett v McKeown is now the leading authority of the House of Lords on this subject, and provides clear guidance on the tracing process.

Foskett v McKeown [2001] 1 AC 102 (HL)

In 1986, Mr Murphy entered into a whole-life insurance policy. The sum assured was £1 million and the annual premium was £10,200. The policy stated that on Murphy's death a specified death benefit became payable, which would be the greater of (1) the sum assured; and (2) the aggregate value of units notionally allocated to the policy under its terms at their bid price on the day of the receipt by the insurers of a written notice of death (the investment element). One of the functions of this investment element was to pay for the cost of life cover. This aspect of the policy was a little complicated, but, essentially, on the receipt of a premium, a notional allocation of units would take place and the insurers would cancel units to meet the cost of life cover for the next year. If premiums ceased to be paid, the policy would be converted into a paid-up policy and units would continue to be cancelled until there were no units left. Once there were no units left the policy would lapse, so that death benefit or surrender value would no longer be available.

The policy and money paid under it were held on an express trust for Murphy's wife and children. Murphy paid five premiums. The first three were paid from his own money, but he then paid two other premiums from another trust, one in 1989 and the other in 1990. The money in this trust had been paid by purchasers to a Mr Deasy in respect of the possible development of land in Portugal. Mr Deasy held this money on trust for the purchasers. Murphy committed suicide and the insurers paid just over £1 million to two remaining trustees of the insurance policy for the benefit of Murphy's children. The purchasers claimed that, since at least two of the five premiums had been paid from money that had been held on trust for them, they should recover at least two-fifths of the £1 million, with the remaining amount being paid to Murphy's children.

A majority of the Court of Appeal [1998] Ch 265 held that the purchasers could recover the value of two of the premiums plus interest but could not receive any share of the proceeds of the policy. The House of Lords, by a bare majority, disagreed, and insisted that the purchasers were entitled to recover two-fifths of the £1 million that was held on trust for the children.

The case raises important issues regarding claims and remedies, which will be considered later; the following extracts principally concern the nature of the proprietary claim and the process of tracing.

---

[44] [2001] 1 AC 102, 128.

Lord Browne-Wilkinson:

The crucial factor in this case is to appreciate that the purchasers are claiming a proprietary interest in the policy moneys and that such proprietary interest is not dependent on any discretion vested in the court. Nor is the purchasers' claim based on unjust enrichment. It is based on the assertion by the purchasers of their equitable proprietary interest in identified property.

The first step is to identify the interest of the purchasers: it is their absolute equitable interest in the moneys originally held by Mr. Deasy on the express trusts of the purchasers' trust deed. ... Like any other equitable proprietary interest, those equitable proprietary interests under the purchasers' trust deed which originally existed in the moneys paid to Mr. Deasy now exist in any other property which, in law, now represents the original trust assets. ... the critical question is whether the assets now subject to the express trusts of the purchasers' trust deed comprise any part of the policy moneys, a question which depends on the rules of tracing. If, as a result of tracing, it can be said that certain of the policy moneys are what now represent part of the assets subject to the trusts of the purchasers' trust deed, then as a matter of English property law the purchasers have an absolute interest in such moneys. There is no discretion vested in the court. There is no room for any consideration whether, in the circumstances of this particular case, it is in a moral sense 'equitable' for the purchasers to be so entitled. The rules establishing equitable proprietary interests and their enforceability against certain parties have been developed over the centuries and are an integral part of the property law of England. It is a fundamental error to think that, because certain property rights are equitable rather than legal, such rights are in some way discretionary. This case does not depend on whether it is fair, just and reasonable to give the purchasers an interest as a result of which the court in its discretion provides a remedy. It is a case of hard-nosed property rights.

Lord Millett:

My Lords, this is a textbook example of tracing through mixed substitutions. At the beginning of the story the plaintiffs were beneficially entitled under an express trust to a sum standing in the name of Mr. Murphy in a bank account. From there the money moved into and out of various bank accounts where in breach of trust it was inextricably mixed by Mr. Murphy with his own money. After each transaction was completed the plaintiffs' money formed an indistinguishable part of the balance standing to Mr. Murphy's credit in his bank account. The amount of that balance represented a debt due from the bank to Mr. Murphy, that is to say a chose in action. At the penultimate stage the plaintiffs' money was represented by an indistinguishable part of a different chose in action, viz. the debt prospectively and contingently due from an insurance company to its policyholders, being the trustees of a settlement made by Mr. Murphy for the benefit of his children. At the present and final stage it forms an indistinguishable part of the balance standing to the credit of the respondent trustees in their bank account. ...

In the present case the plaintiffs do not seek to follow the money any further once it reached the bank or insurance company, since its identity was lost in the hands of the recipient (which in any case obtained an unassailable title as a bona fide purchaser for value without notice of the plaintiffs' beneficial interest). Instead the plaintiffs have chosen at each stage to trace the money into its proceeds, viz. the debt presently due from the bank to the account holder or the debt prospectively and contingently due from the insurance company to the policy holders.

A beneficiary of a trust is entitled to a continuing beneficial interest not merely in the trust property but in its traceable proceeds also, and his interest binds every one who takes the property or its traceable proceeds except a bona fide purchaser for value without notice. In the present case the plaintiffs' beneficial interest plainly bound Mr. Murphy, a trustee who wrongfully mixed the trust money with his own and whose every dealing with the money (including the payment of the premiums) was in breach of trust. It similarly binds his successors, the trustees of the children's settlement, who claim no beneficial interest of their own, and Mr. Murphy's children, who are volunteers. They gave no value for what they received and derive their interest from Mr. Murphy by way of gift. ...

A beneficiary's claim against a trustee for breach of trust is a personal claim. It does not entitle him to priority over the trustee's general creditors unless he can trace the trust property into its product and establish a proprietary interest in the proceeds. If the beneficiary is unable to trace the trust property into its proceeds, he still has a personal claim against the trustee, but his claim will be unsecured. The beneficiary's proprietary claims to the trust property or its traceable proceeds can be maintained against the wrongdoer and anyone who derives title from him except a bona fide purchaser for value without notice of the breach of trust. The same rules apply even where there have been numerous successive transactions, so long as the tracing exercise is successful and no bona fide purchaser for value without notice has intervened.

... In the present case the benefits specified in the policy are expressed to be payable 'in consideration of the payment of the first premium already made and of the further premiums payable'. The premiums are stated to be '£10,220 payable at annual intervals from 6 November, 1985 throughout the lifetime of the life assured'. It is beyond argument that the death benefit of £1 million paid on Mr. Murphy's death was paid in consideration for all the premiums which had been paid before that date, including those paid with the plaintiffs' money, and not just some of them. Part of that sum, therefore, represented the traceable proceeds of the plaintiffs' money.

It is, however, of critical importance in the present case to appreciate that the plaintiffs do not trace the premiums directly into the insurance money. They trace them first into the policy and thence into the proceeds of the policy. It is essential not to elide the two steps. In this context, of course, the word 'policy' does not mean the contract of insurance. You do not trace the payment of a premium into the insurance contract any more than you trace a payment into a bank account into the banking contract. The word 'policy' is here used to describe the bundle of rights to which the policyholder is entitled in return for the premiums. These rights, which may be very complex, together constitute a chose in action, viz. the right to payment of a debt payable on a future event and contingent upon the continued payment of further premiums until the happening of the event. That chose in action represents the traceable proceeds of the premiums; its current value fluctuates from time to time. When the policy matures, the insurance money represents the traceable proceeds of the policy and hence indirectly of the premiums.

...

In my opinion there is no reason to differentiate between the first premium or premiums and later premiums. Such a distinction is not based on any principle. Why should the policy belong to the party who paid the first premium, without which there would have been no policy, rather than to the party who paid the last premium, without which it would normally have lapsed? Moreover, any such distinction would lead to the most capricious results. If only four annual premiums are paid, why should it matter whether A paid the first two premiums and B the second two, or B paid the first two and A the second two, or they each paid half of each of the four premiums? Why should the children obtain the whole of the sum assured if Mr. Murphy used his own money before he began to use the plaintiffs' money, and only a return of the premiums if Mr. Murphy happened to use the plaintiffs' money first? Why should the proceeds of the policy be attributed to the first premium when the policy itself is expressed to be in consideration of all the premiums? There is no analogy with the case where trust money is used to maintain or improve property of a third party. The nearest analogy is with an instalment purchase.

Hobhouse LJ adopted a different approach. He concentrated on the detailed terms of the policy, and in particular on the fact that in the event the payment of the fourth and fifth premiums with the plaintiffs' money made no difference to the amount of the death benefit. Once the third premium had been paid, there was sufficient surrender value in the policy, built up by the use of Mr. Murphy's own money, to keep the policy on foot for the next few years, and as it happened Mr. Murphy's death occurred during those few years. But this was adventitious and unpredictable at the time the premiums were paid. The argument is based on causation and as I have explained is a category mistake derived from the law of unjust enrichment. It is an example of the same fallacy that gives rise to the idea that the proceeds of an ordinary life policy belong to the party who paid the last premium without which the policy would have lapsed. But the question is one of attribution not causation. The question is not whether the same death benefit would have been payable if the last premium or last few premiums had not been paid. It is whether the death benefit is attributable to all the premiums or only to some of them. The answer is that death benefit is attributable to all of them because it represents the proceeds of realising the policy, and the policy in turn represents the product of all the premiums.

In any case, Hobhouse LJ's analysis of the terms of the policy does not go far enough. It is not correct that the last two premiums contributed nothing to the sum payable on Mr. Murphy's death but merely reduced the cost to the insurers of providing it. Life cover was provided in return for a series of internal premiums paid for by the cancellation of units previously allocated to the policy. Units were allocated to the policy in return for the annual premiums. Prior to their cancellation the cancelled units formed part of a mixed fund of units which was the product of all the premiums paid by Mr. Murphy, including those paid with the plaintiffs' money. On ordinary principles, the plaintiffs can trace the last two premiums into and out of the mixed fund and into the internal premiums used to provide the death benefit.

It is true that the last two premiums were not needed to provide the death benefit in the sense that in the events which happened the same amount would have been payable even if those premiums had not been paid. In other words, with the benefit of hindsight it can be seen that Mr. Murphy made a bad investment when he paid the last two premiums. It is, therefore, superficially attractive to say that the plaintiffs' money contributed nothing of value. But the argument proves too much, for if the plaintiffs cannot trace their money into the proceeds of the policy, they should have no proprietary remedy at all, not even a lien for the return of their money. But the fact is that Mr. Murphy, who could not foresee the future, did choose to pay the last two premiums, and to pay them with the plaintiffs' money; and they were applied by the insurer towards the payment of the internal premiums needed to fund the death benefit. It should not avail his donees that he need not have paid the premiums, and that if he had not then (in the events which happened) the insurers would have provided the same death benefit and funded it differently.

Foskett is a complicated case, but these speeches from two judges in the majority show that the claimants could trace their equitable proprietary interest into the insurance premiums and then into the payout from the policy. Tracing is a matter for property law; Lord Browne-Wilkinson's insistence upon 'hard-nosed property rights' emphasizes that there is no room for discretion or considerations of fairness in this exercise. Instead, the focus is upon whether the value inherent in the original proprietary interest can be attributed to the value present in subsequent property, and whether the various stages of the process are 'transactionally linked'.

The majority judges were adamant that the claimants could trace into the payout from the death benefit, although the payout would have occurred even if the claimant's money had not been used to pay the fourth and fifth payment. This was because the payout could be attributed to all the premiums. This conclusion was consistent with the terms of the life insurance policy itself, but was challenged by the minority judges. Lord Steyn thought the lack of a causal link between the death benefit and payment of the final payments was problematic for tracing:[45]

There is in principle no difficulty about allowing a proprietary claim in respect of the proceeds of an insurance policy. If in the circumstances of the present case the stolen moneys had been wholly or

---

[45] [2001] 1 AC 102, 114. See also Evans, 'Rethinking Tracing and the Law of Restitution' (1999) 115 LQR 469.

partly causative of the production of the death benefit received by the children there would have been no obstacle to admitting such a proprietary claim. But those are not the material facts of the case. I am not influenced by hindsight. The fact is that the rights of the children had crystallised by 1989 before any money was stolen and used to pay the 1989 and 1990 premiums. Indeed [in the Court of Appeal] Morritt LJ expressly accepts … that 'in the event, the policy moneys would have been the same if the later premiums had not been paid'. Counsel for the purchasers accepted that as a matter of primary fact this was a correct statement. But he argued that there was nevertheless a causal link between the premiums paid with stolen moneys and the death benefit. I cannot accept this argument. It would be artificial to say that all five premiums produced the policy moneys. The purchasers' money did not 'buy' any part of the death benefit. On the contrary, the stolen moneys were not causally relevant to any benefit received by the children. The 1989 and 1990 premiums did not contribute to a mixed fund in which the purchasers have an equitable interest entitling them to a rateable division. It would be an innovation to create a proprietary remedy in respect of an asset (the death benefit) which had already been acquired at the date of the use of the stolen moneys.

On a slightly different note, the other dissentient, Lord Hope, challenged the conclusion that the payout could be attributed to the fourth and fifth premiums:[46]

The effect of the payment of the first premium was to confer a right on the trustees of the policy as against the insurers to the payment of £1m on the death of the life assured. The effect of the payment of the four remaining premiums up to the date of the life assured's suicide was to reduce the amount which the insured had to provide to meet this liability out by reinsurance or of its own funds. But they had no effect on the right of the trustees to the payment of the sum assured under the terms of the policy, as they did not increase the amount payable on the death.

I do not think that the purchasers can demonstrate on these facts that they have a proprietary right to a proportionate share of the proceeds. They cannot show that their money contributed to any extent to, or increased the value of, the amount paid to the trustees of the policy. A substantially greater sum was paid out by the insurers as death benefit than the total of the sums which they received by way of premium. A profit was made on the investment. But the terms of the policy show that the amount which produced this profit had been fixed from the outset when the first premium was paid. It was attributable to the rights obtained by the life assured when he paid the first premium from his own money. No part of that sum was attributable to value of the money taken from the purchasers to pay the additional premiums.

Foskett v McKeown was not an easy case to decide. The minority approach is defensible: tracing is a matter of evidence, so it might seem odd to ignore evidence of what actually happened and the fact that the premiums paid with the beneficiaries' money were not *necessary* for the death benefit payout. Thus it might appear legitimate to trace into the fourth and fifth premiums, but more difficult to trace from that into the payout because the premiums were not necessary for the payout. However, these arguments were clearly rejected by the majority of the House of Lords. Causation is irrelevant, and the terms of the insurance policy made it clear that the payout from the policy was not linked to a particular premium, but was in consideration of *all* the premiums.

---

[46] [2001] 1 AC 102, 122.

(c) TRACING AT COMMON LAW AND IN EQUITY

It is important to appreciate that, although the fundamental process of tracing is similar at Common Law and Equity, there are important differences between the two. In *Re Diplock*, Lord Greene MR highlighted:[47]

> the materialistic approach of the common law … Equity adopted a more metaphysical approach.

Crucially, the more 'metaphysical' approach of Equity allows tracing into a mixture of money, whereas the more rigid, 'physical' stance of the Common Law does not.[48] The constraints of the Common Law will be considered first, before considering whether this is an area where 'fusion'[49] of tracing rules should occur.

(i) *Tracing at Common Law*

Where the claimant has an existing legal interest in property, which has been misappropriated or transferred to another, he or she will need to rely on the Common Law tracing rules to establish that the interest subsists in substitute property held by the defendant. It is established orthodoxy that the Common Law cannot trace into a mixture. However, it has been persuasively argued that the Common Law has not traditionally been so restricted.[50] For example, the old case of *Taylor v Plumer* has often been thought to decide that the Common Law could not trace into a mixture, on the basis of the following passage from Lord Ellenborough CJ:[51]

> It makes no difference in reason or law into what other form, different from the original, the change may have been made, … for the product of or substitute for the original thing still follows the nature of the thing itself, as long as it can be ascertained to be such, and the right only ceases when the means of ascertainment fail, which is the case when the subject is turned into money, and mixed and confounded in a general mass of the same description. The difficulty which arises in such a case is a difficulty of fact and not of law, and the dictum that money has no ear-mark must be understood in the same way; i.e. as predicated only of an undivided and undistinguishable mass of current money.

This dictum might be thought to support the argument that when an asset is sold and the money deposited in an account, it becomes impossible to trace a legal proprietary interest. However, this reading of *Taylor v Plumer* has been shown to be flawed, since the case itself actually concerned equitable proprietary rights.[52] Millett LJ recognized this subsequently in *Trustee of the Property of FC Jones & Sons v Jones*:[53]

> In *Agip (Africa) Ltd v Jackson* [1990] Ch 265 at 285 I said that the ability of the common law to trace an asset into a changed form in the same hands was established in *Taylor v Plumer* (1815) 3 M & S 562.

---

[47] [1948] Ch 465, 520.

[48] And at Common Law, the claimant is able only to claim the value of the property received by the defendant rather than to recover the property itself: see Torts (Interference with Goods Act) 1977, s. 3, provided at Chapter 18.2, pp. 849–50.

[49] See Chapter 1.2, pp. 8–10.

[50] Smith, 'Tracing in *Taylor v Plumer*: Equity in the Court of King's Bench' [1995] LMCLQ 240; Smith, *Law of Tracing*, ch. 5.

[51] (1815) 3 M&S 562, 575.

[52] Smith, 'Tracing in *Taylor v Plumer*: Equity in the Court of King's Bench' [1995] LMCLQ 240.

[53] [1997] Ch 159, 169–70.

[Millett J cited Lord Ellenborough CJ and continued:]

In this it appears that I fell into a common error, for it has since been convincingly demonstrated that, although *Taylor v Plumer* was decided by a common law court, the court was in fact applying the rules of equity: see Lionel Smith, 'Tracing in *Taylor v Plumer*: Equity in the Court of King's Bench' [1995] LMCLQ 240.

However, Millett LJ did not depart from his reasoning in *Agip*. Rather, he emphasized that the case involved:[54]

no factual difficulties of the kind which proved fatal in this court to the common law claim in *Agip (Africa) Ltd. v. Jackson* [1991] Ch. 547.

This suggests that the insistence in *Agip* that it is impossible at Common Law to trace through a mixture remains good law.[55]

Agip (Africa) Ltd v Jackson [1990] Ch 265; [1991] Ch 547

The claimant had carried out oil explorations in Tunisia in the 1970s and early 1980s, and held an account with the Banque du Sud in Tunis to pay overseas suppliers. The claimant discovered that it had been defrauded of large sums of money by its chief accountant, Mr Zdiri. This action concerned one payment of $518,822, which was made to Baker Oil Services Ltd (Baker Oil), a shell company that immediately before the transfer of the money to it had nothing standing to its credit in the account. Shortly after receiving the money the whole balance was transferred to the account of Jackson & Co., an accountancy firm the partners of which were the first and second defendants. They were also the directors and shareholders of Baker Oil. The third defendant was an employee of the partnership. The money was only held in the partnership account for the benefit of the partnership clients. From there it was then transferred to another company, which held an account at the same branch of Lloyds Bank, before being transferred overseas to the ultimate recipients and organisers of the frauds.

The claimant brought a number of claims against the defendants.[56] The claim at issue in this passage involved reliance on tracing at Common Law.[57]

Millett J:

The common law has always been able to follow a physical asset from one recipient to another. ... But it can only follow a physical asset, such as a cheque or its proceeds, from one person to another. It can follow money but not a chose in action. Money can be followed at common law into and out of a bank account and into the hands of a subsequent transferee, provided that it does not cease to be identifiable by being mixed with other money in the bank account derived from some other source: *Banque Belge pour l'Etranger v Hambrouck* [1921] 1 KB 321. Applying these principles, the plaintiffs claim to follow their money through Baker Oil's account where it was not mixed with any other money and into Jackson & Co's account at Lloyds Bank.

---

[54] Ibid, 168.
[55] See also e.g. *Re Diplock* [1948] Ch 465, 518; *Banque Belge pour l'Etranger v Hambrouck* [1921] 1 KB 321, 330.
[56] For unconscionable receipt and dishonest assistance, see Chapter 19,' 'Third Party Liability'.
[57] [1990] Ch 265, 285.

The defendants deny this. They contend that tracing is not possible at common law because the money was mixed, first when it was handled in New York, and secondly in Jackson & Co's own account at Lloyds Bank.

The latter objection is easily disposed of. … it can be no defence for [the defendant] to show that he has so mixed it with his own money that he cannot tell whether he still has it or not. Mixing by the defendant himself must, therefore, be distinguished from mixing by a prior recipient. The former is irrelevant, but the latter will destroy the claim, for it will prevent proof that the money received by the defendant was the money paid by the plaintiff.

In my judgment, however, the former objection is insuperable. The money cannot be followed by treating it as the proceeds of a cheque presented by the collecting bank in exchange for payment by the paying bank. The money was transmitted by telegraphic transfer. There was no cheque or any equivalent. The payment order was not a cheque or its equivalent. It remained throughout in the possession of the Banque du Sud. No copy was sent to Lloyds Bank or Baker Oil or presented to the Banque du Sud in exchange for the money. It was normally the plaintiffs' practice to forward a copy of the payment order to the supplier when paying an invoice but this was for information only. It did not authorise or enable the supplier to obtain payment. There is no evidence that this practice was followed in the case of forged payment orders and it is exceedingly unlikely that it was.

Nothing passed between Tunisia and London but a stream of electrons. It is not possible to treat the money received by Lloyds Bank in London or its correspondent bank in New York as representing the proceeds of the payment order or of any other physical asset previously in its hands and delivered by it in exchange for the money.[58]

The inability of the Common Law to trace into a mixture is particularly unfortunate in the context of modern-day fraud. It is not uncommon for someone who misappropriates property to sell it and deposit the proceeds in a bank account mixed with other funds. *Agip (Africa) Ltd v Jackson* makes it clear that it is impossible to trace at Common Law through the electrons involved in bank transfers; the Common Law is unable to identify a legal proprietary interest in the money in the bank account. This stands in stark contrast to the more flexible possibilities afforded by tracing in Equity, and drives many claims into the equitable arena. This bifurcation is unnecessarily complicated and a potential source of confusion.[59] The problems involved would be greatly alleviated were there to be only one set of tracing rules.

There is some suggestion that substantive 'fusion' of the tracing rules will occur in the future.

Foskett v McKeown [2001] 1 AC 102, 113 (Lord Steyn)

In truth tracing is a process of identifying assets: it belongs to the realm of evidence. It tells us nothing about legal or equitable rights to the assets traced. In a crystalline analysis Professor Birks ('The Necessity of a Unitary Law of Tracing', essay in *Making Commercial Law, Essays in Honour of Roy Goode* (1997), pp. 239–258) explained, at p. 257, that there is a unified regime for tracing and that 'it allows tracing to be cleanly separated from the business of asserting rights in or in relation to assets successfully traced'. Applying this reasoning Professor Birks concludes, at p. 258:

'that the modern law is equipped with various means of coping with the evidential difficulties which a tracing exercise is bound to encounter. The process of identification thus

---

[58] See also *El Ajou v Dollar Land Holdings plc* [1993] 3 All ER 717; *Bank of America v Arnell* [1999] Lloyd's Rep Bank 399.

[59] Cf. the discussion of the thief in *Westdeutsche Landesbank Girozentrale v Islington LBC* [1996] AC 669: see Chapter 18.2, pp. 849–51.

> ceases to be either legal or equitable and becomes, as is fitting, genuinely neutral as to the rights exigible in respect of the assets into which the value in question is traced. The tracing exercise once successfully completed, it can then be asked what rights, if any, the plaintiff can, on his particular facts, assert. It is at that point that it becomes relevant to recall that on some facts those rights will be personal, on others proprietary, on some legal, and on others equitable.'

I regard this explanation as correct. It is consistent with orthodox principle. It clarifies the correct approach to so called tracing claims. It explains what tracing is about without providing answers to controversies about legal or equitable rights to assets so traced.

In a similar vein, Lord Millett observed:[60]

> Given its nature, there is nothing inherently legal or equitable about the tracing exercise. There is thus no sense in maintaining different rules for tracing at law and in equity. One set of tracing rules is enough. The existence of two has never formed part of the law in the United States: see *Scott on Trusts*, 4th ed (1989), section 515, at pp 605–609. There is certainly no logical justification for allowing any distinction between them to produce capricious results.

Such influential dicta from the House of Lords might give some encouragement that the Common Law/Equity divide regarding tracing will be eliminated. But *Foskett v McKeown* clearly involved tracing an equitable proprietary interest, and so issues of Common Law tracing simply did not arise, so that the *dicta* here were *obiter*. Thus, in *Shalson v Russo* Rimer J was able to state that:[61]

> it cannot be said that *Foskett* … has swept away the long recognised difference between common law and equitable tracing.

In this regard, England appears to be behind some other jurisdictions. Lord Millett mentioned American law, and even more recently the Supreme Court of Canada, in *BMP Global Distribution Inc. v Bank of Nova Scotia*,[62] has recognized the possibility of tracing at Common Law through a clearing system. Deschamps J, giving the judgment of the court, accepted the view advanced by Lord Millett in *Foskett*, given above, and said:[63]

> the clearing system should be a neutral factor: P. Birks, 'Overview: Tracing, Claiming and Defences', in P. Birks, ed., *Laundering and Tracing* (2003), 289, at pp. 302–5. Indeed, I prefer to assess the traceability of the asset after the clearing process and not see that process as a systematic break in the chain of possession of the funds. Just as the collecting bank receives the funds as the payee's agent, the clearing system is only a payment process. Paying through the clearing system amounts to no more than channelling the funds.

This is a sensible approach, which can be contrasted with that taken in *Agip (Africa) Ltd v Jackson*. It better equips the courts to deal with the consequences of commercial fraud, so that it should be possible to trace at law into a mixture.

---

[60] [2001] 1 AC 102, 128.
[61] [2005] Ch 281, [104].
[62] [2005] SCC 15.
[63] Ibid, [83]; D Fox (2010) 68 CLJ 28.

In any event, it is not the case that tracing at Law requires the property to stay in its original form. It is possible to trace through a bank account as long as the account into which money is deposited does not contain any other money, so that there is no mixing.[64] It is even possible to trace at Law into profits made from the original property, as long as there is no mixing. This is illustrated by *Trustee of the Property of FC Jones & Sons v Jones*.

Trustee of the Property of FC Jones & Sons v Jones [1997] Ch 159[65]

The defendant, the wife of a bankrupt, paid £11,700 into an account with a firm of commodity brokers. This money was drawn from a bank account with Midland Bank, which was jointly in her husband's name and in the name of another bankrupt. She used this money to deal in potato futures and paid £50,760 obtained from her deals into a bank deposit account with Raphaels. The trustee in bankruptcy claimed this money. The Court of Appeal held that the money in the husband's bank account belonged to the trustee in bankruptcy, and that the trustee could trace this money into the bank account.

Millett LJ:

In the present case equity has no role to play. The trustee must bring his claim at common law. It follows that, if he has to trace his money, he must rely on common law tracing rules, and that he has no proprietary remedy. But it does not follow that he has no proprietary claim. His claim is exclusively proprietary. He claims the money because it belongs to him at law or represents profits made by the use of money which belonged to him at law.

The trustee submits that he has no need to trace, since the facts are clear and undisputed. The defendant did not mix the money with her own. The trustee's money remained identifiable as such throughout. But, of course, he does have to trace it in order to establish that the money which he claims represents his money. Counsel for the defendant acknowledges that the trustee can successfully trace his money into her account at Raphaels, for his concession in respect of the £11,700 acknowledges this. …

… in my judgment the concession that the trustee can trace the money at common law is rightly made. There are no factual difficulties of the kind which proved fatal in this court to the common law claim in *Agip* … It is not necessary to trace the passage of the money through the clearing system or the London potato futures market. The money which the defendant paid into her account with the commodity brokers represented the proceeds of cheques which she received from her husband. Those cheques represented money in the bankrupts' joint account at Midland Bank which belonged to the trustee.

In *Lipkin Gorman v Karpnale Ltd* [1991] 2 AC 548 at 573 Lord Goff of Chieveley held that the plaintiffs could trace or follow their 'property into its product' for this 'involves a decision by the owner of the original property to assert his title to the product in place of his original property'. In that case the original property was the plaintiffs' chose in action, a debt owed by the bank to the plaintiffs. Lord Goff held, at 574, that the plaintiffs could 'trace their property at common law in that chose in action, or in any part of it, into its product, i.e. cash drawn by Cass from their client account at the bank'.

Accordingly, the trustee can follow the money in the joint account at Midland Bank, which had been vested by statute in him, into the proceeds of the three cheques which the defendant received from her husband. The trustee does not need to follow the money from one recipient to another or follow it through the clearing system; he can follow the cheques as they pass from hand to hand. It is sufficient for him to be able to trace the money into the cheques and the cheques into their proceeds.

---

[64] *Banque Belge Pour L'Etranger v Hambrouck* [1921] 1 KB 321.

[65] See Lord Millett, '*Jones v Jones*: Property or Unjust Enrichment?' in *Mapping the Law* (eds Burrows and Rodger) (Oxford: Oxford University Press, 2006).

...

Given that the trustee can trace his money at Midland Bank into the money in the defendant's account with the commodity brokers, can he successfully assert a claim to that part of the money which represents the profit made by the use of his money? I have no doubt that, in the particular circumstances of this case, he can. There is no need to trace through the dealings on the London potato futures market. If the defendant, as the nominal account holder, had any entitlement to demand payment from the brokers, this was because of the terms of the contract which she made with them. Under the terms of that contract it is reasonable to infer that the brokers were authorised to deal in potato futures on her account, to debit her account with losses and to credit it with profits, and to pay her only the balance standing to her account. It is, in my opinion, impossible to separate the chose in action constituted by the deposit of the trustee's money on those terms from the terms upon which it was deposited. The chose in action, which was vested in the defendant's name but which in reality belonged to the trustee, was not a right to payment from the brokers of the original amount deposited but a right to claim the balance, whether greater or less than the amounted deposited; and it is to that chose in action that the trustee now lays claim.

Because there was a chain of straight substitutions from the money in the partnership account to the chose in action representing the funds deposited at the wife's bank account, it did not matter that the original money paid from the partnership bank account had nearly quintupled in value: the trustee in bankruptcy was entitled to claim this profit simply because it derived from the original money without being mixed with any other money of the wife. This clearly follows from the judgment of the Court of Appeal. However, it is perhaps difficult to see how the money in the husband's bank account belonged to the trustee in bankruptcy at law. After all, the bank had a contract with its customer, and its customer was not the trustee in bankruptcy. Of course, it would seem straightforward to say that the customer held the account on trust for the claimant.[66]

(ii) *Tracing in Equity*

As has already been seen, tracing in Equity is often to be preferred to tracing at Common Law because of Equity's ability to focus not on the physical thing but the 'metaphysical' nature of property. Equity can trace the *value* of misappropriated assets through a mixture, which is particularly important when money is placed in a current account and mixed with funds from other sources. Indeed, it is clear that the court will be prepared to draw certain inferences when deciding whether one asset is a substitute for another.[67] A recent example of this was provided in *Relfo Ltd v Varsani*.[68] The key issue for the purposes of tracing in that case was raised due to a lack of evidence, which meant that certain inferences had to be drawn by the court. The claimant, Relfo, could show that, in breach of fiduciary duty, its director had transferred £500,000 of its money to Mirren, and that, on the same day, a similar sum (minus 1.3 per cent, which was presumably a commission) had been transferred from Intertrade to the account of the defendant, Mr Varsani. But the claimant had difficulties in showing that the money had been transferred from Mirren to Intertrade. The Court of Appeal nevertheless held that the claimant could trace the value of its property into the defendant's account. Arden LJ said:

... the judge was entitled to draw the inference not merely that Relfo's monies had passed into Intertrade's account but that those monies were actually the source of the monies paid to Mr Bhimji Varsani. The payments that the judge inferred were greater in number and scale than those that Millett J inferred in *El*

---

[66] McFarlane and Stevens, 'The Nature of Equitable Property' (2010) 4 JoE 1, 22.
[67] E.g. *El Ajou v Dollar Land Holdings Plc* [1993] 3 All ER 717.
[68] [2014] EWCA Civ 360; [2015] 1 BCLC 14.

Ajou, but the principle is the same. The judge had plenty of material from which to draw the inference. In [77] of his judgment, he refers to the similarity in amount and timing of the Mirren payment and the Intertrade payment, the fact that the amount paid to Mr Bhimji Varsani was the same as the amount of the Relfo/Mirren payment less 1.3%, which might well have been a commission, the fact that Mr Bhimji Varsani gave no consideration for this payment and the fact that on his findings Mr Gorecia authorised the payment from Relfo's account intending that it should lead to a payment to Mr Bhimji Varsani.

I accept [counsel's] submission that the intention of Mr Gorecia would not be enough in itself to make the Intertrade payment substituted property for the purposes of the tracing rules. However intention can be relevant as a factor in the basket of factors from which the judge may draw an inference that it is in fact a substitution.

…

The inference that the judge made means that he found that what had happened was on the following lines. At the start of the chain of transactions, Relfo had money on deposit with its bank, i.e. it had the benefit of a debt owed to it by its bank. It exchanged this right for a debt owed to it by Mirren. The value of this debt lay in the credit balance on this account. Mirren agrees to transfer this balance to another person or person at some future date in exchange for Intertrade making the Intertrade payment.

I therefore accept [counsel's] submission that the fact that Mirren did not reimburse anyone for the Intertrade payment until after the Intertrade payment had been made does not matter. On the judge's findings, the Intertrade payment and the other payments made throughout the chain of substitutions was made on the faith of the arrangement that Mirren would provide reimbursement. By making that arrangement, Mirren exploited and used the value inherent in Relfo's money that had been paid into Mirren's account.

In my judgment, [counsel] is correct in his submission that *Agip* is authority for the proposition that monies held on trust can be traced into other assets even if those other assets are passed on before the trust monies are paid to the person transferring them, provided that that person acted on the basis that he would receive reimbursement for the monies he transferred out of the trust funds. The decision in *Agip* demonstrates that in order to trace money into substitutes it is not necessary that the payments should occur in any particular order, let alone chronological order. As [counsel] submits, a person may agree to provide a substitute for a sum of money even before he receives that sum of money. In those circumstances the receipt would postdate the provision of the substitute. What the court has to do is establish whether the likelihood is that monies could have been paid at any relevant point in the chain in exchange for such a promise. I see no reason in logic or principle why this particular way of proving a substitution should be limited to payments to or by correspondent banks.

I further agree with [counsel] that there is no logical reason why the substituted product of a claimant's money cannot be traced through any number of accounts. There is no limit on the number of substitutions that can in theory take place. However, the number of substitutions and the fact that they do not occur in chronological sequence may make it harder to substitute one asset for another.

This is a sensible approach and helps to combat fraud. It highlights that the equitable rules of tracing are generally much more advantageous than those operating at Common Law. However, there are two principal disadvantages to the equitable jurisdiction, which might favour seeking to trace at Common Law. First, equitable claims are susceptible to the bona fide purchaser defence, which does not affect claims to legal title.[69] Secondly, and more relevant to the process of tracing, orthodoxy demands that the property in which the claimant had an equitable proprietary interest must have passed to the defendant through the hands of a fiduciary in breach of duty. This restriction will be examined first.

---

[69] See Chapter 18.6(a), p. 911.

(a) The fiduciary requirement

The fiduciary requirement for tracing in Equity will be satisfied where, as is usually the case, the property had been held by a trustee or any other type of fiduciary. Importantly, the fiduciary through whose hands the property must have passed in breach of duty need not be the defendant him- or herself.

Re Diplock [1948] Ch 465[70]

By his will, Mr Diplock directed his executors to apply his residuary estate 'for such charitable institutions or other charitable or benevolent object or objects in England' as they should 'in their ... absolute discretion select'. It was assumed that the will created a valid charitable trust; and the executors distributed some £203,000 among 139 different charities before its validity was challenged by the next-of-kin. The House of Lords held the bequest void in *Chichester Diocesan Fund and Board of Finance Inc. v Simpson*.[71] The next-of-kin of the testator, having exhausted their remedy against the executors, made claims to recover the money from the charities.

It was held that the next-of-kin succeeded, both in respect of personal claims[72] and proprietary claims.[73] The right to trace into a mixed fund was not restricted to cases where the defendant was the person who had mixed the moneys, or where the fiduciary relationship existed between the parties to the action.

Lord Greene MR:

First of all, it appears to us to be wrong to treat the principle which underlies *Hallett's* case[74] as coming into operation only where the person who does the mixing is not only in a fiduciary position but is also a party to the tracing action. If he is a party to the action he is, of course, precluded from setting up a case inconsistent with the obligations of his fiduciary position. But supposing that he is not a party? The result cannot surely depend on what equity would or would not have allowed him to say if he had been a party. Suppose that the sole trustee of (say) five separate trusts draws 100*l.* out of each of the trust banking accounts, pays the resulting 500*l.* into an account which he opens in his own name, draws a cheque for 500*l.* on that account and gives it as a present to his son. A claim by the five sets of beneficiaries to follow the money of their respective trusts would be a claim against the son. He would stand in no fiduciary relationship to any of them. We recoil from the conclusion that all five beneficiaries would be dismissed empty-handed by a court of equity and the son left to enjoy what in equity was originally their money.

.....

The starting point of the claim of the depositors was the existence of a fiduciary relationship as between themselves and the directors: that relationship arose from the fact that the depositors had entrusted their money to the directors for the purpose of a business which could not lawfully be carried on, so that the directors must be treated as holding the money on behalf of the depositors. If the directors had paid the money of a depositor into their own banking account he would have had an action against them exactly similar to the action in *Hallett's* case and it would have been correctly said that the

---

[70] Approved by the House of Lords in *Westdeutsche Landesbank Girozentrale v Islington London Borough Council* [1996] AC 669.

[71] [1944] AC 341: see Chapter 5.5(a), pp. 256–7.

[72] This aspect of the case was later affirmed on appeal to the House of Lords in *Ministry of Health v Simpson* [1951] AC 251; see further Chapter 19.3(d)(i), p. 964.

[73] For further discussion, see Chapter 18.3(c)(ii)(c), p. 874 and Chapter 18.6, pp. 917, 921.

[74] *Re Hallett's Estate* (1880) 13 Ch D 696, see Chapter 18.3(c)(ii)(c), p. 871.

directors could not be heard to set up a title of their own to the money standing in the account adverse to the claim of the depositor. But nothing of the sort could be said if the directors paid the money into the account of the society at its bankers. Neither the conscience of the society nor of its liquidator (if it went into liquidation) could ever come into the picture on the basis of a fiduciary relationship since the only parties to that relationship were the directors and the depositors. The society could not have been a party to it, since it had no power to accept the depositor's money. If, therefore, in such a case, the depositor could claim a charge on the society's account with its bankers the claim must have been based on some wider principle.

What can that principle be? In our judgment it must be the principle clearly indicated by Lord Parker,[75] that equity may operate on the conscience not merely of those who acquire a legal title in breach of some trust, express or constructive, or of some other fiduciary obligation, but of volunteers provided that as a result of what has gone before some equitable proprietary interest has been created and attached to the property in the hands of the volunteer.

It is sensible to require misappropriation of the property in order to trace: if the property was properly transferred to another, then there is no reason why the tracing exercise should begin.[76] However, the requirement of a *fiduciary* relationship can pose difficulties. The example of a thief stealing money has already been raised;[77] it is clear that the victim can trace in Equity, but can a thief really be said to be in a fiduciary relationship with the victim of his crime? To do so is somewhat artificial; it is suggested that it would be better to jettison the requirement for a breach of fiduciary duty. This has been done in New Zealand; in *Elders Pastoral Ltd v Bank of New Zealand*,[78] both Cooke P[79] and Somers J[80] cited with approval the following passage from the third edition of Goff and Jones, *The Law of Restitution*:[81]

Equity's traditional rules suggest that it is necessary to discover a fiduciary relationship before a plaintiff can trace his property. Now that law and equity are fused this requirement makes little sense, and it has been recently accepted that 'the receiving of money which consistently with conscience cannot be retained is, in equity, sufficient to raise a trust in favour of the party for whom or in whose account it was received'.

This step has not yet been taken in England. However, it may not be too far away. In *Agip*, Millett J recognized the force of criticisms[82] of the fiduciary requirement:[83]

The only restriction on the ability of equity to follow assets is the requirement that there must be some fiduciary relationship which permits the assistance of equity to be invoked. The requirement has been widely condemned and depends on authority rather than principle, but the law was settled by *Re*

---

[75] In *Sinclair v Brougham* [1914] AC 398. Although this decision was overruled by the House of Lords in *Westdeutsche Landesbank Girozentrale v Islington London Borough Council* [1996] AC 669, it was not because of the analysis of tracing, but rather because of the conclusion that the plaintiffs in *Sinclair v Brougham* had had an equitable proprietary interest. See Chapter 18.3(c)(ii)(c), p. 874.

[76] No equitable title would have been retained, by virtue of overreaching: see Chapter 2.7(d), pp. 56–7.

[77] See Chapter 18.2, pp. 849–51.

[78] [1989] 2 NZLR 180.

[79] Ibid, 185.

[80] Ibid, 193.

[81] *The Law of Restitution* (3rd edn) (London: Sweet & Maxwell, 1986), p. 77, citing Bingham J in *Neste Oy v Lloyds Bank plc* [1983] 2 Lloyd's Rep 658, 665–6.

[82] Including by himself: 'Tracing the Proceeds of Fraud' (1991) 107 LQR 71.

[83] [1990] CL 265, 290. For the facts of this case, see Chapter 18.3(c)(i), p. 861.

Diplock [1948] Ch 465. It may need to be reconsidered but not, I venture to think, at first instance. The requirement may be circumvented since it is not necessary that the fund to be traced should have been the subject of fiduciary obligations before it got into the wrong hands; it is sufficient that the payment to the defendant itself gives rise to a fiduciary relationship: *Chase Manhattan Bank NA v Israel-British Bank (London) Ltd* [1981] Ch 105. In that case, however, equity's assistance was not needed in order to trace the plaintiff's money into the hands of the defendant; it was needed in order to ascertain whether it had any of the plaintiff's money left. The case cannot, therefore, be used to circumvent the requirement that there should be an initial fiduciary relationship in order to start the tracing process in equity.

The requirement is, however, readily satisfied in most cases of commercial fraud, since the embezzlement of a company's funds almost inevitably involves a breach of fiduciary duty on the part of one of the company's employees or agents. That was so in [the] present case. There was clearly a fiduciary relationship between Mr. Zdiri and the plaintiffs. Mr. Zdiri was not a director nor a signatory on the plaintiffs' bank account, but he was a senior and responsible officer. As such he was entrusted with possession of the signed payment orders to have them taken to the bank and implemented. He took advantage of his possession of them to divert the money and cause the separation between its legal ownership which passed to the payees and its beneficial ownership which remained in the plaintiffs. There is clear authority that there is a receipt of trust property when a company's funds are misapplied by a director and, in my judgment, this is equally the case when a company's funds are misapplied by any person whose fiduciary position gave him control of them or enabled him to misapply them.

Millett J is surely right to suggest that the law needs to be reconsidered. For example, in *Chase Manhattan*, a decision he mentioned and which is critically discussed more fully in Chapter 7,[84] Goulding J concluded that a fiduciary relationship existed between two banks when one bank had made a payment to another bank by mistake. But this is also very artificial: why would one bank have to act in the best interests of another, sacrificing its own personal interests, simply because the other bank made a mistake?

Lord Millett was right in *Foskett* to say that:[85]

There is certainly no logical justification for allowing any distinction between [tracing at law and in equity] to produce capricious results in cases of mixed substitutions by insisting on the existence of a fiduciary relationship as a precondition for applying equity's tracing rules. The existence of such a relationship may be relevant to the nature of the claim which the plaintiff can maintain, whether personal or proprietary, but that is a different matter.

Although no English case unambiguously abolishes this requirement for a fiduciary relationship, it seems that it might easily be sidestepped. In *Campden Hill Ltd v Chakrani*, Hart J said:[86]

According to authority which is binding on me the claimant must first establish a fiduciary relationship arising either from a division of the legal and beneficial ownership in the monies sought to be traced or from the very nature of the relationship.

If all that is required is a division of the legal and beneficial ownership, then the fiduciary requirement adds nothing and will always be satisfied where there is an equitable property base. This is

---

[84] Chapter 7.2(a), pp. 731–4.
[85] [2001] 1 AC 102, 128.
[86] [2005] EWHC 911 (Ch), [74].

welcome: once the claimant has established an equitable property right and therefore necessarily a division of legal and equitable title, there should be no further need to establish a fiduciary relationship in order to trace.[87]

(b) Unmixed funds

Tracing in Equity into unmixed funds is relatively straightforward. For example, if a trustee holds land on trust, and in breach of trust sells the land and deposits the proceeds of the sale into a new account with no other funds in it, the beneficiary will have no problems in tracing into the bank account. There has been no mixing: no-one else's property can be identified in the bank account. The money in the bank account can be attributed to the beneficiary's original proprietary interest.

(c) Mixed funds

Tracing into mixed funds is more problematic. So, if the example in the preceding paragraph is modified such that the trustee deposited the proceeds of the sale of land into an account that contained some of the trustee's own money, then that account would constitute a mixed fund. The equitable tracing rules differ according to whose interests are present in the fund. Three principal situations can be discerned: mixing the wrongdoer's property with the innocent beneficiary's property; mixing two or more innocent beneficiaries' assets; and mixing a wrongdoer's property with property belonging to two or more innocent beneficiaries. Each scenario will be considered in turn, but it is important to note that Equity has no qualms in principle about tracing into and through a mixed fund. As Millett J recognized in *El Ajou v Dollar Land Holding*:[88]

> The victims of a fraud can follow[89] their money in equity through a bank account where it has been mixed with other moneys because equity treats the money in such accounts as charged with the repayment of their money. If the money in the account subject to the charge is afterwards paid out of the account and into a number of different accounts, the victims can claim a similar charge of each of the recipient accounts. They are not bound to choose between them ... Equity's power to charge a mixed fund with the repayment of trust moneys ... enables the claimant to follow the money not because it is theirs, but because it is derived from a fund which is treated as if it were subject to a charge in their favour.

MIXING OF THE BENEFICIARY'S MONEY WITH THAT OF THE WRONGDOER   If a trustee wrongly takes money out of the trust fund and deposits it in his or her bank account in which the trustee already has his or her own money, there will be a mixed fund in the account. The beneficiary is able to trace into the account: the value of his or her original equitable proprietary interest can readily be found in the mixture produced. But what if the trustee spends some of this fund on purchasing a new asset: has the trustee spent his or her own money or that of the beneficiary? The logic of tracing as an evidential process does not really help: we *could* say that the value inherent in the beneficiary's original interest is now present in the subsequently acquired asset from the mixed fund, but there is no reason why we *must* say it. The beneficiary's interest may still be present in the remaining money in the account. However, Equity has sensibly developed rules to deal with such situations: given that the claimant beneficiary is entirely innocent, and the trustee a wrongdoer, everything is presumed against the trustee. This is particularly

---

[87] Cf. Virgo, 'Re Hallett's Estate' in *Landmark Cases in Equity* (eds Mitchell and Mitchell) (Oxford: Hart 2012), pp. 381–2. For the difficulties that arise in establishing a fiduciary relationship, see Chapter 14.1, p. 660.

[88] [1993] BCLC 735, 753.

[89] Despite using the language of following, Millett J is actually referring to tracing.

appropriate since the wrongdoing trustee has created the evidential difficulty of identifying whose property has been used to acquire the new asset. In *Re Tilley*, Ungoed-Thomas J observed that:[90]

> If a trustee mixes trust assets with his own, the onus is on the trustee to distinguish the separate assets, and to the extent that he fails to do so they belong to the trust.

A trustee is presumed to act in the best interests of his or her beneficiary, so it is no surprise that the beneficiary can choose either to trace his or her own proprietary interest into an asset purchased from a mixed fund, or to insist that the asset was purchased with the trustee's own money, depending on whichever is the more advantageous to him or her.[91] In *Re Tilley*, the judge cited *Re Hallett's Estate*[92] as authority for allowing the beneficiary to presume that the trustee spent the trustee's own money first, and described *Re Oatway*[93] as 'the converse of the decision in *Re Hallett's Estate*',[94] since it allows the beneficiary to presume that the trust money was spent first.

Re Hallett's Estate [1880] 13 Ch D 696[95]

Mr Hallett was a solicitor. He was trustee of his own marriage settlement, and had paid some money from that trust into his own bank account. He was also solicitor to Mrs Cotterill, and improperly paid some of his client's money into his personal bank account as well. Hallett made various payments from, and into, the account, and also incurred further debts. At the date of his death, the account held sufficient funds to meet the claims of the trustees of the marriage settlement and of Mrs Cotterill, but not his personal debts as well. In an action for the administration of Hallett's estate, the main question was whether the trust and Mrs Cotterill could claim in priority to the creditors.

The Court of Appeal held that both the trust and Mrs Cotterill were entitled to a charge upon the moneys in the bank account in priority to the general creditors; the various payments by Hallett out of the account should be presumed to be payments of his own money and not that of the trust, nor of Mrs Cotterill.

Jessel MR:

Now, first upon principle, nothing can be better settled, either in our own law, or, I suppose, the law of all civilised countries, than this, that where a man does an act which may be rightfully performed, he cannot say that that act was intentionally and in fact done wrongly. A man who has a right of entry cannot say he committed a trespass in entering. A man who sells the goods of another as agent for the owner cannot prevent the owner adopting the sale, and deny that he acted as agent for the owner. It runs throughout our law, and we are familiar with numerous instances in the law of real property. A man who grants a lease believing he has sufficient estate to grant it, although it turns out that he has not, but has a power which enables him to grant it, is not allowed to say he did not grant it under the power.

---

[90] [1967] 1 Ch 1179, 1183. See also *Lupton v White* (1805) 15 Ves Jun 432; *Sinclair Investments (UK) Ltd v Versailles Trade Finance Ltd* [2011] EWCA Civ 347; [2011] 3 WLR 1153, [100] (Lord Neuberger MR).

[91] Subject to doctrines such as the lowest intermediate balance rule: see Chapter 18.3(c)(iii)(b), pp. 879–81.

[92] (1880) 13 Ch D 696.

[93] [1903] 2 Ch 356.

[94] [1967] 1 Ch 1179, 1183.

[95] Virgo, '*Re Hallett's Estate*' in *Landmark Cases in Equity* (eds Mitchell and Mitchell) (Oxford: Hart 2012).

Wherever it can be done rightfully, he is not allowed to say, against the person entitled to the property or the right, that he has done it wrongfully. That is the universal law.

When we come to apply that principle to the case of a trustee who has blended trust moneys with his own, it seems to me perfectly plain that he cannot be heard to say that he took away the trust money when he had a right to take away his own money. The simplest case put is the mingling of trust moneys in a bag with money of the trustee's own. Suppose he has a hundred sovereigns in a bag, and he adds to them another hundred sovereigns of his own, so that they are commingled in such a way that they cannot be distinguished, and the next day he draws out for his own purposes £100, is it tolerable for anybody to allege that what he drew out was the first £100, the trust money, and that he misappropriated it, and left his own £100 in the bag? It is obvious he must have taken away that which he had a right to take away, his own £100. What difference does it make if, instead of being in a bag, he deposits it with his banker, and then pays in other money of his own, and draws out some money for his own purpose? Could he say that he had actually drawn out anything but his own money? His money was there, and he had a right to draw it out, and why should the natural act of simply drawing out the money be attributed to anything except to his ownership of money which was at the bankers[?]

Re Oatway [1903] 2 Ch 356

The trustee, Mr Oatway, paid trust money into his own bank account, which already contained his own money. He then purchased shares in Oceana, which he paid for by a cheque on his bank account, and dissipated the rest of the money. It was held that the beneficiary could trace into the shares, even though, when the shares were purchased, the balance to the credit of the bank account exceeded the value of the shares, so that there would still have been some money credited to the account that could meet the claimant's claim, before that amount was then dissipated. The trustee was not entitled to withdraw anything from the bank account until the trust money had been restored to the trust.

Joyce J:

Trust money may be followed into land or any other property in which it has been invested; and when a trustee has, in making any purchase or investment, applied trust money together with his own, the *cestuis que trust* are entitled to a charge on the property purchased for the amount of the trust money laid out in the purchase or investment. Similarly, if money held by any person in a fiduciary capacity be paid into his own banking account, it may be followed by the equitable owner, who, as against the trustee, will have a charge for what belongs to him upon the balance to the credit of the account. ... It is, in my opinion, equally clear that when any of the money drawn out has been invested, and the investment remains in the name or under the control of the trustee, the rest of the balance having been afterwards dissipated by him, he cannot maintain that the investment which remains represents his own money alone, and that what has been spent and can no longer be traced and recovered was the money belonging to the trust. In other words, when the private money of the trustee and that which he held in a fiduciary capacity have been mixed in the same banking account, from which various payments have from time to time been made, then, in order to determine to whom any remaining balance or any investment that may have been paid for out of the account ought to be deemed to belong, the trustee must be debited with all the sums that have been withdrawn and applied to his own use so as to be no longer recoverable, and the trust money in like manner be debited with any sums taken out and duly invested in the names of the proper trustees. The order of priority in which the various withdrawals and investments may have been respectively made is wholly immaterial. I have been referring, of course, to cases where there is only one fiduciary owner or set of *cestuis que trust* claiming whatever may be left as against the trustee. In the present case there is no balance left. The only investment or property remaining which represents any part of the mixed moneys paid into the banking account is the Oceana shares purchased for £2,137. Upon these, therefore, the trust had a charge for the £3,000 trust money paid into the account. That is to say, those shares and the proceeds thereof belong to the trust. It was objected that the investment in the Oceana shares was made at a time when Oatway's own share of the balance to the credit of the account (if the whole had been then justly distributed) would have exceeded £2,137, the price of the shares; that he was therefore entitled to withdraw that sum, and might rightly apply it for his own purposes; and that consequently the shares should be held to belong to his estate. To this I answer that he never was entitled to withdraw the £2,137 from the account, or, at all events, that he could not be entitled to take the sum from the account and hold it or the investment made therewith, freed from the charge in favour of the trust, unless or until the trust money paid into the account had been first restored, and the trust fund reinstated by due investment of the money in the joint names of the proper trustees, which never was done. The investment by Oatway, in his own name, of the £2,137 in Oceana shares no more got rid of the claim or charge of the trust upon the money so invested, than would have been the case if he had drawn a cheque for £2,137 and simply placed and retained the amount in a drawer without further disposing of the money in any way. The proceeds of the Oceana shares must be held to belong to the trust funds under the will of which Oatway and Maxwell Skipper were the trustees.

Hallett and *Oatway* work in tandem to protect an innocent beneficiary against a wrongdoing fiduciary: a beneficiary can *choose* whether or not to trace into an asset acquired from a fund containing a mixture of his or her own property and that of his or her fiduciary.[96] This explains why, in *Shalson v Russo*, Rimer J said that the beneficiary is entitled to 'cherry pick' between applying either the *Hallett* or *Oatway* presumption.[97] Admittedly, there is little authority about whether this approach should still be applied where there are sufficient funds in the fiduciary's account to give the beneficiary the value of his or property back again, and any argument over substitute assets is in effect between the beneficiary and the wrongdoing fiduciary's creditors. It is possible to argue that cherry picking unduly favours the beneficiary over other creditors, and this might explain why, in *Turner v Jacob*,[98] Patten J expressed the view that a beneficiary cannot cherry pick and trace into purchased assets if there is enough money left in the fund to satisfy the claim. However, on balance it is suggested that it is more consistent with the underlying rules and principles of tracing to allow the innocent beneficiary to cherry pick against the wrongdoing fiduciary even if the latter is insolvent; after all, the creditors should not be in a better position than the fiduciary.

MIXING THE BENEFICIARY'S MONEY WITH THAT OF ANOTHER INNOCENT PARTY The *Hallett* and *Oatway* presumptions are inappropriate where the property in the fund is a mixture of the property of innocent parties: there is no policy reason to favour one party over the other. This sort of mixture might arise where a trustee takes money from two separate trusts and puts it in the same, empty bank account, or the trustee gives misappropriated trust money to an innocent third party who deposits the money in his or her own bank account which already contains his or her own money, for example.

---

[96] Such flexible rules are welcome and consistent with the evidential nature of the tracing process; the suggestion by the House of Lords in *Foskett v McKeown* [2001] 1 AC 102 that proprietary rights become vested at once and do not depend on later events should not be followed.

[97] [2003] EWHC 1637 (Ch); [2005] Ch 281, [144]

[98] [2006] EWHC 1317 (Ch), [102].

In such situations, the wrongdoer has no claim to any of the property, and those who do have a claim are equally innocent.

The general rule is that the mixture belongs to the innocent parties in the proportions by which they contributed to the fund. This approach was adopted by Lord Parker in *Sinclair v Brougham*:[99]

> Suppose the property is acquired by means of money, part of which belongs to one owner and part to another, the purchaser being in a fiduciary relationship to both. Clearly each owner has an equal equity. Each is entitled to a charge on the property for his own money, and neither can claim priority over the other. It follows that their charges must rank pari passu according to their respective amounts. Further, I think that as against the fiduciary agent they could by agreement claim to take the property itself, in which case they would become tenants in common in shares proportioned to amounts for which either could claim a charge. Suppose, again, that the fiduciary agent parts with the money to a third party who cannot plead purchase for value without notice, and that the third party invests it with money of his own in the purchase of property. If the third party had notice that the money was held in a fiduciary capacity, he would be in exactly the same position as the fiduciary agent, and could not, therefore, assert any interest in the property until the money misapplied had been refunded. But if he had no such notice this would not be the case. There would on his part be no misconduct at all. On the other hand, I cannot at present see why he should have any priority as against the property over the owner of the money which had, in fact, been misapplied.[100]

Although much of the reasoning in *Sinclair* has since been departed from,[101] this analysis of tracing remains valid.[102] In *Re Diplock* Lord Greene MR cited Lord Parker's speech in concluding that:[103]

> Where an innocent volunteer (as distinct from a purchaser for value without notice) mixes 'money' of his own with 'money' which in equity belongs to another person, or is found in possession of such a mixture, although that other person cannot claim a charge on the mass superior to the claim of the volunteer he is entitled, nevertheless, to a charge ranking pari passu with the claim of the volunteer. ... Just as a volunteer is not allowed by equity in the case, e.g., of a conveyance of the legal estate in land, to set up his legal title adversely to the claim of a person having an equitable interest in the land, so in the case of a mixed fund of money the volunteer must give such recognition as equity considers him in conscience (as a volunteer) bound to give to the interest of the equitable owner of the money which has been mixed with the volunteer's own. But this burden on the conscience of the volunteer is not such as to compel him to treat the claim of the equitable owner as paramount. That would be to treat the volunteer as strictly as if he himself stood in a fiduciary relationship to the equitable owner which ex hypothesi he does not. The volunteer is under no greater duty of conscience to recognize the interest of the equitable owner than that which lies upon a person having an equitable interest in one of two trust funds of 'money' which have become mixed towards the equitable owner of the other. Such a person is not in conscience bound to give precedence to the equitable owner of the other of the two funds.

Treating the innocent parties equally is the fairest solution. However, some care needs to be taken when the mixed fund is in a current bank account (rather than a deposit account) and money is used

---

[99] [1914] AC 398, 442–3.

[100] 'Ranking equally'.

[101] This case recognized that property which was transferred pursuant to a void transaction would be held on resulting trust for the transferor. However, it was overruled by the House of Lords: *Westdeutsche Landesbank Girozentrale v Islington London Borough Council* [1996] AC 669.

[102] In *Westdeutsche*, Lord Browne-Wilkinson said that the House of Lords 'should not be taken to be casting any doubt on the principles of tracing as established in *Re Diplock*': [1996] AC 669, 714.

[103] [1948] Ch 465, 524.

from that account. Intuitively, it would seem sensible for all innocent claimants to be able to trace into any assets acquired with money from the account, and identify a proprietary interest in that property in the same proportions as were present in the account immediately before the transaction. This would maintain parity between equally innocent parties.

Nevertheless, this is not the traditional approach of the law. In *Clayton's case*, Sir William Grant MR said:[104]

> But this is the case of a banking account, where all the sums paid in form one blended fund, the parts of which have no longer any distinct existence. Neither banker nor customer ever thinks of saying, this draft is to be placed to the account of the £500 paid in on *Monday*, and this other to the account of the £500 paid in on *Tuesday*. There is a fund of £1000 to draw upon, and that is enough. In such a case, there is no room for any other appropriation than that which arises from the order in which the receipts and payments take place, and are carried into the account. Presumably, it is the sum first paid in, that is first drawn out. It is the first item on the debit side of the account, that is discharged, or reduced, by the first item on the credit side. The appropriation is made by the very act of setting the two items against each other. Upon that principle, all accounts current are settled, and particularly cash accounts. When there has been a continuation of dealings, in what way can it be ascertained whether the specific balance due on a given day has, or has not, been discharged, but by examining whether payments to the amount of that balance appear by the account to have been made? You are not to take the account backwards, and strike the balance at the head, instead of the foot, of it.

This passage has led to the 'rule' in *Clayton's case* that the first payment in to the account is presumed to be the first payment out of the account. Given the frequency of transactions through a current account, this presumption has sometimes been thought to be helpful.

However, this 'first in, first out' rule is not obviously fair. Imagine that a trustee takes £500 of A's money and deposits it in an empty current account, and then the following day takes £500 of B's money and deposits that money in the same account as well. If the trustee then uses money from that current account to buy a £500 bike, it is unclear why the law should presume that A's money alone has been used to buy the bike. Indeed, the bike was only bought after B's money was received, so it might be possible to think that B's money was used. But this is also artificial. There is no reason why only one party should be able to trace into the bike. Both A and B should be able to trace into the bike in equal shares. This approach was preferred by the Court of Appeal in *Barlow Clowes International Ltd v Vaughan*.

Barlow Clowes International Ltd v Vaughan [1991] EWCA Civ 11

Barlow Clowes International ('BCI') operated a number of investment portfolios, to which various investors contributed. BCI wrongly dissipated much of the investors' moneys, but some money remained in its account. The question considered in the following passage was whether the remaining money should be held rateably for all investors or whether the rule in *Clayton's case* applied. The Court of Appeal refused to apply *Clayton's case*.

Dillon LJ:

That rule [in *Clayton's case*] will apply to the appropriation of payments between any trader and his customer where there is an account current or running account. But it will not apply unless there is a

---

[104] *Devaynes v Noble, Clayton's case* (1816) 1 Mer 572, 608–9.

running account — see per Lord Halsbury LC in *The Mecca* [1897] AC 286 at page 291— and even in relation to the appropriation of payments it is not, as Lord Halsbury said at page 290, an invariable rule, "… the circumstances of a case may afford ground for inferring that transactions of the parties were not so intended as to come under this general rule". …

[Counsel's] wider submission is to the effect that, while the rule in *Clayton's Case* is valid and useful, subject to the observations in *The Mecca*, where what is in question is the appropriation of payments as between the parties to a running account, it is illogical and unfair to the earlier contributors to apply the rule as between innocent beneficiaries, whose payments to a third party, BCI, have been paid by that third party into a bank account in which, at the end of the day, there are—for whatever reason—not enough moneys left to meet all claims.

[Counsel] submits that it might be more fair to apply the North American method outlined above,[105] but as that is not practicable in the circumstances of this case, the court should fall back on a distribution pari passu between all investors in the proportions of the amounts respectively due to them.

For my part, so far as fairness is concerned, I have difficulty in seeing the fairness to a later investor whose contribution was in all likelihood still included in the uninvested moneys in the Schedule A accounts, of holding that all those moneys must be shared pari passu by all investors early or late if there was no common investment fund. In addition of course the order made by the House of Lords in *Sinclair v Brougham*, on which the order which [counsel] seeks in the present case is modelled, was expressly subject to any tracing application by any individual depositor or shareholder. If the application of *Clayton's Case* is unfair to early investors pari passu distribution among all seems unfair to late investors.

… the decisions of this court, in my judgment, establish and recognise a general rule of practice that *Clayton's Case* is to be applied when several beneficiaries' moneys have been blended in one bank account and there is a deficiency. It is not, in my judgment, for this court to reject that long-established general practice.

Woolf LJ:

[Counsel] refers to the dicta of Judge Learned Hand *In re Walter J Schmidt & Co.* (1923) 298 S 314 at page 316:

> "When the law turns to fiction, it is, or at least it should be, for some purpose of justice. To adopt 'the fiction of first in, first out' … is to apportion a common misfortune to a test which has no relation whatever to the justice of the case."

In my judgment this comment of Judge Learned Hand accurately describes the result of applying the rule in *Clayton's Case* to the "common misfortune" which was shared by the investors in BCI. However it is to be noted that the judge in that case (we are told) later felt compelled by authority to apply the rule. In this case the capricious consequences of applying the rule are underlined by the fact that the dates upon which investments were received by BCI often depended upon agents, such as the 4th and 5th defendants, combining the investments of a number of clients and then forwarding a lump sum to BCI.

In addition to relying upon the arbitrary results which follow from the "mechanistic" application of the rule [counsel] relies upon the expense and time which will be involved in having to apply the rule. With the advent of computer technology it cannot be said the task is impossible but it is clearly complex. The costs involved will result in a depletion of the assets available to the investors. In determining the appropriateness of the machinery used for resolving the claims of the investors among themselves, surely this should be a relevant consideration.

---

[105] See the speech of Woolf LJ, immediately below.

The second solution for resolving the claims of the investors among themselves is the rolling charge or North American solution ("North American" because it is the solution adopted or favoured in preference to the rule in *Clayton's Case* in certain decisions of the courts in the United States and Canada because it is regarded as being manifestly fairer). This solution involves treating credits to a bank account made at different times and from different sources as a blend or cocktail with the result that when a withdrawal is made from the account it is treated as a withdrawal in the same proportions as the different interests in the account (here of the investors) bear to each other at the moment before the withdrawal is made. This solution should produce the most just result, but in this case, as counsel accept it is not a live contender, since while it might just be possible to perform the exercise the costs involved would be out of all proportion even to the sizeable sums which are here involved.

The third solution (and the only other solution canvassed in argument) is the *pari passu ex post facto* solution. This involves establishing the total quantum of the assets available and sharing them on a proportionate basis among all the investors who could be said to have contributed to the acquisition of those assets, ignoring the dates on which they made their investment. [Counsel] submits this is the solution which is appropriate in this case. It has the virtue of relative simplicity and therefore relative economy and also the virtue of being in this case more just than the first solution. It would have the effect of sharing the pool of assets available proportionately among the thousands of investors in a way which reflected the fact that they were all the victims of a "common misfortune".

On the evidence which is available to this court as to the circumstances of this case, I have no doubt that if, as a matter of principle, this court is in a position to adopt the third solution, then that is the solution which is the most appropriate. It is therefore necessary to turn to the authorities to see whether they prevent this court adopting what I would see as being the correct result. ...

... it is settled law that the rule in *Clayton's Case* ... need only be applied when it is convenient to do so and when its application can be said to do broad justice having regard to the nature of the competing claims. *Hallett's case* shows that the rule is displaced where its application would unjustly assist the trustee to the disadvantage of the beneficiaries. In *Re Diplock*, the rule would have been displaced by the trustee subsequently earmarking the beneficiary's funds. It is not applied if this is the intention or presumed intention of the beneficiaries. The rule is sensibly not applied when the cost of applying it is likely to exhaust the fund available for the beneficiaries.

...

[Woolf LJ ultimately concluded:]

1. While the rule in *Clayton's Case* is prima facie available to determine the interests of investors in a fund into which their investments have been paid, the use of the rule is a matter of convenience and if its application in particular circumstances would be impracticable or result in injustice between the investors it will not be applied if there is a preferable alternative.

2. Here the rule will not be applied because this would be contrary to either the express or inferred or presumed intention of the investors. If the investments were required by the terms of the investment contract to be paid into a common pool this indicates that the investors did not intend to apply the rule. If the investments were intended to be separately invested, as a result of the investments being collectively misapplied by BCI a common pool of the investments was created. Because of their shared misfortune, the investors will be presumed to have intended the rule not to apply.

3. As the rule is inapplicable the approach which should be adopted by the court depends on which of the possible alternative solutions is the most satisfactory in the circumstances. If the North American solution is practical this would probably have advantages over the pari passu solution. However the complications of applying the North American solution in this case make the third solution the most satisfactory.

4. It must however be remembered that any solution depends on the ability to trace and if the fund had been exhausted (ie. the account became overdrawn) the investors whose monies were in the fund prior to the fund being exhausted will not be able to claim against monies which were subsequently paid into the fund. Their claims will be limited to following, if this is possible, any of the monies paid out of the fund into other assets before it was exhausted.

Barlow Clowes International v Vaughan highlights that it will often be inappropriate to apply the rule in *Clayton's case*. In fact, the 'rule' of 'first in, first out' is only a presumption, which will often be rebutted either because the intentions of the parties point to a different result, or because it is impracticable. The 'rolling charge' solution should be preferred. This 'North American approach' involves calculating at each stage what proportion of the fund belongs to each contributor. Where there are a number of complicated transactions, this solution might itself be impracticable—as it was in *Barlow Clowes*—and, therefore, the simpler *pari passu* principle may be employed.[106] This requires the fund to be distributed to the parties in the proportions by which they contributed to the fund, regardless of exactly when their money appeared in the mixed fund. As a result, the *pari passu* solution is clearly not as precise in achieving justice between the parties as the rolling charge, which should be adopted wherever possible.[107]

It must also be remembered that *Clayton's case* will not apply where the money has been mixed by a wrongdoer with his or her own money; *Re Hallett* and *Re Oatway* both explicitly rejected the 'first in, first out' rule, since everything should be presumed against the wrongdoing trustee.

The erosion in the application of *Clayton's case* led Lindsay J in *Russell-Cooke Trust Co v Prentis* to observe that:[108]

It is plain from all three of the judgments in *Barlow Clowes* … that the rule can be displaced by even a slight counterweight. Indeed, in terms of its actual application between beneficiaries who have in any sense met a shared misfortune, it might be more accurate to refer to the exception that is, rather than the rule in, *Clayton's case*.

Nevertheless, authority dictates that *Clayton's case* is the starting point of analysis,[109] even though it rarely accords with the justice of any particular case, and the presumption of 'first in, first out' will invariably be rebutted. As Henderson J observed in *Charity Commission for England and Wales v Framjee*:[110]

I can deal briefly with the *Clayton's Case* approach, because nobody submits that it should be followed in the present case. Quite apart from the arbitrary way in which it favours the recipients of later donations over the recipients of earlier donations, the evidence establishes that it would be prohibitively expensive to attempt to reconstruct the accounts of the [Trust] over the last ten years in order to ascertain the precise order in which payments in were matched by payments out. Furthermore, the authorities establish that, although the rule in *Clayton's Case* is probably still the default rule in England and Wales which has to be applied in the absence of anything better, it may be displaced with relative ease in favour of a solution which produces a fairer result…

---

[106] See *Charity Commission for England and Wales v Framjee* [2014] EWHC 2507; [2015] 1 WLR 16.
[107] See e.g. *Shalson v Russo* [2003] EWHC 1637 (Ch); [2005] Ch 281.
[108] [2002] EWHC 2227 (Ch); [2003] 2 All ER 478, [55].
[109] Conaglen, 'Contests between Rival Trust Beneficiaries' [2005] CLJ 45.
[110] [2014] EWHC 2507; [2015] 1 WLR 16, [49]. See too *National Crime Agency v Robb* [2014] EWHC 4384 (Ch); [2015] Ch 520, [64] (Etherton C).

MIXING THE WRONGDOER'S MONEY WITH THAT OF TWO OR MORE INNOCENT PARTIES   The analysis of this third situation follows logically from the analysis of the first two. If a wrongdoing fiduciary takes £100 from beneficiary A, and another £100 from beneficiary B, and puts the money into his or her own account, which has £100 of his or her own money in it, then it would be possible for A and B each to trace into the mixed fund and identify an equitable proprietary right either to one-third of the fund, or to £100, which will be the same unless the value of the fund has increased or decreased. If the fiduciary then spends £100 to purchase an asset from that fund, then both A and B will have the opportunity to elect whether to trace into the acquired asset, or to insist that the fiduciary spent his or her own money on the asset, applying the *Hallett* and *Oatway* presumptions against the wrongdoing trustee. In either event, A and B rank as equals, and between them the rolling charge analysis favoured in *Barlow Clowes* should apply.

(iii) *Limitations on tracing*

(a) *Dissipation*

Where the asset in which the claimant can identify his or her equitable proprietary interest has been dissipated, there will be no specific property into which the claimant can trace. So if a trustee misappropriates the beneficiary's money to buy a boat, which burns in a fire and is destroyed, there is no remaining asset into which the beneficiary can trace. In *Re Diplock*, Lord Greene MR said:[111]

> The equitable remedies pre-suppose the continued existence of the money either as a separate fund or as part of a mixed fund or as latent in property acquired by means of such a fund. If, on the facts of any individual case, such continued existence is not established, equity is as helpless as the common law itself. If the fund, mixed or unmixed, is spent upon a dinner, equity, which dealt only in specific relief and not in damages, could do nothing.

(b) *Lowest intermediate balance rule*

It is important that the claimant be able to establish that the value of his or her original interest can be attributed to particular substitute property. The 'lowest intermediate balance rule' may place a limit on the value that the claimant can trace. For example, if a trustee takes £100 of the claimant's money and mixes it with £100 of his or her own money, and then spends £150 from this fund on a holiday, the claimant would be able to trace into the mixed fund, employ the *Hallett* presumption, and identify the remaining £50 in the account as belonging to him or her in Equity. But if the trustee then later puts another £50 of his or her own money into the account, such that there is now £100 in the account, then the claimant is unable to trace into that 'extra' £50, since it clearly did not derive from the value in his or her original equitable proprietary interest but patently came from the trustee. The amount into which the claimant could trace dipped to £50; from that point onwards, the value of the claimant's interest in the fund could not increase:[112] this is known as the lowest intermediate balance rule.

---

[111] [1948] Ch 465, 521.
[112] Unless that £50 was invested, made a profit, and those profits deposited in the account. But in that situation, it is crucial that the profit is made from the £50 attributable to the claimant's original proprietary interest, and not from any money appearing later on from extraneous sources.

Roscoe v Winder [1915] 1 Ch 62 (Sargant J)

An agreement for the sale of the goodwill of a business provided that the purchaser, Wigham, should collect certain of the book debts and pay that money over to the vendor. Wigham collected the debts and paid part of the money, £455 18*s*. 11*d*., into his private account. A few days later the balance in the account was reduced to £25 18*s*. At the date of Wigham's death, the balance had risen to £358 5*s*. 5*d*. The question was the extent to which the claimants could claim a charge under the rules in *Hallett's* case. The court held that the charge was limited to £25 18*s*., the lowest intermediate balance subsequent to the appropriation.

Sargent J:

But there is a further circumstance in the present case which seems to me to be conclusive in favour of the defendant as regards the greater part of the balance of 358*l*., 5*s*. 5*d*. It appears that after the payment in by the debtor of a portion of the book debts which he had received the balance at the bank on 19 May, 1913, was reduced by his drawings to a sum of 25*l*. 18*s*. only on 21 May. So that, although the ultimate balance at the debtor's death was about 358*l*., there had been an intermediate balance of only 25*l*. 18*s*. The result of that seems to me to be that the trust moneys cannot possibly be traced into this common fund, which was standing to the debtor's credit at his death, to an extent of more than 25*l*. 18*s*., because, although prima facie under the second rule in *Re Hallett's Estate* (1880) 13 Ch D 696 any drawings out by the debtor ought to be attributed to the private moneys which he had at the bank and not to the trust moneys, yet, when the drawings out had reached such an amount that the whole of his private money part had been exhausted, it necessarily followed that the rest of the drawings must have been against trust moneys. There being on 21 May, 1913, only 25*l*. 18*s*., in all, standing to the credit of the debtor's account, it is quite clear that on that day he must have denuded his account of all the trust moneys there—the whole 455*l*. 18*s*. 11*d*.—except to the extent of 25*l*. 18*s*.

… You must, for the purpose of tracing … put your finger on some definite fund which either remains in its original state or can be found in another shape. That is tracing, and tracing, by the very facts of this case, seems to be absolutely excluded except as to the 25*l*. 18*s*.

Then, apart from tracing, it seems to me possible to establish this claim against the ultimate balance of 358*l*. 5*s*. 5*d*. only by saying that something was done, with regard to the additional moneys which are needed to make up that balance, by the person to whom those moneys belonged, the debtor, to substitute those moneys for the purpose of, or to impose upon those moneys a trust equivalent to, the trust which rested on the previous balance. Of course, if there was anything like a separate trust account, the payment of the further moneys into that account would, in itself, have been quite a sufficient indication of the intention of the debtor to substitute those additional moneys for the original trust moneys, and accordingly to impose, by way of substitution, the old trusts upon those additional moneys. But, in a case where the account into which the moneys are paid is the general trading account of the debtor on which he has been accustomed to draw both in the ordinary course and in breach of trust when there were trust funds standing to the credit of that account which were convenient for that purpose, I think it is impossible to attribute to him that by the mere payment into the account of further moneys, which to a large extent he subsequently used for purposes of his own, he intended to clothe those moneys with a trust in favour of the plaintiffs.

Certainly, after having heard *Re Hallett's Estate* (1880) 13 Ch D 696 stated over and over again, I should have thought that the general view of that decision was that it only applied to such an amount of the balance ultimately standing to the credit of the trustee as did not exceed the lowest balance of the account during the intervening period.

Roscoe is a good illustration of the lowest intermediate balance rule. However, the last part of this passage is controversial. When the trustee later paid more money into the account, the court rejected the contention that it was trust money because it was not clear that that was what the trustee *intended*. But this appears to be inconsistent with the general thrust of the presumptions favoured in *Re Hallett*: if everything is presumed against the wrongdoing trustee but in favour of the innocent beneficiary, it might be thought that when the trustee pays more money into the account he or she does so to return the trust fund to the appropriate level. This would seem consistent with the general policy concerns of Equity, but could only be employed against a wrongdoer. Yet such an argument might be rejected in any event on the basis that the extra money put into the account clearly did *not* derive from the claimant's equitable proprietary interest.[113] There is only room for the evidential presumptions of *Hallett* and *Oatway* to operate where the evidence does not clearly establish to whom the property belongs. This was made clear by Lord Toulson, giving the advice of the Privy Council in *Brazil v Durant International Corp*:[114]

> The doctrine of tracing involves rules by which to determine whether one form of property interest is properly to be regarded as substituted for another. It is therefore necessary to begin with the original property interest and study what has become of it. If it has ceased to exist, it cannot metamorphose into a later property interest. Ex nihilo nihil fit: nothing comes from nothing. If the money in a bank account has dwindled from £1,000 to £1, only the remaining £1 is capable of being substituted by something else; the £999 has ceased to exist. This explains 'the lowest intermediate balance' principle.

(c) Tracing through a debt

It has traditionally been said to be impossible to trace through a debt. As Rimer J observed in *Shalson v Russo*:[115]

> it is not possible to trace into and through an overdrawn account, because such an account is not an asset at all: it is a liability. The consequence is that the claimant cannot show that his money has become represented by an asset into which it is possible to trace: all his money has done is to reduce a liability, and so has ceased to exist.

It is possible to quibble with Rimer J's contention that a claimant cannot trace into a debt. This is possible in order to revive the debt through the remedy of subrogation.[116] Indeed, it might be argued that the claimant's proprietary interest in money used to discharge a debt could be traced into the funds now held by the creditor, but this is unlikely to be of much assistance: the creditor has necessarily given value for the property received in becoming a creditor in the first place. Provided he or she has not acted in bad faith or with notice that the money rightfully belonged to the claimant, he or she should be able to avail him- or herself of the bona fide purchaser defence.[117]

A difficult question is whether it should be possible to trace through a debt. Smith has forcefully argued that tracing 'backwards' through a debt should be possible.

---

[113] Cf the discussion of the swollen assets theory, at Chapter 18.3(c)(iv), pp. 887–9.

[114] [2015] UKPC 35; [2015] 3 WLR 599, [17].

[115] [2005] Ch 281, [140]. See too *Diplock*, 521; *James Roscoe (Bolton) Ltd v Winder* [1915] 1 Ch 62; *Re Goldcorp Exchange Ltd* [1995] 1 AC 74; *Bishopsgate Investment Management Ltd v Homan* [1995] Ch 211; *Serious Fraud Office v Lexi Holdings plc* [2009] EWCA Crim 1443; [2009] QB 376, [50] (Keene J); *Re BA Peters Ltd* [2008] EWCA Civ 1604; [2010] 1 BCLC 142, [15] (Lord Neuberger).

[116] Chapter 18.5(c), p. 900.

[117] See Chapter 18.6(a), p. 911.

Smith, 'Tracing Through a Debt' (1995) 54 CLJ 290, 292–4

The simplest case of tracing is the clean substitution, where a new asset is acquired solely with the value being traced. For example, we might be tracing the value inherent in £500 which was stolen from the plaintiff. If the thief uses it to buy a car, then ownership of the £500 can be traced into ownership of the car. Now change the facts slightly, so that the thief buys the car on credit; he takes ownership of the car, but he is the seller's debtor in respect of the purchase price. A day later, the thief pays the debt with the stolen money. Can we trace from the money into the car? It is difficult to see why not. There is no substantial change in the transaction; the period of credit might be reduced to a minute or a second the better to make this point. If that is right, then when money is used to pay a debt, it is traceable into what was acquired in exchange for the incurring of the debt.

...

However the matter is analysed, it seems clear that money which is used to pay a debt can be traced into what was acquired in exchange for the assumption of that debt. The incurring of the debt is the means of acquisition of that item, and the money being traced is the means of 'acquisition' or extinguishment of the debt. This is even clearer in a case in which the transfer of the acquired asset is delayed. Assume that the thief buys the car from the seller under a conditional sales contract. The thief becomes liable for the full price; he owes a debt; but he does not yet own the car. Only when he has paid all of the price does ownership pass. This case is perfectly clear; of course the money can be traced into the car. It shows that the debt is a red herring in the tracing exercise; it is just the means by which the price is paid, with some delay. But the price is paid for the asset bought, and so the price is traceable into that asset.

This approach to tracing might be thought to gain some support from the insistence of the House of Lords in *Foskett v McKeown* that tracing is not based upon 'causation', and so does not necessarily require causal links between the contribution of value and the acquisition. Rather, tracing depends upon being able to 'attribute' value in one asset to another. This process of attribution *could* involve going 'backwards' in time, through a debt, and attributing the value in the property used to discharge a debt as now subsisting in whatever was previously acquired through incurring that debt.

However, Conaglen has argued that although it would be possible to recognize backwards tracing in English law, this would be inappropriate.

Conaglen, 'Difficulties with Tracing Backwards' (2011) 127 54 LQR 432, 448–55

When trust money is used to pay the debt, there is no value inherent in the debt which is capable of being acquired because the debt is a *liability*.

...

The primary justification, in terms of legal policy, for recognising the possibility of tracing backwards is that it involves the 'use [or development of] tracing rules to secure what is perceived to be a just result'.[118] The justice, or fairness, of the case is strongest on the side of the trust beneficiaries who seek to trace the trust assets through the payment of a debt into the asset that was acquired by incurring the debt. One can readily understand the intuitive impulse to say that the trust beneficiaries' money has been used to 'acquire' an asset when it is used to pay off the debt in return for which the asset was first acquired. In a sense, the trust beneficiaries' money has been used to pay the price of the asset.

[118] Virgo, *Principles of the Law of Restitution* (2nd edn) (Oxford: Oxford University Press, 2006), p. 634.

However, that intuitive impulse can provide no more than a very rough guide as to how the law ought to approach the question of attribution, because it ignores the legal mechanism by which the trustee acquired the asset over which the trust beneficiaries now seek to make a claim. When the trustee uses trust funds to pay the debt, the beneficiaries' money has been used to pay the price of the asset only in a loose sense. In return for the asset, the vendor accepted the debtor's obligation to pay the debt: the vendor determined that the purchaser was sufficiently creditworthy that the vendor was prepared to agree to pass title in return for acquiring the benefit of a debt obligation rather than cash. The asset that the vendor accepted in return for agreeing to pass title in the goods to the purchaser was the benefit of the debt, not cash. The debt may later be realised by the payment of cash, but that cash may not come directly from the purchaser, as where the vendor factors the debt. And even where the cash does come from the purchaser, that is satisfaction of the debt rather than payment of the consideration for which the asset was acquired.

…

When the already precarious position of unsecured creditors is weighed against the concomitantly far better protected position of trust beneficiaries, it is suggested that the law ought not to recognise the possibility of tracing backwards. The unsecured creditors should not have their position worsened further by effectively making them insurers for the beneficiaries against trustee defalcations. Trust beneficiaries whose money has been wrongly applied in satisfaction of a debt can stand in the position of the satisfied creditor (by subrogation),[119] but it is a step too far, in policy terms, to allow them to stand in the position of the debtor and act as owners of property that the trustee acquired before the debt was paid.

The position in English law has for some time been unclear. Some limited judicial support for tracing backwards can be found. For example, in *Bishopsgate v Homan*, Dillon LJ said that:[120]

where an asset was acquired by the [defendant company] with moneys borrowed from an overdrawn or loan account and there was an inference that when the borrowing was incurred it was the intention that it should be repaid by misappropriations of [the plaintiff's money]. Another possibility was that moneys misappropriated from [the plaintiffs] were paid into an overdrawn account of [the defendant company] in order to reduce the overdraft and so make finance available within the overdraft limits for [the defendant company] to purchase some particular asset.

… it is at least arguable, depending on the facts, that there ought to be an equitable charge in favour of [the plaintiffs] on the asset in question of [the defendant company].

Dillon LJ's comments were *obiter*, but he raised the potentially significant issue that whether or not the defendant intended to pay off the debt with misappropriated funds might be important. This approach can be discerned in other *dicta*. For example, in the Court of Appeal in *Foskett*, Scott V-C stated that:[121]

it does not seem to me at all obvious that the circumstance that the payment into the account of the purchasers' money was made very shortly after the payment of the premium, rather than before or at the same time as the payment, should be regarded as fatal to the purchasers' equitable tracing claim. The availability of equitable remedies ought, in my view, to depend upon the substance of the transaction in question and not upon the strict order in which associated events happen. … I regard the point

---

[119] See Chapter 18.5(c), p. 900.
[120] *Bishopsgate Investment Management Ltd v Homan* [1995] Ch 211, 216.
[121] [1998] Ch 265, 283–4.

> as still open and, in particular, ... I do not regard the fact that an asset is paid for out of borrowed money with the borrowing subsequently repaid out of trust money as being necessarily fatal to an equitable tracing claim by the trust beneficiaries. If, in such a case, it can be shown that it was always the intention to use the trust money to acquire the asset, I do not see why the order in which the events happen should be regarded as critical to the claim.

Scott V-C cited Smith's article, quoted above, with approval. However, his Lordship's comments above were again *obiter*, not shared by the other judges, and the point remains open: there is no case in which backwards tracing has been explicitly accepted or rejected as part of the *ratio decidendi* in this jurisdiction.

Indeed, the weight of *dicta* on this topic in England and Wales does not seem to favour backwards tracing: both Dillon LJ in *Bishopsgate* and Scott V-C in *Foskett* were isolated in their approach. In *Bishopsgate*, for example, Legatt LJ was adamant that:[122]

> there can be no equitable remedy against an asset acquired *before* misappropriation of money takes place, since ex hypothesi it cannot be followed into something which existed and so had been acquired before the money was received and therefore without its aid.

Similarly, in *Foskett*, Hobhouse LJ insisted that:[123]

> The doctrine of tracing does not extend to following value into a previously acquired asset.

However, it now seems likely that English law will develop in a manner which recognizes backwards tracing. This is because backwards tracing appears to have been recognized to some extent by the Privy Council in the Jersey case of *Brazil v Durant International Corp*.[124]

Brazil v Durant International Corp [2015] UKPC 35; [2015] 3 WLR 599

The municipality of Sao Paolo brought claims against companies controlled by its former mayor and his son. The defendants had accepted bribes and then laundered the money received. The claimant sought to trace the value of the money into the defendants' accounts, but the defendants argued that some of the money was untraceable because it had been paid into their accounts before the bribes were received. The claimant argued that the sums paid into the account were effectively its own money, since similar sums were received as bribes only a few days later. The claimant argued that it was possible to trace backwards from the sums deposited in the account to the money received as a bribe. The Privy Council agreed.

Lord Toulson:

More particularly the respondents submit, as Professor Smith argues, that money used to pay a debt can in principle be traced into whatever was acquired in return for the debt. That is a very broad proposition and it would take the doctrine of tracing far beyond its limits in the case law to date. As a statement of general application, the Board would reject it. The courts should be very cautious before expanding

---

[122] [1995] Ch. 211, 221.
[123] [1998] Ch 265, 289. See also Morritt LJ at 296.
[124] [2015] UKPC 35; [2015] 3 WLR 599.

equitable proprietary remedies in a way which may have an adverse effect on other innocent parties. If a trustee on the verge of bankruptcy uses trust funds to pay off an unsecured creditor to whom he is personally indebted, in the absence of special circumstances it is hard to see why the beneficiaries' claim should take precedence over those of the general body of unsecured creditors.

However there may be cases where there is a close causal and transactional link between the incurring of a debt and the use of trust funds to discharge it. *Agricultural Credit Corpn of Saskatchewan v Pettyjohn* (1991) 79 DLR (4th) 22 (Sask CA) provides a good example. In 1981 and 1984 Mr and Mrs Pettyjohn applied to the credit corporation for loans to purchase cattle. They were informed that their applications were approved and that they could proceed to make the purchases. The Pettyjohns went ahead and bought cattle using a credit line with their bank as their immediate source of funding. About the same time, or shortly afterwards, the loan agreements with the credit corporation were executed, under which the credit corporation was given security over the cattle, and the moneys advanced by the credit corporation were used to pay back the bank. Sometime later the Pettyjohns sold the cattle (without the credit corporation's agreement), bought replacement cattle and used the proceeds of sale to repay the loan for the purchase of the replacement cattle. They then became insolvent.

The credit corporation claimed to have a purchase money security interest in the replacement cattle under the Personal Property Security Act. The claim gave rise to two issues: whether the lender had a right to security over cattle which were purchased after the loan application had been approved but before the loan moneys had been advanced: and, if so, whether the lender was entitled to trace the value of its original security into the replacement cattle.

The Saskatchewan Court of Appeal decided the case in favour of the credit corporation. Its decision on the second point turned on the construction of the provisions of the Act, but its decision on the first point is of general interest. Under the Act it was necessary for the credit corporation to establish that it gave value to the debtor for the purpose of enabling the debtor to acquire rights in personal property (as it undoubtedly did) and, more importantly, that the value was applied to acquire the rights. On that issue the court said at p 38:

> 'The … requirement, that the value have been used to acquire such rights, presents greater difficulties. How can it be said that the moneys advanced were used to acquire rights when the purchase had already taken place and the rights already acquired? It is, however, commercially unreasonable to divide the transactions so minutely. The Pettyjohns used the value given to them to pay off interim financing, but the interim financing had not been obtained as a separate transaction, but always with the view that it would be repaid through the moneys advanced by ACCS. The Pettyjohns used the value given as part of a larger, commercially reasonable transaction to acquire rights in the 1981 and 1984 cattle. The fact that the use of the value given was, due to the nature of the transaction, after the acquisition of rights does not alter the conclusion that the value given was used to acquire those rights.'

On those facts the court was right in the view of the Board not to divide minutely the connected steps by which, on any sensible commercial view, the purchase of the cattle was financed by the credit corporation, but to look at the transaction overall. The interposition of the bank was purely to provide bridging finance to cover the gap in time between the purchase and the credit corporation's funds coming through as previously arranged.

The development of increasingly sophisticated and elaborate methods of money laundering, often involving a web of credits and debits between intermediaries, makes it particularly important that a court should not allow a camouflage of interconnected transactions to obscure its vision of their true overall purpose and effect. If the court is satisfied that the various steps are part of a coordinated scheme, it should not matter that, either as a deliberate part of the choreography or possibly because of the incidents of the banking system, a debit appears in the bank account of an intermediary before a reciprocal credit entry. The Board agrees with Sir Richard Scott V-C's observation in *Foskett v McKeown* that the availability of equitable remedies ought to depend on the substance of the transaction in question and not upon the strict order in which associated events occur.

Similarly, in a case such as *Agricultural Credit Corpn of Saskatchewan v Pettyjohn*, the Board does not consider that it should matter whether the account used for the purpose of providing bridging finance was in credit or in overdraft at the time. An account may be used as a conduit for the transfer of funds, whether the account holder is operating the account in credit or within an overdraft facility.

The Board therefore rejects the argument that there can never be backward tracing, or that the court can never trace the value of an asset whose proceeds are paid into an overdrawn account. But the claimant has to establish a coordination between the depletion of the trust fund and the acquisition of the asset which is the subject of the tracing claim, looking at the whole transaction, such as to warrant the court attributing the value of the interest acquired to the misuse of the trust fund. This is likely to depend on inference from the proved facts, particularly since in many cases the testimony of the trustee, if available, will be of little value.

It is very likely that this decision will have a significant influence on English law. If adopted by the English courts, it would mean that 'backwards tracing' would be possible. But it is important to emphasize that the scope of 'backwards tracing' is restricted by Lord Toulson. In particular, his Lordship emphasized the need for a 'close causal and transactional link', and that 'the claimant has to establish a coordination between the depletion of the trust fund and the acquisition of the asset which is the subject of the tracing claim'. These notions will no doubt be explored further in subsequent cases. They are clearly intended to give the court some flexibility in this area.

Backwards tracing is helpful in helping to combat fraud and money laundering, and the facts of *Brazil v Durant International Corp* are a good example of this. So, where a wrongdoer incurred a debt in order to acquire an asset, and always planned to discharge the debt with a beneficiary's property, then this seems likely to satisfy the 'coordination' and 'close causal and transactional link' requirements demanded by the Privy Council. Moreover, in these circumstances, allowing the claimant to assert a proprietary interest in the acquired asset might not unfairly prejudice the wrongdoer or other creditors since the asset would never have been acquired by the wrongdoer had he or she not known that he or she would be able to exploit the beneficiary's property.

However, the situation might be considered to be different where the trustee unwittingly misappropriated a beneficiary's money in breach of duty, and discharged a debt that he or she had acquired long before. For example, if the trustee paid off the entirety of a mortgage taken many years ago to purchase a house, it might seem unsatisfactory to allow the claimant to trace backwards *through* the debt, into the house, and then assert beneficial ownership of the house. This is because, if the house has risen in value, the claimant would, fortuitously, receive all the benefit of this increase.[125] Such an outcome might be considered to be harsh on the trustee who made the sound investment decision to purchase the house long before, and who might have been able to pay off the mortgage with other funds anyway.[126] In such a situation, it is unlikely that there is any 'coordination' or 'close causal and transactional link' that would enable the claimant to trace backwards. In between these two examples, of course, there may be a range of difficult cases, but nevertheless it is suggested that the judgment in *Brazil v Durant International Corp* is to be welcomed since it allows courts to provide remedies for fraud and money laundering more effectively and in a principled way.

[125] Subject to defences: see Chapter 18.6, p. 911.
[126] This may be especially important since it is not clear whether change of position is a defence to proprietary claims: see Chapter 18.6(b), pp. 916–19.

(iv) *The swollen assets theory*

It has been seen that the tracing exercise requires the claimant to identify his or her proprietary interest in specific substitute assets. It is sometimes suggested that this requirement of specificity is too rigid. For example, a situation might arise where the claimant can trace his or her money into the hands of a defendant, but the defendant spends that money on things he or she would have had to pay anyway, such as bills or tax. Since the property has been dissipated, the claimant cannot trace into any specific asset and will not have a proprietary claim. Yet had the defendant paid the bills with his or her own money—and whether or not he or she did so might simply be a matter of chance—the claimant would be able to trace and assert a proprietary claim. Where there is no proprietary claim, the defendant may be in a better position as a result of the misappropriation of the claimant's property, since the defendant's assets will be greater than they otherwise would have been.

As a result, it has sometimes been suggested that the claimant should be able to trace into the defendants 'swollen assets' generally, without having to identify particular assets into which value can be traced. This would ensure that the defendant does not benefit from his or her wrong, and further protects the claimant. This is crucially important in the event of the defendant's insolvency; if the defendant is solvent, the claimant may obtain satisfaction through a personal claim. The corollary of this is that the 'swollen assets theory' of tracing would adversely affect the position of the insolvent defendant's creditors.

The 'swollen assets theory' received the support of Lord Templeman in the Privy Council in *Space Investments Ltd v Canadian Imperial Bank of Commerce Trust Co. (Bahamas) Ltd*:[127]

> A bank in fact uses all deposit moneys for the general purposes of the bank. Whether a bank trustee lawfully receives deposits or wrongly treats trust money as on deposit from trusts, all the moneys are in fact dealt with and expended by the bank for the general purposes of the bank. In these circumstances it is impossible for the beneficiaries interested in trust money misappropriated from their trust to trace their money to any particular asset belonging to the trustee bank. But equity allows the beneficiaries, or a new trustee appointed in place of an insolvent bank trustee to protect the interests of the beneficiaries, to trace the trust money to all the assets of the bank and to recover the trust money by the exercise of an equitable charge over all the assets of the bank. Where an insolvent bank goes into liquidation that equitable charge secures for the beneficiaries and the trust priority over the claims of the customers in respect of their deposits and over the claims of all other unsecured creditors. This priority is conferred because the customers and other unsecured creditors voluntarily accept the risk that the trustee bank might become insolvent and unable to discharge its obligations in full. On the other hand, the settlor of the trust and the beneficiaries interested under the trust, never accept any risks involved in the possible insolvency of the trustee bank. On the contrary, the settlor could be certain that if the trusts were lawfully administered, the trustee bank could never make use of trust money for its own purposes and would always be obliged to segregate trust money and trust property in the manner authorised by law and by the trust instrument free from any risks involved in the possible insolvency of the trustee bank. It is therefore equitable that where the trustee bank has unlawfully misappropriated trust money by treating the trust money as though it belonged to the bank beneficially, merely acknowledging and recording the amount in a trust deposit account with the bank, then the claims of, the beneficiaries should be paid in full out of the assets of the trustee bank in priority to the claims of the customers and other unsecured creditors of the bank.

But this seems very generous to the claimant, and contrary to general principles of property law. The claimant is unable to identify his or her proprietary right in any particular substitute asset, so should be limited to personal claims. Indeed, English law has refused to adopt the 'swollen assets' theory.

---

[127] [1986] 1 WLR 1072, 1074.

In a later decision of the Privy Council, *Re Goldcorp Exchange Ltd*, Lord Mustill insisted that *Space Investments* should not be followed on this point,[128] and this was accepted by the English Court of Appeal in *Bishopsgate v Homan*, in which Dillon LJ said:[129]

> As I read the judgment of the Privy Council in *In re Goldcorp Exchange Ltd.* delivered by Lord Mustill, it makes it clear that Lord Templeman's observations in the *Space Investments* case [1986] 1 W.L.R. 1072 were not concerned at all with the situation we have in the present case where trust moneys have been paid into an overdrawn bank account, or an account which has become overdrawn. Lord Mustill said in the clearest terms, [1995] 1 A.C. 74, 104–105:
>
> > 'Their Lordships should, however, say that they find it difficult to understand how the judgment of the Board in *Space Investments Ltd. v. Canadian Imperial Bank of Commerce Trust Co. (Bahamas) Ltd.* [1986] 1 WLR 1072, on which the claimants leaned heavily in argument, would enable them to overcome the difficulty that the moneys said to be impressed with the trust were paid into an overdrawn account and thereupon ceased to exist: see, for example, *In re Diplock* [1948] Ch. 465. The observations of the Board in the *Space Investments* case were concerned with a mixed, not a non-existent, fund.'
>
> … Instead the decision of the Court of Appeal in *In re Diplock; Diplock v. Wintle* [1948] Ch. 465 is endorsed. There it was said, at p. 521:
>
> > 'The equitable remedies presuppose the continued existence of the money either as a separate fund or as part of a mixed fund or as latent in property acquired by means of such a fund. If, on the facts of any individual case, such continued existence is not established, equity is as helpless as the common law itself.'

Nevertheless, the swollen assets theory received some academic support. For example, Evans has argued that:[130]

> the normative support for such a requirement of specificity is tenuous. The supposed requirement appears to be driven by the idea that a proprietary remedy is in some sense a continuation or re-representation of the claimant's proprietary interest in an asset of which he or she has been deprived. Just as the claimant's proprietary interest is an interest in some specific asset, so too must be its re-representation in the defendant's hands. Thus Lionel Smith argues that it is in the nature of proprietary rights that they are held in specific assets and that tracing, which never creates proprietary rights, cannot alter their 'specific nature'; and thus, a proprietary remedy may be awarded only when there is some 'specifically surviving enrichment' in the hands of the defendant and not where there is merely a 'generally surviving enrichment'. But it is not the tracing process that creates remedial proprietary rights. It is the claiming rules or (if one accepts the possibility of a truly remedial constructive trust) the order of a court in upholding the claimant's claim and awarding a proprietary remedy. It is therefore not to the point that the tracing process cannot create an interest in generally surviving enrichment, that is, enrichment not represented by a specific asset with a transactional connection to the claimant's wealth. The question is whether courts can recognise or create such an entitlement as a proprietary remedy in response to the claimant's claim.
>
> There is good reason to suppose that they can.
>
> …

---

[128] [1995] 1 AC 74, 105.

[129] *Bishopsgate Investment Management Ltd v Homan* [1995] Ch 211, 218–19.

[130] 'Rethinking Tracing and the Law of Restitution' (1999) 115 LQR 469.

The swollen assets theory of tracing is a further logical development of the restitutionary or causal approach to tracing. It depends on the same assertion as the restitutionary approach, that it is possible to trace the claimant's value into the defendant's assets even where it is not possible to trace the claimant's value into any specific asset, so long as there is a causal connection between the value received and the surviving enrichment. It is important to note that, as a theory of the law of tracing, the swollen assets theory makes no assertions about the claimant's entitlement to a proprietary remedy. The power of the court to award a proprietary remedy, remains based on the antecedent circumstances giving rise to the defendant's enrichment. The swollen assets theory is concerned solely with the subject matter of any claim or remedy.

This provides a sophisticated justification for the 'swollen assets' approach, but it must be rejected as inconsistent with case law and principles of the law of property. Since Evans' article, *Foskett* has made it clear that tracing is not based upon causation, and has nothing to do with unjust enrichment. *Foskett* sets out a clear, logical approach, which should be preferred to that of Evans. This has been emphasized more recently by Keene LJ in *Serious Fraud Office v Lexi Holdings plc (in administration)*:[131]

For the equitable charge to attach it must attach to assets in existence which derive from the misappropriated trust funds. There must be a nexus. Were it otherwise the principles of following and tracing could become otiose. On the contrary, tracing in this area is a vital process: just because it is by that process that the necessary nexus is established and the proprietary remedy, be it by way of constructive trust or equitable charge, made effectual. It is for that reason that if all the misappropriated trust funds in any given case are paid into an account which was and remains overdrawn then the proprietary remedy is lost: for there are no identifiable assets left in existence, deriving from the misappropriated trust funds, to which a constructive trust or an equitable charge could attach …. In such a situation it is not open to a beneficiary to seek to shift the claim for an equitable charge to other assets which do not derive from the misappropriated trust funds.

4. CLAIMING

Claiming should be separated from tracing. As Lord Millett explained in *Foskett*:[132]

Tracing is also distinct from claiming. It identifies the traceable proceeds of the claimant's property. It enables the claimant to substitute the traceable proceeds for the original asset as the subject matter of his claim. But it does not affect or establish his claim. That will depend on a number of factors including the nature of his interest in the original asset. He will normally be able to maintain the same claim to the substituted asset as he could have maintained to the original asset. If he held only a security interest in the original asset, he cannot claim more than a security interest in its proceeds. But his claim may also be exposed to potential defences as a result of intervening transactions. Even if the plaintiffs could demonstrate what the bank had done with their money, for example, and could thus identify its traceable proceeds in the hands of the bank, any claim by them to assert ownership of those proceeds would be defeated by the bona fide purchaser defence. The successful completion of a tracing exercise may be preliminary to a personal claim (as in *El Ajou v Dollar Land Holding plc* [1993] 3 All ER 717) or a proprietary one, to the enforcement of a legal right (as in *Trustees of the Property of FC Jones & Sons v Jones* [1997] Ch 159) or an equitable one.

---

[131] [2008] EWCA Crim 1443; [2009] QB 376, [50].
[132] [2001] 1 AC 102, 128.

Tracing is the process that can be used to support a claim. But tracing (or following) does not necessarily determine the nature of a claim: tracing may lead to both proprietary and personal claims. The latter will be considered in Chapter 19.

Lord Millett was clear that the nature of a proprietary claim corresponds to the nature of the original proprietary right. A legal proprietary right will lead to a legal claim; an equitable right to an equitable claim; a limited right, such as a security interest, cannot lead to a claim for anything more than a security interest. But even if a claimant can trace into a substitute asset, a claim may fail because the defendant might be a bona fide purchaser, for example. The defences to proprietary claims will be considered later.[133]

It is useful here to consider the *nature* of proprietary claims. There is some dispute amongst commentators about whether proprietary claims are simply a question of property, or whether they are based upon unjust enrichment. The House of Lords in *Foskett v McKeown* explicitly addressed this point and concluded that proprietary claims did not fall within the scope of unjust enrichment.[134]

Foskett v McKeown [2001] 1 AC 102

Lord Browne-Wilkinson:[135]

The crucial factor in this case is to appreciate that the purchasers are claiming a proprietary interest in the policy moneys and that such proprietary interest is not dependent on any discretion vested in the court. Nor is the purchasers' claim based on unjust enrichment. It is based on the assertion by the purchasers of their equitable proprietary interest in identified property.

Lord Hoffmann:[136]

... this is a straightforward case of mixed substitution. ... This is not based upon unjust enrichment except in the most trivial sense of that expression. It is, as my noble and learned friend says, a vindication of proprietary right.

Lord Hope (dissenting):[137]

The argument for a claim against them in unjust enrichment fails on causation. The children were not enriched by the payment of these premiums. On the contrary, they would be worse off if they were to be required to share the proceeds of the policy with the purchasers. It is as well that the purchasers' remedy in respect of the premiums and interest does not depend upon unjust enrichment, otherwise they would have had to have been denied a remedy in respect of that part of their claim also.

Lord Millett:[138]

The transmission of a claimant's property rights from one asset to its traceable proceeds is part of our law of property, not of the law of unjust enrichment. There is no 'unjust factor' to justify restitution (unless 'want of title' be one, which makes the point). The claimant succeeds if at all by virtue of his own title, not to reverse unjust enrichment. Property rights are determined by fixed rules and settled

---

[133] See Chapter 18.6, p. 911.
[134] For consideration of unjust enrichment, see Chapter 1.4(b), pp. 13–15.
[135] [2001] 1 AC 102, 108.
[136] Ibid, 115.
[137] Ibid, 126.
[138] Ibid, 127–9.

principles. They are not discretionary. They do not depend upon ideas of what is 'fair, just and reasona-ble'. Such concepts, which in reality mask decisions of legal policy, have no place in the law of property.
... the plaintiffs seek to vindicate their property rights, not to reverse unjust enrichment.

Given the clarity of theses passages from the House of Lords, it might seem surprising that there remains much discussion about the nature of proprietary claims. Their Lordships were agreed that the claim existed to vindicate the claimant's proprietary interest identified in an asset through the process of tracing.

Nevertheless, criticism has been directed at this approach for failing to explain *why* the claimant has a claim to an asset in which he or she never had an interest at the outset. Birks insisted that there needed to be an *event* to create a proprietary right in a substitute asset, and that the only possible event would be unjust enrichment:[139]

In contrasting the categories of property—a category of response—and unjust enrichment—a cat-egory of causative event—their Lordships, in the grip of fiction, must really have intended to contrast causative events. They must have intended to say that the property right in the substitute arose from the original declaration of trust, not from any other event and in particular not from unjust enrichment.

The element of fiction is evident. It is odd to say that a right in a [substitute asset of a] car about which at the time nobody knew anything arose from a declaration of trust of money. It is even more odd when the right itself mutates. The claimant has a choice in relation to the substitute whether to take a beneficial inter-est proportionate to his involuntary contribution or a security interest for the amount of that contribution.

However, even if we accept that an 'event' is required to create a property right in a substitute asset, this could be accommodated by viewing the actions of the defendant as interfering with the claimant's property right. As Grantham and Rickett have written:[140]

while property rights start as a response to some other legally significant event, once in existence, they become an event in themselves. Where a person retains a property right, the law will (and must, if property law is to maintain any independent doctrinal credibility beyond being a 'factor' to be taken into account) respond to any interference with that right.

It is, therefore, doctrinally possible for property rights in the original asset to be the event or source of the property rights in the traceable product. This alone is sufficient to deny the proposition that rights in the traceable product are *always* a response to unjust enrichment. If property rights may generate further rights, then it is entirely plausible that the rights in the traceable product arise as a response to the plaintiff's persisting property rights in the original asset and the interference with those rights.

Nevertheless, Burrows maintains that the 'vindication of property rights' approach favoured by the House of Lords in *Foskett v McKeown* is flawed and that an unjust enrichment analysis is to be preferred:[141]

There is a difference between following and tracing. One is concerned with the creation of new pro-prietary rights over property that does not already belong to the claimant but is rather a substitution of

---

[139] Birks, *Unjust Enrichment* (2nd edn) (Oxford: Oxford University Press, 2005), p. 35.
[140] Grantham and Rickett, 'Tracing and Property Rights: The Categorical Truth' (2000) 63 MLR 905, 909.
[141] Burrows, *The Law of Resitution* (3rd edn) (Oxford: Oxford University Press, 2011), p. 170.

> property previously owned in equity by the claimant. So, in an unauthorised substitution case, if one is entitled to trace from a pig to a horse to a car, one cannot say, without invoking fiction, that one has proprietary rights in the car merely because one owned the pig that is now represented by the car. The truth is that one's proprietary rights in the pig entitle one to new proprietary rights in the car because the holder of the car has been unjustly enriched at one's expense.

The above passage is clearly inconsistent with *Foskett*. And in our view, the House of Lords was correct to reject an analysis based upon unjust enrichment. In order to establish a claim in unjust enrichment, the defendant must be enriched at the claimant's expense, and there must be an unjust factor providing a ground of restitution.[142] It is unclear what the ground of restitution is in these cases. As Lord Millett pointed out, if it is simply 'want of title', then that only highlights that we are here concerned with the law of property. Courts do not refer to unjust enrichment in this area, and are content to rely upon the vindication of property rights. We should feel confident in doing the same. On that basis, it would seem that a proprietary interest can be attributed from one asset to another simply as an incident of the law of property. This explains how claims to substitute assets can arise, and why any analysis based upon unjust enrichment is redundant.

It is important to understand the debate between the competing approaches, particularly as it is prominent in much of the literature. But how significant to the outcome of any given case is choosing between the two analyses? In *Foskett*, Lord Millett thought the correct analysis might be crucial:[143]

> The correct classification of the plaintiffs' cause of action may appear to be academic, but it has important consequences. The two causes of action have different requirements and may attract different defences.
>
> A plaintiff who brings an action in unjust enrichment must show that the defendant has been enriched at the plaintiff's expense, for he cannot have been unjustly enriched if he has not been enriched at all. But the plaintiff is not concerned to show that the defendant is in receipt of property belonging beneficially to the plaintiff or its traceable proceeds. The fact that the beneficial ownership of the property has passed to the defendant provides no defence; indeed, it is usually the very fact which founds the claim. Conversely, a plaintiff who brings an action like the present must show that the defendant is in receipt of property which belongs beneficially to him or its traceable proceeds, but he need not show that the defendant has been enriched by its receipt. He may, for example, have paid full value for the property, but he is still required to disgorge it if he received it with notice of the plaintiff's interest.
>
> Furthermore, a claim in unjust enrichment is subject to a change of position defence, which usually operates by reducing or extinguishing the element of enrichment. An action like the present is subject to the bona fide purchaser for value defence, which operates to clear the defendant's title.

This last paragraph is often considered to be the crucial difference between the approaches based upon vindication of property rights and unjust enrichment. Admittedly, this paragraph is ambiguous, but it might be taken to suggest that the defence of change of position should only be available to claims based upon unjust enrichment, not the vindication of property rights.[144] This will be considered fully later,[145] but it might be noted here that there is no reason in principle why claims based on property law should not also be subject to the defence of change of position. Given the clear guidance from the

---

[142] *Banque Financière de la Cité v Parc (Battersea) Ltd* [1999] 1 AC 221, 227 (Lord Steyn).

[143] [2001] 1 AC 102, 129.

[144] Lord Millett has, extra-judicially, confirmed that he prefers this approach: Lord Millett, 'Proprietary Restitution', in *Equity in Commercial Law* (eds Degeling and Edelman) (Sydney: Law Book Co., 2005), pp. 315, 325.

[145] See Chapter 18.6(b), pp. 916–19.

House of Lords in *Foskett* that these claims do not fall within the umbrella of unjust enrichment, it might now be better to focus on whether this defence should apply to the restitutionary claim, rather than on whether the label of 'unjust enrichment' should be given to the claim.

5. REMEDIES FOR PROPRIETARY CLAIMS

(a) COMMON LAW

Where the claimant has brought a proprietary claim at Common Law, for example, in the tort of conversion, the remedy will usually be a personal one for the value of the property. This is because the Common Law does not generally recognize proprietary remedies.[146] It will be sufficient for the claimant to establish that the defendant has received property in which the claimant has a legal proprietary interest, without needing to show that the defendant has retained this property.

(b) EQUITABLE PROPRIETARY REMEDIES

Various proprietary remedies are available to vindicate a claimant's equitable proprietary right. There are three principal remedies that need to be considered: beneficial ownership under a constructive trust; an equitable charge or lien; and subrogation. Choosing the appropriate remedy depends on the type of case at issue.

(i) *Purchase of substitute asset with the beneficiary's property alone*

If a trustee misappropriates a beneficiary's money from a trust fund and uses only that money to acquire a new asset, then the beneficiary should be able to assert beneficial ownership of that substitute asset.[147] The beneficiary owned the original money in Equity, so should own any asset subsequently acquired with his property. A constructive trust arises by operation of law; the defendant can be forced to transfer the property to the claimant. In *Boscawen v Bajwa*, Millett LJ recognized that:[148]

> The plaintiff will generally be entitled to a personal remedy; if he seeks a proprietary remedy he must usually prove that the property to which he lays claim is still in the ownership of the defendant. If he succeeds in doing this the court will treat the defendant as holding the property on a constructive trust for the plaintiff and will order the defendant to transfer it in specie to the plaintiff.

This can lead to controversial results: for example, if a trustee misappropriates £1 of the beneficiary's money in order to buy a lottery ticket, which wins £1million, then it appears to be relatively straightforward for the beneficiary to trace into the £1million winnings. As Lord Millett explained in *Foskett*:[149]

> Since the manner in which an asset is realised does not affect its ownership, and since it cannot matter whether the claimant discovers what has happened before or after it is realised, the question

---

[146] Save for the action for ejectment to recover land and the discretionary remedy of delivery up of goods under s. 3(3) of the Torts (Interference with Goods) Act 1977, quoted in Chapter 18.2, pp. 849–50.

[147] Subject to any defences: see Chapter 18.6, p. 911.

[148] [1996] 1 WLR 328, 334.

[149] [2001] 1 AC 102, 134.

of ownership can be answered by ascertaining the shares in which it is owned immediately before it is realised. Where A misappropriates B's money and uses it to buy a winning ticket in the lottery, B is entitled to the winnings. Since A is a wrongdoer, it is irrelevant that he could have used his own money if in fact he used B's. This may seem to give B an undeserved windfall, but the result is not unjust. Had B discovered the fraud before the draw, he could have decided whether to keep the ticket or demand his money back. He alone has the right to decide whether to gamble with his own money. If A keeps him in ignorance until after the draw, he suffers the consequence. He cannot deprive B of his right to choose what to do with his own money; but he can give him an informed choice.

In fact, the claimant might be able to trace into all the proceeds even if the defendant was entirely innocent: if it could be established that there was no mixing of property and that the £1 used to purchase the ticket indisputably belonged to the claimant, then all the winnings should equally belong to the claimant in Equity. It is unclear whether a constructive trust over the entirety of the winnings is satisfactory if the defendant would otherwise simply have used his own money to buy the ticket. Although the tracing rules mean that the claimant can identify a proprietary interest in the lottery winnings, that does not mean that the remedy awarded should necessarily allow the claimant to recover the entire amount. Although the claimant might have a remedy over the whole amount, this may be subject to any defence that the defendant might have; this will be considered later.[150]

Such 'clean' substitutions might be distinguished from situations where the claimant's property is mixed with other property.

(ii) *Purchase of substitute asset with mixed funds*

As with the tracing rules, it is helpful to consider separately situations where the claimant's money is mixed with that of a wrongdoing fiduciary, as was the case in *Foskett*, and instances where the claimant's money is mixed with that of an innocent volunteer.

(a) *Defendant is a fiduciary*

In *Re Hallett*, Jessell MR suggested that where the fiduciary held an asset that he had purchased with money from a mixed fund containing both his own property and that of the claimant, the claimant would be limited to claiming an equitable charge or lien over the fund, and would not be able to assert beneficial ownership:[151]

where a trustee has mixed the money with his own, there is this distinction, that the cestui que trust, or beneficial owner, can no longer elect to take the property, because it is no longer bought with the trust-money simply and purely, but with a mixed fund. He is, however, still entitled to a charge on the property purchased, for the amount of the trust-money laid out in the purchase; and that charge is quite independent of the fact of the amount laid out by the trustee.

However, these comments were *obiter* and unsatisfactory. A fiduciary would be able to avoid the imposition of a constructive trust simply by mixing the claimant's money with his own, thereby reducing the claimant's remedy to a charge over the fund, which would clearly be disadvantageous to the innocent claimant if the purchased asset increased in value. It would be odd for the law to favour a fiduciary in this way, given that the presumptions generally operate against the wrongdoing fiduciary.

---

[150] See Chapter 18.6(c), pp. 919–21.
[151] *Re Hallett's Estate* (1879) 13 Ch D 606, 709.

It was therefore no surprise that many cases refused to follow *Hallett*,[152] and in *Foskett* the House of Lords clearly departed from *Hallett* on this point. Lord Millett said:[153]

> Any authority that this dictum might otherwise have is weakened by the fact that Sir George Jessel MR gave no reason for the existence of any such rule, and none is readily apparent. The dictum was plainly obiter, for the fund was deficient and the plaintiff was only claiming a lien. It has usually been cited only to be explained away: see for example *In re Tilley's Will Trusts* [1967] Ch 1179, 1186, per Ungoed-Thomas J … It was rejected by the High Court of Australia in *Scott v Scott* (1963) 109 CLR 649 … It has not been adopted in the United States … In *Frimeau v Granfield* (1911) 184 F 480, 482 Learned Hand J expressed himself in forthright terms: 'On principle there can be no excuse for such a rule.'
>
> In my view the time has come to state unequivocally that English law has no such rule. It conflicts with the rule that a trustee must not benefit from his trust. I agree with Burrows[154] that the beneficiary's right to elect to have a proportionate share of a mixed substitution necessarily follows once one accepts, as English law does, (i) that a claimant can trace in equity into a mixed fund and (ii) that he can trace unmixed money into its proceeds and assert ownership of the proceeds.

However, the appropriate remedy in *Foskett* was difficult to determine. The majority insisted that the claimant's property had been used to acquire the life insurance policy and therefore the payout, so the claimants should obtain a proportionate share of the payout under a constructive trust.

Foskett v McKeown [2001] 1 AC 102, 109–11 (Lord Browne-Wilkinson)

> In the former case (mixing of funds) it is established law that the mixed fund belongs proportionately to those whose moneys were mixed. In the latter case it is equally clear that money expended on maintaining or improving the property of another normally gives rise, at the most, to a proprietary lien to recover the moneys so expended. In certain cases the rules of tracing in such a case may give rise to no proprietary interest at all if to give such interest would be unfair: see *In re Diplock; Diplock v Wintle* [1948] Ch 465, 548.[155]
>
> Both Sir Richard Scott V-C and Hobhouse LJ[156] considered that the payment of a premium on someone else's policy was more akin to an improvement to land than to the mixing of separate trust moneys in one account. Hobhouse LJ was additionally influenced by the fact that the payment of the fourth and fifth premiums out of the purchasers' moneys conferred no benefit on the children: the policy was theirs and, since the first two premiums had already been paid, the policy would not have lapsed even if the fourth and fifth premiums had not been paid.
>
> Cases where the money of one person has been expended on improving or maintaining the physical property of another raise special problems. The property left at the end of the day is incapable of being physically divided into its separate constituent assets, i.e. the land and the money spent on it. Nor can the rules for tracing moneys through a mixed fund apply: the essence of tracing through a mixed fund is the ability to re-divide the mixed fund into its constituent parts pro rata according to the value of the contributions made to it. The question which arises in this case is whether, for tracing purposes, the payments of the fourth and fifth premiums on a policy which, up to that date, had been the sole

---

[152] E.g. *Re Tilley's Will Trusts* [1967] Ch 1179, 1185–9 (Ungoed-Thomas J).
[153] [2001] 1 AC 102, 131.
[154] *The Law of Restitution* (London: Butterworth, 1993), p. 368.
[155] See Chapter 18.6(d), p. 921.
[156] In the Court of Appeal: [1998] Ch 265.

property of the children for tracing purposes fall to be treated as analogous to the expenditure of cash on the physical property of another or as analogous to the mixture of moneys in a bank account. If the former analogy is to be preferred, the maximum amount recoverable by the purchasers will be the amount of the fourth and fifth premiums plus interest: if the latter analogy is preferred the children and the other purchasers will share the policy moneys pro rata.

The speech of my noble and learned friend, Lord Millett, demonstrates why the analogy with moneys mixed in an account is the correct one. Where a trustee in breach of trust mixes money in his own bank account with trust moneys, the moneys in the account belong to the trustee personally and to the beneficiaries under the trust rateably according to the amounts respectively provided. On a proper analysis, there are 'no moneys in the account' in the sense of physical cash. Immediately before the improper mixture, the trustee had a chose in action being his right against the bank to demand a payment of the credit balance on his account. Immediately after the mixture, the trustee had the same chose in action (i e the right of action against the bank) but its value reflected in part the amount of the beneficiaries' moneys wrongly paid in. There is no doubt that in such a case of moneys mixed in a bank account the credit balance on the account belongs to the trustee and the beneficiaries rateably according to their respective contributions.

So in the present case. Immediately before the payment of the fourth premium, the trust property held in trust for the children was a chose in action, i.e. the bundle of rights enforceable under the policy against the insurers. The trustee, by paying the fourth premium out of the moneys subject to the purchasers trust deed, wrongly mixed the value of the premium with the value of the policy. Thereafter, the trustee for the children held the same chose in action (i e the policy) but it reflected the value of both contributions. The case, therefore, is wholly analogous to that where moneys are mixed in a bank account. It follows that, in my judgment, both the policy and the policy moneys belong to the children and the trust fund subject to the purchasers trust deed rateably according to their respective contributions to the premiums paid.

The contrary view appears to be based primarily on the ground that to give the purchasers a rateable share of the policy moneys is not to reverse an unjust enrichment but to give the purchasers a wholly unwarranted windfall. I do not myself quibble at the description of it being 'a windfall' on the facts of this case. But this windfall is enjoyed because of the rights which the purchasers enjoy under the law of property. A man under whose land oil is discovered enjoys a very valuable windfall but no one suggests that he, as owner of the property, is not entitled to the windfall which goes with his property right. We are not dealing with a claim in unjust enrichment.

Moreover the argument based on windfall can be, and is, much over-stated. It is said that the fourth and fifth premiums paid out of the purchasers' moneys did not increase the value of the policy in any way: the first and second premiums were, by themselves, sufficient under the unusual terms of the policy to pay all the premiums falling due without any assistance from the fourth and fifth premiums: even if the fourth and fifth premiums had not been paid the policy would have been in force at the time of Mr. Murphy's death. Therefore, it is asked, what value has been derived from the fourth and fifth premiums which can justify giving the purchasers a pro rata share. In my judgment this argument does not reflect the true position. It is true that, in the events which have happened, the fourth and fifth premiums were not required to keep the policy on foot until the death of Mr. Murphy. But at the times the fourth and fifth premiums were paid (which must be the dates at which the beneficial interests in the policy were established) it was wholly uncertain what the future would bring. What if Mr. Murphy had not died when he did? Say he had survived for another five years? The premiums paid in the fourth and fifth years would in those events have been directly responsible for keeping the policy in force until his death since the first and second premiums would long since have been exhausted in keeping the policy on foot. In those circumstances, would it be said that the purchasers were entitled to 100 per cent of the policy moneys? In my judgment, the beneficial ownership of the policy, and therefore the policy moneys, cannot depend upon how events turn out. The rights of the parties in the policy, one way or another, were fixed when the relevant premiums were paid when the future was unknown.

Lord Browne-Wilkinson highlighted the choice available to the Court in deciding how to vindicate the claimants' equitable proprietary interest in the payout from the death benefit. A proportionate share under a constructive trust was best justified by analogy to the acquisition of an asset. A charge was more appropriate if the analogy was made to maintaining, or perhaps improving, already acquired property. Deciding which approach better suited the facts was not easy. Indeed, Lord Browne-Wilkinson said that:[157]

> at the conclusion of the hearing I considered that the majority of the Court of Appeal were correct and would have dismissed the appeal. However, having read the draft speech of Lord Millett I have changed my mind and for the reasons which he gives I would allow the appeal.

Lord Millett's speech proved to be decisively persuasive. The thrust of his reasoning appears in many of the extracts given already; ultimately, he was adamant that:[158]

> in cases where the wrongdoer has misappropriated the claimant's money and used it to acquire other forms of property which have greatly increased in value the courts have consistently refused to limit the claimant to an equitable lien.

The minority (Lord Steyn and Lord Hope), by contrast, agreed with the Court of Appeal and considered the better analogy was that of maintaining or improving the defendant's property.

Foskett v McKeown [2001] 1 AC 102, 112

Lord Steyn:

the relative moral claims of the purchasers and the children must be considered. …

Given that the moneys stolen from the purchasers did not contribute or add to what the children received, in accordance with their rights established before the theft by Mr Murphy, the proprietary claim of the purchasers is not in my view underpinned by any considerations of fairness or justice. And, if this view is correct, there is no justification for creating by analogy with cases on equitable interests in mixed funds a new proprietary right to the policy moneys in the special circumstances of the present case.

Lord Hope:

The first question is simply one of evidence. This is whether, if the purchasers can show that their money was used to pay any of the premiums, they can trace their money into the proceeds obtained by the trustees from the insurers in virtue of their rights under the policy. The second question is more difficult, and I think that it is the crucial question in this case. As I understand the question, it is whether it is equitable, in all the circumstances, that the purchasers should recover from the trustees a share of the proceeds calculated by reference to the contribution which their money made to the total amount paid to the insurers by way of premium.

…

But the result of the tracing exercise cannot solve the remaining question, which relates to the extent of the purchasers' entitlement. It is the fact that this is a case of mixed substitution which creates the

---

[157] [2001] 1 AC 102, 108.
[158] Ibid, 135.

difficulty. If the purchasers' money had been used to pay all the premiums there would have been no mixture of value with that contributed by others. Their claim would have been to the whole of the proceeds of the policy. As it is, there are competing claims on the same fund. In the absence of any other basis for division in principle or on authority—and no other basis has been suggested—it must be divided between the competitors in such proportions as can be shown to be equitable. In my opinion the answer to the question as to what is equitable does not depend solely on the terms of the policy. The equities affecting each party must be examined. They must be balanced against each other. The conduct of the parties so far as this may be relevant, and the consequences to them of allowing and rejecting the purchasers' claim, must be analysed and weighed up. It may be helpful to refer to what would be done in other situations by way of analogy. But it seems to me that in the end a judgment requires to be made as to what is fair, just and reasonable.

…

Of the other analogies which were suggested in the course of the argument to illustrate the extent of the equitable remedy, the closest to the circumstances of this case seemed to me to be those relating to the expenditure by a trustee of money held on trust on the improvement of his own property such as his dwelling house. This was the analogy discussed by Sir Richard Scott V-C and by Hobhouse LJ [1998] Ch 265, 282 and 289–290. There is no doubt that an equitable right will be available to the beneficiaries to have back the money which was misappropriated for his own benefit by the trustee. But that right does not extend to giving them an equitable right to a pro rata share in the value of the house. If the value of the property is increased by the improvements which were paid for in whole or in part out of the money which the trustee misappropriated, he must account to the trust for the value of the improvements. This is by the application of the principle that a trustee must not be allowed to profit from his own breach of trust. But unless it can be demonstrated that he has obtained a profit as a result of the expenditure, his liability is to pay back the money which he has misapplied.

In the present case the purchasers are, in my opinion, unable to demonstrate that the value of the entitlement of the trustees of the policy to death benefit was increased to any extent at all as a result of the use of their money to keep the policy on foot, as the entitlement had already been fixed before their money was misappropriated. In these circumstances the equities lie with the children and not with the purchasers. I do not need to attach any weight to the fact that the purchasers have already been compensated by the successful pursuit of other remedies. Even without that fact I would hold that it is fair, just and reasonable that the children should be allowed to receive the whole of the sum now in the hands of the trustees after the purchasers have been reimbursed, with interest, for the amount of their money which was used to pay the premiums.

Lord Hope rightly makes a clear distinction between the claim and the remedy. He favoured the analogy of maintaining or improving, rather than acquiring, property on the facts of the case. Choosing whether the view of the minority or the majority is preferable when deciding the appropriate remedy in *Foskett* is largely a matter of judgement. However, the majority approach was consistent with the terms of the policy itself, which said that any payout would be in consideration of the payment of all the premiums: the claimant's money was used to pay the premiums that led to the payout, so it might be said that the claimant's money 'acquired' the payout.

In any event, the minority's invocation of concepts of justice, fairness, and even 'common sense'[159] were clearly rejected. Proprietary remedies do not depend upon such vague considerations. Indeed, it is difficult to know how Lord Hope envisaged the balancing exercise between various rights should be undertaken, and how useful any guidance provided to the lower courts could be. It is better that

---

[159] [2001] 1 AC 102, 124 (Lord Hope).

proprietary remedies rest upon clear and certain principles. Of course, a desire for fairness is entirely appropriate, and too rigid an approach might lead to injustice. However, the better way to introduce some flexibility probably lies in the realm of defences.[160]

The dissentients in *Foskett* thought that the remedy awarded was too hard on the defendants. But it has also been suggested that the remedy was not hard enough. Berg has argued that Mr Murphy was a wrongdoing trustee, and that the claimants should have been able to strip him of *all* the profits he made from his breach of fiduciary duty.

Berg, 'Permitting a Trustee to Retain a Profit' (2001) 117 LQR 366, 371

In *Foskett v. McKeown* it should have been held: First, that a trustee who has invested both his own money and misappropriated trust funds in a particular asset holds the entire profit on a constructive trust; and secondly, that it makes no difference if events eventually turned out so that the profit was obtained on that part of the investment that was made with the trustee's own money. At most, a modest extension—and arguably none at all—would have been required to the rule, as presently applied, that a trustee is accountable for any benefit or gain obtained or received in circumstances in which there existed a conflict between his fiduciary duty and his personal interest[161] ...

It is therefore submitted that the correct response in *Foskett v. McKeown* would have been to order repayment to M's children of the £30,660 of M's own money used for the first three premiums; and to declare that the remaining £969,340 was held on a constructive trust for the trust beneficiaries.

This approach of Berg *might* have been possible on the facts of *Foskett*, but it is a very different type of claim. It does not rest upon the vindication of property rights, but is founded upon the wrong of breach of fiduciary duty. Although this might lead to a full account of profits, it is important to note that the court has a flexible discretion to award an equitable allowance to the fiduciary.[162]

EQUITABLE CHARGE   The majority in *Foskett* made it clear that the claimant is able to elect between an equitable charge and a proportionate share of ownership of an asset that has been acquired from a mixed fund by a wrongdoing fiduciary. But this ability to elect presumably does not exist in situations where the claimant's money has only been used to maintain or improve an asset, in which case the claimant should be limited to a charge. So, if a fiduciary misappropriates the claimant's money, places it in his or her own account, and then spends money from that account on repairing his or her house, it would be too generous to the claimant and too harsh on the fiduciary to allow the claimant a proportionate share of the house: although the claimant's equitable interest may be identifiable in the house, it was not used to acquire it nor own it. A charge is the more appropriate remedy. This approach is logical, supported by previous authority,[163] and consistent with the thrust of the reasoning of the House of Lords in *Foskett*. Indeed, Lord Millett expressly left room for this conclusion:[164]

It is not necessary to consider whether there are any circumstances in which the beneficiary is confined to a lien in cases where the fund is more than sufficient to repay the contributions of all parties. It is sufficient to say that he is not so confined in a case like the present.

---

[160] See Chapter 8.6, p. 911.
[161] See Chapter 14.3, p. 672.
[162] See Chapter 14.5(e), pp. 716–17.
[163] Cf the decision of the Court of Appeal in *Foskett*: [1998] Ch 265.
[164] [2001] 1 AC 102, 132.

(b) Defendant is an innocent volunteer

If the defendant is an innocent volunteer and holds an asset that has been purchased from a fund containing both the claimant's and the defendant's money, then the substitute asset should be held for the claimant and defendant in the appropriate proportions. This was recognized by Lord Millett in *Foskett* when he said that:[165]

> Innocent contributors, however, must be treated equally inter se. Where the beneficiary's claim is in competition with the claims of other innocent contributors, there is no basis upon which any of the claims can be subordinated to any of the others. Where the fund is deficient, the beneficiary is not entitled to enforce a lien for his contributions; all must share rateably in the fund.
>
> The primary rule in regard to a mixed fund, therefore, is that gains and losses are borne by the contributors rateably. The beneficiary's right to elect instead to enforce a lien to obtain repayment is an exception to the primary rule, exercisable where the fund is deficient and the claim is made against the wrongdoer and those claiming through him.

The claimant has no choice but to accept a proportionate share in any asset acquired from a mixed fund where the defendant is equally innocent, and cannot elect to seek a charge if the purchased property has fallen in value.

(c) Subrogation

In *Orakpo v Manson Investments Ltd*, Lord Diplock described subrogation as:[166]

> a convenient way of describing a transfer of rights from one person to another, without assignment or assent of the person from whom the rights are transferred and which takes place by operation of law in a whole variety of widely different circumstances.

Most relevant for present purposes are cases where the claimant can trace his or her proprietary interest into a debt which the defendant discharged. Subrogation operates to 'keep the charge alive', and, effectively, puts the claimant into the shoes of the third party creditor whose debt has been discharged. So where the claimant's money is used by the defendant to discharge a debt owed to a secured creditor, typically a bank as mortgagee, the claimant can be subrogated to the bank's charge and enjoy exactly the same rights as the bank previously had.[167] In effect, the benefit of the charge is treated as though it had been assigned to the claimant.[168]

Boscawen v Bajwa [1996] 1 WLR 328, 335

Abbey National lent money to the purchaser of a house, with the loan being secured by a legal charge. This money was paid to the purchaser's solicitors. In breach of trust, that firm of solicitors transferred the money to the vendor's solicitors before completion and the money was used to

---

[165] Ibid.
[166] [1978] AC 95, 104 (Lord Diplock).
[167] *Cf Cheltenham and Gloucester plc v Appleyard* [2004] EWCA Civ 291; *Filby v Mortgage Express (No. 2) Ltd* [2004] EWCA Civ 759.
[168] *Banque Financière de la Cité v Parc (Battersea) Ltd* [1999] 1 AC 221, 236 (Lord Hoffmann). See also *Boscawen v Bajwa* [1996] 1 WLR 328, 333 (Millett LJ).

discharge the vendor's mortgage with the Halifax. The sale of the house fell through. The creditors of the vendor had obtained a charging order against the property that was sold, with the proceeds of sale paid into court. The creditors claimed the proceeds of sale, but Abbey National claimed that it was entitled by subrogation to the security right of the Halifax, being the vendor's former mortgagee, and so it was entitled to a charge on the proceeds of sale that ranked above the vendor's creditors. The Court of Appeal found for Abbey National.

Millett LJ:

Subrogation, therefore, is a remedy, not a cause of action ... It is available in a wide variety of different factual situations in which it is required in order to reverse the defendant's unjust enrichment. Equity lawyers speak of a right of subrogation, or of an equity of subrogation, but this merely reflects the fact that it is not a remedy which the court has a general discretion to impose whenever it thinks it just to do so. The equity arises from the conduct of the parties on well-settled principles and in defined circumstances which make it unconscionable for the defendant to deny the proprietary interest claimed by the plaintiff. A constructive trust arises in the same way. Once the equity is established the court satisfies it by declaring that the property in question is subject to a charge by the way of subrogation in the one case or a constructive trust in the other.

Accordingly, there was nothing illegitimate in the deputy judge's invocation of the two doctrines of tracing and subrogation in the same case. They arose at different stages of the proceedings. Tracing was the process by which the Abbey National sought to establish that its money was applied in the discharge of the Halifax's charge; subrogation was the remedy which it sought in order to deprive Mr. Bajwa (through whom the appellants claim) of the unjust enrichment which he would thereby otherwise obtain at the Abbey National's expense.

...

The appellants submit that the mere fact that the claimant's money is used to discharge someone else's debt does not entitle him to be subrogated to the creditor whose debt is paid. There must be 'something more:' *Paul v. Speirway Ltd.* [1976] Ch 220, 230, per Oliver J.; and see *Orakpo v Manson Investments Ltd.* [1978] AC 95, 105, where Lord Diplock said:

> 'The mere fact that money lent has been expended upon discharging a secured liability of the borrower does not give rise to any implication of subrogation unless the contract under which the money was borrowed provides that the money is to be applied for this purpose: *Wylie v Carlyon* [1922] 1 Ch 51.'

... In *Butler v Rice* [1910] 2 Ch 277 the fact that the debtor had not requested the claimant to make the payment and did not know of the transaction was held to be immaterial. This is not to say that intention is necessarily irrelevant in a case of the present kind; it is to say only that where the payment was made by a third party and the claimant had no intention to make any payment to or for the benefit of the recipient the relevant intention must be that of the third party.

... If *Butler v Rice* and similar cases are relied upon to support the proposition that there can be no subrogation unless the claimant intended to keep the original security alive for its own benefit save in so far as it was replaced by a new and effective security, with the result that the remedy is not available where the claimant had no direct dealings with the creditor and did not intend his money to be used at all, then I respectfully dissent from that proposition. I prefer the view of Slade LJ in *In re T H Knitwear (Wholesale) Ltd* [1988] Ch 275 that in some situations the doctrine of subrogation is capable of applying even though it is impossible to infer a mutual intention to this effect on the part of the creditor and the person claiming to be subrogated to the creditor's security. In the present case the payment was made by [the solicitors], and it is their intention which matters. As fiduciaries, they could not be heard to say that they had paid out their principal's money otherwise than for the benefit of their principal.

> Accordingly, their intention must be taken to have been to keep the Halifax's charge alive for the benefit of the Abbey National pending completion. In my judgment this is sufficient to bring the doctrine of subrogation into play.

This passage shows that subrogation does not depend upon any mutual intention of the parties, and can put the claimant in the same—but no better—position as the creditor whose debt has been discharged.

Millett LJ clearly refers to subrogation being based upon unjust enrichment. Other judges have subsequently followed this approach.[169] But, for similar reasons to those given already,[170] this is inappropriate, and Lord Millett's subsequent approach in *Foskett* should be preferred.[171] Subrogation should operate to vindicate a claimant's property right, as established through tracing.

However, it now also seems that subrogation may be available even in the absence of a 'tracing link' as a result of the decision of the Supreme Court in *Menelaou v Bank of Cyprus Plc*.[172]

Menelaou v Bank of Cyprus Plc [2015] UKSC 66; [2015] 3 WLR 1334

Rush Green Hall was the Menelaou family home. It was jointly owned by the parents, and subject to two charges in favour of the Bank of Cyprus UK Ltd ('the Bank') worth £2.2 million. The parents decided to sell Rush Green Hall, and instructed Boulters, a firm of solicitors, for this purpose. On 15 July 2008 contracts were exchanged for the sale of the property for £1.9million, and the purchasers paid a 10 per cent deposit. On 24 July 2008, contracts were exchanged for the purchase of Great Oak Court for £875,000. The purchaser of Great Oak Court was Melissa Menelaou, one of the parents' children, and the 10 per cent deposit of £87,500 was paid from the deposit received from the sale of Rush Green Hall. Melissa was to receive Great Oak Court as a gift, and hold it on trust for herself and her two younger siblings. The Bank reluctantly agreed to these arrangements, on the basis that it would release its charge over Rush Green Hall upon receipt of £750,000, and instead take a third party charge over Great Oak Court. The Bank instructed Boulters to ensure that this occurred. Melissa was unaware of these arrangements. When the sale of Rush Green Hall was completed, Boulters received the balance of the purchase price from the purchasers and remitted £750,000 to the Bank and sent £785,000 to the vendors of Great Oak Court. The Bank's charges over the Hall were cancelled and Melissa was registered as proprietor of Great Oak Court. A charge over Great Oak Court was sent to the Bank by Boulters, purportedly signed by Melissa. However, Melissa was unaware of this. In 2010, when seeking to sell Great Oak Court, Melissa claimed that the charge was void as she had not signed it. The Bank argued that it should be subrogated to an unpaid vendor's lien over Great Oak Court. The Supreme Court agreed with the Bank.

Lord Clarke:

It appears to me that this is a case of unjust enrichment. In *Benedetti v Sawiris* [2013] UKSC 50, [2014] AC 938 the Supreme Court recognised that it is now well established that the court must ask itself four questions when faced with a claim for unjust enrichment. They are these: (1) Has the defendant been enriched? (2) Was the enrichment at the claimant's expense? (3) Was the enrichment unjust?

---

[169] E.g. *Anfield (UK) Ltd v Bank of Scotland plc* [2010] EWHC 2374 (Ch); [2011] 1 WLR 2414.
[170] See Chapter 18.4, pp. 889–93.
[171] *Halifax plc v Omar* [2002] EWCA Civ 121; [2002] 2 P & CR 377 [71]; *Bofinger v Kingsway Group Ltd* [2009] HCA 44.
[172] [2015] UKSC 66; [2015] 3 WLR 1334.

(4) Are there any defences available to the defendant? See, for example, *Benedetti* at para 10, following *Banque Financière de la Cité v Parc (Battersea) Ltd* [1999] 1 AC 221 per Lord Steyn at 227 (and per Lord Hoffmann to much the same effect at 234) and *Investment Trust Companies v Revenue and Customs Comrs* [2012] EWCH 458 (Ch), [2012] STC 1150 per Henderson J at para 38 (*ITC*).

In that paragraph Henderson J noted that Professor Andrew Burrows QC said in *The Law of Restitution*, 3rd ed (2011) p 27 that, if the first three questions are answered affirmatively and the fourth negatively, the claimant will be entitled to restitution and that those four elements 'constitute the fundamental conceptual structure of an unjust enrichment claim'. In para 39, Henderson J accepted that approach, although he said that the four questions were no more than broad headings for ease of exposition, that they did not have statutory force and that there may be a considerable degree of overlap between the first three questions. I agree.

In the instant case, there is no doubt that Melissa was enriched when she became the owner of Great Oak Court, which she was given by her parents, albeit on the basis that she would hold it for the benefit of herself and her two younger siblings. As it is correctly put on behalf of the Bank, her obligation to pay the purchase price of Great Oak Court to the vendor was discharged. The essential question is whether she was enriched at the expense of the Bank, since, if she was, there cannot in my opinion have been any doubt that the enrichment was unjust.

I would accept the submission made on behalf of the Bank that the unjust factor or ground for restitution is usually identified in subrogation cases as being, either (1) that the lender was acting pursuant to the mistaken assumption that it would obtain security which it failed to obtain: see eg *Banque Financière* per Lord Hoffmann at p 234H, or (2) failure of consideration: see the fourth and fifth points made by Neuberger LJ in *Cheltenham & Gloucester plc v Appleyard ("C&G")* [2004] EWCA Civ 291, paras 35 and 36; [2004] 13 EG 127 (CS).

On the facts here the Bank expected to have a first legal charge over Great Oak Court securing the debts of the appellant's parents and their companies but, as events turned out, it did not have that security interest. The critical question is therefore whether Melissa was enriched at the expense of the Bank.

[Lord Clarke held that Melissa was unjustly enriched at the expense of the Bank and continued]

The next question is what remedies are available to the Bank. The answer is that the Bank is subrogated to the unpaid seller's lien. Subrogation (sometimes known in this context as restitutionary subrogation) is available as a remedy in order to reverse what would otherwise be Melissa's unjust enrichment. It is important to recognise that a claim in unjust enrichment is different in principle from a claim to vindicate property rights; see eg *Foskett v McKeown* [2001] 1 AC 102 per Lord Browne-Wilkinson at p 108F, Lord Millett at p 129E-F and Lord Hoffmann at p 115F, where he agreed with Lord Millett.

Foskett was a claim to enforce property rights. Lord Millett expressed the distinction between that case and a case of unjust enrichment at p 129F:

> 'A plaintiff who brings an action in unjust enrichment must show that the defendant has been enriched at the plaintiff's expense, for he cannot have been unjustly enriched if he has not been enriched at all. *But the plaintiff is not concerned to show that the defendant is in receipt of property belonging beneficially to the plaintiff or its traceable proceeds.* The fact that the beneficial ownership of the property has passed to the defendant provides no defence; indeed, it is usually the very fact which founds the claim. Conversely, a plaintiff who brings an action like the present must show that the defendant is in receipt of property which belongs beneficially to him or its traceable proceeds, but he need not show that the defendant has been enriched by its receipt. He may, for example, have paid full value for the property, but he is still required to disgorge it if he received it with notice of the plaintiff's interest.'

The sentence which I have put in italics shows that a claim in unjust enrichment does not need to show a property right.

In *C & G* [2004] EWCA Civ 291 Neuberger LJ (giving the judgment of the Court of Appeal) summarised the principles relevant to different types of subrogation concisely in paras 24-49. Like Floyd LJ [in the Court of Appeal in *Menelaou*] at para 44, he set out the principles relevant here at para 25 as follows:

> The principle upon which C&G rely has been nowhere better stated than by Walton J in *Burston Finance Ltd v Speirway Ltd (in liquidation)* [1974] 1 WLR 1648 at p 1652B-C:
>
> > [W]here A's money is used to pay off the claim of B, who is a secured creditor, A is entitled to be regarded in equity as having had an assignment to him of B's rights as a secured creditor. It finds one of its chief uses in the situation where one person advances money on the understanding that he is to have certain security for the money he has advanced, and for one reason or another, he does not receive the promised security. In such a case he is nevertheless to be subrogated to the rights of any other person who at the relevant time had any security over the same property and whose debts have been discharged in whole or in part by the money so provided by him.

Neuberger LJ noted at para 26 that that formulation was cited with approval by (among others) Lord Hutton in *Banque Financière* at p 245C-D.

He further noted at para 36 that in *Banque Financière* the lender bargained for what Lord Hoffmann called at p 229C 'a negative form of protection in the form of an undertaking', which he did not get. He added that this did not prevent his claim to be subrogated to a security, albeit essentially as a personal remedy: see per Lord Steyn at p 228C-D and Lord Hoffmann at p 229C.

The class of subrogation under discussion in this case is known as subrogation to an unpaid vendor's lien. I agree with Floyd LJ at para 15 that it is not a concept which it is particularly straightforward to understand. He puts it thus. What the Bank seeks to achieve is to be placed in a position equivalent to that of the vendor of Great Oak Court at the point where the purchase money has not been paid. At that point the vendor would be able to refuse to convey the title to Great Oak Court, unless the purchase money was paid to him. He added that the lien was explained by Millett LJ in *Barclays Bank plc v Estates & Commercial Ltd* [1977] 1 WLR 415 at pp 419-420, in this way (omitting citations):

> 'As soon as a binding contract for sale [of land] is entered into, the vendor has a lien on the property for the purchase money and a right to remain in possession of the property until payment is made. The lien does not arise on completion but on exchange of contracts. It is discharged on completion to the extent that the purchase money is paid. … Even if the vendor executes an outright conveyance of the legal estate in favour of the purchaser and delivers the title deeds to him, he still retains an equitable lien on the property to secure the payment of any part of the purchase money which remains unpaid. The lien is not excluded by the fact that the conveyance contains an express receipt for the purchase money.
>
> The lien arises by operation of law and independently of the agreement between the parties. It does not depend in any way upon the parties' subjective intentions. It is excluded where its retention would be inconsistent with the provisions of the contract for sale or with the true nature of the transaction as disclosed by the documents.'

Floyd LJ then set out the passage from the judgment of Walton J in *Burston Finance* set out by Neuberger LJ in *C&G* and quoted at para 39 above. I adopt Floyd LJ's description of the position at para 17 of his judgment as follows. A third party who provides some or all of the purchase money for a purchaser, thereby discharging the obligation to the vendor, can claim the benefit of the unpaid vendor's lien by subrogation. This is so even after the lien has been extinguished as between vendor and purchaser. Floyd LJ notes that it is not intuitively clear how, or why, this should be the case and asks how it is that the unpaid vendor's lien transferred from the vendor to the third party. He says with force that it might be thought that once the obligation in question has been extinguished, there is nothing which the vendor could transfer. He further asks by what legal method the transfer takes place, even if there was something to transfer. He notes that there has been no legal assignment and suggests that it was conceptual problems such as these that gave rise to the notion that the vendor's lien was 'kept alive' for the benefit of the subrogated third party.

Floyd LJ resolves this apparent difficulty by adding that in *Banque Financière* at p 236 Lord Hoffmann explained that the phrase 'keeping the charge alive' was not a literal truth but a metaphor or analogy:

> 'In a case in which the whole of the secured debt is repaid, the charge is not kept alive at all. It is discharged and ceases to exist.'

Lord Hoffmann added at p 236E-F:

> 'It is important to remember that, as Millett LJ pointed out in *Boscawen v Bajwa* [1996] 1 WLR 328, 335, subrogation is not a right or a cause of action but an equitable remedy against a party who would otherwise be unjustly enriched. It is a means by which the court regulates the legal relationships between a plaintiff and a defendant or defendants in order to prevent unjust enrichment. When judges say the charge is 'kept alive' for the benefit of the plaintiff, what they mean is that his legal relations with a defendant who would otherwise be unjustly enriched are regulated as if the benefit of the charge had been assigned to him.'

In para 19 Floyd LJ notes that Lord Hoffmann reviewed five authorities, namely *Chetwynd v Allen* [1899] 1 Ch 353, *Butler v Rice* [1910] 2 Ch 277, *Ghana Commercial Bank v Chandiram* [1960] AC 732, *Paul v Spierway* [1976] Ch 220 and *Boscawen v Bajwa* [1996] 1 WLR 328. Having done so, Lord Hoffmann noted at p 233 that in *Boscawen* there was no common intention that the vendor, whose mortgage had been paid off, should grant any security to *Abbey National*.

Lord Hoffmann then said this at pp 233H-234D:

> 'As Millett LJ pointed out, at p 339 [of *Boscawen*], the Abbey National expected to obtain a charge from the purchaser as legal owner after completion of the sale, and, in the event which happened of there being no such completion, did not intend its money to be used at all. This meant that:
>
> "The factual context in which the claim to subrogation arises is a novel one which does not appear to have arisen before but the justice of its claim cannot be denied."
>
> These cases seem to me to show that it is a mistake to regard the availability of subrogation as a remedy to prevent unjust enrichment as turning entirely upon the question of intention, whether common or unilateral. Such an analysis has inevitably to be propped up by presumptions which can verge upon outright fictions, more appropriate to a less developed legal system than we now have. I would venture to suggest that the reason why intention has played so prominent a part in the earlier cases is because of the influence of cases on contractual subrogation. But I think it should be recognised that one is here concerned with a restitutionary remedy and that the appropriate questions are therefore, first, whether the defendant would be enriched at the plaintiff's expense; secondly, whether such enrichment would be unjust; and thirdly, whether there are nevertheless reasons of policy for denying a remedy. An example of a case which failed on the third ground is *Orakpo v Manson Investments Ltd* [1978] AC 95, in which it was considered that restitution would be contrary to the terms and policy of the Moneylenders Acts.'

That appears to me to be an illuminating passage. Lord Hoffmann stresses what are the same questions as those referred to in para 18 above. Moreover, the reference to *Orakpo* seems to me to be of some significance. It demonstrates that, when Lord Hoffmann was referring to 'subrogation as a remedy to prevent unjust enrichment', he was not referring to subrogation to personal rights alone because *Orakpo* was a case concerning subrogation to property rights.

The case of *Orakpo* is also of interest because it shows the broad nature of the doctrine of unjust enrichment. Three examples suffice. Lord Diplock said at p 104E-F:

'My Lords, there is no general doctrine of unjust enrichment recognised in English law. What it does is to provide specific remedies in particular cases of what might be classified as unjust enrichment in a legal system that is based upon the civil law. There are some circumstances in which the remedy takes the form of 'subrogation', but this expression embraces more than a single concept in English law. It is a convenient way of describing a transfer of rights from one person to another, without assignment or assent of the person from whom the rights are transferred and which takes place by operation of law in a whole variety of widely different circumstances. Some rights by subrogation are contractual in their origin, as in the case of contracts of insurance. Others, such as the right of an innocent lender to recover from a company moneys borrowed ultra vires to the extent that these have been expended on discharging the company's lawful debts, are in no way based on contract and appear to defeat classification except as an empirical remedy to prevent a particular kind of unjust enrichment.'

Lord Salmon said this at p 110:

'The test as to whether the courts will apply the doctrine of subrogation to the facts of any particular case is entirely empirical. It is, I think, impossible to formulate any narrower principle than that the doctrine will be applied only when the courts are satisfied that reason and justice demand that it should be.

Finally, Lord Edmund-Davies said at p 112:

'Apart from specific agreement and certain well-established cases, it is conjectural how far the right of subrogation will be granted though in principle there is no reason why it should be confined to the hitherto recognised categories (Goff and Jones, *The Law of Restitution* (1966), pp 376-377).'

Those statements seem to me to support a flexible approach to the remedies appropriate in a particular case. Indeed, the principles have been extended since the decision in *Orakpo* because there is now a general doctrine of unjust enrichment in a way that there was not when Lord Diplock drafted his speech. Lord Hoffmann stresses the importance of the questions identified in para 18 above. It appears to me that, on the facts of this case, if, as here, the first three questions are answered in the affirmative and the fourth in the negative, the appropriate equitable remedy is that the claimant is subrogated to the unpaid vendor's lien as explained in paras 41 and 42 above. On the facts here the Bank is entitled to a lien on the property, which is in principle an equitable interest which it can enforced by sale. In short, by effectively reinstating Melissa's liability under the charge, the remedy of subrogation is reversing what would otherwise be her unjust enrichment.

I would accept the submission made on behalf of the Bank that the analyses in *Banque Financière* have rationalised the older cases through the prism of unjust enrichment. *Banque Financière* was not limited to subrogation to personal rights. The remedy the House fashioned was subrogation to a property right but, as the Bank puts it, it was attenuated so as not to grant RTB a greater right than that for which it had bargained. There is no reason why, on the facts of this case, the remedy should not be subrogation as described above, even if the Bank did not retain a property interest in the proceeds of sale of Rush Green Hall. The remedy simply reverses the unjust enrichment which Melissa would otherwise enjoy by ensuring that the Bank not only has a personal claim against her but also has an equitable interest in Great Oak Court, as it would have had if the scheme had gone through in accordance with the agreement of the Bank and the Menelaou parents. Moreover, but for the proposed remedy the Bank would lose the benefit it was to receive from the scheme, namely a charge on Great Oak Court to replace the charges it had on Rush Green Hall.

This is a difficult judgment. The analysis of the unjust enrichment claim is somewhat controversial,[173] but the most important aspect of Lord Clarke's reasoning for present purposes is that subrogation is available even if it is not possible to assert any proprietary interest in the money used to discharge the unpaid vendor's lien. Unjust enrichment can lead to subrogation. This might be thought to be consistent with the earlier decision of the House of Lords in *Banque Financière de la Cité v Parc*,[174] but, as Lord Clarke rightly observed, that involved subrogation to a security essentially as a personal remedy.[175] This was supported by Lord Neuberger:

Given that the Bank has a claim based on unjust enrichment against Melissa to the extent described above, it is hard to identify a more appropriate remedy for the Bank to obtain against Melissa. Subrogation to the Lien would accord to the Bank, and impose on Melissa, a right very similar to, although rather less in value than, that which the Bank should have had. It would give the Bank a lien instead of a formal charge, and it would be in the sum of £875,000 (plus interest), rather than the larger debt, well over £1m at the time of the purchase of the freehold, owed by the Menelaou parents to the Bank.

An award of financial compensation might seem rather less appropriate. It was never intended that the Bank should have any personal claim against Melissa, merely that the freehold which she owned would be charged with the Menelaou parents' debt to the Bank. Even if the compensation was limited to £875,000 (plus interest), it could prejudice Melissa — for instance, if the freehold declined in value as a result of a fall in the property market subsequent to her acquisition.

However, it is fair to say that the standard response to unjust enrichment is a 'monetary restitutionary award', to use the terminology adopted by in *A Restatement of the English Law of Unjust Enrichment* (Burrows et al, 2012), article 34, in order to reverse the unjust enrichment. In this case, the unjust enrichment could be quantified at £875,000, its value at the time it was conferred, or the difference in the value of the freehold uncharged and subject to the Charge at the date of the assessment of the unjust enrichment (or possibly at some other date). In so far as the quantification would result in an unfair or oppressive sum, the court could adjust the sum to avoid any unfairness or oppression.

…

In those circumstances, it is hard to see why subrogating the Bank to the unpaid vendor's lien is not an appropriate way to remedy the unjust enrichment. I do not consider that the reasoning in *Boscawen v Bajwa* [1996] 1 WLR 328 presents a problem. In that case, at pp 334D and 335C, Millett LJ discussed in instructive detail both tracing, which he explained was 'a process', and subrogation, which he described as 'a remedy'. (On reflection, I wonder whether the distinction, despite the approval of Lord Hoffmann in *Banque Financière* at p 236E of the description of subrogation as a remedy, is as satisfactory as it seems at first sight. It seems to me questionable whether a sharp distinction can satisfactorily be drawn between a process and a remedy, but the point has no effect on the outcome of this case.)

While I accept that Millett LJ treated tracing as the appropriate process to achieve subrogation in *Boscawen*, there are two important caveats for present purposes. First, he nowhere stated that subrogation was an impermissible remedy if tracing was not an available prior process. Secondly, as [counsel] pointed out, at p 339A-B Millett LJ said that it would be 'perilous to extrapolate from one set of circumstances where the court has required a particular precondition to be satisfied before the remedy of subrogation can be granted a general rule which makes that requirement a precondition which must be satisfied in other and different circumstances'. Similarly, at p 334H, Millett LJ described subrogation as a remedy which 'will be fashioned to the circumstances'.

[173] See Chapter 1.4(b), pp. 13–15.
[174] [1999] 1 AC 221.
[175] Ibid, 228 (Lord Steyn), 229 (Lord Hoffmann).

Nor do I think that Lord Millett's statement in *Foskett v McKeown* [2001] 1 AC 102, p 127F about property rights being 'determined by fixed rules' and not being discretionary, casts doubt on my conclusion in this case. His analysis in that case has its critics – see eg Burrows, (2001) 117 LQR 412, 417 and *The Law of Restitution*, 3rd ed (2011), pp 140, 170-171 and 432-434, and Mitchell and Watterson, *Subrogation: Law and Practice* (2007), para 6.50. However, and more to the point, Lord Millett's remarks were directed to proprietary claims not unjust enrichment claims. Lord Millett made that clear in a passage at p 129E-G, where he said, *inter alia*, that one must distinguish between a claim brought 'to vindicate … property rights' and one brought 'to reverse unjust enrichment', and that Foskett was an example of the former. This point was also made by Lord Browne-Wilkinson and Lord Hoffmann at pp 108F and 115G respectively.

Finally on this aspect, it is worth mentioning that Melissa's case represents a triumph of form over substance, or, to use the words of Lord Steyn in *Banque Financière* at 227C, 'pure formalism'. It would have been perfectly open to the Bank to have requested Boulters to pay the whole proceeds of the sale of Rush Green Hall to the Bank, with the Bank then remitting back to Boulters the £875,000 needed to purchase Great Oak Court, on the basis that it would be subject to a charge in favour of the Bank to secure the Menelaou parents' indebtedness. If that had happened, and the Menelaou parents had then directed the transfer of Great Oak Court to Melissa, and the defective Deed had been executed, it is very difficult to see why the Bank could not have claimed subrogation to the unpaid vendor's lien. If Melissa's case on this appeal is right, the fact that the Bank sensibly short-circuited the process, and agreed that the £875,000 could be retained by Boulters to purchase Great Oak Court, would mean that a small and practical change, of no apparent commercial significance, results in a substantially different commercial outcome. Such an outcome is, of course, possible, but its unattractiveness tends to support the conclusion which I have reached.

It therefore seems that the Supreme Court extends subrogation beyond its previously understood limits. No longer is a proprietary interest necessary in order to seek subrogation. It can be awarded as a result of a successful claim in unjust enrichment. This seems to be an unfortunate and unnecessary development: a personal restitutionary remedy would be sufficient to reverse an unjust enrichment. Proprietary remedies should only be awarded where the claimant has a proprietary interest that must be protected. This distinction would give better effect to Lord Millett's approach in *Foskett*, which made a clear distinction between claims to enforce property rights, and (personal) claims to reverse an unjust enrichment.

Indeed, Lord Carnwath would have preferred to reach the same result not by invoking unjust enrichment, but rather focussing on traditional proprietary principles:

I agree that the appeal should be dismissed, but I arrive at that conclusion by a somewhat different route from that taken by my colleagues. In my view the respondent's case can be supported (contrary to the decision of the deputy judge) by a strict application of the traditional rules of subrogation, without any need to extend them beyond their established limits.

I am less convinced with respect of the case for 'rationalising' the older cases 'through the prism of unjust enrichment', as Lord Clarke suggests was done in *Banque Financière (Banque Financière de la Cité v Parc (Battersea) Ltd* [1999] 1 AC 221), thus in effect conflating the two doctrines. As Lord Millett explained in *Foskett v McKeown* [2001] 1 AC 102, 129 (cited by Lord Clarke at para 38), there is a clear distinction of principle between a claim to enforce property rights and a claim for unjust enrichment. Earlier in the same judgment (at p 127F) he had emphasised that property rights are to be determined 'by fixed rules and settled principles', not by discretion or policy. Subrogation to a vendor's lien is a claim to a property right, but it is, as Lord Clarke acknowledges, a less than straightforward concept. It should not be extended, nor should the established rules be distorted, without good reason.

...

In my view, the strict approach advocated by the appellant gains strong support from the judgment of Millett LJ in *Boscawen v Bajwa* [1996] 1 WLR 328. It is the leading modern authority on the application of principles of tracing and subrogation in a context not dissimilar to the present. As has been seen, it was cited with approval by Lord Hoffmann in *Banque Financière* at p 233F ('a valuable and illuminating analysis of the remedy of subrogation').

...

It was clearly regarded by Millett LJ as necessary for the claimants to establish that the money used to pay off the loan was their money. 'Tracing' was the process by which this was done. In the context of subrogation, tracing was not about identifying a particular asset in the hands of the defendant, as belonging notionally to the claimant; but rather as providing the necessary link with the payments made to discharge the relevant mortgage. In the passage quoted above, Millett LJ treated such payments as analogous to money spent in improving property. It was not regarded by him as sufficient to apply a broad causation or 'economic reality' test, such as applied by the Court of Appeal in the present case. ... This aspect of the case is not affected by the decision in *Banque Financière*. Lord Hoffmann noted that there was no difficulty on the facts of that case in 'tracing' the bank's money into the discharge of the relevant debt, since by contrast with *Boscawen* the payment was direct (p 235C-D). I take him to have been using that term in the same sense as Millett LJ. The problem was not so much the right to a proprietary remedy but whether that right should be cut down so as to limit its scope by reference to the limited nature of the initial agreement. The decision itself, and in particular the nature of the remedy (personal, proprietary or hybrid?), have been much discussed (see *Goff & Jones* para 6-30). But it throws no doubt on the importance, in the present context, of establishing a tracing link between the claimant's own money and the payment used to discharge the security.

...

The Court of Appeal felt able to decide the case on the footing that the Bank did not have an interest in the money used to pay off the security. It found it unnecessary to decide whether that assumption was correct. In this court it has been submitted that the Bank did have a sufficient interest on the basis either of the principle in *Buhr v Barclays Bank plc* [2001] EWCA Civ 1223, [2002] BPIR 25, or of a so-called *Quistclose* trust (after *Quistclose Investments Ltd v Rolls Razor Ltd* [1970] AC 567).

Although the *Quistclose* principle does not appear in terms to have been relied on in argument in the courts below, the substance was sufficiently pleaded in the amended counterclaim (para 13), which asserts that the proceeds of the sale of Rush Green Hall released by the defendant Bank were—

> '... held on trust for the defendant, subject to a power for Mr and Mrs Menelaou to use the same to purchase a flat in the joint names of Danielle Menelaou and her partner and also to purchase the Property in the name of the claimant but only on condition that the outstanding debts of Mr and Mrs Menelaou were to be secured by a first legal charge over the Property.'

The issue was also addressed by the judge (paras 14-17), albeit not specifically by reference to the *Quistclose* principle. It does not depend on any further findings of fact. I see no reason therefore why it cannot properly be relied on by the Bank in this court.

The *Quistclose* principle was explained and applied by the House of Lords in *Twinsectra Ltd v Yardley* [2002] 2 AC 164. A solicitor (Sims) had received money, lent by Twinsectra to his client (Mr Yardley) for the purchase of a property, under an undertaking that it would be utilised solely for the acquisition of property and for no other purpose. The money was paid to the defendant solicitor (Mr Leach), acting on behalf of the same client; he paid it out to the client who used it for purposes other than the purchase of the property. A claim against the defendant solicitor for dishonest assistance failed only because dishonesty was not established. The money was held to be subject to a trust in the first solicitor's client account, the terms of which were found in the terms of the undertaking, which made clear that the money 'was not to be at the free disposal of [the client]':

> '… the effect of the undertaking was to provide that the money in the Sims client account should remain Twinsectra's money until such time as it was applied for the acquisition of property in accordance with the undertaking. For example, if Mr Yardley went bankrupt before the money had been so applied, it would not have formed part of his estate, as it would have done if Sims had held it in trust for him absolutely. The undertaking would have ensured that Twinsectra could get it back. It follows that Sims held the money in trust for Twinsectra, but subject to a power to apply it by way of loan to Mr Yardley in accordance with the undertaking …' (paras 12-13, per Lord Hoffmann)

In the present case the critical issue is the status of the money received by Boulters on 12 September 2008, as proceeds of the sale of Rush Green Hall. (I do not understand either party to suggest that the deposit £90,000 should be treated differently from the balance of £785,000.) The judge saw no reason to infer a proprietary interest in the Bank:

> '16. In the present case the agreement or understanding recorded in the Bank's letter of 9 September 2008 did not address the question of ownership or even security rights in the sale proceeds of Rush Green Hall, and had no reason to do so. While the arrival of the sale proceeds from Rush Green Hall and the payment of £785,000 to the vendors of Great Oak Court (or their solicitors) and of £750,000 to the Bank could not have been literally simultaneous, it is unrealistic to suppose that the parties were concerned with the status of the incoming monies in any short interval between them. Critically, the agreement was concerned only with the circumstances in which the charges over Rush Green Hall would be released. So long as they remained in place, there was neither need nor reason for the Bank to have any rights over the proceeds of sale, or thereafter, since the charges were only to be released against substitute security over Great Oak Court. And should there be a defect in that substitute security, the Bank had protected itself by obtaining the undertakings given by Boulters in the Certificate of Title.

With respect to the judge, this analysis (like my own as trial judge in *Twinsectra*) seems to me to start from the wrong end. In the Boulters client account the money was undoubtedly trust money, in the sense that it was held beneficially for their clients (see eg *In re A Solicitor* [1952] Ch 328). That is not affected by the brevity of the period for which it was expected to be held. The relevant questions are: for whose benefit was it so held and on what terms? By this time they were acting for both the Menelaous and the Bank. Their respective interests in the money depended on the arrangements between them and with their solicitors. It is true that the Bank's letter of 9 September 2008 said nothing in terms about an interest in the money to be used for the new purchase. But there is nothing to suggest that the money was treated as freely at the disposal of the Menelaous, which would have been inconsistent with the general purpose of the arrangement.

The terms of the certificate of title provided to the Bank by Boulters on 10 September are also relevant. In it Melissa was named as 'borrower', and the price as £875,000. It included a standard form undertaking –

> 'prior to use of the mortgage advance, to obtain in the form required by you the execution of a mortgage and a guarantee as appropriate by the persons whose identities have been checked in accordance with paragraph (1) above as those of the Borrower, any other person in whom the legal estate is vested and any guarantor ….'

They also undertook to notify the Bank of anything coming to their attention before completion which would render the certificate untrue or inaccurate, and if so to 'defer completion pending your authority to proceed and … return the mortgage advance to you if required …'. I agree with [counsel] that in its context the reference in the certificate of title to the 'mortgage advance' must be read as a reference to the money received by them from the sale of Rush Green Hall. The natural implication of the undertakings was that, if the sale failed, the sum so defined would be paid to the Bank; not simply transferred to the Menelaous.

It follows in my view that there is no difficulty in this case in finding the necessary 'tracing link' between the Bank and the money used to purchase the new property. In this respect it is a much simpler case than *Boscawen*. The Bank's interest in the purchase money was clear and direct. On this relatively narrow ground, I would hold that the appeal should be dismissed.

Lord Neuberger was also 'sympathetic' to this approach,[176] which is the more traditional and orthodox. The Bank had an equitable interest in the monies used to purchase Great Oak Court, so it follows that the Bank should be able to exploit this proprietary base in order to trace into the property, or at least into the unpaid vendor's lien. There was no need in *Menelaou* to distort the principles of unjust enrichment in order to award subrogation. The reasoning of the Supreme Court is very difficult indeed, and it is to be hoped that the scope of the decision will be limited by future cases.

6. DEFENCES

(a) BONA FIDE PURCHASER

In *Foskett*, Lord Millett said that the bona fide purchaser defence operates to 'clear title',[177] such that it gives the defendant good title and defeats the claimant's equitable proprietary interest. For the defence to succeed, the defendant must have purchased legal title to the property for value, in good faith, and without notice of the claimant's equitable interest. If the defendant has only purchased equitable title, then the bona fide purchaser defence will not apply and the dispute will instead be resolved according to the normal equitable priority rules: generally, the interest that was first in time will take priority and therefore the claimant will still be able to assert an equitable interest in the property.[178]

Macmillan Inc. v Bishopsgate Investment Trust plc [1995] 1 WLR 978, 999–1000 (Millett J)

In English law the order of priority between two competing interests in the same property depends primarily on whether they are legal or merely equitable interests. Where both interests are equitable— or both legal, for that matter—the basic rule is that the two interests rank in the order of their creation. In the case of equitable interests the order of priority may be reversed in special circumstances, but 'where the equities are equal, the first in time prevails.' The absence of notice of the earlier interest by the party who acquired the later interest is irrelevant, even if he gave value. He cannot gain priority as a bona fide purchaser of the legal estate without notice if he has not acquired the legal estate.

Where, however, the first is equitable and the second is legal the position is different. A bona fide purchaser for value who obtains the legal estate at the time of his purchase without notice actual or constructive of a prior equitable right is entitled to priority in equity as well as at law: see *Pilcher v. Rawlins* (1872) L.R. 7 Ch.App. 259. But he must have obtained the legal estate, and the question of notice is normally tested at the time when he obtained it.

---

[176] [2015] UKSC 66; [2015] 3 WLR 1334, [100].
[177] [2001] 1 AC 102, 129.
[178] See Chapter 1.5(h), p. 22.

In English law notice in the present context includes not only actual notice (including 'wilful blindness' or 'contrived ignorance,' where the purchaser deliberately abstains from an inquiry in order to avoid learning the truth) but also constructive notice, that is to say notice of such facts as he would have discovered if he had taken proper measures to investigate them. The doctrine of constructive notice has developed in relation to land, where there is a recognised procedure for investigating the title of the transferor. There is no room for the doctrine of notice in the strict conveyancing sense in a situation in which it is not the custom and practice to investigate the transferor's title. But in the wider sense it is not so limited. In *Barclays Bank Plc. v. O'Brien* [1994] 1 A.C. 180 (a case concerned with land, but in which the defect in title—the presence of undue influence—could not be discovered by the routine investigation of title) Lord Browne-Wilkinson said, at pp. 195–196:

> 'The doctrine of notice lies at the heart of equity. Given that there are two innocent parties, each enjoying rights, the earlier right prevails against the later right if the acquirer of the later right knows of the earlier right (actual notice) or would have discovered it had he taken proper steps (constructive notice). In particular, if the party asserting that he takes free of the earlier rights of another knows of certain facts which put him on inquiry as to the possible existence of the rights of that other and he fails to make such inquiry or take such other steps as are reasonable to verify whether such earlier right does or does not exist, he will have constructive notice of the earlier right and take subject to it.'

In this formulation the doctrine is in my judgment of general application.

This passage highlights that the defendant will not have acted in good faith if he or she had actual or constructive notice of the claimant's beneficial interest in the property. The defendant must also have given some value, although this need not necessarily be adequate.[179] The value provided might be the discharge of a debt, and in such circumstances the defendant will not usually be bound to inquire into the manner in which the payer acquired the money.[180] However, it can be difficult to decide whether a defendant had 'notice' of the claimant's proprietary right. This was an issue in *Credit Agricole Corp and Investment Bank v Papadimitriou*.

Credit Agricole Corp and Investment Bank v Papadimitriou [2015] UKPC 13; [2015] 1 WLR 4265

The proceeds of sale of an antique collection worth some $15 million was misapplied in breach of trust. The claimant pursued a proprietary claim against the bank which received the money, and the question for the court was whether the bank had the defence of being a bona fide purchaser for value without notice. The money had been laundered through Panama and Liechtenstein, and the Privy Council held that the bank ought to have made inquiries before proceeding with the transaction. The principal judgment was handed down by Lord Clarke.

Lord Clarke:

… it is important for these purposes to distinguish between three different circumstances. The first is where the bank in fact appreciates that a proprietary right in the property probably exists, so that the bank has actual notice of the right. That is not this case. The second is where a reasonable person with

---

[179] Just as consideration to support a contractual promise must be sufficient but adequate: e.g. *Chappell & Co. Ltd v Nestlé Co. Ltd* [1960] AC 87.

[180] *Thomson v Clydesdale Bank* [1893] AC 282, 287 (Lord Herschell).

the attributes of the bank should have appreciated based on facts already available to it that the right probably existed, in which case the bank has constructive notice of the existence of the right.

The third is where the bank should have made inquiries or sought advice which would have revealed the probable existence of such a right. Here too, the bank would have constructive notice of the right. The question is in what circumstances and to what extent it can properly be said that the bank should have made inquiries or sought advice.

…

Thus, on the one hand, the bank's knowledge of facts indicating the mere possibility of a third party having a proprietary right would not be enough to put the bank on inquiry but, on the other hand, it is not necessary for the bank to conclude that it probably had such a right. The test is somewhere in between. It may be formulated in this way. The bank must make inquiries if there is a serious possibility of a third party having such a right or, put in another way, if the facts known to the bank would give a reasonable banker in the position of the particular banker serious cause to question the propriety of the transaction. This approach seems to the Board to be consistent with that expressed in *Lewin on Trusts,* 19th ed, 2015, at para 41-134 in connection with commercial transactions. They say that in some commercial contexts a purchaser may be fixed with notice in the absence of actual knowledge, but

> 'only where in the particular commercial contract involved he has failed to draw inferences which ought reasonably have been drawn in that context or has been put upon inquiry by knowledge of suspicious circumstances indicative of wrongdoing on the part of the trans-feror, but has failed to make inquiries that are reasonable in the circumstances.'

In the opinion of the Board the principles set out above apply here, subject to this. … it was common ground before the Board (as it was in the courts below) that the respondent is entitled to trace the pro-ceeds of sale of the Collection into the hands of the Bank unless it establishes that it was a bona fide purchaser for value without notice. In short, … it was for the Bank to show that it lacked constructive notice of the impropriety of the relevant arrangements. This approach is consistent with that noted in a not dissimilar context in the well known statement of Collins MR in *In re Nisbet and Potts' Contract* [1906] 1 Ch 386, 404

This is a helpful passage. It emphasizes that the burden of establishing the bona fide purchaser defence lies squarely on the defendant. And there must be a serious possibility that a third party enjoys rights in the property before a defendant will be taken to have notice of the claimant's rights. Lord Sumption, agreeing with Lord Clarke, added that this:[181]

> is a question which has taxed judges for many years. In particular they have been much exercised by the question in what circumstances a person is under a duty to make inquiries before he can claim to be with-out notice of the prior interest in question. Ultimately there is little to be gained from a fine analysis of the precise turns of phrase which judges have employed in answering these questions. They are often highly sensitive to their legal and factual context. The principle is, I think clear. We are in the realm of property rights, and are not concerned with an actionable duty to investigate. The hypothesis is that the claimant has established a proprietary interest in the asset, and the question is whether the defendant has estab-lished such absence of notice as entitles him to assume that there are no adverse interests. The mere pos-sibility that such interests exist cannot be enough to warrant inquiries. There must be something which the defendant actually knows (or would actually know if he had a reasonable appreciation of the meaning of the information in his hands) which calls for inquiry. The rule is that the defendant in this position cannot say that there might well have been an honest explanation, if he has not made the inquiries suggested

---

[181] [2015] UKPC 13; [2015] 1 WLR 4265, [33].

by the facts at his disposal with a view to ascertaining whether there really is. I would eschew words like 'possible', which set the bar too low, or 'probable' which suggest something that would justify a forensic finding of fact. If even without inquiry or explanation the transaction appears to be a proper one, then there is no justification for requiring the defendants to make inquiries. He is without notice. But if there are features of the transaction such that if left unexplained they are indicative of wrongdoing, then an explanation must be sought before it can be assumed that there is none. In the present case, on the facts actually known to the bank, there was no apparent explanation of the interposition of the Panamanian and Liechtenstein entities unless it was to conceal the origin of funds derived from third parties. That was why the bank had to make inquiries before proceeding as if there was an innocent explanation.

The test remains a flexible one which depends very much on the facts of any given case.

In any event, it is possible that, although the defendant may be able to avail him- or herself of the defence of bona fide purchaser at the date of receipt of the property, the defendant may later lose the protection afforded by this defence. This is illustrated by the decision of the Court of Appeal in *Independent Trustee Services Ltd v GP Noble Trustees Ltd*.[182]

Independent Trustee Services Ltd v GP Noble Trustees Ltd [2012] EWCA Civ 195; [2013] Ch 91

In the course of divorce proceedings, Mr Morris agreed to pay certain sums of money to Mrs Morris, and the latter promised, in return, to accept those payments as full and final satisfaction of her claims against Mr Morris. This agreement was the subject of a judicial consent order under the Matrimonial Causes Act 1973; pursuant to the order, Mr Morris paid Mrs Morris nearly £1.5 million in 2008. In the meantime, however, Mrs Morris suspected that Mr Morris had failed to disclose all his assets, so sought to set aside the consent order. The order was set aside in 2009. Mrs Morris was allowed to keep the money already received from Mr Morris, since it was expected that she would receive even more money under a later consent order, given that the value of Mr Morris' assets was far in excess of what had previously been thought.

However, a major problem for Mrs Morris later arose: it transpired that Mr Morris had been involved in fraudulently misappropriating assets from various occupational pension schemes. The money paid to Mrs Morris originally belonged to the pension funds, and Independent Trustee Services ('ITS'), who were trustees of a pension scheme defrauded by Mr Norris, sought to trace its money into Mrs Morris' hands. It was accepted that, at the time of receipt, Mrs Morris would have the defence of bona fide purchaser: she had no notice of the fraud perpetrated by her husband, and had provided valuable consideration under the judicial consent order.[183] However, at the date of the claim, that order had been set aside, so could it still be said that she had provided value for the money received? The Court of Appeal held that Mrs Morris could no longer rely upon the bona fide purchaser defence.

Lloyd LJ:

Undoubtedly the giving of value would normally be determined, one way or the other, as at the moment of acquisition of the legal title. That is because, normally, once value has been given it is not taken away or given back. Transactions by which value passes are not normally set aside at a later stage. However,

---

[182] [2012] EWCA Civ 195; [2013] Ch 91.
[183] See e.g. *Hill v Haines* [2007] EWCA Civ 1284; [2008] Ch 412.

there are circumstances in which a transaction can be set aside, either to recognise that it was void from the start, or if it is voidable for some reason and an aggrieved party with the necessary standing chooses to avoid it. What we have to address on this appeal is the effect of the avoidance of a relevant transaction, where the earlier subsistence of the transaction was what enabled a recipient to show that value was given for the receipt.

...

In relation to the argument that to allow the setting aside of the transaction to be taken into account might render titles precarious even after a long time, it is, of course, possible that a breach of trust might come to light only after some considerable time, so that the rights of the aggrieved beneficiaries might be asserted only after a good deal of time had elapsed. That might, therefore, lead to a transferee's title being challenged after some years. However, if the transferee was innocent, in the sense of having no notice of the breach of trust at the time of acquiring the legal title, intervening dealings with the property before the time when notice was given would not give rise to any claim against the transferee, except to any traceable proceeds of the disposition, and any person who had in the meantime acquired legal title to any part of the property for value without notice would himself be safe in his possession because he himself would have the defence. ...

As it seems to me, if the defence of bona fide purchaser for value without notice depends, as regards value, on a transaction which has been set aside by the time the defence falls to be raised, the fact of the setting aside should be capable of being relevant to whether the defence can be made out. I do not accept ... [that counsel is] correct to speak of the equitable title to the beneficiaries in the original trust being revived or re-vested. Rather, that title has continued to subsist in the meantime and it is no longer capable of being defeated by the bona fide purchaser defence, any more than it would be if the property were again in the hands of the person guilty of the original breach of trust. Neither in principle nor in practice can I see any sound reason for the court being required to shut its eyes to the fact that, by the time the point arises, the transaction on which the recipient of the property depends to show that he or she is a bona fide purchaser for value without notice has been set aside, at the instance of whichever party, on grounds such as misrepresentation, non-disclosure or any other such vitiating factor, so that it is to be treated, as far as possible, as if it had never happened, or at any rate had never had any legal effect.

If, on the facts of the given case, the setting aside of the transaction does deprive the holder of the assets of the defence of bona fide purchaser for value without notice, then I accept that a claim such as that made by ITS in the present case would have a different outcome according to whether it is asserted before or after the setting aside of the transaction by which value was given for the acquisition of the legal title. I do not see this as a valid objection to the principle that the setting aside of such a transaction can be relevant. It is commonly the case that similar proceedings brought at one time or at another may have different outcomes because of changes in circumstances in the meantime. If the beneficiaries' claim is asserted before the transaction is set aside, presumably the recipient will not take any steps to have it set aside, or at any rate the possibility of such a claim being successfully asserted will be taken into account in deciding whether to seek to have it set aside. I assume that it is relatively unlikely in practice that the other party to the transaction would seek to have it set aside, but if there is a proper basis for that to happen, I would have less sympathy with the position of the recipient, being at risk in this way as well.

...

In those circumstances, it seems to me that the setting aside of [the consent] order was relevant both in principle and in practice to the position as between Mrs Morris and ITS thereafter. Before the order ... she was able to assert and establish that she was a bona fide purchaser for value without notice. Afterwards she could not do so, because the transaction under which she had given value had been set aside and was of no effect; as between her and the other party, Mr Morris, it was as if it had not happened.

This approach to the bona fide purchaser defence seems appropriate: the order having been set aside, Mrs Morris could not insist that she had provided value for the money received. But it is important to note that, although the claimants might have a proprietary claim to any of the money Mrs Morris still possessed, and to its traceable proceeds, any of the money that had already been dissipated by Mrs Morris, or which had passed into the hands of a third party bona fide purchaser for value without notice, would be beyond the reach of the claimants. The claimants could not have a proprietary right in property which no longer existed, nor could they exercise such a right against a bona fide purchaser.

By setting aside the judicial consent order, Mrs Morris clearly became exposed to claims from beneficial owners of the property. However, it is clear that defendants who do set aside such orders run certain other risks as well, including that of their spouse's bankruptcy.[184] Significantly, even if Mrs Morris were to be awarded more money under a new order, she would no longer be able to make use of the bona fide purchaser defence, since she had acquired notice of Mr Morris' fraudulent scheme and the fact that the money truly belonged to someone else.

Independent Trustee Services Ltd v GP Noble Trustees Ltd is an important case, which highlights some difficult issues regarding the bona fide purchaser defence that had not previously been addressed. The impact of the decision goes beyond the narrow confines of setting aside a judicial consent order: the same principles should apply where a contract has been rescinded *ab initio*, and a defendant can no longer be said to have provided value for the property received.[185]

(b) CHANGE OF POSITION

The defence of change of position might also be available to defeat a proprietary claim. This defence was recognized in *Lipkin Gorman v Karpnale Ltd*, a case concerning common law claims, in which Lord Goff said:[186]

where an innocent defendant's position is so changed that he will suffer an injustice if called upon to repay or to repay in full, the injustice of requiring him so to repay outweighs the injustice of denying the plaintiff restitution. …

… It is, of course, plain that the defence is not open to one who has changed his position in bad faith, as where the defendant has paid away the money with knowledge of the facts entitling the plaintiff to restitution; and it is commonly accepted that the defence should not be open to a wrongdoer. … the mere fact that the defendant has spent the money, in whole or in part, does not of itself render it inequitable that he should be called upon to repay, because the expenditure might in any event have been incurred by him in the ordinary course of things.

Thus this defence would not be available to a defendant who has simply relied upon receipt of the property to make payments he or she would have had to have made anyway: it would not be unfair

---

[184] Ibid, [123]–[128].
[185] See Häcker, 'The Effect of Rescission on Bona Fide Purchase' (2012) 128 LQR 493.
[186] *Lipkin Gorman (a firm) v Karpnale Ltd* [1991] 2 AC 548, 579–80.

for the defendant to make restitution if all he or she has done is pay bills that he or she would necessarily have had to pay, for example. Nor is the defence available to someone who acts in bad faith, which includes those who undertake commercially sharp practice,[187] but not those who are merely negligent.[188] The defence of change of position will not inevitably defeat a proprietary claim in its entirety: the defence will only be available to the extent to which the defendant actually changed his or her position.

This defence could have an important role to play regarding equitable proprietary remedies, especially for an innocent defendant who has received property in which the claimant can identify an equitable interest. Of course, if the defendant spends that money, then it would be dissipated and a proprietary claim would no longer lie. But it might be that the defendant, relying upon the receipt of the claimant's property, spends his or her *own* money, which he or she already had. In such a scenario, the claimant could still have a claim to the property in the possession of the defendant, but the defendant—or his creditors, if insolvent—might argue that it would be unfair to force him to transfer the property to the claimant, given the defendant's change of position.

There is some judicial support for change of position operating as a defence to proprietary claims. In *Re Diplock*, for example, the executors of the testator's estate mistakenly paid money to the Leaf Homeopathic Hospital for the specific purpose of paying off a secured bank loan. Although it would seem that the claimants could trace their equitable proprietary interest into the discharged debt and seek subrogation, the Court of Appeal held that the claimants had no proprietary claim against the hospital. Lord Greene MR said:[189]

> we think that the effect of the payment to the bank was to extinguish the debt and the charge held by the bank ceased to exist. The case cannot, we think, be regarded as one of subrogation, and if the appellants were entitled to a charge it would have to be a new charge created by the court. The position in this respect does not appear to us to be affected by the fact that the payment off of this debt was one of the objects for which the grant was made. The effect of the payment off was that the charity, which had previously held only an equity of redemption, became the owners of unincumbered property. That unincumbered property derived from a combination of two things, the equity of redemption contributed by the charity and the effect of the Diplock money in getting rid of the incumbrance. If equity is now to create a charge (and we say 'create' because there is no survival of the original charge) in favour of the judicial trustee, it will be placing him in a position to insist upon a sale of what was contributed by the charity. The case, as it appears to us, is in effect analogous to the cases where Diplock money is expended on improvements on charity land. The money was in this case used to remove a blot on the title; to give the judicial trustee a charge in respect of the money so used would, we think, be equally unjust to the charity who, as the result of such a charge, would have to submit to a sale of the interest in the property which it brought in. We may point out that if the relief claimed were to be accepted as a correct application of the equitable principle, insoluble problems might arise in a case where in the meanwhile fresh charges on the property had been created or money had been expended upon it.

The claim failed, even though on the ordinary principles discussed earlier[190] subrogation would appear possible. It may be that the claim failed on a matter of evidence: the evidence could not conclusively

---

[187] *Niru Battery Manufacturing Co. v Milestone Trading Ltd* [2002] EWHC 1425 (Comm); [2002] 2 All ER (Comm) 705, 741. This was endorsed in the Court of Appeal: [2003] EWCA 1446 (Civ); *Abou-Rahmah v Abacha* [2006] EWCA Civ 1492; [2007] 1 All ER (Comm) 827.

[188] *Maersk Air Ltd v Expeditors International (UK) Ltd* [2003] 1 Lloyd's Rep 491, 499.

[189] [1948] Ch 465, 549–50.

[190] See Chapter 18.5(c), p. 900.

show that the claimant's money had been used to discharge the mortgage. However, in *Boscawen v Bojwa*, Millett LJ cited the above passage from *Diplock* and continued:[191]

> The passage is not without its difficulties and is in need of reappraisal in the light of the significant developments in the law of restitution which have taken place in the last 50 years. The second sentence is puzzling. The discharge of the creditor's security at law is certainly not a bar to subrogation in equity; it is rather a precondition. But the court was probably doing no more than equate the remedy to the creation of a new charge for the purpose of considering whether this was justified.
>
> …
>
> Taken as a whole, however, the passage cited is an explanation of the reasons why, in the particular circumstances of that case, it was considered unjust to grant the remedy of subrogation. The hospital had changed its position to its detriment. It had in all innocence used the money to redeem a mortgage held by its bank, which, no doubt, was willing to allow its advance to remain outstanding indefinitely so long as it was well secured and the interest was paid punctually. The next of kin were seeking to be subrogated to the bank's security in order to enforce it and enable a proper distribution of the estate to be made. This would have been unjust to the hospital. It may be doubted whether in its anxiety to avoid injustice to the hospital the court may not have done an even greater injustice to the next of kin, who were denied even the interest on their money. Justice did not require the withholding of any remedy, but only that the charge by subrogation should not be enforceable until the hospital had had a reasonable opportunity to obtain a fresh advance on suitable terms from a willing lender, perhaps from the bank which had held the original.
>
> Today, considerations of this kind would be regarded as relevant to a change of position defence rather than as going to liability. They do not call for further consideration in the present case.

Millett LJ viewed the defence of change of position as being available. As a matter of policy, this view might be supported. Consider, for example, a trustee who wrongly takes £5,000 out of a trust fund, and gives it to his niece as a birthday present. The niece might be a struggling student who opens a new, high-interest bank account in which she deposits the £5,000. But feeling better about her financial situation, and encouraged to 'save a bit, spend a bit' by her parents, she decides to spend £1,000 of her own money on a holiday, which she would not otherwise have done. The beneficiaries of the trust are naturally aggrieved at the trustee taking £5,000 and are able to trace into the £5,000 in the high-interest account. In such a situation, should the law impose a constructive trust on the property in favour of the beneficiaries?

The answer to this question is not obvious, but it might be thought unfair for the niece to have to give back the money. After all, that might leave her unable to pay her rent, and force her to make unexpected sacrifices beyond those she had previously contemplated. Moreover, if the niece does have to give back the money, she will be unable to seek redress from anyone else, whereas the beneficiaries, by contrast, could bring a claim against the trustee for breach of trust. Admittedly, there is a real risk that that claim might be worthless if the trustee is insolvent.

On the other hand, it may be that the property rights of the beneficiaries are sufficiently strong to defeat the niece's claim to the money. After all, the niece has had a holiday, at least, whereas the beneficiaries have only suffered a loss with no benefits at all. This stance is sometimes thought to follow from the 'hard-nosed' approach to property rights shown by the House of Lords in *Foskett v McKeown*.

---

[191] [1996] 1 WLR 328, 340–1.

However, in *Foskett* the House of Lords did not clearly reject change of position as a defence to proprietary claims. The discussion was *obiter*, and the significant statement from Lord Millet, quoted already[192] ambiguous. Nevertheless, in *Armstrong DLW Gmbh v Winnington Networks Ltd*, Stephen Morris QC said:[193]

> As regards change of position, whilst both counsel appear to accept that this too is a defence to a proprietary restitutionary claim, I am less sure. Change of position is essentially a defence to a claim for restitution based on unjust enrichment. Change of position was certainly discussed, and accepted in principle, as a defence in *Lipkin Gorman*. However Lord Goff's consideration of the defence was in the context of his view that the case was to be analysed as one of unjust enrichment. If *Lipkin Gorman* is in substance to be analysed as a proprietary restitutionary claim, then it does not follow, as a matter of principle, that change of position is or should be a defence to the latter form of claim. Lord Millett's analysis in *Foskett* v *McKeown* (at 129H) and *Chitty*, 29–175 support this conclusion. It is hard to see why, if the defendant purchases with notice, he should still be able to rely on change of position to defeat the claimant's legal title.

This rejection of the change of position defence is sometimes thought to result from the rejection of unjust enrichment as being at the root of these claims. But it is far from certain that change of position is a defence particular to unjust enrichment. A major rationale for the defence is to protect the defendant's receipt of property, and that seems equally applicable in this area as in the context of unjust enrichment. In *Kuwait Airways Corp v Iraqi Airways Co. (No. 6)*, Lord Nicholls suggested that the defence of change of position should be recognized where a claim for restitutionary damages is founded upon the tort of conversion, not unjust enrichment.[194] This might support the argument that there is no reason in principle why change of position has to be exclusively linked with unjust enrichment; change of position might have a broader scope. Indeed, if, as the judge suggested in *Winnington Networks*, the House of Lords' decision in *Lipkin Gorman* is a proprietary restitutionary claim,[195] then it would seem odd to deny the availability of a defence of change of position to equitable proprietary claims: *Lipkin Gorman* is often thought to be the leading decision on change of position, and the House of Lords clearly thought that change of position was in principle available to the type of claim at issue in that case. Moreover, if change of position were recognized to be available beyond the context of unjust enrichment, this might alleviate any pressure that may exist artificially to squeeze some claims out of the law of property and into unjust enrichment.

(c) EQUITABLE ALLOWANCE

Just as a fiduciary might be allowed to retain some of the profits he or she has made from a breach of fiduciary duty, to reflect the value of the skill and work of the fiduciary in achieving that profit,[196] so might a similar equitable allowance be granted in the context of proprietary claims. This has received little discussion in the cases, but Lord Millett, writing extra-judicially, has suggested that it might help to deal with the scenario where an innocent volunteer uses the claimant's money to buy a winning lottery ticket.

---

[192] See Chapter 8.4, p. 892.
[193] [2012] EWHC 10 (Ch), [103].
[194] [2002] UKHL 19; [2002] 2 AC 883, [79].
[195] Cf. the discussion of Millett LJ in *Trustee of the Property of FC Jones and Sons (a firm) v Jones* [1997] Ch 159, given in Chapter 18.3(c)(i), pp. 864–5.
[196] See Chapter 14.5(e), pp. 716–17.

Lord Millett, 'Proprietary Restitution' in *Equity in Commercial Law* (eds Degeling and Edelman) (Sydney: The Law Book Co., 2005), pp. 316–17

> But suppose the defendant or his predecessor in title is innocent? Suppose A did not realise that the money belongs to B, that he had sufficient resources of his to buy the ticket, and being an honest man would have used his own money if he had appreciated that the money he did use did not belong to him? In such a case it is mere chance that he used the claimant's money and not his own. It is an affront to our notions of justice that the claimant should recover the winnings if he used the claimant's money but not if he used his own. It makes the law itself a lottery.
>
> The problem is well known, and still unsolved. There are several possible solutions: (i) we could entitle the innocent recipient to all just allowances for his input, whether labour, skill or luck; in the extreme case of the lottery ticket bought for a nominal sum, that arguably amounts to the whole of the winnings, for the contribution made by the money is negligible; or (ii) we could confine the claimant an equitable lien on the winnings to recover his stake. But, as Professor Worthington has observed,[197] abandoning the property analysis and substituting unjust enrichment does not solve the problem. The unjust element is unjust enrichment has nothing to do with fault. It is either always unjust to use another's property without his consent or it is not. I prefer to recognise the flexibility with which equity is capable of manipulating our concepts of property. When determining the nature and extent of the proprietary remedy which it will make available, equity can easily distinguish between wrongful and innocent misapplication of funds.

Although it is true that the claimant's money was used to buy the ticket, the defendant still needed to purchase the ticket and choose the winning numbers. It may therefore be reasonable to recognize that the defendant contributed significantly to the payout. Admittedly, this means that the value of the defendant's contribution can only be judged once the winning numbers are known: choosing a set of losing numbers is worthless, so the purchase of the ticket and defendant's choice of numbers is only valuable if those numbers actually win. But assessing the value of the defendant's contribution at a later date does not seem to be unduly problematic, and might lead to the defendant's receiving a very generous allowance along the lines suggested by Lord Millett. A reluctance to grant a similar allowance to defendants who are wrongdoers is understandable, but in some circumstances it might still be appropriate given the significant input of the defendant to the payout.[198] However, it is clear that Lord Millett views wrongdoers as undeserving of any allowance, given that Equity consistently favours the innocent claimant over wrongdoing defendant.[199]

It is important to appreciate that any potential allowance does not alter the nature of the remedy awarded—a constructive trust—and only allows the defendant to retain any property to the extent to which he or she has contributed to its existence. Its basis is the same as the equitable allowance examined in Chapter 14: if the defendant were not to be recompensed for the value of his or her contribution, that would leave the claimant unjustly enriched. The defendant's causal contribution to the gains made should be recognized. However, it should also be emphasized that it is unclear whether the courts will be prepared to follow Lord Millett's suggestion and award the defendant an equitable allowance in this context of proprietary claims and remedies. It clearly introduces a degree of flexibility and discretion that might undermine the high level of certainty considered to be so important when dealing with property rights. Nevertheless, in *Boardman v Phipps* all the judges were agreed that an equitable allowance was available,[200] even though the remedy at issue appeared to be that of a

---

[197] Worthington, *Equity* (Oxford: Oxford University Press, 2003), pp. 100–1.
[198] See further Chapter 14.5(e), pp. 716–17.
[199] *Foskett v McKeown* [2001] 1 AC 102, 134, quoted at Chapter 18.5(b)(i), pp. 893–4.
[200] See [1967] 2 AC 46; see further Chapter 14.4(d), p. 690.

proprietary constructive trust.[201] So it may be that the courts will be prepared to award an equitable allowance to limit the effect a constructive trust would otherwise have.

In any event, there is clearly some reluctance to allow the beneficiary to recover all the lottery winnings in this scenario. Worthington has suggested that the court should only allow the beneficiary to recover the value of the misappropriated property from an innocent third party:[202]

> if the disloyal fiduciary transfers [misappropriated property] to an innocent donee, the principal can recover her property if she can follow the original asset into the donee's hands. This outcome rests on the priority of competing property interests. But if the donee uses this initial receipt to generate further profitable traceable proceeds, can the principal claim those too? The issue was not material in *Foskett*, but that case suggests a positive answer on the basis that, as a matter of English property law, the principal is entitled to all the traceable proceeds derived from her property. As noted earlier, that is doubted. If the donee owes the principal no fiduciary obligations in relation to the asset, then the principal's claim against the donee is surely restricted to return of the original receipt, or if it is no longer in the donee's hands, then to its value protected by a lien against the traceable investment proceeds.

(d) DEFENCES IN *RE DIPLOCK*

It has already been seen that in *Re Diplock* the Court of Appeal had great sympathy for innocent defendants, particularly charities, who had received misapplied property. The Court of Appeal refused to allow some of the proprietary claims. The reasons given are to some extent unclear, but the results in *Re Diplock* might be explained due to a lack of evidence to establish the claims on the balance of probabilities, or change of position.[203] However, two other possible defences were raised in *Re Diplock*. First, it was suggested that it might sometimes be inequitable to allow the claimant to trace into property held by the defendant.[204] So, for example, one of the charities that received the mistaken payment was Guy's Hospital, which spent £14,000 on reconstructing two children's wards. It was held that it was not equitable to allow the claimant to trace into this property. But tracing is simply a process and should not be subject to discretionary factors. Instead, the defence of change of position and the possibility of an equitable allowance might be used to ensure that restitution be denied to the extent it would be inequitable. Secondly, there is a suggestion that proprietary claims should be subsidiary to claims against wrongdoing fiduciaries, which should be pursued first.[205] However, English law does not generally impose rules regarding priority of suits, and it would be unusual to insist that a personal claim should subordinate a proprietary claim. This suggestion in *Diplock* should not be followed, and has been rejected in Australia.[206]

QUESTION

Tom steals £10,000 from Alan and £10,000 from Bob. Tom puts the money in his bank account, which was overdrawn by £2,000. Tom later deposits £1,000 of his own money into the account.

---

[201] Albeit triggered by a breach of fiduciary duty, rather than resulting from a proprietary claim.

[202] Worthington, 'Fiduciary Duties and Proprietary Remedies: Addressing the Failure of Equitable Formulae' [2013] CLJ 720.

[203] See Chapter 18.6(b), pp. 916–19.

[204] [1998] Ch 465, 546–8.

[205] Ibid, 556.

[206] *Hagan v Waterhouse* (1991) 34 NSWLR 308, 369–70 (NSWSC).

Tom then gives £10,000 from his account to his daughter, Debbie, as a birthday present. Debbie spends £5,000 of that money on a new car she has been dreaming about for years, but never had the money to buy. She opens a new account at the bank with the remaining £5,000. Feeling financially secure, Debbie treats all her friends to an expensive meal at the restaurant, which costs £2,000.

Tom subsequently takes another £3,000 from his account to discharge in full a mortgage he had taken out with Local Bank two years ago, in order to buy some fields close to his house. He had purchased the land for £6,000, with the assistance of a mortgage of £3,000 from Local Bank. He has since acquired planning permission to build flats on the land, which is now worth £18,000.

Tom also gives £5 from the account to his friend, Luke, to say thank you for his kindness in helping Tom to stop smoking. Luke uses that £5 note to buy five lottery tickets. Luke always buys five lottery tickets every week, and always chooses the same numbers. One of the lottery tickets wins the jackpot of £17 million.

Advise Alan and Bob.

FURTHER READING

Birks, 'Overview: Tracing, Claiming and Defences' in *Laundering and Tracing* (ed Birks) (Oxford: Clarendon Press, 1995).

Conaglen, 'Difficulties with Tracing Backwards' (2011) 127 54 LQR 432.

Evans, 'Rethinking Tracing and the Law of Restitution' (1999) 115 LQR 469.

Lord Millet, 'Proprietary Restitution' in *Equity in Commercial Law* (eds Degeling and Edelman) (Sydney: Law Book Co., 2005).

Smith, *The Law of Tracing* (Oxford: Oxford University Press, 1997).

Smith, 'Tracing Through a Debt' (1995) 54 CLJ 290.

Virgo, 'Vindicating Vindication: *Foskett v McKeown* Reviewed' in *New Perspectives on Property Law, Obligations and Restitution* (ed. Hudson) (London: Cavendish Publishing, 2004).

Virgo, '*Re Hallett's Estate*' in *Landmark Cases in Equity* (eds Mitchell and Mitchell) (Oxford: Hart, 2012).

19

THIRD PARTY LIABILITY

CENTRAL ISSUES

1. There are two principal personal claims that a beneficiary or principal might bring against a third party arising from a breach of trust or fiduciary duty: dishonest assistance and unconscionable receipt.

2. Dishonest assistance is a form of accessory liability. It is parasitic to a breach of trust or fiduciary duty. The third party must have assisted, encouraged, or procured the breach dishonestly.

3. Dishonesty is an objective standard of fault, based upon what the defendant knew. Whether dishonesty is a satisfactory fault element is controversial.

4. Unconscionable receipt requires the defendant to have received property for his or her own benefit as a result of a breach of trust or fiduciary duty in circumstances where it would be unconscionable for the recipient to retain the property.

5. Unconscionability requires the recipient to know that the assets received derive from misapplied property. It is a flexible concept, the boundaries of which are not yet fully clear.

6. There is an important debate about whether or not any level of fault *should* be required before making a third party recipient give up the value of property received. There is some strong support in favour of a strict liability receipt-based claim.

1. INTRODUCTION

There are many reasons why a beneficiary might wish to sue someone other than a trustee, or why a principal in a fiduciary relationship may wish to sue a third party rather than the wrongdoing fiduciary him or herself. Most significantly, if the fiduciary is insolvent and would be unable to satisfy any claim, the claimant might search for third parties to sue in order to obtain satisfactory redress. Typically, this means that a claimant will seek a solvent defendant with the means to pay. The third party defendants in this chapter are often, but not necessarily, financial institutions or professionals, such as solicitors, who are backed by insurers with the means to pay.

Chapter 18 considered proprietary claims; this chapter considers personal claims only: the claimant seeks a sum of money from the defendant, but does not assert any right to any particular property. But even where the defendant is solvent and could satisfy a personal claim, a proprietary claim might often be more desirable: if the property has risen in value, then that uplift in value will necessarily benefit the claimant if the claim is proprietary, but not if the claim is personal.[1] However, a personal claim for the value of the property at the time of the third party's wrong might be preferred where the property has fallen in value. Moreover, a personal claim will be the only possible type of claim available to the claimant if the property in question has been dissipated and no longer exists. In such circumstances, a proprietary claim is impossible and a personal claim alone can be pursued.

Third party liability in Equity has been greatly influenced by the following passage from the speech of Lord Selbourne LC in the important case of *Barnes v Addy*:[2]

> in this case we have to deal with certain persons who are trustees, and with certain other persons who are not trustees. That is a distinction to be borne in mind throughout the case. Those who create a trust clothe the trustee with a legal power and control over the trust property, imposing on him a corresponding responsibility. That responsibility may no doubt be extended in equity to others who are not properly trustees, if they are found either making themselves trustees *de son tort*, or actually participating in any fraudulent conduct of the trustee to the injury of the *cestui que trust*. But, on the other hand, strangers are not to be made constructive trustees merely because they act as the agents of trustees in transactions within their legal powers, transactions, perhaps of which a Court of Equity may disapprove, unless those agents receive and become chargeable with some part of the trust property, or unless they assist with knowledge in a dishonest and fraudulent design on the part of the trustees.

This highlights three major causes of action. The first concerns a party who intermeddles with trust affairs and thereby becomes a trustee *de son tort*. But since such an intermeddler is in effect a trustee and not a third party, trusteeship *de son tort* was examined in Chapter 11.[3] This is probably the least important and controversial of the three.

The last two causes of action highlight that difficult and significant claims may exist *either* on the basis of the third party's receipt of trust property, *or* because the third party has assisted a breach of trust. However, care should be taken if using *Barnes v Addy* as a springboard for analysis. That case may be considered to show the *origins* of these claims, but the present law has evolved greatly from the position in *Barnes v Addy*, such that it is no longer an accurate statement of the law. How the law has developed will be explored in this chapter.

Three general issues might be pointed out at this initial stage: (i) a third party will not incur any liability unless he or she is at fault; (ii) a third party might be liable pursuant to any breach of fiduciary duty, not only breach of trust; (iii) the remedy is a personal liability to account or to compensate for loss suffered, and references to a 'constructive trust' are unfortunate.

(a) FAULT

It is clear that the law generally requires a third party to be at fault before liability will be imposed,[4] but the appropriate fault elements are difficult to establish. Crucially, it needs to be determined whether liability should be assessed subjectively, with reference to the defendant's own thought process, or objectively, by reference to a reasonable person. In *Barnes v Addy*, reference was made to

---

[1] Although Lord Neuberger has recently suggested that the rules on personal liability should be more flexible to catch uplifts in value: *Sinclair v Versailles* [2011] EWCA Civ 347; [2012] Ch 453 [90].

[2] (1874) 9 Ch App 244, 251–2.

[3] Chapter 11.2(h)(i), pp. 535–6.

[4] For consideration of the suggestion that receipt-based liability should be strict, see Chapter 19.3(d)(i), pp. 964–8.

knowledge, and in *Baden Delvaux v Société Générale Pour Favoriser le Développement du Commerce et de l'Industrie en France SA*, Peter Gibson J set out the following 'scale' of knowledge:[5]

(i) actual knowledge; (ii) wilfully shutting one's eyes to the obvious; (iii) wilfully and recklessly failing to make such inquiries as an honest and reasonable man would make; (iv) knowledge of circumstances which would indicate the facts to an honest and reasonable man; (v) knowledge of circumstances which would put an honest and reasonable man on inquiry.

Points (ii)–(v) on this scale are examples of *constructive* knowledge: although the defendant did not *actually* have knowledge of the given facts, such knowledge is attributed to him. This *Baden* scale of knowledge was very influential to both receipt- and assistance-based claims. However, distinguishing between the different points on the scale was very difficult, and judges disagreed about the lowest point on the scale required for third party liability. Ultimately, 'knowledge' has been jettisoned as the fault element in both areas: the claims are now better known as 'dishonest assistance' and 'unconscionable receipt', respectively. Nevertheless, discussion of knowledge and the *Baden* scale remains important, as will be seen below.

(b) BREACH OF DUTY

In *Barnes v Addy*, Lord Selborne LC clearly referred to third parties to a breach of *trust*. But the law has now developed such that a third party can be liable following any breach of *fiduciary duty*. Earlier cases that refer to breach of trust alone should now be read such that the principle includes breaches of fiduciary duty beyond the context of a trust. There is no need for trust property to be involved. In *Royal Brunei Airlines Sdn Bhd v Tan*, Lord Nicholls said:[6]

accessory liability is concerned with the liability of a person who has not yet received any property. His liability is not property-based. His only sin is that he interfered with the due performance by the trustee of the fiduciary obligations undertaken by the trustee. These are personal obligations. They are, in this respect, analogous to the personal obligations undertaken by the parties to a contract.

This is sensible. It is unclear why a claim should lie against a third party who dishonestly assists a breach of trust, but not against a third party who dishonestly assists a breach of fiduciary duty not involving a trust. Trustees are clearly not the only persons who undertake fiduciary obligations. If a third party deliberately participates in a solicitor's breach of fiduciary duty, the client of the solicitor might legitimately seek redress from the party to the corruption. In *Novoship (UK) Ltd v Nikitin*,[7] Longmore LJ, delivering the judgment of the Court of Appeal, said:

[cases dealing with this issue] were considered by Peter Smith J *in JD Wetherspoon plc v Van den Berg & Co Ltd* [2009] EWHC 639 (Ch). He concluded at para 518 that misuse of trust property was not a pre-requisite to a liability to account for profits for dishonest assistance in a breach of fiduciary duty. He reasoned thus:

'In my view in a case for accessory liability there is no requirement for there to be trust property. Such a requirement wrongly associates accessory liability with trust concepts.

---

[5] [1993] 1 WLR 509, 575–6.
[6] [1995] 2 AC 378, 387.
[7] [2014] EWCA Civ 908; [2015] QB 499, [87]–[93].

> … Accessory liability does not involve a trust. It involves providing dishonest assistance to somebody else who is in a fiduciary capacity [and] has committed a breach of his fiduciary duties.'
>
> … in addition as we have said it would be a triumph of form over substance if a dishonest assistant escaped liability by entering into a time charter but not if he entered into a demise charter, or took a licence of land rather than a lease. …
>
> We therefore conclude that the remedy of an account of profits is available against one who dishonestly assists a fiduciary to breach his fiduciary obligations, even if that breach does not involve a misapplication of trust property.

In the realm of receipt-based claims, it is perhaps not obvious that liability should be imposed upon third parties if the relevant property has not been received following a breach of trust but 'only' a breach of fiduciary duty. The claimant is likely to be able to trace *because* he is a beneficiary under a trust and there has been a breach of that trust. Nevertheless, the cases suggest that even in the context of receipt-based claims, references to breach of trust should be expanded to include breach of fiduciary duty. For example, in *El Ajou v Dollar Land Holdings plc*, Hoffmann LJ said:[8]

> the plaintiff must show, first, a disposal of his assets in breach of fiduciary duty.

So, if a director misapplies his company's property in breach of his fiduciary duty, the company might be able to bring a receipt-based claim.[9] However, it might be possible to explain this on the basis that the company acquires an equitable proprietary base under a constructive trust following the breach of duty of the director.[10] In *Arthur v Attorney General of the Turks and Caicos Islands*,[11] the Privy Council held that no breach of trust was required for a receipt-based claim to lie. A Minister of the Turks and Caicos Islands transferred freehold property belonging to the Crown to Mr Arthur. A claim was brought against the latter for unconscionable receipt of the property. The Minister who wrongly transferred the property did not act in breach of trust but in breach of fiduciary duty. Nevertheless, this did not prevent a receipt-based claim. Sir Terence Etherton, giving the advice of the Board, said:[12]

> Liability for knowing receipt can also be incurred when property is transferred in breach of a fiduciary duty other than a breach of trust. An obvious example would be the transfer of a company's property in breach of the directors' fiduciary duties, a director not being a trustee of the company's assets. That is also the basis of the claim in the present case since it is not alleged that the Property was held by or for the Crown on trust, but rather that the Minister acted in breach of fiduciary duty to the Crown in authorising the transfer to the appellant.

However, although the duty breached need not be that of a trustee, it is important to emphasize that a duty must actually be breached; if the fiduciary acted in an authorized manner, then the recipient of any property transferred will not be liable for unconscionable receipt.[13]

---

[8] [1994] 2 All ER 685, 700. The same approach has been adopted in Australia: *Kalls Enterprises Pty Ltd (in liq) v Baloglow* [2007] NSWCA 191; (2007) 63 ACSR 557.

[9] Cf. *Russell v Wakefield Waterworks Co.* (1875) LR 20 Eq 474, 479; *CMS Dolphin Ltd v Simonet* [2001] BCLC 704, [104].

[10] See Chapter 7.2, p. 332.

[11] [2012] UKPC 30.

[12] Ibid, [31].

[13] Conaglen and Nolan, 'Contract and Knowing Receipt: Principles and Application' (2013) 129 LQR 359.

(c) NATURE OF LIABILITY

As can be seen from the extract from *Barnes v Addy*, the third party is said to be liable as a 'constructive trustee'.[14] This is, however, misleading: the third party does not necessarily have any property that belongs to the beneficiary, so no proprietary remedy can be awarded. Even if a third party recipient *does* have property into which the claimant can trace for a receipt-based claim, a constructive trust would be the appropriate response to a *proprietary* claim, not the *personal* claim. As regards the claims under present consideration, the third party's liability is not proprietary but personal. For a receipt-based claim, there is no requirement that the defendant retain the property. And for a claim based upon assistance, there is no need for the defendant even to have received the property.

Dubai Aluminium Co Ltd v Salaam [2002] UKHL 48; [2003] 2 AC 366, [141]–[142] (Lord Millett)

Equity gives relief against fraud by making any person sufficiently implicated in the fraud accountable in equity. In such a case he is traditionally (and I have suggested unfortunately) described as a 'constructive trustee' and is said to be 'liable to account as a constructive trustee'. But he is not in fact a trustee at all, even though he may be liable to account as if he were. He never claims to assume the position of trustee on behalf of others, and he may be liable without ever receiving or handling the trust property. If he receives the trust property at all he receives it adversely to the claimant and by an unlawful transaction which is impugned by the claimant. He is not a fiduciary or subject to fiduciary obligations; and he could plead the Limitation Acts as a defence to the claim.

In this second class of case the expressions 'constructive trust' and 'constructive trustee' create a trap. As the court recently observed in *Coulthard v Disco Mix Club Ltd* [2000] 1 WLR 707, 731 this 'type of constructive trust is merely the creation by the court … to meet the wrongdoing alleged: there is no real trust and usually no chance of a proprietary remedy'. The expressions are 'nothing more than a formula for equitable relief': *Selangor United Rubber Estates Ltd v Cradock* (No 3) [1968] 1 WLR 1555, 1582, *per* Ungoed-Thomas J. I think that we should now discard the words 'accountable as constructive trustee' in this context and substitute the words 'accountable in equity'.

Given that there is not necessarily any property belonging to the claimant upon which trust obligations can bite, it seems appropriate to follow Lord Millett's lead and abandon the language of 'constructive trust'.[15] Indeed, Lord Sumption has recently said:[16]

It is clear that Lord Selborne [in *Barnes v Addy*] regarded as a constructive trustee any person who was not an express trustee but might be made liable in equity to account for the trust assets as if he was. The problem is that in this all-embracing sense the phrase 'constructive trust' refers to two different things to which very different legal considerations apply. The first comprises persons who have lawfully assumed fiduciary obligations in relation to trust property, but without a formal appointment. They may be trustees *de son tort*, who without having been properly appointed, assume to act in the administration of the trusts as if they had been; or trustees under trusts implied from the common intention to be inferred from the conduct of the parties, but never formally created as such. These people can conveniently be called de facto trustees. They intended to act as trustees, if only as a matter of objective construction of

---

[14] *Westdeutsche Landesbank Girozentrale v Islington London Borough Council* [1996] AC 669, [705] (Lord Browne-Wilkinson).

[15] Cf. Mitchell and Watterson, 'Remedies for Knowing Receipt' in *Constructive and Resulting Trusts* (Mitchell (ed.)) (Oxford: Hart, 2010), esp. pp. 128–31. See Chapter 19.3(e), p. 968.

[16] *Central Bank of Nigeria v Williams* [2014] UKSC 10; [2014] AC 118, [9].

their acts. They are true trustees, and if the assets are not applied in accordance with the trust, equity will enforce the obligations that they have assumed by virtue of their status exactly as if they had been appointed by deed. Others, such as company directors, are by virtue of their status fiduciaries with very similar obligations. In its second meaning, the phrase 'constructive trustee' refers to something else. It comprises persons who never assumed and never intended to assume the status of a trustee, whether formally or informally, but have exposed themselves to equitable remedies by virtue of their participation in the unlawful misapplication of trust assets. Either they have dishonestly assisted in a misapplication of the funds by the trustee, or they have received trust assets knowing that the transfer to them was a breach of trust. In either case, they may be required by equity to account as if they were trustees or fiduciaries, although they are not. These can conveniently be called cases of ancillary liability. The intervention of equity in such cases does not reflect any pre-existing obligation but comes about solely because of the misapplication of the assets. It is purely remedial. The distinction between these two categories is not just a matter of the chronology of events leading to liability. It is fundamental. In the words of Millett LJ in *Paragon Finance Plc v DB Thakerar & Co (a firm)* [1999] 1 All ER 400, at 413, it is 'the distinction between an institutional trust and a remedial formula – between a trust and a catch-phrase.'

2. DISHONEST ASSISTANCE

Dishonest assistance is a form of accessory liability: the liability of the assister is parasitic to the commission of a 'primary' breach of duty by the trustee or fiduciary. This sort of liability is also sometimes called 'secondary' liability, and for most purposes references to 'accessory' and 'secondary' liability are interchangeable. However, sometimes the language of 'secondary' liability is used to suggest that the remedies available against the assister should inevitably duplicate those available against the wrongdoing fiduciary. This is not necessarily the case, and will be examined in more detail later.[17]

Consistent with general principles of accessory liability, the following must be established:

i)   a primary wrong;

ii) a conduct element;

iii) a mental element.

(a) PRIMARY WRONG

As illustrated already, a person might be liable as an accessory not only to a breach of trust, but also to a breach of fiduciary duty. In *Barnes v Addy*,[18] it was held that the breach of trust itself must be dishonest. This meant that no matter how culpable an accessory was, if the trustee did not realize that a breach of trust was being committed, then the accessory could not be liable. This was clearly unsatisfactory, and the requirement that the breach of trust or fiduciary duty itself be dishonest was rightly jettisoned by the Privy Council in *Tan*:[19]

Take the simple example of an honest trustee and a dishonest third party. Take a case where a dishonest solicitor persuades a trustee to apply trust property in a way the trustee honestly believes is permissible but which the solicitor knows full well is a clear breach of trust. The solicitor deliberately conceals this

---

[17] See Chapter 19.2(d), pp. 947–51.
[18] See Chapter 19.1, p. 924.
[19] [1995] 2 AC 378, 384.

from the trustee. In consequence, the beneficiaries suffer a substantial loss. It cannot be right that in such a case the accessory liability principle would be inapplicable because of the innocence of the trustee. In ordinary parlance, the beneficiaries have been defrauded by the solicitor. If there is to be an accessory liability principle at all, whereby in appropriate circumstances beneficiaries may have direct recourse against a third party, the principle must surely be applicable in such a case, just as much as in a case where both the trustee and the third party have been dishonest. Indeed, if anything, the case for liability of the dishonest third party seems stronger where the trustee is innocent, because in such a case the third party alone was dishonest and that was the cause of the subsequent misapplication of the trust property.

(b) CONDUCT ELEMENT

The conduct element of accessory liability is often said to be 'assistance'; indeed, the cause of action is now commonly called 'dishonest assistance'. 'Assistance' is broadly defined, and includes anything that helps the commission of the breach of duty. However, this can be distinguished from 'procuring', or 'inducing' a breach of duty.[20] Hart and Honoré wrote that an inducement would:[21]

make a given course of action more eligible or desirable in the eyes of the other than it would otherwise have been, or seem more eligible or desirable than it really is.

It might also be added that a procurement tends to give another person an idea he would not otherwise have had, in contrast to most instances of assistance.

Liability for inducing a breach of trust is well-established.[22] As Harpum wrote in a comprehensive survey of this area of the law in 1986:[23]

A stranger who knowingly induces a trustee to commit a breach of trust will be liable as a constructive trustee. The motive for the inducement is irrelevant. It is also immaterial whether the trustee commits the breach of trust innocently or for some ulterior purpose. It is not necessary that the trust property should have passed through the hands of the stranger or that he should have benefited from the breach.

Thus, before the Privy Council in *Tan* departed from the approach in *Barnes v Addy*, the law required that the primary breach itself be dishonest for assistance liability, but not for inducement liability. There was therefore a divide between these two conduct elements. But, in *Tan*, Lord Nicholls followed on from the quotation given earlier by saying:[24]

The position would be the same if, instead of *procuring* the breach, the third party dishonestly *assisted* in the breach. Change the facts slightly. A trustee is proposing to make a payment out of the trust fund to a particular person. He honestly believes he is authorised to do so by the terms of the trust deed. He asks a solicitor to carry through the transaction. The solicitor well knows that the proposed payment would be a plain breach of trust. He also well knows that the trustee mistakenly believes otherwise. Dishonestly he leaves the trustee under his misapprehension and prepares the necessary documentation. Again, if the accessory principle is not to be artificially constricted, it ought to be applicable in such a case.

---

[20] 'Procuring' and 'inducing' tend to be used synonymously.
[21] Hart and Honoré, *Causation in the Law* (2nd edn) (Oxford: Oxford University Press, 1985), pp. 187–8.
[22] See generally Harpum, 'The Stranger as Constructive Trustee' (1986) 102 LQR 114, 267.
[23] Ibid, 115.
[24] [1995] 2 AC 378, 384–5.

Now that the primary wrong need not be dishonest, any divide between inducement and assistance in the law regarding accessory liability in Equity might well disappear; the use of 'dishonest assistance' often seems to include instances of 'dishonest inducement'.[25] The wide definition of the conduct element means that 'dishonest encouragement' should also lead to liability. 'Encouragement' may constitute either inducement or assistance. For example, if a person encourages a fiduciary to breach his obligations and take part in a fraudulent scheme of which the fiduciary was not previously aware, this may be characterized as 'inducement'. But if the fiduciary had approached the defendant to explain his or her intention to take part in the fraudulent scheme, and the defendant only subsequently encouraged the fiduciary to go ahead with such plans, this would not be inducement. Such conduct might, however, be considered to amount to assistance, since it might embolden the fiduciary by, fortifying the fiduciary's resolve to commit the breach of duty, but there is no real need to stretch the language of 'assistance' this far: encouragement, coupled with the requisite mental element, should be sufficient for accessory liability.[26]

In *Baden*, Peter Gibson J said:[27]

> it seems to me to be a simple question of fact, whether or not there has been assistance. ... the assistance ... must not be of minimal importance.

So assistance is to be given its natural meaning and is a question of fact. Peter Gibson J suggests that there is some sort of *de minimis* exception to accessory liability: the acts of the accessory must have had a more than minimal impact upon the primary wrong. This implies that there must be some causative link between the assistance and the infringement of the principal's rights: without any such connection, there is no reason for that particular claimant to sue the particular defendant. Admittedly, the causal link is necessarily weak, given that the primary breach of fiduciary duty was not committed by the assister, and that such a breach of fiduciary duty may ultimately have occurred even if there had been no assistance from a third party. A strict 'but for' test of causation may therefore yield to a broader approach to identifying causal factors.[28] Mance LJ has said that:[29]

> it is inappropriate to become involved in attempts to assess the precise causative significance of the dishonest assistance in respect of either the breach of trust or fiduciary duty or the resulting loss ... it is necessary to identify what breach of trust or duty was assisted and what loss may be said to have resulted from that breach of trust or duty.

Nevertheless, some causal link *is* required: there will be no liability unless the breach of trust *actually* occurs, suggesting some link with the *result* reached is necessary. Nor will there be liability for

---

[25] E.g. *BCCI (Overseas) Ltd v Akindele* [1999] BCC 669, 676 (Carnwath J; this was not considered on appeal: [2001] Ch 437). In *Watson v Dolmark* [1992] 3 NZLR 311, 316, Cooke P considered instances of inducement to be 'perhaps the clearest possible case of knowing assistance'.

[26] This mirrors accessory liability in the criminal law: see e.g. *R v Gnango* [2011] UKSC 59; [2012] 1 AC 827.

[27] *Baden v Société Générale pour Favoriser le Développement du Commerce et de l'Industrie en France SA* [1993] 1 WLR 509, 574. This passage was cited with approval in *Brinks Ltd v Abu-Saleh (No. 3)* [1996] CLC 133.

[28] For further discussion of causation, see Steele, *Tort Law: Text, Cases and Materials* (3rd edn) (Oxford: Oxford University Press, 2014), ch. 4.

[29] *Grupo Torras SA v Al-Sabah* [1999] CLC 1469, 1667. Mance LJ was hearing the case at first instance, and no adverse comment was made regarding this point on appeal: [2001] CLC 221. See also *Casio Computer Co. Ltd v Sayo (No. 3)* [2001] EWCA Civ 661, [15] (Tuckey LJ).

'assistance' when the relevant acts of the third party occurred *after* the primary breach of duty. This was the case in *Brown v Bennett*, in which Morritt LJ commented that:[30]

> if there is no causative effect and therefore no assistance given by the person ... on whom is sought to establish the liability as a constructive trustee, for my part I cannot see that the requirements of conscience require any remedy at all.

In any event, 'assistance' is defined so widely that it is rare for claims in dishonest assistance to fail for lack of the necessary conduct element. But one oft-cited example is *Brinks Ltd v Abu-Saleh (No. 3)*.[31] Rimer J held that a wife simply accompanying her husband on long car journeys did not fulfil the requisite conduct element for accessory liability, even if such journeys were for the purpose of committing a breach of trust by laundering the proceeds of a robbery through a Swiss bank. This result has been criticized as too generous by Mitchell.

Mitchell, 'Assistance' in *Breach of Trust* (eds Birks and Pretto) (Oxford: Hart, 2002), p. 176

> In effect, Rimer J absolved her from liability on the ground that she had passively acquiesced in her husband's activities. This may have been a generous interpretation of her behavior, given that she had actively accompanied him on his trips and in so doing had lent authenticity to the cover story he had offered to Swiss customs officials, that the pair were antique dealers entering Switzerland on business.

(c) MENTAL ELEMENT

For a long time, the requisite mental element for accessory liability in Equity was knowledge, and the *Baden* scale of knowledge, quoted already, was used.[32] Some cases decided that constructive knowledge down to point (v) (knowledge of circumstances that would put an honest and reasonable person on inquiry) was sufficient for accessory liability.[33] Others held that only points (i) to (iii) would lead to liability, since this would ensure actual knowledge or want of probity tantamount to subjective bad faith.[34] The weight of authority tended to favour the latter approach, but in *Tan* the Privy Council rejected knowledge as the mental element, instead favouring 'dishonesty'.

Royal Brunei Airlines Sdn Bhd v Tan [1995] 2 AC 378 (PC)

The claimant airline appointed Borneo Leisure Travel Sdn Bhd ('BLT') to act as its general travel agent. BLT was required to account to the claimant for the proceeds of ticket sales, after deducting commission. The terms of the agreement constituted BLT a trustee of the money for the claimant.

---

[30] [1999] BCC 525, 533.

[31] [1996] CLC 133.

[32] See Chapter 19.1(a), p. 925.

[33] *Selangor United Rubber Estates Ltd v Cradock (No. 3)* [1968] 1 WLR 1555, 1590; *Karak Rubber Co. Ltd v Burden (No. 2)* [1972] 1 WLR 602; *Baden v Société Générale pour Favoriser le Développement du Commerce et de l'Industrie en France SA* [1993] 1 WLR 509n.

[34] *Carl Zeiss Stiftung v Herbert Smith & Co. (No. 2)* [1969] 2 Ch 276; *Belmont Finance Corpn Ltd v Williams Furniture Ltd* [1979] Ch 250; *Agip (Africa) Ltd v Jackson* [1991] Ch 547; *Polly Peck International plc v Nadir (No. 2)* [1992] 4 All ER 769; *Eagle Trust plc v SBC Securities Ltd* [1993] 1 WLR 263, 293.

The money was not paid into a separate bank account, but was used in the business of BLT, which was conceded to be a breach of trust. BLT fell into arrears in accounting to the claimant and the agreement was terminated. As BLT was insolvent, the claimant sought a remedy against Mr Tan, who was the principal shareholder and director of BLT. It was conceded that Tan had assisted in the breach of trust with actual knowledge of it. The Court of Appeal of Brunei Darussalam held him not liable on the ground that the breach of trust in which he had assisted had not been shown to be a dishonest and fraudulent design on the part of BLT, which was considered essential to accessory liability.[35] The Privy Council held that Tan was personally liable for dishonestly assisting in BLT's breach of trust. There was no further requirement of dishonesty on the part of BLT. Lord Nicholls said:

> … what matters is the state of mind of the third party sought to be made liable, not the state of mind of the trustee. The trustee will be liable in any event for the breach of trust, even if he acted innocently, unless excused by an exemption clause in the trust instrument[36] or relieved by the court.[37] But his state of mind is essentially irrelevant to the question whether the third party should be made liable to the beneficiaries for the breach of trust. If the liability of the third party is fault-based, what matters is the nature of his fault, not that of the trustee. In this regard dishonesty on the part of the third party would seem to be a sufficient basis for his liability, irrespective of the state of mind of the trustee who is in breach of trust. It is difficult to see why, if the third party dishonestly assisted in a breach, there should be a further prerequisite to his liability, namely, that the trustee also must have been acting dishonestly. The alternative view would mean that a dishonest third party is liable if the trustee is dishonest, but if the trustee did not act dishonestly that of itself would excuse a dishonest third party from liability. That would make no sense.
>
> …

No liability

The starting point for any analysis must be to consider the extreme possibility: that a third party who does not receive trust property ought never to be liable directly to the beneficiaries merely because he assisted the trustee to commit a breach of trust or procured him to do so. This possibility can be dismissed summarily. On this the position which the law has long adopted is clear and makes good sense. Stated in the simplest terms, a trust is a relationship which exists when one person holds property on behalf of another. If, for his own purposes, a third party deliberately interferes in that relationship by assisting the trustee in depriving the beneficiary of the property held for him by the trustee, the beneficiary should be able to look for recompense to the third party as well as the trustee. Affording the beneficiary a remedy against the third party serves the dual purpose of making good the beneficiary's loss should the trustee lack financial means and imposing a liability which will discourage others from behaving in a similar fashion.

The rationale is not far to seek. Beneficiaries are entitled to expect that those who become trustees will fulfil their obligations. They are also entitled to expect, and this is only a short step further, that those who become trustees will be permitted to fulfil their obligations without deliberate intervention from third parties. They are entitled to expect that third parties will refrain from intentionally intruding in the trustee–beneficiary relationship and thereby hindering a beneficiary from receiving his entitlement in accordance with the terms of the trust instrument. There is here a close analogy with breach of contract. A person who knowingly procures a breach of contract, or knowingly interferes with the due performance of a contract, is liable to the innocent party. The underlying rationale is the same.

---

[35] See *Barnes v Addy*, (1874) 9 Ch App 244; Chapter 19.1, p. 924.
[36] See Chapter 16.2, p. 744.
[37] Trustee Act 1925, s. 61. See Chapter 16.3, p. 760.

Strict liability

The other extreme possibility can also be rejected out of hand. This is the case where a third party deals with a trustee without knowing, or having any reason to suspect, that he is a trustee. Or the case where a third party is aware he is dealing with a trustee but has no reason to know or suspect that their transaction is inconsistent with the terms of the trust. The law has never gone so far as to give a beneficiary a remedy against a non-recipient third party in such circumstances. Within defined limits, proprietary rights, whether legal or equitable, endure against third parties who were unaware of their existence. But accessory liability is concerned with the liability of a person who has not received any property. His liability is not property-based. His only sin is that he interfered with the due performance by the trustee of the fiduciary obligations undertaken by the trustee. These are personal obligations. They are, in this respect, analogous to the personal obligations undertaken by the parties to a contract. But ordinary, everyday business would become impossible if third parties were to be held liable for unknowingly interfering in the due performance of such personal obligations. Beneficiaries could not reasonably expect that third parties should deal with trustees at their peril, to the extent that they should become liable to the beneficiaries even when they received no trust property and even when they were unaware and had no reason to suppose that they were dealing with trustees.

Fault-based liability

Given, then, that in some circumstances a third party may be liable directly to a beneficiary, but given also that the liability is not so strict that there would be liability even when the third party was wholly unaware of the existence of the trust, the next step is to seek to identify the touchstone of liability. By common accord dishonesty fulfils this role. Whether, in addition, negligence will suffice is an issue on which there has been a well-known difference of judicial opinion. The *Selangor* decision [1968] 1 WLR 1555 in 1968 was the first modern decision on this point. Ungoed-Thomas J at 1590, held that the touchstone was whether the third party had knowledge of circumstances which would indicate to 'an honest, reasonable man' that the breach in question was being committed or would put him on inquiry. Brightman J reached the same conclusion in *Karak Rubber Co Ltd v Burden (No 2)* [1972] 1 WLR 602. So did Peter Gibson J in 1983 in the *Baden* case [1993] 1 WLR 509n. In that case the judge accepted a five-point scale of knowledge which had been formulated by counsel.

Meanwhile doubts had been expressed about this test by Buckley LJ and Goff LJ in the *Belmont* case [1979] Ch 250 at 267, 275. Similar doubts were expressed in Australia by Jacobs P in *DPC Estates Pty Ltd v Grey* [1974] 1 NSWLR 443 at 459. When that decision reached the High Court of Australia, the doubts were echoed by Barwick CJ, Gibbs J and Stephen J: see *Consul Development Pty Ltd v DPC Estates Pty Ltd* (1975) 132 CLR 373 at 376, 398, and 412.

Since then the tide in England has flowed strongly in favour of the test being one of dishonesty: see, for instance, Sir Robert Megarry V-C in *Re Montagu's Settlement Trusts* [1987] Ch 264 at 285, and Millett J in *Agip (Africa) Ltd v Jackson* [1990] Ch 265 at 293. In *Eagle Trust plc v SBC Securities Ltd* [1993] 1 WLR 484 at 495, Vinelott J stated that it could be taken as settled law that want of probity was a prerequisite to liability. This received the imprimatur of the Court of Appeal in *Polly Peck International plc v Nadir (No 2)* [1992] 4 All ER 769 at 777, per Scott LJ. [His Lordship then considered the divergent judicial views in New Zealand and continued:]

Dishonesty

Before considering this issue further it will be helpful to define the terms being used by looking more closely at what dishonesty means in this context. Whatever may be the position in some criminal or other contexts (see, for instance, *R* v *Ghosh* [1982] QB 1053), in the context of the accessory liability principle acting dishonestly, or with a lack of probity, which is synonymous, means simply not acting as an honest person would in the circumstances. This is an objective standard. At first sight this may seem surprising. Honesty has a connotation of subjectivity, as distinct from the objectivity of negligence. Honesty, indeed, does have a strong subjective element in that it is a description of a type of conduct assessed in the light of what a person actually knew at the time, as distinct from what a reasonable person would have known or appreciated. Further, honesty and its counterpart dishonesty are mostly concerned with advertent conduct, not inadvertent conduct. Carelessness is not dishonesty. Thus for the most part dishonesty is to be equated with conscious impropriety.

However, these subjective characteristics of honesty do not mean that individuals are free to set their own standards of honesty in particular circumstances. The standard of what constitutes honest conduct is not subjective. Honesty is not an optional scale, with higher or lower values according to the moral standards of each individual. If a person knowingly appropriates another's property, he will not escape a finding of dishonesty simply because he sees nothing wrong in such behaviour …

Negligence

It is against this background that the question of negligence is to be addressed. This question, it should be remembered, is directed at whether an honest third party who receives no trust property should be liable if he procures or assists in a breach of trust of which he would have become aware had he exercised reasonable diligence. Should he be liable to the beneficiaries for the loss they suffer from the breach of trust?

The majority of persons falling into this category will be the hosts of people who act for trustees in various ways: as advisers, consultants, bankers, and agents of many kinds. This category also includes officers and employees of companies, in respect of the application of company funds. All these people will be accountable to the trustees for their conduct. For the most part they will owe to the trustees a duty to exercise reasonable skill and care. When that is so, the rights flowing from that duty form part of the trust property. As such they can be enforced by the beneficiaries in a suitable case if the trustees are unable or unwilling to do so. That being so, it is difficult to identify a compelling reason why, in addition to the duty of skill and care vis-à-vis the trustees which the third parties have accepted, or which the law has imposed upon them, third parties should also owe a duty of care directly to the beneficiaries. They have undertaken work for the trustees. They must carry out that work properly. If they fail to do so, they will be liable to make good the loss suffered by the trustees in consequence. This will include, where appropriate, the loss suffered by the trustees being exposed to claims for breach of trust.

Outside this category of persons who owe duties of skill and care to the trustees, there are others who will deal with trustees. If they have not accepted, and the law has not imposed upon them, any such duties in favour of the trustees, it is difficult to discern a good reason why they should nevertheless owe such duties to the beneficiaries.

There remains to be considered the position where third parties are acting for, or dealing with, dishonest trustees. In such cases the trustees would have no claims against the third party. The trustees would suffer no loss by reason of the third party's failure to discover what was going on. The question is whether in this type of situation the third party owes a duty of care to the beneficiaries to, in effect, check that a trustee is not misbehaving. The third party must act honestly. The question is whether that is enough.

In agreement with the preponderant view, their Lordships consider that dishonesty is an essential ingredient here. There may be cases where, in the light of the particular facts, a third party will owe a duty of care to the beneficiaries. As a general proposition, however, beneficiaries cannot reasonably expect that all the world dealing with their trustees should owe them a duty to take care lest the trustees are behaving dishonestly.

Unconscionable conduct

Mention, finally, must be made of the suggestion that the test for liability is that of unconscionable conduct. Unconscionable is a word of immediate appeal to an equity lawyer. Equity is rooted historically in the concept of the Lord Chancellor, as the keeper of the Royal Conscience, concerning himself with conduct which was contrary to good conscience. It must be recognised, however, that unconscionable is not a word in everyday use by non-lawyers. If it is to be used in this context, and if it is to be the touchstone for liability as an accessory, it is essential to be clear on what, in this context, unconscionable means. If unconscionable means no more than dishonesty, then dishonesty is the preferable label. If unconscionable means something different, it must be said that it is not clear what that something different is. Either way, therefore, the term is better avoided in this context.

The accessory liability principle

Drawing the threads together, their Lordships' overall conclusion is that dishonesty is a necessary ingredient of accessory liability. It is also a sufficient ingredient. A liability in equity to make good resulting loss attaches to a person who dishonestly procures or assists in a breach of trust or fiduciary obligation. It is not necessary that, in addition, the trustee or fiduciary was acting dishonestly, although this will usually be so where the third party who is assisting him is acting dishonestly. 'Knowingly' is better avoided as a defining ingredient of the principle, and in the context of this principle the *Baden* scale of knowledge is best forgotten.

In this passage, Lord Nicholls sets out a clear vision of accessory liability, consisting of a wide conduct element but narrow mental element of dishonesty. Importantly, the standard of dishonesty is set objectively by a reasonable person. However, it remains important to establish what the defendant knew, as a defendant who was genuinely unaware that any breach might be assisted should not incur accessory liability. Thus the essence of the test is whether a reasonable person would consider that the defendant's conduct was dishonest, given what the defendant knew. One advantage of this approach is that the objective standard of honesty may be varied in accordance with the attributes of the defendant: a defendant who is a solicitor, for example, would be expected to meet a higher standard of honesty than others.

Tan was a decision of the Privy Council and therefore not strictly binding on English courts. However, it was adopted as a good statement of English law by the House of Lords in *Twinsectra v Yardley*.[38] Yet, in accepting Lord Nicholls' approach, the majority, led by Lord Hutton, seemed to depart from the test in *Tan* and introduced a further subjective element: the defendant must have realized that what he did would be considered to be dishonest by reasonable people.

Twinsectra Ltd v Yardley [2002] UKHL 12; [2002] 2 AC 164 (HL)

Yardley borrowed money from the claimant to purchase property. It had been agreed that the money would be held by a solicitor, Sims, who undertook that it would only be used for the purchase of property. Yardley borrowed the same amount of money from Barclays Bank without telling the claimant. Yardley's solicitor, Leach, was aware of the arrangement. In breach of his

---

[38] All the Law Lords appeared to accept this: [2002] UKHL 12; [2002] 2 AC 164, [3] (Lord Slynn), [7] (Lord Steyn), [11] (Lord Hoffmann), [26] (Lord Hutton), and [113] (Lord Millett).

undertaking, Sims paid most of the loan to Yardley to discharge the debts he owed to Yardley. The claimant then brought a number of claims to recover its money, one of which was a claim for dishonest assistance against Leach, who had been paid the money by Sims and who paid it out upon Yardley's instructions. A substantial sum of this money was used for purposes other than the acquisition of property. The trial judge held that, although Leach had shut his eyes to the details of the transaction, he had not acted dishonestly because he believed that the money was at the disposal of Yardley. The Court of Appeal substituted a finding of dishonesty. The House of Lords (Lord Millett dissenting) held that Leach had not acted dishonestly.[39] Lord Hutton said:[40]

Whilst in discussing the term 'dishonesty' the courts often draw a distinction between subjective dishonesty and objective dishonesty, there are three possible standards which can be applied to determine whether a person has acted dishonestly. There is a purely subjective standard, whereby a person is only regarded as dishonest if he transgresses his own standard of honesty, even if that standard is contrary to that of reasonable and honest people. This has been termed the 'Robin Hood test' and has been rejected by the courts. As Sir Christopher Slade stated in *Walker v Stones* [2001] QB 902, 939:

> 'A person may in some cases act dishonestly, according to the ordinary use of language, even though he genuinely believes that his action is morally justified. The penniless thief, for example, who picks the pocket of the multi-millionaire is dishonest even though he genuinely considers that theft is morally justified as a fair redistribution of wealth and that he is not therefore being dishonest.'

Secondly, there is a purely objective standard whereby a person acts dishonestly if his conduct is dishonest by the ordinary standards of reasonable and honest people, even if he does not realise this. Thirdly, there is a standard which combines an objective test and a subjective test, and which requires that before there can be a finding of dishonesty it must be established that the defendant's conduct was dishonest by the ordinary standards of reasonable and honest people and that he himself realised that by those standards his conduct was dishonest. I will term this 'the combined test'.

There is a passage in the earlier part of the judgment in *Royal Brunei* which suggests that Lord Nicholls considered that dishonesty has a subjective element. Thus in discussing the honest trustee and the dishonest third party at [1995] 2 AC 378 at 385 he stated:

> 'These examples suggest that what matters is the state of mind of the third party. ... But [the trustee's] state of mind is essentially irrelevant to the question whether the third party should be made liable to the beneficiaries for breach of trust.'

However, after stating, at 387, that the touchstone of liability is dishonesty, Lord Nicholls went on at 389 to discuss the meaning of dishonesty:

> 'Before considering this issue further it will be helpful to define the terms being used by looking more closely at what dishonesty means in this context. Whatever may be the position in some criminal or other contexts (see, for instance, *R v Ghosh* [1982] QB 1053), in the context of the accessory liability principle acting dishonestly, or with a lack of probity, which is synonymous, means simply not acting as an honest person would in the circumstances. This is an objective standard.'

My noble and learned friend Lord Millett has subjected this passage and subsequent passages in the judgment to detailed analysis and is of the opinion that Lord Nicholls used the term 'dishonesty' in a purely objective sense so that in this area of the law a person can be held to be dishonest even though he does not realise that what he is doing is dishonest by the ordinary standards of honest people. This

---

[39] It was held unanimously that the money in Sims' keeping was held on trust for the claimant. See Chapter 8.5, p. 411.
[40] [2002] UKHL 12; [2002] 2 AC 164, [27]–[43].

leads Lord Millett on to the conclusion that in determining the liability of an accessory dishonesty is not necessary and that liability depends on knowledge.

In *R v Ghosh* [1982] QB 1053 Lord Lane CJ held that in the law of theft dishonesty required that the defendant himself must have realised that what he was doing was dishonest by the ordinary standards of reasonable and honest people. The three sentences in Lord Nicholls' judgment, at 389,[41] which appear to draw a distinction between the position in criminal law and the position in equity, do give support to Lord Millett's view. But considering those sentences in the context of the remainder of the paragraph and taking account of other passages in the judgment, I think that in referring to an objective standard Lord Nicholls was contrasting it with the purely subjective standard whereby a man sets his own standard of honesty and does not regard as dishonest what upright and responsible people would regard as dishonest. …

[Lord Hutton cited passages from *Tan* and continued:]

The use of the word 'knowing' [by Lord Nicholls] would be superfluous if the defendant did not have to be aware that what he was doing would offend the normally accepted standards of honest conduct, and the need to look at the experience and intelligence of the defendant would also appear superfluous if all that was required was a purely objective standard of dishonesty. Therefore I do not think that Lord Nicholls was stating that in this sphere of equity a man can be dishonest even if he does not know that what he is doing would be regarded as dishonest by honest people.

…

At 387 Lord Nicholls stated that there is a close analogy between 'knowingly' interfering with the due performance of a contract and interfering with the relationship between a trustee and a beneficiary. But this observation was made in considering and rejecting the possibility that a third party who did not receive trust property should never be liable for assisting in a breach of trust. I do not think that in referring to 'knowingly' procuring a breach of contract Lord Nicholls was suggesting that knowingly assisting in a breach of trust was sufficient to give rise to liability. Such a view would be contrary to the later passage, at 392, dealing directly with this point.

There is, in my opinion, a further consideration which supports the view that for liability as an accessory to arise the defendant must himself appreciate that what he was doing was dishonest by the standards of honest and reasonable men. A finding by a judge that a defendant has been dishonest is a grave finding, and it is particularly grave against a professional man, such as a solicitor. Notwithstanding that the issue arises in equity law and not in a criminal context, I think that it would be less than just for the law to permit a finding that a defendant had been 'dishonest' in assisting in a breach of trust where he knew of the facts which created the trust and its breach but had not been aware that what he was doing would be regarded by honest men as being dishonest.

It would be open to your Lordships to depart from the principle stated by Lord Nicholls that dishonesty is a necessary ingredient of accessory liability and to hold that knowledge is a sufficient ingredient. But the statement of that principle by Lord Nicholls has been widely regarded as clarifying this area of the law and, as he observed, the tide of authority in England has flowed strongly in favour of the test of dishonesty. Therefore I consider that the courts should continue to apply that test and that your Lordships should state that dishonesty requires knowledge by the defendant that what he was doing would be regarded as dishonest by honest people, although he should not escape a finding of dishonesty because he sets his own standards of honesty and does not regard as dishonest what he knows would offend the normally accepted standards of honest conduct.

[His Lordship considered the facts and concluded:]

It is only in exceptional circumstances that an appellate court should reverse a finding by a trial judge on a question of fact (and particularly on the state of mind of a party) when the judge has had the advantage

---

[41] Quoted in Chapter 19.2(c), pp. 933–4.

> of seeing the party giving evidence in the witness box. Therefore I do not think that it would have been right for the Court of Appeal in this case to have come to a different conclusion from the judge and to have held that Mr. Leach was dishonest in that when he transferred the monies to Mr. Yardley he knew that his conduct was dishonest by the standards of responsible and honest solicitors.

Lord Hutton's speech seems to set out a very different test for dishonesty from that envisaged by Lord Nicholls. Despite Lord Nicholls' insisting that the test in Equity was *not* the same as the criminal test in *Ghosh*, Lord Hutton indicates the opposite. Despite his contrary suggestion in the above passage, this does not avoid the 'Robin Hood' problem mentioned: Lord Hutton's additional subjective limb—that the defendant must realize an objective, reasonable observer would consider him dishonest—allows an escape route for defendants such as Robin Hood, who may not have actually thought that reasonable people would have considered it dishonest to rob from the rich to give to the poor.

The inconsistency between Lord Nicholls and Lord Hutton was clearly shown in Lord Millett's powerful dissent in *Twinsectra*.

Twinsectra Ltd v Yardley [2002] UKHL 12; [2002] 2 AC 164, [114]–[117]

In taking dishonesty to be the condition of liability, however, Lord Nicholls used the word in an objective sense. He did not employ the concept of dishonesty as it is understood in criminal cases. …

[His Lordship cited Lord Nicholls in *Tan* and continued:]

Dishonesty as a state of mind or as a course of conduct?

In *R v Ghosh* [1982] QB 1053 Lord Lane CJ drew a distinction between dishonesty as a state of mind and dishonesty as a course of conduct, and held that dishonesty in section 1 of the Theft Act 1968 referred to dishonesty as a state of mind. The question was not whether the accused had in fact acted dishonestly but whether he was aware that he was acting dishonestly. The jury must first of all decide whether the conduct of the accused was dishonest according to the ordinary standards of reasonable and honest people. That was an objective test. If he was not dishonest by those standards, that was an end of the matter and the prosecution failed. If it was dishonest by those standards, the jury had secondly to consider whether the accused was aware that what he was doing was dishonest by those standards. That was a subjective test. Given his actual (subjective) knowledge the accused must have fallen below ordinary (objective) standards of honesty and (subjectively) have been aware that he was doing so.

The same test of dishonesty is applicable in civil cases where, for example, liability depends upon intent to defraud, for this connotes a dishonest state of mind. *Aktieselskabet Dansk Skibsfinansiering v Bothers* [2001] 2 BCLC 324 was a case of this kind (trading with intent to defraud creditors). But it is not generally an appropriate condition of civil liability, which does not ordinarily require a guilty mind. Civil liability is usually predicated on the defendant's conduct rather than his state of mind; it results from his negligent or unreasonable behaviour or, where this is not sufficient, from intentional wrongdoing.

A dishonest state of mind might logically have been required when it was thought that the accessory was liable only if the principal was guilty of a fraudulent breach of trust, for then the claim could have been regarded as the equitable counterpart of the common law conspiracy to defraud. But this requirement was discarded in *Royal Brunei Airlines Sdn Bhd v Tan* [1995] 2 AC 378.

It is, therefore, not surprising that Lord Nicholls rejected a dishonest state of mind as an appropriate condition of liability. …In my opinion, in rejecting the test of dishonesty adopted in *R v Ghosh* [1982] QB 1053, Lord Nicholls was using the word to characterise the defendant's conduct, not his state of mind.

...

Lord Nicholls dealt with the difficult case where the propriety of the transaction is doubtful. An honest man, he considered, would make appropriate enquiries before going ahead. This assumes that an honest man is one who would not knowingly participate in a transaction which caused the misapplication of funds...

In my opinion Lord Nicholls was adopting an objective standard of dishonesty by which the defendant is expected to attain the standard which would be observed by an honest person placed in similar circumstances. Account must be taken of subjective considerations such as the defendant's experience and intelligence and his actual state of knowledge at the relevant time. But it is not necessary that he should actually have appreciated that he was acting dishonestly; it is sufficient that he was....

The modern tendency is to deprecate the use of words like 'fraud' and 'dishonesty' as synonyms for moral turpitude or conduct which is morally reprehensible. There is much to be said for semantic reform, that is to say for changing the language while retaining the incidents of equitable liability; but there is nothing to be said for retaining the language and giving it the meaning it has in criminal cases so as to alter the incidents of equitable liability.

Should subjective dishonesty be required?

The question for your Lordships is not whether Lord Nicholls was using the word dishonesty in a subjective or objective sense in *Royal Brunei Airlines Sdn Bhd v Tan* [1995] 2 AC 378. The question is whether a plaintiff should be required to establish that an accessory to a breach of trust had a dishonest state of mind (so that he was subjectively dishonest in the *R v Ghosh* sense); or whether it should be sufficient to establish that he acted with the requisite knowledge (so that his conduct was objectively dishonest). This question is at large for us, and we are free to resolve it either way.

I would resolve it by adopting the objective approach. I would do so because:

(1) Consciousness of wrongdoing is an aspect of mens rea and an appropriate condition of criminal liability: it is not an appropriate condition of civil liability. This generally results from negligent or intentional conduct. For the purpose of civil liability, it should not be necessary that the defendant realised that his conduct was dishonest; it should be sufficient that it constituted intentional wrongdoing.

(2) The objective test is in accordance with Lord Selborne's statement in *Barnes v Addy* (1874) LR 9 Ch App 244 and traditional doctrine. This taught that a person who knowingly participates in the misdirection of money is liable to compensate the injured party. While negligence is not a sufficient condition of liability, intentional wrongdoing is. Such conduct is culpable and falls below the objective standards of honesty adopted by ordinary people.

(3) The claim for 'knowing assistance' is the equitable counterpart of the economic torts. These are intentional torts; negligence is not sufficient and dishonesty is not necessary. Liability depends on knowledge. A requirement of subjective dishonesty introduces an unnecessary and unjustified distinction between the elements of the equitable claim and those of the tort of wrongful interference with the performance of a contract.

Twinsectra left the law in an uncertain state: the Privy Council rejected *Ghosh*, but the House of Lords, in purporting to adopt the advice of the Privy Council revived the 'hybrid' test and the final subjective limb of *Ghosh* in a manner inconsistent with *Tan*. On the rules of precedent, the decision of the House of Lords was the authoritative pronouncement of the law, but this was weakened to some extent by Lord Millett's clear rejection of the *Ghosh* test, and his lucid demonstration of why *Tan* and

Twinsectra were inconsistent on this point. Commenting on the decision of the House of Lords, Tjio and Yeo wrote:[42]

> The majority holding in the present case requires all previous decisions applying the *Royal Brunei* test of dishonesty to be scrutinised with great care; they cease to have precedential value unless they can be said to have actually applied the combined test. This will not be an easy task. Moreover, while the majority view may have dispelled the cloud of confusion surrounding the definition of the test of dishonesty, in practical terms, the guidance it provides for future decision-making is somewhat murky. One difficulty is that the application of a purely objective test in the first limb of the combined test can be counter-intuitive. Judges may find it difficult to assess whether the defendant's conduct has breached the objective standard of dishonesty without regard to his knowledge and personal attributes; yet Lord Hutton would deal with such matters only in the second limb. The larger difficulty may be that, if, before *Twinsectra*, courts at first instance were torn between measuring the defendant's conduct against objective or subjective standards, it cannot be said with confidence that this tension will vanish as a result of *Twinsectra*. The uncertainty surrounding the role of 'Nelsonian' cognition within the combined test still allows different judges to take approaches of varying objectivity or subjectivity, or at least creates that perception from the vantage of appellate judges, and the objective/subjective debate is likely, with further protracted litigation, to come full circle.

The law on dishonesty was certainly murky, and it was no surprise to find that the issue rose again in the Privy Council in *Barlow Clowes v Eurotrust*.

Barlow Clowes International Ltd v Eurotrust International Ltd
[2005] UKPC 37; [2006] 1 WLR 1476 (PC), [10]–[18][43]

The appellant had been used to operate a fraudulent offshore investment scheme. Clowes, the perpetrator of the scheme, was convicted of fraud. Some of the investors' money had been paid through bank accounts maintained by the defendant company, which was administered from the Isle of Man. The appellant claimed that the defendant and its directors, including Henwood, had dishonestly assisted Clowes to misappropriate the money.

The Privy Council held that the defendants were liable. The test of dishonesty was whether, in the light of the defendant's knowledge, his assistance was contrary to ordinary standards of honest behaviour. The evidenced supported a finding that Henwood had acted dishonestly. Lord Hoffmann said:

> The judge stated the law in terms largely derived from the advice of the Board given by Lord Nicholls of Birkenhead in *Royal Brunei Airlines Sdn Bhd v Tan* [1995] 2 AC 378. In summary, she said that liability for dishonest assistance requires a dishonest state of mind on the part of the person who assists in a breach of trust. Such a state of mind may consist in knowledge that the transaction is one in which he cannot honestly participate (for example, a misappropriation of other people's money), or it may consist in suspicion combined with a conscious decision not to make inquiries which might result in knowledge: see *Manifest Shipping Co Ltd v Uni-Polaris Insurance Co Ltd* [2003] 1 AC 469. Although a dishonest state of mind is a subjective mental state, the standard by which the law determines whether it is dishonest is objective. If by ordinary standards a defendant's mental state would be characterised as dishonest, it is irrelevant that the defendant judges by different standards. The Court of Appeal held this to be a correct state of the law and their Lordships agree.

---

[42] 'Knowing What is Dishonesty' (2002) LQR 502, 507.
[43] Lord Nicholls of Birkenhead, Lord Steyn, Lord Hoffmann, Lord Walker of Gestingthorpe, and Lord Carswell.

The judge found that during and after June 1987 Mr. Henwood strongly suspected that the funds passing through his hands were moneys which Barlow Clowes had received from members of the public who thought that they were subscribing to a scheme of investment in gilt-edged securities. If those suspicions were correct, no honest person could have assisted Mr. Clowes and Mr. Cramer to dispose of the funds for their personal use. But Mr. Henwood consciously decided not to make inquiries because he preferred in his own interest not to run the risk of discovering the truth.

Their Lordships consider that by ordinary standards such a state of mind is dishonest. The judge found that Mr. Henwood may well have lived by different standards and seen nothing wrong in what he was doing. He had an

> 'exaggerated notion of dutiful service to clients, which produced a warped moral approach that it was not improper to treat carrying out clients' instructions as being all-important. Mr. Henwood may well have thought this to be an honest attitude, but, if so, he was wrong.'

Lord Neill of Bladen, who appeared for Mr. Henwood, submitted to their Lordships that such a state of mind was not dishonest unless Mr. Henwood was aware that it would by ordinary standards be regarded as dishonest. Only in such a case could he be said to be consciously dishonest. But the judge made no finding about Mr. Henwood's opinions about normal standards of honesty. The only finding was that by normal standards he had been dishonest but that his own standard was different.

In submitting that an inquiry into the defendant's views about standards of honesty is required, Lord Neill relied upon a statement by Lord Hutton in *Twinsectra Ltd v Yardley* [2002] AC 164, 174, with which the majority of their Lordships agreed. [Their Lordships quoted from Lord Hutton[44] and continued:]

Their Lordships accept that there is an element of ambiguity in these remarks which may have encouraged a belief, expressed in some academic writing, that the *Twinsectra* case had departed from the law as previously understood and invited inquiry not merely into the defendant's mental state about the nature of the transaction in which he was participating but also into his views about generally acceptable standards of honesty. But they do not consider that this is what Lord Hutton meant. The reference to 'what he knows would offend normally accepted standards of honest conduct' meant only that his knowledge of the transaction had to be such as to render his participation contrary to normally acceptable standards of honest conduct. It did not require that he should have had reflections about what those normally acceptable standards were.

Similarly in the speech of Lord Hoffmann, the statement (in para 20) that a dishonest state of mind meant 'consciousness that one is transgressing ordinary standards of honest behaviour' was in their Lordships' view intended to require consciousness of those elements of the transaction which make participation transgress ordinary standards of honest behaviour. It did not also require him to have thought about what those standards were.

On the facts of the *Twinsectra* case, neither the judge who acquitted Mr. Leach of dishonesty nor the House undertook any inquiry into the views of the defendant solicitor, Mr. Leach, about ordinary standards of honest behaviour. He had received on behalf of his client a payment from another solicitor whom he knew had given an undertaking to pay it to Mr. Leach's client only for a particular use. But the other solicitor had paid the money to Mr. Leach without requiring any undertaking. The judge found that he was not dishonest because he honestly believed that the undertaking did not, so to speak, run with the money and that, as between him and his client, he held it for his client unconditionally. He was therefore bound to pay it upon his client's instructions without restriction on its use. The majority in the House of Lords considered that a solicitor who held this view of the law, even though he knew all the facts, was not by normal standards dishonest.

---

[44] See Chapter 19.2(c), p. 936.

> Their Lordships therefore reject Lord Neill's submission that the judge failed to apply the principles of liability for dishonest assistance which had been laid down in the *Twinsectra* case. In their opinion they were no different from the principles stated in *Royal Brunei Airlines Sdn Bhd v Tan* [1995] 2 AC 378 which were correctly summarised by the judge.

The result in *Barlow Clowes* seems satisfactory. An objective approach to dishonesty is taken, akin to that adopted by Lord Nicholls in *Tan*. But some of the reasoning is surprising. The majority in *Twinsectra* did not say the same thing as Lord Nicholls, and Lord Hoffmann's speech in the Privy Council in *Barlow Clowes* might be considered particularly unexpected given that his Lordship agreed with Lord Hutton in *Twinsectra* itself. As Yeo noted:[45]

> In a surprising twist, the Privy Council in *Barlow Clowes International Ltd (in liquidation) v Eurotrust International Ltd* [2005] UKPC 37; [2006] 1 All E.R. 333, PC (Isle of Man) has declared that the majority in *Twinsectra* had not differed from *Royal Brunei*. Of the members of the Judicial Committee, Lord Hoffmann, who delivered its unanimous opinion, had authored one of the leading majority speeches in *Twinsectra* and Lord Steyn was also part of the majority. ... Lord Hoffmann stated that liability for dishonest assistance required a dishonest state of mind, which may consist in knowledge that the transaction was one in which he should not participate, or in suspicion combined with a conscious decision not to make inquiries which might result in knowledge. There was no further test whether the defendant himself realised what ordinary standards of honesty were. The second limb of the combined test, which has been misconstrued by academics, merely required that the defendant should have sufficient subjective knowledge such that his conduct would be regarded as dishonest by ordinary honest people.
>
> ...
>
> However, this 'clarification' of *Twinsectra* is, with respect, unconvincing. It is difficult to understand the role of a *combined* test if the two limbs are testing for the same thing and one limb does not make sense without the other. It is also difficult to see how the question whether a person has realised that he has breached ordinary standards of honest behaviour can be answered without considering his view on what those standards are. The distinction between the majority and minority positions in *Twinsectra* was explained away as a difference of view on the standards of objective honesty. ... If this is right, it was unsporting of the majority to have let Lord Millett waste so many pages arguing against a straw man.

Yet it may be that Lord Hoffmann's approach is defensible pragmatically. *Barlow Clowes* was a decision of the Privy Council. The Privy Council is unable to overrule decisions of the House of Lords and thereby change English law. But by *interpreting* the decision in *Twinsectra*, rather than overruling it, the Privy Council in *Barlow Clowes* may have made the task much easier for English courts in the future. For example, it is now possible for judges in lower courts to say that they are bound by the decision of the House of Lords in *Twinsectra*, but will interpret that decision in the same way as the Privy Council did in *Barlow Clowes*.

This sleight of hand has been adopted by the Courts and revived Lord Nicholls' approach in *Tan*. For example, in *Abou-Rahmah v Abacha*,[46] the Court of Appeal considered, *obiter*, the test of dishonesty for dishonest assistance. For example, Arden LJ said:[47]

> The decision in *Twinsectra* is of course binding on this court and the judge. But the *Barlow Clowes* decision does not involve a departure from, or refusal to follow, the *Twinsectra* case. Rather, the *Barlow*

---

[45] 'Dishonest Assistance: Restatement from the Privy Council' (2006) LQR 171, 172–3.
[46] [2006] EWCA Civ 1492; [2007] 1 All ER (Comm) 827.
[47] Ibid, [68].

Clowes case gives guidance as to the proper interpretation to be placed on it as a matter of English law. It shows how the *Royal Brunei* case and the *Twinsectra* case can be read together to form a consistent corpus of law.

The meaning of dishonesty in the *Twinsectra* case appeared to involve an additional subjective element, namely an awareness on the part of the accessory that his conduct was dishonest. The decision under appeal in the *Barlow Clowes* case was an appeal from the Isle of Man but no distinction was drawn between the law of [the] Isle of Man and the law of England and Wales. It would appear therefore that the Privy Council was also intending to clarify English law since that is the only logical implication from the methodology of interpretation of an English authority. That interpretation could hardly have been an interpretation which only applied in the Isle of Man but not in England and Wales. The approach of the Privy Council was both striking and bold: one writer has referred to it as taking judicial re-interpretation 'to new heights' (Virgo, Mapping the Law, Essays in memory of Peter Birks, ed Burrows and Rodger (2006) (Oxford) chapter 5, page 86). The decision in the *Barlow Clowes* case could probably have been reached without consideration of the *Twinsectra* decision for the purpose of English law, and it is significant that the Privy Council took another course.

Similarly, Rix LJ referred to dishonesty:[48]

in the *Twinsectra* sense, ... as clarified in *Barlow Clowes*.

There is little doubt that the objective approach to dishonesty represents the current approach to English law. For instance, in *Starglade Properties Ltd v Nash*, the Chancellor insisted that:[49]

The relevant standard ... is the ordinary standard of honest behaviour. Just as the subjective understanding of the person concerned as to whether his conduct is dishonest is irrelevant so also is it irrelevant that there may be a body of opinion which regards the ordinary standard of honest behaviour as being set too high. Ultimately, in civil proceedings, it is for the court to determine what that standard is and to apply it to the facts of the case.

This objective approach is much to be preferred. There is no reason why a defendant should be able to avoid liability simply because he or she is of dubious moral character or awareness, and would not have realized that he or she would be considered to be dishonest by reasonable people. The 'Robin Hood' defence should not apply. However, although the objective test of dishonesty is to be preferred to the more subjective approach taken by Lord Hutton in *Twinsectra*, it is not at all clear that 'dishonesty' is the appropriate touchstone for liability in this area.

(i) *Is dishonesty the right mental element?*

The *Tan* test of dishonesty immediately received a warm reception as the fault element for accessory liability.[50] But dishonesty has clearly caused difficulties at the highest level of the judiciary. It is worth considering whether it is the right mental element for accessory liability. Indeed, a person will only

---

[48] Ibid, [40].
[49] [2010] EWCA Civ 1314, [32].
[50] E.g. Nolan, 'From Knowing Assistance to Dishonest Facilitation' (1995) CLJ 505, 505: a very welcome development and clarification of the law. See also Harpum, 'Accessory Liability for Procuring or Assisting a Breach of Trust' (1995) 111 LQR 545. Compare Berg, 'Accessory Liability for Breach of Tort' (1996) 59 MLR 443, and see also Birks, 'Accessory Liability' [1996] LMCLQ 1.

be considered to be dishonest on the basis of what he or she actually knew,[51] so why add an extra layer of complexity with the label of 'dishonest' to the requisite level of 'knowing'? Escaping the need to establish knowledge is impossible: Hirst LJ has stated that:[52]

> dishonesty and knowledge (of some sort) are rather like the chicken and the egg.

Dishonesty is clearly a concept with its roots in the criminal law, where it is a jury question that goes to the culpability of the accused. But even in the context of accessory liability in the criminal law, the requisite mental element is not dishonesty but knowledge of the essential matters that constitute the primary offence.[53] So Equity has borrowed a concept from the criminal law in a context in which it is not employed by the criminal courts. Yet, counter-intuitively, it seems as if the adoption of dishonesty in the civil law might actually have an impact upon the criminal law. In *Starglade Properties Ltd v Nash*, Leveson LJ said:[54]

> I would add a note of concern if the concept of dishonesty for the purposes of civil liability differed to any marked extent from the concept of dishonesty as understood in the criminal law.
>
> … the analysis which has governed the approach of the criminal law may fit more readily into the language of the House of Lords in *Twinsectra* prior to the explanation of the remarks in that case in *Barlow Clowes* in the Privy Council and *Abu Rahman* [*sic*.] in the Court of Appeal. It is all the more important, therefore, that at some stage the opportunity to revisit this issue should be taken by the Court of Appeal (Criminal Division).

It is somewhat odd for the civil law to seek to influence the criminal law on an issue that should really be a jury question. Rather than borrowing a mental element[55] from the criminal law, it may have been wiser to look to the private law and accessory liability in the contractual realm. As Lord Millett pointed out in *Twinsectra*,[56] a better analogy might be made with the Common Law tort of inducing a breach of contract and, in *Abou-Rahmah v Abacha*, Rix LJ even called the equitable action an 'equitable tort'.[57] The Common Law does not require dishonesty, only intention or knowledge.

Lord Millett developed this theme in *Twinsectra*:[58]

> It would be most undesirable if we were to introduce a distinction between the equitable claim and the tort, thereby inducing the claimant to attempt to spell a contractual obligation out of a fiduciary relationship in order to avoid the need to establish that the defendant had a dishonest state of mind. It would, moreover, be strange if equity made liability depend on subjective dishonesty when in a comparable situation the common law did not. This would be a reversal of the general rule that equity demands higher standards of behaviour than the common law.

---

[51] See e.g. *Heinl v Jyske Bank (Gibraltar)* [1999] Lloyd's Bank Rep 511 (Nourse LJ).

[52] *Three Rivers DC v Governor and Company of the Bank of England (No. 3)* [2000] 2 WLR 15, 62 (in the different context of misfeasance in public office).

[53] *Johnson v Youden* [1950] 1 KB 544, 546.

[54] [2010] EWCA Civ 1314, [42]–[44].

[55] Although Lord Millett, suggested dishonesty related to conduct (*Twinsectra Ltd v Yardley* [2002] UKHL 12; [2002] 2 AC 164, [134], quoted immediately below), this is difficult to explain. Lord Hoffmann's approach in *Barlow-Clowes*, clearly establishes dishonesty concerns the mental element, which seems much more satisfactory.

[56] [2002] UKHL 12; [2002] 2 AC 164, [127].

[57] [2006] EWCA Civ 1492; [2007] 1 All ER (Comm) 827, [2].

[58] [2002] UKHL 12; [2002] 2 AC 164, [132]–[134].

> If we were to reject subjective dishonesty as a requirement of civil liability in this branch of the law, the remaining question is merely a semantic one. Should we return to the traditional description of the claim as 'knowing assistance', reminding ourselves that nothing less than actual knowledge is sufficient; or should we adopt Lord Nicholls' description of the claim as 'dishonest assistance', reminding ourselves that the test is an objective one?
>
> For my own part, I have no difficulty in equating the knowing mishandling of money with dishonest conduct. But the introduction of dishonesty is an unnecessary distraction, and conducive to error. Many judges would be reluctant to brand a professional man as dishonest where he was unaware that honest people would consider his conduct to be so. If the condition of liability is intentional wrongdoing and not conscious dishonesty as understood in the criminal courts, I think that we should return to the traditional description of this head of equitable liability as arising from 'knowing assistance'.

Lord Millett brands dishonesty as 'an unnecessary distraction and conducive to error'. One potential distorting feature of dishonesty is the gravity of the label. The significance of this label was also noted by Lord Hutton.[59] It is very serious to call a professional, such as a solicitor, 'dishonest', and the courts may shy away from this in circumstances where 'knowing assistance' would be semantically less problematic.

Dishonesty is not, therefore, an entirely satisfactory mental element. Indeed, dishonesty might be considered to be an unsatisfactory basis of liability since its definition seems somewhat circular. In *Tan*, Lord Nicholls said that dishonesty 'means simply not acting as an honest person would in the circumstances'.[60] But this simply begs the question: what would an honest person have done? The answer appears to be: he would not have acted dishonestly, but this is clearly circular and does not further our understanding of dishonesty.

Lord Millett, at least, would prefer a return to knowledge. However, dishonesty does seem to require something more than knowledge, since even if assisters know that their actions will assist a breach of fiduciary duty, they might not be considered to be dishonest if they had a good reason for this. But if that is all that dishonesty adds, then it would be simpler and more transparent explicitly to recognize a defence of justification. Indeed, such a defence was perhaps hinted at by Lord Nicholls in *Tan* when he acknowledged that:[61]

> Unless there is a very good and compelling reason, an honest person does not participate in a transaction if he knows it involves a misapplication of trust assets to the detriment of the beneficiaries.

This approach suggests that a person should be liable as an accessory if he or she knows that his or her acts will induce or assist a breach of fiduciary duty. But this is only generally true: in some cases, such actions will be justified and no liability should lie.[62] This is the approach adopted at Common Law,[63] and it may be that this is an area where Equity and the Common Law could be fused.[64]

In any event, it is notable that Lord Nicholls did not subject 'knowledge' to rigorous examination as a potential fault element in *Tan*, in contrast to his analysis of other possible tests of fault. Yet,

---

[59] [2002] UKHL 12; [2002] 2 AC 164, [35], quoted in Chapter 19.2(c), p. 937.

[60] [1995] 2 AC 378, 389.

[61] Ibid.

[62] See e.g. Gardner, 'Knowing Assistance and Knowing Receipt: Taking Stock' (1996) LQR 56, 66.

[63] E.g. *OBG v Allan* [2007] UKHL 21; [2008] 1 AC 1, [193] (Lord Nicholls), citing *Edwin Hill and Partners v First National Finance Corpn. plc.* [1989] 1 WLR 225.

[64] Chapter 1.2, p. 8. See also the comments of e.g. Lord Nicholls in *Royal Brunei Airlines v Tan* [1995] 2 AC 378, 387 and *OBG v Allan* [2007] UKHL 21; [2008] 1 AC 1, [189]; Lord Millett in *Twinsectra v Yardley* [2002] UKHL 12; [2002] 2 AC 164, [127].

since dishonesty can only be assessed in light of what the defendant knew, some examination of this requirement of knowledge seems necessary.

(ii) *What level of knowledge must the accessory possess?*

The defendant must actually know something concerning the wrong committed by the fiduciary in order to be considered dishonest: such knowledge is required to establish a lack of probity. However, it seems that Nelsonian knowledge, or 'turning a blind-eye', also suffices. In a different context, Lord Scott stated that:[65]

> 'Blind-eye' knowledge approximates to knowledge. … an imputation of blind-eye knowledge requires an amalgam of suspicion that certain facts may exist and a decision to refrain from taking any step to confirm their existence.

This should be more than just a vague suspicion,[66] and must be actually held: it is not enough that a reasonable person would have been suspicious of wrongdoing being involved. The inclusion of such 'blind-eye' knowledge is appropriate: a defendant should not be able to escape liability by deliberately not thinking about facts of which he was well aware.

(a) *Content of knowledge*

An accessory must know that his or her acts will assist, encourage, or induce a breach of trust or breach of fiduciary obligation. But how specific does the accessory's knowledge have to be regarding that primary breach of duty? In *Brinks Ltd v Abu-Saleh*, Rimer J expressed the view that a defendant must know of the existence of the fiduciary relationship, or the facts giving rise to it, before he or she could be made liable as an accessory.[67] By contrast, Lord Millett in *Twinsectra* thought it sufficient that the defendant be aware that the subject matter of the trust, which was at issue in the case, 'is not at the free disposal of the principal'.[68] It is suggested that a defendant need not know the precise nature of the relationship between the primary wrongdoer and claimant before becoming liable as an accessory. For this reason, the approach of Lord Millett is to be preferred, and this was adopted by the Privy Council in *Barlow Clowes*.

Barlow Clowes International Ltd v Eurotrust International Ltd [2005] UKPC 37; [2006] 1 WLR 1476, [19]–[28] (Lord Hoffmann)

> Their Lordships now address the grounds upon which the Staff of Government Division allowed Mr. Henwood's appeal. Having set out the Acting Deemster's findings at some length, they said that she could not have held Mr. Henwood liable unless she could find that he had 'solid grounds for suspicion, which he consciously ignored, that the disposals in which Mr. Henwood participated involved dealings with misappropriated trust funds'.
>
> Their Lordships think that, on the facts of this case, this was a substantially accurate way of putting the matter, although they will return to the question of whether Mr. Henwood needed to have had any knowledge or suspicions about the precise terms on which the misappropriated moneys were held.

---

[65] *Manifest Shipping Co. Ltd v Uni-Polaris Insurance Co. Ltd (The Star Sea)* [2001] UKHL 1; [2003] 1 AC 469, [112].
[66] *Abou-Rahmah v Abacha* [2006] EWCA Civ 1492; [2007] 1 All ER (Comm) 827. Cf. Lee, 'Changing Position on Change of Position' [2007] RLR 135.
[67] [1996] CLC 133, 151.
[68] [2002] UKHL 12; [2002] 2 AC 164, [135].

The question for the Staff of Government Division was therefore whether there was evidence upon which the Acting Deemster could make her finding that he had the necessary state of mind.

[Their Lordships considered that there was such evidence, and continued:]

The appellate court then went on to say that because Mr. Henwood knew the general nature of the businesses of the members of the Barlow Clowes group, it was not a necessary inference that he would have concluded that the disposals were of moneys held in trust. That was because there was no evidence that Mr. Henwood 'knew anything about, for example, the actual conduct of the businesses of members of the Barlow Clowes group, the contractual arrangements made with investors, the mechanisms for management of funds under the group's control, the investment and distribution policies and the precise involvement of Mr. Cramer in the group's affairs'.

Their Lordships consider that this passage displays two errors of law. First, it was not necessary … that Mr. Henwood should have concluded that the disposals were of moneys held in trust. It was sufficient that he should have entertained a clear suspicion that this was the case. Secondly, it is quite unreal to suppose that Mr. Henwood needed to know all the details to which the court referred before he had grounds to suspect that Mr. Clowes and Mr. Cramer were misappropriating their investors' money. The money in Barlow Clowes was either held on trust for the investors or else belonged to the company and was subject to fiduciary duties on the part of the directors. In either case, Mr. Clowes and Mr. Cramer could not have been entitled to make free with it as they pleased. In *Brinks Ltd v Abu-Saleh* [1996] CLC 133, 155 Rimer J expressed the opinion that a person cannot be liable for dishonest assistance in a breach of trust unless he knows of the existence of the trust or at least the facts giving rise to the trust. But their Lordships do not agree. Someone can know, and can certainly suspect, that he is assisting in a misappropriation of money without knowing that the money is held on trust or what a trust means: see the *Twinsectra* case [2002] 2 AC 164, para 19 (Lord Hoffmann) and para 135 (Lord Millett). And it was not necessary to know the 'precise involvement' of Mr. Cramer in the group's affairs in order to suspect that neither he nor anyone else had the right to use Barlow Clowes money for speculative investments of their own.

(d) REMEDIES

A fundamental reason why a claimant might bring a claim against a third party rather than the wrongdoing fiduciary is the possibility of substantial redress from the accessory in situations where the fiduciary may not be worth suing. Identifying the remedies available is therefore of crucial importance. But the law in this area is difficult. This is partly due to the assister traditionally being said to be liable as a 'constructive trustee'; yet since the assister may not have any property at all to hold on trust, this use of language is inappropriate and misleading.[69] It has been argued that the remedies available against the liability of an accessory is 'secondary' in nature, and that the dishonest assister should incur joint and several liability with the fiduciary.[70] In situations where the principal seeks to recover his or her loss, it does seem appropriate for the principal to be able to sue either the fiduciary or the accessory for the loss. Thus in *Ultraframe Ltd v Fielding*, Lewison J said:[71]

I can see that it makes sense for a dishonest assistant to be jointly and severally liable for any *loss* which the beneficiary suffers as a result of a breach of trust. I can see also that it makes sense for a dishonest assistant to be liable to disgorge any profit which he *himself* has made as a result of assisting in the

---

[69] See Chapter 19.1(c), p. 927.
[70] E.g. Elliott and Mitchell, 'Remedies for Dishonest Assistance' (2004) 67 MLR 16.
[71] [2005] EWHC 1638; [2006] FSR 17, [1600].

breach. However, I cannot take the next step to the conclusion that a dishonest assistant is also liable to pay to the beneficiary an amount equal to a profit which he did not make and which has produced no corresponding loss to the beneficiary. As James LJ pointed out in *Vyse v. Foster* (1872) LR 8 Ch App 309:

> 'This Court is not a Court of penal jurisdiction. It compels restitution of property unconscientiously withheld; it gives full compensation for any loss or damage through failure of some equitable duty; but it has no power of punishing any one. In fact, it is not by way of punishment that the Court ever charges a trustee with more than he actually received, or ought to have received, and the appropriate interest thereon. It is simply on the ground that the Court finds that he actually made more, constituting moneys in his hands "had and received to the use" of the *cestui que trust*.'

This has been an influential passage. Before considering further the approach to gain-based remedies, it is worth noting that if the accessory is thought to be liable for his or her *own* wrong, then it may be inappropriate to talk of 'joint and several liability' even for loss-based claims. If the accessory bears primary liability for his or her own wrong, then it would be more accurate to say that both the fiduciary and accessory are liable to compensate the claimant for his or her loss, and that the fiduciary and accessory can then sue each other in contribution.[72] Generally, this will lead to the same result and have little impact upon claimants. But there clearly needs to be a link between the assistance and the loss suffered, and the accessory may not have contributed to *all* the losses inflicted by a wrongdoing fiduciary. It is suggested that this is the better approach. As Ridge has argued:[73]

> dishonest assistance is best seen as a primary liability based upon [the accessory] D's exploitation of [the claimant] C's vulnerability ... The nature of D's wrongdoing is distinct from that of [the fiduciary] who breaches an obligation of loyalty. The rationale for dishonest assistance liability has both pragmatic and principled features; these support the availability of gain-based remedies as well as loss-based remedies.

Such primary liability is not entirely freestanding, however, and is derivative and parasitic to the breach of fiduciary duty.[74] This can lead to a difficult issue where the claimant sues the accessory for his or her loss because he or she is unable to sue the wrongdoing fiduciary as a result of an exemption clause that protects the fiduciary. Should the accessory also have the benefit of the exclusion clause? This is a difficult question, and there is no clear answer. To allow the claimant to recover all his or her losses against a third party when he or she would not have been able to do so against the fiduciary might seem generous: the participation of the third party fortuitously improves the claimant's position. The claimant might have limited his or her expectations *in all events* by agreeing to the exemption clause, and the unsatisfactory language of 'constructive trustee' might have signified that the accessory was liable *as if* he or she were the trustee, perhaps with the benefit of the exemption clause. However, on balance, the better view seems to be that the accessory's liability is primary, and that the protection afforded by an exclusion clause is personal to the fiduciary and does not extend to

---

[72] For contribution, see Chapter 16.5(b)(i), pp. 775–7. Of course, any claim in contribution might be worthless if either the fiduciary or accessory is insolvent.

[73] 'Justifying the Remedies for Dishonest Assistance' (2008) 124 LQR 445, 467.

[74] It may perhaps be preferable to view accessory liability as straddling primary and secondary liability, as was subsequently acknowledged by Mitchell with Watterson, 'Remedies for Knowing Receipt' in *Constructive and Resulting Trusts* (ed. Mitchell) (Oxford: Hart, 2010).

protect third parties. This argument seems to be strengthened by the fact that the defendant merits little sympathy if he or she is dishonest.[75] The remedies against the fiduciary and accessory will not always be the same.[76]

The quotation from *Ultraframe* given earlier highlights that gain-based measures may differ as between the fiduciary and accessory. For example, if an accessory had to disgorge gains that he did not make but the fiduciary did, that would seem very much like a punitive measure. As Christopher Clarke J said at first instance in *Novoship (UK) Ltd v Nikitin*:[77]

> there is no equity to compel someone who has not made a profit from his breach, or dishonest assistance in that of another, to account for a profit which he has not made and which does not represent a loss which the principal has suffered.

Admittedly, the contrary result has been favoured in Canada,[78] but was sensibly not adopted in this jurisdiction. If punitive awards against accessories are to be permitted, it should be through overt recognition of the principles and policies underpinning punitive remedies,[79] and not obscured by hiding under the banner of 'account of profits'.

Moreover, it has recently been confirmed by the Court of Appeal that an accessory may have to give up gains that he makes from his dishonest assistance, even if the fiduciary does not make any such gains.

Novoship (UK) Ltd v Nikitin [2014] EWCA Civ 908; [2015] QB 499[80]

Mr Mikhaylyuk was the General Manager, Commercial Manager, and later a director of the claimant, Novoship (UK) Ltd. Mr Mikhaylyuk was responsible for negotiating the charters of vessels owned by companies within the Novoship group. Mr Mikhaylyuk defrauded Novoship to the advantage of himself and others. As part of his dishonest scheme, Mr Mikhaylyuk breached his fiduciary duty in directing a third party to pay bribes to himself and Amon International Inc, a company owned and controlled by Mr Nikitin. Mr Mikhaylyuk also used his position to arrange charters of vessels ('the Henriot charters') to Henriot Finance Ltd, a British Virgin Islands company which was owned and controlled by Mr Nikitin. At first instance, Christopher Clarke J held that Mr Mikhaylyuk was clearly in breach of fiduciary duty due to the conflict between his personal interests and duty to his principal; since Mr Nikitin knew of this and nonetheless continued to participate in Mr Mikhaylyuk's schemes, Mr Nikitin was liable for dishonest assistance. Longmore LJ, delivering the judgment of the Court of Appeal, agreed. The following extract concerns the question of the remedy available against Mr Nikitin, who had entered into the Henriot charters at the market rate, and

---

[75] See e.g. *Lewin on Trusts* (19th edn) (eds Mowbray et al.) (London: Sweet & Maxwell, 2014) [40-031]; Gardner, 'Knowing Assistance and Knowing Receipt: Taking Stock' (1996) 112 LQR 56; Ridge, 'Justifying the Remedies for Dishonest Assistance' (2008) 124 LQR 445, 450.

[76] This was highlighted by the Supreme Court in *Central Bank of Nigeria v Williams* [2014] UKSC 10; [2014] AC 1189 in the context of limitation: see Chapter 16.9(b)(ii), pp. 784–7.

[77] [2012] EWHC 3586 (Comm) at [99].

[78] Eg *Canada Safeway Ltd v Thompson* [1951] 3 DLR 295.

[79] See Chapter 17.7, pp. 841–3.

[80] Davies, 'Gain-based Remedies for Dishonest Assistance' (2015) 131 LQR 173; Gummow, 'Dishonest Assistance and Account of Profits' [2015] CLJ 405.

made a profit of almost $109 million from them. The Court of Appeal agreed with the trial judge that in principle a remedy of account of profits was available against an accessory, but—disagreeing with the judge below—held that an account of profits should not be awarded on the particular facts of the case.

Longmore LJ:

We agree with *Snell's Equity* (32nd ed §30–079) that, subject to one qualification to which we will come, both a liability to make good loss and a liability to account for profits 'follow from the premise that the defendant is held liable to account as if he were truly a trustee to the claimant.'

In our judgment this position is supported both by policy and authority. The policy was articulated by Gibbs J in *Consul Development Pty Ltd v. DPC Estates Pty Ltd* (1975) 132 CLR 373, 397. He said:

> 'If the maintenance of a very high standard of conduct on the part of fiduciaries is the purpose of the rule it would seem equally necessary to deter other persons from knowingly assisting those in a fiduciary position to violate their duties. If, on the other hand, the rule is to be explained simply because it would be contrary to equitable principles to allow a person to retain a benefit that he had gained from a breach of his fiduciary duty, it would appear equally inequitable that one who knowingly took part in the breach should retain a benefit that resulted therefrom. I therefore conclude, on principle, that a person who knowingly participates in a breach of fiduciary duty is liable to account to the person to whom the duty was owed for any benefit he has received as a result of such participation.'

If the phrase 'knowingly took part in' is replaced by 'dishonestly assisted in' we cannot see that it undermines the policy as formulated. It is true that in Australia the concept of 'knowing participation' does not correspond precisely to our concepts of knowing receipt and dishonest assistance. However, so far as accounting for profits are concerned, even in Australian law a knowing participant is not generally required to account for profits that he did not make: *Grimaldi v Chameleon Mining NL* (No 2) [2012] FCAFC 6 at para 536.

...

In *Ultraframe* Lewison J said at para 1594 that a dishonest assistant is liable to account 'for any profit that he makes from his dishonest assistance or from the underlying breach of trust'. However, he was not considering the precise nature of the test of causation which was not in issue. We have already referred to the observations of Gibbs J in holding that questions of policy support the availability of the remedy of an account of profits against a dishonest assistant. His Honour concluded that a dishonest assistant is:

> 'liable to account to the person to whom the duty was owed for any benefit he has received *as a result* of such participation.' (Emphasis added)

...

For the reasons we have given we do not agree with the judge that the same considerations that apply to a fiduciary apply to a dishonest assistant who has no fiduciary duties. We agree with the judge that if Mr Nikitin (or his companies) had not entered into the Henriot charters, the profits would not have been made. In other words, 'but for' entry into the charters the profits would not have been made. But in our judgment the simple 'but for' test is not the appropriate test. In our judgment what Mr Nikitin acquired as a result of his dishonest assistance (and also as a result of Mr Mikhaylyuk's breach of fiduciary duty) was the use of the vessels at the market rate. That was merely the occasion for him to make a profit. The real or effective cause of the profits was the unexpected change in the market. As the judge recognised at para 525 Mr Nikitin made the profits 'because he judged the market well'.

> We would therefore hold that there was an insufficient direct causal connection between entry into the Henriot charters and the resulting profits. We must stress, however, that had Mr Nikitin been a true fiduciary, and had entry into the Henriot charters been a breach of fiduciary duty, then the causation test we have adopted would not have applied.

This is a helpful decision that clarifies a difficult but important area of law. Gain-based remedies are personal to any particular defendant, and in principle are rightly considered to be available against an accessory.[81] The Court of Appeal in *Novoship* thought that an accessory has the responsibility of an express trustee,[82] but this formulation is best understood as simply leading to the conclusion that a personal liability to account for profits can exist. However, as the Court of Appeal also pointed out, equitable relief is discretionary and an equitable allowance may feasibly be granted to an accessory in a similar manner to a fiduciary.[83] The most difficult question now concerns the test of causation that should be required before an accessory will have to disgorge gains made. The notion of a 'sufficiently direct causal connection' is somewhat ill-defined and may prove problematic. Nevertheless, the result in *Novoship* seems satisfactory: Mr Nikitin's gain was the opportunity to enter into the Henriot charters, but these were at market rates and not especially advantageous. The profit of $109 million was caused by market fluctuations, which were too remote from the breach of duty. The claimant would have had to establish a proprietary claim in order to strip Mr Nikitin of the uplift in value of the charters, but this was hopeless as the claimant had no proprietary interest in the charters at the outset.

3. UNCONSCIONABLE RECEIPT

Liability in Equity for receiving, but not necessarily retaining, property in breach of trust or fiduciary duty is also considered to be wrong-based: the recipient must be at fault before liability will be imposed. However, this is in itself controversial, the suggestion that liability should be strict, in accordance with the approach at Common Law, has gained influential support and will be examined later.[84]

The classification of recipient liability is not altogether straightforward. Given the necessity of fault, some have considered unconscionable receipt to be another example of accessory liability, which is parasitic upon the primary breach of fiduciary duty.[85] But as Lord Nicholls insisted in *Tan*:[86]

> Different considerations apply to the two heads of liability. Recipient liability is restitution-based, accessory liability is not.

Sheehan has argued that receipt and assistance must be 'disentangled', and that only the latter sanctions participation in a wrong committed by another.

---

[81] Cf Devonshire, 'Account of Profits for Dishonest Assistance' [2015] CLJ 222.
[82] [2014] EWCA Civ 908; [2015] QB 499, [82].
[83] See Chapter 14.5(e), p. 716.
[84] See Chapter 19.3(d)(i), pp. 964–8.
[85] Cf. Finn, 'The Liability of Third Parties for Knowing Receipt or Assistance' in *Equity, Fiduciaries and Trusts* (ed. Walters) (Toronto: Carswell, 1993).
[86] *Tan* [1995] 2 AC 378, 386. See similarly Lord Millett in *Twinsectra*; [2002] UKHL 12; [2002] 2 AC 164, [107]. For further consideration of 'restitution', see Chapter 1.4(b), pp. 13–15.

Sheehan, 'Disentangling Equitable Personal Remedies for Receipt and Assistance' (2008) RLR 41, 58

> Knowing receipt, however, is a different type of wrong from dishonest assistance. It appears to be a hybrid, possibly unique in being parasitic, but non-participatory in any sense. This has caused trouble. Some commentators favour … suggesting that it is the analogue of conversion, and some … suggest merger with assistance. The latter commentators do not appreciate the difference between a parasitic and a participatory wrong and the former do not appreciate the importance of the parasitism.

It seems sensible to differentiate between recipient and assistance liability. Admittedly, in *Novoship (UK) Ltd v Nikitin*, Longmore LJ thought that dishonest assistance and knowing receipt were 'two types of secondary liability',[87] and in *Central Bank of Nigeria v Williams* the Supreme Court treated both as instances of 'ancillary liability',[88] but this is only because they concern the liability of parties who are not themselves trustees or fiduciaries. The liability of knowing recipients and dishonest assisters clearly rest on different bases. The elements necessary for each are different, and merely receiving property is not as active a role in the fiduciary's breach as deliberate assistance. Indeed, in *Agip (Africa) Ltd v Jackson*, Millett J said that knowing receipt is 'concerned with rights of priority in relation to property'.[89] This proprietary basis of a receipt-based claim distinguishes it from assistance-based liability. Conaglen and Goymour have written that:[90]

> The *source* of the claim in knowing receipt is receipt of property that does not belong beneficially to the recipient and the 'wrong' lies in treating property that he knows is not beneficially his own as if it were, whether by dissipating it or otherwise putting it beyond the reach of those to whom it belongs beneficially.

Although unconscionable receipt and dishonest assistance should be considered separately, it should be appreciated that both claims might arise on the same set of facts: a party who assists the breach of fiduciary duty might then receive the misapplied property. A claimant may well be able to sue the same third party for both dishonest assistance and unconscionable receipt.[91]

In order to establish receipt-based liability the claimant must establish:

i)   a proprietary base;

ii) a breach of trust or fiduciary duty;

iii) beneficial receipt of the property;

iv) fault.

These elements will be considered in turn.

(a) PROPRIETARY BASE

The claimant should have an equitable proprietary interest in the property received in order to have any claim in the first place. In order to establish such a proprietary base, the criteria outlined in

---

[87] [2014] EWCA Civ 908; [2015] QB 499, [68].

[88] [2014] UKSC 10; [2014] AC 1189.

[89] [1990] Ch 265, 292.

[90] 'Knowing Receipt and Registered Land' in *Constructive and Resulting Trusts* (ed. Mitchell) (Oxford: Hart, 2010), p. 172.

[91] See e.g. *Abou-Rahmah v Abacha* [2006] EWCA Civ 1492; [2007] 1 All ER (Comm) 827.

Chapter 18 are relevant.[92] The claimant must be able to follow or trace his or her interest into the hands of the recipient in the same way as was analysed in Chapter 18,[93] but we are here considering the *personal* claim against the recipient him- or herself, rather than the proprietary claim against the asset.

(b) BREACH OF TRUST OR FIDUCIARY DUTY

The property must have been misapplied in breach of duty. If the property was lawfully sold to the third party, the claimant's interest in the property will have been overreached and he or she will have no further claim, either personal or proprietary.[94] However, the claimant will be able to follow the property or its traceable product pursuant to *any* breach of trust: there is no need to establish a fraudulent breach of duty.

Clearly, the vast majority of cases in the context of unconscionable receipt will concern a breach of trust, but it is equally possible that claimants can sue in unconscionable receipt where they were not the beneficiaries under a trust but principals in a fiduciary relationship. For example, a company director may transfer the company's property to a defendant in breach of duty. The company might be able to sue the recipient for unconscionable receipt even though the director was not a trustee.[95] It is unclear whether the duty breached by the director must have been a *fiduciary* duty, or any duty.[96] It may be preferable to require that the duty breached be fiduciary, as this would restrict the potential impact of a breach upon third party recipients. However, given that the recipient must be at fault,[97] it is perhaps artificial to restrict a claim to breaches of fiduciary duty alone.[98]

Sometimes the issue of whether or not there has actually been a breach has been obscured with unfortunate results. In *Criterion Properties plc v Stratford UK Properties LLC*,[99] the claimant, Criterion Properties plc, and defendant, Oaktree, formed a limited partnership. Fearing that the claimant might be taken over by another company, the managing director and another director of the claimant signed a so-called 'poison pill' agreement with the defendant. This gave the defendant the right to have its interest in the partnership bought out on favourable terms if another company gained control of the claimant or if the chairman or managing director ceased to be involved in its management. The managing director was dismissed and the defendant sought to exercise its option to be bought out. The issue was whether the 'poison pill' agreement was valid. In the House of Lords, Lord Nicholls said:[100]

> Unfortunately, in the courts below this 'want of authority' issue was approached on the basis that the outcome turned on whether Oaktree's conduct was unconscionable. This seems to have been the test applied by the Court of Appeal in *Bank of Credit and Commerce International (Overseas) Ltd v Akindele* [2001] Ch 437[101] both to questions of 'want of authority' and to liability for what traditionally has been labelled 'knowing receipt'.

---

[92] See Chapter 18.2, p. 849.
[93] See Chapter 18.3, p. 851.
[94] See e.g. Nolan, 'Equitable Property' (2006) 122 LQR 232.
[95] See Chapter 19.1(b), p. 926.
[96] See Chapter 14.2(b), p. 665.
[97] If a strict liability regime were to be adopted, this reasoning may not be satisfactory.
[98] Conaglen, 'The Nature and Function of Fiduciary Loyalty' (2005) 121 LQR 452, 478–9.
[99] [2004] UKHL 28; [2004] 1 WLR 1856.
[100] Ibid, [3]–[4].
[101] See Chapter 19.3(d), pp. 957–61.

> I respectfully consider the Court of Appeal in Akindele's case fell into error on this point. If a company (A) enters into an agreement with B under which B acquires benefits from A, A's ability to recover these benefits from B depends essentially on whether the agreement is binding on A. If the directors of A were acting for an improper purpose when they entered into the agreement, A's ability to have the agreement set aside depends upon the application of familiar principles of agency and company law. If, applying these principles, the agreement is found to be valid and is therefore not set aside, questions of 'knowing receipt' by B do not arise. So far as B is concerned there can be no question of A's assets having been misapplied. B acquired the assets from A, the legal and beneficial owner of the assets, under a valid agreement made between him and A.

(c) BENEFICIAL RECEIPT

A defendant can only be liable for unconscionable receipt if he or she receives the property *beneficially*, for his or her own benefit. Thus a party who receives property as an agent cannot be sued for his or her receipt, since he or she only holds the property *ministerially*, for the benefit of another.

In *Agip Africa Ltd v Jackson*, Millett J said:[102]

> The essential feature … is that the recipient must have received the property for his own use and benefit. That is why neither the paying nor the collecting bank can normally be brought within it. In paying or collecting money for a customer the bank acts only as his agent. It is otherwise, however, if the collecting bank uses the money to reduce or discharge the customer's overdraft. In doing so it receives the money for its own benefit.

However, this raises two significant issues. First, why is beneficial receipt required? And, secondly, why are banks not considered to receive property beneficially?

Intuitively, it might seem obvious that a defendant should not be sued in unconscionable receipt if he or she derives no personal benefit from the property received. After all, this claim is not against the property itself, but the recipient. But why should the recipient *necessarily* be immune if he or she holds the property for the benefit of another? If the recipient has acted unconscionably, then perhaps his or her culpability should lead to liability even if he or she were not the beneficial owner of the property. If made liable, the recipient might then be afforded a defence to any claim brought by the person for whom the property was received: the latter should not be in a better position where the property was received unconscionably. Hiebendaal has argued that:[103]

> It would be artificial to treat the agent as not having received property when the agent has received title to the property. While the law does permit fictions, it should only do so where there is a principled basis for the fiction. There is no obvious and sufficient reason in principle why equity would not intervene when the agent's conscience is affected.
>
> ….
>
> …receipt is simply a factual question, and does not inherently depend on what contractual (or other) obligations the recipient has. … the requirement for beneficial receipt is inapt.

---

[102] [1990] Ch 265, 1390.
[103] 'The Recipient Has No Clothes: Conscience, Conduits and Knowing Receipt' (2011) 5 Journal of Equity 43, 53–8.

This approach would place greater onus on the fault element. This may well seem appropriate at present, but might buckle if the strain exercised by arguments in favour of eliminating fault in the context of receipt-based claims were to prove overwhelming.[104]

In any event, it is clear that beneficial receipt is still a necessary element of unconscionable receipt. In *Attorney-General of Zambia v Meer Care & Desai*, Peter Smith J insisted that:[105]

> Intermediaries who pass on property have never been liable for knowing receipt.

The requirement for beneficial receipt is very well established. However, it is important to note that even if a party does not receive beneficially and therefore cannot be liable for unconscionable receipt, that third party might be liable in dishonest assistance.

The second issue raised by Millett J in *Agip (Africa) Ltd v Jackson* concerns banks' receipt of money. His Lordship suggested that since banks receive money for the benefit of their customers, they do not receive property beneficially but only ministerially. Apparently, the only exception to this analysis is where the bank receives money that is used to pay a client's overdraft, as then the money clearly does go to the bank beneficially because the bank does not have to account for the money to anyone else. But this approach seems unduly narrow. Banks do not generally hold money ministerially for clients; the relationship between a client and bank is that of creditor–debtor, not trustee–beneficiary. Banks can and do invest the money they have as their own, and in parallel accept that there is a liability to pay the client the money owed upon demand.

Gleeson, 'The Involuntary Launderer: The Banker's Liability for Deposits of the Proceeds of Crime', in *Laundering and Tracing* (ed. Birks) (Oxford: Clarendon Press, 1995), pp. 126–7

> The *locus classicus* of the relationship between banker and customer is *Foley v Hill*, where Lord Cottenham said that 'Money, when paid into a bank, ceases altogether to be the money of the principal; it is then the money of the banker … to do as he pleases'.[106]
>
> …
>
> To say that a bank receives merely as minister is to misunderstand fundamentally the nature of banking. A bank does not merely 'hold' moneys paid into an account with it. It takes those moneys and deals with them in the capital markets, lending them at interest or purchasing investments, and takes credit for the profit made on those investments for itself. There is no legal connection between the money of the depositor and the profit made by the bank through its use. Now under these circumstances, to speak of the bank holding these moneys merely as 'minister' is nonsense.

The qualms of Gleeson in this extract have been voiced judicially. Indeed, in the House of Lords in *Foskett v McKeown*, Lord Millett himself seemed to differ from his earlier stance in *Agip* when he said:[107]

> Money paid into a bank account belongs legally and beneficially to the bank and not to the account holder.

[104] See Chapter 19.3(d)(i), pp. 964–8.
[105] [2007] EWHC 952 (Ch), [683].
[106] (1848) 2 HL Cas 28, 36–7.
[107] [2001] 1 AC 102, 128.

It may be that the approach of the courts in this area is evolving. In *Uzinterimpex JSC v Standard Bank plc*, Moore-Bick LJ said:[108]

> a person who receives property merely as an agent has no interest of any kind in it himself and must simply account to his principal for it. Receipt by him is the equivalent of receipt by the principal. When a person opens a current account at a bank he authorises the bank to receive payments from third parties on his behalf and therefore payment by a third party to the customer's account at the bank is payment to the customer. However, it has long been established that the relationship between banker and customer is one of creditor and debtor: see *Foley v Hill* (1848) 11 H.L.C. 28. The customer whose account is in credit lends the money to the bank for use by it in its business. The distinction drawn in *Agip v Jackson* between receipt by a bank into an account that is in credit and receipt into an account that is overdrawn has been criticised on the grounds that the nature of the relationship between banker and customer is such that the bank always has the benefit of using the customer's money for its own purposes until such time as it is called upon to repay the debt: see in particular Bryan, *Recovering Misdirected Money from Banks: Ministerial Receipt at Law and in Equity* published in Restitution and Banking Law (1998), ed. Rose. ...
>
> In my view there is a good deal of force in Dr. Bryan's criticism of the decision in *Agip v Jackson*, but it is unnecessary for the purposes of this appeal to decide whether it is well-founded ...

These comments in *Uzinterimpex* were clearly *obiter*. But the tide may be shifting, and claims for unconscionable receipt against banks might soon be upheld more generally. This could lead to banks having to defend a greater number of receipt-based claims. Such a development may be criticized as placing a drain on the banks' time and resources, but it should be emphasized that a bank will only be liable if it has acted unconscionably. The fault element is well placed to restrict the scope of liability.

Although the focus tends to be upon the receipt of banks, it is worth highlighting that this problem of receipt can arise more generally. For example, in *Trustor v AB Smallbone (No. 2)*,[109] the Court had to consider the nature of a company's receiving property. Given the company's separate legal personality from the identity of those individuals who control the company, a company's receipt would generally, by itself, only lead to the company being sued for receipt. However, where the company has been exploited to conceal another person's own receipt, the corporate veil might be pierced. Sir Andrew Morritt V-C remarked that:[110]

> receipt by a subsidiary company will not count as a receipt by the parent if the subsidiary is acting in its own right, not as agent or nominee, at any rate in the absence of a want of probity or dishonesty.
>
> ...
>
> In my judgment the court is entitled to 'pierce the corporate veil' and recognise the receipt of the company as that of the individual(s) in control of it if the company was used as a device or façade to conceal the true facts thereby avoiding or concealing any liability of those individual(s).

Another difficult issue concerns the receipt of registered land which was transferred in breach of trust. For example, a purchaser may pay valuable consideration to acquire a registered estate. If the land was previously held by the vendor on trust, and the sale of the land was in breach of trust, should the beneficiaries be able to sue the purchaser for a receipt-based claim if the purchaser had the requisite degree of knowledge? This is particularly important since the beneficiaries will no longer have a proprietary

---

[108] [2008] EWCA Civ 819, [39]–[40].
[109] [2001] 1 WLR 1177.
[110] Ibid, at [19]–[23].

claim to the land itself: their beneficial interests will have been overreached.[111] However, the personal, receipt-based claim also depends upon the beneficiaries being able to identify a proprietary interest in the property received by the defendant; the better view[112] appears to be that section 29 of the Land Registration Act 2002 will prevent claims against the purchaser in unconscionable receipt, since that section ensures that once title to the land has been registered, the purchaser takes free of the beneficiaries' unregistered interest under the trust.[113] Such a result helps to further the protection of the integrity of the Land Register, such that purchasers do not have to worry about personal claims from beneficiaries if they provide valuable consideration for the transfer. This is also consistent with the approach of the High Court of Australia to the Australian legislation in *Farah Constructions Pty Ltd v Say-Dee Pty Ltd*.[114] However, in *Arthur v Attorney General of the Turks and Caicos Islands*,[115] the Privy Council held that the legislation in the Turks and Caicos Islands did allow a personal claim in unconscionable receipt to be brought against a purchaser of registered title. But the Privy Council recognized that 'special care' should be taken when considering the relevance and usefulness of judgments based on other jurisdictions.[116] It is suggested that the same approach should not be adopted in this jurisdiction.

(d) FAULT

It is well-established that recipients will only be liable in Equity if they are at fault. Indeed, the fault element is crucial to limiting the scope of receipt-based liability. However, its content is controversial. Previously, the cause of action was called 'knowing receipt', and the focus was upon the recipient's knowledge; cases differed between an objective[117] and subjective[118] test of fault.

We have already seen that Lord Nicholls in *Tan* said that the *Baden* scale of knowledge was 'best forgotten',[119] and it was always unlikely that these comments would be limited to assistance and not affect receipt-based claims. That the courts have generally felt unable to continue to apply a fault element of knowledge in the face of such strong criticisms is therefore unsurprising. Yet a divide between claims based upon receipt and assistance remains: despite Lord Nicholls' speech in *Tan*, the courts have favoured unconscionability rather than dishonesty as the fault element for recipient liability.

Bank of Credit and Commerce International (Overseas) Ltd v Akindele [2001] Ch 437 (CA)

Employees of a company, acting in fraudulent breach of their fiduciary duties, procured the company's entry into an artificial loan agreement with the defendant, pursuant to which the defendant paid US$10 million to the company in exchange for 250,000 shares in its holding company, on the basis that the company would arrange for the shares to be sold at a price which gave the defendant a 15 per cent annual return on his investment. The purpose of this scheme was to make

---

[111] See Chapter 2.7(d), pp. 56–7.

[112] Conaglen and Goymour, 'Knowing Receipt and Registered Land' in *Constructive and Resulting Trusts* (ed. Mitchell) (Oxford: Hart, 2010), p. 172.

[113] Unless the beneficiaries were in actual occupation at the time of the disposition to the purchaser: s. 29(2) and Schedule 3, [2].

[114] [2007] HCA 222, [193]–[198].

[115] [2012] UKPC 30. See Chapter 19.1(b), p. 926.

[116] Ibid, [15].

[117] See e.g. *Karak Rubber Co. Ltd v Burden (No. 2)* [1972] 1 WLR 602; *Belmont Finance Corpn Ltd v Williams Furniture Ltd (No. 2)* [1980] 1 All ER 393; *Polly Peck International plc v Nadir (No. 2)* [1992] 4 All ER 769.

[118] E.g. *Re Montagu's Settlement Trusts* [1987] Ch 264; *Eagle Trust plc v SBC Securities Ltd* [1993] 1 WLR 484; *Cowan de Groot Property Ltd v Eagle Trust plc* [1992] 4 All ER 700; *Eagle Trust plc v SBC Securities Ltd (No. 2)* [1996] 1 BCLC 121.

[119] [1995] 2 AC 378, 392, quoted in Chapter 18.2(c), pp. 932–5.

it appear that the corporate group had more money than was in fact the case. In pursuance of this agreement, the defendant received US$16.679 million from the company. The claimants, who were liquidators of the company, claimed that the defendant was liable to account for this sum because he had received the money knowing of the breach of fiduciary duty.[120]

The Court of Appeal held that to be liable for a receipt-based claim it was not necessary to show that the defendant had acted dishonestly. It was sufficient that the defendant's knowledge of the provenance of the funds which he had received made it unconscionable for him to retain the benefit of the receipt. In this case there was insufficient evidence to conclude that the defendant's knowledge was such that it was unconscionable for him to retain the benefit of the money he had received and so the defendant was held not liable.

Nourse LJ:

… there are two questions which, though closely related, are distinct: first, what, in this context, is meant by knowledge; second, is it necessary for the recipient to act dishonestly? Because the answer to it is the simpler, the convenient course is to deal with the second of those questions first.

Knowing receipt—dishonesty

As appears from the penultimate sentence of his judgment, Carnwath J [in the court below] proceeded on an assumption that dishonesty in one form or another was the essential foundation of the claimants' case, whether in knowing assistance or knowing receipt. That was no doubt caused by the acceptance before him (though not at any higher level) … that the thrust of the recent authorities at first instance was that the recipient's state of knowledge must fall into one of the first three categories listed by Peter Gibson J in *Baden v Société Générale pour Favoriser le Développement du Commerce et de l'Industrie en France SA* [1993] 1 WLR 509 at 575–576, on which basis, said Carnwath J, it was doubtful whether the test differed materially in practice from that for knowing assistance. However, the assumption on which the judge proceeded, derived as I believe from an omission to distinguish between the questions of knowledge and dishonesty, was incorrect in law. While a knowing recipient will often be found to have acted dishonestly, it has never been a prerequisite of the liability that he should.

…

The point was made most clearly by Vinelott J in *Eagle Trust plc v SBC Securities Ltd* [1993] 1 WLR 484 at 497:

> 'What the decision in *Belmont (No 2)* [1980] 1 All ER 393 shows is that in a "knowing receipt" case it is only necessary to show that the defendant knew that the moneys paid to him were trust moneys and of circumstances which made the payment a misapplication of them. Unlike a "knowing assistance" case it is not necessary, and never has been necessary, to show that the defendant was in any sense a participator in a fraud.'

Knowing receipt—the authorities on knowledge

With the proliferation in the last twenty years or so of cases in which the misapplied assets of companies have come into the hands of third parties, there has been a sustained judicial and extrajudicial debate as to the knowledge on the part of the recipient which is required in order to found liability in knowing receipt. Expressed in its simplest terms, the question is whether the recipient must have actual knowledge (or the equivalent) that the assets received are traceable to a breach of trust or whether constructive knowledge is enough. The instinctive approach of most equity judges, especially in this court, has been to assume

---

[120] The claimants also contended that the defendant was liable for dishonest assistance, but the Court of Appeal rejected this claim because the trial judge had correctly concluded that the defendant had acted honestly.

that constructive knowledge is enough. But there is now a series of decisions of eminent first instance judges who, after considering the question in greater depth, have come to the contrary conclusion, at all events when commercial transactions are in point. In the Commonwealth, on the other hand, the preponderance of authority has been in favour of the view that constructive knowledge is enough.[121]

…

Collectively, those observations might be thought to provide strong support for the view that constructive knowledge is enough. But it must at once be said that in each of the three cases in this court (including, despite some apparent uncertainty in the judgment of Goff LJ in *Belmont Finance Corpn Ltd v Williams Furniture Ltd (No 2)* [1980] 1 All ER 393 at 412) actual knowledge was found and, further, that the decisions in *Karak Rubber Co Ltd v Burden (No 2)* [1972] 1 WLR 602 and *Agip (Africa) Ltd v Jackson* [1990] Ch 265 were based on knowing assistance, not knowing receipt. Thus in none of the five cases[122] was it necessary for the question to be examined in any depth and there appears to be no case in which such an examination has been conducted in this court. The groundwork has been done in other cases at first instance. ….

The seminal judgment, characteristically penetrative in its treatment of authority and, in the best sense, argumentative, is that of Sir Robert Megarry V-C in *Re Montagu's Settlement Trusts* [1987] Ch 264. It was he who first plumbed the distinction between notice and knowledge. It was he who, building on a passage in the judgment of this court in *Re Diplock* [1948] Ch 465 at 478–479 first emphasised the fundamental difference between the questions which arise in respect of the doctrine of purchaser without notice on the one hand and the doctrine of constructive trusts on the other. Reading from his earlier judgment in the same case, he said [1987] Ch 264 at 278:

> 'The former is concerned with the question whether a person takes property subject to or free from some equity. The latter is concerned with whether or not a person is to have imposed upon him the personal burdens and obligations of trusteeship. I do not see why one of the touchstones for determining the burdens on property should be the same as that for deciding whether to impose a personal obligation on a [person]. The cold calculus of constructive and imputed notice does not seem to me to be an appropriate instrument for deciding whether a [person's] conscience is sufficiently affected for it to be right to bind him by the obligations of a constructive trustee.'

He added that there is more to being made a trustee than merely taking property subject to an equity.

….

Sir Robert Megarry V-C summarised his conclusions in eight subparagraphs, at 285. I read the first three:

> '(1) The equitable doctrine of tracing and the imposition of a constructive trust by reason of the knowing receipt of trust property are governed by different rules and must be kept distinct. Tracing is primarily a means of determining the rights of property, whereas the imposition of a constructive trust creates personal obligations that go beyond mere property rights.
>
> (2) In considering whether a constructive trust has arisen in a case of the knowing receipt of trust property, the basic question is whether the conscience of the recipient is sufficiently affected to justify the imposition of such a trust.
>
> (3) Whether a constructive trust arises in such a case primarily depends on the knowledge of the recipient, and not on notice to him; and for clarity it is desirable to use the word "knowledge" and avoid the word "notice" in such cases.'

---

[121] His Lordship considered *Karak Rubber Co. Ltd v Burden (No. 2)* [1972] 1 WLR 602, [632] (Brightman J); *Belmont Finance Corpn Ltd v Williams Furniture Ltd (No. 2)* [1980] 1 All ER 393, [405] (Buckley LJ), at 412 (Goff LJ); *Rolled Steel Products (Holdings) Ltd v British Steel Corpn* [1986] Ch 246, [306]–[307] (Browne-Wilkinson LJ); *Agip (Africa) Ltd v Jackson* [1990] Ch 265, [291] (Millett J); *Houghton v Fayers* [2000] 1 BCLC 511, [516] (Nourse LJ).

[122] See the cases in the previous footnote.

The effect of Sir Robert Megarry V-C's decision, broadly stated, was that, in order to establish liability in knowing receipt, the recipient must have actual knowledge (or the equivalent) that the assets received are traceable to a breach of trust and that constructive knowledge is not enough.

The Baden case

It will have been observed that up to this stage I have made no more than a passing reference to the fivefold categorisation of knowledge accepted by Peter Gibson J in *Baden*[123]

....

Reference to the categorisation has been made in most of the knowing receipt cases to which I have referred from *Re Montagu's Settlement Trusts* [1987] Ch 264 onwards. In many of them it has been influential in the decision. In general, the first three categories have been taken to constitute actual knowledge (or its equivalent) and the last two constructive knowledge.

Two important points must be made about the *Baden* categorisation. First, it appears to have been pro-pounded by counsel for the plaintiffs, accepted by counsel for the defendant and then put to the judge on an agreed basis. Secondly, though both counsel accepted that all five categories of knowledge were relevant and neither sought to submit that there was any distinction for that purpose between knowing receipt and knowing assistance (a view with which the judge expressed his agreement: see [1993] 1 WLR 509 at 582), the claim in constructive trust was based squarely on knowing assistance and not on knowing receipt: see at 572. In the circumstances, whatever may have been agreed between counsel, it is natural to assume that the categorisation was not formulated with knowing receipt primarily in mind. This, I think, may be confirmed by the references to 'an honest and reasonable man' in categories (iv) and (v). Moreover, in *Agip (Africa) Ltd v Jackson* [1990] Ch 265 at 293, Millett J warned against over-refinement or a too ready assumption that categories (iv) and (v) are necessarily cases of constructive knowledge only, reservations which were shared by Knox J in *Cowan de Groot Properties Ltd v Eagle Trust plc* [1992] 4 All ER 700 at 761.

Knowing receipt—the recipient's state of knowledge

In *Royal Brunei Airlines Sdn Bhd v Tan* [1995] 2 AC 378, which is now the leading authority on knowing assistance, Lord Nicholls of Birkenhead, in delivering the judgment of the Privy Council, said, at 392, that 'knowingly' was better avoided as a defining ingredient of the liability, and that in that context the Baden categorisation was best forgotten. Although my own view is that the categorisation is often help-ful in identifying different states of knowledge which may or may not result in a finding of dishonesty for the purposes of knowing assistance, I have grave doubts about its utility in cases of knowing receipt. Quite apart from its origins in a context of knowing assistance and the reservations of Knox and Millett JJ, any categorisation is of little value unless the purpose it is to serve is adequately defined, whether it be fivefold, as in the *Baden* case [1993] 1 WLR 509, or twofold, as in the classical division between actual and constructive knowledge, a division which has itself become blurred in recent authorities.

What then, in the context of knowing receipt, is the purpose to be served by a categorisation of knowl-edge? It can only be to enable the court to determine whether, in the words of Buckley LJ in *Belmont Finance Corpn Ltd v Williams Furniture Ltd (No 2)* [1980] 1 All ER 393 at 405, the recipient can 'con-scientiously retain [the] funds against the company' or, in the words of Sir Robert Megarry V-C in *Re Montagu's Settlement Trusts* [1987] Ch 264 at 273, '[the recipient's] conscience is sufficiently affected for it to be right to bind him by the obligations of a constructive trustee'. But, if that is the purpose, there is no need for categorisation. All that is necessary is that the recipient's state of knowledge should be such as to make it unconscionable for him to retain the benefit of the receipt.

---

[123] See Chapter 19.1(a), p. 925.

> For these reasons I have come to the view that, just as there is now a single test of dishonesty for knowing assistance, so ought there to be a single test of knowledge for knowing receipt. The recipient's state of knowledge must be such as to make it unconscionable for him to retain the benefit of the receipt. A test in that form, though it cannot, any more than any other, avoid difficulties of application, ought to avoid those of definition and allocation to which the previous categorisations have led. Moreover, it should better enable the courts to give commonsense decisions in the commercial context in which claims in knowing receipt are now frequently made.

This judgment from Nourse LJ has been very influential, and recast the fault element as requiring 'unconscionability'. The extent to which the approach in *Akindele* differs from *Tan* is revealing. For example, Nourse LJ was of the opinion that the *Baden* scale of knowledge can still be a useful tool when assessing fault, in contrast to Lord Nicholls. As has already been explained in the context of assistance liability, it is impossible to brand somebody 'dishonest' or 'unconscionable' without establishing what the defendant knew, and, although somewhat crude, the *Baden* categories might be a useful aid to help to achieve this.

Despite abandoning knowledge as the fault element in a similar vein to *Tan*, Nourse LJ rejected dishonesty and favoured unconscionability as the fault element. This stands in contrast to *Tan*. It is worth repeating the following passage from *Tan*:[124]

> unconscionable is not a word in everyday use by non-lawyers. If it is to be used in this context, and if it is to be the touchstone for liability as an accessory, it is essential to be clear on what, in this context, unconscionable means. If unconscionable means no more than dishonesty, then dishonesty is the preferable label. If unconscionable means something different, it must be said that it is not clear what that something different is.

Clearly, Nourse LJ thought unconscionability meant something different from dishonesty, but he did not explain precisely *what* that difference is. Admittedly, 'unconscionability' is a more traditional concept in Equity than 'dishonesty', but its content must be made clear. However, it should also be noted that the reasoning of Lord Nicholls in *Tan* persuaded some judges to employ a test of dishonesty in receipt-based claims as well,[125] even after *Akindele*. For example, in *Dubai Aluminium Co. Ltd v Salaam* Lord Millett stated that the:[126]

> case in knowing receipt, like that in dishonest assistance, was founded on the allegations of dishonesty, and was thus also fault-based. Dishonest receipt ... can be based on the defendant's dishonesty.

Nevertheless, references to dishonesty in this context are rare, and the *Akindele* test of unconscionability has established itself as the current law. For example, in *Arthur v Attorney General of the Turks and Caicos Islands*,[127] Sir Terence Etherton, giving the advice of the Privy Council, said that:[128]

> Knowing receipt in the *Akindele* sense is, as [counsel] accepted, not merely absence of notice but unconscionable conduct amounting to equitable fraud. It is a classic example of lack of *bona fides*.

---

[124] [1995] 2 AC 378, 392.
[125] See e.g. Aikens J in *Bank of America v Arnell* [1999] Lloyd's Rep Bank 399, [15].
[126] [2002] UKHL 48; [2003] 2 AC 366, 391.
[127] [2012] UKPC 30. See Chapter 19.1(b), p. 926.
[128] Ibid, [40].

But difficult questions remain. In particular, is unconscionability to be assessed subjectively or objectively? It is suggested that the thrust of Nourse LJ's approach in *Akindele* tends towards a subjective test:[129] the recipient's conscience must actually be affected for a claim to succeed. His conscience will be tainted where he or she actually knew of, or turned a blind eye to, the wrongful circumstances in which the property was received. It is suggested that general suspicion is insufficient, and that the defendant must turn a blind eye to a particular suspicion about a particular transaction.[130]

By contrast, Birks thought that unconscionability should be objectively assessed:[131]

> The unconscionable person as identified by her economic criteria turns out to be the person who could, in the circumstances, have reasonably been expected to discover the trust or fiduciary provenance of the assets received.[132]

Such an approach perhaps gains some support from the comments of Lord Sumption in *Credit Agricole Corp and Investment Bank v Papadimitriou*:[133]

> Whether a person claims to be a bona fide purchaser of assets without notice of a prior interest in them, or disputes a claim to make him accountable as a constructive trustee on the footing of knowing receipt, the question what constitutes notice or knowledge is the same. It is a question which has taxed judges for many years. In particular they have been much exercised by the question in what circumstances a person is under a duty to make inquiries before he can claim to be without notice of the prior interest in question. Ultimately there is little to be gained from a fine analysis of the precise turns of phrase which judges have employed in answering these questions. They are often highly sensitive to their legal and factual context. The principle is, I think clear. We are in the realm of property rights, and are not concerned with an actionable duty to investigate. The hypothesis is that the claimant has established a proprietary interest in the asset, and the question is whether the defendant has established such absence of notice as entitles him to assume that there are no adverse interests. The mere possibility that such interests exist cannot be enough to warrant inquiries. There must be something which the defendant actually knows (or would actually know if he had a reasonable appreciation of the meaning of the information in his hands) which calls for inquiry. The rule is that the defendant in this position cannot say that there might well have been an honest explanation, if he has not made the inquiries suggested by the facts at his disposal with a view to ascertaining whether there really is. I would eschew words like 'possible', which set the bar too low, or 'probable' which suggest something that would justify a forensic finding of fact. If even without inquiry or explanation the transaction appears to be a proper one, then there is no justification for requiring the defendants to make inquiries. He is without notice. But if there are features of the transaction such that if left unexplained they are indicative of wrongdoing, then an explanation must be sought before it can be assumed that there is none.

In any event, a test of 'unconscionability' might be criticized as too vague. It is a slippery concept, which may be manipulated by judges to reach a desired result. This does little to further legal certainty or allow parties to plan their affairs and predict whether or not their actions will lead to their being liable.

---

[129] As does the approach in *Arthur v Attorney General of the Turks and Caicos Islands* [2012] UKPC 30.

[130] Cf *Abou-Rahmah v Abacha* [2006] EWCA Civ 1492; [2007] 1 All ER (Comm) 827.

[131] Birks, 'Receipt' in *Breach of Trust* (eds Birks and Pretto) (Oxford: Hart, 2002) p. 227.

[132] The possibility of an objective approach was also left open, *obiter*, by Lord Neuberger MR in *Sinclair Trade Finance Ltd v Versailles Group plc* [2011] EWCA Civ 347, [2012] Ch 453, [107].

[133] [2015] UKPC 13; [2015] 1 WLR 4265, [33] (see further Chapter 18.6(a), pp. 911–14).

'Unconscionable' gives no guidance. ... 'Unconscionable' indicates unanalyzed disapprobation, thus embraces every position in the controversy.[134]

Birks even described unconscionability as a 'fifth wheel on the coach', and so irrelevant, given that knowledge still needs to be assessed.

Against this, it might be argued that a degree of flexibility allows courts to achieve justice on the particular facts of any given case. And if unconscionability depends upon 'subjective' knowledge, then the ability of potential defendants to predict the outcome of a case improves: a defendant who did not know of any wrongdoing, or have any suspicions, will not be liable. The requirement of unconscionability was robustly defended by the Court of Appeal in *Criterion Properties plc v Stratford UK Properties LLC*.[135] However, the Court did not unambiguously favour a subjective test.[136]

Criterion Properties plc v Stratford UK Properties LLC [2003] EWCA Civ 1783; [2003] 1 WLR 2108, [31]–[38] (Carnwath LJ)[137]

The purpose of the new formulation [in *Akindele*] was to give greater flexibility for the application of common sense in commercial situations.

...

In considering the application in *Akindele* of the distinction between 'dishonesty' and 'unconscionability', it is important to keep in mind the factual context, in particular that it was a case of actual fraud by the BCCI officers. If, at the time of the original offer, the Chief had known of the underlying fraud, it would have been clearly dishonest for him to enter into the agreement; he would have been a co-conspirator. If, on the other hand, having entered into the agreement in good faith, and having learnt subsequently of the fraud, he had then sought to enforce the agreement, his conduct would not necessarily have been 'dishonest'. There need have been nothing underhand about it; he would simply have been seeking to enforce his contract. However, it would have been 'contrary to conscience' for him to do so, at least for more than the return of his investment, because he would have been seeking to take advantage of someone else's fraud. One cannot necessarily apply the same analysis to a simple want of authority. A third party's right to rely on the apparent authority of the agent is not lost, merely because, after contract and before action, he becomes aware of the lack of authority. Nor, in the absence of fraud or the like, is it necessarily 'unconscionable' for him to hold the principal to a bad bargain.

...

Although that discussion was presented as one of 'constructive' as opposed to 'actual' knowledge, it is clear that Nourse LJ was not proposing a rigid division of any kind.

...

I do not see how one can consider the 'consciousability' of the actions of one party to the agreement without considering the position of the other. It is wholly artificial, in the context of this case, to consider the actions and motivations of the directors of Oaktree, and to ignore those of the directors of Criterion, particularly if it was they, through the Chairman Mr Nordström, who were the principal instigators of the SSA.

---

[134] Birks, 'Receipt' in *Breach of Trust* (eds Birks and Pretto) (Oxford: Hart, 2002), p. 226.
[135] See also *Armstrong DLW GmbH v Winnington Networks Ltd* [2012] EWHC 10 (Ch); [2012] 3 WLR 835, [132].
[136] [2003] EWCA Civ 1783; [2003] 1 WLR 2108.
[137] See Chapter 19.3(b), pp. 953–4.

The Court of Appeal[138] suggested that unconscionability depended on factors such as the fault of both parties and the actions and knowledge of the defendant in the context of the commercial relationship as a whole. Further guidance might be gleaned from cases on the defence of change of position,[139] which is barred where the defendant has acted unconscionably. This includes a failure to act in a commercially acceptable way,[140] and wilfully and recklessly failing to make such inquiries as an honest and reasonable person would make,[141] but not negligence.[142] However, some caution should be exercised about using change of position cases in this context: when barring a defence, unconscionability plays a different role than that required when grounding a claim.

(i) Should receipt-based liability be strict?

Deciding what shape receipt-based liability *should* take is further complicated by the fact that disagreements appear not only regarding the appropriate fault element, but also regarding whether there should be any fault element at all. There are powerful calls for strict liability based upon a defendant's receipt.

A strict liability approach would not be without precedent. Looking across to the Common Law, for example, it is well-established that where the defendant has received property belonging to the claimant, but the defendant no longer retains that property or its traceable proceeds, the claimant can bring a personal restitutionary claim for money had and received, which does not depend upon the defendant's fault at all.[143] The defendant's liability is strict. Consequently, the fact that the defendant was unaware of the claimant's proprietary rights is irrelevant, save where the defendant provided consideration for the property and can claim a defence of bona fide purchase. The defendant may also have a defence of change of position. This defence is available where the defendant's position has changed in reliance on the receipt of the benefit such that it is inequitable to require him or her to make restitution to the claimant.[144]

If the Common Law claim for restitution of the value of the claimant's property received by the defendant is a strict liability claim, why does the similar equitable claim of unconscionable receipt require proof of fault? Both claims are grounded on the defendant's receipt of property belonging to the claimant. In fact, Equity does recognize one type of strict liability restitutionary claim. This is where the defendant mistakenly received property belonging to another in the administration of an estate, as in *Ministry of Health v Simpson*.[145] Why should such a strict liability claim not be available more generally in Equity to mirror the equivalent Common Law claim?

What follows in this section concerns suggestions for how the law *might* develop regarding strict liability. It must be remembered that the authorities clearly do require fault, which is presently expressed as 'unconscionability'. The cases do not recognize strict liability for innocent

---

[138] This aspect of the case was unaffected by the decision of the House of Lords: see [2004] UKHL 28; [2004] 1 WLR 1856.

[139] Chapter 18.6(b), p. 916.

[140] *Niru Battery Manufacturing Co. v Milestone Trading Ltd* [2002] EWHC 1425 (Comm); [2002] 2 All ER (Comm) 705, 741; endorsed by the Court of Appeal [2003] EWCA Civ 1446; *Abou-Rahmah v Abacha* [2006] EWCA Civ 1492, [2007] 1 All ER (Comm) 827.

[141] *Papamichael v National Westminster Bank* [2003] Lloyd's Rep 341, 369 (Judge Chambers QC).

[142] *Maersk Air Ltd v Expeditors International (UK) Ltd* [2003] 1 Lloyd's Rep 491, 499. Although compare, *obiter*, *Armstrong DLW GmbH v Winnington Networks Ltd* [2012] EWHC 10 (Ch); [2012] 3 WLR 835, [123].

[143] *Lipkin Gorman v Karpnale Ltd* [1991] 2 AC 548; see Chapter 1.4(b), pp. 13–15.

[144] See Chapter 18.6(b), p. 916.

[145] [1951] AC 251 (the *Diplock* litigation).

volunteers in Equity apart from in rare, particular situations, notably the administration of estates.[146]

Lord Nicholls writing extra-judicially, has influentially supported a strict liability claim.

Lord Nicholls of Birkenhead, 'Knowing Receipt: The Need for a New Landmark' in *Restitution: Past, Present and Future* (eds Cornish, Nolan, O'Sullivan, and Virgo) (Oxford: Hart 1998), pp. 238–44

... equity should now follow the law. Restitutionary liability, applicable regardless of fault but subject to a defence of change of position, would be a better-tailored response to the underlying mischief of misapplied property than personal liability which is exclusively fault-based. Personal liability would flow from having received the property of another, from having been unjustly enriched at the expense of another. It would be triggered by the mere fact of receipt, thus recognising the endurance of property rights. But fairness would be ensured by the need to identify a gain, and by making change of position available as a defence in suitable cases when, for instance, the recipient had changed his position in reliance on the receipt.

....

If recipient liability is to have a firmer basis for the future, the attempt to formulate one single principle of personal liability should be abandoned. Instead, personal liability should be based on the combination of two separate principles of liability. First, ... a principle of strict liability ... would be confined to restoring an unjust gain. Secondly, dishonest recipients should be personally liable to make good losses as well as accounting for all benefits.

Birks has expressed similar views.

Birks, 'Receipt' in *Breach of Trust* (eds. Birks and Pretto) (Oxford: Hart, 2002) p. 239

while a person's wealth remains unjustly swollen the liability to make restitution is utterly independent of fault. There is no argument for keeping what one was never intended to have. After an honest change of position things begin to look different

A strict liability claim would enable 'fusion'[147] in this area of the law: neither the Common Law nor Equity would demand that the recipient be at fault. This may seem harsh on the recipient, who would expect to be able to keep any gift received.[148] The need to protect and further the important principle of the defendant's security of receipt might sensibly be emphasized. But Lord Nicholls and Birks believe that security of receipt is sufficiently protected by the availability of the defence of change of position: if defendants have not changed their position, then there is no reason to strengthen the security of their receipt, since they have not yet relied upon the receipt by changing their position.

However, this may be too quick. Change of position is not all that easy to establish; in *Lipkin Gorman*, the leading case, the House of Lords insisted that the change of position must be 'extraordinary', and some recipients may not yet have done enough to avail themselves of the change of position

---

[146] *Baker (GL) Ltd v Medway Building and Supplies Ltd* [1958] 1 WLR 1216 recognized a strict liability equitable claim where assets were distributed from an *inter vivos* trust. This seems anomalous.

[147] Chapter 1.2, p. 8.

[148] Of course, if the recipient paid for the property, then he or she may avail him- or herself of the defence of bona fide purchaser for value without notice.

defence. Moreover, it might seem better for the law to require the claimant to have to prove fault as an element of the claim; otherwise, it might be too easy for claimants to pick a defendant to sue, and then put the defendant to the trouble of having to defend a claim and prove a change of position. Fault may well become relevant at the defence stage anyway, since change of position cannot be pleaded by a person who has acted in bad faith. It appears that shifting to a strict liability regime would still catch wrongdoers, but would *also* make the innocent recipient personally liable. So, for example, the charities in *Re Diplock*,[149] which received property in breach of trust but did not change their position, *would* be liable for their receipt of the property, despite not being at fault *at all*. The appropriateness of such a result might be doubted: as between the innocent recipient and the innocent claimant, the law might favour the former to protect the important principles of security of receipt and finality of transactions. After all, the claimant will be able to sue somebody else: the wrongdoing fiduciary.

There has thus been much resistance to abandoning fault in this area. Many have pointed to the fact that equitable liability often requires fault, and that equitable property rights are not as well protected as common law property rights, making fusion inappropriate: the bona fide purchaser defence generally applies throughout Equity, for example, but not at Common Law.

Smith, 'Unjust Enrichment, Property, and the Structure of Trusts' (2000) 116 LQR 412, 430–4[150]

The argument which suggests that personal claims based on receipt of trust property must line up with the strict liability in *Lipkin Gorman* seems to ignore a very basic truth: a beneficiary's interest under a trust is not legal ownership. Equitable proprietary rights are not protected in the same way as legal ones. In general, they are protected less well. They are always subject to destruction by bona fide purchase of a legal interest or overreaching, and wrongful interference with them is dependent on fault. Beneficiaries cannot generally sue in conversion when a defendant interferes with the trust property; nor are they owed the duties of care which are owed to the legal owner. The argument for strict liability would make the most sense as part of an agenda which sought the abolition of the trust, and the return to a regime in which only one person can claim to be the owner of a given asset. That would be an odd agenda to pursue, when civilian systems all over the world, aware of the flexibility which the trust device offers, are introducing it in various forms. Certainly as the law is now, the beneficiary's interest under a trust attracts incidents different from legal ownership. It is not clear that it would make sense to abolish some of the characteristics of equitable proprietary rights while leaving others intact. If liability for receiving trust property is strict, why should equitable interests be subject to destruction by the defence of bona fide purchase of a legal interest?

...

The strict liability approach would contemplate that a plaintiff need only allege that a bank received trust property, not that the bank knew or should have known of the trust; with no more than that, the bank would be required to prove its good faith as a defence, or to account for what it had done with this money. In other words, there is no procedure which a bank, be it ever so honest, can adopt in order to ensure that it is not prima facie liable for the receipt of trust funds. Prima facie liability implies potentially extended periods of expense and uncertainty when litigation is pending; and of course it throws on the defendant the risk that even though the elements of some defence are present, they cannot be proved to the satisfaction of the trier of fact. Although there may be no difference in the classroom between fault-based liability and strict liability with defences, there is a great difference in the courtroom.

---

[149] [1948] Ch 465: see Chapter 18.3(c)(ii), p. 867.

[150] See also Low, 'Recipient Liability in Equity: Resisting the Siren's Lure' (2008) RLR 96.

The better view is that strict liability should not be adopted in this area. This has been strongly supported by the High Court of Australia.[151] Nevertheless, the contrary suggestion has been made judicially. For example, in *Twinsectra Ltd v Yardley*, Lord Millett said, *obiter*: [152]

> Liability for 'knowing receipt' is receipt-based. It does not depend on fault. The cause of action is restitutionary and is available only where the defendant received or applied the money in breach of trust for his own use and benefit … There is powerful academic support for the proposition that the liability of the recipient is the same as in other cases of restitution, that is to say strict but subject to a change of position defence.

In *Criterion Properties plc v Stratford UK Properties LLC*, Lord Nicholls voiced similar views after the extract given already:[153]

> If, however, the agreement is set aside, B will be accountable for any benefits he may have received from A under the agreement. A will have a proprietary claim, if B still has the assets. Additionally, and irrespective of whether B still has the assets in question, A will have a personal claim against B for unjust enrichment, subject always to a defence of change of position. B's personal accountability will not be dependent upon proof of fault or 'unconscionable' conduct on his part. B's accountability, in this regard, will be 'strict'.

For Lord Nicholls to adopt this approach is unsurprising, given his earlier extra-judicial comments. Such comments from the House of Lords clearly need to be taken seriously, but it must also be remembered they were *obiter*, given that the House was not persuaded that there had been a breach of duty that would give rise to a claim. The current approach is well-stated by Nourse LJ in *Akindele*, who considered Lord Nicholls' extra-judicial writing and said:[154]

> No argument before us was based on the suggestions made in Lord Nicholls's essay. Indeed, at this level of decision, it would have been a fruitless exercise. We must continue to do our best with the accepted formulation of the liability in knowing receipt, seeking to simplify and improve it where we may. While in general it may be possible to sympathise with a tendency to subsume a further part of our law of restitution under the principles of unjust enrichment, I beg leave to doubt whether strict liability coupled with a change of position defence would be preferable to fault-based liability in many commercial transactions, for example where, as here, the receipt is of a company's funds which have been misapplied by its directors. Without having heard argument it is unwise to be dogmatic, but in such a case it would appear to be commercially unworkable and contrary to the spirit of the rule in *Royal British Bank v Turquand* (1856) 6 E & B 327 that, simply on proof of an internal misapplication of the company's funds, the burden should shift to the recipient to defend the receipt either by a change of position or perhaps in some other way. Moreover, if the circumstances of the receipt are such as to make it unconscionable for the recipient to retain the benefit of it, there is an obvious difficulty in saying that it is equitable for a change of position to afford him a defence.

---

[151] *Farah Constructions Pty Ltd v Say-Dee Pty Ltd* [2007] HCA 292, [155].
[152] [2002] UKHL 12; [2002] 2 AC 164, [105]. See also *Dubai Aluminium Co. Ltd v Salaam* [2002] UKHL 448; [2003] 2 AC 366, 391 (Lord Millett).
[153] [2004] UKHL 28; [2004] 1 WLR 1856; this extract follows on from that given at Chapter 19.3(b), pp. 953–4.
[154] [2001] Ch 437, 456.

Nourse LJ was right to reject the possibility of a change of position defence to unconscionable receipt: since the recipient is a wrongdoer, the recipient cannot have changed his or her position in good faith.[155] This passage also shows that the intervention of the Supreme Court or Parliament will be required if the law is to develop along strict liability lines; this seems unlikely to happen for quite some time, if at all.

Nevertheless, given the weight of support in favour of strict liability, two further points deserve to be raised. First, even if a strict liability claim is recognized, a concurrent fault-based claim for dishonest assistance would still exist. The latter would enable claimants to recover their losses and would not be defeated by the defence of change of position, and the former would focus on the defendant's receipt but would be subject to the change of position defence. The claimant might then be able to choose between the compensatory and restitutionary measure, and may not be disadvantaged by the strict liability claim.

Secondly, many of the proponents of strict liability in this area use the language of 'unjust enrichment'. This is controversial. Admittedly, *Lipkin Gorman*, the leading case at Common Law, was said by the House of Lords to be a case of unjust enrichment, but it might also be analysed as an example of the vindication of legal property rights.[156] Choosing the appropriate means of analyzing these claims was considered in the previous chapter and is equally relevant here.

(a) Defences

If the claimant manages to establish the key elements of unconscionable receipt, it will be very difficult for the defendant to escape liability. It will not matter if the defendant paid for the property, since the defendant will not, *ex hypothesi*, be acting bona fides. And even if a change of position defence were available, for the reasons given already it would not assist a defendant in bad faith. In order to evade the consequences of equitable liability, a defendant would be best advised to dispute one of the necessary elements of a claim. However, it may be that the third party will not be liable if the limitation period has expired; the defence of limitation was considered in Chapter 16.[157]

(e) REMEDIES

In *Novoship (UK) Ltd v Nikitin*,[158] the Court of Appeal said that:

> the knowing recipient … has, in principle, the responsibility of an express trustee.

The most common remedy for unconscionable receipt is a personal restitutionary remedy for the value of the property received. In *Crown Dilmun v Sutton*, Peter Smith J said that the defendant is:[159]

> liable to account for the profits it has received, or will make, by reason of the acquisition of property with notice that it was acquired in breach of fiduciary duty.

155 See Chapter 18.6(b), p. 916.
156 See Chapter 18.6(b), pp. 916–17.
157 See Chapter 16.9(b)(i), pp. 784–7.
158 [2014] EWCA Civ 908; [2015] QB 499, [82].
159 [2004] EWHC 52; [2004] 1 BCLC 468, [204].

Generally, the value of the profits will be assessed at the date of receipt. But Equity is sufficiently flexible to value the gains made by the defendant at a later date.[160] Indeed, the language of 'liable as a constructive trustee' might suggest that the defendant should be liable for any subsequent gains as if he or she were a trustee. However, if the claimant's losses exceed the defendant's gains, then a compensatory remedy should be available; after all, the defendant has committed a wrong and should not be able to deny a duty to compensate. In *Central Bank of Nigeria v Williams*, Lord Sumption said:[161]

> The essence of a liability to account on the footing of knowing receipt is that the defendant has accepted trust assets knowing that they were transferred to him in breach of trust and that he had no right to receive them. His possession is therefore at all times wrongful and adverse to the rights of both the true trustees and the beneficiaries. No trust has been reposed in him. He does not have the powers or duties of a trustee, for example with regard to investment or management. His sole obligation of any practical significance is to restore the assets immediately. It is true that he may be accountable for any profit that would have been made or any loss that would have been avoided if the assets had remained in the hands of the true trustees and been dealt with according to the trust. There may also, in some circumstances, be a proprietary claim. But all this is simply the measure of the remedy. It does not make him a trustee or bring him within the provisions of the Limitation Act relating to trustees.

This emphasizes the distinction between the personal remedies for unconscionable receipt and the proprietary remedies, which is examined in Chapter 18.

An unconscionable recipient will often have to bear the claimant's losses alone: a common reason for bringing a claim against a third party rather than a wrongdoing fiduciary is that the third party is more likely to provide adequate redress. The fiduciary may be insolvent. Nevertheless, in some situations the fiduciary may also be able to satisfy the claim, and in such situations the recipient is able to seek contribution from that fiduciary.

Contribution was examined in Chapter 16.[162] As a reminder, the Civil Liability (Contribution) Act 1978 provides:

> s.1(1) Subject to the following provisions of this section, any person liable in respect of any damage suffered by another person may recover contribution from any other person liable in respect of the same damage (whether jointly with him or otherwise).
>
> …
>
> s.6(1) A person is liable in respect of any damage for the purposes of this Act if the person who suffered it (or anyone representing his estate or dependants) is entitled to recover compensation from him in respect of that damage (whatever the legal basis of his liability, whether tort, breach of contract, breach of trust or otherwise).

Contribution is easy where both parties are liable for the claimant's loss. But in the sorts of situation under present consideration, the remedy for unconscionable receipt will generally be a *restitutionary* remedy for the gains made by the defendant's receipt. Can the 1978 Act still apply? The Court of Appeal in *City Index Ltd v Gawler*[163] answered affirmatively. The Court held that even though the remedy for unconscionable receipt was restitutionary, it could also be characterized as compensatory,

---

[160] Cf. *Sinclair Investments (UK) Ltd v Versailles Trade Finance Ltd* [2011] EWCA Civ 347; [2012] Ch 453.
[161] [2014] UKSC 10; [2014] AC 1189, [31].
[162] See Chapter 16.5(b)(i), p. 775.
[163] [2007] EWCA Civ 1382; [2008] Ch 313.

since the defendant was liable to make good the loss suffered by the trust or principal to the extent of the value that the defendant had received. It followed that a defendant who was liable for unconscionable receipt could be considered to be liable for the 'same damage' as a defendant who was liable for negligence and so a claim for contribution might lie. Carnwath LJ observed:[164]

> I have some sympathy with the observation of Brightman J in *Bartlett v Barclays Bank Trust Co Ltd (No 2)* [1980] Ch 515, 545B, quoted by Sir Andrew Morritt C, that: 'the so-called restitution which the [trustee] must now make to the plaintiffs ... is in reality compensation for loss suffered by the plaintiffs ... not readily distinguishable from damages except with the aid of a powerful legal microscope.' It seems unlikely that the draftsman of the 1978 Act intended its application to depend on such subtle distinctions of nomenclature.

The result is clearly sensible: there is no reason to force a recipient to bear the entire costs of the breach of trust. But squeezing a restitutionary remedy within 'damage' is difficult and unconvincing. However, it is suggested that any discomfort with the reasoning must be overcome on policy grounds.[165]

Even if contribution is available in principle, it still needs to be ascertained to what *extent* contribution should be allowed. The Court of Appeal in *Gawler* considered this issue, and highlighted the court's broad discretion to do what is just and equitable as between the parties. Clearly, the relative levels of fault of the parties must be ascertained: if the fiduciary was negligent but the recipient unconscionable, it might be sensible for the recipient to pay the greater share. The same might well be true if the recipient still has the property in question. However, it seems that any liability to make contribution should operate only to the extent that the value of the claimant's loss corresponds to the value of the defendant's gain,[166] for only then can the parties be considered to be liable for the same damage.

4. LIABILITY OF PARTNERS

Another question that arises concerns the vicarious liability of partners in a partnership for one of their number who is held liable for a wrong. This is relevant to the two principal heads of liability considered in this chapter: dishonest assistance and unconscionable receipt are both wrongs.

PARTNERSHIP ACT 1890

s.10 Liability of the firm for wrongs

Where, by any wrongful act or omission of any partner acting in the ordinary course of the business of the firm, or with the authority of his co-partners, loss or injury is caused to any person not being a partner in the firm, or any penalty is incurred, the firm is liable therefor to the same extent as the partner so acting or omitting to act.

The leading discussion can be found in the decision of the House of Lords in *Dubai Aluminium Co. Ltd v Salaam*,[167] where a partner in a firm of solicitors was held liable for dishonestly assisting a

---

[164] Ibid, [27].
[165] Cf. Gardner, 'Moment of Trust for Knowing Receipt?' (2009) 125 LQR 20, 23.
[166] Goymour, 'A Contribution to Knowing Receipt Liability? (*City Index v Gawler*)' [2008] RLR 113, 118.
[167] [2002] UKHL 48; [2003] 2 AC 366.

fraudulent scheme. In holding that the firm was liable for the acts of the solicitor even though these were unauthorized, because the fraudulent scheme was closely connected with the acts that the dishonest solicitor was authorized to do, Lord Nicholls considered the interpretation of section 10 of the Partnership Act.[168]

> ... There is nothing in the language of section 10 to suggest that the phrase 'any wrongful act or omission' is intended to be confined to common law torts. On the contrary, the reference to incurring a penalty points away from such a narrow interpretation of the phrase. The liability of co-partners for penalties incurred, for instance, for breach of revenue laws was well established when the 1890 Act was passed: see *Lindley on Partnership*, 6th ed (1893), p 160, and *Attorney-General v Stannyforth* (1721) Bunb 97.
>
> In addition to the language the statutory context points in the same direction. Section 10 applies only to the conduct of a partner acting in the ordinary course of the firm's business or with the authority of his co-partners. It would be remarkable if a firm were liable for fraudulent misrepresentations made by a partner so acting, but not liable for dishonest participation by a partner in conduct directed at the misappropriation of another's property. In both cases the liability of the wrongdoing partner arises from dishonesty. In terms of the firm's liability there can be no rational basis for distinguishing one case from the other. Both fall naturally within the description of a 'wrongful act'.
>
> ...
>
> Vicarious liability is concerned with the responsibility of the firm to other persons for wrongful acts done by a partner while acting in the ordinary course of the partnership business or with the authority of his co-partners. At first sight this might seem something of a contradiction in terms. Partners do not usually agree with each other to commit wrongful acts. Partners are not normally authorised to engage in wrongful conduct. Indeed, if vicarious liability of a firm for acts done by a partner acting in the ordinary course of the business of the firm were confined to acts authorised in every particular, the reach of vicarious liability would be short indeed. Especially would this be so with dishonesty and other intentional wrongdoing, as distinct from negligence. Similarly restricted would be the vicarious responsibility of employers for wrongful acts done by employees in the course of their employment. Like considerations apply to vicarious liability for employees.
>
> ... liability for agents should not be strictly confined to acts done with the employer's authority. Negligence can be expected to occur from time to time. Everyone makes mistakes at times. Additionally, it is a fact of life, and therefore to be expected by those who carry on businesses, that sometimes their agents may exceed the bounds of their authority or even defy express instructions. It is fair to allocate risk of losses thus arising to the businesses rather than leave those wronged with the sole remedy, of doubtful value, against the individual employee who committed the wrong. To this end, the law has given the concept of 'ordinary course of employment' an extended scope.

The scope of the reasoning in *Salaam* is not, however, as wide as it might at first appear: a firm of solicitors will not be vicariously liable for a solicitor who has committed a wrong as an express trustee[169] or as a trustee *de son tort*, because it is not within the ordinary scope of a solicitor's practice to act as a trustee.[170]

---

[168] Ibid, [10]–[22].
[169] *Walker v Stones* [2001] QB 902.
[170] *Dubai Aluminium Co. Ltd v Salaam* [2002] UKHL 48; [2003] 2 AC 366, [143] (Lord Millett).

QUESTION

Trevor is the trustee of a family trust for his two nieces, Helen and Rebecca. Trevor asks his solicitor, Sam, for advice about how to manage the trust fund. Sam encourages Trevor to purchase Rob's land as an investment for the trust for £1 million. Trevor thought this might be a good investment because it was possible to build a block of flats on the land. Planning permission for such development has since been refused, and the land is only worth £200,000.

There is a clause in the trust deed that prevents the trustee from purchasing land for the trust. Trevor had forgotten about this. Sam suspected that there might be such a clause in the trust instrument, but did not bother to check. However, Sam did tell Rob, who was a friend of his, that he was worried about whether or not Trevor could purchase the land with trust monies. Rob decided to ignore Sam's fears, and celebrated the sale of his land by investing all the money in a start-up venture which has completely failed.

Trevor also took £1,000 from the trust money and gave it to his sister, Jenna, as a birthday present. This was clearly in breach of trust. Jenna knew that Trevor was the trustee of the settlement for Helen and Rebecca, and thought it surprising that her usually stingy brother was so generous to her.

Advise Helen and Rebecca.

FURTHER READING

Birks, 'Receipt' in *Breach of Trust* (eds Birks and Pretto) (Oxford: Hart, 2002).

Conaglen and Nolan, 'Contract and knowing receipt: principles and application' (2013) 129 LQR 359.

Davies, *Accessory Liability* (Oxford: Hart, 2015) ch. 4.

Elliott and Mitchell, 'Remedies for Dishonest Assistance' (2004) 67 MLR 16.

Harpum, 'The Stranger as Constructive Trustee' (1986) 102 LQR 114 and 267.

Harpum, 'The Basis of Equitable Liability' in *The Frontiers of Liability, Vol 1.* (ed. Birks) (Oxford: Oxford University Press, 1994).

Mitchell, 'Assistance' in *Breach of Trust* (eds Birks and Pretto) (Oxford: Hart, 2002).

Mitchell and Watterson, 'Remedies for Knowing Receipt', in *Constructive and Resulting Trusts* (ed. Mitchell) (Oxford: Hart, 2010).

Lord Nicholls of Birkenhead, 'Knowing Receipt: The Need for a New Landmark' in *Restitution: Past, Present and Future* (eds Cornish, Nolan, O'Sullivan, and Virgo) (Oxford: Hart, 1998), pp. 231.

Ridge, 'Justifying the Remedies for Dishonest Assistance' (2008) 124 LQR 445.

Smith, 'Unjust Enrichment, Property, and the Structure of Trusts' (2000) 116 LQR 412.

Lord Walker, 'Dishonesty and Unconscionable Conduct in Commercial Life—Some Reflections on Accessory Liability and Knowing Receipt' (2005) 27 Sydney LR 187.

PART IX

ORDERS

20

EQUITABLE ORDERS

CENTRAL ISSUES

1. Equitable orders can be granted in support of both legal and equitable rights.

2. Equitable remedies are only available where Common Law remedies (often damages) are inadequate.

3. Failure to comply with equitable orders constitutes contempt of court, which can be punished by imprisonment and fines.

4. The court may refuse to grant equitable relief if innocent third parties would be prejudiced by the equitable order, or if there has been laches or acquiescence.

5. Injunctions direct parties either to do something (mandatory injunctions) or not to do something (prohibitory injunctions). The latter may be granted more readily than the former.

6. The jurisdiction to grant injunctive relief includes the ability to award interim injunctions whilst waiting for the substantive trial.

7. Two particularly important types of interim injunction are freezing orders, by which the court can prevent a party from dealing with his or her assets, and search orders, which force the defendant to allow the claimant to search his or her premises for relevant material.

8. Specific performance is an equitable remedy, which requires a party to perform a particular positive obligation.

9. The Court has a discretion to award damages in lieu of an injunction or specific performance if justice so requires.

10. The remedy of rectification enables mistakes in documents to be corrected and ensures that the document corresponds with the intention of those who entered into the instrument.

11. Rescission is a remedy that enables a transaction to be treated as though it had never come into existence, and the parties are restored to their position prior to the transaction.

1. GENERAL PRINCIPLES

It was seen in Chapter 1 that Equity has a creative function to provide remedies to moderate the rigours of the Common Law. The creative function is illustrated most effectively by the law relating to trusts and trustees, as has been seen through the chapters in this book. But this creativity is also exemplified by a number of equitable orders, the significance of which is not limited to the law of trusts and trustees. This chapter will focus upon the commercially significant remedies of injunctions, specific performance, rectification, and rescission. Given that the latter three are often considered in depth on contract courses and in contract textbooks,[1] we will concentrate predominantly upon injunctions.

Although it is true that damages for the breach of Common Law obligations are available 'as of right', and that equitable remedies are inevitably discretionary, it is important to recognize that such discretion is informed by a number of key principles. Importantly, equitable remedies are only available where Common Law remedies are inadequate: Equity can only intervene where the Common Law fails to do justice. However, equitable orders can be made in support of both legal and equitable rights. Failure to comply with an equitable order constitutes the crime of contempt, the punishment for which may be imprisonment, sequestration of the defendant's assets, or a fine—or a combination of these sentences.

(a) BARS TO EQUITABLE ORDERS

Factors that may lead to particular types of equitable orders not being granted will be considered later in this chapter. However, Equity has developed some general bars to equitable relief. For example, echoing the maxim, 'Equity will not act in vain', Lord Hatherley LC has insisted that the court will not make:[2]

> an idle and ineffectual order. The simplest illustration of this is the case of cutting down timber. It would be idle when the trees have been cut down to make an order not to allow the trees to remain prostrate, and all that can be done in such a case is to leave the parties to their remedy for damages.

The maxim that 'He who comes to Equity must come with clean hands'[3] is similarly applicable; the court is unlikely to grant an order in favour of a claimant who has misled the court.[4] Nor is the court likely to grant equitable relief if to do so would prejudice any third party interests acquired for value and in good faith,[5] or if the claimant is estopped from relying upon his or her right.[6] Acquiescence and lapse of time may also bar equitable relief. Acquiescence requires conduct that shows the claimant has waived his or her rights and is thereby estopped from later asserting those rights, but does not inevitably involve any delay.[7] Laches, on the other hand, simply requires delay and not necessarily acquiescence. In *Lester v Woodgate*, Patten LJ distinguished the two.

Lester v Woodgate [2010] EWCA Civ 199; [2010] 2 P & CR DG 14, [20]–[22]

> Although the Recorder mentions laches and estoppel together in his judgment, they are separate defences with different and distinct consequences. Laches is a general equitable defence which bars the grant of equitable relief when the claimant has been guilty of undue delay in asserting his rights: see the

---

[1] See e.g. McKendrick, *Contract Law: Text, Cases and Materials* (6th edn) (Oxford: Oxford University Press, 2014).
[2] *Attorney-General v Colney Hatch Lunatic Asylum* (1868) 4 Ch App 146, 154 per Lord Hatherley LC.
[3] See Chapter 1.5(b), pp. 16–18.
[4] *Armstrong v Sheppard & Short Ltd* [1959] 2 QB 384. See also *Gonthier v Orange Contract Scaffolding Ltd* [2003] EWCA Civ 873; *Richardson v Blackmore* [2005] EWCA Civ 1356; [2006] BCC 276.
[5] See Chapter 18.6(a), p. 911.
[6] See Chapter 9.4, p. 469.
[7] *Duke of Leeds v Earl of Amherst* [1846] 2 Ph 117, 123.

judgment of Sir Barnes Peacock in *Lindsay Petroleum Company v Hurd* (1874) LR 5 PC 221 at page 239 (recently endorsed by the House of Lords in *Fisher v Brooker* [2009] UKHL 41) where he said:—

> "Now the doctrine of laches in Courts of Equity is not an arbitrary or a technical doctrine. Where it would be practically unjust to give a remedy, either because a party has, by his conduct, done that which might fairly be regarded as equivalent to a waiver of it, or where by his conduct and neglect he has, though perhaps not waiving that remedy, yet put the other party in a situation in which it would not be reasonable to place him if the remedy were afterwards to be asserted, in either of these cases lapse of time and delay are most material. But in every case, if an argument against relief, which otherwise would be just, is founded upon mere delay, that delay of course not amounting to a bar by any statute of limitations, the validity of that defence must be tried upon principles substantially equitable. Two circumstances, always important in such cases, are the length of the delay and the nature of the acts done during the interval, which might affect either party and cause a balance of justice or injustice in taking the one course or the other, so far as relates to the remedy."

The word laches is also sometimes used to denote the type of passive conduct which can amount to acquiescence and so found an estoppel when it can be shown that the party standing by has induced the would-be defendant to believe that his rights will not be enforced and that other party has, as a consequence, acted in a way which would make the subsequent enforcement of those rights unconscionable.

But where the conduct relied on consists of no more than undue delay, it operates only to bar the grant of equitable relief such as an injunction. It does not extinguish the claimants' legal right or bar its enforcement by, for example, the award of common law damages.

2. INJUNCTIONS

(a) TYPES OF INJUNCTION

An injunction is an order of the court directing a party either to do something (mandatory injunction) or to refrain from doing something (prohibitory or negative injunction). An injunction not to stop providing a service might look negative on the surface, but in substance it is a mandatory injunction to continue to provide the service.

An injunction granted before the substantive trial of an action is called an interlocutory, or interim, injunction. Final injunctions are granted after the court has tried the substance of a claim. Final injunctions are sometimes called perpetual injunctions, but they do not necessarily last forever; a final injunction might be granted only until the end of a lease.[8]

An injunction may be granted even though the claimant's rights have not yet been infringed. Such 'quia timet'[9] injunctions can be granted where interference with the claimant's rights is threatened or feared but has not yet occurred. However, the court will not easily grant such injunctions; as Lord Dunedin commented in *A-G for the Dominion of Canada v Ritchie Contracting and Supply Co Ltd*:[10]

> no one can obtain a *quia timet* order by merely saying 'Timeo';[11] he must aver and prove that what is going on is calculated to infringe his rights.

---

[8] *Moore v Ullcoats Mining Co. Ltd* [1908] 1 Ch 575, 585.
[9] The Latin might be translated as: 'because he fears'.
[10] [1919] AC 999, 1005.
[11] The Latin might be translated as: 'I fear'.

In *Fletcher v Bealey*, Pearson J set out further criteria:[12]

> I do not think ... that I shall be very far wrong if I lay it down that there are at least two necessary ingredients for a *quia timet* action. There must, if no actual damage is proved, be proof of imminent danger, and there must also be proof that the apprehended damage will, if it comes, be very substantial. I should almost say it must be proved that it will be irreparable, because, if the danger is not proved to be so imminent that no one can doubt that, if the remedy is delayed, the damage will be suffered, I think it must be shewn that, if the damage does occur at any time, it will come in such a way and under such circumstances that it will be impossible for the Plaintiff to protect himself against it if relief is denied to him in a *quia timet* action.

This raises a point of more general importance: an injunction will not be granted where damages would be an adequate remedy. This was clearly expressed by Lindley LJ in *London and Blackwall Ry v Cross*:[13]

> The very first principle of injunction law is that prima facie you do not obtain injunctions to restrain actionable wrongs for which damages are the proper remedy.

(b) JURISDICTION

The jurisdiction of the courts to grant injunctions is of long-standing, and has now been recognized by statute.

SENIOR COURTS ACT 1981

37. Powers of High Court with respect to injunctions and receivers

The High Court may by order (whether interlocutory or final) grant an injunction. ... in all cases in which it appears to the court to be just and convenient to do so.

(1) Any such order may be made either unconditionally or on such terms and conditions as the court thinks just.

(c) MANDATORY INJUNCTIONS

It is clearly within the courts' power to grant an injunction to force somebody to take positive action where they have an obligation to do so. This was discussed by the House of Lords in *Redland Bricks Ltd v Morris*.[14]

---

[12] (1885) 28 Ch D 688, 698.
[13] (1886) 31 Ch D 354, [369].
[14] [1970] AC 652.

Redland Bricks Ltd v Morris [1970] AC 652, 665–6

The appellant's excavation of clay had left a pit into which the respondent's land was slipping. The respondent obtained an injunction, which required the appellant to restore support to the respondent's land within six months. The appellant appealed to the House of Lords on the grounds that damages were an adequate remedy. In allowing the appeal, the House of Lords considered broader issues concerning the nature of the jurisdiction to grant a mandatory injunction.

Lord Upjohn:

[T]he case … which is before your Lordships' House is typical, where the defendant has withdrawn support from his neighbour's land or where he has so acted in depositing his soil from his mining operations as to constitute a menace to the plaintiff's land. It is in this field that the undoubted jurisdiction of equity to grant a mandatory injunction, that is an injunction ordering the defendant to carry out positive works, finds its main expression, though of course it is equally applicable to many other cases. Thus, to take the simplest example, if the defendant, the owner of land, including a metalled road over which the plaintiff has a right of way, ploughs up that land so that it is no longer usable, no doubt a mandatory injunction will go to restore it; damages are not a sufficient remedy, for the plaintiff has no right to go upon the defendant's land to remake his right of way.

… The grant of a mandatory injunction is, of course, entirely discretionary and unlike a negative injunction can never be 'as of course'. Every case must depend essentially upon its own particular circumstances. Any general principles for its application can only be laid down in the most general terms:

1. A mandatory injunction can only be granted where the plaintiff shows a very strong probability upon the facts that grave damage will accrue to him in the future. … It is a jurisdiction to be exercised sparingly and with caution but in the proper case unhesitatingly.

2. Damages will not be a sufficient or adequate remedy if such damage does happen. This is only the application of a general principle of equity …

3. Unlike the case where a negative injunction is granted to prevent the continuance or recurrence of a wrongful act the question of the cost to the defendant to do works to prevent or lessen the likelihood of a future apprehended wrong must be an element to be taken into account:

   (a) where the defendant has acted without regard to his neighbour's rights, or has tried to steal a march on him or has tried to evade the jurisdiction of the court or, to sum it up, has acted wantonly and quite unreasonably in relation to his neighbour he may be ordered to repair his wanton and unreasonable acts by doing positive work to restore the status quo even if the expense to him is out of all proportion to the advantage thereby accruing to the plaintiff …

   (b) but where the defendant has acted reasonably, though in the event wrongly, the cost of remedying by positive action his earlier activities is most important for two reasons. First, because no legal wrong has yet occurred (for which he has not been recompensed at law and in equity) and, in spite of gloomy expert opinion, may never occur or possibly only upon a much smaller scale than anticipated. Secondly, because if ultimately heavy damage does occur the plaintiff is in no way prejudiced for he has his action at law and all his consequential remedies in equity.

So the amount to be expended under a mandatory order by the defendant must be balanced with these considerations in mind against the anticipated possible damage to the plaintiff and if, on such balance, it seems unreasonable to inflict such expenditure upon one who for this purpose is no more than a potential wrongdoer then the court must exercise its jurisdiction accordingly. Of course, the court does not have to order such works as upon the evidence before it will remedy the wrong but may think it proper

> to impose upon the defendant the obligation of doing certain works which may upon expert opinion merely lessen the likelihood of any further injury to the plaintiff's land. …
>
> 4. If in the exercise of its discretion the court decides that it is a proper case to grant a mandatory injunction, then the court must be careful to see that the defendant knows exactly in fact what he has to do and this means not as a matter of law but as a matter of fact, so that in carrying out an order he can give his contractors the proper instructions.

Lord Upjohn's reasoning clearly sets out the types of factors courts must consider before granting a mandatory injunction. However, caution should be exercised when considering his suggestion that negative injunctions are available 'as of course'. Negative injunctions are also necessarily discretionary, and never available 'as of right'. Indeed, in *National Commercial Bank Jamaica Ltd v Olint Corpn Ltd* Lord Hoffmann insisted that:[15]

> arguments over whether the injunction should be classified as prohibitive or mandatory are barren.

This is because the same principles underpin the discretion to grant both mandatory and prohibitive injunctions. Nevertheless, as Lord Upjohn indicated, it will often be the case that mandatory injunctions are more intrusive than prohibitive injunctions, and there is little doubt that prohibitive injunctions are more common.

(d) PROHIBITORY INJUNCTIONS

A prohibitory injunction does not force a person to do anything, only to refrain from doing something. For this reason, prohibitory injunctions are not thought to interfere with the defendant's freedom of action to such an objectionable degree as mandatory injunctions. Many examples of prohibitory injunctions could be given. For example, where a private nuisance is established, an injunction will often be used to prevent the nuisance from continuing; injunctive relief avoids the inconvenient alternative of numerous actions for damages from different claimants affected by the nuisance. Similarly, injunctions can be particularly helpful in restraining infringements of intellectual property rights.[16]

(i) *Breach of contract*

Of particular commercial significance are injunctions granted to restrain a breach of contract. In general, an injunction is most appropriate where the obligation is negative. If the obligation is positive, specific performance, considered later,[17] will normally be the appropriate remedy. Admittedly, mandatory injunctions are also available to enforce positive obligations, but such injunctions will not be granted if the result would be tantamount to an order of specific performance in circumstances in which specific performance would not be granted.[18]

Prohibitory injunctions are particularly important in the employment context. Restrictive covenants in an employment contract might be very valuable: an employer may well seek to enforce an employee's contractual obligation not to work for a competitor or in a particular area during a

---

[15] [2009] UKPC 16; [2009] 1 WLR 1405, [20].
[16] E.g. Trade Marks Act 1994, s. 14.
[17] See Chapter 20.3, p. 1008.
[18] See *Co-operative Insurance v Argyll Stores* [1998] AC 1, considered at Chapter 20.3, pp. 1009–10. The same bars that apply to the specific performance of a contract also apply to injunctions.

certain period after the termination of his or her employment. Prohibitory injunctions are often granted in support of such restrictive covenants: there is no question of such injunctions being tantamount to specific performance of a positive obligation. But courts are wary about granting injunctions that would, in effect, force a person to perform his contract. As Fry LJ said in *De Francesco v Barnum*:[19]

> I think the Courts are bound to be jealous, lest they should turn contracts of service into contracts of slavery.

Whether or not positive performance of the agreement would be compelled by a negative injunction preventing the defendant from breaching his or her contract in a particular way can be difficult to decide; the court will consider factors such as the need for the defendant to use his or her competencies to earn a living, the length of time the negative covenant is to be enforced, and how many other opportunities are realistically open to the defendant. In *Lumley v Wagner*,[20] Miss Johanna Wagner, an opera singer, contracted to sing for three months at Mr Lumley's theatre. Miss Wagner then made a conflicting agreement to sing at Mr Gye's theatre, and Mr Lumley successfully sought an injunction to enforce Miss Wagner's negative contractual obligation not to sing for anyone else in that period. The Lord Chancellor commented that:[21]

> It was objected that the operation of the injunction in the present case was mischievous, excluding the Defendant J. Wagner from performing at any other theatre while this Court had no power to compel her to perform at [Mr Lumley's] Her Majesty's Theatre. It is true that I have not the means of compelling her to sing, but she has no cause of complaint if I compel her to abstain from the commission of an act which she has bound herself not to do, and thus possibly cause her to fulfil her engagement. The jurisdiction which I now exercise is wholly within the power of the Court, and being of opinion that it is a proper case for interfering, I shall leave nothing unsatisfied by the judgment I pronounce. The effect, too, of the injunction in restraining J. Wagner from singing elsewhere may, in the event of an action being brought against her by the Plaintiff, prevent any such amount of vindictive damages being given against her as a jury might probably be inclined to give if she had carried her talents and exercised them at the rival theatre: the injunction may also, as I have said, tend to the fulfilment of her engagement; though, in continuing the injunction, I disclaim doing indirectly what I cannot do directly.

As the Lord Chancellor recognized, a possible effect of this injunction was that Miss Wagner would sing for Mr Lumley at his theatre. But Miss Wagner was not compelled to do this. Instead, she might have done something else during that period; three months is not an especially long period of time.

In *Warren v Mendy*,[22] by contrast, a negative injunction was refused where its duration would have been two years. That case concerned Frank Warren, a boxing promoter, who had entered into a contract exclusively to manage a fighter, Nigel Benn. Benn became unhappy with Warren, and entered into an agreement with Ambrose Mendy concerning the introduction of commercial opportunities. Warren sought an injunction to prevent Mendy from inducing Benn's breach of contract with Warren and to prevent Mendy from acting as Benn's manager. The Court of Appeal upheld the decision of the trial judge to refuse an injunction: given the short career a boxer has, an injunction over a two-year

[19] (1890) 45 Ch D 430, 438.
[20] (1852) 1 De GM & G 604. See also *Warner Brothers Pictures Inc. v Nelson* [1937] 1 KB 209.
[21] Ibid, 619–20.
[22] [1989] 1 WLR 853.

period would have effectively compelled Benn to work with Warren. This was particularly inappropriate given the breakdown in mutual trust and confidence between the parties. Nourse LJ reviewed the authorities and said:[23]

> consideration of the authorities has led us to believe that the following general principles are applicable to the grant or refusal of an injunction to enforce performance of the servant's negative obligations in a contract for personal services inseparable from the exercise of some special skill or talent. (We use the expressions 'master' and 'servant' for ease of reference and not out of any regard for the reality of the relationship in many of these cases.) In such a case the court ought not to enforce the performance of the negative obligations if their enforcement will effectively compel the servant to perform his positive obligations under the contract. Compulsion is a question to be decided on the facts of each case, with a realistic regard for the probable reaction of an injunction on the psychological and material, and sometimes the physical, need of the servant to maintain the skill or talent. The longer the term for which an injunction is sought, the more readily will compulsion be inferred. Compulsion may be inferred where the injunction is sought not against the servant but against a third party if either the third party is the only other available master or if it is likely that the master will seek relief against anyone who attempts to replace him. An injunction will less readily be granted where there are obligations of mutual trust and confidence, more especially where the servant's trust in the master may have been betrayed or his confidence in him has genuinely gone.

Ultimately, as Nourse LJ indicates in this passage, whether or not an injunction should be granted is a question of fact. But courts are particularly wary about forcing a person to work against his or her will: the dangers inherent in compelling someone to work for another might outweigh the fear that damages are an inadequate remedy.

Nevertheless, where the calculation of damages is impossible or inadequate, and no injustice will be done, the Court may favour injunctive relief. In *Araci v Fallon*,[24] a leading jockey, Kieron Fallon, signed an agreement to ride a particular horse, Native Khan, whenever requested, and not to ride a rival horse in any race in which he had been asked to ride Native Khan. The owners of Native Khan asked Fallon to ride the horse in the Epsom Derby, but Fallon refused and promised to ride a rival horse instead. The Court of Appeal held that the losses that the owners of Native Khan might suffer were Fallon to pip Native Khan to the title on another horse would be tremendously difficult to quantify, and that damages would be an inadequate remedy; the Court of Appeal therefore granted an injunction, even though it might have the effect of depriving Fallon of racing in the Derby—something that the first instance judge had refused to sanction.[25]

However, it would seem that the reluctance of the courts indirectly to compel a party to work for others is greatly reduced if the defendant is a company. In *Lady Navigation Inc. v Lauritzencool AB*,[26] a charterer managed a pool of ships. The owners of two of those vessels argued that the charterer had mismanaged their ships and threatened to remove their vessels from the pool of ships managed by the charterer. This would have been a breach of contract. The charterer sought an injunction to prevent the owners from removing their ships. The Court of Appeal granted this injunction. Mance LJ insisted that this was not tantamount to specific performance, observing that they were 'juristically distinct'.[27] For example, the owners could comply with their obligations by simply allowing the

---

[23] Ibid, 865–8.

[24] [2011] EWCA Civ 668.

[25] In the event, Fallon did not ride in the Derby, and Native Khan finished 5th, one place higher than the horse Fallon was due to ride.

[26] [2005] EWCA Civ 579; [2005] 2 Lloyd's Rep. 63.

[27] Ibid, [10].

vessels to lay idle. Mance LJ cited cases such as *Lumley v Wagner* and *Warren v Mendy*, and expressed the opinion that:[28]

> Even if one is considering a contract for services far more easily described as personal in nature than the present, there is no inflexible principle precluding negative injunctive relief which prevents activity outside the contract contrary to its terms.
>
> …
>
> The present relationships are between business concerns who, in the event of such relief, can be expected to continue to make them work in their own interests, and to sort out any complaints in arbitration if necessary hereafter. …
>
> In conclusion, neither the fact that the contracts involved were for services in the form of a time charter nor the existence under such contracts of a fiduciary relationship of mutual trust and confidence represents in law any necessary or general objection in principle to the grant of injunctive relief precluding the [owners] from employing their vessels outside the pool pending the outcome of the current arbitration. Nor does it afford any such objection to the grant of such relief that the only realistic commercial course which it left to the appellants was, as I am prepared to assume, to do what they have done, namely to continue to provide the vessels to the pool and to perform the charters.

This approach might be more generous to claimants than that taken where the defendant is a particular individual. But if preventing a company from breaching an obligation would simply involve the company's asking its employees or contractor to comply with one set of obligations rather than another, this does not seem so objectionable. Clearly, it is far removed from the spectre of slavery, which is sometimes raised by the courts.

A greater willingness to grant injunctions to restrain a breach of contract might also be discerned from the decision of the Court of Appeal in *AB v CD*.[29] The parties entered into a licensing agreement, under which AB obtained the right to market CD's internet-based platform. A clause in the contract purported to exclude liability for loss of profits in the event of a breach, or of any cause of action, and also to cap the recoverable damages under any head of claim according to a prescribed formula. AB sought an interim injunction[30] to require CD not to terminate the agreement. At first instance, the judge refused to grant an injunction as he considered that AB would be adequately compensated by damages. A unanimous Court of Appeal allowed AB's appeal, insisting that the clause in the contract should be taken into account when deciding whether or not the remedies which would be available at common law were adequate to reflect the substantial justice of the situation. As Underhill LJ put it:[31]

> The primary obligation of a party is to perform the contract. The requirement to pay damages in the event of a breach is a secondary obligation, and an agreement to restrict the recoverability of damages in the event of a breach cannot be treated as an agreement to excuse performance of that primary obligation. I share Mance LJ's rejection of the position advanced by Mowlem [in *Bath and North East Somerset DC v Mowlem Plc* [2004] EWCA Civ 115; [2015] 1 WLR 785] that, even where a provision limited the victim of a breach to damages which bore no relation to its loss, those damages had nevertheless to be regarded an adequate remedy: see the end of para. 14 of his judgment. [Counsel's] stance was the same before us, as logically it had to be: even in the case of the most gross and cynical breach

---

[28] Ibid, [20], [32]–[33].

[29] [2014] EWCA Civ 229; [2015] 1 WLR 771.

[30] See Chapter 20.2(e), p. 987, although the thrust of the reasoning seems equally applicable to final injunctions: see e.g. [2014] EWCA Civ 229; [2015] 1 WLR 771, [32] (Ryder LJ).

[31] [2014] EWCA Civ 229; [2015] 1 WLR 771, [27]–[29].

> of contract, if – as was likely to be the case – the only losses suffered which would sound in damages were of a kind which were excluded by the contract, no injunction would lie and the contract-breaker would be able to walk away from his obligations with impunity. That does not seem to me to be just. The rule – if 'rule' is the right word – that an injunction should not be granted where damages would be an adequate remedy should be applied in a way which reflects the substantial justice of the situation: that is, after all, the basis of the jurisdiction under section 37.
>
> Viewed in this way, there is no question of, as [counsel] contended, the commercial expectations of the parties being undermined. The primary commercial expectation must be that the parties will perform their obligations. The expectations created (indeed given contractual force) by an exclusion or limitation clause are expectations about what damages will be recoverable in the event of breach; but that is not the same thing.
>
> This approach also seems to me to sit better with the acceptance by this Court that an injunction may in an appropriate case be granted even where the loss caused by a threatened breach would not sound in damages. ... That is a separate but similar instance of the court refusing to allow a mechanistic application of the 'damages an adequate remedy' rule to prevent the victim of a breach being able to enforce compliance with the primary obligations under the contract.

The logic of this reasoning is clear. Contracts should be performed, and clauses which limit the amount of damages payable do not undermine this point: such clauses restrict the secondary obligation to pay damages in the event of breach, but not the primary obligation to perform. Injunctive relief therefore remains available, and the court is entitled to consider wider losses which would be irrecoverable if an injunction were not granted. Although parties cannot bind the courts to grant an injunction through their contractual arrangement,[32] *AB v CD* usefully highlights that equitable relief cannot easily be sidelined by a term in the contract.

(ii) *Tort*

Injunctions in tort law tend to be granted to protect property rights. It may be that injunctive relief should be granted for a wider range of torts,[33] but a focus on property torts is understandable. An important aspect of property rights is the ability to choose whether or not to release those rights. Indeed, prohibitory injunctions have even been said to have been awarded 'as of course' in the context of trespass.[34] Similarly, nuisance is a tort against land; it protects property rights.[35] Property rights are concerned with land use rather than land value[36] and, as a result, injunctions should be the prima facie remedy available in response to an ongoing nuisance.

However, in *Coventry v Lawrence*, Lord Sumption said:[37]

> There is much to be said for the view that damages are ordinarily an adequate remedy for nuisance and that an injunction should not usually be granted in a case where it is likely that conflicting interests are engaged other than the parties' interests. In particular, it may well be that an injunction should as a matter of principle not be granted in a case where a use of land to which objection is taken requires and has received planning permission.

---

[32] *Warner Brothers Pictures, Incorporated v Nelson* [1937] 1 KB 209, 221 (Branson J).
[33] Murphy, 'Rethinking Injunctions in Tort Law' (2007) 27 OJLS 509.
[34] *Anchor Brewhouse Developments Ltd v Berkley House (Docklands Developments) Ltd* [1987] 2 EGLR 173, 176 (Scott J); see too *Redland Bricks Ltd v Morris* [1970] AC 652, 665 (Lord Upjohn).
[35] *Hunter v Canary Wharf* [1997] AC 655.
[36] Dixon, 'The Sound of Silence' [2014] Conv 79, 84.
[37] [2014] UKSC 13; [2014] AC 822, [161].

To take such a step would involve a significant re-appraisal of the law of nuisance. Lord Mance in particular was uncomfortable with this idea,[38] and it is inconsistent with the approach of the majority in the Supreme Court. Injunctive relief to restrain a nuisance remains the starting point for a court when determining what remedies to award. However, the law on remedies for nuisance appears to be in a state of flux, and it may be that the notion that equitable relief will generally be granted to restrain a nuisance will come under continued attack. This will be examined further when considering damages in lieu of an injunction later.[39]

(iii) *Breach of confidence and privacy*

Injunctions are also regularly granted in order to protect confidential information. Detailed consideration of confidence is outside the scope of this book,[40] but this area has gained much attention recently, particularly since it has been used to protect a person's right to privacy. Injunctions might be particularly important in this context because confidence, once lost, is lost forever. Damages at Common Law are patently unable to keep something confidential. The equitable jurisdiction has therefore been much relied upon, and this jurisdiction continues to evolve. For example, many injunctions granted in this area have been anonymized, which is a sensible way to ensure that information remains confidential. There are many reasons for anonymity; Eady J has observed that:[41]

> It is important always to remember that the modern law of privacy is not concerned solely with secrets: it is also concerned importantly with intrusion.

A further step has been to prevent even the very reporting of an injunction. Such 'super-injunctions' are granted because disclosure would have the effect of rendering the injunction nugatory: even reporting that an injunction has been granted would allow the confidential information to seep out. These 'super-injunctions' have unsurprisingly received much attention in the press, given the onerous restrictions on freedom of expression that they impose. In *JIH v Newsgroup Newspapers Ltd*,[42] Lord Neuberger MR set out the following principles when deciding whether to grant the claimant an anonymity order or other restraint on publication of details of a case that would normally be in the public domain:

JIH v Newsgroup Newspapers Ltd [2011] EWCA Civ 42; [2011] 1 WLR 1645, [21] (Neuberger MR)

(1) The general rule is that the names of the parties to an action are included in orders and judgments of the court.

(2) There is no general exception for cases where private matters are in issue.

---

[38] Ibid, [168].

[39] See Chapter 20.6, p. 1014.

[40] For full consideration, see Aplin, Bently, Johnson, and Malynicz, *Gurry on Breach of Confidence* (2nd edn) (Oxford: Oxford University Press, 2012).

[41] *CTB v NGN* [2011] EWHC 1326 (QB).

[42] [2011] EWCA Civ 42. See also *Report of the Committee on Super-Injunctions: Super-Injunctions, Anonymised Injunctions and Open Justice*, May 20, 2011 (MR Report 2011) (London: HMSO).

(3) An order for anonymity or any other order restraining the publication of the normally reportable details of a case is a derogation from the principle of open justice and an interference with the Article 10[43] rights of the public at large.

(4) Accordingly, where the court is asked to make any such order, it should only do so after closely scrutinising the application, and considering whether a degree of restraint on publication is necessary, and, if it is, whether there is any less restrictive or more acceptable alternative than that which is sought.

(5) Where the court is asked to restrain the publication of the names of the parties and/or the subject matter of the claim, on the ground that such restraint is necessary under Article 8,[44] the question is whether there is sufficient general, public interest in publishing a report of the proceedings which identifies a party and/or the normally reportable details to justify any resulting curtailment of his right and his family's right to respect for their private and family life.

(6) On any such application, no special treatment should be accorded to public figures or celebrities: in principle, they are entitled to the same protection as others, no more and no less.

(7) An order for anonymity or for reporting restrictions should not be made simply because the parties consent: parties cannot waive the rights of the public.

(8) An anonymity order or any other order restraining publication made by a Judge at an interlocutory stage of an injunction application does not last for the duration of the proceedings but must be reviewed at the return date.

(9) Whether or not an anonymity order or an order restraining publication of normally reportable details is made, then, at least where a judgment is or would normally be given, a publicly available judgment should normally be given, and a copy of the consequential court order should also be publicly available, although some editing of the judgment or order may be necessary.

(10) Notice of any hearing should be given to the defendant unless there is a good reason not to do so, in which case the court should be told of the absence of notice and the reason for it, and should be satisfied that the reason is a good one.

In any given case, the equitable jurisdiction is sufficiently flexible to grant a super-injunction or no injunction at all, and a range of options lie between these two extremes. Injunctions are a powerful weapon in safeguarding a person's right to privacy, but granting an injunction might have an adverse impact upon another's (often a newspaper's) freedom of expression. Balancing these rights is a difficult exercise for the courts,[45] but the courts will strive to provide a proportionate response.[46] Consistent with the general principles underpinning the equitable jurisdiction, an appellate court will generally be reluctant to interfere with the properly exercised discretion of a trial judge.[47]

---

[43] European Convention on Human Rights, Article 10 protects the right to freedom of expression, subject to certain restrictions, which are prescribed by law and necessary in a democratic society.

[44] European Convention on Human Rights, Article 8 provides a right to respect for one's 'private and family life, subject to certain restrictions that are in accordance with law and necessary in a democratic society'.

[45] See e.g. *London Regional Transport v Mayor of London* [2001] EWCA Civ 1491; [2003] EMLR 4; *Campbell v MGN* [2004] UKHL 22; [2004] 2 AC 457; *HRH Prince of Wales v Associated Newspapers Ltd* [2006] EWCA Civ 1776; [2007] 2 All ER 139; *McKennitt v Ash* [2006] EWCA Civ 1714; [2008] QB 73.

[46] *S (A Child) (Identification: restriction on Publication)* [2004] UKHL 47; [2005] 1 AC 593, [17].

[47] See e.g. *McKennitt v Ash* [2006] EWCA Civ 1714; [2008] QB 73.

(e) INTERIM INJUNCTIONS

A court can grant an injunction before a full trial takes place. Such interim, or interlocutory, injunctions normally operate until the trial or an earlier specified date. Interim injunctions have been explained on various bases. In *Jones v Pacaya Rubber and Produce Co. Ltd*, Buckley LJ said:[48]

> In all cases of applications for interlocutory injunctions the governing principle is that pending the settlement of the dispute between the parties the Court will as far as possible keep matters in statu quo.

Whereas in *Smith v Peters*, Sir George Jessel MR had:[49]

> no hesitation in saying that there is no limit to the practice of the Court with regard to interlocutory applications so far as they are necessary and reasonable applications ancillary to the due performance of its functions, namely, the administration of justice at the hearing of the cause. I know of no other limit.

Given the lapse of time that may occur before a full trial, it is appropriate that in some situations the courts are able to grant an interim injunction to prevent injustice. However, it is clear that the court will only grant such injunctions in limited circumstances. In *Fourie v Le Roux*, Lord Scott observed that:[50]

> without the issue of substantive proceedings or an undertaking to do so, the propriety of the grant of an interlocutory injunction would be difficult to defend. An interlocutory injunction, like any other interim order, is intended to be of temporary duration, dependent on the institution and progress of some proceedings for substantive relief....
>
> Whenever an interlocutory injunction is applied for, the judge, if otherwise minded to make the order, should, as a matter of good practice, pay careful attention to the substantive relief that is, or will be, sought. The interlocutory injunction in aid of the substantive relief should not place a greater burden on the respondent than is necessary. The yardstick in section 37(1) of the 1981 Act,[51] 'just and convenient', must be applied having regard to the interests not only of the claimant but also of the defendant.

In *Fourie*, the interim injunction sought[52] was not granted by the House of Lords, because there was no claim for substantive relief that the injunction would support. It is inappropriate to grant an interim injunction if the claimant has no substantive right that he or she seeks to protect.

(i) *Prohibitory injunctions*

The previous approach of English law at the interim stage was for the court to investigate the likelihood that a final injunction would be granted at trial. This led to a mini-trial at which the claimant needed to show a strong prima facie case.[53] However, in 1975 the House of Lords rejected this approach, and insisted that the claimant need only establish a real possibility of success, lowering the initial hurdle in the claimant's path.

[48] [1911] 1 KB 455, 457.
[49] (1875) LR 20 Eq 511, 513.
[50] [2007] UKHL 1; [2007] 1 WLR 320, [32]–[33].
[51] See Chapter 20.2(b), p. 978.
[52] A freezing order: see Chapter 20.2(f), p. 993.
[53] See e.g. *Harman Pictures N.V. v Osborne* [1967] 1 WLR 723.

American Cyanamid Co v Ethicon Ltd [1975] AC 396

The defendants were about to launch on the British market a surgical suture which the claimant alleged infringed its patent. The claimant sought an interlocutory injunction to restrain the product launch. This was granted by the trial judge but reversed by the Court of Appeal on the ground that no prima facie case of infringement of the patent had been established. The House of Lords allowed the appeal, and considered when an interlocutory injunction should be granted.

Lord Diplock:

My Lords, when an application for an interlocutory injunction to restrain a defendant from doing acts alleged to be in violation of the plaintiff's legal right is made upon contested facts, the decision whether or not to grant an interlocutory injunction has to be taken at a time when ex hypothesi the existence of the right or the violation of it, or both, is uncertain and will remain uncertain until final judgment is given in the action. It was to mitigate the risk of injustice to the plaintiff during the period before that uncertainty could be resolved that the practice arose of granting him relief by way of interlocutory injunction; but since the middle of the 19th century this has been made subject to his undertaking to pay damages to the defendant for any loss sustained by reason of the injunction if it should be held at the trial that the plaintiff had not been entitled to restrain the defendant from doing what he was threatening to do. The object of the interlocutory injunction is to protect the plaintiff against injury by violation of his right for which he could not be adequately compensated in damages recoverable in the action if the uncertainty were resolved in his favour at the trial; but the plaintiff's need for such protection must be weighed against the corresponding need of the defendant to be protected against injury resulting from his having been prevented from exercising his own legal rights for which he could not be adequately compensated under the plaintiff's undertaking in damages if the uncertainty were resolved in the defendant's favour at the trial. The court must weigh one need against another and determine where 'the balance of convenience' lies.

In those cases where the legal rights of the parties depend upon facts that are in dispute between them, the evidence available to the court at the hearing of the application for an interlocutory injunction is incomplete. It is given on affidavit and has not been tested by oral cross-examination. The purpose sought to be achieved by giving to the court discretion to grant such injunctions would be stultified if the discretion were clogged by a technical rule forbidding its exercise if upon that incomplete untested evidence the court evaluated the chances of the plaintiff's ultimate success in the action at 50 per cent or less, but permitting its exercise if the court evaluated his chances at more than 50 per cent. ...

The use of such expressions as 'a probability', 'a prima facie case', or 'a strong prima facie case' in the context of the exercise of a discretionary power to grant an interlocutory injunction leads to confusion as to the object sought to be achieved by this form of temporary relief. The court no doubt must be satisfied that the claim is not frivolous or vexatious, in other words, that there is a serious question to be tried.

It is no part of the court's function at this stage of the litigation to try to resolve conflicts of evidence on affidavit as to facts on which the claims of either party may ultimately depend nor to decide difficult questions of law which call for detailed argument and mature considerations. These are matters to be dealt with at the trial. One of the reasons for the introduction of the practice of requiring an undertaking as to damages upon the grant of an interlocutory injunction was that 'it aided the court in doing that which was its great object, viz. abstaining from expressing any opinion upon the merits of the case until the hearing': *Wakefield v Duke of Buccleugh* (1865) 12 LT 628, 629. So unless the material available to the court at the hearing of the application for an interlocutory injunction fails to disclose that the plaintiff has any real prospect of succeeding in his claim for a permanent injunction at the trial, the court should go on to consider whether the balance of convenience lies in favour of granting or refusing the interlocutory relief that is sought.

As to that, the governing principle is that the court should first consider whether, if the plaintiff were to succeed at the trial in establishing his right to a permanent injunction, he would be adequately

compensated by an award of damages for the loss he would have sustained as a result of the defendant's continuing to do what was sought to be enjoined between the time of the application and the time
of the trial. If damages in the measure recoverable at common law would be adequate remedy and
the defendant would be in a financial position to pay them, no interlocutory injunction should normally
be granted, however strong the plaintiff's claim appeared to be at that stage. If, on the other hand,
damages would not provide an adequate remedy for the plaintiff in the event of his succeeding at the
trial, the court should then consider whether, on the contrary hypothesis that the defendant were to
succeed at the trial in establishing his right to do that which was sought to be enjoined, he would be
adequately compensated under the plaintiff's undertaking as to damages for the loss he would have
sustained by being prevented from doing so between the time of the application and the time of the
trial. If damages in the measure recoverable under such an undertaking would be an adequate remedy
and the plaintiff would be in a financial position to pay them, there would be no reason upon this ground
to refuse an interlocutory injunction.

It is where there is doubt as to the adequacy of the respective remedies in damages available to either
party or to both, that the question of balance of convenience arises. It would be unwise to attempt
even to list all the various matters which may need to be taken into consideration in deciding where
the balance lies, let alone to suggest the relative weight to be attached to them. These will vary from
case to case.

Where other factors appear to be evenly balanced it is a counsel of prudence to take such measures
as are calculated to preserve the status quo. If the defendant is enjoined temporarily from doing something that he has not done before, the only effect of the interlocutory injunction in the event of his succeeding at the trial is to postpone the date at which he is able to embark upon a course of action which
he has not previously found it necessary to undertake; whereas to interrupt him in the conduct of an
established enterprise would cause much greater inconvenience to him since he would have to start
again to establish it in the event of his succeeding at the trial.

Save in the simplest cases, the decision to grant or to refuse an interlocutory injunction will cause to
whichever party is unsuccessful on the application some disadvantages which his ultimate success at
the trial may show he ought to have been spared and the disadvantages may be such that the recovery
of damages to which he would then be entitled either in the action or under the plaintiff's undertaking
would not be sufficient to compensate him fully for all of them. The extent to which the disadvantages
to each party would be incapable of being compensated in damages in the event of his succeeding
at the trial is always a significant factor in assessing where the balance of convenience lies, and if the
extent of the uncompensatable disadvantage to each party would not differ widely, it may not be improper to take into account in tipping the balance the relative strength of each party's case as revealed
by the affidavit evidence adduced on the hearing of the application. This, however, should be done only
where it is apparent upon the facts disclosed by evidence as to which there is no credible dispute that
the strength of one party's case is disproportionate to that of the other party. The court is not justified in
embarking upon anything resembling a trial of the action upon conflicting affidavits in order to evaluate
the strength of either party's case.

This is a very important passage, which is at the heart of decisions concerning interim injunctions. It
essentially establishes a series of issues that have to be considered. First, there must be a serious question to be tried. This is not as onerous as having to show a prima facie case, but requires the claimant to
show that he or she has a cause of action that would not be struck out as frivolous or vexatious.[54] If the
claimant fails to show that he or she has a sensible cause of action, the outcome of which is uncertain,
then an interim injunction should not be granted.[55]

[54] E.g. *Mothercare Ltd v Robson Brooks Ltd* [1979] FSR 466.
[55] E.g. *Re Lord Cable* [1977] 1 WLR 7.

It is only if there is a serious question to be tried that a court will consider the balance of convenience. The language in this area has been criticized: for example, in *Francome v Mirror Group Newspapers Ltd*, Sir John Donaldson MR thought it to be:[56]

> an unfortunate expression. Our business is justice, not convenience.

Regardless of this question of semantics, it is clear that Lord Diplock thought a wide range of factors might be relevant at this stage. But he considered it to be crucial that if the claimant could be adequately compensated by damages if he or she were to succeed at trial, then an injunction should not be granted, no matter how strong his or her claim.[57] Lord Diplock also highlighted the flip-side of this: if the defendant were to succeed at trial having been subjected to an interim injunction, but the claimant's undertaking in damages[58] would adequately compensate the defendant, it would seem sensible to grant the injunction.[59] In both situations, the balance of convenience is clear: given that damages will provide a satisfactory remedy if it is later established that an injunction was or was not appropriate, the court should refuse or grant the interim injunction and allow matters to proceed to trial.

If damages may not be adequate, then other factors assume increased importance. Significantly, Lord Diplock suggested that the court might generally favour preserving the *status quo*. In *Garden Cottage Foods Ltd v Milk Marketing Board*,[60] Lord Diplock made it clear what was meant by this:

> The status quo is the existing state of affairs; but since states of affairs do not remain static this raises the query: existing when? In my opinion, the relevant status quo to which reference was made in *American Cyanamid* is the state of affairs existing during the period immediately preceding the issue of the writ claiming the permanent injunction or, if there be unreasonable delay between the issue of the writ and the motion for an interlocutory injunction, the period immediately preceding the motion. The duration of that period since the state of affairs last changed must be more than minimal, having regard to the total length of the relationship between the parties in respect of which the injunction is granted; otherwise the state of affairs before the last change would be the relevant status quo.

In *American Cyanamid*, Lord Diplock also indicated that the court should not embark on a mini-trial of conflicting evidence, but where one party's case is clearly far stronger than the other's, this might help to tip the balance.[61] A robust interpretation of this point was provided by Laddie J in *Series 5 Software v Clarke*:[62]

> In my view Lord Diplock did not intend ... to exclude consideration of the strength of the cases in most applications for interlocutory relief. It appears to me that what is intended is that the court should not attempt to resolve difficult issues of fact or law on an application for interlocutory relief. If, on the other hand, the court is able to come to a view as to the strength of the parties' cases on the credible evidence then it can do so. In fact, as any lawyer who has experience of interlocutory proceedings will know, it is frequently the case that it is easy to determine who is most likely to win the trial on the basis

---

[56] [1984] 1 WLR 892, 898.
[57] *Garden Cottage Foods Ltd v Milk Marketing Board* [1984] AC 130.
[58] See Chapter 20.2(e)(iv), p. 993.
[59] E.g. *Foseco International Ltd v Fordath Ltd* [1975] FSR 507.
[60] *Garden Cottage Foods Ltd v Milk Marketing Board* [1984] AC 130, 140, disapproving on this point *Texaco Ltd v Mulberry Filling Station Ltd* [1972] 1 WLR 814, 831.
[61] See e.g. *The Quaker Oats Co. v Alltrades Distributors Ltd* [1981] FSR 9.
[62] [1996] 1 All ER 853, 865.

of the affidavit evidence and any exhibited contemporaneous documents. If it is apparent from that material that one party's case is much stronger than the other's then that is a matter the court should not ignore. To suggest otherwise would be to exclude from consideration an important factor and such exclusion would fly in the face of the flexibility advocated earlier in *American Cyanamid*.

In *American Cyanamid*, Lord Diplock also noted that:[63]

There may be many other special factors to be taken into consideration in the particular circumstances of individual cases.

There was such a relevant factor in *American Cyanamid* itself: the defendant's medical product was not yet on the market, but if doctors and patients began using the product, then it might become commercially impracticable for the claimant later to insist on a permanent injunction to protect its patent at trial: to do so would clearly have a deleterious effect on its goodwill in the pharmaceutical market.

(ii) *Limits of* American Cyanamid

Although the *American Cyanamid* principles are generally applicable to interim injunctions, in *Cayne v Global Natural Resources plc*, May LJ pointed out that:[64]

a judgment ought not, however eminent the judge, to be construed as if they were an Act of Parliament. … I think that one must be very careful to apply the relevant passages from Lord Diplock's familiar speech in the *Cyanamid* case not as rules but only as guidelines.

The courts should not be too rigid in their approach to the *Cyanamid* guidelines. After all, the jurisdiction to grant injunctions under the Senior Courts Act 1981 is to do what is 'just and convenient', and this chimes well with the Civil Procedure Rules',[65]

overriding objective of enabling the court to deal with cases justly.

However, some situations where the *Cyanamid* guidelines are often sidelined can be highlighted. If it is clear that the claimant is in the right, and the issue is not really arguable, then an injunction should be granted and the balance of convenience is irrelevant.[66] The court might also not use the *Cyanamid* guidelines if the case revolves around a simple question of construction of a document, which can easily be done at the interlocutory stage.[67] If the grant or refusal of an interim injunction will have the practical effect of putting an end to the action, then the court will be very conscious of the fact that an injunction might effectively deny the defendant the right to trial. In such cases, the court will take into account the likelihood of the claimant succeeding at trial.[68]

---

[63] *American Cyanamid Co. v Ethicon Ltd* [1975] AC 396, 409.
[64] [1984] 1 All ER 225, 237.
[65] CPR 1998 r 1.1.
[66] *Patel v WH Smith (Eziot) Ltd* [1987] 1 WLR 853; *Texaco Ltd v Mulberry Filling Station Ltd* [1972] 1 WLR 814.
[67] *Fellowes & Son v Fisher* [1976] QB 122, 141.
[68] *NWL Ltd v Woods* [1979] 1 WLR 1294, 1307 (Lord Diplock).

Particular areas of the law have also developed particular rules that drift away from the *Cyanamid* guidance. For example, statute has intervened in the context of labour disputes,[69] and where freedom of expression might be infringed. Section 12(3) of the Human Rights Act 1998 provides that:

> No … relief is to be granted so as to restrain publication before trial unless the court is satisfied that the applicant is likely to establish that publication should not be allowed.

This is to preserve the important human right of freedom of expression, and clearly requires the claimant to show more than simply a serious issue to be tried. In *Cream Holdings Ltd v Banerjee*,[70] Lord Nicholls said:

> the general approach should be that courts will be exceedingly slow to make interim restraint orders where the applicant has not satisfied the court he will probably ('more likely than not') succeed at the trial.

This is a more challenging threshold than that usually required for interim injunctions. However, it is important to appreciate that even if this threshold is met, the courts retain a discretion to refuse injunctive relief.[71]

(iii) *Mandatory interim injunctions*

The court is particularly wary about granting interim mandatory injunctions, being conscious of the potential waste and needless expenditure that might result from a wrongly granted interim mandatory injunction. However, where the defendant has acted badly in some way, the court might be more willing to grant such an injunction. So, where a defendant speeded up building works after being served with notice of the claimant's proceedings to protect his right of light, the court did order an interim mandatory injunction that that which had been built must be pulled down.[72]

Before the court grants such injunctions, it generally needs to be satisfied that an injunction would be granted at trial. The approach of the courts was summarized by Chadwick J in *Nottingham Building Society v Eurodynamics Systems plc* as follows:[73]

> In my view the principles to be applied are these. First, this being an interlocutory matter, the overriding consideration is which course is likely to involve the least risk of injustice if it turns out to be 'wrong'
>
> …
>
> Secondly, in considering whether to grant a mandatory injunction, the court must keep in mind that an order which requires a party to take some positive step at an interlocutory stage, may well carry a greater risk of injustice if it turns out to have been wrongly made than an order which merely prohibits action, thereby preserving the status quo.
>
> Thirdly, it is legitimate, where a mandatory injunction is sought, to consider whether the court does feel a high degree of assurance that the plaintiff will be able to establish his right at a trial. That is because the greater the degree of assurance the plaintiff will ultimately establish his right, the less will be the risk of injustice if the injunction is granted.

---

[69] See e.g. Trade Union and Labour Relations (Consolidation) Act 1992, s. 221.
[70] [2004] UKHL 44; [2005] 1 AC 253, [22].
[71] *Douglas v Hello! Ltd* [2001] QB 967, [153] (Keene LJ).
[72] *Daniel v Ferguson* [1891] 2 Ch 27.
[73] [1993] FSR 468, 474.

> But, finally, even where the court is unable to feel any high degree of assurance that the plaintiff will establish his right, there may still be circumstances in which it is appropriate to grant a mandatory injunction at an interlocutory stage. Those circumstances will exist where the risk of injustice if this injunction is refused sufficiently outweigh the risk of injustice if it is granted.

(iv) *Bars to interim injunctions*

The same bars[74] that apply to final injunctions and equitable injunctions are relevant to interim injunctions. However, a lesser degree of delay might bar interlocutory relief, since any delay might show a lack of the urgency required for interim orders.[75]

Of significant importance is the requirement that the claimant give an undertaking in damages to pay the defendant if at trial it is decided that an injunction should not be granted.[76] The defendant should clearly be compensated for the claimant's having 'wrongly' prevented the defendant's activity. Although the court will generally ask for evidence that the claimant is able to meet the undertaking in damages,[77] in some circumstances the court might grant an interim injunction despite the claimant's lack of funds to meet his or her potential liabilities satisfactorily. In *Allen v Jambo Holdings Ltd*, Lord Denning MR said:[78]

> I do not see why a poor plaintiff should be denied ... [an] injunction just because he is poor, whereas a rich plaintiff would get it. One has to look at these matters broadly. As a matter of convenience, balancing one side against the other, it seems to me that an injunction should go to restrain [the alleged breach].

Moreover, an undertaking may not be required where a regulatory authority pursues a law enforcement claim under statute and not for its own benefit but for that of the public. In *Financial Services Authority v Sinaloa Gold Plc*[79] the Supreme Court held that any other approach might discourage public bodies with limited resources from pursuing their public duties to bring certain claims.

(f) FREEZING INJUNCTIONS

The creative function of Equity is particularly well illustrated by an important remedy developed in the 1970s to deal with the problem of a defendant who seeks to hide his or her assets or take them out of the jurisdiction to prevent the claimant from enforcing a judgment for damages against him or her. To avoid this problem, Equity was relied upon to create a new form of interim injunction, known then as a '*Mareva* injunction' (after one[80] of the early cases that first recognized it, involving a ship of that name)[81] and now known as a freezing injunction. This is an injunction that can be used by judges to freeze some or all of the defendant's assets to prevent the defendant from removing them

---

[74] Cf. Chapter 20.1(a), p. 976.

[75] *Selbit v Coldwyn Ltd* (1923) 58 LJ News, 305.

[76] See Gee, 'The Undertaking in Damages' [2006] LMCLQ 181.

[77] *Brigid Foley Ltd v Ellott* [1982] RPC 433e.

[78] [1980] 1 WLR 1252, 1257.

[79] [2013] UKSC 11; [2013] 2 AC 28. Cf Turner and Varuhas, 'Injunctions, Undertakings in Damages and the Public-Private Divide' (2014) 130 LQR 33.

[80] The first case to recognize this injunction was *Nippon Yusen Kaisha v Karageorgis* [1975] 1 WLR 1093.

[81] See Chapter 20.2(f), p. 995.

from the jurisdiction, or dissipating them, and so ensure that any judgment can be enforced against the defendant. However, it is crucial to remember that the order operates *in personam* to prevent the defendant from dealing with his or her assets: for example, the order might prohibit the defendant from accessing money credited to his or her bank account. But the order does *not* give the claimant any proprietary interests in the defendant's assets.[82] In *Investment and Pensions Advisory Service v Gray*, Morritt J rightly emphasized that:[83]

> It is well established that it is not the purpose or the function of a *Mareva* order to give the creditor who obtains it security over any particular asset of the defendant or a priority over other creditors of the defendant.

Freezing orders can be granted either before or after[84] judgment has been obtained. Such injunctions have proved to be a significant feature of the English law of civil procedure. Lord Denning has described freezing injunctions as:[85]

> The greatest piece of judicial law reform in my time.

(i) *The jurisdiction to grant a freezing injunction*

The jurisdiction to grant a freezing injunction is now statutory.

SENIOR COURTS ACT 1981

37(3) The power of the High Court under subsection (1)[86] to grant an interlocutory injunction restraining a party to any proceedings from removing from the jurisdiction of the High Court, or otherwise dealing with, assets located within that jurisdiction shall be exercisable in cases where that party is, as well as in cases where he is not, domiciled, resident or present within that jurisdiction.

Such injunctions are now appropriately called freezing injunctions under Civil Procedure Rule r 25.1(1):

> The court may grant the following interim remedies:
>
> ....
>
> (f) an order (referred to as a 'freezing injunction')
>
>   (i) restraining a party from removing from the jurisdiction assets located there; or
>
>   (ii) restraining a party from dealing with any assets whether located within the jurisdiction or not.

These provisions embody the common law principles, which were encapsulated in the case that, for a time, gave these injunctions their name.

---

[82] *Cretanor Maritime Co. Ltd v Irish Marine Maritime Ltd* [1978] 3 All ER 164; *Flightline Ltd v Edwards* [2003] EWCA Civ 63; [2003] 1 WLR 1200.
[83] [1990] BCLC 38, 43. See also *Camdex International Ltd v Bank of Zambia (No. 2)* [1997] 1 WLR 632, 638 (Aldous LJ).
[84] *Babanaft International Co. SA v Bassatne* [1990] Ch 13.
[85] Lord Denning, *The Due Process of Law* (London: Butterworths, 1980), p. 134.
[86] Chapter 20.2(b), p. 978.

Mareva Compania Naviera SA v International Bulkcarriers SA [1975] 2 Lloyd's Rep 509

Shipowners sued the charterers of the Mareva for recovery of hire payments and sought an injunction to restrain them from taking any of the money they had received under the charter from a London bank and out of the jurisdiction. The trial judge granted the injunction until the matter was heard by the Court of Appeal. The shipowners appealed on the basis that the injunction should continue until judgment was obtained. This appeal was successful.

Lord Denning MR:

[The shipowners] have applied for an injunction to restrain the disposal of those moneys which are now in the bank. They rely on the recent case of *Nippon Yusen Kaisha v Karageorgis* [1975] 1 WLR 1093.

…

Now [counsel for the shipowners] has been very helpful. He has drawn our attention … to section 45 of the Judicature Act, 1925, which repeats section 25(8) of the Judicature Act, 1875. It says:

> 'A mandamus or an injunction may be granted or a receiver appointed by an interlocutory order of the court in all cases in which it shall appear to the court to be just or convenient.'

In *Beddow v Beddow* (1878) 9 Ch D 89, Sir George Jessel, the then Master of the Rolls, gave a very wide interpretation to that section. He said:

> 'I have unlimited power to grant an injunction in any case where it would be right or just to do so.'

There is only one qualification to be made. The Court will not grant an injunction to protect a person who has no legal or equitable right whatever. That appears from *North London Railway Co v Great Northern Railway Co* (1883) 11 QBD 30. But, subject to that qualification, the statute gives a wide general power to the Courts. It is well summarized in *Halsbury's Laws of England*, vol. 21, 3rd ed., p. 348, para. 729:

> '… now, therefore, whenever a right, which can be asserted either at law or in equity, does exist, then, whatever the previous practice may have been, the Court is enabled by virtue of this provision, in a proper case, to grant an injunction to protect that right.'

In my opinion that principle applies to a creditor who has a right to be paid the debt owing to him, even before he has established his right by getting judgment for it. If it appears that the debt is due and owing—and there is a danger that the debtor may dispose of his assets so as to defeat it before judgment—the Court has jurisdiction in a proper case to grant an interlocutory judgment so as to prevent him disposing of those assets. It seems to me that this is a proper case for the exercise of this jurisdiction. There is money in a bank in London which stands in the name of these time charterers. The time charterers have control of it. They may at any time dispose of it or remove it out of this country. If they do so, the shipowners may never get their charter hire. The ship is now on the high seas. It has passed Cape Town on its way to India. It will complete the voyage and the cargo discharged and the shipowners may not get their charter hire at all. In face of this danger, I think this Court ought to grant an injunction to restrain the defendants from disposing of these moneys now in the bank in London until the trial or judgment in this action. If the defendants have any grievance about it when they hear of it, they can apply to discharge it. But meanwhile the plaintiffs should be protected. It is only just and right that this Court should grant an injunction. I would therefore continue the injunction.

As Lord Denning MR recognized, the power enjoyed by the courts to grant a freezing injunction is very wide indeed. The sole qualification made in this case was the sensible requirement that the claimant needs to have a substantive legal or equitable right that requires protection.[87] However, given the

---

[87] This must be clearly formulated at least: see *Fourie v Le Roux* [2007] UKHL 1; [2007] 1 WLR 320: see Chapter 20.2(e). p. 987.

wide scope of the court's discretion to do justice, an order might be granted against a range of possible defendants. For example, in *H.M. Revenue & Customs v Egleton*, Briggs J acknowledged that:[88]

> Although in the overwhelming majority of cases freezing orders are sought and obtained against the very defendants from whom the claimant seeks monetary compensation in his existing or anticipated proceedings, it is now well established that such orders may also be made against persons in relation to whom the claimant asserts no cause of action and seeks no money judgment, but in relation to whom there is an arguable case that assets held in their name or under their control are in truth beneficially owned by the defendant against whom the claim is made: see *TSB Private Bank International S.A. –v– Chabra* [1992] 1 WLR 231, and the other cases cited in paragraph 37 of the judgment of Aikens J. in *C Inc. –v– L*.[89]

Indeed, Briggs J went on to consider that in some situations an injunction might be granted against a third party, even if he or she was not holding property for the claimant beneficially. His Lordship cited with approval the decision of the High Court of Australia in *Cardile v LED Builders PTY Ltd*, in which the majority said:[90]

> What then is the principle to guide the courts in determining whether to grant Mareva relief in a case such as the present where the activities of third parties are the object sought to be restrained? In our opinion such an order may, and we emphasise the word 'may', be appropriate, assuming the existence of other relevant criteria and discretionary factors, in circumstances in which:
>
> (i) the third party holds, is using, or has exercised or is exercising a power of disposition over, or is otherwise in possession of, assets, including 'claims and expectancies' [89], of the judgment debtor or potential judgment debtor; or
>
> (ii) some process, ultimately enforceable by the courts, is or may be available to the judgment creditor as a consequence of a judgment against that actual or potential judgment debtor, pursuant to which, whether by appointment of a liquidator, trustee in bankruptcy, receiver or otherwise, the third party may be obliged to disgorge property or otherwise contribute to the funds or property of the judgment debtor to help satisfy the judgment against the judgment debtor.

(ii) *Factors relevant to the granting of a freezing injunction*

A freezing injunction is an interim injunction, so it might be thought that the usual requirements recognized in *American Cyanamid Co v Ethicon Ltd*[91] should be satisfied, namely there be a serious issue to be tried and that the 'balance of convenience' favour the grant of the injunction. However, further guidelines have been identified by Lord Denning MR.

Third Chandris Shipping Corporation v Unimarine SA [1979] QB 645, 666–9 (Lord Denning MR)

> It is just four years ago now since we introduced here the procedure known as *Mareva* injunctions. All the other legal systems of the world have a similar procedure. It is called in the civil law saisie conservatoire. It has been welcomed in the City of London and has proved extremely

---

[88] [2006] EWHC 2313 (Ch); [2007] 1 All ER 606, [12].
[89] [2001] 2 Lloyds Law Reports 459.
[90] [1999] HCA 18, [57]. See also *Yukos Capital Sarl v OJSC Rosneft Oil Company* [2010] EWHC 784 (Comm).
[91] [1975] AC 396.

beneficial. It enables a creditor in a proper case to stop his debtor from parting with his assets pending trial ...

Much as I am in favour of the *Mareva* injunction, it must not be stretched too far lest it be endangered. In endeavouring to set out some guidelines, I have had recourse to the practice of many other countries which have [*sic*] been put before us. They have been most helpful. These are the points which those who apply for it should bear in mind:

(i) The plaintiff should make full and frank disclosure of all matters in his knowledge which are material for the judge to know ...

(ii) The plaintiff should give particulars of his claim against the defendant, stating the ground of his claim and the amount thereof, and fairly stating the points made against it by the defendant.

(iii) The plaintiff should give some grounds for believing that the defendant has assets here ... The existence of a bank account in England is enough, whether it is in overdraft or not.

(iv) The plaintiff should give some grounds for believing that there is a risk of the assets being removed before the judgment or award is satisfied. The mere fact that the defendant is abroad is not by itself sufficient ...

(v) The plaintiff must, of course, give an undertaking in damages—in case he fails in his claim or the injunction turns out to be unjustified. In a suitable case this should be supported by a bond or security: and the injunction only granted on it being given, or undertaken to be given.

In setting out those guidelines, I hope we shall do nothing to reduce the efficacy of the present practice. In it speed is of the essence. Ex parte is of the essence. If there is delay, or if advance warning is given, the assets may well be removed before the injunction can bite.

These considerations are sensible and significant. The first—full and frank disclosure—is obviously important since the injunction is granted without notice to the defendant. If there has been non-disclosure of material facts, the injunction might be discharged regardless of the merits of the case,[92] and the defendant may be entitled to damages.[93]

The second consideration essentially requires a good arguable case. This is higher than the 'serious question to be tried' threshold of *American Cyanamid*, which is appropriate given the stringent nature of freezing orders granted without notice. However, the court need not decide whether or not the substantive claim will succeed,[94] and the claimant must proceed with his substantive claim as quickly as he can.[95] It is now possible to grant freezing orders in relation to proceedings that have been or are about to be commenced abroad.[96]

The third guideline given here represents the initial approach of English courts. Indeed, in *Barclay-Johnson v Yuill*, Megarry V-C commented that:[97]

the heart and core of the *Mareva* injunction is the risk of the defendant removing his assets from the jurisdiction and so stultifying any judgment given by the courts in the action.

---

[92] *Lloyd's Bowmaker Ltd v Britannia Arrow Holdings plc* [1988] 1 WLR 1337; *Swift-Fortune Ltd v Magnifica Marine SA (The Capaz Duckling)* [2007] EWHC 1630 (Comm); [2008] 1 Lloyd's Rep 54. However, if the non-disclosure is unimportant, the court is unlikely to set the order aside: *Memory Corporation v Sidhu* [2000] 1 WLR 1443.

[93] *Ali and Fahd Shobokshi Group Ltd v Moneim* [1989] 1 WLR 710, 722.

[94] *Derby & Co. Ltd v Weldon* [1990] Ch 48.

[95] *Lloyds Bowmarker Ltd v Britannia Arrow Holdings plc* [1988] 1 WLR 1337; *Fourie v Le Roux* [2007] UKHL 1; [2007] 1 WLR 320.

[96] Civil Jurisdiction and Judgments Act 1982, s. 25(1); *Fourie v Le Roux* [2007] UKHL 1; [2007] 1 WLR 320.

[97] [1980] 1 WLR 1259, 1262.

It is undoubtedly right that the presence of assets in England will still be a very good reason to grant a freezing order. But the jurisdiction of the courts has now been extended and 'worldwide' freezing orders can now be granted. These will be considered later.[98]

Megarry V-C's comments in *Yuill* emphasize the fourth consideration; the risk of the assets being removed from the jurisdiction, or dissipated, must be real. A freezing order will not be granted simply to provide a claimant with peace of mind that he or she will be able to gain satisfaction from the defendant; in *Ninemia Maritime Corp v Trave Schiffahrtsgesellschaft mbH und Co. KG*, Kerr LJ observed:[99]

> The machinery of the *Mareva* injunction is extremely useful in appropriate cases. But, as the law stands, this jurisdiction cannot be invoked for the purpose of providing plaintiffs with security for claims, even when these appear likely to succeed—we are speaking generally and not with reference to this case—and even when there is no reason to suppose that an order for an injunction, or the provision of some substitute security by the defendants, would cause any real hardship to the defendants.

The normal undertaking in damages must also be given. This might be extended to cover losses suffered by third parties in appropriate circumstances.[100] However, no injunction will be granted if the claimant already enjoys sufficient security for his or her claim.[101]

It is important to appreciate that although freezing orders were originally granted to restrain foreign defendants from removing their assets from the jurisdiction, they can now be granted against English defendants[102] to prevent the dissipation of assets within this jurisdiction.[103] Freezing orders might relate to particular assets or describe the property in general terms. Such injunctions normally restrict the defendant from dealing with his property up to a specified maximum amount. It is normal for the defendant to be granted an allowance for living expenses[104] and legal expenses,[105] although a limit should ordinarily be imposed.

(iii) *World-wide freezing injunctions*

Civil Procedure Rule r 25.1(1)(f)[106] makes it clear that freezing orders can be granted to restrain the dissipation of assets abroad. This is a logical consequence of the nature of freezing injunctions: since the injunction acts *in personam* upon the defendant, and not *in rem* on the assets themselves, only the defendant, and not the assets, must be subject to the jurisdiction of the court. If that defendant breaches the injunction, the English courts can hold him or her in contempt. Given the emphasis upon defendants being within the jurisdiction of the English courts, care must be exercised when labelling this type of injunction 'worldwide'.

However, the language of 'worldwide' is helpful in that it emphasizes the unusual nature of the order: it has the potential to be considered oppressive and to conflict with principles of comity.

---

[98] See Chapter 20.2(f)(iii), p. 998.
[99] [1983] 1 WLR 1412, 1422.
[100] *Clipper Maritime Co. Ltd of Monravia v Mineralimportexport* [1981] 1 WLR 1262.
[101] *Refco Inc. v Eastern Trading Co.* [1999] 1 Lloyd's Rep 159.
[102] *Barclay-Johnson v Yuill* [1980] 1 WLR 1259.
[103] *Z Ltd v A* [1982] 1 All ER 556.
[104] *A.J. Bekhor & Co. v Bilton* [1981] QB 923.
[105] *A v C (No. 2)* [1981] QB 961n; *PCW (Underwriting Agencies) Ltd v Dixon* [1983] 2 All ER 158, 697n.
[106] See Chapter 20.2(f)(i), p. 994.

Masri v Consolidated Contractors International (UK) Ltd (No. 2) [2008] EWCA Civ 303; [2009] QB 450, [35]–[39] (Lawrence Collins LJ)

Consequently the mere fact that an order is *in personam* and is directed towards someone who is subject to the personal jurisdiction of the English court does not exclude the possibility that the making of the order would be contrary to international law or comity, and outside the subject matter jurisdiction of the English court.

That was why Lord Donaldson of Lymington MR confirmed that the *Mareva* injunction should not conflict with 'the ordinary principles of international law' and that 'considerations of comity require the courts of this country to refrain from making orders which infringe the exclusive jurisdiction of the courts of other countries': *Derby & Co Ltd v Weldon (Nos 3 and 4)* [1990] Ch 65, 82. It was for this reason also that it has been suggested that the extension of the *Mareva* jurisdiction to assets abroad was justifiable in terms of international law and comity provided that the case had some appropriate connection with England, that the court did not purport to affect title to property abroad, and that the court did not seek to control the activities abroad of foreigners who were not subject to the personal jurisdiction of the English court: Collins, 'The Territorial Reach of Mareva Injunctions' (1989) 105 LQR 262, 299.

In *Babanaft International Co SA v Bassatne* [1990] Ch 13, 46 Nicholls LJ emphasised, in relation to the post-judgment worldwide Mareva injunction granted in that case:

> 'The enforcement of the judgment in other countries, by attachment or like process, in respect of assets which are situated there is not affected by the order ... The English court is not attempting in any way to interfere with or control the enforcement process in respect of those assets.'

It was concerns of international comity which led the Court of Appeal in *Babanaft International Co SA v Bassatne* to limit the effect of the *Mareva* injunction on third parties abroad who may have notice of the injunction, by what became known as the *Babanaft* proviso, which Kerr LJ described, at p 37, as 'the internationally appropriate course' and which Lord Donaldson MR indicated was designed to avoid 'an excess of jurisdiction': *Derby & Co Ltd v Weldon (Nos 3 and 4)* [1990] Ch 65, 82–83. The reason, as Nicholls LJ said in *Babanaft International Co SA v Bassatne* [1990] Ch 13, 44, was that

> 'It would be wrong for an English court, by making an order in respect of overseas assets against a defendant amenable to its jurisdiction, to impose or attempt to impose obligations on persons not before the court in respect of acts to be done by them abroad regarding property outside the jurisdiction. That, self-evidently, would be for the English court to claim an altogether exorbitant, extra-territorial jurisdiction.'

Even if the third party with notice of the order is subject to the *in personam* jurisdiction of the English court, there may still be concerns relating to international comity, for example where the defendant has an account abroad at a foreign branch of an English bank, or an account at the head office or foreign branch of a foreign bank with a branch in England: *Baltic Shipping Co v Translink Shipping Ltd* [1995] 1 Lloyd's Rep 673.

Lawrence Collins LJ refers to the *Babanaft* proviso, which provides that worldwide freezing injunctions are not intended to bind third parties who are not subject to the court's jurisdiction. Parties are also able to apply for a '*Baltic* proviso', named after *Baltic Shipping Co. v Translink Shipping Ltd*,[107] which provides that nothing in an order prevents parties from complying with their obligations under the laws of other states.

---

[107] [1995] 1 Lloyd's Rep. 673.

Given the extreme nature of worldwide freezing orders ('WFO'), they are only granted on the basis of cogent evidence. The court will take into account various factors when applying its discretion. In *Dadourian Group International Inc. v Simms*, the Court of Appeal laid down the '*Dadourian* guidelines':[108]

Guideline 1: The principle applying to the grant of permission to enforce a WFO abroad is that the grant of that permission should be just and convenient for the purpose of ensuring the effectiveness of the WFO, and in addition that it is not oppressive to the parties to the English proceedings or to third parties who may be joined to the foreign proceedings.

Guideline 2: All the relevant circumstances and options need to be considered. In particular consideration should be given to granting relief on terms, for example terms as to the extension to third parties of the undertaking to compensate for costs incurred as a result of the WFO and as to the type of proceedings that may be commenced abroad. Consideration should also be given to the proportionality of the steps proposed to be taken abroad, and in addition to the form of any order.

Guideline 3: The interests of the applicant should be balanced against the interests of the other parties to the proceedings and any new party likely to be joined to the foreign proceedings.

Guideline 4: Permission should not normally be given in terms that would enable the applicant to obtain relief in the foreign proceedings which is superior to the relief given by the WFO.

Guideline 5: The evidence in support of the application for permission should contain all the information (so far as it can reasonably be obtained in the time available) necessary to make the judge to reach an informed decision, including evidence as to the applicable law and practice in the foreign court, evidence as to the nature of the proposed proceedings to be commenced and evidence as to the assets believed to be located in the jurisdiction of the foreign court and the names of the parties by whom such assets are held.

Guideline 6: The standard of proof as to the existence of assets that are both within the WFO and within the jurisdiction of the foreign court is a real prospect, that is the applicant must show that there is a real prospect that such assets are located within the jurisdiction of the foreign court in question.

Guideline 7: There must be evidence of a risk of dissipation of the assets in question.

Guideline 8: Normally the application should be made on notice to the respondent, but in cases of urgency, where it is just to do so, the permission may be given without notice to the party against whom relief will be sought in the foreign proceedings but that party should have the earliest practicable opportunity of having the matter reconsidered by the court at a hearing of which he is given notice.

(iv) *Effect on third parties*

A matter of particular significance concerns the effect of freezing orders on third parties. This was considered by the House of Lords in *Customs and Excise Commissioners v Barclays Bank plc*.

Customs and Excise Commissioners v Barclays Bank plc [2006] UKHL 28; [2007] 1 AC 181

The Customs and Excise Commissioners were trying to recover outstanding payments of VAT from two companies and obtained a freezing order in respect of funds held by the companies in the defendant bank. The bank was informed of the orders but failed to prevent payment out of the accounts. The claimant sued the bank for negligence. In holding that the bank did not owe a duty of care to the claimant, the House of Lords considered the nature of the court's jurisdiction to grant injunctions.

---

[108] [2006] EWCA Civ 399; [2006] 1 WLR 2499, [25].

Lord Bingham:[109]

The prescribed standard form contains a penal notice:

'If you [...] disobey this order you may be held to be in contempt of court and may be imprisoned, fined or have your assets seized.

Any other person who knows of this order and does anything which helps or permits the respondent to breach the terms of this order may also be held to be in contempt of court and may be imprisoned, fined or have their assets seized.'

The first of these warnings is addressed to the subject of the order, the second to any party (such as a bank) who knows of it. The form provides that anyone served with or notified of the order may apply to the court to vary or discharge it on notice to the applicant's solicitor. The effect of the order as it affects parties other than the applicant and the subject of the order is again stated:

'It is a contempt of court for any person notified of this order knowingly to assist in or permit a breach of this order. Any person doing so may be imprisoned, fined or have their assets seized.'

The form records an undertaking by the applicant to pay the reasonable costs of any person other than the subject of the order:

'which have been incurred as a result of this order including the costs of finding out whether that person holds any of the respondent's assets and if the court finds that this order has caused such person loss, and decides that such person should be compensated for that loss, the applicant will comply with any order the court may make.' ...

It is very well established that the purpose of a freezing injunction is to restrain a defendant or prospective defendant from disposing of or dealing with assets so as to defeat, wholly or in part, a likely judgment against it. The purpose is not to give a claimant security for his claim or give him any proprietary interest in the assets restrained: *Gangway Ltd v Caledonian Park Investments (Jersey) Ltd* [2001] 2 Lloyd's Rep 715, para 14, per Colman J. The ownership of the assets does not change. All that changes is the right to deal with them.

The court will punish a party who breaches one of its orders if the breach is sufficiently serious and the required standard of knowledge and intention is sufficiently proved. This rule applies to freezing injunctions, as the prescribed form and the notices given to the bank in this case make clear. The leading authority on *Mareva* injunctions leaves no room for doubt. In *Z Ltd v A–Z and AA–LL* [1982] QB 558, 572, Lord Denning MR said: 'Every person who has knowledge of [the order] must do what he reasonably can to preserve the asset. He must not assist in any way in the disposal of it. Otherwise he is guilty of a contempt of court.' He repeated this point at pp 573–574 and 575. Eveleigh LJ devoted his judgment in the case wholly to the requirements of contempt in this context. That the power to punish for contempt is not a mere paper tiger is well illustrated by the judgment of Colman J in *Z Bank v D1* [1994] 1 Lloyd's Rep 656 ...

In 1981 Robert Goff J observed that 'the banks in this country have received numerous notices of [*Mareva*] injunctions which have been granted' (*Searose Ltd v Seatrain UK Ltd* [1981] 1 WLR 894, 895), and there is no reason to think that the pace has slackened since. Thus receiving notice of such injunctions is, literally, an everyday event. And the Commissioners are right that they were not claiming substantive relief against the bank as a claimant seeks it against a defendant. But I think the bank is right to say that that is not the whole story, for three main reasons. First, the effect of notification of the order is to override the ordinary contractual duties which govern the relationship of banker and customer. This is

---

[109] [2006] UKHL 28; [2007] 1 AC 181, [9]–[17].

not something of which a bank can complain or of which the bank does complain. A bank's relationship with its customers is subject to the law of the land, which provides for the grant of freezing injunctions. But the effect is none the less to oblige the bank to act in a way which but for the order would be a gross breach of contract. Such a situation must necessarily be very unwelcome to any bank which values its relationship with its customer. Secondly, the order exposes the bank to the risk that its employees may be imprisoned, the bank fined and its assets sequestrated. Of course, this is only a risk if the bank breaches the order in a sufficiently culpable way. But it is not a risk which exists independently of the order, and not a risk to which anyone would wish to be exposed. ...

The *Mareva* jurisdiction has developed as one exercised by court order enforceable only by the court's power to punish those who break its orders. The documentation issued by the court does not hint at the existence of any other remedy. This regime makes perfect sense on the assumption that the only duty owed by a notified party is to the court.

In a similar vein, Lord Hoffmann said:[110]

A freezing order is an injunction made against the putative debtor to which the bank is not a party. But the existence of the injunction may have an effect upon third parties in two ways. First, it is a contempt of court to aid and abet a breach of an injunction by the party against whom the order was made. Secondly, it is an independent contempt of court to do an act which deliberately interferes with the course of justice by frustrating the purpose for which the order was made: see *Attorney-General v Times Newspapers Ltd* [1992] 1 AC 191 and *Attorney-General v Punch Ltd* [2003] 1 AC 1046 for the general principle and *Z Ltd v A–Z and AA–LL* [1982] QB 558, 578 for an explanation by Eveleigh LJ of its application to *Mareva* injunctions. The purpose of serving the bank with the order is therefore to give the bank notice that payment out of the account will frustrate its purpose and, if done deliberately, will be a contempt of court. However, as Lord Hope of Craighead said in *Attorney-General v Punch Ltd* [2003] 1 AC 1046, 1066, for the third party to be liable for contempt:

'it has ... to be shown there was an intention on his part to interfere with or impede the administration of justice. This is an essential ingredient, and it has to be established to the criminal standard of proof.'

The restrictive approach shown by the House of Lords in this case is clearly appropriate. It would be very inconvenient for a bank to be guilty of contempt of court in situations where it had no knowledge of, and assumed no responsibility for, the need to protect the claimant's assets. Third parties owe no duty of care to the claimant who is granted a freezing order. Freezing orders are personal and operate on the defendant alone. To be liable as an accessory, a third party must know that it is assisting the breach of the order.

(v) *Ancillary orders*

It is common for a freezing order to be accompanied by an ancillary order for disclosure. For example, Civil Procedure Rule 25.1(1)(g) provides that the court may make:

an order directing a party to provide information about the location of assets which are or may be the subject of an application for a freezing injunction.

---

[110] Ibid, [29].

This is sensible: if a claimant does not know what assets the defendant has, any freezing order would be much less effective. Ancillary orders for disclosure may be made against the defendant's bank or other third parties.[111] However, the granting of such ancillary orders is a matter for the court's discretion; generally, an order for disclosure will not be made unless it is necessary. If the relevant information could be obtained more easily and less intrusively from the defendant—for example, by ordering that the defendant appear for cross-examination on affidavits sworn by him—then the court will prefer that course of action.[112]

(g) SEARCH ORDERS

Another significant application of the equitable jurisdiction to supplement domestic and international litigation is the search order, sometimes known as the *Anton Piller* order after one of the first cases[113] to recognize the legitimacy of the order. This order is:[114]

> something of a hybrid between disclosure and an injunction.

It might be thought of as an interim mandatory injunction. It allows the claimant, accompanied by his or her lawyer, to enter the defendant's premises and force the defendant to allow the claimant to inspect documents, and remove those specified in the order.[115]

The ability of the courts to award such injunctions evolved at Common Law, but has since been placed on a statutory footing.

CIVIL PROCEDURE ACT 1997

7. Power of courts to make orders for preserving evidence, etc.

(1) The court may make an order under this section for the purpose of securing, in the case of any existing or proposed proceedings in the court—

   (a) the preservation of evidence which is or may be relevant, or

   (b) the preservation of property which is or may be the subject-matter of the proceedings or as to which any question arises or may arise in the proceedings.

(2) A person who is, or appears to the court likely to be, a party to proceedings in the court may make an application for such an order.

(3) Such an order may direct any person to permit any person described in the order, or secure that any person so described is permitted—

   (a) to enter premises in England and Wales, and

   (b) while on the premises, to take in accordance with the terms of the order any of the following steps.

---

[111] *Bankers Trust Co. v Shapira* [1980] 1 WLR 1274.
[112] *A.J. Bekhor & Co. Ltd v Bilton* [1981] QB 923.
[113] The first reported case to make such an order was *EMI Ltd v Pandit* [1975] 1 WLR 302 (Templeman J).
[114] McGhee (ed.), *Snell's Equity* (33rd edn) (London: Sweet & Maxwell, 2015), pp. [18-090].
[115] However, if copies can be made, then the original documents should be returned to the defendant as soon as possible: *Columbia Picture Industries Inc v Robinson* [1987] Ch 38, 76.

(4) Those steps are—

    (a) to carry out a search for or inspection of anything described in the order, and

    (b) to make or obtain a copy, photograph, sample or other record of anything so described.

(5) The order may also direct the person concerned—

    (a) to provide any person described in the order, or secure that any person so described is provided, with any information or article described in the order, and

    (b) to allow any person described in the order, or secure that any person so described is allowed, to retain for safe keeping anything described in the order, and

(6) An order under this section is to have effect subject to such conditions as are specified in the order.

(7) This section does not affect any right of a person to refuse to do anything on the ground that to do so might tend to expose him or his spouse or civil partner to proceedings for an offence or for the recovery of a penalty.

(8) In this section—

'court' means the High Court, and ' premises' includes any vehicle;

and an order under this section may describe anything generally, whether by reference to a class or otherwise.

The procedure for granting search orders and other related orders is governed by the Civil Procedure Rules.[116]

Civil Procedure Rule r 25.1

The court may grant the following interim remedies: …

(c) an order—

    (i) for the detention, custody or preservation of relevant property;

    (ii) for the inspection of relevant property;

    (iii) for the taking of a sample of relevant property;

    (iv) for the carrying out of an experiment on or with relevant property;

    (v) for the sale of relevant property which is of a perishable nature or which for any other good reason it is desirable to sell quickly; and

    (vi) for the payment of income from relevant property until a claim is decided;

(d) an order authorising a person to enter any land or building in the possession of a party to the proceedings for the purposes of carrying out an order under sub-paragraph (c);

…

(h) an order (referred to as a 'search order') under section 7 of the Civil Procedure Act 1997 (order requiring a party to admit another party to premises for the purpose of preserving evidence etc);

(i) an order under section 33 of the Supreme Court Act 1981 or section 52 of the County Courts Act 1984 (order for disclosure of documents or inspection of property before a claim has been made).

Clearly, such orders are very intrusive and the courts are rightly cautious about exercising their jurisdiction to grant search orders. This caution can be discerned in the judgments in *Anton Piller* itself.

---

[116] See also CPR Practice Direction 25, paras 7 and 8.

Anton Piller KG v Manufacturing Process Ltd [1976] Ch 55

The claimant argued that the defendant company had given confidential information to manu-facturers that was damaging to the claimant's business. The claimant applied for an order for permission to enter the defendant's premises and to remove documents into the custody of the claimant's solicitor. The Court of Appeal granted the order.

Lord Denning MR:

During the last 18 months the judges of the Chancery Division have been making orders of a kind not known before. They have some resemblance to search warrants. Under these orders, the plaintiff and his solicitors are authorised to enter the defendant's premises so as to inspect papers, provided the defendant gives permission.

Now this is the important point: the court orders the defendant to give them permission. The judges have been making these orders on *ex parte* applications without prior notice to the defendant ... it is obvious that such an order can only be justified in the most exceptional circumstances ...

Let me say at once that no court in this land has any power to issue a search warrant to enter a man's house so as to see if there are papers or documents there which are of an incriminating nature, whether libels or infringements of copyright or anything else of the kind. No constable or bailiff can knock at the door and demand entry so as to inspect papers or documents. The householder can shut the door in his face and say 'Get out'. That was established in the leading case of *Entick v Carrington* (1765) 2 Wils KB 275. None of us would wish to whittle down that principle in the slightest. But the order sought in this case is not a search warrant. It does not authorise the plaintiffs' solicitors or anyone else to enter the defendants' premises against their will. It does not authorise the breaking down of any doors, nor the slipping-in by a back door, nor getting in by an open door or window. It only authorises entry and inspection by the permission of the defendants. The plaintiffs must get the defendants' permission. But it does do this: it brings pressure on the defendants to give permission. It does more. It actually orders them to give permission—with, I suppose, the result that if they do not give permission, they are guilty of contempt of court.

This may seem to be a search warrant in disguise. But it was fully considered in the House of Lords 150 years ago and held to be legitimate. The case is *United Company of Merchants of England, Trading to the East Indies v Kynaston* (1821) 3 Bli (OS) 153. Lord Redesdale said, at pp. 163–164:

> 'The arguments urged for the appellants at the Bar are founded upon the supposition, that the court has directed a forcible inspection. This is an erroneous view of the case. The order is to permit; and if the East India Company should refuse to permit inspection, they will be guilty of a contempt of the court. ... It is an order operating on the person requiring the defendants to permit inspection, not giving authority of force, or to break open the doors of their warehouse.'

That case was not, however, concerned with papers or things. It was only as to the value of a warehouse; and that could not be obtained without an inspection. But the distinction drawn by Lord Redesdale af-fords ground for thinking that there is jurisdiction to make an order that the defendant 'do permit' when it is necessary in the interests of justice ...

It seems to me that such an order can be made by a judge *ex parte*, but it should only be made where it is essential that the plaintiff should have inspection so that justice can be done between the parties: and when, if the defendant were forewarned, there is a grave danger that vital evidence will be destroyed, that papers will be burnt or lost or hidden, or taken beyond the jurisdiction, and so the ends of justice be defeated: and when the inspection would do no real harm to the defendant or his case.

Nevertheless, in the enforcement of this order, the plaintiffs must act with due circumspection. On the service of it, the plaintiffs should be attended by their solicitor, who is an officer of the court. They should give the defendants an opportunity of considering it and of consulting their own solicitor. If the defendants wish to apply to discharge the order as having been improperly obtained, they must be allow[ed] to do so. If the defendants refuse permission to enter or to inspect, the plaintiffs must not force their way in. They must accept the refusal, and bring it to the notice of the court afterwards, if need be on an application to commit.

You might think that with all these safeguards against abuse, it would be of little use to make such an order. But it can be effective in this way: it serves to tell the defendants that, on the evidence put before it, the court is of opinion that they ought to permit inspection—nay, it orders them to permit—and that they refuse at their peril. It puts them in peril not only of proceedings for contempt, but also of adverse inferences being drawn against them; so much so that their own solicitor may often advise them to comply. We are told that in two at least of the cases such an order has been effective. We are prepared, therefore, to sanction its continuance, but only in an extreme case where there is grave danger of property being smuggled away or of vital evidence being destroyed.

Ormrod LJ:

I agree with all that Lord Denning MR has said. The proposed order is at the extremity of this court's powers. Such orders, therefore, will rarely be made, and only when there is no alternative way of ensuring that justice is done to the applicant.

There are three essential pre-conditions for the making of such an order, in my judgment. First, there must be an extremely strong *prima facie* case. Secondly, the damage, potential or actual, must be very serious for the applicant. Thirdly, there must be clear evidence that the defendants have in their possession incriminating documents or things, and that there is a real possibility that they may destroy such material before any application *inter partes* can be made.

The form of the order makes it plain that the court is not ordering or granting anything equivalent to a search warrant. The order is an order on the defendant *in personam* to permit inspection. It is therefore open to him to refuse to comply with such an order, but at his peril either of further proceedings for contempt of court—in which case, of course, the court will have the widest discretion as to how to deal with it, and if it turns out that the order was made improperly in the first place, the contempt will be dealt with accordingly—but more important, of course, the refusal to comply may be the most damning evidence against the defendant at the subsequent trial. Great responsibility clearly rests on the solicitors for the applicant to ensure that the carrying-out of such an order is meticulously carefully done with the fullest respect for the defendant's rights, as Lord Denning MR has said, of applying to the court, should he feel it necessary to do so, before permitting the inspection.

Clearly, the defendant is left with little practical option but to comply with the order, even though the first he or she will know about it is when the claimant turns up at his or her property. Given the invasion of the defendant's privacy and property, this sort of order has been described one of the law's two 'nuclear' weapons.[117]

The restrictions highlighted by Ormrod LJ are crucial. The claimant's prima facie case must be extremely strong; he or she must be facing very serious damage; it must be clearly established that the defendant does actually possess incriminating evidence and that there is a real risk that such material will be destroyed. If these conditions are not met, then a without-notice injunction to interfere with the defendant's freedom should not be granted. The existence of these high hurdles to the granting of a search order means that search orders are not necessarily unjustifiable violations of a person's right to

---

[117] *Bank Mellat v Nikpour* [1985] FSR 87, 92 (Donaldson LJ). The other is a freezing injunction.

privacy under Article 8 of the European Convention on Human Rights, although in an extreme case the violation might be unjustifiable.[118]

Search orders have been particularly useful in intellectual property disputes,[119] but are not limited in their application, and have even been granted in proceedings for financial relief following the presentation of a petition for divorce, for example.[120] Since the application is made without notice to the defendant, it is imperative that the applicant disclose all relevant information to the court, and be able to issue the usual undertaking in damages. This is particularly important because, even though the injunction is interlocutory, it is clear that its effects cannot be undone. If the claimant or his solicitors act oppressively or improperly in the execution of the order, then aggravated damages may be awarded.[121]

In *Universal Thermosensors Ltd v Hibben*, Nicholls V-C highlighted some of the procedural safeguards that exist.

Universal Thermosensors Ltd v Hibben [1992] 1 WLR 840, 860–1 (Nicholls V-C)

(1) *Anton Piller* orders normally contain a term that before complying with the order the defendant may obtain legal advice, provided this is done forthwith. This is an important safeguard for defendants, not least because *Anton Piller* orders tend to be long and complicated, and many defendants cannot be expected to understand much of what they are told by the solicitor serving the order. But such a term, if it is to be of use, requires that in general *Anton Piller* orders should be permitted to be executed only on working days in office hours, when a solicitor can be expected to be available. …

(2) If the order is to be executed at a private house, and it is at all likely that a woman may be in the house alone, the solicitor serving the order must be, or must be accompanied by, a woman. …

(3) … Understandably, those who execute these orders are concerned to search and seize and then get away as quickly as possible so as to minimise the risk of confrontation and physical violence. Nevertheless, in general *Anton Piller* orders should expressly provide that, unless this is seriously impracticable, a detailed list of the items being removed should be prepared at the premises before they are removed, and that the defendant should be given an opportunity to check this list at the time.

(4) *Anton Piller* orders frequently contain an injunction restraining those on whom they are served from informing others of the existence of the order for a limited period. This is to prevent one defendant from alerting others to what is happening. There is an exception for communication with a lawyer for the purpose of seeking legal advice. In the present case that injunction was expressed to last for a whole week. That is far too long. I suspect something went awry with the drafting of the order in this case.

(5) … Orders should provide that, unless there is good reason for doing otherwise, the order should not be executed at business premises save in the presence of a responsible officer or representative of the company or trader in question.

(6) … [the claimant in this case] carried out a thorough search of all the documents of a competitor company. This is most unsatisfactory. When *Anton Piller* orders are made … consideration should be given to devising some means, appropriate to the facts of the case, by which this situation can be avoided.[122]

---

[118] *Chappell v United Kingdom* (1990) 12 EHHR 1.
[119] E.g. *Ex p Island Records Ltd* [1978] Ch 122.
[120] E.g. *Tchenguiz v Imerman* [2010] EWCA Civ 908; [2011] Fam 116.
[121] *Columbia Picture Industries Inc v Robinson* [1987] Ch 38.
[122] Search orders should not be used to facilitate a 'fishing expedition'.

(7) *Anton Piller* orders invariably provide for service to be effected by a solicitor. The court relies heavily on the solicitor, as an officer of the court, to see that the order is properly executed. Unhappily, the history in the present case, and what has happened in other cases, show that this safeguard is inadequate. The solicitor may be young and have little or no experience of *Anton Piller* orders. Frequently he is the solicitor acting for the plaintiff in the action, and however diligent and fair minded he may be, he is not the right person to be given a task which to some extent involves protecting the interests of the defendant. I think there is force in some of the criticisms set out in the invaluable article by Professor Dockray and Mr. Hugh Laddie Q.C. on 'Piller Problems' (1990) 106 L.Q.R. 601. It seems to me that the way ahead here, pursuing one of the suggestions made in that article, is that when making *Anton Piller* orders judges should give serious consideration to the desirability of providing, by suitable undertakings and other-wise, (a) that the order should be served, and its execution should be supervised, by a solicitor other than a member of the firm of solicitors acting for the plaintiff in the action; (b) that he or she should be an experienced solicitor having some familiarity with the workings of *Anton Piller* orders, and with judicial observations on this subject ...; (c) that the solicitor should prepare a written report on what occurred when the order was executed; (d) that a copy of the report should be served on the defendants; and (e) that in any event and within the next few days the plaintiff must return to the court and present that report at an inter partes hearing, preferably to the judge who made the order. As to (b), I can see advantages in the plaintiff being required to include in his evidence, put to the judge in support of his application for an *Anton Piller* order, details of the name of the solicitor and of his experience.

A difficult issue concerns the privilege against self-incrimination.[123] In *Rank Film Distributors Ltd v Video Information Centre,* the House of Lords held that this privilege should generally be a legitimate reason for refusing to comply with a search order,[124] but statute means that this privilege is no longer available in the context of intellectual property disputes.[125] However, it may still be pleaded in other contexts where the execution of the search order may assist with a criminal prosecution.[126] But in *C plc v P,*[127] it was held that the privilege did not extend to documents or things that have 'an existence independent of the will' of the person who sought to plead it. It followed in that case that the privilege was not available to a defendant who had been required, pursuant to a search order, to hand over a computer to an independent expert, where the hard drive of the computer contained indecent images of children.

3. SPECIFIC PERFORMANCE

Unlike some other jurisdictions, the primary remedy for breach of contract in English law is dam-ages. Specific performance will only be awarded if damages are an inadequate remedy. This is most likely to be the case where the subject matter of the contract is unique in some way.[128] Thus, specific performance is regularly granted in support of agreements for the transfer of land or shares in private companies.[129]

---

[123] Civil Evidence Act 1968, s. 14(1).
[124] [1982] AC 380.
[125] Supreme Court Act 1981, s. 72. See too Theft Act 1968, s. 31.
[126] E.g. *AT & T Istel Ltd v Tully* [1993] AC 45.
[127] [2007] EWCA Civ 493; [2007] 3 WLR 437.
[128] See Jones and Goodhart, *Specific Performance* (2nd edn) (West Sussex: Tottel Publishing, 1996), pp. 143–54.
[129] Although the usual bars to equitable orders apply: see Chapter 20.1(a), p. 976.

However, in *Co-operative Insurance Society v Argyll Stores (Holdings) Ltd*[130] the House of Lords was cautious about increasing the frequency of awards of specific performance. Lord Hoffmann's speech, given here, must be heeded when seeking this type of equitable relief. Various reasons for the reluctance of English law to grant specific performance might be given, but two seem particularly important: specific performance avoids the usual requirement that the victim of a breach mitigate his or her loss, and specific performance—like all equitable remedies—is enforced by the threat of contempt of court. This means that a person who breaches his or her contract and a subsequent order for specific performance might be fined or sent to prison. Judges tend to find this largely unpalatable in the context of commercial contracts.

Co-operative Insurance Society v Argyll Stores (Holdings) Ltd [1998] AC 1 (HL)

The claimant granted the defendant a lease of a unit in a shopping centre in Sheffield. The defendant covenanted to keep the premises open for retail trade during usual business hours. After a business review, the defendant announced that it would close the shop. The claimant sought specific performance of the covenant. The trial judge granted an order for damages but not specific performance. This was reversed by the Court of Appeal. The defendant successfully appealed to the House of Lords. The court would not grant specific performance or a mandatory injunction to require the business to be carried on.

Lord Hoffmann:

A decree of specific performance is of course a discretionary remedy and the question for your Lordships is whether the Court of Appeal was entitled to set aside the exercise of the judge's discretion. There are well-established principles which govern the exercise of the discretion but these, like all equitable principles, are flexible and adaptable to achieve the ends of equity, which is, as Lord Selborne LC once remarked, to 'do more perfect and complete justice' than would be the result of leaving the parties to their remedies at common law: *Wilson v Northampton and Banbury Junction Railway Co.* (1874) LR 9 Ch App 279, 284.

...

The practice of not ordering a defendant to carry on a business is not entirely dependent upon damages being an adequate remedy. In *Dowty Boulton Paul Ltd v Wolverhampton Corporation* [1971] 1 WLR 204 Sir John Pennycuick V-C refused to order the corporation to maintain an airfield as a going concern because: 'it is very well established that the court will not order specific performance of an obligation to carry on a business': see p. 211. He added: 'it is unnecessary in the circumstances to discuss whether damages would be an adequate remedy to the company': see p. 212. Thus the reasons which underlie the established practice may justify a refusal of specific performance even when damages are not an adequate remedy.

The most frequent reason given in the cases for declining to order someone to carry on a business is that it would require constant supervision by the court. In *JC Williamson Ltd v Lukey and Mulholland* (1931) 45 CLR 282, 297–298, Dixon J said flatly: 'specific performance is inapplicable when the continued supervision of the court is necessary in order to ensure the fulfilment of the contract'.

... [S]upervision would in practice take the form of rulings by the court, on applications made by the parties, as to whether there had been a breach of the order. It is the possibility of the court having to give an indefinite series of such rulings in order to ensure the execution of the order which has been regarded as undesirable.

---

[130] [1998] AC 1.

Why should this be so? A principal reason is that ... the only means available to the court to enforce its order is the quasi-criminal procedure of punishment for contempt. This is a powerful weapon; so powerful, in fact, as often to be unsuitable as an instrument for adjudicating upon the disputes which may arise over whether a business is being run in accordance with the terms of the court's order. The heavy-handed nature of the enforcement mechanism is a consideration which may go to the exercise of the court's discretion in other cases as well, but its use to compel the running of a business is perhaps the paradigm case of its disadvantages and it is in this context that I shall discuss them.

The prospect of committal or even a fine, with the damage to commercial reputation which will be caused by a finding of contempt of court, is likely to have at least two undesirable consequences. First, the defendant, who *ex hypothesi* did not think that it was in his economic interest to run the business at all, now has to make decisions under a sword of Damocles which may descend if the way the business is run does not conform to the terms of the order. This is, as one might say, no way to run a business. ...

Secondly, the seriousness of a finding of contempt for the defendant means that any application to enforce the order is likely to be a heavy and expensive piece of litigation. The possibility of repeated applications over a period of time means that, in comparison with a once-and-for-all inquiry as to damages, the enforcement of the remedy is likely to be expensive in terms of cost to the parties and the resources of the judicial system.

This is a convenient point at which to distinguish between orders which require a defendant to carry on an activity, such as running a business over a more or less extended period of time, and orders which require him to achieve a result. The possibility of repeated applications for rulings on compliance with the order which arises in the former case does not exist to anything like the same extent in the latter. Even if the achievement of the result is a complicated matter which will take some time, the court, if called upon to rule, only has to examine the finished work and say whether it complies with the order ...

... If the terms of the court's order, reflecting the terms of the obligation, cannot be precisely drawn, the possibility of wasteful litigation over compliance is increased. So is the oppression caused by the defendant having to do things under threat of proceedings for contempt. The less precise the order, the fewer the signposts to the forensic minefield which he has to traverse. ...

From a wider perspective, it cannot be in the public interest for the courts to require someone to carry on business at a loss if there is any plausible alternative by which the other party can be given compensation. It is not only a waste of resources but yokes the parties together in a continuing hostile relationship. The order for specific performance prolongs the battle. If the defendant is ordered to run a business, its conduct becomes the subject of a flow of complaints, solicitors' letters and affidavits. This is wasteful for both parties and the legal system. An award of damages, on the other hand, brings the litigation to an end. The defendant pays damages, the forensic link between them is severed, they go their separate ways and the wounds of conflict can heal.

4. RECTIFICATION

By the remedy of rectification, courts are able to correct mistakes in an instrument so that it accords with the true intentions of the party (in a unilateral instrument, such as a will)[131] or parties (in the case of bilateral instruments, such as contracts) who made it. It is important to remember that this doctrine cannot be exploited to improve a bargain made by the parties: only a mistake regarding the language used to record the agreement can be rectified.[132]

---

[131] See e.g. Administration of Justice Act 1982, s. 20(1); *Marley v Rawlings* [2014] UKSC 2; [2015] AC 129.
[132] *Frederick E Rose Ltd v William H Pim & Co. Ltd* [1953] 2 QB 450.

Being an equitable remedy, it is discretionary and the usual bars to equitable relief apply.[133] Given the violence rectification effects upon documents voluntarily executed, the claimant must show convincing proof that the document needs to be rectified.[134] Although the scope of rectification might be considered to be increasingly limited as a result of a more 'liberal' approach to the interpretation of documents,[135] it is clear that rectification is still a necessary remedy. For example, rectification is best able to insert absent clauses, remove erroneous clauses, rely upon pre-contractual negotiations and evidence of the parties' subjective intentions in order to establish the actual substance of a contract, and rectification is also well equipped to protect third party rights.[136]

There are two distinct types of mistake that might lead to rectification of a bargain: common mistake and unilateral mistake. The current approach to common mistake rectification was encapsulated by Etherton LJ in *Daventry DC v Daventry & District Housing Ltd*:[137]

> (1) the parties had a common continuing intention, whether or not amounting to an agreement, in respect of a particular matter in the instrument to be rectified; (2) which existed at the time of execution of the instrument sought to be rectified; (3) such common continuing intention to be established objectively, that is to say by reference to what an objective observer would have thought the intentions of the parties to be; and (4) by mistake, the instrument did not reflect that common intention.

In this passage, Etherton LJ synthesized the requirements of Gibson LJ in *Swainland Builders Limited v Freehold Properties Limited*[138] with the approach of Lord Hoffmann in *Chartbrook Ltd v Persimmon Homes Ltd*.[139] The latter's comments affected the third requirement: Lord Hoffmann thought that the common intention of the parties should be judged objectively by a reasonable observer. Admittedly, his comments were *obiter*, but they were accepted by counsel in *Daventry*.[140] It contrasts with the more traditional approach, which looked to the parties' *actual* intentions: it needed to be shown that *both* parties were *actually* labouring under a mistake for common mistake rectification to be available.[141] It is suggested that this subjective approach is the more preferable approach.[142] After all, the best *objective* evidence of the parties' intentions is the written instrument itself. The only justification for interfering with a formal, written instrument should be in order to accord with the parties' *actual* intentions.[143]

A further difficulty with the objective approach to determining a common mistake is that a common mistake might be *objectively* found, even though only one party was *actually* labouring

---

[133] Cf. Chapter 20.1(a), p. 976.

[134] *Countess of Shelburne v Earl of Inchiquin* (1784) 1 Bro CC 338, 341; *James Hay Pension Trustees Ltd v Kean Hird et al.* [2005] EWHC (Ch) 1093, [81].

[135] Particularly after judgments such as *Investors Compensation Scheme Ltd v West Bromwich Building Society* [1998] 1 WLR 896 and *Chartbrook Ltd v Persimmon Homes Ltd* [2009] UKHL 38; [2009] 1 AC 1101. See Buxton, ' "Construction" and Rectification after Chartbrook' (2010) CLJ 253.

[136] Cf. *Cherry Tree Investments Ltd v Landmain Ltd* [2012] EWCA Civ 736.

[137] [2011] EWCA Civ 1153; [2012] 1 WLR 1333, [80].

[138] [2002] EWCA Civ 560; [2002] EGLR 71, [33].

[139] [2009] UKHL 38; [2009] 1 AC 1101; noted Davies, 'Finding the Limits of Contractual Interpretation' [2009] LMCLQ 420.

[140] Toulson LJ thought it would be 'a bold course' for the Court of Appeal not to follow a unanimous opinion of the House of Lords, even if the point under discussion was *obiter*: *Daventry* [2011] EWCA Civ 1153; [2012] 1 WLR 1333, [108].

[141] See Bromley, 'Rectification in Equity' (1971) 87 LQR 532, who was even critical of the need for an 'outward expression of accord' as a substantive element of a claim for rectification. See too *Agip SpA v Navgazione Alta Italia SpA* [1984] 1 Lloyd's Rep 353; *Munt v Beasley* [2006] EWCA Civ 370.

[142] See e.g. *Crossco No.4 Unlimited v Jolan Ltd* [2011] EWHC 803 (Ch), [253] (Morgan J); *Tartsinis v Navona Management Co* [2015] EWHC 57 (Comm), [90]–[99] (Leggatt J).

[143] See further Davies, 'Rectifying the Course of Rectification' (2012) 75 MLR 412. Cp Smith, 'Rectification of Contracts for Common Mistake, *Joscelyne v Nissen*, and Subjective States of Mind' (2007) 123 LQR 116; Burrows, 'Construction and Rectification' in *Contract Terms* (eds A Burrows and E Peel) (Oxford: Oxford University Press, 2007).

under any mistake. Such cases would be better considered under a doctrine of 'unilateral mistake rectification'. In *Daventry*, the Court of Appeal recognized that Lord Hoffmann's approach had blurred the boundary between unilateral mistake and common mistake. Lord Neuberger MR said: [144]

> (i) there is much to be said for the view that many rectification claims which might previously have been regarded as based on unilateral mistake may now be better treated as being based on common mistake, and (ii) if we were deciding this appeal without the benefit of Lord Hoffmann's analysis, I might not have thought it right to allow the appeal on the ground of common mistake, although I may have done so on the ground of unilateral mistake.

Unilateral mistake rectification is more onerous than common mistake rectification as regards bilateral instruments: since only *one* party was mistaken, rectifying the document will impose upon him a bargain to which he did not agree. A very good reason to do this must be established. A string of Court of Appeal decisions makes it clear that for the defendant's conscience to be affected and equitable relief justified, the defendant must *actually* know of, or at least recklessly turn a blind eye to, the claimant's mistake, and then fail to inform the claimant of that mistake at the date of execution.[145] It is absolutely right that the threshold for relief be so demanding, given the 'drastic'[146] nature of relief.

However, in *Daventry*, Toulson LJ was apparently persuaded[147] by McLauchlan's suggestion that unilateral mistake rectification should be awarded where the defendant *ought* to have been aware of the mistake, and the claimant was led reasonably to believe that the defendant was agreeing to the claimant's interpretation of the bargain.[148] But here again, an objective approach to intention is unsatisfactory. As Hodge has observed, the traditional, subjective approach ought to be maintained:[149]

> Good reason must be demonstrated before holding a contracting party to terms which differ, not only from those which he subjectively intended, but also from those to which he objectively assented by his conduct in signing a document which records those terms.

Rectification for a unilateral mistake should *not* be readily granted. The intervention of equity can only be justified if the *actual* intentions of the parties are such that to stick to the written agreement would be unconscionable.

It should, however, be noted that where the instrument being rectified is not a contract but a unilateral instrument, such as a trust instrument, then it is only the settlor's intention that is relevant and not the intention of the trustees. In *Day v Day*, Etherton C said:[150]

> What is relevant in such a case is the subjective intention of the settlor. It is not a legal requirement for rectification of a voluntary settlement that there is any outward expression or objective communication

---

[144] [2011] EWCA Civ 1153; [2012] 1 WLR 1333, [226].

[145] *A Roberts & Co. Ltd v Leicestershire CC* [1961] Ch 555; *Thomas Bates v Wyndham's* [1981] 1 All ER 1077; *Commission for New Towns v Cooper* [1995] Ch 259.

[146] *Agip SpA v Navigazione Alta Italia SpA*, 'The Nai Genova' [1984] 1 Lloyd's Rep 353, 365 (Slade LJ). Blackburne J has commented that '[i]t is drastic because rectification for unilateral mistake has the result of imposing on the defendant a contract which he did not, and did not intend to, make and relieving the claimant from a contract which he did, albeit did not intend to, make': *George Wimpey UK Ltd v VI Construction Ltd* [2005] EWCA Civ 77; [2005] BLR 135, [75].

[147] [2011] EWCA Civ 1153; [2012] 1 WLR 1333, [173]–[178].

[148] McLauchlan, 'The "Drastic" Remedy of Rectification for Unilateral Mistake' (2008) 124 LQR 608.

[149] Hodge QC, *Rectification: The Modern Law and Practice Governing Claims for Rectification for Mistake* (London: Sweet & Maxwell, para 4-22).

[150] [2013] EWCA Civ 280; [2014] Ch 114, [40].

of the settlor's intention equivalent to the need to show an outward expression of accord for rectification of a contract for mutual mistake … In *Chartbrook Ltd v Persimmon Homes Ltd* [2009] UKHL 38, [2009] 1 AC 1101 the House of Lords agreed with Lord Hoffmann's (obiter) explanation of an objective test for rectification for mutual mistake in the case of a contract so as to bring the final document into line with the parties' prior consensus objectively ascertained. Nothing he said there touched upon the requirements for rectification for unilateral mistake in a non-contract case. Although, as I have said, there is no legal requirement of an outward expression or objective communication of the settlor's intention in such a case, it will plainly be difficult as a matter of evidence to discharge the burden of proving that there was a mistake in the absence of an outward expression of intention.

5. RESCISSION

If a transaction is rescinded, then it is treated as if it had never come into existence and the parties are restored to their original positions. A contract will be voidable—and therefore liable to be rescinded—where the consent of one of the parties was impaired, for example due to misrepresentation, duress, or undue influence. But other transactions can also be rescinded, such as deeds of gift and voluntary settlements; any disposition made in breach of fiduciary duty might be rescinded in Equity.[151]

Unless and until a transaction is rescinded, it is valid and enforceable. Rescission will no longer be possible where it is impossible to restore the parties to their original positions before the contract was made ('*restitutio in integrum*').[152] A claimant will also lose the right to rescind if he or she affirms the contract. However, affirmation only occurs once the claimant knew of the circumstances giving rise to the right of rescission, *and* that he had the legal right to rescind.[153] It is also possible that rescission will be barred through laches.[154] It is often also said that third party rights might bar rescission; although rescission will not be allowed where that would prejudice the rights of third parties, it would seem that rescission might be effected by allowing third party purchasers to keep the asset that was the subject matter of the contract, but requiring the defendant to hand over the proceeds of sale,[155] for example.[156]

Rescission is also possible at Common Law if there has been fraudulent misrepresentation, duress, incapacity, or non-disclosure of a material fact for certain types of contract. Rescission at Common Law is a self-help remedy, which takes effect by the act of the party seeking rescission,[157] which is usually effected by communication to the other party to the contract and does not require a court order.[158] By contrast, rescission in Equity is effected by the court,[159] and is available in a wider range of circumstances. The equitable jurisdiction is broader and more flexible, but some commentators favour maintaining rescission at Common Law because a self-help remedy is useful and appropriate

---

[151] See e.g. *Pitt v Holt* [2011] EWCA Civ 197; [2011] 3 WLR; see Chapter 11.7(g), pp. 577–83.

[152] *Clarke v Dickson* (1858) El Bl & El 148.

[153] *Evans v Bartlam* [1937] AC 473, 479 (Lord Atkin).

[154] *Salt v Stratstone Specialist Ltd (t/a Stratstone Cadillac Newcastle)* [2015] EWCA Civ 745; [2015] CTLC 206; *Erlanger v The New Sombrero Phosphate Co.* (1878) 3 App Cas 1218, 1279 (Lord Blackburn).

[155] *Fox v Mackreth* (1788) 2 Bro CC 44.

[156] See generally O'Sullivan, Elliott, and Zakrzewski, *The Law of Rescission* (Oxford: Oxford University Press, 2008), [20.23]–[20.27].

[157] *Halpern v Halpern (No. 2)* [2006] EWHC 1728 (Comm); [2007] QB 88, [26] (Nigel Teare QC).

[158] *Brotherton v Aseguradora Cobeguros (No. 2)* [2003] EWCA Civ 705; [2003] 3 All ER (Comm) 298, [27] (Mance LJ), [45] (Buxton LJ). See too *Car & Universal Finance Co. Ltd v Caldwell* [1965] 1 QB 525.

[159] *Erlanger v New Sombrero Phosphate Co.* (1878) 3 App Cas 1218.

in cases of fraud, for example.[160] Nevertheless, there is also support for fusion in this area. In this vein, Carnwath LJ commented in *Halpern v Halpern* that:[161]

> 130 years after the 'fusion' of law and equity by the Judicature Act 1873, an argument based on a material difference in the two systems would have faced an uphill task. Section 49 of the [Senior] Court Act 1981 ... reproduces the effect of section 25(11) of the 1873 Act; it states:
>
> > '... wherever there is any conflict or variance between the rules of equity and the common law with reference to the same matter, the rules of equity shall prevail.'

6. DAMAGES IN LIEU OF EQUITABLE ORDERS

The jurisdiction to grant damages in lieu of ordering injunctions or specific performance was available under section 2 of the Chancery Amendment Act 1858, commonly known as 'Lord Cairns' Act'. This has now been replaced by section 50 of the Supreme Court Act 1981:

> Where the Court of Appeal or the High Court has jurisdiction to entertain an application for an injunction or specific performance, it may award damages in addition to, or in substitution for, an injunction or specific performance.

The court is empowered to grant damages in *addition* to an equitable order if the circumstances require, but of particular importance are the principles that underpin the court's discretion to award damages in *substitution* for such orders.[162] The leading decision has long been that of the Court of Appeal in *Shelfer v City of London Electric Lighting Co.*

Shelfer v City of London Electric Lighting Co. [1985] 1 Ch 287

A nuisance was a caused by the defendants carrying out noisy and disruptive work. The claimants sought an injunction to prevent further work continuing the nuisance. Kekewich J, at first instance, thought that an injunction was inappropriate and awarded damages in substitution for the injunction (such damages are sometimes known as 'damages in lieu of an injunction', or simply 'damages in lieu'). The Court of Appeal disagreed, insisting that the threshold for the court's exercising its discretion to award damages in lieu was very high. Even though the defendants had statutory authority to carry out the work, an injunction was the appropriate remedy.

Lord Halsbury:[163]

But there is nothing in this case which to my mind can justify the Court in refusing to aid the legal rights established, by an injunction preventing the continuance of the nuisance. On the contrary, the effect of such a refusal in a case like the present would necessarily operate to enable a company who could

---

[160] See e.g. O'Sullivan, Elliott and Zakrzewski, *The Law of Rescission* (Oxford: Oxford University Press, 2008), ch. 10.

[161] [2007] EWCA Civ 291; [2008] QB 195, [70].

[162] The Court also has a statutory discretion to award damages in lieu of rescission under Misrepresentation Act 1967, s. 2(2). For discussion of this provision, see *William Sindall Plc v Cambridgeshire CC* [1994] 1 WLR 1016; [1994] 3 All ER 932.

[163] [1895] 1 Ch 287, 311.

afford it to drive a neighbouring proprietor to sell, whether he would or no, by continuing a nuisance, and simply paying damages for its continuance.

Lindley LJ:[164]

… ever since Lord Cairns' Act was passed the Court of Chancery has repudiated the notion that the Legislature intended to turn that Court into a tribunal for legalizing wrongful acts; or in other words, the Court has always protested against the notion that it ought to allow a wrong to continue simply because the wrongdoer is able and willing to pay for the injury he may inflict. Neither has the circumstance that the wrongdoer is in some sense a public benefactor (e.g., a gas or water company or a sewer authority) ever been considered a sufficient reason for refusing to protect by injunction an individual whose rights are being persistently infringed. Expropriation, even for a money consideration, is only justifiable when Parliament has sanctioned it. Courts of Justice are not like Parliament, which considers whether proposed works will be so beneficial to the public as to justify exceptional legislation, and the deprivation of people of their rights with or without compensation. Lord Cairns' Act was not passed in order to supersede legislation for public purposes, but to enable the Court of Chancery to administer justice between litigants more effectually than it could before the Act.

…

Without denying the jurisdiction to award damages instead of an injunction, even in cases of continuing actionable nuisances, such jurisdiction ought not to be exercised in such cases except under very exceptional circumstances. I will not attempt to specify them, or to lay down rules for the exercise of judicial discretion. It is sufficient to refer, by way of example, to trivial and occasional nuisances: cases in which a plaintiff has shewn that he only wants money; vexatious and oppressive cases; and cases where the plaintiff has so conducted himself as to render it unjust to give him more than pecuniary relief. In all such cases as these, and in all others where an action for damages is really an adequate remedy—as where the acts complained of are already finished—an injunction can be properly refused.

AL Smith LJ:[165]

Many Judges have stated, and I emphatically agree with them, that a person by committing a wrongful act (whether it be a public company for public purposes or a private individual) is not thereby entitled to ask the Court to sanction his doing so by purchasing his neighbour's rights, by assessing damages in that behalf, leaving his neighbour with the nuisance, or his lights dimmed, as the case may be.

In such cases the well-known rule is not to accede to the application, but to grant the injunction sought, for the plaintiff's legal right has been invaded, and he is prima facie entitled to an injunction.

There are, however, cases in which this rule may be relaxed, and in which damages may be awarded in substitution for an injunction as authorized by this section.

In any instance in which a case for an injunction has been made out, if the plaintiff by his acts or laches has disentitled himself to an injunction the Court may award damages in its place. So again, whether the case be for a mandatory injunction or to restrain a continuing nuisance, the appropriate remedy may be damages in lieu of an injunction, assuming a case for an injunction to be made out.

In my opinion, it may be stated as a good working rule that—

(1) If the injury to the plaintiff's legal rights is small,

(2) And is one which is capable of being estimated in money,

(3) And is one which can be adequately compensated by a small money payment,

---

[164] Ibid, 315–16.
[165] Ibid, 322–3.

> (4) And the case is one in which it would be oppressive to the defendant to grant an injunction:—
>
> then damages in substitution for an injunction may be given.
>
> There may also be cases in which, though the four above mentioned requirements exist, the defendant by his conduct, as, for instance, hurrying up his buildings so as if possible to avoid an injunction, or otherwise acting with a reckless disregard to the plaintiff's rights, has disentitled himself from asking that damages may be assessed in substitution for an injunction.

This case has traditionally been pivotal to judges' decisions whether or not to award damages in substitution for an injunction. Significantly, the starting point is very strongly in favour of an injunction. The 'good working rule' highlighted by AL Smith LJ suggests that it will only be in extreme circumstances that an injunction should be replaced with damages. This seems appropriate: after all, the defendant will generally have breached the claimant's property rights and thereby deprived the claimant of the *choice* whether or not to sell his rights. It is only in extreme circumstances that a court should exercise its discretion by forcing the claimant to 'sell' his rights, rather than grant an injunction and thereby encourage the defendant to negotiate with the claimant to agree a fee for the release of the injunction.

Commenting on Lord Cairns' Act, Jolowicz wrote that:[166]

> while the jurisdiction to award such damages must be exercised with care and with due regard to the plaintiff's legal rights, its existence must not be overlooked, still less denied.

Although many cases continued to apply the *Shelfer* guidelines,[167] other decisions showed a greater willingness to grant damages in lieu of an injunction.[168] The law in this area has now been thrown into some doubt by the decision of the Supreme Court in *Coventry v Lawrence*.[169]

Coventry v Lawrence [2014] UKSC 13; [2014] AC 822

The defendants obtained planning permission for a stadium which was to be used for speedway racing. The stadium was later used for stock car racing. This was very noisy, and the claimants sought an injunction to restrain the nuisance. Richard Seymour QC granted an injunction;[170] the Court of Appeal disagreed;[171] the Supreme Court allowed the appeal. At first instance, the judge was not asked to grant damages in lieu of an injunction, probably because there was little realistic possibility of success if *Shelfer* was applied.[172] However, Lord Neuberger said that the defendants should be free to argue that the injunction granted should be discharged, and damages awarded in lieu. Strictly, the comments of the Supreme Court on this issue were *obiter*, but it is likely that they will prove to be influential.

Lord Neuberger:

In more recent times, the Court of Appeal seems to have assumed that the approach of Lindley and A L Smith LJJ in *Shelfer* represents the law, and indeed that the four tests suggested by A L Smith LJ are

---

[166] 'Damages in Equity—a Study of Lord Cairns' Act' (1975) CLJ 224, 252.
[167] E.g. *Regan v Paul Properties Ltd* [2006] EWCA Civ 1391, [35]–[36].
[168] E.g. *Jaggard v Sawyer* [1995] 1 WLR 269.
[169] [2014] UKSC 13; [2014] AC 822.
[170] [2011] EWHC 360 (QB).
[171] [2012] EWCA Civ 26; [2012] 1 WLR 2127.
[172] [2014] UKSC 13; [2014] AC 822, [149]–[150] (Lord Neuberger).

normally to be applied, so that, unless all four tests are satisfied, there was no jurisdiction to refuse an injunction. That seems to have been the approach of Geoffrey Lane LJ in *Miller* [1977] 1 QB 966 … and of Lawton LJ in *Kennaway* [1981] QB 88 …

In *Watson* [2009] 3 All ER 249, the Court of Appeal reversed the trial judge's decision to award damages instead of an injunction in a case where the nuisance was very similar in nature and cause to that alleged in this case. At para 44, Sir Andrew Morritt C described 'the appropriate test' as having been 'clearly established by the decision of the Court of Appeal in *Shelfer*', namely 'that damages in lieu of an injunction should only be awarded under "very exceptional circumstances"'. He also said that Shelfer 'established that the circumstance that the wrongdoer is in some sense a public benefactor is not a sufficient reason for refusing an injunction', although he accepted at para 51 that 'the effect on the public' could properly be taken into account in a case 'where the damage to the claimant is minimal'.

…

… the approach to be adopted by a judge when being asked to award damages instead of an injunction should, in my view, be much more flexible than that suggested in the recent cases of *Regan* and *Watson*. It seems to me that (i) an almost mechanical application of A L Smith LJ's four tests, and (ii) an approach which involves damages being awarded only in 'very exceptional circumstances', are each simply wrong in principle, and give rise to a serious risk of going wrong in practice. (Quite apart from this, exceptionality may be a questionable guide in any event – see *Manchester City Council v Pinnock (Secretary of State for Communities and Local Government intervening)* [2011] 2 AC 104, para 51).

The court's power to award damages in lieu of an injunction involves a classic exercise of discretion, which should not, as a matter of principle, be fettered, particularly in the very constrained way in which the Court of Appeal has suggested in *Regan* and *Watson*. And, as a matter of practical fairness, each case is likely to be so fact-sensitive that any firm guidance is likely to do more harm than good. On this aspect, I would adopt the observation of Millett LJ in *Jaggard* [1995] 1 WLR 269, 288, where he said:

> 'Reported cases are merely illustrations of circumstances in which particular judges have exercised their discretion, in some cases by granting an injunction, and in others by awarding damages instead. Since they are all cases on the exercise of a discretion, none of them is a binding authority on how the discretion should be exercised. The most that any of them can demonstrate is that in similar circumstances it would not be wrong to exercise the discretion in the same way. But it does not follow that it would be wrong to exercise it differently.'

Having approved that statement, it is only right to acknowledge that this does not prevent the courts from laying down rules as to what factors can, and cannot, be taken into account by a judge when deciding whether to exercise his discretion to award damages in lieu. Indeed, it is appropriate to give as much guidance as possible so as to ensure that, while the discretion is not fettered, its manner of exercise is as predictable as possible. I would accept that the *prima facie* position is that an injunction should be granted, so the legal burden is on the defendant to show why it should not.

…

Where does that leave A L Smith LJ's four tests? While the application of any such series of tests cannot be mechanical, I would adopt a modified version of the view expressed by Romer LJ in *Fishenden* 153 LT 128, 141. First, the application of the four tests must not be such as 'to be a fetter on the exercise of the court's discretion'. Secondly, it would, in the absence of additional relevant circumstances pointing the other way, normally be right to refuse an injunction if those four tests were satisfied. Thirdly, the fact that those tests are not all satisfied does not mean that an injunction should be granted.

As for the second problem, that of public interest, I find it hard to see how there could be any circumstances in which it arose and could not, as a matter of law, be a relevant factor. Of course, it is very easy to think of circumstances in which it might arise but did not begin to justify the court refusing, or, as the case may be, deciding, to award an injunction if it was otherwise minded to do so. But that is not the point. The fact that a defendant's business may have to shut down if an injunction is granted should, it seems to me, obviously be a relevant fact, and it is hard to see why relevance should not extend to the fact that a number of the defendant's employees would lose their livelihood, although in many cases that may well not be sufficient to justify the refusal of an injunction. Equally, I do not see why the court should not be entitled to have regard to the fact that many other neighbours in addition to the claimant are badly affected by the nuisance as a factor in favour of granting an injunction.

It is also right to mention planning permission in this context. In some cases, the grant of planning permission for a particular activity (whether carried on at the claimant's, or the defendant's, premises) may provide strong support for the contention that the activity is of benefit to the public, which would be relevant to the question of whether or not to grant an injunction. Accordingly, the existence of a planning permission which expressly or inherently authorises carrying on an activity in such a way as to cause a nuisance by noise or the like, can be a factor in favour of refusing an injunction and compensating the claimant in damages. This factor would have real force in cases where it was clear that the planning authority had been reasonably and fairly influenced by the public benefit of the activity, and where the activity cannot be carried out without causing the nuisance complained of. However, even in such cases, the court would have to weigh up all the competing factors.

In some such cases, the court may well be impressed by a defendant's argument that an injunction would involve a loss to the public or a waste of resources on account of what may be a single claimant, or that the financial implications of an injunction for the defendant would be disproportionate to the damage done to the claimant if she was left to her claim in damages. In many such cases, particularly where an injunction would in practice stop the defendant from pursuing the activities, an injunction may well not be the appropriate remedy.

Lord Sumption:

The courts might have defended the special treatment of nuisance by pointing to the traditional attitude of equity to land as being unique, an approach which is exemplified in its willingness to grant specific performance of contracts for the sale of land. From this, it might have been concluded that paying the claimant enough to buy a comparable property elsewhere where there was no nuisance was not equivalent to letting him use his existing land free of the nuisance. In fact the *Shelfer* principle was based mainly on the court's objection to sanctioning a wrong by allowing the defendant to pay for the right to go on doing it. This seems an unduly moralistic approach to disputes, and if taken at face value would justify the grant of an injunction in all cases, which is plainly not the law. In his dissenting judgment in the Court of Appeal in *Co-operative Insurance Society Ltd v Argyll Stores (Holdings) Ltd* [1996] Ch 286, 304 (subsequently upheld in the House of Lords [1998] AC 1), Millett LJ said:

> 'The competing arguments in the present case, and the difference in the views of the members of this court, reflect a controversy which has persisted since the dispute between Sir Edward Coke and Lord Ellesmere LC. Sir Edward Coke resented the existence of an equitable jurisdiction which deprived the defendant of what he regarded as a fundamental freedom to elect whether to carry out his promise or to pay damages for the breach. Modern economic theory supports Sir Edward Coke; an award of damages reflects normal commercial expectations and ensures a more efficient allocation of scarce economic resources. The defendant will break his contract only if it pays him to do so after taking the payment of damages into account; the plaintiff will be fully compensated in damages; and both parties will be free to allocate their resources elsewhere. Against this there is the repugnance felt by those who share the view of Fuller CJ in *Union Pacific Railway Co v Chicago, Rock Island and Pacific Railway Co* (1896) 163 US 564, 600 that it is an intolerable travesty of justice that a party should be allowed to break his contract at pleasure by electing to pay damages for the breach. English law has adopted a pragmatic approach in resolving this dispute ... The leading principle is usually

said to be that equitable relief is not available where damages are an adequate remedy. In my view, it would be more accurate to say that equitable relief will be granted where it is appropriate and not otherwise; and that where damages are an adequate remedy it is inappropriate to grant equitable relief.'

In my view, the decision in *Shelfer* is out of date, and it is unfortunate that it has been followed so recently and so slavishly. It was devised for a time in which England was much less crowded, when comparatively few people owned property, when conservation was only beginning to be a public issue, and when there was no general system of statutory development control. The whole jurisprudence in this area will need one day to be reviewed in this court. There is much to be said for the view that damages are ordinarily an adequate remedy for nuisance and that an injunction should not usually be granted in a case where it is likely that conflicting interests are engaged other than the parties' interests.

Lord Mance:

I would only add in relation to remedy that the right to enjoy one's home without disturbance is one which I would believe that many, indeed most, people value for reasons largely if not entirely independent of money. With reference to Lord Sumption's concluding paragraph, I would not therefore presently be persuaded by a view that 'damages are ordinarily an adequate remedy for nuisance' and that " 'an injunction should not usually be granted in a case where it is likely that conflicting interests are engaged other than the parties' interests' – a suggested example of the latter being given as a case where a use of land has received planning permission. I would see this as putting the significance of planning permission and public benefit too high, in the context of the remedy to be afforded for a private nuisance. As already indicated, I agree with Lord Neuberger's nuanced approach.

Lord Clarke:

I entirely agree with Lord Sumption (at para 161) that the decision in *Shelfer v City of London Electric Lighting Co* [1895] 1 Ch 287 is out of date and that it is unfortunate that it has been followed so recently and so slavishly. Indeed, I would so hold now in this appeal, although (in the absence of submissions) I would not now lay down precise principles which should be followed in the future. They must be developed on a case by case basis and in each case all will depend upon the circumstances.

Lord Carnwath:

I agree with Lord Neuberger and the rest of the court that the opportunity should be taken to signal a move away from the strict criteria derived from *Shelfer* [1895] 1 Ch 287. This is particularly relevant to cases where an injunction would have serious consequences for third parties, such as employees of the defendant's business, or, in this case, members of the public using or enjoying the stadium. In that respect, in my view, the Court of Appeal in *Watson* [2009] 3 All ER 249 was wrong to hold that the judge had no power to make the order he did, and to limit public interest considerations to cases where the damage to the claimant is 'minimal'.

…

While therefore I agree generally with the observations of Lord Neuberger and Lord Sumption on this aspect, I have three particular reservations.

First, I would not regard the grant of planning permission for a particular use as in itself giving rise to a presumption against the grant of an injunction. As I have said, the circumstances in which permissions may be granted differ so much as to make it unwise to lay down any general propositions. I would accept however that the nature of, and background to, a relevant planning permission may be an important factor in the court's assessment.

Clearly, the Supreme Court thought a departure from *Shelfer* to be desirable. This is largely because injunctive relief is considered in some situations to be oppressive. But it is important to remember that it might be oppressive to the claimants to deprive them of their choice whether or not to sell their property right.[173] Indeed, the refusal of a claimant to release his or her right for a fee indicates that he or she values the protection of this right very highly,[174] and this might be afforded greater respect.

The emphasis upon considerations of public interest by the courts is difficult. Although it is sometimes suggested that an unwillingness to grant damages in lieu might prevent works beneficial to the public from being carried out, and that the courts should therefore take into account the public interest in the defendant's infringing the claimant's right, this was clearly rejected by the Court of Appeal in *Shelfer* itself. Lindley LJ commented that:[175]

> Expropriation, even for a money consideration, is only justifiable when Parliament has sanctioned it. Courts of Justice are not like Parliament, which considers whether proposed works will be so beneficial to the public as to justify exceptional legislation, and the deprivation of people of their rights with or without compensation.

It is problematic to make a judge the arbiter of what is in the public interest. This seems to involve considerations concerning parties who are not before the court, and may be beyond the competence of any particular judge.[176] It is difficult for a judge to assess wider considerations of public interest in what is essentially a dispute between neighbouring landowners. It is suggested that there is some merit in insisting that defendants who seek to rely upon the public interest in justifying the infringement of a claimant's property rights should not avail themselves of Lord Cairns' Act,[177] but rather should engage the support of local authorities and seek to make the most of the compulsory purchase regime.[178] This should not be too difficult: Government has encouraged local authorities to exploit the opportunities afforded by compulsory purchase,[179] and the House of Lords has recognized the legality of 'back to back' agreements, under which a public body can agree to exercise its powers of compulsory purchase in order to ensure that the land can be developed, and then later give the land back to the developer, in return for the developer's undertaking to indemnify the public authority for the costs incurred in the process.[180]

Similarly, it is suggested that it is inappropriate to place great weight on the granting of planning permission in this area. The planning authorities have no power to authorize a nuisance, and are concerned solely with the negative question of whether there is a good reason, from the 'community perspective', not to allow a proposed development to go ahead. If there is no such reason, planning permission is granted, but that does not necessarily indicate that the authorities positively desire that the development proceed. Nor does planning permission purport to determine the validity or strength of any person's private law rights; such rights require protection from the courts through the

---

[173] Davies, 'Lighting the Way Ahead: The Use and Abuse of Property Rights' in *Modern Studies in Property Law—Volume 6* (ed. Bright) (Oxford: Hart, 2011), p. 48.

[174] Although a willingness to sell does not necessarily mean that injunctive relief should be refused.

[175] [1895] 1 Ch 287, 316.

[176] See too Buckley, 'Injunctions and the Public Interest' (1981) 44 MLR 212, 213.

[177] Unless the public interest is overwhelmingly strong and concerns the defence of the realm: see e.g. *Dennis v Ministry of Defence* [2003] EWHC 793 (QB); [2003] Env LR 34. For a much more relaxed approach see *Miller v Jackson* [1977] QB 966, which has since been doubted: *Kennaway v Thompson* [1981] QB 88.

[178] Particularly given the enlarged powers under the revised section 237 of the Town and Country Planning Act 1990.

[179] Department of Communities and Local Government, 'Compulsory Purchase and the Crichel Down Rules' (Office of the Deputy Prime Minister Circular 06/2004, 31 October 2004).

[180] *Standard Commercial Property Securities Ltd v Glasgow CC* [2006] UKHL 50; [2007] SC (HL) 33.

law of nuisance.[181] It is therefore unsatisfactory for planning permission to be dispositive against an injunction.[182]

In any event, it is important to appreciate that if the comments of the Supreme Court in *Coventry v Lawrence* are followed and *Shelfer* is departed from, then it is unclear what principles should be applied when deciding whether to award damages in lieu of an injunction. This is obviously problematic in a wide variety of situations where injunctive relief might be granted, beyond the context of nuisance. For example, in *Prophet plc v Huggett*[183] the judge said:

> I understand that the *Shelfer* formula is to be applied as no more than the working rule which AL Smith LJ conceived it to be, albeit satisfaction of the four tests will normally lead to a refusal of an injunction in the absence of other relevant circumstances.
>
> *Shelfer* and *Coventry* both concerned claims in nuisance rather than breach of covenant. That means that the negative obligation was imposed by the general law rather than having been voluntarily assumed by the defendant, but the source of the obligation cannot be critical in this regard, and the observations of the Supreme Court as to preserving flexibility in the operation of Lord Cairn's Act are equally apposite. I consider therefore that the restriction to exceptional circumstances and hardship … is now to be treated as unsound. That is not to say that the factors identified in previous cases are not relevant, only that they are neither exhaustive nor to be applied mechanistically.

It is not yet clear how any broad discretion is to be applied,[184] although in *Comic Enterprise Ltd v Twentieth Century Fox Film Corp*,[185] an intellectual property dispute, Roger Wyand QC, sitting as a Deputy High Court Judge, cited passages from Lord Neuberger's speech in *Coventry* and concluded:

> From all of this I extract the conclusion that I have to apply a multifactorial exercise balancing the two competing fundamental rights with no presumption that either one automatically trumps the other. There is, however, a legal burden on the Defendant to show why an injunction should not be granted. It will depend upon the facts of the case.

Such a 'multifactorial' approach allows the court great freedom.[186] But it also makes it difficult to predict what factors the court will consider relevant, and what weight will be placed upon them.

(a) QUANTIFYING DAMAGES AWARDED IN LIEU

One of the very difficult issues that a court faces when exercising its discretion to award damages in lieu of an injunction is quantifying the monetary remedy. Neither Lord Cairns' Act nor its successor provides much guidance. In *Wrotham Park Estate Co. Ltd v Parkside Homes Ltd*,[187] a developer

---

[181] *Coventry v Lawrence* [2014] UKSC 13; [2014] AC 822, [90] (Lord Neuberger).

[182] See too Nolan, 'Nuisance, Planning and Regulation: The Limits of Statutory Authority' in *Defences in Tort* ((eds) Dyson, Goudkamp and Wilmot-Smith) (Oxford: Hart, 2015).

[183] [2014] EWHC 615 (Ch); [2014] IRLR 618, [28] (reversed, not discussing this point: [2014] EWCA Civ 1013; [2014] IRLR 797).

[184] *Higson v Guenault* [2014] EWCA Civ 703; [2014] 2 P&CR DG 13.

[185] [2014] EWHC 2286 (Ch); [2014] ETMR 51.

[186] See too Tromans, 'Nuisance-Prevention or Payment?' [1982] CLJ 87; Clause 2 of the Law Commission's Draft Rights to Light (Injunctions) Bill at Appendix B of *Rights to Light* (Law Com No 356, 2014). The fate of this report is not known at the time of writing.

[187] [1974] 1 WLR 798.

breached a restrictive covenant by building too many flats without the claimant's consent. Brightman J thought that it would be an:[188]

> unpardonable waste of much needed houses to direct that they now be pulled down and I have never had a moment's doubt during the hearing of this case that such an order ought to be refused.

Brightman J was clear that damages ought to be awarded in lieu. When assessing the sum to be awarded, he said:[189]

> I think that in a case such as the present a landowner faced with a request from a developer which, it must be assumed, he feels reluctantly obliged to grant, would have first asked the developer what profit he expected to make from his operations. With the benefit of foresight the developer would, in the present case, have said about £50,000, for that is the profit which Parkside concedes it made from the development. I think that the landowner would then reasonably have required a certain percentage of that anticipated profit as a price for the relaxation of the covenant, assuming, as I must, that he feels obliged to relax it. In assessing what would be a fair percentage I think that the court ought, on the particular facts of this case, to act with great moderation. ... I think that damages must be assessed in such a case on a basis which is fair and, in all the circumstances, in my judgment a sum equal to 5 per cent of Parkside's anticipated profit is the most that is fair.

This approach is sensible and well-established. Essentially, the court must try to decide what price for the release of the right would have been agreed by the parties *if* they had negotiated as reasonable parties willing to reach an agreement. Clearly, this bargain is hypothetical and fictional: in many instances, the claimant simply would not have been willing to enter into such negotiations. Indeed, in *Wrotham Park* itself the claimants would not have been willing to countenance relaxing their restrictive covenants. Given the artificial nature of this bargain, it is unsurprising that courts have struggled to establish clear principles to underpin the quantification of this sort of monetary award.

There has been much debate about whether this remedy should be characterized as compensatory or restitutionary; for example, in *Surrey CC v Bredero Homes*, Steyn LJ thought the award in *Wrotham Park* was restitutionary,[190] whereas in *Jaggard v Sawyer*, both Sir Thomas Bingham MR[191] and Millett LJ[192] were critical of this and thought the award was compensatory. But it is important not to get too bogged down in this debate; any bargain between the parties should take into account both the defendant's gain and the claimant's loss: it would be unrealistic for the claimant to release his or her right for anything less than the value of the loss he or she would suffer, and the most the defendant would pay for the right would be a proportion of the profits he or she would expect to make. Admittedly, in *Coventry v Lawrence* Lord Carnwath was circumspect about assessing the award on the basis of a share of the benefit to the defendants,[193] but such comments were *obiter*, unnecessary for the decision, and clearly not shared by either Lord Neuberger[194] or Lord Clarke.[195]

---

[188] Ibid, 811.
[189] Ibid, 815–16.
[190] [1993] 1 WLR 1361, 1369–70.
[191] [1995] 1 WLR 269, 281–2.
[192] Ibid, 291.
[193] [2014] UKSC 13; [2014] AC 822, [248].
[194] Ibid, [128]
[195] Ibid, [173].

The bargain reached is most likely to produce a figure somewhere between the claimant's loss and defendant's gain. As Lord Lloyd commented in *Inverugie Investments v Hackett*:[196]

> The principle need not be characterised as exclusively compensatory, or exclusively restitutionary; it combines elements of both.

In any event, squeezing the award in *Wrotham Park* under a compensatory or restitutionary banner is much less important than trying to decide *how* the courts reach the awards they do. A helpful attempt to establish some guidelines was provided by Gabriel Moss QC in *Tamares (Vincent Square) v Fairpoint Properties (No. 2)*:[197]

> (1) The overall principle is that the court must attempt to find what would be a 'fair' result of a hypothetical negotiation between the parties.
>
> (2) The context, including the nature and seriousness of the breach, must be kept in mind.
>
> (3) The right to prevent a development (or part) gives the owner of the right a significant bargaining position.
>
> (4) The owner of the right with such a bargaining position will normally be expected to receive some part of the likely profit from the development (or relevant part).
>
> (5) If there is no evidence of the likely size of the profit, the court can do its best by awarding a suitable multiple of the damages for loss of amenity.
>
> (6) If there is evidence of the likely size of the profit, the court should normally award a sum which takes into account a fair percentage of the profit.
>
> (7) The size of the award should not in any event be so large that the development (or relevant part) would not have taken place had such a sum been payable.
>
> (8) After arriving at a figure which takes into consideration all the above and any other relevant factors, the court needs to consider whether the 'deal feels right' [cf. Amec Developments Ltd v. Jury's Hotel Management (UK) Ltd [2001] 1 EGLR 81, 87.]

The last factor indicates how uncertain this area is. But some uncertainty is inevitable given the contrived nature of the bargain being imposed upon the parties. The principles set out in *Tamares* are sensible and have been adopted subsequently.[198] In *Pell Frischmann Engineering Ltd v Bow Valley Iran Ltd*, Lord Walker also dealt with the issue of what events can be taken into account.

Pell Frischmann Engineering Ltd v Bow Valley Iran Ltd [2009] UKPC 45, [50]–[51] (Lord Walker)

> Another issue is how far the court is entitled, in its assessment of *Wrotham Park* damages, to take account of events occurring after the time at which the hypothetical negotiation takes place (and in particular, to take account of how profitable the outcome has been for the contract-breaker). This issue sometimes tends to get confused with the wider issue of whether the court is awarding compensatory or restitutionary damages. Their Lordships consider that the right approach is that of the Court of Appeal in *Lunn Poly* [2006] 2 EGLR 29 in which Neuberger LJ observed, at paras 27–29, after citing the

---

[196] [1995] 1 WLR 713, 717–18.
[197] [2007] EWHC 212 (Ch); [2007] 1 WLR 2167, [22].
[198] E.g. *HKRUK II (CHC) Limited v Marcus Alexander Heaney* [2010] EWHC 2245 (Ch), [81]–[89].

judgment of Mr Anthony Mann QC in *Amec Developments Ltd v Jury's Hotel Management (UK) Ltd* [2001] 1 EGLR 81, paras 11–13:

'27. It is obviously unwise to try to lay down any firm general guidance as to the circumstances in which, and the degree to which, it is possible to take into account facts and events that have taken place after the date of the hypothetical negotiations, when deciding the figure at which those negotiations would arrive. Quite apart from anything else, it is almost inevitable that each case will turn on its own particular facts. ...'

'28. ... it should not, in my opinion, be treated as being generally [right to have regard] to events after the date of breach where the court decides to award damages in lieu on a negotiating basis as at the date of breach. After all, once the court has decided on a particular valuation date for assessing negotiating damages, consistency, fairness, and principle can be said to suggest that a judge should be careful before agreeing that a factor that existed at that date should be ignored, or that a factor that occurred after that date should be taken into account, as affecting the negotiating stance of the parties when deciding the figure at which they would arrive.'

'29. In my view, the proper analysis is as follows. Given that negotiating damages under the Act are meant to be compensatory, and are normally to be assessed or valued at the date of breach, principle and consistency indicate that post-valuation events are normally irrelevant. However, given the quasi-equitable nature of such damages, the judge may, where there are good reasons, direct a departure from the norm, either by selecting a different valuation date or by directing that a specific post-valuation-date event be taken into account.'

In a case (such as *Wrotham Park* [1974] 1 WLR 798 itself) where there has been nothing like an actual negotiation between the parties it is no doubt reasonable for the court to look at the eventual outcome and to consider whether or not that is a useful guide to what the parties would have thought at the time of their hypothetical bargain. But in this case the parties clearly expected, as is apparent from their negotiations, that the contract ... would be much more profitable than it turned out to be. For that reason, it is unnecessary to give a detailed account of the actual outcome.

QUESTION

Ransom Ltd ('Ransom') is a technology company. It has been developing new anti-virus software for computers in conjunction with Compsci Ltd ('Compsci'). Compsci is an American Company with a very small office and limited assets in this jurisdiction. Ransom suspects that Compsci, in breach of contract, has divulged sensitive information to its competitor, Snoop Ltd. Compsci has not replied to the emails or calls of Ransom for over a month.

The offices of Ransom are next to land that has been sold to Builders Ltd ('Builders') for development. In order to facilitate the development, Builders has pulled down a fence, which was actually on the property of Ransom. Ransom wants Builders to put back the fence. Ransom also wants to prevent Builders from carrying out any further work on the land since the proposed development will infringe Ransom's easement of light.

Last year, Ransom licensed one of its products to Quickbuck Ltd ('Quickbuck'). The negotiators for both companies had agreed that Ransom would receive 15 per cent of any subsequent profits made by Quickbuck from selling the product, but the final written contract, signed by the managing directors of both companies, stated that Ransom would receive 10 per cent of the profits. The managing director of Quickbuck had assured his counterpart at Ransom that the contract was exactly what had been agreed during the negotiations.

Advise Ransom.

FURTHER READING

Davies, 'Rectifying the Course of Rectification' (2012) 75 MLR 412.

Devonshire, 'Mareva Injunctions and Third Parties: Exposing the Subtext' (1999) 62 MLR 539.

Dockray and Laddie, 'Piller Problems' (1990) 106 LQR 601.

Gee, 'The Undertaking in Damages' (2006) LMCLQ 181.

Jolowicz, 'Damages in Equity—a Study of Lord Cairns' Act' (1975) CLJ 224.

McGrath, 'The Freezing Order: A Constantly Evolving Jurisdiction' (2012) CJQ 12.

The following texts are aimed mainly at practitioners, but contain much that is useful:

Andrews, Clarke, Tettenborn, and Virgo, *Contractual Duties: Performance, Breach, Termination and Remedies* (London: Sweet & Maxwell, 2011) (Part I, chs 27 and 28).

Gee, *Commercial Injunctions* (5th edn) (London: Sweet & Maxwell, 2005) (especially chs 1, 3, and 6).

Hodge QC, *Rectification: The Modern Law and Practice Governing Claims for Rectification for Mistake* (2nd edn) (London: Sweet & Maxwell, 2015) (especially ch. 1)

Jones and Goodhart, *Specific Performance* (2nd edn) (London; Butterworths, 1996) (especially chs 1 and 2).

O'Sullivan, Elliott, and Zakrzewski, *The Law of Rescission* (2nd edn) (Oxford: Oxford University Press, 2014) (especially chs 1, 10, and 15).

INDEX